Scientific Evidence

Third Edition

PAUL C. GIANNELLI
Albert J. Weatherhead III and Richard W. Weatherhead
Professor of Law

Case Western Reserve University
School of Law
Cleveland, Ohio

EDWARD J. IMWINKELRIED
Professor of Law

University of California at Davis
School of Law
Davis, California

Volume 2

LEXIS®
LAW PUBLISHING

P.O. Box 7587, Charlottesville, VA 22906-7587

www.lexispublishing.com

Customer Service: 800/562-1197

Library of Congress Catalog Card No. 99-67624
Two-Volume Set ISBN 0-327-04985-5
Volume 2 ISBN 0-327-04984-7

SUMMARY OF CONTENTS

Volume 1

Volume 2

TABLE OF CONTENTS

Volume 2

Page

CHAPTER 18

THE DNA GENETIC MARKER*

§ 18-1. In General.

The first edition of this treatise devoted less than two full pages to the topic of DNA typing. When the first edition was released, forensic DNA companies such as Lifecodes were just opening their doors; and DNA evidence had yet to be offered in an American courtroom. In the 13 years since the release of the first edition of this treatise, however, there has been explosion of interest in DNA typing. As the following sections point out, there is now a massive volume of literature analyzing DNA typing; one issue of *Journal of Forensic Sciences* contains eight different articles addressing the topic.[1] In both 1992 and 1996, the National Research Council of the National Academy of Sciences released

*The authors wish to express their appreciation to Dr. George Duncan , DNA Specialist, Crime Laboratory, Broward Sheriff's Office, Fort Lauderdale, Florida, who reviewed this chapter in the second and third editions of this treatise.

1. Vol. 37, No. 2, J. FORENSIC SCI. (Mar. 1992). Jacobs, *Scientific Evidence: Aspects of DNA Fingerprinting, A Selective Bibliography*, 47 THE RECORD OF THE ASS'N OF THE BAR OF THE CITY OF NEW YORK 891 (1992).

substantial studies of the forensic use of DNA.[2] The durability of DNA material and the advent of DNA testing make it possible for the police to solve old crimes; in some cities, the availability of DNA testing "has spurred the creation of cold-crime squads."[3] In 1994, the execution of Timothy Spencer, convicted largely on the basis of DNA evidence, dramatized the importance of the topic,[4] as did both trials of O.J. Simpson.[5] Thanks in part to the efforts of the Innocence Project,[6] over 60 convicts have already been exonerated and obtained post-conviction relief on the basis of exculpatory DNA tests.[7] DNA testing is also being used in an effort to establish the innocence of Dr. Sam Sheppard.[8] For that matter, DNA testing figured in the attempted impeachment of President Clinton.[9]

The topic has assumed such social importance that the National Institute of Justice has created a National Commission on the Future of DNA Evidence.[10] The commission includes academics, judges, and practitioners.[11] The commission's various working groups will soon be issuing formal reports on

---

2. THE EVALUATION OF FORENSIC DNA EVIDENCE (1996); DNA TECHNOLOGY IN FORENSIC SCIENCE (1992).

3. Rovella, *Heating Up Cold Crime Squads*, NAT'L L.J., Mar. 8, 1999, at p. A1.

4. *DNA Convict Executed*, NAT'L L.J., May 9, 1994.

5. Noble, *DNA Debate in the Simpson Trial, Crucial to Case, Is About to Begin*, N.Y. TIMES, May 9, 1995, at A1.

6. Myers, *Cardozo Students Learn to Use DNA Tests to Prove Innocence*, NAT'L L.J., Dec. 12, 1994.

7. Dedman, *Sometimes DNA Testing Provides Path to Freedom*, HOUSTON CHRONICLE, Apr. 19, 1999, at p. 3A (discussing "the 61st and 62nd inmates exonerated by DNA evidence in the United States"); Gross, *Lost Lives: Miscarriages of Justice in Capital Cases*, 42 LAW QUAD. Notes 82, 83 (Spr. 1999) ("Since 1992 at least 53 defendants — mostly convicted rapists — have been exonerated by DNA identification evidence; most of them were released after spending years in prison"); Higgins, *Tough Luck for the Innocent Man*, 85 A.B.A. J. 46, 47 (Mar. 1999) ("DNA evidence has exonerated at least 56 inmates, according to the Innocence Project, an advocacy group at Yeshiva University in New York City. Seventy-four innocent inmates have spent time on death row before being cleared, according to organizers of a national conference in November at Chicago's Northwestern University Law School").

8. Taylor, *New DNA Tests May Clear Dr. Sheppard in '54 Slaying*, SAN FRANCISCO CHRONICLE, Feb. 5, 1997, at A6. The results of the tests indicated that the stains matched neither the profile of Marilyn Sheppard or Sam Sheppard but did match the profile of handyman, Richard Eberling. *DNA Tests Do Not Exonerate Dr. Sam Sheppard*, 21 SCI. SLEUTHING REV. 6 (Winter 1997).

9. The DNA report in question appears at http://cnn.com/icreport/report/volume6/volume6247.html. According to the FBI Laboratory, the chance that the semen on Ms. Lewinsky's dress was "not the President's is one in 7.87 trillion." *A "New" DNA Policy: Statistics Are Out; A Qualified Certainty Is In*, 22 SCI. SLEUTHING REV. 12, 13 (Sum. 1998).

10. 63 Fed. Reg. 9578 (Feb. 25, 1998).

11. *New DNA Commission Holds First Meeting*, 62 CRIM. L. (BNA) 1536 (Mar. 25, 1998) (the membership includes such notables as Chief Justice Shirley Abramson of the Wisconsin Supreme Court, George Clark, the San Diego deputy district attorney who participated in the *Simpson* case, Professor Barry Scheck, one of the defense counsel in *Simpson*, and Judge William Webster.

such topics as DNA databases and post-conviction relief based on exculpatory DNA test results.

The sections of this chapter document the significant evolution of both the science and the law relevant to DNA evidence. Section 18-3 points out that the technology has progressed through three basic generations of tests, initially RFLP, then PCR dot blot, and now tests such as STR which combine the strengths of RFLP and PCR. Likewise, § 18-4 traces the evolution of the case law, particularly the decisions addressing the admissibility of testimony about the statistical significance of DNA matches. As these sections demonstrate, DNA evidence has been one of the "hottest" areas in forensic science since the release of the first edition of this treatise.

§ 18-2. The Biology of DNA.

DNA is the basic building block of life; each person's DNA accounts for his or her individuality. Chapter 17 reviewed the use of genetic markers other than DNA. Many of those markers are the protein products of DNA; and as Chapter 17 noted, they can be useful in narrowing the class of persons who can be the source of the marker. This chapter addresses the techniques for directly analyzing the DNA molecules containing the genetic code that determines each person's characteristics. In truth, several types of DNA can be analyzed. For example, mitochondrial DNA can be tested.[12] That type of DNA is found in the energy-producing material surrounding the cell nucleus.[13] The person inherits mitochondrial DNA solely from his or her mother. However, most current testing techniques analyze nuclear DNA. All of a person's cells that have a nucleus — white blood cells, sperm, buccal (saliva) cells,[14] and the tissue surrounding hair roots[15] — have the code-carrying DNA.[16] Each cell with a nucleus contains the

---

12. Donnelly & Friedman, *DNA Database Searches and the Legal Consumption of Scientific Evidence*, 97 MICH. L. REV. 931, 934 (1999).

13. *Id.* at 934 n.16.

14. Allen, Engstrom, Meyers, Handt, Saldeen, Haeseler, Paabo & Gyllensten, *Mitochondrial DNA Sequencing of Shed Hairs and Saliva on Robbery Caps: Sensitivity and Matching Probabilities*, 43 J. FORENSIC SCI. 453 (1998).

15. Allen, Engstrom, Meyers, Handt, Saldeen, Haeseler, Paabo & Gyllensten, *Mitochondrial DNA Sequencing of Shed Hairs and Saliva on Robbery Caps: Sensitivity and Matching Probabilities*, 43 J. FORENSIC SCI. 453 (1998); Linch, Smith & Prahlow, *Evaluation of the Human Hair Root for DNA Typing Subsequent to Microscopic Comparison*, 43 J. FORENSIC SCI. 305 (1998); Hansen, *A Comeback for Hair Evidence*, 84 A.B.A. J. 66 (May 1998).

16. DNA can be extracted from such material as bone, bone marrow, sweat, nasal secretion, and teeth. Yasuda, Takeshita, Sawazaki, Nadano, Iida, Miyahara & Kishi, *A New Individualization Marker of Sweat: Deoxyribonuclease 1 (DNase 1) Polymorphism*, 41 J. FORENSIC SCI. 862 (1996); Rankin, Narveson, Birkby & Lai, *Restriction Fragment Length Polymorphism (RFLP) Analysis on DNA from Human Compact Bone*, 41 J. FORENSIC SCI. 40 (1996); Tahir, Caruso, Hamby, Sovinski & Tahir, *Restriction Fragment Length Polymorphism (RFLP) Typing of DNA Extracted from Nasal*

entire genetic code although the cell reads only the part of the code needed to perform its distinctive function in the human body. (It comes as a surprise to many laypersons that DNA cannot be extracted from human red blood cells, since they lack a nucleus.) DNA is quite durable and can be obtained from sources such as teeth,[17] dandruff,[18] fingernails,[19] and skeletal remains[20]--even remains that have been charred.[21] For matter, DNA samples can sometimes be obtained from plants[22] and animals[23] other than human beings.

Each human being has 22 pairs of nonsex chromosomes and two sex chromosomes. Half the person's chromosomes come from the father's sperm while the other half come from the mother's ovum. Each chromosome is composed of a DNA molecule. Scientists usually refer to a twisted DNA double spiral or helix--in the courtroom, the common analogies are to a "spiral staircase"

Secretions, 40 J. FORENSIC SCI. 459 (1995); Boles, Snow & Stover, *Forensic DNA Testing on Skeletal Remains from Mass Graves: A Pilot Project in Guatemala*, 40 J. FORENSIC SCI. 349 (1995) (teeth). *See also* Cattaneo, Craig, James & Sokol, *Comparison of Three DNA Extraction Methods on Bone and Blood Stains up to 43 Years Old and Amplification of Three Different Gene Sequences*, 42 J. FORENSIC SCI. 1126 (1997); Evison, Smillie & Chamberlain, *Extraction of Single-Copy Nuclear DNA from Forensic Specimens with a Variety of Postmortem Histories*, 42 J. FORENSIC SCI. 1032 (1997); Scherszinger, Bourke, Ladd & Lee, *DNA Extraction from Liquid Blood Using QIAamp*, 42 J. FORENSIC SCI. 893 (1997).

17. Sweet, Hildebrand & Phillips, *Identification of a Skeleton Using DNA from Teeth and a PAP Smear*, 44 J. FORENSIC SCI. 630 (1999); Sweet & Hilebrand, *Recovery of DNA from Human Teeth by Cryogenic Grinding*, 43 J. FORENSIC SCI. 1199 (1998).

18. Lorente, Entrala, Lorente, Alvarez, Villanueva & Budowle, *Dandruff as a Potential Source of DNA in Forensic Casework*, 43 J. FORENSIC SCI. 901 (1998); Herber & Herold, *DNA Typing of Human Dandruff*, 43 J. FORENSIC SCI. 648 (1998).

19. Starrs, *Fingernail Matching Has Met Its Match: DNA Comes to the Fore — Again*, 22 SCI. SLEUTHING REV. 1 (Spr. 1998).

20. Yamamoto, Uchihi, Kojima, Nozawa, Huang, Tamaki & Katsumata, *Maternal Identification from Skeletal Remains of an Infant Kept by the Alleged Mother for 16 Years with DNA Typing*, 43 J. FORENSIC SCI. 701 (1998).

21. Strom & Rechitsky, *Use of Nested PCR to Identify Charred Human Remains and Minute Amounts of Blood*, 43 J. FORENSIC SCI. 696 (1998).

22. Gigliano, *Preliminary Data on the Usefulness of Internal Transcribed Spacer 1 (ITS1) Sequence in Cannabis sativa L. Identification*, 44 J. FORENSIC SCI. 475 (1999); Weinshilboum, *DNA Testing Gets to Root of Great Grapevine Mix-up*, THE DAVIS ENTERPRISE, June 8, 1999, at A1; Sensabaugh & Kaye, *Non-Human DNA Evidence*, 39 JURIMETRICS J. 1 (Fall 1998).

23. Savolainen & Lundeberg, *Forensic Evidence Based on mtDNA from Dog and Wolf Hairs*, 44 J. FORENSIC SCI. 77 (1999); Howe, *Pet Detective*, 16 U.C. DAVIS MAGAZINE 41 (Sum. 1999) (in an interview, D.V.M. Joy Halverson stated: "The most prominent case . . . was a trial in Seattle. A gang of men burst into this couple's home looking for drugs and cash, killed them and shot their dog. When the suspects were arrested, they had blood stains on their clothing, but the blood stains were from the dog. The dog's DNA was one of the few pieces of physical evidence they had tying these people to the crime"); Wilson & White, *Sex Identification of Elk (Cervus elaphus canadensis), Moose (Alces alces), and White-Tailed Deer (Odocoileus virginianus) Using the Polymerase Chain Reaction*, 43 J. FORENSIC SCI. 477 (1998).

or "twisted ladder." The DNA helix is a six- to nine-foot-long molecule found within the nucleus of the cell.

In turn, the helix is comprised of smaller units called nucleotides. Figure 18-1 is illustrative.

Alternating molecules of sugar and phosphate comprise the strands, the sides of the ladder. The organic bases form the rungs of the ladder, joined by hydrogen bonds. The nucleotides consist of a five-sugar carbon deoxyribose, a phosphate group, and an organic base. The four organic bases are: adenine (A), thymine (T), cytosine (C), and guanine (G). Each rung consists of two bases.

There are bonding rules for the bases. The bases combine together in specified ways. A always attaches to T, and G always attaches to C. A combination is known as a base pair. There are roughly three billion base pairs held within the 46 chromosomes. Many base pair sequences are common to all human beings; approximately 99.9% of the base pairs found in all human beings are the same. However, others vary from person to person; of the approximately three billion base pairs in each DNA molecule, about three million base pairs vary.[24] Although a person's DNA at any given site may not be truly singular, (with the exception of identical twins, triplets, etc.) taken as a whole the person's set of base pairs is unique. The order of the bases along the helix determines the person's genetic code. Thus, a certain sequence or set of sequences may result in a particular trait such as blonde hair. Along the helix the sequences for the various traits are separated by spacer DNA.

Scientists are learning to map the helix which is commonly referred to the human genome.[25] The mapping of parts of the genome has important medical applications.[26] It can assist the genetic counselor to determine disease propensity and the probability of the occurrence of certain traits. For example, suppose that it can be established that a given sequence at a particular locus on the helix predisposes the person to a certain disease.[27] In the future if the physician could detect the predisposition in an infant, he or she might be able to prescribe preventative treatment even before any symptoms materialize. The physician might even be able to treat the condition *in utero*.

---

24. Donnelly & Friedman, *DNA Database Searches and the Legal Consumption of Scientific Evidence*, 97 MICH. L. REV. 931, 935 (1999) ("typically, two unrelated individuals will differ at about one site in a thousand").

25. Botstein, White, Shoknick & Davis, *Construction of a Genetic Linkage Map in Man Using Restriction Fragment Length Polymorphisms*, 32 AM. J. HUM. GENET. 314 (1980).

26. Medline includes many references discussing these potential applications.

27. Wieacker, Horn, Pearson, Wienker, McKay & Ropers, *Menkes Kinky Hair Disease: A Search for Closely Linked Restriction Fragment Length Polymorphisms*, 64 HUMAN GENET. 139 (1983).

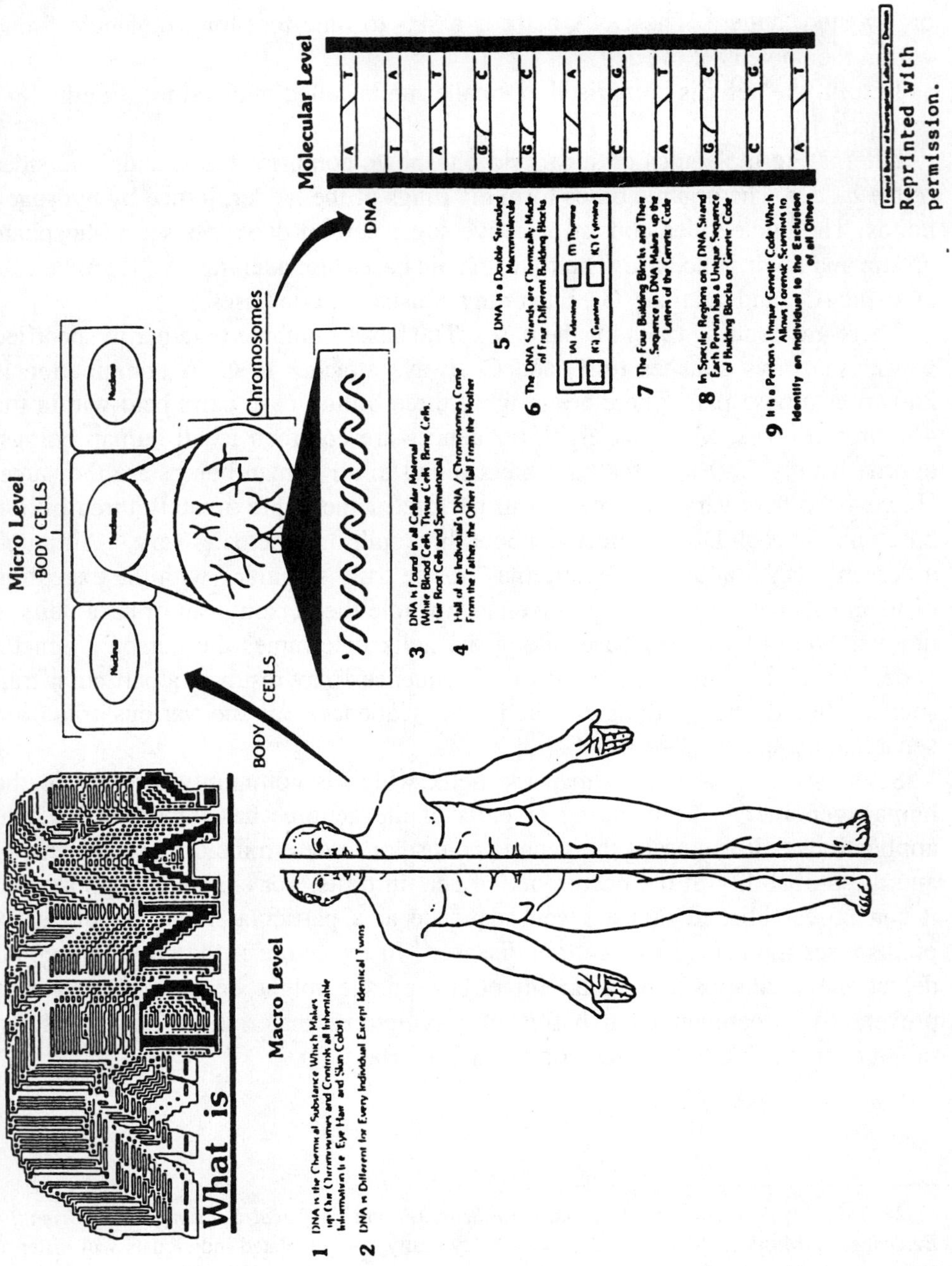
What is DNA?
Macro Level
1 DNA is the Chemical Substance Which Makes up Our Chromosomes and Controls all Inheritable Information (i.e. Eye Hair and Skin Color)
2 DNA is Different for Every Individual Except Identical Twins
BODY CELLS
Micro Level
BODY CELLS
Chromosomes
3 DNA is Found in all Cellular Material (White Blood Cells, Tissue Cells, Bone Cells, Hair Root Cells and Spermatozoa)
4 Half of an Individual's DNA / Chromosomes Come From the Father, the Other Half From the Mother
Molecular Level
DNA
5 DNA is a Double Stranded Macromolecule
6 The DNA Strands are Chemically Made of Four Different Building Blocks
(A) Adenine
(T) Thymine
(G) Guanine
(C) Cytosine
7 The Four Building Blocks and Their Sequence in DNA Makes up the Letters of the Genetic Code
8 In Specific Regions on a DNA Strand Each Person has a Unique Sequence of Building Blocks or Genetic Code
9 It is a Person's Unique Genetic Code Which Allows Forensic Scientists to Identify an Individual to the Exclusion of all Others
Reprinted with permission.

Figure 18-1

§ 18-3. The DNA Typing Techniques.

As the preceding paragraph suggested, until the last 15 years, researchers focused almost exclusively on the medical applications of the techniques for probing DNA sequences such as its use in genetic counseling.[28] However, they have developed forensic applications for their techniques. As previously stated, with the exception of identical twins, each person's DNA is unique; and DNA technology therefore holds out the promise of identifying sequences unique to a particular individual. As Chapter 3 of the 1992 National Academy of Sciences report states, "Unique identification with DNA typing is ... possible provided enough sites of variations are examined." Some experts state that the probability of a chance match is only one in three trillion.[29] The advent of DNA typing not only increases the likelihood of convicting the guilty; it also enhances the likelihood of exculpating the innocent.[30] Chapter 3 of the 1992 N.R.C. report states that the F.B.I. informed the committee that "some 33% of suspects that match evidence samples according to conventional serology turn out to be excluded through DNA typing ...."[31] As previously stated, over 60 wrongfully

28. Lange & Boehnke, *DNA Restriction Fragments*, 35 AM. J. HUMAN GENET. 177 (1982).

29. Dodd, *Editorial — DNA Fingerprinting in Matters of Family and Crime*, 26 MED. SCI. LAW 5 (1986); Gill, Jeffreys & Werrett, *Forensic Applications of DNA "Fingerprints,"* 318 NATURE 577, 579 (1985). McLeod, *English DNA Evidence Held Inadmissible*, 1991 CRIM. L. REV. 583 ("The chances of an innocent, coincidental match were touted as figures as low as 738,000,000,000,000 to one").

30. *New DNA Law May Clear First Man*, NAT'L L.J., Oct. 19, 1998, at p. A9 (the use of DNA evidence in the attempt to obtain post-conviction relief for David Gray).

31. INSTITUTE FOR LAW AND JUSTICE, REPORT ON DNA EXCULPATORY CASES (1996) (28 cases in which accused relied on DNA testing to obtain post-conviction relief); Wenk, *Review of Connors et al. "Convicted by Juries, Exonerated by Science: Case Studies in the Use of DNA Evidence to Establish Innocence after Trial,"* 42 J. FORENSIC SCI. 750 (1997) ("I attempted to quantify the reasons for the initial miscarriage of justice in the cases. About 75% involved identity errors by eyewitnesses."); *The Lazaruses of the Underworld: Resurrected by DNA*, 21 SCI. SLEUTHING REV. 1 (Spring 1997); Stacher v. Pruett, 126 F.3d 561, 569-73 (4th Cir.) (habeas corpus proceeding citing *Netherland, infra*), *cert. denied*, 522 U.S. 1010 (1997); O'Dell v. Netherland, 95 F.3d 1214 (4th Cir.) (habeas corpus proceeding), *aff'd*, 521 U.S. 151 (1997); Kolarik, *DNA, Changed Testimony Gain Acquittal*, 82 A.B.A. J. 34 (Jan. 1996) (Rolando Cruz was acquitted on retrial after spending 11 years on death row in part because "improved DNA tests linked convicted murderer Brian Dugan" to the murder Cruz had previously been found guilty of.); Myers, *Cardozo Students Learn to Use DNA Tests to Prove Innocence*, NAT'L L.J., Dec. 12, 1994 ("The Innocence Project [at Benjamin Cardozo School of Law] has been responsible for freeing eight convicts."); Knight, *More Death Row Inmates Being Freed From Prison: DNA Analysis Produces New Evidence*, SAN FRANCISCO CHRONICLE, July 16, 1997, at A2 ("the relatively new technique of analyzing DNA ... has been able to conclusively prove some death row inmates innocent"); Rovella, *Illinois Expands Right to DNA Testing*, NAT'L L.J., Aug. 11, 1997, at A18 ("[p]rompted by seven exonerations of death row inmates in the past three years, more than any other state," the Illinois legislature enacted a new law regulating inmates' request for post-conviction DNA testing); Bai, *Cold Case*

convicted defendants have obtained post-conviction relief based on exculpatory DNA tests.[32] Understandably, there is a rapidly growing body of literature exploring the forensic utility of DNA techniques.[33] As the literature documents,

---

Confidential: Old Murder Cases Are Being Reopened — and Solved, NEWSWEEK, Jan. 12, 1998, at 70.

32. Dedman, *Sometimes DNA Testing Provides Path to Freedom*, HOUSTON CHRONICLE, Apr. 19, 1999, p. 3A (Dennis Fritz and Ronald Williamson "are the 61st and 62nd inmates exonerated by DNA evidence in the United States, according to the Justice Department"); Gross, *Lost Lives: Miscarriages of Justice*, 42 LAW QUAD. Notes 82, 83 (Spr. 1999) ("Since 1992 at least 53 defendants — most convicted rapists — have been exonerated by DNA identification evidence; most of them were released after spending years in prison").

33. Eriksen, Bertelsen & Svensmark, *Statistical Analysis of the Measurement Errors in the Determination of Fragment Length in DNA-RFLP Analysis*, 52 FORENSIC SCI. INT'L 181 (1992); Gyllensten, Josefsson, Schemschat, Saldeen & Petterson, *DNA Typing of Forensic Material with Mixed Genotypes Using Allele-Specific Enzymatic Amplification (Polymerase Chain Reaction)*, 52 FORENSIC SCI. INT'L 149 (1992); Akane, Seki, Shiono, Nakamura, Hasegawa, Kagawa, Matsubara, Nakahori, Nagtafuchi & Nakagome, *Sex Determination of Forensic Samples by Dual PCR Amplification of an X-Y Homologous Gene*, 52 FORENSIC SCI. INT'L 143 (1992); Hochmeister, Budowle, Borer, Eggmann, Comey & Dirnhofer, *Typing of Deoxyribonucleic Acid (DNA) Extracted from Compact Bone from Human Remains*, 36 J. FORENSIC SCI. 1649 (1991); Walsh, Fildes, Louie & Higuchi, *Report of the Blind Trial of the Cetus AmpliType HLA DQ Forensic Deoxyribonucleic Acid (DNA) Amplification and Typing Kit*, 36 J. FORENSIC SCI. 1551 (1991); Adams, Presley, Baumstark, Hensley, Hill, Anoe, Campbell, McLaughlin, Budowle, Giusti, Smerick & Baechtel, *Deoxyribonucleic Acid (DNA) Analysis by Restriction Fragment Length Polymorphisms of Blood and Other Body Fluid Stains Subjected to Contamination and Environmental Insults*, 36 J. FORENSIC SCI. 1284 (1991); Waye, Michaud, Bowen & Fourney, *Sensitive and Specific Quantification of Human Genomic Deoxyribonucleic Acid (DNA) in Forensic Science Specimens: Casework Examples*, 36 J. FORENSIC SCI. 1198 (1991); Schwartz, Schwartz, Mieszerski, McNally & Kobilinsky, *Characterization of Deoxyribonucleic Acid (DNA) Obtained from Teeth Subjected to Various Environmental Conditions*, 36 J. FORENSIC SCI. 979 (1991); Verbovaya & Ivanov, *"Sexing" Deoxyribonucleic Acid (DNA) on DNA Fingerprint Gel: An Internal Control for DNA Fingerprint Evidence*, 36 J. FORENSIC SCI. 991 (1991); Pascali, Dobosz & Pescarmona, *Estimating Allele Frequencies of Hypervariable DNA Systems*, 51 FORENSIC SCI. INT'L 273 (1991); Westwood & Werrett, *An Evaluation of the Polymerase Chain Reaction Method for Forensic Applications*, 45 FORENSIC SCI. INT'L 201 (1990); Yokoi & Sagisaka, *Haptoglobin Typing of Human Bloodstains Using a Specific DNA Probe*, 45 FORENSIC SCI. INT'L 39 (1990); Shacker, Schneider, Holtkamp, Bohnke, Fimmers, Sonneborn & Rittner, *Isolation of the DNA Minisatellite Probe MZ 1.3 and Its Application to DNA "Fingerprinting" Analysis*, 44 FORENSIC SCI. INT'L 209 (1990); Haglund, Reay & Tepper, *Identification of Decomposed Human Remains by Deoxyribonucleic Acid (DNA) Profiling*, 35 J. FORENSIC SCI. 724 (1990); Medeiros, Macedo & Pena, *M13 Bioprints: Non-Isotopic Detection of Individual-Specific Human DNA Fingerprints with Biotinylated M13 Bacteriophage*, 43 FORENSIC SCI. INT'L 275 (1989); Yokoi & Sagisaka, *Sex Determination of Blood Stains with a Recombinant DNA Probe: Comparison with Radioactive and Non-Radioactive Labeling Methods*, 41 FORENSIC SCI. INT'L 117 (1989); Kobayashi & Matsuzawa, *Sex Determination of Bloodstains by the Use of a Ribonucleic Acid (RNA) Probe*, 34 J. FORENSIC SCI. 1078 (1989); McNally, Shaler, Baird, Balazs, DeForest & Kobilinsky, *Evaluation of Deoxyribonucleic Acid (DNA) Isolated from Human Bloodstains Exposed to Ultraviolet Light, Heat, Humidity, and Soil Contamination*, 34 J. FORENSIC SCI. 1059 (1989) ("under the conditions

several distinct DNA technologies have emerged,[34] and more are on the horizon. The cutting edge today is forecast to be the SNP chip, a small device for analyzing single nucleotide polymarkers. SNP will enable police to do some DNA typing at the crime scene itself. While that technology is just around the corner, several technologies are already mature and in widespread use.

However, before reviewing those technologies, as Chapter 3 of the 1992 N.R.C. report cautions, it must be emphasized that all "the DNA typing [technologies] used today examine only a few sites of variations ...." Section 18-2 pointed out that there are roughly three billion base pairs in the 46 chromosomes. Even the most thorough DNA technologies examine only a very small fraction of the total base pairs. That limitation leaves open the "chance that two persons have DNA patterns (*i.e.*, genetic types) that match at the small number of sites examined." The analyst generally does not testify that a match conclusively identifies a person; rather, as a scientist, the analyst must couch his or her opinion as a probability statement.

Subsection (A) deals with multi locus RFLP testing, the technique originally imported from England and which was sharply criticized in the 1992 National

---

studied, the integrity of DNA is not altered such that false RFLP patterns are obtained"); Honma, Yoshii, Ishiyama, Mitani, Kominami & Muramatsu, *Individual Identification from Semen by the Deoxyribonucleic Acid (DNA) Technique*, 34 J. FORENSIC SCI. 222 (1989); Fowler, Burgoyne, Scott & Harding, *Repetitive Deoxyribonucleic Acid (DNA) and Human Genome Variation — A Concise Review Relevant to Forensic Biology*, 33 J. FORENSIC SCI. 1111 (1988); He, Jiang, Lu, Wang, Zhu, Wang, Shen, Gao, Liu & Wu, *A Study of Sex Identification of Trace, Dried Bloodstains Using a Y-Chromosome-Specific Deoxyribonucleic Acid (DNA) Probe*, 34 J. FORENSIC SCI. 346 (1989); Kobayashi, Nakauchi, Nakahori, Nakagome & Matsuzawa, *Sex Identification in Fresh Blood and Dried Bloodstains by a Nonisotopic Deoxyribonucleic Acid (DNA) Analyzing Technique*, 33 J. FORENSIC SCI. 613 (1988); Fukushima, Hasekura & Nagai, *Identification of Male Bloodstains by Dot Hydridization of Human Y Chromosome-Specific Deoxyribonucleic Acid (DNA) Probe*, 33 J. FORENSIC SCI. 621 (1988); Honma, Yoshi, Ishiyamama, Mitani, Kominami & Muramatsu, *Individual Identification from Semen by the Deoxyribonucleic Acid (DNA) Fingerprint Technique*, 34 J. FORENSIC SCI. 222 (1989); Odelberg, Demers, Westin & Hossaini, *Establishing Paternity Using Minisatellite DNA Probes When the Putative Father is Unavailable for Testing*, 33 J. FORENSIC SCI. 921 (1988); Bar, Kratzer, Machler & Schmid, *Postmortem Stability of DNA*, 39 FORENSIC SCI. INT'L 59 (1988); Sensabaugh, *Forensic Biology — Is Recombinant DNA Technology in its Future?*, 31 J. FORENSIC SCI. 393 (1986); Kantner, Baird, Shaler & Balazs, *Analysis of Restriction Fragment Length Polymorphisms in Deoxyribonucleic Acid (DNA) Recovered from Dried Bloodstains*, 31 J. FORENSIC SCI. 403 (1986); Giusti, Baird, Pasquale, Balazs & Glassberg, *Application of Deoxyribonucleic Acid (DNA) Polymorphisms to the Analysis of DNA Recovered from Sperm*, 31 J. FORENSIC SCI. 409 (1986); Altman, *New DNA Test Offers Biological "Fingerprints" For Crime Fight*, N.Y. TIMES, Feb. 4, 1986, at Y19.

34. *See generally* Thompson & Ford, *DNA Typing: Acceptance and Weight of the New Genetic Identification Tests*, 75 VA. L. REV. 45 (1989); Thompson & Ford, *DNA Typing: Promising Forensic Technique Needs Additional Validation*, 24 TRIAL 56 (Sept. 1988); 15 CRIME LAB. DIGEST (Jan. 1988). It must be emphasized that none of the existing technologies analyze the person's entire sequence of base pairs.

Research Council report. That criticism led to the shift to both single locus RFLP testing and PCR, discussed respectively in subsections (B) and (C). The first part of subsection (C) deals with the early reverse dot blot PCR procedure while the balance of the subsection discusses the now dominant, third generation technologies, notably STR.

§ 18-3(A). Multi Locus Restriction Fragment Length Polymorphism.

As Figure 18-2 indicates, one technology is multi locus restriction fragment length polymorphism (RFLP).[35] This was the first generation DNA test and is generally not used in contemporary forensic testing. However, a discussion of this technology is helpful to an understanding of both the more modern technologies and the reasons why the forensic laboratories shifted to the new technologies.

Alex Jeffreys of the United Kingdom, one of the pioneers in DNA typing, originally used multi locus probes. In the United States, Cellmark Diagnostics of Germantown, Maryland employed this procedure. The use of this procedure requires a relatively large sample, that is, roughly between one and three micrograms of relatively undegraded DNA. After the DNA is extracted from the sample, the procedure entails the use of restriction endonucleases (RE), enzymes which can cleave DNA. The REs have been called biological scissors. The REs cleave DNA only at specific recognition sites; that is, the RE cuts the DNA only if a specific base sequence is present. Thus, the RE HAE III cleaves the DNA only when it recognizes a specific nucleotide sequence, namely, GGCC. HAE III is a naturally occurring product found in specific bacteria. HAE III can be used to cleave the DNA ladder between the G nucleotide and the C nucleotide.[36] If the test is conducted properly, the RE should cut the same person's DNA in the same places every time and, hence, produce the same fragments.

In RFLP testing, the key step is measuring the length of the fragments in the two samples being compared. Different persons tends to have a different number of base pairs between the restriction sites recognized and cut by the RE. The fragments have short sequences of base pairs repeated over and over again — variable number tandem repeats (VNTRs). While "recognized" rung sequences

---

35. Hockmeister, Budowle & Baechtel, *Effects of Presumptive Test Reagents on the Ability to Obtain Restriction Fragment Length Polymorphism (RFLP) Patterns from Human Blood and Semen Stains*, 36 J. FORENSIC SCI. 656 (1991); Zhang, Lan, Huo, Duan & Kobilinsky, *Restriction Fragment Length Polymorphism Analysis of Forensic Science Casework in the People's Republic of China*, 36 J. FORENSIC SCI. 531 (1991).

36. Benzinger, Emerek, Grigsby, Duewer, Lovekamp, Deadman, Thompson, Sallee & Riech, *Products of Partial Digestion with Hae III. Part 1. Characterization, Casework Experience and Confirmation of the Theory of Three-, Four- and Five-Banded RFLP Pattern Origins Using Partial Digestion*, 42 J. FORENSIC SCI. 850 (1997); Duewer & Benzinger, *Products of Partial Digestion with Hae III. Part 2. Quantification*, 42 J. FORENSIC SCI. 864 (1997).

are known to determine visible traits such as hair color and nonvisible traits such as insulin production, VNTRs are "anonymous" sequences; they have not yet been demonstrated to determine any traits. For that reason, VNTRs are sometimes referred to as "junk" DNA. The number of VNTR repetitions between the recognition sites tend to vary among individuals.[37] The cleaved DNA fragments range in size from a few hundred to several thousand base pairs; fragments are measured in kilobases (kb) (thousands of bases).[38]

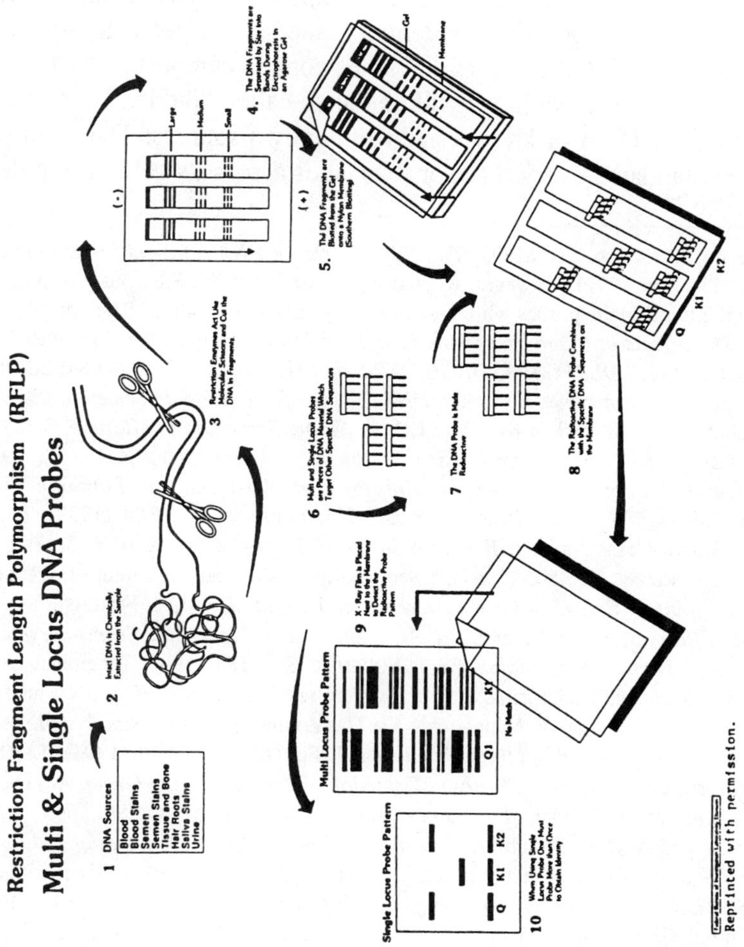

Figure 18-2

37. Thompson & Ford, *Is DNA Fingerprinting Ready for the Courts?*, 125 New Scientist 38, 39 (Mar. 31, 1990).

38. Comment, *DNA Fingerprinting: A Guide to Admissibility and Use*, 57 Mo. L. Rev. 501, 504 n.24 (1992).

After the DNA has been extracted and fragmented, electrophoresis is used to separate the fragments. DNA fragments are negatively charged. The fragments are placed on a gel; the laboratory might use a 14 cm gel length with 1% agarose solution and subject the DNA fragments to 32 volts for 16 hours. Once placed in the gel, the fragments move toward the positive pole or end. The gel plate or sheet is roughly five inches long, four inches wide, and one-quarter inch thick. The longer fragments move more slowly in the gel than the shorter fragments. The analyst usually places more than one sample in the same gel. There are three types of lanes on the gel. One evidential "lane" in the gel will contain the DNA sample being tested. Other evidential lanes contain samples from the suspect and victim. Thirdly, still other lanes will be the so-called "ladder," control, or marker lanes containing DNA of known size from known sources. The laboratory might run marker standards every three or four lanes across its gel.[39] If the defendant is

---

39. The F.B.I. does so. See Miller, *The FBI's Forensic DNA Analysis Program*, 60 F.B.I. LAW ENF. BULL. 11 (July 1991). However, it must be stressed that the F.B.I. uses single locus probes rather than the multi locus probes which are the focus of this subsection. Brauner, Shpitzen, Freund & Manny, *The Effects of Blood Transfusions on PCR DNA Typing at the CSF1PO, TPOX, THO1, D1S80, HLA-DQA1, LDLR, GYPA, HBGG, D7S8 and GC Loci*, 42 J. FORENSIC SCI. 1154 (1997); Skinker, Warnecke, Morrow & Hunsaker, *DNA Typing of Azoospermic Semen at the D1S80 Locus*, 42 J. FORENSIC SCI. 718 (1997); Kreike & Lehner, *Rapid Screening of Multiple Forensic Stains by SSCP Analysis of HLA-DQa Amplification Products*, 42 J. FORENSIC SCI. 715 (1997); Romero, Juston, Ballantyne & Henry, *The Applicability of Formalin-Fixed and Formalin Fixed Paraffin Embedded Tissues in Forensic DNA Analysis*, 42 J. FORENSIC SCI. 708 (1997); Dimo-Simonin, Grange & Brandt-Casadevall, *PCR-Based Forensic Testing of DNA from Stained Cytological Smears*, 42 J. FORENSIC SCI. 506 (1997); Sweet, Lorente, Valenzuela, Lorente & Villanueva, *PCR-Based DNA Typing of Saliva Stains Recovered from Human Skin*, 42 J. FORENSIC SCI. 447 (1997); Shipp et al., *Effects of Argon Laser Light, Alternate Source Light, and Cyano-acrylate Fuming on DNA Typing of Human Bloodstains*, 38 J. FORENSIC SCI. 184 (1993) (chemical treatment of a surface to develop latent fingerprints did not interfere with subsequent PCR DNA analysis of stains on the surface); Hananoka & Minaguchi, *Sex Determination from Blood and Teeth by PCR Amplification of the Alphoid Satellite Family*, 41 J. FORENSIC SCI. 855 (1996); Liechti-Gallati & Neeser, *Efficient and Reliable PCR-Based Detection of the ABO Blood Group Alleles: Genotyping on Stamps and Other Biological Evidence Samples*, 41 J. FORENSIC SCI. 653 (1996); Akane, Yoshimura, Yoshida, Okii, Watabiki, Matsubara & Kimura, *ABO Genotyping Following a Single PCR Amplification*, 41 J. FORENSIC SCI. 272 (1996); Ladd, Bourke, Scherczinger, Pagliaro, Gaensslen & Lee, *A PCR-Based Strategy for ABO Genotype Determination*, 41 J. FORENSIC SCI. 134 (1996); Pai, Chou, Yang & Tang, *Flow Chart HLA-DQA1 Genotyping and Its Application to a Forensic Case*, 40 J. FORENSIC SCI. 228 (1995); Arroyo, Garcia-Sanchez, Gomez-Reino, Cuesta & Vicario, *Prenatal Exclusion of Paternity by PCR-FLP Analysis of VNTR*, 39 J. FORENSIC SCI. 566 (1994); Yamamoto, Tamaki, Kojima, Uchihi & Katsumata, *Potential Forensic Applications of Minisatellite Variant Repeat (MVR) Mapping Using the Poly-merase Chain Reaction (PCR) at D1S8*, 39 J. FORENSIC SCI. 743 (1994); Ivey, Atchison & Georgalis, *Assessment of PCR of the D17S30 Locus for Forensic Identification*, 39 J. FORENSIC SCI. 52 (1994); Akane, Shiono, Matsubara, Nakamura, Hasegawa & Kagawa, *Purification of Forensic Specimens for the Polymerase Chain Reaction (PCR) Analysis*, 38 J. FORENSIC SCI. 691 (1993); Tsongalis, Coleman, Esch, Smith & Kaufman, *Identification of Human DNA in Complex Biological Samples Using the*

suspected to be the source of the unknown DNA sample, known DNA from the defendant will be included in one of the lanes. The end result of the electrophoretic stage is an array of fragments--different sized fragments in various positions in the agarose gel.

The analyst then transfers the array of DNA fragments onto a nylon membrane by a method known as Southern transfer. A reservoir of buffer is placed underneath the gel, and absorbent membrane is positioned on top of the gel. The membrane is placed on top of the gel, and capillary action of the buffer transfers the fragments from the gel onto the membrane where they bind to the membrane in the same positions they previously occupied on the gel.

Before this step of the procedure, the DNA is treated with heat or a chemical which causes the double helix to separate into single strands. This separation is called denaturation; most contemporary laboratories use chemical denaturation rather than heat. The double strand is "unzipped" into single strands.

At this point, the membrane is ready for hybridization. The analyst uses a multi locus probe to identify the DNA fragments present.[40] The probe is a strand of cloned DNA of a known length and nucleotide sequence. The probe acts like a magnet that can bind with specific sequences in the DNA fragments. The probes lock onto or hybridize with complementary DNA fragments. As previously stated, there are bonding rules; A will attach only to T, and C will bind only with G. Thus, when a probe of known sequence bonds with the fragment, the analyst can deduce the sequence of the fragment. To facilitate later visualization, the probes can be tagged with radioactive material such as phosphorous^{32} which gives off beta radiation. In other words, as in this example, the probes were labeled with radioactive isotopes. However, Chapter 1 of the 1992 N.R.C. report pointed out that "attention is increasingly being given to nonisotopic labeling." Chemiluminescent detection is now replacing isotopic labeling,[41] in part because it is simply safer for laboratory personnel to work with non-radioactive material. Chemiluminescence causes the fragments to emit light and allows the fragments to be visualized on the autorad.

After hybridization, the membrane is washed. DNA fragments which have not hybridized will wash away. Only the hybridized fragments remain. To visualize the remaining array, the analyst uses autoradiography. The analyst places the blot

---

Alu Polymerase Chain Reaction, 38 J. FORENSIC SCI. 961 (1993); Roewer & Epplen, *Rapid and Sensitive Typing of Forensic Stains by PCR Amplification of Polymorphic Simple Repeat Sequences in Case Work*, 53 FORENSIC SCI. INT'L 163 (1992); Lee & Chang, *ABO Genotyping by Polymerase Chain Reaction*, 37 J. FORENSIC SCI. 1269 (1992).

40. Nelson, Benzinger, Budzynski, Boodee, Matthews, Buel, Schwartz, von Beroldingen, Wampler, Coons, Bixby, Frank & Metzger, *Validation of Probe EFD52 (D17S26) for Forensic DNA Analysis*, 41 J. FORENSIC SCI. 557 (1996).

41. Johnson & Kotowski, *Chemiluminescent Detection of RFLP Patterns in Forensic DNA Analysis*, 41 J. FORENSIC SCI. 569 (1996).

on a piece of X-ray film; the radioactive tags produce bands, marking the remaining fragments. The marks on the autoradiograph are said to resemble the bar codes in a grocery store although in truth the marks are much less distinct. Multi locus probes may produce 15 or more interpretable bands. The autoradiograph will depict the bands for both the DNA sample being tested and the known DNA in the other electrophoresis lanes.

If two DNA samples originate from the same source, the bands from the two samples should match with respect to *both* their length and their position on the gel; the positions ought to match, and in turn the size of the DNA fragment determines the position of the band on the gel. Simply stated, the key to declaring a match is finding that the same sized fragments are in the same position on both autorads. The analyst must carefully measure each band on the autoradiograph. Some laboratories measure the band twice and record the average value rather than both actual measurements. The analyst must determine whether the bands from the unknown DNA match those from the defendant's DNA. Subsection 18-3(B) discusses the standards which Lifecodes and the F.B.I. laboratory used in the past to declare a match with single locus probes.

Although the development of multi-locus probe RFLP was a major breakthrough, the technique has weaknesses. Due to the large number of bands on autorads produced by multi locus probes, the autorads can be difficult to interpret. Moreover, as we shall see, when the probe hydridizes to proximate sites on the same chromosome, it is doubtful whether there is adequate assurance of the independence of the markers. The markers must be independent if the analyst contemplates using the multiplication or product rule to compute the random match probability. Precisely because of that difficulty and doubt, in its 1992 report the N.R.C. committee recommended the use of single locus probes. In forensic work, multi locus RFLP is practically passé. The 1992 report motivated the forensic laboratories to adopt the technologies described in the ensuing subsections.

§ 18-3(B). Single Locus Restriction Fragment Length Polymorphism.

Another technique is the second generation test, single locus restriction fragment length polymorphism (RFLP).[42] Single locus probe RFLP has largely supplanted the first generation test. Lifecodes Corporation of Stamford, Connecticut relies on single locus RFLP, also illustrated by Figure 18-2. In this

---

42. Schneider, Fimmers, Woodroffe, Werrett, Bar, Brinkman, Eriksen, Jones, Kloosterman, Mevag, Pascal, Rittner, Schmitter, Thomson & Gill, *Report of a European Collaborative Exercise Comparing DNA Typing Results Using a Single Locus VNTR Probe*, 49 FORENSIC SCI. INT'L 1 (1991); Lewis, Kouri, Latorra, Berka, Lee & Gaensslen, *Restriction Fragment Length Polymorphism DNA Analysis by the FBI Protocol Using a Simple, Convenient Hardware System*, 35 J. FORENSIC SCI. 1186 (1990).

procedure, each test produces only one or two bands. The autoradiographs are therefore somewhat easier to interpret than the patterns produced by multi locus RFLP. To generate high probabilities, the analysts run several tests. Each time the analysts search for a different site on a different chromosome. For example, the analyst might use a probe for D2S44–a certain position on the second chromosome.

In the past, Lifecodes has announced the following rule for declaring a match:

> Allele fragment size measurements, expressed in kilobase pairs have a standard deviation of 0.6%. Fragments with measurements that are within approximately 2% of each other (3 standard deviations or 99.7% confidence level) are considered indistinguishable....

Under this rule, two bands are considered matching if their measurements do not differ by more than +/- 1.8%. Thus, a band length of 1,000 kilobases would be deemed or declared to match bands with lengths ranging from 982 kilobase pairs to 1,018 base pairs. Similarly, the F.B.I. laboratory uses a + /- 2.5% window for determining a match.[43] These laboratories employ match windows because as exacting as this process seems, there are limitations to scientific measurements. Each laboratory must validate a match window for its hardware and procedures; in repeated tests, the laboratory determines the difference in measurement to be expected even when fragments from a known same source are being measured. However, reliance on a match window precludes the analyst from testifying that a particular person is definitely the source of the DNA sample. As DNA researcher Professor Robert Tait of the University of California at Davis has pointed out, if the window is between 982 and 1,018, there are actually 36 different sized fragments which fall within the range and would be declared a match.

In 1992 the N.R.C. committee recommended the use of single locus probes. Chapter 2 of the report stressed that such probes produce fewer bands and thereby simplify interpretation of the autorad. Moreover, since with each probe the analyst can test a different chromosome, there is greater assurance that the probes will detect independent alleles. The use of probes targeting different chromosomes reduces the risk of linkage disequilibrium. In most cases, after declaring a match, the laboratory resorts to the multiplication or product rule (discussed in Chapter 15) to generate a statistical evaluation of the significance of the match. It is appropriate to employ that rule only when the individual probabilities being multiplied are independent. According to our reviewer, at one time roughly 90% of the laboratories conducting DNA typing used single locus

---

43. *But see* Grunbaum, *A Foundational Objection to DNA Evidence: A Critique of the FBI's Process for Self-Validation of Methods for Protein and DNA Genetic Marker Typing of Biological Evidence*, 21 CACJ FORUM, No. 3, p. 66 (1994).

probes. The laboratories tested the DNA by using between four or more probes. However, the shift to single locus RFLP was by no means the terminus of the evolution of the technology. The vast majority of laboratories have moved on and now use the PCR techniques detailed in the following subsection.

§ 18-3(C). Polymerase Chain Reaction, including AMP-FLP and STR.

A third technology is the polymerase chain reaction (PCR).[44] DQAlpha PCR testing figured prominently at the criminal trial of O.J. Simpson. Cetus Corporation of Emeryville, California, was the holder of the original patent for this technique, known as polymerase chain reaction (PCR) which essentially amplifies DNA sequences. According to Chapter 2 of the 1992 N.R.C. report, "PCR [was then] a relatively new technique in molecular biology, having come into common use in research laboratories only in the last 4 years." This technique is illustrated by Figure 18-3. Suppose, for example, that the DNA sample is too small to be analyzed by RFLP. On that assumption, PCR could nevertheless be used; this technique requires considerably less biological material than either RFLP procedure.

There are various types of PCR techniques In the final analysis, PCR is simply an amplification technique--a kind of molecular Xeroxing. It must be used in conjunction with an identification procedure such as dot blot or fragment length sizing. Dot blot was the original state of the PCR technology while fragment length sizing, notably STR, has recently become dominant.

Amplification Followed by Dot Blot

The PCR process consists of three steps: denaturation, annealing, and extension. The double helix is separated by heating, yielding two separate single strands of complementary DNA. A primer is then added. A primer is a series of nucleotides of known sequence. The primer anneals to the single strand of DNA produced by denaturation. That strand serves as the mold or template for the

---

44. Matsumoto, Tsuruya, Tsuda, Orihara & Kubo, *Japanese Population Study of a Y-Linked Dinucleotide Repeat DNA Polymorphism*, 44 J. FORENSIC SCI. 588 (1999); Schyma, Huckenbeck & Bonte, *DNA-PCR Analysis of Bloodstains Sampled by the Polyvinyl-Alcohol Method*, 44 J. FORENSIC SCI. 95 (1999); Belgrader, Smith, Weedn & Northrup, *Rapid PCR for Identity Testing Using a Battery-Powered Miniature Thermal Cycler*, 43 J. FORENSIC SCI. 315 (1998); Lee, Pagliaro, Berka, Folk, Anderson, Ruano, Keith, Phipps, Herrin, Garner & Gaensslen, *Genetic Markers in Human Bone: I. Deoxyribonucleic Acid (DNA) Analysis*, 36 J. FORENSIC SCI. 320 (1991); Kasai, Nakamura & White, *Amplification of a Variable Number of Tandem Repeats (VNTR) Locus (pMCT118) by the Polymerase Chain Reaction (PCR) and Its Application to Forensic Science*, 35 J. FORENSIC SCI. 1196 (1990).

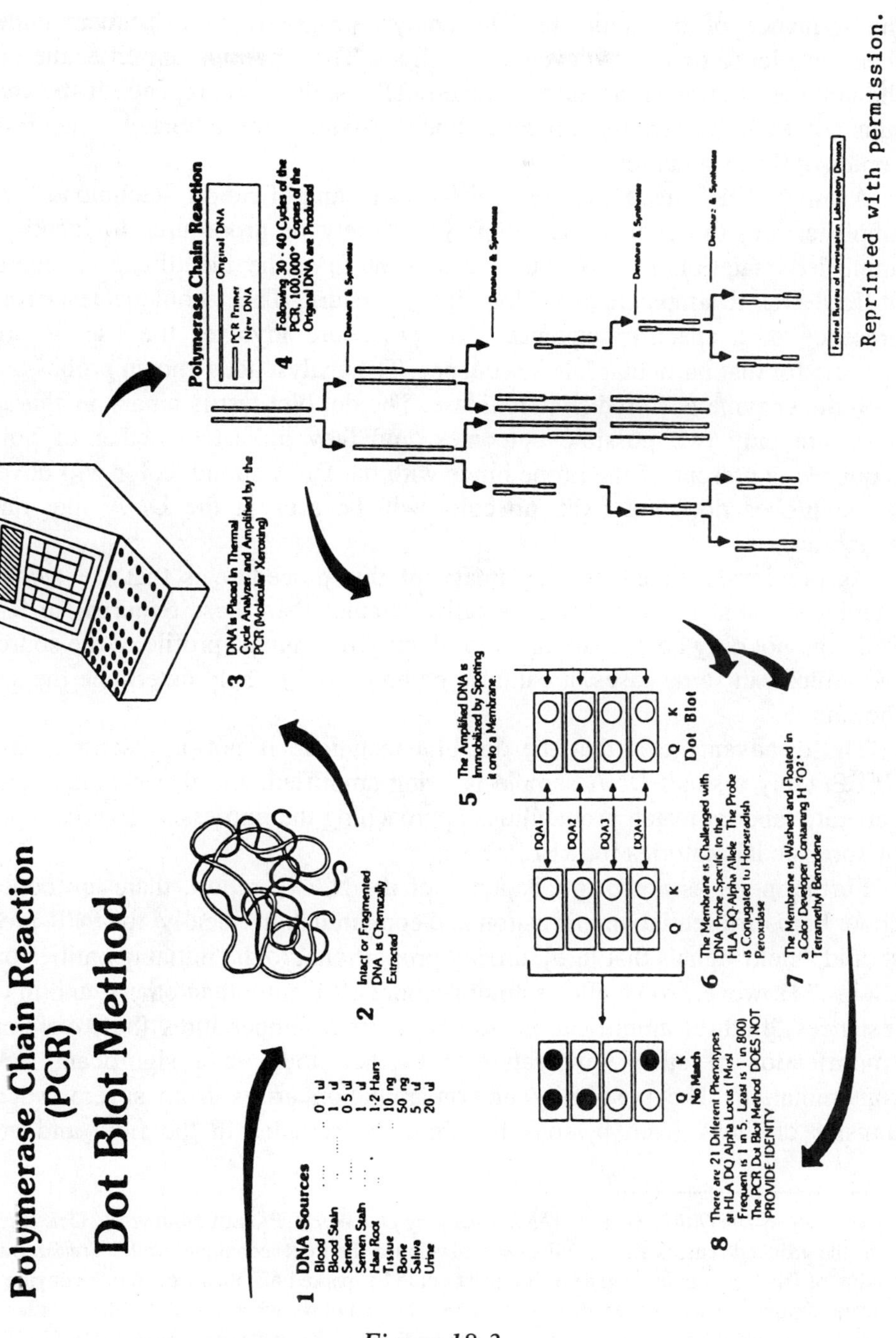

Figure 18-3

amplification process. The addition of the polymerase synthesizes a new DNA strand in the extension step. The sequence of the new DNA strand is dictated by the sequence of the template. The analyst programs an instrument called a thermocycler to repeat this cycle many times. The repetition amplifies the DNA; the number of strands increases geometrically as the cycle repeats. If the analyst runs 20 PCR cycles, the process should produce approximately one million copies of the original template.[45]

Again, PCR itself is essentially an amplification technique. After amplification, the analyst can employ a variety of procedures to identify the amplified material. As previously stated, at first, the identification technique utilized was a simple reverse dot blot procedure. The technique tests for the presence of a specific sequence. The procedure involves the use of probes specific for that particular DNA sequence. The analyst adds known probes tagged with the enzyme horseradish peroxidase. The dot blot test is binary in character; there are only two possible outcomes, and they indicate whether or not the sequence is present. If the probe binds with the DNA strand, color will develop; if the probes does not bind, no color will be seen at the DNA spot on the membrane.

As previously stated, the advantage of this procedure is that the technique enables the analyst to test much smaller samples than those required for RFLP. PCR can not only be used to partially identify the genetic profile of the source of the sample; in some cases, it can also be employed to help determine the sex of the source.[46]

The disadvantage is that the dot blot technique is not as discriminating as RFLP. Only a small DNA sample is being amplified, and the technique cannot generate random match probabilities approaching the impressive figures reported by forensic laboratories for RFLP tests.

Furthermore, as noted in Chapter 2 of the N.R.C. report, there are concerns about both differential amplification and contamination. Ideally, the PCR process should "yield signals that [are] directly proportional to the initial quantities of the alleles." However, some alleles amplify more efficiently than others; and in other instances "faithful amplification occurs at some temperatures [but] differential amplification at other temperatures." Further, there is a significant risk of contamination. The possibility of contamination arises from several sources: transfer of DNA from persons handling the samples in the field and at the

45. Dwyer, *The Quirky Genius Who Is Changing Our World*, PARADE MAGAZINE, Oct. 10, 1993, p. 8 (the article discusses Kary Mullis, who developed the PCR technique; Mullis "realized that a section of DNA containing a gene or fragment could be marked off, then forced into copying itself – using replicating techniques similar to those DNA employs when a cell divides"; "after eight doublings, he would have 256 copies of the gene. By the 20th cycle, he'd have 1,048,576. By the 30th, he'd be up to 1,073,741,824....").

46. Roy & Steffens, *Infrared Fluorescent Detection of PCR Amplified Gender Identifying Alleles*, 42 J. FORENSIC SCI. 452 (1997); Finch, Hope & Daal, *Human Sex Determination Using Multiplex Polymerase Chain Reaction (PCR)*, 36 SCIENCE & JUSTICE 93 (1996).

laboratory, and carryover contamination by PCR products from prior amplifications. In light of these risks, Chapter 2 of the 1992 National Research Council report mentioned the "safeguard" of having "DNA typing independently performed in two laboratories ...." The report recommended "independent replication of results — at least during the early stages of this technology."[47]

PCR technology is no longer in its "early stages." Although the 1992 report was critical of the state of the PCR art, PCR has since gained support. The DNA Commission of the International Society for Forensic Haemogenetics released standardized guidelines for PCR-based technologies.[48] Moreover, 1993 witnessed the publication of a substantial article urging greater judicial receptivity to PCR evidence.[49] The article attempted to meet many of the attacks on PCR, including the criticisms that allelic dropout might exist,[50] there is a serious risk of contamination,[51] initially only a small number of laboratories employed PCR,[52] and on occasion PCR test results can be difficult to interpret.[53] Most importantly, in 1996 the National Research Council of the N.R.C. released a new report entitled *The Evaluation of Forensic DNA Evidence*. Chapter 2 of the report describes the use of PCR testing with dot blot and notes the extensive, post-1992 research.

Polymarker (PM) kits have been used for some time for PCR testing.[54] As in DQAlpha PCR testing, the analyst uses PCR amplification to prepare the sample and then employs the reverse dot blot procedure to determine whether the two

---

47. *But see* Fildes & Reynolds, *Consistency and Reproducibility of AmpliType PM Results Between Seven Laboratories: Field Trial Results*, 40 J. FORENSIC SCI. 279 (1995) ("No samples were typed incorrectly").

48. *Editorial*, 55 FORENSIC SCI. INT'L 1 (1992).

49. MacKnight, *The Polymerase Chain Reaction (PCR): The Second Generation of DNA Analysis Methods Takes the Stand*, 9 COMPUTER & HIGH TECH. L.J. 287 (1993).

50. *Id.* at 314 (controlling the temperature of the test eliminates this risk).

51. *Id.* at 315-18 (the F.B.I. validation study debunks this criticism, and proper laboratory layout can minimize the risk).

52. *Id.* at 319 (there are thirty laboratories conducting PCR testing).

53. *Id.* at 320 (the use of differential analysis and a control dot reduce this problem).

54. Taylor, Challed-Spong & Johnson, *Co-amplification of the Amelogenin and HLA DQa Genes: Optimization and Validation*, 42 J. FORENSIC SCI. 130 (1997); Word, Sawosik & Bing, *Summary of Validation Studies from Twenty-Six Forensic Laboratories in the United States and Canada on the Use of the AmpliType PM PCR Amplification and Typing Kit*, 42 J. FORENSIC SCI. 39 (1997); Tsongalis, Anamani & Wu, *Identification of Urine Specimen Donors by the PM+DQA1 Amplification and Typing Kit*, 41 J. FORENSIC SCI. 1031 (1996); Gross & Guerrieri, *HLA DQA1 and Polymarker Validations for Forensic Casework: Standard Specimens, Reproducibility, and Mixed Specimens*, 41 J. FORENSIC SCI. 1022 (1996); Budowle, Koons & Errera, *Mutiplex Amplification and Typing Procedure for the Loci D1S80 and Amelogenin*, 41 J. FORENSIC SCI. 660 (1996); Grow, Phillips & Reynolds, *Post-Amplification Primer Extension of Heat-Denatured AmpliType PCR Products: Effects on Typing Results*, 41 J. FORENSIC SCI. 497 (1996); Crouse, Nippes & Ritzline, *Confirmation of PM Typing Protocols for Consistent and Reliable Results*, 41 J. FORENSIC SCI. 493 (1996).

samples contain the same DNA allele combinations. PM kits differ from DQAlpha PCR tests, though, in one respect: PM permits the simultaneous testing of five different markers.

Amplification Followed by Sizing Fragment Length

The preceding subsections pointed out the distinctive strengths of RFLP and PCR technology. As previously stated, PCR is an amplification technique pure and simple. The introduction to this chapter noted that today the forensic laboratories have developed new technologies which combine the amplification capability of PCR with the discriminatory power of RFLP.[55] In this technology, the analyst uses PCR amplification in a preliminary stage. However, as in conventional RFLP testing, the analyst then evaluates the amplified samples by sizing the fragments. The principal variations of this mode of PCR are AMP-FLP and STR analysis.

AMP-FLP. One technique is amplified-fragment length polymorphisms (AMP-FLP).[56] This technique analyzes markers such as D1S80. The technique is said to "combine PCR's ability to make many copies of DNA evidence with the resolving power that comes from examining fragment length polymorphisms, the principal strength of RFLP."[57] The technique involves "[a]mplification of fragment length polymorphisms."[58] Again, like PCR, this technique amplifies the sample – hence, the AMP. However, like RFLP, the identification of the markers present is based on "differences in length between alleles"[59] – thus, the FLP as in fragment length polymorphism or differences. In. conventional RFLP testing, the smallest VNTRs are usually 50 to 100 basepairs in length. In D1S80 testing, the

---

55. Ota, Katsuyama, Liu, Arakura & Fukushima, *Validation of HLA-DR Locus Typing in Forensic Specimens by Combining PCR-SSP with PCR-RFLP*, 42 J. FORENSIC SCI. 929 (1997).

56. Wallin, Buoncristiani, Lazaruk, Fildes, Holt & Walsh, *TWGDAM Validation of the AmpFISTR Blue PCR Amplification Kit for Forensic Casework Analysis*, 43 J. FORENSIC SCI. 854 (1998).

57. *DNA Technology Update*, 61 F.B.I. LAW ENF. BULL. 5 (Apr. 1992). *See also* Gross, Carmody & Guerrieri, *Validation Studies for the Genetic Typing of the D1S80 Locus for Implementation into Forensic Casework*, 42 J. FORENSIC SCI. 1140 (1997) (Amplitype PM PCR Amplification); Lorente, Lorente, Alvarez, Budowle, Wilson & Villanueva, *Sequential Multiplex Amplification: Utility in Forensic Casework with Minimal Amounts of DNA and Partially Degraded Samples*, 42 J. FORENSIC SCI. 923 (1997).

58. Cosso & Reynolds, *Validation of AmpliFLP D1S80 PCR Amplification Kit for Forensic Casework Analysis According to TWGDAM Guidelines*, 40 J. FORENSIC SCI. 424 (1995); Tsongalis, Anamani & Wu, *Identification of Urine Specimen Donors by the PM+DQA1 Amplification and Typing Kit*, 41 J. FORENSIC SCI. 1031 (1996); Yun & Yun, *Analysis of the VNTR Locus DXS52 by the Amp-FLP Technique*, 41 J. FORENSIC SCI. 859 (1996).

59. *Id. See also* Fildes & Reynolds, *Consistency and Reproducibility of AmpliType PM Results between Seven Laboratories: Field Trial Results*, 40 J. FORENSIC SCI. 279 (1995).

basic sequence includes 16 basepairs, and it varies from 14 to 41 repeats in length.

STR. Another technique in the vein of AMP-FLP is short tandem repeat (STR) analysis.[60] The STR procedure involves an initial step of simultaneous amplification of several loci.[61] As in D1S80 testing, the subsequent analytic step involves the measurement of the length of the fragment. The STR fragments are even shorter than those used in D1S80 testing; these micro-repeat-units vary from two to five basepairs in length. When 13 STR loci are used, the discriminatory power is comparable to that of four or more RFLP loci. While an RFLP analysis might take three weeks, an STR analysis can completed in as short a time as three days.

In 1996, the National Research Council released a second DNA report. Chapter 4 mentions all of these new techniques. After discussing the STR research, the draft specifically states that "STRs can take their place along with VNTRs as forensic tools."[62] STR research is progressing rapidly to refine the

---

60. Buel, Schwartz & LaFountain, *Capillary Electrophoresis STR Analysis: Comparison to Gel-Based Systems*, 43 J. FORENSIC SCI. 164 (1998); Menotti-Raymond, David, Stephens, Lyons & O'Brien, *Genetic Individualization of Domestic Cats Using Feline STR Loci for Forensic Applications*, 42 J. FORENSIC SCI. 1039 (1997); Kline, Duewer, Newall, Redman, Reeder & Richard, *Interlaboratory Evaluation of Short Tandem Repeat Triplex CTT*, 42 J. FORENSIC SCI. 897 (1997) ("[S]amples typed to the allelic name can now be validly compared regardless of analytical method. Interlaboratory comparison of raw allelic size remains problematic."); Budowle, Moretti, Keys, Koons & Smerick, *Validation Studies of the CTT STR Multiplex System*, 42 J. FORENSIC SCI. 701 (1997); Andersen & Bramble, *The Effects of Fingermark Enhancement Light Sources on Subsequent PCR-STR DNA Analysis of Fresh Bloodstains*, 42 J. FORENSIC SCI. 303 (1997); Pinheiro, Pontes, Gene, Huguet, da Costa & Moreno, *Population Study of the HUMTH01, HUMVWA31A, HUMF13A1, and HUMFES/FPS STR Polymorphisms in the North of Portugal*, 42 J. FORENSIC SCI. 121 (1997); Lucas, Munoz, Pintado & Solano, *Highly Informative Single-Stranded Conformation Polymorphism (SSCP) of Short Tanden Repeats in DNA Identification*, 42 J. FORENSIC SCI. 118 (1997); Micka, Sprecher, Lins, Comey, Koons, Crouse, Endean, Pirelli, Lee, Duda, Ma & Schumm, *Validation of Multiplex Polymorphic STR Amplification Sets Developed for Personal Identification Applications*, 41 J. FORENSIC SCI. 582 (1996); Glock, Schwartz, Schwartz-Jungl & Mayr, *Allelic Ladder Characterization of the Short Tandem Repeat Polymorphism in Intron 6 in the Lipoprotein Lipase Gene and Its Application in an Austrian Caucasian Population Study*, 41 J. FORENSIC SCI. 579 (1996); van Oorschot, Gutowski, Robinson, Hedley & Andrew, *HUMTH01 Validation Studies: Effect of Substrate, Environment, and Mixtures*, 41 J. FORENSIC SCI. 142 (1996).

61. Hochmeister, Budowle, Eisenberg, Borer & Dirnhofer, *Using Multiplex PCR Amplification and Typing Kits for the Analysis of DNA Evidence in a Serial Killer Case*, 41 J. FORENSIC SCI. 155, 157 (1996) (simultaneous amplification at three polymorphic STR loci); Anderson, Greenhalgh, Butler, Kilpatrick, Piercy, Way, Myhill, Wright, Hallett & Parkin, *Further Validation of a Multiplex STR System for Use in Routine Forensic Identity Testing*, 78 FORENSIC SCI. INT'L 47, 48 (1996) (quadruplex system for testing four loci).

62. NAT'L RESEARCH COUNCIL, THE EVALUATION OF FORENSIC DNA EVIDENCE 0-27 (Pre-pub. draft 1996).

technique,[63] including reducing interlaboratory variation in STR analysis[64] and developing population frequencies for the various STR markers.[65] STR testing is so popular that commercial kits are now on the market. At the moment, one of the most popular is the Profiler Plus kit from Perkin-Elmer Corporation.

It is likely that for the next five to ten years, STR will be the paramount DNA technology. Nationwide laboratories appreciate the need for standardization. If they can standardize their procedures, they can collaborate to build large databases which will both improve DNA typing and refine the statistical evaluation of DNA matches. STR analysis is faster than normal RFLP, and STR can generate random match probabilities much greater than those yielded by

---

63. Honda, Roewer & de Knijff, *Male DNA Typing from 25-Year-Old Vaginal Swabs Using Y Chromosomal STR Polymorphisms in a Retrial Request Case*, 44 J. FORENSIC SCI. 868 (1999); Frank & Llewellyn, *A Time Course Study on STR Profiles Derived from Human Bone, Muscle, and Bone Marrow*, 44 J. FORENSIC SCI. 778 (1999); Tun, Honda, Nakatome, Nakamura, Shimada, Ogura, Kuroki, Yamazaki, Terada & Matoba, *Simultaneous Detection of Multiple STR Loci on Sex Chromosomes for Forensic Testing of Sex and Identity*, 44 J. FORENSIC SCI. 772 (1999); Shutler, Gagnon, Verret, Kalyn, Korkosh, Johnston & Halverson, *Removal of a PCR Inhibitor and Resolution of DNA STR Types in Mixed Human-Canine Stains from a Five Year Old Case*, 44 J. FORENSIC SCI. 623 (1999); Foreman, Smith & Evett, *Bayesian Validation of a Quadruplex STR Profiling System for Identification Purposes*, 44 J. FORENSIC SCI. 478 (1999); Watanabe, Umetsu, Yuasa & Suzuki, *Simultaneous Determination of STR Polymorphism and a New Nucleotide Substitution in Its Flanking Region at the CD4 Locus*, 43 J. FORENSIC SCI. 733 (1998). The reader can find a wealth of information about STR at http://ibm4.carb.nist.gov:8800/dna/home.htm.

64. Kline, Duewer, Newall, Redman, Reeder & Richard, *Interlaboratory Evaluation of Short Tandem Repeat Triplex CTT*, 42 J. FORENSIC SCI. 897 (1997).

65. Bassner & Madea, *Allele and Genotype Frequencies for the STR Locus D18S51 in a Western German Population*, 44 J. FORENSIC SCI. 450 (1999); Kupferschmid, Calicchio & Budowle, *Maine Caucasian Population DNA Database Using Twelve Short Tandem Repeat Loci*, 44 J. FORENSIC SCI. 392 (1999); Marco, Martinez-Jarreta, Martinez, Sanchis & Fonseca, *Allele Frequency Distribution of the STR Loci HUMTPOX, HUMTHO1 and HUMVWA in Asturias (North Spain)*, 44 J. FORENSIC SCI. 389 (1999); Yamamoto, Uchihi, Nozawa, Huang, Leong, Tanaka, Miizutani, Tamaki & Katsumata, *Allele Distribution at Nine STR Loci — D3S1358, vWA, FGA, THO1, TPOX, CSF1PO, D5S818, D13S317 and D7S820 — in the Japanese Population by Multiplex PCR and Capillary Electrophoresis*, 44 J. FORENSIC SCI. 167 (1999); Fregeau, Bowen & Fourney, *Validation of Highly Polymorphic Fluorescent Multiplex Short Tanden Repeat Systems Using Two Generations of DNA Sequencers*, 44 J. FORENSIC SCI. 133 (1999); Crouse, Rogers, Amiott, Gibson & Masibay, *Analysis and Interpretation of Short Tandem Reepat Microvariants and Three-Banded Allele Patterns Using Multiple Allele Detection Systems*, 44 J. FORENSIC SCI. 87 (1999); Lins, Micka, Sprecher, Taylor, Bacher, Rabbach, Bever, Creacy & Schumm, *Development and Population Study of an Eight-Locus Short Tandem Repeat (STR) Multiplex System*, 43 J. FORENSIC SCI. 1168 (1998); Klintschar, Al-Hammadi, Lux & Reichenpfader, *Genetic Variation at the Short Tandem Repeat Loci HumvWA, HumFX111B, and HumFES/FPS in the Egyptian and Yemenian Populations*, 43 J. FORENSIC SCI. 805 (1998); Garofano, Lago, Vecchio, Pizzamiglio, Zanon, Virgili, Albonici, Manzari & Budowle, *Italian Population Data on the Polymarkers System and on Five Short Tandem Repeat Loci CSF1PO, TPOX, TH01, F13B, and vWA*, 43 J. FORENSIC SCI. 837 (1998).

traditional PCR analysis. The national Convicted Offender Database Information System (CODIS) is developing a database for 13 STRs. Many states are shifting to the same 13 STR database in order to coordinate with CODIS and accelerate the growth of the CODIS dababase.

§ 18-3(D). Direct DNA Sequencing.

Still another approach is direct DNA sequencing, illustrated by Figure 18-4. As in the case of RFLP and PCR analysis, there are several variations of the technique.

The traditional direct sequencing technique analyzes mitochondrial DNA, the DNA found in the energy producing centers of cells. The DNA sequences in certain portions of the double stranded mitochondrial DNA also appears to be very variable. The procedure is similar to PCR. As in PCR, a primer and a polymerase are used. However, this primer is specially designed:

> [T]he primers are fashioned so that they attach to only one of the two strands and in addition to the four DNA letters that serve as building blocks for the new strands, specially synthesized derivatives of the four letters are present also. Because each of the normal DNA letters is present in the reaction solution as well as the derivative letters, the potential exists for the DNA polymerase to incorporate a derivative letter into the synthesized strand instead of the normal letter. If a derivative letter is inserted, the synthesis of the strand ceases at that point. The termination of the growing DNA strands will occur each time a derivative letter is incorporated. The ratio of normal letters to derivatized letters is such that the synthesis of some strands will be terminated at each letter position in the strand, while other strands will not be terminated because normal letters have been incorporated.[66]

---

66. Baechtel, *A Primer on the Methods Used in the Typing of DNA*, 15 CRIME LAB. DIGEST SUPP. 3, 8-9 (1988). Mitochondrial DNA is robust, in large supply compared to nuclear DNA, highly variable, and amenable to PCR amplification. Savolainen, Rosen, Holmberg, Leitner, Uhlen & Lundeberg, *Sequence Analysis of Domestic Dog Mitochondrial DNA for Forensic Use*, 42 J. FORENSIC SCI. 593 (1997); Melton, Ginther, Sensabaugh, Soodyall & Stoneking, *Extent of Heterogeneity in Mitochondrial DNA of Sub-Saharan African Populations*, 42 J. FORENSIC SCI. 582 (1997); Melton, Wilson, Batzer & Stoneking, *Extent of Heterogeneity in Mitochondrial DNA of European Populations*, 42 J. FORENSIC SCI. 437 (1997) Queralt, Fabregues-Boixar, Adroer, Gene, Catalan, Huguet & Oliva, *Direct Sequencing of the Human Protamine P1 Gene and Application in Forensic Medicine*, 38 J. FORENSIC SCI. 1491 (1993). Two of the leading proponents of the technique are Mark Stoneking, Ph.D., of Penn State and his assistant, Ann Stone. *DNA: A New Kid on the DNA Block; mtDNA Hair Testing Takes Root*, 21 SCI. SLEUTHING REV. 12 (Fall 1997). The technique is especially suitable for hair analysis. The F.B.I. has been a leader in developing the technique although Cellmark Diagnostics is "gearing up" to begin using the technique. *Id.*

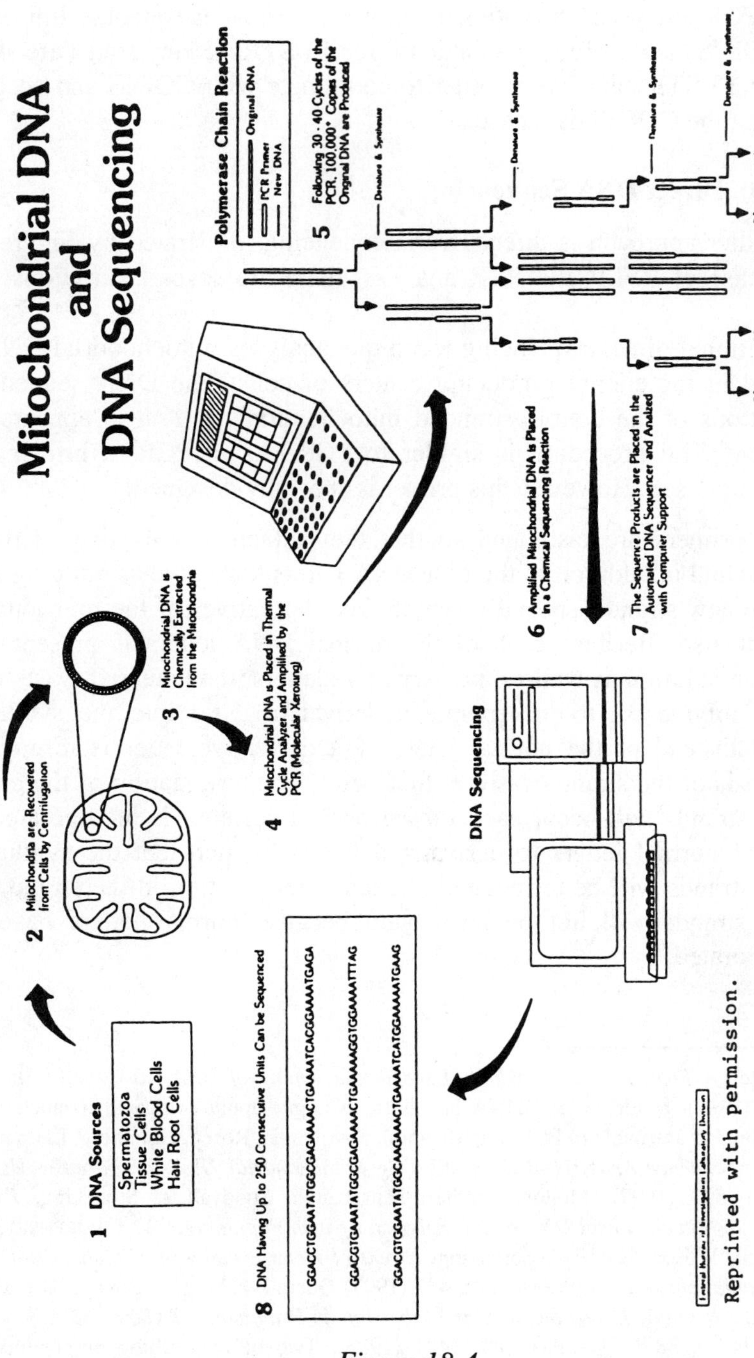

Figure 18-4

"[M]itochondrial DNA can be obtained from the shaft of a hair and not only from a hair root or follicle." *A mtDNA Miscue Exposed*, 21 SCI. SLEUTHING REV. 18 (Winter 1997).

When the synthetic phase ends, several synthesized DNA fragments of differing length will be present in the reaction tube. The last letter in each fragment is a derivative. The analyst then uses electrophoresis to separate the fragments. "The fastest moving fragments will be those whose synthesis was terminated when the DNA polymerase incorporated the first letter into the strand and did so with a derivative letter. The slowest ... will be those fragments (longest) that were not terminated until the last letter in the strand was reached and a derivative was incorporated."[67] In the procedure employed by several companies, as the fragments pass a fixed point in the electrophoretic gel, they are scanned. Each derivative letter is labeled with a distinctive fluorescent molecule, and the scanner identifies each derivative letter as it passes. The scanner thereby generates a complete sequence of the letters. Chapter 2 of the 1992 N.R.C. report speculated that direct sequencing may "ultimately be the optimal method of personal identification, but that is still far from practical."

A new technique, minisatellite variant repeat (MVR), is a variant of direct sequencing.[68] This technique also involves the use of PCR amplification as the preparation stage. However, after amplification, the analyst examines the actual DNA sequence of repeats. This technique determines a repeat "code" order. The technique has limited forensic uses at this time.

§ 18-4. The Potential Weaknesses of DNA Evidence.

DNA testing is not infallible. The purpose of this chapter is to highlight some of the more important potential sources of error in the testing process.

§ 18-4(A). Conducting the Test.

To begin with, as powerful as the various technologies are, there is still the possibility of human error.[69] The procedures such as RFLP and PCR are complex, multi-step techniques.[70] The laboratory technicians must exercise great care to avoid contaminating the samples and committing other mechanical errors. A 1987-88 proficiency study of DNA laboratory dramatized the possibility of

---

67. Baechtel, *supra* note 66, at 9.

68. Jeffreys, Macleod, Tamaki, Neil & Monckton, *Minisatellite Repeat Coding as a Digital Approach to DNA Typing*, 354 NATURE 204 (1991).

69. Van Derbeken, *Attorneys Assail Police DNA Lab*, SAN FRANCISCO CHRONICLE, Dec. 23, 1998, at p. A1 (an attack on the procedures employed at the San Francisco police DNA testing laboratory).

70. Benzinger, Emerick, Grigsby, Lovekamp, Logeman, Sallee, Boster, Rehnstrom, Riech, Small, Glasner, Coons & von Beroldingen, *An Illustrated Guide to RFLP Troubleshooting*, 43 J. FORENSIC SCI. 665 (1998) ("A large number of reagents and steps are required for . . . RFLP analysis, which at times make determining the cause of any observed anomaly difficult. Troubleshooting problems in RFLP analysis is difficult and often the exact cause of a problem cannot be determined").

such error.[71] In this study, Margaret Kuo and Mary Graves of the Orange County Sheriff-Coroner Department sent a batch of 49 or 50 blind samples to Cellmark, Lifecodes, and Cetus. Although Lifecodes correctly typed all 50 samples, Cellmark and Cetus each incorrectly typed one of the samples. "Asked to explain the ... incorrect match ... in the blind test, John Huss, Cellmark's vice president for marketing, says the error occurred because a lab technician incorrectly labeled a vial."[72]

On March 29, 1990 one of the original researchers, Ms. Kuo, together with Bashinski, Hartstrom, and Vukovich released the results of a second blind trial of the three laboratories. On this test, Cetus (Forensic Science Associates) correctly typed all 50 samples. However, Lifecodes could not obtain results on two of the samples; and Cellmark had one incorrect match, two inconclusive results, and five samples on which they could not obtain results. In one forensic case, Lifecodes experts erred in sizing a band on the autorad.[73] Chapter 3 of the 1992 N.R.C. report commented that the "results from [these early] proficiency studies suggested a high rate of false positives due to laboratory error." There are several possible types of laboratory error.

Contamination

There are possibilities for human error at many steps of the procedure. For example, a DNA sample from a crime scene might be mixed with bacterial, viral,

---

71. Thompson, *The Myth of DNA Fingerprints*, 9 CAL. LAW. 34 (Apr. 1989). The results of the test are summarized in an unpublished manuscript, DNA: A BLIND TRIAL STUDY OF THREE COMMERCIAL TESTING LABORATORIES. Professor Imwinkelried has a copy of the manuscript on file in his office. The second proficiency test is summarized in "DNA Committee — Results of Blind Trial #2." A copy of this manuscript is also on file in Professor Imwinkelried's office. Hayes v. State, 660 So. 2d 257 (Fla. 1995) ("a system of quality assurance"); Henderson v. Smith, 128 Idaho 444, 915 P.2d 6 (1996) (the witness, Dr. Foster, was competent to testify about Genetic's laboratory methods and procedures). *See also* King, *DOJ Aware of Problems in FBI's DNA Lab*, 22 THE CHAMPION 9 (Jan./Feb. 1998) (The National Association of Criminal Defense Lawyers contends that there are problems in the FBI's DNA analysis unit (DNAU), including: (1) "Plastic pipettes were used to extract DNA which had been dissolved in chloroform. However, chloroform also dissolves plastic pipettes, which could contaminate the sample"; (2) "Quantities of DNA placed in the testing gel to study band patterns were not measured properly. Amounts too large could cause problems in analysis"; and (3) "Examiners commonly overexposed autoradiographs so that DNA bands appeared football-shaped rather than as a line. This makes it difficult for an examiner to accurately locate the center of a band for analysis."); *FBI Lab's DNA Unit Has Problems, Criminal Defense Group Alleges*, 62 CRIM. L. (BNA) 1215 (Dec. 3, 1997) (quoting N.A.C.D.L. President Gerald B. Lefcourt). The full text of Mr. Lefcourt's remarks can be found at http://www.criminaljustice.org/MEDIA/pr000097.htm.

72. Thompson, *The Myth of DNA Fingerprints*, 9 CAL. LAW. 34 (Apr. 1989).

73. Starrs, *The Fallibility of Forensic DNA Testing: Of Proficiency in Public and Private Laboratories — Part One*, 15 SCI. SLEUTHING REV. 10 (Spring 1990) (discussing People v. Irons, Erie, Illinois).

or other nonhuman DNA; but according to our reviewer, bacterial and viral sequences differ so markedly that their differentiation poses little problem today. Inadvertent contamination can occur at the laboratory itself. To prevent such contamination, the laboratory should implement such procedures as disposing of gloves after the handling of each separate sample and the use of controls during testing.[74] Some laboratories such as Cellmark have implemented a "witnessing" procedure to better ensure the integrity of sample transfers.

Band Shifting

In the older RFLP technologies, band shifting was a problem. If the consistency of the gel used in the electrophoretic stage varies or a particular lane is overloaded with an excessive amount of DNA,[75] the fragments may not travel the correct distance in the gel; the sample in one lane might "run" faster than another. This phenomenon is termed "band shifting." Some researchers claim that band shifting occurred "in perhaps 30% of DNA fingerprinting cases"[76] although our reviewer notes that in his experience, the percentage was much lower. When this phenomenon occurred, even if two DNA samples are from the same person, the bands did not align perfectly on the autoradiograph. In *People v. Caldwell,*[77] despite band shifting, the Lifecodes expert claimed that there was a match; the expert used a correction factor to adjust the alignment of the bands and asserted that the adjusted bands matched. The use of a single correction factor may be valid when the non-alignment is consistent and the relative distance between all the bands has remained the same. However, in the late 1980s "[s]tudies [were] underway to determine if bandshifting requires the application of one uniform correction factor or more than one."[78] Chapter 2 of the 1992 N.R.C. report stated that "[d]ifferent regions of the gel [can] shift by different amounts."

To overcome the problem of band shifting, Lifecodes began employing a "constant" band or monomorphic probe.[79] The probe would always identify DNA

---

74. Frost, *DNA: Breaking Down the Strands of Information for Lawyers and Juries*, THE DAILY RECORDER, June 30, 1998, at p. 5.

75. Thompson & Ford, *The Meaning of a Match: Sources of Ambiguity in the Interpretation of DNA Prints, in* FORENSIC DNA TECHNOLOGY 93, 100 (1991).

76. Norman, *Maine Case Deals Blow to DNA Fingerprinting*, 246 SCIENCE 1556, 1557 (Dec. 22, 1989).

77. No. 8892938, Superior Court of Georgia, Cobb County (1989).

78. *A Momentary Shift in the DNA Bandwagon*, 13 SCI. SLEUTHING NEWSLETTER 10 (Fall 1989).

79. Thompson & Ford, *The Meaning of a Match: Sources of Ambiguity in the Interpretation of DNA Prints, in* FORENSIC DNA TECHNOLOGY 93, 107 (1991). In People v. Harris in California Superior Court and People v. Gent in Ohio, trial judges ruled that the use of monomorphic probes is not a generally accepted technique under the *Frye* test. Scheck & Neufeld, *DNA Task Force Report*, 15 THE CHAMPION 19, 20 (June 1991) (discussing both cases); Bush, *Defense Wins in Dispute Over DNA Testing*, LOS ANGELES DAILY JOURNAL, Jan. 25, 1991, at 1 (discussing *Harris*). Hayes v.

fragments of a certain length and produce a band at a known position. Chapter 2 of the N.R.C. report stated that these probes "detect constant-length fragments that are always in the same position in all people." That band then serves as a benchmark to determine the direction and degree of shift in each gel track. In the words of the 1992 N.R.C. report,

> If several monomorphic fragments are in the same position in both lanes, it is safe to assume that no band shifting occurred. If the monomorphic fragments are in different positions, band shifting is present.

Until more is known about the nature of band shifting, the N.R.C. report recommended the laboratories "adopt the policy of declaring samples that show apparent band shifting to be 'inconclusive.'"

Southern Blotting

Just as bandshifting can occur during the electrophoretic stage, problems can arise during the later Southern blot phase of the test. Chapter 2 of the 1992 N.R.C. report recommended that "[e]very Southern blot procedure be applied to a known DNA sample (in addition to the evidence samples in question) to verify that the hybridization was performed correctly."

The scientific community attempted to surmount problems of test procedure such as bandshifting. The National Institute of Justice asked the National Institute of Standards and Technology (N.I.S.T.) to study the feasibility of developing standard protocols for the DNA laboratories; and Dr. Dennis Reeder, Group Leader of Bioanalytical Techniques at N.I.S.T. conducted studies to evaluate DNA standards. A Technical Working Group in DNA Analysis Methods (TWGDAM), a group of 30 scientists chaired by Mr. James Kearney of the F.B.I., was formed. In September 1990, the American Society of Crime Laboratory Directors (ASCLD) adopted a resolution calling for the development of quality assurance programs, including regular proficiency testing of DNA laboratories.[80] A DNA Commission, formed by the International Society for Forensic Haemogenetics, likewise issued a set of recommendations designed to

---

State, 660 So. 2d 257 (Fla. 1995) (the methodology used by the technician to correct for band shifting was not sufficiently established in light of the position taken by the National Research Council); State v. Quatrevingt, 670 So. 2d 197 (La.), *cert. denied*, 519 U.S. 927 (1996) (Applying the *Daubert* test, the court found that "the practice of using monomorphic probes to correct for band shifting has not been proven reliable."); New York v. Keene, 156 Misc. 2d 108, 591 N.Y.S.2d 733 (Sup. Ct. 1992) (the use of monomorphic probes to correct for band shift is not generally accepted). *But see* Kaye, *DNA Identification in Criminal Cases: Some Lingering and Emerging Evidentiary Issues*, PROCEEDINGS FROM THE SEVENTH INTERNATIONAL SYMPOSIUM ON HUMAN IDENTIFICATION — 1996 at 12, 16 (1997) ("Caldwell v. State, [260 Ga. 278], 393 S.E.2d 436 (Ga. 1990) (monomorphic probe for bandshifting acceptable)").

80. Ferrara, *DNA Testing — The Ball Is in Our Court*, 21 ACADEMY NEWS 7 (Jan. 1991).

ensure the caliber of DNA testing.[81] In Chapter 4 of its 1992 report, the N.R.C. committee singled out the TWGDAM guidelines and encouraged "laboratories engaged in forensic DNA typing [to] adhere to the ... guidelines for quality assurance and proficiency testing ...." The 1996 report adhered to the same recommendation.

§ 18-4(B). Determining Whether There is a Match.

To determine whether there is a match in RFLP testing or PCR/STR analysis, the analyst can either visually compare the two audorads or use a computerized comparison technique.

Visual Comparison

Chapter 2 of the N.R.C. report asserts that each DNA laboratory must have "an objective and quantitative" "match criterion." The critics of DNA evidence contend that there is a large element of subjectivity in determining whether the sets of bands on two autoradiographs match. Sometimes the bands do not clearly resolve or separate during the electrophoresis. The bands may be light and indistinct. "Because DNA results may sometimes be ambiguous or difficult to interpret, the analyst may err in interpreting those results. Determining whether two samples 'match' may involve a subjective judgment."[82] In a late 1991 decision approving the admission of DNA evidence, the Arkansas Supreme Court remarked:

> The evidence established that autoradiographs can sometimes be ambiguous or difficult to interpret and that the analysts can err in measuring the bands and in interpreting the results. Determination whether two samples match can involve subjective judgment.[83]

In light of the risk of misreading the autoradiographs during a visual comparison, the standards of the Parentage Testing Committee of the American Association of Blood Banks (AABB) provide that "[a]utoradiographs or

---

81. *1991 Report Concerning Recommendations of the DNA Commission of the International Society for Forensic Haemogenetics Relating to the Use of DNA Polymorphisms*, 52 FORENSIC SCI. INT'L 125 (1992).

82. Thompson & Ford, *DNA Typing: Acceptance and Weight of the New Genetic Identification Tests*, 75 VA. L. REV. 45, 80 (1989). *See* Thompson & Ford, *The Meaning of a Match: Sources of Ambiguity in the Interpretation of DNA Prints*, *in* FORENSIC DNA TECHNOLOGY ch. 7 (1991) (even when the samples are from the same source, there may be missing, extra, indistinct, or misaligned bands; missing bands — "dropout" — can be caused by degradation of the sample, the presence of extra bands can be caused by contamination, faint bands can be the product of insufficient exposure time during autoradiography, and misaligned bands represent "band shifting").

83. Prater v. State, 307 Ark. 180, 820 S.W.2d 429 (1991).

membranes should be read independently by two or more individuals."[84] The second, independent reading serves as a doublecheck safeguard against subjectivity in the declaration of a match.

Computerized Comparison

In order to minimize the subjectivity of the comparison, most laboratories, including the F.B.I. and Lifecodes, currently employ computerized digitizing systems to make the declaration of a match more objective. The F.B.I. laboratory uses a video system to scan the autoradiographs to measure the bands precisely.[85] After measuring the fragment length, the laboratory applies its match window or criterion. However, there can be imprecisions in even the most careful scientific measurements. For that reason, by repeated tests of fragments from the same source, the laboratory must validate a match window for its hardware and procedures: How much variation in fragment length measurement can be expected even when the fragments come from the same source?

As previously stated, in the past Lifecodes announced a matching rule or window that "[f]ragments with measurements that are within approximately 2% of each other (3 standard deviations of 99.7% confidence level) are considered indistinguishable ...." However, in the *Castro* case in state court in Brooklyn, New York, there was evidence that Lifecodes experts had in fact relied on a visual comparison of the bands.[86] In that case, four experts, Carl Dobkin, Eric Lander, Lorraine Flaherty, and Richard Roberts consulted and then issued the following joint statement:

> According to its published papers and forensic reports to the District Attorney, Lifecodes' standard for declaring a match between two bands involves measuring whether the difference in the position of the bands is less than 3 standard deviations (*i.e.*, 1.8% of the average size of the bands). Although the single bands observed at D2S44 and the lower bands recorded at D17S79 are visually close, the computer sizings indicate that the recorded positions of the bands differ by more than 3 standard deviations. According to Lifecodes' standards, these bands do not match. If the true

84. Note, *DNA Fingerprinting and the Need for a National Data Base*, 17 FORD. URB. L.J. 323, 337 n.89 (1989).

85. Buffrey, Catterick, Greenhalgh, Jones & Russell, *Assessment of a Video System for Scanning DNA Autoradiographs*, 49 FORENSIC SCI. INT'L 17 (1991).

86. Schmeck, *DNA Evidence Faulted in a Bronx Murder Case*, N.Y. TIMES, May 25, 1989, at A17. *But see* People v. Golub, 196 A.D.2d 637, 601 N.Y.S.2d 502 (Sup. Ct. 1993) ("Lifecodes no longer declares a match based on visual inspection of the autorads without confirming the match by quantitative measurement of the bands using a computer. Moreover, Lifecodes now uses the same three-standard-deviation rule to calculate population frequencies that it uses to declare a measured match").

length of the band were 100 base pairs, a 2.5% window would include measurements as low as 97.5 and as high as 102.5.

While Lifecodes uses the 1.8% standard, the F.B.I. laboratory employs a 2.5% tolerance window.

Chapter 2 of the 1992 N.R.C. report added that a laboratory's match criterion "must be based on reproducibility studies that show the actual degree of variability observed when multiple samples from the same person are separated prepared and analyzed under typical forensic conditions." The N.R.C. report asserts that in the past, some laboratories have used matching criteria "based on the average spacing of fragment sizes in each region of the gel ...." The report acknowledged that "other laboratories [have] used purely visual matching criteria." The 1992 N.R.C. committee rejects both approaches as "inadequate." In its judgment, only an objective standard derived from reproducibility studies is acceptable.

§ 18-4(C). Evaluating the Statistical Significance of a Match.

Finally, several questions have arisen about the validity of the statistical evaluations of the significance of a match in DNA types. The proponent of DNA evidence is rarely content to offer the expert's testimony that there is a "match;" in addition, the proponent attempts to introduce testimony to estimate the frequency of the complete multi locus genotype. As Chapter 3 of the 1992 National Research Council report notes, in genetic counseling, that problem almost never arises. In the medical setting, the question is ordinarily whether a parent will pass a particular allele to a child; the genetic counselor can answer that question without knowing the frequency of that allele in the general population. However, in the forensic setting, notably criminal cases, the prosecution is intensely interested in narrowing the class of persons who could be the source of the DNA. Hence, in the typical forensic case, the expert employs the multiplication or product rule to estimate the probability of a random match.[87] After identifying matching DNA markers, the expert determines the frequency of each marker and then multiplies the frequencies together. Although some commentators urge the use of Bayes' theorem and likelihood ratios rather than

87. See the discussion of the multiplication rule in § 15-7(A), *supra*.

the multiplication rule,[88] the multiplication rule is used far more extensively in the courtroom.[89]

However, that rule is properly used only when certain conditions are met. There are three primary conditions: The individual frequencies are trustworthy, the frequency for one marker is independent of the others, and the resulting probability is correctly understood. Section 18-3 pointed out that the technology for analyzing DNA has evolved. As we shall see in this section, there has been a similar evolution of our understanding of the significance of the three conditions in computing DNA random match probabilities. The 1992 and 1996 National Research Council reports figured prominently in this evolution.

Question #1: The Trustworthiness of the Individual Frequencies

One *sine qua non* for using the rule is estimating the frequency of the various DNA markers. Initially, there were only limited databases to estimate the population frequencies of the various DNA sequences. Lifecodes' original base included 2,400 persons while "Cellmark ..., along with its parent corporation ICI in the United Kingdom, [had] performed over 10,000 tests on over 5000 people."[90] Admittedly, these databases were rather small in comparison to the databases for many other genetic markers such as RBC antigens. However, the American Association of Blood Banks has taken the position that a database of 200 individuals within a group ordinarily suffices to generate a valid statistical analysis of frequencies for that group.[91] Chapter 3 of the 1992 N.R.C. report stated that:

> Determining whether an allele has especially high frequency does not require a very large sample. A collection of 100 randomly chosen people provides a sample of 200 alleles, which is quite adequate for estimating allele frequencies.

More importantly, during the 1990s the databases have grown to substantial size.

---

88. Berry, *Inferences Using DNA Profiling in Forensic Identification and Paternity Cases*, 6 STAT. SCI. 175 (1991); Lempert, *Some Caveats Concerning DNA as Criminal Identification Evidence: With Thanks to the Reverend Bayes*, 13 CARDOZO L. REV. 303 (1991). *See* the discussion of the theorem in § 15-7(A), *supra*.

89. Donnelly & Friedman, *DNA Database Searches and the Legal Consumption of Scientific Evidence*, 97 MICH. L. REV. 931, 936 n.20 (1999) (some empirical studies indicate that lay jurors find testimony about likelihood ratios more "baffling" than testimony about random match probabilities).

90. Comment, *DNA Identification Tests and the Courts*, 63 WASH. L. REV. 903, 917 n.64 (1988). However, when our reviewer phoned Mr. Mark Stolorow of Cellmark in mid-1992, Mr. Stolorow informed him that Cellmark's own database includes roughly 1,000 Caucasians, Hispanics, and Blacks.

91. Note, *DNA Fingerprinting and the Need for a National Data Base*, 17 FORD. URB. L.J. 323, 331, 349 (1989).

The Early Controversy

Quite apart from concerns about the size of a data base, there can be serious questions about its representativeness. Research is still ongoing to determine whether the population frequencies developed for the broad racial categories in the American populace (Caucasians, Blacks, and Hispanics) hold true for subpopulations such as Hispanics in Miami (most of whom are Cuban), Hispanics in Houston (most of whom are Mexican), or black persons who live in a relatively isolated, rural community.[92] There is some evidence of an extraordinary degree of intermarriage or inbreeding within these subpopulations. If mating is not random, the subpopulation may not be in so-called Hardy-Weinberg equilibrium; and the frequencies within the subpopulation may deviate from the frequencies obtained in the broader group. The defense raised that issue in the *Castro* case, and the court noted the issue in the *Wesley* case discussed in § 18-5. At the time the N.R.C. prepared its first 1992 report on DNA testing, indications existed that there is some substructuring in DNA frequencies:

> One index of the extent of structuring in the population is the number of homozygotes; that is, the number of individuals who have one rather than two bands for a given probe because they received the same allele from each parent .... If people who are genetically similar tend to mate with each other, the number of homozygotes increases. Several population geneticists have recently examined the databases of Lifecodes and Cellmark. They conclude that these databases contain many times the number of homozygotes that would be expected in a population mating at random. Another indication of population structuring was found in the FBI's Hispanic database, which contained data from Miami and Houston. There

92. Thompson & Ford, *DNA Typing: Acceptance and Weight of the New Genetic Identification Tests*, 75 VA. L. REV. 45, 86 (1989) (noting studies finding "significant differences among races in the frequency of particular alleles"). Harding & Swanson, *Correspondence — DNA Database Size*, 43 J. FORENSIC SCI. 248 (1998) ("There is no clear guidance in the literature on the question of how large a database should be, possibly because there is no simple answer. Published populations for STR loci are generally of the order of either 100 or 200, but sometimes smaller numbers are reported for sub-populations. The International Society of Forensic Haemogenetics has recommended that 100 persons are sufficient.... The Committee on DNA Technology in Forensic Science, when originally reporting the ceiling principle, also suggested databases of 100. More recently, though, in describing databases the Committee suggests at least a few (or several) hundred persons. Several authors (Lander... and Devlin...) have, however, argued that a sample of 100 individuals is too small. Lander, moreover, has suggested that even a database of 500 is too small although he has now given qualified support for a database of 100 individuals. Weir also has implied that samples of 100 individuals are too small because tests for independence of allele frequencies will have low power.").

> were striking differences between the two cities in the frequency of many of the alleles.[93]

Chapter 3 of the 1992 N.R.C. report poses the hypothetical that although an allele might have a 1% frequency in a large population group, it could have a 20% frequency in a specific subgroup. On that hypothetical assumption, "[t]he frequency of homozygotes for the allele would be calculated to be 1 in 10,000" for the large group "but would actually be 1 in 25 for the subgroup."

To deal with the problem of population substructure, the F.B.I. laboratory developed a "fixed bin" procedure to generate its frequencies:

> A bin is an arbitrarily defined range of base pairs. For example, one bin the FBI uses has as its boundaries 872 and 963 base pairs; thus, any allele having a base pair length within that range is classified as belonging to that bin. The FBI then samples a targeted population to establish a data base of allele frequencies. The FBI has compiled, or is in the process of compiling, data bases for Caucasians, Blacks, Asians, and Hispanics. The FBI Caucasian data base ... was derived from blood samples of approximately 225 FBI agents from throughout the United States. The FBI produced autorads for each blood sample, measured the alleles, and categorized them within the appropriate bin. The frequency of occurrence for alleles falling within their respective bins can thus be calculated.[94]

---

93. Thompson & Ford, *Is DNA Fingerprinting Ready for Trial? (An Update)*, 4 CAL. PUBLIC DEFENDER 36, 39-40 (No. 3 1991). *See also* Thompson & Ford, *Is DNA Fingerprinting Ready for the Courts*, 125 NEW SCIENTIST 38, 43 (Mar. 31, 1990); Commonwealth v. Curnin, 409 Mass. 218, 565 N.E.2d 440 (1991) ("there was the question whether there is significant sub structuring (sub-grouping) within racial groups ..."). Allen, Saldeen, Pettersson & Gyllensten, *Genetic Typing of HLA Class II Genes in Swedish Populations: Application to Forensic Analysis*, 38 J. FORENSIC SCI. 554 (1993) (significant allele frequency differences were observed); De Stefano, Casarino, Mannucci, Delfino, Canale & Ferrara, *HLA-DQA1 Allele and Genotype Frequencies in a Northern Italian Population*, 55 FORENSIC SCI. INT'L 59 (1992) (differences from other Caucasian samples).

94. United States v. Jakobetz, 747 F. Supp. 250, 253 (D. Vt. 1990), *aff'd,* 955 F.2d 786 (2d Cir.) *cert. denied,* 506 U.S. 834 (1992). For a discussion of the difference between fixed and floating bins, *see* Weir & Gaut, *Matching and Binning DNA Fragments in Forensic Science*, 34 JURIMETRICS J. 9 (Fall 1993); Herrin, *A Comparison of Models Used for Calculation of RFLP Pattern Frequencies*, 37 J. FORENSIC SCI. 1640 (1992). In 1996, the National Research Council released its new report entitled *The Evaluation of Forensic DNA Evidence*. The new report states that although the floating-bin procedure is generally statistically preferable, certain variations of the fixed-bin procedure ordinarily lead to conservative approximations. *Id.* at ES-6. The draft includes a specific recommendation on binning. Recommendation 5.2 reads: "If floating bins are used to calculate the random-match probabilities, each bin should coincide with the corresponding match window. If fixed bins are employed, then the fixed bin that has the largest frequency among those overlapped by the match window should be used." *Id.* In People v. Venegas, 18 Cal. 4th 47, 954

If the true length of the band were 100 base pairs, a 2.5% window would include measurements as low as 97.5 and as high as 102.5.

The F.B.I. contends that the fixed bin approach produces "a very conservative estimate of allele frequency that more than compensates for potential errors that might result from ... substructure ...."[95] The bin boundaries are more than twice the measurement error calibrated in number of base pairs. According to one expert, "the frequencies of the alleles in each bin are on average at least two times greater ... than the actual frequencies in the sample populations for an allele ... occurring within the bin."[96] In addition, if an allele falls on the boundary of a bin, the F.B.I. categorizes the allele as belonging to the bin with the higher frequency.

Yet some independent experts such as Dr. Lander expressed doubts about the validity of the fixed bin technique. In one case, he testified that "the fact that ...it might turn out to be right doesn't mean that it's got valid scientific method

---

P.2d 525, 74 Cal. Rtpr. 2d 262 (1998), the court discussed the distinction between the two types of binning:

> Like the base-pair measurements of the evidentiary bands, the measurement of bands in a comparative database is ... inexact. For comparison purposes, therefore, the database bands are sorted into ranges of size called "bins." There are two kinds: "floating bins" and "fixed bins."
>
> A floating bin, constructed for each forensic comparison, is a range of sizes at least as large as the match window, centered on the measured size of the evidentiary band in question. The evidentiary band's frequency, *i.e.*, the probability of its appearing in the DNA profile of a randomly selected member of the population underlying the database, is calculated from the ratio of the number of bands in the bin to the total number of bands in the database for that locus.
>
> Fixed bins, on the other hand, compartmentalize the entire spectrum of VNTR base-pair sizes likely to appear as bands on an autorad. The spacing of the fixed-bin boundaries is somewhat uneven because, like the bands in the autorad's sizing-ladder lanes, they are [sometimes] derived from viral DNA that has been exactly measured. A separate fixed-bin table is compiled for each locus in each database. Each database band is entered within the bin that encompasses its base-pair size. To protect a suspect against unduly small frequencies, any bin with four or fewer bands is combined with its neighbor until each bin contains a minimum of five bands. The fixed-bin table shows not only each bin's range of sizes and number of bans, but also each bin's frequency, which is calculated from the ratio of the number of bands in the bin to the total number of bands in the table.
>
> In fixed-bin analysis, the frequency of an evidentiary band is determined by assigning it the frequency of the fixed bin into which its base-pair falls. Special rules may apply when a window around the evidentiary band overlaps multiple bins.

95. *Id.* at 259-60. Monson & Budowle, *A Comparison of the Fixed Bin Method with the Floating Bin and Direct Count Methods: Effect of VNTR Profile Frequency Estimation and Reference Population*, 38 J. Forensic Sci. 1037, 1049 (1993) ("conservative"); People v. Lindsey, 868 P.2d 1085 (Colo. App. 1993) (describing the bin sizes as "conservative"), *aff'd*, 892 P.2d 281 (Colo. 1995).

96. *Id.* at 259.

underlying it."[97] Dr. Lander's doubts were echoed in a 1991 article in *Science* by two population geneticists, Richard Lewontin of the Harvard Museum of Comparative Zoology and Daniel Hartl of Washington University School of Medicine.[98] They pointed out that unless a population group is in Hardy-Weinberg equilibrium, the frequency for that group may not hold true for a subgroup. One of the assumptions of equilibrium is that there is random mating throughout the group. Lewontin and Hartl marshaled evidence of "endogamy," the practice of human populations to marry within one's own group. The authors rejected the bromide that America is a "great melting pot" and argued that the nation more closely resembles "a large salad bowl." They particularly questioned the propriety of applying the frequencies for the large group "Hispanics" to distinct subgroups such as Puerto Ricans, Mexican-Americans, and Meso-Americans who are of Indian descent. The N.R.C. report notes that large groups such as "Hispanics" are "admixture[s] of subgroups with somewhat different allele frequencies."

The same issue of *Science* contained a rebuttal article by Ranajit Chakraborty and Kenneth Kidd.[99] In particular, Chakraborty and Kidd defended the F.B.I.'s use of binned allele frequencies. They contend that that technique tends to advantage the defense; the technique conservatively overstates the frequencies and therefore results in understated probabilities of random match.

Shortly after the publication of this issue of *Science,* William Sessions, the F.B.I. Director, issued a statement about the statistical evaluation of DNA matches.[100] In the statement, Director Sessions

> observed that the concerns raised by Lewontin and Hartl are not new and have been considered by numerous courts that have approved the way the FBI calculates a DNA match. He singled out for particular attention U.S. v. Yee, 48 CrL 1193 (DC N Ohio 1990), which produced a lengthy opinion on the issues surrounding DNA analysis. Lewontin and Hartl testified for the defense in that case, but the court ultimately approved the FBI's results and statistical analysis ....[101]

In the long term, the development of larger databases would moot many of these concerns. A number of jurisdictions are in the process of compiling larger

---

97. United States v. Yee, 134 F.R.D. 161, 182 (N.D. Ohio 1991).

98. Lewontin & Hartl, *Population Genetics in Forensic DNA Typing*, 254 SCIENCE 1745 (Dec. 20, 1991); *Scientists Dispute Validity of Math Used in Reporting Results of DNA Tests*, 50 CRIM. L. REP. (BNA) 1314 (Jan. 8, 1992).

99. Chakraborty & Kidd, *The Utility of DNA Typing in Forensic Work*, 254 SCIENCE 1735 (Dec. 20, 1991).

100. *Scientists Dispute Validity of Math Used in Reporting Results of DNA Tests*, 50 CRIM. L. REP. (BNA) 1314 (Jan. 8, 1992).

101. *Id.* at 1315-16.

databases to permit the formulation of more reliable frequencies. Eventually, the databases would include larger numbers of samples for most subpopulations, and analysts could then compare suspects directly to databases for the subpopulation the suspect belonged to. Most states now require all newly convicted felons or certain categories of convicts such as sex offenders to supply samples for DNA databases.[102] The existence of these databases should permit the development of more precise frequency figures. However, these databases will "take a number of years to compile."[103]

The Release of the 1992 N.R.C. Report

Chapter 3 of the 1992 N.R.C. report addressed this problem in detail. The chapter contains proposals for both the short and the long term. In the long term, the N.R.C. recommended that laboratories use a "ceiling principle" to estimate frequencies. The committee's ceiling principle approach entails the following procedures:

- — Researchers would test 100 persons drawn from 15-20 populations, that is, groups that are relatively homogenous genetically. The committee lists illustrative groups such as English, Germans, Italians, Russians, Navahos, Puerto Ricans, Chinese, Japanese, Vietnamese, and West Africans.
- — In estimating any frequency, the laboratory should generally use the highest frequency discovered for any population. That figure is then raised to the upper 95% confidence limit.[104] That number becomes the ceiling. More specifically, "the largest frequency of any of these populations or 5%, whichever is larger, would be taken as the ceiling frequency."

This procedure was frankly designed to generate conservative frequency estimates which the laboratory can report regardless of the ethnic background of the defendant.

In the short term, the N.R.C. recommended the use of a modified ceiling principle:

- — The laboratory would initially check to see whether the observed multi locus genotype matches any sample in its database. If not, the laboratory can inform the trier of fact that although it searched a database of N

102. Toups, *DNA Ties Genetic, Criminal Codes*, INSIGHT 48, 49 (Feb. 4, 1991) (Virginia is developing a database for all recently convicted felons, while Arizona, California, Florida, Minnesota, and Nevada are compiling databases for sex offenders). *See also* Jones v. Murray, 763 F. Supp. 842 (W.D. Va. 1991) (upholding the constitutionality of the enabling Virginia legislation).

103. *Scientists Dispute Validity of Math Used in Reporting Results of DNA Tests*, 50 CRIM. L. REP. (BNA) 1314, 1315 (Jan. 8, 1992).

104. State v. Johnson, 186 Ariz. 329, __ n.5, 922 P.2d 294, 299 n.5 (1996) (stating the formula for computing the upper 95% confidence limit).

individuals, it could find no match. The report notes that "in a recently reported analysis of the FBI databank, no exactly matching pairs were found in five- locus DNA profiles, and the closest match was a single three-locus match among 7.6 million pairwise comparisons." That type of testimony should give the trier some insight into the rarity of the genotype.

— On certain conditions, the laboratory could then calculate an estimated population frequency "on the basis of a conservative modification of the ceiling principle." The conditions include requirements that the laboratory have tested at least three major races and that the database be tested for Hardy-Weinberg equilibrium.

— The laboratory could then estimate a frequency by "(l) calculating the 95% upper confidence limit for the allele frequency in each of the existing population samples and (2) using the largest of these values or 10%, which is larger."[105]

The Criticism of the 1992 Report

However, the 1992 N.R.C. proposals were sharply criticized. To begin with, critics charged that the ceiling principles were policy judgments masquerading as science. The critics asserted that the committee had decided to overcompensate for the risk of substructuring and had prescribed a pseudo-scientific technique in order to do so. Further, the critics argued that with the exception of a few studies,[106] the most recent research indicates that the 1992 N.R.C. report badly

105. The computation of the upper 95% confidence limit is discussed in State v. Johnson, 922 P.2d 294, 299 n.5 (Ariz. 1996). The footnote sets out the formula for the computation.

106. Liu, Koda, Soejima, Pang, Wang & Kimura, *Lewis (FUT3) Genotypes in Two Different Chinese Populations*, 44 J. FORENSIC SCI. 82, 83 (1999) (reporting some differences not only between Chinese and Japanese populations but also between populations in different areas in China); Budowle, Baechtel & Fejeran, *Polymarker, HLA-DQA1, and D1S80 Allele Frequency Data in Chamorro and Filipino Populations from Guam*, 43 J. FORENSIC SCI. 1195 (1998) (the D1S80 locus in the Chamorro population sample); Budowle, Koons & Moretti, *Subtyping of the HLA-DQA1 Locus and Independence Testing with PM and STR/VNTR Loci*, 43 J. FORENSIC SCI. 657 (1998) (the GYPA locus in the African American samples did not meet Hardy-Weinberg expectations); Busque, Desmaris, Provost, Schumann, Zhong & Chadroborty, *Analysis of Allele Distribution for Six Short Tandem Repeat Loci in the French Canadian Population of Quebec*, 42 J. FORENSIC SCI. 1147 (1998) ("statistically significant deviation from Hardy-Weinberg expectations of genotype frequencies was noted at some loci by one or more tests"); Budowle, Smerick, Keys & Moretti, *United States Population Data on the Multiplex Short Tandem Repeat Loci — HUMTH01, TPOX, and CSF1PO — and the Variable Number Tandem Repeat Locus D1S80*, 42 J. FORENSIC SCI. 846 (1997) (the TPOX locus in the Caucasian population); Mueller, *Commentary on Budowle, Lindsey, Koons, Giusti & Comey, "Validation and Population Studies of the Loci LDLR, GYPA, HBGG, D7S8, and Gc (PM Loci), and HLA-DQ-a Using a Multiplex Amplification and Typing Procedure,"* 40 J. FORENSIC SCI. 45 (1995) (when the author repeated the test for the HBGG locus in the Caucasian population, he "obtained a *p*-value of 0.008, suggesting a highly significant departure from the Hardy-Weinberg equilibrium").

overestimated the risk of substructuring.[107] Moreover, some critics argue that the ceiling principle is so conservative that it does not yield "a good scientific

---

107. Gino, Robino, Torre, Iorio & Peruccio, *LDLR, GYPA, HBGG, D7S8, and GC Allele and Genotype Frequencies in the Northwest Italian Population*, 44 J. FORENSIC SCI. 171 (1999) ("All five loci met Hardy-Weinberg expectations"); Budowle, Baechtel & Fejeran, *Polymarker, HLA-DQA1, and D1S80 Allele Frequency Data in Chamorro and Filipino Populations from Guam*, 43 J. FORENSIC SCI. 1195 (1998) (with one exception, "All loci, in both sample populations, . . . meet Hardy-Weinberg expectations"); Pancorbo, Castro, Fernandez-Fernandez & Garcia-Orad, *Population Genetics and Forensic Applications Using Multiplex PCR (CSF1PO, TPOX, and TH01) Loci in the Basque Country*, 43 J. FORENSIC SCI. 1181 (1998) ("All loci meet Hardy-Weinberg expectations"); Zehner, Mebs & Bratzke, *Population Genetic Study of the Simultaneously Amplified Loci HLA DQA1, LDLR, GYPA, HBGG, D7S8, and GC in a German Population Sample*, 43 J. FORENSIC SCI. 913 (1998) ("All loci are in Hardy-Weinberg equilibrium"); Alessio & Claudio, *The Distribution of DsS80 (pMCT118) Alleles in a Southern Italian Population Sample*, 43 J. FORENSIC SCI. 911 (1998) ("the population was in HWE"); Cariolou, Manoli, Christophorou, Bashiardes, Karagrigoriou & Budowle, *Greek Cypriot Allele and Genotype Frequencies for Amplitype PM-DQA1 and D1S80 Loci*, 43 J. FORENSIC SCI. 661 (1998) ("all loci meet Hardy-Weinberg expectations"); Pelotti, Mantovani, Esposti, Apote, Bragliani, Maiolini, Abbondanza & Pappalardo, *The DRPLA CAG Repeats in an Italian Population Sample: Evaluation of the Polymorphism for Forensic Applications*, 43 J. FORENSIC SCI. 410 (1998) ("The heterozygosity was 0.81 and no significant deviation from Hardy-Weinberg equilibrium was found."); Gene, Fuentes, Huguet, Pique, Bert, Corella, Perez-Perez, Corbella & Moreno, *Quechua Amerindian Population Characterized by HLA-DQa, YNZ22, 3APO B, HUMTH01, and HUMVWA31A Polymorphisms*, 43 J. FORENSIC SCI. 403 (1998) ("No significant deviations between observed and expected numbers were found, thus assuming the Hardy-Weinberg equilibrium."); Jorquera & Budowle, *Chilean Population Data on Ten PCR-Based Loci*, 43 J. FORENSIC SCI. 171 (1998) ("All loci except HBGG and THO1 meet Hardy-Weinberg expectations."); Busque, Desmaris, Provost, Schumann, Zhong & Chakroborty, *Analysis of Allele Distribution for Six Short Tandem Repeat Loci in the French Canadian Population of Quebec*, 42 J. FORENSIC SCI. 1147 (1997) ("Although statistically significant deviation from Hardy-Weinberg expectations of genotype frequencies was noted at some loci by one or more tests, in general the genotype frequencies are well estimated from the product of allele frequencies at all loci."); Ambach, Parson, Hiederstatter & Budowle, *Austrian Caucasian Population Data for the Quadruplex Plus Amelogenin: Refined Mutation Rate for HumvWFA31/A*, 42 J. FORENSIC SCI. 1136 (1997) ("The population data meet Hardy-Weinberg and linkage equilibrium expectations...."); Moura-Neto & Budowle, *Fixed Bin Population Data for the VNTR Loci D1S7, D2S44, D4S139, D5S110, D10S28, and D14S13 in a Population Sample from Rio De Janeiro, Brazil*, 42 J. FORENSIC SCI. 926 (1997) ("The six VNTR loci meet Hardy-Weinberg expectations...."); Medintz, Levine, McCurdy, Chiriboga, Kingston, Desnick, Eng & Kobilinsky, *HLA-DQA1 and Polymarker Allele Frequencies in Two New York City Jewish Populations*, 42 J. FORENSIC SCI. 919 (1997) ("For all loci tested, except HBGG, the 2 subpopulations meet the assumption of Hardy-Weinberg equilibrium."); Tahir, Caruso, Budowle, Azis & Novick, *Distribution of HLA-DQa and Polymarker (LDLR, GC, GYPA, HBGG, and D7S8) Alleles in Arab and Pakistani Populations Living in Abu Dhabi, United Arab Emirates*, 42 J. FORENSIC SCI. 914 (1997) ("No significant departures from HWE expectations were detected."); Klintschar & Crevenna, *HumCD4—Validation of a STR System for Forensic Purposes in an Austrian Caucasian Population Sample*, 42 J. FORENSIC SCI. 907 (1997) ("The observed phenotype distribution is in Hardy-Weinberg equilibrium"); Budowle, Smerick, Keys & Moretti, *United States Population Data on the Multiplex Short Tandem Repeat Loci — HUMTH01, TPOX, and CSF1PO — and the*

Variable Number Tandem Repeat Locus D1S80, 42 J. FORENSIC SCI. 846 (1997) ("All loci, except the TPOX locus in the Caucasian population sample, meet Hardy-Weinberg expectations."); Bell, Budowle, Martinez-Jarreta, Casalod, Abecia & Castellano, *Distribution of Types for Six PCR-Based Loci: LDLR, GYPA, HBGG, D7S8, GC and HLA-DQA1 in Central Pyrenees and Teruel (Spain)*, 42 J. FORENSIC SCI. 510 (1997) ("Results were in agreement with Hardy-Weinberg expectations."); Spinella, Marsala, Biondo & Montagna, *Italian Population Allele and Genotype Frequencies for the AmpliType PM and the HLA-DQ-alpha Loci*, 42 J. FORENSIC SCI. 514, 515 (1997) ("We found that the observed genotype frequencies compared well to the expected genotype frequencies, on the basis of the Hardy-Weinberg equilibrium."); Rousselet, Pfitzinger & Mangin, *A Pentaplex Automated Fluorescent Typing System for Forensic Identification and French Caucasian Population Data*, 42 J. FORENSIC SCI. 500 (1997) ("Statistical calculations for these phenotype distributions met expectations for Hardy-Weinberg equilibrium."); Jin, Underhill, Buoncristiani & Robertson, *Defining Microsatellite Alleles by Genotyping Global Indigenous Human Populations and Non-Human Primates*, 42 J. FORENSIC SCI. 496, 498 (1997) ("It has been shown that Hardy-Weinberg equilibrium generally holds in cosmopolitan populations as well as indigenous populations at almost all microsatellite lock examined...."); Hartmann, Houlihan, Keister & Buse, *The Effect of Ethnic and Racial Population Substructuring on the Estimation of Multi-Locus Fixed-Bin VNTR RFLP Genotype Probabilities*, 42 J. FORENSIC SCI. 232 (1997) ("substructuring of races by major ethnic groups does not lead to large errors"); Budowle, Jankowski, Corey, Swec, Freck-Tootell, Pino, Schwartz, Kelley & Tarver, *Evaluation of Independence Assumptions for PCR-Based and Protein-Based Genetic Markers in New Jersey Caucasians*, 42 J. FORENSIC SCI. 223 (1997) ("All loci meet Hardy-Weinberg expectations."); Park, Lee, Lee, Kim, Koo, Budowle & Rho, *Genetic Variations at Four Tetrameric Tandem Repeat Loci in Korean Population*, 42 J. FORENSIC SCI. 125 (1997) ("satisfy Hardy-Weinberg expectation"); Pinheiro, Pontes, Gene, Huguet, da Costa & Moreno, *Population Study of the HUMTH01, HUMVWA31A, HUMF13A1, and HUMFES/FPS STR Polymorphisms in the North of Portugal*, 42 J. FORENSIC SCI. 121 (1997) ("No deviation from Hardy-Weinberg equilibrium was found."); Liu, Koda, Soejima, Uchida & Kimura, *PCR Analysis of Lewis-Negative Gene Mutations and the Distribution of Lewis Alleles in a Japanese Population*, 41 J. FORENSIC SCI. 1018 (1996) ("in accordance with those expected by the Hardy-Weinberg equilibrium"); Budowle, Woller, Koons, Furedi, Errera & Padar, *Hungarian Population Data on Seven PCR-Based Loci*, 41 J. FORENSIC SCI. 667 (1996) ("do not deviate from Hardy Weinberg expectations"); Glock, Schwartz, Schwartz-Jungl & Mayr, *Allelic Ladder Characterization of the Short Tandem Repeat Polymorphism in Intron 6 of the Lipoprotein Lipase Gene and Its Application in an Austrian Caucasian Population Study*, 41 J. FORENSIC SCI. 579 (1996) ("no deviation from Hardy-Weinberg equilibrium"); Walkinshaw, Strickland, Hamilton, Denning & Gayley, *DNA Profiling in Two Alaskan Native Populations Using HLA-DQA1, PM, and D1S80 Loci*, 41 J. FORENSIC SCI. 478 (1996) (the data "fell well within Hardy-Weinberg expectations"); Rodriguez-Calvo, Bellas, Souto, Vide, Valverde & Carracedo, *Population Data on the Loci LDLR, GYPA, HBGG, D7S8, and GC in Three Southwest European Populations*, 41 J. FORENSIC SCI. 291 (1996) ("All loci met Hardy-Weinberg expectations in the three sampled populations."); Scholl, Budowle, Radecki & Salvo, *Navajo, Pueblo, and Sioux Population Data on the Loci HLA-DQA1, LDLR, GYPA, HBGG, D7S8, Gc, and D1S80*, 41 J. FORENSIC SCI. 47 (1996); Hayes, Budowle & Freund, *Arab Population Data on the PCR-Based Loci: HLA-DQA2, LDLR, GYPA, HBGG, D7S8, Gc, and D1S80*, 40 J. FORENSIC SCI. 888 (1995) ("All loci met Hardy-Weinberg expectations."); Lander & Budowle, *DNA Fingerprinting Dispute Laid to Rest*, 371 NATURE 735 (Oct. 27, 1994); Budowle, Baechtel, Smerick, Presley, Giusti, Parsons, Alevy & Chakraborty, *D1S80 Population Data in African Americans, Caucasians, Southeastern Hispanics, Southwestern Hispanics, and Orientals*, 40 J. FORENSIC SCI. 38 (1995) ("All sample populations met Hardy-Weinberg expectations.");

estimate" of the probability.[108] The DNA Commission of the International Society for Forensic Haemogenetics has challenged the ceiling principle.[109]

The 1996 N.R.C. Report

Most importantly, in its 1996 report on DNA testing, the National Research Council of the N.R.C. changed its position on the ceiling and modified ceiling principles. At several points, the report asserts that in light of the most recent research, it is unnecessary to use either principle.[110] The report states that although some research in the late 1980s created a doubt whether the databases were in Hardy-Weinberg equilibrium, the deviations from equilibrium "turned

---

Budowle, Lindsey, DeCou, Koons, Giusti & Comey, *Validation and Population Studies of the Loci LDLR, GYPA, HBGG, D7S8, and Gc (PM loci), and HLA-DQ@ Using a Multiplex Amplification and Typing Procedure*, 40 J. FORENSIC SCI. 45 (1995) ("All loci meet Hardy-Weinberg expectations."); Budowle, Monson, Giusti & Brown, *The Assessment of Frequency Estimates of Hae III-Generated VNTR Profiles in Various Reference Databases*, 39 J. FORENSIC SCI. 319 (1994); Crouse, Feur, Nippes, Hutto, Barnes, Coffman, Livingston, Ginsberg & Glidewell, *Analysis of HLA-DQ@ Allele and Genotype Frequencies in Populations from Florida*, 39 J. FORENSIC SCI. 731 (1994); Budowle, Monson, Giusti & Brown, *Evaluation of Hinf I-Generated VNTR Frequencies Determined Using Various Ethnic Databases*, 39 J. FORENSIC SCI. 988 (1994); Lorente, Lorente, Budowle, Wilson & Villanueva, *Analysis of the HUMTH01 Allele Frequencies in the Spanish Population*, 39 J. FORENSIC SCI. 1270 (1994) ("The genotype distribution meets Hardy-Weinberg expectations."); Comment, *Admissibility of DNA Statistical Data: A Proliferation of Misconception*, 30 CAL. WEST. L. REV. 145, 176, 178 (1993) ("negligible effect"); Devlin, Risch & Roeder, *Comments on the Statistical Aspects of the NRC's Report on DNA Typing*, 39 J. FORENSIC SCI. 28, 29, 38 (1994); Chow, Tan, Yap & Ng, *The Development of DNA Profiling Database in an HAE III Based RFLP System for Chinese, Malays, and Indians in Singapore*, 38 J. FORENSIC SCI. 874 (1993) (the allele distributions were not significantly different among six groups).

108. The Technical Working Group on DNA Analysis Methods (TWGDAM), *Consensus Approach for Applying the "Ceiling Principle" to Derive Conservative Estimates of DNA Profile Frequencies*, 39 J. FORENSIC SCI. 899 (1994) ("TWGDAM cannot recommend the application of the ceiling principle. The basis of the need for a ceiling principle approach is flawed"): Kaye, *The Forensic Debut of the National Research Council's DNA Report: Population Structure, Ceiling Frequencies and the Need for Numbers*, 34 JURIMETRICS J. 369 (1994) (the courts should "distinguish between policy judgments and scientific assessments"); Kaye, *DNA Evidence: Probability, Population Genetics, and the Courts*, 7 HARV. J. OF LAW & TECH. 101, 168 (1993) ("There is very little evidence, and certainly no scientific consensus, that the impact [of substructuring] is substantial in any known population"). Lempert, *DNA, Science, and the Law: Two Cheers for the Ceiling Principle*, 34 JURIMETRICS J.41, 45 (Fall 1993); Devlin, Risch & Roeder, *Comments on the Statistical Aspects of the NRC's Report on DNA Typing*, 39 J. FORENSIC SCI. 28 (1994). *See also* Jarjoura, Jamison & Androulakakis, *Likelihood Ratios for Deoxyribonucleic Acid (DNA) Typing in Criminal Cases*, 39 J. FORENSIC SCI. 64 (1994).

109. *Editorial*, 59 FORENSIC SCI. INT'L 1 (1993).

110. NAT'L RESEARCH COUNCIL, THE EVALUATION OF FORENSIC DNA EVIDENCE ES-2, ES-3, 0-21, 0-32, 5-32, 5-33 (Pre-pub. draft 1996).

out to be an artifact."[111] With some modifications for special situations, the 1996 report endorses the use of the traditional product rule to compute the random match probability.[112]

Question #2: The Independence of the Markers Identified

The trustworthiness of the individual frequencies is not the only *sine qua non* for invoking the multiplication rule discussed in Chapter 15; there are questions about the independence of the DNA types as well as the reliability of the frequencies for each type. As previously stated, in reporting probabilities, many laboratories utilize the product rule; they multiply the population frequency for each individual type found in the DNA sample to yield an overall probability of a random match. However, the product rule may be used only if the individual factors are independent. The laboratories' claim of independence is plausible, especially when the laboratory uses single locus probes for different sites on different chromosomes.[113] The use of genetic markers on different chromosomes reduces the likelihood that there is any linkage between the markers. Chapter 1 of the 1992 N.R.C. report recommended testing loci on different chromosomes. (Again, the ability to test loci on separate chromosomes is one of the advantages of the single locus probe procedure which the 1992 N.R.C. also recommended.) When forensic DNA testing made its advent in the United States, there had been only limited experimentation to validate the hypothesis of independence; the original British researchers relied on a test involving only 20 Caucasians.[114] In *People v. Wesley,*[115] the court expressed concern about the dearth of hard

---

111. *Id.* at 4-17. *See also* Kaye, *Bible Reading: DNA Evidence in Arizona*, 28 ARIZ. ST. L.J. 1035, 1056 (1996) ("In the early days of DNA population analysis, there appeared to be a clear excess of homozygotes, but it did not take long for an explanation to emerge. [F]or technical reasons, not all heterozygotes can be detected. When the limitations of the laboratory method are taken into account, the excess homozygosity vanishes").

112. *Id.* at ES-4. The report proposes two special modifications. One is for VNTR systems "in which a heterozygous locus can be mistaken for a homozygous one." A second modification is for PCR systems. However, aside from those special modifications, Recommendation 4.1 reads: "In general, the calculation of a profile frequency should be made with the product rule. If the race of the person who left the evidence-sample DNA is known, the database for the person's race should be used; if the race is not known, calculations for all the racial groups to which possible suspects belong should be made."

113. Thompson & Ford, *DNA Typing: Acceptance and Weight of the New Genetic Identification Tests*, 75 VA. L. REV. 45, 85-86 (1989).

114. *Id.* at 83. *See also* Hoeffel, *The Dark Side of DNA Profiling: Unreliable Scientific Evidence Meets the Criminal Defendant*, 42 STAN. L. REV. 465, 488-89 (1990) ("the oft-quoted statistic that the chance that two individuals would have the same DNA profile is one in thirty billion is based on a study of fourteen British Caucasians").

115. 140 Misc. 2d 306, 533 N.Y.S.2d 643 (Albany County Ct. 1988), *aff'd sub nom.* People v. Bailey, 156 A.D.2d 846, 549 N.Y.S.2d 846 (1989).

evidence of the independence of the bands. While in the early cases most courts permitted experts to assume independence and employ the multiplication rule, the assumption has been questioned.[116] Chapter 1 of the 1992 N.R.C. report acknowledged that the assumption was dubious when a multi locus probe tests loci situated closely together on the same chromosome. The report stated that:

> When they are very close on the same chromosome, the phenomenon of linkage disequilibrium can result — a deviation from independent inheritance in which particular alleles at the two sites tend to be transmitted together.

For that reason, the report strongly advocated the use of single locus probe RFLP. That recommendation has been almost universally implemented by forensic DNA laboratories.

Question #3: The True Significance of the Resulting Probability

Assuming that there is a match, the question becomes what is the statistical significance of the match. A number of statistics might be proffered at trial; the list includes, *inter alia*, a random match probability, a source probability, a guilt probability, and a likelihood ratio.

Random Match Probability

Chapter 15 discusses the multiplication or product rule. In most cases, the DNA expert uses that rule to compute a random match probability. If the individual frequencies are reliable and the markers are independent, the witness may properly multiply the frequencies. That multiplication yields the random match probability. How often would you have to dip into the relevant population to randomly find another person with the same set of DNA markers? In effect, the random match probabilities compares the suspect to an arbitrarily chosen member of the defined population.[117] This probability compares the defendant to a random person in the population.

Of course, sometimes that is not the relevant comparison. Suppose, for example, that the evidence indicates that a relative of the defendant – a person

116. Kaye, *DNA Paternity Probabilities*, 24 FAM. L.Q. 279, 299 n.80 (Fall 1990) ("The underlying assumption of statistical independence of bands has been questioned on several grounds").

117. Donnelly & Friedman, *DNA Database Searches and the Legal Consumption of Scientific Evidence*, 97 MICH. L. REV. 931, 938 (1999).

from the same gene pool – was the possible perpetrator. Then the appropriate comparison would be between two persons from the same gene pool.[118]

Another question that has arisen is whether the random match probability should be combined with the error rate for the laboratory which conducted the test. A number of commentators have urged the combination.[119] They argue that without the error rate information, the statistic will mislead the jury[120] and overstate the probative value of the DNA evidence.[121] However in its 1996 report, the National Research Council took the contrary position.[122] It may be difficult to obtain an accurate estimate of laboratory error. It is certainly questionable to use earlier laboratory error rates if laboratory personnel and procedures have changed — and improved — in the interim.[123] An educated guess would be that the courts will "give defendants ... latitude in adducing statistics and pointing to past instances which might be indicative of laboratory error"[124] without requiring the prosecution's experts to factor error rates into their probability computations.

---

118. Note, *My Brother's Keeper: A Challenge to the Probative Value of DNA Fingerprinting*, 23 Am. J. CRIM. L. 195, 213 (1995); Koehler, *DNA Matches and Statistics: Important Questions, Surprising Answers*, 76 JUDICATURE 222, 224, 229 (Feb. – Mar. 1993) (hereinafter cited as Koehler, JUDICATURE); Koehler, *Error and Exaggeration in the Presentation of DNA Evidence at Trial*, 34 JURIMETRICS J. 21, 27 (Fall 1993) (hereinafter cited as Koehler, Jurimetrics) ("the probability that the suspect and his biological brother will share a set of alleles on each of the three probes is approximately ... 1/64").

119. Kaye, *DNA Identification in Criminal Cases: Some Lingering and Emerging Evidentiary Issues*, *in* PROCEEDINGS FROM THE SEVENTH INTERNATIONAL SYMPOSIUM ON HUMAN IDENTIFICATION – 1996 at 12, 17 (1997). *See* Koehler, *One in Millions, Billions, and Trillions: Lessons from People v. Collins (1968) and People v. Simpson (1995)*, 47 J. LEGAL EDUC. 214, 222 (1997); Kaye, *DNA, NAS, NRC, DAB, FRLP, PCR, and More: An Introduction to the Symposium on the 1996 NRC Report on Forensic DNA Evidence*, 37 JURIMETRICS J.395 (1997); Thompson, *Accepting Lower Standards: The National Research Council's Second Report on Forensic DNA Evidence*, *id.* at 405; Lempert, *After the DNA Wars: Skirmishing with NRC II*, *id.* at 439.

120. Kaye, *supra* note 119, at 17.

121. Lempert, *supra* note 119.

122. Koehler, *Why DNA Likelihood Ratios Should Account for Error (Even When a National Research Council Report Says They Should Not)*, 37 JURIMETRICS J.425 (1997).

123. Berger, *Laboratory Error Seen Through the Lens of Science and Policy*, 30 U.C. DAVIS L. REV. 1081 (1997).

124. Kaye, *supra* note 119 at 18. One of the frequently overlooked issues is whether evidence of laboratory error rate is admissible at all. There is a serious question whether the admission of such evidence would violate the character prohibition. Imwinkelried, *Coming to Grips with Scientific Research in Daubert's "Brave New World": The Courts' Need to Appreciate the Evidentiary Differences between Validity and Proficiency Studies*, 61 BROOKLYN L. REV. 1247 (1995). In the final analysis, the theory of logical relevance is: The past errors indicate that the analyst or laboratory is prone to error, and in turn that increases the probability that the analyst or laboratory erred on the occasion in question. That is a classic use of a character trait as circumstantial proof of conduct. In Unmack v. Deaconess Medical Center, 967 P.2d 783 (Mt. 1997), the court went to the very brink of explicitly holding that the character evidence prohibition bars this type of testimony.

The Source Probability

Even when the random match probability is the appropriate computation, that probability must be distinguished from the source probability.[125] To determine that probability, the witness must specify the size of the relevant population.[126] The witness can use Bayes' theorem. The size of the population establishes the prior probability. For instance, if the population includes 1,000 persons, the prior probability would be only 0.1%. The witness would then factor in the genetic information to derive the posterior probability.[127] In short, to compute the source probability, the statistician must know both the population frequency and the population size. If the population frequency is 1 in 100 but there are 1,000 persons in the population, presumably there are 10 persons with the same set of DNA markers. Given that population frequency and size, the defense could argue that the chance is only one in ten that the defendant is the source of the DNA sample.

The rub is that there is an element of arbitrariness in selecting the population size. What is the relevant population--the number of Caucasians in Los Angeles, California, the United States, North America, the New World? There is no scientific criterion for selecting the relevant population. At trial, during cross-examination of the proponent's expert, the opposing counsel can force the expert to assume various populations. With the smallest population, there might be 10 other persons who could be expected to have the same set of DNA markers; with the next smallest population, 100; with the next, 1,000; and so on. That cross-examination technique can diminish the impact of a seemingly impressive random match probability stated during the direct examination.

The Guilt Probability

Both the random match and source probabilities should be distinguished from the guilt probability.[128] "[E]ven if the defendant is the source of the trace, there may be an innocent explanation. Perhaps the defendant innocently left the trace before or after the crime was committed. A Good Samaritan might, for example, run into the woods to save a woman screaming for help, cut himself on a tree branch, and bleed on the woman while trying to save her." To compute this probability, the witness could use Bayes' theorem (discussed in Chapter 15); but

---

125. *Id.* at 27-30; Koehler, JUDICATURE, *supra* note 118, at 224-25.

126. Koehler, JURIMETRICS J., *supra* note 118, at 27-28 ("Absent an estimate of the size of the potential source population, a source probability statement cannot be made").

127. *Id.* (Bayesian analysis; "the size of the population informs one's estimate of the prior odds").

128. *Id.* at 31-32; Koehler, JUDICATURE, *supra* note 118, at 224.

the witness would have to make an assumption as to the nongenetic evidence in the case.[129]

Remaining Issues: "Trawl" Searches and Mixed Samples

Although the 1996 N.R.C. report has laid to rest many of the controversies about the statistical evaluation of a DNA match, other questions remain controversial. One is the proper computation of the probability when the match results from the "trawl" of a database.[130] Both N.R.C. reports distinguish between two situations: (1) "confirmation" cases in which non-scientific evidence gives the police reason to suspect the defendant before they obtain a sample from him or her; and (2) cases in which, before the police "trawl" a database, they have only a crime scene samples. The match in the trawl leads the police to suspect the defendant.

— According to N.R.C. I (1992), in the case of "trawl" searches, [131] the courts should not admit any evidence of the initial match in the "trawl." That match should simply furnish a justification for further testing of the sample at additional loci. Even when the further test also yields a match, at trial the jury should hear only the testimony about a random match probability based on the new loci.

— According to N.R.C. II (1996), [132] in "trawl" cases, the random match probability computed in the traditional fashion should be multiplied by the numbers of persons in the database. Alternatively, if the evidence is presented in the form of a likelihood ratio, the ratio should be divided by the number of profiles in the database. In either event, the final figure will be much less inculpatory than it otherwise would be.

— Leading commentators have sharply criticized both approaches.[133] They argue that when the "trawl" eliminates other possible suspects, the evidence should be deemed more rather than less probative. They concede that in "confirmation" cases, the whole body of evidence might be more probative: After all in "confirmation" cases prior to the DNA test the police had other evidence pointing to the defendant, and there is always the possibility that the result of the DNA test could "taint" the evidence against the defendant which the police obtain later. For instance, if they learn of the DNA test result, at least subconsciously witnesses might be tempted to identify the defendant. However, the commentators argue that

---

129. *Id.* at 225.

130. Donnelly & Friedman, *DNA Database Searches and the Legal Consumption of Scientific Evidence*, 97 MICH. L. REV. 931 (1999).

131. *Id.*at 941-42, 963, 966-67.

132. *Id.*at 942-44.

133. *Id.*

the DNA evidence itself in "trawl" cases is at least as probative as the same test result in a "confirmation" case.

Another issue is the proper statistical method of interpreting DNA mixtures.[134] The 1992 National Research Council report recommended "calculat[ing] only the proportion of the population that is either included or excluded in a mixed stain."[135] The proposal was that "[i]f a suspect's pattern is found within the mixed pattern, the appropriate frequency to assign such a 'match' is the sum of frequencies of all the genotypes that are contained within (*i.e.* that are a subset of) the mixed pattern."[136] Other commentators, though, favor the use of a likelihood ratio.[137] That ratio "compares the probabilities of the evidentiary profile under alternative explanations."[138] The 1996 N.R.C. adopts the latter proposal. The 1996 report criticizes the calculation proposed by the 1992 report on the ground that "it does not make use of some of the information available, namely, the genotype of the suspect."[139]

One final problem warrants mention. In November 1997, the F.B.I. made an announcement which has already proven controversial. On November 12, 1997, the F.B.I. announced that "DNA can now prove with reasonable scientific certainty that DNA in an evidence stain came from a specific person."[140] For that reason, F.B.I. witnesses will no longer simply report "matches."[141] As in the past, once a match is found, the analyst will compare the profile with a database. However, "[i]f that number is exceedingly rare as compared to the number of people in the U.S. population, the individual is declared to be the source of the evidentiary stain."[142] It is predictable that the defense bar will challenge this new practice. Moreover, since current law would permit the analyst to both cite a random match probability and point out the size of the American population, it remains to be seen whether the courts will perceive any legal necessity for allowing F.B.I. witnesses to take this step.[143]

---

134. Koehler, *supra* note 122 at 22-23; Evett, Gill & Lambert, *Taking Account of Peak Areas when Interpreting Mixed DNA Profiles*, 43 J. FORENSIC SCI. 62 (1998).

135. *Quoted in* Weir, Triggs, Starling, Stowell, Walsh & Buckleton, *Interpreting DNA Mixtures*, 42 J. FORENSIC SCI. 213 (1997).

136. *Id.* at 219.

137. *Id.* at 213.

138. *Id.* at 219.

139. *FBI Says It Can Identify Particular Person As Source of DNA Evidentiary Material*, 62 CRIM. L. (BNA) 1170 (Nov. 19, 1997).

140. *Id.*

141. *Id.*

142. *Id.* at 1171; *DNA Profiling Advancement*, 67 F.B.I. LAW ENF. BULL. 24 (Feb. 1998).

143. *A "New" DNA Policy: Statistics Are Out; a Qualified Certainty Is In*, 22 SCI. SLEUTHING 12-13 (Sum. 1998).

§ 18-5. The Judicial and Legislative Response to DNA Evidence.

§ 18-5(A). The Validity of DNA Typing.

There are both cases and statutes dealing with the admissibility of DNA typing evidence.

The Case Law

The jurisprudence on DNA typing has undergone little evolution. The early cases uncritically accepted DNA evidence. However, even today with the benefit of a much more sophisticated understanding of DNA testing, the courts are receptive to DNA evidence.

The Early Case Law

In the early cases, most courts were quite receptive to DNA evidence. Initially, there were only trial court decisions admitting testimony based on the DNA technique.[144] A few years after the advent of DNA testing in the United States, in testimony before the United States Senate Subcommittee on the Constitution of the Judiciary Committee, Professor James Starrs stated that "[b]y all reports some twenty or so criminal cases have been concluded at the trial level in some seven states where DNA matching has been welcomed, with nary a word of judicial dissent anywhere." Many of these trial court decisions were unpublished.

However, there were a few early favorable published opinions as well. The seminal case, *Andrews v. Florida,*[145] arose in Florida. In that case, an intermediate state appellate court ruled DNA evidence admissible. In *Andrews,* the Lifecodes expert "testified to a match between the DNA in the defendant's blood and the DNA from the swab stating that the percentage of the population that would have the DNA bands indicated by the samples would be 0.0000012 percent. In other words, the chance that the DNA strands found in the defendant's blood would be duplicated in some other person's cells was 1 in 839,914,540." In the text of its opinion, the court stated its view that DNA

---

144. Fiatal, *DNA Testing and the Frye Standard,* 59 F.B.I. LAW ENF. BULL. 26, 31 n.20 (June 1990) ("Trial courts have admitted conclusions based upon DNA analysis by examiners from the FBI on over 50 occasions"). Moss, *DNA — The New Fingerprints,* 74 A.B.A. J. 66, 68 (May 1, 1988) describes trial court decisions in Melbourne, Florida, Norman, Oklahoma, New York City, and Scranton, Pennsylvania. The Moss article refers to a *Hill* case in Oklahoma. Another Oklahoma trial court has also admitted DNA testimony. *Admission of DNA Fingerprint Prompts Queries,* NAT'L L.J., Jan. 19, 1988 (describing State v. Andrews, CR87-1659, an Orlando, Florida Circuit Court decision). A California trial court has similarly admitted DNA testimony. Thompson, *DNA Wins in Court,* 9 CAL. LAW. 36 (Oct. 1989) (the trial judge admitted the evidence in People v. Axell, Ventura Super. Ct., No. CR-23911), *aff'd,* 235 Cal. App. 3d 836, 1 Cal. Rptr. 2d 411 (1991).

145. 533 So. 2d 841 (Fla. Dist. Ct. App. 1988). *See* Note, U. ARK. LITTLE ROCK L. REV. 543 (1989-90).

evidence need not satisfy the *Frye* test in Florida; the court read the earlier Florida precedents as adopting the more liberal relevancy test for the admissibility of scientific evidence. However, in dictum in footnote six, the court stated that on the record below, DNA evidence would pass muster under *Frye*.

The second published decision was rendered by a New York trial court in *People v. Wesley*.[146] In ruling the DNA evidence admissible in that case, the court was impressed by prosecution evidence "DNA testing is accurate down to one white in 840 million and one black in 1.4 billion."[147] However, the trial judge did not allow that statistical evidence to be presented to the jury. In *Wesley,* a defense expert pointed to the absence of published data demonstrating that the various alleles are independent.[148] To compensate for the lack of proof of independence, the judge ordered that the prosecution statistics be adjusted downward by a factor of ten before the statistics were presented to the jury.

Thus, the weight of the early authority favored admitting DNA evidence as a matter of course. The precedential value of these cases was somewhat "less compelling than they [at first] appear" because in the vast majority the defense did not mount any sophisticated admissibility attacks on the evidence.[149] Nevertheless, the case law clearly preponderated in favor of the view that DNA evidence is admissible.

As we shall see in the remaining subsections, in the early cases DNA did suffer occasional setbacks. However, those setbacks were not caused by any skepticism on the courts' part about the validity of the underlying technology. In the cases in which the courts excluded DNA testimony, they did so for other stated reasons, namely, either a finding that the analyst had not employed proper procedure in the pending case or a conclusion that the statistical evaluation testimony was flawed. There has been never been any serious disagreement over the validity of the basic theory.

The Status Quo

There are now numerous other published opinions sustaining the admission of DNA typing evidence.[150] Because of the lag time between the introduction of

---

146. 140 Misc. 2d 306, 533 N.Y.S.2d 643 (Albany County Ct. 1988), *aff'd sub nom.* People v. Bailey, 156 A.D.2d 846, 549 N.Y.S.2d 846 (1989).

147. 5 WEST'S CRIMINAL LAW NEWS 2 (Nov. 25, 1988).

148. Thompson & Ford, *DNA Typing: Acceptance and Weight of the New Genetic Identification Tests,* 75 VA. L. REV. 45, 105 (1989).

149. Scheck & Neufeld, *Riding the Double Helix,* 16 THE CHAMPION 31, 32 (Jan./Feb. 1992) (discussing Judge Kennedy's opinion in United States v. Porter et al., No. F06277-89, a District of Columbia Superior Court case).

150. Annot., *Admissibility of DNA identification evidence,* 84 A.L.R.4TH 313 (1991); Nikos, *DNA Takes on Larger Role as Defense Tool,* THE DAILY RECORDER, Sept. 30, 1992, at 5 ('Prosecutors pioneered its use in United States criminal courts in 1987, and now it is used as evidence in criminal courts in every state except North Dakota, FBI officials said. As of July 31, DNA has been admitted as evidence in 756 trials nationwide ..., according to the FBI ...."); *DNA Test Results Generally Admissible in Federal and State Courts When Foundation Requirements Are Met*, 8 CRIMINAL L. NEWS 1 (Feb. 25, 1991); Fiatal, *DNA Testing and the Frye Standard*, 58 F.B.I. LAW ENF. BULL. 26 (June 1990); Starrs, *DNA Profiling*, SCI. SLEUTHING REV. 13 (Winter 1991) ("the swelling rank of those states which have found DNA profiling to be admissible"); Purnell v. City of Akron, 925 F.2d 941 (6th Cir. 1991); Tipps v. Metropolitan Life Ins. Co., 768 F. Supp. 577 (S.D. Tex. 1991); USA v. Young, 754 F. Supp. 739 (D.S.D. 1990); United States v. Jakobetz, 747 F. Supp. 250 (D. Vt. 1990), *aff'd,* 955 F.2d 786 (2d Cir.), *cert. denied,* 506 U.S. 834 (1992); District of Columbia *ex rel.* J.A.B. v. W.R., 60 U.S.L.W. (BNA) 2175, 17 Fam. L. Rep. 1499 (D.C. Super. Ct., Aug. 2, 1991); Yelder v. State, 630 So. 2d 92 (Ala. Crim. App.), *rev'd,* 630 So. 2d 107 (Ala. 1992), *cert. denied*, 510 U.S. 1214 (1994); Snowden v. State, 574 So. 2d 960 (Ala. Crim. App. 1990) (the DNA expert's population frequency calculations were scientifically reliable and admissible); Perry v. State, 586 So. 2d 236 (Ala. Crim. App. 1990) (DNA typing satisfies *Frye*); Prater v. State, 307 Ark. 180, 820 S.W.2d 429 (1991); People v. Axell, 235 Cal. App. 3d 836, 1 Cal. Rptr. 2d 411 (1991); People v. Fishback, 829 P.2d 489 (Colo. App. 1991), *aff'd*, 851 P.2d 884 (Colo. 1993); Martinez v. State, 549 So. 2d 694 (Fla. Dist. Ct. App. 1989) (it was permissible for the expert to state that the probability of a random match was one in 234 billion); People v. Thomas, 137 Ill. 2d 500, 148 Ill. Dec. 751, 561 N.E.2d 57 (1990); Hopkins v. Indiana, 579 N.E.2d 1297 (Ind. 1991); State v. Brown, 470 N.W.2d 30 (Iowa 1991); Smith v. Deppish, 248 Kan. 217, 807 P.2d 144 (1991) ("[s]tatistics based on population studies are admissible and any challenge to the reliability of the testing goes to its weight, not its admissibility"); Cobey v. State, 80 Md. App. 31, 559 A.2d 391 (the single locus probe method satisfies *Frye*; there was no rebuttal evidence in this case, and the court noted that it was not declaring DNA evidence admissible in every case), *cert. denied,* 317 Md. 542, 565 A.2d 670 (1989); State v. Williams, 252 N.J. Super. 369, 599 A.2d 960 (1991); State v. Thomas, 245 N.J. Super. 428, 586 A.2d 250 (1991) (dictum); People v. Shi Fu Huang, 145 Misc. 2d 513, 546 N.Y.S.2d 920 (1989) (the population frequencies were based on a study of 167 blood samples obtained in mainland China); King v. Tanner, 142 Misc. 2d 1004, 539 N.Y.S.2d 617 (Sup. Ct. 1989) (based on the DNA typing evidence, the expert calculated King's probability of paternity as 99.99%); State v. Pennington, 327 N.C. 89, 393 S.E.2d 847 (1990); Comment, *Criminal Procedure — Match Game 1990's: The Admissibility of DNA Profiling — State v. Pennington*, 13 CAMPBELL L. REV. 209 (1991); State v. Blair, 592 N.E.2d 854, (Ohio App. 1990); State v. Lee, 1990 Ohio App. LEXIS 5311, 1990 W.L. 197975 (Ohio App.); State v. Pierce, 1990 Ohio App. LEXIS 2882, 1990 W.L. 97596 (Ohio App.), *aff'd*, 64 Ohio St.3d 490, 597 N.E.2d 107 (1992); State v. Ford, 301 S.C. 485, 392 S.E.2d 781 (1990) (DNA evidence satisfies *Frye*); Vickers v. State, 801 S.W.2d 214 (Tex. App. 1990); Mandujano v. State, 799 S.W.2d 318 (Tex. App. 1990); Kelly v. State, 792 S.W.2d 579 (Tex. App. 1990) (the court applied the relevancy standard), *aff'd,* 824 S.W.2d 568 (Tex. Crim. App. 1992); Glover v. State, 787 S.W.2d 544 (Tex. App. 1990) (the prosecution evidence of the reliability of the technique was unrebutted), *aff'd,* 825 S.W.2d 127 (Tex. Crim. App. 1992); Spencer v. Commonwealth, 238 Va. 275, 384 S.E.2d 775 (1989) (the odds of a random match were one in 135 million), *cert. denied,* 493 U.S. 1036 (1990); State v. Woodall, 385 S.E.2d 253 (W. Va. 1989) (although the court restricted the admissibility of statistical probability testimony, the court held that DNA test results are admissible; the validity of DNA typing is now subject to judicial notice). *See also* Hager, *DNA on Trial as Evidence*, L.A. TIMES, Mar. 27, 1991, at 6 (in *People v. Axell* in Ventura, California, a trial judge admitted DNA testimony over objection); Sherman, *Genetic Testing Criticized*, NAT'L L.J., Apr. 20, 1992, at 1 ("DNA evidence has been admitted in more than 300 cases nationwide").

Some jurisdictions continue to admit DNA evidence under the *Frye* test. Harmon v. State, 908

evidence in a trial court and the subsequent publication of an appellate opinion dealing with the evidence, most of the published opinions deal with RFLP although the vast majority laboratories are now relying primarily on newer technologies. It is fair to say that "an overwhelming majority of the courts" which have passed on DNA testimony have ruled the evidence admissible.[151] Given that majority view, the courts understandably also held that the admission of DNA evidence does not violate due process.[152] According to the F.B.I. crime laboratory, DNA evidence has already been admitted in over 40 states.[153] The latest F.B.I. survey, set out below, indicates that RFLP evidence has been admitted in 258 cases.[154]

P.2d 434 (Alaska App. 1995); State v. Bogan, 183 Ariz. 506, 905 P.2d 515 (App. 1995) (a DNA match between palo verde seed pods found in defendant's truck and a palo verde tree growing at the crime scene); People v. Venegas, 18 Cal. 4th 47, 954 P.2d 525, 74 Cal. Rptr. 2d 262 (1998) (the court approved of the RFLP procedures used by the FBI as well as by Cellmark); Polk v. State, 612 So. 2d 381 (Miss. 1992); Commonwealth v. Rodgers, 413 Pa. Super. 498, 605 A.2d 1228 (1992). Other jurisdictions admit the evidence under the reliability standard, which the Supreme Court adopted in the *Daubert* case. United States v. Coronado-Cervantes, 912 F. Supp. 497 (D.N.M. 1996); Mitchell v. Commonwealth, 908 S.W.2d 100 (Ky. 1995); United States v. Bonds, 12 F.3d 540 (6th Cir. 1993); United States v. Martinez, 3 F.3d 1191 (8th Cir. 1993), *cert. denied*, 510 U.S. 1062 (1994); State v. Wright, 593 So. 2d 759, 764 (La. App.), *cert. denied*, 506 U.S. 922 (1992); State v. Jobe, 486 N.W.2d 407 (Minn. 1992); Note, *Evidence) Novel Scientific Evidence) DNA Profiling Held Admissible Under the Relevancy Standard, Prater v. State, 307 Ark. 180, 820 S.W.2d 429 (1991)*, 15 U. ARK. LITTLE ROCK L.J. 71 (1992).

151. Sylvester & Stafford, *Judicial Acceptance of DNA Profiling*, 60 F.B.I. LAW ENF. BULL. 26 (July 1991); People v. White, 621 N.Y.S.2d 728 (Sup. Ct. App. Div. 1995). *Accord,* State v. Brown, 470 N.W.2d 30 (Iowa 1991) ("the great majority of appellate courts").

152. Spencer v. Murray, 5 F.3d 758 (4th Cir. 1993), *cert. denied*, 510 U.S. 1171 (1994); Reid v. Page, 47 F. Supp. 2d 1008 (C.D. Ill. 1999); Armstead v. State, 342 Md. 38, 673 A.2d 221 (1996).

153. Sherman, *DNA Evidence Dispute Escalates*, NAT'L L.J., Jan. 20, 1992. In his 93-page opinion in United States v. Porter et al., 1991 WL 319015 (Super. Ct., District of Columbia., Sept. 21, 1991), *vacated*, 618 A.2d 629 (U.S. App. D.C. 1992), Judge Kennedy acknowledged that DNA testimony has been accepted in more than 30 states. *No DNA Profiles*, NAT'L L.J., Oct. 7, 1991. Robin, *DNA Evidence in Court*, 9 CRIM. JUST. 8, 56 (Fall 1994) ("Of the forty-seven state courts of last resort that had considered the matter as of June 1993, thirty-eight ruled in favor of admitting DNA evidence. No court has rejected ... the theory, technology, or scientific principles underlying DNA profiling."). In 1994, Chase Foster of the F.B.I.'s Legal Assistance Unit (DNALAU) prepared LEGAL ASPECTS OF FORENSIC DNA EVIDENCE. According to that survey, as of February 2, 1994, RFLP testimony had been admitted in 37 state courts of last resort, five federal appellate courts, 55 state intermediate appellate courts, four published federal trial court opinions, and one reported state trial court opinion. The May 12, 1998 update of the survey indicates that the admission of RFLP testimony has been upheld in 83 state courts of last resort, 12 federal appellate courts, 132 state intermediate appellate courts, five reported federal trial court decisions, and four reported state trial court decisions. *See also* Scheck & Neufeld, *Riding the Double Helix*, 16 THE CHAMPION 31, 32 (Jan. 1992); Sherman, *Genetic Testing Criticized*, NAT'L L.J., Apr. 20, 1992, at 1 ("DNA evidence has been admitted in more than 300 cases nationwide").

154. REPORTED FORENSIC DNA CASES 1 (updated July 28, 1999).

The Illinois Supreme Court has gone to the length of declaring that a trial judge may judicially notice the general reliability of the electrophoretic procedure which, as previously stated, is employed in DNA identification analysis.[155] The Court of Appeals for the Second Circuit, the West Virginia Supreme Court, and the Kentucky Supreme Court are in accord.[156] Given those decisions, Professor Moenssens has predicted that in the future, most courts will judicially notice the general validity of DNA typing.[157] Chapter 6 of the 1992 N.R.C. report asserts that at this point in the evolution of the technology, courts should judicially notice the propositions that: The analysis of DNA polymorphism is a reliable method of comparing samples; with the exception of identical twins, each person's DNA is unique; and the then current laboratory procedure for analyzing DNA "(specifically single-locus probes analyzed on Southern blots without evidence of band shifting)" was "fundamentally sound."

The general validity of DNA typing became so well accepted that some courts were soon requiring the government to fund DNA testing for the defense.[158] Even most of the innovations in DNA testing quickly won judicial acceptance. One federal trial court admitted testimony about an RFLP analysis using

155. People v. Thomas, 137 Ill. 2d 500, 148 Ill. Dec. 751, 561 N.E.2d 57, 63-64 (1990).

156. United States v. Jakobetz, 955 F.2d 786, 799-800 (2d Cir. 1992) ("in future cases ..., a court could properly take judicial notice of the general acceptability of the general theory and the use of these specific techniques"), *cert. denied,* 506 U.S. 834 (1992); Fugate v. Commonwealth, 993 S.W.2d 931 (Ky. 1999); State v. Woodall, 385 S.E.2d 253 (W. Va. 1989).

157. Goldberg, *A New Day for DNA?*, 78 A.B.A. J. 84, 85 (Apr. 1992). United States v. Beasley, 102 F.3d 1440 (8th Cir. 1996) (judicial notice of the reliability of PCR analysis), *cert. denied*, 520 U.S. 1246 (1997); Government of Virgin Islands v. Byers, 941 F. Supp. 513 (D. V.I. 1996) (the trial judge may judicially notice expert testimony offered in earlier cases to support or dispute the merits of a particular scientific procedure); State v. Moore, 323 Ark. 529, 915 S.W.2d 284 (1996); United States v. Jakobetz, 955 F.2d 786, 799 (2d Cir.), *cert. denied*, 506 U.S. 834 (1992); United States v. Coronado-Cervantes, 912 F. Supp. 497, 499 (D.N.M. 1996); State v. Moore, 323 Ark. 529, 915 S.W.2d 284 (1996) ("DNA profiling evidence should no longer be viewed as novel scientific evidence requiring a preliminary showing beyond the showing that the expert properly performed a reliable methodology in creating the DNA profiles"); United States v. Martinez, 3 F.3d 1191 (8th Cir. 1993), *cert. denied*, 510 U.S. 1062 (1994); People v. Adams, 195 Mich. App. 267, 489 N.W.2d 192 (1992), *modified*, 441 Mich. 916, 497 N.W.2d 182 (1993).

158. Cade v. State, 658 So. 2d 550 (Fla. Dist. Ct. App. 1995); *Ex parte* State, 662 So. 2d 1189 (Ala. 1995); Washpon v. New York State Dist. Att'y, Kings County, 625 N.Y.S.2d 874 (1995) (a New York statute authorizes testing at public expense when the defendant is indigent); State v. Dubose, 662 So. 2d 1156 (Ala. Crim. App. 1993), *aff'd*, 662 So. 2d 1189 (Ala. 1995); Polk v. State, 612 So. 2d 381 (Miss. 1992); Commonwealth v. Brison, 618 A.2d 420 (Pa. Super. 1992). *But see* Husske v. Commonwealth, 252 Va. 203, 476 S.E.2d 920 (1996) (to be entitled to a state-paid expert, the defendant must make a "particularized need" for the expert's help; in the instant case, the defendant failed to make the required showing), *cert. denied*, 519 U.S. 1154 (1997); Zollinger, *Defense Access to State-Funded DNA Experts: Considerations of Due Process*, 85 CAL. L. REV. 1803 (1997).

chemiluminescence rather than isotopic labeling,[159] one state trial court and one state appellate court[160] admitted testimony about the analysis of mitochondrial DNA,[161] and two state appellate courts have already sustained the admission of testimony about STR analysis.[162] However, there have been notable exceptions to the norm of quick judicial acceptance. Chapter 6 of the 1992 N.R.C. report added that it is questionable whether the use of monomorphic probes to correct for band shifting is "sufficiently well established to justify admissibility."

Several times each year the Office of General Counsel of the Federal Bureau of Investigation prepares a summary report on forensic DNA profiling. The July 28, 1999 report contains the following summary of the RFLP case law.[163] Although most of the published opinions involve RFLP, according to the F.B.I survey, PCR has been admitted in 98 cases.[164] For example, early on the Virginia Supreme Court approved the admission of testimony based on PCR amplification.[165] The federal District Court for the Southern District of New York is in accord.[166]

---

159. United States v. Lowe, 954 F. Supp. 401 (D. Mass. 1996).

160. State v. Council, 515 S.E. 2d 508 (S.C. 1999).

161. Curriden, *A New Evidence Tool: First use of mitochondrial DNA test in a U.S. criminal trial*, 82 A.B.A. J. 18 (Nov. 1996) ("Traditional DNA typing uses genetic material taken from the nucleus of the cell, which is inherited half from the mother and half from the father. Mitochondrial DNA tests examine genetic material in the cell's more abundant energy-producing mitochrondia, which are inherited completely from the mother"); *New DNA Points to Guilt*, NAT'L L.J., Sep. 16, 1996) (the prosecution of Paul Ware in Chattanooga, Tennessee). *See also* Cohen, *Innovative DNA Test Is an ID Whose Time Has Come for the FBI*, WALL ST. J., Dec. 19, 1997, p. A1 (testimony about mitochondrial DNA tests "has been used by the Federal Bureau of Investigation only since August 1996 and has resulted in six convictions in six attempts. Thanks to the FBI, mitochondrial DNA testing has already occurred in 70 cases that haven't yet reached trial;" "nuclear testing suffers from a major limitation: It can't be used unless the evidence is ... in good shape; crucially, there have to be cell nuclei present, and hair that has been pulled away from its roots doesn't contain any nuclei. In contrast, mitochondrial DNA is located outside of a cell's nucleus.... That means more DNA can be extracted from ... less well-preserved fragments of evidence").

162. People v. Allen, 72 Cal. App. 4th 1093, 85 Cal. Rptr. 2d 655 (1999); Commonwealth v. Rosier, 425 Mass. 807, 685 N.E.2d 739 (1997). However, a California Superior Court prosecution, People v. Botkin, STR evidence was excluded. Superior Court Judge Robert Dondero excluded the evidence "because [the] manufacturer [PE Biosystems of Foster City, California] declined to provide data about the chemical makeup of the DNA test." Slind-Flor, *DNA Testing Routs Trade Secrets*, NAT'L L.J., May 24, 1999, at B4. PE Biosystems claimed that the data was proprietary. Samuel Thummer of Brown & Bain in Phoenix suggested that in the future, such problems could be avoided through the use of protective orders, as in civil cases. *Id.*

163. The full report contains the supporting case citations. Readers can obtain a copy of the latest report by contacting Professor Imwinkelried or Ms. Michelle M. Harwell, Federal Bureau of Investigation, Office of General Counsel, 10th Street and Pennsylvania Avenue, N.W., Room 7879, Washington, D.C. 20535, (202) 324-1420 (telephone), or (202) 324-1043 (FAX).

164. REPORTED FORENSIC DNA CASES 1 (updated July 28, 1999).

165. Spencer v. Commonwealth, 240 Va. 78, 393 S.E.2d 609, *cert. denied,* 498 U.S. 908 (1990); United States v. Hicks, 103 F.3d 837 (9th Cir. 1996), *cert. denied*, 520 U.S. 1193 (1997); United

Table I. RFLP Cases

RFLP	Admissions	Admitted With Limited Statistics or Without Statistics	Remands and/or Exclusions Based Upon DNA Evidence	TOTAL
State Courts of Last Resort	95	21	14	130
Federal Appellate Courts	13	0	1	14
State Intermediate Appellate Courts	141	6	9	156
Reported Federal Trial Courts	5	2	0	7
Reported State Trial Courts	4	2	1	7
Total RFLP Decisions	258	31	25	314

States v. Beasley, 102 F.3d 1440 (8th Cir. 1996), *cert. denied*, 520 U.S. 1246 (1997); United States v. Gaines, 979 F. Supp. 1429 (S.D. Fla. 1997); United States v. Shea, 957 F. Supp. 331 (D.N.H. 1997), *aff'd*, 159 F.3d 37 (1st Cir. 1998), *cert. denied*, 119 S. Ct. 1480 (1999); Brodine v. State, 936 P.2d 545 (Alaska App. 1997); State v. Tankersley, 191 Ariz. 359, 956 P.2d 486 (1998); People v. Wright, 62 Cal. App. 4th 31, 72 Cal. Rptr. 2d 246 (1998); State v. Isley, 262 Kan. 281, 936 P.2d 275 (1997); Commonwealth v. Rosier, 425 Mass. 807, 685 N.E.2d 739 (1997); Commonwealth v. Sok, 425 Mass. 787, 683 N.E.2d 671 (1997); State v. Harvey, 151 N.J. 117, 699 A.2d 596 (1997); People v. Morales, 227 A.D.2d 648, 643 N.Y.S.2d 217 (N.Y. App. 1996); State v. Begley, 956 S.W.2d 471 (Tenn. 1997); People v. Pope, 284 Ill. App. 3d 695, 220 Ill. Dec. 309, 672 N.E.2d 1321 (1996) (DQ-Alpha and polymarker typing); State v. Lyons, 324 Or. 256, 924 P.2d 802 (1996); Harmon v. State, 908 P.2d 434 (Alaska App. 1995); People v. Morganti, 43 Cal. App. 4th 643, 50 Cal. Rptr. 2d 837 (1996); State v. Hill, 257 Kan. 774, 895 P.2d 1238 (1995); People v. Lee, 212 Mich. App. 228, 537 N.W.2d 233 (1995); Seritt v. State, 647 So. 2d 1 (Ala. Crim. App. 1994); Esty v. State, 642 So. 2d 1074 (Fla. 1994), *cert. denied*, 514 U.S. 1027 (1995); State v. Penton, 1993 Ohio App. LEXIS 1937 (Ohio App. Apr. 7, 1993); State v. Lyons, 124 Or. App. 598, 863 P.2d 1303 (1993), *review granted*, 319 Or. 406, 879 P.2d 1284 (1994), *aff'd*, 924 P.2d 802 (Or. 1996); State v. Russell, 125 Wash.2d 24, 882 P.2d 747 (1994), *cert. denied*, 514 U.S. 1129 (1995).

In 1994, Chase Foster of the F.B.I.'s DNA Legal Assistance Unit prepared LEGAL ASPECTS OF FORENSIC DNA EVIDENCE. According to that survey, PCR evidence has been admitted by three state courts of last resort, five state intermediate appellate courts, and one published state trial court opinion. The June 28, 1999 update of the survey indicates that the admission of PCR testimony has been upheld by 39 state courts of last resort, five federal appellate courts, 46 state intermediate appellate courts, and three reported state trial court decisions. *See also* Gibeaut, *Courts Cautiously Explore the Strange, New Tests for DNA*, 84 A.B.A. J. 40 (Apr. 1998) ("The courts' crawl toward a more controversial DNA test called polymerase chain reaction typing is especially cautious. Appeals courts in about 20 states and in two federal circuits have approved PCR evidence since 1990, with the majority of decisions coming after 1995."); Erlich, *The Application of PCR Amplification to Casework Analysis*, 18 CRIME LAB. DIGEST 127 (Oct. 1991) (PCR evidence "has been subjected to 22 admissibility hearings and admitted in 20 cases in the following states: California, Oregon, Kansas, Texas, Florida, Virginia, Michigan, Washington, New Jersey, Ohio and Wisconsin.").

166. United States v. Cuff, 37 F. Supp. 2d 279 (S.D.N.Y. 1999).

There have been dissenting voices on PCR. For instance, a California Superior Court judge ruled that PCR does not yet pass muster under the *Frye* test.[167] Chapter 2 of the 1992 N.R.C. report tended to support that ruling; the report stated that PCR "has not yet achieved full acceptance in the forensic setting." However, the California courts have since reconsidered their position.[168] Modernly, the vast majority of jurisdictions, including federal courts[169] and state courts in such jurisdictions as Arizona,[170] Nevada,[171] New Mexico,[172] and Tennessee,[173] accept PCR evidence. The 1996 N.R.C. report lent its support to the admissibility of PCR testimony. Given that support, the results shown on the F.B.I.'s July 28, 1999 summary PCR chart should come as no surprise:

Table II. PCR Cases

PCR				
State Courts of Last Resort	42	1	4	47
Federal Appellate Courts	5	0	0	5
State Intermediate Appellate Courts	47	2	2	52
Reported Federal Trial Courts	0	2	0	2
Reported State Trial Courts	3	0	0	3
Total PCR Decisions	98	5	6	109
**NOTE: There are 17 decisions that address two or more methods of DNA typing. These cases are counted separately in the individual columns but only counted once in the Total DNA Decisions column.				

167. Towns, *Jury in Trial Over 1987 Murder Will Not Hear DNA Evidence, Local Judge Rules*, SACRAMENTO DAILY RECORDER, Sept. 20, 1991, at 1 (the murder and rape prosecution of Paul Steven Mack). People v. McSherry, 11 Cal. App. 4th 1157, 14 Cal. Rptr. 2d 630, 634 (1992) ("PCR analysis has not been approved by an appellate court as admissible in California under *Kelly-Frye*"; the court distinguished the cases admitting PCR evidence on the ground that they were decided "under a more lenient relevance standard than the *Kelly-Frye* rule followed in California."); People v. Martinez, Case No. A709321 (Los Angeles County Super. Ct. 1989); Murray v. State, 692 So. 2d 157 (Fla. 1997). However, the *McSherry* decision was subsequently depublished.

168. People v. Roybal, 19 Cal. 4th 481, 966 P.2d 521, 79 Cal. Rptr. 2d 487, 499-500 (1998), *modified*, 19 Cal. 4th 1231a (1999).

169. United States v. Shea, 159 F.3d 37, 41 (1st Cir. 1998); United States v. Cuff, 37 F. Supp. 2d 279 (S.D.N.Y. 1999).

170. State v. Tankersley, 191 Ariz. 359, 956 P.2d 486 (1998).

171. Bolin v. State, 114 Nev. 503, 906 P.2d 784 (1998).

172. State v. Stills, 125 N.M. 66, 957 P.2d 51 (1998).

173. State v. Begley, 956 S.W.2d 471 (Tenn. 1997); *Evidence — State v. Begley: When the Tennessee Supreme Court Meets PCR-Method DNA Analysis, It's Love at First Sight*, 28 U. MEM. L REV. 1239 (1998).

The Statutes

In a number of states, the legislatures have intervened. The intervention has taken the form of two different types of statutes.

One type of statute mandates the admission of DNA evidence.[174] For example, in 1989 the Maryland legislature passed House Bill 711, section 10-915 of the Annotated Maryland Courts and Judicial Proceedings Code. That bill declared DNA evidence to be admissible in the courts of that state. There are similar statutes in Louisiana,[175] Michigan,[176] Minnesota,[177] and Missouri.[178] While some statutes are limited to civil paternity suits, others apply in criminal cases. Congress also considered legislation to regulate DNA testing and passed the DNA Identification Act in 1994.[179]

In addition, many states have enacted a type of legislation discussed in Chapter 2 of this treatise, namely, statutes requiring persons convicted of certain

---

174. Note, *"Genetically" Altered Admissibility: Legislative Notice of DNA Typing*, 39 CLEV. ST. L. REV. 415 (1991); *A Defense Counsel's Guide to the Use of DNA Evidence in Virginia*, 2 REGENT UNIV. L. REV. 113, 114 n.6 (1992) (listing state statutes); Note, *DNA Profiling Evidence: The Need for a Uniform and Workable Evidentiary Standard of Admissibility*, 26 VAL. U. L. REV. 595, 620 (1992) (listing state statutes); IND. STAT. 35-37-4-11(b) ("In a criminal trial or hearing, the results of forensic DNA analysis are admissible without antecedent expert testimony that forensic DNA analysis provides a trustworthy and reliable method of identifying characteristics in an individual's genetic material."); Satcher v. Netherland, 944 F. Supp. 1222 (E.D. Va. 1997), *aff'd in part, rev'd in part*, 126 F.3d 561 (4th Cir.), *cert. denied*, 522 U.S. 1010 (1997). In Armstead v. State, 342 Md. 38, 673 A.2d 221 (1996), the court construed a state statute as precluding "generalized" attacks on the admissibility of DNA evidence. Under the statute, the trial judge's power to altogether exclude the evidence is limited to cases in which the evidence is irrelevant or there were such serious laboratory procedure errors that the evidence would be unhelpful to the trier of fact. According to the F.B.I.'s May 12, 1998 update of its DNA evidence survey, such statutes exist in 15 states.

175. Comment, *Beyond People v. Castro: A New Standard of Admissibility for DNA Fingerprinting*, 7 J. CONTEMP. HEALTH L. & POL. 269, 299 (1991) (citing LA. REV. STAT. ANN. § 444.1); Note, *United States v. Two Bulls: Eighth Circuit Addresses Admissibility of Forensic DNA Evidence*, 37 LOY. L. REV. 173, 186 (1991) ("Louisiana has legislatively determined that DNA tests are relevant"). *See also* Fiatal, *DNA Testing and the Frye Standard*, 59 F.B.I. LAW ENF. BULL. 26, 31 nn.22, 29 (June 1990).

176. MICH. STAT. ANN. § 25.496 (1990).

177. MINN. STAT. ANN. § 634.25. *See* the authorities cited in note 175, *supra*.

178. In 1991, the Missouri legislature approved S.B. No. 152. The legislation directs the Missouri Department of Public Safety to establish a "DNA Profiling System." Section 2(3) of the bill provides that various Missouri state crime laboratories will "[p]rovide expert testimony in court on DNA evidentiary issues." *See SB 152 — DNA Profiling*, 26 MISSOURI BAR LEGISLATIVE DIGEST 14-15 (July 1991).

179. *House Prepares to Consider Crime Bill Far Different From That Passed by Senate*, 50 CRIM. L. REP. (BNA) 1063 (Oct. 16, 1991); *Congressional Interest in DNA*, NATIONAL INSTITUTE OF JUSTICE REPORTS 7 (June 1991).

offenses to contribute samples to DNA databanks.[180] Due in part to the financial incentives offered under the DNA Identification Act,[181] every state now has a database.[182] All of the statutes cover sexual assault, roughly half apply to homicide, and approximately a third extend to some juvenile offenses.[183] Louisiana has gone to the length of requiring all arrestees to contribute a sample for its database,[184] and New York and North Carolina are contemplating a similar step.[185] To date, with the exception of one Massachusetts trial court,[186] the courts have uniformly upheld the constitutionality of these statutes.[187] The state

---

180. Robin, *DNA Evidence in Court*, 9 CRIM. JUST. 8, 57 (Fall 1994) ("by October 1993, twenty-two states have enacted or initiated legislation, mostly applicable to sex offenders, making DNA testing a condition of parole or a consequence of conviction for state databank purposes"); Smith & Gordon, *The Admission of DNA Evidence in State and Federal Courts*, 65 FORDHAM L. REV. 2465, 2487-88 (1997). According to the May 12, 1998 update of the F.B.I. survey of DNA evidence, such statutes exist in 48 states. "While all state collection statutes cover sexual assaults, only about half address other crimes such as murder or manslaughter, and only about a third of those statutes cover juvenile crimes." *National DNA Evidence Commission Begins Work On Recommendations Sought by Justice Department*, 66 U.S.L.W. 2593 (Apr. 7, 1998).

181. 42 U.S.C. §§ 3796kk to 3796kk, 14131-14134; Donnelly & Friedman, *DNA Database Searches and the Legal Consumption of Scientific Evidence*, 97 MICH. L. REV. 931, 939 (1999).

182. Donnelly & Friedman, *DNA Database Searches and the Legal Consumption of Scientific Evidence*, 97 MICH. L. REV. 931, 939 (1999).

183. *National DNA Evidence Commission Begins Work on Recommendations Sought by Justice Department*, 66 U.S.L.W. (BNA) 2593 (Apr. 7, 1998).

184. LA. REV. STAT. ANN. § 15:609(A) (effective September 1, 1999).

185. Bernstein, *Oregon Will Add to Its DNA Database*, OREGONIAN ONLINE, Mar. 22, 1999.

186. Landry v. Harshbarger, No. CIV. A.98-462 (Mass. Super. Ct., Aug. 12, 1998) (unpublished order preliminary enjoining enforcement of the Massachusetts statute). Donnelly & Friedman, *Dna Database Searches and the Legal Consumption of Scientific Evidence*, 97 MICH. L. REV. 931, 939 (1999); Schoenberg, *DNA Dragnet*, LEGAL TIMES, May 10, 1999, at a ("A Massachusetts trial court found the state's law unconstitutional on the grounds that it violated both the 4th Amendment and the state constitution as a search without probable cause. But last month the Massachusetts Supreme Judicial Court reversed that decision ...."). *See* Landry v. Attorney General, 429 Mass. 336, 709 N.E.2d 1085 1999).

187. Shaffer v. Saffle, 148 F.3d 1180 (10th Cir.), *cert. denied*, 119 S. Ct. 520 (1998); Hernandez v. Prunty, 129 F.3d 125 (9th Cir. 1997); Schlicher v. Peters, 103 F.3d 940 (10th Cir. 1996) (the Kansas statute); Boling v. Romer, 101 F.3d 1336 (10th Cir. 1996) (the Colorado statute); Rise v. State of Oregon, 59 F.3d 1556 (9th Cir. 1994), *cert. denied*, 517 U.S. 1160 (1996); Gilbert v. Peters, 55 F.3d 237 (5th Cir. 1995); Ewell v. Murray, 11 F.3d 482 (4th Cir. 1993) (Virginia statute), *cert. denied*, 511 U.S. 1111 (1994); *In re* Appeal in Maricopa County Juvenile Action No. JV-512600, 187 Ariz. 419, 930 P.2d 496 (Ariz. App. 1996); Rise v. State, 59 F.3d 1556 (9th Cir. 1995), *cert. denied*, 517 U.S. 1160 (1996); Carey v. City of Richmond, 972 F.2d 338 (4th Cir. 1992); ; Shelton v. Gudmanson, 934 F. Supp. 1048 (W.D. Wis. 1996); Vanderlinden v. State of Kan., 874 F. Supp. 1210 (D. Kan. 1995), *aff'd sub nom.* Schlicher v. Peters, 103 F.3d 940 (10th Cir. 1996) ; Kruger v. Erickson, 875 F. Supp. 583 (D. Minn. 1995), *aff'd*, 77 F.3d 1071 (8th Cir. 1996); Sanders v. Coman, 864 F. Supp. 496 (E.D.N.C. 1994); Ryncarz v. Eikenberry, 824 F. Supp. 1493 (E.D. Wash. 1993); Jones v. Murray, 763 F. Supp. 842 (W.D .Va. 1991); Danzey v. State, 703 So. 2d 1019 (Ala. Crim. App. 1997); In the Matter of the Appeal in Maricopa County Juvenile Action

databases coordinate with the Convicted Offender Database Information System (CODIS) operated by the FBI.[188] As of October 1998, CODIS included more than 250,000 profiles with several hundred thousand more waiting to be analyzed.[189] However, the caveat is that no court has yet to pass on the validity of a statute as sweeping at the Louisiana legislation, requiring arrestees to contribute DNA samples. In jurisdictions which already have DNA databases for convicts, the question will arise as to whether the incremental utility of obtaining samples from arrestees justifies the intrusion.

§ 18-5(B). The Use of Proper Test Procedure.

The cases addressing this issue tend to fall into one of four categories: (1) cases excluding DNA evidence on the basis of improper test procedure; (2) cases requiring proof of test procedure but finding satisfactory proof; (3) cases announcing that deficiencies in test procedure ordinarily cut to weight, not admissibility; and (4) cases adopting a compromise position and requiring a showing of correct procedure in only certain respects.

Category #1

The first category includes cases excluding DNA evidence for the stated reason that the prosecution did not establish that the analyst complied with correct protocol in conducting the test in question. A number of courts have taken the position that the foundation for the admission of DNA evidence must include testimony that the analyst followed proper test procedure in testing the samples in the instant case.[190] By far the most early significant trial court decision banning

---

No. JV 510161, 901 P.2d 1205 (Ariz. App. 1995); Aranjo v. State, 718 So. 2d 266 (Fla. Dist. Ct. App. 1998); Murneigh v. Gainer, 685 N.E.2d 1357 (Ill. 1997); People v. Calahan, 649 N.E.2d 588 (Ill. App. 1995); Doe v. Gainer, 642 N.E.2d 114 (Ill. 1994), *cert. denied*, 513 U.S. 1168 (1995); People v. Wealer, 264 Ill. App. 3d 6, 636 N.E.2d 1129, *appeal denied*, 157 Ill. 2d 519, 642 N.E.2d 1299, 205 Ill. Dec. 182 (1994); State v. Patterson, 963 P.2d 436 (Kan. App. 1998); Murphy v. Dept. of Correction, 429 Mass. 736, 711 N.E.2d 149 (1999) (rejecting an equal protection attack); Landry v. Attorney General, 429 Mass. 336, 709 N.E.2d 1085 (1999); State v. Merkt, 1998 WL 202638 (Minn. App. 1998); Cooper v. Gammon, 943 S.W.2d 699 (Mo. App. 1997); *In re* Nicholson, 1999 WL 61010 (Ohio. App. 1999); State *ex rel.* Juvenile Department of Multnomah County v. Orozco, 878 P.2d 432 (Or. App. 1994); Dial v. Vaughn, 1999 WL 3154644 (Pa. Commw. 1999); State v. Olivas, 856 P.2d 1076 (Wash. 1993). *See also* Mayfield v. Dalton, 109 F.3d 1423 (9th Cir. 1997) (the constitutional challenge was not ripe for review).

188 Donnelly & Friedman, *DNA Databases and the Legal Consumption of Scientific Evidence*, 97 MICH. L. REV. 931, 939-40 (1999).

189. *Id.* at 940.

190. United States v. Two Bulls, 918 F.2d 56 (8th Cir. 1990), *vacated,* 925 F.2d 1127 (8th Cir. 1991); United States v. Jakobetz, 747 F. Supp. 250 (D. Vt. 1990), *aff'd on other grounds,* 955 F.2d 786 (2d Cir.), *cert. denied,* 506 U.S. 834 (1992); *Ex parte* Perry, 586 So. 2d 242 (Ala. 1991) ("Are there current techniques that are capable of producing reliable results in DNA identification and

DNA evidence, for failure to prove this element of the foundation is *People v. Castro.*[191]

In *Castro,* the trial court acknowledged that DNA typing evidence is reliable enough to be admitted so long as the testing laboratory conducts the test by using accepted procedures. However, the trial judge faulted the procedures which Lifecodes used to conduct the test in question. The judge stated that "the defense was successful in demonstrating to this court that the testing laboratory failed in its responsibility to perform the accepted scientific techniques ... in several major respects."[192] The trial judge specifically noted that Lifecodes failed to use its announced matching standard of three standard deviations in evaluating the autoradiographs in *Castro.*[193]

The first appellate opinion excluding DNA evidence was *State v. Schwartz.*[194] Like the *Castro* court, in *Schwartz* the Minnesota Supreme Court conceded the general reliability of DNA typing. However, the court stressed that "specific DNA test results are only as reliable and accurate as the testing procedures used by the particular laboratory."[195] In *Schwartz,* Cellmark was the testing laboratory. After citing TWGDAM's guidelines, the court found several deficiencies in Cellmark's protocol:

> The director of Cellmark's Research and Development Laboratory, Dr. Robin Cotton, admitted that because Cellmark did not meet all the minimum guidelines, such as formal methodology validation and published results of experimental studies in peer review journal, the FBI likely would not consider their test results ready for use in court. The experts also reviewed similar standards for DNA typing developed by CACLD (the California Association of Crime Laboratory Directors). Again, Dr. Cotton acknowledged that Cellmark has not comported with all of these standards.[196]

---

that are generally accepted in the scientific community? In this particular case, did the testing laboratory perform generally accepted scientific techniques without error in the performance or interpretation of the tests?"); State v. Schwartz, 447 N.W.2d 422 (Minn. 1989); People v. Castro, 144 Misc. 2d 956, 545 N.Y.S.2d 985 (Sup. Ct. 1989); State v. Houser, 490 N.W.2d 168 (Neb. 1992). *See generally* Imwinkelried, *The Debate in the DNA Cases Over the Foundation for the Admission of Scientific Evidence: The Importance of Human Error as a Cause of Forensic Misanalysis*, 69 WASH. U. L.Q. 19 (1991); Note, *United States v. Two Bulls: Eighth Circuit Addresses Admissibility of Forensic DNA Evidence*, 37 LOY. L. REV. 173 (1991).

191. 144 Misc. 2d 956, 545 N.Y.S.2d 985 (Sup. Ct. 1989).

192. *Id.* at 996.

193. *Id.* at 998 n.15. *See* Note, *The Admissibility of DNA Typing: A New Methodology*, 79 GEO. L.J. 313, 325-31 (1990); Comment, *DNA Fingerprinting: Is It Ready for Trial?*, 45 U. MIAMI L. REV. 243, 252-55 (1990).

194. 447 N.W.2d 422 (Minn. 1989).

195. *Id.* at 426.

196. *Id.* at 426-27.

In another appellate case, *United States v. Two Bulls,*[197] the original panel of the Court of Appeals for the Eighth Circuit held that the trial judge erred in admitting DNA evidence without determining both whether there are standard procedures for conducting DNA tests and whether the standards were followed in the instant case. The court emphasized that the questions were issues for the trial judge. Before ruling, the trial judge should listen to both sides and then rule on the questions as "a matter of law." The appellate court remanded the case to the trial court for an expanded pretrial hearing addressing the questions overlooked in the initial hearing.[198]

In dictum, the Idaho Supreme Court has stated that in ruling on the admissibility of DNA evidence, trial judges should closely scrutinize the laboratory's test protocol.[199] Chapter 6 of the 1992 N.R.C. report supports the position taken by these courts. That chapter states that "DNA evidence should not be admissible if the proper procedures were not followed."

Category #2

The second category includes cases in which, as a necessary part of the foundation or predicate, the courts demanded proof of correct test procedure but admitted the evidence because the record below contained such proof.[200] In one

197. 918 F.2d 56, 61 (8th Cir. 1990), *vacated,* 925 F.2d 1127 (8th Cir. 1991).

198. *See* Note, *United States v. Two Bulls: Eighth Circuit Addresses Admissibility of Forensic DNA Evidence*, 37 LOY. L. REV. 173 (1991).

199. State v. Horsley, 117 Idaho 920, 792 P.2d 945 (1990); New Development, *State v. Horsley: The Idaho Court's First Look at DNA Printing as Evidence*, 27 IDAHO L. REV. 393 (1990-91).

200. United States v. Coronado-Cervantes, 912 F. Supp. 497, 500 (D.N.M. 1996) (proof of "compliance with standard protocol in applying the RFLP technique is essential and goes to admissibility, rather than merely to the weight of DNA evidence"); *Ex parte* Turner, 1998 Ala. LEXIS 8, 1998 WL 12625, 62 Cr.L. (BNA) 1404 (Ala. Sup. Ct., Jan. 16, 1998); *Ex parte* Perry, 586 So. 2d 242, 250 (Ala. 1991); People v. Venegas, 18 Cal. 4th 47, 954 P.2d 525, 74 Cal. Rptr. 2d 262 (1998) (the court ruled that the trial judge must inquire "whether the procedures actually utilized in this case were in compliance with" accepted methodology; the court held that this inquiry should condition the admissibility of DNA evidence because "[u]nlike fingerprint, shoe track, bite mark, or ballistic comparisons, which jurors essentially can see for themselves, questions concerning whether a laboratory has adopted correct, scientifically accepted procedures for generating autorads or determining a match depend almost entirely on the technical interpretations of experts"; however, the court added that some "derelictions in following the prescribed scientific procedures" do not render the evidence inadmissible; the court explained that "[s]hortcomings such as mislabeling, mixing the wrong ingredients, or failing to follow routine precautions against contamination may well be amenable to evaluations by jurors without the assistance of expert testimony. Such readily apparent missteps" are not fatal to admissibility); People v. Fishback, 829 P.2d 489 (Colo. App. 1991), *aff'd*, 851 P.2d 884 (Colo. 1993); Hopkins v. Indiana, 579 N.E.2d 1297 (Ind. 1991); Jackson v. State, 92 Md. App. 304, 608 A.2d 782, 791, *cert. denied*, 328 Md.

Illinois case,[201] Cellmark was the testing laboratory. In approving the admission of the Cellmark test, the court specifically commented that Cellmark "appears to be learning from past mistakes as seen by the company's adoption of a written protocol and adoption of the TWGDAM [Technical Working Group-Interagency Working Group of DNA Methodology] standards."[202] The court enumerated the procedures which Cellmark has implemented:

> When a case arrives at Cellmark, it is assigned to one person, who is responsible for performing tests and following testing procedures. Cellmark requires its scientists to follow a written protocol in performing tests. Expiration dates ensure chemicals used in the process are fresh .... [I]nstruments and equipment are kept in working order. A second Cellmark employee witnesses all steps in the chain of custody as well as many test procedures. Once the autorads are developed, the molecular biologist presents them to a Ph.D. scientist for review. The Ph.D. scientist reviews the entire case file in interpreting the autorad. Two Ph.D. scientists separately review each case and each writes a report of findings. The reports are combined in the final document sent to the client. A laboratory supervisor reviews the report before it is released to the client.[203]

In an Indiana case,[204] the court admitted the DNA evidence despite the fact that there was testimony that the physical evidence had been improperly handled by persons who were not wearing gloves.

238, 614 A.2d 84 (1992); State v. Davis, 814 S.W.2d 593, 603 (Mo. 1991), *cert. denied*, 502 U.S. 1047 (1992); State v. Houser, 241 Neb. 525, 490 N.W.2d 168, 181 (1992); State v. Moore, 323 Ark. 529, 915 S.W.2d 284 (1996) (the prosecution must show "that the expert properly performed a reliable methodology in creating the DNA profiles"); Armstead v. State, 342 Md. 38, 673 A.2d 221 (1996) (despite a state statute purportedly authorizing the admission of DNA testimony, the trial judge retains power to exclude the evidence when serious laboratory procedure errors render the testimony so flawed that it would be unhelpful to the trier of fact); United States v. Martinez, 3 F.3d 1191 (8th Cir. 1993), *cert. denied*, 510 U.S. 1062 (1994); People v. Lindsey, 868 P.2d 1085 (Colo. App. 1993), *aff'd*, 892 P.2d 281 (Colo. 1995); Polk v. State, 612 So. 2d 381 (Miss. 1992). *See also* People v. Diaz, 3 Cal. 4th 495, 834 P.2d 1171, 11 Cal. Rptr. 2d 353, 364 (1992), *cert. denied*, 508 U.S. 916 (1993). While holding that use of proper test procedures cuts to admissibility and not merely weight, a number of jurisdictions seem to allocate the opponent the burden of proving non-compliance. State v. Pennington, 327 N.C. 89, 393 S.E.2d 847, 854 (1990); State v. Ford, 301 S.C. 485, 392 S.E.2d 781, 784 (1990); State v. Wimberly, 467 N.W. 499, 506 (S.D. 1991); State v. Woodall, 182 W. Va. 15, 385 S.E.2d 253, 260 (1989).

201. People v. Miles, 217 Ill. App. 3d 393, 577 N.E.2d 477, *appeal denied,* 142 Ill. 2d 661, 584 N.E.2d 136 (1991). Note, *State v. Davis: DNA Evidence and the Use of Frye in Missouri*, 60 UMKC L. REV. 577, 592 (1992) ("The court ... did express the view that [deficiency in test procedure] goes to the weight of the evidence and not its admissibility").

202. *Id.* at 403, 577 N.E.2d at 483.

203. *Id.*, 577 N.E.2d at 483-84.

204. Smith v. State, 702 N.E.2d 668 (Ind. 1998).

Category #3

In a third category, the courts have held that deficiencies in test procedure usually affect the weight, but not the admissibility, of DNA evidence. In *United States v. Jakobetz,*[205] the Court of Appeals for the Second Circuit declared that the validity of the theory of DNA typing is now a proper subject for judicial notice. The court then added:

> Beyond such judicial notice, the threshold for admissibility should require only a preliminary showing of reliability of the particular data offered, i.e., some indication of how the laboratory work was done .... Affidavits should normally suffice to provide a sufficient basis for admissibility. DNA profiling evidence should be excluded only when the government cannot show this threshold level of reliability .... The district court should focus on whether accepted protocol was adequately followed in a specific case, but the court, in exercising its discretion, should be mindful that this issue should go more to the weight than to the admissibility of the evidence. Rarely should such a factual determination be excluded from jury consideration.[206]

It appears to be an incipient trend in the case law to treat deficiencies in test procedure as going only to the weight of the evidence.[207] The *Castro* court itself recognized that there was authority for that treatment.[208]

Although the traditional common-law view treats proof of correct test procedure as an essential part of the admissibility foundation, there is a strong statutory construction argument that deficiencies in test procedure cut only to weight. In *Daubert,*[209] the Supreme Court abandoned the traditional, general acceptance test for the admissibility of purportedly scientific testimony. The Court reasoned that Federal Rule of Evidence 402 abolishes uncodified exclusionary rules of evidence.[210] Like the general acceptance test, the requirement for a showing of proper test procedure is a creature of case law. If

---

205. 955 F.2d 786 (2d Cir.), *cert. denied*, 506 U.S. 834 (1992).

206. *Id.* at 799-800.

207. Harmon, *How Has DNA Evidence Fared? Beauty Is In the Eye of the Beholder*, 1 EXPERT EVIDENCE REP. (Shep./McG.-Hill) 149, 150-51 (Feb. 1990); Imwinkelried, *The Debate in the DNA Cases Over the Foundation for the Admission of Scientific Evidence: The Importance of Human Error as a Cause of Forensic Misanalysis*, 69 WASH. U. L.Q. 19, 20-21 (1991).

208. People v. Castro, 144 Misc. 2d 956, 959, 545 N.Y.S.2d 985, 987 (Sup. Ct. 1989) (several courts "have indicated that [this] question goes to the weight of the evidence not the admissibility").

209. Daubert v. Merrell Dow Pharmaceuticals, Inc., 509 U.S. 579 (1993).

210. In its opinion, the *Daubert* Court quoted an article by the Reporter for the Federal Rules, the late Professor Edward Cleary, to the effect that "[i]n principle no common law of evidence remains." 509 U.S. at 587-88.

the general acceptance test did not survive the enactment of the Federal Rules, there is a parallel argument that the adoption of the Federal Rules was also the death knell for the traditional view on this issue.

Category #4

The California Supreme Court's 1998 decision, *People v. Venegas,*[211] created a fourth category of cases. On the one hand, the court held that to some extent in DNA cases, as part of the admissibility analysis the trial judge must inquire "whether the procedures actually utilized in this case were in compliance with" accepted methodology. In this regard, the court emphasized the special character of DNA evidence; "[u]nlike fingerprint, shoe track, bite mark, and ballistic comparisons, which jurors essentially can see for themselves, questions concerning whether a laboratory has adopted correct, scientifically accepted procedures for generating autorads or determining a match depend almost entirely on the technical interpretations of experts." On the other hand, the court added that some "derelictions in following the prescribed scientific procedures" are not fatal to admissibility. The court stated that "[s]hortcomings such as mislabeling, mixing the wrong ingredients, or failing to follow routine precautions against contamination may well be amenable to evaluations by jurors without the assistance of expert testimony. Such readily apparent missteps" do not preclude the introduction of the DNA testimony.

One related question is whether the opponent may introduce proof of prior laboratory errors in order to support the inference that the analyst erred in conducting the test on the occasion in question. Such testimony is certainly logically relevant under Rule 401. However, when the issue is the weight of the evidence, there would appear to be a strong argument that the character evidence prohibition bars the testimony.[212] The underlying theory of logical relevance is seemingly "He or she erred before, therefore it more likely they erred again"—classic, forbidden character reasoning. To date, at least the courts have ignored that issue. One court has gone to the length of holding that the opponent is entitled to cross-examine the witness about errors committed by other analysts at the same laboratory.[213] However, in 1998 the Montana Supreme Court went to

---

211. 18 Cal. 4th 47, 954 P.2d 525, 74 Cal. Rptr. 2d 262 (1998).

212. Imwinkelried, *Coming to Grips with Scientific Research in Daubert's "Brave New World": The Courts' Need to Appreciate the Evidentiary Differences between Validity and Proficiency Studies*, 61 BROOKLYN L. REV. 1247, 1272-81 (1995). Note that there might be other theories of logical relevance for the introduction of particular proficiency test results. The character evidence prohibition comes into plan only when the defense attempts to use the laboratory's or analyst's past errors as circumstantial proof that the error was repeated in the instant case.

213. Williams v. State, 342 Md. 724, 679 A.2d 1106 (1996).

the brink of expressly holding that the character evidence prohibition bars the admission of this type of evidence.[214]

It is quite another matter for the judge to consider such evidence when the judge is determining the admissibility of the DNA testimony. In that setting, the last sentence of Federal Rule 104(a) is applicable. That sentence provides that in determining foundational facts, the trial judge is not bound by technical exclusionary rules of evidence. The wording of Rule 104(a) is broad enough to lift the bar of the character evidence rules when the judge is deciding the admissibility of the DNA testimony.

§ 18-5(C). The Statistical Evaluation of a DNA Match.

Just as the courts are divided over the necessity for proof of proper test protocol, the courts are split over the question of the admissibility of statistical testimony evaluating the significance of a match in DNA markers. Of course, the latter issue is moot if the proponent is content to elicit general testimony that the markers "matched" without proffering a statistical evaluation of the significance of the match.[215] However, in the vast majority of cases the proponent proffers such an evaluation. The case law on this issue has progressed through several phases. There have been four phases. It is an understatement to say that the decisions have "evolved." The development of the case law is more dramatic; it would be more accurate to say that the courts have come full circle. Here too the 1992 and 1996 National Research Council reports have been influential.

The Initial Phase: Uncritical Acceptance of the Statistical Evidence

To be sure, a large number of the early cases — the clear majority of the published opinions — approved the admission of statistical testimony evaluating the significance of a DNA match.[216] The vast majority of the early cases accepted

214. Unmack v. Deaconess Medical Center, 967 P.2d 783 (Mt. 1998).

215. Sholler v. Commonwealth, 969 S.W.2d 706 (Ky.1998).

216. Snowden v. State, 574 So. 2d 960 (Ala. Crim. App. 1990) (the DNA expert's population frequency calculations were scientifically reliable and admissible); Prater v. State, 307 Ark. 180, 820 S.W.2d 429 (1991) ("the probability of selecting a person at random from an unrelated black population and getting the same profile was only 1 in 3,700"); People v. Axell, 235 Cal. App. 3d 836, 1 Cal. Rptr. 2d 411 (1991); District of Columbia *ex rel.* J.A.B. v. W.R., 60 U.S.L.W. (BNA) 2175, 17 Fam. L. Rep. 1499 (D.C. Super. Ct., Aug. 2, 1991) (a 99.93 probability of paternity); Martinez v. State, 549 So. 2d 694 (Fla. Dist. Ct. App. 1989) (it was permissible for the expert to state that the probability of a random match was one in 234 billion); State v. Brown, 470 N.W.2d 30 (Iowa 1991) (the odds of someone possessing the same genetic profile were one in several billion); Smith v. Deppish, 248 Kan. 217, 807 P.2d 144 (1991) ("[s]tatistics based on population studies are admissible and any challenge to the reliability of the testing goes to its weight, not its admissibility"); People v. Shi Fu Huang, 145 Misc. 2d 513, 546 N.Y.S.2d 920 (1989) (the population frequencies were based on a study of 167 blood samples obtained in mainland China);

the statistical evidence in part because the defense did not mount any critical attacks on the evidence.

However, even in the early cases a few courts expressed skepticism about the trustworthiness of statistical evaluations of DNA matches.[217] In one of the earliest published DNA cases, *Wesley,*[218] a New York trial judge admitted DNA evidence after prosecution experts testified that "DNA testing is accurate down to one white in 840 million and one black in 1.4 billion." Yet, the judge did not allow that statistical testimony to be presented to the jury. In *Wesley,* a defense expert pointed to the absence of published data demonstrating that the various alleles are independent.[219] To compensate for the lack of proof of independence, the judge ordered that the prosecution statistics be adjusted downward by a factor of ten before the statistics were presented to the jury.

In an appellate opinion, *Caldwell v. State,*[220] DNA evidence suffered a partial setback, as it did in *Wesley*. In *Caldwell,* the Georgia Supreme Court initially held that DNA identification is based "on sound scientific theory." Moreover, the court ruled that in the instant case, Lifecodes had conducted the test "in an acceptable fashion." However, the court found fault with the statistical testimony offered by the prosecution. In *Caldwell,* Dr. Jung Choi, a molecular geneticist, gave "undisputed" testimony on behalf of the defense that "the populations [in Lifecodes' database] were not in Hardy-Weinberg equilibrium." The Lifecodes expert had estimated that the likelihood of a random match was one in 24,000,000. In contrast, Dr. Choi pointed out that using the database conservatively, the odds might be only one in 250,000. The court barred

---

King v. Tanner, 142 Misc. 2d 1004, 539 N.Y.S.2d 617 (Sup. Ct. 1989) (based on the DNA typing evidence, the expert calculated King's probability of paternity as 99.99%).

Some courts continue to admit the testimony under the *Frye* standard. People v. Wesley, 83 N.Y.2d 417, 633 N.E.2d 451, 611 N.Y.S.2d 97 (1994); People v. Wesley, 183 A.D.2d 75, 589 N.Y.S.2d 197 (1992). Other courts admit the testimony under the reliability standard, which the Supreme Court adopted in the *Daubert* case. Government of the Virgin Islands v. Penn, 838 F. Supp. 1054 (D.V.I. 1993); Prater v. State, 820 S.W.2d 429 (Ark. 1991); State v. Brown, 470 N.W.2d 30 (Iowa 1991); People v. Adams, 489 N.W.2d 192 (Mich. App. 1992), *modified*, 441 Mich. 916, 497 N.W.2d 182 (1993); State v. Houser, 490 N.W.2d 168 (Neb. 1992); State v. Pierce, 64 Ohio St. 3d 490, 597 N.E.2d 107 (1992).

217. *DNA Evidence Finding Stricter Scrutiny, New Uses*, 29 TRIAL 15 (Apr. 1993) ("Controversy over match statistics is keeping DNA evidence out of courts that use the *Frye* test"); People v. Watson, 257 Ill. App. 3d 915, 629 N.E.2d 634, 196 Ill. Dec. 89 (1994); Commonwealth v. Lanigan, 413 Mass. 154, 596 N.E.2d 311 (Mass. 1992); State v. Vandebogart, 136 N.H. 365, 616 A.2d 483 (1992); State v. Anderson, 115 N.M. 433, 853 P.2d 135 (1992), *rev'd*, 118 N.M. 284, 881 P.2d 29 (1994).

218. 140 Misc. 2d 306, 533 N.Y.S.2d 643 (Albany County 1988), *aff'd sub nom.* People v. Bailey, 156 A.D.2d 846, 549 N.Y.S.2d 846 (1989).

219. Thompson & Ford, *DNA Typing: Acceptance and Weight of the New Genetic Identification Tests*, 75 VA. L. REV. 45, 105 (1989).

220. Caldwell v. State, 260 Ga. 278, 393 S.E.2d 436 (1990).

"Lifecodes' enormous claimed power of identity based on its 'assumption' that the relevant population is in Hardy-Weinberg equilibrium," but the court permitted testimony as to "the more conservative figures ...."

Massachusetts v. Curnin[221] reached an outcome similar to that in *Caldwell*. At trial, the prosecution expert from Cellmark testified that the frequency of the defendant's DNA type was only one in 59,000,000. However, the defense expert criticized the prosecution expert's computation:

> The defendant's expert ... testified that Cellmark's data base was not adequate for the purpose of producing an estimate of the frequency of finding a particular genotype in the human population. Cellmark did not have data on missing alleles in certain tests reflected in its data base. Additionally, there was the question of whether there is significant sub structuring (sub-grouping) within racial groups that would affect the probability determinations ....

The court found that the prosecution had made an insufficient showing of "the general acceptance or inherent rationality of the process by which Cellmark concluded that only one person in 59 million would have the same alleles as were shown in the test it conducted ...."

Another defense trial court victory on the statistical evaluation issue occurred in *People v. Despain*[222] a 1991 decision like *Curnin*. In *Despain*, the trial judge excluded the prosecution evidence under *Frye*. In *Despain*, the defense mounted an attack on the F.B.I. method of estimating probabilities of computing a random match. Citing an article by Professor Giannelli, the Yuma County Superior Court ruled that scientific evidence can have such an influence on the jury that "[t]o demonstrate there is no legitimate controversy [over the validity of the scientific technique], the burden on the state must be substantially greater than preponderance of the evidence." The court added that "even under [a] preponderance of the evidence [standard], this court finds the existing controversy to be legitimate and significant. There is not general acceptance within the relevant scientific community of the FBI procedures at this time to permit the test results to be offered in evidence."

The F.B.I. procedures were likewise rejected in *United States v. Porter et al.*, still another 1991 decision.[223] In *Porter*, the court found that there was a sharp controversy over the reliability of the F.B.I.'s procedures for computing

---

221. Commonwealth v. Curnin, 409 Mass. 218, 565 N.E.2d 440 (1991).

222. State v. Despain, No. 15589 (Ariz. Super. Ct., Feb. 12, 1991); Scheck & Neufeld, *DNA Task Force Report*, 15 THE CHAMPION 19, 20 (June 1991).

223. Scheck & Neufeld, *Riding the Double Helix*, 16 THE CHAMPION 31 (Jan./Feb. 1992) (discussing Judge Kennedy's 93-page opinion in United States v. Porter et al., No. F06277-89, Super. Ct., District of Columbia, Sept. 21, 1991).

statistical probabilities of a random match in DNA profile. The court specifically noted questions about the independence of the bands and the reliability of the frequencies for subpopulations. The court ruled that the questions were so substantial that they affected the admissibility and not merely the weight of the DNA evidence.

Although cases such as *Porter* were notable, there were the distinct exception to the rule. The rule followed by the overwhelming majority of the early opinions was that it was permissible to introduce a random match probability computed in the traditional fashion.

The Next Phase: A Shift Toward Inadmissibility, Based in Part on the 1992 N.R.C. Report

The N.R.C. issued its initial DNA report in 1992. In the words of Chapter 3 of the 1992 N.R.C. report, "Some courts have accepted the multiplication rule based on the grounds of allelic independence, others have used various ad hoc corrections to account for nonindependence, and still others have rejected probabilities altogether." In the report, the committee itself leveled several criticisms of the traditional method of computing the random match probability. To begin with, the committee concluded that when the laboratory uses multi locus probe FRLP, there is inadequate assurance of the independence of the factors. Further, the committee was dubious of the individual population frequencies. The frequencies were compiled for broad ethnic groups such as Caucasian, Hispanic, and Afro-American. Given the evidence that some substructuring existed, the committee feared that the frequencies were untrustworthy. Several courts cited the 1992 report's criticisms and, on the basis of that criticism, excluded prosecution statistical testimony.[224] The defense

224. People v. Barney, 8 Cal. App. 4th 798, 10 Cal. Rptr. 2d 731 (1992); Commonwealth v. Lanigan, 413 Mass. 154, 596 N.E.2d 311 (1992); United States v. Bridgett, 61 L.W. (BNA) 2046 (D.C. Super. Ct., May 29, 1992); Murray v. State, 692 So. 2d 157 (Fla. 1997); State v. Boles, 183 Ariz. 563, 905 P.2d 572 (1995) (in *Bible*, *infra*, the Arizona Supreme Court barred the introduction of statistical evaluations; the expert witnesses here violated the spirit of that ruling by testifying that they "had never seen or heard of two unrelated individuals whose DNA autorad matched" and that "to find such a match would require a sample size equal to or greater than the world population"), *vacated*, 188 Ariz. 129, 933 P.2d 1197 (1997) ; State v. Hummert, 183 Ariz. 484, 905 P.2d 493 (App. 1994), *vacated*, 188 Ariz. 119, 933 P.2d 1187 (1997) ; State v. Bible, 175 Ariz. 549, 858 P.2d 1152 (1993), *cert. denied*, 511 U.S. 1046 (1994); People v. Watson, 257 Ill. App. 3d 915, 629 N.E 2d 634, 196 Ill. Dec. 89, *appeal denied*, 157 Ill. 2d 519, 642 N.E.2d 1299, 205 Ill. Dec. 182 (1994), *vacated*, 650 N.E.2d 1037, 209 Ill. Dec. 64 (1995); State v. Carter, 246 Neb. 953, 524 N.W.2d 763 (1994); State v. Buckner, 125 Wash. 2d 915, 890 P.2d 460 (1995), *aff'd*, 133 Wash.2d 63, 941 P.2d 667 (1997).; Recent Decision, *Evidence — The Pennsylvania Supreme Court Defines the Standard of Admissibility for DNA Evidence at Trial — Commonwealth v. Crews, 640 A.2d 395 (Pa. 1994)*, 68 TEMP. L. REV. 953 (although the expert could testify that it was "more probable than

argument was especially potent in *Frye* jurisdictions. The tenor of the report seemed to reflect a controversy over the methodology for computing the probability, and the existence of a sharp controversy arguably precluded a court from finding the general acceptance required by *Frye*.

A Third Phase: Acceptance of Probabilities Computed by the Conservative Modified Ceiling Principle

Some courts not only negatively excluded statistical testimony which does not comply with the N.R.C. recommendations; they also affirmatively admitted probabilities computed in conformity with the modified ceiling principle recommended by the 1992 N.R.C. report.[225] The California Supreme Court did so

---

not" that the crime scene DNA matched the defendant, the expert could not testify to a random match probability).

225. Brim v. State, 695 So. 2d 268 (Fla. 1997); State v. Jones, 130 Wash. 2d 302, 922 P.2d 806 (1996); State v. Johnson, 183 Ariz. 623, 905 P.2d 1002 (1995), *aff'd*, 186 Ariz. 329, 922 P.2d 294 (1996); People v. Venegas, 18 Cal. 4th 47, 954 P.2d 525, 74 Cal. Rptr. 2d 262 (1998) (however, the court held that the prosecution expert erred in making the computation; in particular, the F.B.I. expert used "unduly narrow floating bins"; in its calculation, "the FBI used floating bins of plus or minus 2.5 percent"; "The bins, or ranges of base-pair lengths in the database, must be at least as large as the windows used to match the alleles of the suspect with those of the evidentiary sample"; "Defendant's expert witness, Lawrence Mueller, testified ... that the FBI's floating bins of plus or minus 2.5 percent ... were overly narrow [because] the bins were narrower than the scope of the FBI's matching criterion, which placed windows of plus or minus 2.5 percent around the respective bands of both the evidentiary sample and defendant's known sample and declared a match if the two windows overlapped..."; "The FBI's floating bin of plus or minus 2.5 percent was too narrow because ... it failed to include all the band sizes within the FBI's actual match criterion. [T]hat criterion requires not one but two match windows of plus or minus 2.5 percent, one around the band from the known (defendant's) sample and the other around the questioned evidentiary sample. A match is declared if the windows overlap. If the windows barely overlap, the distance between matched bands may be almost twice 2.5 percent, or 5 percent. Thus, the floating bin should have been plus or minus 5 percent."); People v. Taylor, 33 Cal. App. 4th 262, 40 Cal. Rptr. 2d 132 (1995); Vargas v. State, 640 So. 2d 1139 (Fla. App. 1994); Commonwealth v. Fowler, 425 Mass. 819, 685 N.E.2d 746 (1997); Commonwealth v. Lanigan, 419 Mass. 15, 641 N.E.2d 1342 (1994); State v. Bloom, 516 N.W.2d 159 (Minn. 1994); State v. Vandebogart, 139 N.H. 145, 652 A.2d 671 (1994); United States v. Porter, 618 A.2d 629 (D.C. pp. 1992); United States v. Bridgett, 51 CRIM. L. (BNA) 1304, 61 L.W. (BNA) 2046 (D.C. Super. Ct. May 29, 1992); State v. Montalbo, 828 P.2d 1274 (Haw. 1992); People v. Watson, 257 Ill. App. 3d 915, 629 N.E.2d 634, 196 Ill. Dec. 89 (1994); State v. Alt, 504 N.W.2d 38 (Minn. 1993); Washington v. Cauthron, 120 Wash. 2d 879, 846 P.2d 502 (1993).; Kaye, *Bible Reading: DNA Evidence in Arizona*, 28 ARIZ. ST. L.J. 1035, 1071 (1996) ("If one limits *Johnson* to its face or takes the opinion at face value, the case establishes only that interim-ceiling estimates of the VNTR-profile frequencies made from a database that is not obviously inconsistent with the assumption of Hardy-Weinberg equilibrium are admissible."); Riley, *How Should North Approach the Admissibility of DNA: A Comprehensive Analysis of How Other Courts Approach the Admissibility of DNA*, 72 N.D. L. REV. 609, 613-16 (1996) (describing a computation using the ceiling method).

in 1998 in its *Venegas* decision.[226] The argument ran that if anything, the probability computed in this fashion understated the inculpatory nature of the evidence. Thus, even in a *Frye* jurisdiction, it could be said that the probability was generally accepted as an appropriately conservative estimate.

The Fourth Phase: The Cases Come Full Circle Back to a Norm of Admissibility Due in Part to the 1996 N.R.C. Report

Pointing to the research studies indicating that substructuring is less of a problem than the 1992 N.R.C. report assumed, many courts have now come full circle and are again allowing the introduction of statistics computed in the traditional fashion rather than by the modified ceiling method. Some of these courts are in *Frye* jurisdictions[227] while others are in jurisdictions following *Daubert*.[228] This view appears to be the definite trend in the case law.[229] In 1996, the National Research Council of the N.A.S. released its new DNA report. At several points, the new report states that post-1992 research has rendered it

---

226. 18 Cal. 4th 47, 954 P.2d 525, 74 Cal. Rptr. 2d 262 (1998).

227. People v. Wright, 62 Cal. App. 4th 31, 72 Cal. Rptr. 2d 246 (1998); State v. Freeman, 253 Neb. 385, 571 N.W.2d 276 (1997); Brim v. State, 654 So. 2d 184 (Fla. App. 1995) (although there are differing views of the proper method of statistically estimating the random match probability, each view is generally accepted by a typical cross-section of the relevant scientific community); Keirsey v. State, 106 Md. App. 551, 665 A.2d 700 (Spec. App. 1995) (the statistical testimony is exempt from the *Frye* rule; the rule applies only to scientific techniques controlled by "inexorable, physical laws"), *vacated*, 342 Md. 120, 674 A.2d 510 (1996), *cert. denied*, 520 U.S. 1191 (1997); People v. Chandler, 536 N.W.2d 799 (Mich. App. 1995) (the product rule is not subject to *Frye* scrutiny; a challenge to the statistical evidence cuts to its weight, not its admissibility).

In People v. Venegas, 18 Cal. 4th 47, 954 P.2d 525, 74 Cal. Rptr. 2d 262 (1998), the court expressly ruled only that it is permissible to introduce testimony about a random match probability computed under the modified ceiling principle. However, the court's remand instructions raised the possibility that in the lower court, the prosecution could establish that the computation of the probability in the traditional fashion is now generally accepted:

> In the event of a retrial, the prosecution will be free to introduce one or more recomputed analyses of the relevant DNA data in this case after demonstrating that such statistical results were generated by either of the following means: (1) recalculation of statistical probabilities under the NRC's modified ceiling approach..., or (2) recalculation made ... under any other statistical methodology that is otherwise demonstrated to have gained general acceptance in the relevant scientific community....

228. United States v. Davis, 40 F.3d 1069 (10th Cir. 1994), *cert. denied*, 514 U.S. 108 (1995); United States v. Chischilly, 30 F.3d 1144 (9th Cir. 1994), *cert. denied*, 513 U.S. 1132 (1995); United States v. Bonds, 12 F.3d 540 (6th Cir. 1993); State v. Anderson, 118 N.M. 284, 881 P.2d 29 (1994); State v. Futrell, 112 N.C. App. 651, 436 S.E.2d 884 (1993); State v. Loftus, 573 N.W.2d 167 (S.D. 1997) (a reliable foundation); State v. Buckner, 133 Wash. 2d 63, 941 P.2d 667 (1997).

229. State v. Freeman, 571 N.W.2d 276 (Neb. 1997); Lempert, *After the DNA Wars: A Mopping Up Operation*, 31 ISRAEL L. REV. 536 (1997).

unnecessary for the courts to use the ceiling or modified ceiling principles.[230] The report contains a recommendation expressly stating that "[i]n general, the calculation of a profile frequency should be made with the product rule."[231] The report has accelerated the trend toward admitting random match probabilities computed in the traditional fashion.[232] The courts' renewed faith in the reliability of the statistical testimony has not only removed most of the doubts about the admissibility of the testimony; one court has gone to the length of holding that this type of statistical testimony is legally sufficient to support a conviction even in the face of exculpatory eyewitness testimony.[233]

§ 18-6. The Future of DNA Evidence

Irrespective of the battle over DNA typing, the next step in the evolution of courtroom use of DNA is predictable. When DNA mapping is more complete, experts will be able to identify the sites which determine major features such as eye and hair color. Eventually, experts will attempt to develop a profile of the perpetrator of a crime by using the DNA map to "decode" DNA samples found at crime scenes. As a California criminalist, Larry Ragle, has stated,

> Someday you'll be able to put a drop of blood or sperm from a semen sample into a device, and it'll decode it and give you the range of characteristics of the donor: his color, eye color, maybe even facial characteristics. You'll have an image like the kind our police artists do now.[234]

---

230. NAT'L RESEARCH COUNCIL, THE EVALUATION OF FORENSIC DNA EVIDENCE ES-2, ES-3, 0-21, 0-32, 5-32, 5-33 (Pre-pub. draft 1996).

231. *Id.* at ES-4.

232. United States v. Black Cloud, 101 F.3d 1258 (8th Cir. 1996); United States v. Shea, 957 F. Supp. 331 (D.N.H. 1997), *aff'd*, 159 F.3d 37 (1st Cir. 1998), *cert. denied*, 119 S. Ct. 1480 (1999); People v. Miller, 173 Ill. 2d 167, 670 N.E.2d 721, 219 Ill. Dec. 43 (1996), *cert. denied*, 520 U.S. 1157 (1997); People v. Dalcollo, 218 Ill. Dec. 435, 669 N.E.2d 378 (1996); State v. Kinder, 942 S.W.2d 313 (Mo. 1996), *cert. denied*, 118 S. Ct. 149 (1997); State v. Marcus, 294 N.J. Super. 267, 683 A.2d 221 (App. Div. 1996), *cert. denied*, 157 N.J. 543, 724 A.2d 803 (1998); Commonwealth v. Blasioli, 454 Pa. Super. 207, 685 A.2d 151 (1996), *aff'd*, 552 Pa. 149, 713 A.2d 1117 (1998); State v. Copeland, 130 Wash. 2d 244, 922 P.2d 1304 (1996).

233. People v. Rush, 630 N.Y.S.2d 631 (N.Y. City Crim. Ct. 1995), *aff'd*, 242 A.D.2d 108, 672 N.Y.S.2d 362 (1998).

234. Brown, *DNA and Kelly-Frye: Who Will Survive in California?*, 11 CRIM. JUST. J. 1, 84-85 (1988); Comment, *A New Twist in the Double Helix: Admissibility of DNA "Fingerprinting" in California*, 6 SANTA CLARA COMPUTER & HIGH TECH. L.J. 469, 471 n.13 (1989). DNA analysis is already being used to make sex determinations. Reynolds & Varlaro, *Gender Determination of Forensic Samples Using PCR Amplification of ZFX/ZFY Gene Sequences*, 41 J. FORENSIC SCI. 279 (1996); Casarino, Stefano, Mannucci & Canale, *HLA-DQA1 and Amelogenin Coamplification: A Handy Tool for Identification*, 40 J. FORENSIC SCI. 456 (1995).

§ 18-7. Selected Bibliography.

P. BILLINGS, DNA ON TRIAL (1992).

BUREAU OF JUSTICE STATISTICS, U.S. DEPARTMENT OF JUSTICE, FORENSIC DNA ANALYSIS: ISSUES (1991).

H. COLEMAN & E. SWENSON, DNA IN THE COURTROOM: A TRIAL WATCHER'S GUIDE (1994).

COMMITTEE ON DNA FORENSIC SCIENCE, NATIONAL RESEARCH COUNCIL, AN EVALUATION OF FORENSIC DNA EVIDENCE (National Academy Press 1996).

COMMITTEE ON DNA TECHNOLOGY IN FORENSIC SCIENCE, BOARD ON BIOLOGY, COMMISSION ON LIFE SCIENCES, NATIONAL RESEARCH COUNCIL, DNA TECHNOLOGY IN FORENSIC SCIENCE (National Academy Press 1992).

M. FARLEY & J. HARRINGTON, FORENSIC DNA TECHNOLOGY (1990).

H. GRIFFIN & A. GRIFFIN, PCR TECHNOLOGY: CURRENT INNOVATIONS (1994).

K. INMAN & N. RUDIN, DNA DEMYSTIFIED: SOLVING CRIMES IN THE 90'S (1994).

K. INMAN & N. RUDIN, INTRODUCTION TO FORENSIC DNA ANALYSIS (1997).

H. LEVY, AND THE BLOOD CRIED OUT (1996).

NATIONAL ASSOCIATION OF CRIMINAL DEFENSE LAWYERS DNA TASK FORCE, DNA DEFENSE MATERIALS

OFFICE OF TECHNOLOGY ASSESSMENT, CONGRESS OF THE UNITED STATES, GENETIC WITNESS: FORENSIC USE OF DNA TESTS (1990) (4 vols.)

L. THOMPSON, FORENSIC DNA PROFILING PROTOCOLS (1998).

Hoeffel, *The Dark Side of DNA Profiling: Unreliable Scientific Evidence Meets the Criminal Defendant*, 42 STAN. L. REV. 465 (1990).

Krstulja, *Sample Kelly-Frye Motion Opposing the Introduction of DNA (RFLP) Evidence*, 5 CALIFORNIA PUBLIC DEFENDER 40 (1st Quarter, 1992).

McKenna, Cecil & Coukos, *Reference Guide on Forensic DNA Evidence*, *in* REFERENCE MANUAL ON SCIENTIFIC EVIDENCE (Fed. Jud. Cntr 1994).

Miller, *The FBI's Forensic DNA Analysis Program*, 60 F.B.I. LAW ENF. BULL. 11 (July 1991).

Sylvester & Stafford, *Judicial Acceptance of DNA Profiling*, 60 F.B.I. LAW ENF. BULL. 26 (July 1991).

Thompson & Ford, *DNA Typing: Acceptance and Weight of the New Genetic Identification Tests*, 75 VA. L. REV. 45 (1989).

Comment, *DNA Fingerprinting and Paternity Testing*, 22 U.C. DAVIS L. REV. 609 (1989).

Comment, *DNA Identification Tests and the Courts*, 63 WASH. L. REV. 903 (1988).

CHAPTER 19

PATHOLOGY*

§ 19-1. In General.

The forensic pathologist serves as a medical detective[1] and has a critical role in the forensic investigation of death. The pathologist is one of the most qualified experts on the subject of cause of death, and is the best qualified expert on the manner or mode of death. The pathologist's opinions are vital not only because of his expertise but also because other experts' opinions on these subjects are so often wrong. In one study, researchers contrasted pathologists' opinions after an autopsy with other professionals' opinions formed before the autopsy.[2] In the

*The authors wish to express their appreciation to Dr. Michael Graham, St. Louis University School of Medicine, who reviewed this chapter in all three editions of this treatise.

1. Feegel, *The Medical Detective*, 14 TRIAL 22 (Oct. 1978).

2. Asnaes & Paaske, *The Significance of Medicolegal Autopsy in Determining Mode and Cause of Death*, 14 FORENSIC SCI. INT'L 23 (1979). *See also* Ajiki, Fukunaga, Saijoh & Sumino, *Recent Status of the Medical Examiner System in Japan: Demographic Variation of Medicolegal Deaths in Hyogo Prefecture and Uncertainty in Medicolegal Investigations Conducted by Medical*

case of male decedents, the other professionals' opinions on cause of death were erroneous in 23.4% of the cases, and their opinions on manner of death erred in 46.9% of the cases.[3] Moreover, the forensic pathologist plays a pivotal role coordinating the work of other forensic investigators. During the autopsy, the pathologist may collect samples for analysis by criminalists, serologists, and toxicologists; the pathologist typically provides these other investigators with general guidance as to the type of tests they should conduct. If the pathologist is serving as medical examiner, the other experts may be members of his staff.

This chapter discusses both forensic pathology and the law governing the admission of pathological testimony. After surveying the pathologist's qualifications and the autopsy procedure, the chapter reviews the various scientific determinations made by the pathologist: who — the identity of the decedent; how — in what manner did the decedent die; when — what was the time of death or the onset of an illness or injury; and where — the place of death or injury. Finally, legal limitations on pathologists' testimony are discussed.

The topic of pathologists' testimony has heated up since the May 23, 1995 indictment of Ralph Erdmann, a Texas pathologist who allegedly tampered with evidence in autopsies.[4] Furthermore, in 1997, a New Jersey medical examiner was convicted of witness-tampering while on trial for faking an autopsy report. In 1992, a Texas pathologist entered a no contest plea to faking autopsies in murder cases.[5]

Practitioners, 51 FORENSIC SCI. INT'L 35 (1991); Albreksten & Thomsen, *Detection of Injuries in Traumatoc (sic) Deaths. The Significance of Medico-Legal Autopsy*, 42 FORENSIC SCI. INT'L 135 (1989) (in 34% of 218 deaths investigated, the hospital missed injuries detected in a subsequent autopsy; in 5% of the cases, the overlooked injuries were the cause of death); Segerberg-Konttinen, *Determination of Cause and Mode of Death Before and After Medicolegal Autopsy: A Comparative Study*, 33 J. FORENSIC SCI. 441 (1988).

3. *Id.*

4. *Pathologist Indicted*, NAT'L L.J.., June 5, 1995; Fricker, *Pathologist's Plea Adds to Turmoil: Discovery of Possibly Hundreds of Faked Autopsies Helps Defense Challenges*, 79 A.B.A. J. 24 (Mar. 1993); Hansen, *Body of Evidence*, 81 A.B.A. J. 60, 65 (June 1995); Campbell, *Erdmann Faces New Legal Woes: Pathologist Indicted for Perjury in Texas Murder Trial*, 81 A.B.A. J. 32 (Nov. 1995). *See also* Boyle v. Johnson, 93 F.3d 180, 187 (5th Cir. 1996) ("It was not until 1987 or 1988 ... that the prosecution was alerted to the possibility that Dr. Erdmann had falsified autopsies and committed perjury...."), *cert. denied*, 519 U.S. 1120 (1997). *But see* Fuller v. Johnson, 114 F.3d 491 (5th Cir.) (denying habeas corpus relief from a state conviction resting in part on testimony by Dr. Erdmann), *cert. denied*, 522 U.S. 963 (1997).

5. Castelle, *Lab Fraud: Lessons Learned from the "Fred Zain" Affair*, 23 THE CHAMPION 12, 13 (May 1999).

§ 19-2. The Pathologist.

For centuries scientists have contributed to the resolution of legal disputes, including controversies revolving around deaths.[6] However, before the Middle Ages, scientists' involvement in the legal system was sporadic and informal.[7] During the Middle Ages, two major systems emerged for ensuring scientific input into the investigation of death.[8] One system developed in continental Europe.[9] In Europe, scientific institutes were created to conduct medicolegal investigations; the institutes were relatively free from political influence.[10] By the 18th and 19th centuries, numerous European universities had well-developed curricula in legal medicine.[11] A second, competing model emerged in England. The position of coroner was created in 1194.[12] In contrast to his European counterpart, the English coroner was an appointed political functionary. Soon after the creation of the coroner's office, the coroner was assigned the duty of investigating deaths.[13] Justices of the peace assumed this duty for a period of time; but in the late 19th century, the duty was again assigned to coroners.[14]

When the colonies were founded in North America, they had to establish their own system of death investigation. Since the English represented the majority in most colonies, it was expectable that the colonies initially embraced the English coroner model.[15] The colonies modified the coroner's position by making the office elective.[16] The result was that many coroners had absolutely no legal or medical background.[17]

Eventually the continental medical examiner system gained a foothold in the United States. The first American medical examiner offices were created in Boston's Suffolk County in 1877 and New York City in 1915.[18] The medical examiner is appointed; and to be eligible for appointment, the person must

---

6. Wecht, *Science and the Law: Hard Evidence for the Courtroom*, 19 TRIAL 48 (Jan. 1983).

7. *Id.*

8. *Id.*

9. *Id.*

10. *Id.*

11. *Id.*

12. *Id.*

13. *Id.*

14. *Id.*

15. *Id.* at 49.

16. *Id.*

17. *Id.* Hansen, *Body of Evidence*, 81 A.B.A. J. 60, 64 (June 1995) ("Only four states, Kansas, Louisiana, North Dakota and Ohio, require that a coroner be a doctor. In North Dakota, the requirement only applies to counties with more than 8,000 people. Louisiana makes an exception for parishes in which no doctor is willing to serve. In other states, the qualifications are far more lenient. South Carolina, for example, requires only a high school diploma").

18. *Id.*

possess certain minimum medical qualifications.[19] Twenty-three states have statewide medical examiner systems, and another 13 states have medical examiner offices in particular localities, usually major cities.[20] In most of these states, the appointee must be a pathologist.[21] In the remaining states including Delaware, Iowa, Rhode Island, New Jersey, and Tennessee, there is a preference for forensic pathologists.[22]

Within the medicolegal community, the medical examiner divides the labor of medicolegal death investigation with the coroner.[23] In a jurisdiction employing the coroner system, the coroner may have some legal authority such as subpoena power; but the key tribunal is the jury of inquest.[24] The jury can order an autopsy and, on the basis of that autopsy, issue official rulings on the cause and manner of death.[25] The coroner has administrative responsibility for the presentation of evidence to the inquest jury. The coroner may hire a non-pathologist physician, general pathologist or, occasionally, a forensic pathologist to conduct an autopsy and testify about the autopsy before the jury of inquest.

The forensic pathologist plays a larger role in death investigation in jurisdictions opting for the medical examiner model. To begin with, a medical examiner typically has broader jurisdiction than a coroner.[26] The enabling legislation creating coroner offices usually limits the coroner's jurisdiction to the investigation of unnatural deaths, unattended deaths, and deaths in which no physician is prepared to execute a death certificate.[27] The medical examiner's office has authority over more types of cases. The enabling legislation for such offices frequently contains lengthy, detailed lists of cases such as drownings,

---

19. *Id.* Prahlow & Lantz, *Medical Examiner/Death Investigator Training Requirements in State Medical Examiner Systems*, 40 J. FORENSIC SCI. 55 (1995); Hanzlick, Combs, Parrish & Ing, *Death Investigation in the United States, 1990: A Survey of Statutes, Systems, and Educational Requirements*, 38 J. FORENSIC SCI. 628, 629-30 (1993) ("In 39 of 40 states that utilize medical examiners, the medical examiner is required to hold a medical degree or equivalent....").

20. *Id.*

21. Wecht, *Use of Forensic Pathology in Defending Criminal Cases, in* 2 FORENSIC SCIENCES 25-12 (C. Wecht ed. 1983).

22. *Id.* Hansen, *Body of Evidence*, 81 A.B.A. J. 60, 64-65 (June 1995) ("Only a handful of states and some of the largest urban areas with medical examiner systems require that death investigations be conducted by board-certified or board-eligible forensic pathologists.... Of the nearly 671,000 doctors licensed to practice in the United States, less than 3 percent, or 17,149 doctors, are specialists in pathology.... Only 435 of them are board-eligible forensic pathologists, of whom 335 are board-certified").

23. Gantner, *The Autopsy and the Law*, 69 AM. J. CLIN. PATH. 235 (1978).

24. *Id.* at 236.

25. *Id.*

26. Wecht, *supra* note 21, at 25-12-13.

27. *Id.* at 25-12.

criminal abortions, and electrocutions that the medical examiner must investigate.[28]

Furthermore, the forensic pathologist serving as a medical examiner has greater independence during the investigation. The forensic pathologist: personally conducts the autopsy; directs the investigative efforts of the other forensic investigators in the medical examiner's employ; and personally rules on the cause and manner of death.[29]

Within the medical community, the forensic pathologist shares responsibility for death investigation with the general pathologist.[30]

The broad field of pathology has two major subdivisions: anatomic pathology and clinical pathology.[31] Anatomic pathologists study the structural alterations or changes caused by disease and injury processes.[32] The primary work of clinical pathologists consists of the laboratory examination of samples removed from the body such as blood specimens and other body fluids.[33] To qualify as a pathologist, either anatomic or clinical, a physician must complete five years of specialized training (a residency) after graduating from medical school.[34] After qualifying, the pathologist is capable of performing many types of work, including research. Most will go on to fellowships for an additional one or two years of subspecialty training. However, in fact, many pathologists go to work either in hospital medical schools or on medical examiner staffs.

There is a marked contrast between the orientations of hospital and forensic pathology. It is true that to qualify at all as a pathologist, the hospital pathologist must have four or five years of specialized training. However, even during that extended period, he probably participated in only 100 autopsies. Moreover, albeit specialized, the training does not extensively cover such subjects as wound interpretation, manner of death determination, or time of death in depth. The hospital and forensic pathologists differ not only in their training; they also differ in the nature of their work. In the overwhelming majority of hospital autopsies, the pathologist knows the identity of the decedent and has a relatively exhaustive clinical history, including detailed observations of the person before death.[35] During the autopsy, the hospital pathologist is usually not concerned about the

---

28. *Id.* at 25-13.

29. Gantner, *supra* note 23, at 236.

30. Wecht, *Forensic Pathology: A New Prescription for Civil Cases*, 19 TRIAL 42 (June 1978).

31. A. MOENSSENS, J. STARRS, C. HENDERSON & F. INBAU, SCIENTIFIC EVIDENCE IN CIVIL AND CRIMINAL CASES §12.01 (4th ed. 1995).

32. *Id.*

33. *Id.*

34. *Id.* Smock, Nichols & Fuller, *Development and Implementation of the First Clinical Forensic Medicine Training Program*, 38 J. FORENSIC SCI. 835 (1993) (the new Kentucky program).

35. Wecht, *supra* note 30, at 42.

manner of death; almost all the deaths that he will study are natural deaths.[36] The hospital pathologist is primarily concerned with the extent of the disease, the effects of the disease on the body, and the effect of the treatment of the disease rather than the cause of the disease.[37]

The forensic pathologist has a different background and function. Forensic pathology has been a recognized subspecialty since 1959.[38] In addition to the training that a hospital pathologist receives, a forensic pathologist requires another year of specialized work. In that period, the pathologist receives training beyond his previous training in anatomic pathology or in both anatomic and clinical pathology.[39] There are roughly 40 approved training programs in forensic pathology.[40] The programs vary in content. While most qualify the student to sit for the forensic pathology certification examination in addition to anatomic or anatomic/clinical pathology, other programs lead to combined certification in anatomic and forensic pathology.[41] However, whatever the program of study, the forensic pathologist will be exposed to such subjects as wound interpretation, firearm residue analysis, anthropology, toxicology, trace evidence, serology, and legal causation. By the end of these four or five years of graduate training, the pathologist will probably have observed or participated in 400-500 autopsies. After a minimum of one year of intensive training at an accredited forensic pathology center and performance of autopsies at the center, the candidate who is already board certified in at least anatomic pathology is eligible to sit for the examination for certification as a forensic pathologist by the American Board of Pathology.[42]

During an autopsy, the forensic pathologist is concerned with an entirely different set of questions than the hospital pathologist. The decedent's identity may be unknown, and the forensic pathologist must guide the investigation to uncover the identity.[43] Even if the decedent's identity is established, the forensic pathologist has a different focus than the hospital pathologist. The forensic pathologist must determine the causation and manner of the death.[44]

---

36. *Id.*

37. *Id.* at 42-43.

38. Wecht, *Forensic Pathology for Trial Lawyers, in* SCIENTIFIC AND EXPERT EVIDENCE 1141, 1143 (2d ed. 1981); A. MOENSSENS, J. STARRS, C. HENDERSON & F. INBAU, *supra* note 31, at §12.01.

39. *Id.*

40. AMERICAN MEDICAL ASS'N, GRADUATE MEDICAL EDUCATION DIRECTORY (1996); Feegel, *The Forensic Pathologist as an Expert in Civil Cases, in* 1 FORENSIC SCIENCES 23-6 (C. Wecht ed. 1983).

41. *Id.* at 23-6-7.

42. Wecht, *supra* note 38, at 1143.

43. Wecht, *supra* note 30, at 43.

44. *Id.*

Whenever a serious question as to the cause or manner of a death arises during a legal proceeding, the question should be studied by a certified forensic pathologist.[45] A coroner may have no medical expertise at all, and a hospital pathologist lacks the specialized training and orientation to conduct an optimal investigation. Unfortunately, there is an acute shortage of forensic pathologists in the United States. At the present time, there are approximately 500 forensic pathologists in America, and only half of them work full-time in the field of forensic pathology.

§ 19-3. The Autopsy and Other Procedures.

There are various tools at the pathologist's disposal. The primary tool, the autopsy, is an examination that the pathologist personally conducts. Many of the other tools such as toxicological tests are conducted by consulting experts and members of the medical examiner's staff subject to the pathologist's supervision.

§ 19-3(A). Autopsy.

Obtaining the Body for Autopsy

In some cases, the boy has already been buried; and it must be exhumed for autopsy.[46] In almost all jurisdictions, either by statute or common law, courts have the power to order disinterment.[47] The court may enter the order on the motion of a defendant or an appropriate representative of the state, such as a prosecutor or medical examiner.[48] The party moving for a disinterment order must ordinarily establish the following facts:

First, the condition of the corpse is such that its examination will probably yield certain forensic evidence.[49] If the time lapse is too substantial and decomposition has probably progressed too far, the cadaver may no longer yield forensic evidence.[50]

Second, the forensic evidence will be material to establishing the defendant's guilt or innocence[51] or, in a civil case, liability or not.

Third, the forensic evidence cannot be obtained by any reasonably available, alternative means. The evidence will not be merely cumulative or

---

45. *Id.* at 43.

46. *In re* the Exhumation of Meriwether Lewis, 999 F. Supp. 1066 (M.D. Tenn. 1998) (the applicability of the Archaeological Resources Protection Act).

47. Annot., 63 A.L.R.3D 1294, 1300 (1975). Robertson, *Raising the Dead: Motions to Exhume*, FORUM, Vol. 19, No. 5-6, 21 (1992). FORUM is a publication of California Attorneys for Criminal Justice, headquartered in Culver City, California.

48. Annot., 63 A.L.R.2D 1294, 1302 (1975).

49. *Id.* at 1298.

50. *Id.* at 1299, 1319-20.

51. *Id.* at 1298.

corroborative.[52] The existence of several eyewitnesses may make disinterment unnecessary.[53]

If the body has not been buried yet, the autopsy laws determine whether the body will be delivered to the pathologist for autopsy. Those laws vary widely from jurisdiction to jurisdiction.[54] In a few jurisdictions the autopsy law is set out in the state constitution, but in most states the law has been codified in statute.

These laws require that: Certain types of deaths be reported to the medical examiner; the body be delivered to the medical examiner; and the medical examiner investigate the death to determine its cause and manner. In some jurisdictions, the autopsy law contains a detailed list of the types of reportable deaths, including abortions, electric shock, explosions, industrial deaths, deaths of prisoners and other persons in custody, lightning, medication overdose, poisoning, suffocation, vehicular accidents, and cases in which no physician is willing to sign a death certificate. However, the typical statutory pattern is to list major categories of deaths, notably accidents, homicides, suicides, sudden deaths under suspicious or unusual circumstances, and deaths involving contagious or infectious diseases. In sum, in jurisdictions granting the medical examiner the most expansive jurisdiction, the medical examiner will investigate any death other than an expected death with a known natural cause. In most states, roughly 30% of the deaths fall within the medical examiner's jurisdiction.[55]

---

52. *Id.* at 1299.

53. State v. Whiteaker, 499 S.W.2d 412, 416-17 (Mo. 1973), *cert. denied,* 415 U.S. 949 (1974).

54. For an excellent compilation of the state autopsy laws, *see* Wecht, *Autopsy Laws and Procedures, in* 2 FORENSIC SCIENCES 26-90-212 (C. Wecht ed. 1983). Hanzlick, Parrish & Combs, *Standard Language in Death Investigation Laws*, 39 J. FORENSIC SCI. 637 (1994).

55. Feegel, *supra* note 1, at 23. Autopsy rates vary widely from state to state. The following is a list of the percentage of deaths involving children under age nine which result in autopsies: Rhode Island 67.3%, Vermont 61.3%, New Hampshire 59.1%, Washington 59%, Nebraska 58.4%, Nevada 58.3%, Colorado 58%, Massachusetts 57.8%, Minnesota 57.4%, Alaska 56.7%, Wisconsin 55.6%, Illinois 54.8%, Montana 53.9%, California 53.8%, Iowa 52.6%, Oregon 52.1%, Delaware 50.7%, Washington, D.C. 50.7%, Ohio 50.2%, Michigan 50%, Missouri 50%, Idaho 50.3%, North Dakota 49.7%, Florida 48.8%, New York 48.8%, New Mexico 45.9%, Pennsylvania 45.5%, Texas 45.4%, New Jersey 45%, Utah 44.4%, Maryland 43.8%, Kansas 43.7%, Louisiana 41.5%, Wyoming 41.1%, Connecticut 40.8%, Arizona 40.7%, South Carolina 40.5%, Hawaii 39.4%, North Carolina 39.2%, Oklahoma 38.9%, Maine 38.6%, Alabama 38.5%, South Dakota 37.7%, Indiana 37.5%, West Virginia 37.5%, Georgia 37.1%, Virginia 35.6%, Kentucky 35.4%, Arkansas 31.4%, Mississippi 28.8%, and Tennessee 23.1%. Lundstrom & Sharpe, *Some Parents Getting Away with Murder*, THE SACRAMENTO BEE, Apr. 21, 1991, at A20. There are also marked regional differences in autopsy rates: Pacific 54%, New England 53%, W. North Central 51%, E. North Central 51%, Mountain 49%, Mid-Atlantic 47%, W. South Central 43%, S. Atlantic 42%, and E. South Central 31%. *Id.*

Conducting the Autopsy

After the body is delivered to the forensic pathologist, the pathologist must determine the type and depth of investigation necessary. Autopsy procedures and protocol vary not only from state to state but also from one medical examiner's office to another within the same state.[56] The following is a description of the procedures that many offices follow.

If an exhumation has been authorized, the body and coffin are carefully removed from the ground.[57] Rough handling can cause new damage to the body — artefactual injuries — that may mislead the pathologist during the autopsy.[58] In some cases, when the body and coffin are removed, the investigators will take samples of the surrounding earth and ground water.[59] Toxins in the earth or water may have seeped into the body, and the toxins may result in an error in the toxicological tests ordered by the pathologist.[60]

Whether the body is delivered to the pathologist immediately after discovery or only after exhumation, the pathologist's first task is to decide upon the proper scope of the investigation. Suppose, for example, that the case seems relatively simple and straightforward and all indications are that the death is not a homicide. There is likely to be little dispute over the cause or manner of death.[61] In this event, the pathologist may examine the body externally and remove fluids from only the heart or major blood vessel, eyes, and bladder for toxicological examination.[62] In selected non-homicide cases in which there is little doubt about the circumstances of death, such a limited examination — frequently called a postmortem view — may be warranted.[63]

However, there are often latent clues to the true cause or manner of death that will be discovered only by a more thorough examination.[64] For this reason, experienced pathologists usually err on the side of caution and conduct a more comprehensive investigation.[65] A complete examination also affords the pathologist a better opportunity to assess, among other things, the length of survival and the potential for carrying out activity after an injury.

A comprehensive examination usually begins with a meticulous study of the clothing and personal effects associated with the body. This physical evidence

---

56. *See generally* Wecht, *Autopsy Laws and Procedures, in* 2 FORENSIC SCIENCES ch. 26 (C. Wecht ed. 1983).

57. *Id.* at 26-17.

58. *Id.*

59. *Id.*

60. *Id.*

61. Bucklin, *Forensic Pathology for Attorneys*, 12 CAL. W.L. REV. 197, 199 (1976).

62. *Id.*

63. *Id.*

64. *Id.*

65. *Id.*

can help answer key questions in medicolegal death investigation. Identification in the pocket of a pair of pants may help answer the question of who was the decedent. Soot from the discharge of a firearm on the jacket may be of aid in deciding how the decedent died. Heavy clothing will affect the rate of cooling and be relevant in estimating when death occurred. Trace evidence such as fibers or soil on the body or clothing may assist in identifying the place of death.

After examining the clothing and personal effects, the pathologist makes a careful external examination of the body.[66] This examination should include: scalp, eyes, nose, ears, mouth, neck, thorax, abdomen, back, genitalia, upper extremities, and lower extremities.[67]

An internal examination of the body cavity follows the external examination. Depending upon his preference, the pathologist initially makes a U-, V-, or Y-shaped primary incision to expose the body cavity. The pathologist carefully inspects the following internal areas: the neck, thorax, abdomen, cranial cavity and, when appropriate, the spinal cord.[68] In each area, the pathologist examines the various organs *in situ* (in place). Organs are then removed for more thorough study.[69] The pathologist may remove the organs one by one or *en bloc* (as a group).

While conducting the external and internal examinations, the pathologist gathers samples for other forensic experts on the medical examiner's staff. During the inspection of the decedent's clothing and the external examination, the pathologist gathers samples for the criminalists specialized in trace evidence analysis.[70] The samples may include the clothing itself, hair from various regions of the body, fingernail clippings, and tracings of imprints on the body.[71] During the internal examination, the pathologist collects samples for serologists and toxicologists. The serological samples might include blood and swabbings from the mouth, vagina, and rectum, in cases of suspected rape.[72] Chapter 20 discusses the samples collected for toxicological studies.[73]

During the external and internal examinations, the pathologist should ensure that his observations are recorded in a permanent fashion. Some pathologists dictate to a secretary or assistant during the examinations while others prefer to

---

66. Graham, *The Medicolegal Autopsy: Description of the Process*, *in* MEDICOLEGAL DEATH INVESTIGATION: TREATISE IN FORENSIC SCIENCES (2d ed. 1999).

67. J. WESTON & V. MCCARTY, THE MEDICOLEGAL INVESTIGATION OF DEATH IN NEW MEXICO 99-101.

68. *Id.* at 113-15.

69. Prahlow, Ross, Salzberger, Lott, Guileyardo & Barnard, *Immersion Technique for Brain Removal in Perinatal Autopsies*, 43 J. FORENSIC SCI. 1056 (1998).

70. J. WESTON & V. MCCARTY, THE MEDICOLEGAL INVESTIGATION OF DEATH IN NEW MEXICO 121.

71. *Id.*

72. *Id.* at 122-23.

73. *Id.* at 123-25.

tape record their verbal descriptions or take written notes of the observations simultaneously with the observations. Photographs are also commonly taken for identification and to illustrate pertinent findings.

Memorializing the Autopsy in a Report

Just as autopsy procedures vary widely, the format of autopsy reports varies. Figure 19-1 is a sample autopsy report prepared by a forensic pathologist.[74] The report is typical in the sense that it contains the types of data commonly found in most autopsy reports.

Doe, John AUTOPSY #5000-99

ST. LOUIS CITY MEDICAL EXAMINER

Pathologist: George E. Gantner, M.D.

Pathologist: Michael Graham, M.D.

Name of Deceased: Doe, John
Address: 233 Woodbourne Drive, St. Louis, Mo., 63105
Date and Time of M.E. Notification: 2/10/99//7:30 PM
Date/Time of Pronounced Death: 2/10/99//7:00 PM
Autopsy: 2/10/99 at 9:30 PM
Date and Time of Injury [Best Estimate]: 2/10/99//6:30 PM
Race: White
Sex: Male
Age: 54 years
Appearance of Age: Approximately as stated
Date of Birth: 6/7/44
Occupation: Not Currently Employed
Marital Status: Never Married
History suggests death by: Homicide
Death Certificate by: St. Louis City Medical Examiner
Investigator: Mary Fran Ernst
Depth of Investigation: Toxicology plus Autopsy
Body Initially brought from: vacant lot
Body then DOA: St. Louis University Hospital
Agency: St. Louis City Police Department
The body was identified by accompanying papers which matched the body tags.

---

74. Prepared by Dr. George Gantner, School of Medicine, St. Louis University, St. Louis, Missouri and revised by Dr. Michael Graham.

The police identified the body from eyewitnesses.
Identification by family members.

External Examination: No clothing is present on the body. However, a bag of clothing accompanies the body. The body weight is measured at 150 lbs. (67.50 kgms.). The body length is 67 in. (170.18 cm.). The state of preservation is good in this unembalmed body. Rigor mortis is absent. There is a normal state of nutrition. The abdomen is flat. Lividity is unfixed and is primarily found on the posterior body surfaces and right side of the body. Cyanosis is absent. There is no peripheral edema present. Personal hygiene is good. The hair is brown. This represents the apparent natural color. The hair is worn medium length. The face is normally clean-shaven but has not been recently shaved. The body hair is of normal male distribution. The pupils are round, regular, equal and somewhat dilated. There is bilateral orbital ecchymosis. The irises are hazel. The teeth are in a fair state of repair. The gums are normal in appearance. The oral cavity is normal. The male breasts are normal. The skin is of normal color. An operative scar is present. There is an old scar 2 cm. in diameter located 4 cm. right of the umbilicus. A patent orotracheal airway is in place. Monitor lead connectors are in place. There is a gunshot wound entrance of the chest. There is a contusion of the forehead and neck.

Detailed Description of Specified Injuries

A. There is a gunshot wound entrance of the chest.

(1) This wound is located 2.5 cm. left of midline and 22.0 cm. (8.80 in.) below the level of the left shoulder. The hole is up to 12 mm. (.48 in.) in diameter with liquid blood oozing forth. It is round with the edges inverted and smooth. No tissue protrudes from this hole. The edges show an abrasion/contusion ring up to 16 mm. (.64 in.) in total diameter. Powder stipple is present which measures 25 mm. (1.00 in.) in diameter. This cannot be washed off indicating it is due to powder particles. Powder smudging surrounds the hole for a distance of up to 35 mm. (1.40 in.) from the center. It can be washed away. Dried blood from the wound is copious in amount. The pattern suggests a previous run pattern in the 180 compass direction. An incision into the wound shows extensive deeper hemorrhage. A bullet, seen on the X-rays, is found in the left pleural space and is recovered in evidence. Evaluation of this wound suggests that it is an entrance wound involving close range. X-ray shows the path traced with fine lead particles. This wound is related to the bullet found in the pleural space. The path of the shot is slightly from right to left, front to back and slightly from above, downward assuming the body in the upright position. The bullet passed through the sternum at the level of the fifth rib, pericardium (15 mm), heart (right

ventricle, 12mm, left ventricle, 15 mm), pericardium (20 mm), left lung lower lobe (20 mm) to come to rest in the left pleural cavity.

B. There is a contusion of the:

1) forehead
2) neck

(1) (Forehead) The contusion described measures up to 6.0 cm (2.40 in.) in diameter and is present on the lower left forehead.

(2) (Neck) This contusion is diffuse in outline measuring up to 10.0 cm (4.00 in.) in maximum dimension. It appears to involve deep hemorrhage but is without swelling. The surface is blue and red. The contusion is located on the lower anterolateral right neck.

Body Cavities: The body is opened with the usual Y incision. The abdominal fat layer measures 20 mm (.80 in.) in thickness. Hemorrhage is present to match gunshot wound described above. The peritoneal cavity shows no free fluid or adhesions. Peritoneal adhesions are absent. The right pleural cavity shows no air, fluid or adhesions. The left pleural cavity contains fluid measured at 1650 ml (49.50 fl. oz.). The fluid is bloody. The left pleura shows no adhesions. The pericardial cavity contains fluid measured at 350 ml (10.50 fl. oz.). The fluid is bloody. No adhesions are present.

Neck Organs: The soft tissue of the neck is free of hemorrhage. The hyoid bone is intact. The glottis, laryngeal and tracheal airways are widely patent. The larynx is normal. The thyroid gland is normal. The parathyroids are not identified.

Mediastinum: The thymus gland is grossly normal.

Heart and Thoracic Organs: The heart weighs 475 gms. (16.63 oz.). The surface of the heart shows a gunshot wound. A bullet has entered the midportion of the right ventricle anteriorly causing a round hole 12 mm in diameter. It has then passed through the septum and then exited in the posterior left ventricular wall through a 15 mm diameter round hole. The subepicardial fat is less in amount than normally seen. The left ventricle is hypertrophied. The left ventricular wall measures 26 mm (1.04 in.) and the right 3 mm (.12 in.). The endocardium, cardiac valves and chambers are not remarkable. The circumference of the tricuspid valve is 100 mm (4.00 in.), the pulmonary 85 mm (3.40 in.), the mitral 110 mm (4.40 in.), and the aortic 90 mm (3.60 in.). The coronary arteries are found with partial atheromatous obstruction up to 10%. The cut surface of the myocardium is the normal reddish brown color.

Vascular System: The aorta shows moderate atherosclerosis. The systemic arteries in general are normal. The systemic veins are normal.

Lungs: The lungs together weigh 950 gms. (33.25 oz.). A gunshot wound is found in the left lower lobe. The lung surface is red and purple in color. The lung tissue throughout is increased in firmness and decreased in crepitance. Both lungs show moderate amounts of congestion and edema fluid. The air passages contain bloody material. The pulmonary arteries are free of emboli, thrombi, and other gross lesions.

Liver: The liver weighs 1540 gms. (53.90 oz.). The liver is reddish brown in color and of normal consistency. The surface and cut section are unremarkable.

Biliary Tract: The gallbladder and biliary tract are normal and free of stones.

Pancreas: The pancreas is normal in consistency and in appearance.

Gastrointestinal Tract: The esophagus is normal. The stomach contains undigested food material consisting of corn and green beans. The approximate gastric volume is 300 ml. (9.00 fl. oz.). The gastric mucosa is free of ulcers and other lesions. Both small and large intestines are normal.

Spleen: The spleen weighs 185 gms. (6.48 oz.) and is normal on the surface and cut section.

Lymphatic System: The lymph nodes are normal in size and appearance.

Bone Marrow: The bone marrow is normal.

Adrenals: The adrenals are well supplied with lipoid material and are free of hemorrhage, inflammation, and primary and secondary neoplasms. The medullary portions are not remarkable.

Kidneys: The kidneys appear grossly normal and together weigh 275 gms. (9.63 oz.). The cortex measures 12 mm (.48 in.) in thickness. The renal capsules strip with ease to reveal a normally smooth surface. There are no abnormalities of the cut surface of the kidney. The renal pelvis and ureter are not remarkable.

Urinary Bladder: The bladder contains urine measured at 150 ml (4.50 fl. oz.). The urine is clear and yellow. A diverticulum is present in the dome of the bladder. This is attached by a 2 cm. neck. The diverticulum is 8 cm. in diameter and is roughly spherical. No stones are present.

Male Genital System: The prostate gland is nodular. The cut surface exudes cloudy fluid. Both testes are normal. The penis is normal and circumcised. The scrotum is normal.

Cranial Cavity: The reflected scalp shows no additional evidence of contusion, hematoma, or other lesion. The calvarium and bones at the base of the skull are not remarkable. The dura mater and pia arachnoid are normal in appearance. The weight of the unfixed brain is 1520 gms. (53.20 oz.). The cerebral hemispheres are symmetrical and normal in appearance. No brain injury is detected on careful search. Cut sections of brain substance show essentially normal structures throughout. The circle of Willis and other intracranial vessels are normal. The ventricular system and spinal fluid are normal. The pituitary gland is grossly normal. The pineal gland is not identified.

Spinal Cord: The spinal cord is not examined in this case.

Specimens saved for Toxicology and other studies include: Blood Urine Vitreous.

Doe, John AUTOPSY #5000-99

ST. LOUIS CITY MEDICAL EXAMINER

Final Diagnoses

I. Gunshot Wound of Chest
  A) Entrance anterior left chest (close range)
    1) Track backward, slightly leftward, slightly downward.
    2) Track via Sternum, pericardium, heart, pericardium, left lung to come to rest in the left pleural cavity (bullet recovered).
      a) Hemothorax, left
      b) Hemopericardium

II. Integumentary System and Soft Tissues
  A) Forehead and neck, contusions

III. Cardiovascular System
  A) Heart, left ventricles, hypertrophy.
  B) Aorta, moderate atherosclerosis.

IV. Genitourinary System
  A) Prostate, nodular hyperplasia
  B) Urinary bladder, diverticulum.

Doe, John AUTOPSY #5000-99

ST. LOUIS CITY MEDICAL EXAMINER

Data for Death Certificate

Part I Cause of Death
  (immediate cause): Gunshot wound of chest

Manner of Death: Homicide

Toxicology Notes: Blood: Ethanol - 45 mg/dl (.045% gm%)
Urine: Drug screen--no substances identified

____

George E. Gantner, M.D.

____

Michael Graham, M.D.

Figure 19-1

The first part of the report records demographic data, including such information as to race, sex, age, occupation, marital status, and the time when the person was pronounced dead.

The next section memorializes the external examination of the body. This section begins with the body's uppermost parts and proceeds downward to the lowermost extremities. In the process, the section gives a detailed description of each injury exhibited by the body. The pathologist should provide an especially explicit description of any apparently significant wounds (*e.g.*, gunshot wounds); the pathologist characterizes each wound as entrance or exit, and, among other things, describes its location, appearance (round, stellate, etc.), and states the dimensions of the wound. Any discolorations on the body's surface as well as any marks or scars that could serve as identifying marks are also mentioned. Many pathologists include diagrams of the front and rear views of the body and indicate the location of each wound, mark, or scar on the diagrams. Many medical examiner offices use a set of symbols to signify the wounds on the body. Figure 19-2 is a list of symbols that are commonly used in one medical examiner facility:

The next part of the report describes the results of the internal examination of the body cavities. While writing this part of the report, the pathologist attempts to correlate his observations of internal injuries with the external injuries mentioned in the previous part of the report. If the external injury was a bullet wound, the pathologist provides a detailed description of the pathway of the projectile in the body. The description will include the direction, path, and dimensions of the bullet track.

The next to last section of the report might be a list of final diagnoses. The pathologist would list, often in order of significance, each injury and disease process observed during the autopsy.

The last section of the report includes the data for the death certificate. This section customarily sets out the pathologist's opinions as to the decedent's cause and manner of death. If there have been serological, toxicological, or other studies, the pathologist could list those findings here.

COMMON SYMBOLS TO INDICATE TYPES OF INJURIES[75]

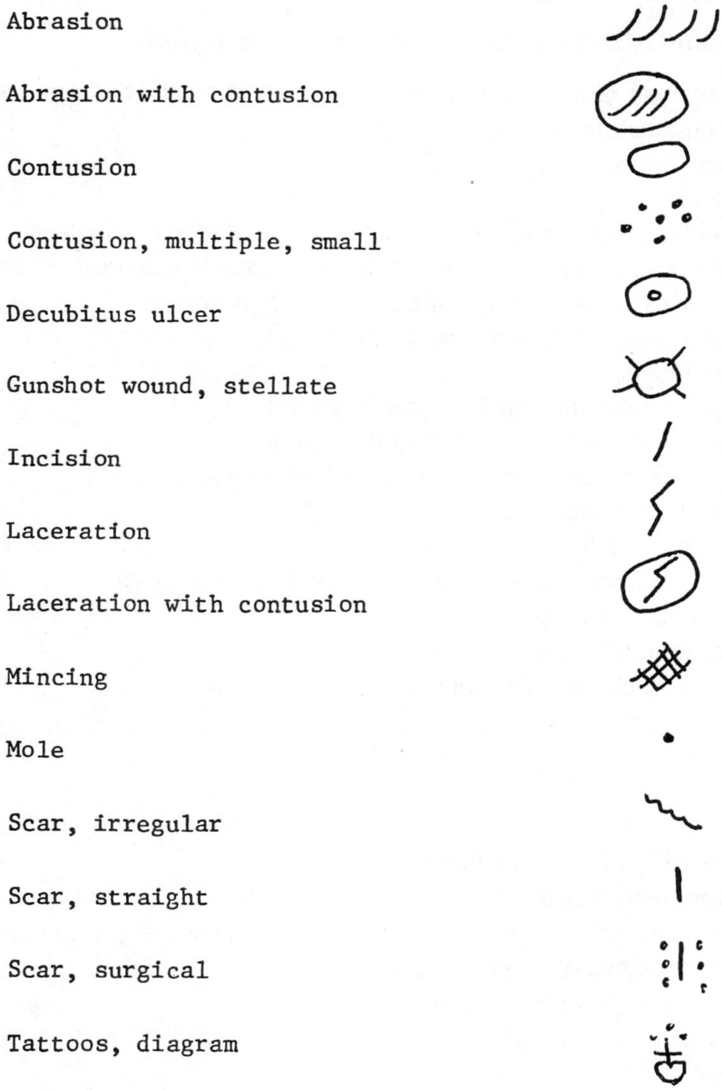

Figure 19-2

---

75. J. Weston & V. McCarty, *supra* note 67, at 104. Reprinted with permission. *See also* Mackauf, *A Key to Medical Terminology*, 13 Trial Law. Q. 99 (Spring 1979).

Although the pathologist frequently sets out the initial demographic data in outline form, the balance of the autopsy report is usually written in complete sentences as a narrative. The narrative is likely to include a good deal of technical terminology. For that reason, while the attorney is reading the report, the attorney should have on his or her desk a medical dictionary or glossary. A list of useful references is included in the bibliography in § 19-11. Figure 19-3 lists some frequently encountered terms and abbreviations.

Glossary of terms in common use in medical records:

Laceration — any tear in the skin or other tissues that is caused by blunt force injury (*e.g.*, dull instrument)
Contusion — any bruise
Abrasion — scrape
Ecchymosis — blue-purple, non-elevated patch of skin due to hemorrhage
PERLA — pupils equal size and reactive to light and accommodation. Normal response of eye during examination of a living person
NSR — normal sinus rhythm — normal heart rhythm
SOB — short of breath
Discomfort — uncomfortable, uneasy; may be painful
Significant Discomfort — readily apparent discomfort
Excoriation — any superficial loss of tissue surface such as a scratch
ETOH — "drinking" alcohol; ethanol
AOB — alcohol on breath
CAP — clear to ausculation and percussion — normal chest exam
Vaginal Vault — vaginal cavity
Introitus — area around vaginal opening
Posterior fornix — back part of vagina at the cervix (uterus)
Anterior — front
Posterior — back
Ventral — front
Dorsal — back
Superior — toward head; situated above
Inferior — toward feet; situated below
Distal — remote; farther from the point of reference (opposite of proximal)
Medial — toward midline of body (opposite of lateral)
Phalanx, Phalanges — finger(s)
Forearm — forearm
Arm — upper arm
Pectoral — breast area
Precordial — middle of chest
Epigastric — stomach area; upper central abdomen
LLQ — left lower quadrant of abdomen

RUQ — right upper quadrant of abdomen
RLQ — right lower quadrant of abdomen
LUQ — left upper quadrant of abdomen
Substernal — mid chest; behind breastbone
Manubrial — mid chest
Mandibular — pertaining to the lower jaw
Maxillary — pertaining to the upper jaw
Orbital — around eye
Pinna — ear
Cervical — neck
Tarsal — having to do with the ankle/foot
Incision — a cut

Figure 19-3[76]

§ 19-3(B). Other Procedures.

As a medical examiner, the pathologist heads or is a part of a multidisciplinary team. The team includes criminalists who conduct trace analyses, bacteriologists, serologists, anthropologists,[77] and toxicologists. Many of these experts will be employees of the medical examiner's office; others serve as independent contractors; and still others work on the staff of other agencies such as police departments. Whatever the employment status of these other experts, the forensic pathologist coordinates their efforts. This coordination is a cooperative partnership; the pathologist collects samples for these other experts, and in turn they analyze the samples and submit their findings to the pathologist. During his or her training and experience, the pathologist comes to learn a good deal about other disciplines such as firearms examination and toxicology. In many cases, in addition to submitting samples for general analysis, the pathologist will suggest that the samples be subjected to particular tests. At the conclusion of the medicolegal investigation, the pathologist must integrate all the experts' findings and arrive at conclusions about cause and manner of death, consistent with those findings.

§ 19-4. Identity of Decedent.

A forensic pathologist can make a unique contribution to the fact-finding process in criminal cases. Attorneys and judges usually call upon the forensic pathologist for aid in answering four basic questions: How did the decedent die

76. WRIGHT, MEDICAL EVIDENCE — OUTLINE FOR TRIAL ADVOCACY FOR PROSECUTORS (unpublished manuscript on file with the National College of District Attorneys, Bates College of Law, University of Houston, Houston, Texas). Reprinted with permission of the National College of District Attorneys.

77. Mann & Ubelaker, *The Forensic Anthropologist*, 59 F.B.I. LAW ENF. BULL. 20 (July 1990).

— the cause, mechanism, or manner of death? When did the decedent die or when did the injury occur? Where did the decedent die or suffer the injury? And who was the decedent?

In most cases, there is little doubt about the identity of the decedent. However, in some instances, even after the initial police investigation, the decedent's identity is unknown or in serious doubt. In those cases, the forensic pathologist must address the question of identity. The pathologist and allied experts can sometimes answer the question definitively; in other cases, they can narrow the class of persons that the decedent belonged to.

§ 19-4(A). Identifying the Decedent.

A number of techniques can lead to the scientific identification of the decedent.[78]

The most well-known technique is fingerprinting, which is discussed in Chapter 16. That technique involves a comparison between prints lifted from the body and antemortem fingerprint records of known individuals. The fingerprint examiner may be able to make a positive identification even though the body has undergone extensive putrefaction.[79] If the epidermis or outer skin surface is still intact, the examiner can inject a special solution under the skin to bring out the prints.[80]

If identity cannot be established by fingerprints, a forensic odontologist, a dentist specializing in medicolegal problems, may be able to identify the decedent. Forensic odontology is discussed in Chapter 13. Human dentition is extremely durable; the teeth can, for instance, survive a fire that would destroy the skin and make fingerprinting impossible. Like fingerprinting, this technique is comparative. The odontologist compares postmortem findings with antemortem dental records.[81]

---

78. Bennett & Rockhold, *Use of an Alternate Light Source for Tattoo Recognition in the Extended Postmortem Interval*, 44 J. Forensic Sci. 182 (1999); Kahana, Hiss & Smith, *Quantitative Assessment of Trabecular Bone Pattern Identification*, 43 J. Forensic Sci. 1144 (1998) ("the trabecular architecture is unique to each individual and stable enough to be used as a forensic marker for positive identification of human remains").

79. Bucklin, *supra* note 61, at 201.

80. *Id.*

81. Robinson, Rueggeberg & Lockwood, *Thermal Stability of Direct Dental Esthetic Restorative Materials at Elevated Temperatures*, 43 J. Forensic Sci. 1163 (1998); Rudnick, *The Identification of a Murder Victim Using a Comparison of the Postmortem and Antemortem Dental Records*, 29 J. Forensic Sci. 349 (1984). *See also* Skinner & Anderson, *Individualization and Enamel History: A Case Report in Forensic Anthropology*, 36 J. Forensic Sci. 939 (1991) ("We report the presence, in the dental enamel of the primary and secondary dentition, of stress markers, termed striae of Retzius, whose locations correspond well with anecdotal reports and ... medical records which describe the timing of specific episodes of stress. The enhanced probability of personal identification from dental histological stress markers is evaluated"); Lorton, Rethman &

If neither fingerprinting nor forensic odontology establishes identity, a forensic radiologist may be able to make an identification based on peculiarities in the recovered portions of the skeleton.[82] (Even when other identification modalities are possible, X-ray identification may be used for convenience or expediency.) This technique has enormous potential. Millions of medical X-rays have been taken and are still available in physicians' and hospitals' files.[83] The

---

Friedman, *The Computer-Assisted Postmortem Identification (CAPMI) System: Sorting Algorithm Improvements*, 34 J. FORENSIC SCI. 996 (1989) (the researchers have refined the CAPMI software algorithms); Williams, Friedman & Lorton, *A New Algorithm for Use in Computer Identification*, 34 J. FORENSIC SCI. 682 (1989) (the researchers revised the CAPMI software to list the records in the database by minimum number of mismatches); Lorton, Rethman & Friedman, *The Computer-Assisted Postmortem Identification (CAPMI) System: A Computer-Based Identification Program*, 33 J. FORENSIC SCI. 977 (1988) (a computerized dental identification software program developed by the U.S. Army Institute of Dental Research (USAIDR)). Byers, Churchill & Curran, *Identification of Euro-Americans, Afro-Americans, and Amerindians from Palatal Dimensions*, 42 J. FORENSIC SCI. 3 (1997); Kogon & MacLeon, *Long-Term Validation Study of Bitewing Dental Radiographs for Forensic Identification*, 41 J. FORENSIC SCI. 230 (1996); MacLean, Kogon & Stitt, *Validation of Dental Radiographs for Human Identification*, 39 J. FORENSIC SCI. 1195 (1994).

82. Angyal & Derczy, *Personal Identification on the Basis of Antemortem and Postmortem Radiographs*, 43 J. FORENSIC SCI. 1089 (1998); Marlin, Clark & Standish, *Identification of Human Remains by Comparison of Frontal Sinus Radiographs: A Series of Four Cases*, 36 J. FORENSIC SCI. 1765 (1991); Jabonlonski & Shum, *Identification of Unknown Human Remains by Comparison of Antemortem and Postmortem Radiographs*, 42 FORENSIC SCI. INT'L 221 (1989); Dailey & Furue, *A Photographic Technique for the Restoration of Damaged Radiographs*, 33 J. FORENSIC SCI. 1273 (1988); Sauer, Brantley & Barondess, *The Effects of Aging on the Comparability of Antemortem and Postmortem Radiographs*, 33 J. FORENSIC SCI. 1223 (1988) ("even though bone is a flexible tissue and changes constantly during life, aspects of the criteria chosen are quite stable and ... even after two-and-a-half decades the ability to make positive identifications from postcranial axial material is not necessarily diminished"); Yoshino, Miyasaka, Sato & Seta, *Classification of Frontal Sinus Patterns by Radiography. Its Application to Identification of Unknown Skeletal Remains*, 34 FORENSIC SCI. INT'L 289 (1987); Messmer, *The Use of Mammographic Equipment in Mass Disaster Identification*, 27 J. FORENSIC SCI. 723 (1982); Murphy & Gantner, *Radiologic Examination of Anatomic and Skeletonized Remains*, 27 J. FORENSIC SCI. 9 (1982); Murphy, Spruill & Gantner, *Radiologic Identification of Unknown Human Remains*, 25 J. FORENSIC SCI. 727 (1980); Sanders, Woesner, Ferguson & Noguchi, *A New Application of Forensic Radiology: Identification of Deceased From a Single Clavicle*, 115 AM. J. ROENT. 619 (1972); Singleton, *The Roentgenological Identification of Victims of the "Noronic" Disaster*, 66 AM. J. ROENT. 375 (1951); Tsunenari, Uchimura, Yonemitsu & Oshiro, *Unusual Personal Identification With Characteristic Features in Chest Roentgenograms*, 3 AM. J. FORENSIC MED. & PATH. 357 (1982).

83. Murphy, Spruill & Gantner, *supra* note 82, at 734. Goldstein, Sweet & Wood, *A Specimen Positioning Device for Dental Radiographic Identification — Image Geometry Considerations*, 43 J. FORENSIC SCI. 185 (1998); Fitzpatrick, Shook, Kaufman, Wu, Kirschner, MacMahon, Levine, Maples & Charletta, *Optical and Digital Techniques for Enhancing Radiographic Anatomy for Identification of Human Remains*, 41 J. FORENSIC SCI. 947 (1996); Riepert, Rittner, Ulmcke, Ogbuihi & Schweden, *Identification of an Unknown Corpse by Means of Computed Tomography (CT) of the Lumbar Spine*, 40 J. FORENSIC SCI. 126 (1995); Hogge, Messmer & Doan, *Radiographic Identification of Unknown Human Remains and Interpreter Experience Level*, 39 J.

number of X-rays may exceed the number of fingerprints and dental records. Radiologic identification has been used successfully in the identification of victims of mass disasters such as the 1949 fire on the Great Lakes liner Noronic, which claimed 119 lives.[84] In a one-year comparative study in the St. Louis metropolitan area, the medical examiner made more identifications through medical X-rays than through fingerprints and dental records combined.[85]

Radiologic identification is similar to fingerprints and forensic odontology in that the technique necessitates locating antemortem X-rays for comparison. The radiologist can attempt to superimpose the antemortem and postmortem X-rays to determine whether there is a match[86] — whether they both contain a unique anatomic feature or evidence of surgical procedure.

Another potentially useful technique is facial reconstruction.[87] Given the shape and dimensions of the skull, including the jaw, cheekbones, and dentition, a

---

FORENSIC SCI. 373 (1994); Kahana & Hiss, *Positive Identification by Means of Trabecular Bone Pattern Comparison*, 39 J. FORENSIC SCI. 1325 (1994); P. SEKHARAN, STUDIES ON CERTAIN FORENSIC ASPECTS OF SKULL IDENTIFICATION AND INDIVIDUALIZATION (1989); Haglund & Fligner, *Confirmation of Human Identification Using Computerized Tomography (CT)*, 38 J. FORENSIC SCI. 708 (1993); Owsley, Mann, Chapman, Moore & Cox, *Positive Identification in a Case of Intentional Extreme Fragmentation*, 38 J. FORENSIC SCI. 985 (1993); Rouge, Telmon, Arrue, Larrouy & Arbus, *Radiographic Identification of Human Remains Through Deformities and Anomalies of Post-Cranial Bones: A Report of Two Cases*, 38 J. FORENSIC SCI. 997 (1993); Owsley & Mann, *Positive Personal Identity of Skeletonized Remains Using Abdominal and Pelvic Radiographs*, 37 J. FORENSIC SCI. 332 (1992).

84. Singleton, *supra* note 82, at 375.

85. Murphy, Spruill & Gantner, *supra* note 82, at 728.

86. Tsunenari, Uchimura, Yonemitsu & Oshiro, *supra* note 82, at 358. *See also* United States v. Webb, 796 F.2d 60, 64 (5th Cir. 1986), *cert. denied*, 479 U.S. 1038 (1987); Nickerson, Fitzhorn, Koch & Charney, *A Methodology for Near-Optimal Computational Superimposition of Two-Dimensional Digital Facial Photographs and Three-Dimensional Cranial Surface Meshes*, 36 J. FORENSIC SCI. 480 (1991); Dong-Sheng, Yu-Wen, Cheng, Run-Ji, Yong-Chuan, Jian-Hai, Wei-Dong & Jiang, *A Study on the Standard for Forensic Anthropologic Identification of Skull-Image Superimposition*, 34 J. FORENSIC SCI. 1343 (1989); Brocklebank & Holmgren, *Development of Equipment for the Standardization of Skull Photographs in Personal Identifications by Photographic Superimposition*, 34 J. FORENSIC SCI. 1214 (1989); Chee & Cheng, *Skull and Photographic Superimposition: A New Approach Using a Second Party's Interpupil Distance to Extrapolate the Magnification Factor*, 34 J. FORENSIC SCI. 708 (1989) (the authors discuss the difficulty of determining the correct magnification factor to use in the superimposition technique); Iten, *Identification of Skulls by Video Superimposition*, 32 J. FORENSIC SCI. 173 (1987); Bastiaan, Dalitz & Woodward, *Video Superimposition of Skulls and Photographic Portraits — A New Aid to Identification*, 31 J. FORENSIC SCI. 1373 (1986). Austin-Smith & Maples, *The Reliability of Skull/Photograph Superimposition in Individual Identification*, 39 J. FORENSIC SCI. 446 (1994); Kumari & Sekharan, *Remote Control Skull Positioning Device for Superimposition Studies*, 54 FORENSIC SCI. INT'L 127 (1992); Ubelaker, Bubniak & O'Donnell, *Computer-Assisted Photographic Superimposition*, 37 J. FORENSIC SCI. 750 (1992).

87. Rhine, *Coming to Terms with Facial Reproduction*, 35 J. FORENSIC SCI. 960 (1990); Venezis, Blowes, Linney, Tan, Richards & Neave, *Application of 3-D Computer Graphics for*

forensic anthropologist can approximate the decedent's facial appearance.[88] American police have already used these techniques as an investigative tool to assist them in identifying an unknown decedent.[89]

Crime laboratories are now using DNA typing to make identifications. Chapter 18 discusses DNA typing in detail.

§ 19-4(B). Narrowing the Class.

In some cases, it is impossible to identify definitively the decedent. Nevertheless, the pathologist and allied experts may be able to furnish the police with valuable information, narrowing the class of persons the decedent belonged to. Specifically, the pathologist may be able to determine whether the remains are human and, if so, the decedent's sex, race, and approximate age and stature.

Human Origin

The initial question facing the anthropologist is whether the remains are of human origin. This question can be troublesome because some bones of bears and some apes are superficially similar to those of human beings. However, a firm conclusion can be based on detailed examination and serologic tests.[90]

Facial Reconstruction and Comparison with Sculpting Techniques, 42 FORENSIC SCI. INT'L 69 (1989) (although anthropologists have traditionally used manual sculpting techniques in facial reconstruction, they are now experimenting with 3-D computer graphics); Stephens & Hegler, *Use of Glue Gun in Forensic Anthropology and Pathologic Bone Reconstruction Cases*, 34 J. FORENSIC SCI. 454 (1989); Mittleman, Souviron, Valor & Lugo, *Facial Reconstruction, Publicity, and Photography Leading to Identification of Deceased Persons*, 52 F.B.I LAW ENF. BULL., 21 (Aug. 1983); Stewart, *The Points of Attachment of the Palpebral Ligaments: Their Use in Facial Reconstructions of the Skull*, 28 J. FORENSIC SCI. 858 (1983); Tyrell, Evison, Chamberlain & Green, *Forensic Three-Dimensional Facial Reconstruction: Historical Review and Contemporary Developments*, 42 J. FORENSIC SCI. 653 (1997); Quatrehomme, Cotin, Subsol, Delingette, Grevin, Fidrich, Bailet & Ollier, *A Fully Three-Dimensional Method for Facial Reconstruction Based on Deformable Models*, 42 J. FORENSIC SCI. 649 (1997); O'Donnell, *Forensic Imaging Comes of Age*, 63 F.B.I. LAW ENF. BULL. 5, 6 (Jan. 1994) (age enhancement technique); Craig, *Facial Reconstruction*, 37 J. FORENSIC SCI. 1442 (1992).

88. Hoffman, McConathy, Coward & Saddler, *Relationship Between the Piriform Aperture and Interalar Nasal Widths in Adult Males*, 36 J. FORENSIC SCI. 1152 (1991); George, *The Lateral Craniographic Method of Facial Reconstruction*, 32 J. FORENSIC SCI. 1305 (1987); Gatliff, *Facial Sculpture on the Skull for Identification*, 5 AM. J. FORENSIC MED. & PATH. 327 (1984); Mittleman, Souviron, Valor & Lugo, *supra* note 87, at 21 Gatliff, *Forensic Sculpture Adapts to Museum Use*, *in* SELECTED PAPERS FROM THE 7TH ANNUAL CONF. OF THE GUILD OF NATURAL SCI. ILLUSTRATORS 13 (1986).

89. *Id. See also* McKenna, Jablonski & Fearnhead, *A Method of Matching Skulls with Photographic Portraits Using Landmarks and Measurements of the Dentition*, 29 J. FORENSIC SCI. 787 (1984).

90. Chilvarquer, Katz, Glassman, Prihoda & Cottone, *Comparative Radiographic Study of Human and Animal Long Bone Patterns*, 32 J. FORENSIC SCI. 1645 (1987).

Sex

Next, the anthropologist can determine the sex of the person who was the source of the skeletal remains.[91] Several anatomic features help to differentiate male from female decedents.[92] The bones of the male tend to be larger, heavier,

---

91. Inoue, *Fourier Analysis of the Forehead Shape of Skull and Sex Determination by Use of Computer*, 47 FORENSIC SCI. INT'L 101 (1990); Johnson, O'Higgins, Moore & McAndrew, *Determination of Race and Sex of the Human Skull by Discriminant Function Analysis of Linear and Angular Dimensions*, 41 FORENSIC SCI. INT'L 41 (1989); Wu, *Sex Determination of Chinese Femur by Discriminant Function*, 34 J. FORENSIC SCI. 1222 (1989) (this technique correctly determined sex in over 80% of the cases); Berrizbeitia, *Sex Determination with the Head of the Radius*, 34 J. FORENSIC SCI. 1206 (1989) (92% sexing accuracy); Holland, *Use of the Cranial Base in the Identification of Fire Victims*, 34 J. FORENSIC SCI. 458 (1989) (the cranial base can be used to sex skeletalized individuals, but some pathologists believe that shrinkage resulting from burning can preclude the use of the technique; these researchers found that the shrinkage caused by a low-temperature burning such as an average hour fire "does not significantly impair" the accuracy of the technique); Taylor, DiBennardo, Linares, Goldman & DeForest, *Metropolitan Forensic Anthropology Team (MFAT) Studies in Identification: 1. Race and Sex Assessment by Discriminant Function Analysis of the Postcranial Skeleton*, 29 J. FORENSIC SCI. 798 (1984); Robling & Ubelaker, *Sex Estimation from the Metatarsals*, 42 J. FORENSIC SCI. 1062 (1997); Pollanen & Ubelaker, *Forensic Significance of the Polymorphism of Hyoid Bone Shape*, 42 J. FORENSIC SCI. 890 (1997); Introna, Di Vella, Campobasso & Dragone, *Sex Determination by Discriminant Analysis of Calcanei Measurements*, 42 J. FORENSIC SCI. 725 (1997); Smith, *Attribution of Foot Bones to Sex and Population Groups*, 42 J. FORENSIC SCI. 186 (1997); Trancho, Robledo, Lopez-Bueis & Sanchez, *Sexual Determination of the Femur Using Discriminant Functions. Analysis of a Spanish Population of Known Sex and Age*, 42 J. FORENSIC SCI. 181 (1997); Kalmey & Rathbun, *Sex Determination by Discriminant Function Analysis of the Petrous Portion of the Temporal Bone*, 41 J. FORENSIC SCI. 865 (1996); Hsiao, Chang & Liu, *Sex Determination by Discriminant Function Analysis of Lateral Radiographic Cephalometry*, 41 J. FORENSIC SCI. 792 (1996); Smith, *Attribution of Hand Bones to Sex and Population Groups*, 41 J. FORENSIC SCI. 469 (1996); Riepert, Drechsler, Schild, Nafe & Mattern, *Estimation of Sex on the Basis of Radiographs of the Calcaneus*, 77 FORENSIC SCI. INT'L 133 (1996); Falsetti, *Sex Assessment from Metacarpals of the Human Hand*, 40 J. FORENSIC SCI. 774 (1995); Iscan, Yoshino & Kato, *Sex Determination from the Tibia: Standards for Contemporary Japan*, 39 J. FORENSIC SCI. 785 (1994); Lazenby, *Identification of Sex from Metacarpals: Effect of Side Asymmetry*, 39 J. FORENSIC SCI. 1188 (1994); Camacho, Pellico & Rodriguez, *Osteometry of the Human Iliac Crest: Patterns of Normality and Its Utility in Sexing Human Remains*, 38 J. FORENSIC SCI. 779 (1993); Scheurer & Elkington, *Sex Determination from Metacarpals and the First Proximal Phalanx*, 38 J. FORENSIC SCI. 769 (1993); Kieser, Moggi-Cecchi & Groeneveld, *Sex Allocation of Skeletal Material by Analysis of the Proximal Tibia*, 56 FORENSIC SCI. INT'L 29 (1992); Mittler & Sheridan, *Sex Determination in Subadults Using Auricular Surface Morphology: A Forensic Science Perspective*, 37 J. FORENSIC SCI. 1068 (1992).

92. Rogers, *A Visual Method of Determining the Sex of Skeletal Remains Using the Distal Humerus*, 44 J. FORENSIC SCI. 57 (1999) (by using four morphological features, the researcher was able to sex the remains with 92% accuracy); King, Iscan & Loth, *Metric and Comparative Analysis of Sexual Dimorphism in the Thai Femur*, 43 J. FORENSIC SCI. 954 (1998) ("maximum head diameter and bicondylar breadth are the optional combination for sex diagnosis and yielded 94.2% accuracy"); Cologlu, Iscan, Yavuz & Sari, *Sex Determination from the Ribs of Contemporary Turks*, 43 J. FORENSIC SCI. 273 (1998) (the sternal extremity of the fourth rib); Garlie & Saunders,

and have more prominent ridges. The female skull is more rounded than that of the male. The shape of the pelvis area is also an important indicator of sex. The male sacrum is curved, long, and narrow; in contrast, the female sacrum is flat, short, and wide.[93] In addition, in the female the sciatic notch is wide at an obtuse angle; the male sciatic notch is small at an acute angle.[94]

If the kidney is intact, the pathologist may order an analysis of the kidney for the presence of Y chromosomes.[95] In the test, the technician examines the nuclei of the cells to determine what percent of the nuclei contain Y chromosomes. Research indicates that a count higher than 10% is strongly indicative that the decedent was male.[96]

Many pathologists consider additional criteria in sexing skulls.[97] For example, the male brow is more developed than that of the female while the male chin is squarer than that of the female. In addition, the rim of the female eye socket is sharper than that of the male. Costal cartilage calcification patterns,[98] nasal

---

Midline Facial Tissue Thicknesses of Subadults from a Longitudinal Radiographic Study, 44 J. FORENSIC SCI. 61 (1999) ("males exhibit greater tissue thickness measurements than females but only significantly so after age 14"); Miller, Walker & O'Halloran, *Age and Sex-Related Variation in Hyoid Bone Morphology*, 43 J. FORENSIC SCI. 1138 (1998).

93. Bucklin, *supra* note 61, at 202; Sutherland & Suchey, *Use of the Ventral Arc in Pubic Sex Determination*, 36 J. FORENSIC SCI. 501 (1991) ("In the present study, focus was placed on the ventral arc which, when used alone, provided 96% accuracy in sex determination"); MacLaughlin & Bruce, *The Accuracy of Sex Identification in European Skeletal Remains Using the Phenice Characters*, 35 J. FORENSIC SCI. 1384 (1990) ("Three documented European skeletal series were examined to assess the accuracy and reliability of the pubic variables described by Phenice for correctly identifying the sex of adult human skeletal remains. The accuracy and objectivity of these variables, as reported by Phenice ..., could not be confirmed on this European material. In general, the subpubic concavity feature, when used alone, proved to be the most reliable variable for sex identification"); Hunt, *Sex Determination in the Subadult Ilia: An Indirect Test of Weaver's Nonmetric Sexing Method*, 35 J. FORENSIC SCI. 881 (1990); Rogers & Saunders, *Accuracy of Sex Determination Using Morphological Traits of the Human Pelvis*, 39 J. FORENSIC SCI. 1047 (1994).

94. Bucklin, *supra* note 61 , at 202; Schulter-Ellis & Hayek, *Sexing North American Eskimo and Indian Innominate Bones with the Acetabulum/Pubis Index*, 33 J. FORENSIC SCI. 697 (1988).

95. Thomsen, *Sex Determination of Severely Burned Bodies*, 10 Forensic Sci. 235 (1977).

96. *Id.* at 241. *See also* Duffy, Skinner & Waterfield, *Rates of Putrefaction of Dental Pulp in the Northwest Coast Environment*, 36 J. FORENSIC SCI. 1492 (1991) (the sex chromatin test).

97. Hsiao, Chang & Liu, *Sex Determination by Discriminant Function Analysis of Lateral Radiographic Cephalometry*, 41 J. FORENSIC SCI. 792 (1996); Inoue, Inoue, Fushimi & Okada, *Sex Determination by Discriminant Function Analysis of Lateral Cranial Form*, 57 FORENSIC SCI. INT'L 109 (1992); Song, Lin & Jia, *Sex Diagnosis of Chinese Skulls Using Multiple Stepwise Discriminant Function Analysis*, 54 FORENSIC SCI. INT'L 135 (1992).

98. Rao & Pai, *Costal Cartilage Calification Pattern — A Clue for Establishing Sex Identity*, 38 FORENSIC SCI. INT'L 193, 201 (1988) (although the authors recommend the use of the test, they emphasize that the method is "best practiced [as] a screening test").

features,[99] the Mandibular Canine Index,[100] crematin weights,[101] and other dental features can be helpful clues.[102]

Race

After identifying the decedent's sex, the anthropologist may attempt to determine the decedent's race.[103] The shapes of the long bones or skull[104] are clues to the decedent's race.[105] The anthropologist can usually differentiate on the basis of the slope and appearance of the facial bones, the breadth and length of the skull, and nasal features. In Caucasians, the shape of the palate tends to be

---

99. Macho, *Descriptive Morphological Features of the Nose — An Assessment of Their Importance for Plastic Reconstruction*, 34 J. FORENSIC SCI. 902 (1989).

100. Rao, Rao, Pai & Koitan, *Mandibular Canine Index — A Clue for Establishing Sex Identity*, 42 FORENSIC SCI. INT'L 249 (1989) ("Accuracy of sex determination identity was found to be 84.3% in the male and 87.5% in the female").

101. Warren & Maples, *The Anthropometry of Contemporary Commercial Cremation*, 42 J. FORENSIC SCI. 417 (1997).

102. DeVito & Saunders, *A Discriminant Function Analysis of Deciduous Teeth to Determine Sex*, 35 J. FORENSIC SCI. 845 (1990).

103. Taylor, DiBennardo, Linares, Goldman & DeForest, *supra* note 85, at 798. Marino, *A Pilot Study Using the First Cervical Vertebra as an Indicator of Race*, 42 J. FORENSIC SCI. 1114 (1997); Hsu, Tsai, Hsiao, Chang, Lin, Liu, Yu & Ferguson, *The Effect of Shovel Trait on Carabelli's Trait in Taiwan Chinese and Aboriginal Populations*, 42 J. FORENSIC SCI. 802 (1997); Smith, *Attribution of Foot Bones to Sex and Population Groups*, 42 J. FORENSIC SCI. 186 (1997); Smith, *Attribution of Hand Bones to Sex and Population Groups*, 41 J. FORENSIC SCI. 469 (1996); Gill, *Challenge on the Frontier: Discerning American Indians from Whites Osteologically*, 40 J. FORENSIC SCI. 783 (1995); Craig, *Intercondylar Shelf Angle: A New Method to Determine Race from the Distal Femur*, 40 J. FORENSIC SCI. 777 (1995); Brace, *Region Does Not Mean "Race"— Reality Versus Convention in Forensic Anthropology*, 40 J. FORENSIC SCI. 171 (1995).

104. Ross, McKeown & Konigsberg, *Allocation of Crania to Groups Via the "New Morphometry,"* 44 J. FORENSIC SCI. 584 (1999).

105. Bucklin, *supra* note 61, at 202; Sledzik & Ousley, *Analysis of Six Vietnamese Trophy Skulls*, 36 J. FORENSIC SCI. 520 (1991); Johnson, O'Higgins, Moore & McAndrew, *Determination of Race and Sex of the Human Skull by Discriminant Function Analysis of Linear and Angular Dimensions*, 41 FORENSIC SCI. INT'L 41 (1989); Holland, *Use of the Cranial Base in the Identification of Fire Victims*, 34 J. FORENSIC SCI. 458 (1989) (the cranial base can be used to determine the race of skeletalized individuals, but some pathologists believe that shrinkage during fire can preclude the application of the technique to fire victims; these researchers found that the average shrinking in a low temperature burning such as the average house fire "does not significantly impair the accuracy" of this identification technique); Iscan, Loth & Wright, *Racial Variation in the Sternal Extremity of the Rib and its Effect on Age Determination*, 32 J. FORENSIC SCI. 452 (1987); Holland, *Race Determination of Fragmentary Crania by Analysis of the Cranial Base*, 31 J. FORENSIC SCI. 719 (1986); Gill, Hughes, Bennett & Gilbert, *Racial Identification from the Midfacial Skeleton with Special Reference to American Indians and Whites*, 33 J. FORENSIC SCI. 92 (1988).

triangular; in members of the Negroid race, the shape is often round or rectangular.[106]

Age

The anthropologist may also be able to furnish a rough estimate of the decedent's age at the time of death.[107] There are numerous indicators of age. Several techniques are based on osteology, or the study of bones.[108]

One technique is based on the analysis of centers or points of ossification.[109] Bones form from these centers. As the years pass, the centers gradually unite with the main portions of the bone. It is said that the epiphysis of the bone fuses.[110] The centers and portions unite in a relatively regular sequence. Until the person reaches 25 years of age, the stage of ossification allows the anthropologist to determine age within a year or two.

---

106. *Bucklin, supra* note 61, at 202. In a lecture outline on file with the National College of District Attorneys, Law Center, University of Houston, anthropologist Hugh Berryman of the University of Tennessee, Memphis, lists some of the differences in skull features. For example, he states that: Europeans tend to have vertical lower faces and narrow faces, interorbital spaces, and nasal apertures; Africans tend to have lower facial prominences and wide interorbital spaces and nasal apertures; and the faces of Asians tend to have an overall flatter appearance. *See also* Burris & Harris, *Identification of Race and Sex from Palate Dimensions*, 43 J. FORENSIC SCI. 959 (1998).

107. *See* Huxley & Angevine, *Determination of Gestational Age from Lunar Age Assessments in Human Fetal Remains*, 43 J. FORENSIC SCI. 1254 (1998). *But see* Ross, Jantz & McCormick, *Cranial Thickness in American Females and Males*, 43 J. FORENSIC SCI. 267, 271 (1998) ("The results of this study do not support previous investigations that cranial thickness increases with age....").

108. M. ISCAN, AGE MARKERS IN THE HUMAN SKELETON (1989); Stout, *The Use of Histomorphology to Estimate Age*, 33 J. FORENSIC SCI. 121 (1988); Ubelker, *Estimating Age at Death from Immature Human Skeletons: An Overview*, 32 J. FORENSIC SCI. 1254 (1987). Houck, Ubelaker, Owsley, Craig, Grant, Fram, Woltanski & Sandness, *The Role of Forensic Anthropology in the Recovery and Analysis of Branch Davidian Compound Victims: Assessing the Accuracy of Age Estimations*, 41 J. FORENSIC SCI. 796 (1996) (the researchers used the following techniques: long bone length, epiphyseal appearance and union, dental development, pubic symphyseal morphology, auricular surface morphology, sternal rib morphology, and degenerative changes; the authors state that "[m]ultiple methods of age estimation based on a variety of age-related structures should be used"); Cool, Hendrikz & Wood, *Microscopic Age Changes in the Human Occipital Bone*, 40 J. FORENSIC SCI. 789 (1995); Pfau & Sciulli, *A Method for Establishing the Age of Subadults*, 39 J. FORENSIC SCI. 165 (1994); T. WHITE & P. FOLKENS, HUMAN OSTEOLOGY (1991).

109. These techniques can sometimes be used even after body has been badly burned. Huxley & Kosa, *Calculation of Percentage Shrinkage in Human Fetal Diaphyseal Lengths from Fresh Bone to Carbonized and Calcined Bone Using Petersohn and Kohler's Data*, 44 J. FORENSIC SCI. 577 (1999).

110. M. ISCAN, AGE MARKERS IN THE HUMAN SKELETON (1989).

In addition, certain divisions in the skeleton disappear as the years pass.[111] For example, the sutures in the skull close.[112] Skull suture fusion is, in general, an unreliable method for determining age with the exception of the basilar suture.

The symphysis in the pubic area is another indicator. The symphysis is the joint between the left and right pubis. Some anthropologists have attempted to devise formulae for predicting age based on an analysis of the symphysis.[113] Other degenerative changes in bones can likewise be helpful clues to the age of the decedent.[114]

The teeth also develop in a predictable progression. Hence, the stage of dentition such as the molars is evidence of age.[115] This is especially reliable in

---

111. Mann, Jantz, Bass & Willey, *Maxillary Suture Obliteration: A Visual Method for Estimating Skeletal Age*, 36 J. FORENSIC SCI. 781 (1991); Gruspier & Mullen, *Maxillary Suture Obliteration: A Test of the Mann Method*, 36 J. FORENSIC SCI. 512 (1991); Mann, Symes & Bass, *Maxillary Suture Obliteration: Aging the Human Skeleton Based on Intact and Fragmentary Maxilla*, 32 J. FORENSIC SCI. 148 (1987); McCormick & Stewart, *Age Related Changes in the Human Plastron: A Roentgenographic and Morphologic Study*, 33 J. FORENSIC SCI. 100 (1988); O'Halloran & Lundy, *Age and Ossification of the Hyoid Bone: Forensic Implications*, 32 J. FORENSIC SCI. 1655 (1987).

112. Galera, Ubelaker & Hayek, *Comparison of Macroscopic Cranial Methods of Age Estimation Applied to Skeletons from the Terry Collection*, 43 J. FORENSIC SCI. 933 (1998).

113. Snow, *Equations for Estimating Age at Death from the Pubic Symphysis: A Modification of the McKern-Stewart Method*, 28 J. FORENSIC SCI. 864 (1983); Klepinger, Katz, Micozzi & Carroll, *Evaluation of Cast Methods for Estimating Age from the Os Pubis*, 37 J. FORENSIC SCI. 763 (1992).

114. Murray & Murray, *A Test of the Auricular Surface Aging Technique*, 36 J. FORENSIC SCI. 1162 (1991).

115. Xiaohu, Philipsen, Jablonski, Weatherhead, Pang & Jiazhen, *Preliminary Report on a New Method of Human Age Estimation From Single Adult Teeth*, 51 FORENSIC SCI. INT'L 281 (1991); Ohtani & Yamamoto, *Age Estimation Using the Racemization of Amino Acid in Human Dentin*, 36 J. FORENSIC SCI. 792 (1991); Kashyap & Rao, *A Modified Gustafson Method of Age Estimation from Teeth*, 47 J. FORENSIC SCI. 237 (1990) (the Gustafson method estimates age based on "certain regressive changes in the hard tissues of the anterior teeth"); Lucy, Aykroyd, Pollard & Solheim, *A Bayesian Approach to Adult Human Age Estimation from Dental Observations by Johanson's Age Changes*, 41 J. FORENSIC SCI. 189 (1996); Lucy & Pollard, *Further Comments on the Estimation of Error Associated with the Gustafson Dental Age Estimation Method*, 40 J. FORENSIC SCI. 222 (1995).

See also Solheim, *A New Method for Dental Age Estimation in Adults*, 59 FORENSIC SCI. INT'L 137 (1993); Mincer, Harris & Berryman, *The A.B.F.O. Study of Third Molar Development and Its Use As an Estimator of Chronological Age*, 38 J. FORENSIC SCI. 379 (1993); Lamendin, Baccino, Humbert, Tavernier, Nossintchouk & Zerilli, *A Simple Technique for Age Estimation in Adult Corpses: The Two Criteria Dental Method*, 37 J. FORENSIC SCI. 1373 (1992); Ohtani & Yamamoto, *Estimation of Age from a Tooth by Means of Racemization of an Amino Acid, Especially Aspartic Acid) Comparison of Enamel and Dentin*, 37 J. FORENSIC SCI. 1061 (1992).

In 1990, the California legislature enacted California Welfare & Institutions Code § 680 reading:

> In any case in which a person is alleged to be a person described in Section 601 or 602, or subdivision (a) of Section 604, and the age of the person is at issue and the court finds that a

infants and children. The baby teeth are referred to as deciduous dentition.[116] The first baby teeth erupt at approximately six months; all the deciduous teeth should have erupted by two years of age. Between the sixth and eleventh year, the typical person begins to replace deciduous teeth with adult dentition. The first molar may erupt at six years, the second at age 12, and the third at 18. Computerized image analysis is now being used to enhance the accuracy of age estimates based on examination of teeth.[117] Age can also be estimated by analyzing the aspartic acid racemization in both enamel and dentine.[118]

> scientific or medical test would be of assistance in determining the age of the person, the court may consider ordering an examination of the minor using the method described in "The Permanent Mandibular Third Molar" from the Journal of Forensic Odonto-Stomatology, Vol. 1: No. 1: January-June 1983.

There is currently a controversy whether by enacting this statute, the legislature manifested its intent that a proponent of testimony estimating age based on an examination of the third molar would not need to lay the normal evidentiary foundation for the testimony. Reply to People's Answer to Minor's Opposition to Court Order Pursuant to Welfare & Institutions Code Section 608, *In the Matter* of Juan Lopez, No. 116-531 (Juv. Div., Cal. Super. Court, San Francisco Cty.). In the *Lopez* case, the prosecution's expert, Dr. Michael Barkin, claimed that the technique was "99.9% accurate at the point of being 6 months within a person's actual age." *Id.* at 5. However, in the article cited in the above statute, the researcher, Dr. Nortje, conceded that "[i]f we estimate the age of an individual child in a given root stage as the average age for that root stage, the resulting estimate may differ from the true age by as much as 29 months in some cases because of the observed statistical variation about the average." 1 J. FORENSIC ODONTO-STOMATOLOGY 31. Further, in FORENSIC DENTISTRY 116 (1976), Dr. Irvin Sopher cautions that in the 14 to 23 year range, "the skeletal structures rate superior to the teeth in relation to chronological age estimation." It remains to be seen whether the courts will interpret the new statute as obviating the need for compliance with normal foundational requirements and, if not, whether this technique will pass muster under the normal standards. *See* Alex, *Welfare and Institutions Code Section 608: A Kelly-Frye Nightmare*, 18 CALIFORNIA ATTORNEYS FOR CRIMINAL JUSTICE FORUM 21 (May/June 1991) ("This statute is dangerous and should not be construed to give Kelly-Frye acceptance to a method whose reliability in the scientific community has not been established. Such results are inconclusive, preliminary in nature, and subject to several variables. For the purpose of age determination, the admissibility of expert testimony based upon the application of this technique does not pass the ... test of Kelly-Frye and, consequently, is not admissible in a court of law ....").

116. BASS, FORENSIC ANTHROPOLOGY (unpublished manuscript on file with the National College of District Attorneys, Bates College of Law, University of Houston, Houston, Texas). *See also* Kumar & Sridhar, *Estimation of the Age of an Individual Based on Times of Eruption of Permanent Teeth*, 48 J. FORENSIC SCI. 1 (1990); Miller, Dove & Cottone, *Failure of Use of Cemental Annulations in Teeth to Determine the Age of Humans*, 33 J. FORENSIC SCI. 137 (1988).

117. Lopez-Nicolas & Luna, *Application of Automatic Image Analysis (IBAS System) to Age Calculation. Efficiency in the Analysis of Several Teeth from a Single Subject*, 50 FORENSIC SCI. INT'L 195 (1991); Kambe, Yonemitsu, Kibayashi & Tsunenari, *Application of a Computer Assisted Image Analyzer to the Assessment of Area and Number of Sites of Dental Attrition and Its Use for Age Estimation*, 50 FORENSIC SCI. INT'L 97 (1991).

118. Ohtani, Ohhira, Watanabe, Ogasawara & Sugimoto, *Estimation of Age from Teeth by Amino Acid Racemization: Influence of Fixative*, 42 J. FORENSIC SCI. 137 (1997); Carolan, Gardner, Lucy & Pollard, *Some Considerations Regarding the Use of Amino Acid Racemization in Human Dentine as an Indicator of Age at Death*, 42 J. FORENSIC SCI. 10 (1997); Ohtani, *Studies on Age*

A microscopic examination of the core of skeletal bones can provide further evidence.[119] The analyst measures the osteons or canals in the core of the bone.[120] Analysis of femoral cores appears to yield more accurate age estimates than the cores of tibia or humeri.[121] An age estimate, based on microscopic techniques, may be accurate to a plus or minus five year range.[122]

Preliminary research indicates that the quantification of certain minerals present in bones (iron, zinc, phosphorous, magnesium, lipids, cholesterol, and proteins) may similarly furnish valuable clues to dating bones.[123]

There has also been research on the question of whether age estimates can be based on the metamorphosis of the rib.[124] The researchers devised a system of nine phases that the extremity progresses through and attempted to correlate ages with the phases. They concluded that an examination of the morphology of the rib is helpful in estimating age. Other researchers are investigating the use of analysis of chest plate X-rays to determine age.[125]

Occupation

Unusual osteological features can also enable the anthropologist to identify the occupation of the decedent.[126] For example, in one case, an osteological

---

Estimation Using Racemization of Aspartic Acid in Cementum, 40 J. FORENSIC SCI. 805 (1995); Mornstad, Pfeiffer & Teivens, *Estimation of Dental Age Using HPLC-Technique to Determine the Degree of Aspartic Acid Racemization*, 39 J. FORENSIC SCI. 1425 (1994). *See also* Ohtani, Matsushima, Kobayashi & Kishi, *Evaluation of Aspartic Acid Racemization Ratios in the Human Femur for Age Estimation*, 43 J. FORENSIC SCI. 949 (1998).

119. Thompson, *Microscopic Determination of Age at Death in an Autopsy Series*, 26 J. FORENSIC SCI. 470 (1981).

120. *Id.* at 471.

121. *Id.*

122. Bucklin, *supra* note 61, at 202.

123. Castellano, Villanueva & von Frenckel, *Estimating the Date of Bone Remains: A Multivariate Study*, 29 J. FORENSIC SCI. 527 (1984).

124. Iscan & Loth, *Determination of Age from the Sternal Rib in White Male: A Test of the Phase Method*, 31 J. FORENSIC SCI. 122, 131 (1986) ("The present study suggests that age can be successfully estimated to within a phase of the actual age of the rib"); Iscan, Loth & Wright, *Age Estimation from the Rib by Phase Analysis: White Females*, 30 J. FORENSIC SCI. 853 (1985); Hoppa & Saunders, *Two Quantitative Methods for Rib Seriation in Human Skeletal Remains*, 43 J. FORENSIC SCI. 174 (1998); Stout, Dietze, Iscan & Loth, *Estimation of Age Using Cortical Histomorphometry of the Sternal End of the Fourth Rib*, 39 J. FORENSIC SCI. 778 (1994); Dudar, Pfeiffer & Saunders, *Evaluation of Morphological and Histological Adult Skeletal Age-at-Death Estimation Techniques Using Ribs*, 38 J. FORENSIC SCI. 677 (1993).

125. Barres, Durigon & Paraire, *Age Estimation from Quantitation of Features of "Chest Plate" X-Rays*, 34 J. FORENSIC SCI. 228, 232 (1989) (the authors assert that this method compares favorably to Iscan's method of determining age on the basis of rib analysis).

126. Weinker & Wood, *Osteological Individuality Indicative of Migrant Citrus Laboring*, 33 J. FORENSIC SCI. 562 (1988).

pathology on the right shoulder of the skeleton helped the anthropologist determine that the decedent had spent significant time working as a citrus fruit picker.[127]

Stature

Finally, the anthropologist can estimate the individual's stature from skeletal remains. The anthropologist measures the dimensions of the long bones and compares the measurements with existing charts.[128] The femur is particularly useful in making the estimate. New research suggests that reliable estimates can likewise be based on the dimensions of the vertebral column.[129] Foot and shoe measurements can also assist in estimating stature.[130]

---

127. *Id.*

128. Bucklin, *supra* note 61, at 202; Giles, *Corrections for Age in Estimating Older Adults' Stature from Long Bones*, 36 J. FORENSIC SCI. 898 (1991) ("Because in the 20th century stature has gradually increased in virtually all populations, the apparent decrease in stature of older people is a composite: an actual stature decrease incident to aging ... and a decrease attributable to the fact that the maximum stature attained by older people is less than that attained by adults born later in the century ...."); Giles & Hutchinson, *Stature- and Age-Related Bias in Self-Reported Stature*, 36 J. FORENSIC SCI. 765 (1991) (after measuring a decedent's stature, the pathologist usually compares it with the reported stature of the suspected decedent; for example, the pathologist may consider the height reported on the suspected decedent's driver's license; however, there are indications that many persons, particularly short persons, overestimate their height when they report it); Willey & Falsetti, *Inaccuracy of Height Information on Driver's Licenses*, 36 J. FORENSIC SCI. 813 (1991); Abdel-Malek, Ahmed, El Sharkawi & El Hamid, *Prediction of Stature from Hand Measurements*, 46 FORENSIC SCI. INT'L 181 (1990) (measurements of hand length and hand breadth); Badkur & Nath, *Use of Regression Analysis in Reconstruction of Maximum Bone Length and Living Stature from Fragmentary Measures of the Ulna*, 45 FORENSIC SCI. INT'L 15 (1990); Simmons, Jantz & Bass, *Stature Estimation from Fragmentary Femora: A Revision of the Steele Method*, 35 J. FORENSIC SCI. 628 (1990); Giles & Klepinger, *Confidence Intervals for Estimates Based on Linear Regression in Forensic Anthropology*, 33 J. FORENSIC SCI. 1218 (1988); Rao, Gupta & Sehgal, *Determination of Length of Human Long Bones of Hands from Their Fragments*, 40 FORENSIC SCI. INT'L 279 (1989); Robbins, *Estimating Height and Weight from Size of Footprints*, 31 J. FORENSIC SCI. 143 (1986); Tibbetts, *Estimation of Stature from the Vertebral Column in American Blacks*, 26 J. FORENSIC SCI. 715 (1981). *But see* Kahane & Thornton, *Discussion of "Estimating Height and Weight from Size of Footprints,"* 32 J. FORENSIC SCI. 9 (1987); Galloway, *Estimating Actual Height in the Older Individual*, 33 J. FORENSIC SCI. 126 (1988); Kodagoda & Jayasinghe, *A Preliminary Test of Pearson's Formula for Estimation of Height of Sri Lankans*, 36 FORENSIC SCI. INT'L 241 (1988); Lundy, *A Report on the Use of Fully's Anatomical Method to Estimate Stature in Military Skeletal Remains*, 33 J. FORENSIC SCI. 534 (1988); Sciulli & Pfau, *A Method for Estimating Weight in Children from Femoral Midshaft Diameter and Age*, 39 J. FORENSIC SCI. 1280 (1994); Holland, *Estimation of Adult Stature from Fragmentary Tibias*, 37 J. FORENSIC SCI. 1223 (1992); Jantz, *Modification of the Trotter and Gleser Female Stature Estimation Formulae*, 37 J. FORENSIC SCI. 1230 (1992); Meadows & Jantz, *Estimation of Stature from Metacarpal Lengths*, 37 J. FORENSIC SCI. 147 (1992).

129. Lundy, *Sacralization of a Sixth Lumbar Vertebra and Its Effect upon the Estimation of Living Stature*, 33 J. FORENSIC SCI. 1045 (1988); Meadows & Jantz, *Allometric Secular Change in*

§ 19-5. Cause of Death.

After identifying the decedent, the pathologist focuses on the question of how the decedent died. This question has three aspects: the cause of death, the mechanism of death, and the manner or mode of death. This section deals with the first aspect, cause of death (COD).

§ 19-5(A). Blunt Force Injuries.

Blunt force injuries produce both external and internal lesions. Although many injuries contain features of all three, individual wounds can usually be subdivided into contusions, abrasions, and lacerations.

A common blunt force lesion is a contusion or bruise. A bruise is caused by blunt trauma generally to the surface of the body. Force can be transmitted internally to cause bruising of internal organs in tissues. Thus, a bruise may be located remote to the point of impact. In this type of injury involving the skin, there is no break in the skin. However, the force disrupts blood vessels below the skin and causes tissue hemorrhage. The blood exits or extravasates from the damaged vessels and infiltrates the tissue. The action of certain enzymes and the decomposition of hemoglobin cause the color of the bruise to change over time. At first, the bruise might appear red to violet. Within three days, the color could change to dark blue. Within five to seven days, the bruise may take on a greenish appearance. Within eight to 10 days, the bruise may turn yellow; and in 13 to 18 days, the skin would return to normal. However, it must be recognized that the healing of a bruise shows considerable individual variability.

The next significant blunt force injury is an abrasion. An abrasion occurs when a blunt force scrapes or compresses the external surface of the body. The force removes the skin surface and denudes or exposes the area. There is ordinarily little bleeding accompanying an abrasion. The most important forensic implication of an abrasion is that it indicates a point of impact. There are four basic types of abrasions. A scratch occurs when a pointed object passes over the

---

the Long Bones from the 1800s to the Present, 40 J. FORENSIC SCI. 762 (1995); Jantz, Hunt & Meadows, *The Measure and Mismeasure of the Tibia: Implications for Stature Estimation*, 40 J. FORENSIC SCI. 758 (1995); Jason & Taylor, *Estimation of Stature from the Length of the Cervical, Thoracic, and Lumbar Segments of the Spine in American Whites and Blacks*, 40 J. FORENSIC SCI. 59 (1995).

130. Giles & Vallandigham, *Height Estimation from Foot and Shoeprint Length*, 36 FORENSIC SCI. INT'L 1134 (1991); Jasuja, Singh & Jain, *Estimation of Stature from Foot and Shoe Measurements by Multiplication Factors: A Revised Attempt*, 50 FORENSIC SCI. INT'L 203 (1991); Gordon & Buikstra, *Linear Models for the Prediction of Stature from Foot and Boot Dimensions*, 37 J. FORENSIC SCI. 771 (1992).

skin and moves a layer of skin in front of the object.[131] Second, an impact (pressure) abrasion occurs when an object is stamped against the skin, as when tire tread moves over skin surface.[132] A friction (sliding) abrasion is caused by linear pressure on the skin if the pressure is accompanied by movement.[133] If a rough object comes in contact with a wide area of skin surface, the abrasion is occasionally termed a brush burn, although it is somewhat of a misnomer.[134]

A third common type of external lesion is a laceration. Here the skin surface and often the underlying tissue are torn. Internal structures can also be lacerated.[135] There are several types of lacerations.[136] Splitting occurs when the skin is crushed between two hard objects such as skull and rock.[137] If the skin is in a relatively fixed position when the force is applied, overstretching resulting in tearing can occur; a kick to the head might cause this type of laceration. Lacerations can also result from grinding compression.[138] When a car runs over a body, the compression might cause avulsion, actual separation of skin from underlying tissue. Simple tearing can be caused by irregular or sharp objects such as a stick.[139] Lastly, chop injuries with features of cuts and lacerations are inflicted by heavy-edged instruments such as hatchets.[140] The shape of the laceration may give a clue to the type of object that caused the laceration.[141] If the object has a blunt round end which strikes the body, the laceration will often have a stellate or star shape. If the object has an edge, as in the case of a hammer, the laceration may have a crescent shape. A linear round object such as a metal rod will produce a linear laceration with a Y at the very end.

Blunt force capable of causing serious external lesions may cause major internal injury. A person can have a serious internal injury from blunt trauma with only mild or no apparent external injury. A common injury would be a fracture of a bone,[142] a break in the bone's continuity. There are several types of fractures.[143] If a fracture produces a single break without other fragmentation of

---

131. CASE, BLUNT FORCE INJURIES (unpublished manuscript on file at Department of Pathology, St. Louis University Medical School).

132. *Id.*

133. *Id.*

134. *Id.*

135. Cohle, Hawley, Berg, Kiesel & Pless, *Homicidal Cardiac Lacerations in Children*, 40 J. FORENSIC SCI. 212 (1995) ("Cardiac lacerations ... are almost never accidental").

136. *Id.* at 3.

137. *Id.*

138. *Id.*

139. *Id.*

140. *Id.*

141. *Id.*

142. Zhi-Jin & Jia-Zhen, *Study of the Microstructures of Skull Fracture*, 50 FORENSIC SCI. INT'L 1 (1991) (the utility of the scanning electron microscope in studying skull fractures).

143. Wecht, *supra* note 21, at 25-29.

the bone, the fracture is termed simple. When there is other fragmentation, the fracture is called multiple or comminuted. If the fracture breaks skin, the fracture is termed open or compound.

In addition to the fracture of bones, blunt trauma may cause internal bleeding by disruption of internal organs or vascular structures. The bleeding itself is termed hemorrhage.[144] If the escaping blood collects in tissue or a body space to form a localized mass, the collection is called a hematoma.[145]

Blunt Force Injuries to the Brain

An understanding of brain injuries requires an appreciation of the composition of the brain and its coverings. The outermost skin covering is often termed the scalp, it covers the skull which encases the brain with its protective membranes. The layer of membrane closest to the inner skull surface is the dura, the next layer the arachnoid, and the final layer the pia mater. These three layers serve as protective coverings for the cerebrum, which is what most laypersons have in mind when they use the expression, "brain." In reality, the brain consists of the cerebellum and brainstem in addition to the cerebrum.

There are numerous types of intracranial injuries. An epidural or extradural hematoma can occur between the skull and the dura.[146] A hematoma in this region is normally caused by a fracture. A fracture tearing the middle meningeal artery can cause severe bleeding, leading to coma and death — in some cases rapidly.[147]

A subdural hematoma can develop in the space between the dura and the arachnoid.[148] Symptoms may not become manifest until days after the trauma.

A subarachnoid hematoma can occur between the arachnoid membrane and the brain. Although subarachnoid hemorrhage commonly occurs in a head injury, extensive subarachnoid hemorrhage often results from natural disease processes affecting the intracranial arteries such as ruptured aneurysms.

Epidural, subdural, and subarachnoid hematoma are sometimes referred to as extracerebral lesions. There are also intracerebral lesions directly involving the cerebrum. A concussion is a state of temporary unconsciousness produced by a head injury. A contusion (a bruise of the brain) is a more severe injury; the period of unconsciousness, if present, is frequently longer, and there may be minor hemorrhaging.[149] The most severe injury would be a full laceration or tearing of

---

144. *Id.*

145. *Id.*

146. *Id.* at 25-23. Collins & Davis, *A Retrospective and Prospective Study of Cerebral Tissue Pulmonary Embolism in Severe Head Trauma*, 39 J. Forensic Sci. 624 (1994).

147. *Id.*

148. *Id.* at 25-54.

149. *Id.* at 25-55.

the brain.[150] Lacerations can lead to intracerebral hematomas.[151] A coup injury occurs on the side of the brain which sustained the impact of the blunt force. However, since the cerebrum has some mobility within the skull, contrecoup injuries are possible. These injuries occur on the side of the head opposite the impact. Predominantly coup injury suggests a moving object striking a stationary head (being struck with a hammer) while predominantly contrecoup injuries suggest that the moving head struck a fixed surface (tripping and striking the head on a sidewalk).

Battered Child and Shaken Baby Syndrome

Children are not only particularly vulnerable to blunt force injuries; child abuse is so widespread that unfortunately, children are frequently subjected to such injuries.[152] The high incidence of multiple fractures and subdural hematoma in children was first noted by Caffey in 1946.[153] In 1962, Kempe coined the term, "battered child syndrome."[154]

There are several different types of abusers.[155] The intermittent abuser batters the child periodically, but there are periods of proper care between batterings. A one-time abuser may be stopped either by his own sense of self-restraint or by the child's death. Constant abusers batter the child frequently because of the abuser's impulsive immature personality or outright hatred for the child.[156] An ignorant abuser inflicts injury on the child because the abuser does not understand the probable effect of his or her conduct on the child.[157] In an example cited by Wecht and Larkin, a mother poured pepper down her child's throat because she had heard that the pepper would stop the child's crying without harming the child.[158]

The injuries inflicted on children by abusers include, among others, abrasions, lacerations, fractures, and contusions.[159] The injured parts of the child's body

---

150. *Id.*

151. *Id.* at 25-56.

152. *See generally* Wecht & Larkin, *The Battered Child Syndrome, in* LEGAL MEDICINE 1980 31 (C. Wecht ed. 1980).

153. *Id.*

154. *Id.*

155. *Id.* at 32.

156. *Id.* at 33.

157. *Id.* at 34.

158. *Id.*

159. *Id.* at 35-38; Paul, *The Medical Examination in Sexual Offences against Children*, 17 MED. SCI. LAW 251 (1977) (the article details the type of examination which the expert should conduct to determine whether the child has been subjected to abuse. Lyon, Gilles & Cory, *Medical Evidence of Physical Abuse in Infants and Young Children*, 28 PAC. L.J. 93 (1996) (an excellent, detailed review of the types of bruises, fractures, and intracranial injuries indicative of child abuse); Walker,

often include the head, abdomen, and chest.[160] The abdomen may be damaged when the abuser delivers a kidney punch to the child.[161] A head injury may result if the abuser shakes the child too hard. If the abuser squeezes the child hard, there may be a chest or abdominal injury. There may also be retinal hemorrhages and subdural hemorrhage of the optic nerve.[162]

As noted in § 19-10, many courts now permit forensic pathologists to testify not only that a child's body exhibited certain injuries but also that those injuries are characteristic of battered child syndrome. Diagnostic radiologists can help establish the cause and date of any bone fractures.[163] Each case must be evaluated

---

Cook & Lambert, *Skeletal Evidence for Child Abuse: A Physical Anthropological Perspective*, 42 J. FORENSIC SCI. 196 (1997).

160. Fossum & Descheneaux, *Blunt Trauma of the Abdomen in Children*, 36 J. FORENSIC SCI. 47 (1991); Wecht & Larkin, *supra* note 152, at 39-41.

161. *Id.* at 41.

162. Riffenburgh & Sathyavagiswaran, *The Eyes of Child Abuse Victims: Autopsy Findings*, 36 J. FORENSIC SCI. 741 (1991); Rao, Smith, Choi, Xiaohu & Kornblum, *Autopsy Findings in the Eyes of Fourteen Fatally Abused Children*, 39 FORENSIC SCI. INT'L 293, 299 (1988) (such hemorrhages "are not common in non-abused children"). Thayer, *Medical Indications of SBS*, 12 CRIM. JUST. 18, 19 (Summer 1997) ("Child abuse experts credit Dr. John Caffey, a pediatric radiologist, as being the first to recognize SBS as an association in infants of subdural hematoma (*i.e.*, internal bleeding in the brain), and retinal hemorrhages with little or no external head injury. In 1972, Dr. Caffey wrote *On the Theory and Practice of Shaking Infants: Its Potential Residual Effects of Permanent Brain Damage and Mental Retardation* (Aug. 1972)"; "Levitt and other SBS experts such as Alexander state that features observed by Caffey, such as subdural hematomas, retinal hemorrhaging, and certain bone fractures (such as broken ribs or other 'long bones'), are not the cause of death in SBS babies, but rather 'markers' or presenting signs and symptoms characteristic of SBS"; "Hematomas in SBS victims result when the perpetrator's shaking causes the infant's head repeatedly to experience such rapid acceleration and deceleration that the baby's brain literally moves about within the brain's three membranes (the pia mater, the arachnoid, and the dura mater), causing a shearing or rupturing of the mass of small bridging veins covering the brain"; "Child abuse experts, especially pediatric radiologists and opthalmologists, have concluded that retinal hemorrhages (RH) are 'highly specific' but not pathognomonic (a definitive symptom) of SBS"); Sargent, Kennedy & Kaplan, *"Hyperacute" Subdural Hematoma: CT Mimic of Recurrent Episodes of Bleeding in the Setting of Child Abuse*, 41 J. FORENSIC SCI. 314 (1996) ("There is a proportionally high incidence of subdural hematoma in cases of child abuse, due in part to the increased susceptibility of the immature brain to trauma."); Gilliland & Folberg, *Shaken Babies — Some Have No Impact Injuries*, 41 J. FORENSIC SCI. 114 (1996) ("Retinal hemorrhages continue to show themselves to be a good marker of infants injured by vigorous, intentional shaking."). However, there is a rare natural disease of infancy, glutaric aciduria, that can result in neurologic symptoms similar to the brain damage caused by violent shaking. *Rare Childhood Disorder Mimics "Shaken Baby" Abuse*, AMER. MED. NEWS, Nov. 11, 1996. However, that disease does not result in retinal hemorrhages.

163. Brown, Fox & Hubbard, *Medical and Legal Aspects of Battered Child Syndrome*, 50 CHI.-KENT L. REV. 45 (1973).

by correlating the investigative and physical findings. Caution is warranted in this area.[164]

Even greater wariness is warranted when the expert relies on shaken baby syndrome.[165] In these cases, there is usually no evidence that the baby suffered prior, repeated injuries. Worse still, there are sometimes no outward signs of physical injury.[166] Nevertheless, experts are sometimes willing to opine that on a specific occasion, the baby was shaken to death. The theory is that "an infant's relatively weak neck muscles and relatively large head ma[k]e him particularly susceptible to brain injuries from shaking . . . ."[167] In the absence of an impact site, the expert searches for "markers," including brain swelling, subdural bleeding, and retinal hemorrhages.[168] However, many forensic experts are dubious that a baby can be literally shaken to death in this manner without leaving outward signs of physical injury.[169] There are other rare conditions, including glutaric aciduria[170] and oxteogensis imperfecta (brittle bone disease)[171] which can account for some of the same signs as the alleged syndrome.

§ 19-5(B). Sharp Force Injuries.

There are three basic types of wounds that can be inflicted by sharp-edged instruments: cuts, stabs, and chops.[172]

A cut is sometimes called an incised wound; it leaves a sharp defect in the skin.[173] In a cut, the length of the wound is generally greater than its depth. Cut wounds are ordinarily relatively superficial.

---

164. Some have asserted that at least some pathologists use the following criteria to determine whether the syndrome is present: The child is under three years of age; there is evidence of several bone injuries sustained at different times; there are subdural hematomas; the case history given the hospital by the child's custodian does not fit the wound pattern; and there is evidence of neglect of the child. MATUSINKA, PROSECUTION OF DOMESTIC VIOLENCE CASES (unpublished manuscript on file with the National College of District Attorneys, Bates College of Law, University of Houston, Houston, Texas). However, our reviewer indicated that he is uncomfortable with that generalization.

165. Hansen, *Why Are Iowa's Babies Dying?*, 84 A.B.A. J. 75 (Aug. 1998).

166. *Id.* at 77.

167. *Id.* at 78.

168. *Id.*

169. *Id.* at 77.

170. This is a rare natural disease of infancy. *Rare Childhood Disorder Mimics "Shaken Baby" Abuse*, AMER. MED. NEWS, Nov. 11, 1996. However, that disease does not result in retinal hemorrhages.

171. Cata, *Child Abuse v. Temporary Brittle Bone Disease*, 22 NAT'L L.J. 16 (Aug. 1998).

172. The signatures of sharp force trauma can sometimes be identified even if the body is badly burned. Herrmann & Bennett, *The Differentiation of Traumatic and Heat-Related Fractures in Burned Bone*, 44 J. FORENSIC SCI. 461 (1999).

173. *See* Clark, Sandusky, Hawley, Pless, Fardal & Tate, *Fatal and Near-Fatal Animal Bite Injuries*, 36 FORENSIC SCI. INT'L 1256 (1991) (bites by pit bulls). Patel, *Artefact in Forensic*

In a stab wound,[174] the depth of the wound usually exceeds its length. A stab can be caused by either a sharp-pointed instrument such as an ice pick or an instrument such as a knife with a sharp edge.

Chopping wounds are inflicted by heavy instruments such as axes, cleavers, and hatchets. Chops are ordinarily larger wounds than either cuts or stabs and are frequently associated with fractures of the underlying bones.

A careful examination of a knife wound may enable the forensic pathologist to reach several conclusions. At the outset, the pathologist may be able to determine whether the instrument that caused the wound had one or two sharp edges.[175] If the instrument had a single sharp edge, the stab wound will have a point at one end, but it will be blunt at the other end.[176] If the instrument had a double-sharp edge, the wound will have two sharp points.[177]

The pathologist may also be able to estimate the length of the instrument that caused the wound.[178] The pathologist measures the depth of the wound, the distance from the skin surface to the apex of the wound. A knife, however, can create a stab wound much longer than its blade.[179] The reason is that when the knife is pushed into the body, the skin tissue compresses. However, it would be difficult for a two-inch knife to create a ten-inch wound. Thus, the pathologist can exclude some weapons with relative confidence, but it is virtually impossible to determine the exact length of the instrument. Obviously, if the blade was only partially inserted, the wound track will be shorter than the blade.

The pathologist can also estimate the width of the blade that caused the knife wound. However, due to skin elasticity, here too the estimate is only a general approximation, not an exact determination. More accurate determinations of the width of the blade can be made if a stab wound through a bone is identified.

The location of some wounds — "defense wounds" — may indicate the victim was trying to defend himself during the assault.[180] However, the pathologist cannot tell if the assailant is right- or left-handed.

The pathologist should be able to determine the direction of the stab. If the stab cuts through thick fat underlying the skin, the slant of the wound canal may

---

Medicine: Postmortem Rodent Activity, 39 J. FORENSIC SCI. 257 (1994) (the results of such activity can sometimes be misinterpreted as homicidal mutilation of the corpse).

174. Hunt & Cowling, *Murder by Stabbing*, 52 FORENSIC SCI. INT'L 107 (1991).

175. Bucklin, *supra* note 61, at 211.

176. *Id.*

177. *Id.*

178. *Id.* at 212. Wayne v. Benson, 89 F.3d 530, 533 (8th Cir. 1996) ("At Wayne's trial, a forensic pathologist testified that the murder weapon probably had a blade about one and a half inches long and one-half inch wide"), *cert. denied*, 519 U.S. 1096 (1997).

179. *Id.*

180. *Id.* ("At Wayne's trial, a forensic pathologist testified that the murder weapon probably had a blade about one and a half inches long and one-half inch wide").

indicate the direction from which the stab came.[181] The wound may be caused by an arrow. An arrow wound can closely simulate a bullet wound.[182] However, arrow wounds have distinguishing features.[183] Bullet wounds are discussed in the immediately following subsection.

§ 19-5(C). Gunshot Wounds.

Pathologists are often called on to analyze gunshot wounds. The Federal Bureau of Investigation estimates that firearms are involved in approximately two-thirds of all homicides in the United States.[184] Any discussion of gunshot wound pathology must begin with the observation that when a pistol or rifle fires, several types of material exit the barrel. The material that travels the farthest is the bullet itself. Powder also leaves the barrel, but it does not travel as far as the bullet. Next, soot exits the barrel. Finally, flames and gases reach a short distance beyond the end of the barrel. These materials help the forensic pathologist to analyze gunshot wounds and, on the basis of that analysis, make certain determinations.

Types of Gunshot Wounds

Gunshot wounds fall into two categories: entrance and exit wounds.

Entrance wounds. Pathologists classify entrance wounds on the basis of the distance between the skin surface and the muzzle when the weapon discharged. At any range, the entry of the bullet into the skin causes two effects: a hole and an abrasion collar[185] or margin. As the bullet stretches the skin and pushes its way into the body through the skin, it scrapes away some of the outer layer of the skin around the edge of the hole. This rim is called the abrasion collar. However, the characteristics of these effects and other features will vary, depending on the range of the shot.

---

181. Wecht, *supra* note 21, at 25-44.

182. Hain, *Fatal Arrow Wounds*, 34 J. FORENSIC SCI. 691 (1989); Downs, Nichols, Scala-Barnett & Lifschultz, *Handling and Interpretation of Crossbow Injuries*, 39 J. FORENSIC SCI. 428 (1994).

183. Randall & Newby, *Comparison of Gunshot Wounds and Field-Tipped Arrow Wounds Using Morphologic Criteria and Chemical Spot Tests*, 34 J. FORENSIC SCI. 579, 585 (1989) (the wounds differ with respect to the shape of the central defect and the presence of both abrasion rings and wipe-off material such as lead deposits); Taupin, *Arrow Damage to Textiles—Analysis of Clothing and Bedding in Two Cases of Crossbow Deaths*, 43 J. FORENSIC SCI. 205 (1998).

184. Bucklin, *supra* note 61, at 203.

185. Randall & Jaqua, *Gunshot Entrance Wound Abrasion Ring Width as a Function of Projectile Diameter and Velocity*, 36 J. FORENSIC SCI.138 (1991) ("The authors postulate that abrasion width is a function of the ratio of projectile velocity and the maximum deformation velocity of the target skin").

One type of wound is a contact wound.[186] If the muzzle is against the surface when the weapon discharges, the flame and gas emitted from the muzzle scorch hair and skin in the area. This scorching is usually termed searing. In some cases, when the muzzle was pressed firmly against the skin, there will also be an imprint or profile of the muzzle. The abrasion ring is round if the shot was head-on but oval if the bullet struck at an angle (although rings with these shapes are not confined to contact wounds). In many cases involving contact wounds of the scalp, the entrance wound is stellate or star-shaped in appearance.[187] In this type of contact wound, the gasses initially blow into the wound; but there is then a backlash, deflecting the gasses back and tearing the edge of the wound. In other instances, though, the hole is circular. First, if the weapon was .22 caliber, the firearm discharges so little gas that there may be no tearing. Second, when the contact occurred over a cavity such as the chest or abdomen, the gasses blow in; but there is little or no backlash. The edges of the hole frequently bevel inward and are often burned. Inside the hole the pathologist should find soot and powder; like the gasses, these materials enter the wound. Many contact wounds have a pinkish tint. The tint results from the presence of carboxyhemoglobin and carboxymyoglobin, created by the mixture of hemoglobin (or myoglobin) and carbon monoxide. Gunsmoke has a high carbon monoxide content, creating a cherry-red discoloration in the wound. This carbon monoxide can also be seen in some close (but not contact) wounds. It also may be seen at the exit wound. Further, there may be backspatter in a contact or close-range wound.[188]

Another type of gunshot wound is a close-range wound, up to perhaps six inches from the skin surface. A key difference between a contact and a close-range wound is the final resting place of the soot. In a contact wound the soot comes to rest inside the wound. In a close-range wound, the soot deposits around the wound. This soot deposit is variously called blackening, fouling, or smudging.

A third kind of gunshot wound is an intermediate range shot, potentially up to 3½ to 4 feet from the skin surface. At this intermediate distance, there would be no soot on the skin surface. Since they have greater mass than the soot, particles

---

186. Bucklin, *supra* note 61, at 204. Smith, Berryman, Symes & LeVaughn, *Identification of Gunpowder in Healed Wounds*, 38 J. FORENSIC SCI. 739 (1993) (a contact wound to the abdomen). *See also* Smith, Symes, Berryman & LeVaughn, *Characteristic Features of Entrance Wounds from Hollow-Point Bullets*, 38 J. FORENSIC SCI. 323 (1993) (characteristic central tags).

187. Alakija, Dowling & Gunn, *Stellate Clothing Defects with Different Firearms, Projectiles, Ranges, and Fabrics*, 43 J. FORENSIC SCI. 1148 (1998) ("The .22-caliber rifle did not produce stellate tearing in these fabrics at any range. The .22-caliber pistol always produced stellate tears at tight contact and loose contact ranges; non-stellate defects were produced by this pistol at ranges of 2 cm or greater. The .30-.30 Winchester rifle produced stellate tears at all contact and close ranges up to and including 8 cm. The 12-gauge shotgun only produced stellate tears at loose contact ....").

188. Burnett, *Detection of Bone and Bone-Plus-Bullet Particles in Backspatter from Close-Range Shots to Heads*, 36 J. FORENSIC SCI. 1745 (1991).

of powder carry farther and imbed in the skin or mark. This phenomenon is termed peppering, stippling, or tattooing. Most handguns using flake powder rarely cause stippling beyond 18 inches. Ball powder can stipple the body up to approximately 3½ to 4 feet.

The last type of wound is a distant shot. Once the distance exceeds that at which stippling occurs, it is difficult to estimate the distance; a shot from six feet may appear the same as a shot from 30 feet. In a distant shot, the hole tends to be circular or oval with a smooth abrasion rim. Because the skin is somewhat elastic, the size of the hole in the skin bears no constant relationship to the caliber of the bullet. In attempting to characterize the wound, the pathologist considers the damage done by the expanding gasses, the bullet, and debris — both on the bullet and in the air which the bullet travels through.[189] In a contact wound, all three types of damage are present. In a near contact wound, the gasses dissipate; and, hence, the damage is caused by the bullet and the debris. In a distant wound, the damage is done by the bullet.

The above paragraphs describe typical wounds. However, atypical wounds are sometimes encountered.[190] The possible causes of such wounds include intermediate targets (such as clothing that the bullet passes through), ricochets, inappropriate weapon/ammunition combinations,[191] poor weapon construction, and the use of misaligned silencers.[192] In addition, if the bullet strikes a bone, most notably the skull, the grazing effect can create an atypical defect in the bone — sometimes called a keyhole lesion.[193]

Shotgun entrance wounds also pose special problems.[194] The number of projectiles in a shotgun shell can vary markedly. If the firer uses 00 buckshot,

---

189. JACHIMCZYK, VIOLENT DEATH INVESTIGATION AND PATHOLOGY (unpublished manuscript on file with the National College of District Attorneys, Bates College of Law, University of Houston, Houston, Texas).

190. Donoghue, Kaleklar, Richmond & Teas, *Atypical Gunshot Wounds of Entrance: An Empirical Study*, 29 J. FORENSIC SCI. 379 (1984); Lantz, Stone, Broudy & Morgan, *Terminal Ballistics of the 9mm with Action Safety Bullet or Blitz-Action-Trauma (BAT) Ammunition*, 39 J. FORENSIC SCI. 612 (1994).

191. Thogmartin & Start, *9 mm Ammunition Used in a 40 Caliber Glock Pistol: An Atypical Gunshot Wound*, 43 J. FORENSIC SCI. 712 (1998).

192. *Id.*; Stone & Petty, *Interpretation of Unusual Wounds Caused by Firearms*, 36 J. FORENSIC SCI. 736 (1991) (interposed targets such as clothing, windows, and body parts can cause confusing patterns and can lead to misidentification of the points of entrance and exit).

193. Dixon, *Keyhole Lesions in Gunshot Wounds of the Skull and Direction of Fire*, 27 J. FORENSIC SCI. 555 (1982).

194. Harruff, *Comparison of Contact Shotgun Wounds of the Head Produced by Different Gauge Shotguns*, 40 J. FORENSIC SCI. 801; Horvath, Gardner & Siegel, *Range of Fire Estimates from Shotgun Pellet Patterns: The Effect of Shell and Barrel Temperature*, 38 J. FORENSIC SCI. 585 (1993). With shotguns, pellet spread increases proportionally to the firing distance. The presence of a wad imprint usually indicates a firing distance of between 10 and 30 feet. However, pellets will disperse with a billiard ball effect if they strike an intermediary target.

there may be only nine to 15 projectiles. However, if the person uses #9 birdshot, there could be 270 projectiles. If the shot is at short range — up to three or four feet, there will be a single hole or defect; and the wadding enters the wound together with the shot. Just beyond four feet, the group of shot begins to separate. Hence, in a medium range shot, there is still a single defect; but the hole has an irregular margin similar to a cookie cutter edging. At longer distances, the group of shot has separated, there will be multiple wounds, and the wadding may create a separate defect. The choke of the shotgun has a significant effect on the shot pattern at a given distance. If the shooter simultaneously discharges both shots from a double-barrel shotgun, externally the wound may simulate a wound made by the discharge of a single barrel.[195]

Exit wounds.[196] In an exit wound, there is no powder stippling or charring around the wound; there should be no powder or gas to impact the skin surface. Typically, there is no rim of abrasion. However, there may be a misleading marginal abrasion if the exit wound was "shored," that is, if the skin was up against a firm material such as concrete, metals or even certain tight garments when the bullet exited. As the skin is pressed between the exiting bullet and the supporting material, a pressure abrasion can be created which sometimes resembles an entry abrasion rim. In an exit wound, the hole in the skull bevels outward.[197] The exit hole tends to be larger than an entrance hole.[198] However, the size of the defect is not a reliable criterion for differentiating between entry and exit wounds. Moreover, the shape of the hole is very variable. As the bullet passes through the body, the bullet may tumble and leave the body sideways. If the bullet fragmented bone, the bone fragments may exit separately, creating secondary exit wounds. The bullet itself could break up into several particles, or

---

195. Medich, Cohle, Burritt & Davison, *Single Wound Produced by Simultaneous Discharge of Both Shells from a Double-Barrel Shotgun*, 35 J. FORENSIC SCI. 473 (1990).

196. Grey, *The Incredible Bouncing Bullet: Projectile Exit Through the Entrance Wound*, 38 J. FORENSIC SCI. 1222 (1993) ("the first reported case that documents findings that prove that the projectile exited through the entrance wound"); Smith, Berryman, Symes, Francisco & Hnilica, *Atypical Gunshot Exit Defects to the Cranial Vault*, 38 J. FORENSIC SCI. 339 (1993).

197. *But see* Peterson, *External Beveling of Cranial Gunshot Entrance Wounds*, 36 J. FORENSIC SCI. 1592 (1991) (although entrance gunshot wounds generally have internal beveling, external beveling can occur; and consequently, an entrance wound can sometimes be mischaracterized as an exit wound; however, our reviewer states that the wound should not be mischaracterized if the examiner identifies the dominant beveling).

198. *But see* Quatrehomme & Iscan, *Characteristics of Gunshot Wounds in the Skull*, 44 J. FORENSIC SCI. 568 (1999) ("In four cases . . . entrances were larger than exits"); *Forensic Mental Health Issues Addressed at NACDL Winter Meeting*, 54 CRIM. L. (BNA) 1584, 1587 (Mar. 23, 1994) ("The idea that a bullet's exit hole is bigger than the entrance hole is 'total garbage,' [Dr. Patrick] Besant-Matthews [, formerly Chief Medical Examiner in Seattle, Washington,] said. One of the many reasons it could be the other way around is 'gas tearing.' He explained that if a gun is fired very close to the body, the pressurized gas that follows the bullet out of the muzzle is enough to tear a hole in the flesh – a hole bigger than the exit wound").

the jacket may separate from the bullet in the body; the bullet fragments and the jacket could leave secondary exit wounds.

In shotgun killings, exit wounds are rare. Unless the firer used very large shot or the shot struck a thin portion of the body (*e.g.*, arm), the shot probably will not have enough energy to pass through the body.

Analysis of Gunshot Wounds

An examination of the gunshot wound will assist in reaching several determinations.

Characterizing the wound as contact, close, intermediate, or distant will aid in determining the range of fire, the muzzle-to-target distance. In addition to studying the characteristics of the wound, the pathologist may rely on certain rules of thumb. Some experts believe that "between three and 10 yards the dispersion of shot is about one inch per yard for a fully choked barrel and between one and two inches per yard for a cylindrical barrel," while others follow the rule that "[t]he diameter of the pellet pattern in inches equals the muzzle distance from the target in yards."[199] Since factors other than range[200] will affect the dispersion of pellets, test firings of the weapon to compare the dispersion found on the body should be conducted if possible. Test firing is one of the firearms identification techniques discussed in Chapter 14.

The pathologist can also estimate the direction or angle of the shot.[201] If the bullet entered the body perpendicularly, the abrasion collar around the hole is circular and of equal width all around the hole.[202] In an angular shot, the abrasion is oval — the greater the angle, the wider the abrasion margin.[203] The pathologist

---

199. Breitenecker, *Shotgun Wound Patterns*, 52 AM. J. CLIN. PATH. 258 (1969); J. MASON, FORENSIC MEDICINE FOR LAWYERS 106 (1978).

200. Even, Bergman, Springer & Klein, *The Effects of Water Soaking on Firing Distance Estimations*, 33 J. FORENSIC SCI. 319 (1988) (soaking of the target by water or blood can affect the gunshot residue and thereby the distance estimation); Zaki & Hanzlick, *Gunshot Wound with Asphalt Related Pseudo-Soot, Pseudo-Tattooing, and Pseudo-Scorching*, 32 J. FORENSIC SCI. 1136 (1987) (contact between the body and an asphalt surface produced artifacts which mimicked the tattooing and soot deposition of a close-range gunshot wound).

201. Bucklin, *supra* note 61, at 206; Suwanjutha, *Direction, Site and the Muzzle to Target Distance of Bullet in the Head and Neck at Close Range as an Indication of Suicide or Homicide*, 37 FORENSIC SCI. INT'L 223 (1988) ("For suicide, the direction of the bullet should be at an angle of elevation in the majority of cases. The position of the handgun in relation to the head in suicide was most often in tight contact and near contact. For homicide, the direction of the bullet should be horizontal in most cases. The bullet was at close range in the majority of cases;" however, our reviewer disagrees with the preceding two sentences); Smith, Berryman & Lahren, *Cranial Fracture Patterns and Estimate of Direction from Low Velocity Gunshot Wounds*, 32 J. FORENSIC SCI. 1416 (1987).

202. W. SPITZ & R. FISHER, THE MEDICOLEGAL INVESTIGATION OF DEATH 204 (1972).

203. *Id.* at 204-05.

can also examine the body's internal organs to determine whether the bullet struck them; the bullet track inside the body helps confirm the angle of entrance. This analysis, however, determines only the anatomic position of the track within the body; the body may not have been upright when the bullet entered the body. Graze wounds of skin or internal organs can indicate the direction the bullet was travelling when it created the wound.[204] Moreover, as a general proposition, the location of an entry wound on a decedent's back indicates that the decedent had his or her back to the shooter at the time the shooter pulled the trigger.[205]

The pathologist can sometimes venture an opinion as to the type of firearm that caused the wound. In a contact wound, the muzzle may have left an impression on the skin. In addition, firearms differ in their capacity to cause damage to body organs.[206] High velocity weapons such as .30-06 and .30-30 hunting rifles can cause massive organ destruction that low velocity firearms of .38, .357, and .45 caliber are incapable of causing. Hence, the extent of damage may be indicative of the kind of weapon used.

Similarly, on occasion the pathologist may be able to surmise the type of ammunition used. Bullets differ in their composition. By carefully removing residue from around and within the wound and subjecting the residue to instrumental analysis such as atomic absorption or neutron activation analysis,

---

204. Dixon, *Determination of Direction of Fire from Graze Gunshot Wounds of Internal Organs*, 29 J. Forensic Sci. 331 (1984); Dixon, *Determination of Direction of Fire from Graze Gunshot Wounds*, 25 J. Forensic Sci. 272 (1980).

205. *But see* Hansen, *Study Says Quick Turns by Suspects Can Account for Gunshot Wounds in Back*, 83 A.B.A. J. 38 (Sep. 1997) ("Conventional wisdom holds that somebody who has been shot in the back must have had his or her back to the person doing the shooting when the decision to pull the trigger was made. But a new study of reaction-response time in a shooting situation suggests that the widely held assumption may not always hold true. It found that a person can turn around in less time than it takes to fire a drawn and pointed weapon. It takes the average person less than a third of a second to turn his or her body 90 degrees, which is about 5/100 of a second faster than the average time it takes to fire a handgun with the finger on the trigger, according to the study. It takes the average person a little more than two-thirds of a second to turn his or her body a full 180 degrees, which is about 1/1000 of a second faster than the average time it takes to fire a gun with a finger outside the trigger guard, the study showed. The results were published in the April 1997 issue of *Wound Ballistics Review*, the journal of the International Wound Ballistics Association").

206. Klatt, Tschirhart & Noguchi, *Wounding Characteristics of .38 Caliber Revolver Cartridges*, 34 J. Forensic Sci. 1387 (1989); Ragsdale & Sohn, *Comparison of the Terminal Ballistics of Full Metal Jacket 7.62-mm M80 (NATO) and 5.56-mm M193 Military Bullets: A Study in Ordnance Gelatin*, 33 J. Forensic Sci. 676, 677 (1988) (the researchers investigate the generalization that the 5.56-mm round creates more severe tissue wounds and conclude that the generalization "is incomplete. Relative wounding potential should be catalogued by specific bullet species and impact velocities rather than weapon type ...."); Jauhari & Bandyopadhyay, *Wound Ballistics: Motion of 9MM, Ball MK2Z, Bullet in Gel*, 5 J. Police Sci. & Admin. 197 (1977); Lantz, Stone, Broudy & Morgan, *Terminal Ballistics of the 9mm with Action Safety Bullet or Blitz-Action-Trauma (BAT) Ammunition*, 39 J. Forensic Sci. 612 (1994).

the pathologist can sometimes single out the type of ammunition. However, our reviewer states that this technique is "controversial."

Moreover, the pathologist may be able to determine the number and sequence of shots.[207] A careful examination of the exit and entrance wounds, internal wound tracks, and the projectiles remaining in the body should permit the pathologist to fix the number of shots striking the body. If while passing through the body the bullets fractured bone, the pathologist may be able to reconstruct the sequence of shots. Fracture lines caused by later shots will stop at fracture lines caused by earlier shots.[208]

§ 19-5(D). Drowning.

Drowning is one of the most difficult causes of death to diagnose.[209] There are several questions that must be considered in any suspected case of drowning.

One question is whether the victim died before entering the water. A killer may attempt to disguise a homicide as an accidental drowning. In resolving this question, some pathologists rely on an examination of the gastrointestinal system. Some pathologists believe that the presence of water in the duodenum (the first part of the small intestine) is evidence that the victim was alive when he or she entered the water. However, other pathologists believe that water in the gastrointestinal tract is not a useful criterion, since water can reach there after death.

If the person was alive upon entry, the next question that arises is whether the cause of the person's death while in the water was drowning. Several tests may aid in answering this question. One test is an ultrasonic[210] or microscopic[211] study for the presence of diatoms, unicellular algae, in the victim's bone marrow. Although in the past some experts claimed that this is a conclusive test for drowning, the current consensus is that the test is nonspecific.[212] Some believe

---

207. Jentzen, Lutz & Templin, *Tandem Bullet Versus Multiple Gunshot Wounds*, 40 J. FORENSIC SCI. 893 (1995); Mann & Owsley, *Human Osteology: Key to the Sequence of Events in a Postmortem Shooting*, 37 J. FORENSIC SCI. 1386 (1992).

208. Dixon, *Pattern of Intersecting Fractures and Direction of Fire*, 29 J. FORENSIC SCI. 651 (1984).

209. Lorente, Lorente & Villanueva, *Postmortem Stability of Lung Surfacant Phospholipids*, 37 J. FORENSIC SCI. 1341 (1992) ("one of the most difficult challenges in forensic pathology").

210. Fukui, Hata, Takahashi & Matsubara, *A New Method of Detecting Diatoms in Human Organs*, 14 FORENSIC SCI. INT'L 67 (1980).

211. Funayama, Aoki, Sebetan & Sagisaka, *Detection of Diatoms in Blood by a Combination of Membrance Filtering and Chemical Digestion*, 34 FORENSIC SCI. INT'L 175 (1987); Bucklin, *supra* note 61, at 220. Pachar & Cameron, *Scanning Electron Microscopy: Application in the Identification of Diatoms in Cases of Drowning*, 37 J. FORENSIC SCI. 860 (1992).

212. *Id.* Pollanen, *The Diagnostic Value of the Diatom Test for Drowning, II. Validity: Analysis of Diatoms in Bone Marrow and Drowning Medium*, 42 J. FORENSIC SCI. 286 (1997); Pollanen, Cheung & Chiasson, *The Diagnostic Value of the Diatom Test for Drowning, I. Utility: A*

that the procedure is characteristic, but not conclusive.[213] Another test analyzes the heart blood to determine whether small cells known as macrophages normally found in the lungs are present.[214] The theory underlying this test is that when the victim drowns, water enters the lungs and causes the air cells or alveoli in the lungs to burst. The rupture of the alveoli permits the rushing water to wash the macrophages from the lungs into the bloodstream. This test is also not specific for drowning. Still another technique is examining the body externally to determine whether there is a mushroom or cone of froth in the mouth and nose and froth in the lower airways. The froth supports a finding of a drowning death.[215] Still another new technique is testing the level of serum strontium.[216] Egyptian researchers have reported their findings, indicating that the serum strontium level can help differentiate between deaths due to drowning and postmortem immersion of a victim.[217] Other techniques for diagnosing drowning are now under study.[218]

A final issue is whether the drowning occurred in fresh or sea water. In the view of some pathologists, the resolution of this question ordinarily requires sampling the blood on the right and left sides of the heart.[219] These pathologists believe that in a fresh water drowning, the level of chloride is often lower in the left heart. In sea water drownings, the reverse is true. To be significant, the difference in chloride levels should exceed 18 milli-equivalents.[220] Freshwater drowning usually results in dilution of the blood, electrolyte imbalance, hemolysis, increased blood volume, and overloading of the heart. Saltwater

---

Retrospective Analysis of 771 Cases of Drowning in Ontario, Canada, 42 J. FORENSIC SCI. 281 (1997); Ludes, Coste, Tracqui & Mangin, *Continuous River Monitoring of the Diatoms in the Diagnosis of Drowning*, 41 J. FORENSIC SCI. 425 (1996).

213. Fukui, Hata, Takahashi & Matsubara, *supra* note 210, at 67.

214. Karkola & Neittaanmaki, *Diagnosis of Drowning by Investigation of Left Heart Blood*, 18 FORENSIC SCI. INT'L 149 (1981). *See also* Jianping & Enshou, *A Study of the Diagnosis of Drowning by Examination of Lung Chlorophyll(a) of Planktons With a Spectrofluorophotometer*, 53 FORENSIC SCI. INT'L 149 (1992).

215. Bucklin, *supra* note 61, at 219-20.

216. Abdallah, Hassan, Kabil & Ghanim, *Serum Strontium Estimation as a Diagnostic Criterion of the Type of Drowning Water*, 28 FORENSIC SCI. INT'L 47 (1985).

217. *See also* Fornes, Pepin, Heudes & Lecomte, *Diagnosis of Drowning by Combined Computer-Assisted Histomorphometry of Lungs with Blood Strontium Determination*, 43 J. FORENSIC SCI. 772 (1998) (there was "no overlap between values found in drowned subjects and those in non-drowned subjects").

218. Jeanmonod, Staub & Mermillod, *The Reliability of Cardiac Haemodilution as a Diagnostic Test of Drowning*, 52 FORENSIC SCI. INT'L 171 (1992); Lorente, Hernandez-Cueto, Villanueva & Luna, *The Usefulness of Long Surfactant Phospholipids (LSPs) in the Diagnosis of Drowning*, 35 J. FORENSIC SCI. 1367 (1990); Yu-Chuan, Zhao-Ke & Jia-Zhen, *The Significance of Detecting Serum Fluorine Level in the Diagnosis of Drowning*, 46 J. FORENSIC SCI. 289 (1990).

219. Bucklin, *supra* note 61, at 219-20.

220. *Id.*

drowning causes hemoconcentration. However, perhaps the majority of pathologists believe that there is no single, simple test.

§ 19-5(E). Hyperthermia, Fire Deaths, and Hypothermia.

Exposure to extremes of heat and cold can result in death. Hyperthermia is an abnormal elevation of the body temperature, usually above 106 degrees F. It has many causes. Various natural disease processes can affect the brain's thermoregulatory center and cause elevated temperature. Hyperthermia can also result from exposure to high environmental temperature and humidity (heat stroke). Fire deaths should be distinguished from hyperthermia deaths.

Deaths occurring in fires may not always be due to actual burning. Suppose, for example, that a person dies during a fire. The thermal burns could have led to death, but there may be a cause other than the burning; for instance, fires create smoke, smoke contains carbon monoxide, and the victim could have died of carbon monoxide poisoning.[221]

When a person has been severely burned, the body's skin may exhibit linear, sharp-edged lesions similar to cuts.[222] These lesions develop because the heat splits the skin and underlying tissue. In addition, the heat causes the body's muscles to shorten, often leaving the body in a pugilistic position.[223] Fire can fracture bones, including the skull.[224] The heat may cause the content in the cranium to expand, literally bursting the skull open. Dry heat may also singe the hair. These heat effects must not be confused with pre-existing injuries.

One of the determinations that a pathologist attempts to make is whether the victim was alive when the fire was in progress. For example, it is important to uncover a fire set by a killer in an attempt to conceal a murder by burning the house with the body in it. Although there are certain exceptions such as flash fire, individuals who were alive during the fire will have soot within the lower airway and will have elevated levels of carbon monoxide. The body should also be examined for the presence of injuries such as gunshots and stabs that are unrelated to the fire.

---

221. *Death by Fire or Trauma? Determinations Using Postmortem Carboxyhemoglobin Levels*, 20 SCI. SLEUTHING REV. 19 (Winter 1996) ("It is generally accepted that a blood carboxyhemoglobin (COHb) level of 50% or greater indicates that a person was alive and breathing during a fire, and further, that such a COHb level is sufficient, in of itself, to cause death"; the article cites new research published in Wirthwein & Pless, *Carboxyhemoglobin Levels in a Series of Automobile Fires, Death Due to Crash or Fire?*, 17 AM. J. FOR. MED. PATH. 117 (1996)).

222. *Id.* at 216; Parks, Noguchi & Klatt, *The Epidemiology of Fatal Burn Injuries*, 34 J. FORENSIC SCI. 399 (1989).

223. Bucklin, *supra* note 61, at 216.

224. *Id.*

Other types of heat produce different types of lesions. For example, wet heat scalds the skin.[225] Or if the burning was caused by electrical current passing through the body, there may be deep scars and yellow-gray, elevated areas of skin.[226] When the current passes through the heart area, death may be due to ventricular fibrillation, in which the heart muscle fibers contract irregularly.[227] Current passing through the brainstem can also cause death.

It is customary to differentiate among several degrees of burns. In first-degree burns such as sunburn, the skin takes on a red color. In second-degree burns, blistering occurs. Elevated, often circular vesicles form on the superficial skin surface. In third-degree burns, the burn affects the entire thickness of the skin. Finally, in fourth-degree burns, charring and loss of body parts can occur.[228]

Like extreme heat, severe cold can cause death. In these cases, the cause of death is hypothermia. Hypothermia is abnormally low body temperature, usually under 95 degrees F.[229] The time lapse preceding death by hypothermia in an exposure victim is affected by such factors as the victim's clothing, the victim's prior state of health and activity, body habitus, and the nature of the exposure (dry cold vs. cold water immersion).

§ 19-5(F). Asphyxia.

Asphyxia is a broad term encompassing numerous conditions in which there is a mechanical or chemical interference with the uptake or utilization of oxygen. Asphyxia can occur in several ways.[230] One way is hanging. Judicial hangings

---

225. United States v. Vretta, 790 F.2d 651, 660-61 (7th Cir.) (the pathologist testified that detached skin was caused by scalding), *cert. denied*, 479 U.S. 851 (1986); McConnel v. Commonwealth, 33 Ky. L. Summary 15 (Ky., Nov. 14, 1986) (expert testified that child appeared to have been held in scalding water).

226. Bucklin, *supra* note 61, at 216-17. L. Geddes, Handbook of Electrical Hazards and Accidents (1995); Mellen, Weedn & Kao, *Electrocution: A Review of 155 Cases with Emphasis on Human Factors*, 37 J. Forensic Sci. 1016 (1992).

227. Hahson, *Electrocution by Low-Voltage*, 9 Forensic Sci. Dig. 85 (1983).

228. Glassman & Crow, *Standardization Model for Describing the Extent of Burn Injury to Human Remains*, 41 J. Forensic Sci. 152 (1996). There is a rule of nines for burns in adults: 18% for the chest and abdomen, 18% for the back and buttocks, 9% each for the front and back of each lower limb, 4.5% each for the front and back of the head and the front and back of each upper limb, and 1% for the genital area. The percentage distribution is somewhat different in infants.

229. J. Weston & V. McCarty, *supra* note 67, at 305; Hirvonen, Huttunen & Hiltunen, *Creatine Phosphokinase in Serum and Cerebrospinal Fluid, and Microscopic Findings in Brain and Heart in Hypothermic Rabbits*, 39 Forensic Sci. Int'l 271, 278 (1988) (based on research with rabbits, the authors suggest that an assay for CPK may be "an additional method of supporting the diagnosis of hypothermia;" however, our reviewer states that postmortem CPK is not a worthwhile test because it is difficult to interpret).

230. Wecht, *supra* note 21, at 25-72; Tamaki & Katsumata, *Enzyme-Linked Immunoabsorbent Assay for Plasma Thyroglobulin Following Compression of the Neck*, 44 Forensic Sci. Int'l 193 (1990) (the results suggest that "Tg was released by mechanical force on the thyroid gland added at

should be distinguished from other types of hangings. In judicial hangings as a method of administering the death penalty, the sudden drop snaps the cervical vertebra.[231] In suicidal hangings, in contrast, death usually results from compression of the blood vessels in the neck, thus preventing blood from getting to or draining from the brain. The object used to compress the neck often leaves a furrow or mark on the neck.[232] In addition, there may be minute hemorrhagic spots (petechial hemorrhages) on the victim's face and eyelids.[233] A non-judicial hanging rarely may be accidental rather than suicidal. Various asphyxial modalities which decrease the supply of oxygen to the brain (hypoxia) apparently heighten sexual gratification.[234] Accidental deaths during autoerotic asphyxial episodes are generally due to hanging and occur almost exclusively in males. If a person engaging in such activity becomes unconscious, he is unable to relieve the pressure on the neck; and death will ensue.[235]

Asphyxia can also be caused by strangulation. If the strangler uses a ligature such as a rope, it typically leaves furrows on the victim's neck.[236] Or the strangulation may be manual throttling. Throttling leaves bruises and occasionally fingernail marks on the neck. More so than ligature strangulation, throttling can cause fractures in the neck area, particularly of the larynx and the hyoid bone, which is located at the base of the tongue.[237]

---

the agonal stage;" the elevated Tg level may therefore be diagnostic for external compression of the neck; our reviewer adds that this suggestion is not generally accepted); Ito & Kimura, *Histological Examination of the Temporal Bone in Medicolegal Cases of Asphyxia*, 44 FORENSIC SCI. INT'L 135 (1990) (an examination of the temporal bone can help the pathologist determine whether the cause of the asphyxia was drowning, strangulation by ligature, or manual strangulation; however, our reviewer states that he would not rest such a determination on the examination of the temporal bone); Gilson, Balko, Blisard & Taylor, *Morphologic Variations of the External Arcuate Nucleus in Infants Dying of SIDS: A Preliminary Report*, 39 J. FORENSIC SCI. 1076 (1994) (in this study, victims of SIDS tended to have differences in the morphology of this region which is thought to be involved in respiratory regulation).

231. Bucklin, *supra* note 61, at 212. James & Nasmyth-Jones, *The Occurrence of Cervical Fractures in Victims of Judicial Hanging*, 54 FORENSIC SCI. INT'L 81 (1992).

232. Bucklin, *supra* note 21, at 213. Clark, Feczko, Hawley, Pless, Tate & Fardal, *Asphyxial Deaths Due to Hanging in Children*, 38 J. FORENSIC SCI. 344 (1993).

233. *Id.*

234. Wecht, *supra* note 21, at 25-76.

235. Bucklin, *supra* note 61, at 214; Garza-Leal & Landron, *Autoerotic Asphyxial Death Initially Misinterpreted as Suicide and a Review of the Literature*, 36 J. FORENSIC SCI. 1753 (1991); Byard, Hucker & Hazelwood, *A Comparison of Typical Death Scene Features in Cases of Fatal Male and Female Autoerotic Asphyxia with a Review of the Literature*, 48 FORENSIC SCI. INT'L 113 (1990).

236. Wenyou, Junzhu & Xinman/Mau, *A New Staining Method for Constriction Marks in Skin*, 50 FORENSIC SCI. INT'L 147 (1991).

237. Bucklin, *supra* note 61, at 214. Maxeiner, *"Hidden" Laryngeal Injuries in Homicidal Strangulation: How to Detect and Interpret These Findings*, 43 J. FORENSIC SCI. 784 (1998); Pollanen & Chiasson, *Fracture of the Hyoid Bone in Strangulation: Comparison of Fractured and*

Finally, the lack of oxygen may be caused by smothering and choking. Smothering and choking entail an obstruction to the passage of air. The obstruction can occur externally (smothering) or internally (choking). Externally, a killer might place a pillow over the airways, including the mouth and nose.[238] Internally, foreign material might be aspirated into the respiratory passage. A "cafe coronary" occurs when a bolus of food blocks the airway, usually lodging at the opening to the larynx.

The previously described occurrences are types of mechanical asphyxia. Various chemicals can also cause asphyxia. Examples of these are carbon monoxide[239] and cyanide.

§ 19-6. Mechanism of Death.

The previous section surveyed some of the leading causes of death. The cause of death differs from the mechanism of death. The cause of death is the injury or disease which initiates the chain of events leading to death. The mechanism of death is the "biochemical or physiologic abnormality produced by the cause of death which [is] incompatible with life."[240] The mechanisms of sudden death fall into three broad categories: exsanguination, sudden heart stoppage, and slow heart stoppage.[241] In exsanguination, the victim bleeds to death. Death in which the heart stops suddenly is often due to conditions in which the lethal physiologic disruption involves the heart directly. Examples include electrocution and sudden coronary artery death. Interference with the respiratory control centers (for example, barbiturate overdose) features the cessation of breathing followed shortly by the cessation of cardiac activity. The recognition of the mechanism which is operative in a given case steers the pathologist to certain groups of causes of death.

Unfractured Hyoids from Victims of Strangulation, 41 J. FORENSIC SCI. 110 (1996); Pollanen, Bulger & Chiasson, *The Location of Hyoid Fractures in Strangulation Revealed by Xeroradiography*, 40 J. FORENSIC SCI. 303 (1995); Ubelaker, *Hyoid Fracture and Strangulation*, 37 J. FORENSIC SCI. 1216 (1992).

238. Avis & Archibald, *Asphyxial Suicide by Propane Inhalation and Plastic Bag Suffocation*, 39 J. FORENSIC SCI. 253 (1994).

239. Yoshida, Adachi, Watabiki, Tatsuno & Ishida, *A Study on House Fire Victims: Age, Carboxyhemoglobin, Hydrogen Cyanide and Hemolysis*, 52 FORENSIC SCI. INT'L 13 (1991). *See also* Avis & Archibald, *Asphyxial Suicide by Propane Inhalation and Plastic Bag Suffocation*, 39 J. FORENSIC SCI. 253 (1994); Wagner, Clark, Wesche, Doedens & Lloyd, *Asphyxial Deaths from the Recreational Use of Nitrous Oxide*, 37 J. FORENSIC SCI. 1008 (1992).

240. WRIGHT, FORENSIC PATHOLOGY 5 (unpublished manuscript on file with the National College of District Attorneys, Bates College of Law, University of Houston, Houston, Texas).

241. *Id. See also* W. CURRAN, A. MCGARRY & C. PETTY, MODERN LEGAL MEDICINE, PSYCHIATRY AND FORENSIC SCIENCE 252-53 (1980).

§ 19-7. Manner or Mode of Death.

The questions of the cause and mechanism of death lie within medical expertise. However, the forensic pathologist must deal with another question, the manner or mode of death. This issue requires medicolegal expertise and is often the most subtle issue facing the pathologist.

In some cases, the indicators of the manner of death are so equivocal that the pathologist must report the manner as "undetermined." However, in the overwhelming majority of cases, the pathologist will be able to assign the death to one of the categories in the "NASH" classification: natural causes — accidental — suicidal — homicidal.[242]

A natural death is one resulting from the inevitable failure of a vital body function due solely to a natural disease process. Most deaths encountered by both hospital and forensic pathologists fall into this classification.[243] If it was clear from the outset that the death was due to a recognized natural disease, it is unlikely that the death would have been reported to the medical examiner, unless the death was sudden and unexpected or fell into one of the other categories of reportable diseases set forth in the particular statute in effect in that medical examiner system.

In accidental death, death is due to trauma but the trauma was not intentionally applied to the body. Even a death caused by a gunshot wound could be accidental. For example, although rare, a person might have inadvertently discharged a firearm while cleaning it.

Death is suicidal if the trauma is intentionally self-induced.[244] Of course, there are many methods of committing suicide.[245] If a person commits suicide with a

---

242. 3 B M. HOUTS & I. HAUT, COURTROOM MEDICINE § 23.01 (1984).

243. DiMaio & DiMaio, *Natural Death as Viewed by the Medical Examiner: A Review of 1000 Consecutive Autopsies of Individuals Dying of Natural Disease*, 36 J. FORENSIC SCI. 17 (1991) ("One of the most common misconceptions ... in regard to medical examiner offices is that the cases handled by these offices are exclusively traumatic in origin. In fact, the largest category of deaths seen in medical examiners' offices are natural deaths").

244. Jobes, Casey, Berman & Wright, *Empirical Criteria for the Determination of Suicide Manner of Death*, 36 J. FORENSIC SCI. 244 (1991) (in 126 cases, the Empirical Criteria for the Determination of Suicide (ECDS) "predicted 100% of the suicides and 83% of the accidents, thus correctly identifying 92% of all cases"); Little & Sparks, *Brain Markers and Suicide: Can A Relationship Be Found?*, 35 J. FORENSIC SCI. 1393, 1400 (1990) (although some have suggested that "some persons who commit suicide have altered neurochemistry in their brains," "neurochemical methods for detecting suicide cannot be considered forensically useful" at present); Rosenberg, Davidson, Smith, Berman, Buzbee, Gantner, Gay, Moore-Lewis, Mills, Murray, O'Carroll & Jobes, *Operational Criteria for the Determination of Suicide*, 33 J. FORENSIC SCI. 1445, 1450-51 (1988) (a working group of coroners, medical examiners, statisticians, and public health officials developed a list of criteria related to the decedent's intent).

245. Morgen, Schramm, Kofoed, Steensberg & Theilade, *Automobile Exhaust as a Means of Suicide: An Experimental Study with a Proposed Model*, 43 J. FORENSIC SCI. 827 (1998); Shaw &

knife, hesitation wounds are often present.[246] Hesitation wounds are typically superficial and are frequently located in the same general area as the fatal wound. The hesitation marks often parallel the fatal wound. Some hesitation wounds are created as trial wounds to find out what the contemplated lethal wound will feel like — the "courage" factor. Other victims desire to suffer some pain before death, possibly to atone for feelings of guilt. If a clever killer used a knife, the killer might make additional wounds in the same vicinity as the fatal thrust to give the appearance of hesitation wounds. These wounds can usually be distinguished from true hesitation wounds, since they will generally have the appearance of wounds inflicted after death or when the blood pressure is low or absent.

Lastly, death can be homicidal. Here a third party intentionally causes the injuries leading to death. This definition is broad enough to include cases in which the third party is lawfully exercising a right of self-defense or defense of others. Accordingly, a homicidal death is not necessarily an unlawful killing.

In knife deaths (and other types of assaultive death), one important type of evidence of the death's homicidal character is the presence of defense wounds. The victim often sustains these cuts on his extremities (such as hands and forearms) as he tries to parry the killer's thrusts and perhaps grab the knife away from the killer. In some suicides, in order to conceal the suicide and ensure that surviving relatives collect insurance proceeds, decedents have feigned defense wounds before killing themselves.

As a practical matter, in the investigation of manner of death, forensic pathologists sometimes use presumptions.[247] For example, many pathologists follow the rule of thumb that deaths caused by firearms are usually intentional, that is, either homicidal or suicidal.[248] The presumption is rebuttable in the pathologist's mind.[249] For example, the location of the wound, the presence of a gun cleaning kit nearby, and traces of gun cleaning chemicals on the decedent's hands might rebut the presumption and lead the pathologist to characterize the death as accidental. However, it should be recognized that in determining manner of death, pathologists rely on their past experience. If that experience has been that a certain type of death is almost always accidental or nearly always homicidal, the past experience may influence the pathologist's judgment.

Hsu, *Horizontal Distance and Height Determining Falling Pattern*, 43 J. FORENSIC SCI. 765 (1998) (distinguishing between a person accidentally falling to death and one intentionally leaping to death).

246. Wecht, *supra* note 21, at 25-46.

247. WRIGHT, *supra* note 240, at 5.

248. *Id.*

249. *Id.*

§ 19-8. Time of Death.

The determination of time of death (TOD) is unfortunately an inexact science.[250] In the words of one expert, the science remains in the "dark ages."[251] Even the best trained and most experienced pathologist cannot positively pinpoint a time of death.[252] In the typical cases, only a gross estimate can be ventured.[253] Moreover, the estimate becomes progressively less reliable as the time frame between death and the autopsy — the postmortem interval — increases. The longer the time lapse, the greater is the margin of error.

The immediate consequences of death occur within five to 10 minutes. They include, *inter alia*: cessation of breathing and circulation, changes in the appearance of the eyes, loss of natural muscle tone (primary flaccidity), and pallor of the skin. The cessation of circulation causes the pallor of the skin; as the blood stops circulating, it drains from the capillaries and venules of the skin.

These immediate consequences lead to two other sets of consequences: the early or short-term changes and the late or long-term changes.[254] Together these changes serve as a postmortem clock which allows the pathologist to gauge the time of death within very broad parameters. Each sign of death, whether early or late, can vary with the conditions prevailing at the time of death.[255] Moreover, on many of the signs, even the leading experts disagree over the correct chronology.[256]

This section describes the various techniques pathologists rely on to estimate time of death. In a given case, the pathologist may employ several techniques. By using multiple techniques, the pathologist can improve the reliability of the estimate;[257] but even then the pathologist's opinion remains merely an estimate.

§ 19-8(A). Short-Term Signs.

As previously stated, the shorter the postmortem interval, the more trustworthy the estimate of time of death is likely to be. Consequently, time estimates based on early signs of death have smaller margins of error than estimates based on the late changes. However, even when the pathologist relies exclusively on the early

---

250. Houts, *Time of Death: Still the Dark Ages of Proof*, 10 TRAUMA 7 (Aug. 1968).

251. *Id.* at 1.

252. *Id.* at 7.

253. *Id.* at 3-4.

254. For charts listing these changes, *see* Wecht, *supra* note 21, at 25-20, 25-22-23.

255. Burton, *Fallacies in the Signs of Death*, 19 J. FORENSIC SCI. 529 (1974).

256. *Id.*

257. Schoenly, Griest & Rhine, *An Experimental Field Protocol for Investigating Postmortem Interval Using Multidisciplinary Indicators*, 36 J. FORENSIC SCI. 1395 (1991); Henssge, Madea & Gallenkemper, *Death Time Estimation in Case Work. II. Integration of Different Methods*, 39 FORENSIC SCI. INT'L 39 (1988) ("it is possible to narrow down a reliable time period for a stated death by means of the lower and upper limits of different criteria").

signs, he cannot pinpoint a given hour as the time of death.[258] Like the long-term changes, the short-term signs are subject to numerous variables; and an opinion based on the short-term signs is at best an approximation. Some experts assert that estimates based on the early signs are subject to a margin of error of two to four hours.[259]

The three leading short-term signs are livor mortis, rigor mortis, and algor mortis — sometimes referred to as the triad of death.[260]

Livor Mortis

Livor mortis, lividity, or hypostasis is the postmortem discoloration of the body. When the person dies, circulation ceases. Gravity draws the blood into the lower or dependent regions of the body, where the blood pools. When the blood sinks to the lower areas, those areas take on a red-purple coloration. Although the stain may superficially resemble a bruise, there is a fundamental difference. In lividity, the blood remains in the vessels. In contrast, when the coloration is due to a bruise, the blood hemorrhages into the tissue.

The onset of the process begins immediately at death, but lividity usually becomes apparent between one and two hours after death.[261] Livor exhibits wide variability. In some severely debilitated individuals it may begin before death. Its appearance can be delayed in anemic persons, and it may never be perceived in some dark-skinned decedents.[262] In its early stage, the coloration is moveable or only partly fixed. If someone presses his finger against the discolored area of skin, the area will blanch or turn white.

In the next stage, the lividity becomes "fixed," maximal, or permanent. In this stage, the color no longer blanches under finger pressure. The experts differ on the time lapse needed for fixation. The most frequent estimates are between six and twelve hours.

Like the other signs, livor mortis can be influenced by several variables. For example, if the decedent were anemic, the lividity might be difficult to detect. High temperatures tend to accelerate the disappearance of lividity.[263]

Rigor Mortis

Rigor mortis is the postmortem rigidity or stiffening of the body. When death occurs, the body immediately loses natural muscle tone — primary flaccidity. At the time of death, a complex series of biochemical alterations takes place. The

258. Camps, *Time of Death*, 10 TRAUMA 9 (Aug. 1968).

259. A. FATTEH, HANDBOOK OF FORENSIC PATHOLOGY 20-29 (1973).

260. Burton, *supra* note 255, at 529.

261. Wecht, *supra* note 21, at 25-20.

262. *See also id.*

263. *Id.*

muscles begin to develop an acid condition, and energy-dependent processes cease. This acid condition is due to a chemical change; the body begins to develop lactic acid. The appearance of rigor is variable. The chemical processes culminating in perceptible rigor start immediately upon death. In most cases, rigor becomes apparent two to four hours after death.[264] The condition may occur within 15 minutes after death or as late as six hours after death.[265] The rigidity first becomes apparent in the eyelids and face and then appears to work its way down the body to the jaw, arms, trunk and legs. The step-wise appearance of rigor from the top of the body to the bottom is only an apparent phenomenon. The process of rigor actually begins in all body muscles at the same time. However, rigor becomes perceptible in the smaller muscles before it does in the larger ones. This accounts for the apparent sequence of the onset and disappearance of rigor mortis. Rigor becomes complete within 12 or 16 hours after death.[266]

However, the condition is merely temporary. As decomposition sets in, the rigor starts to disappear. Rigor ordinarily appears to leave in the apparent order of appearance; it departs first in the face area and works downward. In the body's lower extremities, rigor may persist for between three and five days.[267] If the surrounding temperature is high, rigor may begin to disappear in 24 hours after death; but in most cases, disappearance begins in 36 or 48 hours after death.[268] When the rigor has disappeared, the body is said to be in secondary flaccidity.

Rigor is similar to lividity in that rigor is subject to many factors and, for that reason, "gross variation."[269] Intense emotion or physical activity can hasten the onset of rigor. In fact, if death occurred quickly and the victim realized the impending death, rigor may occur almost instantaneously. This phenomenon is termed cadaveric spasm or cataleptic rigidity. In these cases, the decedent's hand is sometimes found firmly grasping a weapon such as a gun or knife. However, cases of this phenomenon are rare. Some pathologists have never encountered the spasm. High temperatures can cause rigor to appear and disappear earlier than normal.[270] If someone forcibly breaks the rigor, rigor will not return and reestablish itself. If the pathologist does not discover that rigor was broken, he might mistake the broken rigor for its natural disappearance and reach an

---

264. *Id.*

265. *Id.*

266. *Id.*

267. *Id.*

268. *Id.*

269. Camps, *supra* note 258, at 13.

270. Krompecher, *Experimental Evaluation of Rigor Mortis. V. Effect of Various Temperatures on the Evolution of Rigor Mortis*, 17 FORENSIC SCI. INT'L 19 (1981). *See also* Krompecher & Bergerioux, *Experimental Evaluation of Rigor Mortis. VII. Effect of Ante- and Post-Mortem Electrocution on the Evolution of Rigor Mortis*, 38 FORENSIC SCI. INT'L 27 (1988) (electrocution hastens both the onset and passing of rigor mortis).

erroneous conclusion about the time of death. Cold temperatures retard rigor mortis.

Algor Mortis

Algor mortis is the cooling of the body after death. The phenomenon is sometimes colorfully referred to as the chill of death. After death, the body tends to reach thermal equilibrium with the environment; that is, the body temperature declines until it reaches a plateau equaling the ambient temperature.[271]

Over the years experts have advanced several different formulae for calculating the fall of body temperature.[272] At first it was assumed that body cooling follows Newton's Law of Cooling that the rate of heat loss from a warm object cooling in air is directly proportional to the excess of the object's temperature over its surroundings.[273] Researchers subsequently discovered that body cooling does not follow that norm. Many experts now believe that the curve of cooling is a sigmoid or reverse-S shaped curve such as Figure 19-4.[274]

As Figure 19-4 indicates, there is an initial period of slow cooling. Temperature then drops rapidly — practically in a straight line.[275] As the body temperature nears the environmental temperature, the rate slows again.[276] During this last period of slow temperature fall, the rate of decline seems to follow Newton's Law. Over the entire period of decline, the average loss per hour is approximately 1.5 degrees F.[277] However, the range of temperature loss is wide. Two English researchers recently proposed an amendment to Newton's Law to develop a formula — the time dependent Z equation (TDZE) — to estimate postmortem interval based on body temperature data.[278] The TDZE method requires taking two rectal temperatures, approximately an hour apart.

---

271. Wecht, *supra* note 21, at 25-17.

272. Camps, *supra* note 258, at 9. Lynnerup, *A Computer Program for the Estimation of Time of Death*, 38 J. FORENSIC SCI. 816 (1993); Nokes, Flint, Williams & Knight, *The Application of Eight Reported Temperature-Based Algorithms to Calculate the Postmortem Interval*, 54 FORENSIC SCI. INT'L 109 (1992).

273. Sharpe, *The Rate of Cooling as an Index of the Time of Death*, 10 TRAUMA 19 (Aug. 1968).

274. *Id.;* Sopher, *The Law Enforcement Officer and the Determination of the Time of Death*, F.B.I. LAW ENF. BULL. Reprint, Oct. 1973, at 4. Reprinted with the permission of the Federal Bureau of Investigation.

275. Sharpe, *supra* note 273, at 19.

276. *Id.* at 19-20.

277. Sopher, *supra* note 274, at 4.

278. Green & Wright, *Postmortem Interval Estimates from Body Temperature Data Only*, 28 FORENSIC SCI. INT'L 35 (1985); Green & Wright, *The Theoretical Aspects of the Time Dependent Z Equation as a Means of Postmortem Interval Estimation Using Body Temperature Data Only*, 28 FORENSIC SCI. INT'L 53 (1985).

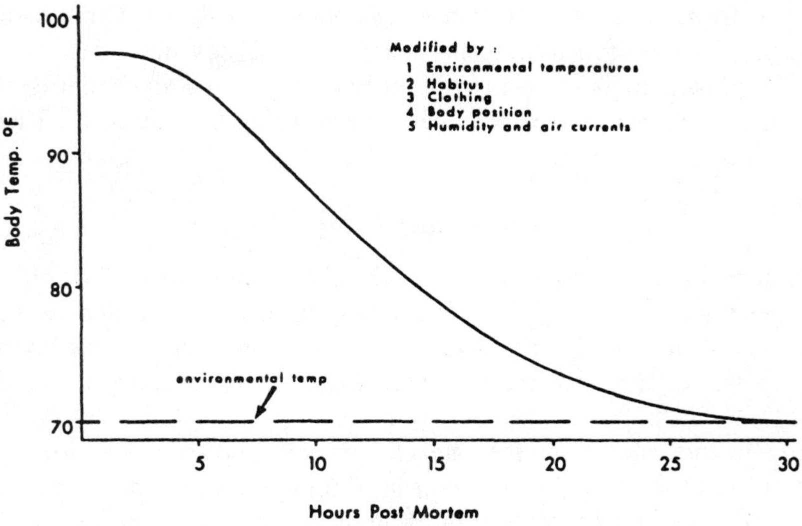

Figure 19-4

Like the other signs in the triad of death, algor mortis is subject to many variables.[279] The state of ventilation of the location of the body can affect the rate of fall. Although the pathologist will usually assume that the body temperature was the normal 98.4 degrees F at the time of death, the assumption may be false; the temperature at that time might have been higher due to an infection or lower if the person was gradually dying for some time.[280] The site at which the pathologist inserts the thermometer can have an effect. The body surface cools before the interior, and there is usually a 1° difference between temperature measured in the mouth and temperature in the rectum.[281] Many European pathologists now insert the thermometer into the brain.[282] Most American pathologists use liver temperatures because of the ease of obtaining measurements. The physical state of the body can have an effect. If the body is

---

279. Camps, *supra* note 258, at 9; Knight, *The Evolution of Methods for Estimating the Time of Death from Body Temperature*, 36 FORENSIC SCI. INT'L 47, 53 (1988) ("the level of accuracy remains low, even in the artificial venue of a controlled environment").

280. Camps, *supra* note 258, at 10.

281. Henssge, *Death Time Estimation in Case Work. I. The Rectal Temperature Time of Death Nomogram*, 38 FORENSIC SCI. INT'L 209 (1988) (the nomogram is based on a single measurement of the rectal temperature). Hensage, *Rectal Temperature Time of Death Nomogram: Dependence of Corrective Factors on the Body Weight Under Stronger Thermic Insulation Conditions*, 54 FORENSIC SCI. INT'L 51 (1992).

282. Burton, *supra* note 255, at 530. *See also* Nokes, Flint, Jaafar & Knight, *The Use of Either the Nose or Outer Ear as a Means of Determining the Postmortem Period of a Human Corpse*, 54 FORENSIC SCI. INT'L 153 (1992).

fat or heavily clothed, the temperature decline will be slower. Other pathologists favor using a series of measurements at a number of body sites.[283]

Although pathologists rely heavily on livor, rigor, and algor mortis, there are other early signs that they can evaluate in estimating time of death. Those other signs include the following.

Stomach Contents

The state of the stomach can be indicative of the time of death.[284] Some experts estimate that a small meal empties in between one and two hours, a medium-sized meal in three to four hours, and a large meal in six hours. Other experts prefer to state that the stomach should empty in between two and four hours.[285]

Many factors can affect the rate of stomach emptying. Abnormal medical conditions such as a drug overdose or head injury can slow or even temporarily stop the digestive process.[286] Fear or excitement can inhibit digestion.[287] The type of food eaten also can influence the rate of digestion.[288]

Age of Bodily Injuries

The age of an injury on the body differs from the time of death. In some cases, there is a typical interval between the occurrence of an injury and the onset of severe symptoms resulting from the injury.[289] If the pathologist has information about the onset of the symptoms, he or she can estimate the time of the occurrence of the causal event. The victim may have suffered the injuries hours before the time of death. However, if the wound would normally be immediately fatal, a determination of the age of the injury is persuasive evidence of the time of death. Many types of injuries follow a normal chronology of color changes.[290] For example, a black eye typically follows this sequence: an initial bluish-red

---

283. Morgan, Nokes, Williams & Knight, *Estimation of the Post Mortem Period by Multiple-Site Temperature Measurements and the Use of a New Algorithm*, 39 FORENSIC SCI. INT'L 89 (1988).

284. J. BOCK, M. LANE & D. MORRIS, IDENTIFYING PLANT FOOD CELLS IN GASTRIC CONTENTS FOR USE IN FORENSIC INVESTIGATIONS — A LABORATORY MANUAL (1988); Suzuki, *Experimental Studies on the Presumption of the Time After Food Intake from Stomach Contents*, 34 FORENSIC SCI. INT'L 83 (1987); Camps, *supra* note 258, at 14.

285. *Id.* at 15.

286. *Id.*

287. *Id.*

288. *Id.*

289. Gilliland, *Interval Duration Between Injury and Severe Symptoms in Nonaccidental Head Trauma in Infants and Young Children*, 43 J. FORENSIC SCI. 723 (1998).

290. Wecht, *supra* note 21, at 25-24. *See also* Langlois & Gresham, *The Ageing of Bruises: A Review and Study of the Colour Changes With Time*, 50 FORENSIC SCI. INT'L 227 (1991).

color; changing to dark violet; turning yellow or yellow-green within a day or two; becoming brown on the fourth or fifth day; and finally disappearing.[291] The injured cells under the discolored area also follow a regular sequence of disintegration and repair. The pathologist can examine the tissues in a microscopic study.[292] The pathologist can also use microscopy to detect healing changes between 24 and 36 hours after a fracture. Within five to seven days after a fracture, calcification can be seen microscopically. It must be remembered that there is wide variation in the rate of resolution of various wounds. The presence of certain markers such as cathespin D can help the pathologist distinguish between a vital wound and one inflicted postmortem.[293] The measurement of other chemical changes such as fluctuations in elemental concentrations can aid the pathologist in determining the time of the infliction of an injury.[294]

Eye Chemistry

Vitreous humor is a fluid in one of the regions of the eye. After death, the glucose and potassium levels, among others, in the vitreous humor change.[295] There has been some research attempting to correlate the changes with the lapse of time postmortem,[296] but many experts remain skeptical of the strength of the correlation.[297] There also has been some research into the phenomenon of corneal

291. Wecht, *supra* note 21, at 25-24.

292. *Id.* at 25-25.

293. Girela, Hernandez-Cueto, Lorente & Villanueva, *Postmortem Stability of Some Markers of Intra-Vital Wounds*, 40 FORENSIC SCI. INT'L 123 (1989).

294. Zhong & Zhen, *Localization and Quantification of Histamine in Injured Skin as Parameters for the Timing of Wounds*, 51 FORENSIC SCI. INT'L 163 (1991); Njau, Epivatianos, Tsoukali-Papadopoulou, Psaroulis & Stratis, *Magnesium, Calcium and Zinc Fluctuations on Skin Induced Injuries in Correlation With Time of Induction*, 50 FORENSIC SCI. INT'L 67 (1991).

295. Pounder, Carson, Johnston & Orihara, *Electrolyte Concentration Differences Between Left and Right Vitreous Humor Samples*, 43 J. FORENSIC SCI. 604 (1998); Madea, Herrmann & Henbge, *Precision of Estimating the Time Since Death by Vitreous Potassium — Comparison of Two Different Equations*, 46 FORENSIC SCI. INT'L 277, 283 (1990) ("equations with a steeper slope than that reported by Sturner should be preferred to avoid systematic overestimations of the time since death"); Coe, *Vitreous Potassium as a Measure of the Postmortem Interval: An Historical Overview and Critical Evaluation*, 42 FORENSIC SCI. INT'L 201 (1989); Madea, Henssge, Honig & Gerbracht, *References for Determining the Time of Death by Potassium in Vitreous Humor*, 40 FORENSIC SCI. INT'L 231 (1989); Stephens & Richards, *Vitreous Humor Chemistry: The Use of Potassium Concentration for the Prediction of the Postmortem Interval*, 32 J. FORENSIC SCI. 503 (1987); Bray, *The Eye as a Chemical Indicator of Environmental Temperature at the Time of Death*, 29 J. FORENSIC SCI. 396 (1984); Bray, Luke & Blackbourne, *Vitreous Humor Chemistry in Deaths Associated with Rapid Chilling and Prolonged Freshwater Immersion*, 28 J. FORENSIC SCI. 588 (1983).

296. Wroblewski, *Estimation of Time of Death by Eye Changes*, 2 FORENSIC SCI. 201 (1973).

297. M. HOUTS, COURTROOM MEDICINE § 1A.04 (1977).

haziness.[298] Corneal hazing which occurs within 10 minutes of death is due to atmospheric drying of the surface of the eye and can be reversed by wetting the eye with water. However, irreversible deeper clouding occurs 10-12 hours after death whether or not the eyes are open.

Enzyme Activities in Muscles

Other researchers have attempted to document that after death, the level of the activity of certain enzymes (protease and creatine phosphokinase) changes.[299] The researchers have attempted to correlate the changes in enzyme activity with the lapse of time postmortem.[300] To date the research has been restricted to rats, but the researchers are hopeful that the technique will also prove applicable to humans.[301]

Retardation of Plant Life Under the Body

If the body comes to rest on ground with plant life, the body may retard the growth of the plants under the body. A consulting botanist may be able to estimate the period of time the body has been resting on top of the plant life by studying the state of retardation of the plants. Alternatively, perennial plants may have begun to grow around the remains of the body. Dendochronology (the study of annual growth rings) may help a botanist estimate the time of death.[302]

---

298. GRADWOHL, LEGAL MEDICINE 81, 94 (F. Camps ed. 3d ed.).

299. Mayer & Neufeld, *Post-Mortem Changes in Skeletal Muscle Protease and Creatine Phosphokinase Activity — A Possible Marker for Determination of Time of Death*, 15 FORENSIC SCI. INT'L 197 (1980); Dachun & Jiazhen, *Localization and Quantification of the Nonspecific Esterase in Injured Skin for Timing of Wounds*, 53 FORENSIC SCI. INT'L 203 (1992). *See also* Kominato, Kumada, Yamazaki & Misawa, *Estimation of Postmortem Interval Using Kinetic Analysis of the Third Component of Complement (C3) Cleavage*, 34 J. FORENSIC SCI. 207 (1989); Kominato, Harada, Yamazaki & Misawa, *Estimation of Postmortem Interval Based on the Third Component of Complement (C3) Cleavage*, 33 J. FORENSIC SCI. 404 (1988); Perry, Bass, Riggsby & Sirotkin, *The Autodegradation of Deoxyribonucleic Acid (DNA) in Human Rib Bone and Its Relationship to the Time Interval Since Death*, 33 J. FORENSIC SCI. 144 (1988); Gallois-Montbrun, Barres & Durigon, *Postmortem Interval Estimation by Biochemical Determination in Birds Muscle*, 37 FORENSIC SCI. INT'L 189 (1988).

300. Mayer & Neufeld, *supra* note 299.

301. *Id.*

302. Willey & Heilman, *Estimating Time Since Death Using Plant Roots and Stems*, 32 J. FORENSIC SCI. 1264, 1265 (1987). *See also* Quatrehomme, Lacoste, Bailet, Grevin & Ollier, *Contribution of Microscopic Plant Anatomy to Postmortem Bone Dating*, 42 J. FORENSIC SCI. 140 (1997) ("This procedure was not based on counting the number of annual rings ... but on demonstrating a completely primary structure without development of secondary formations; this material was considered as a part of a young root system whose development would correspond to about one year").

Infestation of Insects On and Around the Body

After death, insects tend to colonize the body in a particular sequence.[303] The body itself is an inviting microhabitat for many types of insects. Thus, the state of

---

303. Lord, *Collection and Preservation of Forensically Important Entomological Materials*, 28 J. FORENSIC SCI. 936 (1983). *See* Goff, Brown, Hewadikaram & Omori, *Effect of Heroin in Decomposing Tissues on the Development Rate of Boettscherisca peregrina (Diptea, Sarcophagidae) and Implications of This Effect on Estimation of Postmortem Intervals Using Arthropod Development Patterns*, 36 J. FORENSIC SCI. 537 (1991) ("The time required for pupation was significantly greater for colonies fed on tissues from heroin-dosed" specimens); Goff & Flynn, *Determination of Postmortem Interval by Arthropod Succession: A Case Study from the Hawaiian Islands*, 36 J. FORENSIC SCI. 607 (1991); Introna, Suman & Smialek, *Sarcosaprophagous Fly Activity in Maryland*, 36 J. FORENSIC SCI. 238 (1991); Erzinclioglu, *On the Interpretation of Maggot Evidence in Forensic Cases*, 30 MED. SCI. LAW 65 (1990) (in the past, entomologists have often estimated the interval based on the largest maggot present on the corpse; this estimate rests on a misconception about the biology of flies because the first egg may begin to develop even before it is laid on the corpse); Haskell, McShaffrey, Hawley, Williams & Pless, *Use of Aquatic Insects in Determining Submersion Interval*, 34 J. FORENSIC SCI. 622 (1989); Kashyap & Pillay, *Efficacy of Entomological Method in Estimation of Postmortem Interval: A Comparative Analysis*, 40 FORENSIC SCI. INT'L 245 (1989) ("Sixteen insect-infested cadavers were examined and analyzed to evaluate the reliability of the entomological method in estimation of time elapsed since death, in relation to other medicolegal approaches. The entomological method was found statistically more reliable and superior ...."); Introna, Altamura, Dell'Erba & Dattoli, *Time Since Death Definition by Experimental Reproduction of Lucilla Sericata Cycles in Growth Cabinet*, 34 J. FORENSIC SCI. 478 (1989); Scott v. Commonwealth, 685 S.W.2d 184, 185 (Ky. 1984) ("The time of death, the summer of 1982, was determined by insect larvae, which are present only in the summer").here is an excellent paper by Kris Barrett on forensic entomology. The paper was prepared for the "Introduction to Forensic Science" course at American University. The paper can be obtained by writing Mr. Charles Midkiff, National Labortory Center, Bureau of Alcohol, Tobacco and Firearms, 1401 Research Boulevard, Rockville, Maryland. The paper points out that four different types of arthropods are involved: (1) necrophagous species which feed on the carrion itself, the most important category for establishing time of death; (2) predators and parasites on the necrophagous species; (3) omnivorous species which feed on both the carrion and its inhabitants; and (4) adventive/cryptozoic species which use the carrion as an extension of their own environment by sheltering in, on, or under the carcass. The paper also notes the research identifying the various waves of expected arthropod invasions for exposed and buried corpses. Introna, Campobasso & Di Fazio, *Three Case Studies in Forensic Entomology from Southern Italy*, 43 J. FORENSIC SCI. 210 (1998); Goff & Win, *Estimation of Postmortem Interval Based on Colony Development Time for Anoplolepsis longipes (Hymenoptera: Formicidae)*, 42 J. FORENSIC SCI. 1176 (1997); Keiper, Chapman & Foote, *Midge Larvae (Diptera: Chironomidae) as Indicators of Postmortem Submersion Interval of Carcasses in a Woodland Stream: A Preliminary Report*, 42 J. FORENSIC SCI. 1074 (1997); Anderson, *The Use of Insects to Determine Time of Decapitation: A Case-Study from British Columbia*, 42 J. FORENSIC SCI. 947 (1997); K. SMITH, A MANUAL OF FORENSIC ENTOMOLOGY 13-55 (1986); Christopherson & Gibo, *Foraging by Food Deprived Larvae of Neobellieria bullata (Diptera: Sarcophagidae)*, 42 J. FORENSIC SCI. 71 (1997); Anderson & VanLaerhoven, *Initial Studies of Insect Succession on Carrion in Southwestern British Columbia*, 41 J. FORENSIC SCI. 617 (1996); Goff, Brown, Omori & LaPointe, *Preliminary Observations of the Effects of Phencyclidine in Decomposing Tissues on the Development of Parasarcophaga* insect infestation at the time of the body's discovery is a clue to the time of death.[304] A forensic entomologist may be of great aid to the pathologist in evaluating the insect infestation on the body.[305]

There are a number of caveats. The most obvious is that this research is still in its relatively early stages. However, even at this point, it is obvious that given the numerous variables, there are several identifiable dangers. One is that the sequence of infestation probably depends on the geographic region.[306] There can be regional life-cycle differences within a particular insect species. Furthermore, the body may have been deposited at its final resting place some time after death. If the entomologist does not realize this, he or she may underestimate the postmortem interval.[307] Or the insects in question may have gone through more than one growth cycle before the body's discovery. If the entomologist erroneously assumes that there was only one life cycle, again the entomologist may underestimate the interval. When the victim is a baby and the cadaver is found with a diaper containing fecal material, the entomologist might

---

ruficornis (Diptera: Sarcophagidae), 39 J. FORENSIC SCI. 123 (1994); Lord, Goff, Adkins & Haskell, *The Black Soldier Fly Hermetia illucens (Diptera: Stratiomyidae). As a Potential Measure of Human Postmortem Interval: Observations and Case Histories*, 39 J. FORENSIC SCI. 215 (1994); Sperling, Anderson & Hickey, *A DNA-Based Approach to the Identification of Insect Species Used for Postmortem Interval Estimation*, 39 J. FORENSIC SCI. 418 (1994); Greenberg, *Flies as Forensic Indicators*, 28 J. MED. ENTOMOLOGY 565 (1991); E. CATTS & N. HASKELL, ENTOMOLOGY AND DEATH: A PROCEDURAL GUIDE (1990); Goff, Brown, Omori & LaPointe, *Preliminary Observations of the Effects of Amitriptyline in Decomposing Tissues on the Development of Parasarcophaga ruficornis (Diptera: Sarcophagidae) and Implications on This Effect to Estimation of Postmortem Interval*, 38 J. FORENSIC SCI. 316 (1993); Tantawi & Greenberg, *The Effect of Killing and Preservative Solutions on Estimates of Maggot Age in Forensic Cases*, 38 J. FORENSIC SCI. 702 (1993); Goff, Brown & Omori, *Preliminary Observations on the Effect of Methamphetamine in Decomposing Tissues on the Development Rate of Parasarcophaga ruficornis (Diptera: Sacrophagidae) and Implications of this Effect on the Estimations of Postmortem Intervals*, 37 J. FORENSIC SCI. 867 (1992); Schoenly, *A Statistical Analysis of Successional Patterns in Carrion Anthropod Assemblages: Implications for Forensic Entomology and Determination of the Postmortem Interval*, 37 J. FORENSIC SCI. 1489 (1992); Schoenly, Goff & Early, *A BASIC Algorithm for Calculating the Postmortem Interval from Anthropod Successional Data*, 37 J. FORENSIC SCI. 808 (1992).

304. Schrof, *Murder, they chirped: Insect detectives are the latest scientific tool in criminal investigations*, 111 U.S. NEWS & WORLD REP., Oct. 14, 1991, at 67.

305. *See* State v. Needs, 99 Idaho 883, 591 P.2d 130 (1979).

306. VanLaerhoven & Anderson, *Insect Succession on Burned Carrion in Two Biogeoclimatic Zones in British Columbia*, 44 J. FORENSIC SCI. 32 (1999); Avila & Goff, *Anthropod Succession Patterns onto Burnt Carrion in Two Contrasting Habitats in the Hawaiian Islands*, 43 J. FORENSIC SCI. 581 (1998); Rodriguez & Bass, *Insect Activity and Its Relationship to Decay Rates in Human Cadavers in East Tennessee*, 28 J. FORENSIC SCI. 423 (1983); Byrne, Camann, Cyr, Catts & Espelie, *Forensic Implications of Biochemical Differences Among Geographic Populations of the Black Blow Fly, Phormia regina (Meigen)*, 40 J. FORENSIC SCI. 372 (1995).

307. Sopher, *supra* note 274, at 6.

overestimate the interval; the insects may have begun in the fecal material before death, and their maturity might mislead the entomologist.[308] In addition, both the covering of the body[309] and drugs in the system[310] can affect the rate of maturation. Finally, it is ideal if the crime scene investigator collects live, immature specimens.[311] It can be difficult to differentiate among species until they reach adulthood.[312] The laboratory should grow at least two generations to the adult stage.[313] The comparison of the two generations enables the analyst to better estimate the age of the samples found at the scene.

Other researchers are using a related technique, estimating the postmortem interval based on the amount of animal damage to the skeleton.[314]

Other Techniques

Although the above techniques are the leading ones in most widespread use, there is an enormous amount of research into other techniques for estimating postmortem interval.[315]

---

308. Goff, Charbonneau & Sullivan, *Presence of Fecal Material in Diapers as a Potential Source of Error in Estimations of Postmortem Interval Using Arthropod Development Rates*, 36 J. FORENSIC SCI. 1603 (1991).

309. Goff, *Problems in Estimation of Postmortem Interval Resulting from Wrapping of the Corpse: A Case Study from Hawaii*, 9 J. AGRIC. ENTOMOL. 237 (1992).

310. Goff, Miller, Paulson, Lord, Richards & Omori, *Effects of 3,4-Methylenedioxymethamphetamine in Decomposing Tissues on the Development of Parasarcophaga ruficornis (Diptera: Sarcophagidae) and Detection of the Drug in Postmortem Blood, Liver Tissue, Larvae, and Puparia*, 42 J. FORENSIC SCI. 276 (1997) (the presence of some drugs in the system can cause the larvae to develop more rapidly).

311. Goff, *Estimation of Postmortem Interval Using Anthropod Development and Successional Patterns*, 5 J. FORENSIC SCI. 81, 83 (1993).

312. *Id. at* 86.

313. Catts, *Analyzing Entomological Data*, *in* ENTOMOLOGY AND DEATH: A PROCEDURAL GUIDE 131-34 (1990).

314. Willey & Snyder, *Canid Modification of Human Remains: Implications for Time-Since-Death Estimations*, 34 J. FORENSIC SCI. 894 (1989); Haglund, Reay & Swindler, *Canid Scavenging/Disarticulation Sequence of Human Remains in the Pacific Northwest*, 34 J. FORENSIC SCI. 587 (1989) (the researchers identify five sequential steps of animal scavenging of human remains); Haglund, Reay & Swindler, *Tooth Mark Artifacts and Survival of Bones in Animal Scavenged Human Skeletons*, 33 J. FORENSIC SCI. 985 (1988).

315. Introna, DiVella & Campobasso, *Determination of Postmortem Interval from Old Skeletal Remains by Image Analysis of Luminol Test Results*, 44 J. FORENSIC SCI. 535 (1999) (this study indicates that there is "a possible quantitative relationship between the PMI and luminol chemiluminescence in powdered bone"); Brion, Marc, Launay, Gailledreau & Durigon, *Postmortem Interval Estimation by Creatinine Levels in Human Psoas Muscle*, 52 FORENSIC SCI. INT'L 113 (1991); Vanezis, *Assessing Hypostasis by Colorimetry*, 52 FORENSIC SCI. INT'L 1 (1991); Rognum, Hauge, Oyasaeter & Saugstad, *A New Biochemical Method for Estimation of Postmortem Time*, 51 FORENSIC SCI. INT'L 139 (1991); Querido, *In Vitro Loss of Potassium from Erythrocytes During the 0-108 h Postmortem Period in Rats: Relationship Between Potassium Loss and*

§ 19-8(B). Long-Term Signs.

The second group of postmortem changes sets in at a later stage than the signs mentioned in the last subsection.

In a normal environment, the long-term change is the process of decomposition which includes autolysis and putrefaction. There are numerous contributing causes to decomposition, including bacterial activity within the body (putrefaction). Environmental temperature is the single most important factor in determining the rate of decomposition. High temperatures accelerate the putrefaction process while low temperatures slow the process. Doctor Wecht has outlined a general chronology for decomposition:[316]

Postmortem Interval, 51 FORENSIC SCI. INT'L 111 (1991); Nokes, Daniel, Flint & Barasi, *Investigations into the Analysis of the Rate of Decay of the Compound Action Potentials Recorded from the Rat Sciatic Nerve After Death: Significance for the Prediction of the Post-Mortem Period*, 50 FORENSIC SCI. INT'L 75 (1991); Madea & Henssge, *Electrical Excitability of Skeletal Muscle Postmortem in Casework*, 47 FORENSIC SCI. INT'L 207 (1990); Querido, *Linearization of the Relationship Between Postmortem Plasma Chloride Concentration and Postmortem Interval in Rats*, 45 FORENSIC SCI. INT'L 117 (1990); Fneschi, Picchi, Tassini, Valensin & Vivi, *H-NMR Studies of Postmortem Biochemical Changes in Rat Skeletal Muscle*, 44 FORENSIC SCI. INT'L 225 (1990) (changes in perchloric acid extracts); Querido, *Double Logarithmic, Linear Relationship Between Plasma Sodium/Potassium Concentration Ratio and Postmortem Interval During the 6-96-H Postmortem Period in Rats*, 44 FORENSIC SCI. INT'L 125 (1990); Endo, Hara, Kuriiwa & Kano, *Postmortem Changes in the Levels of Monoamine Metabolites in Human Cerebrospinal Fluid*, 44 FORENSIC SCI. INT'L 61 (1990); Nagata, Kage, Kimura, Kudo & Noda, *Sulfide Concentrations in Postmortem Mammalian Tissues*, 35 J. FORENSIC SCI. 706 (1990) (concentrations increased in blood, liver, and kidneys, but there was little or no change in the lung, brain, and muscle); Sparks, Oeltgen, Kryscio & Hunsaker, *Comparison of Chemical Methods for Determining Postmortem Interval*, 34 J. FORENSIC SCI. 197 (1989) (the accumulation or clearance of the dopaminergic metabolite 3-methoxytyramine (3-MT) in the patamen of the brain); Sarkioja, Yla-Herttuala, Solakivi, Nikkari & Hirvonen, *Stability of Plasma Total Cholesterol, Tricylcerides, and Apolipoproteins B and A-1 During the Early Postmortem Period*, 33 J. FORENSIC SCI. 1432 (1988); Sawyer, Steup, Martin & Forney, *Cardiac Blood pH as a Possible Indicator of Postmortem Interval*, 33 J. FORENSIC SCI. 1439 (1988); McKeown & Bennett, *A Preliminary Investigation of Postmortem Tooth Loss*, 40 J. FORENSIC SCI. 755 (1995); Cox, Mitchell & Espinoza, *CompuTOD, A Computer Program to Estimate Time of Death of Deer*, 39 J. FORENSIC SCI. 1287 (1994).

316. Wecht, *supra* note 21, at 25-22.*See also* Yoshino, Kimijima, Sato & Seta, *Microscopical Study on Estimation of Time Since Death in Skeletal Remains*, 49 FORENSIC SCI. INT'L 143 (1991) ("Microradiographic examination revealed no morphological changes in [compact] bonds left in the open air for long periods, except one of 15 years since death. In bones left in the soil, vacuoles of 5-10 mm diameter, which contained a honeycomb-like structure formed by small vacuoles of 0.5-1 mm diameter, were found in the peripheral zone of the substantia compacta approximately 5 years since death .... In bones left in the sea for 4-5 years, vacuoles of 5-10 mm diameter were observed in the outer peripheral zone of the substantia compacta"); Mann, Bass & Meadows, *Time Since Death and Decomposition of the Human Body: Variables and Observations in Case and Experimental Field Studies*, 35 J. FORENSIC SCI. 103, 110 (1990) ("the rate of bodily decay is quite variable"); Galloway, Birkby, Jones, Henry & Parks, *Decay Rates of Human Remains in an Arid*

Sign	*Time of appearance*
Green discoloration of skin,	2 to 3 days
abdomen, trunk	4 to 7 days
Visible purplish-brown color in subcutaneous veins	5 to 7 days
Skin blisters	5 to 7 days
Formation of gas (gastrointestinal tract and tissues)	7 to 9 days
Wet, peeling skin	7 to 9 days
Greenish-purple, swollen face and body	1 to 4 weeks
Easily detached hair and nails	3 to 4 weeks

Suppose that a body is left in water or on very moist soil.[317] The likelihood is that the long-term change will take the form of saponification. In saponification, adipocere[318] forms on the body; acids formed by the body fat give the skin a yellowish color and make the skin waxy or soapy to the touch. Adipocere which is apparent to the naked eye may be seen in as soon as three months after death. The process is usually not developed before five or six months after death.[319] The more warm and moist the environment, the faster will be the process.

Lastly, assume that the body is left in a dry, warm environment. This environment will dry out the body and make the skin taut and leathery. Peripheral mummification involving the hands and feet can be found in people dead two or three days. The process of generalized mummification can begin in one month after death and require a full year for completion. However, in most cases, the process is complete between three and a half and six months after death.[320]

Environment, 34 J. FORENSIC SCI. 607 (1989); Rodriguez & Bass, *Decomposition of Buried Bodies and Methods That May Aid in Their Location*, 30 J. FORENSIC SCI. 836 (1985). Bass has been one of the leading researchers in this field, and his articles are especially worth reading. Shean, Messinger & Papworth, *Observations of Differential Decomposition on Sun Exposed v. Shaded Pig Carrion in Coastal Washington State*, 38 J. FORENSIC SCI. 938 (1993).

317. Haglund, *Disappearance of Soft Tissue and the Disarticulation of Human Remains from Aqueous Environments*, 38 J. FORENSIC SCI. 806 (1993); Spennemann & Franke, *Decomposition of Buried Human Bodies and Associated Death Scene Materials on Coral Atolls in the Tropical Pacific*, 40 J. FORENSIC SCI. 356 (1995).

318. Pfeiffer & Stevenson, *The Natural Decomposition of Adipocere*, 43 J. FORENSIC SCI. 368 (1998).

319. W. SPITZ & R. FISHER, THE MEDICOLEGAL INVESTIGATION OF DEATH 23 (2d ed. 1980); Komar, *Decay Rates in a Cold Climate Region: A Review of Cases Involving Advanced Decomposition from the Medical Examiner's Office in Edmonton, Alberta*, 43 J. FORENSIC SCI. 57 (1998); Mellen, Lowry & Micozzi, *Experimental Observations on Adipocere Formation*, 38 J. FORENSIC SCI. 91 (1993).

320. Wecht, *supra* note 21, at 25-23. Ambach & Ambach, *Is Mummification Possible in Snow?*, 54 FORENSIC SCI. INT'L 191 (1992).

§ 19-9. Place of Death.

The forensic pathologist is often asked to determine the place of death as well as the time of death.[321] The place of death can have critical legal importance. As a preliminary matter, the place of death may determine whether the trial court has jurisdiction and venue over the case. The place of death can also be a hotly contested issue on the historical merits of the case.

In some instances, the forensic pathologist can determine only that the death did not occur where the body was found. Livor and rigor mortis occasionally enable the pathologist to reach this conclusion. Assume, for example, that the pathologist discerns two areas of lividity or that the location of the lividity is inconsistent with the position of the body when the body was discovered.[322] The police may have found the body in a typical, suicidal hanging position; but rather than discovering lividity in the body's lower extremities, the pathologist notes lividity in the chest area. Inconsistent or multiple lividity strongly suggests that the body was moved after death. In the same fashion, the posture of the body's rigor may be inconsistent with the position in which it was found. In the hanging example, assume that the police find the body with the arms flexed rather than hanging straight down. The posture of the rigor will prompt the pathologist to suspect that the decedent died elsewhere and was later moved to the place and into the position in which the police discovered the body.

In other cases, the forensic pathologist and allied experts may be able to affirmatively determine the place of death. The pathologist may request that police laboratory criminalists analyze the trace evidence on the body (fiber, glass, and soil). Chapter 24 describes the various techniques for analyzing trace evidence. Or the pathologist may ask a forensic entomologist for assistance.[323] There are different species of flies in urban and rural areas.[324] The presence of a particular species of insect on the body may give a clue to the place of death.

---

321. Berryman, Bass, Symes & Smith, *Recognition of Cemetery Remains in the Forensic Setting*, 36 J. Forensic Sci. 230 (1991).

322. Burton, *supra* note 255, at 531.

323. Goff, *Comparison of Insect Species Associated with Decomposing Remains Recovered Inside Dwellings and Outdoors on the Island of Oahu, Hawaii*, 36 J. Forensic Sci. 748 (1991); Hawley, Haskell, McShaffrey, Williams & Pless, *Identification of a Red Fiber: Chironomid Larvae*, 34 J. Forensic Sci. 617 (1989) (the pathologist discovered the larva of a common freshwater midge on the body; the discovery indicated the submersion of the body); Prichard, Kossoris, Leibovitch, Robertson & Lovell, *Implications of Trombiculid Mite Bites: Report of a Case and Submission of Evidence in a Murder Trial*, 31 J. Forensic Sci. 301 (1986) (some insects have a discrete geographic distribution); Middleton, *Tale Told by a Fly*, 69 A.B.A. J. 571 (1973).

324. *Id.*

§ 19-10. Pathological Evidence.

§ 19-10(A). Necessity for Pathological Testimony.

Although a forensic pathologist's expertise makes him the best qualified witness on numerous topics, in most jurisdictions other witnesses may also testify on these topics.[325]

In some cases, the courts do not require any expert testimony even to establish cause of death.[326] For example, if a gunshot wound is obviously mortal, even a lay juror can infer that the wound caused death. In one federal case, there was a detailed description of a gunshot wound that passed through the victim's brain and no other signs of injury.[327] On these facts, the court held that expert testimony was unnecessary to establish causation. In a clear-cut case, the inference can be deemed a matter of common knowledge.

In other cases, courts accept testimony from lesser experts, such as police officers, morticians, coroners, and physicians not expert in this area. Sheriffs have sometimes qualified as experts based on limited training and practical experience in investigating homicides.[328] Even when the witness lacked medical training, many courts have allowed forensic chemists,[329] coroners, morticians, embalmers, and chemistry professors to opine on cause of death.[330] The courts have not been at all reluctant to permit physicians[331] and hospital pathologists[332] to testify on such topics as cause[333] and time[334] of death. The courts have even

---

325. Carter v. Fenner, 136 F.3d 1000 (5th Cir.) (the coroner was an expert in forensic pathology with a degree in medicine; the coroner was qualified to offer an opinion about the behavior of people under the influence of alcohol), *cert. denied*, 119 S. Ct. 591 (1998).

326. Annot., 65 A.L.R.3D 283 (1975); Annot., 31 A.L.R.2D 693 (1953). *E.g.,* Parten v. State, 672 S.W.2d 251 (Tex. App. 1984.).

327. Rife v. Blankenship, 721 F.2d 983 (4th Cir. 1983).

328. Brown v. State, 140 Ga. App. 160, 230 S.E.2d 128 (1976), *cert. denied,* 434 U.S. 819 (1977).

329. Massie v. State, 349 Md. 834, 709 A.2d 1316 (App.1998).

330. Annot., 71 A.L.R.3D 1265 (1976); Jackson v. State, 412 So. 2d 302, 305 (Ala. Crim. App. 1982); Woodard v. State, 401 So. 2d 300, 303 (Ala. Crim. App. 1981); Smoot v. State, 381 So. 2d 668, 670-71 (Ala. Crim. App. 1980); State v. Miller, 429 N.W.2d 26 (S.D. 1988) (a forensic pathologist testified about the type of instrument used to inflict certain head wounds on the murder victim).

331. Martin v. Industrial Comm'n, 75 Ariz. 403, 257 P.2d 596 (1953); State v. Vincent, 785 S.W.2d 805 (Mo. App. 1990) (gunshot wounds and injuries); Barber v. State, 628 S.W.2d 104, 108 (Tex. App. 1981), *cert. denied,* 459 U.S. 874 (1982).

332. Annot., 56 A.L.R.2D 1447 (1957).

333. Barber v. State, 628 S.W.2d 104, 108 (Tex. App. 1981), *cert. denied,* 459 U.S. 874 (1982).

334. Martin v. Industrial Comm'n, 75 Ariz. 403, 257 P.2d 596 (1953); Massie v. State, 349 Md. 834, 709 A.2d 1316 (App.1998).

allowed investigators to testify on such subjects as the manner and sequence of the gunshot wounds causing the victim's death.[335]

Although in the past many courts have liberally admitted nonexpert testimony and testimony by minimally qualified experts, more and more courts are embracing the view that testimony on subjects such as cause of death requires at least some medical training.[336] In a growing number of cases, courts have barred testimony by coroners and morticians.[337] Moreover, even in jurisdictions allowing nonpathologists to testify to cause of death, some trial courts take the position that manner of death is such a subtle, evaluative judgment that only qualified pathologists can testify on that subject.

§ 19-10(B). Permissible Subjects for Expert Opinions.

Identity of Decedent

As previously stated, the forensic pathologist must often grapple with the question of the decedent's identity. The pathologist may ask a fingerprint examiner or forensic odontologist to assist in the identification. Chapters 13 and 16 note that fingerprint and dental identification testimony is admissible. Chapter 18 discusses DNA typing. Several jurisdictions have also accepted evidence of radiological identification.[338] In one case, the court admitted the evidence and rejected a *Frye* challenge even though the radiologist conceded that there were only three or four American experts experienced in radiologic identification.[339]

There is little case law dealing with the anthropological techniques used to narrow the class of persons the decedent might belong to. One of the few reported cases is *State v. Needs,*[340] in which an anthropologist estimated the

---

335. State v. Beuke, 38 Ohio St. 3d 29, 526 N.E.2d 274 (1988), *cert. denied*, 489 U.S. 1071 (1989).

336. Annot., 71 A.L.R.3D 1265, 1268 (1976); Evans v. Twin Falls County, 118 Idaho 210, 796 P.2d 87, 91 (1990) (citing Am. Jur. 2d, the court states that "[a] majority of states which have addressed this matter have held that ... [w]here the subject matter regarding the cause of disease, injury, or death of a person is wholly scientific or so far removed from the usual and ordinary experience of the average person that expert knowledge is essential to the formation of an intelligent opinion, only an expert can competently give opinion evidence ...."), *cert. denied*, 498 U.S. 1086 (1991).

337. *Id.*

338. Coleman v. State, 423 So. 2d 276, 278 (Ala. Crim. App. 1982); Commonwealth v. Gilbert, 366 Mass. 18, 24, 314 N.E.2d 111, 115 (1974); Commonwealth v. Devlin, 365 Mass. 149, 310 N.E.2d 353 (1974).

339. Commonwealth v. Devlin, 365 Mass. 149, 310 N.E.2d 353 (1974). However, our reviewer adds that today there are many radiologists qualified to make such identifications.

340. 99 Idaho 883, 591 P.2d 130 (1979).

decedent's age and stature.[341] The witness based the age estimate on an analysis of the decedent's femur bone and pubic symphysis. However, the testimony was evidently admitted without objection. Consequently, the appellate court did not have occasion to reach the question of whether these anthropological techniques satisfied the *Frye* test. In *State v. Klindt,*[342] it was unnecessary for the court to discuss the question because the case arose in Iowa, a jurisdiction which has abandoned *Frye*. However, in the course of sustaining the admission of expert anthropological testimony about the victim's stature, the court stressed that forensic anthropology is "a recognized scientific discipline."[343] In addition to opinions about age and stature, some courts are now admitting testimony about sex based on bone analysis.[344]

Cause and Manner of Death

Forensic pathologists sometimes find themselves in disagreement over a decedent's cause or manner of death.[345] However, possibility of disagreement has not discouraged the courts from routinely admitting pathologists' opinions on cause, mechanism, and manner of injury and death.

The courts allow pathologists to testify on the nature, cause, and effects of wounds and injuries.[346] For example, a pathologist may testify that the pattern of bruises on an alleged rape victim's labia majora and minora is consistent with

---

341. *Id.* at 886, 591 P.2d at 133. *See also* United States v. Ferri, 778 F.2d 985 (3d Cir. 1985), *cert. denied,* 479 U.S. 831 (1986).

342. 389 N.W.2d 670 (Iowa 1986).

343. *Id.* at 673. *See also* People v. Knights, 166 Cal. App. 3d 46, 212 Cal. Rptr. 307 (1985); State v. Bullard, 312 N.C. 129, 322 S.E.2d 370 (1984). *But see* United States v. Dorsey, 45 F.3d 809 (4th Cir.) (the trial judge properly excluded the testimony of a defense forensic anthropologist who proposed testifying that the defendant was not the individual depicted in bank surveillance photographs; the defense had shown neither that the testimony would be helpful to the trier of fact nor that the evidence amounted to "scientific knowledge" under *Daubert*), *cert. denied*, 515 U.S. 1168 (1995).

344. State v. Marra, 1992 WL 140800 (Conn.).

345. *E.g.,* People v. Kent, 111 Ill. App. 3d 733, 67 Ill. Dec. 334, 444 N.E.2d 570 (1982); People v. Ellison, 100 Ill. App. 3d 282, 426 N.E.2d 1058 (1981); Estate of Moran, 67 Ill. App. 3d 576, 24 Ill. Dec. 312, 385 N.E.2d 79 (1978), *aff'd,* 77 Ill. 2d 147, 32 Ill. Dec. 349, 395 N.E.2d 579 (1979).

346. Thomas v. Taylor, 170 F.3d 466, 473-74 (4th Cir. 1999) ("The medical examiner testified that the first shot . . . 'would be lethal'"); Bishop v. Kelso, 914 F.2d 1468 (11th Cir. 1990); Bell v. State, 435 So. 2d 772, 775 (Ala. Crim. App. 1983); United States v. Eagle, 133 F.3d 608 (8th Cir. 1998) (the physician was properly permitted to testify that what he found during the examination would be consistent with the victim's version of the events); Gilbert v. Texas Mental Health & Retardation, 919 F. Supp. 1031, 1037 (E.D. Tex. 1996) ("A pathologist should be expected to comment knowledgeably on the cause of death of a patient...."); McIntosh v. State, 855 S.W.2d 753 (Tex. App. 1993) (a physician testified that the killing was a crime of passion).

forcible insertion of a penis.[347] A pathologist is also permitted to testify on the cause of illnesses such as conditions that may result from by poisoning.[348] Similarly, a pathologist may testify about the effects of the use of illicit drugs such as cocaine.[349] The pathologist's opinions about a decedent's cause of death are also admissible. Pathologists have been permitted to testify to deaths caused by, inter alia: blunt trauma,[350] sharp-edged instruments,[351] strangulation,[352] gunshot wounds,[353] burns,[354] asphyxia,[355] and poisons[356] including arsenic,[357] carbon monoxide,[358] cyanide,[359] and Darvon.[360]

---

347. People v. Chambers, 136 Cal. App. 3d 444, 186 Cal. Rptr. 306 (1982). *See also* United States v. Weeson, 779 F.2d 1443 (9th Cir. 1986) (expert testimony that the victim's injuries were inconsistent with consensual intercourse); Pegg v. State, 183 Ga. App. 668, 359 S.E.3d 678 (1987) (forcible penile entry); People v. Byrd, 206 Ill. App. 3d 996, 565 N.E.2d 176, 151 Ill. Dec. 905 (1990) (the vaginal injuries sustained by the complainant resulted from nonconsensual intercourse), *appeal denied*, 137 Ill. 2d 667, 571 N.E.2d 150, 156 Ill. Dec. 563 (1991); State v. Everett, 98 N.C. App. 23, 390 S.E.2d 160 (1990) (the witness, a pediatrician, not only testified that there had been penetration but also opined as to the number of times sexual penetration had occurred).

348. State v. Jones, 54 N.C. App. 482, 283 S.E.2d 546 (1981); Benedi v. McNeil-P.P.C., Inc., 66 F.3d 1378, 1382 (4th Cir. 1995) (toxicity).

349. Bright v. State, 191 Ga. App. 655, 382 S.E.2d 426 (1989); State v. Rangitsch, 40 Wash. App. 771, 700 P.2d 382 (1985).

350. Guam v. Reyes, 879 F.2d 646 (9th Cir. 1989) (a pathologist was permitted to testify that a bruise on the victim's chest was "most likely" caused by pressure from the tip of a gun); Mitchell v. State, 18 Ala. App. 471, 93 So. 46, *cert. denied,* 208 Ala. 699, 93 So. 923 (1922); People v. Stout, 122 Ill. App. 3d 254, 77 Ill. Dec. 641, 460 N.E.2d 1205 (1984); People v. Gray, 121 Ill. App. 3d 867, 77 Ill. Dec. 298, 460 N.E.2d 354 (1984); People v. Mifflin, 120 Ill. App. 3d 1072, 458 N.E.2d 1343 (1984); People v. Franklin, 119 Ill. App. 3d 899, 75 Ill. Dec. 563, 457 N.E.2d 1005 (1983); People v. Martin, 112 Ill. App. 3d 486, 65 Ill. Dec. 151, 445 N.E.2d 795 (1983); People v. Schreiber, 104 Ill. App. 3d 618, 60 Ill. Dec. 417, 432 N.E.2d 1316 (1982), *cert. denied,* 459 U.S. 1214 (1983); Lufkins v. Leapley, 965 F.2d 1477, 1483 (8th Cir.), *cert. denied*, 506 U.S. 895 (1992).

351. People v. Perez, 100 Ill. App. 3d 901, 56 Ill. Dec. 149, 427 N.E.2d 229 (1981); People v. Paschall, 91 A.D.2d 645, 456 N.Y.S.2d 828 (1982) (but the court forbade the expert from characterizing particular injuries as "defense wounds"); Commonwealth v. Henry, 524 Pa. 135, 569 A.2d 929 (1990) (multiple transverse cuts on the front of the victim's neck were the type generally attributable to threatening or at-bay situations), *cert. denied,* 499 U.S. 931 (1991).

352. Deel v. Jago, 967 F.2d 1079, 1083 (6th Cir. 1992).

353. United States v. Lebron-Gonzalez, 816 F.2d 823 (1st Cir.) (the direction of a fatal shot), *cert. denied*, 484 U.S. 843 (1987); Bryant v. State, 428 So. 2d 641 (Ala. Crim. App. 1982), *cert. denied,* 428 So. 2d 646 (Ala. 1983); Portis v. State, 418 So. 2d 924 (Ala. Crim. App.), *cert. denied,* 418 So. 2d 927 (Ala. 1982); Bright v. State, 191 Ga. App. 655, 382 S.E.2d 426 (1989) (the path of a bullet through the body); People v. Reyes, 102 Ill. App. 3d 820, 57 Ill. Dec. 914, 429 N.E.2d 1277 (1981) (distance determinations); Wissman v. State, 540 N.E.2d 1209 (Ind. 1989) (the angle of entry); State v. Moran, 495 So. 2d 338 (La. App. 1986) (distance from which gun fired); May v. State, 524 So. 2d 957 (Miss. 1988) (the victim's gunshot wound was not a contact wound); People v. Bonilla, 95 A.D.2d 396, 467 N.Y.S.2d 599 (1983), *aff'd sub nom.* People v. Eulo, 63 N.Y.2d 341, 472 N.E.2d 286, 482 N.Y.S.2d 436 (1984); Smith v. Commonwealth, 239 Va. 243, 389 S.E.2d 871 (the presence of gunpowder debris in the back of the victim's head was consistent with a "close gunshot wound"), *cert. denied*, 498 U.S. 881(1990); Annot., 86 A.L.R.2D 611 (1962) (muzzle-to-

The courts allow forensic pathologists to venture beyond the medical questions of cause and mechanism to testify directly on the medicolegal question of manner or mode of death.[361] For example, pathologists have testified that the manner of death was homicidal[362] or accidental.[363] To establish the homicidal

---

target determinations); Smith v. Angelone, 111 F.3d 1126, 1131 (4th Cir.) ("Dr. Frances Field testified that there was powder residue in Sgt. Conner's head wound consistent with 'a close gunshot wound,' meaning within three feet for a pistol and within six feet for a rifle"), *cert. denied*, 521 U.S. 1131 (1997); Burris v. Parke, 948 F. Supp. 1310, 1315 (N.D. Ind. 1996) ("A pathologist, Dr. Robert Ransburg, testified that the body had a gunshot entrance wound in the right temple. Dr. Ransburg stated that the wound was a 'contact wound.' By this he meant that the muzzle would have had to have been held against the temple to create such a wound"), *aff'd*, 116 F.3d 256 (7th Cir.), *superseded*, 130 F.3d 782 (7th Cir.), *cert. denied*, 522 U.S. 990 (1997); People v. Mayfield, 14 Cal. 4th 668, 765, 928 P.2d 485, 542, 60 Cal. Rptr. 2d 1, 58 (On certain assumed facts, "the prosecutor asked Dr. Root [the autopsy surgeon] to give an expert opinion on whether he would necessarily expect to find gunpowder stippling or tattooing around the wound. Dr. Root testified that in his opinion it would be anatomically impossible for Sergeant Wolfley to have held the gun in both hands so that it was aimed toward his face and yet beyond the range at which gunpowder residue would cause stippling or tattooing and therefore he would necessarily expect to find stippling or tattooing around the wound."), *cert. denied*, 118 S. Ct. 116 (1997).

354. Binakonsky v. Ford Motor Co., 133 F.3d 281 (4th Cir. 1998); People v. McNeeley, 77 A.D.2d 205, 433 N.Y.S.2d 293 (1980); State v. Setzer, 42 N.C. App. 98, 256 S.E.2d 485, *cert. denied*, 298 N.C. 571, 261 S.E.2d 127 (1979).

355. Commonwealth v. Pikul, 400 Mass. 550, 511 N.E.2d 336 (1987) (expert testimony that a child's death was due to traumatic sexual asphyxia); People v. Marshall, 15 Cal. 4th 1, 13, 931 P.2d 262, 265, 61 Cal. Rptr. 2d 84, 88 (1997).

356. Sheriff, Clark County v. Morris, 99 Nev. 109, 659 P.2d 852 (1983) (lethal dose); O'Bryan v. State, 591 S.W.2d 464 (Tex. Crim. App. 1979) (fatal dose), *cert. denied*, 446 U.S. 988 (1980).

357. Vaughn v. State, 249 Ga. 803, 294 S.E.2d 504 (1982); State v. Jones, 54 N.C. App. 482, 283 S.E.2d 546 (1981); State v. Barfield, 298 N.C. 306, 259 S.E.2d 510 (1979), *cert. denied*, 448 U.S. 907 (1980); State v. Hunt, 297 N.C. 258, 254 S.E.2d 591 (1979).

358. Manigan v. State, 402 So. 2d 1063 (Ala. Crim. App.), *cert. denied*, 402 So. 2d 1072 (Ala. 1981); Williams v. State, 250 Ga. 553, 300 S.E.2d 301, *cert. denied*, 462 U.S. 1124 (1983); Clifton v. Nardi, 65 Ill. App. 3d 344, 22 Ill. Dec. 194, 382 N.E.2d 514 (1978); State v. Setzer, 42 N.C. App. 98, 256 S.E.2d 485, *cert. denied*, 298 N.C. 571, 261 S.E.2d 127 (1979).

359. O'Bryan v. State, 591 S.W.2d 464 (Tex. Crim. App. 1979), *cert. denied*, 446 U.S. 988 (1980); State v. Hoffman, 106 Wis. 2d 185, 316 N.W.2d 143 (1982).

360. People v. Ellison, 100 Ill. App. 3d 282, 55 Ill. Dec. 733, 426 N.E.2d 1058 (1981).

361. Barrett v. Acevedo, 169 F.3d 1155, 1160 (8th Cir. 1999) ("Dr. Vincent DiMaio, a physician and forensic pathologist, testified that, in his opinion, Willits had been murdered"); State v. Dietz, 390 S.E.2d 15, 23-24 (W. Va. 1990) ("the manner and mode of death").

362. People v. Franklin, 119 Ill. App. 3d 899, 75 Ill. Dec. 563, 457 N.E.2d 1005 (1983); Sippio v. Maryland, 350 Md. 633, 714 A.2d 684 (App. 1998). *But see* State v. Pinero, 70 Haw. 509, 778 P.2d 704, 712 (1989) (the pathologist should not have been permitted to testify that the death was "a homicide;" "The [witness' answers were] plainly beyond the intendment of ... [R]ule 704; the questions were conclusionary, and the answers told the jury what result to reach. Moreover, the opinions were 'phrased in terms of inadequately explored ... criteria' related to criminal homicide. HAW. R. EVID. 704, Commentary").

character of a death, a pathologist may testify that most suicides shoot themselves in areas of the body other than the area where the decedent's wound was located.[364] Similarly, there is substantial authority permitting experts to characterize injuries as "defensive wound[s]."[365] Many courts, including the United States Supreme Court, have already accepted battered child syndrome evidence and allowed pathologists to testify that the decedent child's wound pattern indicates inflicted injury rather than accident.[366] One state has judicially noticed the validity of shaken baby syndrome.[367] One court even allowed a pathologist to characterize a set of wounds as not being the result of a "maniacal attack."[368]

---

363. State v. Jones, 801 P.2d 263, 267 (Wash. App. 1990) (the doctors "were better qualified than jurors to adjudge ... whether the fatal blow was accidental or inflicted. Opinion evidence on these issues is commonly allowed in homicide cases"); Lufkins v. Leapley, 965 F.2d 1477, 1483 (8th Cir.), *cert. denied,* 506 U.S. 895 (1992); Strauch v. Keane, 801 F. Supp. 1271, 1275 (S.D.N.Y. 1992), *aff'd,* 999 F.2d 536 (2d Cir.), *cert. denied,* 510 U.S. 950 (1993). *But see* State v. Cheeks, 253 Kan. 93, 853 P.2d 655 (1993) (a pediatrician should not have been permitted to opine that the victim died as a result of physical abuse rather than as an accident; the expert improperly relied on profiles).

364. May v. State, 524 So. 2d 957 (Miss. 1988).

365. Floyd v. State, 569 So. 2d 1225, 1232 (Fla. 1990).

366. Estelle v. McGuire, 502 U.S. 62 (1991); United States v. Bowers, 660 F.2d 527, 529 (5th Cir. 1981) ("Testimony describing the battered child syndrome has been approved in several state jurisdictions"); Eslava v. State, 473 So. 2d 1143 (Ala. Crim. App. 1985); Bell v. State, 435 So. 2d 772, 776 (Ala. Crim. App. 1983); Boone v. State, 282 Ark. 274, 668 S.W.2d 17 (1984); State v. Heath, 264 Kan. 557, 957 P.2d 449 (1998); Carpenter v. Commonwealth, 771 S.W.2d 822 (Ky. 1989) (a child's injuries were intentionally caused rather than accidental); State v. Durfee, 322 N.W.2d 778 (Minn. 1982); People v. McNeeley, 77 A.D.2d 205, 433 N.Y.S.2d 293 (1980); People v. Kinder, 75 A.D.2d 34, 428 N.Y.S.2d 375 (1980); Commonwealth v. Rodgers, 364 Pa. Super. 477, 528 A.2d 610 (1987), *appeal denied,* 518 Pa. 638, 542 A.2d 1368 (1988); State v. Toennis, 52 Wash. App. 176, 758 P.2d 539 ("The Battered Child Syndrome is a well-recognized medical diagnosis ...."), *review denied,* 111 Wash. 2d 1026 (1988). *See generally* 1 E. IMWINKELRIED, UNCHARGED MISCONDUCT EVIDENCE § 4.06 (rev. ed. 1999); Orfinger, *Battered Child Syndrome: Evidence of Prior Acts in Disguise,* 41 FLA. L. REV. 345, 347 (1989) ("Expert testimony as to battered child syndrome has hardly been a point of judicial contention; every jurisdiction considering such evidence has held it admissible"); People v. Ripley, 291 Ill. App. 3d 565, 685 N.E.2d 362 (1997) (circumstantial evidence alone, including medical evidence regarding the nature of a child's injuries and the force required to inflict them, can be sufficient to prove that the defendant intentionally or knowingly injured a child).

367 Brown v. Commonwealth, __S.W.2d__, 1999 Ky. App. LEXIS 17, 1999 WL 95697 (Ky. App. 1999).

368. People v. Smith, 59 N.Y. 156, 451 N.E.2d 157, 464 N.Y.S.2d 399 (1983). *See also* Hernandez v. State, 772 S.W.2d 274 (Tex. App. 1989) (a pathologist was allowed to testify that a wound was a "deliberate cutting type of wound"); State v. Dietz, 390 S.E.2d 15 (W. Va. 1990) (a pathologist was permitted to testify that the homicide was "of a psychosexual type").

However, other courts have held that even a forensic pathologist may not describe injuries as "defense wounds"[369] or a killing as "murder."[370] In these cases, the courts believed that the pathologist overstepped proper bounds by using terms with specialized legal meanings. In still another case, the appellate court held that the trial judge erred in permitting a physician to testify about the age of a healed cervical tear.[371] The court declared that the opinion embraced the ultimate question of whether the complainant had been abused when she was 10 years old.

Time of Death

The courts recognize that the determination of time of death is an inexact science.[372] Some courts even give the jury a cautionary instruction to that effect.[373] In light of the imprecision inherent in any estimate of time of death, it is not surprising that forensic pathologists occasionally disagree over time of death in the reported cases.[374] However, although the courts realize the fallibility of opinions of time of death, they are also aware that pathologists' opinions on the subject can be helpful to a jury. Consequently, the courts admit pathologists' opinions on time of death,[375] age of injuries,[376] and the sequence of multiple

---

369. West v. State, 485 So. 2d 681 (Miss. 1985), *cert. denied*, 479 U.S. 983 (1986); People v. Paschall, 91 A.D.2d 645, 456 N.Y.S.2d 828 (1982).

370. Bell v. State, 435 So. 2d 772, 778 (Ala. Crim. App. 1983) (error not prejudicial).

371. Brown v. Commonwealth, 812 S.W.2d 502 (Ky. 1991).

372. Gruzen v. State, 276 Ark. 149, 634 S.W.2d 92, *cert. denied,* 459 U.S. 1020 (1982).

373. *Id.*

374. *E.g.,* People v. Trolia, 107 Ill. App. 3d 487, 63 Ill. Dec. 155, 437 N.E.2d 804, (1982), *cert. denied,* 460 U.S. 1044 (1983); People v. Cable, 96 A.D.2d 251, 468 N.Y.S.2d 470 (1983).

375. United States v. Maravilla, 907 F.2d 216 (1st Cir. 1990) (Federal Rule of Evidence 403, permitting the trial judge to balance probative value against probative danger, does not require the exclusion of a forensic pathologist's testimony about the approximate time of death); Gruzen v. State, 276 Ark. 149, 634 S.W.2d 92, *cert. denied,* 459 U.S. 1020 (1982); State v. Needs, 99 Idaho 883, 591 P.2d 130 (1979); People v. Hendricks, 145 Ill. App. 3d 71, 99 Ill. Dec. 20, 495 N.E.2d 85 (1986) (the court rejected the defense argument that time of death estimates are so unreliable that the prosecution's reliance on the estimate necessarily creates a reasonable doubt about the defendant's guilt), *aff'd*, 1988 Ill. LEXIS 194 (1988), *different results reached on reh'g*, 137 Ill. 2d 31, 148 Ill. Dec. 213, 560 N.E.2d 611 (1990); People v. Kent, 111 Ill. App. 3d 733, 67 Ill. Dec. 334, 444 N.E.2d 570 (1982); People v. Trolia, 107 Ill. App. 3d 487, 63 Ill. Dec. 155, 437 N.E.2d 804 (1982), *cert. denied,* 460 U.S. 1044 (1983); State v. Garrett, 627 S.W.2d 635, 642 (Mo.), *cert. denied,*459 U.S. 906 (1982); Felker v. Turpin, 83 F.3d 1303, 1310 (11th Cir. 1996) ("Tillman testified that in his opinion the victim could have been killed as many as fourteen days prior to her body being discovered on December 8, 1981....").

376. People v. Washington, 197 Cal. App. 3d 488, 891, 232 Cal. Rptr. 190, 194 (1986) (abrasions), *superseded,* 235 Cal. Rptr. 302, 733 P.2d 624 (1987); People v. Cable, 96 A.D.2d 251, 468 N.Y.S.2d 470 (1983), *rev'd*, 63 N.Y.2d 270, 471 N.E.2d 447, 481 N.Y.S.2d 675 (1984). *But see* Brown v. Commonwealth, 812 S.W.2d 502 (Ky. 1991) (the age of a healed cervical tear).

deaths.[377] The pathologist may testify on the basis of short-term signs such as stomach contents[378] and rigor[379] as well as long-term changes such as decomposition.[380] However, in one case, the court held that a forensic pathologist's estimate based on insect larvae was inadmissible because the expert conceded that "his methodology is completely untested by other scientists ...."[381] In contrast, most contemporary courts have been receptive to entomologists' testimony on similar subjects.[382]

Place of Death

In most instances, the prosecutor must use trace evidence — fiber, hair, and soil — to determine the place of death. The admissibility of trace evidence is discussed in Chapter 24.

Position of the Body

The expert may also express an opinion on the position of the victim's body when the victim was shot.[383]

§ 19-10(C). Admissibility of Autopsy Reports.

As noted in Chapter 6, courts often admit forensic reports as business entries or public records even when the scientist who prepared the report does not testify at trial. The courts have applied this view to autopsy reports prepared by

---

377. Hitchcock v. Key, 163 Ga. App. 901, 296 S.E.2d 625 (1982); Estate of Moran, 67 Ill. App. 3d 576, 24 Ill. Dec. 312, 385 N.E.2d 79 (1978), *aff'd,* 77 Ill. 2d 147, 32 Ill. Dec. 349, 395 N.E.2d 579 (1979).

378. State v. Pridgen, 313 N.C. 80, 326 S.E.2d 618 (1985).

379. State v. Garrett, 627 S.W.2d 635, 642 (Mo.), *cert. denied,* 459 U.S. 906 (1982).

380. State v. Needs, 99 Idaho 883, 591 P.2d 130 (1979).

381. State v. Miller, 429 N.W.2d 26, 39 (S.D. 1988).

382. Starrs, *Calling All Bugs!*, 19 SCI. SLEUTHING REV. 1, at 4 (Spring 1995) (collecting the following cases: State v. Abbott, 654 S.W.2d 260 (Mo. App. 1983); State v. Benner, 533 N.E.2d 701 (Ohio 1988); Bond v. State, 403 N.E.2d 812 (Ind. 1980); People v. Clark, 86 Cal. Rptr. 106 (Cal. App. 1970); Earhart v. State, 823 S.W.2d 607 (Tex. Cr. App. 1991); State v. Hart, 94 Ohio App.3d 665, 641 N.E.2d 755 (App.), *dismissed*, 70 Ohio St.3d 1446, 639 N.E.2d 114 (Ohio 1994); State v. John, 557 A.2d 93 (Conn. 1989); State v. Keenan, 66 Ohio St.3d 402, 613 N.E.2d 203 (1993); People v. Klafta, 831 P.2d 512 (Haw. 1992); Lee v. State, 545 N.E.2d 1085 (Ind. 1989); Pasco v. State, 563 N.E.2d 587 (Ind. 1990); People v. Rissley, 165 Ill.2d 364, 651 N.E.2d 133, *cert. denied*, 516 U.S. 992 (1995); Scott v. Commonwealth, 685 S.W.2d 184 (Ky. 1984); Taylor v. State, 834 P.2d 1325 (Kan. 1992); People v. Vernon, 152 Cal. Rptr. 765 (Cal. App. 1979); Wilson v. Commonwealth, 836 S.W.2d 872 (Ky. 1992), *cert. denied*, 507 U.S. 1034 (1993).

383. Guam v. Reyes, 879 F.2d 646 (9th Cir. 1989); State v. Jones, 749 S.W.2d 356 (Mo.), *cert. denied*, 488 U.S. 871 (1988); State v. Torres, 99 N.C. App. 364, 393 S.E.2d 535 (1990) (one of the shots fired at the murder victim could have entered the victim's body while the victim was lying on the floor); Terry v. State, 668 So. 2d 954 (Fla. 1996).

pathologists; autopsy reports have qualified as business entries[384] and public records.[385] Since the reports fall within well-recognized hearsay exceptions, most courts hold that their admission does not deny the defendant the right of confrontation.[386] The report is admissible even without sponsoring testimony by the pathologist who authored the report,[387] at least when the record contains foundational evidence that the report's author had the expert qualifications to form the opinions stated in the report.[388]

Moreover, as part of the basis for an expert opinion, one pathologist may rely on a report prepared by a medical examiner's investigator[389] or an autopsy report written by another pathologist.[390] However, the pathologist does not have carte blanche to select the bases for his or her opinion. Under Federal Rule of Evidence 703, the pathologist may rely on hearsay which is not independently admissible only if it is reasonable to do so.[391] In one case the court ruled that it was error for the pathologist to recite that none of his colleagues had given him a persuasive reason to change his opinion.[392] The court found that there had been no showing that it was a reasonable practice for the witness to rely on other experts' concurrence in his opinion. It is one thing to allow a pathologist to rely on a toxicologist's report and build a further inference on the toxicologist's conclusion. It is quite another matter to treat the pathologist's testimony as a conduit for introducing other pathologists' conclusions on the same topic.

---

384. Wiley v. State, 389 So. 2d 604 (Ala. Crim. App. 1980); United States v. Rosa, 11 F.3d 315 (2d Cir. 1993), *cert. denied*, 511 U.S. 1042 (1994). *But see* Segrest v. Gillette, 96 N.C. App. 435, 386 S.E.2d 88 (1989) (a laboratory report describing a test did not fall within the business entry hearsay exception because it was prepared two years and nine months after the test).

385. People v. Wardlow, 118 Cal. App. 3d 375, 173 Cal. Rptr. 500 (1981); United States v. Rosa, 11 F.3d 315 (2d Cir. 1993), *cert. denied*, 511 U.S. 1042 (1994); Ealy v. State, 685 N.E.2d 1047 (Ind. 1997) (Relying on the Indiana version of Federal Rule of Evidence 803(8) (C), the court held that autopsy reports may be admissible; however, the court added that "[t]he [judge] must determine whether the report was prepared for advocacy purposes or in anticipation of litigation. If it was not, then the evidence is admissible."); Garcia v. State, 868 S.W.2d 337 (Tex. Crim. App. 1993); Segrest v. Gillette, 414 S.E.2d 334, 337 (N.C. 1992) (relying on the North Carolina version of Federal Rule of Evidence 803(8) (C)).

386. Wiley v. State, 389 So. 2d 604 (Ala. Crim. App. 1980); United States v. Rosa, 11 F.3d 315 (2d Cir. 1993), *cert. denied*, 511 U.S. 1042 (1994). *But see* Manocchio v. Moran, 708 F. Supp. 473 (D.R.I. 1989) (the admission of a medical examiner's report on the cause of death violated the confrontation clause because the prosecution did not make a good faith effort to produce the examiner at trial), *rev'd*, 919 F.2d 770 (1st Cir. 1990), *cert. denied*, 500 U.S. 910 (1991).

387. People v. Wardlow, 118 Cal. App. 3d 375, 173 Cal. Rptr. 500 (1981).

388. *Id.*

389. United States v. Scarfo, 711 F. Supp. 1315 (E.D. Pa. 1989), *aff'd sub nom.* United States v. Pungitore, 910 F.2d 1084 (3d Cir. 1990), *cert. denied*, 500 U.S. 915 (1991).

390. State v. Gonzalez, 206 Conn. 391, 538 A.2d 219 (1988).

391. United States v. Kennedy, 890 F.2d 1056, 1060-61 (9th Cir. 1989), *cert. denied*, 494 U.S. 1008 (1990).

392. State v. Barrett, 445 N.W.2d 749 (Iowa 1989).

§ 19-11. Selected Bibliography.

In General

L. ADELSON, THE PATHOLOGY OF HOMICIDE (1974).

C. ANDERSON, MANUAL FOR THE EXAMINATION OF BONES (1982).

W. BASS, HUMAN OSTEOLOGY — A LABORATORY AND FIELD MANUAL (3d ed.).

K. BENNETT, A FIELD GUIDE FOR HUMAN SKELETAL IDENTIFICATION (1993).

Bucklin, *Forensic Pathology*, *in* SCIENTIFIC AND EXPERT EVIDENCE 1165 (2d ed. 1981).

W. CURRAN, A. MCGARRY & C. PETTY, MODERN LEGAL MEDICINE, PSYCHIATRY, AND FORENSIC SCIENCE (1980).

Devlin, *The Autopsy in Criminal Cases*, *in* SCIENTIFIC AND EXPERT EVIDENCE 1205 (2d ed. 1981).

D. DIMAIO & V. DIMAIO, FORENSIC PATHOLOGY (1992).

V. DIMAIO, GUNSHOT WOUNDS (1985).

R. Froede, ed., HANDBOOK ON FORENSIC PATHOLOGY (1991).

M. GRAHAM & R. HANZLOCK, FORENSIC PATHOLOGY IN CRIMINAL CASES (1997).

V. GEBERTH, PRACTICAL HOMICIDE INVESTIGATION: TACTICS, PROCEDURES, AND FORENSIC TECHNIQUES (3d ed. 1996).

W. HAGLUND & M. SORG, FORENSIC TAPHONOMY: THE POSTMORTEM FATE OF HUMAN REMAINS (1997).

M. HELPERN & B. KNIGHT, AUTOPSY (1977).

C. HENSSGE, B. KNIGHT, T. KROMPECHER, B. MADEA & L. NOKES, THE ESTIMATION OF THE TIME SINCE DEATH IN THE EARLY POSTMORTEM PERIOD (1995).

C. HIRSCH, R. MORRIS & A. MORITZ, HANDBOOK OF LEGAL MEDICINE (5th ed. 1979).

M. HOUTS & I. HAUT, COURTROOM MEDICINE (1984) (3 vols.).

M. ISCAN, AGE MARKERS IN THE HUMAN SKELETON (1989).

M. ISCAN & K. KENNEDY, RECONSTRUCTION OF LIFE FROM THE SKELETON (1989).

F. JAFFE, A GUIDE TO PATHOLOGICAL EVIDENCE (1976).

C. JOYCE & E. STOVER, WITNESSES FROM THE GRAVE: THE STORIES BONES TELL (1991).

B. LIPSKIN & K. FIELD, DEATH INVESTIGATION AND EXAMINATION: MEDICOLEGAL GUIDELINES AND CHECKLISTS (1984).

J. MASON, FORENSIC MEDICINE FOR LAWYERS (1978).

NATIONAL INSTITUTE OF JUSTICE, U.S. DEPARTMENT OF JUSTICE, NATIONAL GUIDELINES FOR DEATH INVESTIGATION (1997).

K. SELLIER & B. KNEUBUEHL, WOUND BALLISTICS AND THE SCIENTIFIC BACKGROUND (1994).

K. SMITH, A MANUAL OF FORENSIC ENTOMOLOGY (1986).

W. SPITZ & R. FISHER, THE MEDICOLEGAL INVESTIGATION OF DEATH (2d ed. 1980).

Wecht, *Use of Forensic Pathology in Defending Criminal Cases*, *in* 2 FORENSIC SCIENCES 25-1 (C. Wecht ed. 1983).

Wecht, *Autopsy Laws and Procedures*, *in* 2 FORENSIC SCIENCES 26-1 (C. Wecht ed. 1983).

Wecht, *Forensic Pathology for Trial Lawyers*, *in* SCIENTIFIC AND EXPERT EVIDENCE 1141 (2d ed. 1981).

C. WETLI, R. MITTLEMAN & V. RAO, PRACTICAL FORENSIC PATHOLOGY (1988).

C. WETLI, R. MITTLEMAN & V. RAO, AN ATLAS OF FORENSIC PATHOLOGY (1999).

Glossaries

AM. JUR. PROOF OF FACTS, FACT BOOK WITH MEDICAL GLOSSARY (1983).

3 M. HOUTS, LAWYERS GUIDE TO MEDICAL PROOF apps. 2 & 3 (1978) (abbreviations and nomenclature).

F. JAFFE, A GUIDE TO PATHOLOGICAL EVIDENCE 137-58 (1976) (glossary).
A. KERR, MEDICAL HIEROGLYPHS: ABBREVIATIONS AND SYMBOLS (1970).
MCQUADE, ANALYZING MEDICAL RECORDS PART III (1981) (glossary and abbreviations).
STEDMAN'S MEDICAL DICTIONARY (5th ed. 1982).
D. TENNENHOUSE, ATTORNEYS MEDICAL DESKBOOK (2d ed. 1983) (glossary, abbreviations, and symbols).

CHAPTER 20

TOXICOLOGY*

§ 20-1. In General.

Toxicology is the study of poisons (toxins or toxicants) that can cause impairment, poor health, or death. The toxicant might have impaired the victim in a drug-facilitated sexual assault.[1] The toxicant may have been the cause of death. In an attempt to identify the cause of death, the forensic pathologist consults with the toxicologist. During the autopsy the pathologist may collect samples of tissue and body fluid for toxicological analysis. After analyzing the samples to identify any toxicants present, the toxicologist furnishes the test results to the pathologist.

Although the toxicologist usually functions as an adjunct to the pathologist, toxicology itself is a vast field. There are thousands of toxicants that may contribute to or cause death.[2] All the leading texts on forensic science include

---

*The authors wish to express their appreciation to Dr. Alphonse Poklis, Director, Medical College of Virginia Toxicology Laboratory, who reviewed this chapter in all three editions of this treatise.

1. LeBeau, Andollo, Hearn, Baselt, Cone, Finkle, Fraser, Jenkins, Mayer, Negrusz, Poklis, Walls, Raymon, Robertson & Saady, *Recommendations for Toxicological Investigations of Drug-Facilitated Sexual Assaults*, 44 J. FORENSIC SCI. 227 (1999).

2. Poklis, *Forensic Toxicology in Postmortem Investigations*, 10 LAB. MED. 224, 227 (1979).

lengthy sections devoted to toxicology.[3] There are massive treatises and texts devoted solely to toxicology.[4]

The field of toxicology is so broad that this chapter can serve as only a broad brush introduction to the topic. The next section introduces the general procedures toxicologists use to collect, extract, and analyze samples. The following section focuses on the analysis of alcohol, the single most common substance encountered in toxicological analysis. Another section considers the analysis of poisons. The concluding section discusses the legal limitations on the admissibility of toxicological evidence.

Toxicological evidence can be generated by either a clinical (hospital) or forensic laboratory. As Dr. David Stafford of the University of Tennessee Toxicology Laboratory has emphasized in his lectures on this subject, the two types of laboratory differ markedly in many respects:

— A clinical laboratory wants to obtain the minimum information needed for diagnosis or treatment as expeditiously as possible while a forensic laboratory usually seeks more specific, precise information for courtroom use and is largely free of time constraints.

— If a traffic accident results in a fatality and there is a question as to whether a driver was alcohol intoxicated, a clinical laboratory will typically use an enzymatic method on serum extracted from blood. The result would be a serum alcohol (SAC) concentration. In contrast, a forensic laboratory would almost always employ gas chromatography; and the result will be reported on a whole blood rather than a serum basis.

— The approaches of the two types of laboratories similarly differ if there is a suspicion of drug use. The clinical laboratory will ordinarily conduct a drug screen on urine rather than blood and test for a limited number -- perhaps 8-10 -- of commonly abused drug classes. In an emergency department, the doctor may need only to confirm a clinical impression or diagnosis such as a heroin overdose. The patient might have had a history of heroin use and display classic symptoms of an overdose such as pinpoint pupils and respiratory depression. In that situation, there might be no real need for a confirmatory test. If the screen yields a

3. Winek, *Forensic Toxicology*, *in* 2 FORENSIC SCIENCES ch. 31 (C. Wecht ed. 1983); Niyogi, *Toxicology*, *in* SCIENTIFIC AND EXPERT EVIDENCE ch. 15 (2d ed. 1981).

4. B. LEVINE, PRINCIPLES OF FORENSIC TOXICOLOGY (1999); J. ARENA, POISONING: TOXICOLOGY, SYMPTOMS, TREATMENTS (4th ed. 1979); R. CRAVEY, INTRODUCTION TO FORENSIC TOXICOLOGY (1981); L. GOTTSCHALT & R. CRAVEY, TOXICOLOGICAL AND PATHOLOGICAL STUDIES ON PSYCHOACTIVE DRUG-INVOLVED DEATHS (1979); A. CURRY, POISON DETECTION IN HUMAN ORGANS (3d ed. 1976); M. HOUTS, R. BASELT & R. CRAVEY, COURTROOM TOXICOLOGY (1983) (6 vols.); STEWART & STOLLMAN, TOXICOLOGY MECHANISMS AND ANALYTICAL METHODS (1961) (2 vols.); VON OETTINGER, POISONING (1958).

positive result and the physician believes that a confirmatory test is necessary, the result of the screening test can be confirmed by a technique such as mass spectrometry (MS). However, most clinical laboratories lack MS capability; they would have to send the sample to another laboratory for confirmation. A forensic laboratory would have that capability in house. A forensic laboratory will conduct a more comprehensive examination, including quantitation.

— At a clinical laboratory, standards might be run at intervals as long as a month or several months to calibrate the instrumentation or process. Further, the testing may consist of running a control at a single concentration such as 0.10 gms/dl. However, a forensic laboratory anticipates that it will have to defend its analyses in court. Consequently, it may run standards for every batch of specimens. In addition, a forensic laboratory may employ a multipoint calibration curve.

— Finally, forensic laboratory personnel are more conscious of chain-of-custody procedures. At a hospital laboratory, the priority may be obtaining a quick result for diagnostic purposes; and in the rush to obtain a quick result, personnel may slight chain-of-custody considerations.

In short, whenever an attorney encounters a toxicology laboratory report, the attorney must determine the type of laboratory which created the report.

§ 20-2. General Procedures to Identify an Unknown.

In many instances, police officers investigating a death suspect that a poison caused the death, but they have no idea of its identity. In such cases, the toxicology laboratory uses a general screening procedure to identify the unknown toxin. The procedure entails five steps: (1) collecting samples of tissue and body fluid; (2) safeguarding the samples until extraction; (3) extracting the unknown drug from the samples; (4) identifying the drug present --qualitative analysis; and (5) determining the amount of drug present -- quantitative analysis.

§ 20-2(A). Sample Collection.

The samples are usually collected by physicians, pathologists, and police officers. Because of their professional training, the physician conducting a biopsy on a living patient or the pathologist conducting an autopsy have some understanding of the number and types of samples that the toxicologist needs.[5] Unfortunately, police officers often do not appreciate the need for a large quantity and diversity of samples. For example, the investigating police officer may request that the toxicologist test for "all drugs and poisons" but submit only

5. Poklis, *supra* n 2, at 225.

10 milliliters (ml) of blood -- a wholly inadequate sample for comprehensive testing.[6]

The need for a large quantity of sample arises because testing for a general unknown may require numerous tests. Some tests will contaminate or destroy portions of the sample. The toxicologist cannot run all the necessary tests unless a large amount of material is submitted for testing. Furthermore, different toxins have varying affinities for different parts of the body.[7] Different poisons have differing sites of concentration. For example, most metals such as mercury tend to accumulate in the bone, kidney, and liver. Since the various toxins have different storage areas within the body, the person collecting samples must gather samples from a wide variety of body sites. Moreover, as we shall see in § 20-3(C), there is a special need for multiple samples in ethanol cases. In such cases, the analyst often needs to determine the exogenous alcohol--the amount of alcohol which the body gained from external sources such as antemortem consumption or postmortem embalming fluid. However, postmortem the body can synthesize or produce its own ethanol--endogenous ethanol. Obtaining multiple specimens from different anatomical sites--heart blood, peripheral blood (*i.e.* femoral artery), vitreous humor, urine, and bile--can help the analyst determine whether the postmortem synthesis of ethanol has occurred.[8]

The recommended list of samples varies from laboratory to laboratory, but the following list is illustrative. The list was prepared by Mr. Larry Howard, Director, Division of Forensic Sciences, Georgia State Crime Laboratory:

Specimen	Living	Dead
Gastric contents	all	all
Urine	100 cc (cubic centimeters)	all
Breath	plastic bag	tied off lung
Blood	10 cubic centimeters	25 cc or more
Hair	200 mg (milligrams)	200 mg (complete with roots)
Fingernails	clippings	whole nails, if possible
Nasal swabs	as necessary	as necessary
Skin swabs	as necessary	as necessary
Bile	NA	all
Liver	NA	100 gm (grams)

---

6. *Id.*

7. *Id.* at 226.

8. O'Neal & Poklis, *Postmortem Production of Ethanol and Factors that Influence Interpretation*, 17 AM. J. FORENSIC MED. & PATH. 8, 18 (1996).

Kidney	NA	one
Lung	NA	one
Brain	NA	as necessary
Ocular fluid	NA	all
Injection site	NA	as necessary

Figure 20-1[9]

If the source of the samples is a cadaver, the toxicologist should consider collecting larvae from the cadaver. Poisons and other drugs can be extracted from the larvae.[10]

Inadequate quantity or diversity of sample can lead to error. Inadequate sampling can cause a false negative. If there is an insufficient quantity of sample, the toxicologist may run out of sample before conducting the one test that could reveal the presence of the toxicant. Inadequate sampling can also cause a false positive. The toxicologist may consume the entire sample while conducting nonspecific tests and thus be precluded from conducting a specific test to confirm positively the identity of the drug.

§ 20-2(B). Safeguarding Samples.

Whether the person collecting the samples is a police officer or pathologist, that person must initiate a proper chain of custody to protect the samples from contamination and substitution. Each specimen should be placed in a separate container.[11] Although some jurisdictions employ plastic bags as containers, glass jars with screw tops are preferable.[12] The person taking the sample should label

---

9. HOWARD, FORENSIC TOXICOLOGY (unpublished manuscript on file with the National College of District Attorneys, Bates College of Law, University of Houston, Houston, Texas). Reprinted with the permission of the National College of District Attorneys.

10. Hedouin, Bourel, Martin-Bouyer, Becart, Tournel, Deveaux & Gosset, *Determination of Drug Levels in Larvae of Lucila sericata (Diptera: Calliphoridae) Reared on Animal Carcasses Containing Morphine*, 44 J. FORENSIC SCI. 351 (1999); Kintz, Godelar, Tracqui, Mangin, Lugnier & Chaumont, *Fly Larvae: A New Toxicological Method of Investigation in Forensic Medicine*, 35 J. FORENSIC SCI. 204 (1990); Gunatilake & Goff, *Detection of Organophosphate Poisoning in a Putrefying Body by Analyzing Arthropod Larvae*, 34 J. FORENSIC SCI. 714 (1989); Sadler, Robertson, Brown, Fuke & Pounder, *Barbiturates and Analgesics in Calliphora vicina Larvae*, 42 J. FORENSIC SCI. 481 (1997); Miller, Lord, Goff, Donnelly, McDonough & Alexis, *Isolation of Amitriptyline and Nortriptyline from Fly Puparia (Phoridae) and Beetle Exuviae (Dermestidae) Associated with Mummified Human Remains*, 39 J. FORENSIC SCI. 1305 (1994); Nolte, Pinder & Lord, *Insect Larvae Used to Detect Cocaine Poisoning in a Decomposed Body*, 37 J. FORENSIC SCI. 1179 (1992).

11. Poklis, *supra* note 2, at 226.

12. *Id.*; Baselt, Yoshikawa, Chang & Li, *Improved Long-Term Stability of Blood Cocaine in Evacuated Collection Tubes*, 38 J. FORENSIC SCI. 935 (1993).

each container with the name of the decedent, the name of the person taking the sample, the type of sample, and the date and time of the collection.[13]

Some samples require preservatives.[14] For example, sodium fluoride ought to be added to one of the tubes of blood intended for analysis of ethanol and carbonmonoxide.[15] However, no preservative should be added to tissue specimens.[16]

Blood and urine samples should be refrigerated until delivered to the toxicologist.[17] If the samples have to be transported a great distance before delivery, they ought to be packed with dry ice.[18]

Any error in this step can degrade the quality of the samples and contaminate the specimens. The result could be either a false positive or false negative in the subsequent toxicological analysis.

§ 20-2(C). Extraction of Drug.

After receiving samples of tissue and body fluid, the toxicologist must often extract the drugs for testing. There are several methods of extraction.[19]

One classic technique is known as the Stas-Otto method.[20] The method is based on the ability of ethanol to precipitate protein while simultaneously extracting an alkaloidal poison.[21] This method is effective for drugs such as strychnine and codeine but poor for barbiturates.[22]

In contrast, the second technique, tungstic acid, is excellent for extracting barbiturates.[223] However, it is a poor method of isolating other drugs such as imipramine and amitriptyline.[24]

A third method is direct extraction,[25] a relatively new technique,[26] that requires less time and produces better yields for many drugs.[27] Some toxicologists

13. Poklis, *supra* note 3, at 226-27.

14. *Id.* at 226.

15. *Id.*

16. *Id.*

17. *Id.*

18. *Id.*

19. Chen, Hommerson, Zweipfenning, Franke, Harmen-Boverhof, Ensing & de Zeeuw, *Solid Phase Extraction of Morphine from Whole Blood by Means of Bond Elut Certify Columns*, 38 J. Forensic Sci. 668 (1993); Chen, Wijsbeek, Franke & de Zeeuw, *A Single-Column Procedure on Bond Elut Certify for Systematic Toxicological Analysis of Drugs in Plasma and Urine*, 37 J. Forensic Sci. 61 (1992); Ensing, Franke, Temmink, Chen & de Zeeuw, *Application of Empore C-8 Extraction Disks for Screening Urine in Systematic Toxicological Analysis*, 37 J. Forensic Sci. 460 (1992).

20. *Id.;* Niyogi, *supra* note 3, at 346-47.

21. Poklis, *supra* note 2, at 226.

22. *Id.*

23. *Id.;* Niyogi, *supra* note 3, at 347.

24. Poklis, *supra* note 2, at 226.

consider direct extraction the method of choice.[28] However, the technique is unsuited for some drugs, including morphine.[29]

A fourth method is acid digestion.[30] Like the other methods, this technique has strengths and weaknesses. On the one hand, it is an effective technique for extracting morphine and quinine.[31] On the other hand, this method decomposes and destroys other drugs such as cocaine and belladonna alkaloids.[32]

A final technique is ammonium sulfate.[33] This technique has limited utility. For instance, it cannot be used to isolate barbiturates or other acidic poisons.[34]

Just as inadequate sampling can distort the toxicological analysis, the toxicologists choice of an improper extraction method could cause error.[35] The two problems can also work in conjunction to produce an error. Thus, if the officer submits an inadequate quantity of sample, the toxicologist may be unable to use a variety of extraction techniques. The few techniques employed may be ineffective to extract the poison that caused the death.

Some modern analytic techniques do not require extraction.[36] For example, the immunoassay techniques do not necessitate an extraction step.[37] These techniques are discussed in Chapter 23 dealing with drug identification.

§ 20-2(D). Qualitative and Quantitative Analysis.

The toxicologist can employ a wide range of analytic techniques for identifying and quantifying the toxicants present in an extract.[38] Virtually all the chemical and instrumental techniques mentioned in Chapters 23 and 25 have been adapted to toxicological analysis.

It is impossible to screen a general unknown for every conceivable toxin.[39] Limitations of time, money, and sample quantity preclude using every analytic technique. Consequently, each toxicology laboratory develops its own procedure

---

25. *Id.*

26. Niyogi, *supra* note 3, at 348.

27. *Id.*

28. *Id.* at 347.

29. Poklis, *supra* note 2, at 226.

30. *Id.*

31. *Id.*

32. *Id.*

33. *Id.*

34. *Id.*

35. *Id.*

36. Niyogi, *supra* note 3, at 348.

37. *Id.*

38. *See generally* M. HOUTS, R. BASELT & R. CRAVEY, COURTROOM TOXICOLOGY (1983) (vols. 3-6).

39. Winek, *Forensic Toxicology, in* 2 FORENSIC SCIENCES 31-18 (C. Wecht ed. 1983).

or protocol for screening a general unknown.[40] The following description illustrates a screening procedure.

The laboratory might conduct a preliminary screening test to determine the broad category that the extracted drug falls into. Having identified the broad category, the toxicologist then employs a series of tests designed to narrow the number of possible drugs and ideally identify a particular drug.[41] The toxicologist has a wide variety of texts to choose among.[42] The toxicologist might employ these groups of tests:

—For volatile compounds, a number of gas chromatography (GC) tests with different columns, temperatures, and detectors;[43]

—For organic extractable compounds, a number of systems of thin layer chromatography (TLC);[44]

—For strong organic acids, again a series of TLC or GC tests;[45] and

—For inorganic compounds, emission spectrography, atomic absorption spectrometry (AAS), and several GC systems.[46] Like GC, HPLC[47] and ion chromatography[48] can be used in the testing.

---

40. *Id.*

41. *Id.*

42. Chaturvedi, Vu, Ritter & Canfield, *DNA Typing as a Strategy for Resolving Issues Relevant to Forensic Toxicology*, 44 J. FORENSIC SCI. 189 (1999).

43. Winek, *Forensic Toxicology*, *in* 2 FORENSIC SCIENCES 31-20 (C. Wecht ed. 1983); Ishii, Hattori, Seno, Kumazawa & Suzuki, *Sensitive Detection of Strychnine in Biological Samples by Gas Chromatography with Surface Ionization Detection*, 40 J. FORENSIC SCI. 483 (1995); Dam & Daenens, *Microanalysis of Carbon Monoxide in Blood by Head-Space Capillary Gas Chromatography*, 39 J. FORENSIC SCI. 473 (1994); Kuhlman, Magluilo & Smith, *Two Deaths Involving Isoflurane Abuse*, 38 J. FORENSIC SCI. 968 (1993) (GC).

44. Winek, *supra* note 43, at 31-20-23. *See also* Hegge, Franke & de Zeeuw, *Combined Information from Retardation Factor (Rf) Values and Color Reactions on the Plate Greatly Enhances the Identification Power of Thin-Layer Chromatography in Systematic Toxicological Analysis*, 36 J. FORENSIC SCI. 1094 (1991).

45. Winek, *supra* note 43, at 31-23-24.

46. *Id.* at 31-24-25. Quatrehomme, Ricq, Lapalus, Jacomet & Ollier, *Acute Arsenic Intoxication: Forensic and Toxicologic Aspects (An Observation)*, 37 J. FORENSIC SCI. 1163 (1992) (absorption spectrophotometry).

47. Tracqui, Kintz & Mangin, *Systematic Toxicological Analysis Using HPLC/DAD*, 40 J. FORENSIC SCI. 254 (1995); McIntyre, Ruszkiewicz, Crump & Drummer, *Death Following Colchicine Poisoning*, 39 J. FORENSIC SCI. 280 (1994) (HPLC).

48. Kruszyna, Smith & Kruszyna, *Determining Sodium Azide Concentration in Blood by Ion Chromatography*, 43. J. FORENSIC SCI. 200 (1998).

These tests will help identify the drugs present in the extract. The tests yield qualitative findings.[49]

In many cases, the toxicologist must also make quantitative findings. Some poisons are so lethal that their presence in any trace quantity in the tissue or body fluids indicates that the poison caused the death. However, most poisons cause death only if they are present in certain concentrations. Consequently, before concluding the analysis, the toxicologist must quantify the amount of the drug present. Several of the techniques discussed in Chapters 23 and 25, including ultraviolet spectrophotometry (UV) and neutron activation analysis (NAA),[50] have superior quantitative capabilities. However, our reviewer points out that UV is almost never used today. Modernly, gas chromatography/mass spectrometry (GC/MS), which is also discussed in Chapter 23, is in widespread use at toxicology laboratories.[51] Indeed, "[f]or workplace drug testing, GC/MS analysis is required by the Substance Abuse and Mental Health Services Administration (SAMHSA)."[52]

Like the prior steps in the screening procedure, the qualitative and quantitative tests can be sources of error. When only nonspecific tests are employed, the analyst's opinion of the drug's identity could be a false positive. If the analyst conducted only qualitative tests and omitted quantitative findings, the toxicological evidence might be insufficient to prove that the toxicant caused the death.

---

49. Siek & Dunn, *Documentation of a Doxylamine Overdose Death: Quantitation by Standard Addition and Use of Three Instrumental Techniques*, 38 J. FORENSIC SCI. 713 (1993) ("Professional forensic toxicological groups such as the American Academy of Forensic Sciences and Society of Forensic Toxicologists have recently published guidelines for good practice in doing postmortem quantitative determinations."").

50. *See* Poklis & Saady, *Arsensic Poisoning: Acute or Chronic: Suicide or Murder*, 11 AM. J. FORENSIC MED. & PATHOLOGY 226 (1990) (the use of NAA to measure arsenic concentrations in hair strands pulled from a decedent's head).

51. Kupiec & Chaturvedi, *Stereochemical Determination of Selegiline Metabolites in Postmortem Biological Specimens*, 44 J. FORENSIC SCI. 222 (1999); Tanaka, Kasai, Kita & Tanaka, *Distribution of Phenol in a Fatal Poisoning Case Determined by Gas Chromatography/Mass Spectrometry*, 43 J. FORENSIC SCI. 1086 (1998); Moore, Kilbane, Jones, Kunsman, Levine & Smith, *Tissue Distribution of Ketamine in a Mixed Drug Fatality*, 42 J. FORENSIC SCI. 1183 (1997); Jenkins & Goldberger, *Identification of Unique Cocaine Metabolites and Smoking By-Products in Postmortem Blood and Urine Specimens*, 42 J. FORENSIC SCI. 824 (1997); Corburt & Koves, *Gas Chromatography/Mass Spectrometry for the Determination of Cocaine and Benzoylecgonine over a Wide Concentration Range (<0.005-5 mg/dl) in Postmortem Blood*, 39 J. FORENSIC SCI. 136 (1994); Saito, Kojimahara, Aoki & Takeichi, *Detection of Hydroquinone in a Poisoning Case*, 39 J. FORENSIC SCI. 266 (1994).

52. Wu, Hill, Crouch, Hodnett & McCurdy, *Minimal Standards for the Performance and Interpretation of Toxicology Tests in Legal Proceedings*, 44 J. FORENSIC SCI. 516 (1999).

§ 20-3. Procedures to Identify Ethyl Alcohol.

Drinking alcohol is ethanol, grain or ethyl alcohol. Although ethanol is usually not thought of as a poison, it satisfies the definition of a poison: In proper quantities, it can cause poor health and even death.[53] Indeed, ethanol is the single most common substance encountered in toxicological analysis. It can cause death in two ways.

First, ethanol can be an indirect cause; it can contribute to an accident such as traffic mishap that in turn causes death. If a person's blood alcohol concentration reaches 100 mg/100 ml, the person is seven times more likely than a sober driver to become involved in a traffic accident.[54] Each year drunk driving causes 28,000 deaths in the United States.[55]

Second, ethanol can directly cause death. A person can consume so much drinking alcohol that acute alcohol intoxication results.[56] Depending on the individual's tolerance for alcohol, the onset of acute intoxication occurs at a concentration of .35.[57] This level of blood alcohol concentration can be fatal. A concentration of .50 is often fatal. The prognosis is poor if the person's coma persists for more than 12 hours. The mechanism of death is cerebral asphyxia; respiratory arrest occurs because the intoxication depresses the brain's respiratory center.

Given the dangerous character of alcohol and its wide availability, it is critical for toxicologists to be able to identify ethanol in body tissues and fluid samples.[58] Proper identification depends in large part on avoiding the pitfalls described in the following subsections.

§ 20-3(A). Sample Collection.

The collection of samples is troublesome in ethanol analysis; the sampling sites used pose special problems.

If there has been no autopsy, the toxicologist often obtains a blood sample from the heart by injecting a long needle to puncture the chest wall.[59] However,

---

53. Pounder, Stevenson & Taylor, *Alcoholic Ketoacidosis at Autopsy*, 43 J. Forensic Sci. 812 (1998) (the cause of death can be fatal alcoholic ketoacidosis, evidenced by raised blood levels of ketone bodies).

54. Winek, *Forensic Toxicology*, *in* 2 Forensic Sciences 31-27 (C. Wecht ed. 1983).

55. *Id.*

56. Wecht, *Use of Forensic Pathology in Defending Criminal Cases*, *in* 2 Forensic Sciences 25-100 (C. Wecht ed. 1983).

57. Winek, *Forensic Toxicology*, *in* 2 Forensic Sciences 31-28 (C. Wecht ed. 1983) (.35); Wecht, *The Use of Forensic Pathology in Defending Criminal Cases*, *in* 2 Forensic Sciences 25-100 (C. Wecht ed. 1983) (.40).

58. *See generally* Lisko, *Using a Toxicologist in Driving Under the Influence of Alcohol Cases*, 2 Trial Practice Newsletter 1 (Aug. 1988).

59. Poklis, *supra* note 2, at 227.

the use of the needle can cause an erroneous reading; in the process of insertion, the needle may nick the esophagus or an internal injury may rupture the diaphragm and stomach, flooding the thoracic cavity with gastric contents.[60] The contents of the gastrointestinal tract will diffuse and bathe the cavity. Moreover, the ethanol concentration in the heart may differ from that of the blood circulating around the brain where the ethanol induces the clinical symptoms of intoxication.[61] In light of these dangers, some toxicologists recommend that if there has been no autopsy, the blood be drawn from the femoral vein or cerebrospinal fluid from the cisterna magna.[62]

An autopsy allows the pathologist to draw a sample for the toxicologist without the use of a long needle. The pathologist should massage the heart gently before taking the blood sample.[63] The massage helps ensure that the blood is mixed uniformly in the heart's chambers.[64] Although the sample is frequently taken from the heart, many toxicologists prefer a sample from the brain.[65] There are two reasons for the preference. One reason is that there is less risk of contamination. Another reason is that a brain sample may be more probative, since the physiological effects of ethanol are due to its action on the brain. Yet even a brain sample poses problems. Estimating the effect of a given concentration on the behavior of a living person is speculative because there is almost no comparative data for the effect of various concentrations on a living person's brain.[66] Other toxicologists use skeletal muscle as the sample source.[67]

---

60. *Id.*

61. Winek, *Forensic Toxicology, in* 2 FORENSIC SCIENCES 31-16 (C. Wecht ed. 1983).

62. Poklis, *supra* note 2, at 227; Marraccini, Carroll, Grant, Halleran & Benz, *Differences Between Multisite Postmortem Ethanol Concentrations as Related to Agonal Events*, 35 J. FORENSIC SCI. 1360, 1365 (1990) ("In living persons, variation between arterial and venous ethanol concentrations in the absorption-distribution phase is well established. Until recently, the postmortem blood alcohol was assumed to be uniform, irrespective of the sites of sampling, because of ethanol's capacity to diffuse freely through total body water. Studies by others have documented variation in blood ethanol concentrations when sampled from the heart as opposed to other vascular sites. Postmortem blood ethanol concentrations differ between cardiovascular sampling sites. A single blood ethanol measurement is not adequate in certain circumstances to support an opinion of victim impairment. We recommend that multiple cardiovascular site samples ... be analyzed in any case where an interpretation of ethanol impairment is warranted").

63. *Id.*

64. *Id.*

65. Briglia, Bidanset & Dal Cortivo, *The Distribution of Ethanol in Postmortem Blood Specimens*, 37 J. FORENSIC SCI. 991 (1992) (although specimens were obtained from several different sources, there were "no significant differences among the various blood sites tested").

66. Winek, *Forensic Toxicology, in* 2 FORENSIC SCIENCES 31-17 (C. Wecht ed. 1983).

67. Garriott, *Skeletal Muscle as an Alternative Specimen for Alcohol and Drug Analysis*, 36 J. FORENSIC SCI. 60 (1991) ("In certain circumstances, such as decomposition, a valid blood concentration of ... alcohol cannot be determined or results are questionable. In addition, recent studies show that heart blood may have falsely elevated concentrations.... It is for this reason that alternative specimens must sometimes be chosen for analysis ....").

Still other toxicologists prefer samples from bone marrow.[68] Even when other body fluids and tissues are contaminated or damaged, marrow is usually intact. The toxicologist converts the alcohol concentration in the marrow to a blood alcohol level by assuming a constant ratio (such as 1.26) between marrow and blood alcohol concentrations.[69]

§ 20-3(B). Qualitative and Quantitative Tests.

In ethanol analysis, the toxicologist must make both qualitative and quantitative findings. To establish that ethanol contributed to or caused a death, the toxicologist must not only demonstrate the presence of ethanol; he must also quantify the concentration. There are three analytic techniques commonly used for these purposes.[70]

One technique is an oxidative method.[71] In this technique, the toxicologist first separates the alcohol from the body tissue samples by distillation or microdiffusion. The alcohol is then allowed to react with a strong oxidizing agent. The oxidation converts the alcohol into acetic acid. This technique yields reliable quantitative findings; the toxicologist can determine the amount of ethanol present by measuring the amount of oxidizing agent used in the reaction. However, the technique's qualitative findings are nonspecific. Other compounds such as formaldehyde, methanol, and isopropyl alcohol react with the oxidizing agent. Consequently, another chemical test must be conducted to confirm the compound's identity as ethanol. Although it is theoretically possible for the laboratory to use this technique, our reviewer points out that a 1999 survey conducted by the College of American Pathologists revealed that this method is rarely used today.

Another technique is the enzyme method.[72] This method is popular with clinical laboratories. In this method, the toxicologist uses the enzyme alcohol dehydrogenase (ADH) to convert alcohol into acetaldehyde. The amount of acetaldehyde produced by the reaction indicates the quantity of ethanol present. This technique has several advantages over the oxidative method. It is simpler; it can be conducted without the preliminary step of isolating the ethanol by distillation. Furthermore, this method is more specific than the oxidative technique.

---

68. Winek, *Blood Alcohol Levels: Factors Affecting Predictions*, 19 TRIAL 40 (Jan. 1983).

69. *Id.*

70. POKLIS, HOMICIDE INVESTIGATION: DEATH DUE TO POISONING 14 (unpublished manuscript on file at Toxicology Laboratory, St. Louis University School of Medicine).

71. *Id.*

72. *Id.*

Finally, the toxicologist can resort to gas chromatography (GC).[73] According to our reviewer, modernly all forensic specimens are subjected to GC testing. There is a detailed discussion of GC in Chapter 23 devoted to drug identification. GC has several strengths. For example, it is a relatively quick technique for identifying alcohol and yields qualitative and quantitative data. Although GC is not completely specific, some of the common interfering alcohols that may be present have different retention times than ethanol. Hence, GC will separate the interfering alcohols from ethanol.[74]

§ 20-3(C). Possible Errors.

Errors can occur at either the collection or test stages in ethanol analysis. At the collection stage, in the process of injecting the long needle the pathologist may graze the esophagus and thereby cause an erroneously high reading. Or at the test stage, the toxicologist may rely solely on a nonspecific test. Even if these pitfalls are avoided, other sources of error are possible.

In this analysis, the objective is to identify and quantify the amount of ethanol that the subject ingested. However, there are at least two other ways in which ethanol can enter the subject's body. The first method is through embalming fluid injected into the body. Some embalming fluids contain ethanol. The toxicologist should either collect the samples before embalming or ascertain the identity of the embalming fluid to ensure that the fluid used does not contain ethanol.

The second way is postmortem production of endogenous ethanol.[75] The alcohol that the body gains from external sources (antemortem consumption or postmortem embalming fluid) is termed exogenous. However, the body can produce its own ethanol — called endogenous ethanol.[76] Ethanol is formed by

73. *Id.;* Logan, Case & Kiesel, *Differentiation of Diethyl Ether/Acetone and Ethanol/Acetonitrile Solvent Pairs, and Other Common Volatiles by Dual Column Headspace Gas Chromatography*, 39 J. FORENSIC SCI. 1544 (1994).

74. *Id.* POKLIS, *supra* note 70, at 14.

75. O'Neal & Poklis, *Postmortem Production of Ethanol and Factors that Influence Interpretation*, 17 AM. J. FORENSIC MED. & PATH. 8 (1996); O'Neal, Wolf, Levine, Kunsman & Poklis, *Gas Chromatographic Procedures for Determination of Ethanol in Postmortem Blood Using T-Butanol and Methyl Ethyl Ketone as Internal Standards*, 83 FORENSIC SCI. INT'L 31 (1996); Zumwalt, Bost & Sunshine, *Evaluation of Ethanol Concentrations in Decomposed Bodies*, 27 J. FORENSIC SCI. 549 (1982).

76. *Id.* Helander, Beck & Jones, *Distinguishing Ingested Ethanol from Microbial Formation by Analysis of Urinary 5-Hydroxytryptophol and 5-Hydroxyindoleacetic Acid*, 40 J. FORENSIC SCI. 95 (1995); Gilliland & Bost, *Alcohol in Decomposed Bodies: Postmortem Synthesis and Distribution*, 38 J. FORENSIC SCI. 1266 (1993); Saady, Poklis & Dalton, *Production of Urinary Ethanol After Sample Collection*, 38 J. FORENSIC SCI. 1467 (1993); Canfield, Kupiec & Huffine, *Postmortem Alcohol Production in Fatal Aircraft Accidents*, 38 J. FORENSIC SCI. 914 (1993) ("The opinion held by some toxicologists that postmortem alcohol production can be inferred from the presence of acetaldehyde, acetone, butanol, and other volatiles was found to be incorrect"); Levine, Smith,

bacterial or microbial activity during the body's putrefaction.[77] The ethanol created in this fashion may falsely elevate the quantitative finding of exogenous ethanol. The toxicologist can guard against this error. If possible, he should determine the amount of ethanol in the subject's urine.[78] Ethanol ordinarily does not form in urine during putrefaction.[79] Hence, the urine should be free of endogenous ethanol.[80] Unfortunately, in many cases it is impossible to measure the ethanol in the urine because the bladder vacated the urine before sample collection.[81]

Even if the toxicologist cannot avoid this problem by testing the decedent's urine, there are promising techniques that may help minimize the problem. Some researchers have attempted to determine the maximum amount of postmortem ethanol production.[82] If this could be determined, the toxicologist could subtract that figure from the total ethanol detected in the analysis. The subtraction would yield a minimum estimate for the exogenous alcohol. However, different researchers have reached varying conclusions as to the maximum amount of endogenous production.[83]

Other researchers have begun testing the hypothesis that the amount of postmortem production can be correlated with the degree of putrefaction.[84] The initial research indicates a rough correlation between the two factors.[85] By assessing the extent of putrefaction, the toxicologist may be able to estimate the amount of endogenous alcohol. Then, by subtracting that figure from the total ethanol detected, the quantity of exogenous ethanol can be estimated. This technique has promise, but the research is hardly definitive. The database for one experiment included only 130 bodies.[86] Further research is probably needed before this technique can be used in a court of law.

Smialek & Caplan, *Interpretation of Low Postmortem Concentrations of Ethanol*, 38 J. FORENSIC SCI. 663 (1993); Mayes, Levine, Smith, Wagner & Froede, *Toxicologic Findings in the USS Iowa Disaster*, 37 J. FORENSIC SCI. 1352 (1992).

77. Zumwalt, Bost & Sunshine, *supra* note 75.

78. *Id.* at 553.

79. *Id.*

80. *Id.*

81. *Id.*

82. *Id.* at 549.

83. *Id.*

84. *Id.*

85. *Id.*

86. *Id.* at 554.

Still other researchers are investigating a PCR-based technique to detect the presence of a variety of microbes that can cause the endogenous production of ethanol.[87] As the researchers report,

> The sensitivity of the PCR detection method reported here exceeds the level of microbial cells judged to have significant ethanol producing activity in postmortem samples. This degree of sensitivity assures that minimal levels of microbial contamination can be detected, thereby reducing the possibility of a false indication of imbibed alcohol.[88]

Other researchers, including our reviewer, have advanced recommendations for dealing with this problem.[89] The recommendations include the following procedures:[90]

—If the body is evidently decomposed or there are strong indications of putrefaction such as smell, the analyst should assume postmortem synthesis of ethanol.

—Take multiple specimens from different anatomical sites such as heart blood, peripheral blood (*i.e.* femoral artery), vitreous humor, urine, and bile. If there is ethanol in the blood but not in urine and vitreous humor, the analyst ought to presume that postmortem ethanol synthesis has occurred.

—If the analyst relies on gas chromatographic procedures for postmortem ethanol determination, he or she should not use *n*-propanol as the internal standard. That compound is the most commonly reported "other volatile" associated with postmortem ethanol synthesis. It is preferable to utilize *t*-butanol or methyl ethyl ketone as the internal standards.[91]

—If blood is the only available specimen, ethanol findings of 0.03% or lower should be considered negative.

§ 20-4. Procedures to Identify Poisons.

The 16th century physician, Paracelsus, asserted: "All substances are poisons; there is none which is not a poison. The right dose differentiates a poison from a

87. Kupfer, Chaturvedi, Canfield & Roe, *PCR-Based Identification of Postmortem Microbial Contaminants--A Preliminary Study*, 44 J. FORENSIC SCI. 592 (1999).

88. *Id.* at 596.

89. O'Neal & Poklis, *Postmortem Production of Ethanol and Factors that Influence Interpretation*, 17 AM. J. FORENSIC MED. & PATH. 8 (1996).

90. *Id.* at 18.

91. O'Neal, Wolf, Levine, Kunsman & Poklis, *Gas Chromatographic Procedures for Determination of Ethanol in Postmortem Blood Using T-Butanol and Methyl Ethyl Ketone as Internal Standards*, 83 FORENSIC SCI. INT'L 31 (1996).

remedy."[92] Paracelsus was guilty of only a mild overstatement. The term, "poison," can be broadly defined as any substance that taken in sufficient quantity, can cause ill health or death in normal healthy persons. The definition is so broad that literally thousands of substances qualify as poisons.[93] It includes not only classic poisons such as arsenic but also drugs such as barbiturates that can have ill effects in overdosage.[94]

Although all these compounds qualify as poisons, they differ markedly in several respects. For example, they vary in the frequency with which they cause death. Some drugs such as cocaine, heroin, and methadone frequently cause death. Many popular drugs of abuse, including amphetamines and phencyclidine (PCP), occasionally lead to death. Minor tranquilizers such as meprobamate cause death only rarely. Finally, some drugs such as cannabis do not directly cause death, although they still qualify as poisons because they can produce other ill effects on a person's health.

Similarly, poisons vary in their speed or rate of action. Some poisons kill with great rapidity. Phosphorous, carbon monoxide (depending upon the concentration), cyanide, and strychnine share this characteristic.[95] Other poisons have an intermediate rate of action. Carbon tetrachloride and thallium fall into this category.[96] Still other poisons are slow-acting. Depending on the concentration, arsenic and lead can be slow-acting.[97]

Finally, poisons vary in the mechanism of action.[98] Alcohol, barbiturates, cyanide, carbon monoxide, and heroin are depressants or asphyxiants.[99] In contrast, amphetamines, cocaine, and strychnine are stimulants.[100] Ammonia, gasoline, insecticides, lye, magnesium sulfate, mercuric chloride, sodium cyanide, and sulfuric acid are corrosives and irritants.[101]

This long list of chemicals should not mislead the reader. The toxicologist does not rely exclusively on chemical methods of testing. Although most of the balance of this section focuses on chemical tests, non-chemical data plays an important role in toxicological investigation. For instance, the symptoms displayed by the decedent just prior to death are a clue to the identity of the

---

92. *Quoted in* Poklis, *supra* note 2, at 224.

93. *Id.* at 227.

94. *See* Anthony, Hirsch & Moritz, *Poisoning*, *in* HANDBOOK OF LEGAL MEDICINE 84 (5th ed. 1979).

95. HOWARD, *supra* note 9, at 3.

96. *Id.*

97. *Id.* at 4.

98. *Id.*

99. *Id.*

100. *Id. See also* Manhoff, Hood, Caputo, Perry, Rosen & Mirchandani, *Cocaine in Decomposed Human Remains*, 36 J. FORENSIC SCI. 1732 (1991).

101. HOWARD, *supra* note 9, at 4.

poison.[102] When the antemortem symptoms include vomiting, diarrhea, rapid collapse, and weak pulse, the toxicologist will suspect arsenic.[103] If the victim suffered severe convulsions before death, the suspicion may be strychnine.[104] Or if the victim exhibited contracted pupils, the toxicologist may surmise that the poison was a narcotic.[105]

Like the antemortem symptoms, the postmortem pathological lesions exhibited during the autopsy may indicate the identity of the poison.[106] For example, acids and alkalies cause burns around the mouth or on the body surface.[107] Metallic poisons inflict severe damage on the gastrointestinal tract and kidneys.[108] Phosphorous causes degeneration of the liver.[109] The presence of cherry red lividity is indicative of carbon monoxide poisoning. Strychnine poisoning often leads to rigor mortis with the feet extended.

Unfortunately, most poisons do not produce characteristic pathological lesions.[110] Absent such lesions, the toxicologist must resort to the chemical and instrumental tests mentioned in Chapters 23 and 25. For that matter, even when the autopsy discloses lesions, the lesions support only a tentative identification of the poison; the toxicologist must still use chemical tests to confirm the identity of the poison. As in the case of the toxicological analysis of alcohol, there is potential for error at each step in the testing process.

§ 20-4(A). Sample Collection.

If the suspicion of homicide arises after the decedent's embalming and burial, the body may have to be exhumed to obtain the necessary samples. Both the embalming and the burial create problems. Some embalming fluids contain arsenic; other embalming fluids destroy poisons such as cyanide.[111] The toxicologist ought to contact the embalmer to learn the identity of the fluid used and ideally obtain a sample. Burial poses other problems because some poisons, including arsenic, occur naturally in soil. The toxicologist ought to ensure that the soil surrounding the coffin is sampled. By testing the soil, the toxicologist can

---

102. Anthony, Hirsch & Moritz, *supra* note 94, at 84; POKLIS, *supra* note 70, at 1.

103. POKLIS, *supra* note 70, at 1.

104. *Id.*

105. *Id.*

106. *Id.* at 3.

107. *Id.*

108. *Id.*

109. *Id.*

110. *Id.*

111. *See* Takayasu, Holterman, Ohshima & Pounder, *Stability of Tricyclic Antidepressants in Formalim Solutions*, 43 J. FORENSIC SCI. 1213 (1998) (the difficulties encountered in "autopsies performed on bodies embalmed using formalin solutions").

determine whether the earth contains any poisons that could lead to a false positive.

The autopsy must be conducted with care. Each tissue sample should be cut with a different instrument, or the instrument should be completely cleaned before each cutting. Otherwise, the cutting instrument might transfer traces of poison from one organ to another and lead to an erroneous conclusion.

§ 20-4(B). Chemical Tests.

Section 20-2 described the toxicological procedures to screen for a general unknown. At the end of the testing process, the toxicologist must confirm the identity of the poison.[112] To do so, a test or set of tests that is relatively specific for that poison is used. The tests for arsenic are illustrative.

One procedure is the Marsh or Marsh-Berzelin test. The test rests on the principle that the generation of hydrogen in the presence of arsenic results in the formation of arsine. In the Marsh test, the exhaust from burning arsine is aimed at a cold porcelain plate. When the arsine deposits itself on the plate, the deposition forms an arsenic mirror. In the Marsh-Berzelin procedure, the mirror forms in a tube. Although antimony will also form a mirror, the toxicologist can differentiate between antimony and arsenic by adding hypochlorite which dissolves arsenic but not antimony. These tests yield only qualitative findings.

Another test is the Gutzeit procedure. Like the Marsh test, this procedure is based on the production of arsine. In the Gutzeit procedure, the toxicologist uses arsine to reduce mercuric bromide or silicon nitrate on filter paper. The reduction creates a characteristic stain. This test yields both qualitative and quantitative data. The shade of color is proportional to the amount of arsenic present. However, to assess the shade, the analyst must have known standards to compare with the stain. Alternatively, the analyst can use a spectrophotometer to read the optical density of the stain.

Another procedure is a colormetric test using Molybdenum Blue. In this test, when the unknown is arsenic, the reaction produces a blue color. The analyst can visually compare the color with known standards or use a colormeter. Diethyldithiocarbamate is another reagent used in colormetric tests for arsenic. In this test, the reaction produces a red color. There are comparable color tests for other poisons such as the Prussian Blue test for cyanide.

The Reinsch test is another method of confirming a poison's identity as arsenic. In this test, the toxicologist heats the unknown in hydrochloric acid and then adds a copper strip of foil to the solution. If the strip is tarnished brown or black, the tarnish indicates the presence of arsenic, antimony, bismuth silver, or

---

112. de Zeeuw, *Laboratory Guidelines in Analytical Toxicology: How to Approach Qualitative Analysis*, 37 J. FORENSIC SCI. 1437, 1439 (1992) (reviewing various guidelines for qualitative analysis, the author notes the necessity for confirmatory testing).

mercury. The toxicologist can differentiate among those four compounds by further testing. For instance, the toxicologist might remove the tarnish from the strip and gently heat the tarnish in a tube. When so heated, mercury assumes a gobular shape while arsenic takes tetrahedral form.

A final arsenic test is the Bromate procedure. The procedure is used when large quantities of the unknown are available for testing. In this method, the toxicologist mixes the unknown in a hydrazine sulfate-sodium bromide solution. Potassium bromate is then added, at which time a color should appear. The toxicologist adds further bromate one drop at a time until the color disappears. The appearance of the color indicates the unknown's identity as arsenic, and the number of bromate drops needed to eliminate the color indicates the strength or quantity of arsenic present.

In attempting to confirm the poison's identity, the toxicologist is not limited to simple color reactions. For instance, the poison phosphorous has the property of phosphorescence; that is, phosphorous glows in the dark. The toxicologist can examine the subject's feces and vomitus to determine whether they exhibit this property. If a decedent suffered phosphorous poisoning, his liver may display a green glow in a dark room.[113]

As in drug identification testing, the attorney opposing chemical poison testing evidence should not be content with the toxicologist's assertion that the tests used "identify" the poison. The attorney should insist on proof of the specificity of the final tests used to confirm the poison's identity.

§ 20-4(C). Qualitative Findings.

This section catalogues the poisons that the toxicologist is most likely to report in his qualitative findings. There are two broad categories of poisons: inorganics and organics. The inorganic category can be subdivided into three groups: metallics, non-metallics, and corrosives. The organic category can be subdivided into four groups: gaseous, alkaloids, volatiles, and non-volatile, non-alkaloidal organics.

Inorganic Poisons

The common feature of the inorganic poisons is that they lack hydrocarbons in their composition.

Metallics. The poisons in this group have metals in their elemental composition. The group includes arsenic, antimony, beryllium, copper, gold, lead, mercury, silver, and tin.[114] The metals do not decompose in the body.

113. Anthony, Hirsch & Moritz, *supra* note 94, at 115.
114. *Id.* at 97-98, 100, 108, 110.

Consequently, they accumulate in the body and can be detected in postmortem tissue.

Arsenic is perhaps the best known metallic poison. It naturally occurs in ground water and soil. In addition, it has many industrial applications including wood preservation, glass making, weed killers, grasshopper bait, pesticides, and pork and poultry feeds.[115] Since industrial waste is often disposed of in sea water, sea water contains some traces of arsenic. Crustaceans, prawns, shellfish, and some fresh water fish have been found to have arsenic in their tissue. Since human beings are exposed to these industrial products and consume fish, it is becoming common to find trace elements of arsenic in the tissue of persons who have not been poisoned.

Arsenic poisoning can be acute, chronic, or arsine. In acute poisoning, the symptoms appear in as short a time as 30 minutes after ingestion. The symptoms include burning or dryness of the mouth and throat, abdominal pain, vomiting, and bloody diarrhea.[116] The vomiting and diarrhea lead to dehydration and shock. In chronic or subacute poisoning, the symptoms appear over a longer period of time. The fingers and toes gradually weaken. The growing physical weakness can be accompanied by personality changes, headaches, drowsiness, confusion, and memory loss. Hoarseness, coughs, laryngitis, and peeling of the skin can occur. Finally, in arsine poisoning, the victim is exposed to arsenic in gaseous form. In this form, arsenic is extremely toxic, and exposure can be fatal in minutes.

Other common metallic poisons are beryllium, lead, and mercury. Many industrial plants discharge beryllium into the atmosphere.[117] Persons vary in their susceptibility to beryllium.[118] However, if a person inhales in a highly contaminated atmosphere, beryllium poisoning can lead to death within two to five weeks. Lead can cause poisoning when inhaled as fumes, ingested, or absorbed through the skin.[119] Chronic lead poisoning is typically characterized by abdominal pain, physical weakness, and indigestion. The toxicologist can use X-rays to detect lead deposits in bone. Acute mercury poisoning principally affects the kidneys while chronic mercury poisoning impacts the central nervous system. If the toxicologist suspects mercury poisoning, he will usually analyze the subject's urine.[120] Mercury can settle in the colon, kidneys, and liver.

Nonmetallics. The nonmetallic poisons are solid in their stable form. This group includes cyanide, phosphorous, iodine, boron, sodium, and sulphur.

115. *Id.* at 97. *See also* Poklis & Saady, *Arsensic Poisoning: Acute or Chronic Suicide or Murder*, 11 AM. J. FORENSIC MED. & PATHOLOGY 226 (1990).

116. Anthony, Hirsch & Moritz, *supra* note 94, at 98.

117. *Id.* at 100.

118. *Id.*

119. *Id.* at 108.

120. *Id.* at 110.

Cyanide is probably the most notorious poison in this group.[121] It is a quick-acting poison. If the subject ingests or inhales a fatal dose, death often occurs within a matter of minutes.[122] The symptoms preceding death can include convulsions, gasping, and rapid pulse.

Phosphorous is a common ingredient of rat paste.[123] Children sometimes suffer accidental poisoning when they eat food that has been smeared with the paste and left out as rat bait. Death usually ensues in a few hours. The chronology of symptoms is typically nausea and vomiting, followed by coma and culminating in death.

Corrosives. These poisons destroy tissue upon contact. This group includes alkalies such as lye, inorganic acids such as hydrochloric, nitric and sulfuric, as well as compounds such as ammonia, caustic soda, and lysol. Upon contact, these poisons can injure the skin and eyes; they attack the body tissue at the site of contact. Strong alkalies produce a soft mucoid type of skin injury while the other acids often leave a brown or black discoloration on the skin.[124] If the subject inhales fumes from strong acids, the inhalation may injure the air passages and lead quickly to asphyxial death.

Organic Poisons

Except for gaseous poisons, all organic poisons contain the hydrocarbon molecule.

Gasses. These poisons are stable in their gaseous form. This group includes carbon monoxide, carbon dioxide, bromine, chlorine, fluorine, and phosgine. The subject absorbs these poisons through the respiratory system.

Among the gasses, carbon monoxide (CO) has probably attracted the greatest publicity as a poison.[125] The affinity of CO for hemoglobin is roughly 200 times

---

121. *Id.* at 104-05. *See also* B. BALLANTYNE & T. MARRS, CLINICAL AND EXPERIMENTAL TOXICOLOGY OF CYANIDES (1987); Seto, *Stability and Spontaneous Production of Blood Cyanide During Heating*, 41 J. FORENSIC SCI. 465 (1996).

122. Anthony, Hirsch & Moritz, *supra* note 94, at 104.

123. *Id.* at 114. *See also* Kusu, Tsuneta & Takamura, *Fluorometric Determination of Pseudocholinesterase Activity in Postmortem Blood Samples*, 35 J. FORENSIC SCI. 1330 (1990) (the determination may indicate that the death was caused by organophosphorous compounds such as insecticides); Sharma, Jadhav, Saraf & Chandra, *High Performance Liquid Chromatographic Method for the Analysis of Organophosphorous and Carbamate Pesticides*, 48 FORENSIC SCI. INT'L 21 (1990).

124. Anthony, Hirsch & Moritz, *supra* note 94, at 89.

125. *Id.* at 101.; Sato, Tamaki, Hattori, Moore, Tsutsumi, Okajima & Katsumata, *Determination of Total Hemoglobin in Forensic Blood Samples with Special Reference to Carboxyhemoglobin Analysis*, 48 FORENSIC SCI. INT'L 90 (1990) ("The determination of carboxyhemoglobin (COHb) in blood is important to diagnose carbon monoxide (CO) poisoning. The ratio of COHb content ... to total-hemoglobin (Hb) content is considered to be very reliable for the determination of percentage saturation of COHb (COHb%) in forensic blood samples. However, if the total-Hb concentration is

greater than that of oxygen.[126] When the person inhales CO, the CO tends to displace the oxygen in the person's system. The result is oxygen starvation. CO is so toxic that when the concentration in the air is even 1.5%, inhalation can lead to death in between one and three minutes.[127] If a person's blood becomes 20% saturated with CO, the person will experience shortness of breath.[128] At a 30% concentration, the person suffers fatigue, dizziness, and possible collapse.[129] At 40%, the person may die; and at 60%, most victims do die.[130]

Volatiles. This group includes central nervous system depressants such as alcohol, benzene,[131] ether, and toluene. Volatile organics can be lethal if administered internally. Worse still, since they are volatile, they can give up gasses during evaporation. Inhalation of a high concentration of the gasses can likewise lead to death.

Alkaloids. This group includes compounds which have a nitrogenous base in their structure. The group includes opiate derivatives such as nicotine, strychnine, and hemlock.

Nicotine can kill with great speed.[132] The ingestion of nicotine leads almost immediately to unconsciousness. Convulsions follow, and the symptoms culminate in respiratory failure and death. If the toxicologist suspects nicotine poisoning, he should analyze vomitus and gastric contents.

Strychnine works on the central nervous system.[133] Symptoms begin appearing in half an hour after ingestion. One of the initial symptoms is convulsions, which grow in severity and may lead to death within one to three hours. When strychnine is the suspected poison, the toxicologist examines the contents of the blood, liver, stomach, and urine.[134]

---

not correctly determined, the COHb% in blood cannot be correctly calculated"); Levin, Rechani, Gurman, Landron, Clark, Yoklavich, Rodriguez, Droz, de Cabrera & Kaye, *Analysis of Carboxyhemoglobin and Cyanide in Blood from Victims of the Dupont Plaza Hotel Fire in Puerto Rico*, 35 J. FORENSIC SCI. 151 (1990); Lopez-Rivadulla, Fernandez, Cruz & Concheiro, *Direct Carboxyhemoglobin Determination by Derivative Spectroscopy*, 40 FORENSIC SCI. INT'L 261 (1989); Goldbaum, Chace & Lappas, *Determination of Carbon Monoxide in Blood by Gas Chromatography Using a Thermal Conductivity Detector*, 31 J. FORENSIC SCI. 133 (1986) (technique permitting the detection of small quantities of CO in blood).

126. Anthony, Hirsch & Moritz, *supra* note 94, at 101.

127. POKLIS, DRUG AND CHEMICAL TOXICITIES OF SUBSTANCES COMMONLY ENCOUNTERED IN POST MORTEM TOXICOLOGIC ANALYSES 3 (unpublished manuscript on file at Toxicology Laboratory, St. Louis University School of Medicine).

128. *Id.*

129. *Id.*

130. *Id.*

131. Barbera, Bulla & Romano, *A Fatal Case of Benzene Poisoning*, 43 J. FORENSIC SCI. 1250 (1998).

132. Anthony, Hirsch & Moritz, *supra* note 94, at 111.

133. *Id.* at 117.

134. *Id.*

Non-volatile, non-alkaloidal organic poisons. The most commonly encountered poisons in this group were once the barbiturates and the various derivatives of barbituric acid.[135] Today, however, they have been replaced by tricyclic antidepressants such as amitriptyline and imipramine. The benzodiazepines, including diazepam and lorazepam, are frequently encountered. The ingestion of amitriptyline usually causes death only if the person consumes a very large dose -- perhaps fifteen times greater than a therapeutic dose. Death can be rapid.

In § 20-3(C), we saw that there can be an error in alcohol analysis because there can be postmortem production of endogenous ethanol. There can be similar errors in poison analysis. Suppose, for example, that the toxicologist is investigating the possibility that the deceased overdosed on amphetamine. Many other drugs, including clobenzorex, are metabolized to amphetamine.[136]

§ 20-4(D). Quantitative Findings.

Most toxins cause death only if a certain concentration of the toxin is present in the subject's system. For that reason, before reaching an opinion as to the cause of death, the toxicologist must make quantitative findings.

The toxicologist usually reports that one of three different levels of the toxin is present: therapeutic, toxic, or lethal.[137] A therapeutic level is the concentration that would ordinarily result from a person's ingestion of the drug pursuant to a physician's orders.[138] The concentration is high enough to induce the beneficial changes the physician hopes for but low enough not to cause any serious toxic effects. A toxic level is the concentration at which serious toxic symptoms usually emerge.[139] Lastly, at a lethal concentration, the poison can cause death.[140] Here, the toxicologist has either found data indicating that that concentration has been fatal in the past, or the concentration is so far above accepted therapeutic

---

135. *Id.* at 99.

136. Valtier & Cody, *Metabolic Production of Amphetamine Following Administration of Clobenzorex*, 44 J. FORENSIC SCI. 17 (1999).

137. Anthony, Hirsch & Moritz, *supra* note 94, at 88-89; Winek, *Forensic Toxicology, in* 2 FORENSIC SCIENCES 31-65 (C. Wecht ed. 1983); Markiewicz & Chlobowska, *Specific Features of Poisoning*, 46 FORENSIC SCI. INT'L 3 (1990) ("The concept of poison is ... related to a dose and a concentration of a given chemical substance. The fact of the qualitative detection of the substance in biological material does not ... indicate the unequivocal poisoning. The toxicologist has to know the normal, correct, or therapeutic contents of various chemical compounds ... and distinguish them from the toxic or fatal ones"); Druid & Holmgren, *A Compilation of Fatal and Control Concentrations of Drugs in Postmortem Femoral Blood*, 42 J. FORENSIC SCI. 79 (1997); McIntyre, King, Cordner & Drummer, *Postmortem Clomipramine: Therapeutic or Toxic Concentrations*, 39 J. FORENSIC SCI. 486 (1994).

138. *Id.* Winek, *supra* note 137, at 31-65.

139. *Id.*

140. *Id.*

and toxic levels that one can reasonably speculate that the concentration could lead to death.[141]

There are published compilations of therapeutic, toxic, and lethal levels for the common poisons.[142] These reported levels, however, are merely guidelines. Persons vary enormously in their susceptibility to drugs. Moreover, for many poisons, the amount of the poison required for a lethal dose varies, depending on whether the poisoning is chronic (over a long period of time) or acute (a single ingestion) and whether the pathway is inhalation, internal administration, or absorption through the skin. All these factors affect the validity of the ultimate opinion that the poison was present in a lethal concentration.

Some researchers use the following cutoffs: NOEL, ED50, and LD50.[143] NOEL is the no observable effect level. This represents the highest dose of the chemical which can be tolerated by the test subject without any observable adverse effects. ED50 is the level at which 50% of the subjects tested experience some adverse effects. LD50 is the level at which the chemical is fatal to 50% of the subjects.[144] Obviously, this type of in vivo research can be conducted only with animals. (Even with "informed" consent, researchers could not administer potentially lethal doses to human subjects.) On the one hand, many government agencies, including the Environmental Protection Agency, rely heavily on animal studies in, for example, deciding whether to approval pesticides.[145] On the other hand, there are many anatomical and biochemical differences between human beings and other animals. For that reason, "more and more toxicologists are persuaded that toxic effects of drugs and other chemicals in man are not generally predictable from animal studies."[146] As one commentator remarked,

> The results of animal tests are usually of limited value when the data are extrapolated to man; often animal data confuses and misleads with respect to what happens in man. Unexpected toxic effects that do not depend on dosage, occur only occasionally in man, and are not predictable from animal studies, are the greatest concern for clinicians.[147]

---

141. *Id.;* Karch, Stephens & Ho, *Relating Cocaine Blood Concentrations to Toxicity: An Autopsy Study of 99 Cases*, 43 J. FORENSIC SCI. 41 (1998); Logan, Fligner & Haddix, *Cause and Manner of Death in Fatalities Involving Methamphetamine*, 43 J. FORENSIC SCI. 28 (1998).

142. *E.g.*, Winek, *Forensic Toxicology, in* 2 FORENSIC SCIENCES 31-71-90 (C. Wecht ed. 1983); Niyogi, *supra* note 3, at 351-81.

143. Dukes, *Toxicology Made Easy: What Every Trial Advocate Should Know*, 63 DEF. COUNS. J. 338 (1996).

144. Goldstein & Henifin, *Reference Guide on Toxicology, in* REFERENCE MANUAL ON SCIENTIFIC EVIDENCE 181, 188 (1994).

145. Sumner, *Agricultural Chemicals: The Federal Insecticide, Fungicide and Rodenticide Act and a Review of the European Community Regulatory Process, in* REGULATORY TOXICOLOGY 29 (1973).

146. C. WILBER, FORENSIC TOXICOLOGY FOR THE LAW ENFORCEMENT OFFICER 96 (1980).

147. *Id.* at 96-97.

Even prescinding from the problem of extrapolating from animals to human beings, the most recent research underscores that the reported levels must be treated merely as guidelines. For example, there is mounting evidence that postmortem blood-drug concentrations are both site and time dependent.[148] At least for some drugs, "there are several-fold differences in concentration between

---

148. Hillberg, Rogde & Morland, *Postmortem Drug Redistribution--Human Cases Related to Results in Experimental Animals*, 44 J. FORENSIC SCI. 3 (1999); Hilberg, Ripel, Smith, Slordal, Morland & Bjorneboe, *Postmortem Amitripyline Pharmacokinetics in Pigs after Oral and Intravenous Routes of Administration*, 43 J. FORENSIC SCI. 380 (1998); Prouty & Anderson, *The Forensic Science Implications of Site and Temporal Influences on Postmortem Blood-Drug Concentrations*, 35 J. FORENSIC SCI. 243 (1990). *See also* Hearn, Keran, Wei & Hime, *Site-Dependent Postmortem Changes in Blood Cocaine Concentrations*, 36 J. FORENSIC SCI. 673 (1991) ("In medical examiner cases in which scene investigation suggested that the deceased was a cocaine user, blood samples were collected as soon after death as possible. At autopsy, a second set of samples was collected. Analysis of paired samples ... revealed dramatic differences in the cocaine concentration. The magnitude and direction of the change appeared to be site dependent. Usually, but not invariably, cocaine concentration in subclavian vein blood decreases while that in heart, aorta, and femoral vein blood increases ...."); Winek, Westwood & Wahba, *Plasma Versus Bone Narrow Desipramine: A Comparative Study*, 48 FORENSIC SCI. INT'L 49 (1990); Langford, Taylor & Pounder, *Drug Concentration in Selected Skeletal Muscles*, 43 J. FORENSIC SCI. 22 (1998) (comparing concentrations in 12 named muscles and femoral venous blood); Robertson & Drummer, *Postmortem Distribution and Redistribution of Nitrobenzodiazepines in Man*, 43 J. FORENSIC SCI. 9 (1998) ("vitreous concentrations were one-third of blood, while bile concentrations were 5-12 fold higher"); Robertson & Drummer, *Stability of Nitrobenzodiazepines in Postmortem Blood*, 43 J. FORENSIC SCI. 5 (1998) ("These results show that the nitrobenzodiazepines and their metabolites are unstable chemically and metabolically in blood."); Pohland & Bernhard, *Postmortem Serum and Tissue Redistribution of Fluoxetine and Norfluoxetine in Dogs Following Oral Administration of Fluoxetine Hydrochloride (Prozac)*, 42 J. FORENSIC SCI. 812 (1997) ("postmortem serum concentrations appear to be dependent on the sample site"); Moriya & Hashimoto, *Distribution of Free and Conjugated Morphine in Body Fluids and Tissues in a Fatal Heroin Overdose: Is Conjugated Morphine Stable in Postmortem Specimens*, 42 J. FORENSIC SCI. 736 (1997) ("very site dependent"); Skopp, Lutz, Potsch, Ganbmann, Klinder, Schmidt, Aderjan & Mattern, *An In Vitro Experiment for Postmortem Vascular Permeation. The Passage of Morphine and Morphine Glucuronides Across a Vascular Wall*, 42 J. FORENSIC SCI. 486 (1997) ("adsorption to and penetration into the vascular tissue may alter intraluminal blood concentrations even at an early stage of the postmortem time period"); Pounder, Adams, Fuke & Langford, *Site to Site Variability of Postmortem Drug Concentrations in Liver and Lung*, 41 J. FORENSIC SCI. 927 (1996); Levine, Ramcharitar & Smialek, *Stability of Ecgonine Methyl Ester in Postmortem Urine Specimens*, 41 J. FORENSIC SCI. 126 (1996) ("One premise in all forensic toxicological analyses is that analyte concentrations remain unchanged from specimen collection to specimen analysis. However, there are numerous examples in the scientific literature that demonstrate that this premise is not always appropriate."); McKinney, Phillips, Gomez, Brent, MacIntyre & Wataon, *Vitreous Humor Cocaine and Metabolite Concentrations: Do Postmortem Specimens Reflect Blood Levels at the Time of Death*, 40 J. FORENSIC SCI. 102 (1995) (the site and time of collection must be considered); Logan & Luthi, *The Significance of Morphine Concentrations in the Cerebrospinal Fluid in Morphine Caused Deaths*, 39 J. FORENSIC SCI. 699 (1994) ("the site of collection of the CSF must be known"); Quatrehomme, Bourret, Liao & Ollier, *An Experimental Methodology for*

blood samples from different sites."[149] The liver and capillary rich lungs are likely to have especially high concentrations.[150] For that reason, "a calculation of dose from a single postmortem blood-drug concentration" can easily be inaccurate.[151] This problem underscores the need for two blood samples. Moreover, site dependence "undermines the reference value of databases of drug concentrations in post mortem blood samples where the site of origin of the sample is unknown."[152] If the toxicologist uses a database without knowing the site of origin, the toxicologist might erroneously characterize a therapeutic level as a lethal one.

Scientists are developing artificial intelligence (AI) computer software to apply these numerical guidelines.[153]

---

the Study of Postmortem Changes in Toxic Concentrations of Drugs, Using Secobarbital As an Example, 39 J. FORENSIC SCI. 1300 (1994) ("concentrations found at the time of autopsy may be different from concentrations at the time of death"); Yonemitsu & Pounder, *Postmortem Changes in Blood Tranlcypromine Concentration: Competing Redistribution and Degradation Effects*, 59 FORENSIC SCI. INT'L 177 (1993) (site and temporal changes); Browne, Moore, Scheurer, Tebbett & Logan, *A Rapid Method for the Determination of Cocaine in Brain Tissue*, 36 J. FORENSIC SCI. 1662 (1991) ("It has been suggested that brain tissue is a better sampling site than blood for the determination of cocaine concentration."). *But see* Martin & Pounder, *Post-Mortem Toxico-Kinetics of Trazodone*, 56 FORENSIC SCI. INT'L 201 (1992) ("trazodone shows little preferential concentration in solid organs and ... has relatively stable post-mortem blood concentrations with little redistribution artefact"). *See also* Langford & Pounder, *Possible Markers for Postmortem Drug Redistribution*, 42 J. FORENSIC SCI. 88 (1997) (the researchers were investigating to identify a marker indicating that drug redistribution has occurred postmortem; they found that "hepatic enzymes are relatively poor markers for postmortem hepatic drug shifts but amino acids, particularly methionine, may be useful markers for pulmonary drug shifts").

149. Moriya & Hashimoto, *Redistribution of Basic Drugs into Cardiac Blood from Surrounding Tissues during Early-Stages Postmortem*, 44 J. FORENSIC SCI. 10, 15 (1999) ("drug concentrations in left cardiac blood should not be used for toxicological evaluation, even if the postmortem interval is short"); Pounder & Jones, *Post-Mortem Drug Redistribution "A Toxicological Nightmare,"* 45 FORENSIC SCI. INT'L 253, 260 (1990); Logan & Smirnow, *Postmortem Distribution and Redistribution of Morphine in Man*, 41 J. FORENSIC SCI. 221 (1996) ("Ventricular blood morphine concentrations were ... consistently higher than those in the peripheral compartment, represented by either femoral or iliac blood").

150. *Id.* at 261.

151. Prouty & Anderson, *The Forensic Science Implications of Site and Temporal Influences on Postmortem Blood-Drug Concentrations*, 35 J. FORENSIC SCI. 243, 268-69 (1990).

152. Pounder & Jones, *Post-Mortem Drug Redistribution "A Toxicological Nightmare*, 45 FORENSIC SCI. INT'L 253, 262 (1990).

153. Wimbish, Shores & Spiehler, *A Comparison of Three Computer Models for Prediction of Dose in Acute Amitriptyline Overdose*, 36 J. FORENSIC SCI. 153 (1991) ("All the models achieved a high degree of success (77 to 93%) in assigning records to the high-, low-, or middle-dose groups"); Spiehler, *Computer-Assisted Interpretation in Forensic Toxicology: Morphine-Involved Deaths*, 34 J. FORENSIC SCI. 1104 (1989) (the programs include Expert 4, BEAGLE, and Knowledge Master).

§ 20-5. Toxicological Evidence.

The first part of this section addresses the threshold question of the requisite qualifications of an expert testifying on toxicological issues. If the expert qualifies, his opinions may be useful in two ways. First, the opinions may be relevant and admissible in themselves. In that event the toxicologist appears at trial and testifies directly to his opinions. Second, the opinions may serve as the basis for an opinion by another expert such as a forensic pathologist. In some cases, both the toxicologist and the pathologist testify at trial. In other cases, perhaps over a hearsay objection, the pathologist may testify based, in part, on the toxicologist's findings.

§ 20-5(A). Standard of Expertise.

Like many other scientific disciplines, toxicology is developing formal mechanisms for recognizing specialists.[154] Several boards now certify specialists and subspecialists in toxicology: the American Board of Clinical Chemistry (toxicological chemistry), the American Board of Medical Toxicology (only physicians), the American Board of Toxicology, and the American Board of Forensic Toxicology (ABFT).[155] The ABFT certifies toxicologists working in medical examiner offices, alcohol (DWI) programs, and crime laboratories. The board was created in 1975 by the Forensic Science Foundation.

Although certification virtually ensures that the witness will qualify as an expert on toxicology,[156] certification is unnecessary.[157] In most cases, even when the witness lacks certification, the trial court will accept the witness as an expert on toxicology if the witness is either a physician or a degree holder in a natural sciences discipline.[158] The witness need not be a physician or surgeon.[159]

154. Winek, *Forensic Toxicology, in* 2 FORENSIC SCIENCES 31-12 (C. Wecht ed. 1983).

155. *Id.* at note 6, listing the addresses of the boards.

156. Louderback v. Orkin Exterminating Co., 26 F.Supp. 2d 1298 (D. Kan. 1998) (a physician who was board certified by the American Board of Toxicology).

157. Winek, *Forensic Toxicology, in* 2 FORENSIC SCIENCES 31-13 (C. Wecht ed. 1983). *See* Peteet v. Dow Chem. Co., 868 F.2d 1428 (5th Cir.) (if the toxicologist is certified, it is immaterial that the toxicologist is not a specialist in any other field), *cert. denied,* 493 U.S. 935 (1989).

158. Winek, *Forensic Toxicology, in* 2 FORENSIC SCIENCES 31-13 (C. Wecht ed. 1983); Casey v. Ohio Med. Prod., 877 F. Supp. 1380 (N.D. Cal. 1995) (a physician could testify even though the witness was not an expert in toxicology); People v. Coyle, 33 Cal. App. 4th 747, 28 Cal. Rptr. 2d 488 (the witness had extensive knowledge of physiology and pharmacology), *superseded,* 31 Cal. Rptr. 2d 125, 874 P.2d 900 (1994). *But see* Seiden, *Physical Evidence in Criminal Cases,* 28 TRIAL 106, 108 (Aug. 1992) ("Medical examiners seem to be the worst offenders. [U]nfortunately, many are willing to express opinions on areas in which they were never trained. They love to express opinions on ... toxicology.... However, most are unqualified to do so").

159. Genty v. Resolution Trust Corp., 937 F.2d 899, 917 (3d Cir. 1991) ("The only reason given by the trial court for the exclusion of Dr. Brubaker is that he was not a medical doctor. Medical doctors, however, are not the only experts qualified to render an opinion as to the harm caused by

However, the witness should have a bachelor's, master's, or doctorate degree in a field such as chemistry, botany, pharmacy, pharmacology,[160] pharmaceutics, or toxicology.[161] For example, in *Harnage v. State*[162] the witness had completed one and a half years of postgraduate study in biochemistry.[163] The record should contain evidence detailing the witness's credentials.[164] An "unadorned assertion" in the proponent's appellate brief that [the witness] is a scientifically-trained toxicologist holding a Ph.D. is insufficient.[165] In another case, a physician practiced neuropsychology was ruled unqualified absent any further showing of expertise in toxicology.[166]

§ 20-5(B). Tests and Determinations.

Chapter 23 on drug identification and Chapter 25 on instrumental tests review many of the analytic techniques employed by forensic toxicologists. In some cases, the courts mention only that the expert used general toxicological screening tests.[167] Other opinions describe the tests used more specifically. For example, toxicologists have been permitted to testify on the basis of particular nonspecific tests such as microscopic analysis[168] as well as specific tests including atomic absorption[169] and infrared.[170]

---

exposure to toxic chemicals. The trial court's exclusion of Brubaker, without considering his credentials as a doctor of toxicology, simply because he did not possess a medical degree, is inconsistent with expert witness jurisprudence"); People v. Richards, 120 Ill. App. 2d 313, 256 N.E.2d 475 (1970); Stertz v. Briscoe, 184 Kan. 163, 334 P.2d 357 (1959); Winek, *Forensic Toxicology, in* 2 FORENSIC SCIENCES 31-13 (C. Wecht ed. 1983); Shilling v. Mobile Analytical Servs., 602 N.E.2d 1154 (Ohio 1992) (a neurotoxicologist who was not a licensed medical doctor).

160. Ruiz-Troche v. Pepsi Cola of Puerto Rico, 161 F.3d 77 (1st Cir. 1998) (a pharmacologist).

161. Winek, *Forensic Toxicology, in* 2 FORENSIC SCIENCES 31-12-14 (C. Wecht ed. 1983). *See* Loudermill v. Dow Chem. Co., 863 F.2d 566 (8th Cir. 1988) (advanced degrees in toxicology); *In re* Paoli R.R. Yard PCB Litig., 706 F. Supp. 358 (E.D. Pa. 1988) (a toxicologist could not testify about chemical "tracing" of PCBs, since she was untrained in chemistry), *rev'd*, 916 F.2d 829, 855-56 (3d Cir. 1990) (the trial judge erred in barring the toxicologists" testimony "simply because the experts did not have the degree or training which the district court apparently thought would be most appropriate"), *cert. denied*, 499 U.S. 961 (1991).

162. 49 Ala. App. 563, 274 So. 2d 333, *rev'd on other grounds,* 290 Ala. 142, 274 So. 2d 352, *conformed to,* 49 Ala. App. 751, 274 So. 2d 356 (1972), *cert. denied,* 290 Ala. 367, 274 So. 2d 356 (1973).

163. Winek, *Forensic Toxicology, in* 2 FORENSIC SCIENCES 31-14 (C. Wecht ed. 1983). *See also* State v. Cochrane, 114 R.I. 710, 339 A.2d 256 (1975).

164. Genty v. Resolution Trust Corp., 937 F.2d 899, 917 (3d Cir. 1991).

165. *Id.*

166. Louderback v. Orkin Exterminating Co., 26 F.Supp. 2d 1298 (D. Kan. 1998).

167. State v. Barfield, 298 N.C. 306, 259 S.E.2d 510 (1979), *cert. denied,* 448 U.S. 907 (1980).

168. People v. Ellison, 100 Ill. App. 3d 282, 55 Ill. Dec. 733, 426 N.E.2d 1058 (1981).

169. *Id.*

170. *Id.*

In some jurisdictions, on the basis of such test results, toxicologists have been allowed to opine on such judgmental topics as order of death[171] and cause of death.[172] Some states go so far as to permit the toxicologist to conduct the autopsy.[173] However, many trial courts realize that the forensic pathologist has superior qualifications to evaluate such matters as cause, mechanism, and manner of death. In these courts, the toxicologist's testimony may be restricted to stating the test result finding the presence of a certain level of chemicals in the body. The forensic toxicologist has superior expertise in conducting these tests, and the courts routinely allow the toxicologist to testify to the presence of such chemicals as alcohol,[174] arsenic,[175] carbon monoxide (CO),[176] cocaine,[177] cyanide,[178]

---

171. Hitchcock v. Key, 163 Ga. App. 901, 296 S.E.2d 625 (1982).

172. St. John v. State, 358 So. 2d 812 (Ala. Crim. App. 1978). *See also* Peteet v. Dow Chem. Co., 868 F.2d 1428 (5th Cir.) (opinion about cause of cancer and death), *cert. denied*, 493 U.S. 935 (1989); Loudermill v. Dow Chem. Co., 863 F.2d 566 (8th Cir. 1988) (opinion about cause of decedent's cirrhosis of the liver). *But see* Wintz by and through Wintz v. Northrop Corp., 110 F.3d 508 (7th Cir. 1997) (a toxicologist's methodology was insufficient to permit him to opine whether an infants in utero exposure to bromide caused the infant's abnormalities); Berry v. Armstrong Rubber Co., 989 F.2d 822, 828 (5th Cir. 1993) (excluding an opinion by a toxicologist), *cert. denied*, 510 U.S. 1117 (1994); Mancuso v. Consolidated Edison Co. of N.Y., 967 F. Supp. 1437 (S.D.N.Y. 1997) (the internist witness lacked formal training and credentials in toxicology; in conducting his study, the internist should have followed conventional toxicology methods); Cuevas v. E.I. DuPont de Nemours & Co., 956 F. Supp. 1306 (S.D. Miss. 1997).

173. Johnson v. State, 357 So. 2d 162 (Ala. Crim. App.), *cert. denied*, 357 So. 2d 166 (Ala. 1978).

174. Manigan v. State, 402 So. 2d 1063 (Ala. Crim. App.), *cert. denied*, 402 So. 2d 1072 (Ala. 1981); People v. Kent, 111 Ill. App. 3d 733, 67 Ill. Dec. 334, 444 N.E.2d 570 (1982); State v. Setzer, 42 N.C. App. 98, 256 S.E.2d 485, *cert. denied*, 298 N.C. 571, 261 S.E.2d 127 (1979); People v. Forster, 29 Cal. App. 4th 1746, 35 Cal. Rptr. 2d 705 (1994) ("a forensic toxicologist ... opined that Forster had a blood alcohol level of .30 percent at 9:30 p.m. based on the 12:32 a.m. blood test results and absorption and burn-off data"). *See also* Hayes v. State, 514 N.E.2d 332 (Ind. App. 1987) (toxicologist could testify about the conversion of serum ethanol level to an ethanol alcohol level).

175. Vaughn v. State, 249 Ga. 803, 294 S.E.2d 504 (1982); O"Bryan v. Commonwealth, 634 S.W.2d 153 (Ky. 1982); State v. Detter, 298 N.C. 604, 260 S.E.2d 567 (1979); State v. Barfield, 298 N.C. 306, 259 S.E.2d 510 (1979), *cert. denied*, 448 U.S. 907 (1980); State v. Hunt, 297 N.C. 258, 254 S.E.2d 591 (1979); Albanese v. McGinnis, 823 F. Supp. 521 (N.D. Ill. 1993), *aff'd*, 19 F.3d 21 (7th Cir. 1994), *cert. denied*, 513 U.S. 1156 (1995).

176. Robinson v. Smith, 530 F. Supp. 1386 (W.D.N.Y. 1982); United States v. Barnes, 520 F. Supp. 946 (D.D.C. 1981); Johnston v. State, 387 So. 2d 891 (Ala. Crim. App.), *cert. denied*, 387 So. 2d 905 (Ala. 1980); Manigan v. State, 402 So. 2d 1063 (Ala. Crim. App.), *cert. denied*, 402 So. 2d 1072 (Ala. 1981); Williams v. State, 250 Ga. 553, 300 S.E.2d 301, *cert. denied*, 462 U.S. 1124 (1983); Hitchcock v. Key, 163 Ga. App. 901, 296 S.E.2d 625 (1982); *In re* Estate of Moran, 67 Ill. App. 3d 576, 24 Ill. Dec. 312, 385 N.E.2d 79 (1978), *aff'd*, 77 Ill. 2d 147, 32 Ill. Dec. 349, 395 N.E.2d 579 (1979); Clifton v. Nardi, 65 Ill. App. 3d 344, 22 Ill. Dec. 194, 382 N.E.2d 514 (1978); State v. Setzer, 42 N.C. App. 98, 256 S.E.2d 485, *cert. denied*, 298 N.C. 571, 261 S.E.2d 127 (1979); State *ex rel.* Murray v. Shanks, 27 Wash. App. 363, 618 P.2d 102 (1980); Shaffer v. State, 640 P.2d 88 (Wyo. 1982).

dimethylnitrosamine,[179] salt poison,[180] silicone, sodium,[181] strychnine,[182] and trichloral ethanol.[183] Courts also permit the toxicologist to testify about the effects that habitual use of such chemicals[184] or their presence in a person's system can produce in the human body.[185] It must be remembered, though, that after the Supreme Court's 1993 decision in *Daubert v. Merrell Dow Pharmaceuticals, Inc.*,[186] the expert's theory will have to qualify as "scientific knowledge" under the new empirical validation test.[187]

---

177. State v. Cobb, 229 Kan. 522, 625 P.2d 1133 (1981). *See also* Reardon v. Manson, 806 F.2d 39 (2d Cir. 1986), *cert. denied sub nom.* Reardon v. Lopes, 481 U.S. 1020 (1987).

178. O'Bryan v. State, 591 S.W.2d 464 (Tex. Crim. App. 1979), *cert. denied,* 446 U.S. 988 (1980); State v. Hoffman, 106 Wis. 2d 185, 316 N.W.2d 143 (1982).

179. State v. Harper, 208 Neb. 568, 304 N.W.2d 663 (parathion), *cert. denied,* 454 U.S. 882 (1981); Tyler v. State, 247 Ga. 119, 274 S.E.2d 549, *cert. denied,* 454 U.S. 882 (1981); State v. Trimble, 44 N.C. App. 659, 262 S.E.2d 299 (1980).

180. Pudwill v. Brown, 294 N.W.2d 790 (S.D. 1980).

181. People v. Phillips, 122 Cal. App. 3d 69, 175 Cal. Rptr. 703 (1981).

182. State v. Garcia, 102 Idaho 378, 630 P.2d 665 (1981).

183. Sheriff, Clark County v. Morris, 99 Nev. 109, 659 P.2d 852 (1983).

184. United States v. Garcia Abrego, 141 F.3d 142, 172-73 (5th Cir. 1998) (the effects of habitual valium use).

185. *E.g.,* Ruiz-Troche v. Pepsi Cola of Puerto Rico, 161 F.3d 77 (1st Cir. 1998) (the effect of cocaine on a driver's behavior); Genty v. Resolution Trust Corp., 937 F.2d 899, 917 (3d Cir. 1991) ("the harm caused by exposure to toxic chemicals"); Sicarelli v. State Farm Fire & Cas. Co., 556 So. 2d 179 (La. App. 1990) (the effects of alcohol on a person's ability to drive); May v. Strecker, 453 N.W.2d 549 (Minn. App. 1990) (the driver of a vehicle that rear-ended the plaintiff would probably have shown signs of intoxication while at the bar in which he was served alcohol shortly before the accident); Pollard v. State, 549 So. 2d 593 (Ala. Crim. App. 1989) (the effects of a blood alcohol concentration of .134); Burch v. State, 478 So. 2d 1050 (Fla. 1985) (the defendant was attempting to negate the specific intent to commit first-degree murder; the trial judge erred in precluding a toxicologist from testifying about the effects of phencyclidine on the human body delirium, hallucinations, violent behavior, disorientation, and amnesia), *aff'd in part, vacated in part*, 522 So. 2d 810 (Fla. 1988); United States v. Gibson, 105 F.3d 1229, 1235 (8th Cir. 1997) ("the effects that 36% and 57% pure heroin would have upon an individual"); Fierro v. Gomez, 865 F. Supp. 1387, 1395 (N.D. Cal. 1994) (the effects of hydrocyanic gas on the human body), *aff'd*, 77 F.3d 301 (9th Cir.), *vacated*, 519 U.S. 918 (1996); People v. Coyle, 33 Cal. App. 4th 747, 28 Cal. Rptr. 2d 488 (the synergy of cocaine and alcohol and their combined effect on the human body), *superseded,* 31 Cal. Rptr. 2d 125, 874 P.2d 900 (1994). *But see In re* Paoli R.R. Yard PCB Litig., 706 F. Supp. 358 (E.D. Pa. 1988) (it exceeded a toxicologist's expertise to testify that she had chemically "traced" to the railroads PCBS in the bodies of residents who lived near the railroad storage yard; she was untrained in chemistry), *rev'd*, 916 F.2d 829, 855-56 (3d Cir. 1990) (the trial judge erred in excluding the toxicologists" testimony "simply because the experts did not have the degree or training which the district court apparently thought would be most appropriate"), *cert. denied*, 499 U.S. 961 (1991).

186. U.S. 579 (1993).

187. Ruiz-Troche v. Pepsi Cola of Puerto Rico, 161 F.3d 77 (1st Cir. 1998); Cuevas v. E.I. DuPont de Nemours & Co., 956 F. Supp. 1306 (S.D. Miss. 1997) (*Daubert* precluded the toxicologist from testifying that the plaintiff's exposure to a particular herbicide had caused his

Suppose that the toxicologist contemplates basing his or her opinion exclusively on a test report which the judge holds to be independently inadmissible. Is the opinion nevertheless admissible? In one case, a Florida court answered the question in the negative.[188] In that case, the expert intended to rely on a laboratory report which the court ruled to be inadmissible hearsay. The court stated:

> We recognize that experts are generally permitted to express opinions which are based, at least in part, upon inadmissible information. Another line of cases, however, prohibits the use of expert testimony merely to serve as a conduit to place otherwise inadmissible evidence before a jury. In this case, the expert's testimony was merely used as a conduit. In this case, the expert was ... relying exclusively upon information which was not evidence at trial.[189]

§ 20-5(C). Toxicologist's Findings as a Basis for Another Expert's Opinion.

In many cases, the proponent does not offer the toxicologist's findings as an end in themselves. Rather, the proponent invites another expert such as a pathologist to base a further opinion on those findings. The proponent's case may be most impressive if the proponent presents the live testimony of both the toxicologist and the pathologist. However, time or money constraints may make it difficult to produce the toxicologist at trial. When the proponent asks the pathologist to consider the toxicologist's findings or report as part of the basis of the pathologist's opinion, the opponent may object on hearsay grounds. As discussed in Chapter 5, jurisdictions divide over the question of whether the expert may base an opinion on information that is not independently admissible. Chapter 5 noted that the traditional view forbids the expert from doing so but that following the lead of Federal Rule of Evidence 703, perhaps a majority of

---

medical problems.); Cavallo v. Star Enter., 892 F. Supp. 756, 773 (E.D. Va. 1995) (the witness "did not follow the accepted toxicology methodology in formulating his opinion of causation in this case"), *aff'd in part, rev'd in part*, 100 F.3d 1150 (4th Cir. 1996) (the expert had not paid enough attention to settled toxicological methodology), *cert. denied*,502 U.S. 1044 (1998); Casey v. Ohio Med. Prod., 877 F. Supp. 1380, 1385 (N.D. Cal. 1995) (on the one hand, a physician was qualified to testify although the witness was not an expert in toxicology; on the other hand, the case studies the witness contemplated relying on did "not rise to the level of scientific reliability, methodology, or validation required by *Daubert*"; the witness proposed basing an opinion on "a compilation of case reports" rather than "an epidemiological study"); Everett v. Georgia-Pacific Corp., 949 F. Supp. 856 (S.D. Ga. 1996) (the witness physician lacked specialized knowledge or training in toxicology); Cartwright v. Home Depot U.S.A., Inc., 936 F. Supp. 900 (M.D. Fla. 1996) (toxicology studies).

188. Riggins v. Mariner Boat Works, Inc., 545 So. 2d 430 (Fla. App. 1989).

189. *Id.* at 431-32.

jurisdictions now permit the witness to consider any data of a type reasonably relied upon by experts in the particular field in forming opinions or inferences upon the subject.[190] Accordingly, in jurisdictions that have adopted Federal Rule 703, a pathologist may give an opinion based on the findings of a toxicologist.

Even in a jurisdiction that still adheres to the traditional view, the proponent may advance several arguments to persuade the trial court to allow the pathologist to consider the toxicologist's findings.

First, the proponent may introduce a written report of the toxicologist's findings as substantive evidence on the theory that the report qualifies as a business entry or public record.[191] Chapter 6 pointed out that the courts often accept scientific reports on such theories. Federal Rule of Evidence 803(6) expressly sanctions the admission of business entries containing "opinions ... or diagnoses..."[192] The foundation for the admission of the report may be laid without testimony by the scientist who prepared the report.

Second, the proponent could conceivably invite the pathologist to consider the toxicologist's findings without formally introducing the report so long as the proponent demonstrated that the report would be admissible. Even if it is a well-settled rule in the jurisdiction that the bases for an expert's opinion must be independently admissible as substantive evidence, that rule may not require that the report in fact be admitted as substantive evidence.

---

190. FED. R. EVID. 703. *See also* State v. Jones, 54 N.C. App. 482, 283 S.E.2d 546 (1981).

191. *But see* State v. Rivera, 515 A.2d 182 (Del. Super. Ct. 1986) (the admission of a toxicology report prepared by the state medical examiner's office constituted hearsay and violated the accused's confrontation rights). The official Comment to Delaware's version of Rule 803(6) reads: "Rule 803(6) does not make admissible records created for the litigation such as the report of a medical doctor retained to examine a party at the request of the opposing party. Likewise, a toxicologist's report on the presence of drugs would not be admissible because of Rule 803(8)."

192. FED. R. EVID. 803(6). *See* United States v. One 1986 Chevrolet Van, 927 F.2d 39, 42 (1st Cir. 1991) (in a non-jury forfeiture proceeding, "the only concern ... regarding the admission of hearsay evidence is whether the evidence is reliable. We are satisfied that the toxicology report ... [was] reliable.... [T]here is a substantial basis for crediting the reliability of the report. At trial, Officer Campagna identified the report as the one that he filled out, sent to the Rhode Island Toxicology Laboratory and received back with a result"); Timmons v. Hecker, 110 A.D.2d 762, 488 N.Y.S.2d 49 (1985); Yacht Club v. Utah Liquor Control Comm'n, 681 P.2d 1224 (Utah 1984); Gallagher v. National Transp. Safety Bd., 953 F.2d 1214, 1218-19 (10th Cir. 1992) (adequate authentication of a toxicological report). *But see* Meeks v. McBride, 81 F.3d 717 (7th Cir. 1996) (the toxicology report lacked sufficient indicia of reliability to support prison official's decision to deprive an inmate of good-time credit for smoking marijuana). *But see* Grantham v. State, 580 So. 2d 53 (Ala. Crim. App. 1991) (although a toxicologist's report was admissible under state hearsay rules, its receipt violated the defendant's confrontation rights; the report was crucial to the state's case, and the state failed to establish that the toxicologist was unavailable to testify at trial); State v. Carter, 670 S.W.2d 104, 108 (Mo. App. 1984) ("The state's attempt ... to qualify the exhibits under the [Uniform Business Records as Evidence] Act failed because the record is devoid of any testimony describing the mode of preparation. The exhibits contained only conclusions and no specifics detailing exactly what tests were performed to reach the results set forth in the reports").

In most jurisdictions, the trial court has discretion over the order of proof. Federal Rule of Evidence 611(a) provides that "[t]he court shall exercise reasonable control over the ... order of interrogating witnesses and presenting evidence..."[193] The court may permit the proponent to present the pathologist's testimony based in part on the toxicologist's findings if the proponent represents that there will be later live testimony by the toxicologist, subsequent introduction of the report, or at least a later showing of the report's admissibility. In addition, even if the proponent did not invoke the court's discretion to vary the order of proof and the court erroneously permitted the pathologist to testify prematurely, the later introduction of the report might cure the error.[194]

§ 20-5(D). Telephonic Testimony by the Toxicologist.

Some jurisdictions now permit certain witnesses to testify via telephone rather than appearing in person.[195] Defense counsel have challenged this practice on the ground that it violates the defendant's confrontation rights under the sixth amendment. In cases involving children who were allegedly victims of sexual abuse, the Supreme Court has indicated that face-to-face confrontation is not an invariable requirement.[196] The Court has stated that a trial judge may dispense with face-to-face confrontation when there is a case-specific finding that the dispensation will further an important public policy. In two published cases, Colorado prosecutors have attempted to present toxicologist testimony via telephone.[197] In both cases, the Colorado Supreme Court held that the testimony ran afoul of the defendant's confrontation rights. In the first case, *Topping v. People*,[198] the trial judge had allowed the toxicologist to present live testimony over the telephone to accommodate the witness's travel schedule. The court commented that "[m]ere inconvenience of a witness does not constitute unavailability.[199] In the second case, *Gonsoir v. People*,[200] the court reached the same result. In *Gonsoir*, one of the witness's flights had been canceled. However, the court ruled that the witness's travel difficulties fell short of constituting sufficient necessity to override the defendant's confrontation rights. In contrast, in an Iowa case antedating the Supreme Court's confrontation rulings, the state

193. FED. R. EVID. 611(a).

194. Vaughn v. State, 249 Ga. 803, 294 S.E.2d 504 (1982).

195. Annot., *Permissibility of Testimony by Telephone in State Trial*, 85 A.L.R.4TH 476 (1991). Comment, *Telephonic Testimony: Talking with Experts*, 29 U.C. DAVIS L. REV. 413 (1996).

196. Maryland v. Craig, 497 U.S. 836 (1990); Coy v. Iowa, 487 U.S. 1012 (1988).

197. Gonsoir v. People, 793 P.2d 1165 (Colo. 1990); Topping v. People, 793 P.2d 1168 (Colo. 1990).

198. *Id.*

199. *Id.* at 1171.

200. 793 P.2d 1165 (Colo. 1990).

supreme court sustained the admission of a police officers telephonic testimony.[201]

§ 20-6. Selected Bibliography.

B. BALLANTYNE, PERSPECTIVES IN BASIC AND APPLIED TOXICOLOGY (1988).

R. BASELT, ADVANCES IN ANALYTICAL TOXICOLOGY (1984).

R. BASELT & R. CRAVEY, DISPOSITION OF TOXIC DRUGS AND CHEMICALS IN MAN (4th ed. 1995).

M. BRUNDEN, T. VIDMAR & J. MCKEAN, DRUG INTERACTION AND LETHALITY ANALYSIS (1988).

A. CURRY, POISON DETECTION IN HUMAN ORGANS (4th ed. 1988).

M. DERELANO & M. HOLLINGER, HANDBOOK OF TOXICOLOGY (1995).

M. ELLENHORN & D. BARCELOUX, MEDICAL TOXICOLOGY: DIAGNOSIS AND TREATMENT OF HUMAN POISONING (1988).

S. FEINMAN, FORMALDEHYDE: SENSITIVITY AND TOXICITY (1988).

J. HEUVEL, PCR PROTOCOLS IN MOLECULAR TOXICOLOGY (1997).

M. HOUTS, R. BASELT & R. CRAVEY, COURTROOM TOXICOLOGY (1983) (6 vols.).

B. LEVINE, PRINCIPLES OF FORENSIC TOXICOLOGY (1999).

S. MANAHAN, TOXICOLOGICAL CHEMISTRY (2d ed.).

K. MASON, FORENSIC MEDICINE FOR LAWYERS (1978).

N. MULLER & R. DESSING, EUROPEAN DRUG INDEX (4th ed. 1997).

R. NIESINK, J. DE VRIES & M. HOLLINGER, TOXICOLOGY: PRINCIPLES AND APPLICATIONS (1996).

I. SUNSHINE, METHODS FOR ANALYTICAL TOXICOLOGY (3 vols.).

J. YINON, TOXICITY AND METABOLISM (1990).

S. WONG & I. SUNSHINE, ANALYTICAL THERAPEUTIC DRUG MONITORING AND TOXICOLOGY (1997).

Anthony, Hirsch & Moritz, *Poisoning*, *in* HANDBOOK OF LEGAL MEDICINE 84 (5th ed. 1979).

Niyogi, *Toxicology*, *in* SCIENTIFIC AND EXPERT EVIDENCE ch. 15 (2d ed. 1981).

Winek, *Forensic Toxicology*, *in* 2 FORENSIC SCIENCES ch. 31 (C. Wecht, ed. 1983).

Poklis, *Forensic Toxicology in Postmortem Investigations*, 10 LAB. MED. 224 (1979).

---

201. State v. Aldape, 307 N.W.2d 32 (Iowa 1981).

CHAPTER 21

QUESTIONED DOCUMENT EXAMINATION*

§ 21-1. In General.

Although this discipline has traditionally been described as questioned document examination, today practitioners prefer to be referred to as forensic document examiners. Testimony by forensic or questioned document examiners has played a central role in some famous as well as infamous cases. In the renowned *Dreyfus* case, one document expert, Alphonse Bertillon, gave damning evidence against Alfred Dreyfus[1] while another, David Carvalho, was instrumental in Captain Dreyfus' ultimate vindication.[2] In the Lindbergh kidnapping trial, the analysis of the 15 ransom notes by eight leading experts helped seal the fate of Bruno Hauptmann.[3] In the *Hiss* case, testimony by Felix Feehan, an F.B.I. document examiner, was "[t]he single most damaging corroboration" of the defendant's guilt.[4] More recently, questioned document

*The authors wish to express their appreciation to Mr. James Kelly of Kelly and Associates, Decatur, Georgia, who reviewed this chapter in the first two editions of this treatise.

1. A. Moenssens, J. Starrs, C. Henderson & F. Inbau, Scientific Evidence in Civil and Criminal Cases § 5.01, at 546 (4th ed. 1995).

2. White, *Identification and the Document Examiner*, 52 A.B.A. J. 458, 459 (1966).

3. Osborn, *Excerpts and Comments on Testimony by Document Examiners in Regard to State of New Jersey v. Bruno Richard Hauptmann*, 28 J. Forensic Sci. 1049 (1983).

4. *In re* Hiss, 542 F. Supp. 973, 984 (S.D.N.Y. 1982), *aff'd,* 722 F.2d 727 (2d Cir.), *cert. denied,* 464 U.S. 890 (1983).

examination gained notoriety in the battle over the estate of Howard Hughes.[5] Questioned document examiners also played a role in the efforts to determine whether a cadaver buried outside Sao Paulo, Brazil, was the body of Dr. Joseph Mengele, the escaped Nazi SS leader.[6]

It would, however, be a mistake to assume that testimony by expert questioned document examiners is the only legally acceptable method of authenticating a writing. The law permits numerous other methods of authentication. For example, although there is some contrary authority,[7] most jurisdictions allow the lay jurors themselves to compare a questioned document with other exemplars of the alleged author's handwriting.[8] Authentication by juror comparison is permissible in federal practice[9] and in most states.[10] Such comparisons are sanctioned both at common law[11] and by statute.[12] Some jurisdictions even allow the jurors to take the questioned documents and a magnifying glass into the deliberation room.[13]

Moreover, almost all jurisdictions permit lay witnesses, familiar with a person's handwriting style, to give opinions identifying that handwriting.[14] Such testimony is admissible even though its reliability is suspect. In a leading experiment assessing the accuracy of lay handwriting identification,[15] Professor Inbau found that lay opinions suffer from "an appalling degree of inaccuracy."[16] In this study, the highest accuracy score attained by a lay witness was 29%, and

5. A. Moenssens, J. Starrs, C. Henderson & F. Inbau, *supra* note 1, at § 5.06; Cantu, *The Paper Mate Ink on the Howard Hughes "Mormon Will,"* 31 J. Forensic Sci. 360 (1986).

6. Epstein, *Examination of the Joseph Mengele Handwriting*, 32 J. Forensic Sci. 100 (1987).

7. Huff v. State, 437 So. 2d 1087, 1090 (Fla. 1983); State v. LeDuc, 306 N.C. 62, 67-74, 291 S.E.2d 607, 611 (1982).

8. *See* Fed. R. Evid. 901(b)(3); United States v. Brink, 648 F.2d 1140 (8th Cir.), *cert. denied,* 454 U.S. 1031 (1981); United States v. Rich, 580 F.2d 929 (9th Cir.), *cert. denied,* 439 U.S. 935 (1978); United States v. Woodson, 526 F.2d 550 (9th Cir. 1975); Sands v. Cunningham, 617 F. Supp. 1551 (D.N.H. 1985) (rejecting defense argument that the rule permitting lay jurors to compare handwriting samples violates due process).*See also* United States v. Clifford, 704 F.2d 86, 90 n.5 (3d Cir. 1983).

9. *Id.;* Fed. R. Evid. 901(b)(3), 28 U.S.C.A. ("[c]omparison by the trier of fact or by expert witnesses ....").

10. *E.g.,* People v. Roberts, 100 Ill. App. 3d 469, 55 Ill. Dec. 779, 426 N.E.2d 1104 (1981); State v. Fortier, 427 A.2d 1317, 1324-25 (R.I. 1981); Denby v. State, 654 S.W.2d 457, 461 (Tex. Crim. App. 1983).

11. People v. Roberts, 100 Ill. App. 3d 469, 55 Ill. Dec. 779, 426 N.E.2d 1104 (1981).

12. Gross v. State, 161 Ga. App. 489, 288 S.E.2d 733 (1982) (Ga. Code Ann. § 38-709 (1981)); State v. Fortier, 427 A.2d 1317, 1324-25 (R.I. 1981) (R.I. Gen. Laws § 9-19-17 (1969)); Denby v. State, 654 S.W.2d 457, 461 (Tex. Crim. App. 1983) (Tex. Crim. Proc. Code art. 38.27 (1979)).

13. State v. LeDuc, 306 N.C. 62, 71, 291 S.E.2d 607, 613 (1982).

14. Bodiford v. State, 630 S.W.2d 847 (Tex. App. 1982). *See also* C. McCormick, Evidence § 221 (5th ed. 1999); United States v. Tipton, 964 F.2d 650 (7th Cir. 1992).

15. Inbau, *Lay Witness Identification of Handwriting*, 34 Ill. L. Rev. 433 (1939).

16. *Id.* at 435.

the average was only 11%.[17] Based on the study, Professor Inbau proposed banning lay opinions on handwriting identification.[18]

Although no jurisdiction has excluded lay evidence, most courts now prefer testimony by experts when the authenticity of a document is a pivotal issue. In this context, the term "document" has a broad meaning. The document can take the form of impressions on a cowhide, postage stamp, or blueprint[19] or markings on a balloon[20] or skin surface.[21] A wide variety of questions may be involved in an examination: What type of device — typewriter, photocopier, or checkwriter — was used to prepare the document? Who prepared the document? When was the document created? In the case of erased or obliterated writing, what was originally written on the document? Sections 21-2 through 21-6 discuss the techniques that the examiner uses to resolve these questions.[22] Section 21-7 considers the admissibility of expert testimony based on these techniques. As we shall see, just as Professor Inbau assailed the trustworthiness of lay opinions on handwriting comparison, other commentators are now challenging the reliability of testimony by professional forensic document examiners. As in so many other areas of forensic science, the courts are rethinking the admissibility of questioned document expertise under *Daubert.*[23]

§ 21-2. Comparisons Between Styles.

Much of a questioned document examiner's work consists of comparing the questioned document to other exemplars of the suspected author's handwriting or typed document in question. This section first reviews the procedures for gathering the exemplars.[24] Next, the techniques used in making the comparison are discussed.

---

17. *Id.*

18. *Id.* at 440-41.

19. NORWITCH, QUESTIONED DOCUMENTS 1 (unpublished manuscript on file at the National College of District Attorneys, University of Houston College of Law, Houston, Texas).

20. Kelly, *An Unusual Writing Surface — and Considerations*, 6 J. POLICE SCI. & ADMIN. 283 (1978).

21. Taylor & Hnilica, *Investigation of Death Through Body Writing: A Case Study*, 36 J. FORENSIC SCI. 1607 (1991); Totty, *A Case of Handwriting on an Unusual Surface*, 21 J. FORENSIC SCI. SOC'Y 349 (1981).

22. Hilton, *The Evolution of Questioned Document Examination in the Last 50 Years*, 33 J. FORENSIC SCI. 1310 (1988).

23. Daubert v. Merrell Dow Pharmaceuticals, 509 U.S. 579 (1993).

24. *See* Waggoner, *Handwriting Evidence for the Investigator*, 53 F.B.I. LAW ENF. BULL. 22 (June 1984). *See also* Geltzeiler, *The Study of Handwriting as Evidence*, NAT'L L.J., Oct. 14, 1985, at 15.

§ 21-2(A). Exemplars.

In most cases, the questioned document examiner has no previous familiarity with the suspected author's writing or typing style. Consequently, to make the comparison, the examiner must ensure that the investigator collects samples of the author's writing, printing, or correspondence typed during the normal course of business. These samples are termed exemplars or standards. There are two types of samples: collected or nonrequested exemplars and prepared or requested exemplars.

Nonrequested Exemplars

These samples came into existence before (and sometimes after) the dispute over the authenticity of the questioned document arose. There are numerous sources for samples. The following is a partial list of potential sources used by one state crime laboratory's document section:[25]

DOCUMENTS CONTAINING NON-REQUEST SOURCES OF STANDARD HANDWRITING

APPLICATIONS
- auto travel club
- bail bonds
- cable television
- credit, local store accounts
- credit cards, applications
- employment
- enlistment (military)
- family doctor
- health club
- hospital entry
- library card
- licenses (dog, auto, boat, hunting)
- loans
- magazine
- mortgages
- naturalization
- operator's license
- pension

25. This is an updated version of a list appearing in Iowa Criminalistics Document Section 23-24. The authors wish to express their appreciation to criminalists Howard Birnbaum and Jerry Brown, who updated the list.

permits
post office box
professional organizations, applications
reservations
school enrollment, college, preschool[26]
telephone
video club

BUSINESS

account books
building, "after hours" registers
auctions
bank records
blood bank
business associates
business license applications
cancelled checks
contracts
convention registration books
credit union
department receipts
employment applications
gate records
hotel & motel guest register
identification cards
incorporation papers
insurance claims
legal papers
log books (trucks, airplanes)
membership cards
notaries
occupational writings
pension records
personnel office (files)
receipts for pay
receipted bills
registered mail receipts
reports
time cards

---

26. Of course, very old exemplars such as kindergarten writing may be of minimal value. At that point, a person is first beginning to form the habits that will later become characteristic of his or her handwriting style.

- travel reservations
- withholding exemption forms

CONTRACTS

- bills of sale
- deeds
- deeds of trust
- furniture, household appliances
- installment
- insurance (life, car, home, boat, health)
- leases
- loans
- mortgages
- partnership
- purchase
- rental agreements
- utility service (light, water, gas, telephone)

FEDERAL GOVERNMENT

- civil service
- copyrights
- customs
- federal court
- immigration
- loan and grant application for school
- military records (registration, Vet. Adm.)
- naturalization
- other institutions
- passports
- patents
- penitentiary
- pension application and checks
- social security cards — papers
- tax returns
- U.S. post office
- widow's benefits
- withholding forms

LOCAL AND STATE RECORDS

- accident reports
- application for notary public
- baptismal certificates
- building permits
- children's court
- citations

city/county auditor
city clerk
civil proceedings
civil service
complaint bureaus
complaints to law enforcement
court of claims
criminal records
death certificates
fingerprint cards
guardian
jury duty records
marriage certificates
motor vehicle — license and titles
municipal court
permits & licenses (drivers, fishing, hunting)
public assistance
probation & parole records
receipt for returned property
selective service
tax returns
unemployment files
veterans or homestead exemption
voting records
workmen's compensation

PERSONAL

address book
bible entries
bill of sale
bonds
charity pledges
church pledges
cooking recipes
contents of wallet
credit union
department store records
diary
family & friends
funeral attendance register
hotel & motel receipts
health & hospital records
installment contracts

insurance records
legal papers
library cards
membership cards
military discharge papers (records)
passport
pawn ticket
photo album
political organizations
post cards
power of attorney
prescriptions
receipted bills
rent receipts
valentines, greeting cards
wills
death certificates
Bank — cancelled checks
check stubs
deposit slips
microfilm
safe deposit entry
savings withdrawal
signature card
School — autograph albums
athletic contests
application for entrance
clubs and lodges
daily assignments
exams
identification cards
receipts for school supplies
school and college yearbooks
sororities & fraternities
report cards

In gathering nonrequested exemplars, the examiner attempts to locate samples prepared around the time in question and under similar conditions as the questioned document. A person's age and state of health may alter his or her writing style, and it is critical to obtain exemplars that are as comparable as possible to the questioned document.[27] Originals rather than photostats or photographs of original writings are needed. A copy may omit some of the identifying characteristics of the person's handwriting style, such as indications of pen pressure, hesitation points, and other minute pen movements.[28]

Requested Exemplars

Even if nonrequested exemplars are available, to be on the safe side requested exemplars may be sought. These exemplars are prepared for the specific purpose of comparison with the questioned document. Some investigators make it a practice to obtain exemplars from both the suspect and the alleged victim. The samples of the victim's style not only may enable the investigator to eliminate the victim as a possible source of the questioned document;[29] these samples may assist in determining whether the questioned document is a forgery prepared by tracing or simulating a sample of the victim's writing.

As a general proposition, you want to recreate the exact writing conditions. For example, if the questioned writing was written while a person was standing at a bank teller's counter, the exemplars should be collected with the suspect standing at a counter of comparable height. The document sections of police agencies have developed a number of specific guidelines for obtaining exemplars from suspects. The most common guidelines include the following procedures:[30] obtain the exemplars early in the interview with the suspect; obtain most of the exemplars while the suspect is seated in a normal writing position; if the suspect seems to be attempting to disguise his or her true style, request that the suspect stand while writing some exemplars because it may be more difficult to continue the mode of disguise while standing or attempt to break his concentration by discussing a subject such as the weather or football; to prevent the suspect from subsequently claiming that he or she copied the questioned document, keep that document out of the suspect's view while the suspect is executing the exemplars; to the extent possible, duplicate the conditions under which the questioned

---

27. Widla, *The Influence of Spontaneous Writing on Stability of Graphic Features*, 46 FORENSIC SCI. INT'L 63 (1990) ("handwriting ... goes through stages of puberty [and] maturity and finally it shows marks of senility"); Cusack & Hargett, *A Comparison Study of the Handwriting of Adolescents*, 42 FORENSIC SCI. INT'L 239 (1989) ("Normally writers reach graphic maturity after the twentieth birthday. Prior to that time the child passes through three stages which fall roughly into a chronological pattern based on age then reached. From six to nine the writer is imitative, from nine to twelve it is a period of adaptation, and from twelve through adolescence is in a period of fixation"); Masson, *A Study of the Handwriting of Adolescents*, 33 J. FORENSIC SCI. 167 (1988) ("The handwriting of some adolescents changes with bewildering rapidity").

28. Hanna, *Microfilm Documents: What Are the Boundaries in Document Examination?*, 33 J. FORENSIC SCI. 154, 165 (1988) (the microfilm process may cause differences in fine detail).

29. To eliminate the victim, the examiner should obtain exemplars of the victim's writing done prior to the time in question.

30. *See generally* Iowa Criminalistics Document Section, *supra* note 25, at 9-11.

document was written, *e.g.*, the same type of writing instrument, paper, and style (cursive versus printing);[31] do not give the suspect any instructions about spelling, punctuation, or spacing; if the suspect may be attempting to disguise his or her true writing style, vary the speed of dictation from one exemplar to another; direct the suspect to write some exemplars with the unaccustomed hand; as the suspect completes each exemplar, remove the exemplar from the suspect's sight to make it more difficult to maintain a consistent mode of disguise; and at the end of the interview, initial and date the exemplars to assure their admissibility in a subsequent trial.

Some investigators prefer to obtain exemplars that include the same wording as the questioned document. However, to reduce the suspect's nervousness, other investigators customarily obtain exemplars that have different wording but nevertheless include key expressions and combinations of words in the questioned document.[32] There are several forms that may be used to obtain exemplars, including samples of the suspect's method of writing all capital letters, lower case letters, and numerals. The forms include the London Business letter,[33] the Egyptian letter,[34] and the Class of 16 form.[35] Depending upon the

---

31. Waggoner, *supra* note 24, at 24.

32. *Id.* at 22-23.

33. Our London business is good, but Vienna and Berlin are quiet. Mr. D. Lloyd has gone to Switzerland and I hope for good news. He will be there for a week at 1496 Zermott St. and then goes to Turin and Rome and will join Col. Parry and arrive at Athens, Greece, Nov. 27th or Dec. 2d. Letters there should be addressed King James Blvd. 3580. We expect Chas. E. Fuller Tuesday. Dr. L. McQuaid and Robt. Unger, Esq., left on the 'Y.X.' Express tonight. NORWITCH, *supra* note 19, at B.

34. Dear Sam:

> From Egypt we went to Italy, and took a trip through Germany, Holland and England. We enjoyed it all, but Rome and London most. In Berlin we met Mr. John O. Young, of Messars Tackico & Co., on his way to Vienna. His address there is 1497 Upper Zeiss Str., care of Dr. Quincy W. Long. Friday the 18th, we join C. N. Dazet, Esq. and Mrs. Dazet, and leave at 6:30 A.M. for Paris on the "Q.X." Express and early on the morning of the 25th of June start for home on the S.S. King.
>
> Very sincerely yours,

Id. at C.

35. Dear Zach:

> Well, the old class of "16" is through at last. You ask where the boys are to be. Val Brown goes on the 24th to Harvard for Law. Don't forget to address him as "Esq." Ted Updike takes a position with the N.Y.W.H. & H.R.R., 892 Ladd Ave., Fall River, Mass., and Jack McQuade with the D.L. & W. at Jersey City, N.J., 400 E. 6th St. Wm. Fellows just left for a department position in Washington; his address is 735 South G St. At last accounts Dr. Max King was to go to Johns Hopkins for a Ph. D. degree. Think of that! Elliott goes to Xenia, Ohio, to be a Y.M.C.A. secretary. I stay here for the present. What do you do next? How about Idaho?
>
> Yours truly, and goodbye.

Id. at D. *See also Limitations of the "London Business Letter,"* F.B.I. LAW ENF. BULL. Reprint,

nature of the intended document, the examiner can also request that the suspect execute blank forms for a check, credit card purchase, or personal history.

The number of exemplars needed varies with the uniqueness of the writing habits evidenced by the questioned document; the more unique are the habits, the fewer the number of exemplars necessary. Examiners differ over the number of exemplars they prefer, but the following are some of the more commonly cited figures: in the case of a signature, as few as 12 or as many as 30;[36] in the case of a letter, as few as two full pages or as many as six;[37] and in the case of handwriting, 25 exemplars duplicating the questioned document.[38] The investigator might require between half an hour and an hour to obtain all the needed exemplars from the suspect.

A large number of exemplars is vital for two reasons. First, no person writes his or her signature or any word exactly the same way twice. The examiner must determine the range of natural variation in the person's writing style. The limits of the variation of a person's style can be identified only by studying a large number of samples. Second, a large number of examples is important when the suspect attempts to disguise his or her true writing style. The larger the number of exemplars, the more difficult it is to maintain the mode of disguise; sooner or later habits take over, and the suspect will lapse into a normal writing style, especially if each successive exemplar is removed from the suspect's view. A limited number of exemplars is the most common cause of inconclusive findings in questioned document cases.

As in the case of handwriting comparisons, the examiner needs exemplars if the questioned document is typewritten. To obtain representative exemplars, the investigator must obtain exemplars that include all the type characters. In addition, in the past the conventional wisdom was that the investigator should collect exemplars that included the most important combinations of words and numerals in the questioned document. The investigator may take samples or request a typist complete the word or words in question. By increasing the speed, the investigator often forces the typist to abandon a planned mode of disguise. In the case of manual typewriters, obtaining exemplars typed under various pressures ensures that at least some of the exemplars duplicate the conditions under which the questioned document was prepared. Some forensic documents examiners are no longer comfortable attempting to identify a particular typist through the examination of the pressure they apply or the keys on a manual typewriter. These examiners are therefore dubious of the utility of the techniques

---

Feb. 1965; *Correctly Obtaining Known Samples Aids Document Examiner*, F.B.I. LAW ENF. BULL. Reprint, July 1961.

36. Morrill, *The Document Examiner — Scientist or Sciolist?*, 9 THE PROSECUTOR 206 (1973).

37. *Id.*

38. *See also* Waggoner, *supra* note 24, at 25.

outlined in this paragraph. They are much more willing to rely on such bases as the analysis of carbon film ribbons.

§ 21-2(B).Comparison Techniques.

At the outset, the work of questioned document examiners must be distinguished from graphologists and psycholinguists. Graphologists or graphoanalysts attempt to determine the writer's character and personality traits from his handwriting.[39] Psycholinguists attempt to infer the author's psychiatric and demographic characteristics (age, economic status, residence, etc.) from various aspects of the author's linguistic style, such as syntax, punctuation, and spelling.[40] "[A]s electronic writing becomes more common place,"[41] linguistics techniques may become more important; and the importance of traditional questioned document techniques might decline.

However, for the immediate future questioned document techniques will undoubtedly remain the most widely used methods of identifying an author. A forensic document examiner uses different methods and draws different inferences than graphologists or psycholinguists. The two most common tasks facing the examiner are determining whether the author of certain exemplars prepared the questioned document and helping the jury decide whether a document is a forgery. The examiner's methodology varies, depending on whether the questioned document is written or typed.

---

39. Carroll v. State, 276 Ark. 160, 165, 634 S.W.2d 99, 102 (1982).

40. United States v. Clifford, 543 F. Supp. 424, 426 (W.D. Pa. 1982), *rev'd,* 704 F.2d 86 (3d Cir. 1983).One of the leading proponents of forensic linguistics is Robert Ciaffoni. His manuscript, SECRETARY-TYPISTS, CO-APOSTLES OF FORENSIC LINGUISTICS, contains a detailed list of the characteristics such as indentation and hyphenation which forensic linguists rely on. Kenny, *The Expert in Court,* 99 LAW Q. REV. 197, 201-03 (1983) discusses the use of "stylometry" to make "authorship attribution" determinations. The author states his belief that "stylometry, and in particular stylometric authorship attribution, is a genuine science and not a pseudo-science." *Id.* at 202. Mr. Ciaffoni points out that in his Rationale of Judicial Evidence (1827), the British philosopher Jeremy Bentham anticipated linguistics when he wrote that "another mode of impeaching a writing alleged to be genuine" is pointing to a "style, phraseology or mode of spelling dissimilar to those of the individual in question ascertained from other sources." *But see* Hardcastle, *Forensic Linguistics: An Assessment of the CUSUM Method for the Determination of Authorship,* 33 J. FORENSIC SCI. SOC. 95 (1993) (the Cumulative Sum approach to forensic linguistics did not produce reliable results, and testimony based on the approach should not be accepted in court).

41. Kaplan, *Scholars Discuss Judge's Role, Combatting "Junk Science" in Wake of Kumho Decision,* 65 CRIM. L. (BNA) 134, 136 (May 5, 1999) (the articles describes the remarks of Dr. Carole E. Chaski, Executive Director of Linguistic Evidence, Inc., at the National Conference on Science and Law held in San Diego, California, on April 15-16, 1999).

Handwriting and Handprinting

Identification of the author. Handwriting analysis constitutes roughly 75% of the workload of questioned document examiners.[42] In some laboratories, it comprises 90% of the workload. In determining whether the same person authored the questioned document and the exemplars, the examiner makes a meticulous side-by-side, letter-by-letter comparison of the documents. The examiner uses such tools as microscopes and magnification loops to examine minute details. A single handwriting specimen may contain between 500 and 1,000 details,[43] and most of the details are inconspicuous to the untrained eye. These details are categorized as: (1) accidental features caused by the circumstances surrounding the execution of the particular document, (2) class characteristics in the author's writing or printing style, or (3) individual characteristics of the author's style.

Some of the discernible details in the questioned document will not be consistent features in the author's handwriting style. The detail might be attributable to the writing instrument or surface that the author used when the document was executed.[44] For example, if the author used a fountain pen, the examiner may observe a shading in a particular letter in one check, but the shading might not be a regular feature of the author's writing style. The shading may be due to the width of the pen's marking point or the peculiar action of the point when it is applied to the paper.[45] In part, a large supply of exemplars is needed to determine whether a particular detail appears consistently in the person's writing.[46]

Even when the detail appears consistently, it may not be unique to the individual writer. Rather, the detail may be a class characteristic. Class

---

42. Purtell, *Modern Handwriting Instructions, Systems, and Techniques*, 8 J. POLICE SCI. & ADMIN. 66 (1980). Questioned document examiners were earlier called handwriting experts. Our reviewer believes that the 75% figure is an underestimate; he believes that 90% is a more accurate figure.

43. A. MOENSSENS, J. STARRS, C. HENDERSON & F. INBAU, *supra* note 1, at § 5.15.

44. Hilton, *Effects of Writing Instruments on Handwriting Details*, 29 J. FORENSIC SCI. 80, 85 (1984); Masson, *The Effect of Fiber Tip Pen on Signatures*, 53 FORENSIC SCI. INT'L 157 (1992).

45. *Id.*

46. Stinson, *A Validation Study of the Influence of Alcohol on Handwriting*, 42 J. FORENSIC SCI. 411, 415 (1997) (errors, corrections, and omissions increase when the writer is under the influence of alcohol); Vaughan, *Proving False: The Art of Documenting Forgeries*, 13 CAL. LAW. 78, 79 (Oct. 1993) ("When someone is very ill ... the handwriting often becomes erratic, perhaps because of the nature of the medications or the quality of the patient's vision."); Hilton, *Signatures—Review and a New View*, 37 J. FORENSIC SCI. 125 (1992) (the question is "whether the specimen before us is consistent with the variable group of signatures that the person is capable of producing or normally uses to represent himself or herself").

characteristics are subdivided into two categories.[47] Some are system characteristics, caused by the style of penmanship the author learned in school.[48] If the author studied the Palmer method, some of those elements may persist in the author's handwriting style throughout life. Primary schools seem to devoting less time to the teaching of particular penmanship methods, and today many forensic document examiners balk at opining that a class characteristic necessarily originated with a writing system learned in school. Other class characteristics are group details. These details are habits widespread in a certain national or social group such as a particular family.[49] For example, in one case, a questioned document examiner testified that the spelling of a certain word was "characteristic of one familiar with the Swedish language."[50] Arthritic individuals,[51] alcoholics,[52] and blind persons[53] also exhibit class characteristics. Class characteristics help narrow the group of possible authors of the questioned document, but the examiner cannot rely on class characteristics alone to identify a specific person as the author.

To make an identification, the examiner must find individual characteristics. Those characteristics can take several forms: the manner in which the author begins or ends the word, the height of the letters, the slant of the letters, the shading of the letters, or the distance between the words. An identification rarely rests on a single characteristic.[54] It is far more common for the examiner to identify a combination of characteristics that in his or her experience is

---

47. Kelly, *Questioned Document Examination, in* SCIENTIFIC AND EXPERT EVIDENCE 695, 698 (2d ed. 1981).

48. Finch, *Class Characteristics of Alphabetic Speedwriting Shorthand Systems*, 37 J. FORENSIC SCI. 265 (1992).

49. Morgan & Zilly, *Document Examination of Handwriting with a Straightedge or a Writing Guide*, 36 J. FORENSIC SCI. 470 (1991) ("The writing of a blind person is normally not as evenly spaced and precisely formed, and the 't' crossings and 'i' dots are often missing. Such writing is ... identifiable"); Muehlberger, *Class Characteristics of Hispanic Writing in the Southeastern United States*, 34 J. FORENSIC SCI. 371 (1989); Hanna, *A Preliminary Classification of the Writing Elements of Chinese Characters*, 34 J. FORENSIC SCI. 439 (1989); Leung, Tsui, Cheung & Chung, *A Comparative Approach to the Examination of Chinese Handwriting — The Chinese Character*, 25 J. FORENSIC SCI. SOC'Y 255 (1985); Ramsey, *The Cherokee Syllabary*, 39 J. FORENSIC SCI. 1039 (1994) (one of the landmark questioned document cases, Hickory v. United States, 151 U.S. 303 (1894), involved Cherokee writing).

50. Magnuson v. State, 187 Wis. 122, 124-25, 203 N.W. 749, 750 (1925).

51. Miller, *Forensic Examination of Arthritic Impaired Writings*, 15 J. POLICE SCI. & ADMIN. 51 (1987).

52. Beck, *Handwriting of the Alcoholic*, 28 FORENSIC SCI. INT'L 19 (1985).

53. Kerr & Taylor, *Linguistic Evidence Indicative of Authorship by a Member of the Deaf Community*, 37 J. FORENSIC SCI. 1621 (1992) (persons who use the American Sign Language (ASL) tend to have somewhat peculiar syntax); Morgan & Zilly, *Document Examinations of Handwriting with a Straightedge or a Writing Guide*, 36 J. FORENSIC SCI. 470 (1991).

54. Hilton, *How Individual Are Personal Writing Habits?*, 28 J. FORENSIC SCI. 683 (1983).

singular.[55] There is no universally accepted number of points of similarity that the examiner must find before offering an opinion that two writings are identical. Moreover, as in the case of fingerprint analysis, if there is a single, unexplained difference that is basic or fundamental, the examiner cannot venture a definite opinion that the two documents were authored by the same writer. It is true that "certain apparent differences" can have a "logical explanation" such as illness, intoxication, or lack of care.[56] However, when there is no evident explanation for a significant difference between the style of the questioned document and the exemplars, the examiner cannot conclude that the authors are the same "despite extensive similarities."[57] The caveat is that although a single fundamental difference would probably preclude the examiner from opining that there was a positive identification, standing alone the difference would not necessarily dictate an elimination.

Unfortunately, the examiner cannot quantify the probability of a match with any degree of precision.[58] Determining a probability would require data as to the

---

55. Wagonner, *supra* note 24, at 21; Hilton, *supra* note 54, at 684.

56. *Id;* Widla, *The Influence of Spontaneous Writing on Stability of Graphic Features*, 46 FORENSIC SCI. INT'L 63 (1990) ("So far there has been no research aimed at establishing the amplitude of intra-individual variation, so the range of natural variation (*i.e.*, not caused by unnatural factors such as intoxication or by a particularly strong influence of factors accompanying writing) is not known"); Galbraigh, *Alcohol: Its Effect on Handwriting*, 31 J. FORENSIC SCI. 580 (1986).

57. Hilton, *supra* note 54, at 684. Whiting, *The Application of Reasoning to the Evaluation of Fundamental Differences in Handwriting Comparisons*, 41 J. FORENSIC SCI. 634 (1996) ("A cardinal tenet of forensic document analysis is that the existence of a single fundamental difference between questioned and known handwriting samples is a basis for excluding the samples as having come from a common source. But applying that doctrine to actual cases can be difficult because of different interpretations as to what constitutes a true fundamental difference. A review of the literature reveals that there is not just a single classification of a fundamental difference.").

58. Whiting, *Inconclusive Opinions: Refuge of the Questioned Document Examiner*, 35 J. FORENSIC SCI. 938 (1990) ("Document examiners are frequently accused of abdicating their responsibility by too often declaring that they can neither identify nor eliminate an individual as the author of the questioned handwriting. It is the author's contention that characteristics of handwriting comparisons often thwart one's ability to form specific conclusions ...."); Leung & Cheung, *On Opinion*, 42 FORENSIC SCI. INT'L 1, 1-2 (1989) ("A school of workers believes that only three classes of opinions, namely identification, elimination, and inconclusive should be given. There is, however, a greater majority of examiners who maintain that ... the language selected to summarize different sets of facts must vary, some being in positive terms and some in qualified terms"). The Questioned Document Section of the American Academy of Forensic Sciences and the American Board of Forensic Document Examiners recommend the use of the following, standardized terminology for opinions: identification (definite conclusion of identity), strong probability, probable, indications, no conclusion, indications did not, probability did not, strong probability did not, and elimination. McAlexander, Beck & Dick, *The Standardization of Handwriting Opinion Terminology*, 36 J. FORENSIC SCI. 311 (1991).

frequency with which stylistic details recur.[59] That data is currently unavailable.[60] Examiners must rely on professional experience, attempt to remember whether they have encountered this particular combination of characteristics before, and rest the final opinion on their experience and memory. At most, the examiner can say that a particular detail is "very common, [but] this is less so."[61] Examiners cannot reliably quantify the bases for their opinions. It therefore should not come as a surprise that there have been some highly publicized, sharp conflicts among the questioned document examiners, such as the Howard Hughes case. Notwithstanding such notorious conflicts, one study found that disputes among seasoned examiners are rare.[62] In the study, the researchers contacted leading examiners in private practice and government service.[63] The researchers asked the participating examiners how frequently they testified and how often they were opposed by other examiners. The researchers found that the "incidence of opposition runs from a low of 0.006 percent to a 'high' of one percent, with the frequency of disagreement usually being in the hundredths of one percent range."[64] The researchers concluded that "competent and ethical document examiners"[65] rarely disagree.

Some researchers are attempting to computerize signature verification.[66] The researchers describe the signature in a coded, digitized manner. In the reported study, the computer system correctly accepted authentic signatures 90% of the time and correctly rejected inauthentic signatures 97% of the time. Of course, the mere fact that the method has been computerized does not eliminate concerns about the scientific validity of the method. Computerization requires programming decision rules into the software. Depending on the jurisdiction, those rules must pass muster under either *Frye* or *Daubert*.

Forgery determinations. A common variation of the identification task is determining whether a document is a forgery.[67] There are three types of forgeries:

---

59. Hilton, *supra* note 54, at 683.

60. *Id.* at 684-85.

61. *Id.* at 685.

62. Todd, *Do Experts Frequently Disagree?*, 18 J. Forensic Sci. 455 (1973). Our reviewer, Mr. Kelly, points out that on one side, there were three highly experienced examiners. Our reviewer's opinion was that the document was a forgery.

63. *Id.* at 457.

64. *Id.* at 458.

65. *Id.* at 459.

66. Brocklehurst, *Computer Methods of Signature Verification*, 25 J. Forensic Sci. Soc'y 445 (1985). *See also* Huber & Headrick, *Let's Do It By Numbers*, 46 Forensic Sci. Int'l 209 (1990).

67. Forensic scientists sometimes have to determine whether objects other than conventional documents have been forged. Springer & Bergman, *Applications of Non-Destructive Testing (NDT) in Vehicle Forgery Examinations*, 39 J. Forensic Sci. 751 (1994) (forgery of vehicle identification numbers); Waterman, Those Fabulous Fakes: A Look at Forgery in the Field of Fine Art, Hemispheres 74 (July 1994) (art forgeries).

unskilled spurious forgeries, skilled traced forgeries, and skilled freehand forgeries.[68] In a spurious forgery, the forger makes no attempt to mimic the purported author's handwriting. In a traced forgery, the forger literally traces an authentic sample of the purported author's signature. There are several methods of tracing.[69] The forger can: (1) hold the authentic sample against glass, position a source of illumination under the glass, place a blank sheet of paper over the authentic sample, and trace the authentic signature onto the blank sheet; (2) position carbon paper under the original and a blank sheet under the carbon, trace the signature on the original and impress it onto the blank sheet, retrace the carbon impression in ink, and erase any excess carbon; or (3) place the original on top of a blank sheet, position that sheet on top of a soft substance such as a tablet, trace the original signature with enough pressure to leave an indentation on the blank sheet, and finally write over the indentation. In skilled freehand forgery, the forger sometimes repeatedly practices writing the authentic signature. When the forger is confident that he or she has mastered the author's style, the forger writes the signature freehand.[70] In doing so, the forger consciously attempts to adopt the purported author's style and suppress his or her own personal writing habits.

The examiner looks for a number of telltale signs of forgery. One sign is a pen lift.[71] In attempting to duplicate a stroke in an authentic signature, the forger may start the line, lift the pen, and complete the stroke in a second motion. The lift may be evident under a low-powered microscope. Another clue is the presence of hesitation marks.[72] If the forger is attempting to make a freehand copy of a model, he or she may hesitate. Rather than completely lifting the pen off the paper, the forger may simply pause before completing the motion. The pause will leave an excessive amount of ink on the paper. A third common sign of forgery is a retracing, patching, or retouching.[73] The forger may write over a line twice to ensure that the line is complete. A microscopic examination may reveal that there are two strokes in the line. The examiner pays special attention to the lower case letters; while most forgers are attentive when writing capital letters, many are careless when copying small letters.[74]

---

68. *See generally* D. GRAY, METHODS TO DETECT FORGED SIGNATURES 4-5 (1983). Leung, Cheng, Fung & Poon, *Forgery I) Simulation*, 38 J. FORENSIC SCI. 402 (1993).

69. *Id.* Leung, Fung, Cheng & Poon, *Forgery II) Tracing*, 38 J. FORENSIC SCI. 413 (1993).

70. *Id.* at 5.

71. *Id.* at 6. Beck, *Sources of Error in Forensic Handwriting Evaluation*, 40 J. FORENSIC SCI. 78, 80 (1995) ("forensic handwriting comparison is not just an analysis of forms but, more importantly, a consideration of the writing movements behind those forms. These essential movement characteristics may consist of minute hesitation points or penlifts or delicate retouchings that constitute primary signs of simulation").

72. *Id.*

73. *Id.* at 7.

74. A. MOENSSENS, J. STARRS, C. HENDERSON & F. INBAU, *supra* note 1, at § 5.05.

If the forger used a carbon copy tracing technique, there may be either bits of carbon remaining on the paper or signs of erasure.[75] When the forger traces over an indentation, there will be grooves on the paper. Oblique angle lighting techniques may be used to detect the presence of the grooves.[76] Like grooves, tremor lines — slight deviations from the stroke — can occur when a forger is attempting to trace an authentic signature.[77] Or a match might be too perfect. If the examiner can locate the authentic signature that was traced, a perfect match between the questioned document and the authentic signature is evidence of forgery by tracing. As previously stated, a person never writes the same word in precisely the same manner twice; some variation is natural and expectable. When there is no variation, the exactness of the match gives rise to a suspicion of forgery.

Although the above signs are helpful clues to forgery, the examiner must be careful to differentiate between true signs of forgery and illusions of tracing.[78] For example, "sister lines" can create the illusion.[79] A sister line is a line near the primary line, resulting from contact between the paper and the housing of a ballpoint pen. Sister lines can occur in authentic writings and may be difficult to distinguish from tracings characteristic of forgeries. Similarly, a rough writing surface can cause details that may easily be mistaken for tremor lines.[80] In the case of laminated documents, that is, documents enclosed in plastic lamination to protect them against wear, the lamination might create the illusion of lines on the enclosed paper; and those lines may be mistaken for signs of forgery.[81] Some experts assert that "an illusion of tracing will contain at least one contradiction of handwriting identification axioms;"[82] but before inferring forgery from a set of signs of forgery, the examiner must ensure that there are no factors present that could create illusions of tracing and furnish an alternative, innocent explanation for the appearance of the signs.

In some cases, it is relatively easy for the examiner to both determine that there has been a forgery and identify the forger.[83] For example, if the forgery is of the unskilled spurious type and the forger made no attempt to simulate the purported author's signature, the forgery will be in the forger's own handwriting style. However, when the forgery is skilled, the forger makes a conscious effort

---

75. D. GRAY, *supra* note 68, at 7.

76. *Id.* at 8.

77. *Id.* at 8-9.

78. Vastrick, *Illusions of Tracing*, 27 J. FORENSIC SCI. 186 (1982).

79. *Id.*

80. *Id.* at 189.

81. *Id.* at 190.

82. *Id.* at 191.

83. Muehlberger, *Identifying Simulations: Practical Considerations*, 35 J. FORENSIC SCI. 368 (1990) ("[S]hould the forger attempt to 'write' a simulation, there is a good possibility some of her or his own handwriting characteristics will be incorporated in the forgery").

to disguise personal writing habits. In rare cases, the forger is so unsuccessful in suppressing the habits that there are enough similarities between the forged document and samples of the forger's writing to identify the forger.[84] However, in many cases the forger is at least partially successful in suppressing his or her own writing style. In those cases, it is difficult to identify the forger.

Typewriting

At the zenith of the popularity of typewriters, the world population of typewriters exceeded 50,000,000, and over 500 models were produced.[85] The examiner can possibly make three findings about typewritten material: Which make and model of typewriter produced the material? Which specific typewriter produced the material? In the case of manual typewriters, who was the typist?[86]

Make and model of typewriter. A well-equipped document section will maintain an extensive reference collection of the typefaces of the various commercially available typewriters, including domestic and foreign typewriters and models that have been discontinued but are still in widespread use. The reference collection enables the examiner to identify the class, group, or system characteristics of the type.[87]

To facilitate the identification of class characteristics, several police agencies have developed classification systems for typewriters.[88] One of the first, the Schneeberger formula, was developed in Switzerland.[89] Schneeberger collected and classified examples of the type of all the typewriters popular in Switzerland during World War II. The American Society of Questioned Document Examiners

---

84. *E.g.*, People v. Hoover, 87 Ill. App. 3d 743, 43 Ill. Dec. 195, 410 N.E.2d 195 (1980).

85. Mathyer, *Problem of the Identification of Typewriter Makes and Models*, 11 FORENSIC SCI. 1, 2 (1978).

86. Although these three determinations represent the most common tasks which questioned document examiners have to perform with respect to typewriting, there are other tasks which examiners can perform. For example, in some cases examiners are called upon to reconstruct the text typed. Hunton & Puckett, *Restoring Texts of Typewriter Ribbons: A Reliability Study of the RAW-1 Ribbon Analysis Workstation*, 39 J. FORENSIC SCI. 21 (1994); Sperry, *Platen Information Revealed: A Technique for Locating Latent Text on Typewriter (or Printer) Platens*, 39 J. FORENSIC SCI. 223 (1994).

87. In one incident, ABC News purchased the rights to a book supposedly proving an affair between the late President John F. Kennedy and Marilyn Monroe. Thomas, Hosenball & Isikoff, *The JFK-Marilyn Hoax*, NEWSWEEK, Oct. 6, 1997, at 36. The author of the book relied on certain documents as proof of the affair. However, questioned document examiners unmasked the documents as "fakes." *Id.* The examiners pointed out that "the typewriter and correcting tape used on the papers were not invented until a decade after the documents were purported produced." *Id.* at 37.

88. *Id.* at 1; Noblett, *Image Processing and Statistical Analysis as an Aid in the Comparison of Typewritten Impressions*, 32 J. FORENSIC SCI. 963 (1987).

89. Mathyer, *supra* note 85, at 4.

has proposed a classification scheme,[90] as has the International Criminal Police Organization (Interpol).[91] The French National Police are largely responsible for the Interpol system. They prepared over 1,300 cards representing different makes and models of typewriters.[92] None of the current systems is ideal.[93] However, some such as the Bouffard Classification System are useful and can help single out the type on the questioned document.

In most cases, the identification of the type permits the examiner to determine the make and model of machine that produced the typewritten material. However, that identification is becoming an increasingly difficult task. Type is more standardized now than it was 30 years ago.[94] Moreover, following the example of their European counterparts, many American manufacturers no longer manufacture their own type; rather, they purchase type from common suppliers. For that reason, different models and even makes of typewriters may have the same class characteristics; there may be two manufacturers, each with three different models, that use the same generic type.

Identification of a specific typewriter. In handwriting analysis, it is rarely possible to identify the particular pen or pencil that the author used. However, typewriters are far more complex instruments than pens or pencils; the average typewriter has roughly 2,000 parts, and 200 parts are activated whenever the typist strikes a character.[95] A typewriter leaves many more identifying marks on paper than either a pen or a pencil. Whether the typewriter is a conventional instrument with the characters on a typebar or a device like an IBM Selectric typewriter with the type on a ball, the examiner may be able to identify the specific typewriter that produced a page of material.

In the case of conventional typewriters, there are several kinds of characteristics that the examiner searches for. One is the design, size, and space of the characters.[96] Some typestyles mimic printing or handwriting. There can be between six and 16 characters per inch; the more common are ten (pica) and twelve (elite).[97] Spacing can also vary; many typewriters leave approximately the

---

90. *Id.* at 5.

91. *Id.* at 6.

92. *Id.* at 20.

93. *Id.* at 29.

94. Anthony, *Comparison of Modern Typestyles*, 31 J. FORENSIC SCI. 710 (1986).

95. Carpenter, *Questioned Typewriting*, 20 AM. JUR. PROOF OF FACTS 265, 324-25 (1968). In the potential trial of the Unabomber suspect, Theodore Kaczynski, the prosecution contemplated attempting to introduce testimony that the Unabomber manifesto was prepared on a typewriter found in the suspect's mountain cabin. Reske, *A Circumstantial Case: Low-tech typewriter may help convict Unabomber suspect*, 82 A.B.A. J. 18 (June 1996).

96. *Id.* at 274.

97. *Id.* at 275; Catterick, Hickman & Russell, *The Classification of Printwheel Typestyles by Measuring the Size of Characters with an Image Processing System. An Initial Evaluation Using*

same distance between each letter, but proportional-spacing machines leave more width for "fat" letters such as "m" and "w."[98]

Another individual characteristic is vertical or horizontal alignment. No typebar has perfect alignment. At the end of the manufacturing process, most typewriters are manually adjusted; and this human manipulation introduces some misalignment.[99] In the case of manual typewriters, subsequent use of the machine introduces additional misalignment. The bottom of each character should strike a hypothetical base line, but many characters are out of vertical alignment. Since each key has two characters, both characters on the key will be out of proper alignment. When a typed letter is not in alignment, it is sometimes said to be "off its feet." Defects in horizontal alignment can cause the letters to appear too close to or too far apart from each other.[100] Foreign material in the typewriter carriage can cause drag with the result that the characters tend to stack up on each other on the page.[101] A grid can be used to analyze the alignment exactly.[102]

Another identifying characteristic is the weight of the impression left on the page.[103] When the key hits the roller or platen perfectly at the striking center, each part of the impression should be equally dark. However, numerous mechanical problems can cause one part of the impression to be darker than another part. If the key hits the roller above or below the striking center, the top or bottom will be unduly dark.

The most useful characteristic is often a defect on the typeface.[104] Grit may mar the typeface during the manufacturing process. Constant wear and tear on

---

Courier 10 and Elite 12 Printwheels, 43 FORENSIC SCI. INT'L 125 (1989) (image process systems can be used to measure the height, width, and number of characters).

98. Carpenter, *supra* note 95, at 275.

99. *Id.* at 276. Catterick & Keenlyside, *Quantitative Measurement of Misalignments in Typed Documents*, 59 FORENSIC SCI. INT'L 89 (1993).

100. Carpenter, *Questioned Typewriting*, 20 AM. JUR. PROOF OF FACTS278 (1968).

101. *Id.* at 279.

102. Hicks, *Electronic Typewriter Grids*, 44 J. FORENSIC SCI. 187 (1999).

103. Carpenter, *Questioned Typewriting*, 20 AM. JUR. PROOF OF FACTS 265, 279 (1968).

104. *Id.* at 280; Alen & Hardcastle, *The Distribution of Damage Defects Among Characters of Printwheel Typing Elements*, 47 FORENSIC SCI. INT'L 249, 257 (1990) (during manufacture, microscopic metal beads can be imparted to the surface of "golfball" printing elements and can lead to defects in the typescripts; "damage defects do not develop in a purely random manner. However, their occurrence is not simply correlated to the frequency of use of characters; the printing surface of the characters and the presence of weaker sections may be contributory factors"); Stoney & Thornton, *Multivariate Analysis of Typeface Damage Frequencies*, 34 J. FORENSIC SCI. 673 (1989) (both letter-use frequency and letter area, that is basket or keyboard position, show statistically significant positive correlation with typeface damage frequencies); Hardcastle, *Progressive Damage to Plastic Printwheel Typing Elements*, 30 FORENSIC SCI. INT'L 267 (1986). *But see* Behrendt, *Class Defects in Printwheel Typescript*, 33 J. FORENSIC SCI. 328, 334 (1988) ("class defects are present in printwheel typescripts. Class defects may ... appear ... highly individualistic, yet must be accorded the same relative value as other class characteristics. Accurate differentiation

the machine develop further defects. When keys stack up on each other during typing, the back of one key could leave a minute defect on the face of another key.[105]

As in the case of handwriting analysis, the final determination whether the same typewriter produced the questioned document and the exemplars is an evaluative judgment. No data is available on the frequency of incidence of particular defects. The expert must rely on his experience and memory. Although in theory "[e]ven one defect can serve to identify the work of a machine,"[106] before seizing on a single defect as the basis for an identification, the examiner must consider several caveats. The examiner may attempt to determine that the defect observed is a product of the typewriter rather than the typist's style. Just as a large number of handwriting exemplars are needed to ensure that the stylistic detail is habitual, the examiner requires numerous typewriting exemplars to be certain that the defect consistently appears in material prepared on the typewriter. Moreover, a single, unexplained basic difference between the questioned document and the exemplars precludes a finding of identity.[107] One fundamental dissimilarity prevents a conclusion of identity "no matter how uncommonly coincidental the similarities might appear."[108]

Selectric typewriters pose even greater problems. Rather than placing the characters on individual keys, the manufacturer places all the characters on a ball or typehead. Half the sphere is upper case while the other half is lower case.[109] The balls are interchangeable. Hence, a single ball could be used to type on several typewriters.

Electronic typewriters (ET) also pose problems for the examiner. However, an electronic typewriter may leave the impression from its printer on the paper; the typewriter may be missing a printwheel spoke.[110] The impression might be highly distinguishable and enable the examiner at the very least to identify the manufacturer.[111] In addition, the examiner may be able to use the typewriter

---

between class and individual defects must be predicated on an examination of the printwheel. Without examining the printwheel, an examiner is apt to effect an identification on the presence of class characteristics").

105. Carpenter, *supra* note 95, at 280-81.

106. *Id.* at 281.

107. Osborne, *"Explainable" Differences Revealed by Supplementary Typewriting Standards*, 5 J. POLICE SCI. & ADMIN. 393, 394 (1977).

108. *Id.* at 396.

109. Carpenter, *Questioned Typewriting*, 20 AM. JUR. PROOF OF FACTS 265, 283 (1968).

110. Anthony, *Letter Quality Impact Printer Hammer Impressions*, 33 J. FORENSIC SCI. 779 (1988).

111. *Id.*

ribbon system, including the correcting tape, to associate a particular typewriter with a document.[112]

Although the use of typeheads makes typewriter identification more difficult,[113] it is not impossible.[114] Alignment defects can still serve as identifying characteristics.[115] Alignment defects occur most often when the ball is in an extreme tilt or rotation position.[116] In one experiment, the researcher concluded that alignment defects permit differentiation among Selectric typewriters even if the typewriters have had very similar histories of prior use.[117] Furthermore, the examiner may be able to identify the ball that produced the type.[118] During the manufacturing process, minute beads sometimes form accidentally on the print surface of the ball.[119] The pattern of beads on the surface could help to identify the element that produced the typed material.[120]

Identification of a typist. Finally, the examiner may be able to suggest the person who typed the material. The examiner compares the questioned document and the exemplars to determine whether the typist makes characteristic errors.[121] The errors could include misspellings such as the transposition of letters,[122] punctuation errors such as the misuse of semicolons,[123] the style of using spaces and margins,[124] or peculiar solecisms.[125] It is easier to find identifying peculiarities in the work of persons who are poor typists and poorly educated.[126] The better educated the person, the less likely the person is to misspell terms or misuse punctuation. Similarly, the more skilled the typist, the less likely the person is to commit mechanical errors while typing. There is ordinarily little individuality in the typing of a literate, proficient typist, and thus it is more difficult for the examiner to identify such a typist.

---

112. Gerhart, *Methods of Associating Typewriter Ribbons and Correcting Tapes with a Questioned Text*, 34 J. FORENSIC SCI. 1183 (1989).

113. Attenberger & Kanaska, *Examination of a Typewritten Document*, 50 F.B.I. LAW ENF. BULL. 22 (June 1981); Levinson, *Single Element Typewriters*, 13 FORENSIC SCI. INT'L 15 (1979).

114. Miller, *An Analysis of the Identification Value of Defects in IBM Selectric Typewriters*, 29 J. FORENSIC SCI. 624 (1984).

115. *Id.* at 625.

116. *Id.*

117. *Id.*

118. Leslie, *Identification of the Single Element Typewriter and Type Element — Part I Type Elements*, 10 CAN. SOC'Y FORENSIC SCI. J. 87 (1977).

119. *Id.*

120. *Id.*

121. Carpenter, *Questioned Typewriting*, 20 AM. JUR. PROOF OF FACTS 265, 315 (1968).

122. *Id.*

123. *Id.* 315-17.

124. *Id.* at 315.

125. *Id.* at 315-17.

126. *Id.* at 316.

Other Devices That Leave Impressions

Typewriters are not the only devices that leave impressions on surfaces such as paper. Other devices that can impart impressions include adding machines, autopens,[127] cachets (stamping devices),[128] checkwriters,[129] notary seals,[130] photocopiers,[131] facsimile machines,[132] computer printers,[133] binding machines,[134] label makers,[135] word processing software,[136] and punches.[137] Although the

---

127. McCarthy & Winchester, *The Autopen*, 18 J. FORENSIC SCI. 441 (1973).

128. Levinson & Perelman, *Examination of Cachet Impressions*, 28 J. FORENSIC SCI. 235 (1983).

129. Jackson, *Identification of a Checkwriter Based on Ink Deposit Pattern*, 36 J. FORENSIC SCI. 257 (1991) (the checkwriter's impressions had "unusually heavy ink patterns, ... the result of accumulated debris in the typeface of the checkwriter"); Vastrick & Smith, *Checkwriter Identification — Individuality*, 27 J. FORENSIC SCI. 161 (1982).

130. Tang, *A Computer-Aided Seal Discriminating System*, 33 J. FORENSIC SCI. 969 (1988); Vastrick, *The Examination of Notary Seals*, 27 J. FORENSIC SCI. 899 (1982).

131. Gerhart, *Identification of Photocopiers from Fusing Roller Defects*, 37 J. FORENSIC SCI. 130 (1992); Shiver & Nelson, *Nondestructive Differentiation of Full-Color Photocopies*, 36 J. FORENSIC SCI. 145, 152 (1991) ("all seven of the types of [full-color] copiers tested can be distributed from one another by nondestructive examination of their copies"); Totty, *The Examination of Photocopy Documents*, 46 FORENSIC SCI. INT'L 121 (1990) (questioned document examiners are sometimes called upon to determine whether "a particular photocopy document has been produced on a particular photocopy machine" or whether "a particular photocopy was produced ... on a particular date"; to make these determinations, examiners use "simple techniques which are in everyday use by forensic scientists" (such as low power microscopic examination), "techniques which are frequently used in forensic science laboratories ... but which are rarely applied to document examination" (such as scanning electron microscopy and infrared spectroscopy), and "techniques which are well developed within particular fields ... but which are rarely ... used in forensic science" (such as detailed analysis of paper fibres)); Morton, *A Look at Newer Photocopiers*, 34 J. FORENSIC SCI. 461 (1989) (although the early view was that an examiner could never reach "definite findings" about the identity of an office copier, many modern examiners no longer subscribe to that view); Munson, *The Classification of Photocopies by Pyrolysis Gas Chromatography-Mass Spectrometry*, 34 J. FORENSIC SCI. 352 (1989); James, *The Classification of Office Copy Machines from Physical Characteristics*, 32 J. FORENSIC SCI. 1293 (1987); Hilton, *Detecting Fraudulent Photocopies*, 13 FORENSIC SCI. INT'L 117 (1979).

132. Owens, *A Look into Facsimile Transmission*, 35 J. FORENSIC SCI. 112 (1990). *See also* Gernandt, *Document Image Transmission by Telecommunication*, 35 J. FORENSIC SCI. 975 (1990) (the Immigration and Naturalization Service uses a Photophone, a video telephone similar to a fax machine).

133. Blanco, *Identifying Documents Printed by Dot Matrix Computer Printers*, 59 FORENSIC SCI. INT'L 35 (1993); Behrendt & Muehlberger, *Printwheel Typescript Variations Caused by the Manufacturing Process*, 32 J. FORENSIC SCI. 629 (1987).

134. Vanstratt & Ricci, *Identification Properties of the Office Binding Machine*, 27 FORENSIC SCI. INT'L 41 (1985).

135. Mason & Grose, *The Individuality of Toolmarks Produced by a Label Maker Used to Write Extortion Notes*, 32 J. FORENSIC SCI. 137 (1987).

136. Vastrick, *The Forensic Value of Right-Hand Justification*, 46 FORENSIC SCI. INT'L 269, 274 (1990) ("class characteristic differentiation of word processing software packages is feasible

examiner encounters these instruments less often than typewriters, roughly the same procedures and techniques are used in analyzing impressions created by these devices. The examiner searches for class and individual characteristics. A photocopier may have a particular set of defects on its glass.[138] Individual characteristics are commonly found in impressions left by custom-designed punches because they are hand filed and fitted.[139] If the notary's name and county are hand stamped onto the notary seal, the seal will have identifying characteristics.[140]

§ 21-3. Analysis of Paper.

The last section discussed the comparison of the style on the questioned document and the exemplars. This section considers the analysis of the paper that the writing appears on. Most paper is composed of cellulose fiber, bonded by being pressed into thin sheets. The examiner can make several determinations based on a study of the paper sheet. For example, if the paper of the questioned document matches that of the exemplars, the paper may have a similar origin, perhaps the same manufacturer. Or if the examiner can demonstrate that the paper of the questioned document was not marketed until after the purported date of the questioned document, the document is exposed as a forgery. These determinations necessitate an analysis of the physical and chemical properties of the paper.

There are numerous physical properties that the examiner can study. For instance, the examiner can ascertain whether the questioned document and the exemplars have the same watermark. Many manufacturers place a watermark on their product; at one point in the manufacturing process, a dandy roll covered with wire cloth rolls over the sheet and impresses the watermark onto the sheet.[141](Although the paper pulp is approximately 97% water, it goes over the top of the dandy, not the other way around.) Some manufacturers change their watermark from year to year, and thus the watermark is helpful in dating the sheet. In addition, if the examiner suspects that the sheet was torn from a pad or tablet, the edges of the sheet may match with the tears in the pad; unless some

---

through different right-hand justification spacing allotments when the printer used does not have proportional spacing capabilities. The test is, however, preliminary in nature as there are numerous different word processing software packages on the market").

137. Kraemer & Voorhees, *The Manufacture and Examination of Hand-Operated Custom-Design Punches*, 28 J. FORENSIC SCI. 273 (1983).

138. Kelly, *Identifying the Copying Machine Used in Preparation of Simulated Forgeries*, 18 J. FORENSIC SCI. 410, 411 (1973).

139. Kraemer & Voorhees, *supra* note 137, at 274.

140. Vastrick, *supra* note 136, at 903.

141. Radiographic instruments can be used to detect the watermark. Kerr & Gallant, *Large Area Tritium Sources for Forensic Document Radiography*, 28 FORENSIC SCI. INT'L 221 (1985).

paper fell off when the tear was made, the two sets of edges should fit into each other. The examiner can study the length, width, thickness, weight per unit area, color, texture, gloss, finish, and opacity of the paper.[142] These physical properties can be measured without substantially altering the document. When the examiner has a sufficient quantity of the questioned material, he or she can also use tests that will change the document — for example, bursting strength — determining the amount of pressure necessary to burst a hole in the sheet; folding endurance — how many times the sheet can be folded before breaking; and accelerated aging tests — the effects of heat or artificial light on the sheet.[143]

The chemical composition of the paper can also be studied. The examiner can stain the sheet with dyes; the reaction between the paper and the dye may be indicative of the composition of the sheet.[144] The various chromatographic techniques, detailed in Chapter 23 on drug identification, also apply to paper analysis.[145] A chromatographic procedure, inverse paper chromatography, has been developed for paper examinations.[146] In the conventional use of paper chromatography, the paper is the known, and the analyst uses the migration of the liquid on the paper to identify the unknown liquid. In inverse paper chromatography, the analyst applies a known mixture of dyestuffs onto the unknown paper.[147] The paper serves as the sorbent medium; and by comparing migratory behavior of the dyes on the paper with known standards, the analyst may be able to identify the paper.[148]

Some laboratories employ several chemical tests in addition to the standard chromatographic techniques. Most paper includes a "sizing" such as rosin or starch.[149] Chemical reagents can be used to identify the sizing in the questioned paper.[150] Similarly, in addition to its fiber and sizing, most paper includes a loading material; this material can be identified by burning part of the sheet and examining the ash.[151] The examiner can also subject the paper to absorption procedures and tests for paraffin, mineral coating, and acidity.[152]

---

142. F.B.I., SOME SCIENTIFIC ASPECTS OF DOCUMENT EXAMINATION 5-7 (1946).

143. *Id.* at 9-10.

144. Ganguly, *Identification of Mutilated Lottery Ticket by Examination of Its Dye*, 7 J. POLICE SCI. & ADMIN. 14 (1979).

145. *Id.*

146. Ziderman, *A Simple Technique for Comparing Paper Samples by Their Performance as a Chromatographic Sorbent (Inverse Paper Chromatography)*, 26 J. FORENSIC SCI. 387 (1981).

147. *Id.*

148. *Id.*

149. F.B.I., *supra* note 142, at 3.

150. *Id.* at 11.

151. *Id.*

152. *Id.* at 11-12. Blackledge & Gernandt, *The pH Pen — A Means of Comparing Paper Products*, 38 J. FORENSIC SCI. 134 (1993) (analyzing the pH level of paper).

Finally, the examiner can use sophisticated instrumental techniques, including many of the techniques mentioned in Chapter 25 on instrumental analysis. Both infrared and ultraviolet instruments have been adapted to use in paper analysis. Some laboratories utilize the most advanced techniques, including neutron activation analysis (NAA) and scanning electron microscopy (SEM).[153] NAA can assist in determining the trace elements present in the paper.[154] SEM enables the examiner to visualize properties of the sheet that are invisible to both the naked eye and the normal microscope. Used in conjunction with energy dispersive X-ray analysis (EDX), SEM can also be employed to determine the elemental composition of paper. Polish researchers have used an RC oscillator to make comparative measurements of the vibration frequency of paper to determine the authenticity of writings.[155]

The above techniques can be utilized to analyze almost any type of paper. There are special types of paper that lend themselves to unique tests. One example is safety paper.[156] Safety paper is employed to protect the document against alteration; it is designed so that a stain or a word such as "Void" appears if someone applies a mechanical eraser or a chemical eradicator to the surface of the paper.[157] Safety paper is often used to manufacture check forms. To analyze a unique type of sheet such as safety paper, the examiner must learn as much as possible about the special manufacturing procedures.[158] The peculiarities of the manufacturing process will help in deciding whether special tests are appropriate.

§ 21-4. Analysis of Ink, Ribbon Dye, or Pencil Lead.

Section 21-2 dealt with the style of the markings on the questioned document, and § 21-3 addressed the topic of the paper the markings are impressed upon. This section considers the ink, dye, or lead with which the markings are made. Like paper analysis, ink examination can help answer such questions as whether the questioned document was backdated. If the document bears a date in 1974 but the manufacturer did not introduce the ink until 1982, at the very least the date has probably been altered. As in the case of paper analysis, there is a wide variety of techniques for analyzing the lead, dye, or ink.

---

153. Ziderman, *supra* note 146, at 388.

154. Blanchard, *Trace Element Profiles and Ratios Determined by Instrumental Neutron Activation Analysis for Fine Paper Identification*, 23 J. FORENSIC SCI. 679 (1978).

155. Grzeszyk, Struzewski & Szymanski, *A New Method for Comparison of Paper Samples*, 46 FORENSIC SCI. INT'L 101 (1990) (this technique is non-destructive).

156. Davis, *Safety Paper*, 7 J. POLICE SCI. & ADMIN. 80 (1979).

157. *Id.*

158. *Id.* at 81-82.

Pencil Lead

Pencil "lead" is actually composed of graphites, clays, and waxes.[159] There are chemical and instrumental techniques for differentiating among pencil leads. If the laboratory has an adequate reference collection, the laboratory can usually discriminate among manufacturers and can often identify the specific type of pencil used to make the markings on the questioned document.[160]

Typewritten Ribbon Dyes

In typewriting with a fabric ribbon, the mark on the questioned document is a trace of the dye in the ribbon. There are several methods of identifying the type of ribbon used to make the mark.[161] Ribbon thread counts vary from 250 to 320 threads per square inch, and a microscopic examination of a clear typed mark may enable the examiner to estimate the number of threads per square inch in the ribbon that made the mark.[162] The density of the color of the mark is another indicator.[163] Densities range from light to extra dark. At least when the ribbon is fresh and well impregnated with the ink, the examiner can determine the density by comparing the mark on the questioned document with known standards. The ribbon typically contains a toner to darken the color left on the paper.[164] Manufacturers use different toners, and the examiner can employ several chemical tests to differentiate among the toners.[165] One of the most popular chemical tests for typewriter ribbon impressions is thin layer chromatography (TLC).[166] Some laboratories use TLC to test typewriter impressions,[167] specifically to differentiate various typewriters.[168]

Writing Inks

At one time an estimated 75% of the questioned documents received by the F.B.I. Laboratory was written in ink.[169] That statistic reflects the great popularity

---

159. Cain, Cantu, Brunelle & Lyter, *A Scientific Study of Pencil Lead Components*, 23 J. FORENSIC SCI. 637 (1978).

160. *Id.*

161. Carpenter, *Questioned Typewriting*, 20 AM. JUR. PROOF OF FACTS 265, 291 (1968).

162. *Id.*

163. *Id.* at 292.

164. *Id.* at 293.

165. *Id.*

166. F.B.I., *A Scientific Look at Typewriter Ribbon Inks*, F.B.I. LAW ENF. BULL. Reprint, June 1965.

167. *See English, Dye Composition of Typewriter Inks as an Indication of Date of Typing*, 6 J. POLICE SCI. & ADMIN. 74 (1978).

168. Brunelle, Negri, Cantu & Lyter, *Comparison of Typewriter Ribbon Inks by Thin-Layer Chromatography*, 22 J. FORENSIC SCI. 807 (1977).

169. F.B.I., *A Scientific Look at Writing Inks*, F.B.I. LAW ENF. BULL. Reprint, Feb. 1964.

of ink instruments, especially ballpoint pens.[170] The examiner may occasionally analyze documents with disappearing ink.[171] At first, forensic laboratories used simple microscopic techniques to study the physical properties of ink on questioned documents.[172] However, the recent trend has been to employ more sophisticated techniques, some similar to those developed for drug analysis.[173] Some techniques are destructive, but others are not. The examiner attempts to avoid resort to destructive tests; but when he or she decides that they must be used, any pertinent non-destructive tests are conducted first.

Those techniques include chemical tests. The two preliminary chemical tests are solubility and the spot test.[174] In a solubility test, the analyst extracts a small plug of the ink from the writing with a hypodermic needle and then measures the relative solubility of the ink in various solvents. The test results are observed under a low-powered microscope.[175] In a chemical spot test, as in a solubility test, the analyst initially removes a small plug of ink sample from the writing and allows the plug to react with known chemical and then assesses the color reaction.[176] The resulting colors indicate the composition of the ink.

Physical tests that measure the reaction of ink to various wavelengths of light are often employed to differentiate ink writings. Two of the most commonly used are infrared reflectance and luminescence. These non-destructive procedures involve the illumination of the questioned writing with intense light and, through the use of filters and video technology, the recording of differential changes to the writing based on the composition of the ink. These procedures are not completely discriminating and may be unable to distinguish two different ink formulations. However, it is possible to determine rather conclusively that two writings were prepared with different inks. In the performance of these techniques, though, circumstances can arise which would cause errors.[177]

---

170. *Id.*

171. Throckmorton, *Disappearing Ink: Its Use, Abuse, and Detection*, 35 FORENSIC SCI. INT'L 199, 203 (1990) (the examiner used "[a] weak solution of Drano (sodium hydroxide) crystals mixed with water" to cause the writing to reappear).

172. *See generally* Lyter, *Ink Analysis: A Key Element in Questioned Document Examination*, 19 TRIAL 53 (Jan. 1983).

173. Brunelle, *Novel Techniques for the Examination of Physical Evidence — Their Admissibility as Evidence*, 56 J. ASS'N OFF. ANAL. CHEM. 1391, 1397 (1973); Rohde, McManus, Vogt & Heineman, *Separation and Comparison of Fountain Pen Inks by Capillary Zone Electrophoresis*, 42 J. FORENSIC SCI. 1004 (1997).

174. Brunelle & Pro, *A Systematic Approach to Ink Identification*, 55 J. ASS'N OFF. ANAL. CHEM. 823, 824 (1972).

175. *Id.*

176. *Id.*

177. Lyter, *supra* note 172, at 54; Horton & Nelson, *An Evaluation of the Use of Laser-Induced Infrared Luminescence to Differentiate Writing Inks*, 36 J. FORENSIC SCI. 838 (1991); Moore, *Abnormalities Encountered in Infrared Examinations of Ball Pen Writing Over Correction Fluid*, 45 J. FORENSIC SCI. INT'L 265 (1990); Sensi & Cantu, *Infrared Luminescence: Is It a Valid Method*

More recent chemical testing includes the use of chromatographic procedures.[178] Paper chromatography,[179] thin layer chromatography (TLC),[180] gas liquid chromatography (GLC),[181] and high performance or high pressure liquid chromatography (HPLC)[182] all have been utilized successfully to analyze inks.

In addition to chromatography, other instrumental techniques are used such as infrared and ultraviolet spectroscopy as well as electrophoretic procedures.[183] Ultraviolet techniques have long been used in ink analysis.[184] Infrared analysis is also useful.[185] The electrophoretic procedures, discussed in Chapter 17 on genetic markers, are being employed in ink analysis.[186] The use of laser techniques is

---

to Differentiate Among Inks?, 27 J. FORENSIC SCI. 196 (1982); Chowdry, Gupta & Bami, *Ink Differentiation with Infrared Techniques*, 18 J. FORENSIC SCI. 418 (1973).

178. Lyter, *supra* note 172, at 54.

179. Brunelle & Pro, *supra* note 174, at 823.

180. *Id.;* Lyter, *supra* note 172, at 54; Lewis, *Thin-Layer Chromatography of Writing Inks — Quality Control Considerations*, 41 J. FORENSIC SCI. 874 (1996); Aginsky, *Forensic Examination of "Slightly Soluble" Ink Pigments Using Thin-Layer Chromatography*, 38 J. FORENSIC SCI. 1131 (1993); Aginsky, *Comparative Examination of Inks by Using Instrumental Thin-Layer Chromatography and Microspectrophotometry*, 38 J. FORENSIC SCI. 1111 (1993); Harris, *Developments in the Analysis of Writing Inks on Questioned Documents*, 37 J. FORENSIC SCI. 612 (1992) (the use of TLC by the Royal Canadian Mounted Police); Fanali & Schudel, *Some Separations of Black and Red Water-Soluble Fiber-Tip Pen Inks by Capillary Zone Electrophoresis and Thin-Layer Chromatography*, 36 J. FORENSIC SCI. 1192 (1991); Jasuga, Singla & Seema, *Thin-Layer Chromatographic Analysis of Indian Stamp Pad Inks*, 42 FORENSIC SCI. INT'L 255 (1989); Krantz, *Technique for Transferring Ink from a Written Line to a Thin-Layer Chromatographic Sheet*, 31 J. FORENSIC SCI. 655 (1986).

181. Brunelle & Pro, *supra* note 174, at 825.

182. Lofgren & Andrasko, *HPLC Analysis of Printing Inks*, 38 J. FORENSIC SCI. 1151 (1993); Tebbett, Chen, Fitzgerald & Olson, *The Use of HPLC with Multiwavelength Detection for the Differentiation of Non Ball Pen Inks*, 37 J. FORENSIC SCI. 1149 (1992); Keto, *Characterization of Alkali Blue Pigment in Counterfeit Currency by High Performance Liquid Chromatography*, 29 J. FORENSIC SCI. 198 (1984); Coldwell & Karger, *Ball-Point Pen Ink Examination by High Pressure Liquid Chromatography*, 60 J. ASS'N. OFF. ANAL. CHEM. 613 (1977).

183. Fanali & Schudel, *Some Separations of Black and Red Water-Soluble Fiber-Tip Pen Inks by Capillary Zone Electrophoresis and Thin-Layer Chromatography*, 36 J. FORENSIC SCI. 1192 (1991).

184. Gupta, Mukhi & Bami, *Differentiation of Inks on Documents by Dequenching of Ultraviolet Fluorescence: A Case Report*, 12 FORENSIC SCI. INT'L 61 (1978).

185. Andrasko, *Microreflectance FTIR Techniques Applied to Materials Encountered in Forensic Examination of Documents*, 41 J. FORENSIC SCI. 812 (1996); Merrill & Bartick, *Analysis of Ballpoint Pen Inks by Diffuse Reflectance Infrared Spectrometry*, 37 J. FORENSIC SCI. 528 (1992); Trzcinska, *Infrared Spectroscopy of Ballpen Paste*, 46 FORENSIC SCI. INT'L 105 (1990); Olson, *Color Comparison in Questioned Document Examination Using Microspectrophotometry*, 31 J. FORENSIC SCI. 1330 (1986).

186. Brunelle & Pro, *supra* note 174, at 823; Fanali & Schudel, *Some Separations of Black and Red Water-Soluble Fiber-Tip Pen Inks by Capillary Zone Electrophoresis and Thin-Layer Chromatography*, 36 J. FORENSIC SCI. 1192 (1991).

also under study.[187] These procedures can often differentiate ink even when chromatographic procedures cannot effect separation.[188] Other techniques are also being adapted to questioned document examination.[189]

In recent years there has been an intensive effort to develop a systematic approach to ink identification.[190] This effort has taken three forms. First, many laboratories have expanded the number of tests they use in analyzing ink.[191] A given laboratory's or private examiner's routine testing protocol might include subjecting the ink sample to microscopic examination, infrared reflectance and luminescence, solubility test, chemical spot tests, thin layer chromatography, and spectrophotometry.[192] Second, the Bureau of Alcohol, Tobacco, and Firearms amassed a large Standard Ink Library of known standards.[193] The library has since been transferred to the Secret Service Laboratory. The library currently includes the formulas for seven thousand inks.[194] Third, in the early 1970s the Bureau began encouraging ink manufacturers to add identifiers — "tags" — to their products.[195] As a practical matter, most manufacturers have tended to use an ink formulation for approximately three years.[196] Six major ink manufacturers participated in the voluntary tagging program and changed their formulations and taggants annually.[197] These manufacturers account for between 40 and 50% of the domestic production of ink.[198]Although these programs are no longer active, the amount of "tagged" ink in existence and the range of documents examined makes these programs a valuable contribution to the state of the art of ink

---

187. Horton & Nelson, *An Evaluation of the Use of Laser-Induced Infrared Luminescence to Differentiate Writing Inks*, 36 J. FORENSIC SCI. 838 (1991); Sinor, Wilde, Everse & Menzel, *Lasers and Optical Spectroscopy in Questioned Document Examination*, 31 J. FORENSIC SCI. 825 (1986).

188. Brunnelle & Pro, *supra* note 174, at 823.

189. Rohde, McManus, Vogt & Heineman, *Separation and Comparison of Fountain Pen Inks by Capillary Zone Electrophoresis*, 42 J. FORENSIC SCI. 1004 (1997); Cassidy & Allen, *Application of the Microdroplet Method of X-Ray Analysis to the Characterization of Inks*, 38 J. FORENSIC SCI. 40 (1993); Zeichner & Glattstein, *Some Special Observations Regarding Visible Transmission Spectra of Inks and an Improved Method for Their Discrimination by Microspectrophotometry*, 37 J. FORENSIC SCI. 738 (1992).

190. *Id.*

191. *Id.;* Lyter, *supra* note 172, at 54; Sensi & Cantu, *supra* note 177, at 196.

192. Brunelle & Pro, *supra* note 174, at 824-25.

193. Lyter, *Examination of Ball-Point Pen Ink by High Pressure Liquid Chromatography*, 27 J. FORENSIC SCI. 154 (1982).

194. A. MOENSSENS, J. STARRS, C. HENDERSON & F. INBAU, *supra* note 1, at § 5.12 (the Bureau of Alcohol, Tobacco, and Firearms (ATF) founded the Standard Ink Library; the ATF later transferred the library to the U.S. Secret Service; "At present it contains approximately 7000 different ink standards from all over the world").

195. *Id.*

196. Lyter, *supra* note 172, at 54.

197. *Id.*

198. *Id.*

examination. Under ideal conditions — proper equipment, adequate standards, and a tagged ink -- the examiner might be able to determine the type of ink, the manufacturer, and even the batch of production.[199]

Toners

Photocopy machines use toners. Like an ink or dye, toner can be analyzed and identified.[200] However, the identification of the toner may have little probative value, since the toner used in conjunction with a photocopy machine can be changed from time to time.

Computer Printers and Carbon Paper

Documents generated by computer printers[201] and with carbon paper[202] also lend themselves to analysis by the techniques described in this section.

§ 21-5. Age Determinations.

In the previous sections, several techniques for dating a document were mentioned. For example, if a document bears the date 1976 but the document is written in an ink that was not marketed until 1981, the earliest possible date for the creation of the document is 1981. This evidence indicates that a forger either created the entire document or at least altered the date. Dating techniques are vital in exposing forgeries. The examiner can be working with a large or small time frame. In the above hypothetical, the time frame spans years. In other cases,

---

199. Lyter, *supra* note 193, at 156-60.

200. Mizrachi, Aizenshtat, Levy & Elkayam, *Classification and Identification of Color Photocopiers by FT-IR and GC/MS*, 43 J. FORENSIC SCI. 353 (1998); Mazzella, Lennard & Margot, *Classification and Identification of Photocopying Toners by Diffuse Reflectance Infrared Fourier Transform Spectroscopy (DRIFTS): II. Final Report*, 36 J. FORENSIC SCI. 820 (1991); Mazzella, Lennard & Margot, *Classification and Identification of Photocopying Toners by Diffuse Reflectance Infrared Fourier Transform Spectroscopy (DRIFTS): I. Preliminary Results*, 36 J. FORENSIC SCI. 449 (1991); Zimmerman, Mooney & Kimmett, *Preliminary Examination of Machine Copier Toners by Infrared Spectrophotometry and Pyrolysis Gas Chromatography*, 31 J. FORENSIC SCI. 489 (1986); Levy & Wampler, *Applications of Pyrolysis Gas Chromatography/Mass Spectrometry to Toner Materials from Photocopiers*, 31 J. FORENSIC SCI. 258 (1986); Merrill, Bartick & Mazzella, *Studies of Techniques for Analysis of Photocopy Toners by IR*, 41 J. FORENSIC SCI. 264 (1996); Tandon, Jasuja & Sehgal, *Thin Layer Chromatography Analysis of Photocopy Toners*, 73 FORENSIC SCI. INT'L 149 (1995); Andrasko, *A Simple Method for Sampling Photocopy Toners for Examination by Microreflectance Fourier Transform Infrared Spectrophotometry*, 39 J. FORENSIC SCI. 226 (1994); Chang, Huang & Giang, *An Improvement on Pyrolysis Gas Chromatography for the Differentiation of Photocopy Toners*, 38 J. FORENSIC SCI. 843 (1993).

201. Kaur, Jasuja & Singla, *Thin Layer Chromatography of Computer Printer Ribbon Inks*, 53 FORENSIC SCI. INT'L 51 (1992).

202. Davis & Lyter, *Comparison of Typewritten Carbon Paper Impressions*, 27 J. FORENSIC SCI. 424 (1982).

the time frame is short, and the question is whether a forger added a stroke to a check five minutes after receiving it.

§ 21-5(A). Sequence of Marks.

There are techniques for determining the sequence of strokes on a questioned document even when the strokes intersect.[203]

First, if the writer used a pencil to make a series of strokes, it may be shown that the last written line will have an uninterrupted graphite deposit.[204]

Second, when the writer used wet ink in a fountain pen, the last aqueous stroke will tend to spread or feather out along the earlier line.[205]

Third, if the writer employed a ball-point pen, there may be several clues to the order in which the strokes were made.[206] The width of the second line ordinarily narrows where it crosses the earlier line.[207] Furthermore, the second stroke tends to drag a small amount of the ink from the previous line with it and carry it in the direction of the second line.[208] Some researchers believe that the configuration of the groove pattern at the intersection between the two strokes can provide positive evidence of the sequence of the strokes.[209] Infrared instruments are used to visualize the groove pattern.[210] The Igoe-Reynolds lift is a technique that may be of assistance in determining stroke sequence.[211] It is tempting to assume that the stroke that appears darker to the naked eye is the uppermost or last stroke.[212] However, that appearance is sometimes the result of an optical illusion.[213] The Igoe-Reynolds technique involves applying an adhesive paper to the writing, impressing an image of the strokes onto the paper,

203. Radley, *Determination of Sequence of Writing Impressions and Ball Pen Inkstrokes Using the ESDA Technique*, 33 J. FORENSIC SCI. SOC. 69 (1993) (although the analysts could reliably identify inkstrokes over impressions, the converse situation produces a fair number of false negatives); Giles, *Extending ESDA's Capability: The Determination of the Order of Writing and Impression Using the Technique of Electrostatic Detection*, 59 FORENSIC SCI. INT'L 163 (1993); Strach, *Establishing the Sequence of Intersecting Ball-Point Pen Strokes*, 11 FORENSIC SCI. 67 (1978). *See also* Foley, *Characteristics of Synchronous Sequential Signatures*, 32 J. FORENSIC SCI. 121 (1987).

204. Morrill, *supra* note 36, at 206.

205. *Id.* Our reviewer cautions that it can be very difficult to make this determination.

206. Strach, *supra* note 203, at 67.

207. *Id.* at 68-69.

208. *Id.* at 69-70.

209. Radley, *Determination of Sequence of Ball-Point Pen Writing Utilizing Infared Luminescence Techniques*, 22 J. FORENSIC SCI. SOC'Y 373 (1982).

210. *Id.*

211. Godown, *Recent Developments in Writing Sequence Determination*, 20 FORENSIC SCI. INT'L 227 (1982).

212. *Id.*

213. *Id.*

and then lifting the image by removing the paper. Kromekote, manufactured by Champion Paper Company, is the lift off paper commonly used. This method permits a more objective evaluation of the continuity of the strokes,[214] but it is somewhat destructive of the paper. Indian researchers have developed another lifting technique involving the use of photographic glossy paper treated with pyridine.[215] When handwriting and typewriting intersect, some researchers recommend careful flaking of the carbon from the paper at the point of intersection.[216]

Many laboratories and private examiners employ the stereo microscope as the basic instrument in determining the sequence of marks. The stereo microscope enables the examiner to study the length, breadth, and depth of each line on the paper. Other laboratories are using image enhancement systems as an aid in determining the sequence of strokes.[217]

Still other laboratories utilize the laser scanning confocal microscope (LSCM) for this purpose.[218] In one experiment, the use of the LSCM enabled the researchers to accurately determine the writing sequence in 75% of the cases.[219]

§ 21-5(B). Dating in a Large Time Frame.

It is usually impossible for an examiner to determine the precise date on which a document was prepared. However, techniques exist which can indicate that a document could not have been prepared on the date it bears. In some cases, the examiner can also approximate the date of preparation for a document. The techniques usually involve the analysis of ink, paper, typeface, or pencil marks.

Ink

As the types and composition of writing inks have changed, the techniques available for determining the age of ink writing have similarly evolved. Inks commonly used in the pre-Revolutionary time period and found in the examination of documents prepared until the 1940's are composed of iron gallotanate. These inks garner their color from the oxidation of iron upon exposure to air and often contained blue dyes to impart color prior to this

---

214. *Id.*

215. Gupta, Rai & Chugh, *Determination of Writing Sequence of Strokes of Ball-Point Pen Versus Ball-Point Pen and Other Conventional Writing Instruments*, 34 FORENSIC SCI. INT'L 217 (1987).

216. Hart & Carney, *Typewriting Versus Writing Instrument: A Line Intersection Problem*, 34 J. FORENSIC SCI. 1329, 1334 (1989).

217. Schuetzner, *Examination of Sequence of Strokes with an Image Enhancement System*, 33 J. FORENSIC SCI. 244 (1988).

218. Cheng, Chao, Jeng & Lee, *A New Method of Identifying Writing Sequence with the Laser Scanning Confocal Microscope*, 43 J. FORENSIC SCI. 348 (1998).

219. *Id.* at 349.

oxidation process.[220] This oxidation process frequently follows an orderly sequence with maximum darkness occurring within a few weeks or months and gradual fading over years until only a rust colored deposit remains.[221] This color change was often associated with the age of the writing; but due to the various formulations of ink available and the effect of environmental conditions on the oxidation rate, these age assessments are prone to error. One attempt to quantify this process relied on measuring the extent to which the iron ions have migrated from the written line.[222] This process proceeds with some regularity. Thus, comparative analysis between a questioned document and known standards would provide a likely time frame, within 20 years, for the preparation of the document.

With the introduction of fountain pen inks in the early 1900's and their routine use in the 1920's, the examination schemes evolved to include both physical and chemical testing. Physical testing usually included microscopy while chemical tests frequently entailed solubility tests or spot tests, as previously noted. In addition, researchers from various parts of the world began to investigate the question of how long ink had been on a document by measuring the ability to extract or solubilize the ink line as a function of age. These methods used qualitative or semi-quantitative measurement techniques to arrive at a relative date of preparation for the examined writings.[223]

Several other procedure are also possible with fountain pen inks. These are commonly referred to as ion migration tests.[224] As time passes, the ions of chloride and sulfate diffuse from the ink stroke.[225] The distance the ions travel from the stroke is an indication of the age of the writing.[226] There are several limitations to this test. To begin with, the age limit for the test appears to be two years; after that time, migration is minimal or unpredictable.[227] Moreover, many modern inks do not contain sufficient quantities of these ions, and hence the tests may have outlived their usefulness.[228] Even when the ink contains sufficient chlorides, a number of factors can affect the rate of chloride migration. The factors include the paper the ink is applied to, the density of the ink, and the

---

220. F.B.I., *supra* note 142, at 20.

221. *Id.*

222. McNeil, *Scanning Auger Microscopy for Dating of Manuscript Inks*, *in* ARCHAEOLOGICAL CHEMISTRY III, ADVANCES IN CHEMISTRY SERIES, No. 205, p. 255 (A.C.S. 1984).

223. Mitchell, *Estimation of the Age of Ink in Writing*, THE ANALYST, vol. XLV, No. 435, p. 246 (July 1922); Kikuahi, *Estimation of the Age of Writing in Blue Black Ink (III)*, JAPANESE POL. SCI. REP., vol. 16, No. 1, p. 83 (1963).

224. F.B.I., *supra* note 142, at 23.

225. *Id.*

226. F.B.I., *supra* note 169, at 2.

227. *Id.*

228. *Id.*

humidity under which the document was stored.[229] "Unless these factors are known . . ., the reliability of the chloride migration tests may be questionable."[230] Some experts assert that today the sulfate migration test is of no value.

The introduction of ball pen inks, initially in the 1940's as oil-based formulations and later as glycol-based formulations, and felt or porous inks in the 1960's led to the use of examination methodologies similar to those employed for other chemical analysis, such as pharmaceuticals or textiles. These analytic techniques involved the use of chromatographic and spectroscopic methods previously described.[231] By amassing standard libraries it became possible to determine the identity of a particular ink formulation on a questioned document by comparison of analysis results. If the commercial availability of the standard ink found to match the questioned ink is known, it is possible to assign a date of first availability to the questioned writing. The validity of this process is based upon the completeness of the standard library. Since at first the libraries were limited, the initial attempts to use this procedure in court were greeted with skepticism.[232] However, since the early proffers of testimony in the 1970's, most examiners employing this procedure have amassed larger libraries with sufficient representation of non-domestic products to gain routine acceptance by trial courts. The added presence of "tags" in writing inks has increased the utility of this procedure and more precisely defined the possible time period for preparation of the examined writing.[233] For example, if the questioned ink contains a tag which the manufacturer first added in 1984, the presence of the tag establishes that the document could not have been executed before that year. The early research performed on fountain pen ink has been extended to both ball pen and felt or porous point pen inks in the form of relative aging examinations.[234]

---

229. *Id.*

230. *Id.*

231. *See* notes 178-89, *supra.*

232. In the Spring 1997 issue of SCI. SLEUTHING REV., Professor Starrs discusses Richard Brunelle's testimony in United States v. Bruno, 333 F. Supp. 570 (E.D. Pa. 1971). Professor Starrs states that federal District Judge Masterson found that Mr. Brunelle's "ink library" was so incomplete that it was impossible for him to exclude a great number of inks which he had never examined. He conceded that he had no foreign ink library. In particular, the library did not include Japanese inks.

233. *E.g.*, Commonwealth v. Johnson, 399 Pa. Super. 266, 582 A.2d 336 (1990); *The Case of the Doctor Who Doctored the Documents*, 15 SCI. SLEUTHING REV. (Wint. 1991).

234. Lyter, *supra* note 172, at 54; Aginsky, *A Microspectrophotometric Method for Dating Ballpoint Inks—A Feasibility Study*, 40 J. FORENSIC SCI. 475 (1995); Aginsky, *Some New Ideas for Dating Ballpoint Inks—A Feasibility Study*, 38 J. FORENSIC SCI. 1134 (1993); Brunelle, *Ink Dating—The State of the Art*, 37 J. FORENSIC SCI. 113 (1992); Brunelle & Lee, *Determining the Relative Age of Ballpoint Ink Using a Single-Solvent Extraction, Mass-Independent Approach*, 34 J. FORENSIC SCI. 1166 (1989); Cantu, *Comments on the Accelerated Aging of Ink*, 33 J. FORENSIC SCI. 744 (1988); Brunelle, Breedlove & Midkiff, *Determining the Relative Age of Ballpoint Inks Using a Single-Solvent Extraction Technique*, 32 J. FORENSIC SCI. 1511 (1987); Brunelle & Cantu, *A*

These procedures determine the relative age of writing by comparing the rate and extent to which solvents can extract the ink from the paper. As time passes, the ink becomes drier and more difficult to extract. Thus, the difficulty of extraction is a rough indicator of the age of the ink mark.[235] These procedures involve the comparative examination of both questioned and known writings. For a valid comparison, the questioned and known writings must have certain common surrounding circumstances, including the same type of paper and storage conditions.

The absence of known, dated standards had spurred interest in attempts to develop "absolute" aging methods. However, controversy exists over the validity of these methods.[236] These techniques rely on the use of artificial aging and have been sharply criticized in the scientific community. However, continued research and collaboration with the legal community may eventually provide adequate assurance of the reliability of the technique and guidelines for applying the technique.

In addition to the examination of writing ink for extractability, it is possible to study the volatile components.[237] As inks dry, they lose their volatile components.[238] Therefore, an older ink will either have less of a specific volatile component or a smaller relative amount of the component.

The above techniques are available when the writer used a pen to apply the ink. The examiner can also analyze ink or dyes applied by typewriter fabric ribbons. For example, the examiner may extract or elute the toners from the dye mark left by the typewriter ribbon and subject the eluted toner to thin layer chromatography (TLC).[239] By gathering exemplars of the typewriter's work produced during the same time period as the questioned document and comparing the toners in the dye marks on the paper, the examiner might be able to demonstrate that the questioned document was prepared at a different time. If the toners do not match, the difference is strong evidence that the page was typed when the typewriter had a different ribbon.[240] The quality of the inking left on the paper may also indicate the date of the document's preparation.[241] "This determination is based on the fact that a new ribbon deposits a heavier amount of

---

Critical Evaluation of Current Ink Dating Techniques, 32 J. FORENSIC SCI. 1522 (1987); Cantu & Prough, *On the Relative Aging of Ink—The Solvent Extraction Technique*, 32 J. FORENSIC SCI. 1151 (1987).

235. Lyter, *supra* note 172, at 54.

236. Stewart & Fortunato, *Distinguishing Between Relative Ink Age Determination and the Accelerated Aging Technique*, 2 INT'L J. FORENSIC DOC. EXAM., No. 1, at 10-15 (Jan./Mar. 1996).

237. Lyter, *supra* note 172, at 54.

238. *Id.* at 54-55.

239. English, *supra* note 167, at 74-75. Tebbett, *Chromatographic Analysis of Inks for Forensic Science Applications*, 3 FORENSIC SCI. REV. 71 (1991) (listing references).

240. *Id.* at 76.

241. F.B.I., *supra* note 169, at 5.

ink than one which has experienced long and heavy usage. Standards for such a comparison should be obtained from records prepared at different times...."[242]

Paper

The watermark is not only useful in identifying the manufacturer and determining whether the questioned document and exemplars have a similar source, it can also be helpful in dating the document.[243] Some paper manufacturers change their watermark from year to year, and a number of laboratories have built up reference files of paper watermarks.[244] Moreover, as the dandy roll is used over and over again, wear creates defects in the watermark. Identifying those defects in the watermark can help to further narrow the time period in which the paper could have been manufactured.[245] Unfortunately, not all paper contains watermarks.[246] Unless the examiner can find a watermark, there may be little the examiner can do to date the paper. Most components of paper such as wood pulp and filler do not exhibit "any measurable effect of age."[247]

Typewriting Style

Since 1932 the Federal Bureau of Investigation has maintained a file of typestyles marketed in the United States.[248] The file lists when each typestyle was first introduced. By comparing the type on the questioned document with the standards in the reference file, the examiner can determine whether the style was available when the document was purportedly typed. Moreover, by gathering samples of other typing by the same typewriter, the examiner can develop a chronology or history of the defects on the characters.[249] The examiner should collect exemplars prepared over a substantial time period, including dates before and after the purported date of the questioned document.[250]

---

242. *Id.* at 6.

243. *Id.* at 2.

244. *Id.* at 2-3.

245. F.B.I., *supra* note 142, at 26.

246. *Id.*

247. *Id.* at 31.

248. F.B.I., *supra* note 169, at 5. *The approximate age of a Document*, F.B.I. LAW ENF. BULL. Reprint, Feb. 1966, at 5.

249. *Id.* at 6; Armistead, *The Use of Minor Typescript Variations in Age-Dating Material*, 16 J. POLICE SCI. & ADMIN. 217 (1988) ("defects in typescript often more narrowly circumscribe the period during which a questioned document could have been typed").

250. *Id. See also* Hilton, *Establishing the Date of Selectric Typewriting: A Case Study*, 10 J. POLICE SCI. & ADMIN. 178 (1982).

Pencil Marks

There is very little the examiner can do to date a pencil mark. The mark is composed primarily of graphite and clay deposits.[251] These components are chemically inert, and "the passing of time registers no effect by means of which the age of a document may be measured."[252]

Photocopy Machines

If the examiner can demonstrate that a copy displays the characteristic of a particular photocopy machine, the copy could not have been made before the date of introduction (DOI) of the machine into the market. Examiners have collected data on the characteristics of the various machines and their respective dates of introduction.[253]

§ 21-6. Altered Documents.

Forgers often attempt to alter documents by adding or subtracting marks on the face of the paper. When the examiner suspects alteration, he or she faces two tasks: deciding whether an alteration has been made and, if so, determining the document's original language before the alteration. Numerous techniques are available for these tasks;[254] the techniques chosen depend upon the nature of the suspected alteration.

Erasures

To eliminate a mark on the paper, the forger may employ a mechanical eraser, a sharp instrument such as a pen knife, or a chemical eradicator.[255] Whatever the

251. F.B.I., *supra* note 142, at 31.

252. *Id.* at 32.

253. Crown, *Dates of Introduction of Specific Photocopy Machines*, 34 J. FORENSIC SCI. 110 (1989). *See also* Shiver & Nelson, *Nondestructive Differentiation of Full-Color Photocopies*, 36 J. FORENSIC SCI. 145, 147 (1991) (listing the dates of introduction of full-color copiers).

254. *E.g.*, Srinivasan & Thirunavukkarasu, *Decipherment of an Obliterated Vehicle Identification Number*, 41 J. FORENSIC SCI. 163 (1996) ("microscopical study replaced the usual etching techniques in establishing the true identity of the stolen vehicle"); Harris, *Radiography and Passport Examinations*, 23 CAN. SOC'Y FORENSIC SCI. 25 (1990) (radiography can be used to examine passports suspected of being altered).

255. Abulafia, Brown & Abramovich-Bar, *A Fraudulent Case Involving Novel Ink Eradicating Methods*, 42 J. FORENSIC SCI. 300 (1997) (the use of two stain removers and paint remover to eradicate ink on checks); Slotter, *Check Fraud: A Sophisticated Criminal Enterprise*, 65 F.B.I. LAW ENF. BULL. 1, 5 (Aug. 1996) ("Chemical alteration is commonly referred to as 'check washing.' Check washers use a variety of acid-based chemical solutions to erase amount and payee information while maintaining the integrity of the preprinted information. They then dry the check and inscribe a new payee and a significantly higher dollar amount before presenting it to a bank for payment").

technique used, the erasure will abrasively disturb the paper surface.[256] At the erasure site, the paper should be thinner and roughened.[257] The erasure site can be identified by measuring the thickness of the paper at several points on its surface or determining the amount of light transmitted through the paper at the various points.[258] The examiner can sometimes visualize the site by fuming the surface of the paper with iodine.[259] He or she may also use powders, including graphite and ultraviolet fluorescent powder, to locate the site.[260] For example, Mathyer's powder tends to adhere to paper surfaces disturbed by the action of a rubber erasure.[261] Similarly, Lycode powders will stick to minute traces of grease on the paper surface; an india rubber eraser characteristically leaves grease traces at the erasure site.[262]

Instrumental techniques are also available. The easiest and quickest method is often microscopy. Examiners sometimes use infrared[263] and ultraviolet[264] instruments to detect erasures. The use of a new technique, betagraphy, is under study.[265] Beta particles are negative electrons.[266] The surface mass of a sheet of paper determines the paper's ability to absorb beta particles.[267] When a particular site on the paper is thinner than other sites, as it would be if the site has been erased, it will absorb a different amount of beta particles than the other parts of the sheet. The examiner places the sheet between a source of particles and

---

256. Morrill, *supra* note 36, at 206. *See also* Zimmerman, Doherty & Mooney, *Erasable Felt Tip Writing Instrument Detection*, 33 J. FORENSIC SCI. 709, 711 (1988) (the manufacturers of some new felt tip writing instruments claim that the attached eraser "erases like magic"; researchers found, however, that "all of these pens and their erasures could be detected by some method"); O. HILTON, DETECTING AND DECIPHERING ERASED PENCIL WRITING, reviewed in Allen, *Book Review*, 50 FORENSIC SCI. INT'L 141 (1991).

257. Moore, *Evaluation of a Method Using Powder to Detect the Site of Rubber Erasures*, 26 J. FORENSIC SCI. 724, 725-26 (1981).

258. *Id.* at 725.

259. F.B.I., *supra* note 142, at 34.

260. Moore, *supra* note 257, at 724. *See also* Riker & Lewis, *Methylene Blue Revisited: The Search for a Trouble-Free Erasure Sensitive Powder*, 33 J. FORENSIC SCI. 773, 777 (1988) ("The toner powder/bicarbonate of soda combinations equals or surpasses the sensitivity of the methylene blue/starch mixture ....").

261. Moore, *supra* note 257,at 725.

262. Kind & Dobbs, *The Use of Lycode Powders for the Detection of Erasures*, 19 J. FORENSIC SCI. SOC'Y 175 (1979).

263. Noblett, *The Use of a Scanning Monochromator as a Barrier Filter in Infrared Examinations of Documents*, 27 J. FORENSIC SCI. 923 (1982); Hilton, *New Dimensions in Infrared Luminescence Photography*, 26 J. FORENSIC SCI. 319 (1981).

264. Morrill, *supra* note 36, at 206.

265. Buquet, *New Techniques for the Detection of Alterations in Documents*, 10 FORENSIC SCI. 185 (1977).

266. *Id.*

267. *Id.*

photographic film. The film will pinpoint the erasure site by showing that that site has absorbed a different quantity of particles.[268]

Obliterations

The forger may lack the skill to attempt to completely erase the mark from the paper surface. In that event, he or she may resort to the cruder tactic of attempting to obliterate the mark.[269] When the forger does so, the examiner has several options.

One option is to attempt to remove the obliterating material such as the ink with which the forger wrote over the original mark.[270] It is not enough to find a chemical or mechanical means that will effectively remove the opaquing material; the means must not disturb the original mark underneath the material.[271] If the forger is careful or lucky enough to have attempted the obliteration with the same ink or dye present in the original mark, the chemical that eliminates the opaquing material may also destroy the original mark. In the past, some examiners use freon to read through white opaquing fluid; but there are now new and better fluids such as Liquid Window--SP to render questioned documents transparent for obliteration study.

The second option is to attempt to penetrate the overlaying material.[272] The examiner may use ultraviolet[273] or infrared[274] when the ink of the original mark and the opaquing material react differently to the radiation.[275] The most novel approach to penetrating the obliterating material is the use of lasers.[276] Chapter 16 pointed out that lasers are now being used to excite luminescence in fingerprints that cannot be detected by other means. Some of the same technology, including the argon laser, has been adapted to document examination. If the underlying, original material luminesces under laser excitation, the laser technique can be employed to penetrate the overlaying material obscuring the original mark.[277]

---

268. *Id.* at 186.

269. Maldonado & Sierra, *Crayon Obliteration over Ballpoint Pen Writing*, 37 J. FORENSIC SCI. 1679 (1992).

270. Morrill, *supra* note 36, at 206.

271. *Id.*

272. *Id. See also* Waggoner, *Examination of Correction Fluid Obliteration*, 32 J. FORENSIC SCI. 539 (1987) (photography with transmitted light).

273. Morrill, *supra* note 36, at 206.

274. Noblett, *supra* note 263, at 923.

275. Waggoner & Spradlin, *Obliterated Writing — An Unconventional Approach*, 28 J. FORENSIC SCI. 686, 687 (1983).

276. Dalrymple, *Visible and Infrared Luminescence in Documents: Excitation by Laser*, 28 J. FORENSIC SCI. 692 (1983).

277. *Id.* at 693; Blacklock, *The Laser: A Tool for Questioned Document Examination*, 15 J. POLICE SCI. & ADMIN. 125 (1987).

Although the preceding paragraphs describe the most popular techniques, they do not exhaust the possibilities. Another possibility is photographing the paper from the reverse side.[278] In addition, the F.B.I. has adapted computer technology to the task. The F.B.I. was called upon to decipher a scratched out portion of a letter from Thomas Jefferson.[279] To do so, the laboratory employed a computer with a digital airbrush attachment. Even though "none of the 'normal protocols'" was "adequate" to the task, the digital airbrush enabled the laboratory to identify the obliterated writing.[280]

The preceding paragraphs discuss the common situation in which markings on a writing are obliterated. However, the relevant marking might have been made on another surface. For instance, a marking could have been made on a bathroom wall.[281] In one such case, the markings had been physically scrubbed off the wall. Nevertheless, the examiners successfully employed an Alternate Light Source to recover the obliterated writing.

Additions

To determine whether a forger added a mark after the execution of the original document, the examiner may use several techniques previously discussed.[282] Section 21-4 mentioned the various techniques for differentiating between inks and typewriter ribbon dyes. If the examiner can show that the mark in question is composed of a different ink or dye than the rest of the writing on the document, the difference suggests that the mark is a subsequent addition. Section 21-5 listed several methods of dating marks on the surface of the questioned document. When the examiner can demonstrate that the other marks on the sheet are older than the mark in question, the age difference is cogent evidence of forgery.

Indentations

There are several ways to visualize an indentation left on a sheet of paper that was under the sheet on which something was written. Sometimes in the past the examiner simply shaded the sheet with a pencil. However, today a forensic document examiner would not rely on that technique. It is not just that shading with a pencil might be detrimental to the paper fibers; further, there are more

---

278. Curfman & Oleksow, *Decipherment of Opaqued Writing with Acetate-Assisted Photocopying*, 37 J. FORENSIC SCI. 1684 (1992).

279. *The F.B.I. Finds a Way: A "New" Document Examination Method Using the Computer as an Eraser*, 22 SCI. SLEUTHING 6-7 (Wint. 1998).

280. *Id.*

281. Leaver & Smith, *Using an Alternate Light Source to Restore Writing*, 44 J. FORENSIC SCI. 653 (1999).

282. Furtunato & Stewart, *Sentence Insertions Detected Through Ink, ESDA, and Line Width Analysis*, 37 J. FORENSIC SCI. 1702 (1992).

sophisticated techniques than pencil shading. The most widespread technique is the use of oblique, reflected, or side lighting.[283] The oblique light creates a shadow effect, and the examiner can see the indentation in relief.[284] Oblique lighting is not the only technique available. Iodine fuming is another, well-accepted method.[285]

The prior paragraph describes the traditional techniques for identifying indentations. However, examiners are now experimenting with advanced instrumental methods. Some are employing scanning electron microscopy and X-ray imaging.[286] Others are using autoradiography.[287] An indented surface will absorb more radioactive 35-sulphur dioxide gas than an undamaged surface. By exposing the sheet to the gas, the examiner can develop a positive image of the indented characters.[288]

The new technique that has garnered the most publicity is probably the electrostatic detection apparatus (ESDA).[289] With the ESDA, the examiner places the questioned document on a brass plate and covers the document with a thin

---

283. Foster & Morantz, *An Electrostatic Imaging Technique for the Detection of Indented Impressions in Documents*, 13 FORENSIC SCI. INT'L 51 (1979); Caywood, *Decipherment of Indented Writings — A New Technique*, 1 J. POLICE SCI. & ADMIN. 50, 52 (1973).

284. A. MOENSSENS, J. STARRS, C. HENDERSON & F. INBAU, *supra* note 1, at § 5.07.

285. Baier, *Application of Experimental Variables to the Use of the Electrostatic Detection Apparatus*, 28 J. FORENSIC SCI. 901 (1983).

286. Given, *Techniques for Visualization of Indented Writings*, 27 IDENT. NEWS 3 (Apr. 1977).

287. Wells, *A Novel Method for Revealing Unintended Handwriting Impressions on Underlying Layers of Paper*, 16 J. FORENSIC SCI. SOC'Y 201 (1976).

288. *Id.*

289. Baier, *supra* note 285, at 901; Riebeling & Kobus, *Some Parameters Affecting the Quality of ESDA Results*, 39 J. FORENSIC SCI. 15 (1994); Giles, *Extending ESDA's Capability: The Determination of the Order of Writing and Impressions Using the Technique of Electrostatic Detection*, 59 J. FORENSIC SCI. 163 (1993); Wanxiang & Xiaoling, *A Study of the Principle of the Electrostatic Imaging Technique*, 28 J. FORENSIC SCI. SOC'Y 237 (1988); Hart & Hart, *Photographically Subtracting Interfering Images from ESDA Print*, 34 J. FORENSIC SCI. 1405 (1989) (ESDA sometimes visualized both the indentations and other, interfering writing on the reverse side; the examiner can subtract the overlapping image from the reverse side by making a positive transparency of the writing on the reverse side and sandwiching the transparency with the ESDA negative); Tolliver, *The Electrostatic Detection Apparatus (ESDA): Is It Really Non-Destructive to Documents?*, 44 FORENSIC SCI. INT'L 7 (1989) (with some pencil writing on certain types of paper, ESDA may remove a small amount of the graphite from the document; however, this would not have a significant impact on the appearance of the document or any developed indented impressions); Gupta, Lal & Misra, *Electrostatic Detection of Secret Writings*, 41 FORENSIC SCI. INT'L 17 (1989) (ESDA can be used to develop documents written with secret ink); Horan & Horan, *How Long After Writing Can an ESDA Image Be Developed?*, 39 FORENSIC SCI. INT'L 119 (1988); Moore, *The Electrostatic Detection Apparatus (ESDA) and Its Effects on Latent Prints on Paper*, 33 J. FORENSIC SCI. 357 (1988); Noblett & James, *Optimum Conditions for Examination of Documents Using an Electrostatic Detection Apparatus (ESDA) Device to Visualize Indented Writings*, 28 J. FORENSIC SCI. 697 (1983); Ellen, *The Use of Electrostatic Imaging in the Detection of Indented Impressions*, 15 FORENSIC SCI. INT'L 53 (1980).

film of insulating polymer. By moving an electric wire above the document, the examiner creates an electrostatic charge over the surface. The examiner then spreads a powder over the surface by a cascade or cloud method. When the powder settles on the surface, indentations appear as black images against a light gray background.[290] In the conventional method, the examiner preserves the images by covering them with protective adhesive tape or recording the images photographically.[291] Researchers are experimenting with a technique for fixing or fusing the images on the polymer film to produce a permanent record.[292] The examiner can use ESDA in conjunction with an image processing system.[293]

Just as an indentation may be left on a sheet of paper, an indentation might remain on a typewriter correction ribbon. There are techniques for identifying indentations on the ribbon surface.[294] Infrared luminescence can also be used to analyze indentations and, in some cases, detect the alteration of a document.[295]

Charred Documents

If the combustion is complete and the document is entirely reduced to ashes, the examiner cannot reconstruct the original writing. However, when the combustion is only partial, the examiner might be able to determine the original marks. In many laboratories, it is standard procedure to prepare the document for analysis by treating it in a moisture chamber. After treatment, several techniques

---

290. *Id.*

291. Jasuja & Singla, *Preserving Electrostatic Detection Apparatus (ESDA) Images: A New Approach*, 52 FORENSIC SCI. INT'L 21 (1991).

292. *Id.*

293. Houde, *Image Enhancement for Document Examination Using the Personal Computer*, 38 J. FORENSIC SCI. 143 (1993); Behnen & Nelson, *Additional Applications of Digital Image Processing to Forensic Document Examinations*, 37 J. FORENSIC SCI. 797 (1992); Black, *Application of Digital Image Enhancement Software with the Macintosh Computer to Questioned Document Problems*, 37 J. FORENSIC SCI. 783 (1992); Wenderoth, *Application of the VSC-1/Atari 1040ST Image-Processing System to Forensic Document Problems*, 35 J. FORENSIC SCI. 439, 445 (1990).

294. Grantham, *Identification of Indented Typewritten Entries with Characters Present on a Lift-Off Correction Ribbon*, 37 J. FORENSIC SCI. 1610 (1992).

295. Sharf, Gabbay & Brown, *Infrared Luminescence of Indented Writing as Evidence of Document Alteration*, 42 J. FORENSIC SCI. 729, 732 (1997) ("The origin of the luminescence might be the transfer of components of the writing ink, such as the vehicle, to the undersheet, or the transfer of components of the paper, such as a coated layer. In many cases, ... the exact reason cannot be determined as the original document that produced the indented writing is not available for examination. In the case reported here, [however,] indented impressions were found on the two documents submitted for examination. The impressions on each one were found to originate from writing on the other"; the luminescence "enabled the determination of the sequence of the various entries, and therefore to conclude that the entries in question were made at a later stage with respect to the rest of the text.").

can be used to determine the original writing. Some inks do not burn,[296] and the examiner may employ an infrared microscope to read the remaining ink marks.[297] Another method is placing the document in contact with the emulsion side of a photographic plate for between one and three weeks.[298] An image of the original writing transfers to the photographic plate. Other chemical methods include spraying, painting, and bathing the document.[299]

None of the techniques listed in this section has a 100% success rate. The examiner must choose a technique or combination of techniques tailored to the alteration that the examiner suspects has occurred. It is generally easier for the examiner to determine that an alteration has occurred than it is to decipher the original markings.[300] In a given case, the examiner may be able to demonstrate almost conclusively that there has been an alteration, but it could prove to be impossible to determine the original writing.[301]

Water-Soaked Documents

There are also techniques for restoring water-soaked documents.[302]

§ 21-7. Questioned Document Evidence.

The previous sections summarized the scientific aspects of questioned document examination. This section reviews the legal restrictions on testimony by questioned document examiners.

§ 21-7(A). Admissibility — In General.

As previously noted, the questioned document examiner ordinarily compares the questioned document with exemplars. The comparison is the basis for the examiner's testimony.

---

296. Moon, *Identification of Wrinkled and Charred Counterfeit Currency Offset Printing Plate by Infrared Examination*, 29 J. FORENSIC SCI. 644 (1984).

297. F.B.I., *Evidence or Ashes*,F.B.I. LAW ENF. BULL. Reprint 4, June 1964.

298. *Id.;* F.B.I., *supra* note 142, at 42.

299. *Id.* at 41.

300. Carpenter, *Questioned Typewriting*, 20 AM. JUR. PROOF OF FACTS 265, 298 (1968).

301. *Id.*

302. Taylor, *The Restoration and Identification of Water-Soaked Documents*, 31 J. FORENSIC SCI. 1113 (1986) (freeze dehydration).

The Courts' Early Skepticism

At early common law, testimony based on such a comparison was inadmissible. One of the leading federal cases announcing that view is *Strothers v. Lucas,*[303] an 1832 decision in which the court declared:

> It is a general rule that evidence by comparison of hands is not admissible, where the witness has had no previous knowledge of the handwriting, but is called upon to testify merely from a comparison of hands.[304]

The common law preferred testimony by lay witnesses familiar with the alleged author's handwriting style. This view persisted past the turn of the century.[305]

The Initial Inroads on the Early View

The courts soon made limited inroads on the early view. Sometimes lay witnesses familiar with the author's handwriting are unavailable; lay witnesses are frequently unavailable when the document is ancient. The unavailability of lay witnesses created a special necessity to resort to expert testimony, and that necessity overcame the courts' skepticism about the expert testimony. Likewise, a few trial courts initially deviated from the strict, common law view by admitting expert testimony about the authenticity of old documents.[306] In that situation, it is unlikely that the proponent could locate a lay witness to the execution of the document. Again, a species of necessity justified turning to the expert testimony.

The Shift to Judicial Receptivity

As the courts became more accustomed to working with such expert testimony and the questioned document profession gained recognition, courts gradually became more receptive to examiners' testimony. In 1913, Congress sanctioned the admission of expert comparison testimony by enacting 28 U.S.C. § 1731. However, even at this point, judicial acceptance of expert testimony was grudging. For example, many courts declared that although admissible, the testimony was "generally of slight weight."[307]

---

303. 6 Pet. 763, 8 L. Ed. 573 (1832).

304. *Id.* at 767, 8 L. Ed. at 575.

305. *E.g.,* Withaup v. United States, 127 F. 530, 535 (8th Cir. 1903).

306. COSTAIN, QUESTIONED DOCUMENTS AND THE LAW: HANDWRITING EVIDENCE IN THE FEDERAL COURT SYSTEM 4 (paper presented by the American Academy of Forensic Sciences Annual Meeting, San Diego, California, February 15-18, 1977, copy on file with Prof. Imwinkelried).

307. Rinker v. United States, 151 F. 755, 761 (8th Cir. 1907).

Today, however, testimony by document examiners is common. Furthermore, although some courts still purport to adhere to the view that this testimony carries no greater weight than lay testimony,[308] numerous reported cases acknowledge that "expert testimony to forgery may outweigh eyewitness testimony to genuineness ...."[309]

The Modern Dispute Over Admissibility

In most jurisdictions, the courts are still receptive to expert questioned document testimony. However, in the past 15 years, a controversy has arisen over the reliability of opinions by questioned document examiners. The genesis of the controversy was a presentation on August 14, 1986 by Professor Mark Denbeaux of Seton Hall Law School. On that date, Professor Denbeaux spoke on the admissibility of questioned document evidence at the National Association of Criminal Defense Lawyers convention in Monterey, California. He made two points. First, he argued that courts should reconsider this issue and exclude the evidence. He asserted that "the so-called discipline rests on unverified assumptions."[310] He cited cases such as *Phoenix Fire Insurance v. Philip*, 13 Wend. 81 (1834), as examples of the courts' tendency in the 19th century to exclude the evidence altogether. He then pointed to decisions such as *Hoag v. Wright*, 174 N.Y. 36, 66 N.E. 579 (1903), as proof that as recently as the turn of the century, the courts still distrusted questioned document evidence. He contended that the favorable publicity for the questioned document testimony in the Lindberg kidnapping trial changed the public perception of questioned document examiners, but he asserted that there is no empirical research to validate the examiners' underlying assumptions.

---

308. Welfert v. Boatmen's Bank of Jefferson County, 671 S.W.2d 355 (Mo. App. 1984).

309. C. McCormick, Evidence § 205, at 502 n.80 (2d ed. 1972) (citing Boyd v. Gosser, 78 Fla. 64, 82 So. 758 (1919) (a striking fact case); *cf. In re* Estate of Krugle, 134 So. 2d 860 (Fla. App. 1961); Hoover v. Hoover, 238 Iowa 88, 26 N.W.2d 98 (1947); Reffert v. Hughes, 396 S.W.2d 786 (Ky. 1965); *In re* Estate of Simon, 381 Pa. 284, 113 A.2d 266 (1955); *In re* Young's Estate, 347 Pa. 457, 32 A.2d 901 (1943); Adams v. Ristine, 138 Va. 273, 122 S.E. 126 (1924)). *See also* Annot., 154 A.L.R. 649 (1945); Annot., 31 A.L.R. 1431 (1924).

310. Denbeaux, *Questioning Questioned Document Examiners: How to Expose Expert Handwriting Witnesses* 1 (copy on file with Prof. Imwinkelried). *See also* Huber & Headrick, *Let's Do It By Numbers*, 46 Forensic Sci. Int'l 209, 210-11 (1990) ("Kirk condemned handwriting identification for the lack of statistical data on which to properly value the significance of handwriting characteristics. 'Handwriting analysis ... cannot be truly scientific until such serious omissions ... are repaired.' Rhodes, at the first International Meeting of Questioned Document Examiners (1986), stated: 'In the present state of our knowledge, it is impossible to prove the identity of any handwriting.' Thornton and Rhodes criticized document examination as a field which has progressed more by judicial acceptance than by any attempts to elevate the practice to a more scientific discipline").

Second, he urged courts to hold that if questioned document evidence is admissible, the opponent has a right to test the examiner's competency by requiring the examiner to submit to in-court experiments. He cited *Johnson Harvester Co. v. Miller*, 72 Mich. 265, 40 N.W. 429 (1888) and *State v. Bulna*, 46 N.J. Super. 313, 134 A.2d 738 (1957), *aff'd*, 27 N.J. 93, 141 A.2d 529 (1958), as authority for his position.

In 1989, Professor Denbeaux and two coauthors published a now famous University of Pennsylvania Law Review article[311] elaborating his views and detailing the results of empirical studies of the proficiency of questioned document examiners.[312] The studies in question reveal alarmingly high error rates.[313] In one study, only 13% of the examiners reached the correct conclusion.[314] The error rates documented in the article added force to Professor Denbeaux' criticism of the courts' currently receptive attitude toward questioned document testimony.

Despite the publication of that article in 1989, during the early 1990's the courts maintained their favorable attitude toward questioned document evidence. At this juncture, there were no indications that the courts were seriously rethinking their stance on the admissibility of such evidence. However, in 1993, the Supreme Court handed down its decision in *Daubert v. Merrell Dow Pharmaceuticals, Inc.*.[315] In *Daubert*, the Court abandoned the traditional acceptance test and announced a new empirical validation standard to determine

---

311. Risinger, Denbeaux & Saks, *Exorcism of Ignorance as a Proxy for Rational Knowledge: The Lessons of Handwriting Identification "Expertise,"* 137 U. PA. L. REV. 731 (1989).

312. *Id.* at 738-51.

313. *Id.*

314. *Id.* at 746. *But see* Kam, Fielding & Conn, *Writer Identification by Professional Document Examiners*, 42 J. FORENSIC SCI. 778 (1997) (the article describes "a comprehensive test administered to more than 100 professional document examiners.... Each examiner made 144 pair-wise comparisons of freely-created original handwritten documents. The task was to determine whether or not a 'match' was detected, namely whether or not the two documents were written by the same hand"; "Unlike the professional examiners, the nonprofessional tends to grossly over-associate. They erroneously 'matched' many documents that were created by different writers, mismatching almost six times as many unknown documents to database documents as the professionals did (38.3% vs. 6.5% of the documents). The results of our test lay to rest the debate over whether or not professional document examiners possess writer-identification skills absent in the general population. They do."); Kam, Wetstein & Conn, *Proficiency of Professional Document Examiners in Writer Identification*, 39 J. FORENSIC SCI. 5 (1994) (in this study, "[t]he hypothesis that professionals and nonprofessionals are equally proficient in performing writer identification was found ... to have the probability of less than 0.001. These findings give indication that handwriting identification expertise indeed exists, and calls into question the conclusions of previous studies...."); Dillon, *Further Commentary on "Proficiency of Professional Document Examiners in Writer Identification,"* 40 J. FORENSIC SCI. 724 (1995) (criticizing the design of the proficiency test); *Author's Response*, 40 J. FORENSIC SCI. 724 (1995) (responding to the criticism).

315. 509 U.S. 579 (1993).

the admissibility of purportedly scientific testimony. Significantly, in footnote 11 of his lead opinion, Justice Blackmun suggested that the new test applied to both conventional and novel scientific techniques. The opinion and footnote raised the possibility that the lower courts would apply the new test to questioned document examination and perhaps find it lacking.

That possibility soon came to pass in early 1995. In *United States v. Starzecpyzel*,[316] the court approvingly cited the 1989 article. The court held that questioned document testimony does not qualify as "scientific knowledge" under *Daubert*. Ultimately, the court decided to admit the testimony as "technical" knowledge under Federal Rule 702; the court was impressed by an empirical study indicating that questioned document examiners could resolve identification questions more accurately than laypersons.[317] However,the court decided to give the jury a cautionary instruction; the court stated that "the jury will be instructed that [questioned document examiners] offer practical rather than scientific expertise." Again in 1995, the Army Court of Appeals concluded that "handwriting analysis evidence is best treated under [Military Rule of Evidence] 702 as 'technical, and other specialized knowledge.'"[318] The court ruled the evidence admissible even though it did not satisfy all the reliability factors listed in *Daubert*. In still another 1995 case, a defense attorney attempted to call one of the authors of the article as an expert witness to testify to the shortcomings of questioned document examination. The trial judge barred the testimony, but the appellate court held the exclusion to be error.[319]

In 1996, like the military and *Starzecpyzel* courts, the Sixth Circuit concluded that forensic document examination does not amount to "scientific knowledge."[320] The parallel to *Starzecpyzel* continues, since as in the former case

---

316. 880 F. Supp. 1027 (S.D.N.Y. 1995). The Fall 1995 (Vol. 4, No. 2), Spring 1996 (Vol. 5, No. 1), and Fall 1996 (Vol. 5, No. 2) issues of the JOURNAL OF QUESTIONED DOCUMENT EXAMINATION contain a detailed review of the expert testimony presented at the *Daubert* hearing in the *Starzecpyzel* case.

317. The court cited an early article by Dr. Kam and his colleagues, namely, Kam, Welstein & Conn, *Proficiency of Professional Document Examiners in Writers Identification*, 39 J. FORENSIC SCI. 5 (1994).The researches have since published two additional articles, Kam, Fielding & Conn, *Writer Identification by Professional Document Examiners*, 42 J. FORENSIC SCI. 778 (1997) and Kam, Fielding & Conn, *Effects of Monetary Incentives on Performance of Nonprofessionals in Document-Examination Proficiency Tests*, 43 J. FORENSIC SCI. 1000 (1998).The later articles also indicate that forensic document examiners can significantly outperform laypersons. The last, 1998 article finds that forensic document examiners are markedly more accurate even when the laypersons are given a monetary reward for accuracy.

318. United States v. Ruth, 42 M.J. 730, 732 (Arm. Ct. App. 1995), *aff'd on other grounds*, 46 M.J. 1 (U.S.C.A.A.F. 1997).

319: United States v. Velasquez, 64 F.3d 844 (3d Cir. 1995); Starrs, *In the Wake of Harbor Pilots: Document Examiners Given the Twice-Over in Federal Courts*, 19 SCI. SLEUTHING REV. 1, 5-6 (Sum. 1995).

320. United States v. Jones, 107 F.3d 1147 (6th Cir.), *cert. denied*, 521 U.S. 1127 (1997).

the Sixth Circuit ruled that the forensic document evidence was nevertheless admissible as non-scientific testimony. In the Oklahoma bombing prosecution of Timothy McVeigh, the trial judge, Judge Matsch, echoed the Sixth Circuit; he expressed serious reservations about questioned document examination testimony.[321]

Still in 1996, two of the leading critics, Professors Risinger and Saks, released another article contributing to the debate.[322] In their article, the authors conceded that "a skill probably exists in some people for certain tasks, but probably involves a large amount of inherent talent."[323] However, they argued that the extant research does not permit a court to identify all the subtasks in which the skill can be exercised dependably.[324] Further, they added a caveat:

> [T]here is reason to believe that, like eyewitness identification, handwriting identification is strongly influenced by context cuing. In other words, the presentation of extraneous information to the examiner which indicates the answer desired and reasons beyond handwriting for its being the correct conclusion may affect the document examiner's conclusion.... [T]he founding fathers of the area were more sensible.... Hagan, Ames, and Osborn all took strong positions that it was the professional duty of the examiner to insist that such information not be presented and to take steps to step up modes of consultation to insure against such contamination.[325]

In 1997, the American Bar Association Journal published an article devoted to the controversy over the status of questioned document examination.[326] The article is based in part on an interview with Professor Andre Moenssens. On the one hand, Moenssens conceded that expert handwriting analysis is "an art" rather than a scientific discipline.[327] On the other hand, he argued that the analysis can be reliable and ought to be admissible.

---

321. Rudolf & Widenhouse, *Daubert Redux: Oklahoma City Bomb Case*, 21 THE CHAMPION 24, 25-26 (May 1997) The judge remarked, "I don't think there is any such scientific knowledge. And that's why I don't think that ... these people can express such opinions." The judge added:

> There are no agreed standards for the terminology. There is no confidence level that's been agreed upon.... We do not have any body of scientific knowledge of which I am aware that says that there are such identifying characteristics every time a person puts pencil or pen to paper that you can say that's who it is.... And they do it by experience. There is no academy of training for these people. They just say, I've done enough of that that now, I'm a self-declared expert at it.

322. Risinger & Saks, *Science and Nonscience in the Courts: Daubert Meets Handwriting Identification Expertise*, 82 IOWA L. REV. 21 (1996).

323. *Id.* at 63.

324. *Id.* at 64.

325. *Id.*

326. Hansen, *John Hancock*, 83 A.B.A. J. 76 (May 1997).

327. *Id.* at 77.

If anything, the dispute heated up in 1998.To begin with, 1998 witnessed the publication of a lengthy article by Professor Moenssens on the subject.[328] In the article, Professor Moenssens expanded on the views he expressed in the 1997 interview with the A.B.A. Journal. He emphasized the research conducted by Dr. Kam.[329] Professor Moenssens explained that the F.B.I. hired Dr. Kam, the head of the Drexel University Data Fusion Laboratory, to devise a method to search through questioned document databases. In order to do so, Dr. Kam had to "explore the question of whether these [document] examiners were capable of doing what they said they were." Dr. Kam concluded that on most tasks, "there was a meaningfully statistical difference between the experts and the nonexperts.... The error rates showed that the expert document examiners made, on global average, 6.5% matching errors and the nonexperts made 38.6% errors."

More broadly, Professor Moenssens pointed to a large body of scientific literature supposedly establishing the existence of questioned document expertise. He pointed out that there are articles in numerous journals devoted to the topic, including Journal of the American Society of Questioned Document Examiners, International Journal of Forensic Document Examiners, Journal of Forensic Sciences, Journal of Forensic Identification, Forensic Science International, Journal of Police Science and Administration, Journal of Forensic Science Society, and Canadian Society of Forensic Science Journal. There is now a Questioned Document Article Database (QDAQ) "containing thousands of articles on every aspect of document examination." Further, "[a]fter more than ten years of research..., some 80,000 writings have been collected at the *Bundeskriminalamt* in Germany in a computer data base which has been called FISH in this country."

Later in 1998 after the release of Professor Moenssens' article, Dr. Kam published another study.[330] As Professor Moenssens had noted, Dr. Kam's earlier research had indicated a "performance gap between professionals and nonprofessionals."[331] In the latest phase of his research, Dr. Kam investigated to determine whether the poor performance by nonprofessionals could be attributed to their lack of significant monetary incentive. Using different incentive schemes, his concluded that "the performance of nonprofessionals . . . was relatively insensitive to the monetary incentive scheme."[332] That conclusion suggests that the professional examiner's superior performance is due to superior skill.

---

328. Moenssens, *Handwriting Identification Evidence in the Post-Daubert World: Identifying the Genuine Article and the Genuine Legal Issue: Broader Standards Need for "Scientific Knowledge,"* 66 U.M.K.C. L. REV. 251 (1997).

329. *See supra* note 317.

330. Kam, Fielding & Conn, *Effects of Monetary Incentives on Performance of Nonprofessionals in Document Examination Proficiency Tests*, 43 J. FORENSIC SCI. 1000 (1998).

331. *Id.*

332. *Id.*

On the other hand, 1998 also witnessed the publication of several articles critical of the scientific claims of questioned document examination,[333] including another article by Risinger, Denbeaux, and Saks.[334] Their latest article is a detailed, point-by-point rebuttal of Professor Moenssens' 1998 article.

The criticisms of the scientific premises of questioned document examination have merit; and, as this subsection notes, the criticisms have won some recent judicial converts. However, it is still fair to say that most courts accept such testimony on such theories as characterizing the subject as non-scientific, technical evidence, and hence exempt from close scrutiny under *Daubert*.[335] For instance, many courts continue to receive questioned document testimony about signatures and typewriter impressions.[336]

1999 witnessed further developments on this front. The Supreme Court's early 1999 decision in *Kumho Tire Co., Ltd. v. Carmichael*[337] lends some support to the argument that the lower courts should admit questioned document testimony as non-scientific evidence. In *Kumho*, on the one hand, the Court announced that like scientific testimony, nonscientific expert testimony is subject to a "*Daubert* style scrutiny" of reliability. On the other hand, the Court added that nonscientific expert testimony can qualify for admission even if it does not satisfy one or several of the *Daubert* criteria. Moreover, in his lead opinion, Justice Breyer approvingly mentioned the Solicitor General's Amicus Brief which listed "handwriting analysis" as an illustration of admissible, non-scientific expert testimony. To be sure, *Kumho* is not a square holding that questioned document testimony qualifies for admission on that theory. However, combined with Dr. Kam's research indicating the superior ability of questioned document examiners to accurately perform identification tasks, the *Kumho* Court's approving reference is ammunition for the proponents of that type of testimony. It might be appropriate to give the jury a cautionary instruction such as the one drafted in *Starzecpyzel*, but it seems wrong-minded to altogether bar questioned document testimony.

In a 1999 post-*Kumho* decision,[338] *Paul*, the Court of Appeals for the Eleventh Circuit--the lower court reversed by *Kumho*--upheld the admission of questioned document testimony. The court found that the prosecution witness qualified. The

---

333. Beecher-Monas, *Blinded by Science: How Judges Avoid the Science in Scientific Evidence*, 71 TEMP. L. REV. 55 (1998).

334. Risinger, Denbeaux & Saks, *Brave New "Post-Daubert World"— A Reply to Professor Moenssens*, 29 SETON HALL L. REV. 405 (1998).

335. Beecher-Monas, *Blinded by Science: How Judges Avoid the Science in Scientific Evidence*, 71 TEMP. L. REV. 55, 56 (1998).

336. Bout v. Bolden, 22 F. Supp. 2d 653, 655 (E.D. Mich. 1998).

337. 119 S. Ct. 1167 (1999).

338. United States v. Paul, 175 F.3d 906 (11th Cir. 1999).

court also concluded that his testimony was both reliable and helpful to the jury. The court stated:

> [T]he ability of the jury to perform the same visual comparisons as the expert cuts against the danger of undue prejudice from the mystique attached to "experts." [The expert] specifically identified points of comparison that he recognized between the writing of the extortion note and the handwriting examples that Paul provided. The jury was free to conduct its own comparison and reach its own conclusion regarding the author of the extortion note.[339]

Further, on cross-examination the expert had frankly "acknowledged . . . that no licensing board existed for questioned document examiners, and [that] the profession is not subject to standards that quantify or measure the work of individual examiners." Given those concessions, there was minimal risk that the jury would mistakenly conclude that the testimony was "unassailable" as scientific.

The *Paul* court upheld the trial judge's decision to exclude defense testimony by Professor Denbeaux. The court acknowledged that he had written on the subject of forensic document examiner. However, the court remarked:

> The record reflects that Denbeaux had no skill, experience, training or education in the field of handwriting analysis. His skill, experience, training and education as a lawyer did not make him any more qualified to testify as an expert on handwriting analysis than a lay person who read the same articles.[340]

The most recent decision, *United States v. Hines*,[341] was handed down by the District Court for Massachusetts in mid-1999. Like *Paul*, the court cites *Kumho*. The court decided to treat two types of proffered testimony differently. On the one hand, the court admitted "testimony as to similarities and differences between the handwriting on the note and that of the defendant." The court acknowledged the criticism that "handwriting comparison has never been subjected to 'meaningful' validity testing that compares the results of examiners' conclusions with actual outcomes." However, the court found that "although lay people are capable of making handwriting comparisons without the assistance of an expert, experts are probably better at it than lay persons and their testimony can be of assistance to a trier of fact." On the other hand, the court excluded "testimony as to the expert's conclusion that the defendant was the author of the

---

339. *Id.* at 911.

340. *Id.* at 912.

341. 65 Cr.L. (BNA) 404 (D. Mass., June 11, 1999).

note." The court found inadequate "empirical validation" that forensic document examiners can reliably reach conclusions which are that precise.

§ 21-7(B). Admissibility — Specific Techniques.

In § 21-2(B), questioned document examiners were distinguished from graphologists and psycholinguists. Most courts have refused to admit testimony by either of the latter types of experts. A number of courts have refused to permit graphologists to testify about the state of mind of the author of a document.[342] The courts have been equally negative in their attitude toward psycholinguistics. Although the discipline of psycholinguistics has some scholarly support,[343] the courts have almost uniformly excluded testimony by psycholinguists,[344] whether the evidence was offered by the prosecution[345] or the defense.[346]

---

342. United States v. Bourgeois, 950 F.2d 980, 986-87 (5th Cir. 1992); People v. Hester, 39 Ill. 2d 489, 512, 237 N.E.2d 466, 480 (1968), *cert. dismissed,* 397 U.S. 660 (1970) ("speculative and ... incompetent"); State v. Anderson, 379 N.W.2d 70 (Minn. 1985), *cert. denied*, 476 U.S. 141 (1986); Cameron v. Knapp, 137 Misc. 2d 373, 520 N.Y.S.2d 917 (Sup. Ct. 1987); Daniels v. Cummins, 66 Misc. 2d 575, 580-82, 321 N.Y.S.2d 1009, 1014-16 (1971) (citing the rejection of graphology by Osborn and Harrison).

343. Arens & Meadow, *Psycholinguistics in the Confession Dilemma*, 56 COLUM. L. REV. 19 (1956).

344. As previously stated, one of the leading proponents of forensic linguistics is Mr. Robert Ciaffoni of Canonsburg, Pennsylvania. In his manuscript, SECRETARY-TYPISTS, CO-APOSTLES OF FORENSIC LINGUISTICS, Mr. Ciaffoni argues that the Pennsylvania Supreme Court decision in *In re* Covington Estate, 348 Pa. 1, 33 A.2d 235 (1943), supports the admissibility of forensic linguistic testimony. In evaluating the genuineness of a writing, the court specifically commented about "the style of the sentences" (*id.* at 13), "the grammatical construction," (*id.* at 16), and the "literary craftsmanship" of the document. *Id.* Kenny, *The Expert in Court*, 99 LAW Q. REV. 197, 202-04 (1983) points out that stylometry testimony was admitted in the Raymond prosecution in England. However, the author questions whether the tests which the expert relied on "had ... been sufficiently tried for their use in court to be justified." *Id.* at 203. The author approvingly refers to the *Hearst* court's decision to exclude psycholinguistic testimony. *Id.* at 204. The only American case admitting such testimony is New York v. Mulvey, Indictment No. 24,728 (Erie County, N.Y., Jan. 1955), cited in United States v. Hearst, 412 F. Supp. 893, 895 (N.D. Cal. 1976), *aff'd,* 563 F.2d 1331 (9th Cir. 1977), *cert. denied,* 435 U.S. 1000 (1978).

The vast majority of American authority excludes the testimony. *See* Comment, *Stylistics Evidence in the Trial of Patricia Hearst*, 1977 ARIZ. ST. L.J. 387; United States v. Edelman, 873 F.2d 791, 795 (5th Cir. 1989) (upholding the exclusion of proposed testimony by Dr. Robert Shuy, a linguistics expert, about conversations in murder-for-hire cases); United States v. Aguon, 851 F.2d 1158, 1171 (9th Cir. 1988) (upholding the exclusion of psycholinguistics testimony), *cert. denied sub nom.*, Boylan v. United States, 498 U.S. 849 (1990); World Boxing Council v. Cosell, 715 F. Supp. 1259, 1264 (S.D.N.Y. 1989) (in excluding linguistics testimony about an author's alleged misuse of certain published articles, the court stated that the expert relied on "virtually incomprehensible pseudo-scientific jargon"). *But see* G. MCMENAMIN, FORENSIC STYLISTICS (1993). A version of the text appears as pages 1-250 of a Special Issue of 58 Forensic Science International (1993). Chapter 5 (pp. 76-110) of the text collects numerous cases in which, to some

Although the courts are more hospitable to expert testimony by questioned document examiners, the admissibility of the testimony in a particular case largely turns on the proponent's proof of the validity and acceptance of the specific technique used by the examiner. For example, in a leading ink case, *United States v. Bruno,*[347] the government attempted to prove that a particular document was a forgery through chromatographic analysis of the ink on the document.[348] The prosecution expert conceded that his library of ink standards was incomplete and further that several unknown factors could have affected the condition of the ink and, hence, the test outcome.[349] The court concluded that "the state of the art in this field of ink identification is not yet sufficiently advanced to be reasonably scientifically certain that an ink of unknown composition is the same as a known ink."[350] The court cited *Frye* as authority.[351] The state of the art of ink identification has progressed significantly since 1971 when *Bruno* was decided,[352] but *Bruno* is a clear signal that many courts are discriminating in their analysis of proffered questioned document testimony. It is not enough that the technique falls within the questioned document examiner's general domain; the court will scrutinize the reliability and acceptability of the specific technique.

The admissibility of many questioned document techniques is well established in *Frye* jurisdictions. Testimony that handwriting styles match and opinions that

---

extent, the courts permitted a witness to rest an identification on stylistic factors.

345. United States v. Clifford, 543 F. Supp. 424 (W.D. Pa. 1982), *rev'd on other grounds,* 704 F.2d 86 (3d Cir. 1983).

346. United States v. Schmidt, 711 F.2d 595 (5th Cir. 1983), *cert. denied,* 464 U.S. 1041 (1984); United States v. Hearst, 412 F. Supp. 893 (N.D. Cal. 1976), *aff'd,* 563 F.2d 1331 (9th Cir. 1977), *cert. denied,* 435 U.S. 1000 (1978).

347. 333 F. Supp. 570 (E.D. Pa. 1971).

348. *Id.* at 572.

349. *Id.* at 573. Midkiff & Starrs, *Ink Dating — In the Footsteps of Cold Fusion?*, SCI. SLEUTHING, Vol. 18, No. 1, p. 1, 2 (Spr. 1994) (the incompleteness of reference libraries "has seen the courts reject the ink dating analysis of a Treasury Department expert in U.S. v. Bruno, (333 F. Supp. 570 (D. Penn. 1971)) where the expert's library of inks did not include any ink samples from Japan. Similarly an F.B.I. expert who compared the unknown ink only to samples from one manufacturer of ink, Formulab, (concededly a major and dominant manufacturer) and not to the 15 to 20 others he recognized existed was deemed to have tendered unacceptable evidence in an Indiana forgery trial. (Eifler v. State, 570 N.E.2d 70 (Ind. 1991))").

350. *Id. See also* United States v. Colasurdo, 453 F.2d 585 (2d Cir. 1971), *cert. denied,* 406 U.S. 917 (1972) (where comparative chromatographic ink analysis testimony was admitted without objection).

351. *Id.* at 574.

352. A. MOENSSENS, J. STARRS, C. HENDERSON & F. INBAU, *supra* note 1, § 5.19. Janopoulos v. Harvey L. Walner & Assocs., 866 F. Supp. 1086, 1095-97 (N.D. Ill. 1994) (the use of TLC to date an ink sample qualifies for admission under *Daubert* even though the expert could not define "the potential error rate;" "[r]ates of error ... are only one factor to consider in determining admissibility of an expert's testimony").

a questioned document was typed on a particular machine are admissible.[353] Similarly, an opinion that the defendant intended to disguise his natural handwriting style was held admissible.[354] However, when the expert had no hard data about the frequency of defects in typeface, a New York court refused to permit the expert to couch the opinion in probabilistic terms.[355] The ink analysis techniques that are in widespread use are gaining the same acceptability as the conventional methods of analyzing typing.[356] Ink analysis testimony has been admitted "into federal, state, and local, and military courts in more than 20 states and abroad."[357] In the first test case for ESDA, the court held testimony based on the technique admissible.[358] Other novel techniques such as the Igoe-Reynolds lift have yet to surface in the reported appellate cases, although at least in Florida and Georgia, some experts have relied on such methods during their trial testimony.

In a *Daubert*[359] jurisdiction, the focus should be on the validity of the specific technique used by the expert. In some cases such as ESDA, there has been extensive empirical research into the validity of the technique. In that event, the technique would qualify as reliable "scientific . . . knowledge" within the intendment of that expression in Federal Rule 702. If the technique in question fails to satisfy the empirical validation standard, the testimony might nevertheless be admissible on the alternative ground that it is reliable nonscientific evidence. In *Kumho*,[360] the Court indicated that reliable nonscientific testimony is admissible under Rule 702. If, for instance, Dr. Kam's research demonstrates that the technique enables a questioned document examiner to resolve a forensic question more accurately than a layperson, the trial judge could admit the evidence as reliable nonscientific "technical . . . knowledge" under Rule 702. If the judge feared that the jury might overestimate the probative worth of the evidence, rather than excluding the testimony, the judge could give a strongly worded cautionary instruction, as in *Starzecpyzel*.[361]

---

353. *Id.* § 5.18, citing State v. Swank, 99 Or. 571, 195 P. 168 (1921). *See also* United States v. Weger, 709 F.2d 1151 (7th Cir. 1983); Kramer v. State, 605 S.W.2d 861 (Tex. Crim. App. 1980).

354. State v. Deutsch, 103 N.M. 752, 713 P.2d 1008 (Ct. App. 1985), *cert. denied*, 476 U.S. 1183 (1986).

355. People v. Risley, 214 N.Y. 75, 108 N.E. 200 (1915).

356. Lyter, *supra* note 172, at 55.

357. *Id.,* citing United States v. Hopkinson, 631 F. 2d 665 (10th Cir. 1980), *cert. denied,* 450 U.S. 969 (1981); Stoller v. United States, 320 F.2d 340 (Ct. Cl. 1963).

358. State v. Barrett, 401 N.W.2d 184 (Iowa 1987).

359. Daubert v. Merrell Dow Pharmaceuticals, Inc., 509 U.S. 579 (1993).

360. Kumho Tire Co., Ltd. v. Carmichael, 119 S. Ct. 1167 (1999).

361. United States v. Starzecpyzel, 880 F. Supp. 1027 (S.D.N.Y. 1995).

§ 21-7(C). Degree of Certitude.

Most contemporary courts do not insist that the expert vouch for his opinion as a conclusive certainty.[362] The expert may admit to a degree of uncertainty,[363] state a reservation,[364] or characterize the opinion as inconclusive.[365] It is also permissible for the expert to phrase the opinion as a likelihood[366] or degree of probability.[367] In a decision of dubious wisdom, one court permitted the expert to testify that he was "90% sure" although the expert evidently lacked any statistics to justify quantifying the probability in that fashion.[368]

§ 21-7(D). Admissibility of Exemplars.

As noted in the last subsection, well-accepted questioned document techniques such as the examiner's comparison of a document with exemplars are admissible. However, the opponent may nevertheless object to the testimony on the ground that the proposed exemplars are inadmissible. Such an objection may rest on one of five grounds.

Constitutional Objections

First, the opponent may attack the manner in which the exemplars were obtained. Chapter 2 discusses the constitutional limitations on the acquisition of physical evidence such as handwriting exemplars. In light of the case law summarized in that chapter, most courts have held that neither the fourth[369] nor

---

362. United States v. Daughenbaugh, 49 F.3d 171 (5th Cir. 1995); United States v. Stone, 9 F.3d 934 (11th Cir. 1993), *cert. denied*, 513 U.S. 833 (1994); United States v. McGlory, 968 F.2d 309, 346 (3d Cir.) (the testimony was admissible although "the expert could not make a positive statement that the handwriting on all of the receipts" was the defendant's), *cert. denied sub nom.* Hauser v. United States, 506 U.S. 956 (1992); United States v. Glover, 846 F.2d 339, 343 (6th Cir.), *cert. denied*, 488 U.S. 982 (1988); United States v. Herrera, 832 F.2d 833, 837 (4th Cir. 1987); Doe v. State, 634 So. 2d 613 (Fla. 1994). *See* McAlexander, *The Meaning of Handwriting Opinions*, 5 J. POLICE SCI. & ADMIN. 43 (1977).

363. United States v. Fleishman, 684 F.2d 1329, 1336-37 (9th Cir.), *cert. denied,* 459 U.S. 1044 (1982).

364. United States v. Galvin, 394 F.2d 228, 229 (3d Cir. 1968).

365. United States v. Hardrich, 707 F.2d 992 (8th Cir.), *cert. denied,* 464 U.S. 991 (1983).

366. United States v. Weger, 709 F.2d 1151, 1153 (7th Cir. 1983).

367. United States v. Tovar, 687 F.2d 1210 (8th Cir. 1982); United States v. Massa, 686 F.2d 526, 527 (7th Cir. 1982).

368. State v. Hartfield, 45 Or. App. 639, 643, 609 P.2d 390, 393 (1980), *rev'd on other grounds,* 290 Or. 583, 624 P.2d 588 (1981).

369. United States v. Mara, 410 U.S. 19 (1973); Bell v. State, 582 S.W.2d 800, 806-07 (Tex. Crim. App. 1979), *cert. denied,* 453 U.S. 927 (1981).In Burns v. State, 729 So. 2d 203(Miss. 1998), the court held that the exemplar is admissible even if the police obtain the exemplar by false pretenses. In *Burns*, a jail administrator asked the defendant to write out and sign a list of the

the fifth amendment[370] bars court orders compelling the defendant to supply handwriting exemplars. On occasion, courts have rejected fifth amendment challenges even when the police requested the defendant to execute a *literatim* exemplar, that is, a sample that literally duplicated the language of the questioned document.[371] One court ruled that "[a]sking the defendant to write the words which were written on the forged instrument merely provided more reliable physical evidence; it did not change the nature of the evidence."[372] However, there is currently a split of authority whether a court order for an exemplar violates the fifth amendment when the government wants to learn the defendant's spelling idiosyncrasies as well as the defendant's writing style.[373]

---

people he wished admitted on visiting days. The court ruled that the administrator had no obligation to inform the defendant of the intended use of the writing.

370. Schmerber v. California, 384 U.S. 757 (1966); United States v. McDougal, 137 F.3d 547, 559 (8th Cir. 1998); United States v. Tanoue, 94 F.3d 1342, 1345 (9th Cir. 1996); United States v. Yusufu, 63 F.3d 505, 515 (7th Cir.) (the defendant's refusal to supply a handwriting sample or attempt to disguise his handwriting style can amount to obstruction of justice), *cert. denied*, 516 U.S. 1015 (1995); United States v. McVeigh, 896 F. Supp. 1549 (W.D. Okla. 1995) (there was no fifth amendment barrier to the entry of an order memorializing the defendant's refusal to provide an exemplar of his cursive handwriting); People v. Tai, 37 Cal. App. 4th 990, 44 Cal. Rptr. 2d 253 (1995) (the fifth amendment did not prohibit the admission of expert testimony that while supplying a court-ordered exemplar, the defendant attempted to disguise his handwriting); People v. Clark, 5 Cal. 4th 950, 857 P.2d 1099, 22 Cal. Rptr. 2d 689 (1993), *cert. denied*, 512 U.S. 1253 (1994). *See also* State v. Bertram, 591 A.2d 14 (R.I. 1991) (construing the corresponding provision of the state constitution).

371. United States v. Rogers, 475 F.2d 821 (7th Cir. 1973); Ringer v. United States, 463 F.2d 1083 (8th Cir. 1972); United States v. Doe (Schwartz), 457 F.2d 895 (2d Cir.), *cert. denied,* 410 U.S. 941 (1972). *Compare* United States v. Ghidoni, 732 F.2d 814 (11th Cir. 1984) (court order that the defendant execute a consent allowing a foreign bank to release incriminating documents to the government), *cert. denied*, 469 U.S. 932 (1984).

372. Ringer v. United States, 463 F.2d 1083, 1085 (8th Cir. 1972).

373. *Compare* United States v. Campbell, 732 F.2d 1017, 1021 (1st Cir. 1984) (violation), United States v. Matos, 990 F. Supp. 141 (E.D.N.Y. 1998) (the provision of exemplars by dictation was testimonial in nature where one incriminating aspect was the content of the writing, specifically the spelling of a certain word), United States v. Butler, 44 Crim. L. Rep. (BNA) 2082 (D.C. Super. Ct., Sept. 30, 1988) (the handwriting exemplar may not be a form asking questions about potentially incriminating subjects), *and* Nadworny v. Fair, 744 F. Supp. 1194, 1202-03 (D. Mass. 1990) (a defendant's handwriting exemplars were testimonial in the sense that they revealed that the defendant was right handed; consequently, the use of the exemplars violated the defendant's privilege against self-incrimination) *with* United States v. Jacobowitz, 877 F.2d 162, 169 (2d Cir. 1989) (a suspect may be asked to provide a handwriting exemplar by writing the name of an alleged alias), *cert. denied*, 493 U.S. 866 (1990), *In re* Special Federal Grand Jury Empanelled October 31, 1985 (John Doe), 809 F.2d 1023 (3d Cir. 1987) (a grand jury witness may be compelled to provide a handwriting exemplar with a backward slant), *and* United States v. Pheaster, 544 F.2d 353 (9th Cir. 1976), *cert. denied sub nom.*, Inciso v. United States, 429 U.S. 1099 (1977) (no violation); United States v. Watkins, 60 Crim. L. (BNA) 1317, 1996 WL 712665 (D. Colo. Dec. 5, 1996) (citing *Campbell* and noting the split of authority, the court ruled that a writing's spelling of a dictated word is testimonial in nature); United States v. Wade, 57 Crim. L.

The Government's Prior Possession of an Ample Number of Exemplars

Secondly, there are non-constitutional grounds for resisting motions for court orders. For example, one court denied the government's motion when the government already had an ample supply of the defendant's handwriting.[374]

Acceptable Types of Exemplars

A third ground for objection is that the document is not an acceptable type of exemplar. The common-law standards governing permissible types of exemplars have undergone extensive evolution.[375] At first, courts limited the proponent to documents that were already in the case for an independent reason.[376] The proponent could use a pleading[377] or a document already introduced into evidence[378] as an exemplar. At the next stage in the doctrine's evolution, courts permitted the proponent to use any document that the opponent admitted to be or treated as genuine. Some jurisdictions codified the rule:

> Evidence respecting the handwriting may also be given by a comparison made by a witness skilled in these matters, or the jury, with writings admitted or treated as genuine by the party against whom the evidence is offered.[379]

Several jurisdictions extended the rule to the situation in which the opponent was for some reason estopped from denying the exemplar's authenticity.[380] However, in jurisdictions following this rule, the proponent could not use other exemplars "no matter how strong the circumstantial evidence is that defendant's writing was contained in the" proposed exemplar.[381]

This restrictive rule is obviously at odds with modern concepts of relevance and authentication. Initially, some courts broadened the test by accepting exemplars that could be authenticated by direct evidence, that is, the testimony of

---

(BNA) 1465, 1995 WL 464908 (S.D.N.Y. Aug. 4, 1995) (citing *Campbell*, *infra*, the court states that "[b]y dictating the exemplar, the Government seeks not only samples of Wade's penmanship but also evidence [of] spelling, 'a testimonial message in addition to a physical display'").

374. United States v. Green, 282 F. Supp. 373 (S.D. Ind. 1968).

375. *See* Annot., 41 A.L.R. 575 (1955).

376. Withaup v. United States, 127 F. 530, 535 (8th Cir. 1903).

377. *Id.*

378. F.B.I., *Admissibility of Standard Writings*, F.B.I. LAW ENF. BULL. Reprint 1, May 1966.

379. OR. REV. STAT. § 42.070 (repealed 1981), quoted in State v. Hartfield, 45 Or. App. 639, 643, 609 P.2d 390, 393 (1980), *rev'd*, 290 Or. 583, 624 P.2d 588 (1981).

380. State v. LeDuc, 306 N.C. 62, 69, 291 S.E.2d 607, 612 (1982).

381. State v. Hartfield, 45 Or. App. 639, 645, 609 P.2d 390, 393-94 (1980).

"a person who saw the party sign the standard."[382] Most courts gradually moved toward the view that an exemplar is admissible whether the proponent uses direct or circumstantial evidence to authenticate the exemplar.[383]

There is some modern authority that to be admissible as an exemplar, a document must have been created *ante litem motam,* that is, before the dispute began.[384] The rationale for this limitation is that if the party prepares the exemplar *post litem motam,* after the controversy arises, the exemplar will be self-serving and suspect.[385] However, "[m]odern court decisions have generally abandoned the prohibition against *post litem motam* exemplars."[386] At modern common law, the prevailing view appears to be that the proponent may use any standard of handwriting or typing[387] so long as the proponent presents sufficient direct or circumstantial evidence of authentication. Former 28 U.S.C. § 1731 referred to "any admitted or proved handwriting."[388] The current provision, Federal Rule of Evidence 901(b)(3), uses language that is equally broad, "specimens which have been authenticated."[389] Rule 901(b)(2) states that to be a qualified skilled lay observer, the witness cannot have acquired his or her familiarity with the alleged author's handwriting style "for purposes of the litigation." If Congress had intended to bar exemplars prepared for purposes of the litigation, it seemingly would have done so expressly. It is especially dubious to continue to enforce the common-law restriction in light of the *Daubert* Court's endorsement of the general norm that the Rules abolish uncodified exclusionary rules.[390]

---

382. State v. Farmer, 612 S.W.2d 442, 446 (Mo. App. 1981); Rauenzahn v. Sigman, 383 Pa. 439, 119 A.2d 312 (1956).

383. Scharfenberger v. Wingo, 542 F.2d 328 (6th Cir. 1976); People v. Ramos, 30 Cal. 3d 553, 639 P.2d 908, 180 Cal. Rptr. 266 (1982), *rev'd on other grounds,* 463 U.S. 992 (1983); State v. Clark, 592 S.W.2d 709, 717 (Mo. 1979), *cert. denied,* 449 U.S. 847 (1980).

384. United States v. Lam Muk Chiu, 522 F.2d 330 (2d Cir. 1975); Ramsey, *The Cherokee Syllabary,* 39 J. FORENSIC SCI. 1039, 1045-46 (1994) (in Hickory v. United States, 151 U.S. 303 (1894), the Supreme Court held that the trial judge properly excluded a specimen volunteered post litem motam).

385. *Id.*

386. A. MOENSSENS, J. STARRS, C. HENDERSON & F. INBAU, *supra* note 1, at § 5.16.

387. Register v. State, 34 Ala. App. 505, 42 So. 2d 519, *cert. denied,* 252 Ala. 659, 42 So. 2d 525 (1949); Grant v. Jack, 116 Me. 342, 102 A. 38 (1917); People v. Risley, 214 N.Y. 75, 108 N.E. 200 (1915).

388. F.B.I., *supra* note 378, at 1.

389. FED. R. EVID. 901(b)(3). Since the statutory text does not codify the post litem motam restriction, there is a strong argument that the restriction did not survive the enactment of the Federal Rules. Imwinkelried, *Federal Rule of Evidence 402: The Second Revolution,* 6 REV. LITIG. 129 (1987).

390. In Daubert v. Merrell Dow Pharmaceuticals, Inc., 509 U.S. 579 (1993), the Court held that the enactment of the Federal Rules overturned the traditional general acceptance test even though the seminal, *Frye* decision dated back to 1923.The Court approvingly quoted the statement of the

A Normal Authentication Objection

If the proposed exemplar is an acceptable type of standard, another ground for objection is that the exemplar does not satisfy the rules for relevance, specifically, the authentication doctrine. In a given case, those rules might require the exclusion of the proposed exemplar.

To ensure the probative worth of the exemplar, "the trial judge must ... be satisfied that there is enough similarity between the genuine handwriting and the disputed handwriting that the jury could reasonably infer that the disputed handwriting was also genuine."[391] The judge makes a preliminary, visual comparison of the questioned document and the proposed exemplar. If the judge believes that there are insufficient similarities between the two documents to support an inference of common authorship, the judge excludes the exemplar.

Even if on its face the exemplar has sufficient similarities to the questioned document, the opponent may challenge the adequacy of the exemplar's authentication. Most jurisdictions now subscribe to the general proposition that the proponent may rely on direct or circumstantial evidence to authenticate the exemplar.[392] However, some jurisdictions recognize an exception to this rule; these courts hold that "opinion evidence by an expert cannot establish the genuineness of a standard by comparing it with another exemplar."[393] Thus, the proponent may use any method of authenticating the exemplar other than expert comparison with another exemplar. If the proponent employs a permissible method of authentication, the court will usually hold the foundation adequate because the standard is minimal. Federal Rule of Evidence 901(a) provides that the authentication requirement "is satisfied by evidence sufficient to support a finding that the matter in question is what its proponent claims."[394] Rule 901(a) states the majority view, but in criminal cases a few authorities insist that the prosecutor establish the authenticity of an exemplar by proof beyond a reasonable doubt.[395] The traditional view is that the trial court rules finally on the

---

late Professor Edward Cleary, the Reporter for the Advisory Committee, that "in principle no common law of evidence remains." If the *Frye* standard did not survive the adoption of the Federal Rules, by parity of reasoning the *post litem motam* limitation should have been overturned.

391. State v. LeDuc, 306 N.C. 62, 74, 291 S.E.2d 607, 614 (1982).

392. *See* F.B.I., *supra* note 378, at 1-2.

393. A. Moenssens, J. Starrs, C. Henderson & F. Inbau, *supra* note 1, at § 5.16. *See* Archer v. United States, 9 Okla. 569, 60 P. 268 (1900) and Rauenzahn v. Sigman, 383 Pa. 439, 119 A.2d 312 (1956).

394. Fed. R. Evid. 901(a).

395. Dean v. United States, 246 F. 568, 576 (5th Cir. 1917); State v. Fortier, 427 A.2d 1317, 1324 (R.I. 1981). *See also* R. v. Ewing, 2 All E.R. 645, 650-51 (1983) (an English decision construing the Criminal Procedure Act as requiring proof beyond a reasonable doubt of the exemplar's authenticity in a criminal case).

admissibility of the exemplars;[396] this practice simplifies the jury's task. However, there is some authority at common law[397] and under the Federal Rules of Evidence[398] that the jury makes the final decision. In the view of these authorities, the proper procedure is as follows: The court decides only whether the proponent's foundational evidence has sufficient probative value to support a permissive inference of the exemplar's authenticity, the opponent presents any controverting evidence to the jury, and the jury finally decides the exemplar's genuineness.[399]

An Objection Premised on Federal Rule of Evidence 403

Even if the opponent cannot exclude the proposed exemplar on logical relevance grounds, he or she may be able to block its admission under the "legal" relevance doctrine. Rule 403 states the modern federal version of the doctrine.[400] Rule 403 permits the court to balance the probative value of the evidence against countervailing dangers such as unfair prejudice. The exemplar could have little probative value if it was made years before the questioned document.[401] The proponent's attempt to introduce an exemplar can create unfair prejudice if the exemplar suggests some misconduct by the defendant. Suppose, for example, that the exemplar is a prison record,[402] a conviction record,[403] a parole report,[404] or any document suggesting the defendant's prior arrest or imprisonment.[405] Although such documents are not per se inadmissible as exemplars,[406] if the government has other exemplars, under Rule 403 the court may exclude the exemplar suggesting the defendant's uncharged misconduct. Alternatively, the court might direct the prosecutor to mask or redact the portions of the record that suggest the misconduct. If the exemplar surmounts these hurdles, the proponent may mark it for identification, use it during the questioning of the examiner, and

---

396. *E.g.,* Scharfenberger v. Wingo, 542 F.2d 328 (6th Cir. 1976); State v. Clark, 592 S.W.2d 709, 717 (Mo. 1979), *cert. denied,* 449 U.S. 847 (1980).

397. Annot., 41 A.L.R.2d 575, 581 (1955).

398. 5 J. Weinstein & M. Berger, Weinstein's Evidence &901(a)[01], at 901-15-23 (1993).

399. *Id.* Texas amended its version of Rule 901(b)(3) to reinstate the earlier practice. The Texas version of that subdivision concludes with the language, "which have been found by the court to be genuine." *See* Wellborn, *Authentication and Identification Under Article IX of the Texas Rules of Evidence,* 16 St. Mary's L.J. 371, 378-79 (1985).

400. Fed. R. Evid. 403.

401. However, the courts have been lax and often admit exemplars that are years old. *E.g.,* State v. Bostwick, 222 Neb. 631, 385 N.W.2d 906 (1986) (nine-year-old exemplars).

402. United States v. Mauchlin, 670 F.2d 746 (7th Cir. 1982).

403. Smith v. State, 489 S.W.2d 920 (Tex. Crim. App. 1973).

404. State v. Martinez, 94 N.M. 50, 607 P.2d 137 (Ct. App. 1980).

405. United States v. White, 444 F.2d 1274, 1280 (5th Cir.), *cert. denied,* 404 U.S. 941 (1971); Hardy v. United States, 199 F.2d 704 (8th Cir. 1952).

406. Hilliard v. United States, 121 F.2d 992, 997 (4th Cir.), *cert. denied,* 314 U.S. 627 (1941).

present it to the jury for inspection. The exemplar need not be an original, and it need not be formally admitted into evidence.[407]

§ 21-7(E). Examiner Qualifications.

In the past, courts have allowed bank cashiers,[408] principals of business colleges,[409] and handwriting teachers[410] to testify to handwriting comparisons. These witnesses are merely secondary experts.[411] Their qualifications to testify on the subject are suspect.[412] Some leading authorities assert that examinations by secondary experts "cannot result in better than fifty percent accuracy."[413] The failure to consult a primary expert can amount to ineffective assistance of counsel.[414]

A primary expert would be a true forensic document examiner, a person whose principal occupation is using the techniques and making the determinations outlined in this chapter. No college or university offers a degree program in questioned document examination. Few institutions of higher learning offer even a single course in the subject.

Although there is no uniform curriculum for forensic document examiners, most examiners agree upon the profile of a qualified examiner.[415] To begin with, the person ought to have a B.S. degree in a physical science.[416] After obtaining that degree, the individual should serve a two-year apprenticeship under an experienced examiner.[417] During the apprenticeship, the individual should not only learn an examiner's day-to-day work; the individual should also make "a detailed study of the literature" on questioned document examination, notably the "major textbooks, including Evidential Documents by V.P. Conway, Suspect Documents by Wilson Harrison, Scientific Examination of Documents by

---

407. United States v. Shields, 573 F.2d 18 (10th Cir. 1978).

408. Ausmus v. People, 47 Colo. 167, 107 P. 204 (1910); State v. Wickett, 230 Iowa 1182, 300 N.W. 268 (1941); Continental Royalty Co. v. Marshall, 239 S.W.2d 837 (Tex. Civ. App. 1951); C. McCormick, *supra* note 309, at § 205, at 500 n.69.

409. First Galesburg Nat'l Bank & Trust Co. v. Federal Reserve Bank, 295 Ill. App. 524, 15 N.E.2d 337 (1938); C. McCormick, *supra* note 309, at § 205, at 500 n.69.

410. *Id.* at 500.

411. *Id.* § 205.

412. State v. LeDuc, 306 N.C. 62, 68, 291 S.E.2d 607, 611 (1982).

413. *Qualifications of Examiner of Questioned Documents*, 16 Am. Jur. Proof of Facts 481, 432 (1965).

414. United States v. Tarricone, 996 F.2d 1414 (2d Cir. 1993).

415. Behrendt, *The Status of Training for Questioned Document Examiners in the United States*, 34 J. Forensic Sci. 366 (1989).

416. *Id.* at 484; McGuire, Selecting an Expert Witness (unpublished manuscript on file with the National College of District Attorneys, Bates College of Law, University of Houston, Houston, Texas).

417. Kelly, *supra* note 47, at 705.

Ordway Hilton, and Questioned Documents by A.S. Osborn."[418] During the apprenticeship, the individual also ought to obtain training in the use of optical equipment such as microscope and infrared and ultraviolet instruments.[419] In some laboratories, questioned document trainees must complete a two-year internship "before their first word of actual testimony is ever given."[420]

As this consensus on the proper training of an examiner has emerged, there has been an effort to upgrade the professionalism of forensic document examiners. The American Academy of Forensic Sciences has a Documents Section, and there is a separate American Society of Questioned Document Examiners. In 1977, the Section helped create the American Board of Forensic Document Examiners. The Board certifies examiners. Such examiners usually have two years' training. At present, there are fewer than 200 active, certified Diplomates. One authority asserts that "[m]ost reputable forensic examiners are associated with the American Academy of Forensic Sciences or the American Society of Questioned Document Examiners. These organizations probably recognize fewer than 500 bona fide questioned document examiners in the United States ...."[421]

Until recently, most courts were relatively liberal in holding that persons qualified as questioned document examiners. For example, in *Heller v. Murray,*[422] the court held that the witness qualified even though his only formal training in questioned document examination was "a mail order degree." *Miller v. United States*[423] is also instructive. The *Miller* court sustained the witness's qualifications although the witness admitted that "he had not given much attention to the matter, and had had no experience in examining handwritings, except for his own satisfaction; ... that he did not consider himself an expert, but

---

418. *Id.*

419. QUALIFICATIONS OF EXAMINER OF QUESTIONED DOCUMENTS, *supra* note 413, at 485.

420. MCGUIRE, *supra* note 416, at 2.

421. Stone, *Capabilities of Modern Forensic Laboratories*, 25 WM. & MARY L. REV. 659, 660 (1984). *See also* Behrendt, *The Status of Training for Questioned Document Examiner in the United States*, 34 J. FORENSIC SCI. 366 (1989) (arguing that there are several deficiencies in the current reliance on on-the-job training as the primary instructional method for questioned document examiners).

422. 112 Misc. 2d 745, 746-47, 447 N.Y.S.2d 348, 351 (1981), *aff'd,* 118 Misc. 2d 508, 464 N.Y.S.2d 391 (1983). *See also* People v. Yu, 166 A.D.2d 249, 564 N.Y.S.2d 300 (a handwriting expert was qualified to testify to his analysis of a Chinese character signature even though he could not read or speak Chinese), *appeal denied*, 76 N.Y.2d 992, 565 N.E. 2d 530, 563 N.Y.S.2d 781 (1990); First Coppell Bank v. Smith, 742 S.W.2d 454 (Tex. App. 1987) (although the witness was a graphoanalyst, he also had training and experience in analysis of questioned documents, including forgeries).

423. 277 F. 721 (4th Cir. 1921).*See also* United States v. Tipton, 964 F.2d 650, 653-54 (7th Cir. 1992).

might be called an expert, but not of the first class; [and] that he could identify handwritings as well as the ordinary man, and probably a little better...."

Many courts still pay lipservice to the rule that a person can qualify as an examiner by study without practice or practice without study.[424] Recent cases, however, indicate that some courts are beginning to adopt a more critical attitude. By way of illustration, courts have held witnesses unqualified when: The witness has minimal practical experience;[425] the witness's training was merely self-study and a correspondence school course;[426] the witness's specialty was graphology and had a very limited background in questioned document examination,[427] and the witness regarded questioned document examination as a hobby rather than his profession.[428]

§ 21-7(F). Sufficiency of Evidence.

The virtually unanimous view of the courts is that the normal rules apply in assessing the sufficiency of expert questioned document. However, several jurisdictions have adopted special rules.

By way of example, in Texas there is a special statutory rule for criminal cases.[429] A Texas statute provides:

> It is competent to give evidence of handwriting by comparison, made by experts or by the jury. Proof of comparison only shall not be sufficient to establish the handwriting of a witness who denies his signature under oath.[430]

---

424. A. Moenssens, J. Starrs, C. Henderson & F. Inbau, *supra* note 1, § 5.21.

425. Carroll v. State, 276 Ark. 160, 634 S.W.2d 99 (1982).

426. United States v. King, 532 F.2d 505 (5th Cir.), *cert. denied,* 429 U.S. 960 (1976).

427. State v. Livanos, 151 Ariz. 13, 725 P.2d 505 (Ct. App. 1986). *See also* United States v. Bourgeois, 950 F.2d 980, 986-87 (5th Cir. 1992) (a masters degree in graphoanalysis); Graves v. State, 547 N.E.2d 881 (Ind. App. 1989) (although the witness was a member of the International Graphoanalysis Society, the record did not detail the organization's membership standards; and the record also failed to indicate how the witness's training prepared her to compare writings to determine authorship).*But see* Henry v. State, 533 So. 2d 182 (Miss. 1988); Hooten v. State, 492 So. 2d 948 (Miss. 1986); Starrs, *Recent Developments in Federal and State Rules Pertaining to Medical and Scientific Expert Testimony*, 34 Duq. L. Rev. 813, 843 (1996).

428. Keys v. Keys, 23 Tenn. App. 188, 129 S.W.2d 1103 (1939).*See also* United States v. Paul, 175 F.3d 906, 912 (1st Cir. 1999) (upholding the exclusion of testimony by a law professor who has written about questioned document examination).

429. Denby v. State, 654 S.W.2d 457, 461 (Tex. Crim. App. 1983).

430. Tex. Crim. Proc. Code Ann. art. 38.27 (1979), *quoted in* Denby v. State, 654 S.W.2d 457, 461 (Tex. Crim. App. 1983).

The special statutory rule does not come into play unless the witness "denies his signature under oath." However, if the witness does so, the statute mandates corroboration of the expert's testimony.[431]

Moreover, some jurisdictions have special statutory rules in will cases. For example, a Virginia statute provides:

> If the will be wholly in the handwriting of the testator, that fact shall be proved by at least two distinterested witnesses.[432]

In one case, the proponent of a holographic will relied solely on expert testimony comparing the alleged will with exemplars of the decedent's handwriting. The court held that the expert testimony was insufficient absent a disinterested witness's testimony that the exemplars themselves were in the testator's handwriting.[433]

§ 21-8. Selected Bibliography.

Qualifications of Examiners of Questioned Documents, 16 AM. JUR. PROOF OF FACTS 481 (1965).

Carpenter, *Questioned Typewriting*, 20 AM. JUR. PROOF OF FACTS 265 (1968).

J. CONWAY, EVIDENTIAL DOCUMENTS (1959).

D. ELLEN, THE SCIENTIFIC EXAMINATION OF DOCUMENTS (1989).

FEDERAL BUREAU OF INVESTIGATION, SOME SCIENTIFIC ASPECTS OF DOCUMENT EXAMINATION (1946).

W. HARRISON, SUSPECT DOCUMENTS (1966).

O. HILTON, SCIENTIFIC EXAMINATION OF QUESTIONED DOCUMENTS (rev. ed 1982).

O. HILTON, SCIENTIFIC EXAMINATION OF QUESTIONED DOCUMENTS (rev. ed. 1992).

R. A. HUBER & A. M. HEADRICK, HANDWRITING IDENTIFICATION: FACTS AND FUNDAMENTALS (1999).

A. OSBORN, QUESTIONED DOCUMENTS PROBLEMS (rev. ed. 1944).

E. SMITH, PRINCIPLES OF FORENSIC HANDWRITING IDENTIFICATION AND TESTIMONY (1984).

Brunelle & Pro, *A Systematic Approach to Ink Identification*, 55 JOURNAL OF OFFICIAL ANALYTICAL CHEMISTS 823 (1972).

Kelly, *Questioned Document Examination*, SCIENTIFIC AND EXPERT EVIDENCE 695 (2d ed. 1981).

Lyter, *Ink Analysis: A Key Element in Questioned Document Examination*, 19 TRIAL 53 (Jan. 1983).

Morrill, *The Document Examiner – Scientist or Sciolist?*, 9 THE PROSECUTOR 206 (1973).

Waggoner, *Handwriting Evidence for the Investigator*, 53 F.B.I. LAW ENF. BULL. 20 (June 1984).

---

431. *See* Camacho v. State, 765 S.W.2d 431 (Tex. Crim. App. 1989); Turner v. State, 636 S.W.2d 189 (Tex. Crim. App. 1982); Russell v. State, 598 S.W.2d 238 (Tex. Crim. App.), *cert. denied*, 449 U.S. 1003 (1980); Cadd v. State, 587 S.W.2d 736 (Tex. Crim. App. 1979).

432. VA. CODE § 64.1-49.

433. Bowers v. Huddleston, 241 Va. 83, 86-88, 399 S.E.2d 811, 813-14 (1991) ("the expert testimony did nothing to accomplish the statutory requirement of proof, by a second disinterested witness ....").

CHAPTER 22

ALCOHOL TESTING*

§ 22-1. In General.

Drunk driving exacts a huge toll in the United States every year. Some estimate that the annual economic losses resulting from alcohol-related collisions total $5,000,000,000.00.[1] In the typical year, there are one million arrests for drunk driving.[2] In some years alcohol-related collisions have accounted for 40,000 fatalities[3] and nearly a million personal injuries.[4]

---

*The authors wish to express their appreciation to Dr. Kurt Dubowski, Distinguished Professor of Medicine, University of Oklahoma, who reviewed this chapter in all three editions of this treatise.

1. Lauter, *The Drunk Driving Blitz*, NAT'L L.J., March 22, 1982, p. 1.

2. Joye, *Drunk Driving: Recommendations for Safer Highways*, 19 TRIAL 60 (June 1983).

3. Caplan, *The Determination of Alcohol in Blood and Breath*, *in* FORENSIC SCIENCE HANDBOOK 592, 593 (R. Saferstein ed. 1982). *But see Drunk Driving Deaths Drop to '75 Level*, SAN FRANCISCO CHRONICLE, May 15, 1998, at p. A8 (in 1997 "fatalities from drunken driving fell to their lowest level in more than 20 years. There were 16,250 alcohol-related traffic fatalities in 1997, the lowest level since the government began keeping records in 1975. In percentage terms, 39.3%

In the past, the legal response to drunk driving took the form of two types of statutes. One is an implied consent statute. Such a statute provides that as a condition to obtaining a driver's license, the driver consents to the administration of alcohol tests if lawfully stopped on suspicion of drunk driving.[5] In most states, the statutes provide further that when a driver wrongfully refuses to submit to a test, the refusal allows the state to administratively revoke the person's driving privilege; in a few states, the refusal itself is a crime, typically a misdemeanor.[6]

The second type of statute enacted in most jurisdictions prescribes the evidentiary effect of alcohol test results. The traditional statutes typically create a three-zone classification with differing presumptions for each zone. In 1938, the National Safety Council (NSC) and the American Medical Association (AMA) recommended the following classification: If the driver has less than .05% alcohol in his blood, he is presumed sober[7]; when the driver's blood alcohol

---

of the fatalities were alcohol-related, the first time that figure had fallen below 40 percent"); Dilworth, *Reduced Incidence of Drunk Driving Deaths Encourages Tougher Laws*, 30 TRIAL 111 (Oct. 1994) ("The National Highway Traffic Safety Administration . . . reported recently that fatal crashes involving alcohol dropped by 2 percent in 1993. There were 17,461 fatalities in alcohol-related crashes during the year, the lowest numbers since the agency began tracking them"); "*runken Driving Takes Its Toll*, 19 AIDE MAGAZINE, Aug. 1988, at 6 ("However, the number of alcohol-related deaths has been going down since the beginning of the decade. In 1980, 51,091 people died on America's highways, with about 28,000 of these alcohol-related victims. By contrast, in 1986, the last year for which figures are available, there were 46,056 traffic fatalities, of which 23,990 involved alcohol").

4. Lauter, *supra* note 1, at 1.

5. ALA. CODE § 32-5-192; ALASKA STAT. § 28.35.031; ARIZ. REV. STAT. ANN. § 28-691; ARK. STAT. ANN. § 5-65-202; CAL. VEH. CODE § 13353; COLO. REV. STAT. § 42-4-1202; CONN. GEN. STAT. ANN. § 14-227b; DEL. CODE ANN. tit. 21, § 2740; D.C. CODE ANN. § 40-502; FLA. STAT. ANN. § 322.261; GA. CODE ANN. § 68B-306; HAW. REV. STAT. § 286-151; IDAHO CODE § 18-8002; ILL. REV. STAT. ch. 625, § 5/11-501.1; IND. CODE ANN. § 9-11-4-1; IOWA CODE ANN. § 321B.4; KAN. STAT. ANN. § 8-1001; KY REV. STAT. ANN. § 186.565; LA. REV. STAT. ANN. § 32.661; ME. REV. STAT. ANN. tit. 29, § 1312; MD. TRANSP. CODE ANN. § 16-205.1; MASS. GEN. LAWS ANN. ch. 90, § 24(f); MICH. COMP. LAWS ANN. § 257.625c; MINN. STAT. § 169.123.2 (Supp. 1984); MISS. CODE ANN. § 63-11-5; MO. REV. STAT. § 577.020; MONT. CODE ANN. § 61-8-402; NEB. REV. STAT. § 39-669.08; NEV. REV. STAT. 484.382; N.H. REV. STAT. ANN. 265.84; N.J. STAT. ANN. § 39:4-50.2; N.M. STAT. ANN. § 66-8-107; N.Y. VEH. & TRAF. LAW § 1194; N.C. GEN. STAT. § 20-16.2; N.D. CENT. CODE § 39-20-01; OHIO REV. CODE ANN. § 4511.19.1; OKLA. STAT. ANN. tit. 47, § 751; OR. REV. STAT. § 487.805; PA. CONS. STAT. ANN. tit. 75, § 1547; R.I. GEN. LAWS § 31-27-2.1; S.C. CODE § 56-5-2950; S.D. CODIFIED LAWS ANN. § 32-23-10; TENN. CODE ANN. § 55-10-406; TEX. REV. CIV. STAT. ANN. art. 6701L-5; UTAH CODE ANN. § 41-6-44.10; VT. STAT. ANN. tit. 23, § 1202; VA. CODE § 18.2-268.2; WASH. REV. CODE ANN. § 46.20.308; W. VA. CODE § 17C-5A-1; WIS. STAT. § 343.305.

6. Note, *To Submit or Not to Submit — Where Is My Attorney?: The Right to Counsel Before Submission to Chemical Testing in a DWI Proceeding*, 63 NEB. L. REV. 373, 374 (1984).

7. Vasquez v. National Car Rental, Inc., 24 F. Supp. 2d 197, 201 (D.P.R. 1998) (under P.R. Laws Ann. tit. 9 § 1041(b)(1), "if at the time of the analysis there was less than ten (10) hundredths of one (1) percent of alcohol per volume . . . in the driver's blood, it shall be conclusively presumed

concentration falls between .05% and .15%, there is no presumption of sobriety or intoxication; and if the concentration exceeds .15%, the driver is presumed under the influence of alcohol.[8] In 1960, a joint NSC-AMA committee recommended that the third zone be lowered to .10%.[9] In 1962, the Uniform Vehicle Code was amended to implement the recommendation.[10] Most states eventually adopted the Uniform Vehicle Code's presumptions.[11]

Recent Developments

The 1980s and 1990s witnessed an intensified national campaign to eradicate drunk driving. There was a broad concern about the extent to which alcohol contributed to the commission of crime.[12] In particular, three groups pressed for drunk driving reform legislation: MADD (Mothers Against Drunk Drivers), SADD (Students Against Driving Drunk), and Remove Intoxicated Drivers (RID).[13] Due in part to the lobbying efforts of these groups, major legislative changes have occurred. The third zone under the Uniform Vehicle Code has been lowered further to 0.08.[14] Sixteen states and the District of Columbia have adopted that standard.[15] Many states have adopted a tiered system. By way of example, some have a lower threshold for operators of commercial vehicles.[16] A

---

that the driver was not under the influence of intoxicating drinks at the time the alleged violation was committed"); People v. Andersen, 26 Cal. App. 4th 507, 31 Cal. Rptr. 2d 826 (discussing California's rebuttable statutory presumption), *modified*, 32 Cal. Rptr. 2d 442 (App. 1994); Lundy, *The Jury Instruction Corner*, CACJ FORUM, Vol. 21, No. 4, p. 17 (1994).

8. Joye, *supra* note 2, at 61.

9. *Id.*

10. Carlson, *Defending Drunk Driving Cases: Evidence Problems, in* 3 CRIMINAL DEFENSE TECHNIQUES § 51.02[1], at 51-4 (S. Bernstein ed. 1982).

11. 10th Annual Criminal Advocacy Institute (Practicing Law Institute 1978) collects the statutes from throughout the United States.

12. Skolnik, *The Battle with the Bottle: DOJ Launches Crackdown on Alcohol-Related Crime*, LEGAL TIMES, Jan. 18, 1999, at p. 1. *See also* Egelhoff v. Montana, 518 U.S. 37 (1996) (state legislation limiting the voluntary intoxication defense).

13. *Drunk Driving in America*, THE ATLANTIC, Oct. 1983, at 18-19; *The War Against Drunk Drivers*, NEWSWEEK, Sept. 13, 1982, at 34.

14. UNIFORM VEHICLE CODE AND MODEL TRAFFIC ORDINANCE § 11-902,1(b), Supp. IV (1984). *See Senate OKs Drunk Driving Limit*, SAN FRANCISCO CHRONICLE, Mar. 5, 1998, p. A4 (15 states now use the .08 standard); Foster, *It May Be Legal, But It Can Still Be Unsafe*, THE DAVIS ENTERPRISE, Nov. 17, 1991, at D-1 ("Five states--California, Oregon, Utah, Maine, and Vermont--already have reduced their legal limits to 0.08 percent . . . . Most states already set 0.04 percent as the legal limit for drivers of buses, trucks, and other commercial vehicles").

15. *President Clinton to Resume Efforts to Enact Stricter Drunk Driving Standard*, 64 CRIM. L. (BNA) 256, 257 (Jan. 6, 1999).

16. In California, the level for commercial operators is 0.04%.

number of states have adopted a lower threshold for repeat offenders.[17] Other states have tiered their system on a different basis, namely, age; in these jurisdictions, for drivers under 21, the threshold level has been lowered to 0.02.[18] Penalties have been stiffened at the same time that the offenses have been broadened. Since 1982, roughly half the states have increased the sanctions for drunk driving.[19] Twenty-five state legislatures have enacted statutes providing mandatory confinement for first offenders.[20]

As a result of this national campaign, implied consent and presumption statutes have been joined by a third type of legislation: In over 40 states, the legislatures have adopted statutes making it a per se offense to drive with a certain blood or breath alcohol concentration, such as 10%.[21] Under these statutes, the prosecutor does not have to invoke a presumption of intoxication; the offense is simply driving with a specified blood (BAC) or breath alcohol concentration (BrAC). Indeed, in a few states the offense includes driving with a metabolite of a drug in the operator's body.[22] The prosecutor need not show any signs (perceived effects) of intoxication such as slurred speech or lack of coordination. The per se statutes do not repeal the presumptive statutes, and the prosecutor can charge the defendant with either the traditional offense of driving under the influence or the new per se crime. Although there have been some

---

17. *E.g.*, State v. Robinson, 1999 Tenn. Crim. App. LEXIS 49, 64 Cr.L. (BNA) 351 (Tenn. Crim. App., Jan. 19, 1999) (discussing TENN. CODE ANN. 55-10-408(b); under that statute, while the standard for first-time offenders is 0.10, the standard for repeat offenders is 0.08).

18. Barnett v. State, 270 Ga. 472, 510 S.E.2d 527 (1999) (the legislation is justified by the legitimate interests in protecting the public safety and safeguarding the physical well being of children); Commonwealth v. Howard, 969 S.W.2d 700 (Ky. 1998). *See also* People v. Goslar, 70 Cal. App. 4th 270, 82 Cal. Rptr. 2d 558 (1999) (upholding the constitutionality of a gross vehicular manslaughter statute recognizing a lower standard for persons under 21 years of age).

19. NAT'L HIGHWAY TRAFFIC SAFETY AD., U.S. DEP'T TRANS., DWI SANCTIONS: THE LAW AND THE PRACTICE III-2 (1983).

20. *Id.* at 2.

21. Footer, *Driving While Intoxicated: A Prosecutor's Perspective*, 20 TRIAL 42 (Oct. 1984) (41 states); Lauter, *Do Breath, Blood Tests Stand Up?*, NAT'L L.J., Mar. 22, 1982, at 23. ERWIN, CREATIVE TECHNIQUES PRESENTING THE DRUNK DRIVER, IN CALIFORNIA ATTORNEYS FOR CRIMINAL JUSTICE CRIMINAL LAW SEMINAR 111-16 (1984) compiles the statutes. The compilation includes statutes from: Alabama, Alaska, California, Delaware, Florida, Minnesota, Missouri, Nebraska, New Hampshire, New York, North Carolina, Oregon, South Dakota, Utah, Vermont, Washington, and Wisconsin. *See also* Forte v. State, 686 S.W.2d 744, 746 n.2 (Tex. App. 1985), *aff'd in part, rev'd in part*, 707 S.W.2d 89 (Tex. Crim. App. 1986); Thompson, *The Constitutionality of Chemical Test Presumptions of Intoxication in Motor Vehicle Statutes*, 20 SAN DIEGO L. REV. 301, 333 n.122 (1983). Our reviewer points out that it would be more correct scientifically to state the concentration as g/dL blood or g/210L breath.

22. State v. Hammonds, 192 Ariz. 528, 968 P.2d 601(1998).

attacks on the constitutionality of per se statutes,[23] the courts have almost uniformly upheld them.[24]

The Importance of Scientific Intoxication Testing

The advent of per se statutes and enhanced sanctions for drunk driving make the topic of this chapter, chemical intoxication testing, all the more important. On the one hand, there is no legal requirement that the prosecution always present scientific evidence of the chemical intoxication tests discussed in this chapter.[25] The prosecution can offer other evidence such as videotapes of the defendant's post-arrest behavior at the police station[26] and the arresting officer's testimony about the results of the simple, traditional field sobriety tests such as walking a straight line,[27] walk-and-turn, one-leg-stand, and finger-to-nose.[28]

---

23. People v. Alfaro, 143 Cal. App. 3d 709, 192 Cal. Rptr. 184 (1983), *withdrawn*; Commonwealth v. Barud, 545 Pa. 297, 681 A.2d 162 (1996) (The state variation of the per se offense makes it a crime to have a BAC above 0.10 within three hours after operating a motor vehicle; the court struck the statute down as vague and overbroad; the statute encompasses lawful as well as unlawful conduct and fails to provide a reasonable standard by which persons may gauge their conduct.). *Contra* United States v. Skinner, 973 F. Supp. 975 (W.D. Wash. 1997); Sereika v. State, 114 Nev. 175, 955 P.2d 175 (1998). While these cases discuss overbreadth and vagueness challenges, in Commonwealth v. Myron E. Howard, No. 97-XX-0003 (Davis County Circuit Ct., Div. No. 1, Ky., Feb. 28, 1997), District Judge Gene Lanham invalidated a state statute on equal protection grounds. The statute in question prescribed a .02 level for drivers younger than 21 years of age. The judge concluded that the statute created a suspect class based solely on age without a rational basis. *.02 for Under 21 Ruled Unconstitutional*, 19 THE ADVOCATE 63 (Nov. 1997).

24. Fuenning v. Superior Court of County of Maricopa, 139 Ariz. 590, 680 P.2d 121 (1983); Burg v. Municipal Court, 35 Cal. 3d 257, 673 P.2d 732, 198 Cal. Rptr. 145 (1983), *cert. denied*, 466 U.S. 967 (1984); People v. Ziltz, 98 Ill. 2d 38, 74 Ill. Dec. 40, 455 N.E.2d 70 (1983); Annot., *Validity, construction, and application of statutes directly proscribing driving with blood-alcohol level in excess of established percentage*, 54 A.L.R.4TH 149 (1987).

25. United States v. Channel, 423 F. Supp. 1017, 1021 (D. Md. 1976).

26. Palmer v. State, 604 P.2d 1106 (Alaska 1979).

27. Taylor, *Drunk Driving Defense: Field Evidence in Drunk Driving Cases*, 9 CRIM. DEF. 21 (Mar./Apr. 1982); Bell, *Exposing FSTs for What They Are: "Cutting the Fig Leaf,"* 21 THE CHAMPION 37, 38 (Nov. 1997) (The National Highway Traffic Safety Administration Manual for field sobriety testing states "considered independently, the nystagmus test was the most accurate of the three. Among subjects who exhibited four or more clues 82 percent had BAC's of 0.10 or higher. However, the other two tests were nearly as accurate (80 percent for Walk and Turn, 78 percent for One-Leg Stand). When the nystagmus and Walk and Turn results were jointly interpreted using the decision table, 83 percent of the subjects were classified correctly."); Lerman & Day, *Field Sobriety Testing and Dr. Spurgeon Cole's Challenge*, 17 THE CHAMPION 23 (July 1993) ("In ... 1992, Dr. Spurgeon Cole of Clemson University conducted a study involving 21 male subjects and two groups of seven police officers to test the accuracy and validity of six field sobriety tests.... Dr. Cole's research found that the police officers were wrong in their judgment of defendants' impairment due to alcohol 46 percent of the time. Recently, Dr. Cole testified in a Collier County, Florida court on behalf of a defense motion to exclude the Finger to Nose Test, Counting Backwards Test and the Romberg Alphabet Test. On April 8, 1993, the Honorable Judge

For that matter, the prosecution may also attempt to present evidence of novel, more sophisticated field testing techniques such as the controversial horizontal gaze nystagmus (HGN) procedure.[29] In this procedure, the officer starts with an object in front of the subject's nose and then moves the object in a horizontal plane to the side of the subject's face. During the process, the officer observes the movement of the subject's eyes. If the eye movement fluctuates back and forth, HGN has occurred. The officer notes both the occurrence of the fluctuation and the angle (lateral to the nose) at which the jerking movement began. While some officers uses a protractor to measure the angle of onset of nystagmus, today in the field many officers rely on their unaided eye. As a general proposition, if the eye jerking begins before an angle of 45 degrees, the subject is suspected of intoxication.[30] Many police agencies using the HGN test employ a six point scoring system. The first criterion is whether HGN occurs at an angle of less than 45 degrees. If it does, the suspect receives a score of two points. In addition, the officer asks the subject to move his or her eyes laterally as far as possible; the

---

Cynthia A. Ellis issued an order prohibiting the introduction into evidence of these three commonly used field sobriety tests in DUI cases without first establishing scientific reliability."). Cole, Kulis & Nowacczyk, *NHTSA and FST's: True Lies and False Advertising*, 12 DWI J. 1 (Mar. 1997) is coauthored by Dr. Cole. The article mentions the Florida case. In addition, the article discusses the 1981 NHTSA study which is often cited "as evidence of an 80 percent accuracy rate with the use of the FST battery." *Id.* at 2. The article states that 78% of the subjects had extreme BACs. "Only 22 percent of the subjects were in the critical BAC level range around 0.10." *Id.* at 3. Since "over two-thirds of the decisions [were] 'gimmies,'" and "the officers [had] a 50/50 chance of being correct just on the basis of guessing," "the reported 80% accuracy rate does not look exceptionally good." *Id.* There are common sense doubts about the probative worth of field sobriety test results. After all, these techniques use "abnormal tests to test faculties." Reiff, *.10% Solution*, 22 THE CHAMPION 37 (Jan./Feb. 1998). When the officer learned the tests at the academy, he or she was asked to perform the tests on a level surface in a well lit area without complicating factors such as bad weather or cars passing nearby. Further, the officer does not know the suspect's baseline, that is, how the suspect would perform on the tests if the suspect were completely sober. In the Walk and Turn (WAT) test, the officer usually asks the suspect to place his arms to his side. That posture is unnatural; normally, when persons try to maintain their balance, they spread their arms out. The One Legged Stand (OLS) is certainly a difficult position for anyone, even a completely sober person, to maintain for 30 seconds. Nevertheless, the courts continue to be receptive to testimony about the results of field sobriety tests. United States v. Everett, 972 F. Supp. 1313 (D. Nev. 1997) (a Drug Recognition Evaluation (DRE) protocol); Williams v. State, 710 So. 2d 24 (Fla. Dist. Ct. App. 1998) (the DRE protocol).

28. State v. Brown, 321 Or. 285, 298, 899 P.2d 663, 675 (1995).

29. The test was developed by DARTS (Drug-Alcohol Recognition Training Seminars), 1410 E. Glenoaks Boulevard, Glendale, California. Nystagmus is a jerking motion of the eyes. Horizontal gaze nystagmus occurs when the eye attempts to follow an object slowly moving to the suspect's side. The DARTS researchers contend that the angle of onset of the jerking motion correlates with the suspect's blood alcohol concentration. DARTS' press releases claim the following correlation: 45 degrees--.05% BAC, 40 degrees--.10%, 35 degrees--.15%, and 30 degrees--.20%.

30. State v. Bresson, 51 Ohio St.3d 123, 554 N.E.2d 1330 (1990).

degree of nystagmus is then assessed again. Moderate nystagmus in the far lateral position results in a score of one while severe nystagmus receives a score of two. In addition, the officer assesses the eye tracking of an object. Smooth tracking receives a score of zero, but inconsistent tracking can result in a maximum score of two points. A score of four or more points is said to correlate with a blood alcohol level exceeding 0.01 per cent.[31]

On the other hand, in the overwhelming majority of cases the prosecutor relies primarily on a chemical test to prove the defendant's BAC. A prosecutor who relied exclusively on field tests would run the risk of the court concluding that the prosecutor had not sustained the initial burden of going forward and directing an acquittal. Even when the prosecutor escaped a directed verdict, during summation the defense could point to the lack of a "truly scientific" chemical test to prove the defendant's guilt and invite the jury to treat that gap as a source of reasonable doubt. If the jury found that argument plausible, the result could be a not guilty verdict. Thus, despite the availability of nonscientific types of evidence, the prosecutor is under practical pressure to lay a convincing foundation for evidence of a scientific intoxication test.

This chapter initially surveys the scientific aspects of alcohol testing, including an analysis of the pharmacology of alcohol and the various chemical tests for intoxication. Those tests determine the concentration of ethyl alcohol in the analyzed substance (breath, blood, etc.) at the time of the sampling, some time after the legally relevant event such as the collision. For that reason, in many cases the prosecutor asks the expert to retroactively estimate the defendant's BAC at the time of the relevant event. In addition, the technology for preserving breath and blood samples for independent retesting is discussed.

The second half of the chapter focuses on the law governing intoxication tests, including the witness's qualifications, the admissibility of the various tests and BAC computations, and the statutory presumptions of intoxication based on BAC findings.

The state of the science and law frequently permit successful defense in a drunk driving prosecution. The acquittal rate for jury trials in that type of case exceeds the average rate for all types of prosecutions.[32] In that light, it is critical for counsel in this type of litigation to develop a thorough grasp of the scientific and legal framework. This chapter sketches that framework.

---

31. *Id.*, citing U.S. Dept. of Transp., Nat'l Highway Traffic Safety Admin., Improved Sobriety Testing (1984).

32. Head, *Five Myths About Defending Accused Drunk Drivers*, 29 Trial 64, 66 (Mar. 1993) ("Where jury trials are available, success rates for acquittal are surprisingly good. The national average for acquittals is about 50 percent for those accused of drunk driving if their cases are heard by juries. In some jurisdictions, only about 20 percent to 30 percent of all drunk-driving arrests lead to a conviction....").

§ 22-2. Pharmacology of Alcohol.

As the next section points out, blood and breath are the two materials usually analyzed in intoxication testing. Urine is sometimes analyzed as well. To understand why these substances are used for testing, the pharmacology and metabolism of alcohol must be reviewed. As a person consumes alcohol, the alcohol passes into the stomach. A small quantity of the alcohol passes directly from the stomach into the blood stream. However, most of the alcohol passes from the stomach into the upper region of the small intestine and then into the blood stream. After entering the blood stream through either route, the alcohol passes through the liver.[33]

Once the alcohol reaches the liver, one of two things happens. Most of the alcohol — 90 to 95% — is absorbed into the liver tissue and then metabolized.[34] The enzyme alcohol dehydrogenase catalyzes a reaction, and later steps in the reaction eventually yield carbon dioxide (CO_2) and water.[35] While most of the alcohol is thus eliminated through metabolism, the balance of the alcohol — five to 10% — is excreted.[36] The kidneys excrete some alcohol in urine while the lungs eliminate other alcohol in breath.

Before being excreted in breath, the alcohol is carried by the blood to the lung walls near the pulmonary blood supply.[37] There are hundreds of millions of small alveoli (air sacs) in this area of the lungs.[38] This is the region where the alveolar air is in most intimate contact with the blood.[39] Because of the contact, Henry's law comes into play. One writer has described the law in the following, somewhat simplistic fashion: "When a volatile chemical (alcohol) is dissolved in a liquid (blood) and is brought into contact with a closed air space (alveolar breath), an equilibrium is formed and there exists a fixed ratio between the concentration of the volatile compound (alcohol) in air (alveolar breath) and its concentration in the liquid (blood) and this ratio is constant for a given temperature."[40] In a general way, that law governs the amount of alcohol that diffuses into the air in contact with the liquid. Breath normally leaves the human mouth at 34 C.[41] In court, some witnesses assume for purposes of testifying that

---

33. Houts, *Impeaching the Clinical Laboratory: The Blood-Alcohol Blood Test*, 10 TRAUMA 33 (June 1968) (quoting the testimony of John Clegg, M.D.).

34. Caplan, *supra* note 3, at 597.

35. Houts, *supra* note 33, at 3.

36. Caplan, *supra* note 3, at 597.

37. Hensel, *Forensic Tests for Blood Alcohol: Where Do We Stand Today?*, 18 TRAUMA 30 (Oct. 1976).

38. *Id.*

39. *Id.*

40. Caplan, *supra* note 3, at 602.

41. *Id.*

the ratio between alcohol in the blood and alcohol in the air is 2,100/1;[42] that is, there is the same amount of alcohol in one part of blood as there is in 2,100 parts of breath. As the next section notes, however, this ratio can vary from person to person and, for a given person, it may vary from time to time. Dr. Kurt Dubowski of the University of Oklahoma College of Medicine is one of the leading authorities in the world on the subject and a past president of the American Academy of Forensic Sciences. Mason and Dubowski believe that the proper mean value for the population is approximately 1/2,300 under certain defined conditions. For that matter, Dubowski maintains that there is no such thing as a "normal" ratio between alcohol in blood and in expired alveolar breath. The ratio is not a constant. In any event, the ratio is a mathematical expression applying to a particular defined population, but not necessarily a given individual.

There is not only a relationship between the amount of alcohol in alveolar air and the amount in pulmonary blood; there is also a relationship between blood in the various parts of the body. After alcohol is absorbed into the blood, it distributes itself to the various organs in proportion to their water content and blood supply.[43] If we assign alcohol in the blood stream a value of 1.00 (the blood alcohol concentration or BAC), alcohol in the urine would have an approximate value of 1.30 and the alcohol in the brain 0.90.

Moreover, there is a relationship between the percent alcohol in the body as a whole (the whole body alcohol concentration) and the percent alcohol in the blood (the BAC). In the 1930s, Professor Erik Widmark of the University of Lund, Sweden, investigated this relationship.[44] Widmark termed this ratio the r factor, % alcohol in body (WBC)/% alcohol in blood (BAC).[45] Like the 2,100/1 ratio, the r factor is a variable. Widmark found that the average r factor is 0.68 for men, but he discovered a wide range of values even with his small data base

---

42. *Id.* Jones & Andersson, *Variability of the Blood/Breath Alcohol Ratio in Drinking Drivers*, 41 J. FORENSIC SCI. 916 (1996) (the study involved 799 drinking drivers; "During 1992, 1993, and 1994, the mean blood/breath ratios of alcohol were remarkably constant, being 2409 , 2407..., and 2421. ").

43. Winek, *Blood Alcohol Levels: Factors Affecting Predictions*, 19 TRIAL 40 (Jan. 1983).

44. Fitzgerald & Hume, *Erroneous Expert Opinions in the Civil and Criminal Trial of Intoxication Cases: Widmark Revisited*, THE CHAMPION, Dec. 1983, at 6.

45. *Id.* at 18. Kuwatch, *A New and Easier Method for Hand-Calculating BACs*, 5 DWI J. 1, 2-3, 8 n.3 (Oct. 1990) ("alcohol does not spread evenly throughout the body. Almost all of it is dissolved in the water-rich tissues of the body. Therefore, in order to calculate blood alcohol concentration, we must divide the weight of the alcohol by the weight of only that portion of the body that holds alcohol, rather than by the weight of the entire body. Widmark's original research, still valid today, found that the average man's body can hold alcohol in even distribution in 68% of its weight. Widmark called this '0.68' the 'r' factor. It varies from person to person, but research has shown that among normal men the range of values is from 0.50 to 0.90, with an average value of 0.68. For normal women, the range of values is from 0.45 to 0.63, with an average value of 0.55. Men and women have different average 'r' values because of sex-related differences in the proportion of body fat;" "The 'r' stands for 'reduzierte korpermasse,' or 'reduced body mass'").

of only 30 subjects.[46] The spread for male subjects was from 0.52 to 0.86, and the range for female subjects ran from 0.47 to 0.64.[47] The values were not closely bunched.[48]

The alcohol that reaches the brain and nervous system induces the observable effects of intoxication.[49] Ethanol acts as a central nervous system depressant. Alcohol initially affects the higher functions such as judgment. Alcohol next affects the more autonomic functions including muscular coordination. It can produce ataxia (muscular incoordination, delirium, drowsiness, flushed face, and vertigo.[50] Alcohol tends to release a person's inhibitions; this tendency accounts for the widespread popular misconception that alcohol is a stimulant rather than a depressant.

Researchers have developed a rough correlation between the extent of the observable effects and degree of intoxication. Dr. Dubowski has prepared the following chart:[51] These correlations have been tested in numerous controlled studies. In using the chart, however, the reader should bear in mind two caveats. One is that persons vary markedly in their tolerance to alcohol.[52]At a particular blood-alcohol concentration such as 0.07%, an inexperienced drinker might display many observable effects of intoxication while a chronic drinker might appear entirely sober. Second, these signs and symptoms are not specific to intoxication; many pathological conditions other than intoxication can cause similar symptoms.[53]

---

46. *Id.* at 19.

47. *Id.*

48. *Id.*

49. K. Dubowski, The Technology of Breath-Alcohol Analysis 5 n 2 (1991) ("while the blood sampled for enforcement purposes is necessarily venous, it is the arterial blood reaching the brain that brings about alcohol-related impairment").

50. Knoll, *Scientific Evidence of Intoxication*, The Advocate, Nov. 1970, at 7.

51. Copyright 1997 by Kurt M. Dubowski, Ph.D. Reprinted with permission.

52. Simpson, *Concentration Tolerance and the Influence of Alcohol*, 15 J. Anal. Tox. 47 (1991); Simpson, *Medicolegal Alcohol Determination: Comparison and Consequences of Breath and Blood Analysis*, 13 J. Anal. Tox. 361 (1989); Sullivan, Hauptman & Bronstein, *Lack of Observable Intoxication in Humans with High Plasma Alcohol Concentrations*, 32 J. Forensic Sci. 1660 (1987).

53. A new test, contrast sensitivity, can help identify a defendant's vision problems that may account for some of the symptoms. The new test can seemingly detect problems that escape the traditional E chart vision test. Moss, *Special vision test, court Breathalyzer ruling*, 73 A.B.A. J. 38 (May 1, 1987); Edwards, *A New Defense for DUI Cases: The Autointoxication Syndrome*, 17 The Champion 41 (Nov. 1993) (Japan has long recognized this syndrome; persons suffering from the syndrome "may develop" "drunken symptoms" "even when little or no alcohol has been consumed. These symptoms include alcoholic odor on the breath, drowsiness, staggering, and cloudiness of the conscious"; the syndrome "is caused by the yeast candida albicans (a yeast fungus) fermenting sugar and other simple carbohydrate foods in the gastrointestinal tract; the article cites a number of scientific articles discussing the syndrome").

The pharmacology of alcohol is a vast, complex subject that would warrant a separate text. Indeed, several exist. For our purposes, it is sufficient to understand that: After ingestion, alcohol finds its way into the blood, urine, and breath; there are ratios that generally determine the relationship between the alcohol concentrations in the whole body, blood, urine, and breath; and there is also a correlation between the various concentrations and the extent of a driver's observable effects of intoxication and impairment.

STAGES OF ACUTE ALCOHOLIC INFLUENCE / INTOXICATION

BLOOD-ALCOHOL CONCENTRATION grams/100 mL.	STAGE OF ALCOHOLIC INFLUENCE	CLINICAL SIGNS/SYMPTOMS
0.01-0.05	Subclinical	Influence/effects not apparent or obvious Behavior nearly normal by ordinary observation Impairment detectable by special tests
0.03-0.12	Euphoria	Mild euphoria, sociability, talkativeness Increased self-confidence; decreased inhibitions Diminution of attention, judgment and control Some sensory-motor impairment Slowed information processing Loss of efficiency in critical performance tests
0.09-0.25	Excitement	Emotional instability; loss of critical judgment Impairment of perception, memory and comprehension Decreased sensitory response; increased reaction time Reduced visual acuity, peripheral vision and glare recovery Sensory-motor incoordination; impaired balance Drowsiness
0.18-0.30	Confusion	Disorientation, mental confusion; dizziness Exaggerated emotional states (fear, rage, grief, etc.) Disturbances of vision (diplopia, etc.) and of perception of color, form, motion, dimensions Increased pain threshold Increased muscular incoordination; staggering gait; slurred speech Apathy, lethargy
0.25-0.40	Stupor	General inertia; approaching loss of motor functions Markedly decreased response to stimuli Marked muscular incoordination; inability to stand or walk Vomiting; incontinence of urine and feces Impaired consciousness; sleep or stupor
0.35-0.50	Coma	Complete unconsciousness; coma; anesthesia Depressed or abolished reflexes Subnormal temperature Impairment of circulation and respiration Possible death
0.45+	Death	Death from respiratory arrest

KURT M. DUBOWSKI, Ph.D., D.A.B.C.C., D.A.B.F.T
The University of Oklahoma
Department of Medicine
Oklahoma City, Oklahoma

Figure 22-1

§ 22-3. Starting Points for Estimating Blood Alcohol Concentration.

For most purposes under the substantive law, the critical alcohol concentration is the defendant's concentration at the time of the legally relevant event such as an accident.[54] Unfortunately, the police cannot administer a test to the defendant at that instant. A test is not administered until some later time. To estimate the defendant's alcohol concentration at the legally relevant time, the expert will choose one of two starting points and then extrapolate to the legally relevant time. The next section analyzes the extrapolation. This section deals with the two starting points most commonly used. The expert can start with the amount of alcohol consumed by the defendant before the legally relevant event and work forward in time to the relevant event. Alternatively, the expert can start with the indicated alcohol concentration at the time of the subsequent test and work backward in time to the relevant event.

§ 22-3(A). Amount of Alcohol Consumed.

One possible starting point is testimony about the amount of alcohol the defendant consumed. The source of this testimony could be the defendant's trial testimony, the defendant's pretrial admissions, or the testimony of a bartender, social host, or drinking companion. If the defendant's social host or companion knows only the quantity and type of beverage the defendant consumed and the court is unwilling to judicially notice the proof of the beverage, the prosecutor may have to call an expert (a bartender or liquor salesperson) to establish the proof. The expert must know both the quantity of liquid consumed and the proof of the beverage. Those two figures permit the expert to compute the amount of alcohol the defendant ingested. The expert first divides the proof by two. For example, 86 proof represents 43% alcohol by volume.[55] The expert next multiplies the number of ounces of beverage ingested by the percent of the beverage that is alcoholic, as in this computation:

10 ounces (beverage consumed)	×	50% alcoholic (½ of 100 proof)	=	5 ounces of alcohol consumed

54. Some jurisdictions have criminalized having a certain alcohol concentration within a specified number of hours *after* driving. Section 22-4 of this chapter discusses such legislation. In one jurisdiction, the courts have invalidated that type of legislation as being unconstitutionally overbroad. State v. Baker, 720 A.2d 1139 (Del. Sup. 1998).

55. Winek, *supra* note 43, at 42.

(This computation assumes that the defendant has no renal or liver disease, which can alter the volume of distribution or metabolism of ethanol.[56])

The next step in the computation is to determine the whole body alcohol concentration (WBC). To do so, the expert converts the defendant's body weight into the same unit of measurement as the amount of alcohol consumed. For example, if the expert determined the amount of alcohol consumed in ounces, the expert would convert the defendant's weight from pounds to the same unit of measurement, ounces. When the defendant weighs 200 pounds, the expert would convert that weight into 3,200 ounces. The expert then divides the amount of alcohol consumed by the defendant's body weight:

$$\frac{\text{5 ounces alcohol consumed}}{\text{3,200 ounces weight}} = \text{WBC}$$

After Hours	1 Drink				2 Drinks				3 Drinks				4 Drinks			
	4	3	2	1	4	3	2	1	4	3	2	1	4	3	2	1
Weight (lbs.) 80	—	—	—	.02	—	—	.05	.08	.07	.10	.10	.10	.12	.12	.15	.15
100	—	—	—	.02	—	—	.04	.06	.05	.07	.08	.09	.09	.10	.12	.13
120	—	—	—	.02	—	—	.03	.04	.03	.04	.06	.08	.06	.08	.09	.11
140	—	—	—	.01	—	—	.02	.04	.02	.03	.05	.06	.04	.06	.08	.09
160	—	—	—	.01	—	—	.02	.03	.01	.02	.04	.05	.03	.04	.06	.08
180	—	—	—	.01	—	—	.01	.03	—	.02	.03	.04	.02	.04	.05	.07
200	—	—	—	—	—	—	.01	.02	—	.01	.03	.04	.01	.03	.04	.06

After Hours	5 Drinks				6 Drinks				7 Drinks				8 Drinks			
	4	3	2	1	4	3	2	1	4	3	2	1	4	3	2	1
Weight (lbs.) 80	.17	.17	.19	.20	.19	.22	.22	.25	.25	.27	.27	.30	.29	.30	.32	.33
100	.13	.14	.16	.17	.16	.18	.19	.21	.20	.22	.23	.25	.24	.25	.27	.28
120	.09	.11	.13	.14	.13	.14	.16	.17	.15	.17	.19	.20	.19	.20	.22	.23
140	.07	.09	.10	.12	.10	.12	.13	.15	.13	.14	.16	.17	.15	.17	.18	.20
160	.06	.07	.09	.10	.08	.09	.11	.13	.10	.12	.13	.15	.13	.14	.16	.17
180	.04	.06	.07	.09	.06	.08	.09	.11	.09	.10	.12	.13	.11	.12	.14	.15
200	.03	.04	.05	.08	.05	.07	.08	.09	.07	.09	.10	.12	.09	.10	.12	.13

Figure 22-2

56. Rohrer, McMillen & Reed, *Calculation of Blood Alcohol Concentrations in Criminal Defendants*, 22 AM. J. TRIAL ADVOC. 177, 187 (1998).

The final step is converting from WBC into blood alcohol concentration (BAC). As stated in the last section, there is a general relationship between the two concentrations. The relationship is expressed by Widmark's r factor.[57] The WBC/BAC ratio is usually assumed to be 0.68.[58] However, as previously noted, 0.68 is an average, not a constant. In Widmark's study, there was a wide range of values for r; and the values reported were not bunched closely together.[59]

The final product of this computation is a BAC figure. The figure represents the BAC the defendant will attain when the alcohol ingested is completely absorbed. Unfortunately, this computation does not tell the expert when the defendant will achieve total absorption or what the defendant's BAC would be at any time other than complete absorption. To estimate those figures, the expert must extrapolate from this starting point. Extrapolation is discussed in § 22-4. The National Highway Traffic Safety Administration has released the charts, set out on the previous page, stating generalizations about the BAC level which persons of various weights should attain after consuming a particular number of drinks.[60]

§ 22-3(B). Alcohol Concentration Indicated by Test Administered After Event.

The expert can also estimate the BAC from a different starting point. When the test itself is not the legally relevant event, the expert can begin with the result of a test conducted after the legally relevant event and then, using extrapolation techniques, retroactively estimate the concentration at the time of the event. In the past 60 years, over 300 different methods have been developed for analyzing alcohol concentrations.[61] Dr. Dubowski estimates that in the past 140 years or so, well over 1,000 methods have been developed.[62] Most of the techniques analyze the body materials discussed in § 22-2: blood, urine, and breath. It is impossible to review all the techniques in a chapter of this size. We shall concentrate on the most popular techniques now in use.

Blood Analysis

Blood specimens are sometimes used for alcohol determinations. The alcohol concentration in the brain tissue (cells) is the concentration that induces the

---

57. Fitzgerald & Hume, *supra* note 44, at 18.

58. *Id.*

59. *Id.* at 19.

60. For purposes of these charts, "one drink" is a 12-ounce beer, a 4-ounce glass of wine, or a 1¼-ounce shot of 80-proof liquor.

61. Knoll, *supra* note 50, at 9.

62. K. Dubowski, The Technology of Breath-Alcohol Analysis 3 (1991) (hundreds of methods).

symptoms of intoxication experienced by the drinker and the signs observed by third parties. The scientist can use blood alcohol concentration to approximate the alcohol concentration inside the cell (but more commonly relies on established information on the relationship of alcohol concentration in various body materials to impairment and performance). There are several methodologies for measuring the alcohol concentration in blood.

Initially, the analyst obtains the blood sample; in some cases the analyst obtains the sample directly from the subject, but more often a third party obtains the sample and then delivers it to the analyst. When other sources for obtaining the sample are unsuitable, a qualified collector can extract vitreous humour.[63] Some techniques require a preliminary separation of the alcohol from the blood.[64] The separation can be accomplished by distillation, aeration, or diffusion.[65] In distillation, the alcohol is vaporized. Some laboratories use simple steam distillation[66] while a few laboratories employ the more sophisticated Kozelka-Hine apparatus.[67] In aeration, the expert utilizes a vacuum pump.[68] The apparatus consists of several test tubes connected by a chain of rubber tubing, and the pump separates the alcohol by sucking it out of the specimen.[69] Years ago the Southgate[70] and Bogen methods were used to modify the technique.[71] Finally, the analyst can effect separation by employing a diffusion or microdiffusion technique.[72] Widmark discovered that if blood is placed in a closed jar with acid dichromate but separated from it, vapors of alcohol in the blood pass from the blood to the compartment containing the acid dichromate.[73] The diffusion usually requires two hours.

After the preliminary separation, the alcohol can be analyzed by a technique called titration.[74] The analyst allows the separated alcohol to react with a reagent

63. Yip & Shum, *A Study on the Correlation of Blood and Vitreous Humour Alcohol Levels in the Late Absorption and Elimination Phases*, 30 MED. SCI. LAW 29 (1990); Harper, *A Comparative Study of the Microbiological Contamination of Postmortem Blood and Vitreous Humour Samples Taken for Ethanol Determination*, 43 FORENSIC SCI. INT'L 37 (1989) (even when other blood sources are contaminated by bacteria or fungi, vitreous humour may be free from contamination); Fernandez, Adulla, Linares, Tato & Bermejo, *A Comparative Pharmacokinetic Study of Ethanol in the Blood, Vitreous Humour and Aqueous Humour of Rabbits*, 41 FORENSIC SCI. INT'L 61 (1989).

64. Hensel, *supra* note 37, at 18.

65. *Id.* at 18-22.

66. *Id.* at 20.

67. *Id.* at 21. Our reviewer informs us that virtually no one uses this technique today.

68. *Id.* at 22.

69. *Id.* Our reviewer tells us that this technique is no longer popular.

70. *Id.*

71. *Id.* at 23.

72. *Id.* at 22.

73. *Id.* at 25.

74. Tarantino, *The .10 Percent Solution*, THE CHAMPION, July 1984, at 37.

such as potassium dichromate.[75] The alcohol will reduce the potassium dichromate, and the amount of potassium reduced reflects the amount of alcohol present.[76] By measuring the amount of potassium dichromate reduced, the amount of alcohol present in the sample can be calculated.

All of the above methods have been used in the past. However, in contemporary practice many of those methods are now of purely historical interest. For all practical purposes today alcohol is measured in liquid or solid biological materials by only two methodological principles: enzymatic oxidation methods or gas chromatography.[77]

As just stated in addition to traditional distillation, aeration, and diffusion techniques, enzymatic techniques can be used.[78] This technique also involves the destruction of the alcohol. An enzyme sometimes used is alcohol dehydrogenase. The enzyme catalyzes a reaction with alcohol[79] in the presence of diphosphopyridine nucleotide or nicotinamide adenine.[80] The reaction results in the conversion or destruction of the nucleotide or adenine.[81] The analyst then employs a spectrophotometer to measure the amount of nucleotide or adenine remaining.[82]

Still other laboratories use the gas chromatograph (GC) to analyze the alcohol concentration in blood. Some prefer GC as the method of choice.[83] Our reviewer tells us that GC is one of the most, if not the most, widely used method in current practice. Today in clinical practice enzymatic oxidation is the most extensively used technique while GC dominates forensic practice. Chapter 23, devoted to drug identification, contains a discussion of GC.

Blood analysis has limitations. The most obvious disadvantage for law enforcement agencies is that blood collection requires more highly trained personnel such as a physician, laboratory technician, or nurse. In fact, many state statutes provide that blood samples for intoxication may be taken only by such persons. The need for a medically trained phlebotomist raises a further problem. To obtain the blood sample, the police will usually have to transport the defendant to a clinic or hospital staffed by such personnel. The transportation consumes time that may make the expert's extrapolation less reliable.

---

75. Hensel, *supra* note 37, at 18.

76. *Id.*

77. K. Dubowski, The Technology of Breath-Alcohol Analysis 3 (1991) (listing chemical oxidation and gas chromatography).

78. Tarantino, *supra* note 74, at 37.

79. Hensel, *supra* note 37, at 27.

80. Tarantino, *supra* note 74, at 37.

81. Hensel, *supra* note 37, at 27. Our reviewer tells us that, in reality, the reaction results in a conversion rather than destruction.

82. *Id.*

83. Knoll, *supra* note 50, at 11. *But see* Laferty, *Ethyl Chloride: Possible Misidentification As Ethanol*, 39 J. Forensic Sci. 261 (1994) (using headspace gas chromatography).

A further problem is that the method of extracting the blood sample can render the blood analysis inadmissible at trial. The physician customarily sterilizes the area of skin before extracting the blood sample and may inadvertently use a sterilizing solution containing alcohol. Both scientists and courts are divided over the effect of the use of a solution containing alcohol. Some experiments indicate that the technician would have to be "excessively sloppy" in swabbing the area with the solution before the solution would cause any significant contamination.[84] A study by Dubowski and Essary urges that technicians withdrawing blood specimens follow certain precautions (such as using only dry sterile gauze pads for covering the puncture site) but concludes that contamination of blood specimens for analysis is today "a rare event."[85] Other writers assert flatly that the use of alcohol to sterilize the arm can render the blood test worthless.[86]As discussed later, courts are similarly split. Some hold that the use of an alcohol sterilizing solution affects only the weight of the blood analysis evidence, but others exclude the analysis when the physician employs an alcohol solution.[87]

Urine Analysis

Urine analysis is an indirect method of determining the subject's blood alcohol concentration. It is still sometimes used in states such as California, Minnesota, and Ohio. The determination of blood alcohol concentration from urinalysis requires the use of a conversion factor between BAC and alcohol concentration in blood. The factors cited most often are 1.3 and 1.33; the BAC is assigned a value of 1.00, and the concentration in urine is expected to be roughly a third higher.[88]

As an indicator of the BAC, the alcohol concentration in urine suffers from several weaknesses. To begin with, there is a controversy in the scientific community over the proper ratio.[89] Some writings cite urine/blood conversion

---

84. Winek, *supra* note 43, at 41.

85. Dubowski & Essary, *Contamination of Blood Specimens for Alcohol Analysis During Collection*, 4 ABSTRACTS & REVIEW IN ALCOHOL & DRIVING 7 (Apr.-June 1983).

86. Houts, *supra* note 33, at 8.

87. Tarantino, *supra* note 74, at 38.

88. Caplan, *supra* note 3, at 606; Hensel, *supra* note 37, at 31.

89. *Id.;* Hutton, *Cross-Examination of a Urine Test*, CACJ FORUM, Vol. 21, No. 2, at 81 (1994) (the author quotes Dr. Dubowski as writing that "the only urine specimen which could, in theory, be confidently employed for alcohol analysis for purposes of estimating the co-existing BAC is ureteral urine) clearly an impractical specimen for law enforcement purposes" and "[t]here is massive documentation that the blood alcohol concentration cannot be established sufficiently reliably for forensic purposes from the alcohol concentration of a pooled bladder urine specimen because of the extensive variability of the blood:urine ratio of alcohol"); Jones, *Ethanol Distribution Ratios Between Urine and Capillary Blood in Controlled Experiments and in Apprehended Drunk Drivers*, 37 J. FORENSIC SCI. 1992) ("the UAC/BAC ratio of ethanol varied widely").

factors ranging from 0.8:1 to 2.0:1.[90] The reported range of conversion factors is even wider than those citations.[91] In one Irish study, the researchers compared direct blood alcohol readings with blood alcohol concentrations indirectly estimated from urine.[92] In a third of the cases, the indirect estimate exceeded the actual BAC.[93] In one case in which the actual BAC was only .11%, the BAC estimated from urine was over .18%.[94]

One potential source of error in urinalysis is that the analyst might collect a urine sample including a urinary bladder accumulation.[95] The longer the person retains urine in the bladder, the greater is the risk of error. In one reported case, in which the subject retained urine for six hours, the BAC was under .08%; but the BAC estimated from urine was almost 0.16%.[96] To compensate for this source of error, the collector should direct the subject to attempt to empty his bladder before collecting the specimen for analysis.[97] The first urine sample ought to be discarded, and the second specimen submitted for analysis.[98]

Because of the doubts about BAC estimated from urine, the National Highway Traffic Safety Administration has discouraged the use of urine tests.[99] Some experts recommend that urinalysis be used only when a blood or breath sample is unavailable or contaminated.[100] A few states have adopted that recommendation.[101]

---

90. 2 R. Erwin, Defense of Drunk Driving Cases § 25.01, at 25-2.3 (3d ed. 1984).

91. Winek & Esposito, *Comparative Study of Ethanol Levels in Blood Versus Bone Marrow, Vitreous Humor, Bile and Urine*, 17 Forensic Sci. Int'l 27, 28, 35 (1981).

92. R. Erwin, *supra* note 90, at 25-3.

93. *Id.*

94. *Id.*

95. *Id.* at 25-2.1.

96. *Id.*

97. *Id.* at 25-4. Some persons cannot completely empty their bladder. Kessler v. Department of Motor Vehicles, 9 Cal. App. 4th 1134, 12 Cal. Rptr. 2d 46 (1992) (an administrative regulation, Title 17, § 1219.2(a), California Code of Regulations, requires that the officer have the suspect void the bladder at least twenty minutes before collecting a urine sample).

98. *Id.*

99. Nat'l Highway Traffic and Safety Ad., U.S. Dep't Transp., Highway Safety Program Manual No. 8, *quoted in* R. Erwin, *supra* note 90, at 25-1-2. Hutton, *Cross-Examination of a Urine Test*, CACJ Forum, Vol. 21, No. 2, p. 81 (1994) ("several states have repealed laws that authorized urine as a test for blood alcohol, and legislation is periodically introduced in California to abolish use of the test").

100. Winek & Esposito, *supra* note 91, at 27.

101. Sher, *That's All She Wrote*, Forum, vol. 24, no. 4, p. 8 (1998) ("The [California] legislature made several major changes in DUI law this year. Starting next year, urine testing will no longer be available for most persons arrested for DUI offenses . . . . Urine testing will still be allowed if a blood or breath test is not available, and remains an option where the officer has reasonable cause to believe the person is under the influence of a drug other than alcohol").

Breath Analysis

In 1927, it was first proposed that police use breath testing devices to measure BAC.[102] The proposal had great appeal because it opened up the possibility of tests administered by police at the time of arrest. That possibility was more attractive than blood and urine tests which sometimes necessitated transporting the subject to a hospital and the consequent delay.[103] Breath tests can be conducted in a non-laboratory setting. Since 1927, breath devices have proliferated.[104] Many, like the Drunkometer developed by Harger, are no longer in use. Some devices such as the Portable Intoximeter and the Vacu-Sampler used in the past were not true testing devices; the instruments merely capture and preserve breath samples for subsequent analysis. However, most of the instruments commonly referred to as breath tests actually analyze the breath sample. This section discusses three conventional devices, the Breathalyzer, the Gas Chromatograph, and the Intoxilyzer, as well as a newer device, the passive alcohol sensor.

The Breathalyzer

The Breathalyzer was first developed by then Lieutenant R.F. Borkenstein of the Indiana State Police. It operates on the basis of a chemical reaction between alcohol and potassium dichromate. In Borkenstein's model of the Breathalyzer, the test process begins when the subject exhales into the device. The device captures 52.5 ml of air.[105] "The ideal specimen for breath-alcohol analysis is expired alveolar air . . . ."[106] The operator then turns a knob that releases the breath sample into tubing leading to an open ampoule containing a solution of potassium dichromate in sulfuric acid.[107] If the breath contains alcohol, the alcohol will react with and reduce the potassium dichromate. The result of the reaction is that the solution loses some of its yellow color[108] and that the light can

---

102. Hensel, *supra* note 37, at 33.

103. Our reviewer points out that the sample is often collected in jail.

104. Hensel, *supra* note 37, at 33.

105. *Id.* at 38.

106. K. Dubowski, The Technology of Breath-Alcohol Analysis 5 (1991).

107. Doctor Dubowski explains the sampling method in this manner. The approach uses the heated, metal piston-cylinder type of sample chamber found in manual Breathalyzers. It traps a fixed volume (52.5 mL) of end expiratory breath in the chamber and delivers the entire sample as a bubble stream to a test ampoule through the action of a descending weighted pistol. This arrangement collects only the terminal portion of whatever breath traverses the vertical cylinder; excess breath exits through ports near the top of the chamber. *Id.* at 6; Feldman & Cohen, *The Questionable Accuracy of Breathalyzer Tests*, 19 Trial 54 (June 1983).

108. K. Dubowski, The Technology of Breath-Alcohol Analysis 10 (1991) ("Oxidation of the alcohol to acetic acid produces a proportional change in reagent color from its original yellow to shades of yellow-green or green").

then transmit more easily through the solution. The device measures the change in the transmittance of light or optical density.[109] Breathalyzers use a tungsten lamp and a blue filter that passes light through the solution. The amount of light transmitted through the solution is gauged by a photocell (a selenium photovoltaic cell).[110]

The Breathalyzer has several advantages. The instrument produces a test result quickly; the chemical reaction is complete within 90 seconds.[111] Furthermore, the instrument can be operated by a police officer at the scene. Forty hours of training are normally adequate to familiarize an officer with the instrument's operation. In addition, there is substantial evidence that the breath concentration correlates with the blood concentration.[112]

However, the Breathalyzer is not infallible. The critics of the Breathalyzer point to three major sources of error in breathalyzer testing.

Uncertainty in Breathalyzer measurements of breath alcohol concentration. One potential source of error is the uncertainty in the measurement of the breath alcohol concentration by the Breathalyzer. In one of Dr. Dubowski's studies, Breathalyzer measurements were checked against gas chromatograph measurements.[113] He found that the Breathalyzer reading sometimes differed from the gas chromatograph measurement.

Imprecision in the ratio used to convert breath alcohol concentration to blood alcohol concentration. A second source is the 1:2,100 ratio or partition coefficient used to convert breath alcohol concentration to blood alcohol concentration. The ratio assumes that the amount of alcohol in one part of blood is equivalent to the alcohol in 2,100 parts of alveolar air. The ratio was originally derived by applying Henry's law to the alcohol escaping from the blood and entering the lung area. However, subsequent research revealed that for several reasons, the ratio may not be valid for a particular defendant.[114] (The questions

---

109. Feldman & Cohen, *The Questionable Accuracy of Breathalyzer Tests*, 19 TRIAL 54 (June 1983).

110. Bergh & Rodgers, *On the Choice of Color Filters for the Breathalyzer*, 19 J. FORENSIC SCI. 684-85 (1974).

111. Feldman & Cohen, *supra* note 109, at 55.

112. Pribor, Campbell, Hebb & Trost, *Ethanol and Vehicular Safety: The Nashville Experience: Part II. Breath-/Blood-Alcohol Correlation*, CLIN. FORUM 21, 24 (June 1985) ("[A]t a breath alcohol level of 0.10%, 95 out of 100 persons will be legally intoxicated; at a breath alcohol level of 0.12%, 997 persons out of 1,000 will be intoxicated; and at a breath alcohol level of 0.13%, 99,994 persons out of 10,000 will be DUI").

113. K. DUBOWSKI, ALCOHOL, DRUGS AND TRAFFIC SAFETY 637-47 (L. Goldberg ed. 1981).

114. Gerstenzang, *Breath Issues — Partition Ratio or Blood-Breath Presumption*, 23 THE CHAMPION 52, 53-54 (Jan./Feb. 1999); Smith, *Science, The Intoxilyzer, and Breath Alcohol Testing*, 11 THE CHAMPION 8, 15 (May 1987) (Henry's Law applies to systems that have attained equilibrium; "[a]n unknown amount of time is required for fresh air introduced to the lung to attain an equilibrium concentration of alcohol"). Some of the relevant physical factors are biological

about the validity of the ratio help explain why so many states have amended their penal laws to redefine the criminal offense as driving with a certain breath alcohol concentration.).

The ratio might not hold true because the defendant's breath sample was not comprised solely of alveolar or deep lung air. In controlled studies, because of illness or lung weaknesses, some persons produced breath samples that contained only 60% alveolar air; the deep lung air was mixed with shallow air.[115] The correct partition ratio for such a sample might be 1:3,200 rather than 1:2,100.[116]

A complicating factor is that a person's ratio can vary from time to time.[117] One researcher reported that subjects' ratios varied as much as 24% during an

---

variables. Simpson, *Accuracy and Precision of Breath-Alcohol Measurements for a Random Subject in the Postabsorptive State*, 33 CLIN. CHEM. 261 (1987). There is evidence that the greatest inaccuracy occurs during the absorptive stage. Simpson, *Accuracy and Precision of Breath Alcohol Measurements for Subjects in the Absorptive State*, 33 CLIN. CHEM. 753 (1987); Simpson, *Incorrect Overestimates of Blood Alcohol Concentration from Breath Test Results*, 14 J. ANAL. TOX. 263 (1990). *See also* Logan & Gullberg, *Lack of Effect of Tongue Piercing on an Evidential Breath Alcohol Test*, 43 J. FORENSIC SCI. 239 (1998) ("For the purposes of breath alcohol testing, oral jewelry should be treated in the same manner as dental work, and may be left in place during the test without affecting the outcome."); Logan, Distefano & Case, *Evaluation of the Effect of Asthma Inhalers and Nasal Decongestant Sprays on a Breath Alcohol Test*, 43 J. FORENSIC SCI. 197 (1998) ("The only preparation which produced any effect on the instrument was Primatene Mist which contains 34% ethyl alcohol. The alcohol was, however, eliminated from the breath in the usual pattern of mouth alcohol elimination, and after 5 min there was no longer any effect.").

115. 1 R. ERWIN, DEFENSE OF DRUNK DRIVING CASES § 16.02(2)(a) (2d ed. 1966); Gerstenzang, *Breath Issues — Partition Ratio or Blood-Breath Presumption*, 23 THE CHAMPION 52, 55-56 (Jan.-Feb. 1999) ("Hyperventilization for 20 seconds before performing the ABT causes an 11 percent reduction in BrAC. Three deep breaths before the sample breath reduce BrAC by 4 percent. After breath holding for 15 s. before exhalation, the BrAC increases by 12% (for a minimum exhalation) and 6 percent (for a maximum exhalation). A 30 s. breath hold before exhalation increases BrAC by 16 percent").

116. *Id.*; Belotti, *The Preparation and Trial of a Drunken Driving Case Involving a Breathalyzer, in* SCIENTIFIC AND EXPERT EVIDENCE 195, 209 (2d ed. 1981). *See generally* 1 R. ERWIN, DEFENSE OF DRUNK DRIVING CASES ch. 18 (3d ed. 1984); Heifer, *Breathalcohol-Concentration/Bloodalcohol-Concentration: Utopia of a forensically usable means of evidence*, 23 BLUTALKOHOL 229 (July 1986).

117. Comment, *Breath Alcohol Analysis: Can It Withstand Modern Scientific Scrutiny?*, 5 NO. KY. L. REV. 207, 215 (1978). *See also* Scott, *A Short Discussion of McDonald*, 16 C.A.C.J. FORUM 21-22 (Sept.-Oct. 1989) (attacking the factual assumption that a person's partition ratio does not change); Wade, *DUI Statistics Often Don't Add Up*, 13 THE ADVOCATE 20, 21 (Apr. 1991) ("Even more problematic for presumptive statutes are findings that the blood:breath ratio is not even stable for a given individual. [S]tudies have found that BAC and BrAC measurements ... fluctuate 0.03% or more over short time periods. When repeated measurements of the combined blood:breath ratios were taken over longer time periods, variations as great as 1100 to 3100 were found within the same person. Consequently, it is debatable whether a person's 'true' blood:breath ratio can ever be determined ....").

experiment.[118] A British research team reached the same conclusion.[119] The British researchers declared that "even in the same person there were significant discrepancies" and that the ratio "varies ... widely in the same person with time."[120] However, a caveat is in order: The British study has been subjected to severe criticism. Dr. Dubowski believes that many of the results in the experiments were caused by instrumental problems and the failure to use fully (expired) alveolar air samples. It is clear, however, that the ratio varies from person to person. Values as low as 1,142 and as high as 7,000 have been reported.[121] The true average probably lies somewhere between 1,900 and 2,400.[122] Moreover, some claim that that the male average differs from the female average[123] although our reviewer states that the claim has proven to be unfounded.

The cumulative effect of these variations in the ratio is that in some cases, the use of the 1:2,100 ratio results in an erroneously high blood alcohol concentration estimate. In 1980, Dr. Dubowski discussed the problem in testimony in a trial in Anchorage, Alaska.[124] In his testimony, Dr. Dubowski stated that in his experiments using instruments relying on the 1:2,100 ratio, in 86% of the cases the instruments yielded results lower than independently

---

118. Comment, *Breath Alcohol Analysis: Can It Withstand Modern Scientific Scrutiny?*, 5 No. KY. L. REV. 207, 215 (1978).

119. Alobaidi, Hill & Payne, *Significance of Variations in Blood: Breath Partition Coefficient of Alcohol*, 1976 BRIT. MED. J. 1479. Our reviewer adds the caveat that there are serious questions about the methodology of this research.

120. *Id.* at 1481.

121. Frajola, *How to Cross Examine the Operator of a Breathtesting Machine*, *in* NAT'L ASS'N CRIM. DEF. LAWYERS 1985 ANNUAL MEETING 8; ERWIN, *supra* note 21, at 51; Tarantino, *The .10 Percent Solution*, THE CHAMPION, May 1985, at 41.

122. Mason & Dubowski, *Breath Alcohol Analysis: Uses, Methods, and Some Forensic Problems — Review and Opinion*, 21 J. FORENSIC SCI. 9, 24 (1976); Thompson, *supra* note 14, at 328. Labianca & Simpson, *Statistical Analysis of Blood- to Breath-Alcohol Ratio Data in the Logarithm-Transformed and Non-Transformed Modes*, 34 EUR. J. CLIN. CHEM. CLIN. BIOCHEM. 111 (1996) (in the opinion of the authors, the data "is a refutation of the argument that breath-alcohol analyzers relying on a 2100:1 blood/breath ratio tend to underestimate the blood-alcohol concentrations of driving-while-intoxicated arrestees because the commonly accepted mean postabsorptive ratio is 2300:1. In fact, whenever the absorption status of a driving-while-intoxicated arrestee at the time of a breath test cannot be definitively established, the results of this work support the application of a relative error rate of -40% to +28% for 95% of the population...."); Giguiere & Simpson, *Medicolegal Alcohol Determination: In Vivo Blood/Breath Rations*, *in* PROCEEDINGS, 27TH MEETING INT'L ASS'N FORENSIC TOXICOLOGISTS 494 (V. McLinden & D. Honey, eds., 1990) ("the post-absorptive mean blood/breath ratio is approximately 2300:1").

123. Woodford, *Sex Bias in the DWI Scale for Blood Alcohol Testing*, 3 D.W.I. J. 4 (July 1988) ("By measuring a woman using the male scale, she will inevitably score as though she had consumed more alcohol than in fact she has"). Our reviewer states that this claim rests on a misinterpretation of the available data.

124. ERWIN, *supra* note 21, at 7.

determined blood alcohol concentrations at the same time.[125] In 14% of the cases the underestimate did not occur. Dr. Dubowski has pointed out, however, that it would be fallacious to leap to the conclusion that the use of the ratio leads to an overestimate in 14% of the cases. As he has explained, the 14% figure includes estimates identical to the actual blood-alcohol concentration, harmless overestimates in the third decimal place which were eliminated by truncating, and finally a much smaller percentage of true overestimates.

In a 1990 New Jersey case, *State v. Downie,*[126] Dr. Dubowski clarified and extended his earlier testimony:

> In another study of subjects in the post-absorptive phase, involving 388 paired venous blood/breath samples, Dr. Dubowski found that in 86% of the cases, the Breathalyzer underestimated the blood-alcohol level. In 14% of the cases, it did not underestimate the blood-alcohol level. Of that 14%, in 2.3% of the cases the Breathalyzer stated exactly the blood-alcohol content. In 9.4% of the cases, the Breathalyzer overestimated the blood-alcohol level at the third decimal level, where it has no impact on the subject's Breathalyzer reading. In only 2.3% of cases did the Breathalyzer materially overestimate the blood-alcohol level potentially to the detriment of an accused.

---

125. *Id.* at 8. *See also* Gullberg, *An Application of Probability Theory to a Group of Breath-Alcohol and Blood-Alcohol Data*, 35 J. FORENSIC SCI. 1342, 1351 (1990) (the overestimation of blood alcohol from breath alcohol "is a very unlikely event"); Harding, Laessig & Field, *Field Performance of the Intoxilyzer 5000: A Comparison of Blood- and Breath-Alcohol Results in Wisconsin Drivers*, 35 J. FORENSIC SCI. 1022, 1027 (1990) ("the Intoxilyzer 5000 is likely to underestimate blood alcohol concentrations in the driving population"); Frankvoort, Mulder & Neuteboom, *The Laboratory Testing of Evidential Breath Testing Machines*, 35 FORENSIC SCI. INT'L 27 (1987) (although the results in general were good, the researchers observed that the results tended to underestimate actual concentration); Harding & Field, *Breathalyzer Accuracy in Actual Enforcement Practice: A Comparison of Blood- and Breath-Alcohol Results in Wisconsin Drivers*, 32 J. FORENSIC SCI. 1235, 1239 (1987) ("Breathalyzer and blood-alcohol results correlated well and ... blood-alcohol concentration tended to be underestimated by the Breathalyzer"). *But see* Simpson, *Incorrect Overestimates of Blood Alcohol Concentration from Breath Test Results*, 14 J. ANAL. TOX. 263 (1990); Simpson, *Medicolegal Alcohol Determination: Widmark Revisited*, 34 CLIN. CHEM. 888 (1988) (emphasizing the magnitude of the risk of overestimation).

126. 117 N.J. 450, 569 A.2d 242, *cert. denied,*498 U.S. 819 (1990). *See also* Harding, Laessig & Field, *Field Performance of the Intoxilyzer 5000: A Comparison of Blood- and Breath-Alcohol Results in Wisconsin Drivers*, 35 J. FORENSIC SCI. 1022, 1027 (1990) ("Compared with the blood-alcohol result, Intoxilyzer 5000 results were lower by more than 0.01g/210L 67% of the time, within 0.01g/210L 31% of the time, and higher by more than 0.01g/210L 2% of the time"; "the Intoxilyzer 5000 is likely to underestimate blood-alcohol concentrations in the driving population"). *See also* Friel, Logan & Baer, *An Evaluation of the Reliability of Widmark Calculations Based on Breath Alcohol Measurements*, 40 J. FORENSIC SCI. 91 (1995) ("At the 95% confidence level, the calculated dose at 105 and 125 min. did not overestimate the true dose....").

Hence, this source of error should work to the defendant's material detriment in only a small fraction of cases.

Nevertheless, on balance Dr. Dubowski has strongly recommended that the results of analyses for alcohol in breath be reported in terms of the actual, measured breath-alcohol concentration, rather than the supposedly equivalent blood-alcohol concentration:

> The latter practice relies on an assumed equivalence or conversion factor which is neither the mean value of the blood/breath alcohol concentration ratio for the population at large, nor is it known to apply to the tested subject to the requisite degree of certainty for criminal . . . judicial proceeding (i.e. beyond a reasonable doubt).[127]

The National Safety Council Committee on Alcohol and Other Drugs, the Uniform Vehicle Code, and many states have adopted this recommendation.[128]

The susceptibility of the Breathalyzer to interference. A third potential source of error in Breathalyzer analysis is the alleged susceptibility of the Breathalyzer to radio frequency interference (RFI) or electromagnetic interference (EMI). Many models have sophisticated electronic circuitry, which might make them vulnerable to interference. In September 1981, the Dade County, Florida police department notified one of the leading manufacturers of alcohol testing devices, Smith & Wesson Electronics, that interference from police radios had caused some of its Breathalyzers to register erratic readings.[129] That notice prompted Smith & Wesson to investigate the susceptibility of its products to RFI.

In January 1982, Smith & Wesson issued a customer advisory informing purchasers of its products that its Model 1000 was subject to RFI but that a modification of the model would make it relatively immune to RFI.[130] In the same advisory, Smith & Wesson asserted that its other models were resistant to RFI. The advisory read: "The Breathalyzer series 900 and 900A, and our new Infrared Breathalyzer Model 2000 are not sensitive to radio frequency interference."[131] The Model 1000 (which is no longer on the market) had more elaborate circuitry than either the 900 or the 900A, and it makes sense that the Model 1000 would be more vulnerable to RFI.

On September 10, 1982, Smith & Wesson issued another customer advisory. The company acknowledged that further experiments indicated that the models 900 and 900A were also sensitive to RFI. The second recall bulletin had much more impact than the first. Smith & Wesson had marketed only a few Model

---

127. K. DUBOWSKI, THE TECHNOLOGY OF BREATH-ALCOHOL ANALYSIS 22 (1991).

128. *Id.*

129. Lauter, *Breathalyzer Defect Jeopardizes Many Drunk Driving Convictions*, NAT'L L.J., June 7, 1982.

130. Joye, *supra* note 2, at 62.

131. *Id.*

1000s, but it had sold over 6,000 Model 900s and 2,000 Model 900As.[132] (At one time, those models represented roughly half the nationwide market for breath-testing equipment, but even they are no longer in production.)

Smith & Wesson's two customer advisories triggered private and government research into the RFI problem. One research study was released in early 1983.[133] That publication reported that:

— Model 900 is "quite resistant to RFI";[134] and
— Model 900A is "very sensitive to RFI and unsuitable for use as a reliable indicator of percentage of blood alcohol."[135]

At roughly the same time the National Highway Traffic Safety Administration directed the Law Enforcement Standards Laboratory of the National Bureau of Standards to investigate the RFI phenomenon.[136] In May 1983 the Laboratory released its report entitled "Limited Electromagnetic Interference Testing of Evidentiary Breath Testers."[137] That report initially surveys test programs conducted in Arizona, Illinois, Maryland, Michigan, Minnesota, New York, North Carolina, South Carolina, and Texas.[138] The report summarizes the results of those programs by declaring that "these ... programs indicate that less than one percent of the devices tested were found to be susceptible to RFI in the environments where they were used."[139] The report then describes the Laboratory's own research. The report states: "[T]his issue is not of the magnitude it was first alleged to be. RFI susceptibility among EBTs (evidential breath testers) in the field is minimal."[140]

Although the Laboratory's report did much to allay the fears caused by the Smith & Wesson customer advisories, the report came under fire.[141] A Minneapolis firm, Nichols, Kruger, Starks & Carthers, received information indicating that the final Laboratory report downplayed concerns expressed in the report's preliminary drafts.[142] The firm filed a Freedom of Information Act

---

132. *Id.*

133. Feldman & Cohen, *supra* note 109, at 54.

134. *Id.* at 57.

135. *Id.* at 58.

136. *Id.* at 64.

137. Reprinted in ERWIN, *supra* note 21, at 84.

138. *Id.* at 87.

139. *Id.*

140. *Id.* Indeed, the report may overstate the magnitude of the problem. According to our reviewer, the NIST borrowed a simulator from the Colorado state authorities. The researchers did not realize that the alcohol concentration in the simulator decreases as it is used repeatedly.

141. Kaster, *RFI Testing on Breath Alcohol Measuring Devices: The NBS-NHTSA Cover-Up*, THE CHAMPION, May 1984, at 8.

142. *Id.* at 12.

request for the preliminary drafts.[143] The government initially denied the request; but many of the documents were subsequently disclosed after the firm filed suit in Federal District Court in Minneapolis.[144] The documents were revealing. The draftsman of the preliminary versions of the report, John Adams, evidently did not sign the Final Report.[145] The original version of the report did not contain the language, "minimal effect."[146] The Laboratory tested only 16 of the 28 evidential breath testers in general use in the United States.[147] The Final Report refers to the tested devices only by code, but the documents divulged in the FOIA suit explain the code.[148] Furthermore, the original draft of the report contained several recommendations for procedures to protect EBTs from RFI that were omitted in the Final Report.[149] Some critics charged that the Final Report "can be seen as nothing less than a coverup of the actual test data."[150]

In light of the controversy over RFI, several states prescribed procedures that their police departments and highway patrols had to use to minimize the possibility of RFI.[151] Several states implemented the procedures recommended by Smith & Wesson.[152] However, "none of the states followed the recommendations made in the [original version of the Laboratory] Report to rectify potential RFI problems,"[153] and the critics assailed the procedures recommended by Smith & Wesson as being "inadequate, incomplete, and possibly scientifically unsound."[154] To a degree, the controversy surfaced in the state courts. As noted later, courts in Massachusetts, Minnesota, New Jersey, and Rhode Island found the evidence of RFI sufficiently impressive to justify imposing new limitations on the admissibility of breathalyzer evidence. In Ohio, an administrative regulation requires that intoxilyzers be tested for RFI.[155]

Dr. Dubowski has cautioned that the so-called RFI problem is a "red herring." He points out that no one has ever demonstrated that RFI has ever produced a single incorrect breath-alcohol analysis result in field practice. He dismisses the National Bureau of Standards report. He believes that the NBS researchers failed to distinguish between the unavoidable variation among successive simulator test results, the inevitable changes in results due to alcohol depletion of the simulator

---

143. *Id.* at 13.
144. *Id.*
145. *Id.*
146. *Id.* at 14.
147. *Id.* at 10.
148. *Id.* at 15.
149. *Id.* at 16.
150. *Id.* at 30.
151. *Id.* at 11-13.
152. *Id.* at 11.
153. *Id.*
154. *Id.* at 13.
155. State v. Yoder, 613 N.E.2d 626 (Ohio 1993) (OHIO ADMIN. CODE 3701-53-02(C)).

solution, and true "interference" from electromagnetic sources. Furthermore, their definition of "susceptibility" was so broad that it included all these sources of variation and systematic error. Dr. Dubowski concludes that there is insufficient evidence that a serious RFI problem exists.[156] In his view, the RFI issue has largely disappeared from the scene; and for that reason, his laboratory no longer follows the original Smith & Wesson recommendations.

Practical limitations. There are practical limitations on the Breathalyzer. Its turnaround time is seven to eight minutes, longer than that of many other devices.[157] Furthermore, it is "more operator-dependent for correct and properly sequenced purging, breath sampling, and analysis."[158] As a consequence, it is now used primarily at "low-test volume locations or test sites that have irregular patterns of test activity."[159] In the field today, gas chromatograph and infrared devices are dominant.

Gas Chromatography

Since the mid-1970s, the gas chromatograph has become increasingly popular as a technique for measuring alcohol concentration. The GC-based devices such as the GC-Intoximeter Mark IV are in use in Arizona and California and abroad in such countries as New Zealand. Chapter 23, devoted to drug identification, discusses GC.

As a breath testing device, GC has strengths and weaknesses. A strength is its relative specificity.[160] The GC can differentiate between ethanol and closely related chemicals such as methanol, acetone, and acetaldehyde.[161] However, GC suffers from some of the same weaknesses as the Breathalyzer models. Like the Breathalyzer, the GC measures the breath alcohol concentration; and that the older breath-alcohol GC devices converted that figure into a blood concentration on the basis of the 1:2,100 ratio.[162] As previously noted, an individual's partition coefficient varies from time to time, and the coefficient varies widely from individual to individual. Similarly, there have been claims that some GC breath

---

156. Samija, Shajani & Wong, *Radio Frequency Interference (RFI) Effects on Evidentiary Breath Testing Using the Breathalyzer Models 900 and 900A*, J. CAN. SOC'Y FORENSIC SCI. 211 (1986).

157. K. DUBOWSKI, THE TECHNOLOGY OF BREATH-ALCOHOL ANALYSIS 13 (1991).

158. *Id.*

159. *Id.*

160. Jones, *The Precision and Accuracy of a Gas Chromatograph Intoximeter Breath Alcohol Device, Part I — In Vitro Experiments*, 18 J. FORENSIC SCI. 75 (1978). *See also* Senkowski & Thompson, *The Accuracy of Blood Alcohol Analysis Using Headspace Gas Chromatography When Performed on Clotted Samples*, 35 J. FORENSIC SCI. 176 (1990).

161. *Id.*

162. Hutton, *Cross-Examination of a Criminalist in a Gas Chromatograph Case*, *in* SCIENTIFIC AND EXPERT EVIDENCE 221, 231 (2d ed. 1981).

testing devices, including the Alco-Analyzer Gas Chromatograph (now out of production) , were subject to RFI.[163] One police sergeant asserted that RFI can affect both the chart and the digital readout of the Alco-Analyzer GC.[164]

Infrared Instruments

Just as infrared instruments have been adapted to drug identification, such instruments are now used in intoxication testing.[165] Early in this decade IR devices became "the most common new or replacement devices for law enforcement (and many clinical and research) applications."[166] Several IR instruments such as the BAC DataMaster and Intoxilyzer Models 1400 and 5000[167] are commercially available. They typically employ a nonlaser source of infrared light.[168] The subject blows into a cell or chamber where the breath is captured. The instrument directs a beam of infrared light through the chamber.[169] Any ethanol in the breath will absorb light at the wavelength of 3.39 microns.[170] When the light passes through the chamber, it falls on a photocell,[171] which measures the infrared light at the 3.39 micron wavelength. By measuring the light falling on the cell, the instrument can determine how much light of that wavelength was absorbed by the breath.[172]

---

163. Freed, *Radio Frequency Interference with the Model 1000SA Alco-Analyzer Gas Chromatograph*, 28 J. Forensic Sci. 985 (1983).

164. *Id.* at 986, 991.

165. *See generally* Smith, *Science, the Intoxilyzer, and Breath Alcohol Testing — Part I,* 11 The Champion 8 (May 1987); Smith, *Science, the Intoxilyzer, and Breath Alcohol Testing,* 11 The Champion 5 (June 1987).

166. K. Dubowski, The Technology of Breath-Alcohol Analysis 16 (1991).

167. *Id.* at 3.

168. Hensel, *supra* note 37, at 40.

169. *Id.*

170. *Id.* at 39; K. Dubowski, The Technology of Breath-Alcohol Analysis 17 (1991) ("IR absorption spectrometry uses wavelengths between 770 nm and 12,000 nm. When a substance absorbs IR radiation, vibrational or rotational motion is excited or intensified in the molecules of that substance").

171. Hensel, *supra* note 37, at 40. The Intoximeter Model 3000 isolates an absorption band at 3.45 microns.

172. *Id. See also* Gullberg, *Developing a New Computerized Breath Test Program: Washington's Experience with the BAC Verifier Datamaster*, 16 J. Police Sci. & Admin. 1, 6 (1988) ("Beer's law, which makes transmittance a function of concentration, is the controlling principle"); Cowan, *Does the Intoxilyzer 4011AS-A Conform to the Beer-Lambert Law?*, 28 J. Forensic Sci. Soc'y 179 (1988) (the Intoxilyzer instruments tested showed excellent conformity with the law).

Infrared breath testing devices have numerous advantages. They are nondestructive.[173] An IR analysis is also rapid; the test can be complete in 90 seconds. Its turnaround time is a fraction of that of the old Breathalyzer. Furthermore, laboratory personnel can quickly be trained to operate IR devices; some devices require only six hours of training. Moreover, researchers report that the leading Intoxilyzers meet or exceed the United States Department of Transportation's model specifications for evidential breath-alcohol devices.[174]

However, like the other breath testing devices, IR instruments are fallible. Like the Breathalyzer and the GC, the older IR instruments relied on the 1:2,100 partition coefficient.[175] (More precisely, the instruments measure breath alcohol concentration; and then a coefficient was used to convert that concentration into a blood alcohol concentration.) However, even before analysts shifted to the practice of reporting direct breath measurements, no court sustained an admissibility attack on IR evidence, based on the use of the coefficient; but counsel could still point to the reliance on the coefficient as the basis for a weight attack. It has also been claimed that IR instruments are subject to RFI.[176]

In addition, there have been contentions that the Intoxilyzer Model 5000/64's cell chamber gradually loses integrity and, as a result, can register "apparent alcohol readings" or "ghosting."[177]

Further, Software Evaluation Associates of Kingston, Washington, is critical of the software employed by the BAC DataMaster System.[178]

---

173. Wilkinson, Sockrider, Bartsch, Kataoka & Zettle, *The Trapping, Storing, and Subsequent Analysis of Ethanol in In-Vitro Samples Previously Analyzed by a Nondestructive Technique*, 26 J. FORENSIC SCI. 671, 672 (1981).

174. Goldberger & Caplan, *Infrared Quantitative Evidential Breath-Alcohol Analyzers: In Vitro Accuracy and Precision Studies*, 31 J. FORENSIC SCI. 16 (1986). In 1973 and 1975, the U.S. Department of Transportation established mandatory standards for both testing devices and the calibrating units. However, in December 1984 the mandatory standards were converted into mere model specifications. K. DUBOWSKI, THE TECHNOLOGY OF BREATH-ALCOHOL ANALYSIS 25 (1991).

175. Hensel, *supra* note 37, at 40.

176. Balderaz v. Porter, 578 F. Supp. 1491 (S.D. Ohio 1983).

177. Sapir, *Flaking or Flaky: CMI's Intoxilyzer Model 5000*, 14 DRINKING/DRIVING LAW LETTER 345, 346 (Nov. 10, 1995) (a claim by Byron Wesley, the head of the Kentucky State Police Breath Alcohol Testing program). The loss of integrity consists of flaking, pitting, or scarring caused by two to three years of regular use. The same author adds further criticisms of the Model 5000 in *First Draw Your Curves — Then Plot Your Readings: Oregon and The Intoxilyzer Model 5000 Under Daubert*, 13 DRINKING/DRIVING LAW LETTER 189 (July 1, 1994). The author asserts that the manufacturer has made claims "without validating data." *Id.* at 193.

178. Software Evaluation Associates submitted its report entitled *Software Reliability Analysis for the BAC DateMaster System* (Doc. No. SEA-EN-1, Mar. 17, 1995) to Marjorie Tedrick, a defense attorney whose offices are located at 4508 Auburn Way North, Suite C, Auburn, Washington 98002. In part, Software Evaluation Associates concluded that "the software never was passed through an appropriately stringent set of tests either before release or after. QA methods currently in use by the Washington State Patrol are inadequate to detect the kinds of failure we encountered in the lab."

Lastly, some critics assert that IR breath testers are not as specific as GC devices. One critic alleges that acetone absorbs IR light at the same wavelength as ethanol.[179] Diabetics and athletes may have significant amounts of acetone in their breath.[180] Dr. Dubowski dismisses the acetone problem as another "red herring." In his experience, he has never encountered sufficient acetone from endogenous sources in the breath to significantly affect a quantitative evidential breath-alcohol analyzer employing infrared spectrometry and presently marketed in the United States. However, he adds:

> By its nature, infrared measurement at one wavelength--or at any small number of IR absorption bands--cannot be absolutely specific for any given chemical entity, including ethanol. To differentiate between two IR-absorbing components and to quantitate one of them correctly requires at least two wavelengths plus, usually, a third isobestic point in the spectrum. (An isobestic point is one of equal absorbance common to the two components.) More components require proportionately more wavelengths for proper differentiation.[181]

Passive Alcohol Sensors

The other instruments discussed in this section are active devices; that is, the analyst somehow invades the suspect's body to obtain the sample. For that reason, the courts often required an antecedent fourth amendment justification before the analyst may subject the suspect to the alcohol test. However, passive

---

179. 33 Crim. L. Rep. (BNA) 2384 (Aug. 10, 1983) and 52 U.S.L.W. (BNA) 2064 (Aug. 2, 1983) (citing John Tarantino); Caldwell & Kim, *The Response of the Intoxilyzer 5000 to Five Potential Interfering Substances*, 42 J. FORENSIC SCI. 1080 (1997) (the substances tested included toluene, *m*-xylene, *o*-xylene, methanol, and isopropanol; "All compounds tested were found to be capable of inducing false positive readings for ethanol...."); Logan, Gullberg & Elenbaas, *Isopropanol Interference with Breath Alcohol Analysis: A Case Report*, 39 J. FORENSIC SCI. 1107 (1994) ("The presence of interfering substances, particularly acetone, has historically been a concern in the forensic measurement of ethanol in human breath."). *See also* Jones, *Observations on the Specificity of Breath-Alcohol Analyzers Used for Clinical and Medicolegal Purposes*, 34 J. FORENSIC SCI. 842 (1989) ("Methanol could not be distinguished from ethanol with" the IR Intoximeter 3000). *But see* Cowan, McCutcheon & Weathermon, *The Response of the Intoxilyzer 4011AS-A to a Number of Possible Interfering Substances*, 35 J. FORENSIC SCI. 797, 811 (1990) (the authors attempted to determine whether 11 chemicals, including acetone, would interfere with the test result; "only three — isopropanol, toluene, and methyl ethyl ketone — could reasonably interfere with the test, and then only under unusual circumstances. Those circumstances result in a slight additive effect to a breath alcohol concentration near the level required for prosecution. Any substantial additive effect from these three substances would illuminate the interference light, which invalidates the test").

180. 52 U.S.L.W. (BNA) 2064 (Aug. 2, 1983). *But see* Dubowski & Essary, 8 J. ANAL. TOX. 205 (1984).

181. K. DUBOWSKI, THE TECHNOLOGY OF BREATH-ALCOHOL ANALYSIS 19 (1991).

alcohol sensors are now being marketed.[182] Some sensors are built into standard police flashlights.[183] The officer holds the sensor near a motorist's face. The sensor samples the exhaled air; a pump draws the air from in front of the person being tested. The Insurance Institute for Highway Safety helped develop the technology in collaboration with Protypes, Inc., in Maryland and Lion Industries, Ltd., in the United Kingdom. Some sensors register a digital display of breath alcohol concentration. Passive sensors rely on fuel cells.[184] Results are "clearly distance-related."[185] "Accuracy and precision of most fuel cell-based devices do not match those of manual Breathalyzers or automatic IR-based devices . . . ."[186]

Prosecutors are now arguing that police may rely on these displays at least as part of the basis for finding reasonable suspicion or probable cause. The Indiana court has held that under its statutory scheme, although the display test result is inadmissible at trial, the result is admissible at a suppression hearing to show probable cause.[187]

§ 22-4. Extrapolation From Starting Points.

As noted in the last section, the starting points for the expert analysis establish the defendant's eventual peak blood alcohol concentration (based on an analysis of the amount of alcohol ingested) or the defendant's concentration at the time of the test. Due to the particular wording of their statutes, a few jurisdictions have held that extrapolation testimony is neither necessary nor even permitted; these courts construe their statutes as proscribing a certain blood alcohol concentration

---

182. O'Neill, *Detecting Drunk Drivers by Using a Passive Alcohol Sensor, in* DRUNK DRIVING LAWS & ENFORCEMENT: AN ASSESSMENT OF EFFECTIVENESS 57 (A.B.A. 1986); Jones & Lund, *Detection of Alcohol-Impaired Drivers Using a Passive Alcohol Sensor*, 14 J. POLICE SCI. & ADMIN. 153 (1986); Couric, *Light Tests Drivers' Sobriety*, 71 A.B.A. J. 25 (Nov. 1985).

183. Others look like a hand-held breath-alcohol tester.

184. K. DUBOWSKI, THE TECHNOLOGY OF BREATH-ALCOHOL ANALYSIS 26 (1991). Dr. Dubowski described the technology in this manner:

> A fuel cell is basically an electromechanical device for continuously converting a fuel and an oxidant into direct current. Typically, it consists of two or more conductor electrodes separated by an ion-conducted electrolyte layer, with provisions to move fuel and oxidant into the cell and reaction products out of the cell. The process can be used to measure alcohol in breath, using alcohol as fuel and atmospheric oxygen as the oxidant . . . . One monitors the electrical current generated by electrochemical oxidation of ethanol to acetic acid . . . . Under controlled conditions, the current flow thus generated is proportional to the concentration of alcohol in the breath sample . . . .

Id at. 14.

185. *Id. at* 27.

186. *Id. at* 14.

187. State v. Johnson, 503 N.E.2d 431 (Ind. App. 1987).

at the time of the test — rather than at the time of driving.[188] However, in the majority of jurisdictions, the issue is the accused's concentration at the time of driving, that is the legally relevant time. Consequently, extrapolation evidence is admissible. In the majority of these jurisdictions, although extrapolation evidence is permitted, it is not required; the courts accept the expert analysis even if the prosecutor stops there and does not ask the expert to extrapolate to the time of the legally relevant event such as the accident. For example, in *State ex rel. Williams v. City Court of Tucson,*[189] the court held that evidence of the defendant's concentration at the time of the test was material and admissible even without the extrapolation.[190] However, there is substantial support for a minority view

---

188. United States v. Skinner, 973 F. Supp. 975 (W.D. Wash. 1997) (upholding the constitutionality of a state statute making it a crime to have a breath or blood alcohol concentration of 0.10 percent or higher within two hours of driving); State v. Tischio, 107 N.J. 504, 527 A.2d 388 (1987), *app. dismissed,* 484 U.S. 1038 (1988); Fargo, N.D. v. Stensland, 492 N.W.2d 591 (N.D. 1992) ("The precise blood-alcohol content at the time of operation ... is not an element of the per se offense. The legislature could reasonably conclude that those who drive a vehicle with blood-alcohol content that is .10% or greater, within two hours after relinquishing control of a vehicle, pose an unreasonable risk to public safety."). *But see* Haines, *Under the Influence*, 139 N.J. L. J., Mar. 13, 1995 (this article excerpts an article appearing in volume 6 of ST. THOMAS LAW REVIEW, Spring 1994; the author criticizes the *Tischio* case for eliminating the extrapolation defense; the author contends that the case was "a judicial embarrassment" because it relied on a "strained" interpretation of the governing New Jersey statute). *But see* State v. Baker, 720 A.2d 1139 (Del. Sup. 1998) (invalidating such a statute as being unconstitutionally overbroad).

An Idaho statute, IDAHO CODE § 18-8004(2), provides that "[a]ny person having an alcohol concentration of less than [the legal limit] as shown by an analysis of his blood, urine, or breath, by a test requested by a police officer shall not be prosecuted for driving under the influence of alcohol" unless a specified exception applies. The Idaho Supreme Court has ruled that the prosecution cannot defeat the application of the statute by proffering extrapolation testimony that the defendant had a prohibited concentration at the time of driving. State v. Daniel, 979 P.2d 103 (Idaho 1999).

189. 15 Ariz. App. 229, 487 P.2d 766 (1971).

190. *See also* United States v. Sauls, 981 F. Supp. 909, 926 (D. Md. 1997) (the test must be administered within a reasonable period of time after the defendant was driving; "a reasonable period of time will ordinarily be a test administered within three hours of the time of driving. However, a test administered beyond the three hour time limit will not necessarily preclude the admissibility of the test result or the application of the appropriate permissible inferences"); Akerberg v. Metropolitan Rail, 773 F. Supp. 111, 114 (N.D. Ill. 1991) ("A blood test, such as that taken of Akerberg shortly after the accident, is admissible to prove intoxication in a personal injury case. *See also* Cuellar v. Hout, 168 Ill. App. 3d 416, 421-22, 118 Ill. Dec. 867, 870, 522 N.E.2d 322, 325 (can prove intoxication at time of accident by subsequent blood test and 'retrograde extrapolation'), *app. denied,* 122 Ill. 2d 572, 125 Ill. Dec. 214, 530 N.E.2d 242 (1988)"); McDougall v. Riddel, 169 Ariz. 117, 817 P.2d 62 (Ct. App. 1991) (the absence of "relation back" evidence does not preclude the prosecution's expert from basing an estimate on the number of drinks which the accused consumed); Desmond v. Superior Court of Maricopa County, 161 Ariz. 522, 779 P.2d 1261 (1989) (if the test result is not related back to the arrest, the officer may testify that the test indicated the presence of alcohol in the blood but may not state the percentage of alcohol; if the test result is not related back to the time of the operation of the vehicle, the

demanding that the prosecutor offer the extrapolation as well to make out a submissible case for the jury.[191]

---

prosecution lacks a prima facie case that the defendant was under the influence at the time); Ransford v. District of Columbia, 583 A.2d 186 (D.C. App. 1990) (if the test is completed "within a reasonable time after operation of the vehicle," the prosecution need not present expert testimony relating the test result back to the time of operation; however, the defense may present retrograde extrapolation evidence even when the prosecution does not do so); State v. Banoub, 700 So. 2d 44 (Fla. Dist. Ct. App. 1997) (a four hour delay was not unreasonable); Miller v. State, 597 So. 2d 767 (Fla. 1991) (the test must be taken within a reasonable time after the defendant is stopped); State v. Miller, 555 So. 2d 391 (Fla. Dist. Ct. App. 1989) (retrograde extrapolation is unnecessary if the test is performed within a reasonable time after the defendant's stop); State v. Sutliff, 97 Idaho 523, 547 P.2d 1128, 1129 (1976); Commonwealth v. Wirth, 936 S.W.2d 78 (Ky. 1996); Commonwealth v. Andrew, No. 94-T-376 (Carroll Dist. Ct., Ky., Dec. 6, 1994) (The April 1995 issue of THE ADVOCATE reprints the trial court order entered by Judge Stan Billingsley; the judge dispensed with the necessity for expert extrapolation testimony by "taking judicial notice" of certain facts about absorption and elimination; however, the judge acknowledged that in decisions such as Commonwealth v. Price, 94-XX-00030, Kenton Circuit Court, "[o]ther courts take a different view and place upon the Commonwealth a . . . burden" to produce extrapolation evidence); State v. Shepard, 481 N.W.2d 560 (Minn. 1992); State v. Kubik, 235 Neb. 612, 456 N.W.2d 487 (1990) ("matters of delay between driving and testing are properly viewed as going to the weight of the breath test results, rather than to the admissibility of the evidence .... In some cases, the delay may be so substantial as to render the test results nonprobative of the accused's impairment or breath alcohol level while driving. In this case, however, the breath test was given less than 1 hour after the defendant was stopped"; after surveying numerous decisions from other jurisdictions, the court characterizes its position as the majority view in the United States); State v. Taylor, 132 N.H. 314, 566 A.2d 172 (1989) (the test was performed within a reasonable time after the defendant's operation of the motor vehicle); Commonwealth v. Kasunic, 620 A.2d 525 (Pa. Super. 1993) (the test was taken 50 minutes after the defendant was discovered, and the test revealed a 0.21% BAC, more than twice the legal limit; the court distinguished earlier cases requiring extrapolation testimony on the ground that those cases involved readings, 0.114 and 0.108, very close to the legal limit); State v. Lusi, 625 A.2d 1350 (R.I. 1993) (there is no need for extrapolation testimony if the test is "taken within a reasonable time" after the defendant was driving his vehicle); State v. McDonald, 421 N.W.2d 492 (S.D. 1988); LaRocca, *Admissibility of Delayed Blood Test Results — Commonwealth v. Gonzalez, 519 Pa. 116, 546 A.2d 26 (1988)*, 62 TEMP. L. REV. 757, 762-63 (1989) ("Most courts have concluded that delays between vehicle operation and blood alcohol testing do not create a need for the use of extrapolation evidence ...."); Stowell & Stowell, *Estimation of Blood Alcohol Concentrations after Social Drinking*, 43 J. FORENSIC SCI. 14 (1998) ("Many believe that ... estimates [based on blood samples taken some hours after the time of interest] are not reliable...." However, in this experiment, "most BACs measured about an hour after cessation of drinking were within or very close to the predicted range based on back extrapolation from the actual ... BAC result.").

191. People v. LaPlante, 81 Misc. 2d 34, 365 N.Y.S.2d 392 (Just. Ct. 1975). *See also* Desmond v. Superior Court of Maricopa County, 161 Ariz. 522, 779 P.2d 1261 (if the prosecution does not present relation-back testimony, the officer may not state the percentage of alcohol found in the breath or blood) (1989); State *ex rel.* Ross v. Nance, 165 Ariz. 286, 798 P.2d 1295 (1990) (relation-back evidence is required in criminal prosecutions under *Desmond, supra,* but not in a license suspension proceeding); McDougall v. Riddel, 169 Ariz. 117, 817 P.2d 62 (Ct. App. 1991), *aff'd*, 171 Ariz. 34, 827 P.2d 1129 (1992); State v. Geisler, 215 Conn. 819, 576 A.2d 547 (1990) (the

The extrapolation is an estimate based on a blood alcohol curve. The curve usually consists of a sharp rise in concentration, a peak, and then a slow decline, as illustrated by Figure 22-3.

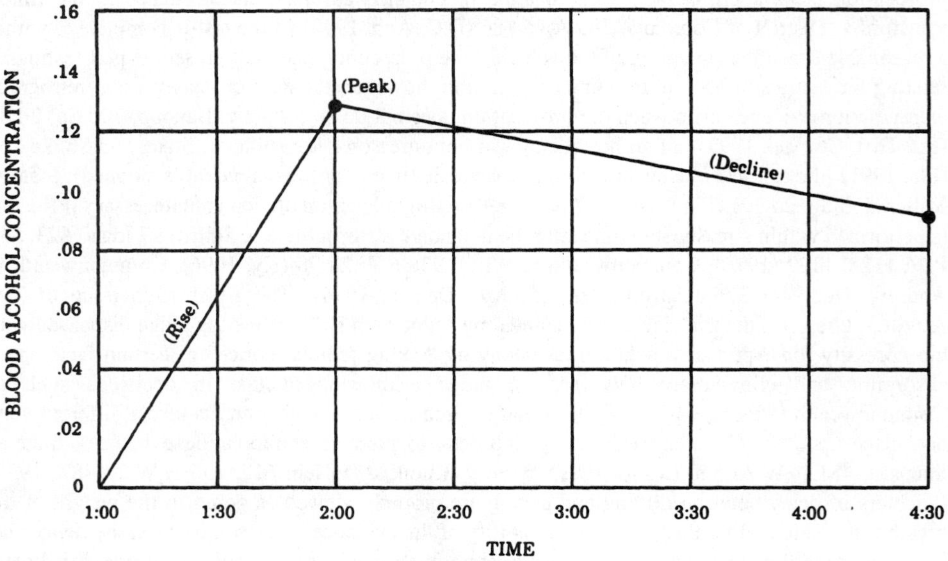

Figure 22-3

---

state is obligated to adduce evidence relating the defendant's BAC at the time of the test back to the time of his operation of the vehicle), *vacated*, 498 U.S. 1019 (1991); People v. LaPlante, 81 Misc. 2d 34, 365 N.Y.S.2d 392 (Just. Ct. 1975); Commonwealth v. Murray, 1999 Pa. Super. 34, 1999 Pa. Super. LEXIS 135, 64 Cr.L. (BNA) 473 (Pa. Super. Ct., Feb. 18, 1999) (in some cases, Pennsylvania law requires that the prosecution introduce expert testimony relating a defendant's post-driving test results back to the time of driving); State v. Ladwig, 434 N.W.2d 594 (S.D. 1989) (the State did not present sufficient evidence to enable the jury to extrapolate or relate the test result back to the time of driving); Mireles v. Texas Dept. Of Public Safety, __S.W.2d__, 1998 Tex. App. LEXIS 6858, 1998 W.L. 758032 (Tex. App. 1998) (evidence that a motorist failed field sobriety texts and had an alcohol concentration exceeding the legal limit one hour after he was stopped did not constitute even a scintilla of evidence that the motorist operated a vehicle with a prohibited concentration; the state must prove the concentration at the time of the operation of the vehicle); Vermont v. Dumont, 146 Vt. 252, 499 A.2d 787 (1985); State v. Fortier, 149 Vt. 599, 547 A.2d 1327 (1988) (applying *Dumont*). *See also* Essen & Hine, *Retrograde Extrapolation Evidence: Convincing the Courts of Its Importance*, 5 D.W.I. J. 2 (Feb. 1990); Tarantino, *Obtaining an Acquittal Through the Use of Retrograde Extrapolation*, 4 D.W.I. J. 7 (July 1989); Trichter, *A Motion in Limine: Keeping Out Breath Test Results Where There Are No Extrapolation Facts*, 15 THE CHAMPION 43 (Sept./Oct. 1991). *See also* State v. Zumbo, 601 A.2d 986, 989-90 (Vt. 1991) (the defense claimed that under VT. STAT. ANN. tit. 23, § 1204(a)(1), it was entitled to an instruction that if the defendant's BAC was found to be 0.05% or less, the jury could presume that the defendant was not intoxicated; to gain the benefit of the presumption, the defense had to present extrapolation testimony).

Suppose, for example, that the defendant began drinking at 1:00 p.m., that the defendant finished drinking at 1:30 p.m., and that, based on the starting point of the amount of alcohol the defendant consumed, the expert estimates that the eventual peak BAC would have been .14%. The expert might assume that the typical person would reach that BAC at 2:00 p.m. The accident in question occurred at 1:45 p.m. The expert would place the assumed peak BAC on a chart, as in Figure 22-4,

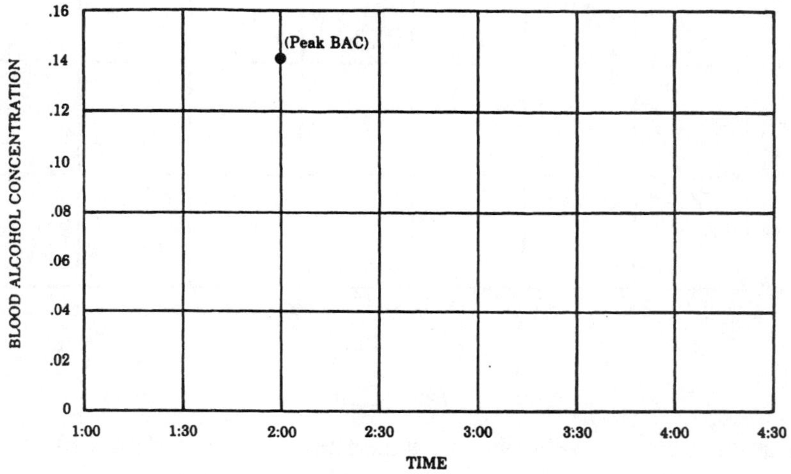

Figure 22-4

then draw the first part of the curve connecting 0 concentration with the peak BAC concentration, as in Figure 22-5,

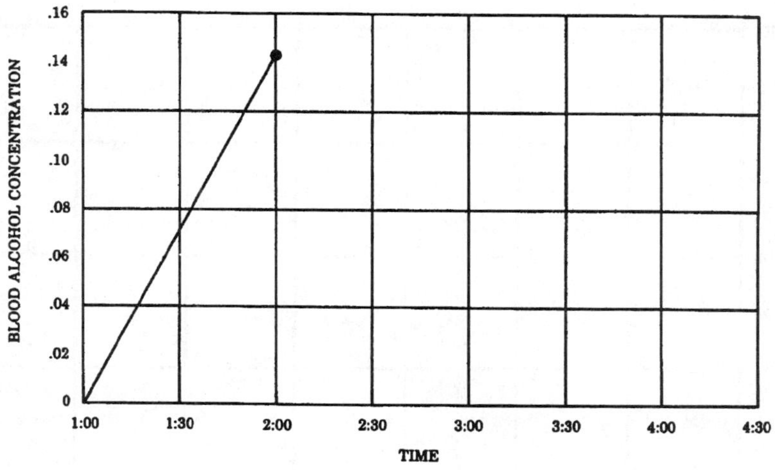

Figure 22-5

and finally locate the BAC value at the 1:45 p.m. point on the horizontal axis, as in Figure 22-6.

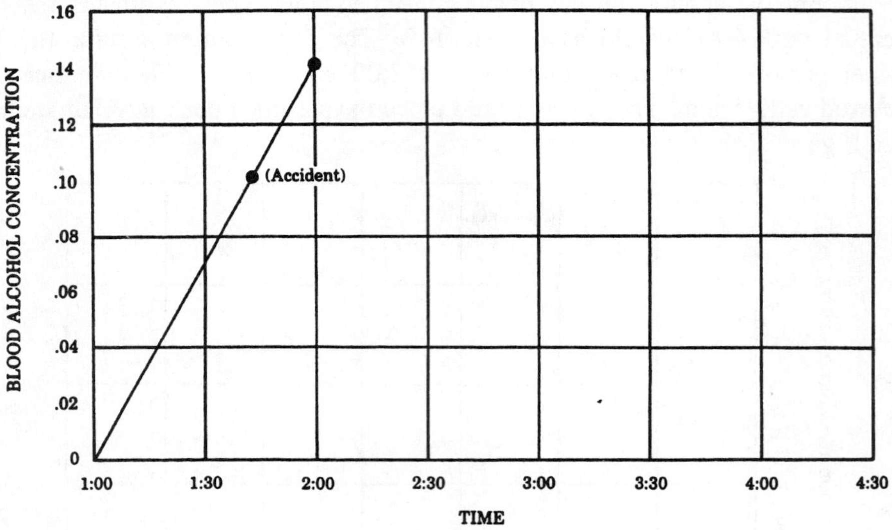

Figure 22-6

Now assume alternatively that the expert uses the defendant's blood alcohol concentration at the time of the test as the starting point. Suppose, for example, that the test at 4:30 p.m. revealed a BAC of .14%. The testimony indicates that the defendant stopped drinking at 3:00 p.m. The expert begins the extrapolation by placing the .14 value on the chart at the 4:30 p.m. point on the horizontal axis, as in Figure 22-7.

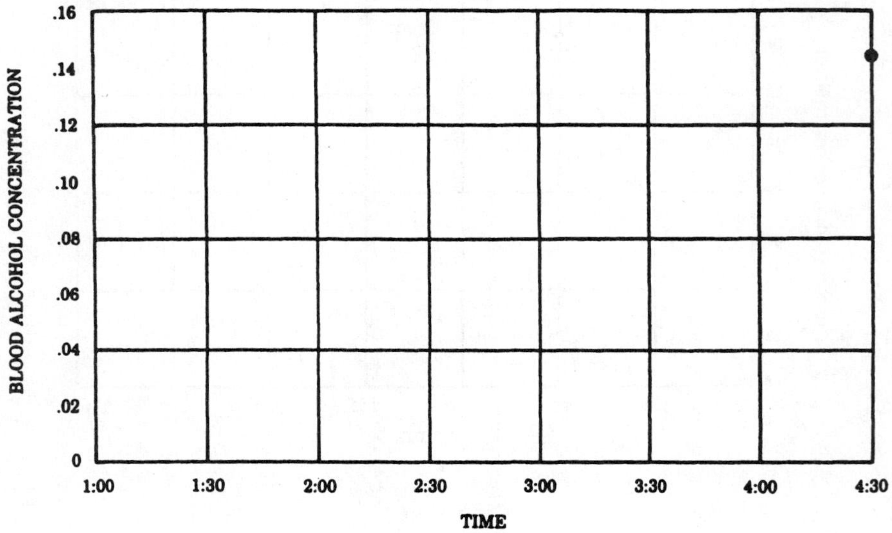

Figure 22-7

Next the expert uses the assumed elimination rate to draw a line back toward an earlier, peak BAC. The rate determines the slope of the line. Suppose the expert assumes that the peak occurs an hour after the end of drinking (here 4:00 p.m.) and that the elimination rate is a constant .02% per hour. In our hypothetical, half an hour elapsed between the assumed peak BAC and the time of the test, 4:30 p.m. During that half an hour, the BAC should have declined .01%. Thus, the peak BAC at 4:00 p.m. would have been .15%, as shown in Figure 22-8.

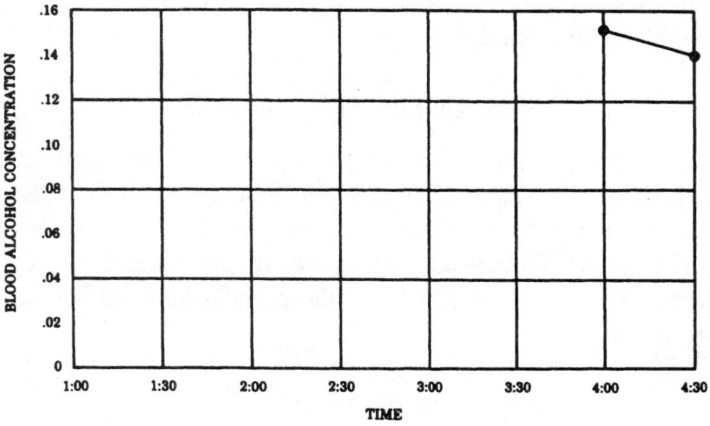

Figure 22-8

The expert completes the extrapolation by locating the time of the accident, 4:15 p.m., along the horizontal axis, as in Figure 22-9.

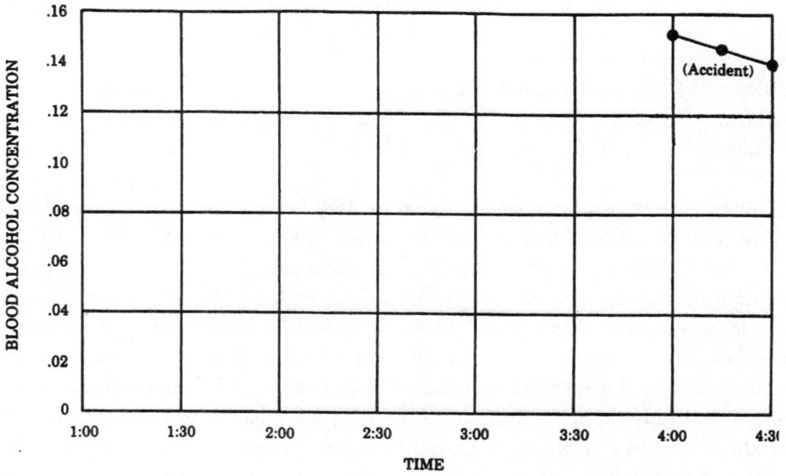

Figure 22-9

The above extrapolation is based on flawed assumptions. The concentration is not static; it rises and falls. Some writers assert that with the exception of the peak value, each value will appear twice on the curve — once during the rise and again during the fall.[192] Dr. Dubowski goes farther and characterizes a curve showing a steady rise and decline as fictional. His research and other research at Indiana University indicates that depending upon the individual's characteristics, there will be "zigzagging" in the curve; there will be many positive and negative spikes from the trend line — a phenomenon he terms the "steeple effect." Extrapolations based on the curve are imprecise[193] because the absorption curve involves several questionable premises.

Straight Line Rises and Falls

In the prior examples, the expert assumes that BAC both rises and falls in a straight line fashion. The expert assumes that the increase or decrease is linear in nature. Although there is an element of truth in this generalization, it is an oversimplification. Dr. Dubowski's discovery of the "steeple effect" undercuts the assumption. A sizeable proportion of the population does not follow a zero-order (linear) curve.

A Constant Absorption Rate

Another assumption is the time required for absorption. In the reported cases, the prosecution expert usually states that maximum absorption requires roughly an hour plus or minus 15 minutes, that is, between 45 and 75 minutes.[194] The absorption period, however, is variable.[195] It differs from person to person. Some

---

192. Fitzgerald & Hume, *supra* note 44, at 8.

193. Ullman v. Overnite Transp. Co., 563 F.2d 152 (5th Cir. 1977); Poulnot v. District of Columbia, 608 A.2d 134 (D.C. App. 1992) (it is improper to judicially notice alcohol absorption rates).

194. Gullberg & McElroy, *Comparing Roadside with Subsequent Breath Alcohol Analyses and Their Relevance to the Issue of Retrograde Extrapolation*, 57 FORENSIC SCI. INT'L 193, 194 (1992) ("the rising BrAC defense"); *Presenting the Medical Evidence: Sources of Error in Gas Chromatograph Intoximeter Breath Test for Breath Alcohol*, 18 TRAUMA 47-48 (Dec. 1976). *See also* Jones, Jonson & Neri, *Peak Blood-Ethanol Concentration and the Time of Its Occurrence After Rapid Drinking on an Empty Stomach*, 36 J. FORENSIC SCI. 376, 384 (1991) ("A large body of evidence can be mustered to support the notion that most drunk drivers have passed the peak BEC and are most probably in the postabsorptive phase of ethanol metabolism when biological specimens are obtained for analysis of ethanol in traffic-law enforcement. This conclusion comes from evaluating a large number of double blood specimens (30 to 60 min. apart) from apprehended drunk drivers. The change in BEC per unit of time almost always showed a decreasing trend. [It is] highly likely that the peak BEC was indeed passed at the time specimens were obtained").

195. Poulnot v. District of Columbia, 608 A.2d 134 (D.C. App. 1992) (it is improper to judicially notice an elimination rate).

writers report absorption periods as short as 30 minutes,[196] but other researchers have discovered periods as long as two,[197] two and a half,[198] or three[199] hours. Dr. Dubowski has documented peak BACs within 12 minutes of the end of drinking and absorption peaks as long as four hours after the end of drinking.

There is even evidence that the absorption rate of an individual can vary from time to time. Absorption is a complex, nonlinear uptake phenomenon. The available data indicates that the rate can depend upon the meal consumed at the time of drinking[200] and the type and concentration of beverage consumed. However, some writers dispute that the drinker's stomach contents have any significant effect on the person's absorption rate.[201]

Peak

Another assumption is that the concentration will peak once after absorption, level off at an equilibrium for a short time, and then steadily decline. In a given case, that assumption could be false. In some cases, a person's concentration will peak at least twice; the concentration can rise, fall, and rise again.[202]

---

196. *Presenting the Medical Evidence: Sources of Error in Gas Chromatograph Intoximeter Breath Test for Breath Alcohol, supra* note 194; Radlow & Hurst, *Delayed Blood Alcohol Determinations in Forensic Applications*, 2 CRIM. JUST. J. 281, 284 (1979).

197. Comment, *Driving With 0.10% Blood-Alcohol: Can the State Prove It?*, 16 U.S.F. L. REV. 817, 823 (1982).

198. Radlow & Hurst, *supra* note 196, at 284.

199. Wade, *DUI Statistics Often Don't Add Up*, 5 CRIM. JUST. 18, 20 (Spring 1990) ("an individual may not reach his or her peak alcohol concentration for more than three hours"); Simpson, *Do Breath Tests Really Underestimate Blood Alcohol Concentration?*, 13 J. ANAL. TOX. 120 (Mar./Apr. 1989) ("fully postabsorptive status may not occur until more than three hours after drinking").

200. Comment, *supra* note 197, at 824. Jones & Jonsson, *Food-Induced Lowering of Blood-Ethanol Profiles and Increased Rate of Elimination Immediately After a Meal*, 39 J. FORENSIC SCI. 1084 (1994); Watkins & Adler, *The Effect of Food on Alcohol Absorption and Elimination Patterns*, 38 J. FORENSIC SCI. 285 (1993) ("The average elimination rate of ethanol was found to be significantly lower after a meal....").

201. Scherotter, *California Vehicle Code Section 23152(B): A Guessing Game for California Drivers*, 5 CRIM. JUST. J. 249, 254, 262 (1982).

202. Comment, *supra* note 197, at 827. Jakus, Shajani & Image, *Consumption of a Large Dose of Alcohol in a Short Time Span*, 56 FORENSIC SCI. INT'L 113, 124 (1992) ("In consumption patterns atypical of social drinking, *i.e.* bolus consumption of fast and deliberate consumption of alcoholic beverages ..., plateauing of BAC does occur for a variable and unpredictable time interval").

Clearance

In the reported cases, the prosecution experts have testified that the typical elimination clearance or detoxification rate per hour is either 0.015%[203] or 0.020%.[204] However, like the absorption period, the clearance rate is variable. An individual's clearance rate can vary from time to time.[205] Furthermore, the rate varies from individual to individual. In his original research, Widmark referred to the elimination rate as the b or Beta factor.[206] Widmark concluded that the rate was relatively constant for the individual from day to day but that the rate varied considerably from individual to individual.[207] He discovered a wide range of Beta values; the values were not tightly grouped.[208] Subsequent research confirms Widmark's early findings. Dr. Dubowski reports that the blood-alcohol decline can vary from 0.006% to 0.04% per hour.[209]

---

203. United States v. Du Bois, 645 F.2d 642, 643 (8th Cir. 1981). One court has judicially noticed a .015 percent per hour rate. O'Neil, Mertz & Squire, *Strategies in Defending the Drunk Driver*, 12 OHIO N.U. L. REV. 1, 7 n.16 (1985) (citing Bryn v. Collins, No. WMS 84-9 (William Cty., Ohio Ct. App., July 27, 1984)).

204. Comment, *supra* note 197, at 821. *See also* Fitzgerald & Hume, *supra* note 33, at 7 n.10, citing Greiner v. State, 157 Tex. Crim. 479, 249 S.W.2d 601 (1952) (0.02%), and Toms v. State, 95 Okla. Crim. 60, 239 P.2d 812 (1952) (0.015%). Feldstein, *On the Rate of Elimination of Alcohol*, 9 DWI J. 1, 9 (Dec. 1994) (it has been suggested that "alcohol burns off at the rate of 0.02% per hour. The American Medical Association ..., however, correctly reported that 'in man, the average utilization rate is equivalent to a drop in blood alcohol level of 0.018% w/v (18 mgt/100 ml) per hour. 0.018% should be used as an average;" the author cites AMERICAN MEDICAL ASSOCIATION, COMMITTEE ON MEDICOLEGAL PROBLEMS, ALCOHOL AND THE IMPAIRED DRIVER: A MANUAL ON THE MEDICOLEGAL ASPECTS OF CHEMICAL TEXTS FOR INTOXICATION WITH SUPPLEMENT ON BREATH/ALCOHOL TESTS 22 (1976)).

205. Gullberg, *Variation in Blood Alcohol Concentration Following the Last Drink*, 10 J. POLICE SCI. & ADMIN. 289, 292 (1982); Comment, *supra* note 161, at 826. Barron, Perry & Ferslew, *The Effect of Ibuprofen on Ethanol Concentration and Elimination Rate*, 37 J. FORENSIC SCI. 432 (1992).

206. Fitzgerald & Hume, *supra* note 44, at 18.

207. *Id.* Feldstein, *On the Rate of Elimination of Alcohol*, 9 DWI J. 1, 9 (Nov. 1994) (citing AMERICAN MEDICAL ASSOCIATION, COMMITTEE ON MEDICOLEGAL PROBLEMS, ALCOHOL AND THE IMPAIRED DRIVER: A MANUAL ON THE MEDICOLEGAL ASPECTS OF CHEMICAL TESTS FOR INTOXICATION WITH SUPPLEMENT ON BREATH/ALCOHOL TESTS 22 (1976), the author states that "[v]ariations occur within the range of 0.01% w/v (10 mg/100 ml) to 0.025% w/v (24 mg/100 ml) per hour"); Jones & Andersson, *Influence of Age, Gender, and Blood-Alcohol Concentration on the Disappearance Rate of Alcohol from Blood in Drinking Drivers*, 41 J. FORENSIC SCI. 922 (1996) (in this study, women had a higher elimination rate than men).

208. Fitzgerald & Hume, *supra* note 44, at 20-21. Jones, *Disappearance Rate of Ethanol from the Body of Human Subjects: Implications in Forensic Toxicology*, 38 J. FORENSIC SCI. 104, 115 (1993) (Widmark's estimate of the Beta slope as 16 mg/dL/h "still remains a valid and realistic value for male moderate drinkers"; however, there can be "wide variation" in the slope, "as low as 8 mg/dL/h or as high as 36 mg/dL/h").

209. Radlow & Hurst, *supra* note 196, at 284; Jones, *Excretion of Alcohol in Urine and Diuresis in Healthy Men in Relation to Their Age, the Dose Administered and the Time After Drinking*, 45

There have been a number of proposals to deal with the problem of the variability of the factors in the hypothetical blood alcohol curve. One proposal is to require that the test be administered within a certain period of time after the legally relevant event. The longer the time lapse, the greater is the risk that the variability of the factors will distort the final estimate. To reduce that risk, this proposal would require that the police or medical personnel administer the test within a short time after the event such as the two hour period prescribed by statute in New York.[210] Even absent a statutory prescription, some courts have rejected extrapolations based on tests taken two and a half hours after the accident.[211] In a 1992 case involving a "not insignificant" delay of one hour, the Pennsylvania court ruled that without relation-back evidence, the record was legally insufficient to support a conviction.[212] Other jurisdictions are more tolerant of delays and hold that the delays affect the weight but not the admissibility of the extrapolation.[213]

FORENSIC SCI. INT'L 217 (1990) ("Ethanol-induced diuresis showed large inter-subject variations"); Neutebroom & Jones, *Disappearance Rate of Alcohol from the Blood of Drunk Drivers Calculated from Two Consecutive Samples: What Do the Results Really Mean?*, 45 FORENSIC SCI. INT'L 107 (1990) (the researchers observed a "wide range of alcohol elimination rates"); McKinley, *Proving a Violation of Vehicle Code Section 23152(b): Rabbit Tracks in the Snow or Roulette?*, 5 CRIM. JUST. J. 223, 253 (1982).

210. *See* N.Y. VEH. & TRAF. LAW § 1194 (McKinney's Supp. 1983-84); People v. D'Angelo, 124 Misc. 2d 1050, 478 N.Y.S.2d 538 (Sup. Ct. 1984); People v. Keane, 76 A.D.2d 963, 428 N.Y.S.2d 972 (1980). *But see* People v. McGrath, 135 A.D.2d 60, 524 N.Y.S.2d 214 (the two-hour limitation is inapplicable to court-ordered chemical tests), *aff'd,* 73 N.Y.2d 826, 534 N.E.2d 318, 537 N.Y.S.2d 480 (1988).

211. United States v. Du Bois, 645 F.2d 642 (8th Cir. 1981).

212. Commonwealth v. Jarman and Commonwealth v. Modaffare, 529 Pa. 92, 601 A.2d 1229 (1992). However, the result has been overturned by statute. Commonwealth v. Brehm, 444 Pa. Super. 138, 663 A.2d 712 (1995).

213. State *ex rel.* Romley v. Brown, 168 Ariz. 481, 815 P.2d 408 (1991) (relation-back evidence is unnecessary in a prosecution for reckless manslaughter); Funk v. Department of Motor Vehicles, 1 Cal. App. 3d 449, 81 Cal. Rptr. 662 (1969); Miller v. State, 1991 Fla. LEXIS 1657, 1991 W.L. 138307 (Fla.) (if the test is administered within a reasonable time after the accused ceases operating the motor vehicle, the inability of the prosecution to relate the blood alcohol concentration back to the time of driving goes only to the weight of the evidence), *superseded*, 597 So. 2d 767 (Fla. 1991); State v. Kelly, 430 N.W.2d 427 (Iowa 1988) (a delay beyond the statutory period did not preclude the admission of the test result); Tyner v. State, 503 N.E.2d 444 (Ind. App. 1987); State v. Harris, 670 S.W.2d 73 (Mo. App. 1984). *See also* Akerberg v. Metropolitan Rail, 773 F. Supp. 111, 114 (N.D. Ill. 1991) ("[a] blood test ... taken shortly after the accident ...."); LaRocca, *Admissibility of Delayed Blood Test Results — Commonwealth v. Gonzalez, 519 Pa. 116, 546 A.2d 26 (1988)*, 62 TEMP. L. REV. 757, 761 (1989) ("In Commonwealth v. Trefey, [249 Pa.[Super.] 117, 375 A.2d 786 (1977)], the Superior Court of Pennsylvania held that a one and one-half hour delay ... did not render the results inadmissible .... In Commonweath v. Tylwalk, [258 Pa.[Super.] 506, 393 A.2d 473 (1978)], the superior court ... held that a four and one-half hour delay ... affected the weight but not the admissibility of the blood test results").

Another proposal is to mandate two tests. It has been argued that if two tests were taken, the expert could compute the defendant's personal clearance rate. This proposal has several proponents,[214] including the National Safety Council.[215] Michigan adopted an administration regulation requiring the administration of at least two breath tests. The Michigan Court of Appeals has declared that "where [this] administrative rule ... [has] not been complied with, the accuracy of [the] test is sufficiently questionable to preclude the test results from being admitted into evidence."[216] The North Carolina statute similarly requires "the testing of at least duplicate sequential breath samples."[217] Dr. Dubowski believes that requiring two tests would not greatly enhance the reliability of an extrapolation. As previously stated, he has discovered considerable "zigzagging" in the trend line. Given the steeple effect, the expert could not confidently determine whether the concentration was on the rise or fall even with two tests.[218] (Distinguish this proposal from the recommendation that two tests be conducted as a quality assurance (QA) method. That method enjoys widespread acceptance.)[219]

---

214. Gullberg, *A Concern Associated with Single Breath Alcohol Analysis for Forensic Purposes*, 38 J. FORENSIC SCI. 1263 (1993); Nichols, *Toward a Coordinated Judicial View of the Accuracy of Breath Testing Devices*, 59 N.D. L. REV. 329, 348 (1983); *Estimating the Second Breath Alcohol Measurement from the First: A Model Refinement*, 36 J. FORENSIC SCI. 634 (1991); Gullberg, *Predicting the Second Breath Alcohol Measurement from the First: An Application of Regression Analysis*, 36 J. FORENSIC SCI. 10 (1991); Gullberg, *Duplicate Breath Testing: Some Statistical Analyses*, 37 FORENSIC SCI. INT'L 205 (1988) (citing both the recommendation of the National Safety Council Committee on Alcohol and Drugs and the new program in the State of Washington); Fitzgerald & Hume, *The Single Chemical Test for Intoxication: A Challenge to Admissibility*, 66 MASS. L. REV. 23 (1981); Radlow & Hurst, *supra* note 196, at 285.

215. NAT'L SAFETY COUNCIL, TRAFFIC SAFETY MONOGRAPH NO. 2: TESTING THE DRUNK DRIVER (1970).

216. People v. Willis, 180 Mich. App. 31, 446 N.W.2d 562 (1989).

217. N.C. GEN. STAT. § 20-139.1.

218. *But see* Commonwealth v. Neal, 392 Mass. 1, 464 N.E.2d 1356 (1984) and Romano v. Kimmelman, 96 N.J. 66, 474 A.2d 1 (1984) (both cases list two tests as one of the procedures for compensating for radio frequency interference).

219. K. DUBOWSKI, THE TECHNOLOGY OF BREATH-ALCOHOL ANALYSIS 8-9 (1991) states:

> Replication is an accepted step in quality assurance (QA) of chemical analysis methods, usually by repeated analysis of separate aliquots from a single original specimen. Collection of at least two separate breath specimens and their sequential analysis has . . . become an accepted practice. It facilitates detection of contaminated breath specimens, or demonstrates that the individual, uncontaminated breath specimens possess acceptably uniform biological and chemical characteristics. Extensive studies have demonstrated that duplicate alcohol analyses on separate consecutive breath samples can be expected to yield BrAC results corresponding within 0.009g/210L for 95 percent of such results.

The National Safety Council's Committee on Alcohol and Other Drugs supports this practice. *Id.* Dr. Dubowski adds that the collection interval should be between two and 10 minutes and that "consecutive BrAC results within 0.02g/210L" is "deemed to be in acceptable agreement." *Id. at* 9.

§ 22-5. Test Sample Preservation.

As noted earlier, there are inherent imprecisions in the computations used to generate the expert's starting point and extrapolation. Moreover, human and machine error are possible in the administration of the test.[220] In light of these last two sources of error, there has been interest in preserving blood, urine, and breath samples for subsequent retesting. A later retest might disclose that the initial test was erroneous.

There are techniques such as the use of fluoride for preserving blood and urine samples.[221] For example, when 0.2% fluoride is added to a urine sample, "[t]his has been shown to prevent any change in alcohol concentration for two weeks even when subjected to hot weather in storage in car trunks during the summer. No significant changes in alcohol content were noted in samples containing fluoride stored in the refrigerator for as long as ten months."[222] Some studies indicate that even without the addition of special preservatives, the blood alcohol concentration in blood and urine samples remains stable so long as the samples are stored suitably.[223]

At one time, there was a major controversy over the possibility of preserving breath samples for subsequent retest. Some contended that preservation is possible. There is agreement that if the sample was initially tested in an ampoule, the ampoule and the solution inside the ampoule can be saved.[224] Some claim that an analyst could test these materials to determine whether the ampoule had any optical defects or imperfections and whether the total quantity of solution in the ampoule was correct.[225] The issue that divided scientists was whether the alcohol concentration is stable or whether the changes in the concentration can be correlated with the passage of time. If not, it makes no sense to require that the breath sample be preserved; a subsequent retest would not shed any light on what the correct reading should have been at the time of the earlier test.

On the one hand, some researchers believed that with proper precautions, the alcohol concentration in a breath sample can be stabilized. Jones and Volpe take this position.[226] They recommended that the ampoules be placed in tightly capped, dark glass bottles and refrigerated at minus one degree centigrade within

---

220. Bellotti, *supra* note 116, at 207-10.

221. Caplan, *supra* note 3, at 607.

222. *Id.*

223. *Id.*

224. Note, *The Defendant's Right to Independent Analysis of the Breathalyzer Ampoule: The Probable Virginia Response*, 21 WM. & MARY L. REV. 219, 236 (1979).

225. *Id.* Our reviewer states that the quantity of solution changes unpredictably over time from evaporation or water-vapor absorption.

226. Jones & Volpe, *Storage Properties of Breath Ampuls*, 40 J. STUD. ALCOHOL 1039, 1043-44 (1979); Nichols, *supra* note 214, at 341.

one hour of the original test.[227] One biochemistry professor at the University of Oregon reached the same conclusion.[228] An industry, companies manufacturing breath preserving devices, emerged.[229] Companies, including Federal Signal Corporation in Park Forest South, Illinois, marketed devices such as the Toxtrap throughout the United States. Some devices captured the breath sample in a metal capsule made of indium while others passed the breath through a tube containing a solid absorbant such as silica gel which retains the alcohol.[230] Legislation in Canada and some American states required the use of these devices.[231]

On the other hand, some experts asserted that it is impossible to stabilize the solution and that the changes in the solution do not correlate with the passage of time. After reviewing expert testimony, the New Mexico Supreme Court concluded that "there is no substantial evidence ... that an independent breath alcohol sample could be accurately retested after capture and preservation on the machines currently in use."[232] In another case involving conflicting expert testimony, the New York Supreme Court ruled that a retest would not yield any "scientifically reliable evidence."[233]

Dr. Dubowski reported that his research indicates that the solution in the ampoule is subject to "unpredictable changes" that do "not correlate with time sufficiently well to permit scientifically valid and forensically acceptable conclusions regarding the validity of the original Breathalyzer test result."[234] He believed that no examination of a Breathalyzer ampoule or its content at any time other than a few moments after the initial test can reveal information validly bearing on what the initial test result was or should have been. The Wisconsin Supreme Court upheld Dr. Dubowski's position in 1984 in *State v. Walstad.*[235] On October 2, 1975, the Committee on Alcohol and Drugs of the National Safety Council issued a Formal Statement, asserting that "at the present time, a scientifically valid procedure is not known to be available for the re-examination of a Breathalyzer ampoule that has been used in the breath test for ethanol, in order to confirm the accuracy and reliability of the original breath analysis." This statement was unanimously approved by both the Committee and its Executive

---

227. *Id.*

228. State v. Michener, 25 Or. App. 523, 527 n.5, 550 P.2d 449, 451 n.5 (1976). *See also Comeau, Indium Encapsulation of Breath Samples for Alcohol Content: A Review and Report,* 11 CAN. FORENSIC SCI. J. 261 (1978).

229. Caplan, *supra* note 3, at 625-26.

230. Cohen, *Chemical Testing Expert and the Lawyer,* THE CHAMPION, May 1984, at 17, 20-21.

231. Caplan, *supra* note 3, at 625-26.

232. Montoya v. Metropolitan Court, 98 N.M. 616, 651 P.2d 1260 (1982).

233. People v. Santiago, 116 Misc. 2d 340, 455 N.Y.S.2d 511 (Sup. Ct. 1982).

234. DUBOWSKI, BOOK OF ABSTRACTS: 28TH ANNUAL MEETING, AMERICAN ACADEMY OF FORENSIC SCIENCES 96 (1976).

235. 119 Wis. 2d 483, 351 N.W.2d 469 (1984).

Board. The Committee and its Board reaffirmed this position in 1984 and periodically since then. .

More to the point, ampoules are used in Breathalyzers; and as previously stated, Breathalyzers have been phased out. In field work, GC and IR-based devices now dominate. The shift to such devices has largely mooted the question of ampoule preservation.

§ 22-6. Evidentiary Requirements.

There is an extensive body of case law[236] and law review[237] literature detailing the elements of the foundation for an intoxication test, including the question of whether it is necessary to adduce proof that the testing instrument was in working order.[238] Many of the cases and articles propose foundation checklists.[239] For example, in one case, the Nebraska Supreme Court listed the following elements: The device was in proper working order at the time of the test;[240] the person

236. People v. Anselmo, 74 Cal. App. 3d Supp. 8, 141 Cal. Rptr. 694 (1977), *withdrawn*; Clinton v. Kammerich, 642 S.W.2d 353, 356 (Mo. App. 1982); State v. Powell, 618 S.W.2d 47 (Mo. App. 1981); State v. Gerber, 206 Neb. 75, 291 N.W.2d 403 (1980); State v. Salhus, 220 N.W.2d 852 (N.D. 1974); Mullan v. State, 668 S.W.2d 427 (Tex. App.1984).

237. Sapir, Giangrande & Peters, *Breath Alcohol Machines: Evidence Foundation Requirements in Illinois*, 22 J. MARSHALL L. REV. 1 (1988); Comment, *Statutory DWI and Its Interpretation by Texas Courts*, 14 HOUS. L. REV. 1082, 1098 (1977).

238. People v. Morris, No. 5-96-0787 (Ill. App. Ct., 5th Dist., Aug. 5, 1998) ("The State relies on People v. Kirkpatrick, 216 Ill. App. 3d 875, 576 N.E.2d 546 (1991), in which our colleagues on the Second District Appellate Court held, in the face of the statutory scheme and regulation requiring a certain margin of error, that a machine with a greater margin of error did not violate this requirement. Specifically, the court held that although the State statutory scheme requires a margin of error no greater than 0.01 and although a reading of two digits of .09 as in Kilpatrick resulted in a margin of error of .0ll, the machine nevertheless complied with the State regulations. [W]e respectfully decline to follow our colleagues' decision in Kikpatrick. It sub silentio establishes a standard of substantial compliance, rather than the strict compliance intended by the clear language of . . . the statute . . . ."); Commonwealth v. Barbeau, 411 Mass. 782, 585 N.E.2d 1392 (1992); State v. Wittenbarger, 124 Wash. 2d 467, 880 P.2d 517 (1994) (the police shifted from the Breathalyzer to the BAC Veriner DataMaster; the maintenance protocol for the Breathalyzer required the tester to record specific data for initial voltage values, adjusted voltage values, and calibration factors; the maintenance protocol for the DataMaster merely required the tester to indicate that certain tests had been performed with satisfactory results; it was not a violation of due process under either the state or national constitution for the police to make this shift. *See also* Dubowski, *Quality Assurance in Breath-Alcohol Analysis*, 18 J. ANAL. TOX. 306 (Oct. 1994).

239. *See* the cases and articles cited in notes 236-37, *supra.* Davenport v. Director, DMV, 6 Cal. App. 4th 133, 7 Cal. Rptr. 2d 818 (1992), *modified* (May 8, 1992).

240. Breath-alcohol simulators are typically used to calibrate the machine. Simulators are prepared by equilibrating a flowing gas such as air with an aqueous alcohol solution of known concentration, at a fixed temperature. The resultant vapor effluent has a predictable and controllable alcohol concentration.

conducting and interpreting the test was qualified and held a valid permit; the test was conducted in a manner approved by the Department of Health; and there was compliance with other statutory requirements.[241]

Courts have allowed the sponsoring witness to authenticate a written checklist, showing that he or she followed the required procedures.[242] It is ideal if the

---

K. DUBOWSKI, THE TECHNOLOGY OF BREATH-ALCOHOL ANALYSIS 24 (1991). *See also* Dubowski & Essary, *Vapor-Alcohol Control Tests with Compressed Ethanol-Gas Mixtures: Scientific Basis and Actual Performance*, 20 J. ANAL. TOX. 484 (1996); Dubowski & Essary, *Evaluation of Commercial Breath-Alcohol Simulators: Further Studies*, 15 J. ANAL. TOX. 272 (1991).

241. State v. Friedrich, 681 So. 2d 1157 (Fla. Dist. Ct. App. 1996) (although there were demonstrated variations in the alcohol concentrations in the solution bottles used to test the breath testing machines, the results of the tests were still admissible; there was testimony that it would probably take more than a year for the alcohol concentration in the solution to change significantly and that the stock solution was consumed in a matter of a few months); State v. Gerber, 206 Neb. 75, 291 N.W.2d 403 (1980); State v. Beardsley, Case No. 97 TRC 4176-01 (Mun. Ct., Washington County, Ohio, Oct. 24, 1997) (Nuzum, J.) (the prosecution expert, Dr. Craig Sutheimer, was the Deputy Director of the Ohio Department of Health and the Chief of Alcohol Testing for the State of Ohio; he conceded that the calibration tests run by the Ohio Department of Health "were inadequate to independently determine and certify the actual alcohol concentration of the batch being certified. The number of samples selected from each batch ... did not constitute a statistically significant number..."; further, "he testified that the manufacturers of this solution..., Repco Laboratories and Stiefeel Laboratories, have refused to give him access to the manufacturer's own quality control protocol for the manufacturer's independent testing of the solutions"; the manufacturers claimed that the information was proprietary; "The Court concludes ... that the calibration checks obtained from the use of this solution are not trustworthy. The Court finds the Motion to Suppress is well taken. The results of the BAC test obtained by the law enforcement agency of this Defendant's breath are deemed by this Court inadmissible at trial."); Commonwealth v. Thill, 612 A.2d 1043 (Pa. Super. 1992) (the county failed to comply with a state regulation mandating that the simulator solution used to calibrate its breath-testing devices be certified "by a laboratory independent of the manufacturer"); Dubowski & Essary, *Evaluation of Commercial Breath-Alcohol Simulators: Further Studies*, 15 J. ANAL. TOX. 272 (Sept./Oct. 1991); Stamm, *The State's Weak Link: Simulator Solutions*, 22 THE CHAMPION 39 (Apr. 1998) (the article discusses Commonwealth v. Brosnick, 530 Pa. 158, 607 A.2d 725 (1992); in that case, a nine-month investigation by the state Auditor General found deficiencies in the procedures for verifying the accuracy of the simulator solution). *See also* State v. Schwalk, 430 N.W.2d 317 (N.D. 1988) (the foundation was inadequate because the State did not explain the effect of omitting a step contained in the state toxicologist's directions for collecting blood samples); State v. Sivesind, 439 N.W.2d 530 (N.D. 1989) (the prosecution failed to comply with *Schwalk* when the prosecution neglected to introduce the written instructions for correct blood-sample collection); State v. Watson, 51 Wash. App. 947, 756 P.2d 177 (1988) (evidence that the machine was working properly nine days after the test was inadequate to prove that it was working at the time of the test).

242. Snelgrove v. Department of Motor Vehicles, 194 Cal. App. 3d 1364, 240 Cal. Rptr. 281 (1987); People v. Angelino, 160 Ill. App. 3d 632, 112 Ill. Dec. 523, 513 N.E.2d 1132 (1987); Cissell v. Director of Revenue, 737 S.W.2d 522 (Mo. App. 1987); State v. Bush, 595 S.W.2d 386 (Mo. App. 1980); State v. Shephard, 639 S.W.2d 258 (Mo. App. 1982); State v. Hamaker, 524 S.W.2d 176 (Mo. App. 1975); State v. Sutton, 253 Or. 24, 450 P.2d 748 (1969).

witness has personal knowledge of the facts showing compliance with the required procedures,[243] but maintenance records are similarly admissible to show that the instrument in question was properly calibrated.[244] Depending on the foundation, the records could qualify for introduction as substantive evidence under the past recollection recorded,[245] business entry,[246] or official record[247] hearsay exceptions. Documentary evidence is not only admissible to establish the foundational element that the test instrument was in good working order; in many jurisdictions, hearsay law permits the admission of documentary evidence of the test result indicating the defendant's intoxication.[248] Although the process of

243. State v. McCormack, 92 Or. App. 84, 756 P.2d 1281 (although the witness did not administer the test, the witness was present and observed the administration of the test), *rev. denied,* 306 Or. 661, 763 P.2d 152 (1988).

244. United States v. Wilmer, 799 F.2d 495 (9th Cir. 1986), *cert. denied,* 481 U.S. 1004 (1987); People v. Kinne, 71 N.Y.2d 879, 522 N.E.2d 1052, 527 N.Y.S.2d 754 (1988); State v. Hughes, 713 S.W.2d 58 (Tenn. 1986); Triplett v. Schwendiman, 754 P.2d 87 (Utah App. 1988); State v. Beardsley, Case No. 97 TRC 4176-01 (Mun. Ct., Washington County, Ohio, Oct. 24, 1997) (Nuzum, J.) (the prosecution expert, Dr. Craig Sutheimer, was the Deputy Director of the Ohio Department of Health and the Chief of Alcohol Testing for the State of Ohio; he conceded that the calibration tests run by the Ohio Department of Health "were inadequate to independently determine and certify the actual alcohol concentration of the batch being certified. The number of samples selected from each batch ... did not constitute a statistically significant number..."; further, "he testified that the manufacturers of this solution..., Repco Laboratories and Stiefeel Laboratories, have refused to give him access to the manufacturer's own quality control protocol for the manufacturer's independent testing of the solutions"; the manufacturers claimed that the information was proprietary; "The Court concludes ... that the calibration checks obtained from the use of this solution are not trustworthy. The Court finds the Motion to Suppress is well taken. The results of the BAC test obtained by the law enforcement agency of this Defendant's breath are deemed by this Court inadmissible at trial."); State v. Friedrich, 681 So. 2d 1157 (Fla. Dist. Ct. App. Sept. 12, 1996) (although there were demonstrated variations in the alcohol concentrations in the solution bottles used to test the breath testing machines, the results of the tests were still admissible; there was testimony that it would probably take more than a year for the alcohol concentration in the solution to change significantly and that the stock solution was consumed in a matter of a few months); Commonwealth v. Thill, 612 A.2d 1043 (Pa. Super. 1992) (the county failed to comply with a state regulation mandating that the simulator solution used to calibrate its breath-testing devices be certified "by a laboratory independent of the manufacturer"); Dubowski & Essary, *Evaluation of Commercial Breath-Alcohol Simulators: Further Studies*, 15 J. ANAL. TOX. 272 (Sept./Oct. 1991); Stamm, *The State's Weak Link: Simulator Solutions*, 22 THE CHAMPION 39 (Apr. 1998) (the article discusses Commonwealth v. Brosnick, 530 Pa. 158, 607 A.2d 725 (1992); in that case, a nine-month investigation by the state Auditor General found deficiencies in the procedures for verifying the accuracy of the simulator solution). *See also* State v. Garlick, 313 Md. 209, 545 A.2d 27 (1988) (a hospital report of the results of blood and urine tests fell within the business entry hearsay exception); FED. R. EVID. 803(6), 803(8), 28 U.S.C.A.

245. FED. R. EVID. 803(5), 28 U.S.C.A..

246. *Id.* at FED. R. EVID. 803(6).

247. *Id. at* FED. R. EVID. 803(8).

248. United States v. Farmer, 820 F. Supp. 259 (W.D. Va. 1993) (business records exception); Lake v. Reed, 16 Cal. 4th 448, 940 P.2d 311, 65 Cal. Rptr. 2d 860 (1997) (upholding the admission

laying the foundation is ordinarily routine, some foundational elements often prove troublesome. The following subsections highlight those elements.

§ 22-6(A). Witness Qualifications.

If the witness merely testifies to the administration of a scientific intoxication test, including the digital readout, the opponent may object to the witness's qualifications on two grounds.

One objection is that there has been no showing of the witness's training in chemistry or engineering. A person should not be considered an expert simply because he or she has a title such as "Drug Recognition Examiner."[249] A few courts have sustained objections to the witness's alleged expert status,[250] but most courts summarily overrule these objections.[251] By way of example, some hold that: Only two days' training in the use of a Breathalyzer suffices;[252] training in chemistry is unnecessary;[253] and the witness need not understand the machine's

---

of an unsworn forensic laboratory report in an administrative proceeding to suspend a driver's license); Gananian v. Zolin, 33 Cal. App. 4th 634, 39 Cal. Rptr. 2d 384 (1995); Love v. Garcia, 634 So. 2d 158 (Fla. 1994); Bell v. Department of Motor Vehicles, 11 Cal. App. 4th 304, 13 Cal. Rptr. 2d 830, 832 (1992); Wilson v. Zolin, 9 Cal. App. 4th 1104, 11 Cal. Rptr. 2d 870 (1992) (a sworn statement of the officer who administered the test was admissible as an official record in a proceeding to suspend a driver's license); Burge v. Department of Motor Vehicles, 5 Cal. App. 4th 384, 7 Cal. Rptr. 2d 5 (1992) (business record hearsay exception), *modified* (May 5, 1992); Imachi v. Department of Motor Vehicles, 2 Cal. App. 4th 809, 3 Cal. Rptr. 2d 478 (1991), *modified* (Feb. 11, 1992); ILL. VEHICLE CODE § 11-501.4 ("admissible in evidence as a business record exception to the hearsay rule"); People v. Hoke, 213 Ill. App. 3d 263, 157 Ill. Dec. 124, 571 N.E.2d 1143 (1991); Judd v. Louisiana, 663 So. 2d 690 (La. 1995) (LA. REV. STAT. ANN. § 13:3714).

249. Sapir, *Proper Voir Dire: Qualifying the Expert Witness*, DWI J: LAW AND SCIENCE, Dec. 1998, at p. 6.

250. People v. Leahy, 17 Cal. Rptr. 2d 359 (Cal. Super. 1992) (a police officer was unqualified to establish the scientific validity of the HGN field sobriety test), *withdrawn*; People v. Williams, 3 Cal. App. 4th 1326, 5 Cal. Rptr. 2d 130 (1992); People v. Morgan, 236 N.Y.S.2d 1014 (Cty. Ct. 1962); State v. Helms, 127 N.C. App. 375, 490 S.E.2d 565 (1997) (the foundational witness for testimony about an HGN test must qualify as an expert), *rev'd*, 345 N.C. 578, 504 S.E.2d 293 (1998); State v. Garvick, 98 N.C. App. 556, 392 S.E.2d 115, 120 (although the witness was a chemistry professor, he had never run a Breathalyzer test and neither was aware of nor had conducted any experimentation with respect to the effect of a smudge on the vial), *app. dismissed*, 327 N.C. 142, 394 S.E.2d 182, *aff'd*, 327 N.C. 627, 398 S.E.2d 330 (1990).

251. *See* Desmond v. Superior Court, 161 Ariz. 522, 779 P.2d 1261 (1989) (the witness was a police officer who was properly certified to conduct the test); State v. Murphy, 451 N.W.2d 154 (Iowa 1990) (the witness was a police officer who had received training through a state law enforcement agency in administering the HGN test and was certified as an instructor in field sobriety tests). *See also* Carter v. Fenner, 136 F.2d 1000 (5th Cir. 1998) (a medical doctor was permitted to testify about the conduct of persons acting under the influence of alcohol).

252. Omohundro v. Arlington County, 194 Va. 773, 75 S.E.2d 496 (1953).

253. French v. State, 484 S.W.2d 716 (Tex. Crim. App. 1972). *See also* Washington v. State, 194 Ga. App. 756, 391 S.E.2d 718 (1990) (a chemist who had performed research on the physical

internal engineering.[254] The appellate courts commit the ruling on the witness's qualifications to the trial court's discretion and reverse the ruling only when there has been a clear abuse of the discretion.[255] These decisions are justifiable, since in most jurisdictions the validity of the underlying theory and the reliability of the instrumentation are judicially noticeable. Since the prosecutor does not have to elicit foundational testimony on the theory and instrument, the witness can qualify so long as he or she is adequately trained to operate the device.

A second, more substantial objection is that the witness lacks a qualification specified by statute. Several jurisdictions have statutes providing that only a licensed physician, registered nurse, or medical technologist can collect a blood or urine test.[256] The vast majority of states have statutes or administrative regulations requiring that the person operating the instrument be certified or have a permit to conduct a breath test.[257] The courts divide on the effect of a violation of these statutory provisions. If a blood or urine sample is withdrawn by someone who does not fall within a statutory list of qualified personnel, some courts

---

and behavioral effects of alcohol on persons under varying degrees of intoxication qualified as an expert on that subject); State v. Young, 795 P.2d 285, 290 (Haw. App.) (a certified operator supervisor of the Intoxilyzer was competent to testify about the partition coefficient), *cert. denied*, 71 Haw. 669, 833 P.2d 901 (1990). *But see* State v. Gibson, 515 So. 2d 556 (La. App. 1987) (training in chemistry is necessary when the police officer attempts to testify about the meaning of a breath-alcohol reading); State v. Priester, 301 S.C. 165, 391 S.E.2d 227 (1990) (a laboratory technologist was competent to conduct the test but not to testify about the effect of a certain level of alcohol on the human system, that is, whether a person with a blood-alcohol reading exceeding 100 milligrams per deciliter is intoxicated).

254. Beck v. State, 651 S.W.2d 827, 829 (Tex. App. 1983).

255. State v. Rector, 630 S.W.2d 603 (Mo. App. 1982).

256. Carlson, *supra* note 10, at 51-24. *See* Spears v. Commonwealth, 37 K.L.S. 15 (Ky. App., Dec. 21, 1990) (a Kentucky statute, KRS 189.520(6), uses the following language to describe the persons who may draw blood from a suspect: "Only a physician, registered nurse or qualified medical technician, duly licensed in Kentucky, acting at the request of the arresting officer, can withdraw any blood of any person submitting to a test under this section or KRS 186.565"; the court held that the phrase, "duly licensed in Kentucky," does not have the effect of prohibiting unlicensed medical personnel such as paramedics or phlebotomists from drawing blood; the court reasoned that the licensing requirement applies only to those categories of medical personnel who can be licensed); State v. Barnick, 477 N.W.2d 200 (N.D. 1991) (the statute requires that the person drawing the blood sample be a "qualified technician"; the witness was a self-styled phlebotomist without medical credentials or supervision). Provision I.A.1.a. of the Rules and Regulations of the Colorado Board of Health Relating to Tests for Alcohol and Other Drugs, 5-CCR-1005-2, states that "[b]lood samples shall be collected by venipuncture by a physician, registered nurse, certified paramedic, certified emergency medical technician, certified medical technologist, or a person whose normal duties include withdrawing blood samples under the supervision of a physician or registered nurse."

257. AMERICAN MED. ASS'N, ALCOHOL AND THE IMPAIRED DRIVER 162 (1970). *E.g.*, State v. Powell, 618 S.W.2d 47 (Mo. App. 1981) (construing the Missouri statute).

routinely exclude the test results.[258] One court even ruled that when the defense requests, the person performing the analysis must produce his or her certificate in court.[259] However, even when the person does not fall within the list, other courts admit the evidence so long as the person had medical training[260] or there is no evident prejudice resulting from the statutory violation.[261]

The courts also divide over the significance of the operator's lack of a permit or certificate. Some hold that proof of the operator's possession of a permit or certificate is a necessary part of the foundation.[262] Other courts refuse to suppress the evidence when the governing statute does not expressly provide that a violation of the statute leads to the inadmissibility of the resulting analysis.[263] Still other courts admit the evidence when the witness testifies that a certified operator was present and observed the test.[264]

§ 22-6(B). Validity of Instrument.

The opponent can attack the instrument or technique on two grounds.

Failure to Satisfy Frye *or* Daubert

One ground is that the proponent has not established the technique's scientific validity under *Daubert* or general acceptability under the *Frye* test discussed in Chapter 1. This attack is rarely successful. On numerous occasions, the courts have admitted blood tests,[265] field sobriety tests,[266] urine tests,[267] and breath tests,

---

258. Carlson, *supra* note 10, at 51-24. *See* Otte v. State, 172 Neb. 110, 108 N.W.2d 737 (1961); State v. Hilton, 49 Or. App. 927, 620 P.2d 970 (1980).

259. Comment, *Admissibility Under Louisiana Law of the Results of Chemical Tests of a Person's Blood Alcohol Concentration*, 35 LOY. L. REV. 1402, 1414 (1990) ("In the case of State v. Jones, [316 So. 2d 100 (La. 1975)] the Louisiana Supreme Court held that the statutory best evidence rule requires that, if the defendant insists, the person performing the analysis must produce his or her certificate in court for the test results to be admissible. Since *Jones* was decided, the Louisiana Legislature has repealed the best evidence statute in favor of a set of articles in the Louisiana Code of Evidence .... In this writer's opinion, the change in the statutory law legislatively overrules the best evidence portion of the *Jones* decision).

260. State v. Groulx, 109 N.H. 281, 249 A.2d 690 (1969); State v. Stowers, 649 S.W.2d 607 (Tenn. Crim. App. 1983).

261. Nicholas v. State, 268 Ark. 541, 595 S.W.2d 237 (1980).

262. State v. Gerber, 206 Neb. 75, 291 N.W.2d 403 (1980).

263. People v. Rawlings, 42 Cal. App. 3d 952, 117 Cal. Rptr. 651 (1974).

264. Watson v. Frierson, 272 Ark. 316, 613 S.W.2d 824 (1981).

265. Woolley v. Hafner's Wagon Wheel, Inc., 22 Ill. 2d 413, 176 N.E.2d 757 (1961). *Compare* People v. Campbell, 73 N.Y.2d 481, 539 N.E.2d 584, 541 N.Y.S.2d 756 (1989) (the prosecution must establish the reliability of the DuPont Automatic Clinical Analyzer) *with* Hammond v. State, 569 A.2d 81 (Del. 1989) (no foundation is needed for the Analyzer other than proof that it is a hospital instrument used by physicians for therapeutic purposes).

including the Drunkometer,[268] the Breathalyzer,[269] the gas chromatograph,[270] and infrared tests.[271]

The only tests currently struggling to gain judicial acceptance are the acoustic analysis of audiotapes of allegedly intoxicated persons,[272] the horizontal gaze nystagmus (HGN) test discussed in § 22-1, and portable breath tests. There is a four-way split of authority over the admissibility of testimony based on horizontalgaze nystagmus.[273] In a National Highway Traffic Safety

---

266. People v. Sides, 199 Ill. App. 3d 203, 145 Ill. Dec. 160, 556 N.E.2d 778 (1990) (in a case involving the finger-to-nose, walk-and-turn, and one-leg-stand tests, the court commented that "[n]o expert testimony is needed nor is a showing of scientific principles required before a jury can be permitted to conclude that a person who performs badly on the field-sobriety tests may have his mental or physical faculties ... impaired ...."); New York v. Quinn, 153 Misc.2d 139, 580 N.Y.S.2d 818 (N.Y. Dist. Ct. 1991) (a battery of field sobriety tests, including the one-leg stand, the finger-to-nose, and horizontal gaze nystagmus), *rev'd*, 158 Misc.2d 1015, 607 N.Y.S.2d 534 (A.D. 1993).

267. Bunderdeanu v. England, 219 A.2d 104 (D.C. App. 1966).

268. Woolley v. Hafner's Wagon Wheel, Inc., 22 Ill. 2d 413, 176 N.E.2d 757 (1961); People v. Bobczyk, 343 Ill. App. 504, 99 N.E.2d 567 (1951); State v. Roberts, 102 N.H. 414, 158 A.2d 458 (1960); State v. Greul, 59 N.J. Super. 34, 157 A.2d 44 (1959); McDonald v. Ferguson, 129 N.W.2d 348 (N.D. 1964); Toms v. State, 95 Okla. Crim. 60, 239 P.2d 812 (1952); State v. Baker, 56 Wash. 2d 846, 355 P.2d 806 (1960).

269. State v. Bush, 595 S.W.2d 386 (Mo. App. 1980).

270. State v. Tiernan, 206 N.W.2d 898 (Iowa 1973).

271. Watson v. Frierson, 272 Ark. 316, 613 S.W.2d 824 (1981); State v. Crea, 119 Idaho 352, 806 P.2d 445, 447 (1991) ("scientific acceptance of the Intoximeter 3000 is well established in Idaho and many other jurisdictions, including Alaska, Georgia, New Hampshire, New York, Tennessee, Wisconsin, Wyoming, and country-wide acceptance in England"); Schultz v. Commissioner of Pub. Safety, 393 N.W.2d 373 (Minn. App. 1986); People v. Flynn, 129 Misc. 2d 176, 492 N.Y.S.2d 882 (1985); People v. Gallagher, 132 Misc. 2d 195, 503 N.Y.S.2d 500 (1986); Dayton v. Schenck, 63 Ohio Misc. 14, 16 Ohio Op. 3d 97, 409 N.E.2d 284 (1980); Gandara v. State, 661 S.W.2d 749 (Tex. App. 1983); State v. Brooks, 643 A.2d 226 (Vt. 1993). *But see* Sapir, *First Draw Your Curves; Then Plot Your Readings: Oregon and The Intoxilyzer Model 5000 Under Daubert*, 13 DRUNK DRIVING LAW LETTER 189, 193 (July 1, 1994) ("Oregon accepted the new Intoxilyzer Model 5000/568G without [the] validating data" necessary to satisfy the *Daubert* standard).

272. Tanford, Pisoni & Johnson, *Novel Scientific Evidence of Intoxication: Acoustic Analysis of Voice Recordings from the Exxon Valdez*, 82 J. CRIM. L. & CRIMINOLOGY 579 (1991).

273. The test was developed by DARTS (Drug-Alcohol Recognition Training Seminars), 1410 E. Glenoaks Boulevard, Glendale, California. Nystagmus is a jerking motion of the eyes. Horizontal gaze nystagmus occurs when the eye attempts to follow an object that the officer slowly moves to the suspect's side. The DARTS researchers contend that the angle of onset of the jerking motion correlates with the suspect's blood alcohol concentration. DARTS' press releases claim the following correlation: 45° — .05% BAC, 40 — .10%, 35 — .15%, and 30 — .20%. On behalf of the National Highway Traffic Safety Administration, the Southern California Research Institute of Los Angeles has studied the technique. ERWIN, *supra* note 15, at 26. Although the Institute found some evidence of a correlation between the BAC and the angle of onset, the Institute concluded that the nystagmus can be caused by other factors such as brain damage. *Id.* at 33. In one published opinion on the test, the court held the evidence inadmissible. People v. Loomis, 156 Cal. App. 3d

Supp. 1, 203 Cal. Rptr. 767 (1984). The court held that there was insufficient proof of the test's reliability and of the officer's qualifications as an expert on the subject. *See also* Umeda & Sakata, 87 ANN. OTOLOGY, RHINOLOGY & LARYNGOLOGY 392 (1978).

The test was originally used by the Los Angeles Police Department. *TAP Bulletin Describes Test to Identify Drug-Impaired Drivers*, N.I.J. REPORTS 28 (Summer 1990). In State v. Superior Court of County of Cochise, 149 Ariz. 269, 718 P.2d 171 (1986), the court not only held that the test is sufficiently reliable to be used in establishing probable cause for a motorist's arrest; the court also indicated that at trial, testimony about the test is admissible to corroborate a chemical test result. *See also* Ballard v. State, 955 P.2d 931 (Alaska App.1998) (the test "is premised on generally accepted scientific theory;" however, the prosecution may make "no attempt to correlate the HGN test with any particular blood-alcohol level, range of blood-alcohol levels, or level of impairment"); State v. Grier, 791 P.2d 627 (Alaska App. 1990) (an HGN test result may be used to establish probable cause for an arrest for drunk driving); Williams v. State, 710 So. 2d 24 (Fla. Dist. Ct. App. 1998) (standing alone, an HGN test neither triggers a presumption of impairment nor establishes a blood alcohol level of 0.08% or more); State v. Edman, 452 N.W.2d 169 (Iowa 1990) (citing *Murphy, infra,* the court holds that HGN test results are now admissible without a foundation establishing the scientific validity of the test); State v. Murphy, 451 N.W.2d 154 (Iowa 1990) ("The Iowa Law Enforcement Academy and the U.S. Department of Transportation view the HGN test as [a] ... reliable indicator[] of intoxication and recommend its use as a field sobriety test"; a police officer trained in administering the test may testify about the test results at trial even if the record does not contain any scientific testimony about the reliability of the test; the court analogized the test to other field sobriety tests); State v. Armstrong, 561 So. 2d 883 (La. App.) (the HGN test is generally accepted by the relevant scientific community), *cert. denied,* 568 So. 2d 1077 (La. 1990); People v. Quinn, 153 Misc.2d 139, 580 N.Y.S.2d 818 (Dist. Ct. 1991) ("HGN is generally accepted by the scientific community"); State v. Nagel, 30 Ohio App. 3d 80, 506 N.E.2d 285 (1986); State v. Chiodo, 80 Or. App. 453, 722 P.2d 58, *review denied,* 302 Or. 461, 730 P.2d 1251 (1986); State v. Edmundson, 379 N.W.2d 835 (S.D. 1985); Howard v. State, 744 S.W.2d 640 (Tex. App. 1987) (the test is admissible for qualitative rather than quantitative purposes).

But see United States v. Van Griffin, 874 F.2d 634, 638 (9th Cir. 1989) (when the federal prosecutor adduced testimony about an HGN test, the defense was entitled to introduce a Department of Transportation manual "in order to show the measures that are necessary to be taken in order to have a reliable test for nystagmus"; although the manual was hearsay, it was admissible as "a party admission by the United States under FED. R. EVID. 801(d)(2)(D)"); *In re* Malone, 575 So. 2d 106 (Ala. 1990) (the admission of testimony about an HGN test was error because the prosecution failed to demonstrate either the test's reliability or the scientific principles which the test is based on); State *ex rel.* Hamilton v. City Court of Mesa, 165 Ariz. 514, 799 P.2d 855 (1990) (an officer may testify that the HGN test indicates a possible neurological dysfunction, but the officer may not estimate BAC based on the test); People v. Ojeda, 225 Cal. App. 3d 404, 275 Cal. Rptr. 472 (1990) (the officer may testify that the test result indicates that the defendant was under the influence of alcohol; but without a special showing of scientific expertise, the officer may not state that the test result indicates a particular BAC level); People v. Dakuras, 172 Ill. App.3d 865, 122 Ill. Dec.791, 527 N.E.2d 163, *appeal denied,* 123 Ill. 2d 561, 128 Ill. Dec. 894, 535 N.E.2d 405 (1988) (the Illinois statute precludes the prosecution from introducing the test at trial); People v. Vega, 145 Ill. App. 3d 996, 99 Ill. Dec. 808, 496 N.E.2d 501 (1986); State v. Borchardt, 224 Neb. 47, 395 N.W.2d 551 (1986); State v. Helms, 348 N.C. 578, 504 S.E.2d 293 (1998) (the state has yet to demonstrate that the underlying scientific principle is reliable); State v. Bresson, 51 Ohio St. 3d 123, 554 N.E.2d 1330 (1990) (the court quotes a U.S. Department of Transportation manual stating that the HGN test is "the single most accurate field test to use in determining whether a person is alcohol impaired"; while a qualified expert may testify about HGN at both a suppression hearing and trial, the expert may not base a BAC estimate on HGN); State v. Reed, 83 Or. App. 451, 732 P.2d 66 (1987) (the prosecution failed to present expert testimony establishing the relationship between nystagmus and alcohol consumption); Commonwealth v. Miller, 367 Pa. Super. 359, 532 A.2d 1186 (1987) (the police officer's testimony was insufficient to establish general acceptance of the underlying principle within the scientific community); State v. Barker, 366 S.E.2d 642 (W. Va. 1988) (the court refused to judicially notice the validity of the HGN test, and the prosecution had failed to offer scientific evidence to establish its validity; moreover, even if the test is valid, the witness may not base a BAC estimate on the test alone); Annot., *Horizontal gaze nystagmus test: use in impaired driving prosecution*, 60 A.L.R.4TH 1129 (1988); Pangman, *Horizontal Gaze Nystagmus: Voodoo Science*, 2 DWI JOURNAL 1 (Mar. 1987); Rouleau, *Unreliability of the Horizontal Gaze Nystagmus Test*, 4 AM. JUR. PROOF OF FACTS 3D 439 (1989); Tarantino, *Combatting Gaze Nystagmus Test*, 1 D.W.I. JOURNAL 1 (July/Aug. 1986).

The upshot is that there is currently a four-way split of authority over the admissibility of HGN evidence.

The four basic views are: HGN test evidence is inadmissible for any purpose; HGN evidence is admissible for the limited purpose of establishing probable cause at a pretrial suppression hearing; HGN evidence is admissible at trial, but the expert may not base an estimate of breath or blood alcohol concentration on an HGN test; and HGN evidence is fully admissible at trial. In this test, the officer holds a pencil, penlight, or similar object 12-15 inches in front of the suspect's face and moves it to the suspect's extreme left and then back to the extreme right. TRANSP. SAFETY INST., NAT'L HIGHWAY TRAFFIC SAFETY ADMIN., DRUG EVALUATION AND CLASSIFICATION TRAINING PROGRAM: THE DRUG RECOGNITION EXPERT SCHOOL IV-9 (1993). The formula, (BA = 50 - Angle), yields the BAC estimate. *Id.* at IV-13.

Although there are four basic views, in truth the cases take a wide range of views on the admissibility of HGN testimony. People v. Kirk, 289 Ill. App. 3d 326, 681 N.E.2d 1073 (1997) (the defendant was entitled to a hearing to determine whether the test satisfies *Frye*); State v. Murphy, 953 S.W.2d 200 (Tenn. 1997) (the prosecution must lay a foundation showing that the test is admissible under Rule 702); Meaney, *Horizontal Gaze Nystagmus: A Closer Look*, 36 JURIMETRICS J. 383 (Summer 1996) ("All ten state supreme courts that have directly considered the admissibility of HGN testimony to show that a defendant was operating under the influence have decided in favor of admissibility. However, two recent state supreme courts have questioned this result." The author believes that "despite being generally accepted by some scientific communities for some purposes, HGN is not scientifically valid as a field sobriety test."); Honts & Amato-Henderson, *Horizontal Gaze Nystagmus Test: The State of the Science in 1995*, 71 N.D. L. REV. 671, 674-75 (1995). The following cases generally sustain the admission of HGN testimony: People v. Joehnk, 35 Cal. App. 4th 1488, 42 Cal. Rptr. 2d 6 (1995); Zimmerman v. State, 693 A.2d 311 (Del. 1997) (the test result is admissible to establish probable cause and as substantive evidence of intoxication); State v. Beam, 2 Fla. L. Weekly Supp. 444 (County Ct. Dade County Aug. 22, 1994) (after surveying the cases, the court concludes that the evidence is admissible in part because the *Frye* test is inapplicable); State v. Williams, 3 Fla. L. Weekly Supp. 70 (County Ct, Dade County Jan. 19, 1995) (the test results are admissible "to establish (1) that the defendant was impaired; and/or (2) that the defendant was over the legal limit; and/or (3) the defendant's specific breath or blood alcohol level at the time he performed the test"); State v. Taylor, 694 A.2d 907 (Me. 1997) (although evidence of the test is admissible to support probable cause and as substantive proof of intoxication, the administering officer may not testify to a particular blood alcohol level); Schultz v. State, 106 Md. App. 145, 664 A.2d 60 (Spec. App. 1995) (it is judicially noticeable that if properly administered by a qualified officer, an HGN test is sufficiently reliable to be admissible); People v.

Administration test of HGN, the researchers found a substantial margin of error.[274] Given that finding, a split of authority is expectable. As the cases cited in footnote indicate, there is authority supporting each of the following views: HGN testimony is inadmissible for any purpose; HGN is admissible for the limited purpose of establishing probable cause at a pretrial suppression hearing; HGN is admissible at trial, but the expert may not base an estimate of breath or blood alcohol concentration on an HGN test; and HGN test is fully admissible at trial both to show intoxication and to quantify the suspect's BAC. The case law is in flux, and any generalization is hazardous. However, it is probably fair to say that although a few jurisdictions judicially notice the validity of the HGN test,[275] most

---

Berger, 217 Mich. App. 213, 551 N.W.2d 421 (1996); State v. Klawitter, 518 N.W.2d 577 (Minn. 1994) (Drug Recognition Protocol); State v. Hill, 865 S.W.2d 702 (Mo. App. 1993) (the prosecution expert testified that the test is used by law enforcement in all fifty states); People v. Quinn, 153 Misc.2d 139, 580 N.Y.S2d 818 (Dist. Ct. 1991), *rev'd*, 158 Misc.2d 1015, 607 N.Y.S.2d 534 (Sup. Ct. 1993). The following cases admit HGN for the limited purpose of establishing the presence of alcohol, but not in order to prove that the defendant had a particular BAC: State v. Superior Court of County of Cochise, 149 Ariz. 269, 718 P.2d 171 (App. 1986); People v. Burning, 592 N.E.2d 1222 (Ill. App. 1992); Whitson v. State, 863 S.W.2d 794 (Ark. 1993); State v. O'Key, 321 Or. 285, 899 P.2d 663 (1995); City of Fargo v. McLaughlin, 512 N.W.2d 700 (N.D. 1994); Emerson v. State, 880 S.W.2d 759 (Tex. Crim. App.), *cert. denied*, 513 U.S. 931 (1994), ; State v. Barker, 366 S.E.2d 642 (W.Va. 1988).. The following cases hold HGN evidence inadmissible: People v. Leahy, 8 Cal. 4th 587, 882 P.2d 321, 34 Cal. Rptr. 2d 663 (1994) (inadequate foundation); State v. Meador, 674 So. 2d 826 (Fla. Dist. Ct. App. 1996); State v. Witte, 251 Kan. 313, 836 P.2d 1110 (1992) (relying on *Frye*); Commonwealth v. Sand, 424 Mass. 184, 675 N.E.2d 370 (1997); Young v. Brookhaven, 693 So. 2d 1355 (Miss. 1997) (the HGN test is not generally accepted in the scientific community); Commonwealth v. Moore, 430 Pa. Super. 575, 635 A.2d 625 (1993), *appeal denied*, 656 A.2d 118 (Pa. 1995); Commonwealth v. Apollo, 603 A.2d 1023 (Pa. Super. 1992) (the proffered expert was a behavioral optometrist who described his personal observations but was unaware of any studies questioning the accuracy of the HGN technique); State v. Cissne, 72 Wash. App. 677, 865 P.2d 564, *review denied*, 124 Wash.2d 1006, 877 P.2d 1288 (1994); Simpson, *The Effect of Daubert on the Admissibility of HGN and Direct Breath Test Evidence*, DWI J., Vol. 9, No. 5, at 5 (May 1994). Of course, the foundational witness must qualify as an expert. State v. Helms, 127 N.C. App. 375, 490 S.E.2d 565 (1997), *rev'd*, 345 N.C. 578, 504 S.E.2d 293 (1998). To date, the courts have been relatively lax in evaluating the witness's credentials. Columbus v. Anderson, 74 Ohio App. 3d 768, 600 N.E.2d 712 (1991) (a three day course on HGN); State v. Earley, 1986 Ohio App. LEXIS 5878, 1986 WL 2998 (Ohio App. Mar. 10, 1986) (a three or five day special training program).

274. Bell, *.10% Solution*, 23 THE CHAMPION 65, 67 (Apr. 1999) (an N.H.T.S.A. manual states: "Considered independently, the nystagmus test was the most accurate of the three [field tests] . . . . 82 percent [of the persons who tested positive on the HGN test] had BACs of 0.10 or higher").

275. The jurisdictions are Iowa, Ohio, and Texas. Russell, *Note and Comment: Judicial Notice of the Validity of the Horizontal Gas Nystagmus Test in Texas: Emerson v. State*, 2 TEX.WESLEYAN L. REV. 355, 356 (1996); State v. Nagel, 30 Ohio App.3d 80, 506 N.E.2d 285 (1986); State v. Witte, 251 Kan. 313, 318, 836 P.2d 1110, 1112 (1992). In State v. Ito, 65 Cr.L. (BNA) 178 (Haw. Intermed. App. Ct., Apr. 29, 1999), after noting the split of authority, the court upheld a trial judge's decision to judicially notice the reliability of the HGN test. However, the court limited its ruling to cases in which the prosecution offers the HGN test result "as evidence that the police had

states require that the proponent present live expert testimony to lay the foundation and hold that without special scientific training, a police officer is unqualified to present the necessary testimony.[276] Further, while the majority of courts would permit the use of HGN testimony at a pretrial suppression hearing, at trial "the overwhelming majority of courts that have faced the issue"[277] preclude the officer from basing an opinion about a "specific blood alcohol content" on an HGN test result.

As reflected in the cases cited in footnote, there is also a sharp division of judicial sentiment over the passive alcohol sensor.[278] Each of the following views

---

probable cause to believe that a defendant was DUI." The court stopped short of addressing the issue of whether HGN is admissible at trial to prove intoxication.

276. Brunson v. State, 580 So. 2d 62 (Ala. Crim. App. 1991); Zimmerman v. State, 693 A.2d 311 (Del. 1997); State v. Meador, 674 So. 2d 826 (Fla. Dist. Ct. App. 1996); Commonwealth v. Sands, 675 N.E.2d 370 (Mass. 1997); Hulse v. State, 63 Cr.L. (BNA) 194 (Mont. Sup. Ct., May 5, 1998); State v. Borchardt, 395 N.W.2d 551 (Neb. 1986); State v. Torres, 976 P.2d 20 (N.M.1999) (the court expressly stated that in adopting this position, it was following the majority view; the arresting officer testified that the National Highway Traffic Safety Administration accepted the test, that the test was nationally certified, and that the test was routinely given; the court ruled that the officer's testimony was an inadequate foundation); State v. Helms, 490 S.E.2d 565 (N. C. Ct. App. 1997); Commonwealth v. Stringer, 678 A.2d 1200 (Pa. Super. Ct. 1996); State v. Murphy, 953 S.W.2d 200 (Tenn. 1997); State v. Cissne, 865 P.2d 564 (Wash. Ct. App. 1994); Bianchi, *Eye Test for Drunk Drivers Requires Expert Testimony*, LAWYERS WEEKLY USA, Mar. 22, 1999.

277. Wilson v. State, 124 Md. App. 543, 723 A.2d 494 (1999).

278. As in the case of HGN test evidence, the courts are badly divided. *See* the discussion of the four-way split of authority over HGN evidence in note 21, *supra*. Some courts have held that the passive alcohol sensor test result cannot be admitted at trial as substantive evidence of intoxication. Trousdale v. State, 500 So. 2d 1329 (Ala. Crim. App. 1986); Boyd v. Montgomery, 472 So. 2d 694 (Ala. Crim. App. 1985); People v. Davis, 296 Ill.App3d 923, 695 N.E.2d 1363, 231 Ill. Dec. 244 (1998) (at a suppression hearing, the prosecution could introduce testimony about the results of a preliminary breath screening test in order to show that the defendant's arrest was supported by probable cause; the dissent argued that the statute, 625 I.L.S.C. 5/11-501.5 clearly forbids the state from introducing PBT evidence in court for any purpose); State v. Deshaw, 404 N.W.2d 156 (Iowa 1987); State v. Ifill, 574 A.2d 889 (Me. 1990) (testimony about the Alcohol Level Evaluation Roadside Tester (ALERT) is usually inadmissible, but the defense can open the door); People v. Tracy, 186 Mich. App. 171, 463 N.W.2d 457 (1990) (the result of a PBT test may be used to establish probable cause in an affidavit for a search warrant authorizing the taking of a blood sample; a Michigan statute provides that "in a criminal prosecution, [a PBT test may be used] solely to assist the court ... in determining a challenge to the validity of an arrest"); People v. Thomas, 121 A.D.2d 73, 509 N.Y.S.2d 668 (1986); People v. Thomas, 70 N.Y.2d 823, 517 N.E.2d 1323, 523 N.Y.S.2d 437 (1987) (the Alco-Sensor test results were offered to establish reasonable grounds to give the defendant a Breathalyzer test, but it was irrelevant on that theory, since reasonable cause is not in issue at trial); State v. Schimmel, 409 N.W.2d 335 (N.D. 1987); Commonwealth v. Myrtetus, 397 Pa. Super. 299, 580 A.2d 42 (1990) (the result of a preliminary breath test may serve only as an aid to the police in determining probable cause for arrest; at trial, the defendant therefore could not introduce the test result). *But see* Patrick v. State, 295 Ark. 473, 750 S.W.2d 391 (1988) (although the prosecution may use the test results only to establish probable cause, the defense may employ the results as exculpatory evidence at trial). There is even authority

enjoys some judicial support: The test result cannot be admitted at trial as substantive evidence of intoxication; the test result may be used pretrial to establish probable cause; and the test result is altogether inadmissible both at trial and pretrial hearings. At this juncture in the evolution of the case law, the majority of cases probably follow the second view. In an early 1999 decision, the Arkansas Supreme Court surveyed the case law and concluded that nearly every state that has confronted the issue has refused to admit the test result for any

---

that the test may not be used for the limited purpose of establishing probable cause. State v. Green, 217 Neb. 70, 348 N.W.2d 429 (1984). However, most courts approve that limited use of the test result. Turrentine v. State, 176 Ga. App. 145, 335 S.E.2d 630 (1985); State v. Johnson, 503 N.E.2d 431 (Ind. App. 1987); State v. Smith, 218 Neb. 201, 352 N.W.2d 620 (1984); State v. Le Beau, 144 Vt. 315, 476 A.2d 128 (1984). Kuwatch, *Preliminary Alcohol Screening Devices*, 23 C.A.C.J. FORUM 47 (Oct. 1996) ("An active device ... requires the cooperation of the test subject who must blow into it enough to cause a ... B.A.C. reading. A passive device merely tests the air in its vicinity for the presence of alcohol...."); Granick, *"PAS" or Fail: Use and Abuse of the Preliminary Alcohol Screening Device*, 20 THE CHAMPION 40 (Apr. 1996) (in this article, the terminology is preliminary alcohol screening (PAS) test rather than PBT; the author cites Bokor v. Department of Licensing, 874 P.2d 168 (Wash. App. 1994) as excluding PAS test results even for the limited purpose of showing probable cause; however, the author concedes that "though PAS results are often excluded from trial, the law generally allows courts to consider the test results for probable cause"); Porche v. State, 217 Ga. App. 325, 457 S.E.2d 578 (1995); Whiteley v. State, 188 Ga. App. 129, 372 S.E.2d 296 (1988), *cert. denied* (Sep. 16, 1988); Dotson v. State, 213 Ga. App. 7, 443 S.E.2d 650 (1994); People v. Rose, 268 Ill. App. 3d 174, 643 N.E.2d 865, 205 Ill. Dec. 574 (1994) (the court concludes that although the prosecution may introduce the results of a preliminary breath test to prove probable cause for an arrest, PBT test results are inadmissible at trial to prove intoxication; the court rests its conclusion on the construction of ILLINOIS VEHICLE CODE § 11-501.5); Commonwealth v. Reed (Grant Dist. Ct., Ky., Dec. 23, 1993) (the February 1994 issue of THE ADVOCATE sets out the order by Judge Stanley Billingsley; in the order, the judge rules that the prosecution may not introduce PBT results without foundational testimony showing compliance with certain standards prescribed by Ky. Rev. Stat. 189A.103 and 189A.105; in the instant case, the judge suppressed the test results because the prosecution's showing was deficient); Commonwealth v. Stanley, 629 A.2d 940 (Pa. Super. 1993) (excluding evidence of a preliminary breath test). ILLINOIS VEHICLE CODE § 11-501.5 provides that police may rely on the result of a preliminary breath screening test to determine whether to require a suspect to submit to a chemical test. The statute adds that the test result "may be used by a defendant as evidence in any administrative or court proceeding...." *But see* Commonwealth v. Allen, 684 A.2d 633 (Pa. Super. Ct. 1996) (although the results are inadmissible in prosecutions for drunk driving, they may be considered in a prosecution for underage drinking); Stacy v. Commonwealth, 22 Va. App. 417 (App. 1996) (although the results are inadmissible at trial, they may be considered at a pretrial hearing on whether there was probable cause for an arrest); People v. Bury, 41 Cal. App. 4th 1194, 49 Cal. Rptr. 2d 107 (1996) (testimony about PAS testing is admissible without an evidentiary hearing on its scientific reliability, since the test is not a novel scientific technique); Coniglio v. Department of Motor Vehicles, 39 Cal. App. 4th 666, 46 Cal. Rptr. 2d 123 (1995) (the PAS test is not subject to the regulatory standards for forensic alcohol analysis; hence, evidence of a PAS test can be admitted without a showing of compliance with those standards); People v. Halsey, 209 Ill. Dec. 894, 652 N.E.2d 434 (App. 1995) (PBT results are admissible subject to the usual standards for admissibility).

purpose other than establishing probable cause.[279] In another 1999 decision, the Court of Appeals for the Eighth Circuit stated that "almost every state that has addressed the issue has refused to admit the results of the test for purposes other than probable cause."[280]

Failure to Comply with Statutory or Administrative Requirements

As the preceding paragraphs indicate, on occasion a *Daubert* or *Frye* objection will block the admission of the testimony. However, to be frank, a second objection is more promising. The objection is that the operator did not employ an instrument or technique approved by the appropriate state agency. As early as 1970, twenty states[281] had statutes or administrative regulations providing that the operator must use an instrument approved by a state agency such as the department of health or public safety.[282] Many jurisdictions have adopted similar provisions since then. For example, the Missouri statute reads that the test "shall be performed according to methods approved by the state division of health . . ."[283] Courts split on the effect of the operator's use of an unapproved method.[284] While some admit the evidence if the operator used a scientifically valid instrument, other jurisdictions insist that the operator employ an approved device.[285]

---

279. Munhall v. State, 337 Ark. 41, 986 S.W.2d 863 (1999).

280. United States v. Iron Cloud, 171 F.3d 587, 590 (8th Cir. 1999).

281. At one time, the U.S. Department of Transportation issued mandatory standards for both testing devices and instruments used to calibrating the devices. K. DUBOWSKI, THE TECHNOLOGY OF BREATH-ALCOHOL TESTING 25 (1991). However, even when those regulations were in place, they were merely conditions to federal funding. For example, a state could federal funding only if it used the funds to purchase a testing device on the conforming products list. However, in December 1984, the mandatory standards were converted into mere "model specifications." *Id.*

282. American Med. Ass'n, *supra* note 257, at 162. *E.g.,* OR. REV. STAT. § 487.545 (1979), quoted in State v. Hilton, 49 Or. App. 927, 620 P.2d 970 (1980).

283. MO. REV. STAT. § 577.020.2, quoted in State v. Powell, 618 S.W.2d 47, 49 (Mo. App. 1981); State v. Squires, 426 S.E.2d 738 (S.C. 1992) (infrared spectroscopy is a "chemical test" within the meaning of the state implied consent statute).

284. Annot., 96 A.L.R.3D 745 (1979); State v. Crea, 119 Idaho 352, 806 P.2d 445 (1991) (notwithstanding the deactivation of the Taguchi cell, the Intoximeter 3000 was an approved alcohol testing instrument); State v. Erickson, 517 N.W.2d 646 (N.D. 1994) (although a recorder integrator was a necessary component of a gas chromatography, the integrator was not a "device" that had to be approved by the State Toxicologist).

285. Nick v. Department of Motor Vehicles, 12 Cal. App. 4th 1407 n.6, 16 Cal. Rptr. 2d 305, 311 n.6 ("these tests are not performed on equipment licensed for the purpose of establishing blood-alcohol tests and, accordingly, there is no foundation for admitting the results"), *cert. denied,* 510 U.S. 950 (1993); State v. Polak, 598 So. 2d 150 (Fla. App. 1992) (the bypass of the Taguchi Sensor Cell on an intoximeter was such a substantial modification of the instrument that the modified instrument was no longer an approved instrument); State v. Salhus, 220 N.W.2d 852 (N.D. 1974); Ohio v. Ripple, 70 Ohio St.3d 86, 637 N.E.2d 304 (1994); State v. Baldwin, 569

As the prior paragraph points out, in some cases the defense can invoke a statutory requirement as a basis for excluding prosecution testimony. However, these statutory requirements can be a two-edged sword from the defense perspective. Assume that the prosecution can satisfy the requirement. Some jurisdictions hold that if the operator uses an approved device, the defense in a driver's license suspension hearing may not even present expert testimony that the allowed error margin is too great.[286]

§ 22-6(C). Validity of Formula.

The proponent might not be content to offer the test result; the proponent might go farther and may invite the expert to extrapolate to the time of the legally relevant event. The extrapolation not only requires that the witness have different expertise; it also raises the question of the validity of the formula used to make the extrapolation. Typically the expert uses a hypothetical blood alcohol curve, entailing assumptions about absorption, the peak, and elimination. On the one hand, the courts recognize the inexactitude of extrapolations.[287] On the other hand, they have held that as a general proposition, the assumptions have sufficient scientific validity to render the extrapolation admissible.[288] In a specific case, of course, the extrapolation computation might be so speculative that it is inadmissible.[289]

§ 22-6(D). Test Conditions.

As noted in § 22-3(B), there were claims that many breath testing devices were vulnerable to RFI. Several courts responded to these claims by excluding evidence produced by devices that have not been tested for RFI vulnerability or adding new elements to the prosecution's foundation.

N.W.2d 37 (Wis. App. 1997) (if the breath alcohol test results are obtained by using an unapproved instrument, the results are not entitled to automatic admissibility or even a prima facie presumption of accuracy), *rev'd*, 576 N.W.2d 904 (Wis. 1998).

286. Owens v. Motor Vehicles Div., 319 Or. 259, 875 P.2d 463 (1994).

287. Ullman v. Overnite Transp. Co., 563 F.2d 152 (5th Cir. 1977).

288. *Id.*; United States v. DuBois, 645 F.2d 642, 643 (8th Cir. 1981); Lopez v. State, 478 So. 2d 1110 (Fla. App. 1985); Shuman v. State, 489 N.E.2d 126 (Ind. App. 1986); State v. Allen, 212 N.J. Super. 276, 514 A.2d 879 (1986); State v. Catoe, 78 N.C. App. 167, 336 S.E.2d 691 (1985), *cert. denied,* 316 N.C. 380, 344 S.E.2d 1 (1986). *But see* State v. Tischio, 107 N.J. 504, 527 A.2d 388 (1987) (the two necessary elements of the per se offense, the operation of a motor vehicle and the proscribed blood alcohol concentration, need not occur simultaneously; therefore, extrapolation testimony is neither required nor permitted), *app. dismissed,* 484 U.S. 1038 (1988).

289. LaRocca, *Admissibility of Delayed Blood Test Results — Commonwealth v. Gonzalez, 519 Pa. 116, 546 A.2d 26 (1988)*, 62 TEMP. L. REV. 757, 758-59, 765 (1989) (the expert admitted that the lack of information about the time of the defendant's last drink precluded a more definite opinion).

In one of the first RFI cases, *State v. Gallagher,*[290] the trial judge ordered a statewide ban on the use of the Breathalyzer. The Minnesota Supreme Court later vacated the ban.[291] The state police then implemented new testing procedures to ensure that its devices are immune to RFI. A Minnesota trial court held that those procedures "are effective means of preventing RFI from affecting Breathalyzer readings in the future."[292]

The issue was litigated in Rhode Island in a case entitled *Durand v. City of Woonsocket.*[293] A civil suit was filed on behalf of a class of persons who had been charged with drunk driving on the basis of Breathalyzer tests. The complaint alleged that the conviction of the plaintiffs on the basis of Breathalyzer tests subject to RFI deprived them of their constitutional and civil rights.[294] The complaint requested an injunction against the use of untested Breathalyzers. The plaintiffs presented expert testimony of the susceptibility of the Breathalyzer to RFI.[295] The court entered a consent order enjoining the introduction of evidence of tests conducted with Breathalyzers that had not been specifically tested for RFI.[296]

The other leadiang RFI decisions originated in Massachusetts, New Jersey, Ohio,[297] and Alaska. In *Commonwealth v. Neal*[298] the Massachusetts Supreme Judicial Court grappled with the RFI problem. The court acknowledged that the "body of knowledge regarding the precise effect of RFI ... is not yet well developed ...."[299] However, the court added that "the evidence [of] ... the potential effect of RFI is sufficient to require that the admission of test results be conditioned on a demonstration to the judge of the accuracy of the particular unit at the time the test was performed."[300] The court stated that the prosecutor could show either that the police had tested the device with the procedures recommended by Smith & Wesson or that the police administered two tests.[301]

290. No. 82-1258 (Minn. 1982), cited in 68 A.B.A. J. 1552 (1982).

291. *Id.*

292. Heeden v. Dirkswager, Ramsey County, Second Judicial Court, Minn., *quoted in* LAW ENFORCEMENT STANDARDS LAB., NAT'L BUREAU OF STANDARDS, LIMITED ELECTROMAGNETIC INTERFERENCE TESTING OF EVIDENTIARY BREATH TESTERS 2 (1983).

293. C.A. No. 82-4808 (Super. Ct., Providence Cty.), discussed in DRINKING/DRIVING LAW LETTER, Vol. 2, No. 2, Jan. 21, 1983.

294. Tarantino & Kelly, *How to Get the State to Dismiss Your Case and Pay Your Attorney Fees*, THE CHAMPION, Sept./Oct. 1983, at 9.

295. *See* Feldman & Cohen, *supra* note 109, at 59.

296. Tarantino & Kelly, *supra* note 294, at 10.

297. State v. Symes, 96 Ohio App. 3d 156, 644 N.E.2d 729 (1994).

298. 392 Mass. 1, 464 N.E.2d 1356 (1984).

299. *Id.* at 17, 464 N.E.2d at 1367.

300. *Id.* at 19, 464 N.E.2d at 1368.

301. *Id.*

For its part, in *Romano v. Kimmelman,*[302] the New Jersey Supreme Court differentiated between the Model 900 and the Model 900A. The court was persuaded that the Model 900 is "highly insensitive to RFI."[303] For that reason, the court refused to revise the foundation for tests based on the Model 900. In contrast, the court concluded that the Model 900A is vulnerable to RFI and gave the police the option of conducting two Model 900A tests on each defendant or following special procedures including "the removal of hand-held transmitters, keeping police car transmitters away from close proximity to the testing room, and using extra care in shielding the instrument from outside interference."[304]

In the Alaska decision, *Thayer v. Anchorage,* the court held that "when a timely and appropriate challenge to admissibility of a Breathalyzer test result is made, the municipality must ... demonstrate that the Breathalyzer instrument in question was tested successfully for RFI at least once in a manner substantially complying with Smith & Wesson's recommendations ...."[305]

Many leading authorities, however, considered the so-called RFI problem to be a "red herring." As noted in § 22-3(B), Dr. Dubowski pointed out that RFI has never been shown to have produced a single incorrect breath-alcohol analysis result in the field. The defense counsel arguing to the contrary sometimes rely on the National Bureau of Standards study, but Dr. Dubowski rejects that study on the ground that the study did not distinguish true electromagnetic interference from other causes of variation in the tests.

More importantly today the problem is largely moot. The RFI claims related primarily to Breathalyzers. As emphasized at several points in this chapter, in field practice Breathalyzers have now been supplanted by GC and IR-based devices.

§ 22-6(E). Test Procedures.

There is currently a split of authority over the question of whether proof of correct test procedures is an essential element of the foundation for introducing scientific evidence.[306] However, in a substantial number of jurisdictions, just as

302. 96 N.J. 66, 474 A.2d 1 (1984).

303. *Id.* at 84, 474 A.2d at 11.

304. *Id.*

305. 686 P.2d 721, 727-28 (Alaska App. 1984).

306. Imwinkelried, *The Debate in the DNA Cases Over the Foundation for the Admission of Scientific Evidence: The Importance of Human Error as a Cause of Forensic Misanalysis*, 69 WASH. U. L.Q. 19 (1991); People v. Venegas, 18 Cal. 4th 47, 954 P.2d 525, 74 Cal. Rptr. 2d 262 (1998) (the court ruled that at least in some cases, as part of the admissibility analysis the trial judge should inquire "whether the procedures actually utilized in this case were in compliance with" accepted methology; the court mandated that inquiry in DNA analysis because "[u]nlike fingerprint, shoe track, bite mark, or ballistic comparisons, which jurors essentially can see for themselves, questions concerning whether a laboratory has adopted correct, scientifically accepted

the qualifications and the technique can be attacked on both scientific and statutory grounds, the admissibility of the testimony can also be challenged for improper test procedure at common law as well as under statutory requirements.[307]

The test procedures used may be scientifically unacceptable. For example, when the technique used is a blood test, the technician should not use a solution containing alcohol to sterilize the defendant's arm.[308] In some jurisdictions, if a cleansing solution containing ethanol is used, the technician's error affects the weight but not the admissibility of the analysis.[309] However, other jurisdictions frown upon the use of a sterilizing solution containing any alcohol, even isopropyl. In these jurisdictions, the use of an improper sterilizing solution renders the analysis inadmissible.[310] As a further illustration, some authorities

---

procedures for generating autorads or determining a match depend almost entirely on the technical interpretations of experts;" however, the court added that even in DNA analysis, some "derelictions in following the prescribed scientific procedures" do not render the evidence inadmissible; the court explained that "[s]hortcomings such as mislabeling, mixing the wrong ingredients, or failing to follow routine precautions against contamination may well be amenable to evaluations by jurors without the assistance of expert testimony. Such readily apparent missteps" are not fatal to admissibility); Coniglio v. Department of Motor Vehicles, 39 Cal. App. 4th 666, 46 Cal. Rptr. 2d 123, 132 (1995) (due process demands a showing that the test was properly administered). *But see* Roelfsema v. Dep't Motor Vehicles, 41 Cal. App. 4th 871, 48 Cal. Rptr. 2d 817 (1995) (in this jurisdiction, there is a statutory presumption that public officials properly perform their duties; the presumption applies to a police officer administering a blood alcohol test); City of Dublin v. Young, 75 Ohio St. 3d 472, 663 N.E.2d 1270 (1996) (state law requires that the junior operator conduct a chemical breath test under the "general direction" of the senior operator; that requirement does not necessitate that the senior operator occasionally check the junior operator's performance).

307. People v. Venegas, 18 Cal. 4th 47, 954 P.2d 525, 74 Cal. Rptr. 2d 262 (1998) (in a DNA case, the court ruled that the trial judge must inquire "whether the procedures actually utilized in this case were in compliance with" accepted methodology; the court held that this inquiry should condition the admissibility of DNA evidence because "[u]nlike fingerprint, shoe track, bite mark, or ballistic comparisons, which jurors can essentially see for themselves, questions whether a laboratory has adopted correct, scientifically accepted procedures for generating autorads or determining a match depend almost entirely on the technical interpretations of experts;" however, the court added that some "derelictions in following the prescribed scientific procedures" do not render the evidence inadmissible; the court explained that "[s]hortcomings such as mislabeling, mixing the wrong ingredients, or failing to follow routine precautions against contamination may well be amenable to evaluations by jurors without the assistance of expert testimony. Such readily apparent missteps" are not fatal to admissibility).

308. Winek, *supra* note 43, at 41; Tarantino, *Compromising BAC Test Equipment*, 14 THE CHAMPION 39 (Apr. 1990) (the following swabs have tested positive for ethanol on gas chromatograph: the Zephiran swab, PDT antiseptic towelette, Triad antiseptic towelette, and Clinipad antiseptic towelette; these swabs all contain benzalkonium chloride).

309. Kaufman v. State, 632 S.W.2d 685 (Tex. App. 1982).

310. State v. Alderson, 435 N.E.2d 614 (Ind. App. 1982); State v. Setter, 763 S.W.2d 228 (Mo. App. 1988) (the foundation must include proof that a sterile needle was used to withdraw a blood sample; the defendant need not raise the issue by presenting contrary evidence). Roehrenbeck &

recommend that the test procedures include a measurement of mouth temperature before any breath sampling; mild hyperthermia can elevate the BAC registered in the test.[311] However, to date, no court has excluded test evidence for lack of such a measurement.

If the jurisdiction in question permits the opponent to attack the admissibility of the evidence on the ground of improper test procedure, the procedures used are not immune from attack simply because they are the procedures authorized by the applicable administrative regulations.[312] Good science may require more than the administrative bureaucracy has mandated. Indeed, the test procedure may also be assailable on the ground that statutory or administrative requirements were not followed. For example, police officers sometimes violate a statutory or administrative requirement that they wait 15 or 20 minutes before administering a breath test.[313] The effect of the violation depends on whether the provision prescribed substantive procedures or merely clerical requirements.

Substantive Requirements

If the procedure violated was substantive, the courts divide on the effect of the violation. In some jurisdictions, courts demand strict, virtually literal, compliance

---

Russell, *Blood Is Thicker Than Water: What You Need to know to challenge a Serum Blood Alcohol Result*, 8 CRIM. JUST. J. 14, 15 (Fall 1993) ("State regulations often specify that prior to drawing a blood sample, the staff shall clean the skin with nonalcoholic antiseptic solution. In emergency settings, hospital staff may use an alcohol-based antiseptic to clean the skin, or staff may hook the patient up to an IV solution before drawing blood. [T]he former procedure could raise the blood alcohol count, while the latter could lower it").

311. Gerstenzang, *Breath Issues — Partition Ratio or Blood-Breath Presumption*, 23 THE CHAMPION 52, 54 (Jan.-Feb. 1999) ("Essentially, the 1:2,100 relationship depends upon the temperature of the air leaving the defendant's mouth being 34 degrees C. If the temperature exceeds 34 degrees C, it will artificially and erroneously raise the test result obtained. This defense was so effectively utilized that in one jurisdiction, the police started taking the temperature of the defendant being tested"); Wade, *DUI Statistics Often Don't Add Up*, 13 THE ADVOCATE 20, 22 (Apr. 1991) ("Every degree of increase in body temperature (1 degree C or 1.8 degrees F) can cause an increase of 7% to 9% in BrAC"); Fox & Hayward, *Effect of Hyperthermia on Breath-Alcohol Analysis*, 34 J. FORENSIC SCI. 836 (1989) (the researchers found that a degree of C increase in core body temperature can result in an 8.62% increase in breath alcohol concentration).

312. State v. Benoit, 570 So. 2d 490 (La. App. 1990) (the Department of Public Safety regulations did not go far enough to assure the repair and maintenance of the gas chromatograph equipment or the accuracy of the samples used for calibration); State v. Rowell, 517 So. 2d 799 (La. 1988) (the Louisiana administrative regulations were inadequate to ensure the integrity and reliability of blood alcohol analyses).

313. K. DUBOWSKI, THE TECHNOLOGY OF BREATH-ALCOHOL ANALYSIS 2 (1991) ("[e]stablished scientific safeguards (*e.g.* a 15-minute pretest 'deprivation period')"); Dubowski, *Quality Assurance in Breath-Alcohol Analysis*, 18 J. ANAL. TOX. 306 (1994) ("a pretest deprivation-observation period of at least 15 minutes").

with statutorily prescribed procedures.[314] The court is especially likely to demand strict compliance when just before listing the prescribed procedures, the statute in question uses prefatory language such as, "To be admissible" or "To be valid."[315] Strong statutory language of that nature seems to manifest a legislative intent to condition the admissibility of the testimony on compliance with the prescribed procedures.

However, in other jurisdictions, it is well-settled that the standard is substantial, rather than strict, compliance.[316] In still other jurisdictions, standing alone even a statutory violation affects the weight but not the admissibility of the evidence.[317] These courts stress that the "statute ... does not specifically provide

---

314. *E.g.,* United States v. Plumer, 920 F. Supp. 151, 152 (D. Kan. 1996) (applying Kansas law requiring that the officer check the driver's mouth to determine whether there are any foreign substances in the mouth before administering an Intoxilyzer breath test); Gargone v. State, 503 So. 2d 421 (Fla. App. 1987); State v. Rolison, 733 P.2d 326 (Haw. App. 1987) (waiting period); State v. Nakahara, 5 Haw. App. 575, 704 P.2d 927 (1985); People v. Morris, No. 5-96-0787 (Ill. Ct. App., 5th Dist., Aug. 5, 1998) (a "strict compliance" standard is both "intended by the clear language of . . . the statute and the applicable regulation and endorsed by our supreme court in" People v. Orth, 124 Ill.2d 326, 530 N.E.2d 210 (1988)); People v. Haney, 155 Ill. App. 3d 44, 405 N.E.2d 230 (1987) (waiting period); State v. Fairleigh, 490 So. 2d 490 (La. App. 1986); State v. Westbrook, 385 So. 2d 13 (La.), *on reh'g,* 392 So. 2d 1043 (La. 1980); Woodall v. Director of Revenue, 795 S.W.2d 419 (Mo. App. 1990) (a state administrative regulation required that breath analyzer machine operators perform maintenance checks at intervals not exceeding 35 days; compliance with the regulation was mandatory, and noncompliance required exclusion of test results); State v. Balderson, 138 Or. App. 531, 910 P.2d 1138 (1996) (statutory requirement that "[t]he operator must make certain that the subject has not taken anything by mouth ..., vomited, or regurgitated liquid from his stomach into his mouth, for at least 15 minutes before taking the test"); State v. Sensing, 843 S.W.2d 412 (Tenn. 1992) (20- minute waiting period).

315. For example, S.D. CODIFIED LAWS § 32-23-14.-1 begins with the phrase, "To be considered valid under the provisions of this chapter ...." *See* United States v. McMillan, 820 F.2d 251, 254 (8th Cir.), *cert. denied,* 484 U.S. 898 (1987).

316. Herter v. State, 715 P.2d 274 (Alaska App. 1986); Watson v. Frierson, 272 Ark. 316, 613 S.W.2d 824 (1981); Almobarak v. State, 22 Ark. App. 69, 733 S.W.2d 422 (1987) (waiting period); People v. Bowers, 716 P.2d 471 (Colo. 1986); People v. McDonough, 132 A.D.2d 997, 518 N.Y.S.2d 524 (1987) (waiting period); People v. DeMarasse, 85 N.Y.2d 842, 647 N.E.2d 1353, 623 N.Y.S.2d 845 (1995) (an Intoxilyzer reading was admissible even though the device displayed "deficient sample"). For an explanation of "substantial compliance," *see* Marshall v. Warwick, 155 F.3d 1027, 1031 (8th Cir. 1998).

317. United States v. McMillan, 820 F.2d 251, 255 (8th Cir.), *cert. denied,* 484 U.S. 898 (1987); People v. Rawlings, 42 Cal. App. 3d 952, 117 Cal. Rptr. 651 (1974); State v. Christie, 70 Haw. 158, 766 P.2d 1198 (1988) (the police may test an Intoxilyzer for accuracy by means of a quartz crystal "Beam Attentuator" supplied by the manufacturer although the state administrative rules state that the verification must be accomplished by using a suitable reference sample of known alcohol concentration), *cert. denied,* 490 U.S. 1067 (1989); State v. Litterell, 800 S.W.2d 7 (Mo. App. 1990) (an administrative regulation required a maintenance check within 35 days; although there was no record of successive inspections of the Breathalyzer machine at least once every 35 days, there was no other evidence that the machine in question had malfunctioned); Salter v. Hjelle,

that evidence shall be excluded for failure to comply with said statute."[318] That argument is persuasive in jurisdictions with a provision similar to Federal Rule of Evidence 402. That rule provides that unless excluded by the Constitution, statute, or rule, relevant evidence is admissible.[319] In one federal case, the Court of Appeals for the Ninth Circuit ruled that the results of even an uncompleted breathalyzer test can be admitted.[320] Although the Ninth Circuit did not expressly cite Rule 402, Rule 402 certainly lends support to the ruling in the case.

Clerical Requirements

Although courts split sharply over the significance of a violation of a substantive provision, they almost uniformly hold that violation of a clerical requirement does not warrant exclusion of the analysis. Suppose, for instance, that the person conducting the test neglects to complete the required checklist furnished by a state agency[321] or the manufacturer.[322] The courts generally concur that this violation does not call into question the accuracy of the test result and, hence, does not necessitate the exclusion of the analysis.

---

415 N.W.2d 801 (N.D. 1987) (compliance with the statutory procedures is not the exclusive method of proving the fair administration of the test).

318. People v. Rawlings, 42 Cal. App. 3d 952, 117 Cal. Rptr. 651 (1974).

319. FED. R. EVID. 402; Imwinkelried, *Federal Rule of Evidence 402: The Second Revolution*, 6 REV. LITIG. 129 (1987); United States v. De Water, 846 F.2d 528 (9th Cir. 1988) (although the facts giving rise to the prosecution arose in Hawaii, the federal court was not obliged to apply the Hawaii Health Department Rules governing Intoxilyzer tests); United States v. Hambsch, 748 F. Supp. 343, 344 (D. Md. 1990) ("state rules of evidence ... governing such things as admissibility of alcohol test results are inapplicable in federal prosecutions for drunk driving, in that only the substantive law of the state is intended to be assimilated, not its evidentiary or procedural law").

320. United States v. Brannon, 146 F.2d 1194 (9th Cir. 1998).

321. Pate v. State, 512 So. 2d 138 (Ala. Crim. App. 1987); Oveson v. Municipality of Anchorage, 574 P.2d 801 (Alaska 1978); People v. French, 77 Cal. App. 3d 511, 143 Cal. Rptr. 782 (1978); State v. Holcomb, 99 Or. App.156, 781 P.2d 396 (1989) (the arresting officer printed the Intoxilyzer test result on a test which was not blank at the time of the test; "[o]ur cases distinguish between procedures that affect the actual performance of the test, and thus the admissibility of the results, and procedures that simply record the fact that the operator performed the correct procedure"); State v. Olson, 88 Or. App. 271, 744 P.2d 1327 (1987). *But see* Bowman v. State, 564 N.E.2d 309 (Ind. App. 1990) (the court reversed where the Breathalyzer operator failed to record the test ampoule control number as required by a rule promulgated by the State Department of Toxicology; the court rejected the argument that the recordation requirement was a mere "administrative housekeeping duty" rather than a mandatory "technique used in the test"), *aff'd*, 577 N.E.2d 569 (Ind. 1991).

322. State v. Jackson, 643 S.W.2d 74 (Mo. App. 1982). Trichter, McKinney & Pena, *Demonstrative Evidence in DUI Cases*, 19 THE CHAMPION 4, 7 (May 1995) (the authors argue that the manufacturer's manual should be admissible under Federal Rule of Evidence 803(18), the learned treatise exception; "[a]s a practical matter, any expert, or the court for that matter, would have a difficult time not declaring that the manufacturer was the authority concerning the service and operation of its own breath test device").

§ 22-7. Privileges and Exclusionary Rules.

Even when the proponent can lay an otherwise complete foundation, exclusion of the evidence may result if some privilege or exclusionary rule bars the admission of the evidence. Given appropriate facts, virtually every evidentiary rule can be used to exclude scientific proof.[323] However, there are a number of privileges and rules that repeatedly apply in intoxication cases.

§ 22-7(A). Physician-Patient and Related Privileges.

Many states have a statutory physician-patient privilege. However, in most jurisdictions, the privilege does not apply in criminal cases.[324]

In some jurisdictions, even though the literal language of the statute seems to bar evidence of blood tests conducted by physicians, the courts have carved out an exception for drunk driving cases and related prosecutions such as death-by-auto.[325] However, in other jurisdictions, the privilege may exclude the results of a blood or urine sample obtained at a hospital.[326] Suppose that after an accident, an

---

323. *See generally* E. IMWINKELRIED, THE METHODS OF ATTACKING SCIENTIFIC EVIDENCE ch. 2 (3d ed. 1997).

324. *E.g.*, State v. Smith, 84 Wash. App. 813, 929 P.2d 1191 (1997).

325. State v. Dyal, 97 N.J. 229, 478 A.2d 390 (1984). *See also* Fisher v. Cincinnati, 753 F. Supp. 692, 694 (S.D. Ohio 1990) (under Federal Rule of Evidence 501, the court refused to recognize a medical privilege for the results of a blood alcohol test); Oxford v. Hamilton, 297 Ark. 512, 763 S.W.2d 83 (1989) (the results of a blood alcohol test ordered by a motorist's attending physician after an automobile accident were not confidential communications protected by the physician-patient privilege); State v. Waring, 779 S.W.2d 736 (Mo. App. 1989); State v. Schreiber, 122 N.J. 579, 585 A.2d 945 (1991) (the state patient-physician privilege is inapplicable to drunk driving prosecutions; under N.J. STAT. ANN. § 2A:84A-22.2, the privilege applies only to prosecutions for "crimes," and motor vehicle violations, including drunk driving offenses, are not crimes within the meaning of that expression in the statute).

326. *See* 1 R. ERWIN, *supra* note 90, at ch. 13; Annot., 80 A.L.R.3D 456, 485-86 (1977); Village of Arlington Heights, Illinois v. Bartelt, 211 Ill. App. 3d 747, 156 Ill. Dec. 192, 570 N.E.2d 668 (1991) (a state statute excepted certain written medical records from the medical privilege, but the exception did not apply to an oral report by a hospital employee to the police; the police consequently could not use the report to help establish probable cause to arrest the driver); State v. Elwell, 132 N.H. 599, 567 A.2d 1002 (1990) (the blood sample and the medical report of the test of the sample both were privileged); State v. Schreiber, 240 N.J. Super. 507, 573 A.2d 942 (1990) (in violation of the patient-physician privilege, a physician disclosed the results of a blood-alcohol test to the police; the police could not use the disclosure to obtain a subpoena for the test results), *rev'd*, 122 N.J. 579, 585 A.2d 945 (1991); Dillinbeck v. Hess, 73 N.Y.2d 707, 536 N.E.2d 1126, 539 N.Y.S.2d 707 (1989); Tarantino, *Physician-Patient Privilege*, 14 THE CHAMPION 28 (May 1990); State v. Henneberry, 558 N.W.2d 708 (Iowa 1997) (the court refused to recognize a public policy exception to the statutory privilege); State v. Vandergrift, 1997 S.D. 5, 558 N.W.2d 862 (1997) (the defendant motorist had not waived her privilege). *See also* State v. Conrad, 1997 WL 409469 (Tex. App.) (although the state had repealed the doctor-patient confidentiality privilege in criminal cases, the motorist retained a reasonable expectation of privacy in the medical records reflecting her blood test results; hence, the seizure of the records violated the Fourth Amendment), *superseded*, 1997

injured defendant is taken to an emergency room for treatment and the physician on duty has a blood sample taken without any request from the police. Given these facts, the statutory physician-patient privilege may apply and preclude the admission of the results of a subsequent analysis of the alcohol concentration of the blood sample.[327]

Now assume that the blood sample was extracted from the body of a deceased driver. In that situation, another privilege can come into play. Some jurisdictions have Coroner Acts that contain special privileges for evidence obtained during official autopsies; the evidence may be used only in connection with the autopsy and inadmissible in other legal proceedings.[328] If the pathologist or toxicologist obtains a blood or urine sample during an autopsy, the Coroner Act may bar the admission of a subsequent analysis of the alcohol concentration of the sample.[329]

There are federal statutes limiting the use of certain records maintained in connection with programs and activities relating to substance abuse. Defense counsel have urged that the courts should construe those statutes as manifesting a legislative intent to create an evidentiary privilege. However, in one case, a state court ruled that the statutes did not prohibit the disclosure of the results of a blood alcohol test result performed at a hospital.[330] The defendant was not in the hospital to obtain substance abuse treatment.

§ 22-7(B). Statutory Extensions of Fourth Amendment.

As noted earlier, most jurisdictions have implied consent laws. The laws provide that by accepting a license, the defendant impliedly consents to the administration of intoxication tests and that if the defendant wrongfully refuses to submit to a test, he or she forfeits the license. However, suppose that when the officer requests the defendant to submit to the test, the defendant refuses.[331] May the officer resort to normal fourth amendment doctrines and obtain a warrant for a sample or take a warrantless sample on the ground of exigency?[332]

WL 764527 (Tex. App. Dec. 11, 1997), *cert. denied,* 119 S. Ct. 1462 (1999). *Contra* State v. Hardy, 963 S.W.2d 516 (Tex. Crim. App. 1997).

327. State *ex rel.* Mehle v. Harper, 643 S.W.2d 643 (Mo. App. 1982). *See also* Gonzenbach v. Ruddy, 645 S.W.2d 27 (Mo. App. 1982).

328. *E.g.,* Illinois Coroner's Act, ILL. REV. STAT., ch. 31, § 10(e), *construed in* Bearce v. United States, 433 F. Supp. 549 (N.D. Ill. 1977).

329. Bearce v. United States, 433 F. Supp. 549 (N.D. Ill. 1977).

330. State v. Williams, 94 Ohio Misc.2d 113, 703 N.E.2d 1284 (Com. Pl. 1998).

331. Ruppel v. Ramseyer, 33 F. Supp. 2d 720, 724 (C.D. Ill. 1999) ("A simple blood-alcohol test is so safe, painless and commonplace that a state can legitimately compel the suspect, against his will to accede to the test").

332. In some jurisdictions, to an extent the implied consent law tends to moot this issue. For example, the Michigan implied consent law provides that if hospital personnel have performed a blood alcohol test on the defendant during the course of medical treatment, the prosecution can obtain the test result without a showing of probable cause. People v. Perlos, 436 Mich. 305, 462

In several jurisdictions, the answer is yes.[333] In some of these jurisdictions, although the statute seemingly prohibits nonconsensual blood extraction, courts limit that prohibition to drunk driving cases; the prohibition does not apply in other prosecutions, such as negligent homicide cases.[334] Other courts reason that the statute does not preclude the police from using alternative methods to obtain the sample. For example, in these jurisdictions, even though the defendant withholds actual consent, the police may obtain a warrant based on probable cause to obtain a blood sample from the defendant.[335] Or since the alcohol concentration dissipates rapidly, the police can invoke the emergency doctrine and make a warrantless seizure based on probable cause.[336]

However, in a significant number of jurisdictions, the answer is no.[337] These courts construe their implied consent statutes to mean that the administrative

---

N.W.2d 310 (1990) (construing MICH. COMP. LAWS § 257.625a(9), MICH. STAT. ANN. § 9.2325(1)(9); State v. Smith, 84 Wash. App. 813, 929 P.2d 1191 (1997). Of course, the fourth amendment applies only to searches conducted by government officials and their de jure or de facto agents. State v. Vandergrift, 535 N.W.2d 428 (S.D. 1995) (the implied consent law was inapplicable to private blood samples taken by treating physicians and their agents for medical purposes). *But see* Commonwealth v. Danforth, 395 Pa. Super. 1, 576 A.2d 1013 (1990) (holding unconstitutional the provision of the Pennsylvania implied consent law authorizing taking a blood alcohol test whenever an automobile accident results in death or serious injury, regardless of whether there is probable cause to believe that the driver was intoxicated).

333. *See* Annot., 14 A.L.R.4TH 690 (1982); State v. Nagel, 320 Or. 24, 880 P.2d 451 (1994) (although requiring the defendant to submit to a field sobriety test was a search, exigency made a warrant unnecessary).

334. State v. Thompson, 207 Mont. 433, 674 P.2d 1094 (1984).

335. People v. Reynolds, 895 P.2d 1059 (Colo. 1995) (standing alone, the defendant's admission that he had consumed three beers within six to nine hours before the accident did not give rise to probable cause for a nonconsensual extraction of the defendant's blood); People v. Cords, 75 Mich. App. 415, 254 N.W.2d 911 (1977). *Compare* Note, *State v. Seibel: Wisconsin Police Now Need Only a Reasonable Suspicion to Search a Suspect's Blood Incident to an Arrest*, 1993 WIS. L. REV. 523 *with* Pennsylvania v. Kohl, 532 Pa. 152, 615 A.2d 308 (1992) (a statute permitting an alcohol test of any motorist involved in an accident resulting in death or serious bodily injury violates the fourth amendment; there must be probable cause to believe that the motorist in question is intoxicated).

336. United States v. Reid, 929 F.2d 990, 992-93 (4th Cir. 1991); State v. Dittel, 464 N.W.2d 601 (Minn. App. 1991) ("vital evidence (blood alcohol) burns away"); Commonwealth v. Danforth, 395 Pa. Super. 1, 576 A.2d 1013 (1990) ("evidence of blood alcohol diminishes with time"); Hayes v. State, 634 S.W.2d 359, 363 (Tex. App. 1982); Aliff v. State, 627 S.W.2d 166 (Tex. Crim. App. 1982); Note, *Shed Thou No Blood: The Forcible Removal of Blood Samples from Drunk Driving Suspects*, 60 S. CAL. L. REV. 1115 (1987); Note, *North Carolina Invalidates the Warrantless Seizure of Blood from an Unconscious Suspect*, 21 WAKE FOREST L. REV. 1071 (1986). Of course, there must also be probable cause to believe that the person is intoxicated. *Commonwealth v. Danforth, supra;* Commonwealth v. Kohl, 395 Pa. Super. 73, 576 A.2d 1049 (1990) (applying *Danforth*).

337. Annot., 14 A.L.R.4TH 690, 695 (1982); Combs v. Commonwealth, 965 S.W.2d 161 (Ky. 1998) (the court construed the state statute as barring the issuance of a search warrant to obtain

revocation of the defendant's license is the only authorized sanction for refusal to consent to the test. The Florida[338] and Maryland[339] courts have reached this conclusion. Likewise, the New Mexico courts have found that their implied consent statute contains a "prohibition against any search without consent, warrant or not ...."[340] The Iowa Supreme Court not only reached the same result but also described its position as the majority view in the United States.[341]

§ 22-7(C). Privilege Against Self-Incrimination.

The application of the fifth amendment privilege to intoxication testing raises three issues: Does the process of obtaining the sample constitute compelled incrimination in violation of the privilege? Does the privilege at least forbid the introduction of a videotape of the test? And if the defendant refuses to submit to the test, does the privilege forbid the prosecutor and court from commenting on the defendant's refusal or using the refusal as evidence of consciousness of guilt?[342]

Obtaining Samples

Chapter 2 analyzes the constitutional limitations on the admissibility of scientific evidence. As that chapter points out, the Supreme Court under the fifth amendment and most state supreme courts under the corresponding provisions in their state constitutions have concluded that the privilege protects against only communicative or testimonial incrimination. Applying that standard to intoxication testing, the courts have uniformly held that the involuntary extraction of samples for testing does not constitute compulsory incrimination.[343]

---

blood alcohol evidence from an unwilling driver in a situation involving neither death nor physical injury; the court upheld the statute against a separation-of-power challenge). *See also* State v. Burnett, 536 So. 2d 375 (Fla. App. 1988) (although the motorist's injuries made the administration of a breath test impractical, the officer could not require the motorist to submit to a blood test).

338. Sambrine v. State, 386 So. 2d 546 (Fla. 1980).

339. State v. Loscomb, 291 Md. 424, 435 A.2d 764 (1981).

340. State v. Steele, 93 N.M. 470, 471, 601 P.2d 440, 441 (Ct. App. 1979).

341. State v. Hitchens, 294 N.W.2d 686 (Iowa 1980).

342. Of course, other fifth amendment issues can arise. One issue, for example, is whether stopping a driver on suspicion of driving under the influence is custody requiring the administration of *Miranda* warnings. Stone v. City of Huntsville, 656 So. 2d 404 (Ala. Crim. App. 1994) (no); State v. Prickett, 324 Or. 489, 930 P.2d 221 (1997) (under the state constitution, whether a police officer's questioning of a drunk driving suspect after the administration of field sobriety tests is sufficiently "compelling" to require rights warnings turns on the totality of the circumstances; the state supreme court rejected a lower court's per se rule that such warnings are always required for interrogation after field sobriety tests).

343. Anderson v. Cozens, 60 Cal. App. 3d 130, 131 Cal. Rptr. 256 (1976); Rodriguez v. State, 631 S.W.2d 515 (Tex. Crim. App. 1982).

Videotaped Sobriety Tests

The defense has argued that the prohibition of compulsory incrimination restricts the ability of the police to videotape an arrestee's conduct during field sobriety tests. In *Pennsylvania v. Muniz,*[344] the Supreme Court largely rebuffed the argument. The Court held that the slurred speech and lack of muscular coordination which the arrestee displayed during the sobriety tests amounted to non-testimonial incrimination. However, the Court ruled that it violated the arrestee's privilege against self-incrimination to introduce into evidence the arrestee's videotaped response to the question of whether he knew the date of his sixth birthday. The response was logically relevant to prove the arrestee's impaired mental faculties, but the answer was testimonial in character. The answer expressly asserted a fact or belief. The lower courts are currently split over the question whether the privilege against self-incrimination permits the police to require the suspect to recite the alphabet.[345]

Comment on Refusal to Submit to Testing

In *Griffin v. California*[346] the Supreme Court held that at trial, neither the prosecutor nor the judge may comment adversely on the defendant's failure to testify. By refusing to testify, the defendant implicitly invokes the fifth

---

344. 496 U.S. 582 (1990); People v. Bugbee, 201 Ill. App. 3d 952, 147 Ill. Dec. 381, 559 N.E.2d 554 (1990) (evidence of a motorist's response to an officer's request that the motorist recite the alphabet was non-testimonial); State v. Nielsen, 147 Or. App. 294, 936 P.2d 374 (1997) (even though field sobriety tests require the defendant to reveal something about his mental faculties, the tests are not testimonial under the state constitution); Commonwealth v. Hayes, 674 A.2d 677 (Pa. 1996) (the self-incrimination clause of the state constitution does not give the defendant a right to refuse to perform field sobriety tests). *Compare* Vickers v. State, 878 S.W.2d 329 (Tex. App. 1994) (admission of the videotape of the defendant's recitation of the alphabet from "f" to "w" and counting backwards from 90 to 75 was testimonial) and Allred v. Florida, 622 So. 2d 984 (Fla. 1993) (although the court cites *Muniz,* the court relies on the state constitution in forbidding the police from requiring the arrestee to recite part of the alphabet) *with* State v. Diandrea, 602 So. 2d 1322 (Fla. App. 1992) (reciting part of the alphabet is nontestimonial). *But see* Commonwealth v. Bruder, 365 Pa. Super. 106, 528 A.2d 1385 (1987) (reciting the alphabet as a field sobriety test constituted communicative incrimination, requiring *Miranda* warnings), *rev'd on other grounds,* 488 U.S. 9 (1988); Commonwealth v. Conway, 368 Pa. Super. 488, 534 A.2d 541 (1987) (the trial judge suppressed the audio track of the videotape of the defendant's performance of field sobriety tests; the appellate court found the suppression justified on two grounds, including the theory that the defendant's statements during the test were testimonial in character), *appeal denied,* 520 Pa. 581, 549 A.2d 914 (1988); Essen, *Suppressing Videotape Evidence on Fifth Amendment Grounds,* 3 D.W.I. J. 1 (Feb. 1988).

345. *Compare* State v. Maze, 16 Kan.App.2d 527, 825 P.2d 1169 (1992) (yes) *with* State v. Devlin, 980 P.2d 1037 (Mont. 1999) (citing *Muniz,* the court rules that neither counting nor reciting the alphabet constitutes a testimonial act) and Commonwealth v. Conway, 534 A.2d 541 (Pa. Super. 1987) (in a case antedating *Muniz,* the court answered the question in the negative).

346. 380 U.S. 609 (1965).

amendment privilege; and the government may not make the defendant's lawful invocation of the privilege costly by attempting to draw adverse inferences from his silence. The question then arises whether the *Griffin* rule forecloses adverse comment on the defendant's pretrial refusal to submit to testing.

Initially, the scope of the question must be defined. The question is the permissibility of comment on the defendant's *wrongful* refusal to submit to testing. In some cases, the defendant's refusal is lawful. For example, some jurisdictions afford the defendant a right to consult with counsel before deciding whether to submit to the test.[347] In these jurisdictions, the defendant may lawfully refuse to submit to a test until he has an opportunity to contact counsel, and the prosecutor may not comment adversely on that limited refusal.[348] Furthermore, some jurisdictions insist that the police give the defendant certain warnings before asking the defendant to submit to the test.[349] In those jurisdictions, if the police omit required warnings before the defendant's refusal, an exclusionary rule comes into play; and again the prosecutor may not comment on the refusal.[350] We are assuming *arguendo* that the defendant has been given any necessary warnings and afforded any right to counsel. When the police afford the defendant all mandatory procedural safeguards and the defendant nevertheless wrongfully refuses to be tested, may the prosecutor invite the trier of fact to draw an adverse inference from the refusal?

Until 1983, there was a sharp split of authority over the question of whether the prosecutor may comment on an unlawful refusal to submit to the test. In some states, statute specifically permits comment.[351] Even absent an authorizing statute, perhaps a majority of courts held comment permissible.[352] This position

---

347. Annot., 97 A.L.R.3D 852 (1980).

348. *Id.* at 855-57.

349. *See* § 22-7(F) *infra*.

350. *Id.*

351. *See* Nevarez v. State, 671 S.W.2d 90 (Tex. App. 1984). TEX. TRANS. CODE 724.061 reads: "A person's refusal of a request by an official to submit to the taking of a specimen of a breath or blood, whether the refusal was express or the result of an intentional failure to give the specimen, may be introduced into evidence at the person's trial."

352. Welch v. District Court of Vermont Unit No. 5, 594 F.2d 903 (2d Cir. 1979); Hill v. State, 366 So. 2d 318 (Ala. 1979); People v. Municipal Court (Gonzalez), 137 Cal. App. 3d 114, 186 Cal. Rptr. 716 (1982); State v. Taylor, 648 So. 2d 701 (Fla. 1995); State v. Duke, 378 So. 2d 96 (Fla. App. 1979); Wessels v. State, 169 Ga. App. 246, 312 S.E.2d 361 (1983); State v. Willis, 332 N.W.2d 180 (Minn. 1983); State v. Wright, 116 N.M. 832, 867 P.2d 1214 (1994); People v. Thomas, 46 N.Y.2d 100, 385 N.E.2d 584, 412 N.Y.S.2d 845 (1978); People v. Morales, 161 Misc. 2d 128, 611 N.Y.S.2d 980 (N.Y. City Crim. Ct. 1994); Parks v. State, 666 S.W.2d 597 (Tex. App. 1984). *But see* State v. Satrom, 524 N.W.2d 92 (N.D. 1994) (the officer's testimony must be limited to the fact of refusal; the question should be "Did he refuse?," and the answer should be restricted to "Yes"); State v. Beaton, 516 N.W.2d 645 (N.D. 1994) (although the fact of the defendant's refusal is admissible, his actual statements constituting the refusal are inadmissible unless the defendant earlier received *Miranda* warnings).

was well-reasoned. Beginning with the premise that there is no fifth amendment right to refuse to be tested, these courts argued that as a corollary, a refusal is not an invocation of the fifth amendment. Referring to the refusal is thus not a comment on the privilege.

However, before 1983, a significant minority of jurisdictions rejected this reasoning and found either a constitutional or statutory ban on commenting. A handful of courts rested the ban on constitutional grounds.[353] These courts contended that although the process of affirmatively obtaining a sample is not compelled incrimination, the defendant's negative refusal is testimonial — "a tacit or overt expression."[354] A somewhat larger number of courts based the ban on statutory construction.[355] Some of these courts stressed that the implied consent statute described the defendant's right to refuse in absolute terms[356] while others noted that the only explicit sanction for refusal was administrative license revocation and thus the legislature implicitly forbade any other sanction such as adverse comment.[357]

In 1983, the Supreme Court finally confronted the issue. In that year the Court decided *South Dakota v. Neville.*[358] In an opinion by Justice O'Connor, a seven-justice majority announced that "a refusal to take a blood-alcohol test, after a police officer has lawfully requested it, is not an act coerced by the officer, and thus is not protected by the privilege against self-incrimination."[359] The Court noted that under *Schmerber v. California*[360] the state could have legitimately compelled Neville to submit to an involuntary test. Justice O'Connor added that "the action became no less legitimate when the state offers a second option of refusing the test, with the attendant penalties for making that choice."[361]

Neville thus resolves the question of the propriety of comment under the fifth amendment to the national constitution. Since *Neville,* most state courts passing on the issue have permitted comment.[362] However, a state may still forbid

---

353. State v. Jackson, 195 Mont. 185, 637 P.2d 1, *vacated,* 460 U.S. 1030 (1981), *on remand,* 206 Mont. 338, 672 P.2d 255 (1983); State v. Neville, 312 N.W.2d 723 (S.D. 1981).

354. State v. Neville, 312 N.W.2d 723, 726 (S.D. 1981), *rev'd,* 459 U.S. 553 (1983).

355. Puller v. Anchorage, 574 P.2d 1285 (Alaska 1978); State v. Wilson, 5 Kan. App. 130, 613 P.2d 384 (1980); St. Joseph v. Johnson, 539 S.W.2d 784 (Mo. App. 1976); Commonwealth v. Charles, 270 Pa. Super. 280, 411 A.2d 527 (1979).

356. St. Joseph v. Johnson, 539 S.W.2d 784 (Mo. App. 1976).

357. Puller v. Anchorage, 574 P.2d 1285 (Alaska 1978).

358. 459 U.S. 553 (1983).

359. *Id.* at 564.

360. 384 U.S. 757 (1966).

361. South Dakota v. Opperman, 459 U.S. 553, 563 (1983).

362. State v. Superior Court, 154 Ariz. 574, 744 P.2d 675 (1987); State v. Superior Court of State, 154 Ariz. 275, 742 P.2d 286 (1987); Spicer v. State, 32 Ark. App. 209, 799 S.W.2d 562 (1990) (the defendant's refusal to submit to a Breathalyzer test is admissible as other crimes evidence to show consciousness of guilt); State v. Taylor, 648 So. 2d 701 (Fla. 1995); State v.

comment on an independent state ground such as a state constitution[363] or statutory grounds.[364] Indeed, on remand in *Neville,* the South Dakota Supreme Court again suppressed the evidence of Neville's refusal under the due process clause of the state constitution.[365] (The South Dakota Supreme Court receded from that view in a later decision.[366])

Leroy, 15 Kan. App. 2d 68, 803 P.2d 577 (1990); Commonwealth v. Hager, 702 S.W.2d 431 (Ky. 1986); McDonnell v. Commissioner of Pub. Safety, 473 N.W.2d 848 (Minn. 1991) (citing *Neville,* the court upholds the constitutionality of a state statute imposing criminal penalties on a drunk driving arrestee's refusal to submit to a blood alcohol test); State v. Stever, 107 N.J. 543, 527 A.2d 408, *cert. denied,* 484 U.S. 954 (1987); State v. Wright, 116 N.M. 832, 867 P.2d 1214 (1993); People v. Morales, 161 Misc.2d 128, 611 N.Y.S.2d 980 (N.Y. City Crim. Ct. 1994); Commonwealth v. McConnell, 404 Pa. Super. 439, 591 A.2d 288 (1991) (*Muniz* deals with blood alcohol tests, but the rule announced in *Muniz* extends to field sobriety tests); Thomas v. State, 723 S.W.2d 696 (Tex. Crim. App. 1986); Sandy City v. Larson, 733 P.2d 137 (Utah 1987); Farmer v. Commonwealth, 49 Crim. L. Rep. (BNA) 1115 (Vt. Ct. App., Apr. 23, 1991) (evidence of a drunk driving suspect's refusal to perform a sobriety test is admissible at trial). *But see* State v. Sartor, 524 N.W.2d 92 (N.D. 1994) (the officer's testimony must be limited to the fact of refusal; the question should be "Did he refuse?," and the answer should be restricted to "Yes"); State v. Beaton, 516 N.W.2d 645 (N.D. 1994) (although the fact of the defendant's refusal is admissible, his actual statements constituting the refusal are inadmissible unless the defendant earlier received *Miranda* warnings).

363. *See* Commonwealth v. McGrail, 419 Mass. 774, 647 N.E.2d 712 (1995); Commonwealth v. Zevitas, 418 Mass. 677, 639 N.E.2d 1076 (1994); Commonwealth v. Lydon, 597 N.E.2d 36 (Mass. 1992) (the Massachusetts Declaration of Rights); Opinion of the Justices, 591 N.E.2d 1073 (Mass. 1992); State v. Jackson, 195 Mont. 185, 637 P.2d 1 (1981) (citing Montana constitution as well as the national constitution), *vacated,* 460 U.S. 1030 (1983); Farmer v. Commonwealth, 10 Va. App. 175, 390 S.E.2d 775, *reh'g granted,* 1990 Va. App. LEXIS 110 (1990) (en banc), *reh'g,* 12 Va. App. 337, 404 S.E.2d 371 (1991); State v. Fish, 321 Or. 48, 893 P.2d 1023 (1995) (admitting evidence of the refusal would violate Article I, § 12 of the state constitution, at least when the officer requests the motorist to take all the field sobriety tests; the evidence is testimonial because the complete set of tests involves counting, reciting the alphabet, estimating a period of time, and providing information about residence and date of birth). Commonwealth v. McGrail, 419 Mass. 774, 647 N.E.2d 712 (1995). *But see* Note, *SJC Steers Off Course: DUI Breath Test Refusals Inadmissible*, 28 NEW ENGL. L. REV. 1169 (1994) (criticizing the position of the Supreme Judicial Court).

364. Puller v. Anchorage, 574 P.2d 1285 (Alaska 1978); State v. Wilson, 5 Kan. App. 130, 613 P.2d 384 (1980); Krauss v. State, 322 Md. 376, 587 A.2d 1102 (1991) (section 10-309(a) of the Maryland Transportation Code provides that "[t]he fact of refusal is admissible as evidence of trial" but that "[n]o inference or presumption concerning either guilt or innocence arises because of refusal to submit"; the court construed the statute as precluding the prosecution from offering evidence of a motorist's refusal to submit to a breath test unless the refusal is material to some issue other than guilt or innocence such "as ... when a defendant claims enforcement authorities did not properly afford an opportunity to take the test"); St. Joseph v. Johnson, 539 S.W.2d 784 (Mo. App. 1976); Commonwealth v. Charles, 270 Pa. Super. 280, 411 A.2d 527 (1979).

365. State v. Neville, 346 N.W.2d 425 (S.D. 1984). *But see* State v. Hoenscheid, 374 N.W.2d 128 (S.D. 1985).

366. State v. Hoenscheid, 374 N.W.2d 128 (S.D. 1985).

As in South Dakota, the state constitution has played a role in the case law in Massachusetts. In 1995, under its state constitution, the Massachusetts Supreme Judicial Court barred admission of evidence of a defendant's refusal to submit to field sobriety tests.[367] In 1998, an intermediate appellate court in the same state ruled that the bar is not limited to explicit refusals and extended to "negotiation" over whether to perform the test.[368]

Like the state constitution, state statute can also impact the propriety of comment in a given jurisdiction. For instance, under the statutory scheme adopted in 1983--the very year of the *Neville* decision-- the Washington Supreme Court adopted a general rule barring comment, but the court did so on evidentiary rather than constitutional grounds.[369] The court stated that evidence of the defendant's refusal is admissible only when the defendant raises an issue on which the evidence is probative — such as whether the arresting officer followed normal procedures. However, the court has since concluded that under the new statutory scheme as amended in 1986, "refusal evidence is now generally admissible."[370] To muddy the waters further, in 1998, an intermediate appellate court in Washington held that a driver's refusal to perform a voluntary field sobriety test (FST) is testimonial and protected by the privilege against self-incrimination.[371]

§ 22-7(D). Right to Retest Sample.

In *Brady v. Maryland*[372] the Supreme Court recognized a limited defense right to discover exculpatory information in the government's possession. Early on defense counsel invoked the *Brady* rationale in an attempt to create a due process right to inspect Breathalyzer ampoules and conduct retests. The leading defense precedent is *People v. Hitch,*[373] a 1974 decision by the California Supreme Court. In its opinion, the California Supreme Court declared that: "[T]he test ampoule, its contents and the reference ampoule customarily used in the test constitute material evidence on the issue of the driver's guilt or innocence of the charge of driving a vehicle under the influence of intoxicating liquor. We conclude that the investigative agency involved has a duty to preserve and disclose the evidence."[374]

---

367. Commonwealth v. McGrail, 647 N.E.2d 712 (Mass. 1995).

368. Commonwealth v. Grenier, 45 Mass. Ct. App. 58, 695 N.E.2d 1075 (1998).

369. State v. Zwicker, 105 Wash. 2d 228, 713 P.2d 1101 (1986).

370. State v. Long, 113 Wash. 2d 266, 778 P.2d 1027 (1989).

371. City of Seattle v. Stralsbroten, __P.2d__, 65 Cr.L. (BNA) 426, 1998 W.L. 263543 (Wash. App. 1998).

372. 373 U.S. 83 (1963).

373. 12 Cal. 3d 641, 527 P.2d 361, 117 Cal. Rptr. 9 (1974).

374. *Id.* at 652, 527 P.2d at 369, 117 Cal. Rptr. at 17.

The *Hitch* decision triggered a sharp split of authority. The majority of courts rejected *Hitch* and refused to impose a duty on the police to preserve the ampoule. Most of these courts reasoned that there was no *Brady* violation because it is pure speculation that a retest would yield favorable evidence exculpating the defendant.[375] Other courts reached this result on the theory that retesting was not generally accepted and, hence, would not pass muster under *Frye.*[376]

Oregon adopted a compromise position. In *State v. Michener*[377] the Oregon court indicated that the prosecution has an obligation to produce the ampoule for retesting only if other evidence in the case affirmatively raises a doubt about the defendant's intoxication. In *Michener* the police videotape showed the defendant easily passing physical coordination and dexterity tests. The results of those tests gave the court reason to question the accuracy of the Breathalyzer test. In a subsequent case,[378] the Oregon court suggested that a lay eyewitness's testimony that the defendant was sober might suffice to trigger the government's duty to produce under *Michener.*

Still other courts embraced *Hitch* wholeheartedly. Some did so as a matter of constitutional law,[379] while one court reached the same result by construing state rules of criminal procedure.[380] Some courts even went beyond *Hitch.* Several applied the *Hitch* rationale to mandate the preservation of blood samples.[381]

---

375. Edwards v. Oklahoma, 429 F. Supp. 668 (W.D. Okla. 1976), *rev'd,* 577 F.2d 1119 (10th Cir. 1978); People v. Godbout, 42 Ill. App. 3d 1001, 1 Ill. Dec. 583, 356 N.E.2d 865 (1976); People v. Stark, 73 Mich. App. 332, 251 N.W.2d 574 (1977); State v. Preston, 585 S.W.2d 569 (Mo. App. 1979); State v. Shutt, 116 N.H. 495, 363 A.2d 406 (1976); State v. Teare, 135 N.J. Super. 19, 342 A.2d 556 (1975); State v. Bryan, 133 N.J. Super. 369, 336 A.2d 511 (1974); Montoya v. Metropolitan Court, 98 N.M. 616, 651 P.2d 1260 (1982); People v. Santiago, 116 Misc. 2d 340, 455 N.Y.S.2d 511 (Sup. Ct. 1982); State v. Larson, 313 N.W.2d 750 (N.D. 1981); State v. Watson, 48 Ohio App. 2d 110, 2 Ohio Op. 3d 79, 355 N.E.2d 883 (1975); State v. Grose, 45 Ohio Misc. 1, 74 Ohio Op. 2d 13, 340 N.E.2d 441 (1975); Edwards v. State, 544 P.2d 60 (Okla. Crim. 1975); Turpin v. State, 606 S.W.2d 907 (Tex. Crim. App. 1980).

376. State v. Canaday, 90 Wash. 2d 808, 585 P.2d 1185 (1978). *But see* Parker & Green, *Delayed Ethanol Analysis of Breath Specimens: Long-Term Field Experience with Commercial Silica Gel Tubes and Breathalyzer Collection,* 35 J. FORENSIC SCI. 1353, 1358 (1990) ("Overall, the performance of the commercial collection tubes containing silica gel and the Breathalyzer as a collection device permitted the confirmation of most (81%) of the direct results").

377. 25 Or. App. 523, 550 P.2d 449, *review denied,* 276 Or. 211 (1976).

378. State v. Reaves, 25 Or. App. 745, 550 P.2d 1403, *review denied,* 276 Or. 211 (1976).

379. Scales v. City Court, 122 Ariz. 231, 594 P.2d 97 (1979); Garcia v. District Court, 21st Judicial Dist., 197 Colo. 38, 589 P.2d 924 (1979); State v. Booth, 98 Wis. 2d 20, 295 N.W.2d 194 (Ct. App. 1980). *See also* State v. Humphrey, 104 Wis. 2d 97, 310 N.W.2d 641 (Ct. App. 1981), *rev'd,* 107 Wis. 2d 107, 318 N.W.2d 386 (1982).

380. Lauderdale v. State, 548 P.2d 376 (Alaska 1976) (construing Alaska Criminal Rule 16(b)(7)).

381. McNutt v. Superior Court, 133 Ariz. 7, 648 P.2d 122 (1982); Brown v. Municipal Court for Los Angeles Judicial Dist., 86 Cal. App. 3d 357, 150 Cal. Rptr. 216 (1978).

Others demanded that the police preserve breath samples in connection with infrared tests even though the infrared instruments do not require ampoules.[382]

This was the divisive state of the law when the Supreme Court reached the merits of the issue in 1984 in *California v. Trombetta.*[383] The California court had mandated breath sample preservation even though the police used an Intoxilyzer which does not require ampoules. The Supreme Court reversed in a unanimous opinion written by Justice Marshall. The Court was impressed by the evidence of the accuracy of the Intoxilyzer. Justice Marshall wrote:

> In all but a tiny fraction of cases, preserved breath samples would simply confirm the Intoxilyzer's determination that the defendant had a high level of blood-alcohol concentration at the time of the test. Once the Intoxilyzer indicated that respondents were legally drunk, breath samples were much more likely to provide inculpatory than exculpatory evidence.[384]

Although the case involved an infrared test and not a Breathalyzer or a gas chromatograph, the Court chose sweeping language, suggesting that the holding applies to all breath testing devices: "We conclude, therefore, that the Due Process Clause of the Fourteenth Amendment does not require that law enforcement agencies preserve breath samples in order to introduce breath-analysis tests at trial."

The *Trombetta* decision has not ended the controversy over the *Hitch* doctrine. In a 1984 decision, the Arizona Supreme Court distinguished *Trombetta* and found a due process violation when the police destroyed a second breath sample after the defendant was told that the charges against him had been dismissed.[385] Furthermore, as in the case of the *Neville* decision discussed in the prior subsection, state courts can continue to follow *Hitch* on independent grounds. Some courts premised their *Hitch* analysis on the state constitution rather than the national constitution.[386] Other *Hitch* precedents rested on state rules of criminal

---

382. Baca v. Smith, 124 Ariz. 353, 604 P.2d 617 (1979); People v. Haslam, No. 29904-0 (Cal. Mun. Ct., Oct. 8, 1980), *cited in* 23 A.T.L.A. Rep. 457 (1980). The police may comply with *Baca* either by offering the suspect a choice between replicate breath testing (which involves two samples but preserves neither) and a blood test which preserves a sample. Dean v. City Court of Tucson, 163 Ariz. 510, 789 P.2d 180 (1990); Arizona v. Kemp, 166 Ariz. 339, 802 P.2d 1038 (Ct. App. 1990) (rather than preserving a sample for the defendant, the police may simply inform him that he has the right to be given a part of the sample for independent testing); State v. Velasco, 165 Ariz. 480, 799 P.2d 821 (1990) (the silica gel method of preserving a sample of a defendant's breath is satisfactory although it is less accurate than the Intoxilyzer device used to conduct the primary test; the method has been certified by the state health department).

383. 467 U.S. 479 (1984).

384. *Id.* at 489.

385. Oshrin v. Coulter, 142 Ariz. 109, 688 P.2d 1001 (1984).

386. Anchorage v. Serrano, 649 P.2d 256 (Alaska App. 1982). *See also* People v. Alvarez, 70 N.Y.2d 375, 515 N.E.2d 898, 521 N.Y.S.2d 212 (1987) (as a matter of state constitutional law, the

procedure.[387] Still other states have to some extent codified a retention requirement.[388] However, the trend in the decided cases is toward the *Trombetta* view.[389]

§ 22-7(E). Right to Counsel.

Just as the courts have analyzed the application of the fourth and fifth amendments to intoxication testing, they have addressed the application of the sixth amendment right to counsel.[390] Here again there is a wide split of authority.

Some courts have adopted a flat rule that there is no right to counsel at the time of the intoxication test; the defendant has neither an absolute right to have counsel present nor even a limited right to a reasonable opportunity to contact counsel. This view has adherents among federal[391] and state courts.[392]

---

court decides to follow *Trombetta*). As previously stated, some jurisdictions have also adopted a broader interpretation of the privilege against self-incrimination provisions in their state constitutions. Commonwealth v. McGrail, 419 Mass. 774, 647 N.E.2d 712 (1995); Commonwealth v. Zevitas, 418 Mass. 677, 639 N.E.2d 1076 (1994); Commonwealth v. Lydon, 597 N.E.2d 36 (Mass. 1992) (the Massachusetts Declaration of Rights); Opinion of the Justices, 591 N.E.2d 1073 (Mass. 1992); State v. Fish, 321 Or. 48, 893 P.1d 1023 (1995) (admitting evidence of the refusal would violate Article I, § 12 of the state constitution, at least when the officer requests the motorist to take all the field sobriety texts; the evidence is testimonial because the complete set of tests involves counting, reciting the alphabet, estimating a period of time, and providing information about residence and date of birth). *But see* Note, *SJC Steers Off Course: DUI Breath Test Refusals Inadmissible*, 28 NEW ENGL. L. REV. 1169 (1994) (criticizing the position of the Supreme Judicial Court).

387. Lauderdale v. State, 548 P.2d 376 (Alaska 1976).

388. *E.g.*, VT. STAT. ANN. tit. 23, § 1203(a).

389. Gundersen v. Anchorage, 792 P.2d 673 (Alaska 1990) (although the defendant has a due process right to challenge the results of a police breath test by introducing evidence of an independent test, that right does not require the government to preserve a breath test so long as the government affords the defendant a reasonable opportunity to have an independent test performed); Moss v. Superior Ct. of La Paz Cty., 857 P.2d 400 (Ariz. App. 1993) (given the advances in breath testing technology, the devices are now so reliable that there is no need to retain a sample for later retesting); State v. Anderson, 724 A.2d 1231 (Me. 1999).

390. Carlson, *supra* note 10, at 51-20-23; Forte v. State, 686 S.W.2d 744, 753 n.6 (Tex. App. 1985) (discussing the split of authority).

391. McVeigh v. Smith, 872 F.2d 725 (6th Cir. 1989); Langelier v. Coleman, 861 F.2d 1508 (11th Cir. 19 Woods v. Lemonds, 804 F. Supp. 1106 (E.D. Mo. 1992), *aff'd*, 991 F.2d 802 (8th Cir. 1993); Logan v. Shealy, 500 F. Supp. 502 (E.D. Va. 1980), *aff'd in part, rev'd in part*, 660 F.2d 1007 (4th Cir. 1981).

392. State v. Cichowski, 203 Conn. 97, 523 A.2d 503 (1987); State v. Hoch, 500 So. 2d 597 (Fla. App. 1986), *review denied*, 509 So. 2d 1118 (Fla. 1987); Steward v. State, 436 N.E.2d 859 (Ind. App. 1982); Davis v. State, 174 Ind. App. 433, 367 N.E.2d 1163 (1977); State v. Bristor, 236 Kan. 313, 691 P.2d 1 (1984); Commonwealth v. Cornell, 37 K.L.S. 11, 14 (Ky. Ct. App., Sept. 21, 1990); Elkin v. Commonwealth, Dep't of Transp., Bureau of Vehicle Reg., 646 S.W.2d 45 (Ky. App. 1982); State v. Jones, 457 A.2d 1116 (Me. 1983); Commonwealth v. Brazelton, 404 Mass. 783, 537 N.E.2d 142 (1989) ("The moment at which a person must decide to take or to refuse to

At the other extreme, a number of courts have found a right to counsel although they differ over the source of the right. Some courts derive the right from state rules of criminal procedure,[393] while others rely on state statute.[394] A few courts have found a right to counsel originating in the constitution. Some of these courts believe that the sixth amendment right to counsel attaches at the stage of the administration of the test.[395] These courts often reason that the test can have such a momentous impact on any subsequent prosecution that the test constitutes a critical stage for sixth amendment purposes.[396] Other courts purport

---

take a breathalyzer test is not a critical stage in the criminal process"); Connolly v. Commissioner of Pub. Safety, 373 N.W.2d 352 (Minn. App. 1985); State v. Foster, 95 Or. App. 452, 769 P.2d 790 (1989) (although under the state constitution the right to counsel is triggered whenever a suspect is in formal custody, a traffic stop does not constitute custody); Commonwealth v. West, 370 Pa. Super. 365, 536 A.2d 447, *appeal denied,* 518 Pa. 655, 544 A.2d 1342 (1988); Jamial v. State, 787 S.W. 2d 380 (Tex. Crim. App.) (there is no right under either the state or the national constitution to consult with counsel before deciding whether to submit to a breath test), *cert. denied,* 498 U.S. 853 (1990); McCambridge v. State, 778 S.W.2d 70 (Tex. Crim. App. 1989), *cert. denied,* 495 U.S. 910 (1990); Forte v. State, 759 S.W.2d 128 (Tex. Crim. App. 1988); Growe v. State, 675 S.W.2d 554 (Tex. App. 1984); State v. Schulze, 116 Wash. 2d 154, 804 P.2d 566 (1991) (there is no sixth amendment or state constitutional right to counsel before submitting to a blood test); Wheeler v. State, 705 P.2d 861 (Wyo. 1985); Casenote, *D.W.I. Suspects Do Not Have Right to Consult with Counsel Before Intoxilyzer Test Under Texas Constitution Because Test Is Not a "Critical Stage" in Proceedings*, 21 ST. MARY'S L.J. 233 (1989); State v. Frazier, 914 S.W.2d 467 (Tenn. 1996) (a person's blood alcohol rapidly dissipates over time, and delaying the test while awaiting counsel could compromise the accuracy of the test); State v. White, 504 N.W.2d 211 (Minn. 1993).

393. Kameroff v. State, 926 P.2d 1174 (Alaska App. 1996); Copelin v. State, 659 P.2d 1206 (Alaska 1983) (ALASKA CRIM. R. 5(b)); State v. Schulze, 116 Wash. 2d 154, 804 P.2d 566 (1991) (the right to counsel is granted by state court rule, Criminal Rule 3.1).

394. Annot., 18 A.L.R.4TH 705 (1982); Annot., 97 A.L.R.3D 852 (1980); Heles v. South Dakota, 530 F. Supp. 646, 650-51 (D.S.D.), *vacated as moot,* 682 F.2d 201 (8th Cir. 1982) (collecting the cases); Copelin v. State, 659 P.2d 1206 (Alaska 1983); State v. McAteer, 290 N.W.2d 924 (Iowa 1980); Prideaux v. State, Dep't of Pub. Safety, 310 Minn. 405, 247 N.W.2d 385 (1976); Kuntz v. State Hwy. Comm'r, 405 N.W.2d 285 (N.D. 1987); State v. Duff, 136 Vt. 537, 394 A.2d 1145 (1978); State v. Marquez, 100 Wash. 2d 824, 677 P.2d 599 (1984).

395. Government of Virgin Islands v. Quinones, 301 F. Supp. 246 (D.V.I. 1969); State v. Bristor, 9 Kan. App. 2d 404, 682 P.2d 122, *rev'd,* 236 Kan. 313, 691 P.2d 1 (1984); Prideaux v. State, Dep't of Pub. Safety, 310 Minn. 405, 247 N.W.2d 385 (1976) (dictum); People v. Shaw, 127 Misc. 2d 607, 486 N.Y.S.2d 607 (Vill. Ct. 1984), *rev'd,* 133 Misc. 2d 862, 508 N.Y.S.2d 844 (1986); Commonwealth v. Waggoner, 373 Pa. Super. 23, 540 A.2d 280 (the sixth amendment right attached to the audiotaping of the defendant's field test), *appeal denied,* 520 Pa. 616, 554 A.2d 509 (1988), *cert. denied,* 490 U.S. 1031 (1989). *See also* Friedman v. Commissioner of Pub. Safety, 473 N.W.2d 828 (Minn. 1991) (under Article I, § 6 of the state constitution, the decision whether to take a breath test is a "critical stage"); State v. Spencer, 305 Or. 59, 750 P.2d 147 (1988) (the court premised the right to counsel on Article I, § 11 of the state constitution, the Oregon analogue to the sixth amendment); Casenote, *Implied Consent: Minnesota's Twist on the Constitutional Right to Counsel in DWI Proceedings. (Friedman v. Commissioner of Pub. Safety, 473 N.W.2d 828, Minn. 1991)*, 15 HAMLINE L. REV. 195 (1991).

to find the right rooted in due process.[397] These courts reason that the decision to submit to a test and, in some states, the choice of a test are so complex and critical that fundamental fairness demands affording the defendant the guiding hand of counsel.[398] Many of these courts go farther and recognize a right to counsel of the defendant's choice; the police cannot force the defendant to be content with a public defender.[399]

Even the courts recognizing a counsel right hold that the right is limited. The defendant does not have an absolute right to counsel's presence at the time of the test. Rather the defendant has a limited right to a reasonable opportunity to contact counsel.[400] A telephone conversation between the defendant and the counsel ordinarily suffices.[401] As one court commented, "If the attorney cannot

---

396. *E.g.,* State v. Nielsen, 530 N.W.2d 212 (Minn. App. 1995) (the right to counsel does not extend to the investigatory stage of chemical testing); People v. Shaw, 127 Misc. 2d 607, 486 N.Y.S.2d 607 (1984), *rev'd,* 133 Misc. 2d 862, 508 N.Y.S.2d 844 (1986). *See also* Friedman v. Commissioner of Pub. Safety, 473 N.W.2d 828 (Minn. 1991) (relying on the state constitution); Casenote, *Implied Consent: Minnesota's Twist on the Constitutional Right to Counsel in DWI Proceedings. (Friedman v. Commissioner of Public Safety, 473 N.W.2d 828, Minn. 1991),* 15 HAMLINE L. REV. 195 (1991).

397. Heles v. South Dakota, 530 F. Supp. 646 (D.S.D.), *vacated as moot,* 682 F.2d 201 (8th Cir. 1982) (due to the plaintiff's death); Sites v. State, 300 Md. 702, 481 A.2d 192 (1984); Hall v. Secretary of State, 60 Mich. App. 431, 231 N.W.2d 396 (1975); Troy v. Curry, 36 Ohio Misc. 144, 65 Ohio Op. 2d 194, 303 N.E.2d 925 (1973).

398. Heles v. South Dakota, 530 F. Supp. 646 (D.S.D.), *vacated as moot,* 682 F.2d 201 (8th Cir. 1982) (due to the plaintiff's death).

399. Delmore v. Commissioner of Pub. Safety, 499 N.W.2d 839 (Minn. App. 1993).

400. *Id.*; Saltz v. Dept. of Public Safety, Driver Imp. Bur., 942 P.2d 1151 (Alaska 1997) (the police officer did not violate the motorist's statutory right to counsel; although the officer provided the motorist with a telephone directory, the officer did not read aloud the names of the attorneys in the directory; the motorist could not read the entries because his glasses were back in his vehicle); Copelin v. State, 659 P.2d 1206 (Alaska 1983); State v. Juarez, 161 Ariz. 76, 775 P.2d 1140 (1989); Kunzler v. Pima County Superior Court, 154 Ariz. 568, 744 P.2d 669 (1987) ("It is only when the exercise of that right will hinder an ongoing investigation that the right to an attorney must give way in time and place to the investigation by the police"); Davis v. Commissioner of Public Safety, 517 N.W.2d 901 (Minn. 1994) (the consultation must not unreasonably delay administration of the test); People v. Martin, 143 Misc. 2d 341, 540 N.Y.S.2d 412 (1989) (the defendant's exercise of the right may not unreasonably interfere with the testing procedures); State v. Brazil-Kay, 907 P.2d 1116 (Or. App. 1995) (the defendant's limited right to counsel does not require that testing be delayed beyond the required 15-minute observation period); Note, *To Submit or Not to Submit — Where Is My Attorney?: The Right to Counsel Before Submission to Chemical Testing in a DWI Proceeding,* 63 NEB. L. REV. 373, 385 (1984).

401. Note, *To Submit or Not to Submit — Where Is My Attorney? The Right to Counsel Before Submission to Chemical Testing in a DWI Proceeding,* 63 NEB. L. REV. 373, 386 (1984), citing State v. Fitzsimmons, 93 Wash. 2d 436, 610 P.2d 893, *vacated,* 449 U.S. 977, *on remand,* 94 Wash. 2d 858, 620 P.2d 999 (1980). *See also* Saltz v. State, Dep't of Public Safety, Driver Imp. Bur., 942 P.2d 1151 (Alaska 1997) (the police officer did not violate the motorist's statutory right to counsel; although the officer provided the motorist with a telephone directory, the officer did not read aloud

be contacted within a reasonable time the suspect must decide without the advice of counsel, whether to take the breathalyzer test."[402] There is precedent that if the suspect contacts an attorney by telephone, the police must give the suspect a reasonable opportunity to consult privately with the attorney.[403] There is likewise respectable precedent for the view that the police must allow the suspect to attempt to contact the attorney at the attorney's residence as well as at the attorney's office.[404] There is also authority that as a corollary to the right to counsel, the defendant has a right to a private breath test before deciding whether to take a state-administered test.[405]

Some defense counsel have argued for the right to consult persons other than attorneys. For instance, in one case, the suspect was deaf, and the defense contended that the police should have honored the suspect's request for a sign-language interpreter. The defense premised its contention on the provisions of the Americans With Disabilities Act. However, the Illinois appellate court rejected the contention.[406]

---

the names of the attorneys in the directory; the motorist could not read the entries because his glasses were back in his vehicle); Davis v. Commissioner of Public Safety, 517 N.W.2d 901 (Minn. 1994) (the consultation must not unreasonably delay administration of the test); State v. Karau, 496 N.W.2d 416 (Minn. App. 1993); State v. Brazil-Kay, 907 P.2d 1116 (Or. App. 1995) (the defendant's limited right to counsel does not require that testing be delayed beyond the required 15-minute observation period).

402. Copelin v. State, 659 P.2d 1206, 1212 (Alaska 1983); *Compare* Goss v. People, 209 Ill. Dec. 105, 650 N.E.2d 1078 (App. 1995) (the police allowed the defendant only a one-minute consultation with his attorney before being forced to decide whether to undergo a blood alcohol test) and Kuhn v. Commissioner of Pub. Safety, 488 N.W.2d 838 (Minn. App. 1992) (the police gave the defendant only twenty-four minutes to contact an attorney) *with* Parsons v. Commissioner of Pub. Safety, 488 N.W.2d 500 (Minn. App. 1992) (the defendant was given a phone directory, called a friend to contact an attorney, and forty minutes later was told that she had to decide on her own).

403. Farrell v. Anchorage, 682 P.2d 1128 (Alaska App. 1984). *See also* State v. Holland, 147 Ariz. 453, 711 P.2d 592 (1985); State v. West, 151 Vt. 140, 557 A.2d 873 (1988) (the unjustified presence of police would have a chilling effect on the consultation).

404. People v. Cole, 178 Misc.2d 166, 681 N.Y.S.2d 447 (Co. Ct. 1998).

405. Brosan v. Cochran, 307 Md. 662, 516 A.2d 970 (1986); *Compare* City of Mandan v. Jewett, 517 N.W.2d 640 (N.D. 1994) (the statute does not absolutely guarantee that the consultation will be conducted in private; if the defendant presents a security or flight risk, an officer may be justified in staying within earshot), Gildroy v. Motor Vehicles Div., 132 Or. App. 235, 888 P.2d 64 (1995) (no right to private consultation with counsel) and State v. Penrod, 892 P.2d 729 (Or. App. 1995) (there is a right to a private consultation).

406. People v. Long, 296 Ill. App. 3d 127, 693 N.E.2d 1260, 230 Ill. Dec. 509 (1998).

§ 22-7(F). Failure to Administer Required Warnings.

In *Miranda v. Arizona,*[407] the Supreme Court decreed that law enforcement officers must administer certain warnings to a person before subjecting that person to custodial interrogation. In many states, defense counsel have urged the courts to mandate *Miranda*-like warnings to defendants before subjecting them to intoxication tests.[408] These urgings have met with limited success.[409]

A Right to Warnings of the Consequences of Refusing a Test

In some cases, defense counsel have argued that the defendant is entitled to warnings of the right to refuse to be tested and the consequences of refusal. The Kansas courts have considered and rejected that argument. In one case,[410] a Kansas court held that the police are not obliged to advise suspected drunk drivers that they have a right to refuse a blood alcohol test. In another case,[411] the Kansas Supreme Court held that the police have no duty to inform the driver of the potential consequences of a refusal to submit to the test.

In other jurisdictions, courts have found a statutory requirement to inform the suspect of "his or her right ... to refuse to submit" and the "administrative penalties for failure to submit to the test."[412] Perhaps the most interesting decision is *Graham v. State,*[413] decided by the Alaska Supreme Court. In *Graham* the court announced "that where an arrested person refuses to submit to a breathalyzer test, the administering officer must inquire into the nature of the

---

407. 384 U.S. 436 (1966); Moos v. Norton, 789 F. Supp. 352 (D. Kan. 1992) (a breath test is not custodial interrogation requiring *Miranda* warnings).

408. People v. Wegielnik, 605 N.E.2d 487 (Ill. 1992) (the defendant does not have a right to an interpreter to translate the warnings); McAvoy v. State, 314 Md. 509, 551 A.2d 875 (1989) (the police need not give a suspect *Miranda* warnings before asking the suspect to submit to a chemical sobriety test); Commonwealth v. Mordan, 615 A.2d 102 (Pa. Super. 1992) (although the defendant was deaf and did not read lips, he had no right to have the warnings translated into sign language), *aff'd,* 633 A.2d 588 (Pa. 1993); King v. State, 598 S.W.2d 834 (Tenn. Crim. App. 1980).

409. People v. Berg, 92 N.Y.2d 701, 708 N.E.2d 979, 685 N.Y.S.2d 906 (1999) (the defendant's refusal to submit to a field sobriety test was admissible even though the police had not administered *Miranda* warnings; the refusal was not compelled, since the officers in fact wanted the defendant to take the test).

410. State v. Menzins, 4 Kan. App. 2d 292, 605 P.2d 159 (1980).

411. Hazlett v. Motor Vehicle Dep't, 195 Kan. 439, 407 P.2d 551 (1965).

412. State v. Loscomb, 291 Md. 424, 435 A.2d 764 (Spec. App. 1981) (construing Maryland Court and Judicial Proceedings Article § 16-205(c)); Commonwealth v. Hipp, 380 Pa. Super. 345, 551 A.2d 1086 (1988). *But see* Jessup v. State, 935 S.W.2d 508 (Tex. App. 1996) (although there is a state statutory right to a warning of the consequences of a failure to submit to a blood alcohol test, the violation did not render evidence of the motorist's breath test refusal inadmissible; there was no evidence of a causal connection between the motorist's refusal and the officer's failure to give written warnings after the refusal).

413. 633 P.2d 211 (Alaska 1981).

refusal and, if it appears that the refusal is based on a confusion about the person's rights, the officer must clearly advise that person that the rights contained in the *Miranda* warning do not apply to the breathalyzer examination."[414]

A Right to a Warning That the Suspect Has a Right to Counsel

In other cases, defense counsel have contended that the police must inform the suspect of the right to consult counsel. Even in the jurisdictions recognizing a right to counsel, the courts divide over the question of whether the police must inform the defendant of the right to counsel before administering a test. In 1980, the Washington court recognized that the sixth amendment right attaches at the time of an intoxication test.[415] Nevertheless, in subsequent decisions, the Washington courts have held that the police need not tell drunk driving suspects that they have a right to consult counsel before submitting to the test.[416]

However, the Vermont court reached a contrary conclusion in *State v. Duff.*[417] The court noted that its statute unambiguously provides that the suspect "shall have the right to consult with an attorney."[418] The court concluded that the only way to adequately implement the statutory policy is to require police to inform suspects of the existence of the right.

A Right to a Warning That the Suspect Has No Right to Consult Counsel

At the other extreme, one court has held that the police must expressly inform an arrestee that he has no right to consult counsel in connection with a request that he submit to a breath test.[419] The court pointed out that in the instant case, as

414. *Id.* at 215. Fee v. State, 825 P.2d 464 (Alaska App. 1992) (the defendant had a mistaken belief that he had the right to decline or to insist upon the presence of an attorney).

415. State v. Fitzsimmons, 93 Wash. 2d 436, 610 P.2d 893, *vacated,* 449 U.S. 977, *on remand,* 94 Wash. 2d 858, 620 P.2d 999 (1980).

416. State *ex rel.* Juckett v. Evergreen Judicial Dist. Court, 32 Wash. App. 49, 645 P.2d 734 (1982), *remanded,* 100 Wash. 2d 824, 675 P.2d 599 (1984); State v. Wurm, 32 Wash. App. 258, 647 P.2d 508 (1982), *aff'd in part,* 100 Wash. 2d 824, 675 P.2d 599 (1984).

417. 136 Vt. 537, 394 A.2d 1145 (1978).

418. *Id.* at 538, 394 A.2d at 1146.

419. Roberts v. Maine, 48 F.3d 1287 (1st Cir. 1995) (there was a violation of due process when the defendant was given misleading information); Commonwealth v. Danforth, 608 A.2d 1044 (Pa. 1992) (citing O'Connell, the court states that "[t]here is overwhelming unfairness inherent in the situation where an arrestee is initially told that he has a right to consult with an attorney, and then in conjunction with a request for chemical testing is told that a refusal will result in suspension of driving privileges without being informed that his right to counsel is inapplicable"); Pennsylvania Dep't of Transp. v. Sorg, 147 Pa. Commw. 82, 606 A.2d 1270 (1992) (discussing *O'Connell*); Pennsylvania Dep't of Transp. v. Hoover, 606 A.2d 1264 (Pa. Commw. Ct. 1992) (discussing *O'Connell*); Commonwealth v. Dep't of Transp., Bur. of Traffic Safety v. O'Connell, 521 Pa. 242, 555 A.2d 873 (1989).

often occurs, the police informed the arrestee that he had a right to counsel and then requested that he submit to a test. The court noted that under state law, the suspect had no right to counsel in connection with the test. A layperson might mistakenly assume that the right to counsel applied to the test and refuse to submit until counsel was furnished. The court therefore announced: "[W]here an arrestee requests to speak to or call an attorney ... when requested to take a breathalyzer test, we insist that ... the police instruct the arrestee that such rights are inapplicable to the breathalyzer test and that the arrestee does not have the right to consult with an attorney ... prior to taking the test."[420] Although in the seminal case the police themselves engendered the arrestee's confusion, a subsequent decision has extended the requirement for advice to fact situations in which the police do not make misleading statements.[421] In 1991, the Hawaii Supreme Court came to the same conclusion.[422]

A Right to a Warning About the Right to a Scientific Intoxication Test

In still other cases, the defense counsel have argued that the police must inform the defendant of the right to a scientific intoxication test or to choose among various tests such as breath, urine, and blood. This argument has been made in two contexts.

In the first context, the police do not administer any scientific test, the conviction rests on the testimony of the police and lay witnesses about the defendant's apparently intoxicated behavior, and the defense argues that the failure to advise the defendant of a right to a scientific intoxication test necessitates reversal. "The courts that have considered the question have held that, absent a specific provision in the implied consent law requiring that the arrested person be informed of the provisions of the law and offered a test thereunder, the failure of a law enforcement officer to offer a suspect a chemical sobriety test did not bar a prosecution on a charge of driving while under the influence of intoxicating liquor or a similar offense."[423] A Texas decision,

420. *Id.*

421. Wilson v. Pennsylvania Dep't Transp., 135 Pa. Commw. 339, 581 A.2d 252 (1990) (the government was "not correct in its contention that proof of the giving of *Miranda* warnings before a breath test is absolutely required to make *O'Connell* applicable. [W]here an arrestee requests to speak to an attorney or anyone else when requested to take a breathalyzer test, the police must tell him that [counsel] rights are not applicable to the test").

422. State v. Taniguchi, 815 P.2d 24 (Haw. 1991) (once the arrestee manifests the belief that he is entitled to counsel, the arresting officer must advise the arrestee that he or she has no such right).

423. Annot., 95 A.L.R.2D 710, 711 (1979). *But see* State v. McNichols, 76 Wash. App. 283, 884 P.2d 620 (1994) (dismissal of charges is the appropriate remedy for jail personnel's interference with a DWI arrestee's statutory right to an independent scientific test of his blood alcohol concentration), *rev'd*, 128 Wash. 2d 242, 906 P.2d 329 (1995).

Crawford v. State,[424] typifies the attitude of most courts. In that case, the police neglected to inform the defendant that he could request a scientific intoxication test; and at trial, the prosecution relied on lay testimony about the defendant's alcohol breath, slurred speech, swaying, and his difficulty focusing his eyes. The defendant argued that the police officer's failure to advise the defendant of his statutory right to a blood test required reversal. The court stated that it encouraged police to inform suspects of the right and regarded such advice as "the better practice." Yet, absent more explicit language in the Texas statute, the court affirmed the conviction.

In the second context, the police neglect to inform the defendant that he or she has a choice among three different scientific tests, the police administer one test, and the defendant contends that the police neglect requires the suppression of the evidence of the test administered. The courts vary in their receptivity to this argument. The California courts have concluded that the defendant has neither a statutory[425] nor a constitutional[426] right to be informed of all three tests. The Maryland court is contra. That court stated:

> A police officer who detains an operator of a motor vehicle on the basis that the operator was driving or attempting to drive while intoxicated ... must offer the detained individual a choice of a blood test or a breath test, or no test at all. If an officer is permitted to order ... [the test] obtained by some subterfuge, and use the results at trial, the statutory right of the individual to select the type of test, if any, to which he will submit, is rendered absolutely meaningless.[427]

§ 22-8. Sufficiency of Evidence.

In the typical drunk driving case, the prosecutor initially presents evidence of a scientific intoxication test and then invokes one of the presumptions mentioned earlier in this chapter, such as the presumption of intoxication if the blood alcohol concentration exceeds 0.10%. If the prosecutor has charged the defendant under a per se statute, resort to the presumption is unnecessary. However, in practice, most prosecutors charge the defendant under both the per se statute and the more traditional driving under the influence (DUI) statute. When the two charges are prosecuted together at the same trial, the presence of the DUI charge in the case forces the prosecutor to rely on the presumption statute. Critics have

---

424. 643 S.W.2d 178 (Tex. App. 1982).

425. Skinner v. Silas, 58 Cal. App. 3d 591, 130 Cal. Rptr. 91 (1976).

426. People v. Brannon, 32 Cal. App. 3d 971, 108 Cal. Rptr. 620 (1973).

427. Loscomb v. State, 45 Md. App. 598, 611, 416 A.2d 1276, 1283 (1980); State v. Rivard, 80 Wash. App. 633, 910 P.2d 520 (1996) (if the officer elects to request a sample from the defendant, the officer must inform the defendant of his right to an independent test), *rev'd*, 131 Wash. 2d 63, 929 P.2d 413 (1997).

attacked both the scientific evidence and the presumptions that the prosecutor relies on to make out a submissible case.

§ 22-8(A). Probative Value.

A Generalized Attack

One writer, Marshall Houts, contends that the courts have lost sight of the point that determining whether a person is "under the influence" is a medical question.[428] Houts charges that the courts have allowed the police to commit "medical heresy"[429] by converting the intoxication tests into a "conclusive diagnostic tool."[430] Houts does not believe that intoxication tests are entitled to such great weight. He asserts:

> It is a fundamental tenet in medicine that no laboratory aid should ever be considered diagnostic per se. The laboratory procedures are to be considered as nothing more than diagnostic aids, or diagnostic tools.[431]

More specifically, he argues that "when the clinical (observable) evidence and the laboratory findings are in conflict, the clinical evidence controls and not the laboratory findings."[432] If the test results and the defendant's seemingly sober behavior are contradictory, the test results must yield to "the clinical findings."[433] The defense sometimes argues that "The test has to be wrong" when the test indicates a high level of intoxication but "the police officer does not recall strong signs of impairment in the manner in which" the defendant "spoke, walked, and functioned . . . ."[434]

Dr. Dubowski rejoins that the effect of exogenous chemical agents on human subjects is a question of toxicology, not medicine, and adds that Houts' contention misses the point under modern per se statutes, since under those statutes no clinical findings are necessary.

---

428. Houts, *supra* note 33, at 4.

429. *Id.* at 5.

430. *Id.*

431. *Id.*

432. *Id.*

433. *Id.*

434. Gerstenzang, *Breath Issues — the Big Blow Out of the Prosecution's Case*, 22 The Champion 49-50 (Nov. 1998) ("establish all of the things that the police officer did not see: the defendant did not have slurred speech, did not have blood shot eyes, etc. Go through the whole laundry list of everything that was not there to eliminate the common law symptoms of intoxication that should clearly have been there if the defendant really did have the high blood alcohol concentration that has been reported by the instrumentation").

Chapter 23 discusses the Supreme Court's decision in *Jackson v. Virginia.*[435] There the Court toughened the standard for determining whether the prosecution has sustained its initial burden of going forward. The prosecution must now demonstrate that its evidence has sufficient cumulative probative value to remove any lingering doubt from the mind of a hypothetical, rational juror; it is no longer sufficient to eke out a mere permissive inference of the existence of each element of the charged crime. In *Trombetta,*[436] the Court's decision on the duty of the police to preserve breath samples, the Court commented in a footnote:

> [I]f the Intoxilyzer were truly prone to erroneous readings, then Intoxilyzer results without more might be insufficient to establish guilt beyond a reasonable doubt. Jackson v. Virginia, 443 U.S. 307 (1979).[437]

Together *Jackson* and the footnote in *Trombetta* may lead to attacks on the legal sufficiency of the prosecution's scientific evidence of intoxication.

On the one hand, these attacks have plausibility. Assume the defendant is charged with driving under the influence. Suppose further that the defense counsel presents expert testimony about the limitations of alcohol testing devices and the defendant's behavior suggested sobriety. The defense would have a colorable right to an acquittal. On the other hand, it is unlikely that the courts will accept this argument. In *Trombetta*[438] the Court seemed impressed by the evidence of the accuracy of breath testing. The Court pointed out that the Intoxilyzer has "passed accuracy requirements established by the National Highway Traffic Safety Administration."[439] The Court believed that the Intoxilyzer is so accurate that "[i]n all but a tiny fraction of cases," a second,

---

435. 443 U.S. 307 (1979).

436. California v. Trombetta, 467 U.S. 479 (1984).

437. *Id.* at 489-90 n.10. *See also* Sapir, Giangranda & Peters, *Breath Alcohol Machines: Evidence Foundation Requirements in Illinois*, 22 J. MARSHALL L. REV. 1, 31 (1988) (discussing the application of *Jackson* to breath alcohol cases); Commonwealth v. Renninger, 452 Pa. Super. 421, 682 A.2d 356 (1996) (evidence of the alcohol content of the supernatant of a motorist's blood, rather than of the alcohol content of the whole blood, was insufficient to support a DUI conviction; the prosecution did not offer any testimony as to the formula for converting alcohol content in supernatant into alcohol content in whole blood). *See also* Moore v. State, 645 N.E.2d 6 (Ind. App. 1994) (evidence that the defendant had a given amount of cannabinoids in his urine was insufficient to establish that he was operating a motor vehicle with a controlled substance in his blood; the presence of marijuana in the defendant's urine did not necessarily mean that there was marijuana in his blood; it was possible that the marijuana would be detectable in his urine even though it was no longer in his blood); Kuwatch, *Drug-Related Driving Offenses: Rolling Stoned*, 24 C.A.C.J. FORUM, Vol. 24, No. 1, 28 (1997) (some drug tests are so sensitive that they can detect, for example, a negligible amount of THC metabolite even if the defendant smoked marijuana "several days prior").

438. 467 U.S. at 489.

439. *Id.* at 489 n.9.

independent test would merely confirm the accuracy of the original test.[440] Moreover, although the RFI cases suggest that the courts may now be more sensitive to distortions caused by the conditions under which intoxication testing devices are used, the courts do not appear prepared to generally reappraise the probative value of scientific intoxication tests. The defense will be able to attack the weight of the tests before the jury, but it will be a rare case in which the trial court rules the evidence insufficient as a matter of law.[441]

A More Specific Attack Based on a Need to Adjust the Measured BAC

In several cases, defense counsel have contended that in order to be legally sufficient to establish that the accused had a certain blood alcohol concentration such as .10%, the Breathalyzer reading must exceed .10 by a specified margin — a margin needed to compensate for either the uncertainty in Breathalyzer measurements or the imprecision in converting from breath alcohol concentration to blood alcohol concentration.[442] Some defense counsel have argued that there should be a 0.03% subtraction factor for uncertainty in Breathalyzer measurements and a 0.025% subtraction factor for the blood/breath ratio. Counsel derive these subtraction factors by taking the standard deviation in reported experiments (either experiments comparing Breathalyzer and gas chromatograph measurements or research comparing blood alcohol and breath alcohol measurements) and multiplying by three. Three standard deviations

---

440. *Id.* at 489. *But see* Soloway, *Due Process vs. Lab Process*, PATHOLOGIST, Mar. 1985, at 24 ("To professional laboratorians it is apparent that the testing process is more prone to error than the Supreme Court was led to believe").

441. People v. Randolph, 213 Cal. App. 3d Supp. 1, 262 Cal. Rptr. 378, 380 (1989) (the court rejected a defense argument that the prosecution should be permitted to introduce only "chemical tests so far above 0.10 percent that the range of the margin of error cannot extend below 0.10 percent"); People v. Gustafson, 194 Ill. App. 3d 910, 141 Ill. Dec. 639, 551 N.E.2d 826 (the statute mandating the use of an alcohol partition ratio of 2,100:1 is constitutional although the ratio is the subject of scientific debate), *app. denied,* 133 Ill. 2d 564, 149 Ill. Dec. 329, 561 N.E.2d 699 (1990); People v. Davis, 180 Ill. App. 3d 749, 129 Ill. Dec. 488, 536 N.E.2d 172 (1989) (the Breathalyzer has an industrial tolerance level of 0.01 percent, but that level does not dictate the conclusion that a finding of exactly 0.10 percent breath alcohol is insufficient to justify a license suspension; the provisions of the state code "refer to alcohol concentrations as revealed by chemical tests or other analyses," not absolute values); State v. Downie, 117 N.J. 450, 569 A.2d 242 (the opinion contains a detailed discussion of Dr. Dubowski's testimony about partition ratios; "the Breathalyzer, with a maximum overestimation error margin of 2.3 percent, is not only the best practical tool, but the tool the legislature intended to carry out its will. The reliability of the Breathalyzer results will continue to be the subject of judicial notice in drunk-driving cases"), *cert. denied,* 498 U.S. 819 (1990).

442. Annot., *Challenges to use of breath tests for drunk drivers based on claim that partition or conversion ratio between measured breath alcohol and actual blood alcohol is inaccurate*, 90 A.L.R.4TH 155 (1991).

statistically yield 99.7% confidence, ensuring that in 997 out of 1,000 cases, the actual blood alcohol concentration will be at least .10%.[443]

On occasion, the courts have sustained these defense arguments.[444] For instance, in *State v. Burling,*[445] the Nebraska Supreme Court adopted the defense bar's argument that there is imprecision in converting from breath to blood. In *Burling,* the expert testimony convinced the court that the conversion ratio could be as high as 1:3,400 or as low as 1:1,100. The court stated that it was "concerned ... with the degree by which the machine may overstate defendant's blood alcohol level. A 1:1,100 breath-to-blood distribution ratio is 52.38 percent of the 1:2,100 ratio assumed by the formula built into the machine. Therefore, ... the Intoxilyzer result must be reduced to 52.38 percent of .164 of 1 percent, that is, to .086. Consequently, the Intoxilyzer test result fails to establish that defendant had 'ten-hundredths of 1 percent by weight of alcohol in his blood' and therefore fails to establish a violation ...."[446] However, in two later cases, the court retreated from the sweeping language in *Burling.* In *State v. Hvistendahl,*[447] the court stated that the jury need not adjust the ratio in all cases. When there is a conflict in the record over the margin of error, the trier of fact may base its verdict on either margin. In *State v. Babcock,*[448] the court asserted that in *Burling,* "this court did not intend to . . . rule that as a matter of law a reading of the test

---

443. Labianca, *The Chemical Basis of the Breathalyzer*, 67 J. CHEM. EDUC. 259, 261 (1990).

444. Gerztenzang, *Breath Issues — Partition Ratio or Blood-Breath Presumption*, 23 THE CHAMPION 52, 53 (Jan./Feb. 1999).

445. 224 Neb. 725, 400 N.W.2d 872 (1987).

446. *Id.*, 400 N.W.2d at 876-77. *See also* Labianca, *The Chemical Basis of the Breathalyzer*, 67 J. CHEM. EDUC. 259, 261 (1990) ("If the use of the Breathalyzer continues, then the recommendation of Dubowski that 0.055% should be subtracted from any raw test result, should be ... implemented. This adjustment includes both the 0.025% safety factor ... for results reported in terms of BAC, and an additional 0.03% error factor stemming from a study conducted by Dubowski in which 43% of the Breathalyzer readings that exceeded 0.10% were actually below 0.10%"); Lara v. Tanaka, 1995 Haw. App. LEXIS 48, 58 Cr. L. (BNA) 1151 (Haw. App. Oct. 20, 1995) (in evaluating the legal sufficiency of the evidence to support an administrative revocation of a driver's license, the court must consider the margin of error; in this case the prohibited BAC was 0.10 percent, and the defendant's test result was only 0.107 percent), *rev'd. depublished*, 83 Haw. 24, 924 P.2d 192 (1996); Haynes v. Alaska Dep't of Public Safety, 865 P.2d 753 (Alaska 1993) (as a matter of due process, the inherent margin of error in the Intoxilyzer 3000 machine must be applied in the defendant's favor).

447. 225 Neb. 315, 405 N.W.2d 273 (1987). *See also* People v. Rangel, 204 Cal. App. 3d Supp. 10, 251 Cal. Rptr. 638 (1988) (a defense expert testified that given the inherent inaccuracies of chemical testing, the defendant's blood alcohol concentration could have been between .09 and .121 at the time of the test; based on the testimony, the defense requested an instruction that if the scientific evidence about the error margin showed that the defendant's concentration could have been below .10, as a matter of law the jury was required to find the defendant not guilty; however, since the jury could have rejected the testimony as lacking credibility, the court held that the judge did not have to grant the request).

448. 227 Neb. 649, 419 N.W.2d 527 (1988).

results from an Intoxilyzer . . . should automatically be adjusted. Whether an adjustment is required is dependent upon the credible evidence in each case."

§ 22-8(B). Presumption of Intoxication.

Suppose that the charging document alleges only driving under the influence (DUI) or DUI in addition to a per se offense. In a DUI case, the prosecution must demonstrate that the defendant operated a motor vehicle while impaired, intoxicated, or under the influence. It is neither necessary nor, strictly speaking, sufficient for the prosecutor to prove that the defendant had a blood alcohol concentration exceeding 0.10% or 0.15%. That proof becomes sufficient evidence only by virtue of the older statutory presumptions mentioned in the first section of this chapter. Absent those presumptions, to make out a DUI charge, the prosecutor would have to present expert testimony that the defendant's blood alcohol concentration was high enough to impair the defendant's ability to drive.[449] The prosecutor could present testimony by a doctor, pathologist, biologist, hematologist, physiologist, biochemist, or toxicologist.[450] If the prosecutor omits such testimony and the defense counsel can persuade the trial court that the jurisdiction's statutory presumption is inapplicable, the court may rule peremptorily in the defendant's favor.

Determining the applicability of the statutory presumption can raise several issues. Six issues are noteworthy. Each of these issues relates to a potential condition to applying the presumption, and the defense can prevent the presumption from coming into play by prevailing on any one of the six issues. For the most part, in a given jurisdiction, the resolution of the issue turns on the precise wording of the legislation and the court's approach to statutory interpretation.[451]

The Right Type of Case

One issue is that the statute be invoked in the right type of case. The statutes in most jurisdictions apply in only certain types of proceedings. For example, some statutes are confined to criminal cases. Suppose that a civil defendant in a torts suit contended that the plaintiff was guilty of contributory negligence and was intoxicated at the time of the accident. The civil defendant could not invoke the

---

449. People v. Morgan, 236 N.Y.S.2d 1014 (Co. Ct. 1962).

450. *Id.* at 1017.

451. Courts differ in their approach to statutory interpretation. While some stress the primary of the text of the statute, others are more willing to turn to extrinsic legislative history material and to allow such material to trump the apparent plain meaning of the text. Imwinkelried, *Moving Beyond "Top Down" Grand Theories of Statutory Construction: A "Bottom Up" Interpretive Approach to the Federal Rules of Evidence*, 75 ORE. L. REV. 389 (1996).

statutory presumption.[452] Some statutes are even more narrowly confined to drunk driving prosecutions. Assume that a criminal defendant is on trial for negligent homicide. If the presumption attaches only in DUI cases, the prosecutor cannot resort to the presumption.[453]

Proof of the Working Order of the Equipment

Another issue involves the proper working order of the equipment. In some states, the prosecutor must demonstrate that the instrument had been checked within a specified calibration period; if the calibration period passed without proper maintenance, the presumption cannot be used.[454] Similarly, in some jurisdictions, the courts condition the presumption on proof that the test ampoules were spot checked before the test.[455]

The Timing of the Administration of the Test

Other jurisdictions follow the view that the presumption arises only if the police administer the test within a certain time period after the end of drinking. For example, the time limit is two hours in Delaware, Iowa, Maryland, New York, Ohio, Oklahoma, Virginia, West Virginia, and Wisconsin;[456] three hours in Hawaii; and four hours in Minnesota.[457] In some states, tests administered later do not raise the statutory presumption.[458]

---

452. Bach v. Penn Central Transp. Co., 502 F.2d 1117 (6th Cir. 1974) (construing OHIO REV. CODE § 4511.19).

453. State v. Williams, 375 So. 2d 931 (La. 1979).

454. Cossey v. State, 267 Ark. 679, 590 S.W.2d 60 (1979).

455. State v. Graham, 360 So. 2d 853 (La. 1978), *writ of review granted,* 375 So. 2d 374 (La. 1979); State v. Goetz, 374 So. 2d 1219 (La. 1979).

456. *But see* People v. Wager, No. 113712 (Mich. Sup. Ct., June 15, 1999) (if the statute does not impose a time limitation, "no sound reason exists to engraft a 'reasonable time' element onto the clear language of the statute"); *Blood Test Given Two Hours After Accident Is Admissible at Trial,* LAWYERS WEEKLY USA, July 28, 1999, at 8 (describing the *Wager* decision).

457. American Med. Ass'n, *supra* note 257, at 162. Corrigan v. Zolin, 47 Cal. App. 4th 230, 54 Cal. Rptr. 2d 634 (1996); Jackson v. Department of Motor Vehicles, 22 Cal. App. 4th 730, 27 Cal. Rptr. 2d 712 (1994); Yordamlis v. Zolon, 11 Cal. App. 4th 655, 14 Cal. Rptr. 2d 225, 228 (1992) (under the California Vehicle Code, the presumptions "apply only if the chemical test was performed 'within three hours after the driving'"); OHIO STAT. § 14-224(c) ("the test was commenced within two hours of operation"). *See also* United States v. Sauls, 981 F. Supp. 909, 926 (D. Md. 1997) ("a reasonable period of time will ordinarily be a test administered within three hours of the time of driving. However, a test administered beyond the three hour time limit will not necessarily preclude … the application of the appropriate permissive inferences.").

458. *Id. See also* Briscoe v. State, 60 Md. App. 42, 479 A.2d 1385, *cert. denied,* 302 Md. 8, 485 A.2d 149 (1984).

The Adjustment of the Test Result for the Margin of Error

The overwhelming majority of jurisdictions impose the three requirements mentioned above. However, a few jurisdictions impose a fourth condition. In Hawaii and Nebraska, the state courts have been persuaded that like any scientific instrument, breath testing devices are subject to an error factor. The Hawaii court has found that the factor is 0.0165%.[459] The Nebraska Supreme Court has concluded that the Breathalyzer has an inherent tolerance for error.[460] Both courts hold that to trigger the statutory presumption, the prosecutor must prove a reading that exceeds the sum of the 0.10% concentration plus the inherent margin of error.[461] The Alaska court has held that the trial judge must at least permit the defendant to present expert testimony about the margin of error.[462]

A Requirement for Relation Back Testimony

Some courts such as the Arizona Supreme Court has imposed a fifth condition. In *Desmond v. Superior Court,*[463] the court held that the blood alcohol test will not trigger the presumption unless the prosecution presents expert testimony relating the concentration at the time of the test back to the time of the arrest. The court ruled that "[t]he proper procedure to be followed when a party offers the BAC result into evidence without any relation-back testimony is for the court to admit the portion of the test result that indicates the presence of alcohol in the blood — but not the percentage ...."

---

459. State v. Boehmer, 1 Haw. App. 44, 613 P.2d 916 (1980).

460. State v. Bjornsen, 201 Neb. 709, 271 N.W.2d 839 (1978).

461. Nichols, *supra* note 214, at 335-36. *See also* State v. McGinley, 229 N.J. Super. 191, 550 A.2d 1305 (1988) (since the Breathalyzer has a substantial error margin, the blood alcohol concentration estimate must be adjusted), *overruled on other grounds,* State v. Downie, 117 N.J. 450, 569 A.2d 242 (1990).

462. Barcott v. State, Dep't of Pub. Safety, Div. of Motor Vehicles, 741 P.2d 226 (Alaska 1987). *See also* Imwinkelried & Scofield, *The Recognition of an Accused's Constitutional Right to Introduce Expert Testimony Attacking the Weight of Prosecution Scientific Evidence: The Antidote for the Supreme Court's Mistaken Assumption in California v. Trombetta,* 33 ARIZ. L. REV. 59 (1991) (collecting the cases, the authors point out that some courts bar such defense testimony; but they argue that when scientific evidence constitutes an important part of the prosecution case and the defense rebuttal testimony is reliable, the accused has a constitutional right to introduce the testimony). *But see* State of Oregon v. Allen, 104 Ore. App. 622, 802 P.2d 690 (1990) (such testimony "is an attempt to challenge the validity and reliability of the scientific principles underlying alcohol breath tests. Those tests have been approved by the legislature and defendant's argument can only be addressed to that body").

463. 161 Ariz. 522, 779 P.2d 1261 (1989).

The Right Type of Test

Of course, it is a condition that the police administer the right type of test to the motorist. In some jurisdictions, such as Illinois, the test must be of whole blood.[464] An analysis of blood serum will not trigger the presumption.[465]

§ 22-8(C). Constitutionality of Presumption.

Even if the presumption applies, the defense attorney may argue that the presumption is unconstitutional. There are imprecisions in estimating the defendant's blood alcohol concentration at the time of the legally relevant event. When the prosecution expert relies on a breath test administered after the event, the defense counsel can point to the margin of error in: using the 1:2,100 conversion ratio, employing the estimate of one hour for absorption, assuming that the concentration peaks only once, and relying on 0.015% as the elimination rate. Given these sources of possible error, some commentators have attacked the constitutionality of presumption statutes.[466] These attacks take the form of two arguments.

The Argument that the Statute Embodies a Presumption Which Runs Afoul of the Constitutional Standard Prescribed by County Court of Ulster County v. Allen

The first argument is that these statutes do not satisfy the constitutionally mandated standard for the creation of presumptions. The starting point for one argument is the Supreme Court's 1979 decision in *County Court of Ulster County v. Allen.*[467] The Court's earlier precedents left unsettled the question of the test for determining the constitutionality of a presumption in a criminal case. It was unclear whether the foundational facts had to have sufficient probative value to establish the presumed fact beyond a reasonable doubt, or rather whether it was sufficient that the foundational fact make the presumed fact more likely than not.[468] In *County Court,* the Supreme Court attempted to clarify this area of law.

---

464. People v. Green, 294 Ill. App. 3d 139, 689 N.E.2d 385 (1997) (construing ILLINOIS VEHICLE CODE § 11-501.2(b)).

465. *Id.*

466. Thompson, *supra* note 21, at 301; Cowan, *Guilt by Presumption*, 4 CRIM. JUST., Spring 1989, at 4; Simpson, *Due Process and Drinking Driving Statutes: A Constitutional Attack on Alcohol Testing*, 3 D.W.I. J. 1 (Aug. 1988).

467. 442 U.S. 140 (1979).

468. *Compare* Leary v. United States, 395 U.S. 6, 36 (1969) ("more likely than not to flow from the proved fact on which it is made to depend") *with* Barnes v. United States, 412 U.S. 837, 843 (1973) ("the reasonable doubt standard"). *See also* Thompson, *supra* note 15, at 309-10; Bass, Gesser & Mount, *Scientific Statistical Methodology and the Doctrine of "Reasonable Doubt" in Criminal Law (With Specific Reference to the Breath Analysis for Blood Alcohol); Empirical Fact or Legal Fiction?*, 5 DALHOUSIE L.J. 350 (1979).

Writing for the majority, Justice Stevens announced that the stricter, beyond-a-reasonable-doubt test applies if the presumption is mandatory, that is, when the presumption directs the jury to find the presumed fact after finding the foundational fact.[469] Moreover, even a permissive presumption must satisfy the rigorous beyond-a-reasonable-doubt standard if that presumption is the "sole ... basis" for supporting a finding of the existence of an essential element of the crime.[470]

Based on *County Court,* the critics' first argument proceeds in several steps. The initial step is characterizing the 1:2,100 ratio as a presumption. The critics argue that the statutes sanction the use of breath testing devices, employing the ratio, to prove blood alcohol concentration and that, therefore, the "ratio effectively operates as a presumption .... [I]t is the effect of an evidentiary device and not its designation that is controlling."[471]

In several cases, the Supreme Court has invoked the so-called irrebuttable presumption doctrine.[472] In these cases, the Court treated substantive rules of law as if they were conclusive evidentiary presumptions and analyzed their constitutionality in those terms.[473] The irrebuttable presumption doctrine lends

---

469. County Court of Ulster County v. Allen, 442 U.S. 140, 159-60, 166-67 (1979).

470. *Id.* at 166-67.

471. Thompson, *supra* note 21, at 324-25; Simpson, *The New "Direct Breath" Statutes: Both Bad Law and Bad Science*, 6 D.W.I. J. 1, 3 (Apr. 1991) (the author argues that the legislation rests on an implicit presumption because "the available laboratory studies of impairment involved blood testing"; "[s]tudies to determine the BrAC at which people are impaired drivers during the first one or two hours after the end of drinking appear to be totally nonexistent"). Our reviewer disagrees with the preceding sentence.

Some jurisdictions have, in effect, mooted this constitutional issue by making it clear that their "presumptions" operate merely as permissive inferences. For example, the 1990 revised California instruction, CALJIC 12.61, reads:

> If the evidence establishes beyond a reasonable doubt that at the time of the chemical analysis of the defendant's blood, breath or urine test there was ... 0.10 percent ... or more by weight of alcohol in the defendant's blood, you may but are not required to infer that the defendant was under the influence of an alcoholic beverage at the time of the alleged offense.

In Barnes v. People, 735 P.2d 869 (Colo. 1987), the court construed the language, "it shall be presumed," as creating merely a permissive inference. *See also* Bouleware v. State, 557 So. 2d 1320 (Ala. Crim. App. 1989); State v. Rolle, 560 So. 2d 1154 (Fla.), *cert. denied,* 498 U.S. 867 (1990); People v. Reding, 191 Ill. App. 3d 424, 445-49, 138 Ill. Dec. 689, 703-05, 547 N.E.2d 1310, 1324-26 (1989).

472. *E.g.,* Cleveland Bd. of Educ. v. LaFleur, 414 U.S. 632 (1974); Vlandis v. Kline, 412 U.S. 441 (1973); Stanley v. Illinois, 405 U.S. 645 (1972). For general analyses of the doctrine, *see* Bezanson, *Some Thoughts on the Emerging Irrebuttable Presumption Doctrine*, 7 IND. L. REV. 644 (1974); Sewell, *Conclusive Presumptions and/or Substantive Due Process of Law*, 27 OKLA. L. REV. 151 (1974).

473. Bezanson, *supra* note 472, at 644; Sewell, *supra* note 472, at 151.

support to the characterization of the breath testing statutes as evidentiary presumptions.

Assuming *arguendo* that the ratio functions as an implicit, evidentiary presumption, the critics' next step is contending that in many cases, the presumption should be tested by the stricter standard. If the trial court treats the statutory presumption as mandatory or if the presumption is the only evidence of intoxication (the prosecutor relies exclusively on the scientific intoxication test and presents no lay testimony about the defendant's inebriated behavior or appearance), *County Court* seems to require that the court apply the beyond-a-reasonable-doubt standard to assess the constitutionality of the presumption.[474]

The final step in the first attack is contending that the 1:2,100 ratio is too imprecise to satisfy the beyond-a-reasonable-doubt standard. The critics assert that the range of reported ratios is so wide and there is so little hard evidence of the frequency distribution of ratios that "it is simply not true beyond a reasonable doubt that a given breath concentration of X percent means a concurrent BAC of 2100X percent. This is not to say that there is not a growing body of evidence to suggest a reasonably accurate relationship between blood and breath levels at a distribution of 2100:1. Nevertheless, reasonable accuracy would not appear to be sufficient for a system which requires proof 'beyond a reasonable doubt' ...."[475]

The two key weaknesses in this line of argument are the initial and final steps. The initial step in this attack has common-sense appeal although it is hazardous to invoke the irrebuttable presumption doctrine when no fundamental right is at stake. The intermediate step seems to be a proper reading of the *County Court* decision. However, like the initial step, the final step is highly debatable. The courts have had little experience applying the standards announced in *County Court*. It is too early to speculate as to the ultimate impact of this attack on the constitutionality of the intoxication presumptions. Several courts have already

474. Thompson, *supra* note 21, at 325-26.

475. *Id.* at 326-27, 329-30; Simpson, *Due Process and Drinking Driving Statutes: A Constitutional Attack on Alcohol Testing*, 3 D.W.I. J. 1, 3 (Aug. 1988) ("the 2100 figure is based on the population average blood/breath ratio .... Dubowski ... reports an average of 2280, and Jones reports an average of 2180 for the post-absorptive state. Mathematically, assuming a normal distribution, it can be proven that there is a probability of less than 8% that a person has a value the same as the average; there is about a 51% probability that a person will have a value the same as or greater than the average post-absorptive blood/breath ratio. At best then, there is a 51% likelihood that the breath analyzer result is the same as or less than the actual BAC. Fifty-one percent probability does not meet a reasonable doubt standard. If the average blood/breath ratio from Dubowski is used ..., there is about a 77% probability that the breath analyzer result is the same or less than the actual BAC ... if the subject is post-absorptive. This, too, would not appear to meet a reasonable doubt standard"). *But see* Biasotti, *The Role of the Forensic Scientist in the Application of Chemical Tests for Alcohol in Traffic Law Enforcement*, 29 J. FORENSIC SCI. 1164 (1984) (defending the general validity of the 1:2,100 conversion ratio). Our reviewer concurs with Biasotti and states that there are numerous reported studies of the frequency distribution of ratios.

brushed aside arguments that the state statutes in question constitute unconstitutional conclusive[476] or irrebuttable[477] presumptions.

The Alternative Argument That the Statute Creates a Mandatory Rebuttable Presumption in Violation of Francis v. Franklin

Assume that the statute satisfies the constitutional standard for creating a presumption. The critics have advanced a second, more sweeping attack based on the contention that the presumptions in question have a constitutionally forbidden effect. The argument rests on the Supreme Court's decision in *Francis v. Franklin.*[478] That decision contains broad language attacking mandatory rebuttable presumptions. Construing *Francis,* some lower courts have concluded that a mandatory inference may not operate against a criminal defendant.[479] Two commentators specifically contend that *Francis* invalidates mandatory inferences operating against a defendant in drunk driving cases.[480] Several cases have embraced the argument.[481] The Supreme Court's 1989 decision in *Carella v. California*[482] seems to strengthen this attack.

---

476. Steele v. State, 284 Ark. 340, 681 S.W.2d 354 (1984).

477. State v. Tanner, 15 Ohio St. 3d 1, 472 N.E.2d 689 (1984); Scherlie v. State, 689 S.W.2d 294 (Tex. App. 1985).

478. 471 U.S. 307 (1985).

479. Coleman v. Butler, 816 F.2d 1046, 1048 (5th Cir. 1987); Potts v. Kemp, 814 F.2d 1512 (11th Cir. 1987). *See also* Santiago Sanchez Defuentes v. Dugger, 923 F.2d 801, 804 (11th Cir. 1991) ("A mandatory presumption violates the due process clause if it relieves the state of the burden of persuasion on an element of the offense").

480. Cowan, *Guilt by Presumption*, 4 CRIM. JUST. 4 (Spring 1989); Essen, *When Per Se Statutes Create Mandatory Rebuttable Presumptions: The Defense Response*, 3 D.W.I. J. 1, 4 (June 1988).

481. Cowan, *supra* note 480, at 7, 37 (citing, inter alia, Barnes v. People, 735 P.2d 869 (Colo. 1987)); Wilhelm v. State, 568 So. 2d 1 (Fla. 1990) (the trial judge instructed the jury that if they determined that the defendant had .10% or more by weight of alcohol in his blood, a prima facie case was established; since the judge did not explain "prima facie case," the jury could have interpreted the instruction as relieving the prosecution of its burden of proof on an element of the offense); Rolle v. State, 528 So. 2d 1208 (Fla. Dist. Ct. App. 1988) (the trial judge violated *Francis* by giving the jury the following instruction: "If you find from the evidence that the Defendant had a blood alcohol level of .10 percent or more, that evidence would be sufficient by itself to establish that the Defendant was under the influence of alcohol to the extent that his normal faculties were impaired"), *rev'd,* 560 So. 2d 1154 (Fla. 1990) (the supreme court construed the language as creating merely a permissive inference); State v. Leverett, 245 Mont. 124, 799 P.2d 119, 47 Mont. St. Rep. 1753 (1990) (the jury instruction stated that a blood alcohol concentration of 0.10 or more creates a presumption that the defendant was under the influence "unless and until" contrary evidence is introduced; the instruction placed the burden of production on the defendant in violation of due process); *Federal Court Strikes Down Mandatory Presumption of Intoxication*, 9 DRINKING/DRIVING LAW LETTER 1 (Apr. 27, 1990) ("The United States District Court for the Middle District of Florida struck down a state statute, and a jury instruction based on that statute, as creating a mandatory presumption of intoxication in violation of the constitutional right to due process of law. Defuentes v. Dugger (Case No. 89-669-CIV-ORL-19), _ F. Supp. _ (1989)");

The courts and legislatures are becoming more conscious of the existence of these constitutional attacks. To eliminate the argument that the statutes represent unconstitutional conclusive presumptions, several courts have interpreted their statutory schemes as according the accused the right to present rebuttal evidence. For example, the New York court has construed its blood alcohol statute as permitting the defendant to introduce evidence to contradict the result of a breath alcohol test.[483] The court held that a breathalyzer reading exceeding .10 prima facie establishes a violation, but the court added that "[t]o foreclose a defendant's introduction of evidence seeking to establish that his BAC while operating was less than .10 may raise doubt as to constitutionality."[484]

McLean v. Moran, 963 F.2d 1306 (9th Cir. 1992) (invalidating a mandatory conclusive presumption created by Nevada statute); State v. Crowe, 598 N.E.2d 293 (Ill. App. 1992) (contrasting People v. Haas, 203 Ill. App. 3d 779, 560 N.E.2d 1365 (1990) and People v. Atteberry, 213 Ill. App. 3d 851, 572 N.E.2d 434 (1991), the court notes a split of authority over the question of the propriety of using the expression "prima facie evidence"); Commonwealth v. Sloan, 414 Pa. Super. 400, 607 A.2d 285 (1992) (the use of the term "presume" in the instruction was erroneous).

482. 491 U.S. 263 (1989). In prior cases, including *Franklin,* the defense attempted to rebut the presumed fact. For that reason, in instructing the jury, the judge would have occasion to tell the jury that if they found the foundational facts, they must infer the presumed fact unless the defense rebutted the presumed fact. The clause beginning with "unless" would have the effect of shifting a burden to the accused. *See* State v. Leverett, 245 Mont. 124, 799 P.2d 119, 47 Mont. St. Rep. 1753 (1990). However, in *Carella,* the defense evidently did not attempt to rebut the presumed fact. Given that state of the record, the judge would have to tell the jury only that if they found the foundational facts, they must infer the presumed fact. If the jury instruction in *Carella* violates *Franklin* — as the Court clearly held — the *Franklin* line of cases may invalidate all mandatory inferences of the existence of an element of the charged offense. *But see* Morgan v. Shirley, 958 F.2d 662 (6th Cir. 1992) (the use of a rebuttable presumption did not unconstitutionally shift the burden of persuasion to the defendant); State v. Korhn, 41 Conn. App. 874, 678 A.2d 492 (1996) (there was a state statutory rebuttable presumption that a defendant's BAC was the same at the time of the operation of the motor vehicle as it was at the time of the test; the presumption did not impermissibly shift the burden of proof on the issue of intoxication).

483. People v. Mertz, 68 N.Y.2d 136, 497 N.E.2d 657, 506 N.Y.S.2d 290 (1986).

484. *Id.*; People v. Bransford, 8 Cal. 4th 885, 884 P.2d 70, 35 Cal. Rptr. 2d 613 (1994) (evidence of the variability of the partition ratio is inadmissible), *cert. denied*, 514 U.S. 1130 (1995); People v. Ireland, 33 Cal. App. 4th 680, 39 Cal. Rptr. 870 (1995); People v. Thompson, 215 Cal. App. 3d Supp. 7, 265 Cal. Rptr. 105 (1989) (the defense may offer general evidence about the accuracy and variability of blood-to-breath partition ratios); People v. Lepine, 215 Cal. App. 3d 91, 263 Cal. Rptr. 543 (1989) (the defense may offer general evidence about the range of partition ratios without showing the defendant's personal partition ratio); People v. Cortes, 214 Cal. App. 3d Supp. 12, 263 Cal. Rptr. 113 (1989) (it is error to instruct the jury that the defendant has the burden of raising a reasonable doubt about his partition ratio); People v. McDonald, 206 Cal. App. 3d 877, 254 Cal. Rptr. 384 (1988) (the defendant was charged with both a per se offense and driving under the influence; the trial judge instructed the jury that it should presume that the defendant had a 2100:1 blood-to-breath partition ratio unless the defendant presented contrary evidence about his personal ratio; the court held that the instruction impermissibly nullified defense expert testimony about the range of blood-to-breath partition ratios); State v. Lowther, 740 P.2d 1017 (Haw. App. 1987) (due process entitles the defendant to introduce evidence tending to show the general

In addition, a number of courts have mooted the defense attack on mandatory intoxication inferences by ruling that the "presumptions" operative in their jurisdictions are merely permissive inferences.[485]

Further, to remove the constitutional attack based on the conversion of breath alcohol concentration into blood alcohol concentrations, a number of states have adopted statutes that criminalize driving with a certain breath alcohol concentration.[486] If the statute directly penalizes driving with a particular breath alcohol concentration, the statute arguably eliminates any need to rely on the 1:2,100 conversion ratio. Several state courts have upheld the constitutionality of direct breath statutes.[487]

---

unreliability of the Intoxilyzer); State v. Cothran, 120 N.C. App. 633, 463 S.E.2d 423 (1995) ("our legislature has adopted a breath alcohol per se offense as an alternative method of committing a driving while impaired offense;" evidence of the variability of the ratio is therefore "immaterial"); Commonwealth v. Davis, 8 Va. App. 291, 381 S.E.2d 11 (1989) ("the accused may challenge the test results by competent evidence such as, for example, that he had not consumed enough alcohol in the relevant time to reach the level indicated by the chemical test results ...."); Imwinkelried & Scofield, *The Recognition of an Accused's Constitutional Right to Introduce Expert Testimony Attacking the Weight of Prosecution Scientific Evidence: The Antidote for the Supreme Court's Mistaken Assumption in California v. Trombetta,* 33 ARIZ. L. REV. 59 (1991); Scott, *A Short Discussion of McDonald,* 16 C.A.C.J. FORUM 21-22 (Sept./Oct. 1989) (it is unfair to allocate to the defendant the burden of proving his or her personal ratio because the research shows that the ratio varies from time to time).

But see People v. Oliver, 215 Cal. App. 3d Supp. 1, 264 Cal. Rptr. 89 (1989) (the trial judge may require the defendant to establish his personal ratio); People v. Herst, 197 Cal. App. 3d Supp. 1, 243 Cal. Rptr. 83 (1987) (the defendant may not present expert testimony that partition ratios vary and differ from the statutory ratio without first presenting evidence as to her partition ratio); People v. Pritchard, 162 Cal. App. 3d Supp. 13, 209 Cal. Rptr. 314 (1984) (since the defendant has superior access to the information about his personal ratio, he has the initial burden of producing evidence on the issue).

485. *See* authorities collected in note 471, *supra.*

486. Alaska § 28.35.030; Colo. § 42-4-1201; D.C. § 40-716; ILL. MOTOR VEH. CODE ch. 625, § 5/11-501.1; Minn. §§ 169.01(61), 169.121(d); N.C. §§ 20-4.01, 20-138.1; Ohio Title 45, § 45-11.19(a)(3); Okla. Title 47, § 11-902; Tex. art. 6701L-1; Wash. § 46.61.502(1); Wis. §§ 885.235(1), 346.63. People v. Branson, 19 Cal. Rptr. 2d 595, 601 n.4 (listing all the state statutes), *superseded,* 856 P.2d 1131, 22 Cal. Rptr. 2d 275 (1993).

487. Vanbrunt v. State, 646 P.2d 872 (Alaska App. 1982); People v. Graven, 124 Ill. App. 3d 990, 80 Ill. Dec. 149, 464 N.E.2d 1132 (1984); State v. Bock, 357 N.W.2d 29 (Iowa 1984); Forte v. State, 686 S.W.2d 744 (Tex. App. 1985); State v. McManus, 152 Wis. 2d 113, 447 N.W.2d 654 (1989) (since the statute creates a per se breath-alcohol offense, evidence of the defendant's breath-to-blood ratio is irrelevant and inadmissible). *See also* Simpson, *Medicolegal Alcohol Determination: Comparison and Consequences of Breath and Blood Analysis,* 13 J. ANAL. TOX. 361, 362 (Nov./Dec. 1989) ("Mason and Dubowski ... maintain that by criminalizing either blood test results in g/100 ml or breath test results in g/210 L, the need for conversion from BrAcC to BAC is eliminated and the uncertainty associated with such a conversion no longer need to be considered"); Imwinkelried, *The Basic Legal Challenges to Per Se Statutes: Admissibility, Sufficiency and Constitutionality,* 1 D.W.I. J. 77, 88-94 (1986) (arguing that since the statutes do not regulate constitutionally protected activity such as first amendment speech, the legislature may

However, the defense bar contends that since the alcohol in the bloodstream is the alcohol that induces the symptoms of intoxication, even purported breath statutes rest on an implicit, conclusive presumption of a relationship between breath alcohol and blood alcohol. In a Washington state trial court, the judge struck down a breath statute. Judge Phillip Killien wrote:

> The court concludes that Chapter 153, Sections 2-5 impermissably (*sic*) infringes upon a defendant's due process rights under the Fourteenth Amendment to the United States Constitution by creating a conclusive presumption that breath alcohol equals blood alcohol, and hence substitutes the judgment of a machine for the judgement of the jury. [T]aken as a whole, the Chapter violates the due process clause of the Fourteenth Amendment ... by violating principles of fundamental fairness.[488]

The Washington Supreme Court, however, rejected Judge Killien's reasoning.[489] The court upheld the constitutionality of the breath statute. The court argued that the statute did not create any conclusive presumptions. In the court's view, the statute merely defined an alternative method of committing the offense of drunk driving.

§ 22-9. Selected Bibliography.

S. BRENT & S. STILLER, HANDLING DRUNK DRIVING CASES (1985).
K. DUBOWSKI, THE TECHNOLOGY OF BREATH-ALCOHOL ANALYSIS (1991).
R. ERWIN, DEFENSE OF DRUNK DRIVING CASES (3d ed. 1991).
E. FITZGERALD & D. HUME, INTOXICATION TEST EVIDENCE: CRIMINAL AND CIVIL (1987).
W. GORELICK, CALIFORNIA DRIVING UNDER THE INFLUENCE OF ALCOHOL CASES (3d rev. ed. 1988).
J. HINGSON, HOW TO DEFEND A DRUNK DRIVING CASE (3d ed. 1988).
R. JOYE & J. LOVETT, DRUNK DRIVING (1985) (3 vols.).
D. NICHOLS, DRINKING/DRIVING LITIGATION: CRIMINAL AND CIVIL (1985) (4 vols.).
R. REIFF, DRUNK DRIVING AND RELATED VEHICULAR OFFENSES (1997).

---

exercise its plenary police power to proscribe driving with a certain breath alcohol concentration; the legislature needs only a rational basis for believing that such driving has a dangerous tendency to lead to a substantive evil the legislature can prohibit).

488. State v. Brayman, No. 46546897 (King Cty. Dist. Ct., Wash., Dec. 4, 1986). Labianca & Simpson, *Medicolegal Alcohol Determination: Variability of the Blood-to-Breath-Alcohol Ratio and Its Effect on Reported Breath-Alcohol Concentrations*, 33 EUR. J. CLIN. CHEM. CLIN. BIOCHEM. 919 (1995) ("The enactment of direct breath-alcohol statutes ... has not eliminated the need to correct for the experimental error stemming from the conversion of breath- into blood-alcohol concentration via multiplication of the former by a constant blood/breath ratio. [T]he enactment of such statutes has ... resulted in the legislation of incorrect science").

489. State v. Brayman, 110 Wash. 2d 183, 751 P.2d 294 (1988). *See also* People v. Bransford, 8 Cal. App. 4th 885, 884 P.2d 70, 35 Cal. Rptr. 2d 613 (1994), *cert. denied*, 514 U.S. 1130 (1995); People v. Ireland, 33 Cal. App. 4th 680, 39 Cal. Rptr. 2d 870 (1995); Lerman, *The Legislative Hocus Pocus of BrAC Statutes and Finding the Back Door*, 17 THE CHAMPION 41-42 (May 1993) (citing *Brayman* and State v. Morlock, 588 N.E.2d 165 (Ohio App. 1990)).

J. TARANTINO, DEFENDING DRUNK DRIVERS (2d ed.).

J. TARANTINO, DWI DEFENSE FORMS AND CHECKLISTS (1984).

L. TAYLOR, DRUNK DRIVING DEFENSE (3d ed. 1992).

L. TAYLOR, CALIFORNIA DRUNK DRIVING DEFENSE (1988).

E. WIDMARK, PRINCIPLES AND APPLICATIONS OF MEDICOLEGAL ALCOHOL DETERMINATIONS (1981).

L. TAYLOR, DRUNK DRIVING DEFENSE (4th ed. 1995).

J. WIGMORE, A BIBLIOGRAPHY OF FORENSIC ASPECTS OF ALCOHOLS (1872-1991).

Bellotti, *The Preparation and Trial of a Drunken Driving Case Involving a Breathalyzer, in* SCIENTIFIC AND EXPERT EVIDENCE 195 (2d ed. 1981).

Caplan, *The Determination of Alcohol in Blood and Breath, in* FORENSIC SCIENCE HANDBOOK 592 (R. Saferstein, ed. 1982).

Dubowski & Essary, *Contamination of Blood Specimens for Alcohol Analysis During Collection*, 4 ABSTRACTS & REVIEWS IN ALCOHOL & DRIVING 3 (Apr.-June 1983).

Hensel, *Forensic Tests for Blood Alcohol: Where Do We Stand Today?*, 18 TRAUMA 3 (Oct. 1976).

Imwinkelried, *The Basic Legal Challenges to Per Se Statutes: Admissibility, Sufficiency, and Constitutionality*, 1 D.W.I.J. 77 (July/Aug. 1986).

Mason & Dubowski, *Breath-Alcohol Analysis: Uses, Methods and Some Forensic Problems – Review and Opinion*, 21 J. FORENSIC SCI. 33 (1976).

Radlow & Hurst, *Delayed Blood Alcohol Determinations in Forensic Applications*, 2 CRIM. JUST. J. 281 (1979).

Sapir & Kling, *Cross-Examination of Breath Alcohol Machine Operators*, 13 S. ILL. U. L.J. 83 (1988).

Simpson, *The New "Direct Breath" Statutes: Both Bad Law and Bad Science*, 6 D.W.I.J. 1, 3 (Apr. 1991).

Simpson, *Due Process and Drunk Driving Statutes: A Constitutional Attack on Alcohol Testing*, 3 D.W.I.J. 1, 3 (Aug. 1988).

Winek, *Blood Alcohol Levels: Factors Affecting Predictions*, 19 TRIAL 38 (Jan. 1983).

CHAPTER 23

DRUG IDENTIFICATION*

§ 23-1. In General.

The widespread abuse of illicit drugs in the United States has had a pervasive impact on our society.[1] The phenomenon of drug abuse has had an especially marked effect on the American criminal justice system. A National Institute of Justice study found that seven out of every ten arrestees in major cities test positive for drugs.[2] In other words, there is a strong suggestion that drug abuse contributes to the commission of crimes other than drug offenses. For that matter, drug cases themselves represent a large part of the workload of the courts,

---

*The authors wish to express their gratitude to Professor Jay Siegel, School of Criminal Justice, Michigan State University, who reviewed this chapter in the third edition of this treatise. The authors would also like to thank Mr. Joseph Bono, Supervisory Chemist, Drug Enforcement Administration Special Testing and Research Laboratory, who reviewed this chapter in the second edition, and Provost Robert Shapiro, United States Naval Academy, who reviewed this chapter in the first edition.

1. On September 5, 1990, William Bennett, Director of the Office of National Drug Control Policy, stated that "figures show a declining number of cocaine-related cases showing up in hospital emergency rooms, a drop in the number of workers testing positive for drugs, ... and a diminishing number of individuals reporting drug use. Yet ... the number of cocaine users reporting 'frequent' use has increased ...." *Preliminary Statistics Show Declines in Drug Use, Availability, Drug Czar Says*, 47 CRIM. L. REP. (BNA) 1478 (Sept. 12, 1990).

2. *Drug Abuse: Seven in Ten Arrested Test Positive*, 25 TRIAL 98 (Sept. 1989).

prosecutors, and public defenders.[3] The scientific analysis of suspected contraband drugs constitutes more than 50% of the caseload of many American crime laboratories.[4] Moreover, drug testing has become a widespread practice in the private sector.[5] In large part, the legal system devotes so much attention to illicit drugs because they can have severe deleterious effects on the human body. Each of the three leading categories of drugs of abuse — hallucinogens, stimulants, and depressants — can produce these effects.

The hallucinogenic or psychomimetic drugs include such potent substances as LSD, mescaline, and DMT and such milder compounds as marijuana. The hallucinogens can distort sensory perception, both auditory and visual. They cause delusions and illusions; some hallucinogens, notably LSD, lead to flashbacks. The use of these drugs can have long-term effects; the use of harder hallucinogens such as mescaline can lead to physical tolerance while frequent abuse of softer hallucinogens such as marijuana seems to induce psychological dependence and personality changes. In large dosages, use of hallucinogens triggers paranoid states and suicidal tendencies.

Central nervous system stimulants include drugs such as cocaine and the various amphetamines. Drug abusers prefer these stimulants because they release normal inhibitions. Long-term abuse can lead to paranoid states and severe

---

3. NAT'L COMM'N ON MARIJUANA AND DRUG ABUSE, DRUG ABUSE IN AMERICA: PROBLEM IN PERSPECTIVE (1973).

4. J. PETERSON, FORENSIC SCIENCE AND THE POLICE: THE EFFECT OF SCIENTIFIC EVIDENCE ON CRIMINAL PROSECUTIONS 174 (1983); Soni, *Drug Laboratory Efficiency: Shifting Paradigms*, 63 F.B.I. LAW ENF. BULL. 15 (Aug. 1994) ("the department's Drug Analysis Unit (also referred to as the laboratory) confronted an enormous caseload, one that has doubled since 1982. In 1993, the laboratory analyzed a record number of controlled dangerous substances (CDS) cases–18,010, containing 235,485 total drug units. CDS submissions increased nearly 40 percent over 1990 figures, while total drug units increased over 65 percent").

5. Willner v. Thornburgh, 928 F.2d 1185, 1191-92 (D.C. Cir.) ("A recent study by the Bureau of Labor Statistics found that drug-testing programs have become fairly common in the nation's largest firms. The study showed that the larger the work force, the more likely the employer would have a drug-testing program. Almost 60 percent of private employers with 5,000 or more employees had such programs and another 11 percent were considering implementing one. Some of the nation's largest employers, including American Telephone & Telegraph, Dupont, Exxon, Federal Express, Trans World Applicants, and United Airlines, have drug-testing programs for job applicants. Between 1982 and 1985 the number of FORTUNE 500 corporations having drug-testing programs more than doubled"), *cert. denied*, 502 U.S. 1020 (1991); Blum, *State Drug Test Results Are Varied*, NAT'L L.J., Dec. 16, 1991, at 1 ("Jackson Lewis, which surveyed 922 Fortune 500 officials in 1990 and 484 to date in 1991 on workplace issues, notes that 67 percent consider drugs the primary labor and employment problem today. Its 1990 survey found 39 percent do substance abuse testing, and of those who test: 88 percent test applicants, 52 percent test employees for suspicion, 22 percent test after accidents and 12 percent do random testing. The 1991 figures show those who test rose to 58 percent; of those that do, 81 percent on applicants, 18 percent at random, 61 percent on reasonable suspicion and 35 percent after accidents").

depression. Large dosages trigger palpitation of the heart, increased blood pressure, and panic. Overdoses, resulting in death, are possible.

Central nervous system depressants constitute the final major category of drugs of abuse. This category includes the opiates such as morphine and heroin and the various barbiturates. Drug abusers are attracted to these substances because they have a sedative impact and cause euphoria. The opiates are truly narcotic; they cause addiction or physical dependence. As the dependence grows, the body needs larger doses of the drug. If the needs are not satisfied, the subject undergoes a painful withdrawal. As in the case of stimulants, the depressants can cause overdoses; the mechanism of death is often paralysis of the respiratory center.

Since drugs play such a prominent role in criminal trials, it becomes vital for crime laboratories to develop techniques for identifying drugs of abuse. This chapter analyzes those techniques. The next two sections review the scientific state of the art. The following two sections address the law governing the admissibility and legal sufficiency of drug identification evidence. The sheer volume of drug cases makes it imperative that the legal limitations on drug identification evidence be carefully scrutinized.

Furthermore, there are indications that drug identification testimony is sometimes erroneous or worse. Despite the extensive experience testing drugs, there seems to be a significant error rate in the drug testing conducted by some American laboratories, particularly urine screening laboratories.[6] In a Centers for Disease Control proficiency test of urine screening laboratories, one laboratory was found to have an error rate of 60%.[7] A San Francisco scandal also focused public attention on this subject. "As many as 1,000 San Francisco drug convictions may be in jeopardy, after an undercover police sting operation caught a laboratory technician cutting corners on critical lab tests...."[8] Moreover, "Anne Castillo, a veteran Drug Enforcement Administration ... chemist, was suspected in June [1996] after admitting that she had been filing false test results in her work at the Dallas laboratory."[9]

---

6. Miike & Hewitt, *Accuracy and Reliability of Urine Drug Tests*, 36 KAN. L. REV. 641, 651-57 (1988) (summarizing the results of proficiency tests, the authors assert that "error rates continue to be high"); Hansen, Caudill & Boone, *Crisis in Drug Testing: Results of CDC Blind Study*, 253 J. AM. MED. ASS'N 2382 (1985). *But see* Clark, *Drug Testing: The Weeding-Out Process*, 16 LAW ENF. NEWS, Mar. 31, 1990, at 1 ("A blind sampling of 31 labs conducted in 1988 by the American Association of Clinical Chemistry found a 97-percent accuracy rate, with no false positives ....").

7. Hansen, Caudill & Boone, *Crisis in Drug Testing: Results of CDC Blind Study*, 253 JAMA 2382 (1985).

8. Matier & Ross, *S.F. Police Drug Tests in Question: Lab technician removed from job*, SAN FRANCISCO CHRONICLE, Sep. 15, 1994, p. 1.

9. Schoenburg & McCue, *Veteran DEA Chemist Falsified Test Results for Years*, 20 THE CHAMPION 34 (Dec. 1996).

§ 23-2. Nonspecific Tests.

There are a large number of tests for analyzing suspected illicit drugs. Some tests are biological. For instance, when morphine is injected into a laboratory mouse, a distinctive, S-shaped curve appears in the mouse's tail. There is also a rapid eye test (RET).[10] In RET, the examiner considers such factors as the subject's ability to remain cross-eyed and see peripheral objects[11] and the reaction of the subject's pupils to light.[12] In contrast, there are sophisticated drug analytic techniques such as fluorescence spectroscopy,[13] X-ray diffraction,[14] ion mobility spectrometry,[15] and free zone capillary electrophoresis.[16] There are far too many techniques to cover them all in a single chapter in a treatise of this size. There are entire treatises which comprehensively review the techniques.[17] This chapter includes only a broad brush introduction to the most common techniques.

Initially, two concepts in drug analysis must be understood: specificity and the false positive. A test result is specific for a particular drug if the result occurs only when that drug is present; no other drug can trigger the same test result. When attempting to identify a suspected contraband drug, a forensic laboratory should nearly always use a test specific for that drug. Properly conducted and interpreted, a specific test yields a positive test result for a certain drug only when the unknown is in fact that drug. Unfortunately, most drug analysis techniques are nonspecific; a positive test result is indicative of the drug's identity, but other drugs could yield the same result — the same color or number. Nonspecific tests thus can lead to false positive results, a finding of one drug's presence when in fact another drug is present.[18] All the drug analysis techniques discussed in this section are nonspecific. Nonspecific techniques are suitable for preliminary *screening* rather than positive identification. If the test result is negative, indicating that the unknown was not a contraband drug, the analyst might not test further; but when the test result is positive, indicating that the

---

10. Comment, *Making the Grade: Can Student Drug Testing Programs in Public Schools Pass a Legal Challenge?*, 25 WILLAMETTE L. REV. 165, 170-71 (1989).

11. *Id.*

12. Semore v. Pool, 217 Cal. App. 3d 1087, 1098, 266 Cal. Rptr. 280, 286-87 (1990).

13. Stein, Laessig & Indriksons, *An Evaluation of Drug Testing Procedures by Forensic Laboratories and the Qualifications of Their Analysts*, 1973 WIS. L. REV. 730, 740, 758-59.

14. AMERICAN LAW INSTITUTE-AMERICAN BAR ASSOCIATION, DEFENSE OF DRUG CASES 112 (1970).

15. Reese & Harrington, *The Analysis of Methamphetamine Hydrochloride by Thermal Desorption Ion Mobility Spectrometry and SIMPLISMA*, 44 J. FORENSIC SCI. 68 (1999).

16. Krawczeniuk & Bravenec, *Quantitative Determination of Cocaine in Illicit Powders by Free Zone Capillary Electrophoresis*, 43 J. FORENSIC SCI. 738 (1998).

17. 3-6 M. HOUTS, R. BASELT & R. CRAVEY, COURTROOM TOXICOLOGY (1983). Volumes 3-6 contain an alphabetical list of various chemicals and drugs commonly encountered in forensic analysis. For each drug, the treatise lists acceptable screening and confirmatory tests.

18. Of course, the other possibility is that no drug is present.

unknown might be a contraband drug, the analyst would then resort to further confirmatory tests. Specific techniques for drug *identification* are discussed in the next section.

§ 23-2(A). Morphological Tests.

Many drugs of abuse such as marijuana are derived from plants. If the police recover the suspected contraband in plant form, the forensic scientist may attempt to analyze the plant by its appearance. This analytic procedure is often termed a morphological or physical examination.

The marijuana plant in particular has several characteristic features.[19] The hairs on the upper or dorsal surface of the leaf have a bearclaw appearance and are true cystolith hairs. There is a crystal of calcium carbonate at the base of the hair. The lower or ventral surface of the leaf has a fuzzy appearance due to longer, wavy hairs on that side of the leaf. Moreover, there are visible veins on the ventral surface. Finally, the edge of the leaf is serrated or notched.

The function of classifying plants based on their appearance is a task that falls within the disciplines of plant taxonomy and botany. Nevertheless, most trial courts permit any experienced drug identification analyst to testify to these plant features even if the analyst lacks training in plant taxonomy or botany.

The morphological procedure for identifying marijuana is a nonspecific test. There are other, related plants that exhibit the same gross appearance. A morphological test should be used as a preliminary, screening technique. When the plant does not exhibit the appearance of marijuana, in all likelihood it is not marijuana. However, even if the plant exhibits the gross features of marijuana's appearance, the plant may not be marijuana. For example, common hemp has roughly the same outward appearance as marijuana. A tentative identification based on morphology should be confirmed by a more specific test.

§ 23-2(B). Color Change Tests.

One of the most popular types of nonspecific tests for drugs is the color change test. A sample of the unknown substance is placed on a porcelain spot plate or in a test tube. A known reagent is added to the plate or tube. When the known and unknown mix, a chemical reaction occurs, producing a color change or a series of changes. The change occurs when a feature of the molecule of the principal component of the reactant (the substance to be identified) interacts with a feature of the molecule of the principal component of the reagent. The feature of the reactant (such as conjugate double bands or special groups of atoms) is called a chromophore while the feature of the reagent is termed a chromogen.

---

19. Taylor, Lydon & Anderson, *Anatomy and Viability of Cannabis sativa Stem Cuttings With and Without Adventitious Roots*, 39 J. Forensic Sci. 769 (1994).

The change is a clue to the identity of the unknown drug. There are color change tests for numerous drugs, including codeine,[20] cocaine,[21] barbiturates,[22] heroin,[23] and morphine.[24] The tests include, *inter alia*: cobalt thiocyanate,[25] Dille-Koppanyi, Duquenois-Levine, ferric chloride, Froehde's reagent, KN reagent, Mandelin's reagent, Marquis' reagent, Mayer's reagent, Mecke's reagent, modified Ehrlich reagent, nitric acid, sulfuric acid, and Zwikker's reagent.

Kits for color change tests are available commercially from manufacturers such as Hoffman LaRoche[26] and ODV, Inc.[27] The manufacturers' literature includes detailed descriptions of the content of each reagent and charts listing the colors that various drugs should yield when mixed with the reagent.

The early color change tests were single-step procedures. When the reagent and unknown mixed, a color emerged in the spot plate. However, the laboratories have also developed more sophisticated, multiple-step tests. For example, the Drug Enforcement Administration's South Central Regional Laboratory developed a three-step procedure as a field test to screen for cocaine. In the first step, the analyst adds five drops of reagent #1, a pink solution, to the unknown. If cocaine is present, a blue precipitate forms and falls to the bottom of the test tube. The analyst next adds one or two drops of reagent #2, concentrated hydrochloric acid. When cocaine is present, the blue precipitate dissolves, leaving a pink solution. The third and last step is adding several drops of reagent #1 to the pink solution. If cocaine is present, the blue color reappears in the lower chloroform layer. This description holds true only for cocaine in its salt form. When free base (crack) is used, no precipitate forms with reagent #1. Instead, the precipitate forms when reagent #2 is initially added. The precipitate then goes away.

A step beyond multiple-step tests is integrating a number of tests into a testing scheme. For example, ODV, Inc., recommends a sequence of testing. In the recommended sequence, the analyst first uses Mayer's reagent. If that test result is positive, the analyst next uses the Marquis reagent. However, when the Mayer's result is negative, the analyst uses the Dille-Koppanyi reagent. The

---

20. A. Moenssens, J. Starrs, C. Henderson & F. Inbau, Scientific Evidence in Civil and Criminal Cases § 14.12 (4th ed. 1995).

21. *Id.*

22. *Id.* at § 14.14.

23. *Id.* at § 14.12.

24. *Id.*

25. Logan, Nichols & Stafford, *A Simple Laboratory Test for the Determination of the Chemical Form of Cocaine*, 34 J. Forensic Sci. 678 (1989) (a new test based on the widely accepted cobalt thiocyanate color reaction).

26. McKibben, *Simple and Rapid Color Screening Tests for Flunitrazepam (Rohypnol)*, 44 J. Forensic Sci. 396 (1999).

27. ODV manufactures Drug Identification Kits. Its headquarters are in South Paris, Maine.

entire scheme includes nine reagents and assists in identifying the general group to which any unknown might belong.

Although color change tests are both easy and fast to conduct, they have major weaknesses. To begin with, no one has yet figured out the exact chemical reaction that occurs in any of these spots tests. Moreover, color change tests are nonspecific:

> If we assume that there are 20 distinguishable colors, then there are 8,000 possible responses in three-color tests and 160,000 possible responses in four color tests. Statistically, 250 different compounds (out of 2,000,000) would give the same three-color tests, and 12 would give the same four-color tests.[28]

Color tests are often used as a preliminary screening procedures in the laboratory as well as the field. When the police seize a suspected drug, they can conduct a color change test to determine whether there is probable cause to believe that the substance is a contraband drug. If the test is positive, the substance may be forwarded to a crime laboratory for further analysis. A good forensic laboratory would not rely solely on the color test to identify the unknown; rather, the laboratory would conduct further specific tests to confirm the tentative identification of the substance. In some laboratories, upon further analysis twenty to thirty percent of the positive field color tests turn out to be false positives.[29]

There is also an element of subjectivity in the interpretation of the test results. One analyst might characterize a color as a light red while another analyst would record the test result as a pink. There are techniques for dealing with this problem. Many manufacturers furnish color charts that can be placed next to the plate or tube for direct comparison. In addition, the Inter-Society Color Council-National Bureau of Standards (ISCC-NBS) has developed a set of color charts for the same purpose.[30] Finally, the analyst can photograph the test result with high

---

28. Shapiro, *Chemical Defenses in Drug Cases*, 2 NAT'L J. CRIM. DEF. 131, 132 (1976); Martorano & Solomon, *Drug Evidence and Scientific Testimony: Rigorous Advocacy Put to the Test*, 14 CORNERSTONE 1, 7 (Winter 1992/1993) (on the Marquis reagent, "No one knows how many of the one or two million uncontrolled organic substances turn purple"). CORNERSTONE is a publication of the National Legal Aid and Defender Association.

29. Stall, *Unreliability of Field Tests as Means of Identifying Controlled Substances*, 14 THE ADVOCATE 398 (1982); Martorano & Solomon, *Drug Evidence and Scientific Testimony: Rigorous Advocacy Put to the Test*, 14 CORNERSTONE 1, 7 (Winter 1992/1993) ("The Cobalt Thiocyanate Test which is designed to detect cocaine and heroin may ... reveal the presence of demerol and a variety of other non-controlled drugs. Similarly, a positive result on a Duquesnois-Levine Test ... may be obtained when using a sample of Advil or Nuprin"). CORNERSTONE is a publication of the National Legal Aid and Defender Association.

30. Velapoldi & Wicks, *The Use of Chemical Spot Test Kits for the Presumptive Identification of Narcotics and Drugs of Abuse*, 19 J. FORENSIC SCI. 636, 637 (1974). THE NATIONAL INSTITUTE

quality color film. The production of the charts and photograph at trial enables the trier of fact to make a direct comparison and double-check the analyst's evaluation of the test result.

§ 23-2(C). Microcrystal Tests.

Microcrystalline tests are similar to color change tests. In the latter type of test, the only response in the test result is a color. In the former type of test, there are two responses: both a pattern and a color. With Wagner's reagent, morphine forms red, overlapping plate-like crystals.[31] With Marme's reagent, morphine produces colorless needles.[32] An issue of the Journal of Criminal Law, Criminology and Police Science contains a set of diagrams, depicting the crystals that various barbiturates form with Wagenaar's reagent, Davis' silver reagent, potassium hydroxide and phosphoric acid, and sulfuric acid and water.[33]

The weaknesses of the microcrystalline tests are comparable to those of the color change tests. Microcrystalline tests are arguably more specific than color change tests, since they rely on two responses rather than one. Indeed, there are analysts who consider microctystalline tests to be dispositive for some drugs. However, in many cases microcrystalline tests are also subject to false positives. Likewise, there is an element of subjectivity in interpreting the results. The analyst may mistake the shape or pattern or misread the color. As in color change tests, it is advisable to photograph the test result for production at trial.

§ 23-2(D). Chromatography.

The chromatographic techniques are means of separating and tentatively identifying drugs. Chromatography's separation capability is even more important than its identification capability. As discussed in the next section, many of the more specific drug identification tests require relatively pure samples for analysis. Most street drugs are impure and contaminated. Consequently, before using a specific drug identification technique such as the infrared spectroscopy test, the analyst must purify the sample. The

---

OF STANDARDS AND TECHNOLOGY (NIST) HAS PREPARED STANDARD CENTROID COLOR CHARTS (Standard #2106, publication 260, Winter 1992).

31. A. MOENSSENS, J. STARRS, C. HENDERSON & F. INBAU, *supra* note 20, at § 14.12; Wieblo & Tebbett, "*The Use of Microcrystal Tests in Conjunction with Fourier Transform Infra Red Spectroscopy for the Rapid Identification of Street Drugs*, 37 J. FORENSIC SCI. 1134 (1992).

32. *Id.*

33. Davis, *Barbiturate Differentiation by Chemical Microscopy*, 52 J. CRIM. L., CRIMINOLOGY & POLICE SCI. 459, 461-67 (1961). *See also* Simpson, Simpson & Liu, *Microcrystalloscopic Differentiation of 3,4-Methylenedioxyamphetamine and Related Amphetamine Derivatives*, 36 J. FORENSIC SCI. 908 (1991); Julian, *Microcrystalline Identification of Drugs of Abuse: The Psychedelic Amphetamines*, 35 J. FORENSIC SCI. 821 (1990).

chromatographic techniques are effective purification procedures because of their separation capability.

The separation capability is a byproduct of the two basic phases of any chromatographic technique: the stationary or fixed phase and the mobile phase. The stationary phase is usually a liquid or solid adsorbent. The moving phase may be a gas that carries the suspected illicit drug over the stationary phase. Different chemicals have varying affinities for or attractions to the two phases. Due to these varying affinities, different chemicals require different periods of time in which to migrate across the stationary phase — differential migration. If a substance has a great affinity for the stationary phase, less of it stays in the moving phase. Since the moving phase pushes the substance across the stationary phase, the greater the substance's affinity for the stationary phase the longer the time the substance requires to complete the migration. The smaller the substance's affinity for the stationary phase, the more of the substance that remains in the moving phase, and the shorter the period of time needed to complete the journey.

There are several different chromatographic techniques, including paper chromatography, thin layer chromatography (TLC), gas chromatography (GC or GLC), and high pressure or high performance liquid chromatography (HPLC).[34] Although a forensic laboratory can resort to all chromatographic techniques, the last three — TLC, GC, and HPLC — are in common use today.

Paper Chromatography

In this technique, the stationary phase is an adsorbent coated on filter paper. The unknown is spotted near the bottom of the page of filter paper; and the paper is then placed in a solution, the moving or carrier phase. The filter paper acts like a blotter and soaks up the moving phase. As the moving phase ascends the page, the phase carries the unknown with it. After a certain period of time elapses, the analyst removes the page from the solution. The result of the movement of the solution up the page is the production of a streak of a certain color and length. The length is measured and converted into an Rf value — the ratio to front. The distance traveled by the solvent front, the moving phase, is assigned the numerical value of 1.00. The Rf value is the ratio of the distance covered by the unknown to the distance traveled by the moving phase. Thus, if the unknown covered only half the distance traveled by the solvent front, the Rf value would be 0.50.

34. *See* Kanel, Vickery, Waldner, Monahan & Diamond, *Automated Extraction of Lysergic Acid Diethylamide (LSD) and N-demeythl-LSD from Blood, Serum, Plasma, and Urine Samples Using the Zymark RapidTrace with LC/MS/MS Confirmation*, 43 J. Forensic Sci. 622 (1998) (liquid chromatography (LC)).

The advantages of paper chromatography are that the technique is rapid, simple, and inexpensive. Its disadvantages parallel the weaknesses of the color change and microcrystalline tests: nonspecificity and subjectivity in the interpretation of the test results. The nonspecificity of paper chromatography will become evident when we discuss thin layer chromatography. The cause of the subjectivity of paper chromatography is the necessity for relying on the analyst's sometimes subtle identification of the color of the streak on the filter paper. As previously stated, in contrast to the next three chromatographic techniques, paper chromatography is no longer in widespread use in forensic laboratories. While paper chromatography was once used extensively in forensic laboratories, today it is rarely utilized. It has been largely supplanted by thin layer chromatography.

Thin-layer Chromatography (TLC)

Thin-layer chromatography is closely akin to paper chromatography. TLC was first used by two Russian scientists, Ismailov and Shraiber, in 1938. American researchers, notably Meinhard and Hall, adapted the technique to the separation of terpenes in oils. TLC is now a widely used forensic screening technique. As in paper chromatography, the primary purpose of TLC is to effect the separation (or "fractionation" or "partition") of the components of the sample analyzed.

In TLC, a small portion of the unknown is extracted and placed on a glass plate. The plate is small; it can be two inches by four inches or three inches by five inches or five cm by 10 cm. The plate is coated with the stationary phase, an adsorbent such as silica gel. The unknown is spotted near the bottom of the plate at a point termed the base line or point of origin, as in Figure 23-1.

TLC PLATE

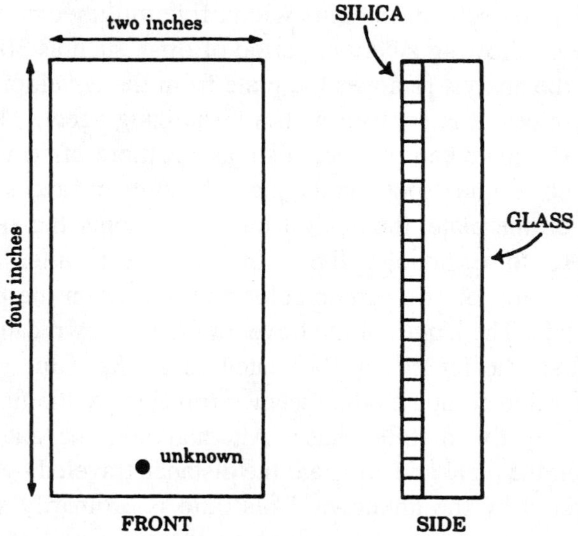

Figure 23-1.[35]

The plate is next placed in a vessel, chamber, or tank containing the development solution or moving phase. The tank sometimes contains up to 200 milliliters of the solution, but the quantity of the solution varies with the test. Only the plate's lower edge rests in the solution. The moving phase or solvent front creeps up the plate by capillary action; the front moves in much the same way as a solution creeps up a blotter. The rate of movement of the unknown up the plate depends on its solubility in the moving phase, and in turn its solubility depends on the polarity of the unknown compound. Polarity describes the distribution of electrical charge between two bonding atoms.[36] In most bonds between two different elemental atoms, bonding electrons are more strongly attracted to one of the two nuclei and thus spend more time near that atom. An unequally shared pain of bonding electrons is a polar bond. Since electrons have negative charges, the atom which attracts more electrons bears a small partial negative charge; and the other atom bears an equal positive charge. Like the unknown compound, the moving and stationary phases will have charges. Opposites attract rather than repel. If due to its polarity the unknown is more attracted to the moving phase, it will be more soluble[37] in that phase and move up

35. This chart is modeled after an audio-visual aid developed by Provost Robert Shapiro. Ensing & de Zeeuw, *Detection, Isolation, and Identification of Truxillines in Illicit Cocaine by Means of Thin-Layer Chromatography and Mass Spectrometry*, 36 J. FORENSIC SCI. 1299 (1991).

36. D. EBBING, GENERAL CHEMISTRY, 342 (4th ed. 1993).

37. L. WADE, ORGANIC CHEMISTRY 60-64 (3d ed. 1995).

the plate faster. In contrast if its polarity causes the unknown to be more attracted to the stationary phase, it will be less soluble and move up the plate more slowly.

After permitting the solvent to come within five millimeters of the end of the silica gel surface or allowing a certain period of time, such as 30 minutes for the capillary action, the analyst removes the plate from the development tank. If the compound is colorless, it is sprayed with a visualizing agent. The movement of the unknown up the plate can produce a streak or, more often when the TLC is properly conducted, a tight "spot" on the plate. In some instances, to visualize the unknown's spot on the plate, the analyst must both apply the spray and subject the sprayed plate to ultraviolet light. In any event, after completing the visualizing process, a spot of a certain color will appear on the plate at a certain position on the plate. The length of the travel of the unknown can be expressed in two fashions. First, the length can be stated as an Rf value. As Figure 23-2 indicates, the Rf value compares the distance traveled by the unknown with the distance covered by the mobile phase. Alternatively, the analyst can spot a known solution on the plate and compare the distance traveled by the known with the distance covered by the unknown. This ratio is ordinarily stated as the Rx value. Thus, if a known sample of cocaine on the sample plate travels the very same distance as the unknown, the unknown is said to have an Rx value of 1.00.

TLC DEVELOPMENT

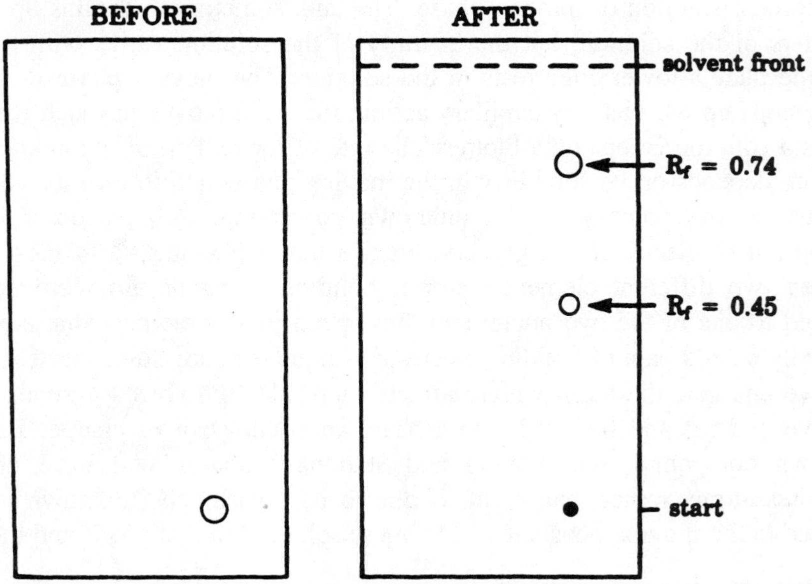

Figure 23-2[38]

38. This chart was also developed by Provost Robert Shapiro.

The color and Rf or Rx value of the spot are the primary clues to the unknown's identity. There have been numerous TLC experiments, and there is an extensive body of literature documenting the Rf value of illicit drugs in certain systems of stationary and moving phases (that is, particular combinations of adsorbents and solvent fronts). For example, under certain conditions (temperature, humidity, coating on the plate, etc.) in silica gel TLC, an analyst would expect the following compounds to produce the listed Rf values:[39]

Drug	Rf
Heroin	76
Methadone	99
Morphine	11
Meperidine	09

The analyst can strengthen the tentative identification of the unknown by running the unknown in several mobile phases. By way of illustration, many laboratories routinely subject unknowns to three different TLC systems.

The advantages of TLC are similar to those of paper chromatography. The technique is quick and inexpensive. However, TLC has major weaknesses. Most fundamentally, standing alone it cannot be used for identification. Even slight variations in the conditions--the age of the plate, the moisture content, and the ambient humidity--can affect the outcome of the test. Rf values are valid only for particular sets of conditions, namely, particular combinations of adsorbent and solvent front. Unless the analyst knows the conditions under which a published Rf value was produced, he or she cannot use that value for comparison with the Rf value in a test run in the laboratory. If the published Rf value was obtained with a different adsorbent or solvent, the comparison is invalid.

Moreover, TLC tests are nonspecific:

> The probability that two different substances (out of the domain of two million) will have the same Rf value in a single TLC experiment is high, and such an experiment does not constitute proof of identity. The typical TLC plate is about four inches long, which means that statistically, assuming an even distribution, 500,000 compounds will fall within one of the inches; 250,000 per 1/2 inch; 125,000 per 1/4 inch; 62,500 per 1/8 inch;

---

39. 1 D. Bernheim, Defense of Narcotics Cases § 4.08, at 4-53 (1983). *See also* A. Moffatt, J. Franke, A. Stead, R. Gill, B. Finkle, M. Moeller, R. Muller, F. Munsch & R. de Zeeuw, Thin Layer Chromatographic Rf Values of Toxicologically Relevant Substances on Standardized Systems (a compilation of the Rf values of 1,100 substances in 10 standardized TLC systems); Nishikawa, Tatsuno, Suzuki & Tsuchihashi, *Analysis of Methylbenactyzium Bromide in Human Urine by Thin-Layer Chromatography and Pyrolysis Gas Chromatography*, 49 Forensic Sci. Int'l 197 (1991); Lavayna & Baggi, *An Improved Thin-Layer Chromatographic Method for the Detection and Identification of Cannabinoids in Cannabis*, 47 Forensic Sci. Int'l 165 (1990).

> 31,250 per 1/16 inch; 15,625 per 1/32 inch; and 7,812 per 1/64 inch. In other words, statistically, again assuming an even distribution, 7,812 compounds could have the same Rf as amphetamine.[40]

(Our reviewer, Mr. Bono, points out, though, that this argument assumes that all of the two million substances will move on the TLC plate. He states that that assumption is erroneous; he informs us that in truth, roughly 99% of the substances will not move at all on the plate.)

Finally, there is an element of subjectivity in interpreting the test results. The analyst must characterize the color to identify the unknown. Several companies that manufacture TLC equipment supply color charts for comparison, and some laboratories routinely photograph the TLC plate to enable the trier of fact to make an independent comparison at trial.

Gas Chromatography (GC, GSC, or GLC)

GC is a method of separating the components of a mixture. There are several different modes of GC. Three of the most common are gas solid chromatography (GSC), gas liquid chromatography (GLC), and capillary gas chromatography. The basis of classification is the location of the stationary phase. In GSC, the stationary phase is a solid material such as granular silica, alumina, or carbon in a column. In GLC, the stationary phase is a liquid coated onto a solid material in a column. The solid material itself is inert, and its solitary function is to serve as a base for spreading the liquid. In capillary GC, the liquid stationary phase is applied directly onto the walls of the column. Capillary columns are best suited for analyzing very small samples.[41] Although capillary GC is now more popular,

---

40. R. SHAPIRO & J. ACKERMAN, A GUIDE TO THE ANALYTICAL MANUAL 6 (1975).

41. G. EWING, INSTRUMENTAL METHODS OF CHEMICAL ANALYSIS 366 (4th ed. 1975). *See also* Ramcharitar, Levine & Smialek, *Benzoylecgonine and Ecgonine Methyl Ester Concentrations in Urine Specimens*, 40 J. FORENSIC SCI. 99 (1995) Lau, Wong & Chan, *The Use of a Packed Column for the Determination of Bupivacaine in Human Plasma by Gas Chromatography: An Application in a Pharmacokinetic Study of Bupivacaine*, 53 FORENSIC SCI. INT'L 125 (1992); Casale & Waggoner, *A Chromatographic Impurity Signature Profile Analysis for Cocaine Using Capillary Gas Chromatography*, 36 J. FORENSIC SCI. 1312 (1991); DePace, Verebey & ElSohly, *Capillary Gas-Liquid Chromatography Separation of Phenethylamines in Amphetamine-Positive Urine Samples*, 35 J. FORENSIC SCI. 1431 (1990); Nakamura, Meeks & Stall, *Solid-Phase Extraction, Identification, and Quantitation of 11-Nor-Delta-9-Tetrahydrocannabinol-9-Carboxylic Acid*, 35 J. FORENSIC SCI. 792 (1990); Tsuchihaski, Nakajima, Nishikawa, Suzuki, Oka & Otsuki, *Screening Test of Stimulants in Human Urine Utilizing Headspace Gas Chromatography for Field Test*, 45 FORENSIC SCI. INT'L 181 (1990) (the researchers developed a small, micro-gas chromatograph for field use); Kintz, Tracqui, Mangin, Lugnier & Chaumont, *A Simple Gas Chromatographic Identification and Determination of 11 CNS Stimulants in Biological Samples. Application on a Fatality Involving Phendimetrazine*, 40 FORENSIC SCI. INT'L 153 (1989); Jones & Schuberth, *Computer-Aided Headspace Gas Chromatography Applied to Blood-Alcohol Analysis: Importance*

GLC is still an extensively used mode of gas chromatography.[42] The rest of this discussion focuses on GLC.

GC* requires that the sample be in its gaseous state to effect the separation. The separation occurs as the vaporized sample traverses a column comprised of a coated packing. The column is housed within a tubing; indeed, it can be said that the tubing is the column. The sample is converted into a gas and swept onto and through the column by a carrier gas stream (the mobile phase). The sample is broken down into its components as the gas stream carries it through the coated packing. The column, or coated packing, consists of a solid support coated with a liquid. The solid support is inert; its only function is to provide a surface for coating with the liquid component of the column. The liquid component (the liquid or stationary phase) is non-volatile. The separations obtained depend upon the properties of the stationary phase. Thus, the GC system includes: (1) the sample, (2) a carrier gas, (3) tubing, (4) solid support material, and (5) a liquid phase.

A small quantity of the sample (usually 0.001-100 micrograms) is dissolved in a few microliters of solvent. The analyst uses a hypodermic syringe to introduce the dissolved sample into the GC system through an injection port, a silicone rubber diaphragm. Because GC requires that the sample be analyzed in its gaseous state, the injection port temperature is maintained above the sample's boiling point to effect the sample's vaporization. In the case of some volatile compounds, the sample is inserted into a heated magazine before injection. The magazine vaporizes the sample. An equilibrium — headspace — then occurs between the sample and the vapor phase. The mobile phase or carrier gas sweeps the sample into the GC column.

---

of Online Process Control, 34 J. FORENSIC SCI. 1116 (1989); Klys & Brandys, *Wide-Bore Capillary Column Gas Chromatography in Toxicological Analysis of Biological Samples from Multidrug Overdose Fatalities*, 38 FORENSIC SCI. INT'L 38 (1988) ("proper column selection is the most critical factor in optimizing GC analytical procedures"); Barnfield, Burns, Byrom & Kemmenoe, *The Routine Profiling of Forensic Heroin Samples*, 39 FORENSIC SCI. INT'L 107 (1988) (gas chromatography on a capillary column using flame-ionization detection).

42. Tanaka, Ohmori & Inoue, *Analysis of Impurities in Illicit Methamphetamine*, 56 FORENSIC SCI. INT'L 157 (1992); Ensing, Racamy & de Zeeuw, *A Rapid Gas Chromatographic Method for the Fingerprinting of Illicit Cocaine Samples*, 37 J. FORENSIC SCI. 446 (1992); Fuelster, *Quantitation of Sugars in Street Drug Samples*, 37 J. FORENSIC SCI. 77 (1992); Janzen, Walter & Fernando, *Comparison Analysis of Illicit Cocaine Samples*, 37 J. FORENSIC SCI. 436 (1992); DePace, Vereby & El Sohly, *Capillary Gas-Liquid Chromatography Separation of Phenethylamines in Amphetamine-Positive Urine Samples*, 35 J. FORENSIC SCI. 1431 (1990); Verebey & DePace, *Rapid Confirmation of Enzyme Multiplied Immunoassay Technique (EMIT) Cocaine Positive Urine Samples by Capillary Gas-Liquid Chromatography/Nitrogen Phosphorous Detection (GLC/NPD)*, 34 J. FORENSIC SCI. 46 (1989).

*The balance of the discussion of GC is based in part on Bleser & Imwinkelried, *Gas Chromatography/Mass Spectrometry (GC/MS)*, THE CHAMPION, Nov. 1983, at 6. Reprinted with the permission of the National Association of Criminal Defense Lawyers.

A high pressure gas cylinder serves as the source of the mobile phase. The most frequently used carrier gasses are helium, nitrogen, carbon dioxide, and hydrogen. The mobile phase should be inert to avoid interaction with the sample or the liquid phase. The column is housed in tubing, usually made of copper, stainless steel, aluminum, or glass. The column is packed within the tubing while the tubing is straight, but then the tubing is coiled or bent. The column length may vary from a few inches to more than 50 feet. In the past most columns were three to ten feet in length, but today capillary columns of between 10 and 30 meters are commonly used. The diameter of the column can also vary from 0.01 to 2.0 inches.

The solid support portion of the column plays no active role in the GC process; the material merely provides a base for spreading the liquid phase. Diatomaceous earth, powdered Teflon, alumina, or micro glass beads make effective solid supports.

The liquid or stationary phase is a thin layer of coating covering the solid support material. Common coatings include silicone polymers, polyesters, and polyethylene glycols. As noted above, the successful separation of the illicit component from the street mixture depends upon the properties of the liquid phase. It is the interaction of the sample with the liquid phase that causes the separation.

When the mobile phase sweeps the sample into the column, the separation process begins. The components of the sample mixture have differing affinities for the liquid phase. Some components will be attracted to the liquid phase and will be more soluble in that phase than other components. A component which is highly soluble in the liquid phase dissolves into that phase; and, at any given time, a greater percentage of its molecules will be in the liquid phase than in the mobile phase. Components travel through the column only while they are in the mobile phase. Consequently, a component with a great affinity for the liquid phase will take longer to traverse the column than other components. The components, with their differing affinities for the liquid phase, emerge or elute from the column at different times, and the desired separation is thereby effected.

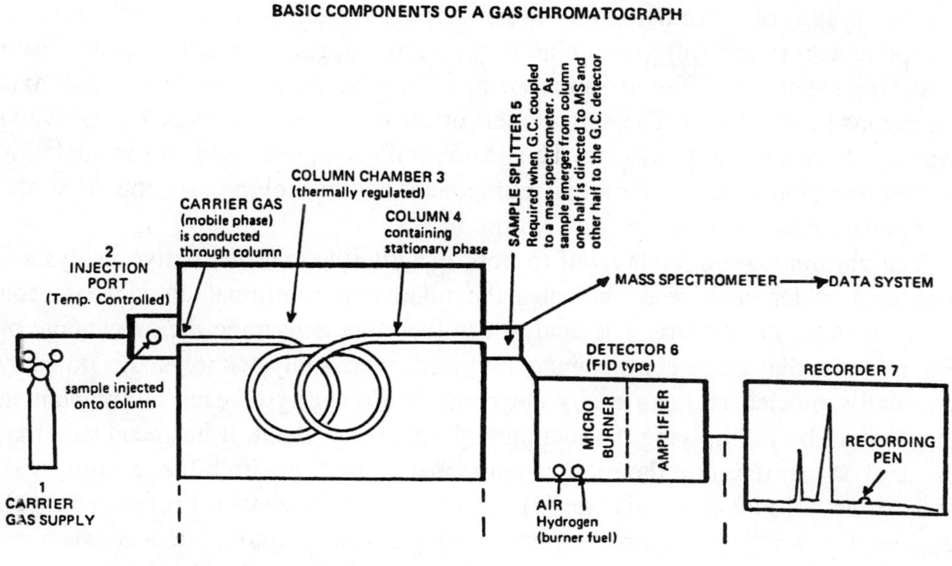

Figure 23-3[43]

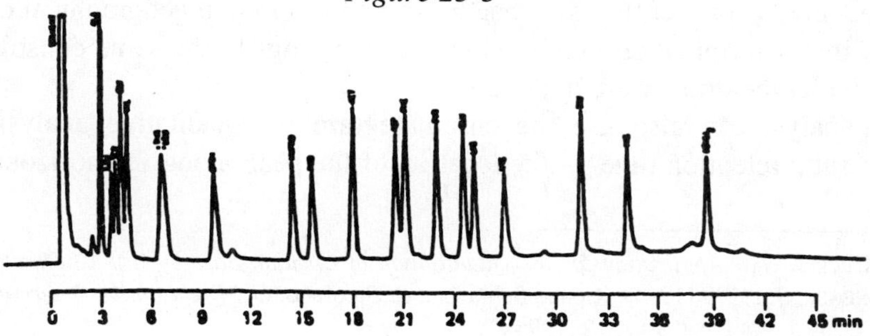

Figure 23-4[44]

When the component emerges from the tubing, it enters a detector. There are various types of detectors. Some are called flame ionization detectors (FID). Other varieties are electron-capture (EC), nitrogen-phosphorus detectors (NPD), hot wire (HWD), and Hall detectors. (As we shall see in § 23-3(C), the GC can be conjoined to a mass spectrometer (MS). The MS can function as a detector.) The common purpose of all detectors is to detect and measure the component as it emerges from the tube. A recorder translates the detector's data into a graph or chromatogram such as Figure 23-4.

---

43. Bleser & Imwinkelried, *Gas Chromatography/Mass Spectrometry (GC/MS)*, THE CHAMPION, Nov. 1983, at 7. Reprinted with permission of the National Association of Criminal Defense Lawyers.

44. *Id.* at 8. Reprinted with permission of the National Association of Criminal Defense Lawyers.

The graph or chromatogram plots response against time. Each time a component emerges from the column, the chromatogram records a peak. Each peak represents a different component of the mixture. The horizontal axis represents time elapsed. The extreme left of the chromatogram is zero time when the sample was initially injected. The position of each peak on the horizontal axis is the retention time (Rt) of that component in the column — the time the component required to travel the column.

The chromatogram lends itself to both quantitative and qualitative analysis.[45] The area under each peak indicates the relative proportional amount of each component in the mixture. The analyst can therefore determine the percentage of the mixture that each component comprised. The analyst knows the quantity originally injected and can easily determine the quantity of each component in the mixture by multiplying the total quantity by the percent. It has been said that the analyst can measure the relative component quantity within the mixture with an accuracy of plus or minus one (1) percent, but our reviewer, Professor Siegel, is doubtful whether the procedure is that precise. Quantitative analysis may enable the expert to determine whether different drug samples were manufactured as part of the same batch[46] or had a common geographical origin.[47] In turn, that determination might help tie all the drugs to the same conspiracy or establish that the drugs were imported.

The analyst can also use the chromatogram for qualitative analysis. The component's retention time — the location of the peak along the horizontal axis

---

45. Krueger, *New Application for the Quantitation of Cocaine Base by Gas Chromatography*, 39 J. FORENSIC SCI. 177 (1994); Ripani, Schiavone & Garofano, *GC Quantitative Determination of Illicit LSD*, 39 J. FORENSIC SCI. 512 (1994).

46. Besacier, Guilluy, Brazier, Chaudron-Thozet, Girard & Lamotte, *Isotopic Analysis of 13C as a Tool for Comparison and Origin Assignment of Seized Heroin Samples*, 42 J. FORENSIC SCI. 429 (1997); Jonson & Stromberg, *Computer Aided Retrieval of Common-Batch Members in Leukart Amphetamine Profiling*, 38 J. FORENSIC SCI. 1472 (1993).

47. Bermejo-Barrera, Moreda-Pineiro, Moreda-Pineiro, Bermejo-Barrera & Bermejo-Barrera, *A Study of Illicit Cocaine Seizure Classification by Pattern Recognition Techniques Applied to Metal Data*, 44 J. FORENSIC SCI. 270 (1999); Moore & Casale, *Cocaine Profiling Methodology — Recent Advances*, 10 FORENSIC SCI. REV. 1 (1998) (impurity signature profiles); Horrocks, Bedford & Morgan-Smith, *The Filtering Effects of Various Household Fabrics on the Pollen Content of Hash Oil (Cannabis Extract)*, 42 J. FORENSIC SCI. 256 (1997) (the same source); Casale & Moore, *3, 4, 5-Trimethoxy-Substituted Analogs of Cocaine, Cis-/Trans-Cinnamoylcocaine and Tropacocaine: Characterization and Quantitation of New Alkaloids in Coca Leaf, Coca Paste and Refined Illicit Cocaine*, 39 J. FORENSIC SCI. 462 (1994); Tanaka, Ohmori, Inoue & Seta, *Impurity Profiling Analysis of Illicit Methamphetamine by Capillary Gas Chromatography*, 39 J. FORENSIC SCI. 500 (1994); Casale & Moore, *Detection and Determination of Pseudococaine in Coca Leaves and Illicit Cocaine Samples*, 39 J. FORENSIC SCI. 1537 (1994); Moore & Cooper, *The Application of Capillary Gas Chromatography-Electron Capture Detection in the Comparative Analyses of Illicit Cocaine Samples*, 38 J. FORENSIC SCI. 1286 (1993); Moore, Meyers & Jiminez, *The Anatomy of a Cocaine Comparison Case: A Prosecutorial and Chemistry Perspective*, 38 J. FORENSIC SCI. 1305 (1993).

— indicates the identity of the component. However, GC qualitative analysis is not specific. Several different chemicals may have the identical retention time. Because retention times can be duplicated, it is dangerous to rely solely on GC as a method of determining the sample's elemental composition. One commentator has remarked that GC is "one of the quickest ways of getting the wrong answer — in qualitative analysis."[48]

A further weakness of GC's qualitative capability is that like Rf values, retention times are valid only for a particular set of experimental conditions.[49] Before comparing an observed retention time with a published retention time, the following information about the experiment that generated the published retention time is needed: the temperature of the oven, the age of the column (columns gradually wear out), the flow rate of the carrier gas, and the stationary phase used in the experiment. The analyst must know these column conditions before using the published Rt.

It is important to distinguish between the two methodological applications of GC. When GC is used as a method of identification, it has limited forensic value. GC is a non-specific test; several chemicals can have the same retention time and thus produce a peak at the very same point along the horizontal axis of the chromatogram.[50] However, when used as a method of separation, GC is unsurpassed. It is an excellent technique for separating the components of a complex organic mixture. GC's separation capability explains why it can be used so effectively in conjunction with mass spectrometry (MS). Subsection 23-3(C) discusses that conjunction.

Our reviewer, Professor Siegel, adds a caveat about GC. GC is generally not good with some polar drugs, notably amphetamines. Peak quality is poor even with capillary systems unless the drug is derivatized first. Acetic anhydride is commonly used for amphetamines to form an amide.

High Pressure or Performance Liquid Chromatography (HPLC)

The chromatographic technique attracting the most recent publicity is high pressure or high performance liquid chromatograph (HPLC).[51] This technique is

---

48. D. AMBROSE, GAS CHROMATOGRAPHY 235 (1971).

49. Franke, Wijsbeek & de Zeeuw, *Interlaboratory Reproducibility of Retention Indeces in Capillary Gas Chromatography*, 35 J. FORENSIC SCI. 813 (1990); Japp, Gill & Osselton, *Comparison of Drug Retention Indices Determined on Packed, Wide Bore Capillary and Narrow Bore Capillary Columns*, 32 J. FORENSIC SCI. 1574, 1575 (1987) (only "a few studies have been carried out ... to determine whether existing data based on packed columns may be used with various types of capillary columns").

50. Kurzman & Fullerton, *Drug Identification*, *in* SCIENTIFIC AND EXPERT EVIDENCE 521, 539-44 (2d ed. 1981).

51. Iwanicki, Maier, Zlotnick, Liu, Kuo & Tagliaro, *Separation of Enantiomeric Ephedrine and Pseudoephedrine — High Pressure Liquid Chromotography and Capillary Electrophoresis*, 44 J.

FORENSIC SCI. 470 (1999); White, Kidd & Webb, *The Determination of Lysergide (LSD) in Urine by High-Performance Liquid Chromatography-Isotope Dilution Mass Spectrometry (IDMS)*, 44 J. FORENSIC SCI. 375 (1999); Bergemann, Geier & von Meyer, *Determination of Lysergic Acid Diethylamide in Body Fluids by High-Performance Liquid Chromatography and Fluorescence Detection — A More Sensitive Method Suitable for Routine Use*, 44 J. FORENSIC SCI. 372 (1999); He, Parissis & Kiratzidis, *Determination of Benzodiazepines in Forensic Samples by HPLC with Photo-Diode Array Detection*, 43 J. FORENSIC SCI. 1061 (1998); Mesmer & Satzger, *Determination of Gamma-Hydrozybutyrate (GHB) and Gamma-Butyrolactone (GBL(by HPLC/UV-VIS Spectrophotometry and HPLC/Thermospray Mass Spectrometry*, 43 J. FORENSIC SCI. 489 (1998); Kretschmer & Helbig, *Chemical Analysis of Macromolecular Particles Using Two-Dimensional High-Performance Liquid Chromatography (HPLC), Illustrated by Polymeric Automobile Direction Indicator Lenses (DILS)*, 36 J. FORENSIC SCI. 1010 (1991); Singh, McArdle, Granley, Mishra & Gordon, *Evaluation of High Performance Liquid Chromatography (HPLC), Enzyme Linked Immunosorbent Assay (ELISA) and Particle Concentration Fluorescence Immunoassay (PCFIA) Methods for the Screening, Quantitation and Pharmacokinetic Study of Furosemide in Horses*, 47 FORENSIC SCI. INT'L 1 (1990); Logan & Stafford, *High-Performance Liquid Chromatography with Column Switching for the Determination of Cocaine and Benzoylecogonine Concentrations in Vitreous Humour*, 35 J. FORENSIC SCI. 1303 (1990); Chiarotti & Fucci, *HPLC Analysis of Cocaine Diasteroisomers by Chiral Stationary Phase*, 44 FORENSIC SCI. INT'L 37 (1990); Logan & Stafford, *Direct Analysis of Anticonvulsant Drugs in Vitreous Humour by HPLC Using a Column Switching Technique*, 41 FORENSIC SCI. INT'L 125 (1989); Harris, Guerra & Wallace, *Assay of Free and Total Tocainide by High Performance Liquid Chromatography (HPLC) with Ultraviolet (UV) Detection*, 34 J. FORENSIC SCI. 912 (1989); Sawyer, Waterhouse, Doedens & Forney, *Heroin, Morphine, and Hydromorphone Determination in Postmortem Material by High Performance Liquid Chromatography*, 33 J. FORENSIC SCI. 1146 (1988) (this technique permits simultaneous determination of the three drugs); Shankar, Damodaran & Sekharan, *Barbiturate Analysis in Tissue by Enzymic Digestion and High-Performance Liquid Chromatography*, 40 FORENSIC SCI. INT'L 45 (1989) (HPLC is the method of choice); Tebbett & McCartney, *A Rapid Method for the Extraction of Cocaine and Benzoylecgonine from Body Fluids*, 39 FORENSIC SCI. INT'L 287 (1988); LeBelle, Lauriault, Callahan, Latham, Chiarelli & Beckstead, *The Examination of Illicit Cocaine*, 33 J. FORENSIC SCI. 662 (1988); Sottolano, *The Quantitation of Phenyl-2-Propanone Using High-Performance Liquid Chromatography*, 33 J. FORENSIC SCI. 1415 (1988); Noggle & Clark, *Resolution of Some Enantiomeric Amines of Forensic Interest by High-Performance Liquid Chromatography*, 31 J. FORENSIC SCI. 732 (1986); Alburges & Peat, *Profiles of 9-Tetrahyrocannabinol Metabolites in Urine of Marijuana Users: Preliminary Observations by High Performance Liquid Chromatography-Radioimmunoassay*, 31 J. FORENSIC SCI. 695 (1986); Selavka, Krull & Lurie, *An Improved Method for the Rapid Screening of Illicit Cocaine Preparations Using High Performance Liquid Chromatography with Electrochemical Detection*, 31 FORENSIC SCI. INT'L 103 (1986); O'Neil & Gough, *Illicitly Imported Heroin Products: Some Physical and Chemical Features Indicative of Their Origin. Part II*, 30 J. FORENSIC SCI. 681 (1985); Reuland & Trinler, *The Use of Absorbance Ratios in High-Performance Liquid Chromatography for the Identification of Drugs of Abuse*, 37 FORENSIC SCI. INT'L 37 (1988); White, Etherington & Catterick, *An HPLC Method Using Absorbance Ratioing for the Identification of Diamorphine in Illicit Heroin Samples*, 37 FORENSIC SCI. INT'L 55 (1988); O'Neil, Baker & Gough, *Illicitly Imported Heroin Products: Some Physical and Chemical Features Indicative of Their Origin*, 29 J. FORENSIC SCI. 889 (1984) (use of HPLC); I. LURIE & J. WITTWER, HIGH-PERFORMANCE LIQUID CHROMATOGRAPHY IN FORENSIC CHEMISTRY (1983); Smith, *Forensic Application of High-Performance Liquid Chromatography*, *in* FORENSIC SCIENCE HANDBOOK 28

particularly well-suited for compounds with high molecular weight.[52] HPLC has wide applications to drugs such as cannabis, cocaine, barbiturates, LSD, and opium.[53]

The major difference between GC and HPLC is that in HPLC, the moving phase is a liquid solvent or solvent mixture. A pump forces the solvent into and through the column. In HPLC, as in GC, the separation occurs as the unknown migrates down the column in the moving phase; but in HPLC, the separation is caused by the differing solubilities of compounds in the solvent.[54] The substances traveling in the moving phase are called the solutes. The detector notes the sequence in which the solutes elute from the column.[55] The chromatogram is similar to the graph produced by a GC instrument. The HPLC chromatogram charts the detector response against the time lapse.[56] If the detector was an ultraviolet detector, the vertical axis of the graph would measure the degree to which each solute absorbed ultraviolet light.[57] The horizontal axis measures the number of minutes elapsed, as in Figure 23-5.

(R. Saferstein ed. 1982); Tracqui, Kintz & Mangin, *HPLC/MS Determination of Buprenorphine and Norbuprenorphine in Biological Fluids and Hair Samples*, 42 J. FORENSIC SCI. 111 (1997); Webb, Baker, Cassells, Francis, Johnston, Lancaster, Minty, Reed & White, *The Analysis of Lysergide (LSD): The Development of Novel Enzyme Immunoassay and Immunoaffinity Extraction Procedures Together with an HPLC-MS Confirmation Procedure*, 41 J. FORENSIC SCI. 938 (1996); Ohtsuji, Lai, Binder, Kondo, Takayasu & Ohshima, *Use of REMEDiHS in Emergency Toxicology for a Rapid Estimate of Drug Concentrations in Urine, Serum, and Gastric Samples*, 41 J. FORENSIC SCI. 881 (1996); Lurie, Sperling & Meyers, *The Determination of Anabolic Steroids by MECC, Gradient HPLC, and Capillary GC*, 39 J. FORENSIC SCI. 74 (1994); Veress, *Study of the Extraction of LSD from Illicit Blotters for HPLC Determination*, 38 J. FORENSIC SCI. 1105 (1993); Moore, Browne, Tebbett, Negrusz, Meyer & Jain, *Determination of Cocaine and Benzoylecgonine in Human Amniotic Fluid Using High Flow Solid-Phase Extraction Columns and HPLC*, 56 FORENSIC SCI. INT'L 177 (1992); Hernandez, Moliz, Gil, Gonzalvo & Villanueva, *Application of the Combined Use of HPLC/Diode Array Detection and Capillary GC/Nitrogen Phosphorous Detection for the Rapid Analysis of Illicit Heroin and Cocaine Samples*, 37 J. FORENSIC SCI. 1276 (1992); Koves & Wells, *Evaluation of a Phototide Array/HPLC-Based System for the Detection and Quantitation of Basic Drugs in Postmortem Blood*, 37 J. FORENSIC SCI. 42 (1992); Larsen & Tebbett, *Direct Analysis of Cocaine in Urine by High-Performance Liquid Chromatography (HPLC) Using a Column-Switching Technique*, 37 J. FORENSIC SCI. 636 (1992).

52. Smith, *Forensic Application of High-Performance Liquid Chromatography*, *in* FORENSIC SCIENCE HANDBOOK 29 (R. Saferstein ed. 1982).

53. *Id.* at 57-63.

54. *Id.* at 30.

55. *Id.* at 33.

56. *Id.* at 31.

57. Sottolano & Lurie, *The Quantitation of Psilocybin in Hallucinogenic Mushrooms Using High Performance Liquid Chromatography*, 28 J. FORENSIC SCI. 929 (1983).

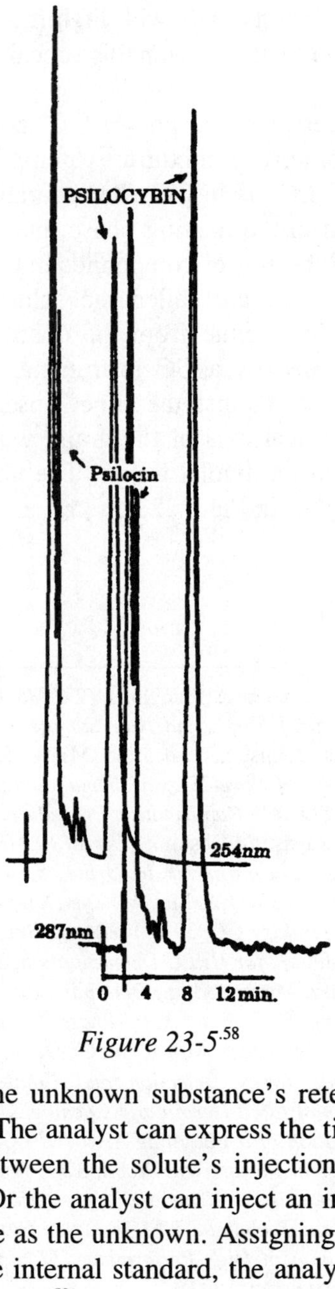

Figure 23-5[58]

The analyst can state the unknown substance's retention volume or time in absolute or relative terms. The analyst can express the time absolutely in terms of the number of minutes between the solute's injection into the column and its elution from the column. Or the analyst can inject an internal standard, a known substance, at the same time as the unknown. Assigning the numerical value 1.00 to the retention time of the internal standard, the analyst can compute a relative retention time for the unknown.[59]

---

58. *Id.* at 934. Copyright, ASTM, 100 Barr Harbor Drive, West Conshohocken, PA. Reprinted with permission.

59. Smith, *supra* note 52, at 52.

HPLC has numerous advantages. It is a superior method for analyzing substances with high molecular weight. Moreover, it is a rapid method of analysis. Some HPLC analyses can be conducted in one to three minutes.[60] In addition, HPLC can be run in "reverse phase" where the column is less polar than the mobile phase. This facilitates some separations.

Yet HPLC suffers from some of the same limitations as GC. GC retention times are meaningful only if the column conditions, including gas flow and temperature, are known. Similarly, the analyst can compare an observed HPLC retention time with a published retention time only if the analyst knows the conditions of the published experiment. In particular, the analyst must know the solvent and temperature.[61] HPLC results seem to be more variable than GC results; in general, HPLC retentions are not as reproducible as GC retention times.[62]

Moreover, like GC, HPLC can yield nonspecific test results. In one study involving 75 drugs of forensic interest, the researchers reported that GC retention times distinguished 45% of the drugs while HPLC retention times distinguished only 9%.[63] The difficulties with HPLC are understandable. The laboratories have somewhat limited experience with HPLC, since it did not become available until 1969.[64] It did not gain wide popularity until five or six years later.[65]

§ 23-2(E). Immunoassay.

An even more recent development in drug analysis than HPLC is the advent of immunoassay techniques. Although these techniques are relatively novel, they are already employed extensively. The armed services use these techniques in their urinalysis testing programs. In 1983, the armed services conducted over two million immunoassay tests.[66] The same tests are being used by civilian police laboratories in California, Florida, Massachusetts, Nevada, Tennessee, Texas,

---

60. DiCesare, Dong & Ettre, *Very-High-Speed Liquid Column Chromatography, The System and Selected Applications*, 14 Chromatographia 257 (1981). *But see* Walker, Krueger, Lurie, Marche & Newby, *Analysis of Heroin Drug Seizures by Micellar Electrokinetic Capillary Chromatography (MECC)*, 40 J. FORENSIC SCI. 6 (1995) ("HPLC does not require derivatization but compared to GC, lacks resolution and speed").

61. Smith, *supra* note 52, at 30, 33.

62. Reuland & Trinler, *The Use of Absorbance Ratios in High-Performance Liquid Chromatography for the Identification of Drugs of Abuse*, 37 FORENSIC SCI. INT'L 37, 37-38 (1988) ("the reproducibility from laboratory to laboratory is not good"); Lurie, *Problems in Using High Performance Liquid Chromatography for Drug Analysis*, 29 J. FORENSIC SCI. 607, 609 (1984).

63. *Id.*

64. Smith, *supra* note 52, at 29.

65. *Id.*

66. Zeese, *Marijuana Urinalyses Tests*, 1 DRUG L. REP. 25 (May-June 1983).

and Utah. A number of manufacturers produce immunoassay test kits;[67] and Syva Company of California, Hoffman LaRoche of New Jersey, Collaborative Research, Inc., of Massachusetts, and Guildhay Antisera of England market their immunoassay products throughout the United States.

There are several varieties of immunoassay: radioimmunoassay (RIA), enzyme multiplied or multiple immunoassay (EMIT), and free radical assay (FRAT).[68] All are based on immunological principles. Immunology is the study of the body's mechanisms for developing defenses or immunities to diseases. The carrier of the disease, the substance invading the body, is called an antigen (Ag). The body's immune response is to counteract the antigen by developing a protective antibody (Ab).

Immunoassay techniques capitalize on these immunological principles to identify illicit drugs. When the drug (the antigen) is injected into a goat or rabbit, the animal's immune response is to create antibodies that specifically counteract that drug or antigen. Several months later the analyst bleeds the animal to withdraw the serum containing the antibody. The antibody can be used to detect the presence of the drug (the antigen) in a person suspected of abusing that drug.

A simple example will suffice. The analyst obtains a sample of the suspect's urine. The police believe that the suspect has recently ingested a drug and that, consequently, the drug or antigen will be present in the urine sample. After the person consumes the drug, it becomes metabolite in his body. The analyst mixes the urine samples with: (1) the antibody specific for that drug; and (2) known drug or antigen labeled with either a radioactive isotope (in RIA) or lysozyme (in EMIT). If the suspect's urine contains the drug, that drug and the labeled drug compete to bind with the antibody — competitive binding. Both the drug and the labeled drug are ligands; that is, they tend to bind or combine with the antibody.

---

67. Kunsman, Levine & Smith, *Vistamin B2 Interference with Tdx Drugs-of-Abuse Assays*, 43 J. FORENSIC SCI. 1225 (1998) (the Abbott TDx); Felscher, Gastmeier & Dressler, *Screening of Pharmaceuticals and Drugs in Synovial Fluid of the Knee Joint and in Vitreous Humor by Fluorescence Polarization Immunoassay (FPIA)*, 43 J. FORENSIC SCI. 619 (1998) (Abbott's fluorescence polarization immunoassay); Levine & Smialek, *Considerations in the Interpretation of Urine Analyses in Suspected Opiate Intoxications*, 43 J. FORENSIC SCI. 388 (1998) (Roche Diagnostic Systems' Abuscreen).

68. Altunkaya, Clatworthy, Smith & Start, *Urinary Cannabinoid Analysis: Comparison of Four Immunoassays with Gas Chromatography-Mass Spectrometry*, 50 FORENSIC SCI. INT'L 15 (1991); Cone & Mitchell, *Validity Testing of Commercial Urine Cocaine Metabolite Assays: II. Sensitivity, Specificity, Accuracy, and Confirmation by Gas Chromatography/Mass Spectrometry*, 34 J. FORENSIC SCI. 32, 43 (1989) ("the KDI Quik Test assay ... was not a reliable indicator for the presence of cocaine-related metabolites in urine"); Cone, Menchen, Paul, Mell & Mitchell, *Validity Testing of Commercial Urine Cocaine Metabolite Assays: I. Assay Detection Times, Individual Excretion Patterns, and Kinetics After Cocaine Administration to Humans*, 34 J. FORENSIC SCI. 15 (1989) ("a commercial spot test (KDI Quik Test) ... produced both false positives and false negatives ... and was not considered to be a valid test for detection of cocaine metabolite").

The more unlabeled drug present in the suspect's urine, the more labeled drug that will be left free or unbound. The analyst can measure either the bound labeled antigen or the unbound labeled antigen. Either measurement indicates the amount of unlabeled drug present in the urine sample.

The immunoassay techniques have become popular in a short time. The tests are rapid, inexpensive, and more portable than many more conventional tests. However, the immunoassay tests have weaknesses. They are nonspecific. The tests are said to be "cross-reactive" with other drugs. Consequently, false positives are possible.[69] Paradoxically, one of the strengths of immunoassay

---

69. Taylor v. O'Grady, 888 F.2d 1189, 1192 n.4 (7th Cir. 1989) ("EMIT ... is ... one of the least accurate of the urinalysis tests. EMIT is primarily useful as an initial test ...."); United States v. Bentley, 875 F.2d 1114, 1123 n.9 (5th Cir. 1989) ("Many of the tests for identifying marihuana are not specific. Two of the common tests for detecting marihuana use, the EMIT and RIA tests, produce inconclusive results that require corroboration by other testing means"); Burka v. New York City Transit Auth., 739 F. Supp. 814, 832 n.11 (S.D.N.Y. 1990) ("Experts agree that the gas chromatography/mass spectrometry (GC/MS) test used in Skinner and Van Raab is more reliable than ... EMIT ...."); National Fed'n of Fed. Emps. v. Carlucci, 680 F. Supp. 416, 428 (D.D.C. 1988) ("the most technologically advanced urine test cannot distinguish between a heroin user and a person who eats poppy seed strudel"); Mirsky, *From the Scientific to the Farcical in Drug Screening Avoidance Schemes*, 14 SCI. SLEUTHING REV. 1, 4 (Fall 1990) ("Cody's research reveals that the EMIT screening procedure... can be beaten by adulterating the urine specimen with bleach..., detergent ..., drano ..., salt ..., liquid soap ..., vinegar and visine ...."); Midkiff, *Countering the "Poppy Seed Defense": No Piece of Cake*, SCI. SLEUTHING REV. 4, 13 (Spring 1990) (poppy seeds are common in certain types of pastries and dishes typical of central Europe; "[t]wo hours after ingestion of only two cookies [containing poppy seeds], EMIT results were well above the cutoff levels established for a urine screening program"); Cone, Yousefnejad & Dickerson, *Validity Testing of Commercial Urine Cocaine Metabolite Assays: IV. Evaluation of the EMIT d.a.u. Cocaine Metabolite Assay in a Quantitative Mode for Detection of Cocaine Metabolite*, 35 J. FORENSIC SCI. 786 (1990); Bugusz, Aderjan, Schmitt, Nadler & Neureither, *The Determination of Drugs of Abuse in Whole Blood by Means of FPIA and EMIT-dau Immunoassays — A Comparative Study*, 48 FORENSIC SCI. INT'L 27, 36 (1990) (EMIT proved to be the inferior technique); Gjerde, Christophersen, Skuterud, Klemetsen & Morland, *Screening for Drugs in Forensic Blood Samples Using EMIT Urine Assays*, 44 FORENSIC SCI. INT'L 179 (1990) (in amphetamine assays, the false positive rate was 9%); *False Positive Tests for Methamphetamine*, 2 THE FORENSIC DRUG ABUSE ADVISOR 1 (Feb. 1990) ("Writing in the JOURNAL OF ANALYTICAL TOXICOLOGY, Fitzgerald et al described a study of three, non-drug using males who used a Vicks inhaler three times an hour for six hours. Urine samples were collected over the next twenty-four hours. Specimens tested positive with ... the Syva-EMIT ..., but not with RIA Abuscreen ...."). Northwestern University researchers reported that one of the widely used immunoassay tests yielded 25% false positives. Edwards, *Mandatory Workplace Drug Testing: Liberties Lost by Increments*, LEGAL TIMES, Sept. 1, 1986, at 11. A New Jersey Department of Corrections study similarly found a 25% error rate. Peranzo v. Coughlin, 608 F. Supp. 1504, 1511 (S.D.N.Y. 1985), *aff'd*, 850 F.2d 125 (2d Cir. 1988); Redeker & Segal, *How to Protect Employers Who Test for Drug and Alcohol Abuse*, 33 PRAC. LAW. 13, 22 (Apr. 1987) ("for example, therapeutic cold medicines, such as Contac and Sudafed, can create a false positive for amphetamine use"); Dunham, Lewis & Alpert, *Testing the Police for Drugs*, 24 CRIM. L. BULL. 155, 159 (1988) ("False positive tests for opiates (such as morphine or heroin) may happen as a

causes one of its weaknesses. The strength is that the more modern immunoassay techniques are extremely sensitive; they can detect very small, trace quantities of the drug. This strength gives rise to a weakness because research indicates that a suspect can have trace amounts of the drug metabolite in his urine even when he did not unlawfully ingest the drug. For instance, several studies suggest that a person may have trace quantities of the metabolite of marijuana (11-nor-THC-carboxylic acid) in his or her urine even if the person has not smoked a marijuana cigarette.[70] If a person remains in the presence of an individual smoking a marijuana cigarette, the person may inhale minute quantities of the smoke.[71] Some state-of-the-art immunoassays are so sensitive that they can detect these

---

result of taking chloropromazine (Thorazine R) — a medication used to treat schizophrenia — or from taking over-the-counter cough medicines containing dextromethorphan. It is also reported in the medical literature that amoxicillin — an antibiotic — can cause a false positive test for cocaine"); Chaney v. Southern R.R., 847 F.2d 718, 721 (11th Cir. 1988) ("Dr. Woodford ... testified that black people disproportionately obtain false positives for drug use on the EMIT test because they have higher levels of melanin, the substance responsible for dark skin tone, in their urine than do white people. According to Dr. Woodford, the EMIT test misreads melanin fragments as ingested THC fragments"); Pella v. Adams, 702 F. Supp. 244 (D. Nev. 1988) ("Even when an initial positive test is confirmed through a second EMIT test, such confirmation does not guarantee that the tested individual has been using marijuana or hashish. A second positive test simply confirms that the proper technical procedures were followed in performing the tests. The same non-THC compound or other mystery factor that caused a false positive result in an initial EMIT test could also produce a false positive in the second EMIT test"); Miike & Hewitt, *Accuracy and Reliability of Urine Drug Tests*, 36 KAN. L. REV. 641, 651-57, 666-72 (1988) (the text summarizes the results of proficiency tests; the appendix identifies other substances which the various tests are cross-reactive with); Buchan, Walsh & Leaverton, *Evaluation of the Accuracy of On-Site Multi-Analyte Drug Testing Devices in the Determination of the Prevalence of Illicit Drugs in Drivers*, 43 J. FORENSIC SCI. 395 (1998) (the researchers tested four on-site kits which test for tetrahydrocannabinol (THC), cocaine metabolites (COC), and opiates (OPI); "Accuracy ranged from 94.0% to 98.3% for THC, 97.4% to 98.0% for COC, and 99.7% to 100% for OPI"); Crouch, Cheever, Andrenyak, Kuntz & Loughmiller, *A Comparison of ONTRAK TESTCUP, Abuscreen ONTRAK, Abuscreen ONLINE, and CG/MS Urinalysis Test Results*, 43 J. FORENSIC SCI. 35 (1998) ("ONTRAK had a 91% agreement with GC/MS ... for testing of samples that contained BZE. The least agreement ... was found when testing samples that contained THC-COOH. The agreement was 89%.); Singh, Granley, Misrha, Naeem, White & Jiang, *Screening and Confirmation of Drugs in Urine: Interference of Hordenine with the Immunoassays and Thin Layer Chromatography Methods*, 54 FORENSIC SCI. INT'L 9 (1992) (cross-reactivity with hordenine); *False Positive Amphetamine Screens*, 5 FORENSIC DRUG ABUSE ADVISOR 27 (Apr. 1993).

False negatives are also possible. Browne, Moore, Negrusz, Tebbett, Covert & Dusick, *Detection of Cocaine, Norcocaine, and Cocaethylene in the Meconium of Premature Neonates*, 39 J. FORENSIC SCI. 1515 (1994); *Bleach Beats Urine Tests*, FORENSIC DRUG ABUSE ADV., Vol. 6, No. 5, p. 38 (May 1994) (by adding household bleach (sodium hypochlorite) to their urine specimen, marijuana users can reduce the amount of measured THC concentration by between 14% and 45%).

70. Perez-Reyes, DiGuiseppi, David, Schindler & Cook, 31 CLIN. PHARMA. THERAP. 617 (1982); Zeidenberg, Bourdon & Nahas, *Marijuana Intoxication by Passive Inhalation: Documentation by Detection of Urinary Metabolites*, 134 AM. J. PSYCH. 76 (1977).

71. *Id.*

minute levels of metabolite.[72] It has been claimed that passive inhalation of "crack" smoke can have the same effect. Hence, the laboratory must establish a cutoff level — a minimum level such as 50 or 100 nanograms of metabolite per milliliter (ng/ml) of urine below which the laboratory reports a negative finding.[73] There is an element of arbitrariness in fixing the cutoff value, and various laboratories use different cutoff values.

Radioimmunoassay (RIA)

Yallow and Benson developed RIA in 1960 as a method for detecting insulin. A number of companies, including Roche Diagnostics, Inc., have adapted the methodology for detecting illicit drug metabolites in urine specimens. Like the other immunoassays, RIA rests on the principle of competitive binding. The manufacturer supplies the analyst with both antibody and antigen (the known drug sample) labeled with a radioactive isotope. The most commonly used isotopes are I^{125}(radioactive iodine), H^3, and C^{14}. The antibody and labeled drug are mixed with the suspect's urine. Figure 23-6 illustrates the possible reactions.

Each row of diagrams in Figure 23-6 represents a different set of circumstances. In the top row, the suspect's urine contains no unlabeled antigen or drug. Perhaps the suspect passively inhaled marijuana smoke from another person, or a substantial period of time elapsed since the suspect smoked a marijuana cigarette. In this event, there will be competition between the labeled and unlabeled antigen to bind with the antibody. The net result is that there is a bit more unbound labeled antigen at the end of the reaction.

In the bottom row, the suspect's urine contains a good deal of unlabeled drug; the suspect has recently smoked marijuana. Once again, there is competition. Since there is more unlabeled antigen in this variation of the hypothetical, there is even more free labeled antigen after the reaction.

To produce these reactions, the analyst must allow the urine sample, antibody, and labeled drug to incubate for a predetermined period such as an hour. The labeled and unlabeled drug or antigen are equally reactive with the antibody, and the period of time allows the solution to attain an equilibrium.

---

72. *Id.*

73. The cutoff can vary from drug to drug.

RADIOIMMUNOASSAY

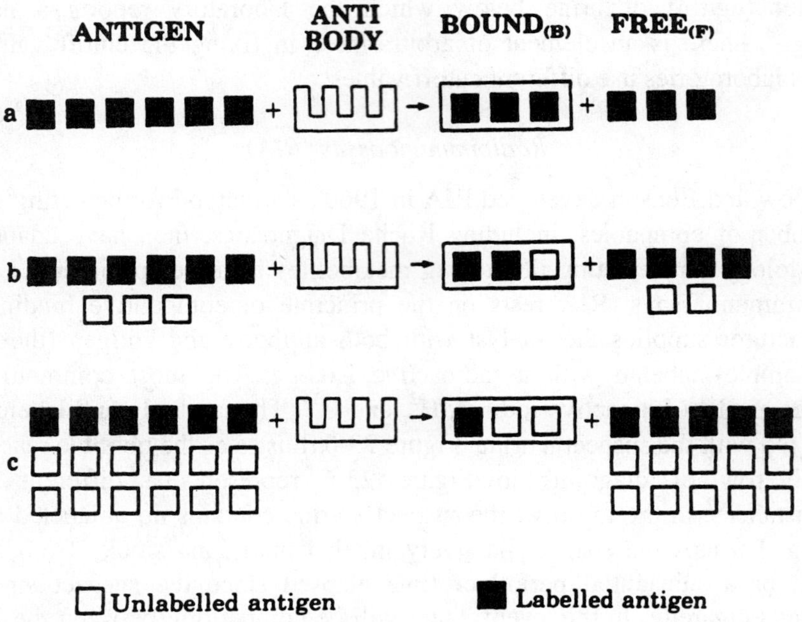

Figure 23-6[74]

After the lapse of this time period, the analyst separates the solution, for instance, by centrifugation. Centrifuging the solution causes the solution to separate into pellets (representing the bound antibody) and fluid or supernatant (including the unbound antigen). The analyst can measure the radioactivity of the pellets or of the supernatant. The measuring instrument depends upon the type of radioactive label employed. If the isotope was I^{125}, the analyst uses a gamma counter. On the other hand, when the isotope employed is H^3, the analyst typically resorts to a scintillation counter. The counters register counts per minute (CPM). When the analyst measures the radioactivity of the pellets, a positive finding for the drug requires that the registered CPM be less than the cutoff

---

74. Prepared by Terrence Brown, Esq. of Gamble, Rich, Webster, David & Green in Des Moines, Iowa. Wu, Forte, Casella, Sun, Hemphill, Foery & Schanzenbach, *CEDIA for Screening Drugs of Abuse in Urine and the Effect of Adulterants*, 40 J. FORENSIC SCI. 614 (1995) (closed enzyme donor immunoassay (CEDIA)); Budgett, Levine, Xu & Smith, *Comparison of Abbott Fluorescence Polarization Immunoassay (FPIA) and Roche Radioimmunoassay for the Analyses of Cannabinoids in Urine Specimens*, 37 J. FORENSIC SCI. 632 (1992); Smith & Kidwell, *Isomeric Amphetamines) A Problem for Urinalysis?*, 50 FORENSIC SCI. INT'L 153 (1991).

value. If the analyst gauges the supernatant's radioactivity, a positive result requires that the registered CPM exceed the cutoff value.[75]

In this fashion, the analyst can conduct a qualitative analysis and reach a conclusion as to whether the urine sample contains the metabolite of the illicit drug. In addition, the analyst can make quantitative findings. The analyst compares the registered CPM with a standard curve to quantify the metabolite.[76]

Immunoassay techniques, [77] including radioimmunoassay, are being used to study patterns of drug abuse evidenced in hair.[78] The Ianus Foundation of Los

---

75. Collison, Spiehler, Guluzian & Sedgwick, *Setting Cutoff Concentrations for Immunoassay Screening of Postmortem Blood*, 43 J. FORENSIC SCI. 390 (1998); Fuller, *A Statistical Approach to the Prediction of Verifiable Heroin Use from Total Codeine and Total Morphine Concentrations in Urine*, 42 J. FORENSIC SCI. 685 (1997) (the researcher attempted to identify "a criterion that would indicate a high probability of detecting 6-acetylmorphine in a specimen and thus confirming heroin use").

76. Lorenzo, *Radioimmunoassay (RIA)*, *in* METHODOLOGY FOR ANALYTICAL TOXICOLOGY 403-04 (I. Sunshine ed. 1975). *See also* Ward, McNally, Rusynik & Salamone, *1251 Radioimmunoassay for the Dual Detection of Amphetamine and Methamphetamine*, 39 J. FORENSIC SCI. 1486 (1994); Mirsky, *From the Scientific to the Farcical in Drug Screening Avoidance Schemes*, 14 SCI. SLEUTHING REV. 4 (Fall 1990) (Cody's research indicates that "the effectiveness of RIA ... analysis [can be undermined] with ammonia ... and bleach ...."); Baugh, Allen, Liu, Langner, Fentress, Chadha, Cook & Walia, *Evaluation of Immunoassay Methods for the Screening of Cocaine Metabolites in Urine*, 36 J. FORENSIC SCI. 79 (1991) (ARIA generated several unconfirmed presumptive positives); Weaver, Gan, Ellen, Baugh, Liao, Langner, Walia & Cook, *Correlations of Radioimmunoassay, Fluoresence Polarization Immunoassay, and Enzyme Immunoassay of Cannabis Metabolites with Gas Chromatography/Mass Spectrometry Analysis of 11-Nor-delta-9-Tetrahydrocannabinol-9-Carboyxlic Acid in Urine Specimens*, 49 FORENSIC SCI. INT'L 43, 55 (1991) ("None of the three test initial methods produces an ideal correlation of the immunoassay result with the GC/MS concentration .... However, significant correlations do exist ...."); Altunkaya & Smith, *Aberrant Radioimmunoassay Results for Cannabinoids in Urine*, 47 FORENSIC SCI. INT'L 195 (1990) (although they happen infrequently, false positive and negative results do occur); Altunkaya & Smith, *Evaluation of a Commercial Radioimmunoassay Kit for the Detection of Lysergide (LSD) in Serum, Whole Blood, Urine and Stomach Contents*, 47 FORENSIC SCI. INT'L 113 (1990); Burnett, Oliver & Smith, *Radioreceptor Assay and Radioimmunoassay of Triazolam in Urine Samples from Racing Greyhounds*, 43 FORENSIC SCI. INT'L 199 (1989); McCurdy, Callahan & Williams, *Studies on the Stability and Detection of Cocaine, Benzoylecgonine, and 11-Nor-Delta-9-Tetrahydrocannabinol-9-Carboxylic Acid in Whole Blood Using Abuscreen Radioimmunoassay*, 34 J. FORENSIC SCI. 858 (1989); Nagao, Takatori, Terazawa, Wu, Wakasugi, Masui & Ikeda, *Development and Application of Immunoassay for Paraquat: Radioimmunoassay*, 34 J. FORENSIC SCI. 547 (1989).

77. Moore, Deitermann, Lewis, Feeley & Niedbala, *The Detection of Cocaine in Hair Specimens Using Micro-Plate Enzyme Immunoassay*, 44 J. FORENSIC SCI. 609 (1999).

78. Reuschel & Smith, *Benzoylecgonine (Cocaine Metabolite) Detection in Hair Samples of Jail Detainees Using Radioimmunoassay (RIA) and Gas Chromatography/Mass Spectrometry (GC/MS)*, 36 J. FORENSIC SCI. 1179 (1991); Arnold, *The Determination of Drugs and Their Substitutes in Human Hairs*, 46 FORENSIC SCI. INT'L 17 (1990) ("With the aid of hair analysis it is possible to examine the drug career of a drug addict for up to 1 year ...."); Offidani, Carnevale & Chiarotti, *Drugs in Hair: A New Extraction Procedure*, 41 FORENSIC SCI. INT'L 35 (1989);

Angeles, California, is one of the leaders in the research. The foundation's Scientific Director, Dr. Werner Baumgartner, points out that "[h]ead hair grows at approximately 1.0-1.3 centimeters per month. Thus a 12-centimeter-long hair provides a drug history of 9-12 months."[79] In January 1989, the National Institute of Justice held a Workshop on Hair Analysis near Washington, D.C. One of the purposes of the workshop was to disseminate information about radioimmunoassay of hair. The proponents of RIA-H (radioimmunoassay-hair) contend that the use of the test reduces the risk of a false positive "because another sample is readily available, inasmuch as the substances are retained in the hair for extended periods."[80] However, there is currently a controversy over the validity of the technique.[81] Some critics assert that it is impossible to properly evaluate the claim that the technique is scientifically valid because Psychemedics, the leading American company using the test, has taken the position that some of its test procedures are proprietary secrets.[82]

Baumgartner, Hill & Blahd, *Hair Analysis for Drugs of Abuse,* 34 J. FORENSIC SCI. 1433 (1989); Bost, *Analysis of Hair for Drugs of Abuse*, 20 ACADEMY NEWS 1, 9 (Sept. 1990) (in a publication of the American Academy of Forensic Sciences, the author states that "[o]ver the last ten years, researchers in the United States, West Germany, Italy, Japan, and Greece have been performing analyses of hair specimens for numerous classes of drugs"); Miike & Hewitt, *Accuracy and Reliability of Urine Drug Tests*, 36 KAN. L. REV. 641, 664 (1988); T. MIECZKOWSKI, H. LANDRESS, R. NEWEL & S. COLETTI, TESTING HAIR FOR ILLICIT DRUG USE (1993) (a National Institute of Justice monograph, NCJ 138539); Gropper & Reardon, *Developing Drug Testing by Hair Analysis*, NAT'L INSTIT. JUST. J. 8, 10 (Apr. 1993) ("In at least three States – Massachusetts, Ohio, and New Jersey – hair testing is being used in correctional settings"). *See* § 24-2, *infra.*

79. *See* RESEARCH REPORT, MONITORING OF SUBSTANCE ABUSE THROUGH HAIR ANALYSIS: A BREAKTHROUGH IN MEDICAL AND FORENSIC SCIENCES, IANUS FOUNDATION (Dec. 1984).

80. Mooney & Neigus, *The Problems of Drug Testing in the Private Workplace*, 37 PRAC. LAW. 57, 64 (Apr. 1991).

81. *Drug Free Workplace Conference: Speaker Rebuts Common Drug Testing Myths and Severely Criticizes Hair Testing*, 2 THE FORENSIC DRUG ABUSE ADVISOR 1, 2 (Dec. 1990); Bost, *Analysis of Hair for Drugs of Abuse*, 20 ACADEMY NEWS 1, 9 (Sept. 1990) ("Several have assumed that drug molecules will be stationary within the hair shaft once they enter the shaft, but no one has substantiated this assumption. No adequate procedure for interlaboratory comparison or proficiency specimen studies has yet been devised ...."); Poppe, *Martinez Pushed Backers' Unproven Drug-Test Technique*, LEGAL TIMES, Dec. 10, 1990, p. 2, 18 ("In June, the National Institute on Drug Abuse and the Food and Drug Administration pronounced hair testing unreliable and said that more studies were needed before regulators would approve the drug-testing method"); Smith & Kidwell, *A Discussion of Opiate Concentrations in Hair*, 39 J. FORENSIC SCI. 301 (1994) (in a previous article, other authors "acknowledge[d] that drugs in sweat, perspiration, or urine can be incorporated in hair. Yet, in the same article they describe forensic applications where their hair testing has determined chronic drug use. If drug (or metabolite) associated with sweat, perspiration, or urine can irreversibly contaminate hair, it remains to be shown how acute drug exposure would be distinguished from chronic use").

82. Needleman, *Further Discussion of "Hair Analysis for Drugs of Abuse,"* 36 J. FORENSIC SCI. 629 (1991) ("the very core of the scientific method is hidden behind the veil of 'proprietary secret'"); Sauls, *Discussion of "Hair Analysis for Drugs of Abuse,"* 35 J. FORENSIC SCI. 778 (1990)

Enzyme Multiplied Immunoassay Technique (EMIT)

EMIT is analogous to RIA. Syva Corporation in Palo Alto, California, has made EMIT equipment available throughout the United States.

The primary difference between RIA and EMIT is the use of a different label. In RIA, the known drug or antigen is labeled with a radioactive isotope. In contrast, in the EMIT procedure, the label is an enzyme, often lysozyme. The urine sample, antibody, and labeled drug are placed in a bacterial cell wall suspension. Lysozyme serves as a catalyst for the hydrolysis or decomposition of the bacterial cell wall suspension. Thus, in its free state, lysozyme would tend to clear the suspension. However, when it is bound, the lysozyme is rendered inactive; and no hydrolysis occurs. The analyst can detect whether and how much hydrolysis has taken place. A spectrophotometer may be used for this purpose. The spectrophotometer measures whether the suspension absorbs the energy generated by the spectrophotometer. The presence of the unlabeled drug or antigen determines whether the lysozyme is free to trigger the hydrolysis. The hydrolysis determines whether the bacterial cell wall suspension clears. Finally, the density of the suspension determines whether and how much energy is absorbed.[83]

There are several advantages to EMIT. By way of example, unlike RIA, EMIT does not require a discrete separation step, thereby eliminating one possible source of human error in the procedure.

However, the risk of false positives is even greater with EMIT than it is with RIA.[84] Many substances include natural lysozyme; that is, lysozyme may be

---

(it is "awkward to argue that the method has achieved a general acceptance within the relevant scientific community when that community has been denied an opportunity to examine it in detail").

83. Lorenzo, *supra* note 76, at 401. Baker, Murphy, Shepp, Royo, Caldarone, Escoto & Salamone, *Evaluation of the Abuscreen Online Assay for Amphetamines on the Hitachi 737: Comparison with EMIT and GC/MS Methods*, 40 J. FORENSIC SCI. 108 (1995); Armbruster, Schwarzhoff, Pierce & Hubster, *Method Comparison of EMIT II and OnLine with RIA for Drug Screening*, 38 J. FORENSIC SCI. 1326 (1993); Smith, *A Discussion of "Method Comparison of EMIT II and OnLine with RIA for Drug Screening,"* 39 J. FORENSIC SCI. 909 (1994); Poklis, Fitzgerald, Hall & Saady, *EMIT) d.a.u. Monoclonal Amphetamine/Methamphetamine Assay. II. Detection of Methylenedioxyamphetamine (MDA) and Methylenedioxymethamphetamine (MDMA)*, 59 FORENSIC SCI. INT'L 63 (1993); Poklis, Hall, Eddleton, Fitzgerald, Saady & Bogema, *EMIT) d.a.u. Monoclonal Amphetamine/Methamphetamine Assay. I. Stereoselectivity and Clinical Evaluation*, 59 FORENSIC SCI. INT'L 49 (1993); Vidal, Ting, Perez, Taylor & Le, *Robotic Method for the Analysis of Morphine and Codeine in Urine*, 37 J. FORENSIC SCI. 1283 (1992).

84. Eichorst, *Phenethylamine Causes False Positive Amphetamines in Post Mortem Specimens When Tested by Syva EMIT*, 50 FORENSIC SCI. INT'L 139 (1991); Allen, *Side Effects*, CAL. LAW., Oct. 1985, at 21 ("The error rate ... can go up to 25 percent"); K. ZEESE, DRUG TESTING LEGAL MANUAL D2-1 through -3 (1994) lists generic lawful drugs and the illicit drugs they are sometimes mistakenly identified as in an EMIT test: ibuprofen — marijuana; fenoprofen — marijuana, amphetamines, barbiturates, benzodiazepines, and methaqualone; naproxen — marijuana;

"exogenous" to the substance. The presence of the natural enzyme may lead to a positive finding.[85] Leading analytical toxicologists recommend that positive RIA and EMIT findings be confirmed by other procedures.[86] Even a confirmatory test result can be misleading if the analyst cannot differentiate exogenously produced lysozyme.

§ 23-2(F). Ultraviolet Spectrophotometry (UV).

The next few subsections discuss several types of spectrophotometry. All the various species of spectrophotometry are based upon features of the electromagnetic spectrum, set out in Figure 23-7. Different types of energy along the spectrum have varying effects on matter. The identification and measurement of those effects are the bases for ultraviolet (UV) and infrared (IR) spectrophotometry and nuclear magnetic resonance (NMR).

Although it is seldom used today, at one time ultraviolet spectrophotometry was the most commonly used type of spectrophotometry. In one survey, 90% of the laboratories reporting responded that they have ultraviolet equipment.[87] This finding is hardly surprising. Ultraviolet equipment is less expensive and complicated than some other spectrophotometric instruments, and the technique is sensitive and nondestructive. The technique's nondestructive character made it an ideal initial test in criminal cases. Since it does not consume or destroy the sample analyzed, the sample can be made available to the defendant and retests can be conducted.

Stated in nanometers, the UV spectrum runs from 10 to 400 nm. Many commercial UV spectrophotometers use only the 200-350 nm portion of the spectrum. When UV energy of a particular wavelength strikes the unknown sample, the energy induces a chemical change or electronic transition. If the amount of energy exactly equals the difference between the ground (lower or normal) and excited (higher) energy level of the molecule's electrons, the UV energy will be absorbed. The electrons are promoted to the higher energy level,

---

ephedrine — amphetamines; phenylopromanolamine — morphine; and dextromethorphan — heroin, opiates, and morphine.

85. Lorenzo, *supra* note 76, at 400.

86. *Id.* at 404. *See also* Gjerde, *Screening for Cannabinoids in Blood Using EMIT: Concentrations of Delta-9-Tetrahydrocannabinol in Relation to EMIT Results*, 50 FORENSIC SCI. INT'L 121 (1991) ("A high EMIT result gave a high probability of finding a high THC concentration in the subsequent confirmation analysis"); Frederick, Green & Fowler, *Comparison of Six Cannabinoid Metabolite Assays*, 9 J. ANAL. TOX. 116 (May/June 1985); Visher & McFadden, *A Comparison of Urinalysis Technologies for Drug Testing in Criminal Justice*, NATIONAL INSTITUTE OF JUSTICE RESEARCH IN ACTION 1, 5 (June 1991) ("Confirmation of initial immunoassay positives by an alternate method–preferably GC or GC/MS–is recommended by the NIDA guidelines.... [C]onfirmation by GC/MS provides the best protection....").

87.. Watkins & Watkins, *Identification of Substances by Instrumental Analysis*, 22 AM. JUR. PROOF OF FACTS 385, 451.

resulting in a reorganization of the electrons in the molecule. Thus, the molecule's structure determines the wavelengths of UV energy that the molecule can absorb. The molecule's UV absorption is an indicator of the identity of the molecule.

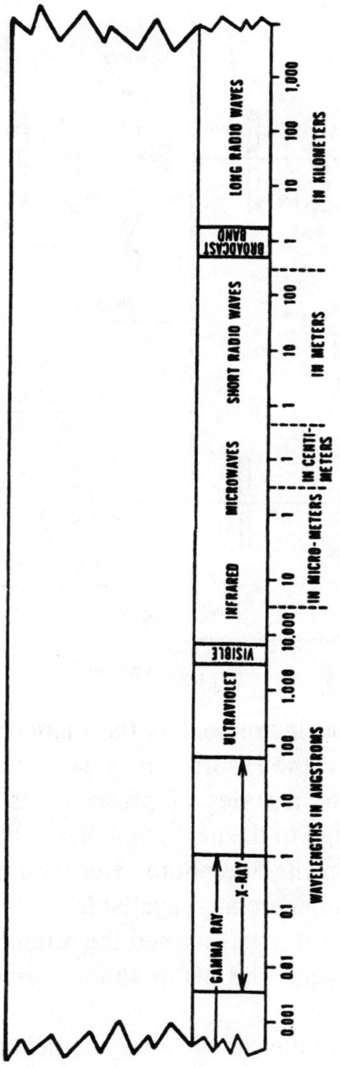

Figure 23-7: [88]

88. Watkins & Watkins, *supra* note 87 at 424-25 (1969); Potsch & Moeller, *On Pathways for Small Molecules Into and Out of Human Hair Fibers*, 41 J. FORENSIC SCI. 121, 122 (1996) (a Perkin Elmer Lambda-5 UV/VIS spectrophotometer). Reprinted with permission.

Figure 23-8 depicts a typical UV spectrophotometer.

The instrument has five basic components. The first is a radiation source. The source could be a hydrogen discharge tube or a tungsten incandescent lamp·

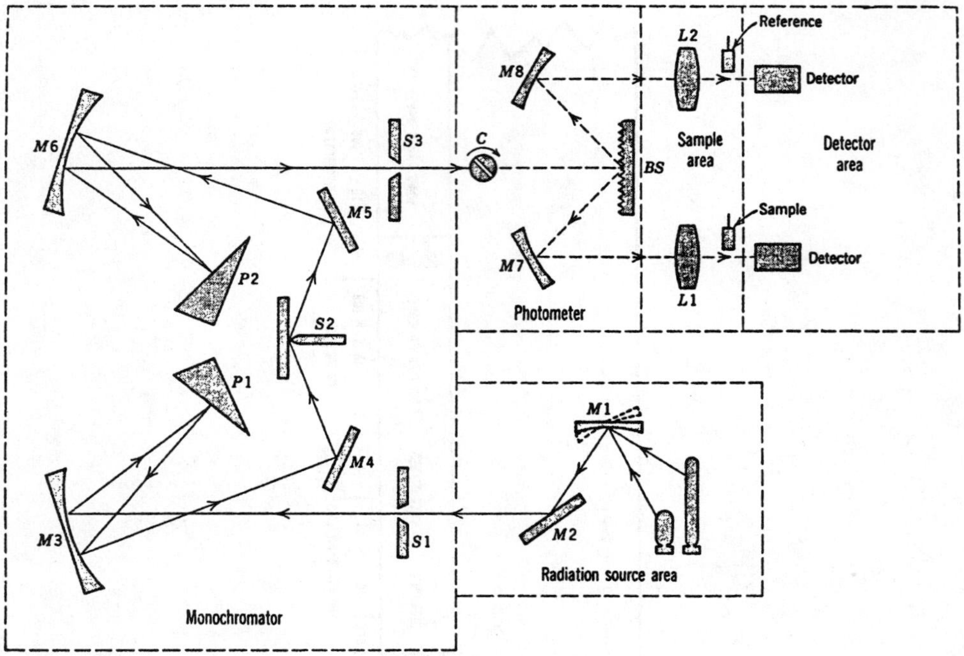

Figure 23-8[89]

The next element of the instrument is the monochromator. This component disperses the light from the source into separate UV wavelengths. The monochromator consists of a series of prisms, slits, and grates. It sends one wavelength at a time through to the next component, the photometer.

In the older UV instruments, the photometer's purpose was to split the beam into two beams. Most commercially available UV spectrophotometers had a double beam design. One beam was termed the reference beam while the second was called the sample beam. The beam splitter aimed the two beams at two different targets.

The targets are located in the sample area, the next to last component of a UV spectrophotometer. The sample is the unknown. The reference is a blank, which should allow all the UV energy to be transmitted through to the last component, the detector.

---

89. *Figure 5*, R. SILVERSTEIN & G. BASSLER, SPECTROMETRIC IDENTIFICATION OF ORGANIC COMPOUNDS (2d ed.). Reprinted by permission of John Wiley & Sons, Inc.

The detector measures the light transmitted through to the detector area. All the light aimed at the reference ought to be transmitted while some energy aimed at the sample will be absorbed. By measuring the amount of energy that was aimed at the sample and transmitted into the detector area, the detector can determine the converse, namely, the amount of UV energy absorbed by the sample. The end product of the instrument is a UV spectrum such as Figure 23-9. This spectrum is called an absorption curve and has several features such as peaks (maxima) and minima.

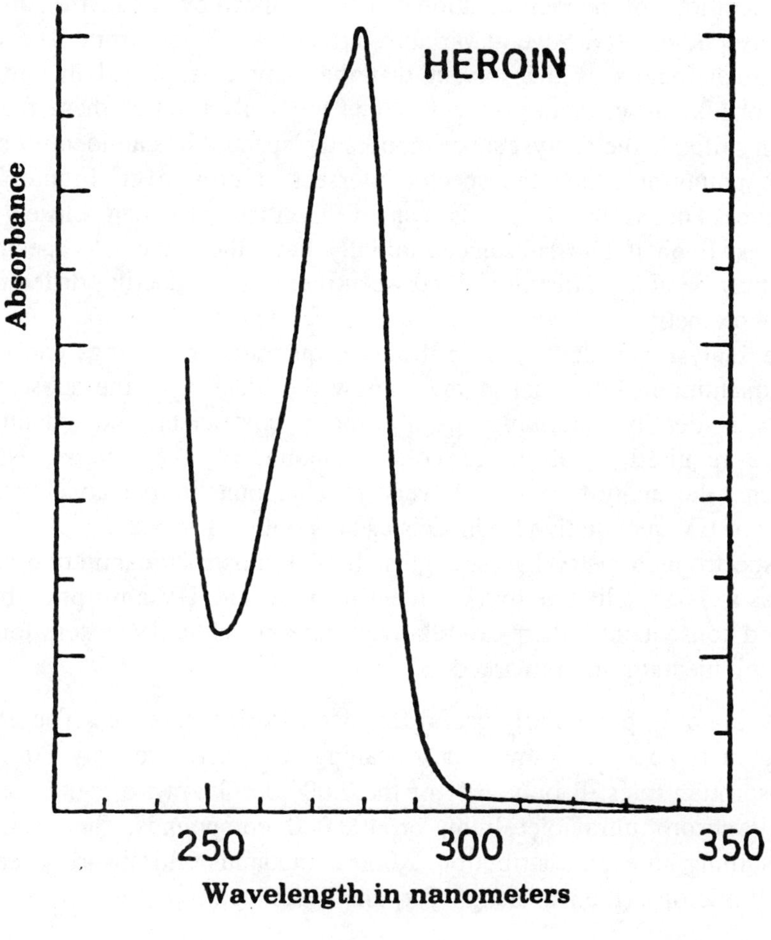

Figure 23-9[90]

90. R. SAFERSTEIN, CRIMINALISTICS: AN INTRODUCTION TO FORENSIC SCIENCE 111 (1981). Reprinted with permission.

The spectrum enables the analyst to make a tentative, qualitative identification of the substances present in the unknown sample relative to a standard. There are numerous compilations of UV spectra that may be used as standards for comparison: the American Petroleum Institute's Ultraviolet Spectral Data, Hershenson's Ultraviolet and Visible Absorption Spectra Index for 1930-45, Kamlet and Ungnade's Organic Electronic Spectral Data, Sadler Research Laboratories' Sadler Ultraviolet Spectra, Friedel and Orchin's Ultraviolet Spectra of Aromatic Compounds, and spectra available from the American Society for Testing Materials in Pennsylvania.

The specificity of the identification can be enhanced by conducting differential UV spectrophotometry. Several variables affect the UV spectrum. The variables include such factors as the solvent that the sample is placed in and the pH (acidity or alkalinity) of the solvent. When the analyst varies these factors, the spectrum shifts. If the analyst superimposes the spectra, he can identify so-called isobestic points at which the spectra intersect or cross-over. Figure 23-10 is illustrative. The isobestic points can differentiate between closely related substances. Even if two substances initially have the same UV spectrum, the analyst may be able to distinguish between them by conducting differential UV spectrophotometry.

If the analyst can identify the substance, quantitative findings can be made. Before quantitating, the analyst must know the identity of the substance. The substance's identity determines its absorption coefficient: the amount of the substance required to absorb a certain amount of UV energy. Using the coefficient, the analyst can reach very reliable quantitative conclusions. The accuracy of UV quantitative findings is usually within 1 to 3%.

UV spectrophotometry has strengths. It is a superior quantitative assay. Its weakness is as a qualitative tool for identification. The UV absorption bands are wide; and consequently there are relatively few possible UV absorption values. As one commentator has remarked:

> UV is not ... particularly useful for identification purposes. The entire UV region is about 200 nm wide, meaning that there are only 200 possible absorption rates. If only 20% of the 2,000,000 known organic compounds will absorb ultraviolet light, or 400,000 compounds, then statistically, assuming an even distribution, 2,000 compounds will absorb at about 258 millimicrons, (the wavelength for) amphetamine....[91]

A UV spectrum lacks the fine detail found in IR and NMR spectra. Even if differential spectrophotometry is conducted, the analyst can usually identify only the substance's functional group, not its precise composition.

---

91. R. SHAPIRO & J. ACKERMAN, *supra* note 40, at 5.

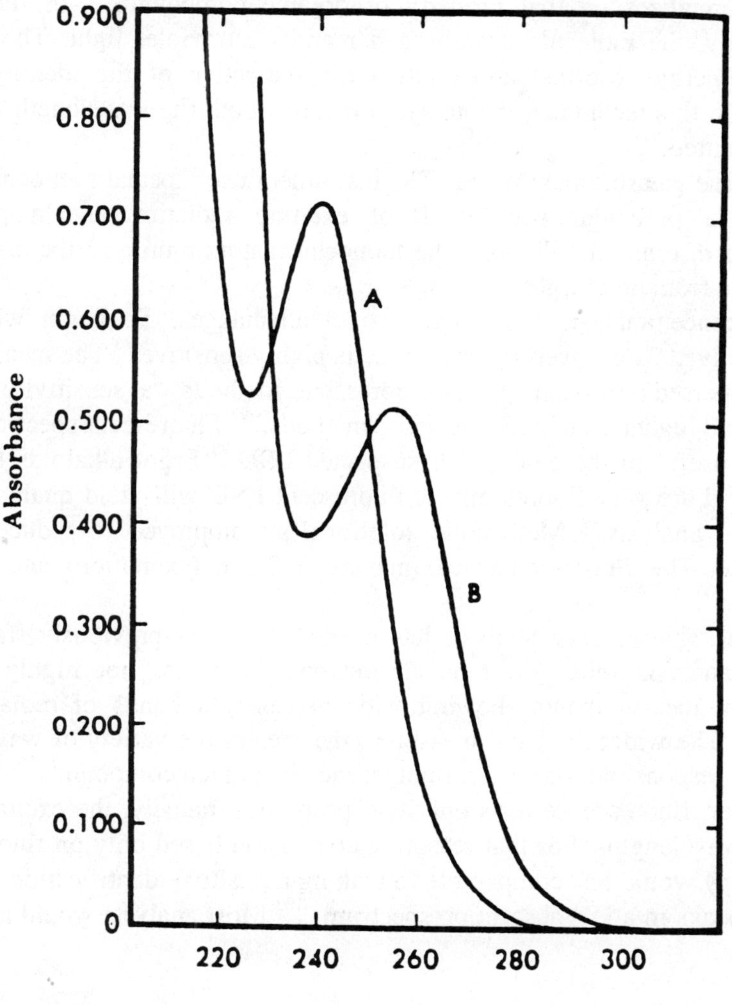

Figure 23-10[92]

§ 23-2(G). Fluorescence Analysis.

After absorbing radiant energy from an external source, some organic compounds emit energy of a different wavelength or frequency. Fluorescence

92. Poklis, *Forensic Toxicology, in* INTRODUCTION TO FORENSIC SCIENCE (W. Eckert, ed. 1980). Reprinted with permission.

analysis capitalizes on that property of organic compounds.[93] In fluorescent spectroscopy, the molecule absorbs and reemits ultraviolet light. The specific levels of energy absorbed and emitted are indicative of the identity of the molecule. In this technique, the analyst measures both the wavelength absorbed and that emitted.[94]

How is the measurement made? The instrument uses special monochromators to isolate a particular wavelength of exciting radiation and a particular wavelength of emitted radiation. The monochromators minimize the problem of interference from other light sources.

Fluorescence analysis has some distinct advantages. To begin with, it is nondestructive.[95] Moreover, the technique is highly sensitive.[96] The measurement of the dispersed emissions gives fluorescent methods "a sensitivity often a thousandfold higher than visible and UV methods."[97] Fluorescent spectroscopy is especially useful in the analysis of suspected LSD.[98] Ergot alkaloids based on lysergic acid are very fluorescent. A fluorescent LSD will yield qualitative and quantitative analysis.[99] Methanolic solutions are employed to reduce Raman interference. The fluorescence maxima are 320 nm (excitation) and 400 nm (emission).[100]

However, fluorescence analysis has it limitations. As previously stated, this mode of analysis relies on monochromators. They are not highly precise, resulting in measurements showing wide wavelength bands of radiation and emission. "The wider the band measured, the greater the variety of wavelengths potentially responsible for the . . . fluorescence in a given compounds . . . ."[101]

Moreover, fluorescence tests only two properties, namely, the excitation and emission wavelengths. For that reason, a conclusion based only on fluorescence spectroscopy would be "comparable to making a positive identification based on only two peaks in a UV absorption spectrum."[102] Most analysts would agree that

---

93. Stein, Laessig & Indriksons, *An Evaluation of Drug Testing Procedures Used by Forensic Laboratories and the Qualifications of Their Analysis*, 1973 WIS. L. REV. 727, 758-59.

94. *Id.* at 759.

95. Siegel, *Forensic Identification of Controlled Substances, in* 2 FORENSIC SCIENCE HANDBOOK 107 (R. Saferstein, ed. 1988).

96. *Id.*

97. Stein, Laessig & Indriksons, *An Evaluation of Drug Testing Procedures and the Qualifications of Their Analysis*, 1973 WIS. L. REV. 727, 759.

98. Siegel, *Forensic Identification of Controlled Substances, in* 2 *Forensic Sciences Handbook* 107 (R. Saferstein, ed. 1988).

99. *Id.*

100. *Id.*

101. Stein, Laessig & Indriksons, *An Evaluation of Drug Testing Procedures and the Qualifications of Their Analysts*, 1973 WIS. L. REV. 727, 759.

102. *Id.*

that basis "is not sufficient for a reliable identification of a compound."[103] Consequently, fluorescence should "be relied upon only to corroborate data produced by other more specific identification methods" such as infrared spectrophotometry.[104] Another limitation is that only a relatively few organic compounds undergo fluorescence. Hence, it is not applicable to all drugs.

§ 23-3. Specific Tests.

The tests mentioned in the last section are subject to a fairly large number of false positive results.[105] For that reason, they are "nonspecific tests." These tests are often used as preliminary, screening procedures before confirmation or positive identification by one or more of the tests discussed in this section.[106] These tests are described as "specific" procedures because they are subject to few, if any, false positive results.

§ 23-3(A). Infrared Spectrophotometry (IR).

Infrared spectrophotometry is akin to ultraviolet spectrophotometry. Both techniques are based on principles of the electromagnetic spectrum. As Figure 23-7 demonstrates, the infrared and ultraviolet spectra bracket the visible light spectrum; they are on opposite sides of the spectrum. There are numerous wavelengths in the infrared spectrum. Most organic chemists work with the part of the spectrum between 4,000 cm-1 and 666 cm-1. However, there has been increasing use of the near infrared region (16,668-4,000 cm-1) and the far infrared region (700-200 cm-1).

As noted in the last subsection, the identity of a substance determines the discrete amount of UV light that the substance will absorb before making an electronic transition. IR spectrophotometry rests on similar principles. However, in the case of IR spectrophotometry, the substance absorbs a photon of light. The effect of the absorption is to change the vibrations within the molecule. The

---

103. *Id.*

104. *Id.*

105. Hansen, Caudill & Boone, *Crisis in Drug Testing: Results of CDC Blind Study*, 253 JAMA 2382 (1985).

106. American Fed'n of Gov't Emps. v. Skinner, 885 F.2d 884, 888 (D.C. Cir. 1989) ("the Department considers a test result positive for proscribed drugs only if it is positive on each of two separate tests, an initial test using immunoassay methods and a confirmatory test using ... GC/MS ... techniques"), *cert. denied*, 495 U.S. 923 (1990); American Fed'n of Gov't Emps., Local 1533 v. Cheney, 754 F. Supp. 1409 (N.D. Cal. 1990) ("All urine samples will be initially screened using the Radio-Immuno-Assay ('RIA') technique. If this test is positive for the presence of drugs, a more accurate gas chromatography/mass spectometry ('GC/MS') confirmatory test will be performed. HHS Guideline § 2.4(g)(2)"), *aff'd*, 944 F.2d 503 (9th Cir. 1991); National Treas. Emps. Union v. Lyng, 706 F. Supp. 934, 937-38 (D.D.C. 1988) ("All specimens identified as positive on the initial test shall be confirmed using the ... GC/MS ... technique ....").

energy of the radiation absorbed equals the difference between two vibrational states. The phenomenon is quantized; the substance absorbs a discrete amount of energy before moving into a new vibrational state.

Figure 23-11 is a schematic diagram of an infrared spectrophotometer:

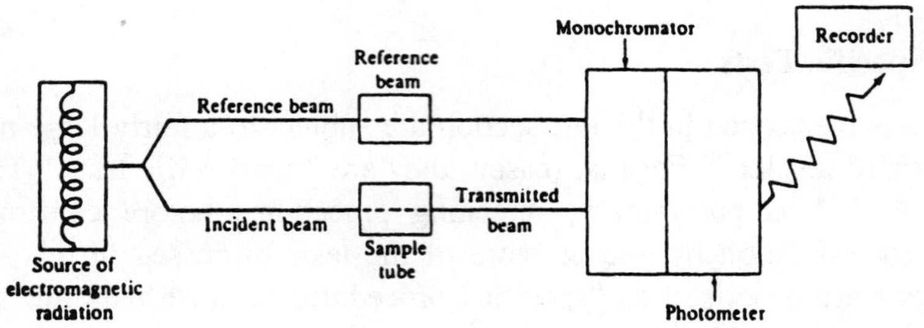

Figure 23-11[107]

The first component, shown on the left-hand side of the diagram, is a source of electromagnetic radiation. The source is usually a Nernst glower, a Globar, or an incandescent wire. The source is the origin of the radiation energy aimed at the sample to be analyzed.

Like the UV spectrophotometers previously discussed, many older IR spectrophotometers used a double beam design. (Today the vast majority of IR instruments in laboratories are based on Fourier Transform technology[108] and have a single beam.) As Figure 23-11 shows, a traditional spectrophotometer split the beam from the source into two beams: the reference beam and the incident beam. The entire reference beam was transmitted through to the photometer. That beam should register 100% transmission. However, the incident beam was aimed at the tube containing the sample. The sample's identity determined how much radiation energy is absorbed by the sample and, conversely, how much energy is transmitted through to the photometer. The monochromator utilized a system of slits, grates, and prisms to permit one wavelength of IR energy at a time to pass through to the photometer. The photometer served as a detector. Most photometers used thermal or heat detectors (thermocouples, bolometers, or Golay cells) to compare the intensities of the reference and incident beams. The recorder finally converts the photometer's measurements into a visual display.

The end product of the IR spectrophotometer is an IR spectrum such as Figure 23-12:

107. *Figure 9.1*, N. ALLINGER, M. CAVA, D. DEJONGH, C. JOHNSON, N. LEBEL & C. STEVENS, ORGANIC CHEMISTRY, Worth Publishers, Inc., New York, New York, 1976. With permission.

108. *See* § 25-4.

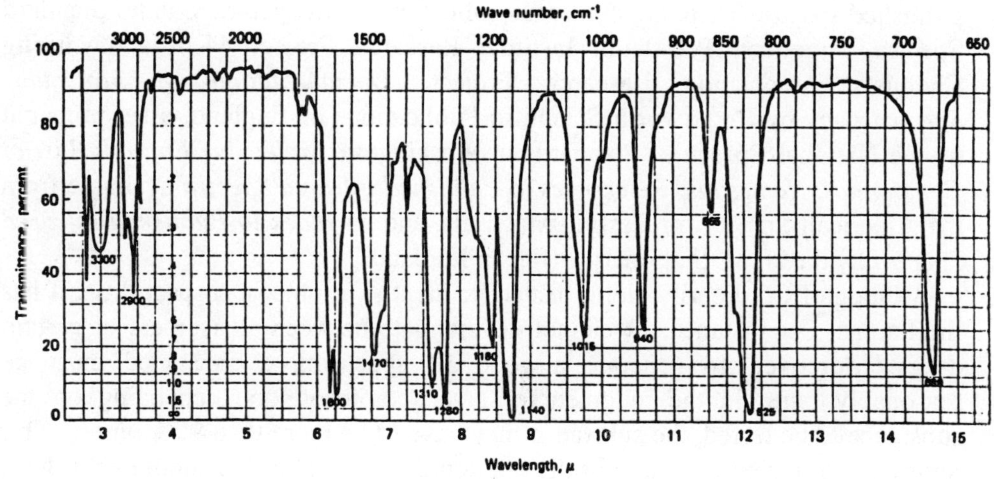

Figure 23-12[109]

Although UV spectrophotometers register the amount of energy absorbed at particular wavelengths, most IR spectrophotometers can register the amount of energy transmitted and absorbed. Figure 23-12 is illustrative. The vertical axis records transmission while the horizontal records the wavelength. This spectrum lends itself to both qualitative and quantitative analysis.

IR is a superior technique for qualitative analysis. Some commentators refer to a molecule's IR spectrum as its fingerprint. For many substances, IR analysis yields a positive, unequivocal, and unmistakable identification. Even some of the harshest critics of drug identification evidence concede the specificity of IR analysis.[110] IR analysis is so powerful in part because of the complexity of the spectrum. The IR region has a wide range of bands arising from complex, interacting vibrations within the molecule. The IR spectrum usually includes between 25 and 75 peaks, and the analyst makes a peak-by-peak comparison with

---

109. CATALOG OF SELECTED ULTRAVIOLET SPECTRAL DATA, THERMODYNAMICS RESEARCH CENTER DATA PROJECT, Thermodynamics Research Center, Texas A & M University, College Station, Texas. Loose-leaf data sheets, extant 1975, with permission.

110. Shapiro, *Chemist in the Courtroom: An Interview with Professor Robert Shapiro About Drugs, Forensic Chemists, and the Law*, 3 NAT'L J. CRIM. DEF. 235, 249 (1977); Levy, Ravreby, Meriovich & Shapira-Heiman, *A Survey and Comparison of Heroin Seizures in Israel During 1992 by Fourier Transform Infrared Spectrometry*, 41 J. FORENSIC SCI. 6 (1996); Lopez-Artiguez, Camean & Repetto, *Unequivocal Identification of Several Common Adulterants and Diluents in Street Samples of Cocaine by Infrared Spectroscopy*, 40 J. FORENSIC SCI. 602 (1995); Lee, *The Identification of Cathinone in Khat (Catha edulis): A Time Study*, 40 J. FORENSIC SCI. 116 (1995). *See also* Suzuki, *Studies on Fentanyl and Related Compounds: II. Spectrometric Discrimination of Five Monomethylated Fentanyl Isomers by Gas Chromatography/Fourier Transform-Infrared Spectrometry*, 43 FORENSIC SCI. INT'L 15 (1989); Raverby & Gorski, *Variations in the Infrared Spectra of Heroin Base*, 34 J. FORENSIC SCI. 918 (1989).

published spectra. There are numerous collections of IR spectra: Sadtler Standard Spectra, American Petroleum Institute Research Project 44, Manufacturing Chemists Association Research Project, *Documentation of Molecular Spectroscopy* by Butterworth Scientific Publications of England, a set prepared by the National Bureau of Standards in Washington, *Molecular Formula List of Compounds, Names and References to Published Infrared Spectra* available from the American Society for Testing Materials, and an *Index to Published Infrared Spectra* by the H. M. Stationary Office in England.[111]

Although IR ordinarily yields a specific identification of a suspect drug, it has limitations. For instance, IR cannot differentiate between all isomers of certain drugs. Moreover, to generate a good IR spectrum, a substance must be reasonably pure. In the judgment of some commentators, depending on the substance to be tested, the substance may have to be more than 90% pure.[112] Our reviewer, Professor Siegel, is of the opinion that the substance should be at least 95% pure. Although samples obtained from pharmaceutical houses are that pure, most street drugs are not.[113] Consequently, the analyst must employ purification procedures such as chromatographic separation before subjecting the substance to IR analysis. Finally, until relatively recently, IR could be used only on large samples.[114] However, a modification of IR, diamond cell IR, is one of several methods which the analyst can use IR to examine much smaller samples.[115] By mounting the sample between a pair of diamonds or sapphires, even a single

---

111. Modernly, most IR spectrometers are controlled by computer. After the instrument produces the infrared pattern, the computer searches a drug reference library stored on one of the computer's drives until it finds a match. The computer might list five or 10 "best matches" and indicate the probability that the unknown is a particular drug. *But see* Shellow, *The Application of Daubert to the Identification of Drugs*, 2 SHEPARD'S EXPERT & SCI. EVID. Q. 593, 600, 621-24, 627 (Wint. 1996) ("spectrometers are now equipped with computerized matching systems. Infrared and mass spectrometers contain algorithms capable of comparing the spectrum of an unknown substance with thousands of spectra in spectrial libraries and then calculating the probability that any given match is correct. However, forensic analysts in crime laboratories typically do not utilize this feature of the instrument, but rely exclusively on their subjective judgment;" "The computer is programmed to generate a list of compounds whose spectra are most similar to that of the suspected drug. The computer will rank order these spectra and attach to each an estimate of the similarity between the spectrum of the suspected drug and the reference standard").

112. Shapiro, *supra* note 110, at 250.

113. *Id.*

114. Midkiff, Washington & Kopec, *Diamond and Sapphire Cell Infrared Spectroscopy — A Powerful New Tool in the Forensic Laboratory*, 7 J. POLICE SCI. & ADMIN. 426 (1979); Pettit & Suzuki, *An Antistatic Device for Use When Sampling with a Diamond Anvil Cell*, 39 J. FORENSIC SCI. 904 (1994).

115. *Id.* at 429-30.

crystal of a drug can be analyzed.[116] With Fourier Transform IR, still smaller samples can be evaluated.[117]

§ 23-3(B). Nuclear Magnetic Resonance (NMR).

Nuclear magnetic resonance (NMR) can also be used in drug analysis. In reality, it is rarely utilized, since only a few laboratories have the necessary instrumentation. Nuclear magnetic resonance shares a common denominator with UV and IR; like those two techniques, NMR is based on the principles of the electromagnetic spectrum. In particular, NMR uses the radio frequency waves to the right of the IR spectrum on Figure 23-7. In NMR, the substance absorbs electromagnetic radiation in the radio frequency region of the spectrum. In the presence of a magnetic field, the nuclei of atoms assume an orientation or spin. For example, they may assume an orientation parallel to the field. However, the absorption of radio frequency waves can cause the nuclei to flip from a low energy, parallel orientation into a high energy, antiparallel orientation. NMR measures the absorptions of radio frequency waves that cause the transitions between orientations or spin states.

Figure 23-13 depicts an NMR instrument.

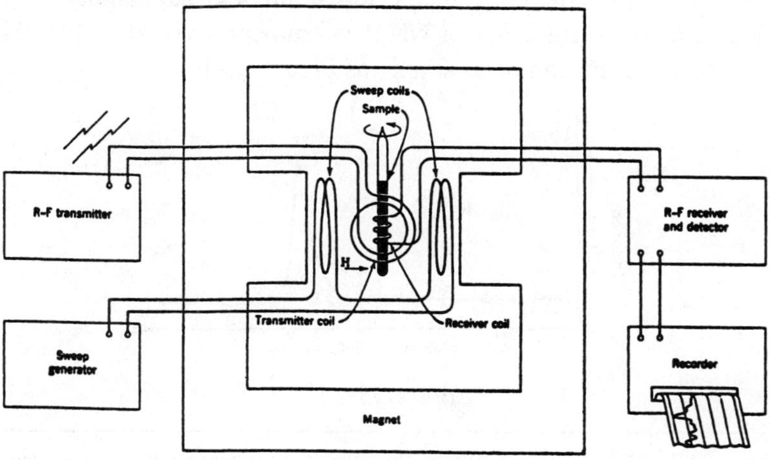

Figure 23-13[118]

116. *Id.* at 429.

117. Kohn & Jeger, *Identification of Drugs by Their Near Infrared Spectra*, 37 J. FORENSIC SCI. 35 (1992); Suzuki, *Fourier Transform Infrared Analyses of Some Particulate Drug Mixtures Using a Diamond Anvil Cell with a Beam Condenser and an Infrared Microscope*, 37 J. FORENSIC SCI. 467 (1992); Minagawa, Suzuki & Suzuki, *Analysis of Benzophenones by Gas Chromatography/Fourier Transform-Infrared Spectrometry*, 51 FORENSIC SCI. INT'L 179 (1991); Harris & Kane, *A Method for Identification of Lysergic Acid Diethylamide (LSD) Using a Microscope Sampling Device with Fourier Transform Infrared (FT/IR) Spectroscopy*, 36 J. FORENSIC SCI. 1186 (1991).

A key NMR component is the magnet surrounding the sample. The magnet generates the magnetic field that the nuclei are oriented towards. The field strength could be set at 1.41 Tesla (T). In that field, protons will precess or move about. The magnetic field is kept homogeneous throughout the test. Although the field is kept homogeneous and uniform around the sample, the field varies during the test. The magnetic field sweep generator increases the field automatically and linearly. The generator does so without causing the field to lose homogeneity.

The next component is the source of the radio frequency energy, namely, the transmitter. The transmitter is a radio frequency oscillator which feeds its signal into a pair of coils mounted at a right angle to the magnetic field. The oscillator's output is kept constant during the test. A fixed oscillator of 60 Megahertz (MHz) is usually employed. 60 MHz is the frequency of energy necessary to cause a precessing proton to jump into the antiparallel direction.

The output is aimed at the unknown sample. The unknown is located in a sampling area in the heart of the NMR apparatus. There is also a radio frequency receiver and detector in the NMR. When the radio frequency waves cause the nuclei in the sampling area to resonate or flip into a new spin state, the nuclei produce a radio frequency signal. The receiver includes a coil that detects this signal. Finally, the recorder converts the signal into a visual display.

Like UV and IR instruments, an NMR instrument's visual display is called a spectrum. The spectrum can be as simple as Figure 23-14:

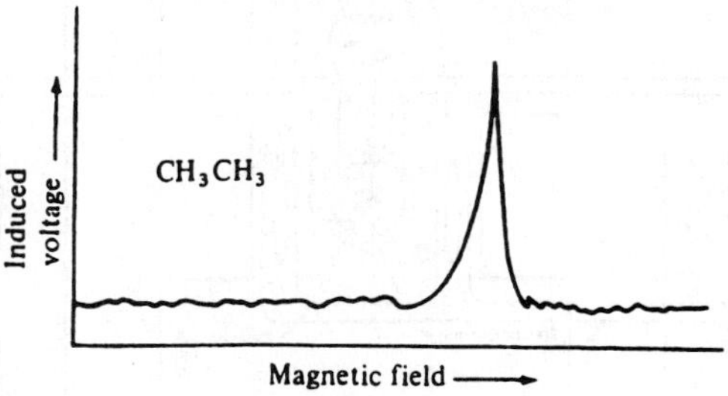

Figure 23-14 [119]

118. *Figure 7-7*, D. SKOOG & D. WEST, PRINCIPLES OF INSTRUMENTAL ANALYSIS. Reprinted with permission of Holt, Rinehart & Winston, Inc.; Cyr, Dawson, By, Neville & Shurvell, *Structural Eludication of Unusual Police Exhibits. II. Identification and Spectral Characterization of N-(2-Hydroxyethyl)amphetamine Hydrochloride*, 41 J. FORENSIC SCI. 608 (1996); Dawson, Black, Lavoie & LeBelle, *Nuclear Magnetic Resonance Identification of the Phenylalklamine Alkaloids of Khat Using a Chiral Solvating Agent*, 39 J. FORENSIC SCI. 1026 (1994); Angelos, Lankin, Meyers & Raney, *The Structural Identification of a Methyl Analog of Methaqualone via 2-Dimensional NMR Techniques*, 38 J. FORENSIC SCI. 455 (1993); Kram & Lurie, *The Determination of Enantiomeric Composition of Methamphetamine by H-NMR Spectroscopy*, 55 FORENSIC SCI. INT'L 131 (1992).

119. *Figure 5.3*, N. ALLINGER, M. CAVA, D. DEJONGH, C. JOHNSON, N. LEBEL & C. STEVENS, ORGANIC CHEMISTRY. Reprinted with permission of Worth Publishers, Inc., New York, New York, 1976.

The horizontal axis plots the magnetic field. As previously stated, the magnetic field (H_o) is slowly increased during the test. The sweep varies the field and is synchronized with the recorder plotting the horizontal axis. The vertical axis measures induced voltage. The induced voltage results from the absorption of radio frequency energy which occurs when the nuclei are excited and flip into a new orientation or spin state.

Although the analyst occasionally uses instruments that produce a spectrum such as Figure 23-14, more sophisticated instruments yield a different, more informative spectrum such as Figure 23-15.

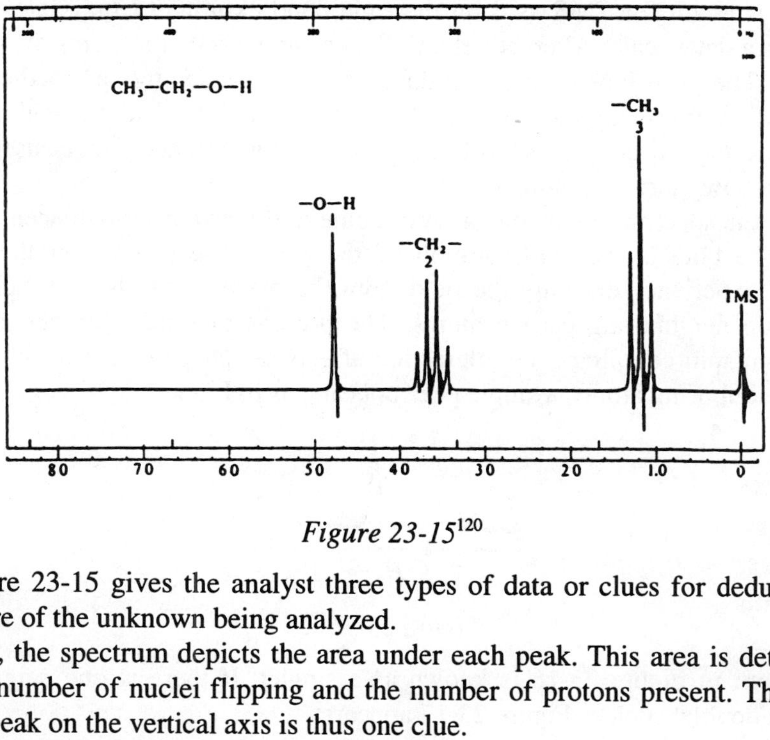

Figure 23-15[120]

Figure 23-15 gives the analyst three types of data or clues for deducing the structure of the unknown being analyzed.

First, the spectrum depicts the area under each peak. This area is determined by the number of nuclei flipping and the number of protons present. The height of the peak on the vertical axis is thus one clue.

Second, the horizontal axis gives the analyst a clue to the number of electrons present. In fact, there are two horizontal axes, one at the top of the spectrum and one at the bottom. The line at the top of the chart depicts the magnetic field. This line corresponds to the horizontal axis on Figure 23-14. The bottom line on Figure 23-15 uses a different unit of measurement.

The magnetic field required to flip the nuclei does not depend solely on the number of protons present. The electrons circulating around the proton generate their own magnetic field. This secondary field is opposed to the external field

---

120. *Figure 5.11*, N. ALLINGER, M. CAVA, D. DEJONGH, C. JOHNSON, N. LEBEL & C. STEVENS, ORGANIC CHEMISTRY. Reprinted with permission of Worth Publishers, Inc., New York, New York, 1976.

applied by the magnet and sweep. To some extent, the secondary field generated by the electrons shields the protons from the primary field applied by the magnet and sweep. Thus, the number of electrons present (the "environment" of the protons) affects the location of the absorption peak along the horizontal axis.

The location of the peak is often measured as a chemical shift on modern instruments. The chemical shift is the difference between the field strength at which the unknown proton absorbs and the field strength at which the protons of a known, TMS, absorb. TMS (tramethylsilane) serves as the standard. The unknown is compared to TMS. As in Figure 23-15, the horizontal axis records the field strength for TMS as 0 on the right-hand extreme of the scale. This is known as a delta scale. Alternatively, the scale can be stated in terms of parts per million. The instrument can produce a ppm scale by a mathematical manipulation, involving the division of the chemical shift. Scales stated in terms of ppm are termed tau scales. Although tau scales were once widely used, delta scales are now more common.

Third, the spectrum gives the analyst a clue to the protons on adjacent carbon atoms. The clue is the configuration of the peak. The protons in the nuclei analyzed experience not only the field from the magnet but also the field from protons on neighboring carbon atoms. The protons interact — a phenomenon called spin-spin coupling. The interaction affects the shape of the peak. If there are no neighboring atoms, a single peak appears, as in Figure 23-16:

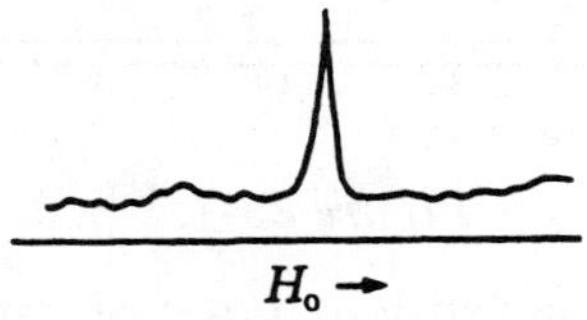

Figure 23-16[121]

The pattern in Figure 23-16 is known as a singlet. If there is one neighboring proton, a doublet such as Figure 23-17 appears:

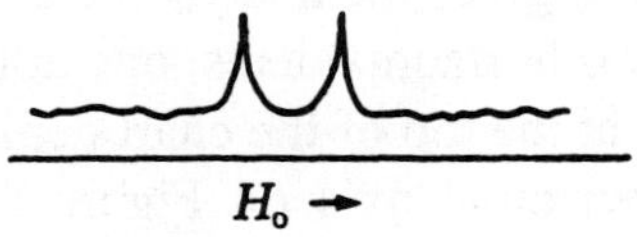

Figure 23-17[122]

---

121. *Figure 5.8*, N. ALLINGER, M. CAVA, D. DEJONGH, C. JOHNSON, N. LEBEL & C. STEVENS, ORGANIC CHEMISTRY. Reprinted with permission of Worth Publishers, Inc., New York, New York, 1976.

122. *Id.* Reprinted with permission.

When there are two neighboring protons, the peak takes the form of a triplet shown in Figure 23-18:

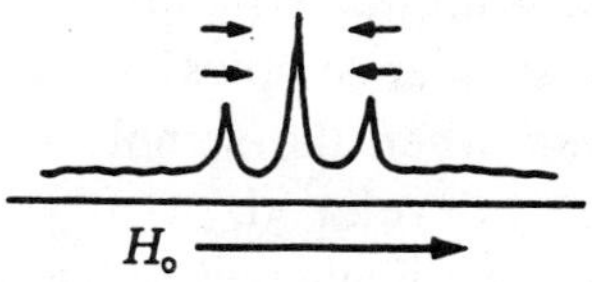

Figure 23-18[123]

The shape of each peak, its "multiplicity," indicates the number of protons on adjacent carbon atoms.

Given the three features of the NMR spectrum, the spectrum can lead to a positive identification of the unknown.[124] An NMR spectrum can even differentiate among isomers of many drugs. The analyst identifies the unknown by comparing the NMR spectrum with published NMR spectra. There are several volumes of published NMR spectra, including compilations by Sadtler and Varian Associates. The NMR technique has another advantage; it is nondestructive.

Although the NMR technique has major strengths, it also has weaknesses. For example, the instrumentation is so sophisticated that it must be meticulously maintained and calibrated. Some instruments need daily or weekly adjustments.[125] Moreover, with the older 60 and 200 mega hertz instruments, the analyst needed relatively large, pure samples to conduct an NMR test. University research laboratories often have expensive instruments with superconducting electromagnets; and those instruments can analyze samples in the one microgram

---

123. *Id.* at Figure 5.9. Reprinted with permission.

124. Avdovich, Lebelle, Savard & Wilson, *Nuclear Magnetic Resonance Identification and Estimation of Solvent Residues in Cocaine*, 49 Forensic Sci Int'l 225 (1991); Brewster & Davis, *Appearance of Aminorex as a Designer Analog of Methylaminorex*, 36 J. FORENSIC SCI. 587 (1991); Angelos, Janovsky & Raney, *The Identification and Quantitation of Pharmaceutical Preparations by Nuclear Magnetic Resonance Spectroscopy*, 36 J. FORENSIC SCI. 358 (1991); Casale, *Detection of Psuedoecogonine and Differentiation from Ecgonine in Illicit Cocaine*, 47 FORENSIC SCI. INT'L 277 (1990); Cantrell, John, Johnson & Allen, *A Study of Impurities Found in Methamphetamine Synthesized from Ephedrine*, 39 FORENSIC SCI. INT'L 39 (1988) (the researchers used two-dimensional NMR to identify peculiar impurities in drug samples to show conspiracy links); Clark, *The Identification of Nitromethaqualone and Its Differentiation from Some Positional Isomers*, 33 J. FORENSIC SCI. 1035 (1988); Hatzis & Rothchild, *Enhanced Quantitative Analytical Capability with a Nuclear Magnetic Resonance (NMR) Spectrometer by Use of an External Integrating Recorder*, 32 J. FORENSIC SCI. 396 (1987); Beazley, *Analytical Characterization of Isoheroin*, 30 J. FORENSIC SCI. 915 (1985); Allen, Cooper & Moore, *1H Nuclear Magnetic Resonance of Heroin's D Ring*, 30 J. FORENSIC SCI. 908 (1985); Harada, Shimizu & Maeiwa, *H-NMR of Human Saliva. An Application of NMR Spectroscopy in Forensic Science*, 34 FORENSIC SCI. INT'L 189 (1987).

125. W. KEMP, ORGANIC SPECTROSCOPY 131 (3d ed. 1991).

range. However, the less expensive instruments sometimes require larger samples of at least ten micrograms. The analyst may have to purify the sample before subjecting it to an NMR test. With modern 300 and 500 mega hertz instruments, however, the analyst can test smaller samples; and the peaks can be so sharp that identification is possible even when the sample is impure. Six hundred mega hertz instruments are now being developed.

Finally, the analyst might have neglected to use a Lanthide Shift Reagent.[126] Two protons can have very similar shifts. Depicted on a normal spectrum, the two peaks may merge and appear as one. However, the addition of a Lanthide Shift Reagent will spread the spectrum out. The use of the reagent makes differentiation possible. Thus, if the analyst relies on a single peak, the attorney should inquire whether used the reagent to determine whether there are indeed two peaks.

§ 23-3(C). Gas Chromatography/Mass Spectrometry (GC/MS).

The previous section devoted to nonspecific tests discussed gas chromatography (GC). A GC is often conjoined with a mass spectrometer (MS) to form a GC/MS.[127] When used in conjunction with an MS, GC is a preparatory

126. *Id.* at 169.

127. Hall, Parikh & Brodbelt, *Aqueous Phase Hexylchloroformate Derivatization and Solid Phase Microextraction: Determination of Benzoylecgonine in Urine by Gas Chromatography-Quadrupole Ion Trap Mass Spectrometry*, 44 J. Forensic Sci. 527 (1999); Deng, Kurosu & Pounder, *Detection of Anabolic Steriods in Head Hair*, 44 J. Forensic Sci. 343 (1999); Cremese, Wu, Cassella, O'Connor, Rymut & Hill, *Improved GC/MS Analysis of Opiates with Use of Oxime-TMS Derivatives*, 43 J. Forensic Sci. 1220 (1998); Garside, Ropero-Miller, Goldberger, Hamilton & Maples, *Identification of Cocaine Analytesin Fingernail and Toenail Specimens*, 43 J. Forensic Sci. 974 (1998); Dasgupta, Hart, Humphrey & Blackwell, *Gas Chromatography-Electron Ionization and Chemical Ionization Mass Spectrometric Analysis of Urinary Phenmetrazine After Derivatization with 4-Carbethoxyhexafluorobutyryl Chloride — a New Derivative*, 43 J. Forensic Sci. 636 (1998); Dasgupta, Handler & Nine, *A Convenient Derivatization Method for Gas Chromatography/Mass Spectrometric Determination of Phenmetrazine in Urine Using 2,2,2-Trichloroethyl Chloroformate*, 43 J. Forensic Sci. 630 (1998); Negrusz, Perry & Moore, *Detection of Cocaine on Various Denominations of United States Currency*, 43 J. Forensic Sci. 626 (1998); Gan, Baugh, Liu & Walia, *Simultaneous Analysis of Amphetamine, Methamphetamine, and 3,4-Methylenedioxymethamphetamine (MDMA) in Urine Samples by Solid-Phase Extraction, Derivatization, and Gas Chromatography/Mass Spectrometry*, 36 J. Forensic Sci. 1331 (1991); Gjerde, Fongen, Gundersen & Christophersen, *Evaluation of a Method for Simultaneous Quantification of Codeine, Ethylmorphine and Morphine in Blood*, 51 Forensic Sci. Int'l 105 (1991); Gaillard & Pepin, *Evidence of Polydrug Use Using Hair Analysis: A Fatal Case Involving Heroin, Cocaine, Cannabis, Chloroform, Thiopental and Ketamine*, 43 J. Forensic Sci. 435 (1998); Casale, Moore & Odeneal, *Comparative Determination of 2-Carbo-methoxy-3-Alkyloxy-and Heteroaroyloxy-Substituted Tropanes in Illicit South American Cocaine Using Capillary Gas Chromatography-Single Ion Monitoring*, 43 J. Forensic Sci. 125 (1998); Crouch, Cheever, Andrenyak, Kuntz & Loughmiller, *A Comparison of ONTRAK TESTCUP, Abuscreen ONTRAK, Abuscreen ONLINE, and GC/MS Urinalysis Test Results*, 43 J. Forensic Sci. 35 (1998);

Meatherall, *GC/MS Confirmation of Barbiturates in Blood and Urine*, 42 J. FORENSIC SCI. 1160 (1997); Musshoff, Daldrup & Ritsch, *Black Market in Anabolic Steroids —Analysis of Illegally Distributed Products*, 42 J. FORENSIC SCI. 1119 (1997); Hart & Dasgupta, *A Novel Derivatization of Phenol after Extraction from Human Serum Using Perfluorooctanoyl Chloride for Gas Chromatography-Mass Spectrometric Confirmation and Quantification*, 42 J. FORENSIC SCI. 693 (1997); Dasgupta & Mahle, *Determination of Phenmetrazine in Urine by Gas Chromatography-Mass Spectrometry after Liquid-Liquid Extraction and Derivatization with Perfluoroooctanoyl Chloride*, 42 J. FORENSIC SCI. 937 (1997); Smith, *Identification of Butyl Cannabinoids in Marijuana*, 42 J. FORENSIC SCI. 610 (1997); Kintz, Tracqui & Mangin, *Sweat Testing for Benzodiazepines*, 41 J. FORENSIC SCI. 851 (1996); Conn, Dawson, Baker, Keegan & Fryirs, *Identification of N-Acetylmethamphetamine in a Sample of Illicitly Synthesized Methamphetamine*, 41 J. FORENSIC SCI. 645 (1996); Moore, Daniel, Fierro, Mozayani & Poklis, *The Detection of a Metabolite of a Benzyl-N-Methylphenethylamine Synthesis in a Mixed Drug Fatality Involving Methamphetamine*, 41 J. FORENSIC SCI. 524 (1996); Dasgupta, Mahle & McLemore, *Elimination of Fluconazole Interference in Gas Chromatography/Mass Spectrometric Confirmation of Benzoylecgonine, the Major Metabolite of Cocaine Using Pentafluoropropionyl Derivative*, 41 J. FORENSIC SCI. 511 (1996); Pelders & Ros, *Poppy Seeds: Differences in Morphine and Codeine Content and Variation in Inter- and Intra-Individual Excretion*, 41 J. FORENSIC SCI. 209 (1996); Jonsson, Kronstrand & Hatanpaa, *A Convenient Derivation Method for the Determination of Amphetamine and Related Drugs in Urine*, 41 J. FORENSIC SCI. 148 (1996); Skopp, Potsch & Aderjan, *Experimental Investigations on Hair Fibers as Diffusion Bridges and Opiates as Solutes in Solution*, 41 J. FORENSIC SCI. 117 (1996); Kintz & Mangin, *Simultaneous Determination of Opiates, Cocaine and Major Metabolites of Cocaine in Human Hair by Gas Chromatography/Mass Spectrometry (GC/MS)*, 73 FORENSIC SCI. INT'L 93 (1995); Kintz, Cirimele & Mangin, *Testing Human Hair for Cannabis II. Identification of THC-COOH by GC-MS-NCI As a Unique Proof*, 40 J. FORENSIC SCI. 619 (1995); Andrews, *Ephedra's Role As a Precursor in the Clandestine Manufacture of Methamphetamine*, 40 J. FORENSIC SCI. 551 (1995); Kumar & Kiser, *Identification and Quantitation of Norcocaine in Illicit Cocaine Samples*, 40 J. FORENSIC SCI. 464 (1995); Couper, McIntyre & Drummer, *Detection of Antidepressant and Antipsychotic Drugs in Postmortem Human Scalp Hair*, 40 J. FORENSIC SCI. 87 (1995); Tracqui, Kintz, Ludes, Jamey & Mangin, *The Detection of Opiate Drugs in Nontraditional Specimens (Clothing): A Report of Ten Cases*, 40 J. FORENSIC SCI. 263 (1995); Romberg & Past, *Reanalysis of Forensic Urine Specimens Containing Benzoylecgonine and THC-COOH*, 39 J. FORENSIC SCI. 479 (1994); Liu, McKeehan, Edwards, Foster, Bensley, Langner & Walia, *Improved Gas Chromatography/Mass Spectrometry Analysis of Barbiturates in Urine Using Centrifuge-Based Solid-Phase Extraction, Methylation, with d5-Pentobarbital as Internal Standard*, 39 J. FORENSIC SCI. 1504 (1994); Gerlits, *GC/MS Quantitation of Benzoylecgonine Following Liquid-Liquid Extraction of Urine*, 38 J. FORENSIC SCI. 1210 (1993); Gibb, Cockerham, Goldfogel, Lawson & Raisys, *Substance Abuse Testing of Urine by GC/MS in Scanning Mode Evaluated by Proficiency Studies, TLC/GC, and EMIT*, 38 J. FORENSIC SCI. 124 (1993); Moeller, Doerr & Warth, *Simultaneous Quantitation of Delta-9-tetrahydro-cannabinol (THC) and 11-Nor-9-carboxy-delta-9-tetrahydrocannabinol (THC-COOH) in Serum by GC/MS Using Deuterated Internal Standards and Its Application to a Smoking Study and Forensic Cases*, 37 J. FORENSIC SCI. 969 (1992); Chiarotti, Fucci & Fernari, *Comparative Analysis of Illicit Heroin Samples*, 50 FORENSIC SCI. INT'L 47 (1991); Janzen, *Ethylbenzoylecgonine: A Novel Component in Illicit Cocaine*, 36 J. FORENSIC SCI. 1224 (1991). This discussion of GC/MS is based in part on Bleser & Imwinkelried, *Gas Chromatography/Mass Spectrometry (GC/MS)*, THE CHAMPION, Nov. 1983, at 6. Reprinted with permission of the National Association of Criminal Defense Lawyers.

step to the MS analysis. MS can specifically identify the components of a sample mixture.[128] However, the components must be in pure form. GC can be employed to purify and separate components. The sample components emerging from the GC column may be fed directly into the MS. However, because MS does not require as large a sample as GC, a stream splitter is typically employed. In the older instruments, as each component emerged from the GC column, the stream was split. Half the stream entered the GC detector while the other half entered the MS. In most modern instruments, there is only an MS detector.

MS identifies the components that the GC has separated by measuring the mass of the component compound and its fragments. MS is a specific identification test because when a molecule of pure substance fragments, the resulting fragmentation pattern is peculiar to the compound. By studying the fragmentation pattern, the component elements of the sample can be positively identified. To effect the fragmentation, the MS relies on: (1) an ion source or ionization chamber, (2) an analyzer tube and magnet, (3) a detector, and (4) a recorder.

The stream splitter feeds the sample into the ionization chamber of the MS. When the compound enters the chamber, it is bombarded by an electron beam. When bombarded, the compound is ionized and acquires a positive charge. The ionization is accompanied by a fission or partial fragmentation of the compound. Every compound breaks apart in a unique, individual manner. The resulting array of fragments or "pieces" is termed the compound's fragmentation pattern.

The MS then forces the ionized sample and its fragments into the analyzer tube and magnet region. The analyzer tube is a curved metal, magnetic field. As the sample and its fragments pass through the tube, they separate according to their masses. The separation occurs because the radius of a fragment's path or trajectory through the curved tube depends upon its mass. Larger fragments are

---

128. The United States Supreme Court has stated that "the combination of EMIT and GC/MS tests ... is highly accurate ...." National Treas. Emps. Union v. Von Raab, 489 U.S. 656, 673 n.2 (1989); Buchan, Walsh & Leaverton, *Evaluation of the Accuracy of On-Site Multi-Analyte Drug Testing Devices in the Determination of the Prevalence of Illicit Drugs in Drivers*, 43 J. FORENSIC SCI. 395, 397 (1998) ("the 'Gold Standard'"). *See also* Taylor v. O'Grady, 888 F.2d 1189, 1192 n.4 (7th Cir. 1989) ("GC/MS ... is probably the most accurate of the urinalysis tests; surveys have rated it as nearly infallible"); Tanks v. Greater Cleveland Reg'l Transit Auth., 739 F. Supp. 1113, 1116 (N.D. Ohio 1990) (the GC/MS "test ... provides a 'fingerprint' of the molecular structure of the metabolites ...."), *aff'd*, 930 F.2d 475 (6th Cir. 1991); Baugh, Liu & Walia, *Simultaneous Gas Chromatography/Mass Spectrometry Assay of Methadone and 2-Ethyl-1,5-Dimethyl-3,3-Diphenylpyrrolidine (EDP) in Urine*, 36 J. FORENSIC SCI. 548 (1991) ("gas chromatography/mass spectrometry (GC/MS) procedures are considered the most reliable and are the preferred confirmatory method"); Riley, *Toward a Drug Free Military*, 5 CRIM. JUST. 10, 12 (Winter 1991) ("GC/MS is the drug test of choice or the 'gold standard' in urinalysis"); Martin, *Why Not Understand Drug Testing?*, 23 NEW ENG. L. REV. 651, 655 (1988-89) ("The 'gold standard' in analytical chemistry is ... GC-MS ....").

less affected by the magnetic force. Thus, the smaller the fragment, the more deflected the ion will be by the magnet, and the more curved the path the ion will take through the analyzer tube.

As each fragment emerges from the analyzer tube, it enters the detector. When the fragment strikes the detector, it loses the charge it acquired while passing through the ion beam. The loss of the charge causes a current to activate the recorder. The record produces a spectrum such as Figure 23-19.

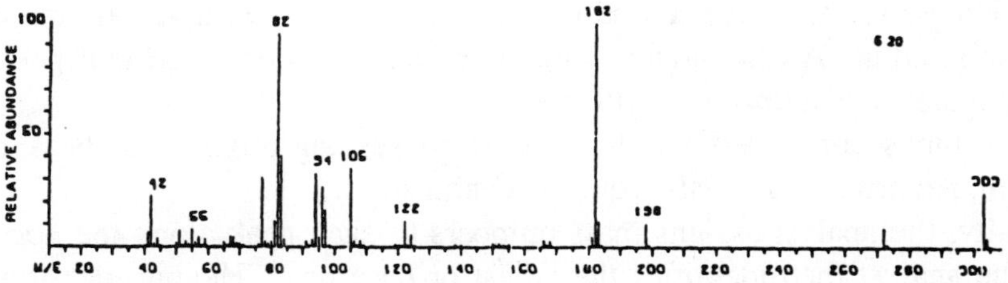

Figure 23-19[129]

As in the case of a GC chromatogram, to understand an MS spectrum, we must appreciate the significance of the horizontal and vertical axes. The horizontal axis is the mass/charge (m/c). If the fragment has lost two electrons, its m/c will be one half of its mass. This axis is unmarked. The analyst must assign numbers to each peak on the spectrum. The analyst typically starts at the left, low mass end of the spectrum and counts the peaks to the right until he reaches the last recorded peak. Some detector/recorder systems mark a faint ion current at each mass unit. That mark helps the analyst assign numbers to the peaks along the horizontal axis.

The vertical axis indicates the intensity or concentration of each peak. The tallest peak is called the base peak and is assigned an intensity value of 100%. All other peaks are compared to that peak. In the final interpretation of the spectrum, the analyst must account for every peak with 3% or greater intensity. The other critical peak is the "parent". The parent peak is the unfragmented ion. If present, it will yield the molecular weight of the drug.

---

129. Bleser & Imwinkelried, *supra* note 43, at 9. Reprinted with permission of the National Association of Criminal Defense Lawyers. *See also* Nakahara, Takahashi, Shimamine & Takeda, *Hair Analysis for Drug Abuse: 1. Determination of Methamphetamine and Amphetamine in Hair by Stable Isotope Dilution Gas Chromatography/Mass Spectrometry Method*, 36 J. FORENSIC SCI. 70 (1991); Clatworthy, Oon, Smith & Whitehouse, *Gas Chromatographic-Mass Spectrometric Confirmation of Radioimmunoassay Results for Cannabinoids in Blood and Urine*, 46 FORENSIC SCI. INT'L 219 (1990); Nakahara, Takahashi, Takeda, Konuma, Fukui & Tokui, *Hair Analysis for Drug Abuse, Part II. Hair Analysis for Monitoring of Methamphetamine Abuse by Istope Dilution Gas Chromatography/Mass Spectrometry*, 46 FORENSIC SCI. INT'L 243 (1990).

The most crucial task in GC/MS analysis is the interpretation of the mass spectrum. The spectrum is a visual display of the sample's fragmentation pattern. The pattern is unique to the compound. If the analyst properly interprets the spectrum, he should be able to positively identify the compound. There are two methods of interpreting the spectrum.

One method is to compare the spectrum with commercially prepared tables. The tables illustrate the spectrum for each compound. The analyst can juxtapose the spectrum and the table to determine whether the fragmentation patterns match. Unless the spectrum and table are of the same size, a visual comparison can be misleading. A comparison is likely to be much more reliable if performed by a computer with a library of MS spectra.

Under the second method, the analyst makes an original analysis of the spectrum. An original analysis requires several steps.

Initially, the analyst assigns mass numbers to each peak along the horizontal axis. The analyst then identifies the tallest or base peak. Having identified that peak, the analyst assigns it an intensity value of 100% and compares it with all the other peaks recorded on the spectrum. As previously styated, some authorities assert that the final analysis must account for every peak with an intensity value of 3% or greater.

In the "full spectrum" or "full scan" mode of analysis, the analyst considers all the peaks on the spectrum.[130] However, there is another mode; "[a]lternatively, the GC/MS can be operated in the selected ion monitoring mode in which the mass spectrometer monitors the ion currents at only a few masses which are characteristic of a specific drug. This mode of operation affords far higher sensitivity, but provides a less specific pattern for identification."[131] This alternative mode is sometimes termed selective ion monitoring (SIM).[132] When a

---

130. Hawks, *Analytical Methodology*, *in* NIDA RESEARCH MONOGRAPH 73: URINE TESTING FOR DRUGS OF ABUSE 30, 35 (1986).

131. *Id*; Robein, *Marshalling Expert Testimony Against Drug Testing*, 35 PRAC. LAW. 79, 81 (Sept. 1989) ("Arguably, there are notable differences in the degrees of reliability between the results of less expensive ... GC/MS ... techniques that monitor one or more mass ions and forensic identification analyses using full mass spectra. *See* A. McBay, Cost Effective, Forensic Quality Testing (unpublished paper delivered to the Drug Policy Foundation, Washington, D.C., May 7, 1988)"); McKay & Mason, *Forensic Science Identification of Drugs of Abuse*, 34 J. FORENSIC SCI. 1471 (1989) ("The use of a full-spectrum GC/MS method should make the results admissible under the *Frye* Standard and the Federal Rules of Evidence, whereas ion monitoring methods could be challenged effectively").

132. Hawks, *supra* note 130. *See also* Casale, Moore & Odeneal, *Comparative Determination of 2-Carbo-methoxy-3-Alkyloxy- and Heteroaroyloxy-Substituted Tropanes in Illicit South American Cocaine Using Capillary Gas Chromatography-Single Ion Monitoring*, 43 J. FORENSIC SCI. 125 (1998); Ishikawa, Suzuki & Hattori, *Positive- and Negative-Ion Mass Spectrometry and Rapid Clean-Up of 19 Phenothiazines*, 44 FORENSIC SCI. INT'L 93 (1990) (SIM); Ho, Liu, Nichols & Kumar, *Isotopic Analog as the Internal Standard for Quantitative Determination: Evaluation of

laboratory relies on SIM, the laboratory scans for only selected ions. The laboratory does so on the assumption that that set of ions is characteristic of the drug in question. Of course, that assumption represents a scientific hypothesis. Consequently, under *Daubert*,[133] the laboratory should be required to provide data empirically validating that hypothesis.

Next, the parent peak is identified. The parent peak is the peak with the highest mass number and indicates the total mass or weight of the unknown compound. Identifying the parent peak is critical because all the compound's fragments must fit into the molecular weight indicated by the parent peak.

At this point, if the analyst has properly assigned mass numbers to the peaks and correctly identified the parent peak, the base peak, and every peak with 3% or greater intensity, the analyst has all the pieces of a jigsaw puzzle. The parent peak tells the analyst the total molecular weight that all the fragments must fit into, and the analyst knows the mass number of each individual fragment that must be accounted for. However, even at this point, like a jigsaw puzzle, the spectrum is not self-explanatory. After tabulating all this data, the analyst must further interpret the spectrum. To identify the compound, the analyst must know not only its composition but also its structure. Most illegal substances are not straight chain compounds. To identify the compound, the analyst must apply molecular structure and bonding theory. There are norms such as the nitrogen rule and the ring and double bond formula which help determine the structure of the compound fragmented in the MS.

Although GC/MS evidence can be a potent testimony in a drug prosecution, it is not infallible. The instrumentation can malfunction. The injection port septum might be worn. A septum should last between 100 and 200 injections.[134] However, high injection port temperatures can shorten the septum's lifespan. A leaking septum can affect the instrument's sensitivity.[135] In particular, if a portion of the specimen leaks back out of the septum, any quantitation would be erroneous. Further, the analyst must select the correct injection port temperature. The temperature must be high enough to instantly vaporize a liquid specimen.[136] If the temperature is too low, the separation will be poor; and broad spectral peaks might result. If the temperature is too high, the specimen might decompose or change its structure. Most importantly, an analyst must operate the instrumentation and interpret both the GC chromatogram and the MS spectrum. To paraphrase Professor Melvin Lewis, "It is no more correct to say that (GC/MS) detects (cocaine) than to say that a violin produces music.

Mass Spectra of Commonly Abused Drugs and Their Deuterated Analogs, 35 J. FORENSIC SCI. 123 (1990) (SIM).

133. Daubert v. Merrell Dow Pharmaceuticals, Inc., 509 U.S. 579 (1993).

134. G. BENDER, PRINCIPLES OF CHEMICAL INSTRUMENTATION 230 (1987).

135. *Id.*

136. *Id.* at 229.

Unfortunately, ... it is much easier for unsound scientific opinion to appear valid than for the product of an incompetently manipulated violin to sound euphonic."[137] The GC/MS analyst may commit a number of errors that will render the ultimate opinion unsound.[138] Some critical errors are highlighted below.

Interpreting the MS spectrum is like working a jigsaw puzzle. To solve the puzzle, all the right pieces are needed, and they must fit into the puzzle. The jigsaw puzzle analogy helps us to understand many of the potential errors in GC/MS evidence.

First, the analyst may not have all the pieces of the puzzle. Suppose, for example, that some peaks on the chromatogram overlap. Overlapping peaks indicate that several different components eluted simultaneously from the column. Such a chromatogram calls into question the reliability of the MS evidence. MS analysis requires pure samples. The GC purifies the samples by separating components of the mixture in the GC column. If the GC peaks overlap, the separation and purification required for MS analysis have not been attained. If the sample's components have not been completely separated, the mass spectrum will display the fragmentation pattern of two or more compounds. There are several possible causes of lack of separation on the chromatogram. The analyst may have made a poor choice of mobile phase, flow rate, solid support material, or liquid phase. Whatever the cause, when the GC does not separate the sample into its component parts, the sample has not been properly prepared for MS analysis.

Second, the analyst may have the wrong puzzle pieces. In some of the older instruments the original printout of the spectrum was unmarked. The analyst had to assign mass unit numbers to the various peaks. There might not be a peak at every unit; an MS spectrum could have widely spaced peaks and many blanks along the horizontal axis. The blanks heightened the danger that the analyst would miscount and misassign mass unit numbers. The danger was especially acute when the background trace of the electrical current on the spectrum was indistinct. The analyst often used the trace as a guide in counting consecutively along the horizontal axis. If the detector/recorder was of poor quality and produced a faint trace, the chance of error increased.

Third, the analyst may be unable to fit every piece of the puzzle into his proposed solution. The analyst must account for all peaks with 3% or greater

---

137. Lewis, *The Element of Subjectivity in Interpreting Instrumental Test Results*, *in* SCIENTIFIC AND EXPERT EVIDENCE 409, 430 (2d ed. 1981).

138. Hawks, *supra* note 130. To minimize the risk of such errors, the 1988 Ad Hoc Committee on Forensic GC/MS has developed a detailed set of *Recommended Guidelines for Forensic GC/MS Procedures in Toxicology Laboratories Associated with Offices of Medical Examiners and/or Coroners*, 35 J. FORENSIC SCI. 236-42 (1990).

intensity;[139] the analyst must fit each peak of such intensity into the puzzle. If the analyst disregards even one peak, he or she has not solved the puzzle and identified the drug. If the spectrum is of poor quality, it may be difficult to determine the intensity of an indistinct peak. On cross-examination, the defense counsel may be able to force the prosecution expert to admit that it was a judgment call to disregard a particular peak on the spectrum and that the analyst's opinion would be different if he or she had had to fit that peak into the puzzle solution. Selective peak reliance can distort the analyst's ultimate opinion.

Fourth, the analyst may choose the wrong parent peak. There may be a cluster of peaks at the high end (the right side) of the MS spectrum. The last peak is not necessarily the true parent peak. The explanation for this phenomenon is that an isotope of the chemical element may be present — a species of the chemical element with the same atomic number but a different mass number. The analyst must be knowledgeable and skillful enough to differentiate the true parent peak from the parent's isotopic peaks. This differentiation can also be a subtle, judgment call. The analyst's call has a tremendous impact on the final opinion. The parent peak represents the total molecular weight that all the fragments must fit into. If the analyst chooses the wrong parent peak, interpreting the MS spectrum will be like attempting to assemble the puzzle pieces into a different picture.

The complexity of the task of interpreting an MS spectrum has triggered two trends in GC/MS technology. One trend is a movement away from conventional electron impact (EI) GC/MS and toward chemical ionization (CI) MS.[140] In EI GC/MS, the high energy electrons make a direct impact on the sample molecules. EI GC/MS produces very complex spectra.[141] The spectrum may include 50 to 200 peaks or points of comparison. The higher the number of peaks, the greater is the risk of interpretive error; unless the instrument is finely tuned, the spectrum may be difficult for the analyst to interpret. In CI MS, the high energy electrons initially ionize a reagent gas, and in turn the reagent gas ionizes the sample.[142] CI GC/MS produces simpler spectra that are nevertheless sufficient to identify many drugs. An additional advantage of CI MS is that the sample need not be separated

---

139. Our reviewer, Professor Siegel, goes farther and insists that all the peaks should be accounted for.

140. .*E.g.*, Clark, *The Specificity of Electron Impact Mass Spectroscopy for the Identification of N-Ethyl-1-Phenylcyclohexylamine (PCE)*, 32 J. FORENSIC SCI. 917 (1987); Hattori, Suzuki, Sato, Mizutani & Yamada, *Positive- and Negative-Ion Mass Spectrometry of 24 Benzodiazepines*, 35 FORENSIC SCI. INT'L 165 (1987).

141. Saferstein, Chao & Manura, *Identification of Drugs by Chemical Ionization Mass Spectroscopy — Part II*, 19 J. FORENSIC SCI. 463 (1974).

142. *Id.* at 464.

by GC before MS analysis.[143] EI MS can be used only as a confirmatory analysis and must be conjoined with an instrument such as the GC.[144]

Another trend is the use of automated and computerized data systems.[145] The trend is more noticeable in EI GC/MS than in CI MS.[146] Since CI MS spectra are simpler than EI GC/MS spectra, it is feasible to manually search for a matching, published spectrum.[147] The complexity of EI GC/MS spectra makes computerization more imperative.

§ 23-3(D). Mixed Melting Point Test.

Each drug has a characteristic melting point. The analyst can melt the unknown and compare its melting point with the published melting points for known drugs. The melting point is reported as a range such as between 78.1 and 78.6. However, more than one drug can have the same melting point. Consequently, a simple melting point test is nonspecific.

The analyst can attain greater specificity by conducting a mixed melting point test. This test rests on the principle that a compound's melting point is depressed if it is impure. One commentary describes the test in this fashion:

> The mixed melting point test uses this principle by comparing the melting points of three samples: a sample of the unknown, a sample of a known, and a sample of a mixture of equal parts of the unknown and the known materials. Since a specific known sample is required, the test can only be performed after a tentative identification is made. If, for example, the unknown is tentatively identified as pentobarbital, then the melting points of the unknown, a known sample of pentobarbital, and a sample of the mixture of the unknown and pentobarbital samples are experimentally derived. All three samples must melt at the same temperature for a positive identification. If the unknown sample were pentobarbital, all three would have the same melting point. If the unknown were not pentobarbital but had the same melting point as pentobarbital, the known and unknown samples

143. *Id.* at 463, 465.

144. *Id.* at 463.

145. Kelly & Martz, *Accelerant Identification of Fire Debris by Gas Chromatography/Mass Spectrometry Techniques*, 29 J. Forensic Sci. 714 (1984) (minicomputer system); Griesemer, Liu, Budd, Raftogianis & Noguchi, *The Determination of Cocaine and its Major Metabolite, Benzoylecgonine, in Postmortem Fluids and Tissues by Computerized Gas Chromatography/Mass Spectrometry*, 28 J. Forensic Sci. 894 (1983); Liu, Ku, Tsay, Fitzgerald & Kim, *Approaches to Drug Sample Differentiation. III: A Comparative Study of the Use of Chiral and Achiral Capillary Column Gas Chromatography/Mass Spectrometry for the Determination of Methamphetamine Enantiomers and Possible Impurities*, 27 J. Forensic Sci. 39 (1982); Mobarak, Bieniek & Korte, *Some Chromatographic Aspects of Hashish Analysis. II*, 11 Forensic Sci. 189 (1978).

146. Saferstein, Chao & Manura, *supra* note 141, at 465-66.

147. *Id.*

> would obviously melt at the same temperature. However, the mixture of the pentobarbital and the unknown would then most probably melt at a temperature below that of the other two samples tested separately, thus indicating that the unknown was not pentobarbital. In this way, the mixed melting point test minimizes the possibility of false identification.[148]

Our reviewer, Professor Siegel, points out that in some cases, the mixed melting point is actually higher rather than lower.

This test has numerous advantages. It is inexpensive and easy to perform. Although the test also furnishes good evidence of a drug's identity, the test result is not completely specific.[149] Moreover, the test cannot be used on all drugs. For instance, as a botanical substance, marijuana cannot be tested in this fashion.

§ 23-4. Admissibility of Drug Analysis Evidence.

The past two sections reviewed the specific and nonspecific tests used for drug analysis. Suppose that the proponent wants to use a test result as proof of the identity of a drug.[150] This section documents the extent to which the courts permit these tests to be used in prosecutions if the witness is a qualified expert[151] and the testimony is otherwise unobjectionable.[152]

---

148. Stein, Laessig & Indriksons, *supra* note 13, at 763-64.

149. *Id.*

150. There are other permissible uses of references to a drug test. For example, at a suppression hearing the prosecution might proffer testimony about the result of a field test in order to establish the justification for a Fourth Amendment intrusion. If that is the setting and the limited purpose for mentioning the test result, the prosecution will not have to lay a normal *Daubert* foundation. United States v. Klimavicius-Viloria, 144 F.3d 1249 (9th Cir. 1998) ("As to the spray test, there was no need for a Daubert hearing. The government did not use the test as scientific evidence that the vessel contained twelve tons of cocaine but to explain Coast Guard activities").

151. *See* United States v. Paiva, 892 F.2d 148 (1st Cir. 1989) (a police detective was qualified to conduct a field test for cocaine); People v. Crose, 194 Ill. App. 3d 97, 141 Ill. Dec. 56, 550 N.E.2d 1102 (1990) (the witness had a bachelor's degree in biology with a minor in chemistry, belonged to two professional societies, had five years' experience with a police forensic service bureau, and had analyzed controlled substances "several thousand times"); Lester v. State, 82 Md. App. 391, 571 A.2d 897 (1990) (the witness had a college degree in forensic science, more than one-half year of experience as a forensic chemist, and state certification for testing marijuana); People v. Curry, 157 A.D.2d 623, 550 N.Y.S.2d 641 (1990) (the witness was a police chemist who had performed more than 1,200 tests for PCP during 13 years on a police laboratory staff). *But see* People v. Park, 72 Ill. 2d 203, 380 N.E.2d 795 (1978), *discussed in* Nance, *Missing Evidence*, 13 CARDOZO L. REV. 831, 842 (1991).

152. The testimony can raise issues of statistical sampling, discussed in Chapter 15 of this treatise. We shall assume, for example, that the analyst has tested either the entire drug specimen or a representative sample. Random sampling procedures are "universally accepted by the courts and have been upheld under challenge." Frank, Hinkley & Hoffman, *Representative Sampling of Drug Seizures in Multiple Containers*, 36 J. FORENSIC SCI. 350, 350-51 (1991) (collecting the cases);

United States v. Dent, 149 F.3d 180, 191 (3d Cir. 1998) ("(1) proper random selection procedure was employed; (2) the chemical testing method conformed with an accepted methodology; (3) the tested and untested samples were sufficiently similar in physical appearance; and (4) the tested and untested samples were contemporaneously seized at the search scene"); United States v. Fitzgerald, 89 F.3d 218, 223 n.5 (5th Cir.) ("Random sampling is generally accepted as a method of identifying the entire substance whose quantity has been measured."), *cert. denied*, 519 U.S. 987 (1996); United States v. Garcia, 66 F.3d 851, 859 (7th Cir. 1995) (the quantity estimates were "not mathematically precise figures. We have held that relying on such estimates is an appropriate way for the district court to determine the quantity of drugs involved in an offense. United States v. Duarte, 950 F.2d 1255, 1265 (7th Cir. 1991) (as long as 'nebulous eyeballing' is avoided, 'factual determinations under the [Sentencing] Guidelines need not emulate the precision of Newtonian physics')"); People v. Peneda, 32 Cal. App. 4th 1022, 38 Cal. Rptr. 2d 312 (1995) (the court sustained the admission of a probability extrapolation; the jury could determine whether the tested samples were representative); Taylor v. Commonwealth, 984 S.W.2d 482 (Ky. App. 1998) (chemical testing of only six out of 98 seized plants); State v. Robinson, 517 N.W.2d 336 (Minn. 1994) (a chemist's analysis of seven of 13 packets allegedly containing cocaine was insufficient to establish beyond a reasonable doubt that all 13 packets contained crack; the material was contained in individually wrapped plastic packages), *review denied* (May 25, 1995); Azoury, Grader-Sageev & Avraham, *Evaluation of a Sampling Procedure for Heroin Street Doses*, 43 J. FORENSIC SCI. 1203 (1998) (the procedure used by the Analytical Chemistry Laboratory in Israel); Hatcher & Ryan, *Response to Claim of Error by Drug Enforcement Administration (DEA) Chemist in Calculating Quantity of Methadone Synthesized from Precursor Chemicals*, 42 J. FORENSIC SCI. 963 (1997) ("the theoretical yield in the reaction to synthesize methadone using diphenylacetonitrile as a precursor was calculated based on a 100% conversion of the precursor to the final product. To the extent a defendant can present evidence via expert testimony that a particular technique would yield less than 100%, he or she is free to introduce that testimony, and the court will make the ultimate decision whether to sentence based on the Government's 100% yield, the defendant's lesser yield, or on a figure someplace in the middle. *See* United States v. Ramsdale, 61 F.3d 825 (11th Cir. 1995); United States v. Carroll, 6 F.3d 735 (11th Cir. 1993), *cert. denied*, 510 U.S. 1183 (1994). But because we cannot predict the competency of the individual actually engaged in the manufacturing process, we must base our calculation on 100% conversion"); Chow, Lee, Saw, Soon & Ng, *The Homogenization of Illicit Heroin Samples: An Empirical and Statistical Approach*, 38 J. FORENSIC SCI. 885 (1993); Colon, Rodriquez & Diaz, *Representative Sampling of "Street" Drug Exhibits*, 38 J. FORENSIC SCI. 641 (1993); Tzidony & Ravreby, *A Statistical Approach to Drug Sampling: A Case Study*, 37 J. FORENSIC SCI. 1541 (1992) (a method for calculating total weight of a drug present in a population within a given confidence interval); United States v. McCutchen, 992 F.2d 22 (3d Cir. 1993) (a police chemist's extrapolation in order to determine the amount of drugs in a Sentencing Guidelines case); United States v. Uwaeme, 975 F.2d 1016 (4th Cir. 1992) (the expert's determination of the amount of heroin involved was reliable even though the expert did not know the standard deviation of the drug sample tested). *See also* United States v. Smith, 964 F.2d 1221 (D.C. Cir. 1992) (the bases of the witness' testimony satisfied Federal Rule of Evidence 703); People v. Bynum, 257 Ill. App. 3d 502, 629 N.E.2d 724, 196 Ill. Dec. 179 (1994). *But see* State v. Wallace, 80 Haw. 382, 910 P.2d 695 (1996) (the prosecution's showing of the net weight of the cocaine was inadequate because there was no competent evidence of the calibration of the balance). In appropriate circumstances, the testimony can be admitted in hearsay form. United States v. Garnett, 122 F.3d 1016 (11th Cir. 1997) (relying on the business entry hearsay exception codified in Federal Rule of Evidence 803(6)); Minner v. Kerby, 30 F.3d 1311 (10th Cir. 1994) (the notes recorded the results of mechanically objective tests

One technique mentioned in the previous section, nuclear magnetic resonance (NMR), is quite sophisticated and the availability of the instrumentation is so limited that there are no reported criminal cases discussing its admissibility. With that exception, however, evidence of the scientific tests discussed in the last sections is routinely admitted. For example, there is a wealth of case law admitting and considering: morphological tests,[153] color change tests,[154] crystal tests,[155] thin layer chromatography,[156] high pressure liquid chromatography,[157] gas chromatography,[158] radioimmunoassay,[159] EMIT,[160] fluorescein polarization

---

and were prepared contemporaneously); Fischer v. Powers, 957 F.2d 609 (8th Cir. 1992) (the admission of a certified copy of a laboratory report did not violate the defendant's confrontation rights); People v. Parker, 8 Cal. App. 4th 110, 10 Cal. Rptr. 2d 38 (1992) (the official record exception to the hearsay rule). *But see* Kettle v. State, 641 So. 2d 746 (Miss. 1994) (when the state crime laboratory test result is admitted, under the confrontation clause the defendant is entitled to have the analyst testify in person; although the laboratory report may satisfy the requirements of the state's business entry hearsay exception, its admission violated the confrontation clause). *But see* Greenberg, *Are DEA Lab Reports Fraudulent?*, 15 THE CHAMPION 16 (Aug. 1991) (the author makes the controversial charge that "[t]he process ... is statistical quackery").

153. United States v. Arias, 639 F.2d 1183, 1184 n.1 (5th Cir. 1981).

154. United States v. Berkowitz, 662 F.2d 1127, 1131 (5th Cir. 1981); United States v. Wilburn, 549 F.2d 734, 736 (10th Cir. 1977); United States v. Hollman, 541 F.2d 196, 200 (8th Cir. 1976); Rupert v. State, 54 Ala. App. 578, 580, 310 So. 2d 501, 503 (1975); *In re* Robert B., 172 Cal. App. 3d 763, 218 Cal. Rptr. 337 (1985); People v. Flores, 128 Cal. App. 3d 512, 518, 180 Cal. Rptr. 368, 371 (1982); People v. Gomez, 198 Colo. 105, 108, 596 P.2d 1192, 1194 (1979), *cert. denied,* 455 U.S. 943 (1982); People v. Vance, 74 Ill. App. 3d 446, 449, 30 Ill. Dec. 436,438, 393 N.E.2d 91, 93 (1979); People v. Bertram, 45 Ill. App. 3d 70, 72, 3 Ill. Dec. 672, 674, 358 N.E.2d 1357, 1359 (1977); Schmitt v. State, 160 Ind. App. 109, 114, 310 N.E.2d 73, 76 (1974), *cert. denied,* 420 U.S. 929 (1975); State v. Miller, 240 Kan. 733, 732 P.2d 756 (1987); State v. Moore, 47 Ohio App. 2d 181, 185, 1 Ohio Op. 3d 267, _, 353 N.E.2d 866, 871 (1973); State v. Stewart, 56 Wis. 2d 278, 281, 201 N.W.2d 754, 755 (1972); State v. Barnes, 52 Wis. 2d 82, 84, 187 N.W.2d 845, 846 (1971); United States v. Lusk, 21 M.J. 695 (A.C.M.R. 1985).

155. People v. Gomez, 198 Colo. 105, 108, 596 P.2d 1192, 1194 (1979), *cert. denied,* 455 U.S. 943 (1982); State v. Mata, 1 Hawaii App. 31, 613 P.2d 919, 926 (1980); State v. Barnes, 52 Wis. 2d 82, 84, 187 N.W.2d 845, 846 (1971).

156. United States v. Ammar, 714 F.2d 238, 261 (3d Cir. 1983), *cert. denied sub nom.* Stillman v. United States, 464 U.S. 936 (1983); United States v. Vitale, 549 F.2d 71, 73 (8th Cir. 1977); People v. Gomez, 198 Colo. 105, 108, 596 P.2d 1192, 1194 (1979), *cert. denied,* 455 U.S. 943 (1982); People v. Brisco, 78 Ill. App. 3d 282, 284, 33 Ill. Dec. 827, 829, 397 N.E.2d 160, 162 (1979); People v. Vance, 74 Ill. App. 3d 446, 449, 30 Ill. Dec. 436,438, 393 N.E.2d 91, 93 (1979); People v. Bertram, 45 Ill. App. 3d 70, 72, 3 Ill. Dec. 672, 674, 358 N.E.2d 1357, 1359 (1977); State v. Miller, 240 Kan. 733, 732 P.2d 756 (1987); State v. Stewart, 56 Wis. 2d 278, 281, 201 N.W.2d 754, 755 (1972); United States v. Bynum, 3 F.3d 769, 772-73 (4th Cir. 1993), *cert. denied*, 510 U.S. 1132 (1994).

157. United States v. Vitek Supply Corp., 144 F.3d 476, 485 (7th Cir. 1998); Ashland Oil v. Delta Oil Products, 212 U.S.P.Q. 508 (E.D. Wis. 1981), *rev'd*, 685 F.2d 175 (7th Cir. 1982), *cert. denied*, 460 U.S. 1081 (1983).

158. United States v. Ammar, 714 F.2d 238, 261 (3d Cir.), *cert. denied sub nom.* Stillman v. United States, 464 U.S. 936 (1983); United States v. Distler, 671 F.2d 954, 962 (6th Cir. 1981);

United States v. Arias, 639 F.2d 1183, 1184 n.1 (5th Cir. 1981); United States v. Orzechowski, 547 F.2d 978, 981 (7th Cir. 1976), *cert. denied,* 431 U.S. 906 (1977); United States v. Hollman, 541 F.2d 196, 200 (8th Cir. 1976); People v. Brisco, 78 Ill. App. 3d 282, 284, 33 Ill. Dec. 827, 829, 397 N.E.2d 160, 162 (1979); State v. Stewart, 56 Wis. 2d 278, 281, 201 N.W.2d 754, 755 (1972); Model Imperial Supply v. Westwind Cosmetics, 829 F. Supp. 35, 38-40 (E.D.N.Y. 1993). *But see* United States v. Lee, 25 F.3d 997, 999 (11th Cir. 1994) (a remand was necessary; on remand, the trial judge should determine whether gas chromatographic chemiluminescence and ion mobility spectrometry satisfy the *Daubert* test).

159. *In re* Brown, 17 Cal. 4th 873, 876-77 n.12, 952 P.2d 715 n.12, 72 Cal.Rptr. 2d 698, 709 n.12 ("the testimony of both experts in this case demonstrates that . . . the RIA would meet the requisite standard of admissibility"), *cert. denied,* 119 S. Ct. 438 (1998); State v. McDougall, 308 N.C. 1, 301 S.E.2d 308, *cert. denied,* 464 U.S. 865 (1983); United States v. Bush, 44 M.J. 646 (A.F. Ct. Crim. App. 1996), *aff'd,* 47 M.J. 2305 (U.S.C.A.A..F. 1997), *cert. denied,* 118 S. Ct. 1048 (1998); Gropper & Reardon, *Developing Drug Testing by Hair Analysis,* NAT'L INSTIT. OF JUST. J. 8, 10 (Apr. 1993) (in United States v. Medina, 749 F. Supp. 59 (E.D.N.Y. 1990), the court concluded that "radioimmunoassay is an effective and accurate method of detecting the presence of various compounds including narcotics;" in Koch v. Harrah's Club, No. 23740 (9th Dist. Ct., Nev., Sep. 12, 1990), the court upheld the inclusion of RIAH testing in an employee substance abuse policy). *But see* United States v. Nimmer, 43 M.J. 252 (C.A.A.F. 1995) (the defense offered a negative RIA test, confirmed by GC/MS, to rebut the prosecution's allegation of one-time use of cocaine; the court conceded that a negative test would be admissible to disprove chronic cocaine use; however, the court remanded for the lower court to determine under *Daubert* whether there has been sufficient validation of the proposition that a negative test result disproves one-time cocaine use), *rev'g,* 39 M.J. 924 (N.M.C.M.R. 1994).

The Ianus Foundation of Los Angeles states that radioimmunoassay of hair (RIAH) has already been accepted by trial courts. The Foundation's literature reads: "Hair analysis was challenged in the following four cases and succeeded in being admitted as evidence. We have had approximately a dozen cases where it was not challenged and about 30 cases where it was used in preparing the case:

People v. Mart Meiel, Case A804003, Los Angeles Superior Court 1985
People v. Robert Korner, Case 154558, Santa Barbara Superior Court 1985
United States v. James Boyle II, CR 85981R, United States District Court
Alaska v. Richard Gene Madjic, 3K081-367R, 3rd Judicial District at Kokiak, May 1982.

The New York Appellate Division has affirmed a lower court order that a party in a custody dispute submit to an RIAH test. Burgel v. Burgel, 141 A.D.2d 215, 533 N.Y.S.2d 735 (1988). However, the court emphasized that it was not ruling on the ultimate admissibility of the evidence at trial: "The ... concern about the novelty of the test is relevant to admissibility, not to discovery. We express no opinion in regard to whether the test results would be admissible, but leave that issue for trial." *Id.*, 533 N.Y.S.2d at 736-37. In United States v. Medina, 749 F. Supp. 59 (E.D.N.Y. 1990), Judge Jack Weinstein upheld the admission of an RIAH test result in a probation revocation proceeding. *But see* Needleman, *Further Discussion of "Hair Analysis for Drugs of Abuse,"* 36 J. FORENSIC SCI. 629 (1991) (the author describes a court-martial in North Carolina in which the trial judge excluded testimony about the technique); Poppe, *Martinez Pushed Backers' Unproven Drug-Test Technique,* LEGAL TIMES, Dec. 10, 1990, at 2, 18 ("A Nevada judge ruled in September that Psychemedics' test 'has not, at this stage, developed sufficiently to form a basis for termination of current employees").

160. Jones v. United States, 548 A.2d 35 (D.C. App. 1988) (although there was no expert testimony as to the reliability of EMIT tests in the record below, the court relied on decisions from

immunoassay (FPIA),[161] ultraviolet spectrophotometry,[162] infrared spectrophotometry,[163] gas chromatography/mass spectrometry,[164] mass

---

other jurisdictions and expert testimony as to 98% accuracy in the record of a District of Columbia Superior Court trial, United States v. Roy, 111 Daily Wash. L. Rep. 2317 (Nov. 15, 1985)). *See also* Burka v. New York City Transit Auth., 739 F. Supp. 814, 842 (S.D.N.Y. 1990) (quoting an expert affidavit that "its accuracy [is] said to be from 95 to in excess of 98% effective").

161. Koenig v. Vannelli, 971 F.2d 422 n.1 (9th Cir. 1992).

162. Rupert v. State, 54 Ala. App. 578, 310 So. 2d 501, 503 (Ala. Crim. App. 1975); People v. Gomez, 198 Colo. 105, 108, 596 P.2d 1192, 1194 (1979), *cert. denied,* 455 U.S. 943 (1982); State v. Herrera, 365 So. 2d 399, 400 (Fla. App. 1978), *cert. denied,* 373 So. 2d 459 (Fla. 1979); State v. Mata, 1 Hawaii App. 31, 613 P.2d 919, 927 (1980); People v. Gustowski, 102 Ill. App. 3d 750, 752, 430 N.E.2d 317, 318 (1981); People v. Ayala, 96 Ill. App. 3d 880, 881, 52 Ill. Dec. 446, 447, 422 N.E.2d 127, 128 (1981); People v. Brisco, 78 Ill. App. 3d 282, 284, 33 Ill. Dec. 827, 829, 397 N.E.2d 160, 162 (1979); Schmitt v. State, 160 Ind. App. 109, 114, 310 N.E.2d 73, 76 (1974), *cert. denied,* 420 U.S. 929 (1975); State v. Bright, 229 Kan. 185, 186, 623 P.2d 917, 919 (1981); State v. Brooks, 217 Kan. 485, 487, 536 P.2d 1365, 1367 (1975); State v. Brodrick, 190 Neb. 19, 20, 205 N.W.2d 660, 661 (1973); State v. Crump, 107 N.H. 62, 63, 217 A.2d 183, 184 (1966); People v. Quackenbush, 44 A.D.2d 736, 354 N.Y.S.2d 458 (1974); State v. Jackson, 280 N.C. 563, 567, 187 S.E.2d 27, 29 (1972); State v. Moore, 47 Ohio App. 2d 181, 185, 1 Ohio Op. 3d 267, _, 353 N.E.2d 866, 872 (1973); State v. Stewart, 56 Wis. 2d 278, 281, 201 N.W.2d 754, 755 (1972); State v. Barnes, 52 Wis. 2d 82, 84, 187 N.W.2d 845, 846 (1971).

163. United States v. Ammar, 714 F.2d 238, 261 (3d Cir. 1983), *cert. denied sub nom.* Stillman v. United States, 464 U.S. 936 (1984); United States v. Arias, 639 F.2d 1183, 1184 n.1 (5th Cir. 1981); United States v. Wilburn, 549 F.2d 734, 736 (10th Cir. 1977); United States v. Vitale, 549 F.2d 71, 73 (8th Cir.), *cert. denied,* 431 U.S. 907 (1977); United States v. Hollman, 541 F.2d 196, 200 (8th Cir. 1976); United States v. Larry, 522 F.2d 264, 266 (10th Cir. 1975); People v. Gustowski, 102 Ill. App. 3d 750, 752, 58 Ill. Dec. 375, 376, 430 N.E.2d 317, 318 (1981); People v. Ayala, 96 Ill. App. 3d 880, 881, 52 Ill. Dec. 446, 447, 422 N.E.2d 127, 128 (1981); People v. Otten, 91 Ill. App. 3d 692, 694, 47 Ill. Dec. 106, 108414 N.E.2d 1222, 1224 (1980).

164. National Treas. Emps. Union v. Von Raab, 489 U.S. 656, 673 n.2 (1989) ("the combination of EMIT and GC/MS tests ... is highly accurate"); United States v. Vitek Supply Corp., 144 F.3d 476, 485 (7th Cir. 1998); United States v. Orzechowski, 547 F.2d 978, 981 (7th Cir. 1976), *cert. denied,* 431 U.S. 906 (1977); Burka v. New York City Transit Auth., 739 F. Supp. 814, 831 (S.D.N.Y. 1990) ("in Skinner and Von Raab, ... the ... EMIT plus GC/MS tests were stipulated as producing highly accurate results"); Dimeo v. Griffin, 721 F. Supp. 958, 964 (N.D. Ill. 1989) ("GC/MS isolates an individual drug or metabolite and identifies it by a characteristic fragmentation pattern similar to a fingerprint"), *aff'd,* 924 F.2d 664 (7th Cir.), *vacated,* 931 F.2d 1215 (7th Cir.), *rev'd,* 943 F.2d 679 (7th Cir. 1991); Edwards v. United States, 483 A.2d 682 (D.C. 1984); People v. Brisco, 78 Ill. App. 3d 282, 284, 33 Ill. Dec. 827, 829, 397 N.E.2d 160, 162 (1979); State v. Lawson, 393 So. 2d 1260, 1265 (La. 1981); State v. Price, 731 S.W.2d 287 (Mo. App. 1987) ("The reported decisions and authorities confirm that the mass spectrometry and gas chromatography technique is an extremely reliable specific test for the measurement, separation, and identification of particular organic compounds;" the opinion collects the authorities); State v. Smith, 656 S.W.2d 297 (Mo. App. 1983); State v. Cannady, 660 S.W.2d 33, 35 (Mo. App. 1983); Jones v. State, 716 S.W.2d 142 (Tex. App. 1986) (GC/MS satisfies the *Frye* test); Koenig v. Vannelli, 971 F.2d 422 n.2 (9th Cir. 1992).

spectrometry,[165] and the polarimeter technique.[166] Many tests are so well accepted that the court will judicially notice the validity of the test.[167]

We shall examine the admissibility of drug tests on four different assumptions: (1) The courts conclude that the *Frye* test, discussed in Chapter 1, is no longer good law, adopt the *Daubert* standard, but require only that the proponent validate the test as a tool for identifying the drug in question; (2) the courts adopt the *Daubert* test but insist that the proponent validate the test as, standing alone, sufficient to identify the drug in question; (3) the courts continue to enforce *Frye* and interpret *Frye* as demanding proof that drug tests are generally accepted in the scientific community as fact-finding techniques; and (4) the courts not only continue to adhere to *Frye* but also construe *Frye* as necessitating proof that drug tests are generally accepted as identification techniques rather than merely as helpful fact-finding tools.

On the first assumption, drug test results would be readily admissible. Numerous experts have already written and would testify that in their opinion, these tests have been empirically validated as helpful in determining whether a substance is a contraband drug.[168] Such testimony would satisfy the *Daubert* standard discussed in Chapter 1.[169] *Daubert* requires empirical validation, but there is a wealth of research available to the proponent of the various drug identification tests.

On the second assumption, it might prove difficult to justify admitting evidence about nonspecific tests. To be sure, there is broad language in some opinions suggesting that to be admissible, a scientific opinion must be sufficient to sustain the finding of fact in question.[170] However, that reading of *Daubert* is unsound. In *Daubert*, Justice Blackmun carefully distinguished admissibility from legal sufficiency. An item of scientific testimony can be relevant and

---

165. United States v. Vitek Supply Corp., 144 F.3d 476, 485 (7th Cir. 1998); United States v. Bush, 47 M.J. 305 (U.S.C.A.A.F. 1997), *cert. denied*, 522 U.S. 1114 (1998).

166. United States v. Arias, 639 F.2d 1183, 1184 n.1 (5th Cir. 1981).

167. Davis, *A Quantitative and Descriptive Survey of Evidence Law in the Kansas Appellate Courts*, 37 KAN. L. REV. 715, 771 (1989) (discussing judicial notice of certain marijuana identification tests in State v. Miller, 240 Kan. 733, 732 P.2d 756 (1987)).

168. *See* 3-6 M. HOUTS, R. BASELT & R. CRAVEY, COURTROOM TOXICOLOGY (1983).

169. United States v. $141,770.00 in U.S. Currency, 157 F.3d 600, 605 (8th Cir. 1998) (the applicability of the Daubert test); United States v. Vitek Supply Corp., 144 F.3d 476, 485 (7th Cir. 1998) (the court states that the fourier transform infrared spectrometry, gas chromatography/mass spectrometry, high performance liquid chromatography, and electrospray liquid chromatography tandem mass spectrometry tests "are widely used and generally accepted in the fields of analytical and forensic chemistry;" the court added that the use of blanks and spiked samples "may be an appropriate means of ensuring both reliability and accuracy").

170. *See* the discussion of Daubert v. Merrell Dow Pharmaceuticals, Inc., 43 F.3d 1311 (9th Cir.), *cert. denied*, 516 U.S. 869 (1995) and Hall v. Baxter Healthcare Corp., 947 F. Supp. 1387 (D. Or. 1996) in Imwinkelried, *Forensic Science: The Second Prong of the Daubert Test: Disturbing Implications of Two Recent Civil Cases*, 33 CRIM. L. BULL. 570 (Nov.-Dec. 1997).

admissible without being legally sufficient to support a judgment. Hence, this reading of *Daubert* would permit the admission of testimony about nonspecific tests so long as they had been empirically validated.

Now turn to the third assumption. If a jurisdiction applies *Frye*, the proponent must demonstrate the general acceptance of the scientific technique. On this assumption, at the very least the prosecutor offering drug test results would have to show that the tests are generally accepted as fact-finding tools. The courts distinguish between the general acceptance of scientific techniques for clinical and investigative purposes. For example, in a leading case applying *Frye*, the California Supreme Court drew that distinction. In *People v. Shirley*[171] the California court analyzed the admissibility of testimony by witnesses with hypnotically enhanced memories. The court acknowledged that hypnosis is widely accepted in medical circles as a therapeutic tool. However, the court stressed that to satisfy *Frye*, a scientific technique must be accepted as a fact-finding tool. The same distinction has been made in a Michigan case, *People v. Gonzales,*[172] and two Minnesota cases, *State v. Saldana*[173] and *State v. McGee.*[174]

The drug tests previously mentioned in this chapter can satisfy these standards.[175] Some texts assert that even nonspecific tests such as GC can provide "prima facie evidence of the identity of a compound."[176] Virtually the entire scientific community attests to the utility of IR and GC/MS as tools for identifying drugs.[177]

However, on the fourth and last assumption, it is doubtful whether the nonspecific test results would be admissible. The fourth assumption is the analogue to the second assumption under *Daubert.* The fourth assumption is that the courts will not only apply *Frye* but enforce an extreme version of *Frye*, namely, a requirement that the scientific technique be accepted as an identification test rather than a screening procedure. A few trial courts have embraced this view and excluded evidence on that ground.[178] One appellate court has similarly excluded EMIT evidence on the ground that EMIT testing for cannabinoids in urine is not generally accepted as reliable in the scientific

---

171. 31 Cal. 3d 18, 723 P.2d 1354, 181 Cal. Rptr. 243 (1982).

172. 415 Mich. 615, 329 N.W.2d 743 (1982).

173. 324 N.W.2d 227 (Minn. 1982).

174. 324 N.W.2d 232 (Minn. 1982).

175. A. DELAAT, PRIMER OF SEROLOGY 108 (1976); H. EISEN, IMMUNOLOGY: AN INTRODUCTION TO MOLECULAR AND CELLULAR PRINCIPLES OF THE IMMUNE RESPONSE 395 (1974); Lorenzo, *Radioimmunoassay (RIA), in* METHODOLOGY FOR ANALYTICAL TOXICOLOGY 404 (I. Sunshine ed. 1975).

176. G. EWING, *supra* note 41, at 364.

177. Stein, Laessig & Indriksons, *supra* note 13, at 727.

178. *E.g.*, Kane v. Fair, 33 Crim. L. Rep. (BNA) 2492 (Mass. 1983) (EMIT test). Comment, 20 WAKE FOREST L. REV. 391 (1984), seems to support this version of the Frye test.

community.[179] If this interpretation of *Frye* were sound, it would be difficult to justify introducing nonspecific test results. One commentator asserts that RIA is so nonspecific that "there is great need to confirm all positive (RIA) results by some other procedure" to adequately identify a drug.[180] Stein, Laessig, and Indriksons state "without qualification that retention times [in GC tests] are not proof of identification unless they are supported by other evidence."[181] They assert that GLC should "not be relied on for identification."[182] It is frequently observed that "chromatography is a means of separation, not of identification."[183] If as a condition precedent to admission the proponent must demonstrate the general acceptance of the technique as an identification test, probably evidence of only specific tests such as IR, GC/MS, and NMR, would be admissible.

However, this interpretation of *Frye* is unsound. The *Shirley, Gonzales, Saldana,* and *McGhee* cases go as far as any appellate courts have gone in extending *Frye*, and even they require only that the proponent show that the scientific technique is generally accepted as a fact-finding tool. These precedents do not demand that the proponent establish that the result of the individual technique be generally accepted as sufficient to prove the fact in issue. This version of *Frye* confuses the tests for admissibility and sufficiency. To sustain a conviction, the prosecutor must show that the cumulative probative value of the prosecution evidence — the combined weight of the prosecution evidence — is sufficient to meet the government's burden of going forward. However, the present focus is the admissibility of an individual item of scientific evidence — not the question whether the defense is entitled to a directed verdict or judgment as a matter of law at the close of the prosecution's case-in-chief.

Unless the courts ultimately adopt this extreme version of *Frye,* even nonspecific test results should be admissible. Experts can truthfully testify that these techniques are helpful fact-finding tools in attempting to identify illicit substances. Thus, unless the drug testing technique is a new one which will have difficulty passing muster under *Frye,*[184] testimony about the technique should be admissible.

---

179. Lahey v. Kelly, 125 A.D. 923, 510 N.Y.S.2d 187, *rev'd*, 71 N.Y.2d 135, 518 N.E.2d 924, 524 N.Y.S.2d 30 (1986).

180. Lorenzo, *supra* note 76, at 404.

181. Stein, Laessig & Indriksons, *supra* note 13, at 752.

182. *Id.* at 753.

183. Kurzman & Fullerton, *Winning Strategies for Defense of Marijuana Cases: Chemical and Botanical Issues*, 1 NAT'L J. CRIM. DEF. 487, 529 (1975).

184. *E.g.*, Semore v. Pool, 217 Cal. App. 3d 1089, 1099 n.7, 266 Cal. Rptr. 280, 287 n.7 (1990) ("At least one court has apparently ruled that a pupillary reaction test is not an accepted test for detecting cocaine usage under ... *Frye* .... (Cocaine-Detection Method Disallowed Under ... *Frye,* Los Angeles Daily Journal, Dec. 15, 1989, at 3.)").

§ 23-5. Legal Sufficiency of Drug Identification Evidence.

Even if all of the drug tests discussed above are admissible, the prosecution may nevertheless suffer a directed verdict. The court may conclude that even considered cumulatively, the individual tests do not have sufficient probative value to establish the identity of the suspected drug. For that reason, the law governing the legal sufficiency of the evidence must be analyzed.*

Typically, courts almost summarily reject attacks on the sufficiency of prosecution drug identification evidence.[185] For example, the courts generally do not even require a scientific analysis of the substance seized from the defendant.[186] There are, however, a few exceptions.[187] For example, a handful of

---

*This discussion is based in part on Imwinkelried, *Jackson v. Virginia: Reopening the Pandora's Box of the Legal Sufficiency of Drug Identification Evidence*, 73 KY. L.J. 1 (1984-85). Reprinted with permission.

185. Annot., 75 A.L.R.3D 717, 721 (1977); United States v. Michael, 788 F. Supp. 1, 3-4 (D.D.C. 1992) (the defendant unsuccessfully argued that the test could not distinguish between cocaine base and cocaine hydrochloride), *rev'd*, 10 F.3d 838 (D.C. Cir. 1993).

186. United States v. Robinson, 144 F.3d 104, 108 (1st Cir. 1998) ("proof based upon scientific analysis or expert testimony is not required to prove the illicit nature of a substance"); United States v. James, 40 F.3d 850, 869 (7th Cir. 1994) ("no chemical testing was performed;" "scientific verification of the identity of the substance is not a prerequisite"), *cert. denied sub nom.* Williams v. United States, 513 U.S. 1132 (1995); Griffin v. Spratt, 969 F.2d 16, 22 (3d Cir. 1992) ("evidence of this nature — *e.g.*, non-scientific evidence indicating that certain substances were illegal drugs — is sufficient to prove guilt beyond a reasonable doubt in a criminal trial"); United States v. Valencia-Lucena, 925 F.2d 506, 512 (1st Cir. 1991) ("proof based upon scientific analysis or expert testimony is not required to prove the illicit nature of a substance"); United States v. Paiva, 892 F.2d 148 (1st Cir. 1989) (the testimony of a knowledgeable lay witness); United States v. McMahon, 861 F.2d 8, 12 (1st Cir. 1988) (collecting cases upholding the legal sufficiency of the evidence absent proof of a laboratory analysis of the drug); United States v. Schrock, 855 F.2d 327, 334 (6th Cir. 1988) ("To our knowledge, no court has held that scientific identification of a substance is an absolute requisite to conviction for a drug-related offense, and we too are unwilling to announce such a rule"); United States v. Pace, 898 F.2d 1218 (7th Cir.), *cert. denied sub nom.* Cialoni v. United States, 497 U.S. 1030 (1990); United States v. Sanchez DeFundora, 893 F.2d 1173, 1175 (10th Cir.) ("The government need not introduce scientific evidence to prove the identity of a substance"), *cert. denied*, 495 U.S. 939 (1990); United States v. Everett, 972 F. Supp. 1313 (D. Nev. 1997) (the Drug Recognition Evaluation (DRE) protocol); United States v. Brazier, 845 F. Supp. 1435 (D. Kan. 1994) (lay opinion testimony about the identity of the substance), *aff'd*, 85 F.3d 641 (10th Cir. 1996); People v. Montiel, 5 Cal. 4th 877, 855 P.2d 1277, 21 Cal. Rptr. 2d 705, 727-28 (1993) (the defendant's own extrajudicial statement), *cert. denied*, 512 U.S. 1253 (1994); Williams v. State, 710 So. 2d 24 (Fla. Dist. Ct. App. 1998) (the Drug Recognition Expert (DRE) protocol); State v. Haller, 363 S.E.2d 719, 724 (W. Va. 1987); Blanchard & Chin, *Identifying the Enemy in the War on Drugs: A Critique of the Developing Rule Permitting Visual Identification of Indescript White Powder in Narcotics Prosecutions*, 47 AMER. U. L. REV. 557, 562-65 (1998) (collecting cases); Note, *The Admissibility of Drug Recognition Expert Testimony in the Prosecution of Individuals Driving Under the Influence of a Controlled Substance: State v. Klawitter, 518 N.W.2d 577 (Minn. 1994)*, 18 HAMLINE L. REV. 261 (1994) (testimony by police officers trained as Drug Recognition Experts (DREs)). *But see* Robinson v. State, 348 Md. 104, 702

courts accepted the species defense in marijuana cases that: Some statutes proscribe only one species of marijuana, Cannabis sativa; there are several species of marijuana; and the tests used by most laboratories cannot differentiate among the species.[188] A somewhat larger number of courts accepted the

---

A.2d 741 (1997) (a police officer's lay opinion based on the substance's appearance was inadmissible; the court asserted that "a lay witness could not rationally identify a substance as crack cocaine based upon visual inspection alone").

187. Annot., 75 A.L.R.3D 717 (1977); United States v. Stone, 139 F.3d 822 (11th Cir.1998) (proof of the identity of the substance as cocaine base is an element of the crime under 21 U.S.C. § 844(a), not merely a sentencing factor; hence, the government must prove the identity of the substance beyond a reasonable doubt); United States v. Fulton, 960 F. Supp. 479 (D. Mass. 1997) (a substance can constitute "crack" for sentencing purposes even if the chemical analysis does not detect any trace of sodium bicarbonate); United States v. Greene, 955 F. Supp. 125, 127 (D.D.C. 1997) ("Any cocaine hydrochloride can be made into cocaine base by neutralizing the acid with something, such as sodium bicarbonate or baking soda."); United States v. Johnson, 976 F. Supp. 284 (D. Del. 1997) (even cumulatively, the defendant's admission that the substance he possessed was "known on the street as 'crack'" and an experienced police officer's testimony that the substance was "crack" were insufficient to meet the government's burden of proving that the substance was "crack" under the Sentencing Guidelines; the defendant cited United States v. James, *infra*), *aff'd*, __F.3d__ (3d Cir. 1999); *A Crack Appears in Crack Sentencing*, 21 SCI. SLEUTHING REV. 11-12 (Fall 1997) ("Perspicacious defense attorneys latched on to [the] dispute between the Sentencing Commission and Congress along with the definition of cocaine base in Guideline 2D1.1 to carry the day in United States v. James, 78 F.3d 851 (3d Cir. 1996). James held that ... the government must prove that crack other than other forms (coca paste, free base cocaine) of cocaine base was involved in a criminal transaction for sentencing to be aggravated.... But what proof must the government produce? Since crack is defined as 'usually prepared' with sodium bicarbonate, then laboratory testing which reveals the presence of sodium bicarbonate together with the presence of cocaine will suffice. (United States v. Culpepper, 916 F. Supp. 1257 (N.D. Ga. 1995) *vacated without opinion, remanded without opinion*, 116 F.3d 1493 (11th Cir. 1997)[, *cert. denied*, 118 S. Ct. 729 (1998)]"). *See also* United States v. Booker, 70 F.3d 488, 489-93 (7th Cir. 1995) ("The scientific evidence ... shows that the terms 'cocaine' and 'cocaine base' refer to the same substance — a base with the [same] chemical formula"; "All forms of freebase cocaine, including crack, have the same chemical formula as cocaine"; "Despite the extensive scientific evidence ... that cocaine and cocaine base are actually the same substance [scientifically], the legislative history of § 841(b) demonstrates that Congress intended the terms to have different meanings"; Congress evidently concluded that in a different form, the drug can be put to more dangerous uses), *cert. denied*, 517 U.S. 1111 (1996); Robinson v. State, 702 A.2d 741 (Md. 1997) (although a police officer could testify that the substance looked like crack cocaine, the judge erred in permitting the expert to opine that the substance was in fact crack cocaine); McBay, *Cocaine Sentencing*, 41 J. FORENSIC SCI. 3 (1996); United States v. Davis, 864 F. Supp. 1303 (N.D. Ga. 1994) (although the pertinent federal sentencing statute sets significantly higher sentences for offenses involving "cocaine base" than for offenses involving the same amount of "cocaine," there is no scientific basis for the distinction); *see also* United States v. Bowen, 127 F.3d 9, 14 (1st Cir. 1997) (conflicting expert testimony as to the characteristics of "hashish oil").

188. G. UELMEN & V. HADDOX, DRUG ABUSE AND THE LAW SOURCEBOOK § 4.6, at 4-31 (1983), citing United States v. Lewallen, 385 F. Supp. 1140 (W.D. Wis. 1974); United States v. Collier, 14 Cr.L. (BNA) 250 (D.C. 1974); United States v. One 1966 Chevrolet Sedan, 14 Cr.L. (BNA) 2387

analogous isomer theory in cocaine cases and required the prosecution to prove the use of a relatively specific test such as the polarimeter.[189] Likewise, there is some authority that the plane polarized light test must be conducted to differentiate between the isomers, d-methamphetamine and d,1-methamphetamine.[190] Moreover, a few jurisdictions adopted a generally skeptical attitude toward prosecution drug identification evidence. In one Washington case, the court rejected a city chemist's opinion identifying a substance as LSD when the opinion rested solely on a modification of the Van Urk color change test.[191] In a Texas case, the court overturned a probation revocation order based on a finding that the probationer possessed heroin.[192] The court acknowledged that the standard for upholding a probation revocation is lower than the threshold for sustaining a conviction.[193] Nevertheless, the court concluded that the prosecution's sole evidence, a Marquis reagent test, was too flimsy to satisfy even that relaxed standard.[194]

(S.D. Fla. 1974). The authors assert that the cited decisions are "the only reported cases recognizing the species defense." *Id.*

189. United States v. Luschen, 614 F.2d 1164 (8th Cir.), *cert. denied,* 446 U.S. 939 (1980). *See also* Chappee v. Vose, 843 F.2d 25, 26-27 (1st Cir. 1988), *rev'g* Chappee v. Massachusetts, 659 F. Supp. 1220 (D. Mass. 1987) (state trial judge violated defendant's right to present a defense by excluding expert witnesses who would have testified to isomer defense). *But see* Best v. State, 79 Md. App. 241, 556 A.2d 701 (to raise the cocaine isomer defense, the accused must do more than suggest the theoretical possibility of the existence of a synthetic isomer not covered by the state statutes; the accused must present some evidence that a nontraditional isomer was actually present in the case; once the accused does so, the burden shifts to the prosecution to negate the defense by proof beyond a reasonable doubt), cert. denied, 317 Md. 70, 562 A.2d 718 (1989).

190. United States v. Loveless, 139 F.3d 587, 593 (8th Cir. 1998) (the court notes that "[u]nder the applicable sentencing guidelines, a sentence for d-methamphetamine is greater than a sentence for l-methamphetamine by a factor of 25"); United States v. O'Bryant, 136 F.3d 980 (5th Cir. 1998); Reece v. United States, 119 F.3d 1462 (11th Cir. 1997); United States v. Trout, 68 F.3d 1276, 1281 n.4 (11th Cir. 1995), *cert. denied*, 516 U.S. 1153 (1996). *See also* United States v. Glover, 97 F.3d 1345 (10th Cir. 1996) (it was inadequate representation for defense counsel to fail to raise the prosecution's neglect to prove whether the offense involved D-methamphetamine or L-methamphetamine); United States v. Seyfert, 67 F.3d 544 (5th Cir. 1995); United States v. Blankenship, 906 F. Supp. 461 (C.D. Ill. 1995); Schoenburg, *Sure It Was Speed — But Which Speed?*, 18 THE CHAMPION 28 (Nov. 1994) ("Under the Federal Sentencing Guidelines, there are two different forms of methamphetamine: L-methamphetamine, an inert form with little or no physiological effect; and D-methamphetamine, which has the active physiological effects characteristic of the drug. What makes this ... particularly interesting is that early DEA lab reports and many state crime lab reports did not distinguish between" the two forms; in United States v. Patrick, 983 F.2d 206 (11th Cir. 1993), "the Eleventh Circuit reversed ... and remanded for a determination by the district court of [the] specific form of methamphetamine").

191. State v. Portrey, 6 Wash. App. 380, 492 P.2d 1050 (1972).

192. Curtis v. State, 548 S.W.2d 57 (Tex. Crim. App. 1977).

193. *Id.* at 58.

194. *Id.* at 58-59.

The number of cases accepting defense attacks on prosecution drug identification evidence is dwarfed by the volume of decisional law rejecting the attacks. The overwhelming majority of courts have repudiated the species[195] and isomer[196] defenses, and courts have sustained convictions based on conclusory prosecution testimony including little or no scientific proof of the specificity of the tests used.[197]

In sustaining these convictions, the courts seem satisfied with the prosecution analysts' testimony[198] or assertion that the tests identify the drug in question.[199] If the expert testifies "unequivocally"[200] or "clearly and unequivocally,"[201] the courts accept the testimony at face value. They appear more concerned about the definiteness of the testimony than the specificity of the tests. The cases are legion in which courts sustained the prosecution evidence even though there was no indication of the identity of the tests used.[202] The opinions often contain vague, unilluminating references to a "chemical analysis."[203] In a similar vein, courts have upheld convictions when all the tests used were nonspecific.[204] The courts

---

195. "[E]very federal circuit with the exception of the Seventh" and "most state courts" rejected the species defense. G. Uelmen & V. Haddox, *supra* note 143, at 4-31. 17 Crim. L. Rep. (BNA) 2503 refers to the "great majority of jurisdictions" rejecting the species defense. *See also* Winters v. State, 646 P.2d 867, 871 (Alaska App. 1982) ("the great weight of authority").

196. United States v. Hall, 552 F.2d 273 (9th Cir. 1977) (unnecessary to perform polarimeter test); United States v. Orzechowski, 547 F.2d 978 (7th Cir. 1976), *cert. denied,* 431 U.S. 906 (1977). *See* United States v. Ortiz, 610 F.2d 280, 281-82 (5th Cir.), *cert. denied,* 495 U.S. 930 (1980).

197. United States v. Burden, 497 F.2d 385, 387 (8th Cir. 1974); United States v. Haro-Espinosa, 619 F.2d 789 (9th Cir. 1979); People v. Chavez, 182 Colo. 216, 219, 511 P.2d 883 (1973); Stevens v. State, 165 Ga. App. 814, 302 S.E.2d 724 (1983); People v. Park, 72 Ill. 2d 203, 20 Ill. Dec. 586, 380 N.E.2d 795 (1978); Barrett v. State, 164 Ind. App. 460, 463, 329 N.E.2d 58, 63 (1975); State v. Keys, 328 So. 2d 154, 156 (La. 1976); State v. Mosier, 83 N.M. 213, 216, 490 P.2d 471, 474 (1971); Carrizal v. State, 138 Tex. Crim. 103, 105, 134 S.W.2d 287, 289 (1939); Valdez v. State, 135 Tex. Crim. 201, 202, 117 S.W.2d 459, 461 (Tex. Crim. App. 1938); State v. Montague, 73 Wash. 2d 381, 391, 438 P.2d 571, 577 (1968); State v. Garcia, 69 Wash. 2d 546, 558, 419 P.2d 121, 128 (1966); State v. Wind, 60 Wis. 2d 267, 208 N.W.2d 357 (1973).

198. State v. Keys, 328 So. 2d 154, 156 (La. 1976).

199. People v. Chavez, 182 Colo. 216, 219, 511 P.2d 883, 884 (1973).

200. Valdez v. State, 135 Tex. Crim. 201, 202, 117 S.W.2d 459, 461 (1938).

201. United States v. Burden, 497 F.2d 385, 387 (8th Cir. 1974).

202. *E.g.,* United States v. Haro-Espinosa, 619 F.2d 789 (9th Cir. 1979); Stevens v. State, 165 Ga. App. 814, 302 S.E.2d 724 (1983).

203. Barrett v. State, 164 Ind. App. 460, 463, 329 N.E.2d 58, 63 (1975); State v. Mosier, 83 N.M. 213, 216, 490 P.2d 471, 474 (1971); State v. Garcia, 69 Wash. 2d 546, 558, 419 P.2d 121, 128 (1966).

204. Carrizal v. State, 138 Tex. Crim. 103, 105, 134 S.W.2d 287, 289 (Tex. Crim. App. 1939); State v. Montague, 73 Wash. 2d 381, 391, 438 P.2d 571, 577 (1968); State v. Wind, 60 Wis. 2d 267, 208 N.W.2d 357 (1973); United States v. Sanchez, 50 C.M.R. 450 (A.F.C.M.R. 1975).

have even gone to the length of affirming convictions in cases in which the prosecution presented evidence of only a single, nonspecific test.[205]

Standard for Legal Sufficiency

At first blush, it may seem surprising that the courts have been so tolerant of relatively feeble drug identification evidence. However, this tolerance is understandable in light of the fact that before the Supreme Court's 1979 decision in *Jackson v. Virginia*[206] many courts employed a lax standard for judging the legal sufficiency of the prosecution proof. Although proof beyond a reasonable doubt was universally employed as the measure of the ultimate burden of persuasion in the United States,[207] that standard was not the test for evaluating the legal sufficiency of the evidence.[208] As triers of fact, the jurors use the standard of proof beyond a reasonable doubt to determine whether the prosecution had met its ultimate burden of persuasion.[209] The jurors resolve all questions of credibility and decide whether the prosecution's case is factually sufficient to meet the final burden. However, the initial burden of going forward is the burden the trial judge applies in deciding whether the prosecution's evidence is legally sufficient.[210] Prior to *Jackson,* there was a three-way split of authority over the question of the proper standard for assessing the legal sufficiency of the prosecution evidence:[211] the scintilla rule,[212] the *Curley* view,[213] and the substantial evidence doctrine.[214]

---

205. People v. Park, 72 Ill. 2d 203, 20 Ill. Dec. 586, 380 N.E.2d 795 (1978) (Duquenois-Levine test). *See* Cheronis, *Tentative and Rigorous Proof in the Identification of Organic Compounds and Application of these Concepts to the Detection of Active Principals of Marijuana*, 4 MICROCHEM. J. 555, 558 (1960) (color tests are only "functional group tests. [S]uch proof is merely tentative and not admissible as reliable evidence").

206. 443 U.S. 307 (1979); Zeese, *The Use and Abuse of Drug Tests*, 5 CRIM. JUST. 2, 6 (Winter 1991) ("The key case regarding sufficiency of evidence is *Jackson v. Virginia* ....").

207. C. MCCORMICK, EVIDENCE § 341 (5th ed. 1999); E. IMWINKELRIED, P. GIANNELLI, F. GILLIGAN & F. LEDERER, COURTROOM CRIMINAL EVIDENCE § 2919 (3d ed. 1998).

208. C. MCCORMICK, *supra* note 207, at §§ 336, 338; E. IMWINKELRIED, P. GIANNELLI, F. GILLIGAN & F. LEDERER, *supra* note 207, at § 2919.

209. C. MCCORMICK, *supra* note 207, at § 341; E. IMWINKELRIED, P. GIANNELLI, F. GILLIGAN & F. LEDERER, *supra* note 207, at §§ 2916, 2925.

210. C. MCCORMICK, *supra* note 207, at §§ 336, 338; E. IMWINKELRIED, P. GIANNELLI, F. GILLIGAN & F. LEDERER, *supra* note 207, at § 2902.

211. *Circuit Note*, 61 GEO. L.J. 275, 431 (1972).

212. C. MCCORMICK, *supra* note 207, at § 338; Hoffman, *Alabama's Scintilla Rule*, 28 ALA. L. REV. 592 (1977); Comment, *Federal Review of the Evidence Supporting State Convictions: Jackson v. Virginia*, 79 COLUM. L. REV. 1577 (1979); Recent Decision, *Criminal Law — Habeas Corpus — Due Process Requires a Federal Habeas Corpus Court to Consider Whether There Was Sufficient Evidence to Justify a Rational Trier of Fact Finding Guilt Beyond a Reasonable Doubt in a State Court Conviction. Jackson v. Virginia, 443 U.S. 307 (1979)*, 10 CUM. L. REV. 849, 858 (1980); Recent Development, *Criminal Law and Procedure — Due Process — Evidentiary Review in Federal Habeas Corpus*, 47 TENN. L. REV. 456, 467 (1980); Comment, *Criminal Procedure:*

Under the scintilla rule, the prosecution's case is legally sufficient if there is a scintilla of relevant evidence on each element of the charged offense.[215] The courts have used various expressions to describe the rule: The motion for a directed verdict must be denied if the record contains any[216] or some[217] relevant evidence; the motion must be denied if there is a modicum[218] or scintilla[219] of evidence; the motion can be granted only if the record is totally[220] devoid[221] of evidence and there is no[222] evidence of an essential element.

Especially in criminal cases, it was expectable that many courts would abandon the scintilla rule.[223] Even before *Jackson v. Virginia*,[224] numerous jurisdictions overruled the scintilla doctrine.[225] Some jurisdictions decided that as a matter of policy, the standard for the initial burden in criminal cases should be enhanced in the same fashion as the ultimate burden.[226] A large number of jurisdictions,[227] state[228] and federal,[229] required that in ruling on a motion for a

---

Sufficiency of Evidence Now Reviewable in Habeas Corpus Proceeding, 19 WASH. L.J. 616, 617 (1980).

213. Curley v. United States, 160 F.2d 229 (D.C. Cir.), *cert. denied*, 331 U.S. 837 (1947); Riggs v. United States, 280 F.2d 949 (5th Cir. 1960); State v. Rocker, 52 Haw. 336, 475 P.2d 684 (1970); 2 C. WRIGHT, FEDERAL PRACTICE AND PROCEDURE: CRIMINAL §§ 466-67 (1982); C. MCCORMICK, *supra* note 207, at § 338; 9 J. WIGMORE, EVIDENCE § 2494 (3d ed. 1940); Comment, *The Jackson v. Virginia Standard for Sufficiency of the Evidence*, 65 IOWA L. REV. 799, 806 (1980).

214. United States v. Feinberg, 140 F.2d 592, 594 (2d Cir.), *cert. denied,* 322 U.S. 726 (1944); United States v. Masiello, 235 F.2d 279, 286 (2d Cir.), *cert. denied,* 352 U.S. 882 (1956); United States v. Orrico, 599 F.2d 113 (6th Cir. 1979); United States v. Green, 548 F.2d 1261, 1266 (6th Cir. 1977); Hays v. United States, 231 F. 106 (8th Cir. 1916), *aff'd sub nom.* Caminetti v. United States, 242 U.S. 470 (1917); Wilson v. Harris, 496 F. Supp. 746 (E.D. Wis. 1980); People v. White, 89 Cal. App. 3d 143, 152 Cal. Rptr. 312 (1979); People v. Houts, 86 Cal. App. 3d 1012, 150 Cal. Rptr. 589 (1978); *In re* T., 79 Cal. App. 3d 382, 144 Cal. Rptr. 856 (1978); State v. Nutley, 24 Wis. 2d 527, 129 N.W.2d 155 (1964); 2 C. WRIGHT, *supra* note 167, at §§ 466-67; Recent Development, *supra* note 212, at 466.

215. C. MCCORMICK, *supra* note 207, at § 338.

216. Comment, *Criminal Procedure: Sufficiency of Evidence Now Reviewable in Habeas Corpus Proceeding*, 19 WASH. L.J. 616, 617 (1980).

217. Comment, *Federal Review of the Evidence Supporting State Convictions: Jackson v. Virginia*, 79 COLUM. L. REV. 1577 (1979).

218. Comment, *supra* note 216, at 621; Recent Development, *supra* note 212, at 467.

219. 9 J. WIGMORE, *supra* note 213, at § 2494.

220. Comment, *supra* note 217, at 1577.

221. Recent Decision, *supra* note 212, at 858.

222. Comment, *supra* note 217, at 1579.

223. 9 J. WIGMORE, *supra* note 213, at § 2494.

224. 443 U.S. 307 (1979).

225. 9 J. WIGMORE, *supra* note 213, § 2494, at 384.

226. 2 C. WRIGHT, *supra* note 213, at §§ 466-467.

227. *Id.*

228. State v. Rocker, 52 Haw. 336, 475 P.2d 684 (1970). *See* C. MCCORMICK, *supra* note 207, at § 338, at 953 n.5.

directed verdict, the trial court inquire whether a rational juror could find the existence of every element of the charged offense beyond a reasonable doubt.[230] The prosecution had not made out a submissible case if its evidence supports a mere permissive inference of the existence of all elements of the offense.[231] This view came to be known as the *Curley*[232] doctrine.

While the *Curley* view had a wide following,[233] a large number of jurisdictions opted for a third, compromise position, the substantial evidence rule.[234] These jurisdictions acknowledged that the scintilla rule afforded the defendant inadequate protection. Yet they refused to incorporate the test of proof beyond a reasonable doubt into the standard for the initial burden of going forward. The compromise rule required the court find only that the prosecution evidence is adequate[235] to fairly[236] or rationally[237] support a permissive[238] inference[239] or conclusion.[240] If a rational juror could find that the evidence preponderates[241] and that the fact's existence is more likely or probable than not,[242] the prosecution had sustained the initial burden. In that event, the court should deny the motion for a directed verdict even when the court was convinced that the evidence would be insufficient to convince a rational juror beyond a reasonable doubt.[243]

Prior to *Jackson v. Virginia,* these jurisdictions felt no constitutional compulsion to opt for the *Curley* view. Before *Jackson,*[244] the controlling Supreme Court precedent was *Thompson v. Louisville,*[245] decided in 1960.

---

229. Riggs v. United States, 280 F.2d 949 (5th Cir. 1960); Curley v. United States, 160 F.2d 229 (D.C. Cir.), *cert. denied,* 331 U.S. 837 (1947); 2 C. WRIGHT, *supra* note 213, at §§ 466-467.

230. Riggs v. United States, 280 F.2d 949 (5th Cir. 1960); Curley v. United States, 160 F.2d 229 (D.C. Cir.), *cert. denied,* 331 U.S. 837 (1947); 2 C. WRIGHT, *supra* note 213, at §§ 466-467.

231. Comment, *supra* note 213, at 806.

232. The leading authority for this proposition is Curley v. United States, 160 F.2d 229 (D.C. Cir.), *cert. denied,* 331 U.S. 837 (1947).

233. 2 C. WRIGHT, *supra* note 213, at §§ 466-467.

234. Circuit Note, *supra* note 211, at 431. *See* People v. White, 89 Cal. App. 3d 143, 152 Cal. Rptr. 312 (1979); People v. Houts, 86 Cal. App. 3d 1012, 150 Cal. Rptr. 589 (1978); *In re* T., 79 Cal. App. 3d 382, 144 Cal. Rptr. 856 (1978).

235. Wilson v. Harris, 496 F. Supp. 746 (E.D. Wis. 1980).

236. Recent Development, *supra* note 212, at 466.

237. United States v. Green, 548 F.2d 1261, 1266 (6th Cir. 1977).

238. State v. Nutley, 24 Wis. 2d 527, 547-48, 129 N.W.2d 155, 163 (1964), *cert. denied,* 380 U.S. 918 (1965).

239. *Id.*

240. United States v. Orrico, 599 F.2d 113 (6th Cir. 1979).

241. United States v. Masiello, 235 F.2d 279, 287 (2d Cir.), *cert. denied,* 352 U.S. 882 (1956); United States v. Feinberg, 140 F.2d 592, 594 (2d Cir.), *cert. denied,* 322 U.S. 726 (1944).

242. United States v. Masiello, 235 F.2d 279, 286 (2d Cir.), *cert. denied,* 352 U.S. 882 (1956).

243. Hays v. United States, 231 F. 106 (8th Cir. 1916), *aff'd sub nom.* Caminetti v. United States, 242 U.S. 470 (1917).

244. 443 U.S. 307 (1979).

245. 362 U.S. 199 (1960).

Thompson was a direct appeal from a state court conviction.[246] *Thompson* had been convicted of disorderly conduct, but there was no evidence of disruptive behavior in the record of trial. The *Thompson* Court declared that it is "a violation of due process to convict and punish a man without evidence of his guilt."[247] The *Thompson* doctrine became known as the "no evidence" rule: The defense is entitled to a directed verdict only when the record contains no evidence of an essential element of the offense.[248]

In 1979 in *Jackson v. Virginia*,[249] Justice Stewart authored the lead opinion that overruled *Thompson.* In *Jackson*, the Court granted a writ of certiorari to consider the question of the impact of *Winship* on *Thompson.* In 1970, in *In re Winship*[250] the Court had announced that due process requires that in a criminal case, the trier of fact use the burden of persuasion of proof beyond a reasonable doubt. According to Stewart, the "central purposes" served by *Winship* not only require the jury to use the proof beyond a reasonable doubt standard during its deliberations; the same policies also demand that the court police the jury's administration of the standard.[251] In Justice Stewart's view, the court has a constitutional responsibility to ensure that the jury operates within the parameters established by *Winship.*[252] To discharge that responsibility, the court must use a standard stricter than *Thompson*: "The *Thompson* doctrine simply fails to supply a workable or even a predictable standard for determining whether the due process command of *Winship* has been honored."[253] Justice Stewart closed by proclaiming the Court's holding: "We hold that in a challenge to a state criminal conviction brought under 28 U.S.C. § 2254 ... the applicant is entitled to habeas corpus relief if it is found that upon the record evidence adduced at the trial no rational trier of fact could have found proof of guilt beyond a reasonable doubt."[254]

Drug Identification Evidence

Even at this late juncture, the impact of *Jackson* on drug prosecutions is unsettled. Relatively few courts have explicitly recognized that *Jackson* is pertinent to the question of the legal sufficiency of prosecution drug

---

246. Comment, *supra* note 216, at 617, 621, 623-24.

247. Thompson v. Louisville, 362 U.S. 199, 206 (1960).

248. Note, *Jackson v. Virginia: The Advent of the Reasonable Doubt Standard in Habeas Corpus Proceedings*, 25 S.D. L. Rev. 372, 372-75 (1980).

249. 443 U.S. 307 (1979).

250. 397 U.S. 358 (1970).

251. Jackson v. Virginia, 443 U.S. 307, 317-20 (1979).

252. *Id.*

253. *Id.* at 320.

254. *Id.* at 324. *See also* Pilon v. Bordenkircher, 444 U.S. 1 (1979).

identification evidence.[255] Many courts continue to pass on the legal sufficiency of such evidence without so much as a citation to *Jackson*.[256] However, it is arguable that *Jackson* should have at least one effect in drug cases: When the defense establishes through judicial notice that all the prosecution's drug identification tests are nonspecific, the prosecution's drug identification evidence is legally insufficient unless the prosecution presents proof of the substance's identity in addition to the analyst's conclusory assertion that the tests identify the substance. The reasoning underlying this argument is straightforward. The scientific concept of specificity and the nonspecific status of many drug identification tests are judicially noticeable facts. When judicial notice establishes that all the prosecution's tests are nonspecific, an analyst's conclusory identification is insufficient to satisfy *Jackson*.

Although matter of common knowledge was the traditional basis for judicial notice, another independent basis has emerged: verifiable certainty.[257] Federal Rule of Evidence 201(b) codifies the modern common law by recognizing alternative bases for judicial notice: "A judicially noticed fact must be one not subject to reasonable dispute in that it is either (1) generally known within the territorial jurisdiction of the trial court or (2) capable of accurate and ready determination by resort to sources whose accuracy cannot reasonably be questioned."[258] Although the courts sometimes use "verifiable certainty" as the shorthand expression for this doctrine, the statute does not require that the proposition be a full-fledged certainty. In *Daubert*, Justice Blackmun commented that "arguably, there are no certainties in science."[259] If anything, post-*Daubert* the courts should apply Rule 201(b)(2) more liberally than in the past.[260]

The courts have frequently invoked the verifiable certainty theory as the basis for noticing scientific data.[261] In particular, the courts have been willing to judicially notice definitions of scientific terms.[262] Numerous scientific dictionaries and texts set out the definition of specificity. It seems patent that the definition of the term, "specificity," is proper subject-matter for judicial notice.

---

255. Chouinard v. State, 96 N.M. 783, 635 P.2d 986 (Ct. App. 1980), *rev'd,* 96 N.M. 658, 634 P.2d 680 (1981), *cert. denied,* 456 U.S. 930 (1982).

256. *E.g.,* United States v. Posey, 647 F.2d 1048 (10th Cir. 1981).

257. C. McCormick, *supra* note 207, at § 330; E. Imwinkelried, P. Giannelli, F. Gilligan & F. Lederer, *supra* note 207, at § 3005.

258. Fed. R. Evid. 201(b).

259. Daubert v. Merrell Dow Pharmaceuticals, Inc., 509 U.S. 579 (1993).

260. Imwinkelried, *Evidence Law Visits Jurassic Park: The Far-Reaching Implications of the Daubert Court's Recognition of the Uncertainty of the Scientific Enterprise*, 81 Iowa L. Rev. 55, 71-73 (1995).

261. Melong v. Micronesian Claims Comm'n, 643 F.2d 10 (D.C. Cir. 1980); Miller Brewing Co. v. G. Heileman Brewing Co., 427 F. Supp. 1204 (W.D. Wis. 1977).

262. *E.g.,* United States v. Sims, 529 F.2d 10 (8th Cir. 1976) (the definition of heroin hydrochloride).

It is equally justifiable to judicially notice the nonspecific status of many drug identification tests. In the past, the courts have noticed the principles underlying scientific tests.[263] In the case of fingerprints[264] and palmprints,[265] the courts have noticed the fact that the tests are specific; as one court remarked, it is judicially noticeable that "no two sets of fingerprints or palmprints are exactly alike."[266] By parity of reasoning, the courts should notice the nonspecificity of such drug identification procedures as color tests and thin layer chromatography. The evidence of the nonspecificity of such widely used drug identification procedures as color tests,[267] thin layer chromatography[268] immunoassay, and ultraviolet spectrophotometry[269] is extensive. Consequently, like the definition of "specificity," the nonspecific status of such tests ought to be judicially noticed.

Assume this scenario. On direct examination, the prosecution's drug identification witness testifies that she subjected the suspected drug to color and ultraviolet tests and that on the basis of those test results, her opinion is that the substance is cocaine, as alleged in the indictment. The witness gives no indication that she used more specific procedures to confirm these tests.[270] In the past before *Jackson* in many jurisdictions that testimony would be legally sufficient to meet the prosecution's initial burden of going forward.[271] The question now arises: After *Jackson*, is that testimony sufficient if the defense has established through judicial notice that both tests are nonspecific for cocaine? There is a strong argument that that testimony falls short of complying with *Jackson*.

It is true that in our scenario, the prosecution's evidence is probably strong enough to create a permissive inference that the drug is cocaine. Although the

---

263. 1 F. WHARTON, CRIMINAL EVIDENCE § 81 (12th ed. 1955).

264. State v. Inman, 350 A.2d 582, 588 (Me. 1976).

265. *Id.*

266. *Id.*

267. R. SHAPIRO & J. ACKERMAN, *supra* note 40, at 5; Shapiro, *supra* note 28, at 137; Stall, *supra* note 29, at 398; Stein, Laessig & Indriksons, *supra* note 13, at 756-57, 762, 785.

268. R. SHAPIRO & J. ACKERMAN, *supra* note 40, at 6; Stein, Laessig & Indriksons, *supra* note 13, at 733-35, 747-49.

269. R. SHAPIRO & J. ACKERMAN, *supra* note 40, at 5; Shapiro, *supra* note 28, at 136; Stein, Laessig & Indriksons, *supra* note 13, at 737-38, 779.

270. In 1991, the Institute of Bill Rights of the College of William and Mary issued its proposal on Drug Testing in the Workplace. Section 4(a)(1) provides that "[n]o disciplinary actions may be taken by an employer against an employee or an applicant based on a positive substance abuse test result unless ... the test result has been confirmed by a second," more sophisticated test.

271. United States v. Haro-Espinosa, 619 F.2d 789 (9th Cir. 1979); Stevens v. State, 165 Ga. App. 814, 302 S.E.2d 724 (1983); People v. Park, 72 Ill. 2d 203, 20 Ill. Dec. 586, 380 N.E.2d 795 (1978); Barrett v. State, 164 Ind. App. 460, 463, 329 N.E.2d 58, 63 (1975); State v. Mosier, 83 N.M. 213, 216, 490 P.2d 471, 474 (Ct. App. 1971); Carrizal v. State, 138 Tex. Crim. 103, 105, 134 S.W.2d 287, 289 (1939); State v. Montague, 73 Wash. 2d 381, 391, 438 P.2d 571, 577 (1968); State v. Garcia, 69 Wash. 2d 546, 558, 419 P.2d 121, 128 (1966).

two tests are nonspecific,[272] both techniques are fact-finding tools for identifying drugs; and both tests yielded the result indicative of cocaine. Given that state of the record, a rational juror could conceivably draw the inference that it is more likely than not that the drug is cocaine. The two test results are consistent with that inference, and there is no test result definitely pointing to a contrary conclusion. Hence, this testimony would satisfy the "substantial evidence" test.[273] However, a mere permissive inference is insufficient to satisfy *Jackson.*[274] A rational juror might find a permissive inference and yet balk at concluding that there was adequate certitude to banish all reasonable doubt from the case.[275]

A lingering, reasonable doubt may be present in our scenario. In the scenario, the key issue is the accuracy of the identification of the unknown substance. While the witness has given conclusory testimony that the two tests identify the cocaine, the judicially noticeable facts would give any rational juror pause and furnish good ground for questioning the testimony. This ground constitutes reasonable doubt. In the cases analyzing the propriety of jury instructions explaining reasonable doubt, the courts have refined the definition of that term. In some jurisdictions, a reasonable doubt must be substantial.[276] This doubt is substantial. The judicially noticeable facts raise substantive doubts in two senses: questions about both the heart of the analyst's testimony and an essential element of the charged offense. The same case law tells us that a doubt can be reasonable and preclude conviction even if the jurors cannot specifically identify[277] or

---

272. R. SHAPIRO & J. ACKERMAN, *supra* note 40, at 5; Shapiro, *supra* note 28, at 132, 136; Stein, Laessig & Indriksons, *supra* note 13, at 737-38, 741-47, 779.

273. United States v. Feinberg, 140 F.2d 592, 594 (2d Cir.), *cert. denied,* 322 U.S. 726 (1944); United States v. Masiello, 235 F.2d 279, 286 (2d Cir.), *cert. denied,* 352 U.S. 882 (1956); United States v. Orrico, 599 F.2d 113 (6th Cir. 1979); United States v. Green, 548 F.2d 1261, 1266 (6th Cir. 1977); Hays v. United States, 231 F. 106 (8th Cir. 1916), *aff'd sub nom.* Caminetti v. United States, 242 U.S. 470 (1917); Wilson v. Harris, 496 F. Supp. 746 (E.D. Wis. 1980); People v. White, 89 Cal. App. 3d 143, 152 Cal. Rptr. 312 (1979); People v. Houts, 86 Cal. App. 3d 1012, 150 Cal. Rptr. 589 (1978); *In re* T., 79 Cal. App. 3d 382, 144 Cal. Rptr. 856 (1978); State v. Nutley, 24 Wis. 2d 527, 547-48, 129 N.W.2d 155, 163 (1964), *cert. denied,* 380 U.S. 918 (1965); Circuit Note, *supra* note 211, at 431; Recent Development, *supra* note 212, at 466.

274. Cosby v. Jones, 682 F.2d 1373 (11th Cir. 1982); Comment, *supra* note 213, at 806.

275. R. TRAYNOR, THE RIDDLE OF HARMLESS ERROR 29 (1970) ("It (the court) should determine whether the trier of fact could reasonably conclude that the alleged fact was ... in criminal cases, almost certain").

276. Many jurisdictions apply a test even more favorable to the defense; in these jurisdictions, it is error to instruct the jury that the doubt must be substantial. United States v. Bridges, 499 F.2d 179 (7th Cir.), *cert. denied,* 419 U.S. 1010 (1974); United States v. Cotten, 10 M.J. 260 (U.S.C.M.A. 1981) (Federal courts have almost universally condemned instructions equating reasonable and substantial doubt). In these jurisdictions, even an insubstantial doubt can mandate an acquittal.

277. People v. Garcia, 54 Cal. App. 3d 61, 126 Cal. Rptr. 275 (1975), *cert. denied,* 426 U.S. 911 (1976).

articulate[278] the doubt; it is error to instruct the jury that they can acquit only if they can verbalize their nagging doubt about the prosecution's case.[279] In our scenario, the doubt is obvious and staring any rational juror in the face. The tests' nonspecificity injects the doubt into the case; and the prosecution has presented no additional evidence — proof of scientific literature accepting the combination of tests as an identification of cocaine, or an experiment verifying the hypothesis that combined, the two tests can determine the presence of cocaine — to dispel the doubt.

There are signs that the courts are taking a fresh look at the issue of the legal sufficiency of prosecution drug identification evidence. The use of the immunoassay drug tests gave the courts an opportunity to revisit this issue. In some judicial tests of immunoassay,[280] courts adopted a stance of healthy skepticism about the specificity of immunoassay.[281] Moreover, in a New Mexico

---

278. Dunn v. Perrin, 570 F.2d 21 (1st Cir.), *cert. denied,* 437 U.S. 910 (1978).

279. *Id.*

280. Storms v. Coughlin, 600 F. Supp. 1214 (S.D.N.Y. 1984); Wykoff v. Resig, 613 F. Supp. 1504 (D. Ind. 1985) (confirmation required); Kane v. Fair, 33 Crim. L. Rep. (BNA) 2492 (Mass. 1983) (EMIT test must be confirmed by an alternative method of analysis); Isaacks v. State, 646 S.W.2d 602 (Tex. App. 1983) (Standing alone, EMIT test result insufficient to revoke probation). *See also* Comment, *Admissibility of Biochemical Urinalysis Testing Results for the Purpose of Detecting Marijuana Use,* 20 WAKE FOREST L. REV. 391 (1984).

281. Although Jensen v. Lick, 589 F. Supp. 35 (D.N.D. 1984), indicated that it would sustain prison disciplinary actions based on EMIT tests, there are two caveats about the opinion. First, the case involved prison disciplinary actions rather than criminal trials. There is a lax standard of proof in such actions. *Id.* at 38. Second, the court found EMIT testing satisfactory only after the government presented a new Center for Disease Control study reporting that EMIT testing procedures are "97 to 99% accurate." *Id.* The court did not accept an expert's conclusory assertion that EMIT tests are adequate to identify illegal drugs. Rather, the court evidently demanded scientific proof of the validity of the EMIT technique. The same caveats apply in Peranzo v. Coughlin, 608 F. Supp. 1504 (S.D.N.Y. 1985). In Higgs v. Wilson, 616 F. Supp. 226 (W.D. Ky. 1985), a federal magistrate recommended the issuance of a preliminary injunction against prison disciplinary actions based solely on Syva EMIT tests. *Reliability of Urinalysis in Prison Questioned,* THE ADVOCATE, Oct. 1984, at 12. THE ADVOCATE is a publication of the Kentucky Department of Public Advocacy. The injunction issued in Higgs v. Wilson, 616 F. Supp. 226 (W.D. Ky. 1985); United States v. McNickles, 948 F. Supp. 345, 349 (D. Del. 1996) ("it is well established in the Third Circuit that one positive drug test result is sufficient to revoke probation"); Gropper & Reardon, *Developing Drug Testing By Hair Analysis,* NAT'L INSTIT. JUST. J. 8,10 (Apr. 1993) (in Koch v. Harrah's Club, No. 23740 (9th Dist. Ct., Nev., Sept. 12, 1990), the Ninth Judicial Court of Nevada "ruled that hair testing alone (by RIAH) was insufficient to form the basis for termination"). *But see* United States v. Young, 41 F.3d 1184 (7th Cir. 1994) (the test results supported the finding that the defendant had possessed cocaine in violation of a condition of his supervised release); United States v. Clark, 30 F.3d 23 (4th Cir.), *cert. denied,* 513 U.S. 1027 (1994); Allen v. Purkett, 5 F.3d 1151, 1153 (8th Cir. 1993) (in a prison discipline case, "prison officials are not required to provide second urinalysis tests to satisfy the Due Process Clause"), *cert. denied,* 513 U.s. 829 (1994); People v. Swamp, 84 N.Y.2d 725, 646 N.E.2d 774, 622 N.Y.S.2d 472 (App. 1995) (a preliminary field test was legally sufficient to support a grand jury

case, *Chouinard v. State*,[282] the court acknowledged *Jackson* as the standard for evaluating the legal sufficiency of the drug identification. Significantly, although the prosecution had presented some expert testimony supposedly identifying a substance as cocaine, the court suggested that the evidence was not the sort of "definitive chemical analysis" that *Jackson* contemplates.[283] In a 1998 decision, an Illinois court ruled that without more, a field test was insufficient to establish the identity of a controlled substance beyond a reasonable doubt.[284]

In part, the legal sufficiency of the evidence depends on the proposition which the prosecution is attempting to prove.[285] First, assume that the prosecutor offers an immunoassay test to prove only that there was a contraband substance in the person's urine sample. It is true that immunoassay tests are subject to false positives;[286] but if the test result is confirmed by a method such as GC/MS, the confirmed test is certainly legally sufficient to establish the identity of the substance found in the urine sample.[287] Next, suppose that the prosecutor wishes to demonstrate that the person actively ingested or consumed the illicit substance. Although passive inhalation of marijuana (and possibly crack cocaine) smoke can produce detectable levels of metabolite in the person's system, "inhalation

---

indictment). *See generally* Mazo, *Yellow Rows of Test Tubes: Due Process Constraints on Discharges of Public Employees Based on Drug Urinalysis Testing*, 135 U. PA. L. REV. 1623, 1644-45 (1987) (collecting the cases).

282. 96 N.M. 783, 635 P.2d 986 (Ct. App. 1980), *rev'd*, 96 N.M. 658, 634 P.2d 680 (1981), *cert. denied*, 456 U.S. 930 (1982).

283. 96 N.M. 783, 635 P.2d 986 (Ct. App. 1980), *rev'd*, 96 N.M. 658, 634 P.2d 680 (1981), *cert. denied*, 456 U.S. 930 (1982).

284. People v. Hagberg, 300 Ill.App.3d 491, 703 N.E.2d 793, 234 Ill. Dec. 873 (1998).

285. Imwinkelried, *Immunoassay Drug Testing*, 12 THE CHAMPION 10, 13-15 (Aug. 1988); United States v. Smith, 978 F.2d 181, 182 (5th Cir. 1992) ("admission of use of a contraband substance, as well as positive urinalysis test results, may constitute circumstantial evidence of possession of a controlled substance...."); United States v. Gordon, 961 F.2d 426, 429 (3d Cir. 1992) ("drug use indicated by urinalysis is only circumstantial evidence of drug possession").

286. Soto v. Lord, 693 F. Supp. 8, 13 (S.D.N.Y. 1988) ("The National Health Laboratories report states in bold print, in the center of the page and just beneath the positive result: 'A positive cannabinoid result should be confirmed by an alternate method'"); Giardino, *An Indoor Air Quality-Pharmacokinetic Simulation of Passive Inhalation of Marijuana Smoke and the Resultant Buildup of 11-Nor-Delta-9-Tetrahydrocannabinol-9-Carboxylic Acid in Urine*, 42 J. FORENSIC SCI. 323 (1997) ("the United States Air Force ... has DOD cut-off levels established to remove any real possibility of a positive due to passive inhalation. Nonetheless, the [good soldier] defense is [sometimes] successfully used").

287. National Treas. Emps. Union v. Von Raab, 489 U.S. 656, 673 n.2 (1989) ("the combination of EMIT and GC/MS tests ... is highly accurate ..."). Statutes in Connecticut, Iowa, Minnesota, Montana, Rhode Island, Utah, and Vermont require confirmation. Note, *State Drug Testing Statutes: Legislative Attempts to Balance Privacy and Productivity*, 14 J. CORP. LAW 721, 746-47, 754 (1989).

typically produces quantities much lower than those resulting from ingestion."[288] The laboratory can probably set the cutoff value high enough to differentiate between quantities produced by consumption and levels that realistically could be caused by mere exposure and inhalation. Several courts have already held that a positive immunoassay test is legally sufficient to sustain a conviction for wrongful marijuana use.[289]

---

288. Imwinkelried, *Some Preliminary Thoughts on the Wisdom of Governmental Prohibition or Regulation of Employee Urinalysis Testing*, 11 NOVA L. REV. 563, 591 (1987); Copeland v. Philadelphia Police Dep't, 840 F.2d 1139, 1141 n.1 (3d Cir. 1988), *cert. denied*, 490 U.S. 1004 (1989); Baggs v. Eagle-Picher Indus., 750 F. Supp. 264, 267 (W.D. Mich. 1990); Dimeo v. Griffin, 721 F. Supp. 958, 963 (N.D. Ill. 1989) (one state agency uses the following cutoff values: marijuana metabolites — 100 ng/ml, cocaine metabolite — 300 ng/ml, opiates — 300 ng/ml, amphetamines — 1,000 ng/ml, and barbituates — 300 ng/ml), *aff'd*, 924 F.2d 664, 669 (7th Cir.), *vacated*, 931 F.2d 1215 (7th Cir.), *rev'd*, 943 F.2d 679 (7th Cir. 1991); Burka v. New York City Transit Auth., 680 F. Supp. 590, 611 (S.D.N.Y. 1988); National Fed'n of Fed. Emps. v. Carlucci, 680 F. Supp. 416, 427 (D.D.C.), *modified*, 3 BNA IER Cas. 128 (D.D.C. 1988); Bozin v. Secretary of Navy, 657 F. Supp. 1463, 1471 (D.D.C. 1987). *See also* Selavka, *Poppy Seed Ingestion as a Contributing Factor to Opiate-Positive Urinalysis Results: The Pacific Perspective*, 36 J. FORENSIC SCI. 685 (1991) ("Poppy seed cakes, bagels, muffins, and rolls did not contain sufficient quantities of poppy seeds to give rise to opiate positive specimens by U.D. Department of Defense ... GC-MS cutoff levels ... although a number of specimens were positive by National Institute of Drug Abuse ... cutoff levels ...."); Mule, Lomax & Gross, *Active and Realistic Passive Marijuana Exposure Tested by Three Immunoassays and GC/MS in Urine*, 12 J. ANAL. TOX. 113, 116 (May/June 1988) ("Our passive inhalation experiments were conducted to determine the concentration on an accurate mass/volume basis of urine cannabinoids under conditions likely to be encountered in social activities. Despite the high concentration of THC in the air ..., cannabinoids in urine obtained 24 hours after exposure from all subjects were less than 6 ng/ml"). State statutes in Minnesota and Vermont require the establishment of cutoff values. Note, *State Drug Testing Statutes: Legislative Attempts to Balance Privacy and Productivity*, 14 J. CORP. LAW 721, 748, 754 (1989).

289. Andrews v. Webb, 685 F. Supp. 579, 587 (E.D. Va. 1988) ("It is well settled as a matter of law that evidence consisting solely of urinalysis laboratory results is sufficient to prove wrongful marijuana use in a criminal case beyond a reasonable doubt"); United States v. Murphy, 33 M.J. 248 (U.S.C.M.A. 1991) (the trial judge took judicial notice that "[t]he human body does not produce the cocaine metabolite, benzoylecgonine, without the ingestion of cocaine"); United States v. Ford, 23 M.J. 332 (U.S.C.M.A. 1987); United States v. Murphy, 23 M.J. 310 (U.S.C.M.A. 1987); United States v. Harper, 22 M.J. 157 (U.S.C.M.A. 1986). *See also* United States v. Blackston, 940 F.2d 877 (3d Cir.) (during the sentencing phase, "three positive urine samples" were sufficient to establish the defendant's possession of drugs), *cert. denied*, 502 U.S. 992 (1991); Harrison v. Dahm, 911 F.2d 37, 41-42 (8th Cir. 1990) (in a prison disciplinary proceeding, a single, unconfirmed EMIT test is sufficient to support a finding of fact); Higgs v. Bland, 888 F.2d 443, 449 (6th Cir. 1989) (in a prison disciplinary proceeding, "[t]he question . . . is whether the EMIT test results constitute 'some evidence' . . . . The reliability of the EMIT test has repeatedly been found to meet due process standards"); Pella v. Adams, 723 F. Supp. 1394 (D. Nev. 1989) ("this court [has] determined that the test itself — ...EMIT ... — and the manner in which the test was conducted, were sufficiently reliable to satisfy the 'some evidence' standard applicable to the review of decisions by a prisoner disciplinary committee. Superintendent, Mass. Correctional Inst. v. Hill, 472 U.S. 445, 457 ... (1985)"); Fowler v. New York City Dep't of Sanitation, 704 F. Supp.

However, lastly assume that the prosecutor wants to show that the person consumed the drug at a particular time or was intoxicated at a certain time as a result of their consumption of the drug. "[T]he test cannot prove that. The test does not establish impairment or intoxication. The test does not detect the drug the [person] was originally exposed to; rather, it measures a metabolite formed later by the chemical processes of the [person's] body. However, the metabolite is not the psychoactive or intoxicating ingredient of the original drug. By the time the metabolite forms, the intoxicating ingredient has disappeared. The metabolite's presence does not even support an inference that the [person] was recently impaired. The available data indicates that the metabolite can remain in the person's body between two weeks and a full month after initial ingestion."[290] Some courts have already concluded that standing alone, an immunoassay test is legally insufficient to prove the time of either use or impairment.[291]

1264, 1272 (S.D.N.Y. 1989) ("Use of only one EMIT test has been determined to have an accuracy rate of better than 95% percent;" the court collects the cases upholding the legal sufficiency of EMIT tests to sustain prison disciplinary actions); Bernstein v. United States, 699 F. Supp. 484 (E.D. Pa. 1988) (a finding of use as the basis for a notation of drug use on a military discharge form); Adkins v. Martin, 699 F. Supp. 1510 (W.D. Okla. 1988) (a finding of use in a prison disciplinary proceeding); Amalgamated Transit Union Local 1277 v. Sunline Transit Agency, 663 F. Supp. 1560, 1570 (C.D. Cal. 1987) (collecting the EMIT cases); Lahey v. Kelly, 71 N.Y.2d 135, 518 N.E.2d 924, 524 N.Y.S.2d 30 (1987) (a finding of use in a prison disciplinary proceeding); *In re* Johnston, 109 Wash. 2d 493, 745 P.2d 864 (1987) (finding of use in a prison disciplinary proceeding); Riley, *Toward a Drug Free Military*, 5 CRIM. JUST. 10, 13 (Winter 1991).

290. Imwinkelried, *supra* note 288, at 590.

291. Skinner v. Railway Labor Executives' Ass'n, 489 U.S. 602 (1989) (the Federal Railroad Administration took the position that blood samples are "the only available body fluid that can provide a clear indication not only of the presence of alcohol and drugs but also their current impairment effects;" "the agency concedes that ... urine tests — unlike blood tests — do not measure current impairment and therefore cannot differentiate on-duty impairment from prior drug .. use which has ceased to affect the user's behavior"); Railway Labor Executives' Ass'n v. Burnley, 839 F.2d 575, 589 (9th Cir. 1988) ("[T]he state of the art drug tests currently used can discover only the metabolites of various drugs, which are not evidence of current intoxication and may remain in the body for days or weeks after the ingestion of the drug"); Jones v. McKenzie, 833 F.2d 335 (D.C. Cir. 1987) (the defendant school system conceded that a positive EMIT test does not establish that the subject used or was under the influence of an illicit drug at any particular time), *vacated on other grounds sub nom.* Jenkins v. Jones, 490 U.S. 1001 (1989); Amalgamated Transit Union, Div. 1279 v. Cambria County Transit Auth., 691 F. Supp. 898, 903 (W.D. Pa. 1988) ("the defendant conceded that the EMIT test could not determine the time of use or degree of impairment"); American Fed'n of Gov't Emps., Council 33 v. Meese, 688 F. Supp. 547, 553 (N.D. Cal. 1988) ("the government concedes that urinalysis testing cannot demonstrate current impairment"); Schaill v. Tippecanoe County Sch. Corp., 679 F. Supp. 833, 857 (N.D. Ind.) ("little, if anything, can be inferred from" a positive test), *aff'd*, 864 F.2d 1309 (7th Cir. 1988); Anable v. Ford, 663 F. Supp. 149, 153 (W.D. Ark. 1985) ("Because the urine tests available are unable to reveal the pharmacological effects of marijuana on the user or the approximate date of use, they cannot determine whether a student has possessed, used, or appeared at school under the influence of marijuana. The utmost that the most precise or urine tests can reveal is that a student has

§ 23-6. Selected Bibliography.

D. AMBROSE, GAS CHROMATOGRAPHY (1971).

F. BAILEY & H. ROTHBLATT, HANDLING NARCOTIC AND DRUG CASES (1972).

D. BERNHEIM, DEFENSE OF NARCOTICS CASES (1983) (2 vols.).

R. DECRESCE, A. MAZURA, M. LIFSHITZ & J. TILSON, DRUG TESTING IN THE WORKPLACE (1989).

D. EVANS, DRUG TESTING LAW, TECHNOLOGY AND PRACTICE (1990).

G. EWING, INSTRUMENTAL METHODS OF CHEMICAL ANALYSIS (4th ed. 1975).

M. GILBERT, HIGH PERFORMANCE LIQUID CHROMATOGRAPHY (1987).

T. GOUGH, THE ANALYSIS OF DRUGS OF ABUSE (1991).

R. GUPTA, CRC HANDBOOK OF CHROMATOGRAPHY: DRUGS (1988).

E. HORWOOD, ANALYTICAL METHODS IN FORENSIC CHEMISTRY (1990).

M. HOUTS, R. BASELT & R. CRAVEY, COURTROOM TOXICOLOGY (1983) (6 vols.).

S. KARCH, DRUG ABUSE HANDBOOK (1997).

P. KINTZ, DRUG TESTING IN HAIR (1996).

T. MILLS, J. ROBERSON, W. WALL, K. LOTHRIDGE, W. MCDOUGALL & M. GILBERT, INSTRUMENTAL DATA FOR DRUG ANALYSIS (1996) (seven vols.).

G. UELMAN & V. HADDOX, DRUG ABUSE AND LAW SOURCEBOOK (1984).

C. VISHER & K. MCFADDEN, A COMPARISON OF URINALYSIS TECHNOLOGIES FOR DRUG TESTING IN CRIMINAL JUSTICE (1991).

J. YINON, FORENSIC MASS SPECTROMETRY (1987).

K. ZEESE, DRUG TESTING LEGAL MANUAL (1988).

Kurzman & Fullerton, *Drug Identification, in* SCIENTIFIC AND EXPERT EVIDENCE 521 (2d ed. 1981).

Lorenzo, *Radioimmunoassay (RIA), in* METHODOLOGY FOR ANALYTICAL TOXICOLOGY 401 (I. Sunshine ed. 1975).

Smith, *Forensic Applications of High-Performance Liquid Chromatography, in* FORENSIC SCIENCE HANDBOOK 28 (R. Saferstein ed. 1982).

Shapiro, *Chemical Defenses in Drug Cases*, 2 NAT'L J. CRIM. DEF. 131 (1976).

Stein, Laessig & Indriksons, *An Evaluation of Drug Testing Procedures by Forensic Laboratories and the Qualifications of Their Analysts*, 1973 WIS. L. REV. 730.

Watkins & Watkins, *Identification of Substances by Instrumental Analysis*, 22 AM. JUR. PROOF OF FACTS 385 (1969).

---

ingested marijuana at some time in the preceding days or weeks"), *modifying* 653 F. Supp. 22, 39-40 (W.D. Ark. 1985); McKay, *Interpretation of Blood and Urine Cannabinoid Concentrations*, 33 J. FORENSIC SCI. 875, 876 (1988) ("There is general agreement in the scientific community that urine concentrations of cannabinoids cannot be correlated with performance, health, or safety"); Note, *State Drug Testing Statutes: Legislative Attempts to Balance Privacy and Productivity*, 14 J. CORP. LAW 721, 734-35 (1989). *But see* Harmon v. Meese, 690 F. Supp. 65, 67 (D.D.C.) (the government claimed that with a high cutoff, a confirmed immunoassay test could show that "the subject has used drugs relatively recently"), *cert. denied*, 488 U.S. 934 (1988); National Fed'n of Fed. Emps. v. Carlucci, 690 F. Supp. 46, 49 (D.D.C. 1988) (the government claimed that off-duty drug use could have "hangover effects" but admitted that "the scientific evidence of hangover effects is 'inconclusive'"); National Fed'n of Fed. Emps. v. Cheney, 884 F.2d 603 (D.C. Cir. 1989), *cert. denied*, 493 U.S. 1056 (1990).

CHAPTER 24

TRACE EVIDENCE*

---

*The authors wish to express their appreciation to Mr. John Wilson, Chief Criminalist, Kansas City Police Crime Laboratory, who reviewed this chapter in all three editions of this treatise.

§ 24-1. In General.

Crime scenes frequently yield physical evidence that can be used to link a suspect to the offense. In one study, researchers concluded that physical evidence — which could readily generate scientific proof — is present at nine out of every 10 crime scenes.[1] This scientific proof, based on an analysis of physical evidence at the scene, is often termed associative or trace evidence. The evidence is used so extensively in part because it can take a myriad of forms[2]. For example, criminalists might examine metal particles[3], plastic fragments,[4] tape,[5] arson debris,[6] explosives residue,[7] or paint specks[8] discovered at the scene.

---

1. B. PARKER, PHYSICAL EVIDENCE UTILIZATION IN THE ADMINISTRATION OF CRIMINAL JUSTICE (1972). *See also* Gruza & Tomaszewski, *Preservation and Use of Traces Revealed During the Search of the Scene of Burglary*, 46 FORENSIC SCI. INT'L 153 (1990); Holyst, *Theoretical and Practical Problems of Traces*, 46 FORENSIC SCI. INT'L 77 (1990); Mueller & Nadasi, *Experience of the Institute of Technical Expertise in the Examination of Criminalistic Traces*, 46 FORENSIC SCI. INT'L 23 (1990); Kolecki, *Identification Features of Traces*, 46 FORENSIC SCI. INT'L 7 (1990); He, *Application of Trace Evidence in Forensic Medical Examination*, 34 J. FORENSIC SCI. 391 (1989); Lewis, *Crime Scene Investigations*, 19 THE CHAMPION 16 (Mar. 1995) (describing the varieties of trace evidence and discussing the risks of loss and contamination of crime scene trace evidence).

2. Lentini, *Differentiation of Asphalt and Smoke Condensates from Liquid Petroleum Distillates Using GC/MS*, 43 J. FORENSIC SCI. 97 (1998); Shimoyama, Hamanaga & Ninomiya, *The Nondestructive Identification of Ivory-Live Seal Materials*, 42 J. FORENSIC SCI. 434 (1997); Blackledge, *Condom Trace Evidence: A New Factor in Sexual Assault Investigations*, 65 F.B.I. LAW. ENF. BULL. 12 (May 1996); Poolman & Pistorius, *The Possibility of Using Elemental Analysis to Identify Debris from the Cutting of Mild Steel*, 41 J. FORENSIC SCI. 998 (1996); Bodziak, *The Manufacture, Examination, and Identification of Die Cut Corrugated Boxes*, 41 J. FORENSIC SCI. 990 (1996); Fitzpatrick, *Foiling Crooks with Magnetic Fingerprints*, WASHINGTON 17 (Spring 1996) (Two researchers at Washington University in St. Louis "discovered that all magnetic media — from credit cards, bank checks, card keys, and security cards to tapes, computer disks, and magnetic ink — are marked with unique, permanent electronic signatures that are virtually impossible to forge.").

3. McDermott, *Metal Particles as Evidence in Criminal Cases*, 39 J. FORENSIC SCI. 1552 (1994).

4. Kirkwood & Isaacs, *The Analysis of Vehicle Sidelight Plastics*, 43 FORENSIC SCI. INT'L 51 (1989).

5. Williams & Munson, *The Comparison of Black Polyvinylchloride (PVC) Tape by Pyrolysis Gas Chromatography*, 33 J. FORENSIC SCI. 1163 (1988).

6. Dietz, *Improved Charcoal Packaging for Accelerant Recovery by Passive Diffusion*, 36 J. FORENSIC SCI. 111 (1991); Biley, *The Archaeological Water Separation Machine in Fire Investigation*, 35 J. FORENSIC SCI. 1201 (1990); Mann & Gresham, *Microbial Degradation of Gasoline in Soil*, 35 J. FORENSIC SCI. 913 (1990); Chambers, *Determination of the Causes of Fires*

This type of evidence is not only widely used; it has also figured in some of the most famous trials in this century. For instance, in the prosecution of Bruno Richard Hauptmann for the kidnapping of Charles Lindbergh's baby, a forestry expert testified that the ladder found at the crime scene was made of wood which matched the floorboard from the defendant's home.[9] Hair and fiber evidence was

---

and Explosions by the Analysis of Biological Materials, 46 FORENSIC SCI. INT'L 47 (1990); Tranthim-Fryer, *The Application of a Simple and Inexpensive Modified Carbon Wire Absorption/Solvent Extraction Technique to the Analysis of Accelerants and Volatile Organic Compounds in Arson Debris*, 35 J. FORENSIC SCI. 271 (1990). *See also* United States v. Triplett, 922 F.2d 1174 (5th Cir.) (testimony by an arson investigator), *cert. denied*, 500 U.S. 945 (1991).

7. Glattstein, Landau & Zeichner, *Identification of Match Head Residues in Post-Explosion Debris*, 36 J. FORENSIC SCI. 1360 (1991); Kolla, *Trace Analysis of Explosives from Complex Mixtures with Sample Pretreatment and Selective Detection*, 36 J. Forensic 1342 (1991); Fetterolf, Mudd & Teten, *An Enzyme-Linked Immunosorbent Assay (ELISA) for Trinitrotoluene (TNT) Residue on Hands*, 36 J. FORENSIC SCI. 343 (1991); Lloyd & King, *One-Pot Processing of Swabs for Organic Explosives and Firearms Residue Traces*, 35 J. FORENSIC SCI. 956 (1990); Baran, *Identification of Explosive Materials*, 46 FORENSIC SCI. INT'L 139 (1990); Nowicki & Pauling, *Identification of Sugars in Explosive Residues by Gas Chromatography-Mass Spectrometry*, 33 J. FORENSIC SCI. 1254 (1988).

8. *E.g.*, United States v. Cook, 580 F. Supp. 948 (N.D. W. Va. 1983), *aff'd*, 782 F.2d 1037 (4th Cir. 1984); Vowkertchian, *Quantitative Analysis of Organic Pigments in Forensic Paint Examination*, 40 J. FORENSIC SCI. 823 (1995); Allen, *The Examination of Thin Sections of Coloured Paints by Light Microscopy*, 57 FORENSIC SCI. INT'L 5 (1992); Zeichner, Levin & Landau, *A Study of Paint Coat Characteristics Produced by Spray Paints from Shaken and Nonshaken Spray Cans*, 37 J. FORENSIC SCI. 542 (1992); Allen & Schnetz, *The Removal of Paint Smears from Tools and Clothing for Microscopical Examination and Analysis*, 52 FORENSIC SCI. INT'L 101 (1991); *Paint Examination Techniques Utilized in F.B.I. Laboratory*, F.B.I. LAW ENF. BULL. Reprint, April 1973; Laing, *Paint Examination Using Thin Paint Sections*, 46 FORENSIC SCI. INT'L 37 (1990); Ionescu, *Authenticity Judgment with the Help of Paint-Brush Traces*, 46 FORENSIC SCI. INT'L 33 (1990); Dabdoub & Severin, *The Identification of Domestic and Foreign Automobile Manufacturers Through Body Primer Characterization*, 34 J. FORENSIC SCI. 1395 (1989); Bates, Allinson & Bal, *Capillary Pyrolysis Gas Chromatography: A System Employing a Curie Point Pyrolyser and a Stationary Phase of Intermediate Polarity for the Analysis of Paint Resins and Polymers*, 40 FORENSIC SCI. INT'L 25 (1989); Wilkinson, Locke & Laing, *The Examination of Paints as Thin Sections Using Visible Microspectrophotometry and Fourier Transform Infrared Microscopy*, 38 FORENSIC SCI. INT'L 43 (1988); Locke, Wilkinson & Hanford, *A Data Collection of Vehicle Topcoat Colours. 2. The Measurement of Colour Samples Used in the Vehicle Refinishing Industry*, 37 FORENSIC SCI. INT'L 177 (1988); Taylor, Cousins, Holding, Locke & Wilkinson, *A Data Collection of Vehicle Topcoat Colours. 3. Practical Considerations for Using a National Database*, 40 FORENSIC SCI. INT'L 131 (1989); Cousins, Holding, Locke & Wilkinson, *A Data Collection of Vehicle Topcoat Colours. 4. A Trial to Assess the Effectiveness of Colour Identification*, 43 FORENSIC SCI. INT'L 183 (1989).

9. Adelman, Peterson & Sorger, *Identification of Wood Instrument by Scanning Electron Microscopy from Splinters Left in Victim*, 33 J. FORENSIC SCI. 787 (1988); Graham, *Anatomy of the Lindbergh Kidnapping*, 42 J. FORENSIC SCI. 368 (1997) ("A hand-made wooden ladder left at the scene provided some of the most critical evidence connecting Bruno Richard Hauptmann to the crime. The information was supplied by Arthur Koehler, wood technologist for the U.S. Forest

presented in the Williams ("child killing") prosecution in Atlanta and played a major role in the application for post-conviction relief by Jeffrey McDonald, the Green Beret doctor in the Fatal Vision case.[10] Of course, together with DNA testimony, trace evidence analysis was the backbone of the prosecution case against O. J. Simpson.

Until the acquittal in the *Simpson* prosecution, the widespread public perception was that trace evidence is both reliable and highly persuasive to juries. The acquittal came as a shock to the forensic science community. After the *Simpson* acquittal, forensic scientists intensified their efforts to refine trace evidence analysis. In June 1996, in San Antonio, Texas, the Forensic Science Training Unit of the F.B.I. Laboratory Division hosted an International Symposium on the Forensic Examination of Trace Evidence in Transition. In addition, an ongoing Scientific Working Group for Materials Examination (SWGMAT) was formed. Edward Bartick of the F.B.I. laboratory was the first chair of the group. The group includes subgroups for fiber and paint analysis.

At the same time, perhaps encouraged by the *Simpson* acquittal, the defense bar is questioning trace evidence more aggressively.[11] During the *Simpson* prosecution, former F.B.I. chemist, Dr. C. Frederick Whitehurst, publicly questioned some of the trace evidence analyses conducted by the F.B.I..[12] In 1997 and 1998, the National Association of Criminal Defense Lawyers pressed the Department of Justice to release the documents compiled during the Office of Inspector General (OIG) investigation of the operation of the F.B.I. laboratory.[13] The investigation raised questions about the caliber of analyses done by the Hair and Fibers Unit.[14] The N.A.C.D.L. contemplated using the material gathered by the OIG to attack the quality of trace evidence testimony given by F.B.I.

Service.... Koehler traced part of the ladder's wood from its mill source to a lumberyard near the kidnapper's home through faint machine planing marks even before the suspect was known. After Hauptmann's arrest, Koehler demonstrated by wood anatomical comparisons that one of the side rails of the ladder previously had been part of a floorboard in Hauptmann's attic. Finally, he established that Hauptmann's hand plane had been used to dress the edges of several ladder parts;" in addition, four square nail holes aligned perfectly between rail 16 of the ladder and a rafter in the attic).

10. In that case, the theory of the defense was that the members of McDonald's family had been slain by intruders. McDonald alleges that the prosecution suppressed hair and fiber evidence which would have supported the defense theory. SUPPLEMENTAL MEMORANDUM OF THE UNITED STATES at 1, United States v. McDonald, No. 75-26-CR-3 (E.D.N.C.).

11. *Clean Bill of Health Eludes FBI Crime Lab*, LEGAL TIMES, July 27, 1998, at p. 12.

12. JOHN F. KELLY & PHILLIP K. WEARNE, TAINTING EVIDENCE: INSIDE THE SCANDALS AT THE FBI CRIME LAB (1998).

13. *DOJ Sets New Date for FBI Lab Documents*, 22 THE CHAMPION 8 (Apr. 1998); *FBI Lab Documents Trickle In*, 21 THE CHAMPION 10 (Dec. 1997).

14. Rovella, *Lab Scandal? What Scandal?*, NAT'L L.J., Apr. 27, 1998, at p. Bl.

analysts,[15] but to date "the number of convictions overturned as a result of the lab scandal is zero."[16] In Canada, a similar official investigation called into question the quality of hair and fiber analysis proffered in the notorious murder prosecution of Guy Paul Morin.[17] All of these recent developments make it imperative that judges and attorneys carefully scrutinize the caliber of trace evidence proffered in court.

§ 24-2. Hair Analysis.

Section 24-4 discusses the exchange principle: Substances such as hair adhere to surfaces such as clothing; and when surfaces come into contact, there can be an exchange of hairs between surfaces. Hence, if one person attacks another and the two struggle, there could be a mutual exchange of hairs. There have been numerous studies of the transfer of human[18] and animal[19] hair. When the analyst finds suspected hair, in the current state of the art an analyst can employ a number of techniques to evaluate a hair sample.[20]

§ 24-2(A). Identification of Hair.

The threshold determination for the analyst is whether a sample is a hair at all, rather than vegetable or synthetic fiber.[21] The analyst may use chemical, macroscopic, or microscopic techniques to make that determination.

A potential chemical technique is a test of the hair's ability to burn. Vegetable fibers burn rather easily, emit a smell like burnt wood, and leave a sharply burnt

---

15. Burger, *FBI Crime Lab Faces Key Tests*, LEGAL TIMES, May 25, 1998, at p. 2; Matthew, *Effectively Cross-Examining an FBI Witness at Trial: Remembering the Basics*, 22 THE CHAMPION 22 (Jan./Feb. 1998).

16. Rovella, *Lab Scandal? What Scandal?*, NAT'L L.J., Apr. 27, 1998, at p. B1.

17. King, *The Ordeal of Guy Paul Morin*, 22 THE CHAMPION 8, 64 (Aug. 1998) (the analyses in the case had been conducted by forensic scientists on the staff of the Ontario Centre of Forensic Sciences (CFS); "Stephanie Nyznyk, a former CFS examiner ,... told the commission that she was under pressure from police and prosecutors to overstate her evidence. Nyznyk admitted that she may have misled authorities — who then unwittingly misled the court — about the value of the hair and fiber samples").

18. Exline, Smith & Drexler, *Frequency of Pubic Hair Transfer During Sexual Intercourse*, 43 J. FORENSIC SCI. 505 (1998).

19. D'Andrea, Fridez & Coquoz, *Preliminary Experiments on the Transfer of Animal Hair During Simulated Criminal Behavior*, 43 J. FORENSIC SCI. 1257 (1998).

20. Sections 24-2 and 24-3 are based in part on Imwinkelried, *Forensic Hair Analysis: The Case Against the Underemployment of Scientific Evidence*, 39 WASH. & LEE L. REV. 41 (1982). Reprinted with permission. *See also* Imwinkelried, *Forensic Science: Hair Analysis*, 27 CRIM. L. BULL. 447 (Sept.-Oct. 1991).

21. A. MOENSSENS, J. STARRS, C. HENDERSON & F. INBAU, SCIENTIFIC EVIDENCE IN CIVIL AND CRIMINAL CASES § 9.08 (4th ed. 1995); *Hair*, 5 AM. JUR. PROOF OF FACTS 569, 571 (1960).

end.[22] In contrast, it is difficult to set hair aflame.[23] Additionally, burning hair creates a smell like burning feathers, and burnt hair usually has a fused or rounded shaft end.[24] However, these tests are destructive and, when conducted, preclude further testing. For that reason, these tests are rarely used.

There is also a macroscopic technique for distinguishing hair from fibers. Hairs ordinarily grow singly without branching.[25] Vegetable fibers are readily distinguishable because they often grow in tight bunches and exhibit branching.[26] These characteristics can be detected even without the benefit of a microscope.

However, the microscopic technique is probably the most trustworthy method of determining whether the sample is hair. If the lengthwise (full-mount or longitudinal) view of a hair strand is examined, the analyst can observe a tip end, a shaft, and a bulb or root end.[27] When the analyst uses optical sectioning[28] or a cross-sectional or transverse view is taken, three concentric rings can be seen. The core is the medulla, containing cellular debris and pigment granules of melanin.[29] The middle ring is the cortex, which also includes pigment.[30] It is composed of flat, elongated cells that give the strand its pliability.[31] The outermost layer is the surface cuticle,[32] consisting of overlapping scales[33] that are transparent[34] and point toward the tip end of the hair strand.[35]

§ 24-2(B). Human or Animal Hair.

Using one of several methods, the analyst can also determine whether a hair strand is of human or animal origin. To begin with, several micro-measurements are helpful in the differentiation.[36] One measurement is the diameter of the hair. The nonhuman primate maximum diameters exceed human averages at both the low and high ends of the range, but there is some overlap between human and

---

22. *Id.* at 571.

23. *Id.*

24. *Id.*

25. *Id.*

26. *Id.*

27. A. MOENSSENS, J. STARRS, C. HENDERSON & F. INBAU *supra* note 21, at § 9.08; *Don't Miss A Hair*, F.B.I. LAW ENF. BULL. Reprint, Dec. 1968, at 2.

28. *Preliminary Report — Committee on Forensic Hair Comparison*, 12 CRIME LAB. DIGEST 50 (July 1985).

29. A. MOENSSENS, J. STARRS, C. HENDERSON & F. INBAU, *supra* note 21, at § 9.08.

30. *Id.*

31. *Id.*

32. *Id.*

33. *Don't Miss A Hair*, *supra* note 27, at 2.

34. Our reviewer points out that this characteristic enables the analyst to tell whether the hair has been dyed. *See* § 24-2(G), *infra*.

35. A. MOENSSENS, J. STARRS, C. HENDERSON & F. INBAU *supra* note 21, at § 9.08.

36. Rosen, *Identification of Primate Hair*, 19 J. FORENSIC SCI. 109 (1974).

nonhuman primate diameters.[37] The analyst may also measure the cross-section area, but again there is overlap, particularly between human hair and that of Old World monkeys.[38] The cuticle scale count (the number of cuticle scales per unit of measure) is yet another indicator, but the analyst cannot discriminate between human and animal hair solely on the basis of scale count.[39] Other features, such as cuticle scale width, are indicative of human origin.[40] Nevertheless, "[t]he metrical features of human head hair are not distinct enough from those of other primates to use micro-measurement as a sole means of hair identification."[41]

In addition to the micro-measurement technique, macroscopic and microscopic methods of differentiating human and animal hair are available. The macroscopic technique involves examining the hair's gross characteristics. Animal hair varies in type; many animals have both heavy guard hair and finer fur hair.[42] Human hair is unitary in type.[43]

The most reliable technique is microscopy. The microscope enables the analyst to detect distinctive characteristics in the cuticle, cortex, and medulla. Human hair tends to have a narrow central medullary canal.[44] The human medulla is normally fragmented[45] and has no obvious cell pattern.[46] It approximates one-third of the width of the cortex.[47] Animal hair differs in each respect. The hairs of lower animals have a broad medulla, display a clear cellular structure, and usually have medullas more than half as broad as the cortical shell.[48]

The human cortex layer contains the majority of the pigment granules while most pigment is located in the medulla in other mammals.[49] There are other differences as well. In the human cortex, the pigment granules are packed most densely toward the peripheral areas.[50] There is frequently a central accumulation of pigment cells in animal hair.[51]

The cuticle or scale shell also aids in distinguishing between human and animal hair. The scales of human hair overlap smoothly, but those of other

---

37. *Id.*
38. *Id.*
39. *Id.* at 110.
40. *Id.* at 111.
41. *Id.* at 112.
42. *Don't Miss A Hair*, *supra* note 27, at 2.
43. *Id.*
44. *Hair*, 5 AM. JUR. PROOF OF FACTS 569, 572 (1960).
45. A. MOENSSENS, J. STARRS, C. HENDERSON & F. INBAU, *supra* note 21, at § 9.11.
46. *Hair*, *supra* note 44, at 572.
47. *Id.*
48. *Id.*
49. A. MOENSSENS, J. STARRS, C. HENDERSON & F. INBAU, *supra* note 21, at § 9.11.
50. *Hair*, *supra* note 44, at 572.
51. *Id.*

mammalian species often protrude roughly.[52] None of these characteristics is exclusively human, but the cumulative presence of these characteristics makes it almost certain that the hair is human in origin.[53]

These hair characteristics can be observed with a conventional microscope. By employing scanning electron microscopy (SEM),[54] French researchers believe that they have discovered new minute features in the medulla "that absolutely differentiate human hairs from all other animal hairs...."[55]

In some cases, the analyst can also determine the particular animal species. For example, under even the conventional microscope, it is possible to detect differences among horse, deer, antelope, and beef hairs.[56] One text on animal hair identification contains photomicrographs of seventy-six mammalian species and describes the unique diagnostic features of each species.[57] Over the years, the techniques for sectioning hairs have improved,[58] and these improved techniques have resulted in better transverse views of the diagnostic traits of the various animal families.[59] Isoelectric fousing of hair keratins has also been used to make species identifications.[60]

§ 24-2(C). Male or Female Hair.

There are a number of techniques for determining the sex of the person who was the source of the human hair strand. The oldest method relies upon the strands' gross characteristics. Male hair is generally larger in diameter, shorter in

---

52. A. Moenssens, J. Starrs, C. Henderson & F. Inbau, *supra* note 21, at § 9.11.

53. *Hair, supra* note 44, at 572.

54. *See* §25-2.

55. Clement, Hagege, Pareux, Connet & Gastaldi, *New Concepts About Hair Identification Revealed by Electron Microscope Studies*, 26 J. Forensic Sci. 447, 457 (1981).

56. *Laboratory Solves Variety of Crimes With Animal Hairs*, F.B.I. Law Enf. Bull. Reprint, Mar. 1960, at 2. Curriden, *New Questions on Atlanta Murders: Did Prosecutors Withhold Evidence of Klan Involvement in Children's Deaths?*, 78 A.B.A. J. 36 (May 1992) (some now contend that Ku Klux Klan member Charles Sanders was responsible for at least some of the killings which Wayne Williams was convicted of; "A police report by a University of Georgia veterinarian concluded that dog hairs found on victims' bodies could only have come from a Siberian husky or an Alaskan malamute. Sanders owned a Siberian husky while Williams owned a German shepherd. At Williams' trial, prosecutors told jurors that the dog hairs were consistent with those of a German shepherd").

57. H. Brunner & B. Coman, The Identification of Mammalian Hair (1974).

58. *See* Cooper & Kirk, *An Improved Technique for Sectioning Hair*, 44 J. Crim. L., Criminology & Police Sci. 124, 124-27 (1953).

59. *Id.* at 127.

60. Carracedo, Concheiro & Requena, *The Isoelectric Focusing of Keratins in Hair Followed by Silver Staining*, 29 Forensic Sci. Int'l 83 (1985).

length, and more wiry in texture.[61] The average diameter of male human hair is $^1/_{350}$ inch while that of female hair is approximately $^1/_{450}$ inch.[62]

Until the last two decades, women routinely manipulated their hair more extensively than men by pinning, curling, brushing, and combing. The manipulation frequently caused the tip ends of female hair to split.[63] More broadly, most cosmetic treatments cause the shaft to evidence some form of damage.[64] Within the past two decades, however, men have begun to treat their hair more frequently, and consequently the presence of a split end now has much less evidentiary value.[65]

Fortunately, more reliable techniques have emerged for making sex determinations. One technique is the test for the X-chromatin body in the hair root sheath.[66] Roughly sixty percent of the cells of a normal woman will include the chromatin body.[67] The corresponding figure for male cells is two percent.[68] The presence of X-chromatin bodies is a specific test, since the frequencies do not overlap; the smallest reported percentage for a female is higher than the greatest recorded percentage for a male.[69]

However, there are times when the analyst cannot use the X-chromatin test. Conducting the test requires hair strands with an intact root sheath.[70] Some crime scenes do not yield strands with their sheath. Hair is likely to lack its sheath, for example, when it has been severed by a weapon.[71] This problem led to the development of another technique for analyzing sheathless hair strands: the Y-chromosome test.[72] The experimental data indicate that when properly stained,

---

61. *Don't Miss A Hair, supra* note 27, at 4.

62. *Id.*

63. *Id.*

64. J. W. HICKS, MICROSCOPY OF HAIR (1977).

65. *Don't Miss a Hair, supra* note 27, at 4.

66. A. MOENSSENS, J. STARRS, C. HENDERSON & F. INBAU, *supra* note 21, at § 9.11; Nagamori, Ohno, Uchima, Kaiwara, Nakazato, Une & Takeda, *Sex Determination from Buccal Musoca and Hair Root by the Combined Treatment of Quiacrine Staining and the Fluorescent Feulgen Reaction Using a Single Specimen*, 31 FORENSIC SCI. INT'L 119 (1986); Nagamori & Takeda, *Sex Determination From Plucked Human Hairs Without Epithelial Root Sheath*, 17 FORENSIC SCI. INT'L 85, 86 (1981).

67. A. MOENSSENS, J. STARRS, C. HENDERSON & F. INBAU, *supra* note 21, at § 9.11.

68. Nagamori & Takeda, *supra* note 66, at 86.

69. Nagamori, *Sex Determination From Plucked Human Hairs Without Epithelial Root Sheath*, 12 FORENSIC SCI. INT'L 167 (1978).

70. *Id.*

71. *Id.*

72. *Id.;* Prahlow, Lantz, Cox-Jones, Rao & Pettenati, *Gender Identification of Human Hair Using Fluorescence in Situ Hybridization*, 41 J. FORENSIC SCI. 1035 (1996); Thomsen & Buchhave, *The Effect of Various Fixatives on Y-Chromosome Detection in Leucocytes*, 29 FORENSIC SCI. INT'L 21 (1985).

the Y-chromosome in the hair cortex nuclei fluoresces.[73] In one experiment, the average frequency for male hairs was 59.4 percent while the figure for female hair was only 5.3 percent.[74] As in the case of the X-chromatin test, the frequencies do not appear to overlap.[75] In another Y-chromosome experiment, there were no false positives.[76]

Finally, although most laboratories do not routinely use neutron activation analysis (NAA), NAA[77] aids in distinguishing male from female hair. There are differences in trace element concentrations between male and female hair.[78] One estimate is that the trace element concentration differences permit the determination of the sex of the source of the hair samples approximately ninety percent of the time.[79] This test is not as conclusive as the X-chromatin or Y-chromosome test, but it is a helpful, confirmatory procedure.

§ 24-2(D). Race of Source.

The hair analyst cannot determine race as positively as sex, but he or she nevertheless can make a relatively confident finding as to the race of the human hair source.[80] The analyst can categorize the hair into one of four groups: Caucasian, Negroid, Mongoloid (including Asiatics and Indians), or mixed.

Caucasian hair has the widest range of color differences.[81] The pigment is evenly distributed.[82] Cross-sections of Caucasian hair are typically oval to round in shape.[83] The hair is usually straight or wavy but not tightly curled.[84]

Negroid hair has dark pigment distributed unevenly.[85] The pigment often clumps along the periphery of the cortex.[86] In a cross-section view, the hair appears flat or oval.[87] The hair is frequently kinky.[88]

---

73. Nagamori, *supra* note 69.

74. *Id.* at 169.

75. *Id.*

76. Kringsholm, Thomsen & Henningsen, *Fluorescent Y-Chromosomes in Hairs and Blood Stains*, 9 FORENSIC SCI. 117, 123 (1978). *See also* Mudd, *The Determination of Sex from Forcibly Removed Hairs*, 29 J. FORENSIC SCI. 1072 (1984).

77. Comment, *The Evidentiary Uses of Neutron Activation Analysis*, 59 CALIF. L. REV. 997, 1054 (1971).

78. *See* Chapter 11.

79. *Id.*

80. *Don't Miss A Hair*, *supra* note 27, at 3; A. MOENSSENS, J. STARRS, C. HENDERSON & F. INBAU, *supra* note 21, at § 9.11.

81. *Hair*, *supra* note 44, at 572.

82. *Don't Miss A Hair*, *supra* note 27, at 3.

83. *Id.*

84. *Id.*

85. *Id.*

86. *Hair*, *supra* note 44, at 573.

87. *Don't Miss A Hair*, *supra* note 27, at 3.

Like Negroid hair, Mongoloid hair has dense pigment.[89] However, as with Caucasian hair, the pigment of Mongoloid hair is rather evenly distributed.[90] Under a cross-section view, its shaft has a circular or triangular shape.[91] Mongoloid hair tends to be coarse and straight.[92]

It has been asserted that if a person is of mixed race, his hair will display the characteristics of the ethnic group that predominates in the person's physical appearance.[93] On that assumption, when the person is of mixed race but had predominantly Negroid features, the person's hair will similarly display Negroid characteristics. However, our reviewer is unaware of any study supporting that assertion, and he is frankly dubious of the validity of the assertion.

According to Professor James Starrs of the George Washington University, research is ongoing to base racial determinations on DNA extracted from the hair shaft.

§ 24-2(E). Body Region.

Microscopy also can enable the analyst to determine the topical site or part of the human body that a hair strand came from. Scalp or crown hair tends to be soft and long.[94] Scalp hair ordinarily displays less diameter variation and more even pigment distribution than hair from other regions of the body.[95] Eyebrow, eyelash, and nostril hairs are short, stiff, and thick.[96] They have wide medullas and taper very quickly to a fine point.[97] Beard and moustache hairs are the thickest.[98] Beard hair is very curved and coarse.[99] These hairs are irregular in shape and have a triangular cross section.[100]

Hairs from the chest or back seem immature.[101] They are generally fine, short, and flexible.[102] Hairs from legs and arms are short, fine, and contain little pigment.[103] Pubic and axillary (armpit) hairs are wiry.[104] They have numerous twists[105] and abruptly change their diameters.[106]

---

88. Hair, *supra* note 44, at 573.
89. *Don't Miss A Hair, supra* note 27, at 3.
90. *Id.*
91. *Hair, supra* note 44, at 573.
92. *Don't Miss A Hair, supra* note 27, at 3.
93. *Id.*
94. *Hair, supra* note 44, at 574.
95. A. Moenssens, J. Starrs, C. Henderson & F. Inbau, *supra* note 21, at § 9.11.
96. *Don't Miss A Hair, supra* note 27, at 4; *Hair, supra* note 44, at 574.
97. *Don't Miss A Hair, supra* note 27, at 4.
98. *Hair, supra* note 44, at 574.
99. A. Moenssens, J. Starrs, C. Henderson & F. Inbau, *supra* note 21, at § 9.11.
100. *Hair, supra* note 44, at 574.
101. A. Moenssens, J. Starrs, C. Henderson & F. Inbau, *supra* note 21, at § 9.11.
102. *Hair, supra* note 44, at 574.
103. A. Moenssens, J. Starrs, C. Henderson & F. Inbau, *supra* note 21, at § 9.11.

§ 24-2(F). Adult or Child Hair.

There are two techniques for determining the age of the human hair source. Unfortunately, neither technique is specific.

The first method is microscopy.[107] Children's hairs are finer, thinner, and less well-developed.[108] However, the state of the art does not enable the analyst to be more specific. The analyst cannot even rely on graying or balding as the basis for a finding that the person was elderly rather than middle-aged, since both graying and balding can occur prematurely.[109] One clue is the variety in the size, shape, and pigmentation of a person's scalp hair; the older the person is, the greater the variety.[110]

The other technique is a chemical test. The test involves dissolving the hair in a solution of caustic potash.[111] The faster the roots dissolve, the younger the human hair source.[112] The speed of dissolution is relative and varies, and for that reason the caustic potash test does not permit an exact age estimate.[113]

In part, the imprecision of these techniques accounts for the reluctance of most experts to offer age estimates in court. Another factor is the destructive nature of these tests. Like the burning tests previously mentioned, these tests consume the sample and foreclose further testing.

§ 24-2(G). Natural or Dyed Hair.

Natural hair can be distinguished from dyed hair microscopically.[114] The cuticle is colorless, and hence the addition of dye is evident. Dyed hair has a duller appearance, and the inner margin of its cuticle is obscured.[115] Moreover, since hair grows at the rate of approximately 1/2 inch per month,[116] there often is a sharp contrast between the previously dyed portion of the hair strand and the new natural growth.[117] Instrumental techniques can also be utilized to analyze

---

104. *Hair, supra* note 44, at 574. According to our reviewer, "buckles" are a primary diagnostic feature for this purpose. J. W. HICKS, MICROSCOPY OF HAIR (1977).

105. A. MOENSSENS, J. STARRS, C. HENDERSON & F. INBAU, *supra* note 21, at § 9.11.

106. *Hair, supra* note 44, at 574.

107. *Don't Miss A Hair*, *supra* note 27, at 3-4.

108. *Hair, supra* note 44, at 575.

109. *Don't Miss A Hair*, *supra* note 27, at 3-4.

110. *Hair, supra* note 44, at 575-76.

111. *Id.* at 575.

112. *Id.*

113. *Id.*

114. *Don't Miss A Hair*, *supra* note 27, at 5.

115. A. MOENSSENS, J. STARRS, C. HENDERSON & F. INBAU, *supra* note 21, at § 9.12.

116. *Don't Miss A Hair*, *supra* note 27, at 5.

117. A. MOENSSENS, J. STARRS, C. HENDERSON & F. INBAU, *supra* note 21, at § 9.12.

hair dyes.[118] These techniques can sometimes succeed in identifying the specific brand of hair dye used.[119]

§ 24-2(H). Fallen or Pulled Out Hair.

The appearance of a pulled hair differs markedly. Hair that falls out will have a clean appearance.[120] The pulled strand will seem mutilated, and the bulb may have a portion of the sheath clinging to it.[121]

It is sometimes said that the mere presence of a root is strong evidence that the hair fell out due to natural causes or a disease.[122] It is true that if hair falls out naturally, the strand will tend to have its root end.[123] However, our reviewer emphasizes that the appearance of the root is the key. The presence of follicular material is an indication that the hair did not fall out naturally. The hair may have been pulled out even if the root is present.

§ 24-2(I). Presence of Poisons or Other Drugs.

If a person was killed by arsenic poisoning, there will be an arsenic residue in the hair.[124] Proof of the arsenic residue can be important evidence of the homicidal character of the death. Chloroquine, an antimalarial drug, can also cause fatal poisonings.[125] By the use of such techniques as thin layer chromatography (TLC), gas chromatography (GC), and mass spectrometry (MS), an analyst can detect minute quantities of the drug in hair samples from a decedent.[126]

Like poisons, drugs of abuse can be detected in human hair samples. Analysts have, for example, employed gas chromatography/mass spectrometry (GC/MS) to determine whether a person had ingested amphetamine, methamphetamine,

---

118. Tanada, Kashimura, Kageura & Hara, *Practical GC/MS Analysis of Oxidation Dye Components in Hair Fiber as a Forensic Investigative Procedure*, 44 J. FORENSIC SCI. 292 (1999); Tanada, Kageura, Hara, Hieda, Takamoto & Kashimura, *Identification of Human Hair Stained with Oxidation Hair Dyes by Gas Chromatographic-Mass Spectrometric Analysis*, 52 FORENSIC SCI. INT'L 5 (1991).

119. *Don't Miss a Hair, supra* note 27, at 11.

120. *Id.*

121. *Id.;* State v. Head, 79 N.C. App. 1, _, 338 S.E.2d 908, 914 ("Hairs matching hers from the slacks and one of the shoes were crushed and tissue adhering to the roots, indicating forcible removal"), *review denied*, 316 N.C. 736, 345 S.E.2d 395 (1986).

122. *Don't Miss a Hair, supra* note 27, at 4.

123. *Id.*

124. *Hair, supra* note 44, at 575-76. Guinn & Demiralp, *Arsenic in Hair by NAA)A Major Recent Murder Case*, 168 J. RADIOANAL. NUCL. CHEM. 249 (1993).

125. Viala, Deturmeny, Aubert, Estadieu, Durand, Cano & Delmont, *Determination of Chloroquine and Monodesethylchloroquine in Hair*, 28 J. FORENSIC SCI. 922 (1983).

126. *Id.*

cocaine, morphine, phencyclidine, amitriptyline, imipramine, and nicotine.[127] Radioimmunoassay (RIA) can also be used to detect drugs in hair.[128]

The location of the various drugs in the strand may indicate the sequence in which the person ingested the drugs.[129]

---

127. Potsch & Moeller, *Influence of Pigmentation on the Codeine Content of Hair Fibers in Guinea Pigs*, 42 J. FORENSIC SCI. 1095 (1997); Kidwell, *Analysis of Phencyclidine and Cocaine in Human Hair by Tandem Mass Spectrometry*, 38 J. FORENSIC SCI. 272 (1993); Suzuki, Hattori & Asano, *Detection of Methamphetamine and Amphetamine in a Single Human Hair by Gas Chromatography/Chemical Ionization Mass Spectrometry*, 29 J. FORENSIC SCI. 611 (1984); Ishiyama, Nagai & Toshida, *Detection of Basic Drugs (Methamphetamine, Antidepressants, and Nicotine) from Human Hair*, 28 J. FORENSIC SCI. 380 (1983); Baumgartner, Jones & Black, *Detection of Phencyclidine in Hair*, 26 J. FORENSIC SCI. 576 (1981); Valente, Cassini, Pigliapochi & Vansetti, *Hair as the Sample in Assessing Morphine and Cocaine Addiction*, 27 CLIN. CHEM. 1952 (1981).

128. Smith & Liu, *Detection of Cocaine Metabolite in Perspiration Stain, Menstrual Bloodstain, and Hair*, 31 J. FORENSIC SCI. 1269 (1986). In United States v. Nimmer, 43 M.J. 252 (C.A.A.F. 1995), *rev'g*, 39 M.J. 924 (N.M.C.M.R. 1994), the defense attempted to introduce a negative RIA test result, confirmed by GC/MS, to rebut a charge of one-time cocaine use. The court conceded that a negative test result would be admissible to rebut an allegation of chronic cocaine use. However, the court remanded to the lower court with instructions to determine under *Daubert* whether it has been validated that a negative test result disproves an allegation of one-time cocaine use.

The Ianus Foundation, P. O. Box 85473, Los Angeles, California 90073, has experimented extensively with radioimmunoassay of hair (RIAH). The foundation has a National Institute of Justice grant to test the technique on federal probationers and parolees. In testimony before the Subcommittee on Human Resources of the House Committee on Post Office and Civil Service, Ianus Scientific Director, Dr. Werner Baumgartner, pointed out that "[h]ead hair grows at approximately 1.0-1.3 centimeters per month. Thus, a 12-centimeter-long hair provides a drug history of 9-12 months." Literature from the foundation states that "[h]air analysis was challenged in the following four cases and succeeded in being admitted as evidence. We have had approximately a dozen cases where it was not challenged and about 30 cases where it was used in preparing the case:

People v. Mart Meiel, Case A804003, Los Angeles County Superior Court, 1985.
People v. Robert Korner, Case 154558, Santa Barbara Superior Court, 1985.
United States v. James Boyle III, CR 8591R, United States District Court.
Frederick Paul Smith, Alaska v. Richard Gene Madjic, 3K081-367CR, 3rd Judicial District at Kodiak, May 1982."

See United States v. Medina, 749 F. Supp. 59, 61 (E.D.N.Y. 1990) ("Extensive scientific writings on RIA hair analysis establishes both its reliability and its acceptance in the field of forensic toxicology when used to determine cocaine use. [R]adioimmunoassay is an effective and accurate method of detecting the presence of various compounds including narcotics"); Burgel v. Burgel, 141 A.D.2d 215, 533 N.Y.S.2d 735 (1988) (in a custody dispute, the husband contended that the wife was an unfit mother because she frequently used drugs; the court ordered the wife to submit to an RIAH test; the court emphasized that "[w]e express no opinion in regard to whether the test results would be admissible, but leave that issue for trial"); Cox, *Analysis of Hair Traces Drug Use*, NAT'L L.J., July 27, 1987, at 3.

129. Baumgartner, Jones & Black, *supra* note 127, at 576.

Most of the research to date has focused on the identification of drugs within the hair strand itself. However, it is also possible to identify shampoo residues on the surface of the strand.[130]

§ 24-2(J). Cut or Crushed Hair.

The analyst can also make a finding as to whether the hair was cut or crushed. If the hair was cut, the cortical cells of the shaft will display a clean, smooth slice.[131] However, when the assailant used a blunt instrument, the cortical cells have a jagged, crushed, or rough appearance.[132]

§ 24-2(K). Blood Grouping.

During the past quarter century, the general field of serology or blood analysis progressed as rapidly as any scientific discipline.[133] The same holds true for the specific application of serology to hair analysis. In certain circumstances, the analyst can determine the ABO blood grouping of the human hair source.[134] Japanese researchers have perfected techniques for detecting numerous enzyme types including ES-D, PGM_1, PGM_2, and PGM_3 from hair samples.[135] Even more recently, researchers have typed the proteins or keratins in the cortex of human hair.[136]

In the past, relying on microscopic examination, the hair analyst could express only the opinion that hair samples are "similar" or that their characteristics are "consistent" with the hypothesis that they originated from a common source.[137]

---

130. Andrasko & Stocklassa, *Shampoo Residue Profiles in Human Head Hair*, 35 J. FORENSIC SCI. 569 (1990).

131. *Don't Miss A Hair*, *supra* note 27, at 4.

132. *Id.*

133. *See* Wraxall, *Forensic Serology*, *in* SCIENTIFIC AND EXPERT EVIDENCE 897 (2d ed. 1981).

134. Lincoln & Dodd, *Mixed Agglutination as a Method for the Determination of A, B, and H Blood Groups of Hair*, 8 MED., SCI. & L. 38 (1968). *See also* Shijun, *Examinations of ABO Bloodgroupings of Human Hair*, 36 FORENSIC SCI. INT'L 173 (1988); Tanabe, Ishiyama & Itakura, *An Improved Method for the Histological Preparation of Single Hairs and Dust Samples — Morphological and Immunological Examination*, 33 J. FORENSIC SCI. 767 (1988).

135. Lawton & Kerr, *Phosphoglucomutase Types in Blood and Hair Roots Taken from Post-Transfusion Subjects*, 29 J. FORENSIC SCI. 445 (1984); Yoshida, Abe & Nakamura, *Studies on the Frequencies of PGM1, PGM2, and Es-D Types From Hair Roots in Japanese Subjects and the Determination of These Types From Old Hair Roots*, 14 FORENSIC SCI. INT'L 1 (1979). *See also* Gillespie & Klement, *Methods and Future Prospects for Forensic Identification of Hairs by Electrophoresis*, 25 J. FORENSIC SCI. Soc'y 57 (1985); Yuasa, Tamaki, Inoue & Okada, *Esterase D Phenotyping of Bloodstains and Hair Roots by Low Voltage Isoelectric Focusing*, 28 FORENSIC SCI. INT'L 63 (1985).

136. *See generally* Lee, Ludwig & Baden, *Matrix Proteins of Human Hair as a Tool for Identification of Individuals*, 11 FORENSIC SCI. 115 (1978).

137. *See* text accompanying notes 228-33 *infra*.

The analyst could not quantify the opinion with any precision. The importance of the serological breakthroughs is that data exists on the population frequencies with which the various blood, enzyme, and protein groups occur.[138] We know, for instance, what percentage of the population falls into the type A blood grouping.[139] The application of serological techniques to hair analysis enables analysts to define the probative value of their findings quantitatively.

In particular, analysts now apply DNA typing techniques in hair analysis. Chapter 18 discusses DNA typing. The polymerase chain reaction (PCR) method of DNA typing is proving to be especially useful because it permits the genetic typing of small samples such as individual hair strands. As Chapter 18 points out, there is a distinction between mitochondrial (mtDNA) and nuclear DNA testing. The PCR procedure which the laboratories currently employ is a form of nuclear DNA testing; but according to our reviewer, mtDNA may come "on line" in many laboratories within the next two years.

§ 24-2(L). Identity of Human Source.

The finding of most interest to the criminal justice system is, of course, the identification of the specific person who was the source of the human hair. The current state of the art does not allow the hair analyst to make a conclusive identification,[140] but there are several techniques that the analyst can use to narrow the class of possible sources. Two of the techniques, the conventional microscope and NAA, have already gained judicial acceptance, but several other promising techniques are vying for acceptance in the courtroom.

New Techniques

One new technique, ion microprobe, failed its first judicial test in *United States v. Brown.*[141] This technique depends upon the measurement of the number and mass of ions that the sample releases when the sample is struck by an ion beam.[142] The instrumentation consists of two mass spectrometers. One spectrometer generates a magnetic field. The field is aimed as a beam at the sample. When the beam strikes the sample, the sample casts off ions of varying

---

138. Wraxall, *supra* note 133, at 940-41.

139. A. Moenssens, J. Starrs, C. Henderson & F. Inbau, *supra* note 21, at § 13.10.

140. State v. Hunt, 53 Wis. 2d 734, 750-51, 193 N.W.2d 858, 867-68 (1972); A. Moenssens, J. Starrs, C. Henderson & F. Inbau, *supra* note 21, at § 13.10; Turner, *Identification of Hit-and-Run Vehicle and Driver*, 27 Am. Jur. Proof of Facts 287, 307 (1971); Petraco, Fraas, Callery & DeForest, *The Morphology and Evidential Significance of Human Hair Roots*, 33 J. Forensic Sci. 68 (1988) ("Although many instrumental approaches to the individualization of human hair have been tried in recent years, these have not proved to be useful or reliable").

141. 557 F.2d 541 (6th Cir. 1977).

142. *Id.* at 555.

mass and numbers. These ions are collected and analyzed by the second mass spectrometer. The analysis yields the concentration of trace elements in the sample.

In *Brown,* the prosecution witnesses relied on ion microprobic analysis as the basis for their conclusion that the hair samples had a common origin.[143] The trial court admitted the evidence, but the Sixth Circuit reversed.[144] The court cited *Frye v. United States*[145] as authority for its decision.[146] As Chapter 1 points out, *Frye* is the landmark case announcing that a novel scientific technique must have gained general acceptance within the relevant scientific field in order to be admissible.[147] In *Brown* the record indicated that there were no prior cases admitting ion microprobic hair analysis and that there were no technical articles discussing the application of ion microprobe to hair examination.[148] Given *Frye,* the record condemned the ion microprobe evidence to inadmissibility.

Three other novel hair examination techniques have yet to surface in the courtroom. One is pyrolysis gas chromatography (PGC).[149] Chromatography techniques are designed to separate the constituent chemicals in compounds. In PGC, a pyrolyser decomposes the sample into fragments. The fragments (the pyrolysate) are then swept into the PGC column. Each chemical element requires a unique period of time to migrate through the column — its retention time or Rt.[150] As each element exits the column, the instrumentation marks a peak on a chart or chromatogram. The chart depicts the spectrum of the compound; a peak appears on the chart as each element leaves the column.[151]

Researchers believe that PGC has tremendous potential as a method of individualizing human hair.[152] However, at present, PGC is far from realizing that potential. Even neighboring hairs from the same human head produce different spectra on gas chromatograms.[153] In addition, researchers have accumulated only a limited number of reference PGC spectra for comparison purposes.[154] Finally,

---

143. *Id.*

144. *Id.*

145. 293 F. 1013 (D.C. Cir. 1923).

146. 557 F.2d at 557.

147. 293 F. at 1014. *See* Giannelli, *The Admissibility of Novel Scientific Evidence: Frye v. United States, A Half Century Later*, 80 COLUM. L. REV. 1197, 1205 (1980). For a discussion of *Frye, see* Chapter 1.

148. 557 F.2d at 557.

149. *See* Watkins & Watkins, *Identification of Substances by Instrumental Analysis*, 22 AM. JUR. PROOF OF FACTS 95-96 (Supp. 1991).

150. *See* Rudzitis, *New Techniques for Pyrolysis Gas Chromatography and Possible Other Forensic Applications*, 62 J. CRIM. L., CRIMINOLOGY & POLICE SCI. 298, 299 (1971).

151. *Id.*

152. Watkins & Watkins, *supra* note 149, at 95-96 (Supp. 1991).

153. *Id.* at 87.

154. Rudzitis, *supra* note 150, at 298.

many agents such as sprays, shampoos, rinses, dyes, and bleaches are applied to human hair, and little is known about the effect of these agents on gas chromatograms.[155]

Like PGC, pyrolysis mass spectrometry (Py-MS) may ultimately prove to be of great value in individualizing human hair.[156] As in PGC, the process begins with the breakdown of the sample into a pyrolysate of fragments.[157] The difference is that in Py-MS, the pyrolysate next enters a mass spectrometer. The fragments are ionized and analyzed. The end product is a mass pyrogram, indicating the components present in the sample.[158]

The proponents of Py-MS argue that it has several advantages over PGC. They claim that Py-MS is a faster technique and that Py-MS instrumentation is more standardized, permitting one analyst to easily duplicate and doublecheck the analysis performed by another analyst.[159] However, there has been little research on Py-MS. For that reason, it is often difficult to properly interpret the pyrogram to deduce the identity of the pyrolysate.[160] Like PGC, Py-MS has not yet advanced to the point that the analyst can confidently individualize hair samples on the basis of Py-MS alone.

A third technique is scanning electron microscopy (SEM).[161] SEM represents a quantum leap in microscopy. Even with the best conventional optical microscopes, the greatest possible magnification is a power of 2,000.[162] SEM is a fundamentally different methodology and can attain much greater magnification. In SEM, the sample is scanned with a beam of electrons.[163] The scan causes the sample to emit secondary electrons. SEM collects and analyzes these electrons. The analysis converts the electrons into a point-by-point image of the sample.[164] This electrical image magnifies the sample by a power of 300,000 although most forensic work uses lower magnification.[165] Thus, the analyst can observe objects and characteristics that were previously invisible to both the naked eye and the best optical microscope.

---

155. Watkins & Watkins, *supra* note 149 at 95-96 (Supp. 1991).

156. *See* Hughes, Wheals & Whitehouse, *Pyrolysis Mass Spectrometry, A Technique of Forensic Potential?*, 10 FORENSIC SCI. 217, 218 (1977).

157. *Id.* at 217.

158. *Id.*

159. *Id.* at 218.

160. *Id.*

161. *See* Verhoeven, *The Advantages of the Scanning Electron Microscope in the Investigative Studies of Hair*, 63 J. CRIM. L., CRIMINOLOGY & POLICE SCI. 125 (1972).

162. People v. Palmer, 80 Cal. App. 3d 239, 251 n.2, 145 Cal. Rptr. 466, 471 n.2 (1978).

163. Judd, *Scanning Electron Microscopy as Applied to Forensic Evidence Analysis*, *in* SCIENTIFIC AND EXPERT EVIDENCE 873 (2d ed. 1981).

164. *Id.*

165. *Id.* at 879-80.

SEM specialists have begun to apply SEM to hair examination.[166] This application creates the possibility of detecting minute hair characteristics peculiar to the individual human source. SEM researchers, though, have not as yet claimed that capability. However, as previously noted, French researchers have asserted that SEM enables the analyst to observe detailed anatomical features that will conclusively differentiate human from animal hairs.[167] In the long run, SEM may hold the greatest promise for modernizing the science of hair analysis.[168]

Traditional Techniques

Although hair analysis by ion microprobe, PGC, Py-MS, and SEM have not yet won judicial sanction, there are two techniques that are well accepted: conventional microscopy and NAA. Researchers are attempting to perfect both techniques by developing data bases to quantify the individuation of the hair samples.

Conventional microscopists concede that their technique cannot conclusively identify the human hair source.[169] There is an element of subjectivity in the microscopic examination of hair examples.[170] However, hair analysts are conducting several research projects to develop better systems for evaluating the significance of the data yielded by conventional microscopy.[171]

One research project involves scale counts. Two researchers claimed that: (1) the scale count of even a single hair strand is nearly always representative of all scalp hairs;[172] and (2) while the average or mean scale count is constant for the individual, the count differs significantly from person to person.[173] One commentator has expressed skepticism about the utility of scale counts to

---

166. Clement, Hagege, Pareux, Connet & Gastaldi, *supra* note 55, at 447; Verhoeven, *supra* note 161, at 125.

167. Clement, Hagege, Pareux, Connet & Gastaldi, *supra* note 55, at 447.

168. *Id.*

169. *See* text accompanying note 227 *infra.*

170. Wickenheiser & Hepworth, *Further Evaluation of Probabilities in Human Scalp Hair Comparisons*, 35 J. FORENSIC SCI. 1323, 1324, 1327-29 (1990) (the researchers reported not only that "[t]he classification of hair varied between examiners" but also that "each examiner had considerable day-to-day variation in hair feature classification"); Miller, *Procedural Bias in Forensic Science Examinations of Human Hair*, 11 LAW & HUM. BEHAV. 157 (1987) (the author compared lineups of hair samples with conventional hair examinations in which the analyst compares a known and a questioned sample; the conventional procedure yielded 30.4% incorrect conclusions while the lineup technique produced only 3.8% incorrect findings).

171. *See* Saferstein, *Criminalistics — A Look Back at the 1970s, a Look Ahead to the 1980s*, 24 J. FORENSIC SCI. 925, 925-30 (1979).

172. Gamble & Kirk, *Human Hair Studies II. Scale Counts*, 31 J. AM. INST. CRIM. L. & CRIMINOLOGY 627, 629 (1941).

173. *Id.* at 631. *See also* Kirk & Gamble, *Further Investigation of the Scale Count of Human Hair*, 33 J. CRIM. L. & CRIMINOLOGY 276, 280 (1942).

individualize human hair sources.[174] To begin with, this critic points out that the research project had a very limited data base — initially only thirty-nine hair samples.[175] The critic conducted his own independent tests to doublecheck the findings of the proponents of the scale count technique, and his test results seemingly contradict the proponents' findings.[176] He concluded that "the value of the scale count in eliminating or 'individualizing' an evidence hair with one from the suspect is to be seriously questioned."[177]

A second research project was conducted in Canada. Canadian researchers catalogued twenty-three different characteristics such as color, pigment distribution, maximum diameter, shaft length, and scale count that microscopists have relied on in the past to differentiate hair sources.[178] For each characteristic, the researchers developed subcategories.[179] For instance, characteristic *O,* length, is subdivided into five groups, depending on the strand's length in inches.[180] The researchers found that if two samples of scalp hair matched in all respects, the odds were only one in 4,500 that the samples originated from different human hair sources.[181] Their estimate for pubic hair is one in 800.[182] As in the case of case of the scale count project, this project involved a small data base: only 100 persons.[183] Even within that small sample, the researchers found several indistinguishable hair samples from different persons.[184] Additionally, the researchers acknowledge that some of the categorization is subjective; for example, the analyst must exercise subjective judgment in categorizing hair samples under factor *A,* color, and factor *E,* texture.[185]

The one in 4,500 estimate has triggered controversy in the scientific community. The critics of the estimate point out that in the study the researchers

---

174. Beeman, *The Scale Count of Human Hair,* 32 J. CRIM. L. & CRIMINOLOGY 572, 574 (1942).

175. *Id.* at 572. *See* Gamble & Kirk, *supra* note 173, at 631.

176. Beeman, *supra* note 174, at 572.

177. *Id.* at 574. *See also* Beeman, *Further Evaluation of the Scale Count of Human Hair,* 33 J. CRIM. L. & CRIMINOLOGY 422, 424 (1943); Bruschweiler, *Forensic Value of the Cuticle of Human Hair, in* PROCEEDINGS OF THE INTERNATIONAL SYMPOSIUM ON FORENSIC HAIR COMPARISON 173 (1985).

178. Gaudette & Keeping, *An Attempt at Determining Probabilities in Human Scalp Hair Comparison,* 19 J. FORENSIC SCI. 599, 601-02 (1974).

179. *Id.*

180. *Id.* at 602.

181. *Id.* at 604-05.

182. Gaudette, *Some Further Thoughts on Probabilities and Human Hair Comparisons,* 23 J. FORENSIC SCI. 758, 760 (1978).

183. Gaudette & Keeping, *supra* note 178, at 599.

184. *Id.* at 603.

185. *Id.* at 605; Aitken & Robertson, *The Value of Microscopic Features in the Examination of Human Hairs: Statistical Analysis of Questionnaire Returns,* 31 J. FORENSIC SCI. 546 (1986) (British experts question the objectivity of the categorization process).

compared hair samples from different persons and attempted to determine how frequently such samples are indistinguishable.[186] The research thus most directly establishes the probability, P(M/notS), that is, the probability (P) of an apparent match (M) when it is given that the hairs do not come from the same person (not S).[187] The critics argue that it is fallacious to use the estimate even as circumstantial evidence of P (not S/M), namely, the probability (P) that the hairs came from different persons (not S) given the apparent match (M).[188] The critics contend that the estimate is "virtually meaningless with respect to hair individualization."[189] The researchers counter that their study is highly probative of an accidental match,[190] and other researchers have come to the same conclusion.[191] Still other researchers are attempting a Bayesian approach to this statistical problem.[192]

Two courts have permitted an analyst to testify to the one in 4,500 estimate,[193] but two other courts have held that there has been insufficient experimental verification of that estimate.[194] In one federal habeas corpus proceeding, while not passing on the wisdom of admitting the 4,500 estimate, the Seventh Circuit

---

186. Note, *Admissibility of Mathematical Evidence in Criminal Trials*, 21 AM. CRIM. L. REV. 55, 57-66 (1983). *See also* Aitken & Robertson, *A Contribution to the Discussion of Probabilities and Human Hair Comparisons*, 32 J. FORENSIC SCI. 684 (1987).

187. *Id.* at 65-66.

188. *Id.;* Burnett & Ogle, *Probabilities and Human Hair Comparison*, 27 J. FORENSIC SCI. 272 (1982).

189. *Id.* at 274. *See also* Ogle, *Discussion of "Further Evaluation of Probabilities in Human Scalp Hair Comparison,"* 36 J. FORENSIC SCI. 971 (1991) ("the experiment conducted by these authors has not provided an answer to the question, 'Once a match between a questioned hair and the exemplar specimen from one individual has been effected, what is the probability that the questioned hair would also match the hair exemplar from another individual in the relevant population?' Until experiments based on 'comparison' data are replaced by scientific research efforts directed toward frequency of occurrence data for the microscopic hair 'features' and hair 'types' present in the various human populations, no hard data will be available for statistical evaluation. The most sophisticated statistical treatment of data derived from invalid experiments cannot produce meaningful probability estimates").

190. Gaudette, *A Supplementary Discussion of Probabilities and Human Hair Comparisons*, 27 J. FORENSIC SCI. 279, 285 (1982).

191. Wickenheiser & Hepworth, *Further Evaluation of Probabilities in Human Scalp Hair Comparisons*, 35 J. FORENSIC SCI. 1323, 1329 (1990) (the authors essentially replicated the original study by Gaudette and Keeping; these authors concluded that "[i]f two hairs are microscopically indistinguishable from root to tip and thus show no significant differences ...., the probability of incorrect association is remote").

192. Hoffman, *Statistical Evaluation of the Evidential Value of Human Hairs Possibly Coming from Multiple Sources*, 36 J. FORENSIC SCI. 1053 (1991).

193. United States v. Jefferson, 17 M.J. 728, 731 (N.C.M.R. 1983); People v. DiGiacomo, 71 Ill. App. 3d 56, 58, 27 Ill. Dec. 232, 234, 388 N.E.2d 1281, 1281-83 (1979).

194. United States v. Massey, 594 F.2d 676, 680 (8th Cir. 1979); State v. Carlson, 267 N.W.2d 170, 176 (Minn. 1978).

held that the admission of the evidence did not deny the defendant any constitutional right.[195] The court remarked that "we know of no constitutional principle by which its admission could be held improper."[196]

In short, the attempts to quantify the data generated by conventional microscopy have met with only limited success. Somewhat more progress has been made toward quantifying the data generated by NAA.[197] In NAA, the sample is placed in a nuclear reactor and bombarded with neutrons. The bombardment makes the sample artificially radioactive. In that condition, the sample emits gamma rays. The instrument collects and measures the gamma rays. The gamma ray energy levels are peculiar to the chemical elements present in the sample. By analyzing the gamma rays, NAA yields both qualitative and quantitative data; NAA enables the analyst to both identify and measure the trace elements present.[198] NAA instruments can measure a quantity as small as one ten millionth of a microgram.[199]

There has been substantial NAA research to determine the occurrence of trace elements in human hair.[200] The research has given many observers hope that NAA will allow far more reliable individualization than in the past. The problem that has arisen is that even among the hairs of a single person, there are hair-to-hair variations in trace element concentrations.[201] Research efforts have focused on the attempt to determine mean values and standard deviations in hair trace element concentrations that will permit conclusive individualization.[202] However, our reviewer points out that even today NAA is not in widespread use in hair analysis.

---

195. United States *ex rel.* DiGiacomo v. Franzen, 680 F.2d 515 (7th Cir. 1982).

196. *Id.* at 519.

197. *See Identification of Substances by Neutron Activation Analysis*, 15 AM. JUR. PROOF OF FACTS 115-23 (1964); Krishman, *Neutron Activation Analysis and Atomic Absorption Spectrometry, in* SCIENTIFIC AND EXPERT EVIDENCE 279 (2d ed. 1981).

198. United States v. Stifel, 433 F.2d 431, 436 (6th Cir. 1970), *cert. denied,* 401 U.S. 994 (1971).

199. *Identification of Substances by Neutron Activation Analysis, supra* note 197, at 124.

200. *Id.* at 131. *See, e.g.,* Cornelis, *Is It Possible to Identify Individuals by Neutron Activation Analysis of Hair?*, 12 MED., SCI. & L. 188 (1972); PERKONS, INDIVIDUALIZATION OF HUMAN HEAD HAIR, IN PROCEEDINGS OF THE FIRST INT'L CONF. ON FORENSIC ACTIVATION ANALYSIS 221 (V. Guinn ed. 1967); PERKONS & JERVIS, HAIR INDIVIDUALIZATION STUDIES, IN PROCEEDINGS OF THE 1965 INT'L CONF. ON MODERN TRENDS IN ACTIVATION ANALYSIS 295 (1965); LIMA, SHIBATA & ATALLA, ACTIVATION ANALYSIS APPLIED TO FORENSIC INVESTIGATION: SOME OBSERVATIONS ON THE PROBLEM OF HUMAN HAIR INDIVIDUALIZATION, IN I RADIOCHEMICAL METHODS OF ANALYSIS 119 (Int'l Atomic Energy Agency 1965).

201. *See* Comment, *Evidentiary Uses of Neutron Activation Analysis*, 59 CALIF. L. REV. 977, 1039 (1971).

202. *Id.* at 1039-42.

§ 24-3. Admissibility of Hair Evidence.

Cases Excluding Hair Evidence

Until recently, the cases in which courts have excluded hair evidence were so rare that they literally amounted to only a handful of precedents. In *United States v. Brown,* ion microprobic hair analysis was excluded because there was no evidence of compliance with *Frye.*[203] In another case, the court found the analyst's testimony too vague and speculative to be helpful to the jury.[204] In two remaining cases, in which the prosecution offered statistical evidence to quantify the individualization of the hair samples, the courts concluded that the prosecution's foundation was inadequate.[205] In two other cases, the courts held that it exceeded the state of the art of comparative hair microscopy for the analyst to positively identify the defendant as the source of the hair strand.[206]

Although such decisions were formerly rarities, since the rendition of the *Daubert* decision in 1993 some jurisdictions have adopted a more skeptical attitude toward hair analysis. In 1995, applying the *Daubert* test, a federal district court held that "[t]he state of the art of hair analysis has not reached a level of certainty to permit such testimony" to qualify as scientific evidence.[207] The court noted "the scarcity of scientific studies regarding the reliability of hair comparison testing."[208] The court also pointed out that in the Laboratory Proficiency Testing Program conducted in the 1970s, "the police laboratories'

---

203. *See* text accompanying notes141-48 *supra.*

204. People v. Roff, 67 A.D.2d 805, 805-06, 413 N.Y.S.2d 43, 44-45 (1979).

205. United States v. Massey, 594 F.2d 676, 681 (8th Cir. 1979); State v. Carlson, 267 N.W.2d 170, 176 (Minn. 1978).

206. State v. Faircloth, 99 N.C. App. 685, 691-93, 394 S.E.2d 198, 202-03 (1990) ("Unlike fingerprints, ... comparative microscopy of hair is not accepted as reliable evidence to positively identify a person;" although it was permissible for the analyst to testify that the hair "could have originated from" the defendant, the analyst could not state that "it would be improbable that these hairs would have originated from another individual"); McCarty v. State, 765 P.2d 1215, 1218 (Okla. Crim. 1988) ("in response to Assistant District Attorney ... Albert's question based on her expertise and examination of the forensic science as to whether Ms. Gilchrist had 'an opinion as to whether Mr. Carty was physically present during the time violence was done to Ms. Willis,' Gilchrist replied, 'he [McCarty] was in fact there.' We find that the admission of this opinion testimony was error, because Ms. Gilchrist did not, and could not, testify that such opinion was based on facts or data 'of a type reasonably relied upon by experts in the particular field' in forming such an opinion. *See* 12 O.S. 1981, § 2703. Ms. Gilchrist herself testified that forensic science techniques had not advanced to the point where a person could be positively identified through ... hair examination").

207. Williamson v. Reynolds, 904 F. Supp. 1529, 1558 (E.D. Okla. 1995), *rev'd on other grounds,* 110 F.3d 1508, 1522-23 (10th Cir. 1997).

208. *Id.* at 1556.

performance was weakest in the area of hair analysis. The "error" rates[209] on hair analysis were as high as 67% on individual samples, and the majority of the police laboratories were incorrect on 4 out of 5 hair samples analyzed. Such an accuracy level was below chance."[210] Finally, the court stressed that "the evaluation of hair evidence remains subjective" because there are no objective "standards ... for human hair identification."[211]

In 1996, an Indiana state court reached a conclusion similar to that in the 1995 federal decision.[212] The court pointed out that the prosecution had not shown that the analyst's technique has been empirically tested or subjected to peer review. The same year witnessed the publication of a substantial article attacking the reliability of hair analysis.[213] The article reviewed the state of the empirical research into hair analysis. The article conceded that testimony about hair analysis "has been generally accepted by our courts for many years. "[214] However, based on their independent review of the data, the authors concluded that until further research improves the state of the scientific art, "forensic hair comparison analysis should be excluded altogether from criminal trials."[215]

---

209. Our reviewer adds a caveat to the court's reasoning. He points out that in this study, inconclusive outcomes were considered "errors." Thus, the court's opinion is somewhat misleading.

210. *Id.*

211. *Id.* However, on appeal, the Court of Appeals for the Tenth Circuit reversed the grant of habeas relief. Williamson v. Ward, 110 F.3d 1508, 1522-23 (10th Cir. 1997). The appellate court reasoned that the trial judge had used "the wrong [legal] standard" in deciding whether to grant habeas relief. In the court's view, in effect the trial judge had erroneously inquired whether the testimony would have been admissible in federal court under *Daubert.* Rather, the question was "whether the error, if any, was so grossly prejudicial that it fatally infected the trial and denied the fundamental fairness that is the essence of due process." *Microscopic Hair Analysis — Has It Taken a Judicial Trimming? Not Yet, Says the 10th Federal Circuit,* 21 SCI. SLEUTHING REV. 8 (Fall 1997).

212. McGrew v. Indiana, 673 N.E.2d 787 (Ind. App. 1996), *vacated,* 683 N.E.2d 592 (Ind.) , *aff'd in part, rev'd in part,* 682 N.E.2d 1289 (Ind. 1997). . *See also Hair Analysis in Indiana,* 21 SCI. SLEUTHING REV. 11 (Spring 1997) (the Indiana court reversed the conviction due to "the lack of any evidence that the microscopic method upon which it was founded is reliable"; however, "the court put on record that it was 'not establishing a per se rule of inadmissibility of microscopic hair analysis'"). However, as in the case of the federal grant of habeas relief, the reviewing court disagreed with the lower court. On appeal, the Indiana Supreme Court upheld the trial judge ruling admitting the testimony. McGrew v. State, 682 N.E.2d 1289 (Ind. 1997). The court observed:

> This conclusion is not unlike our recent statement in Jervis [v. State] that the evidence at issue was more a "matter of the observations of persons with specialized knowledge" than "a matter of 'scientific principles' governed by Indiana Evidence Rule 702(b)." 679 N.E.2d [875] at 881 [Ind. Sup. Ct. 1997].

213. Smith & Goodman, *Forensic Hair Comparison Analysis: Nineteenth Century Science or Twentieth Century Snake Oil?,* 27 COLUM. HUM. RTS. L. REV. 227 (1996).

214. *Id.* at 231.

215. *Id.*

In 1997, the Hawaii Supreme Court upheld the admission of hair comparison evidence.[216] However, the court did not rule that the testimony constitutes full-fledged "scientific" evidence. The court used a rationale striking similar to the reasoning by the federal district court in *United States v. Starzecpyzel*[217] involving questioned document examination. The Hawaiian court distinguished between "scientific knowledge" and nonscientific "technical knowledge." The court asserted that hair comparison evidence qualifies as the latter type of knowledge because it is "well-established and of proven reliability." Further, in the instant case, the court found "no indication that the manner in which the hair ... analysis was conducted ... was technically deficient."

In 1999, the United States Supreme Court handed down its decision in *Kumho Tire Co., Ltd. v. Carmichael.*[218] In *Kumho*, the Court ruled that the trial judge must conduct a "*Daubert* style inquiry into the reliability of all types of expert testimony, nonscientific as well as scientific. In federal court and any state opting to follow *Kumho*'s reading of Rule 702, the proponent of hair evidence will be required to make a showing of the reliability of the evidence, whether the proponent characterizes as nonscientific or scientific expertise. The *Kumho* Court acknowledged that some of the factors mentioned in *Daubert*, such as a quantifiable margin of error, may be inapplicable to nonscientific testimony. However, the opponent will be entitled to insist that the proponent make some foundational showing of the reliability of the proffered hair testimony. *Kumho* will likely encourage the opponents of hair evidence to continue to press the attack begun in 1995.

Cases Admitting Hair Evidence

In contrast to the few cases excluding hair evidence, it is still fair to say that a large body of case law reflects the receptivity of most courts to hair analysis.[219] Courts unhesitatingly permit analysts to opine on the threshold question whether

---

216. State v. Fukusaka, 85 Haw. 462, 946 P.2d 32 (1997) (citing this treatise).

217. 880 F. Supp. 1027 (S.D.N.Y. 1995).

218. 119 S. Ct. 1167 (1999).

219. *See generally* Annot., 23 A.L.R.4TH 1199 (1983); United States v. Bush, 44 M.J. 646 (A.F. Ct. Crim. App. 1996) (mass spectrometric analysis of the chemicals in hair), *aff'd*, 47 M.J. 305 (U.S.C.A.A.F. 1997), *cert. denied*, 118 S. Ct. 1048 (1998); United States v. Matta-Ballesteros, 71 F.3d 754, 766-67 (9th Cir. 1995), *amended*, 98 F.3d 1100 (9th Cir. 1996), *cert. denied*, 519 U.S. 1118 (1997); People v. Pride, 3 Cal. 4th 195, 833 P.2d 643, 10 Cal. Rptr. 2d 636, 661-62 (1992) (citing numerous cases, the court declared that "California courts have long assumed that hair comparison evidence of the sort admitted here has some logical bearing on defendant's commission of the charged crimes" and that "[h]air comparison evidence that identifies a suspect or victim as a possible donor has been routinely admitted in California for many years without any suggestion that it is unreliable under *Kelly/Frye*"), *cert. denied*, 507 U.S. 935 (1993).

the material is hair.[220] Courts also allow analysts to testify on more particular issues such as whether the hair is of human origin,[221] the age of the human hair source,[222] the source's race,[223] and the region of the body in which the hair strand originated.[224]

Most courts have been equally liberal in admitting evidence offered to individualize the human hair source.[225] Repeatedly, courts have permitted the prosecution analyst to express an opinion based on conventional microscopy without demanding any explanation for the analyst's failure to use other techniques,[226] even when the analyst admits the inconclusive nature of

---

220. Murray v. State, 202 Miss. 849, 852-53, 32 So. 2d 789, 790 (1947), *vacated,* 333 U.S. 879 (1948); State v. Harris, 241 Or. 224, 243, 405 P.2d 492, 500-01 (1965).

221. Harnage v. State, 49 Ala. App. 563, 577-80, 274 So. 2d 333, 348-50, *rev'd on other grounds,* 290 Ala. 142, 274 So. 2d 352 (1972), *cert. denied,* 290 Ala. 367 (1973); Ward v. Music, 257 S.W.2d 516, 520 (Ky. 1953); Acrey v. Commonwealth, 312 Ky. 732, 735, 229 S.W.2d 748, 751 (1950); Wright v. State, 422 S.W.2d 184, 188 (Tex. Crim. App. 1967), *vacated,* 408 U.S. 934 (1972).

222. Commonwealth v. McGarty, 323 Mass. 435, 439, 82 N.E.2d 603, 606 (1948).

223. Siripongs v. Calderon, 133 F.3d 732, 735 (9th Cir.) ("As to the unidentified hair samples, none bore Asian characteristics ...."), *cert. denied,* 119 S. Ct. 101 (1998); Harnage v. State, 49 Ala. App. 563, 577-80, 274 So. 2d 333, 348-49, *rev'd on other grounds,* 290 Ala. 142, 274 So. 2d 352 (1972), *cert. denied,* 290 Ala. 367 (1973); Thomas v. State, 374 So. 2d 508, 514 (Fla. 1979), *cert. denied,* 445 U.S. 972 (1980); People v. Kirkwood, 17 Ill. 2d 23, 32, 160 N.E.2d 766, 772 (1959), *cert. denied,* 363 U.S. 847 (1960); State v. Wilson, 217 La. 470, 478, 46 So. 2d 738, 741 (1950), *aff'd,* 341 U.S. 901 (1951); State v. Ray, 274 N.C. 556, 574, 164 S.E.2d 457, 468 (1968); Benton v. State, 86 Okla. Crim. 137, 145-46, 190 P.2d 168, 172 (1948).

224. Harnage v. State, 49 Ala. App. 563, 577-80, 274 So. 2d 333, 348-49, *rev'd on other grounds,* 290 Ala. 142, 274 So. 2d 352 (1972), *cert. denied,* 290 Ala. 367 (1973); Commonwealth v. McGarty, 323 Mass. 435, 439, 82 N.E.2d 603, 606 (1948); State v. Golladay, 78 Wash. 2d 121, 144, 470 P.2d 191, 205 (1970).

225. Watson v. State, 64 Wis. 2d 264, 219 N.W.2d 398 (1974).

226. United States v. Brady, 595 F.2d 359, 362-63 (6th Cir.), *cert. denied,* 444 U.S. 862 (1979); United States v. Cyphers, 553 F.2d 1064, 1072-73 (7th Cir.), *cert. denied,* 434 U.S. 843 (1977); State v. Blazak, 114 Ariz. 199, 203, 560 P.2d 54, 58 (1977), *cert. denied,* 459 U.S. 882 (1982); People v. Carter, 48 Cal. 2d 737, 743, 312 P.2d 665, 668 (1957); Thompson v. State, 539 A.2d 1052, 1057 (Del. Super. 1988) (a microscopic examination of hair is admissible to establish probable cause, but standing alone a microscopic finding cannot serve as a basis for a finding of probable cause; "it is now universally recognized that although fingerprint comparisons can result in the positive identification of an individual, hair comparisons are not this precise"); Ward v. Music, 257 S.W.2d 516, 520 (Ky. 1953); State v. Wilson, 217 La. 470, 478, 46 So. 2d 738, 741 (1950), *aff'd,* 341 U.S. 901 (1951); Commonwealth v. Tarver, 369 Mass. 302, 310-11, 345 N.E.2d 671, 677 (1975); People v. Watkins, 78 Mich. App. 89, 95-96, 259 N.W.2d 381, 384-85 (1977); State v. Carlson, 267 N.W.2d 170, 175 (Minn. 1978); People v. Allweiss, 48 N.Y.2d 40, 396 N.E.2d 735, 421 N.Y.S.2d 341 (1979); State v. Faircloth, 99 N.C. App. 685, 691-93, 394 S.E.2d 198, 202-03 (1990) (the court initially held that Agent Worsham's testimony that the hair "could have originated from" the defendant was admissible because "[h]air-analysis is admissible if relevant;" however, the court added that "[u]nlike fingerprints, ... comparative microscopy of hair is not accepted as reliable evidence to positively identify a person. 'Rather, it serves to exclude

microscopic identification.[227] The analyst is allowed to give such vague testimony as the hair samples "match,"[228] are "compatible,"[229] "similar,"[230] "of the same general character,"[231] "consistent" with the assumption of a common

---

classes of persons and is conclusive, if at all, only to negative identity.' Agent Worsham's testimony that 'it would be improbable that these hairs would have originated from another individual' was, effectively, a positive identification of defendant derived from hair evidence. Agent Worsham's opinion ... was an expression of opinion as to defendant's guilt and then violated Rule 702 of the North Carolina Rules of Evidence"); Moore v. State, 788 P.2d 387, 388 (Okla. Crim. App.) ("The admission of expert testimony on microscopic comparison of hair ... samples has been implicitly, if not explicitly, approved"), *cert. denied,* 498 U.S. 881 (1990); State v. Kersting, 50 Or. App. 461, 623 P.2d 1095 (1981), *aff'd,* 292 Or. 350, 638 P.2d 1145 (1982); State v. Earley, 118 R.I. 205, 209, 373 A.2d 162, 165 (1977); State v. Andrews, 86 R.I. 341, 345, 134 A 2d 425, 430-31, *cert. denied,* 355 U.S. 898 (1957); Skinner v. Commonwealth, 212 Va. 260, 262, 183 S.E.2d 715, 727 (1971); State v. Golladay, 78 Wash. 2d 121, 144, 470 P.2d 191, 205 (1970).

227. United States v. Brady, 595 F.2d 359, 362-63 (6th Cir.), *cert. denied,* 444 U.S. 862 (1979); Harnage v. State, 49 Ala. App. 563, 577-80, 274 So. 2d 333, 348-49, *rev'd on other grounds,* 290 Ala. 142, 274 So. 2d 352 (1972), *cert. denied,* 290 Ala. 367 (1973); People v. Allen, 41 Cal. App. 3d 196, 201, 115 Cal. Rptr. 839, 842 (1974); Fultz v. State, 265 Ind. 626, 634-35, 358 N.E.2d 123, 128 (1976); State v. Huckaby, 368 So. 2d 1059, 1063-64 (La. 1979); State v. Wilson, 217 La. 470, 478, 46 So. 2d 738, 741 (1950), *aff'd,* 341 U.S. 901 (1951); People v. Allweiss, 48 N.Y.2d 40, 396 N.E.2d 735, 421 N.Y.S.2d 341 (1979); Benton v. State, 86 Okla. Crim. 137, 145-46, 190 P.2d 168, 172 (1948); State v. Harris, 241 Or. 224, 243, 405 P.2d 492, 500-01 (1965); State v. Vargus, 118 R.I. 113, 126-27, 373 A.2d 150, 156-57 (1977); State v. Batten, 17 Wash. App. 428, 437-38, 563 P.2d 1287, 1292-93 (1977); State v. Bauman, 77 Wash. 2d 938, 940-41, 468 P.2d 684, 686 (1970); State v. Suddreth, 412 S.E.2d 126 (N.C. App.) (the expert could not rule out the possibility that the hair originated from a source other than the defendant), *rev'd on additional issues,* 331 N.C. 281, 417 S.E.2d 68 (1992).

228. Garland v. Maggio, 717 F.2d 199, 207 n.9 (5th Cir. 1983); State v. Melson, 638 S.W.2d 342, 349 (Tenn. 1982), *cert. denied,* 459 U.S. 1137 (1983).

229. State v. Daniels, 655 S.W.2d 106, 108 (Mo. App. 1983).

230. United States v. Brady, 595 F.2d 359, 362-63 (6th Cir.), *cert. denied,* 444 U.S. 862 (1979); Harnage v. State, 49 Ala. App. 563, 577-80, 274 So. 2d 333, 348-50, *rev'd on other grounds,* 290 Ala. 412, 274 So. 2d 352 (1972); State v. Blazak, 114 Ariz. 199, 203, 560 P.2d 54, 58 (1977); People v. Abbott, 47 Cal. 2d 362, 368, 303 P.2d 730, 734 (1956); People v. Schultz, 99 Ill. App. 3d 762, 55 Ill. Dec. 94, 425 N.E.2d 1267 (1981); People v. Kirkwood, 17 Ill. 2d 23, 32, 160 N.E.2d 766, 772 (1959), *cert. denied,* 363 U.S. 847 (1960); Acrey v. Commonwealth, 312 Ky. 732, 735, 229 S.W.2d 748, 751 (1950); State v. Huckaby, 368 So. 2d 1059, 1063 (La. 1979); State v. Wilson, 217 La. 470, 478, 46 So. 2d 738, 741 (1950), *aff'd,* 341 U.S. 901 (1951); State v. Carlson, 267 N.W.2d 170, 175 (Minn. 1978); State v. Perryman, 520 S.W.2d 126, 130 (Mo. App. 1975); State v. Caplin, 592 A.2d 188, 192 (N.H. 1991) (in earlier cases, "the expert witness testified that the hair samples at issue were similar in all fifteen recognized microscopic characteristics"); Benton v. State, 86 Okla. Crim. 137, 145-46, 190 P.2d 168, 172 (1948); State v. Lerch, 296 Or. 377, 677 P.2d 678 (1984); State v. Kersting, 50 Or. App. 461, 623 P.2d 1095 (1981), *aff'd,* 292 Or. 350, 638 P.2d 1145 (1982); Postell v. State, 663 S.W.2d 552, 553 (Tex. App. 1983), *aff'd,* 693 S.W.2d 462 (Tex. Crim. App. 1985); Wright v. State, 422 S.W.2d 184, 188 (Tex. Crim. App. 1967), *vacated,* 408 U.S. 934 (1972); Skinner v. Commonwealth, 212 Va. 260, 262, 183 S.E.2d 725, 727 (1971).

231. State v. Baldwin, 47 N.J. 379, 392, 221 A.2d 199, 206, *cert. denied,* 385 U.S. 980 (1966).

source,[232] or "could" have come from the same origin.[233] The massive body of case law,[234] liberally admitting even hair evidence of low probative value, dwarfs the few handfuls of cases excluding hair evidence.

The courts often allow the analyst to add that in his or her experience, they have never found matching hair samples from different persons.[235] The courts are also increasingly receptive to testimony couched as probability statements. Two courts have already sustained the admission of the one in 4,500 estimate.[236] Two

---

232. People v. Allen, 41 Cal. App. 3d 196, 201, 115 Cal. Rptr. 839, 842 (1974); State v. Smith, 637 S.W.2d 232, 236 (Mo. App. 1982); State v. Watley, 788 P.2d 375 (N.M. App. 1989) ("microscopically consistent," "consistent," "twin," and "identical"). *See also* Coleman v. Calderon, 150 F.3d 1105 (9th Cir. 1995) (a criminal defense attorney was guilty of ineffective representation in failing to present to the jury evidence that a hair strand found on the victim's hand was "inconsistent" with the defendant's hair).

233. United States v. Cyphers, 553 F.2d 1064, 1072 (7th Cir.), *cert. denied,* 434 U.S. 843 (1977); State v. Faircloth, 99 N.C. App. 685, 691-93, 394 S.E.2d 198, 202 (1990); State v. Batten, 17 Wash. App. 428, 437-38, 563 P.2d 1287, 1292-93 (1977). *The State of the Profession: The Caducity of Truth in the Forensic Sciences*, SCIENTIFIC SLEUTHING, Vol. 18, No. 2, pp. 1, 4 (Sum. 1994) (in the 1980 Georgia murder trial of Gary Nelson, "Roger Parian testified for the prosecution that he had examined the hair in question and that he had concluded that they were consistent with having the same origin, to wit Gary Nelson. Indeed Parian went even further. There was, in his view, a 'high probability' that the hair from the crime scene had come from Nelson. And on cross-examination he propounded the insupportable opinion that only about 120 persons in the Savannah area would have the same hair type as that from the crime scene;" in contrast, an F.B.I. analyst concluded that the hair samples were "not suitable for significant comparison purposes;" in 1991 Nelson's conviction was set aside, and charges against him were dismissed); State v. Suddreth, 412 S.E.2d 126 (N.C. App.) (the expert stated that it was "quite likely" that the hair came from the defendant), *rev'd on additional issues*, 331 N.C. 281, 417 S.E.2d 68 (1992).

234. Notes 219-33, *supra,* collect cases from over 20 jurisdictions.

235. *E.g.*, Pierce v. State, 786 P.2d 1255, 1265 (Okla. Crim. App. 1990) ("Ms. Gilchrist testified ... that in the years during which she had been involved with hair analysis, she had never seen hairs from different people that were microscopically similar in all characteristics. She testified that although she had never seen two people with microscopically consistent hair characteristics, the possibility could not be ruled out. She testified based upon her own experience ...."); People v. Campbell, 163 Ill. App. 3d 1023, 115 Ill. Dec. 8, 516 N.E.2d 1364 (1987) (the expert testified that he had conducted over 25,000 hair examinations and had yet to find head or pubic hair matching his own). *But see* McCarty v. State, 765 P.2d 1215, 1216 (Okla. Crim. 1988) (as in *Pierce*, the witness was Ms. Gilchrist; however, the court ruled that she exceeded the state of the art of "hair examination" in testifying that the defendant was definitely present at the place where the victim was injured). Our reviewer is highly critical of such testimony. He points out that during their training, forensic hair examiners are often presented with relatively unremarkable samples of gray or blond hair . In these procedures, there will almost always be some matches between samples from different sources.

236. United States v. Jefferson, 17 M.J. 728, 731 (N.C.M.R. 1983); People v. DiGiacomo, 71 Ill. App. 3d 56, 58, 27 Ill. Dec. 232, 234, 388 N.E.2d 1281, 1281-83 (1979). *See also* Tatum v. Armontrout, 669 F. Supp. 1496, 1498, 1500 (W.D. Mo. 1987) (in an earlier state court trial, the prosecution expert testified "that statistical studies have concluded that only one person in 5,400 would have the same hair;" in a federal habeas corpus proceeding, the court held that the admission

neutron activation analysis cases are even more remarkable. In one case, although the probability testimony was not proffered, the court seemed impressed by a study indicating that "when the test yields seven comparable concentrations of component elements, the probability is 4,250,000 to 1 that they are from the same source."[237] In another NAA case, the expert was permitted to testify that "the chances of the resemblance he found between the hair samples occurring at random was 1.5 in 10^{10} (1 in 15,000,000,000)."[238]

§ 24-4. Fiber Analysis.

In the early 1900s, the French microscopist, Edmond Locard, championed the exchange principle: Substances such as hair and fibers adhere to surfaces such as clothing; and when two surfaces come into contact, there will be an exchange of hairs and fibers between the surfaces.[239] After the exchange or transfer, the hairs and fibers will persist on the surface for an indefinite period of time. The quantity of hair or fiber found later depends on the intensity of the contact between the surfaces, the new surface's adherent qualities, and subsequent conduct such as the washing of recipient clothing.[240] Secondary transfers are also possible;[241] a criminal may pick up a fiber at one crime scene and leave it at another scene.

Some criminalists assert that fiber is the most commonly encountered type of trace evidence.[242] Fiber evidence played a prominent role in the highly publicized trials of Theodore Bundy in Florida, Wayne Williams in Georgia, Jeffrey

---

of the expert's testimony was not so prejudicial that its introduction denied the defendant due process); Bevill v. State, 556 So. 2d 699, 707 (Miss. 1990) (the defense attacked "the hair analysis ... as to ... the witness ... giving statistical probability based upon a Canadian study. The [trial] judge ... should be guarded in the use of statistics in buttressing an expert witness's testimony, although probability analyses may be admissible in appropriate and carefully circumscribed instances"); State v. Seaton, 674 S.W.2d 214, 215 (Mo. App. 1984). Our reviewer points out that the prosecution testimony in *Armontrout* misstated Gaudette's research.

237. State v. Smith, 637 S.W.2d 232, 235 n.1 (Mo. App. 1982).

238. Lopez v. State, 643 S.W.2d 431, 433 (Tex. App. 1982).

239. *See* Bresee & Annis, *Fiber Transfer and the Influence of Fabric Softener*, 36 J. FORENSIC SCI. 1699 (1991); Mann, *Hair Transfers in Sexual Assault: A Six-Year Case Study*, 35 J. FORENSIC SCI. 951 (1990); Grieve, Dunlop & Haddock, *Transfer Experiments with Acrylic Fibres*, 40 FORENSIC SCI. INT'L 267 (1989). *See also* Lowrie & Jackson, *Recovery of Transferred Fibres*, 50 FORENSIC SCI. INT'L 111 (1991).

240. Palmer, *The Retention and Recovery of Transferred Fibers Following the Washing of Recipient Clothing*, 43 J. FORENSIC SCI. 502 (1998).

241. Gaudette & Tessarolo, *Secondary Transfer of Human Scalp Hair*, 32 J. FORENSIC SCI. 1241 (1987); Taupin, *Hair and Fiber Transfer in an Abduction Case — Evidence from Different Levels of Trace Evidence Transfer*, 41 J. FORENSIC SCI. 697 (1996) (describing secondary and tertiary transfers).

242. Grieve, *The Role of Fibers in Forensic Science Examinations*, 28 J. FORENSIC SCI. 877 (1983).

McDonald, the Green Beret doctor in the so-called Fatal Vision case,[243] and the O.J. Simpson prosecution.

In some cases, the analyst assesses damage to a victim's clothing to determine the type of implement which caused the damage.[244] However, in the typical case, the analyst's principal objective is to identify the type of fiber. There are a number of types of fiber that the criminalist may encounter. First, there is animal fiber, known as hair. Animal fiber is characterized by the presence of the scales described in § 24-2. This category includes: wool, goat, (common, mohair, and cashmere), silk, camel, llama (alpaca, vicuna, and guanaco), rabbit, cow, and yak.[245] Wool is the most common animal fiber, although even wool comprises less than 1% of all the fiber material used in clothing manufacture in the United States. The subject of animal fiber has generated extensive literature, notably Wildman's *The Microscopy of Animal Textile Fibres* and Appleyard's *Guide to the Identification of Animal Fibers.*

The next category is plant fiber. This category has four subdivisions:

— seed: cotton, akund, kapok, and linen;
— bast which can be obtained from the stems of several plants such as jute, flax, Hibiscus, Urena, hemp, sunn, and ramie;
— leaf: sisal, abaca, and phorminum; and
— fruit which is used in ropes, mats, auto seats, and mattresses.[246]

Cotton is the most widely available plant fiber, accounting for 24% of the total American textile fiber production. Catling and Grayson coauthored one of the leading texts on the subject, *Identification of Vegetable Fibers.*

The third fiber category is mineral. This category includes such fibers as glass wool and asbestos. Asbestos takes several forms: corcidolite (blue), chrysotile (white), and amosite (brown).[247]

The last category, man-made fibers, is the most important today. This category comprises three quarters of the total textile production in the United States. Man-made fibers fall into two subdivisions, regenerated and synthetic. Regenerated

---

243. United States v. MacDonald, 966 F.2d 854 (4th Cir.) (discussing testimony about three blond synthetic hairs found at the crime scene), *cert. denied*, 506 U.S. 1002 (1992). *See also* United States v. MacDonald, 979 F. Supp. 1057 (E.D.N.C. 1997) (the court denied the defendant's motion to reopen proceedings), *aff'd*, 161 F.3d 4 (4th Cir. 1998).

244. Taupin, *Comparing the Alleged Weapon with Damage to Clothing — The Value of Multiple Layers and Fabrics*, 44 J. FORENSIC SCI. 205 (1999); Taupin, *Damage to a Wire Security Screen: Adapting the Principles of Clothing Damage Analysis*, 43 J. FORENSIC SCI. 897 (1998); Taupin, *Testing Conflicting Scenarios — A Role for Simulation Experiments in Damage Analysis of Clothing*, 43 J. FORENSIC SCI. 891 (1998).

245. Miller, *An Introduction to Fiber Evidence*, 1983 THE PRACTICAL PROSECUTOR 19, 20.

246. *Id.*

247. *Id.*

fibers are manufactured from cellulose, a fibrous substance found in plants.[248] In contrast, synthetic fibers are manufactured from chemicals.[249] The synthetic manufacturing process has been described in this fashion:

> [C]hemicals are mixed in [a] reactor. Then [the] liquid is extruded through [a] small opening in [a] device called [a] spinnaret which gives [the] fiber its cross-sectional shape. [The] spinnaret nozzle determines the shape of [the] material. [The] shape is chosen for some manufacturing benefit or consumer appeal. Delustering agents [are] sometimes used to reduce shiny appearance.[250]

The synthetic category includes such familiar fibers as acrylics (Orlon, Acrilan, and Creslan), nylons (Nylon 6 and 66), and polyesters (Dacron, Fortrel, Kodel, and Dacron 64).[251]

There are numerous techniques for analyzing these categories of fiber, and these techniques enable the analyst to reach several conclusions about fiber samples.

§ 24-4(A). Techniques.

There are a large number of techniques for analyzing fibers.[252] The following list includes the methods that are most often employed by crime laboratories.

---

248. *Id.*

249. *Id.*

250. *Id.*

251. *Id. See also* Grieve & Cabiness, *The Recognition and Identification of Modified Acrylic Fibers*, 29 FORENSIC SCI. INT'L 129 (1985). *See also* Clayson & Wiggins, *Microfibers — A Forensic Perspective*, 42 J. FORENSIC SCI. 842 (1997).

252. THE TEXTILE INSTITUTE, IDENTIFICATION OF TEXTILE MATERIALS (7th ed. 1975); E. KORNREICH, INTRODUCTION TO FIBERS AND FABRICS (1966). *See also* State v. Head, 79 N.C. App. 1, 12, 338 S.E.2d 908, 914 ("the fiber evidence was ... analyzed with a high degree of precision and accuracy. Special Agent Bendure, an expert in fiber identification and analysis, testified that variables examined in relation to the fibers included the amount of dye absorbed, the amount, particle size, and distribution of delustriant (soil-hiding chemicals), the shape of the fiber (which would be round, star-shaped, triangular, multi-lobed, etc.), color, detail (such as striations on the fiber), light-polarizing characteristics and solubility characteristics"), *rev. denied*, 316 N.C. 736, 345 S.E.2d 395 (1986); Keen, White & Fredericks, *Characterization of Fibers by Raman Microprobe Spectroscopy*, 43 J. FORENSIC SCI. 82 (1998); Fong, *Analytical Methods for Developing Fibers as Forensic Science Proof: A Review with Comments*, 34 J. FORENSIC SCI. 295 (1989) (an excellent, concise overview of the available techniques); Grieve, *Discussion of "Fiber Evidence: Laboratory Methods and Observations from Casework,"* 29 J. FORENSIC SCI. 955 (1984).

Burning Test

This "heat and flame" procedure is a chemical test; it assesses the reaction between the test substance and flame. Different fibers react differently to a flame; some burn, others melt, and still others form beads. In addition to observing the substance's reaction while it approaches the flame and is in the flame, the analyst observes the reaction when the substance is removed from the flame; some fibers continue to burn while others stop burning shortly after withdrawal from the flame. Finally, the analyst notes the smell produced by the reaction. The odor is another clue to the fiber's identity.

When vegetable fiber burns, the end of the fiber becomes sharp; and the odor is similar to burnt wood. Synthetic fiber usually becomes soft and pliable under the flame. Animal fiber continues to burn after withdrawal from the flame; the fiber swells during burning and emits a smell like that of sulphur.

The analyst can quickly and easily conduct a burning test. The disadvantages of this test are that it is destructive and yields little information about the fiber's identity. The substance's reaction during the burning helps determine the gross category of the fiber (*e.g.*, animal versus plant), but the analyst must use more sophisticated techniques to make subtler discriminations.

Solubility Test

The solubility procedure is another chemical test. The analyst immerses the fiber in a chemical and observes the reaction. Some fibers dissolve, others swell, and the chemical may have little noticeable effect on still other fibers. Like the burning test, the solubility test enables the analyst to make only gross differentiations; the test permits the identification of the generic fiber category such as nylon or rayon. It has several weaknesses. Even if the chemical does not dissolve the fiber and destroy it, the immersion may contaminate the fiber and interfere with other test procedures.

Specific Gravity

The specific gravity value is the ratio of fiber mass to the mass of an equal volume of water at four degrees Celsius.[253] The measurement of the specific gravity of a fiber can help distinguish asbestos and Teflon from other fibers.[254] However, this test is of limited value; several different fibers can share the same specific gravity.

---

253. K. HATCH, TEXTILE WORLD 124 (1993).

254. *Specific Gravities,* 13 AM. JUR. PROOF OF FACTS 690 (1963).

Dye Test

Another rarely used chemical test is the dye test.[255] The analyst applies a dye stain to the fiber and observes the resulting color. There are over 7,000 dyes, and the resultant color can vary with the amount of dye formulation used. Hence, the dye test sometimes allows the analyst to make a more specific identification of the fiber.

However, the dye test has its limitations. It can ordinarily be applied only to light-colored fibers. Furthermore, the identification of the resulting color is a subjective determination. Finally, since the dye test can contaminate the sample, the analyst must have a large sample of the fiber before conducting a dye test.

Thin Layer Chromatography (TLC)

As noted in Chapter 23, drug analysts frequently resort to TLC. Fiber analysts do likewise.[256] The analyst can run the dye in several different solvent systems. The analyst should ensure that independent solvent systems that have low correlation coefficients are used; the more independent the solvent systems, the more significance the analyst can attach to the fact that the unknown fiber matches a known fiber in the two or three systems.[257]

---

255. *See* Golding & Kobot, *Comparison of Dyes from Transferred Fibers by Scanning Densitometry*, 35 J. Forensic Sci. 1310, 1321 (1990) ("The Camag scanning densitometer can ... provide all the information about a dye component on a TLC plate that is normally obtained by visual observation; that is, the position, color, and relative proportions of the various components obtained by densitometry are semi-quantitative and thus reduce the errors caused by ... visual comparison. The data obtained by using the ... densitometer are objective, and the variations in interpretation that can occur with subjective visual observations are significantly reduced or eliminated"); Grieve, Dunlop & Haddock, *An Investigation of Known Blue, Red, and Black Dyes Used in the Coloration of Cotton Fibers*, 35 J. Forensic Sci. 301 (1990) (thin layer chromatography often discriminates between dyes which match spectrally); Golding & Kobot, *The Selection of Noncorrelated Thin-Layer Chromatographic (TLC) Solvent Systems for the Comparison of Dyes Extracted from Transferred Fibers*, 34 J. Forensic Sci. 1156 (1989) (to maximize the comparative information, the analyst should use systems which are not correlated; the analyst should use correlation coefficients to determine whether systems are related); Wiggins, Cook & Turner, *Dye Batch Variations in Textile Fibers*, 33 J. Forensic Sci. 998 (1988).

256. Wiggins, Crabtree & March, *The Importance of Thin Layer Chromatography in the Analysis of Reactive Dyes Released from Wool Fibers*, 41 J. Forensic Sci. 1042 (1996); Beattie, Roberts & Dudley, *Thin-Layer Chromatography of Dyes Extracted from Polyester, Nylon, and Polyacrylonitrile Fibres*, 17 Forensic Sci. Int'l 57 (1981); Home & Dudley, *Thin-Layer Chromatography of Dyes Extracted from Cellulosic Fibres*, 17 Forensic Sci. Int'l 71 (1981); Resua, DeForest & Harris, *The Evaluation and Selection of Uncorrelated Paired Solvent Systems for Use in the Comparison of Textile Dyes by Thin-Layer Chromatography*, 26 J. Forensic Sci. 515 (1981).

257. *Id.* at 528.

The shortcoming of TLC is that even when the analyst conducts several TLC tests with independent solvent systems, the identification is nonspecific.[258] To make a more specific identification, the analyst must employ more advanced techniques.

High-Performance Liquid Chromatography (HPLC)

Like TLC, HPLC can be used to analyze fibers as well as drugs. HPLC has been utilized to determine the manufacturer of a particular fiber.[259]

Pyrolysis Gas Liquid Chromatography (Py-GLC)

Section 24-2 noted that pyrolysis techniques can be used to analyze hair. The same techniques have been adapted to analyze fiber.[260] In pyrolysis, the analyst employs heat to decompose the fiber. The pyrolyzed product is then inserted into a gas chromatograph, and the retention time in the GC is a clue to the fiber's identity.

There are different modes of pyrolysis in fiber analysis. In one mode, the analyst injects the fiber into a large vaporizer tube. The tube contains a heating unit. A gas is injected around the heating unit. As the heat decomposes the fiber, the gas picks up the pyrolyzed products and sweeps them into the GC. Alternatively, the analyst can use an electrical probe to heat the fiber. The analyst places the fiber between the ends of the probe and inserts the probe into the GC. When current runs through the probe, the sample is pyrolyzed and immediately enters the GC.

Some commentators caution against relying on pyrolysis techniques as the exclusive bases for a fiber identification.[261] They point out that in the reported studies, different laboratories have reported varying retention times for the same fibers.[262]

Stereo-Binocular Microscope

Analysts routinely utilize microscopes to examine the physical properties of fiber. The analyst can study the fiber to identify the following characteristics,

---

258. Beattie, Roberts & Dudley, *supra* note 256, at 64.

259. Kretschmer & Helbig, *Differentiation of Commercial Polyester Fibers Using Two-Dimensional High-Performance Liquid Chromatography (HPLC) and Multivariate Pattern Recognition Techniques*, 37 J. FORENSIC SCI. 727 (1992).

260. Janiak & Danerau, *The Application of Pyrolysis and Programmed Temperature Gas Chromatography to the Identification of Textile Fibers*, 59 J. CRIM. L., CRIMINOLOGY & POLICE SCI. 434 (1968).

261. Rowen & Reeve, *A Comparison and Evaluation of Techniques for Identification of Synthetic Fibers*, 15 J. FORENSIC SCI. 415, 418-19 (1970).

262. *Id.* at 417.

inter alia: color, size (diameter and coarseness), shape (cross section), the presence of delustering agents, surface characteristics, surface debris, and damage.[263] The stereo-microscope is perhaps the most commonly used microscope.[264] It is a relatively low-powered microscope. However, it produces a three-dimensional image of the fiber — length, width, and depth. This image frequently enables the analyst to determine the general group of the fiber, that is, whether the fiber is animal hair, plant fiber, etc..

Compound Microscope

This is a normal light microscope. Like the stereo-binocular microscope, it allows the analyst to observe the fiber's physical properties. This microscope is suitable for simple longitudinal and cross-sectional views of the fiber.

Comparison Microscope

The comparison microscope is an ideal tool for comparative analysis of known and unknown fiber samples to determine whether the samples match. The microscope consists of two microscopes with identical optical systems.[265] The microscopes are bonded together with an optical bridge. The microscope has two stages on which the two samples are mounted. The images of the two samples are visualized side by side; one sample appears to be a continuation of the other.

Fluorescent Microscope

A fluorescent microscope is equipped with an ultraviolet light source. Under ultraviolet light, the dyes[266] in some fibers fluoresce. The fiber's fluorescent quality is an indication of its identity.[267]

---

263. Deadman, *Fiber Evidence and the Wayne Williams Trial (Part I)*, 53 F.B.I. LAW ENF. BULL. 16 (March 1984).

264. A. MOENSSENS, J. STARRS, C. HENDERSON & F. INBAU, *supra* note 21, at § 9.05.

265. *Id.*

266. Laing, Dudley, *Hartshorne & Rickard, The Extraction and Classification of Dyes from Cotton and Viscose Fibres*, 50 FORENSIC SCI. INT'L 23 (1991); Hartshorne & Laing, *Microspectrofluorimetry of Fluorescent Dyes and Brighteners on Single Textile Fibres: Part 1 — Fluorescence Emission Spectra*, 51 FORENSIC SCI. INT'L 203 (1991); "*Part 2 — Colour Measurements*, 51 FORENSIC SCI. INT'L 221 (1991); *Part 3 —Fluorescence Decay Phenomena*, 51 FORENSIC SCI. INT'L 239 (1991).

267. Cartier, Roux & Grieve, *A Study to Investigate the Feasibility of Using X-Ray Fluorescence Microanalysis to Improve Discrimination Between Colorless Synthetic Fibers*, 42 J. FORENSIC SCI. 1019 (1997); Koons, *Comparison of Individual Carpet Fibers Using Energy Dispersive X-Ray Fluorescence*, 41 J. FORENSIC SCI. 199 (1996); French & Toribara, *X-Ray Fluorescence: With Special Application to Scanning Single Hair Strands*, 13 CRIME LAB. DIGEST 5 (1986).

Hot-Stage Microscope

This type of microscope allows the analyst to examine the effect of heat on the fiber. The sample is placed in a sealed tube. In turn, the tube is positioned in a heating jacket filled with heated oil. A thermometer is inserted into the oil. The analyst observes the thermometer and the sample through the eyepiece. The fiber's behavior can be correlated with changes in temperature. The analyst studies the fiber to note whether the fiber melts and, if so, the melting point, that is, the temperature at which melting occurs. Some natural fibers will not melt; most synthetic fibers, including polymers, do. The melting point allows further differentiation among the fibers that do melt.

Scanning Electron Microscope (SEM)

SEM is discussed in Chapter 25.[268] The SEM produces much greater magnifications than the other microscopes mentioned in this chapter. It is capable of producing magnification exceeding 300,000x. Thus, the SEM yields a tremendously enhanced image of the surface topography of the sample. Moreover, modern SEM instruments are linked to computers with the capability of storing and retrieving reference libraries of images of known fiber samples. The instrument can place the known and unknown images side by side to permit comparison, much in the same fashion as a comparison microscope.

Even the SEM has limitations. It does not depict the color of the fiber. In addition, even when the instrumentation allows side-by-side comparison of the SEM photomicrograms, the analyst must exercise subjective judgment in deciding whether the two fiber samples "match."

Small Angle Light Scattering (SALS)

In SALS, the analyst beams light from the visible portion of the electromagnetic spectrum onto the fiber. As the beam strikes the fiber, the fiber scatters the light. A polarizer or analyzer measures and photographs the angles at which the light scatters. The scattering pattern indicates the identity of the fiber.[269]

As a fiber analysis technique, SALS has promise. In some published studies, SALS analysts have differentiated between fibers within the same generic groups as well as determining whether the fiber had been subjected to such common

---

268. Castro, Galbreath, Pecko, Hellman & Rowe, *Use of the Scanning Electron Microscope to Examine Fiber Impressions on Typewriter Correction Tape*, 40 J. FORENSIC SCI. 291 (1995).

269. Bresee & McCullough, *Discrimination Among Acrylic Fiber Types by Small-Angle Light Scattering of Single Fibers*, 26 J. FORENSIC SCI. 184 (1981); Bresee & Crews, *Using Small-Angle Light Scattering to Discriminate Among Fibers Subjected to Consumer-Like Uses*, 26 J. FORENSIC SCI. 51 (1981); Bresee & Donelson, *Small-Angle Light Scattering for Analysis of a Single Fiber*, 25 J. FORENSIC SCI. 413 (1980).

occurrences as extensive outdoor exposure, mild, low-temperature hand wash, or vigorous, high-temperature machine wash.[270] However, much remains to be learned about SALS. It is unclear whether and to what extent fiber dyes interfere with the scattering pattern.[271] To date, it has not been demonstrated that SALS can discriminate between fibers produced by different manufacturers.

Viscometry

Viscometry measures the manner in which a fiber alters the flow properties of a solvent.[272] The analyst dissolves the fiber in the solvent. The analyst already knows how much time (usually a few tens of seconds) that the solvent would require to pass through a small glass capillary tube. The tube is called a viscometer. The period of time is termed the solvent's efflux time. When the fiber solution and solvent mix, the mixture changes the solvent's viscosity or flow properties. The analyst then sends the mixture through the capillary tube and measures its efflux time. The viscosity of the mixture is expressed as a relative viscosity, that is, the efflux time of the solution compared to the efflux time of the pure solvent.

Some analysts have used viscometry to successfully differentiate among commercially prepared fibers.[273] However, the technique is of relatively recent vintage, and more research is needed. Moreover, published viscosity numbers and relative viscosities are meaningless unless the analyst knows the solvent and temperature used in the published experiment.[274]

Microscopic Photometry

Chapter 23 discusses the use of spectrophotometry in drug analysis. Many of the same techniques can be adapted to fiber analysis.[275] In the past, the

---

270. Bresee & Crews, *supra* note 269, at 51-52.

271. Bresee & McCullough, *supra* note 269, at 188-89.

272. Bresee & Streit, *Dilute Solution Viscometry of Single Polyester Fibers*, 17 FORENSIC SCI. INT'L 167 (1981).

273. *Id.* at 167.

274. *Id.* at 169.

275. Cho, Reffner, Gatewood & Wetzel, *A New Method for Fiber Comparison Using Polarized Infrared Microspectroscopy*, 44 J. FORENSIC SCI. 275 (1999); White, *A Simple High-Pressure Anvil and Template Device for the Production of Infrared Spectra from Microfiber Samples*, 37 J. FORENSIC SCI. 620 (1992); Hartshorne & Laing, *An Absorption Standard for Microspectrophotometry: Results of a Collaborative Exercise*, 51 FORENSIC SCI. INT'L 263 (1991); Hartshorne & Laing, *Color Matching Within a Fiber Data Collection*, 33 J. FORENSIC SCI. 1345 (1988) (the use of chromaticity coordinates to describe absorbance spectra data produced by the microspectrophotometer); Grieve, Dunlop & Haddock, *An Assessment of the Value of Blue, Red, and Black Cotton Fibers as Target Fibers in Forensic Science Investigations*, 33 J. FORENSIC SCI. 1331 (1988) (color is particularly important in the analysis of cotton fibers); Hartshorne & Laing,

microspectrophotometers (MSP) used in fiber analysis have included the entire visible spectrum and the near parts of ultraviolet and infrared spectra.[276] Analysts employ MSP to assess the hue and degree of saturation of color in a fiber. With the inclusion of the UV and IR spectra, the microspectrophotometer enables the analyst to distinguish between colors that appear identical to the naked eye. The use of the microspectrophotometer removes some of the subjectivity inherent in the other fiber analysis techniques; and since this technique is nondestructive, the other tests can be conducted after this technique. However, even with a conventional microspectrophotometer, the analyst can differentiate only between fibers in major categories such as plant and mineral and some subtypes within the major categories.

The Metropolitan Police Forensic Science Laboratory in London has pioneered the use of IR in fiber analysis.[277] The laboratory has developed two techniques to prepare fiber samples for IR analysis.

One technique is the lead foil procedure. This technique is very effective for small samples, for example, less than five millimeters in size.[278] The analyst subjects a cube of lead to great pressure between two die pellets. The pressure reduces the cube to a lead foil. The analyst cuts a square hole in the foil. Next, the analyst subjects the fiber to the pressure. The analyst then cuts the flattened fiber into small pieces. A dissecting needle is used to transfer the pieces into the hole in the foil. The hole is covered with potassium bromide. The fiber mounted on the foil is now ready for IR analysis.

The second preparation technique is the solvent cast method.[279] This method is suitable for larger samples. The fiber sample is dissolved in a solvent and transferred onto a petri dish. The dish is allowed to dry until the solvent evaporates, leaving a film. The analyst next positions a quantity of potassium bromide on a die pellet. The film is then placed on top of the potassium bromide and more potassium bromide is added on top of the film. The sample can then be subjected to IR analysis. This procedure seems to result in less absorption than the lead foil technique.[280]

The Definition of Colour for Single Textile Fibres by Microspectrophotometry, 34 FORENSIC SCI. INT'L 34 (1987).

276. Tungol, Bartick & Montaser, *Analysis of Single Polymer Fibers by Fourier Transform Infrared Microscopy: The Results of Case Studies*, 36 J. FORENSIC SCI. 1027 (1991).

277. Cook & Patterson, *New Techniques for the Identification of Microscopic Samples of Textile Fibers by Infrared Spectroscopy*, 12 FORENSIC SCI. 237 (1978); Fox & Schuetzman, *The Infrared Identification of Microscopic Samples of Man-Made Fibers*, 13 J. FORENSIC SCI. 397 (1968). *See also* Was, Knittel & Schollmeyer, *The Use of FTIR Microspectroscopy for the Identification of Thermally Changed Fibers*, 41 J. FORENSIC SCI. 1005 (1996).

278. Cook & Patterson, *supra* note 277, at 240.

279. Garger, *An Improved Technique for Preparing Solvent Cast Films from Acrylic Fibers for the Recording of Infrared Spectra*, 28 J. FORENSIC SCI. 632 (1983).

280. Cook & Patterson, *supra* note 277, at 239-42.

IR analysis has great potential. Using the technique, analysts have made refined discriminations between subtypes such as classes of polyesters[281] and polymers.[282] The researchers have even attempted to distinguish between different daily production batches at the same plant. However, like the other fiber techniques, IR has its limitations. For example, in some tests, infrared spectroscopy did not discriminate among rayons.[283]

Polarized Light Microscope

The fiber analysis techniques previously mentioned examine the chemical and physical properties of fiber. The analyst may also gauge the sample's optical properties,[284] such as refractive index, birefringence, and dichroism.

To measure refracture index, the fiber is obliquely struck by a light team. When the beam of light passes through a sample, the beam slows. The refractive index of a fiber represents the difference between the speed of light through the fiber and the speed of light through a vacuum. The polarized light microscope allows the analyst to measure the refractive index (RI) of the fiber.

Some fibers are isotropic; that is, they have the same optical properties in all directions. However, most textile fibers are anisotropic; when tested on different axes, the fibers display different optical properties. The RI of the fiber parallel to a plane of polarized light is designated n_{11}. The fiber's RI perpendicular to the plane is designated n_{1}. The difference between the two indices, $n_{11} — n_{1}$, is the birefringence of the fiber.[285]

A third optical property of the fiber, its dichroism, can also be studied. Dichroism is the ability of a fiber to absorb light differently in two different orientations.

Fourier Transform Infrared Spectroscopy

Our reviewer points out that Fourier Transform Infrared Spectroscopy (FTIR) plays an important role in modern fiber analysis.[286] Many forensic laboratories routinely employ FTIR in fiber examinations.

---

281. Cho, Reffner & Wetzel, *Forensic Classification of Polyester Fibers by Infrared Dichroic Ratio Pattern Recognition*, 44 J. FORENSIC SCI. 283 (1999).

282. Cook & Patterson, *supra* note 277, at 239-42.

283. Rowen & Reeve, *supra* note 261, at 417.

284. Deadman, *supra* note 263, at 16. Stoeffler, *A Flowchart System for the Identification of Common Synthetic Fibers by Polarized Light Microscopy*, 41 J. FORENSIC SCI. 297 (1996).

285. Miller, *supra* note 245, at 19, 21.

286. There is an excellent discussion of the technique by Suzuki, *Forensic Applications of Infrared Spectroscopy*, Chapter 3 in Volume 3 of the Saferstein treatise on forensic science.

§ 24-4(B). Possible Findings.

The last subsection discussed the numerous techniques used to assess a fiber's chemical, physical, and optical properties. What is the forensic significance of findings of these properties?

Dr. Larry Howard, Director of the Georgia Bureau of Investigation (GBI) Crime Laboratory, has been quoted as stating that fiber evidence can be nearly as valuable as fingerprint evidence in identifying a criminal.[287] The use of the adverb, "nearly," is well-advised because, in the current state of the art, the fiber analyst cannot single out a criminal as confidently as a fingerprint or DNA analyst.[288]

The hair analyst certainly can determine which major category (animal, plant, mineral, or man-made) the sample falls into. Moreover, some techniques such as IR allow the analyst to differentiate among subtypes such as types of polymers within the major categories. In a few cases, it is even feasible to identify the fiber's manufacturer. As researchers perfect the techniques and accumulate a larger data base, it may become possible to determine the production batch in which the fiber was manufactured.

Once the analyst has identified the manufacturer, the chain of distribution from the manufacturer to a retail outlet accessible to the defendant may be traced. For example, in the Wayne Williams case, the fiber analysts concluded that the carpet fiber involved in that case had been manufactured at a West Point Pepperell mill in Dalton, Georgia.[289] By tracing the chain of distribution to the Atlanta area, a prosecution expert was permitted to testify that only one house in every 8,000 homes in the Atlanta area would have green carpet containing the fiber.[290] Similarly, the fiber analysts concluded that another fiber was from the carpet of a Chevrolet station wagon.[291] Tracing that chain of distribution, the analyst opined that only one car in every 3,800 automobiles in the Atlanta area would have similar carpet.[292] The analyst used data from manufacturers[293] and the Atlanta Regional Commission[294] as the bases for the probability estimates. To dramatize the fiber evidence, the analyst prepared charts linking the fiber

287. ATLANTA JOURNAL AND CONSTITUTION, Dec. 11, 1983, at 15E.

288. Bresee, *Evaluation of Textile Fiber Evidence: A Review*, 32 J. FORENSIC SCI. 510, 520 (1987) ("[A]n analyst ... usually estimates the number of fibers examined during his career, and states that he has never ... or rarely ... examined a fiber of the type in question").

289. Kadish, Davis & Kadish, *Law in the Future: Criminal Law*, 19 TRIAL 93 (Sept. 1983).

290. *Id.*

291. *Id.*

292. *Id.*

293. Deadman, *Fiber Evidence and the Wayne Williams Trial (Conclusion)*, 53 F.B.I. LAW ENF. BULL. 13 (May 1984).

294. *Id.*

evidence to the charged victims, Payne and Cater,[295] and to 10 other victims Williams allegedly killed.[296]

There are several types of cases in which the prosecution expert may be able to narrow the class of possible sources of the fiber. In one type of case, after checking with the manufacturer, the expert learns that only a small quantity of the fiber was originally manufactured.[297] The carpet fiber in the *Williams* case is an example.[298] In another type of case, the fiber was manufactured years ago.[299] As years pass, the quantity currently in use becomes smaller and smaller. In the *Williams* case, the bedroom carpet had not been manufactured since December 1971.[300] Finally, the source of the fiber may be the type of object a person rarely comes into contact with.[301] Another fiber used in the *Williams* case was fiber from the trunk liner of Williams' car.[302]

One researcher, Smalldon, experimented with a new technique for systematizing fiber identification.[303] Smalldon proposed numerically coding the various properties of fiber. Each fiber would have a code number. For example, in Smalldon's system, the code number for Acrilan 41 would be 5:1:2:1.23.[304] The four numbers represent respectively: composition, surface appearance, cross-sectional shape, and absorbance ratio. This classification scheme has potential for making fiber analysis more systematic in the future. The success of the system will depend upon refining the subdivisions for each characteristic and accumulating more data about the incidence of the various characteristics.[305] Other researchers are attempting to evaluate the statistical significance of fiber matches.[306]

---

295. *Id.* at 15.

296. *Id.* at 16.

297. Deadman, *supra* note 263, at 17.

298. *Id. See also* State v. Buell, 22 Ohio St. 3d 124, 489 N.E.2d 795, *cert. denied*, 479 U.S. 871 (1986) (the prosecutor traced the carpeting to J.P. Stevens Company and established that the company had manufactured only 12,015 square yards of the carpeting).

299. Deadman, *supra* note 263, at 17.

300. *Id.*

301. *Id.*

302. *Id.* at 17-18.

303. Smalldon, *The Identification of Acrylic Fibers by Polymer Composition as Determined by Infrared Spectroscopy and Physical Characteristics*, 18 J. Forensic Sci. 69 (1973).

304. *Id.* at 77.

305. Laing, Hartshorne, Cook & Robinson, *A Fiber Data Collection for Forensic Scientists — Collection and Examination Methods*, 32 J. Forensic Sci. 364 (1987) (the Inter-Laboratory Advisory Committee (Fibres) of the U.K. Home Office Forensic Science Services has begun collecting data).

306. Fong & Inami, *Results of Study to Determine the Probability of Chance Match Occurrences Between Fibers Known to be from Different Sources*, 31 J. Forensic Sci. 65, 71 (1986) (overall the study showed a 1/41 probability of a chance match occurrence; if blue cotton fiber is excluded, the probability increases to 1/130); Palmer & Chinherende, *A Target Fiber Study*

§ 24-5. Admissibility of Fiber Evidence.

The courts have treated fiber evidence in much the same fashion as hair evidence. As in the case of hair evidence, there is a huge body of decisional law routinely admitting fiber testimony.[307] In the cases, fiber experts have testified on the basis of the following tests, *inter alia:* dyes,[308] delustering agents,[309] solvents,[310] microscopic examination,[311] thin layer chromatography,[312] gas

---

Using Cinema and Car Seats as Recipient Items, 41 J. FORENSIC SCI. 802 (1996) (the researchers purchased two garments from a major British clothing retail chain; they then attempted to match the fibers from the garments with fibers found on seats in randomly chosen cinema and car seats; "[t]he results of this study show that the chances of finding a particular fiber color/type at random, in the population, is unlikely"). *But see* Gaudette & Binder, *Discussion of "Results of Study to Determine the Probability of Chance Match Occurrences Between Fibers Known to Be from Different Sources,"* 33 J. FORENSIC SCI. 607 (1988) (criticizing the Fong and Inami article).

307. *E.g.,* Maxwell v. State, 236 Ark. 694, 370 S.W.2d 113 (1963); State v. Brown, 168 Conn. 610, 362 A.2d 910 (1975); People v. Mackins, 17 Ill. App. 3d 24, 308 N.E.2d 92 (1974), *cert. denied,* 419 U.S. 1111 (1975); Tomolillo v. State, 4 Md. App. 711, 245 A.2d 94 (1968); State v. Hollander, 201 N.J. Super. 453, 493 A.2d 563 (the fibers analysis technique used were generally accepted within the scientific community), *cert. denied,* 101 N.J. 335, 501 A.2d 983 (1985); State v. Woods, 286 N.C. 612, 213 S.E.2d 214 (1975), *vacated,* 428 U.S. 903 (1976); State v. Walker, 6 N.C. App. 447, 170 S.E.2d 627 (1969); State v. Coolidge, 109 N.H. 403, 260 A.2d 547 (1969), *rev'd on other grounds,* 403 U.S. 443 (1971); State v. Breest, 116 N.H. 734, 367 A.2d 1320 (1976); Hunter v. State, 468 S.W.2d 96 (Tex. 1971); Miller, *supra* note 245, at 21. *But see* Hughes v. Commonwealth, 18 Va. App. 510, 446 S.E.2d 451 (1994) (the prosecution expert found a particular type of fiber in both the kidnapping defendant's car and on a nightshirt belonging to the alleged victim; at the intermediate appellate court level, the majority of the initial panel ruled that since that type of fiber is "used in virtually every kind of nylon carpet," the testimony had little probative value and should not have been admitted; the dissent contended that the common nature of the fiber reduced the weight of the evidence but did not destroy its logical relevance; the en banc appellate court adopted the dissent's view).

308. Harper v. State, 249 Ga. 519, 292 S.E.2d 389 (1982); State v. Sandlin, 61 N.C. App. 421, 300 S.E.2d 893, *app. denied,* 308 N.C. 679, 304 S.E.2d 760, *cert. denied,* 464 U.S. 995 (1983); State v. Coble, 20 N.C. App. 575, 202 S.E.2d 303, *app. dismissed,* 285 N.C. 236, 204 S.E.2d 21 (1974); State v. Nelson, 84 S.D. 218, 169 N.W.2d 533 (1969).

309. United States v. Preston, 331 F. Supp. 457, 458 (D.D.C. 1971).

310. State v. Woods, 286 N.C. 612, 213 S.E.2d 214 (1975), *vacated,* 428 U.S. 903 (1976).

311. Johnson v. United States, 426 F.2d 651 (D.C. Cir. 1970), *cert. dismissed,* 401 U.S. 846 (1971); United States v. Mobley, 421 F.2d 345 (5th Cir. 1970); United States v. Stone, 401 F.2d 32 (7th Cir. 1968); United States v. Phillips, 607 F.2d 808 (8th Cir. 1979); United States v. Curtis, 568 F.2d 643 (9th Cir. 1978); Sanchez v. Heggie, 531 F.2d 964 (10th Cir.), *cert. denied,* 429 U.S. 849 (1976); United States v. Brumley, 466 F.2d 911 (10th Cir. 1972), *cert. denied,* 412 U.S. 929 (1973); Julius v. State, 407 So. 2d 141 (Ala. Crim. App. 1980), *rev'd,* 407 So. 2d 152 (Ala. 1981); Harnage v. State, 49 Ala. App. 563, 274 So. 2d 333, *rev'd,* 290 Ala. 142, 274 So. 2d 352 (1972), *cert. denied,* 290 Ala. 367 (1973); Dorman v. State, 622 P.2d 448 (Alaska 1981); State v. Wallace, 181 Conn. 237, 435 A.2d 20 (1980); State v. Brown, 168 Conn. 610, 362 A.2d 910 (1975); State v. Kraft, 96 Idaho 901, 539 P.2d 254 (1975), *app. dismissed,* 99 Idaho 214, 579 P.2d 1197 (1978); People v. Washington, 68 Ill. 2d 186, 369 N.E.2d 57 (1977), *cert. denied,* 435 U.S. 981 (1978); People v. Carbona, 27 Ill. App. 3d 988, 11 Ill. Dec. 603, 327 N.E.2d 546 (1975), *cert. denied,* 424

chromatography,[313] refractive index,[314] neutron activation analysis,[315] spectrography,[316] mass spectrometry,[317] infrared spectroscopy,[318] and scanning electron microscopy.[319]

In most of the reported cases, the expert offers testimony strikingly similar to the opinions normally admitted in hair cases. The expert testifies that he or she

---

U.S. 914 (1976); People v. Parra, 35 Ill. App. 3d 240, 340 N.E.2d 636 (1975); People v. Gorsuch, 19 Ill. App. 3d 60, 310 N.E.2d 695 (1974); People v. Mackins, 17 Ill. App. 3d 24, 308 N.E.2d 92 (1974), *cert. denied,* 419 U.S. 1111 (1975); Baker v. State, 260 Ind. 618, 298 N.E.2d 445 (1973); State v. McClain, 216 Kan. 602, 533 P.2d 1277 (1975); Commonwealth v. Perez, 357 Mass. 290, 258 N.E.2d 1 (1970); Commonwealth v. Smith, 350 Mass. 600, 215 N.E.2d 897 (1966); State v. Maxie, 513 S.W.2d 338 (Mo. 1974), *cert. denied,* 420 U.S. 930 (1975); State v. Daniels, 655 S.W.2d 106 (Mo. App. 1983); State v. Stout, 591 S.W.2d 225 (Mo. App. 1979); McGuinn v. State, 177 Mont. 215, 581 P.2d 417 (1978); People v. Travato, 309 N.Y. 382, 131 N.E.2d 557 (1955); State v. Fincher, 309 N.C. 1, 305 S.E.2d 685 (1983); State v. Woods, 286 N.C. 612, 213 S.E.2d 214 (1975), *vacated,* 428 U.S. 903 (1976); State v. Rhodes, 275 N.C. 584, 169 S.E.2d 846 (1969); State v. Coble, 20 N.C. App. 575, 202 S.E.2d 303, *app. dismissed,* 285 N.C. 236, 204 S.E.2d 21 (1974); State v. Cooper, 52 Ohio St. 2d 163, 6 Ohio Op. 3d 377, 370 N.E.2d 725 (1977), *vacated,* 438 U.S. 911 (1978); State v. Martin, 164 Ohio St. 54, 57 Ohio Op. 84, 128 N.E.2d 7 (1955); Moore v. State, 788 P.2d 387, 398 (Okla. Crim. App.) ("The admission of expert testimony of microscopic comparison of ... fiber samples has been implicitly, if not explicitly, approved"), *cert. denied,* 498 U.S. 881 (1990); Driskell v. State, 659 P.2d 343 (Okla. Crim. App. 1983); Commonwealth v. Holzer, 480 Pa. 93, 389 A.2d 101 (1978); Commonwealth v. Thomas, 448 Pa. 42, 292 A.2d 352 (1972); Commonwealth v. Petrisko, 442 Pa. 575, 275 A.2d 46 (1971); Commonwealth v. Urbina, 290 Pa. Super. 117, 434 A.2d 157 (1981); Commonwealth v. Paterick, 239 Pa. Super. 1, 361 A.2d 715 (1976); State v. Jefferson, 116 R.I. 124, 353 A.2d 190 (1976); State v. Nelson, 84 S.D. 218, 169 N.W.2d 533 (1969) (degree and direction of twist); Robinson v. Commonwealth, 212 Va. 136, 183 S.E.2d 179 (1971); State v. Jones, 19 Wash. App. 850, 578 P.2d 71 (1978); State *ex rel.* Kanieski v. Gagnon, 54 Wis. 2d 108, 194 N.W.2d 808 (1972). Citing this treatise, the Hawaii Supreme Court has upheld the admission of testimony about microscopic fiber analysis. State v. Fukusaka, 85 Haw. 462, 946 P.2d 32 (1997). The court pointed out that Rule of Evidence 702 distinguishes between "scientific knowledge" and nonscientific "technical knowledge." The court concluded that the testimony was admissible as the latter type of expert evidence; the court asserted that the technique is "well-established and of proven reliability."

312. State v. Woods, 286 N.C. 612, 213 S.E.2d 214 (1975), *vacated,* 428 U.S. 903 (1976).

313. Commonwealth v. Stickle, 484 Pa. 89, 398 A.2d 957 (1979).

314. Driskell v. State, 659 P.2d 343 (Okla. Crim. App. 1983).

315. National Research Dev. Corp. v. Great Lakes Carbon Corp., 410 F. Supp. 1108 (D. Del. 1975); State v. Smith, 637 S.W.2d 232 (Mo. App. 1982).

316. State v. Rhone, 555 S.W.2d 839 (Mo. 1977); Commonwealth v. Paterick, 239 Pa. Super. 1, 361 A.2d 715 (1976).

317. National Research Dev. Corp. v. Great Lakes Carbon Corp., 410 F. Supp. 1108 (D. Del. 1975).

318. People v. Carbona, 27 Ill. App. 3d 988, 327 N.E.2d 546 (1975), *cert. denied,* 424 U.S. 914 (1976).

319. National Research Dev. Corp. v. Great Lakes Carbon Corp., 410 F. Supp. 1108 (D. Del. 1975).

can detect no difference between the fiber samples[320] and that the samples have the same,[321] identical,[322] or indistinguishable properties.[323] On the one hand, the expert may acknowledge that he or she cannot positively conclude that the samples came from the same source.[324] On the other hand, the expert will maintain that since the samples' properties match,[325] the samples are alike[326] or similar[327] and, hence, consistent with the hypothesis of a common source.[328]

---

320. State v. Head, 79 N.C. App. 1, 12, 338 S.E.2d 908, 914 ("there were no inconsistencies in any of the details examined"), *review denied,* 316 N.C. 736, 345 S.E.2d 395 (1986); State v. Martin, 164 Ohio St. 54, 57 Ohio Op. 84, 128 N.E.2d 7 (1955).

321. Johnson v. United States, 426 F.2d 651 (D.C. Cir. 1970), *cert. dismissed,* 401 U.S. 846 (1971); People v. Washington, 68 Ill. 2d 186, 369 N.E.2d 57 (1977), *cert. denied,* 435 U.S. 981 (1978); State v. Coble, 20 N.C. App. 575, 202 S.E.2d 303 (1974); State v. Cooper, 52 Ohio St. 2d 163, 6 Ohio Op. 3d 377, 370 N.E.2d 725 (1977), *vacated,* 438 U.S. 911 (1978); State v. Royster, 48 Ohio St. 2d 381, 2 Ohio Op. 3d 489, 358 N.E.2d 616 (1976); *vacated,* 438 U.S. 911 (1978); Commonwealth v. Urbina, 290 Pa. Super. 117, 434 A.2d 157 (1981); Robinson v. Commonwealth, 212 Va. 136, 183 S.E.2d 179 (1971).

322. United States v. Mobley, 421 F.2d 345 (5th Cir. 1970); United States v. Stone, 401 F.2d 32 (7th Cir. 1968); United States v. Curtis, 568 F.2d 643 (9th Cir. 1978); Julius v. State, 407 So. 2d 141 (Ala. Crim. App. 1980), *rev'd,* 407 So. 2d 152 (Ala. 1981); State v. Wallace, 181 Conn. 237, 435 A.2d 20 (1980); Dorman v. State, 622 P.2d 448 (Alaska 1981); People v. Parra, 35 Ill. App. 3d 240, 340 N.E.2d 636 (1975); People v. Mackins, 17 Ill. App. 3d 24, 308 N.E.2d 92 (1974), *cert. denied,* 419 U.S. 1111 (1975); State v. Post, 255 Iowa 573, 123 N.W.2d 11 (1963); Pilcher v. State, 296 So. 2d 682 (Miss. 1974), *cert. denied,* 420 U.S. 938 (1975); In Interest of M., 487 S.W.2d 502 (Mo. 1972); State v. Rhodes, 275 N.C. 584, 169 S.E.2d 846 (1969); Commonwealth v. Paterick, 239 Pa. Super. 1, 361 A.2d 715 (1976); State v. Jefferson, 116 R.I. 124, 353 A.2d 190 (1976); State v. Jones, 19 Wash. App. 850, 578 P.2d 71 (1978); State *ex rel.* Kanieski v. Gagnon, 54 Wis. 2d 108, 194 N.W.2d 808 (1972).

323. Baker v. State, 260 Ind. 618, 298 N.E.2d 445 (1973); Commonwealth v. Petrisko, 442 Pa. 575, 275 A.2d 46 (1971).

324. United States v. Preston, 331 F. Supp. 457, 458 (D.D.C. 1971); Garr v. Commonwealth, 463 S.W.2d 109, 110 (Ky.), *cert. denied,* 403 U.S. 910 (1971); State v. Jefferson, 116 R.I. 124, 353 A.2d 190 (1976) (not categorically); State v. Jones, 19 Wash. App. 850, 578 P.2d 71 (1978).

325. People v. Trujillo, 32 Cal. 2d 105, 194 P.2d 681, *cert. denied sub nom.* Woodmansee v. California, 335 U.S. 887 (1948); State v. Kraft, 96 Idaho 901, 539 P.2d 254 (1975); Garr v. Commonwealth, 463 S.W.2d 109 (Ky.), *cert. denied,* 403 U.S. 910 (1971); State v. Wade, 83 S.D. 337, 159 N.W.2d 396 (1968).

326. Sanchez v. Heggie, 531 F.2d 964 (10th Cir.), *cert. denied,* 429 U.S. 849 (1976).

327. United States v. Phillips, 607 F.2d 808 (8th Cir. 1979); Harnage v. State, 49 Ala. App. 563, 274 So. 2d 333, *rev'd,* 290 Ala. 142, 274 So. 2d 352 (1972); People v. Nunez, 7 Cal. App. 3d 655, 86 Cal. Rptr. 707 (1970); Felker v. State, 252 Ga. 351, 314 S.E.2d 621, *cert. denied,* 469 U.S. 873 (1984); People v. Popely, 36 Ill. App. 3d 828, 345 N.E.2d 125 (1976); People v. Gorsuch, 19 Ill. App. 3d 60, 310 N.E.2d 695 (1974); People v. Mackins, 17 Ill. App. 3d 24, 308 N.E.2d 92 (1974), *cert. denied,* 419 U.S. 1111 (1975); Commonwealth v. Perez, 357 Mass. 290, 258 N.E.2d 1 (1970); Commonwealth v. Nunes, 351 Mass. 401, 221 N.E.2d 752 (1966); State v. Scarlett, 121 N.H. 37, 426 A.2d 25 (1981); People v. Travato, 309 N.Y. 382, 131 N.E.2d 557 (1955); Commonwealth v. Thomas, 448 Pa. 42, 292 A.2d 352 (1972); Robinson v. Commonwealth, 212 Va. 136, 183 S.E.2d 179 (1971).

Consequently, the samples could share the same origin.[329] In one case, the expert testified that it was "extremely likely" that the fibers came from the defendant's carpeting.[330] Post *Daubert*, it seems doubtful that that type of phrasing is acceptable at least without additional empirical support. Even if the expert professes to be relying primarily on his or her own experience and the proponent characterizes the testimony as nonscientific expert evidence, under *Kumho*[331] the proponent will be required to make a foundational showing of the reliability of the testimony.

In some past cases, even when the expert did not cite any supporting population frequency studies, courts allowed the expert to embellish the testimony. Thus, in *State v. Woods*[332] the expert added that the red polyester fibers found in that case were reasonably rare. In the *Breest* case[333] the expert asserted that there was a "high degree of probability" that the victim had made contact with the defendant.[334] Other expert witnesses have declared that there was a strong probability of a common origin[335] or that conversely, it is unlikely that the samples have different sources.[336] Some experts flatly assert that the samples have a common origin[337] or came from the crime scene[338] or the same company.[339]

In the most extreme cases, courts have allowed the expert to quantify the probability. The last section pointed out that the trial judge permitted the prosecution experts to testify to some probabilities in the Wayne Williams case.

---

328. State v. Brown, 168 Conn. 610, 362 A.2d 910 (1975); Felker v. State, 252 Ga. 351, 314 S.E.2d 621, *cert. denied,* 469 U.S. 873 (1984); Commonwealth v. Perez, 357 Mass. 290, 258 N.E.2d 1 (1970); State v. Daniels, 655 S.W.2d 106 (Mo. App. 1983); State v. Fincher, 309 N.C. 1, 305 S.E.2d 685 (1983).

329. United States v. Brumley, 466 F.2d 911 (10th Cir. 1972), *cert. denied,* 412 U.S. 929 (1973); State v. Wallace, 181 Conn. 237, 435 A.2d 20 (1980); McGuinn v. State, 177 Mont. 215, 581 P.2d 417 (1978); State v. Woods, 286 N.C. 612, 213 S.E.2d 214 (1975), *vacated,* 428 U.S. 903 (1976); Commonwealth v. Holzer, 480 Pa. 93, 389 A.2d 101 (1978); State *ex rel.* Kanieski v. Gagnon, 54 Wis. 2d 108, 194 N.W.2d 808 (1972).

330. State v. Buell, 22 Ohio St. 3d 124, 22 Ohio B. 203, 489 N.E.2d 795, *cert. denied,* 479 U.S. 871 (1986).

331. Kumho Tire Co., Ltd. v. Carmichael, 119 S. Ct. 1167 (1999).

332. 286 N.C. 612, 213 S.E.2d 214 (1975), *vacated,* 428 U.S. 903 (1976).

333. State v. Breest, 116 N.H. 734, 367 A.2d 1320 (1976).

334. *Id.* at 748-50, 367 A.2d at 1331-32. *See also* State v. Maxie, 513 S.W.2d 338, 342 (Mo. 1974) ("high probability"), *cert. denied,* 420 U.S. 930 (1975).

335. People v. Mackins, 17 Ill. App. 3d 24, 308 N.E.2d 92 (1974), *cert. denied,* 419 U.S. 1111 (1975).

336. State v. Woods, 286 N.C. 612, 213 S.E.2d 214 (1975), *vacated,* 428 U.S. 903 (1976).

337. State v. Smith, 637 S.W.2d 232 (Mo. App. 1982).

338. State v. Rhone, 555 S.W.2d 839 (Mo. 1977).

339. United States v. Bangert, 645 F.2d 1297 (8th Cir.), *cert. denied,* 454 U.S. 860 (1981).

State v. Coolidge[340] is a step beyond *Williams.* In *Coolidge* the expert analyzed 40 sets of fibers from the victim's clothes and the defendant's car. He concluded that 27 sets were indistinguishable and asserted that the probability of finding a similar fiber in car sweepings is one in ten. The expert finally declared that the odds of finding 27 matches were one in ten to the twenty-seventh power.[341] In other cases, fiber experts have testified that the odds of coincidental matches were one in 3,200,000[342] and one in a hundred billion.[343] Courts should allow such testimony only when the expert can establish the validity of the statistical formula used and the reliability of the sources of the data used to apply the formula. Absent that foundation, such testimony should be inadmissible in any jurisdiction which takes *Daubert* seriously.

§ 24-6. Glass Identification.

Glass fragments are almost as ubiquitous as hairs and fibers. In one study, researchers examined 100 men's suits at a dry cleaning establishment;[344] 63 suits contained glass fragments. In a subsequent study, researchers surveyed men's footwear at a thrift store.[345] Of the 650 pairs of shoes examined, 261 contained glass fragments.

Given the availability of glass fragments, it is not surprising that crime laboratories use such fragments as associative evidence. Glass fragments can serve as associative evidence in two different ways. First, the analyst can demonstrate that the physical properties of a glass fragment on the defendant's person match the properties of glass found at the crime scene. Second, the analyst can show that a fragment found on the defendant mechanically fits with a fragment remaining at the crime scene — suggesting that at one time, the two fragments were joined.

§ 24-6(A). Properties of Glass Fragments.

Glass is a hybrid substance. It has been described both as a non-crystalline solid and as a super-cooled liquid. In the manufacturing process, glass cools and solidifies from its molten state without being permitted to crystallize. As glass cools, the molecules fix in place without forming crystals. The lack of crystallization helps to make the glass transparent, durable, and individualized.

---

340. 109 N.H. 403, 260 A.2d 547 (1969), *rev'd on other grounds,* 403 U.S. 443 (1971).

341. *Id.* at 421-22, 260 A.2d at 558-61.

342. State v. McClain, 216 Kan. 602, 533 P.2d 1277 (1975).

343. People v. Trujillo, 32 Cal. 2d 105, 194 P.2d 681, *cert. denied sub nom.* Woodmansee v. California, 335 U.S. 887 (1948).

344. Pearson, May & Dabbs, *Glass and Paint Fragments Found in Men's Outer Clothing — Report of a Survey,* 16 J. Forensic Sci. 183 (1971).

345. Davis & Dehann, *A Survey of Men's Footwear,* 17 J. Forensic Sci. Soc'y 271 (1977).

Ninety-five percent of the glass manufactured in the United States has a soda-lime-silica formulation. Silica represents 75% of the glass. The formula includes 10% soda because soda lowers the melting point of the compound. The remaining 15% of the compound consists of lime, added to make glass insoluble in water. There are numerous special types of glass such as safety glass and headlamps; each has a particular chemical composition. For example, bakeware glass includes boron to make the glass heat-resistant. Lead crystal glass such as fine stemware contains lead oxide. Thus, the chemical composition of the glass fragment is a clue to the type of glass.[346]

Although the manufacturer deliberately varies the chemical composition of glass to serve different commercial purposes, other characteristics of glass fragments — "defects" — find their way into the fragment accidentally. The forensic glass analyst encounters three chief types of defects. Cord or ream are parallel lines or striae in the fragment. Cord can appear on the glass surface or internally. Next, the fragment may include stones. Stones are solid, crystalline impurities. Molten glass is heated in a furnace, and fragments of the furnace lining occasionally break off to form impurities. Finally, the fragment could contain a seed defect. A seed is a gas bubble left in the glass, due to insufficient heating during the melting process.

Given the variations in chemical composition and defects among glass fragments, the analyst can study a large number of each fragment's properties such as color and hardness. However, the four most commonly studied properties are: the density of the fragment, its optical qualities, its trace element concentration, and its fluorescence.

Density or Specific Gravity

The density of a glass fragment is its weight per volume at a specified temperature.[347] Density is usually expressed as the number of grams per cubic centimeter (gm/cc) at 20 degrees C.[348] The formula for the specific gravity of the glass specimen is:

$$\frac{\text{density of the substance}}{\text{density of water}}$$

---

346. *See generally* Stone & Thornton, *Glass Evidence, in* SCIENTIFIC AND EXPERT EVIDENCE 239 (2d ed. 1981).

347. *Id.* at 258. The F.B.I. has a computer printout of glass density data that it has distributed to other crime laboratories. Espinoza & Thornton, *Three-Dimensional Presentation of Glass Density Versus Refractive Index Data*, 31 J. FORENSIC SCI. 687 (1986).

348. Stone & Thornton, *supra* note 346, at 258.

There are several methods of determining the specific gravity of a glass fragment. The method of Archimedes is used for large fragments.[349] The fragment is initially weighed in air and then reweighed while immersed in a water of a given temperature. The fragment's specific gravity can be calculated from the two weight measurements.[350]

Another technique is the sink-float method.[351] In this technique, the analyst mixes two liquids of known density until the mixture holds the glass fragment in suspension; the fragment neither sinks nor floats. At that point, the mixture and the fragment have equal density.

A final method is the density gradient technique.[352] The analyst prepares a special liquid column, a gradient tube. There is a graduation of density in liquid along the length of the column. When the fragment is inserted into the column, its level of descent is noted.[353] The fragment comes to rest at a level at which its specific gravity equals the specific gravity of the liquid. This point is called the fragment's equilibrium.[354]

Optical Properties

A fragment's specific gravity correlates strongly with some of the fragment's optical properties such as refractive index (RI).[355] Thus, when the analyst measures both specific gravity and refractive index, there is an overlap of

---

349. *Id.*

350. *Id.*

351. *Id.* at 259; Kahane & Thornton, *Estimation of the Absolute Density of Glass Following the Sink/Float Technique*, 32 J. FORENSIC SCI. 87 (1987).

352. Stone & Thornton, *supra* note 346, at 258. *See also* Thornton, Langhauser & Kahane, *Correlation of Glass Density and Refractive Index — Implications to Density Gradient Construction*, 29 J. FORENSIC SCI. 711 (1984).

353. Fong, *Value of Glass as Evidence*, 18 J. FORENSIC SCI. 398, 400 (1973).

354. Roche & Kirk, *Differentiation of Similar Glass Fragments by Physical Properties*, 38 J. CRIM. L., CRIMINOLOGY & POLICE SCI. 168, 169 (1947).

355. Stone & Thornton, *supra* note 346, at 269; Zeichner & Feingold, *Improved Sample Holder for Refractive Index Measurements of Small, Single Glass Fragments*, 34 J. FORENSIC SCI. 1003 (1989); Zoro, Locke, Day, Badmus & Perryman, *An Investigation of Refractive Index Anomalies at the Surfaces of Glass Objects and Windows*, 39 FORENSIC SCI. INT'L 127, 141 (1988) ("RI anomalies may be observed at, or near to, the surfaces of glass objects when the oil immersion method of RI determinations is used. Many of the anomalies are large and forensic scientists would therefore be well advised to examine glass fragments carefully under a microscope to locate any original surfaces before carrying out RI determinations. Edges at an original surface should be excluded from comparison with the bulk glass"); Lambert & Evett, *The Interpretation of Refractive Index Measurements. VI: The Computer Program Rung*, 28 FORENSIC SCI. INT'L 251 (1985) (a computer program, RUNG, has been developed to assign glass into different groups based on refractive index measurements); Dabbs & Pearson, *Some Physical Properties of a Large Number of Window Glass Specimens*, 17 J. FORENSIC SCI. 70, 77 (1972).

information.[356] However, the overlap is only partial; the measurement of RI provides additional information.[357]

The concept of refractive index is discussed in § 24-4(A) dealing with fiber evidence. The refractive index of a glass fragment is the ratio between the velocity of light in a vacuum and its velocity in the medium, namely, the glass fragment. There are two methods of determining the fragment's RI.

The more traditional technique is the microscopical immersion or Becke line method. When a glass fragment is immersed in a solution, a halo around the glass — the Becke line — is observable. However, in light of a particular wavelength (often light of 5893 Å from a sodium lamp) (an Å or Angstrom is one ten-billionth of a meter), the halo and glass disappear if the fragment and the liquid in which the fragment is immersed have the exact RI.[358] The analyst immerses the fragment in a liquid with a calibrated RI on a microscope slide and observes the immersed fragment through a microscope to determine whether the halo disappears. The manual, Becke line method is a laborious technique for measuring RI.

Many laboratories use a device known as a refractometer to measure RI.[359] However, some types of glass yield poor readings on a refractometer.[360] Moreover, the refractometer cannot be used on small samples; and most samples submitted to crime laboratories fall into that category. The RI of these types of glass must be determined by the Becke line technique.[361]

In the past, analysts were content to identify one RI for a glass fragment. However, recent research indicates that a given glass fragment might exhibit several refractive indices.[362]A single fragment may have three different indices: one on its top surface, another on the opposite surface, and a third for the bulk of the fragment.[363] This discovery provides additional parameters in determining whether two glass fragments match.[364]

---

356. Stone & Thornton, *supra* note 346, at 269.

357. *Id. See also* Thornton, Langhauser & Kahane, *supra* note 315, at 711; Stoney & Thornton, *The Forensic Significance of the Correlation of Density and Refractive Index in Glass Evidence*, 29 FORENSIC SCI. INT'L 147 (1985) (in one study, the correlation coefficient between the two measurements was 0.93).

358. Miller, *A Rapid Method for the Comparison of Glass Fragments*, 10 J. FORENSIC SCI. 272, 273 (1965).

359. Dabbs & Pearson, *supra* note 355, at 70.

360. *Id.* at 71.

361. *Id.*

362. Davies, Dudley & Smalldon, *An Investigation of Bulk and Surface Refractive Indices for Flat Window Glasses, Patterned Window Glasses and Windscreen Glasses*, 16 FORENSIC SCI. INT'L 125 (1980).

363. *Id.* at 126.

364. *Id.* at 136.

In addition to determining the RI of the glass fragment, the analyst can measure its dispersion. A fragment's dispersion is its ability to exhibit various refractive indices for different wavelengths of light.[365] The analyst typically measures the RI of the fragment under sodium light (5893 Å or N_d), blue light (4861 Å or N_f), and red light (6583 Å or N_c). The dispersion number expresses the relationship between the various indices. The formula[366] for dispersion is customarily stated as

$$N_f - N_c$$

or

$$\frac{(Nd - 1)}{N_f - N_c}$$

Some analysts use a k value to incorporate both the RI of the glass fragment and its density.[367] The pertinent formula is

$$k = V / D$$

In the formula, V is dispersion and D is density. The k value is a summary statistic, helping the analyst determine whether glass fragments share a common source.

Trace Element Concentration

As previously stated, manufacturers vary the chemical composition of the different types of glass, depending on the intended commercial use of the glass. Therefore, the analyst can differentiate among some types of glass on the basis of the fragment's elemental composition. There are several techniques for analyzing the elemental composition of the fragment. Most of the techniques are covered in detail in Chapters 11 and 25. These techniques are mentioned only in passing in this section. One technique is atomic absorption spectroscopy (AAS).[368] Although there is a strong correlation between density and refractive index,[369] there appears to be little correlation between RI and trace element concentrations

---

365. Miller, *A Rapid Method for the Comparison of Glass Fragments*, 10 J. FORENSIC SCI. 272, 273 (1965).

366. *Id. See also* Locke, Underhill, Russell, Cox & Perryman, *The Evidential Value of Dispersion in the Examination of Glass*, 32 FORENSIC SCI. INT'L 219 (1986); Graber & Principe, *Identification of Glass Fragments by Measurement of Refractive Index and Dispersion*, 8 J. FORENSIC SCI. 54 (1963).

367. Thornton, *The Use of k Values in the Interpretation of Glass Density and Refractive Index Data*, 34 J. FORENSIC SCI. 1323 (1989). *But see* Koons, *Discussion of "The Use of k Values in the Interpretation of Glass Density and Refractive Index Data,"* 35 J. FORENSIC SCI. 1261 (1990) (criticizing the use of k values).

368. Hughes, Catterick & Southeard, *The Quantitative Analysis of Glass by Atomic Absorption Spectroscopy*, 8 FORENSIC SCI. 217 (1976).

369. *Id.*

such as the level of magnesium in glass fragments.[370] Since RI and the elemental concentration are largely independent, the measurement of the trace element concentration is highly informative. Like AAS, mass spectrometry can be employed to analyze the elemental composition of glass fragments.[371]

There have been numerous reported studies on the use of neutron activation analysis (NAA) to measure the trace element concentration.[372] NAA yields a gamma ray spectrum, indicating the type and quantity of elements present.[373] The spectrum may depict 70 or more peaks useful in identifying not only the type of glass but also the manufacturer.[374]

Other laboratories have successfully applied energy dispersive X-ray (EDX) to analyze the composition of glass fragments.[375] Some use EDX in conjunction with measurements of density and RI. Even if two fragments have matching densities and indices, EDX may enable the analyst to differentiate between the fragments.[376]

Still other researchers have employed emission spectroscopy.[377] A laboratory can integrate emission spectroscopy in a multi-technique identification system. For example, if two fragments match in density, RI, and EDX analysis, the analyst may sometimes discriminate between the samples by the use of emission spectroscopy.[378]

Trace element concentration analyses can be combined with tests of other parameters of the glass. It is becoming increasingly hazardous for an analyst to

---

370. *Id.* at 225.

371. Parouchais, Eng, Warner, Palmer & Kobus, *The Analysis of Small Glass Fragments Using Inductively Coupled Plasma Mass Spectrometry*, 41 J. FORENSIC SCI. 351 (1996).

372. *Id.* at 223; Pitts & Kratochvil, *Statistical Discrimination of Flat Glass Fragments by Instrumental Neutron Activation Analysis Methods for Forensic Science Applications*, 36 J. FORENSIC SCI. 122 (1991). Blacklock, Rogers, Wall & Wheals, *The Quantitative Analysis of Glass by Emission Spectrography: A Six Element Survey*, 7 FORENSIC SCI. 121 (1976); Schmitt & Smith, *Identification of Origin of Glass by Neutron Activation Analysis in a Forensic Case*, 15 J. FORENSIC SCI. 252 (1970); Ruch, Buchanan, Guinn, Bellanca & Pinker, *Neutron Activation Analysis in Scientific Crime Detection — Some Recent Developments*, 9 J. FORENSIC SCI. 119 (1964).

373. Schmitt & Smith, *supra* note 372, at 258.

374. *Id.* at 259.

375. Andrasko & Maehly, *The Discrimination Between Samples of Window Glass by Combining Physical and Chemical Techniques*, 23 J. FORENSIC SCI. 250 (1978).

376. *Id.*

377. *Id.;* Blacklock, Rogers, Wall & Wheals, *supra* note 334, at 121; Schmitt & Smith, *supra* note 305, at 253; Hickman, *Glass Types Identified by Chemical Analysis*, 33 FORENSIC SCI. INT'L 23 (1987); Koons, Fiedler & Rawalt, *Classification and Discrimination of Sheet and Container Glasses by Inductively Coupled Plasma-Atomic Emission Spectrometry and Pattern Recognition*, 33 J. FORENSIC SCI. 49, 50 (1988) (Britain's Metropolitan Police Forensic Science Laboratory uses inductively coupled plasma-atomic emission spectrometry (ICP-AES) to determine the elemental composition of glass samples).

378. Andrasko & Meahly, *supra* note 375, at 250.

rely on a single parameter of a glass sample as the basis for his or her opinion. "[A]necdotal evidence suggests that improvements in quality control in glass manufacturing have resulted in a decrease in the range of indices observed among glass products."[379] Thus, rather than relying exclusively on a refractive index measurement, an analyst might also consider the concentration of perhaps ten elements.[380] Doing so greatly increases the analyst's ability to differentiate between samples from different sources.

Fluorescence

The trace impurities present in some glass fragments can cause the fragment to fluoresce.[381] In this technique, the analyst irradiates the fragment with ultraviolet light.[382] A fluorescence spectrometer might be used to produce a spectrum,[383] but most laboratories simply observe the color of the fluorescence.

As the previous discussion of emission spectroscopy indicated, some researchers have attempted to integrate the various analytic techniques into glass identification systems.[384] A system is already in use at the Metropolitan Police Forensic Science Laboratory in London.[385] In this system, the fragment's RI and the concentrations of manganese, iron, magnesium, aluminum, and barium are measured.[386] This system has enabled the MPFSL analysts to distinguish among sheet glass, containers, tableware, and headlamps.[387] Another glass identification system integrates the techniques of measuring density and RI with EDX and emission spectroscopy.[388]

§ 24-6(B). Mechanical Fit Between Fragments.

Matching the chemical, optical, and physical properties of two glass fragments is only one method of demonstrating that the fragments match and, ergo, could share a common origin. Another method of demonstrating common origin is to mesh or fit two fragments together.[389] In general, if the several fragments fit

---

379. Koons & Buscaglia, *The Forensic Significance of Glass Composition and Refractive Index Measurements*, 44 J. FORENSIC SCI. 496 (1999).

380. *Id.*

381. Stone & Thornton, *supra* note 346, at 257.

382. Lloyd, *Fluorescence Spectrometry in the Identification and Discrimination of Float and Other Surfaces on Window Glasses*, 26 J. FORENSIC SCI. 325 (1981).

383. *Id.* at 326-29.

384. Hickman, *A Classification Scheme for Glass*, 17 FORENSIC SCI. INT'L 265 (1981).

385. *Id.*

386. *Id.*

387. *Id.*

388. Andrasko & Maehly, *supra* note 375, at 250.

389. Stone & Thornton, *supra* note 346, at 252; Thornton, *Fractal Surfaces as Models of Physical Matches*, 31 J. FORENSIC SCI. 1435 (1986).

together — the shapes, angles, and curvatures mesh — the fit is evidence that at an earlier time, the fragments were joined together. This type of evidence has both a common sense and a visual appeal to jurors. The analyst judges the fit in two respects.

First, the analyst determines whether the sides of the fragments match. If one fragment has a projection, the matching fragment should have a depression that fits the projection. As discussed in § 24-8, the process of glass fracture propagation causes certain markings on the sides of fragmented glass. For example, the fracture face may display conchoidal markings, shell-shaped arcs.[390] In addition, the face may exhibit straight markings called hackle.[391] When two fragments were once joined side by side, the markings on the matching fracture faces should complement each other.

Second, the analyst examines the surface of the fragments to determine whether the surface topography is continuous.[392] When there are ream striae on the surface of the two fragments, the lines should continue from one fragment to another. Some striae are invisible to the naked eye. However, an argon ion laser or photographic techniques can be used to visualize the lines.[393]

§ 24-7. Admissibility of Glass Evidence.

Glass evidence has been admitted in numerous cases. The courts have accepted evidence of the following glass identification techniques, *inter alia:* density or specific gravity,[394] color,[395] refractive index,[396] dispersion,[397] neutron

---

390. Stone & Thornton, *supra* note 346, at 250-52.

391. *Id.* at 252.

392. *Id.* at 253.

393. *Id.*

394. Dardy v. State, 347 So. 2d 584 (Ala. Crim. App. 1977); Barton v. State, 57 Ala. App. 167, 326 So. 2d 695, 698 (1975), *cert. denied,* 295 Ala. 391, 326 So. 2d 699 (1976); State v. Bradley, 99 Ariz. 328, 409 P.2d 35 (1965); People v. Gallegos, 4 Cal. 3d 242, 481 P.2d 237, 93 Cal. Rptr. 229 (1971); People v. Gardner, 71 Cal. 2d 843, 457 P.2d 575, 79 Cal. Rptr. 743 (1969); People v. Hall, 62 Cal. 2d 104, 396 P.2d 700, 41 Cal. Rptr. 284 (1964); People v. Miner, 156 Cal. App. 2d 360, 319 P.2d 385 (1957); People v. Crosby, 139 Cal. App. 2d 101, 292 P.2d 922 (1956); People v. Columbo, 118 Ill. App. 3d 882, 455 N.E.2d 733 (1983), *cert. denied,* 467 U.S. 1208 (1984); People v. Dailey, 15 Ill. App. 3d 214, 304 N.E.2d 156 (1973); State v. Mobley, 369 S.W.2d 576 (Mo. 1963); State v. Armstrong, 361 S.W.2d 811 (Mo. 1962); State v. Menard, 331 S.W.2d 521 (Mo. 1960); State v. Wright, 619 S.W.2d 822 (Mo. App. 1981); State v. Worthon, 585 S.W.2d 143 (Mo. App. 1979); State v. Kirksey, 547 S.W.2d 149 (Mo. App. 1977); State v. Bishop, 529 S.W.2d 165 (Mo. App. 1975); State v. Bell, 22 N.C. App. 348, 206 S.E.2d 356 (1974); Commonwealth v. Paterick, 239 Pa. Super. 1, 361 A.2d 715 (1976).

395. People v. Fairchild, 28 Ill. App. 3d 427, 328 N.E.2d 361 (1975); State v. Roberts, 579 S.W.2d 685 (Mo. App. 1979); State v. Menard, 331 S.W.2d 521 (Mo. 1960); State v. Kirksey, 547 S.W.2d 149 (Mo. App. 1977).

396. Varner v. State, 420 So. 2d 841, 842 (Ala. Crim. App. 1982); Dardy v. State, 347 So. 2d 584 (Ala. Crim. App. 1977); Barton v. State, 57 Ala. App. 167, 326 So. 2d 695 (1975), *cert. denied,*

activation analysis,[398] spectroscopy,[399] X-ray spectrography,[400] and mechanical fit.[401]

Opinions on glass identification are usually couched in terms very similar to the opinions on fiber and hair identification. For example, experts have testified that the glass fragments: had the same characteristics;[402] had corresponding properties;[403] were similar;[404] possessed indistinguishable characteristics;[405] were identical;[406] match;[407] and match exactly.[408] Some experts have gone farther and

---

295 Ala. 391, 326 So. 2d 699 (1976); People v. Gallegos, 4 Cal. 3d 242, 481 P.2d 237, 93 Cal. Rptr. 229 (1971); People v. Gardner, 71 Cal. 2d 843, 457 P.2d 575, 79 Cal. Rptr. 743 (1969); People v. Harris, 105 Cal. App. 3d 204, 164 Cal. Rptr. 296 (1980); People v. Miner, 156 Cal. App. 2d 360, 319 P.2d 385 (1957); People v. Crosby, 139 Cal. App. 2d 101, 292 P.2d 922 (1956); People v. Columbo, 118 Ill. App. 3d 882, 74 Ill. Dec. 304, 455 N.E.2d 733 (1983), *cert. denied,* 467 U.S. 1208 (1984); People v. Hairston, 86 Ill. App. 3d 295, 408 N.E.2d 382 (1980); People v. Noascono, 80 Ill. App. 3d 921, 400 N.E.2d 720 (1980); People v. Johnson, 58 Ill. App. 3d 169, 373 N.E.2d 1086 (1978); People v. Dailey, 15 Ill. App. 3d 214, 304 N.E.2d 156 (1973); People v. Nelson, 127 Ill. App. 2d 238, 262 N.E.2d 225 (1970); People v. Eddington, 387 Mich. 551, 198 N.W.2d 297 (1972); State v. Hjerstrom, 287 N.W.2d 625 (Minn. 1979); State v. Mobley, 369 S.W.2d 576 (Mo. 1963); State v. Armstrong, 361 S.W.2d 811 (Mo. 1962); State v. Wright, 619 S.W.2d 822 (Mo. App. 1981); State v. Roberts, 579 S.W.2d 685 (Mo. App. 1979); State v. Bishop, 529 S.W.2d 165 (Mo. App. 1975); State v. Bell, 22 N.C. App. 348, 206 S.E.2d 356 (1974).

397. People v. Noascono, 80 Ill. App. 3d 921, 400 N.E.2d 720 (1980); State v. Hjerstrom, 287 N.W.2d 625 (Minn. 1979).

398. State v. Cox, 542 S.W.2d 40 (Mo. App. 1976).

399. State v. Bradley, 99 Ariz. 328, 409 P.2d 35 (1965); State v. Earley, 192 Kan. 167, 386 P.2d 189 (1963).

400. Stone v. People, 157 Colo. 178, 401 P.2d 837 (1965).

401. Preston v. State, 444 So. 2d 939 (Fla. 1984), *vacated,* 564 So. 2d (Fla. 1990); People v. Columbo, 118 Ill. App. 3d 882, 455 N.E.2d 733 (1983), *cert. denied,* 467 U.S. 1208 (1984); State v. Leavitt, 103 R.I. 273, 237 A.2d 309, *cert. denied,* 393 U.S. 881 (1968).

402. Commonwealth v. Gordon, 431 Pa. 512, 246 A.2d 325 (1968), *cert. denied,* 394 U.S. 937 (1969); State v. Wade, 83 S.D. 337, 159 N.W.2d 396 (1968).

403. People v. Horace, 157 Cal. App. 2d 395, 321 P.2d 64 (1958).

404. People v. Hairston, 86 Ill. App. 3d 295, 408 N.E.2d 382 (1980); People v. Johnson, 58 Ill. App. 3d 169, 373 N.E.2d 1086 (1978); State v. Beltowski, 281 Minn. 28, 160 N.W.2d 705, *cert. denied,* 393 U.S. 988 (1968); State v. Silvacarvalho, 193 Neb. 447, 227 N.W.2d 602 (1975); Commonwealth v. Bosurgi, 411 Pa. 56, 190 A.2d 304, *cert. denied,* 375 U.S. 910 (1963); Commonwealth v. Capone, 282 Pa. Super. 458, 422 A.2d 1383 (1980); Schroeder v. State, 543 S.W.2d 382 (Tex. Crim. App. 1976).

405. People v. Harris, 105 Cal. App. 3d 204, 164 Cal. Rptr. 296 (1980); State v. Edwards, 310 N.C. 142, 310 S.E.2d 610 (1984).

406. State v. Bradley, 99 Ariz. 328, 409 P.2d 35 (1965); People v. Cole, 148 Cal. App. 2d 25, 306 P.2d 49 (1957); People v. Ross, 139 Cal. App. 2d 706, 294 P.2d 174 (1956); People v. Eddington, 387 Mich. 551, 198 N.W.2d 297 (1972); State v. Mobley, 369 S.W.2d 576 (Mo. 1963); Garcia v. State, 522 S.W.2d 203 (Tex. Crim. App. 1975).

407. People v. Atkins, 128 Cal. App. 3d 564, 180 Cal. Rptr. 440 (1982); People v. Gallegos, 4 Cal. 3d 242, 481 P.2d 237, 93 Cal. Rptr. 229 (1971); People v. Crosby, 139 Cal. App. 2d 101, 292 P.2d 922 (1956); People v. Pruitt, 16 Ill. App. 3d 930, 307 N.E.2d 142, *cert. denied,* 419 U.S. 968

opined that the fragments came from the same source[409] or had a common origin.[410] Although a few experts assert that the identification is conclusive,[411] most express qualified opinions.[412] For instance, many experts state only that: The fragments could have the same source;[413] or there is a reasonably good possibility,[414] a probability,[415] a good probability,[416] or a high probability[417] of a common origin. Some experts candidly acknowledge the possibility that the fragments could come from another source.[418]

In a few cases, the experts have cited statistics to give the trier of fact better insight into the significance of a match. For example, in *People v. Harris*[419] the expert asserted that the two samples had the same refractive index. The expert added that there were approximately 8,000 identifiable refractive indices. In

---

(1974); Bruce v. State, 268 Ind. 180, 375 N.E.2d 1042, *cert. denied,* 439 U.S. 988 (1978); State v. Cameron, 604 S.W.2d 653 (Mo. App. 1980); State v. Roberts, 579 S.W.2d 685 (Mo. App. 1979); State v. Bishop, 529 S.W.2d 165 (Mo. App. 1975); State v. Duvall, 50 N.C. App. 684, 275 S.E.2d 284, *rev'd on other grounds,* 304 N.C. 557, 284 S.E.2d 495 (1981); Stamper v. Commonwealth, 220 Va. 260, 257 S.E.2d 808 (1979), *cert. denied,* 445 U.S. 972 (1980).

408. People v. Noascono, 80 Ill. App. 3d 921, 400 N.E.2d 720 (1980).

409. Dardy v. State, 347 So. 2d 584 (Ala. Crim. App. 1977); People v. Gardner, 71 Cal. 2d 843, 457 P.2d 575, 79 Cal. Rptr. 743 (1969); People v. Columbo, 118 Ill. App. 3d 882, 455 N.E.2d 733 (1983), *cert. denied,* 467 U.S. 1208 (1984); People v. Thiele, 114 Ill. App. 3d 189, 70 Ill. Dec. 147, 448 N.E.2d 1025 (1983); People v. Noascono, 80 Ill. App. 3d 921, 400 N.E.2d 720 (1980); People v. Dailey, 15 Ill. App. 3d 214, 304 N.E.2d 156 (1973); State v. Menard, 331 S.W.2d 521 (Mo. 1960); State v. Wright, 619 S.W.2d 822 (Mo. App. 1981); State v. Bishop, 439 A.2d 255 (R.I. 1982); State v. Spring, 48 Wis. 2d 333, 179 N.W. 2d 841 (1970).

410. Varner v. State, 420 So. 2d 841, 843 (Ala. Crim. App. 1982); People v. Nelson, 127 Ill. App. 2d 238, 262 N.E.2d 225 (1970); Roach v. State, 451 N.E.2d 388 (Ind. App. 1983); People v. Burse, 62 Mich. App. 204, 233 N.W.2d 232 (1975); State v. Menard, 331 S.W.2d 521 (Mo. 1960); State v. Cox, 542 S.W.2d 40 (Mo. App. 1976).

411. Lupro v. State, 603 P.2d 468 (Alaska 1979).

412. Marcouiller, *A Revised Glass Annealing Method to Distinguish Glass Types*, 35 J. FORENSIC SCI. 554 (1990) ("The ultimate goal is to turn glass from a 'comparison' type of evidence to an 'identification' type, something not yet possible"). *See also* Ryland, *Discussion of "A Revised Glass Annealing Method to Distinguish Glass Types,"* 36 J. FORENSIC SCI. 14 (1991).

413. Varner v. State, 420 So. 2d 841, 842 (Ala. Crim. App. 1982); People v. Columbo, 118 Ill. App. 3d 882, 74 Ill. Dec. 304, 445 N.E.2d 733 (1983), *cert. denied,* 467 U.S. 1208 (1984); People v. Thiele, 114 Ill. App. 3d 189, 448 N.E.2d 1025 (1983).

414. State v. Wright, 619 S.W.2d 822 (Mo. App. 1981).

415. People v. Burse, 62 Mich. App. 204, 233 N.W.2d 232 (1975).

416. People v. Bryant, 131 Ill. App. 3d 1011, 87 Ill. Dec. 91, 476 N.E.2d 793 (1985), *aff'd,* 113 Ill. 2d 497, 101 Ill. Dec. 825, 499 N.E.2d 413 (1986).

417. Barton v. State, 57 Ala. App. 167, 326 So. 2d 695 (1975), *cert. denied,* 295 Ala. 391, 326 So. 2d 699 (1976); People v. Noascono, 80 Ill. App. 3d 921, 400 N.E.2d 720 (1980); People v. Dailey, 15 Ill. App. 3d 214, 304 N.E.2d 156 (1973).

418. State v. Austad, 197 Mont. 70, 641 P.2d 1373 (1982).

419. 105 Cal. App. 3d 204, 164 Cal. Rptr. 296 (1980).

People v. Columbo,[420] the expert testified that the fragments had the same degree of tolerance and that in only five times in 1,000 previous glass tolerance tests had fragments with the same degree come from different sources. Similarly, in *People v. Hjerstrom*[421] the expert concluded that the samples matched in both refractive index and dispersion. The expert declared that only 5% of all glass in the United States had this combination of refractive index and dispersion.

A few experts had taken the final step and testified to probabilities. In *Roach v. State*[422] the laboratory technician testified that "mathematically the odds are one in one thousand that the glass from the bottom of [defendant's] shoes came from other than a common source."[423] In *State v. Menard*[424] the expert cited a number of probabilities of common origin: one in one thousand, one in ten thousand, one in a hundred thousand, one in a million, and one chance in a billion.[425] The most extreme case to date, however, is *People v. Mann.*[426] There an optometrist analyzed all the properties of a set of prescription glasses. The expert testified, over defense objection, to the "astronomical" figure that "the odds against glasses of defendant's prescription being prescribed for someone else [were] one to four trillion."[427] Without a solid empirical foundation, *Daubert* would seem to preclude the admission of this type of testimony. *Daubert* and the DNA cases have taught the courts to more closely scrutinize that type of statistical evidence.

§ 24-8. Glass Fracture Analysis.

Glass is brittle and frangible. For that reason, it fractures readily. Glass does not break randomly. Rather, the laws of physics explain the fracture process.[428] An analysis of the fractures may help reconstruct the breaking force. The following subsection presents an overview of the fracture process.

---

420. 118 Ill. App. 3d 882, 74 Ill. Dec. 304, 455 N.E.2d 733 (1983), *cert. denied,* 467 U.S. 1208 (1984).

421. 287 N.W.2d 625 (Minn. 1979).

422. 451 N.E.2d 388 (Ind. App. 1983).

423. *Id.* at 391.

424. 331 S.W.2d 521 (Mo. 1960).

425. *Id.* at 523.

426. 30 Ill. App. 3d 508, 333 N.E.2d 467 (1975).

427. *Id.* at 511, 333 N.E.2d at 469.

428. McJunkins & Thornton, *Glass Fracture Analysis: A Review*, 2 FORENSIC SCI. 1 (1973); Stone & Thornton, *supra* note 346, at 248; Locke & Unikowski, *Breaking of Flat Glass — Part 1: Size and Distribution of Particles from Plain Glass Windows*, 51 FORENSIC SCI. INT'L 251 (1991); Thornton & Cashman, *Glass Fracture Mechanism — A Rethinking*, 31 J. FORENSIC SCI. 818 (1986) (the authors assert that the current theories of glass fracture analysis are flawed because they emphasize deformation of the glass which might not occur and they do not account for the cratering phenomenon observed under conditions of sharp dynamic loading).

§ 24-8(A). Fracture Propagation Process.

Fractures in glass can be created by low-velocity, blunt forces, high-velocity forces such as bullets, and thermal heat.

Low-Velocity, Blunt Force Fractures

Figure 24-1 depicts the process by which fractures are created or propagated.

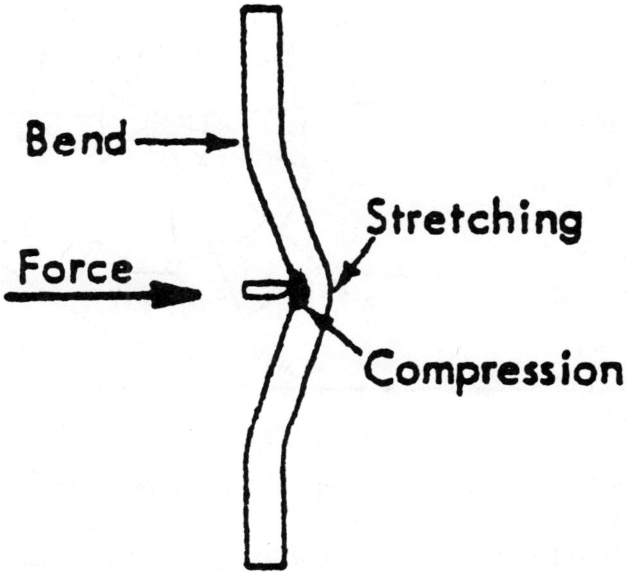

Figure 24-1

In Figure 24-1, the blow strikes the left-hand side of the glass. The striking applies force to the glass. The application of force to the left-hand side of the glass causes tension on the right-hand side, which forces that side of the glass to stretch or bend. The glass bends until it reaches its elastic limit, at which time it begins to fracture. Hence, the fracture initiates first on the far or right-hand side of the glass.

Although the fracture initiates on the far side, the fracture progresses to the left-hand side, the side on which force was initially applied. While the right-hand or far side undergoes tension and stretching, the left-hand side experiences compression. As the fracture moves from right to left, it propels fragments in the same direction. Thus, the fragments are propelled toward the origin of the force applied to the glass. This phenomenon explains why there will normally be glass fragments on the person and clothing of a criminal who breaks a glass window to gain entrance to a building.[429]

As previously stated, the fractures initiate on the right-hand or far side of the glass. On that side, the analyst can expect to find radial fractures as shown in Figure 24-2:

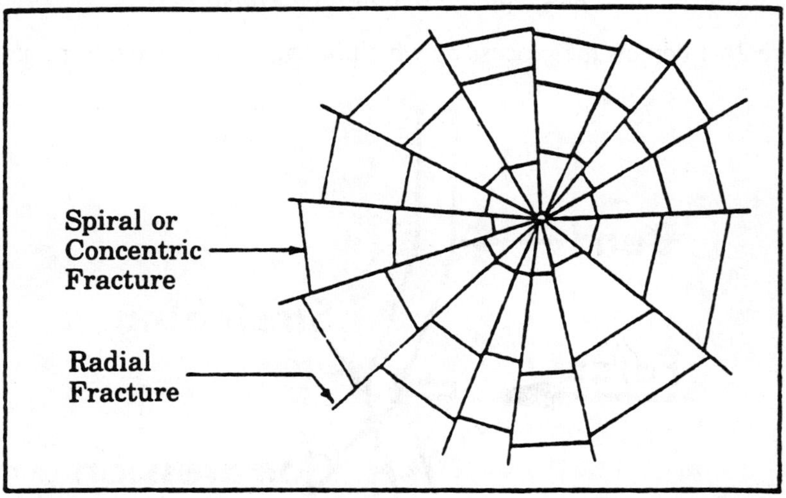

Figure 24-2

These fractures begin at the central point of fracture propagation and radiate out from that point.

There may also be concentric or spiral fractures. As the fracture moves from the far side to the impact side, the force pushes in on the segments between the radial fractures, causing secondary fractures, the concentric or spiral fractures. Such fractures are not always created. If a frame is firmly holding all sides of the sheet of glass, concentric fractures may not occur.

High-Velocity Fractures

High-velocity fractures can be caused by bullets, steel balls, or pebbles. In these fractures, the glass exhibits a cone bevelled toward the exit side. As Figure 24-3 indicates, when the bullet strikes the left-hand, impact side of the glass, it causes a cone-shaped plug to be ejected on the far side. The side with the smaller diameter hole is the entrance side; the side with the larger diameter hole is the exit side.

If the object is traveling at a high speed, the impact will cause a round hole. At a somewhat lower speed, the hole will be irregular. At a very low velocity, there

429. Pounds & Smalldon, *The Distribution of Glass Fragments in Front of a Broken Window and the Transfer of Fragments to Individuals Standing Nearby*, 18 J. FORENSIC SCI. SOC'Y 197 (1979).

may be no hole; the glass simply shatters. Just as there is sometimes no hole, occasionally there are no concentric fractures. These fractures are often missing when the force was high energy but localized.

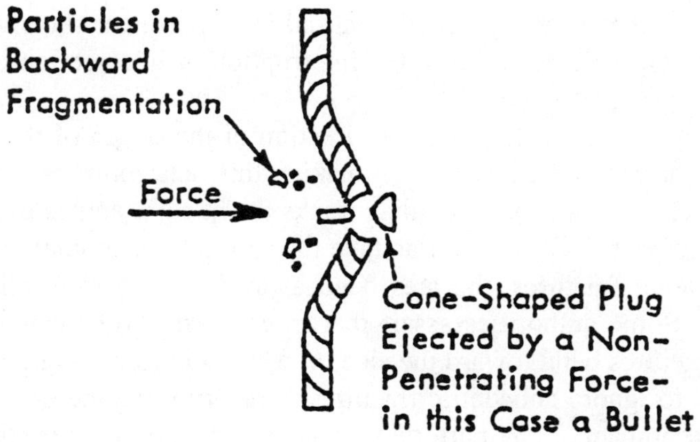

Figure 24-3

Since there is such great variance in high-velocity fractures, the analyst rarely relies solely on an examination of the glass fragments and generalizations about fractures. In most cases, the analyst attempts to locate the same or a similar weapon and glass and conduct test firings. The test firing should be conducted with glass of the same age. The age of the glass sheet can affect its fragmentation pattern.

Thermal Fractures

Heat fractures have distinctive features. If the glass was untempered, the crack is usually curved with a smooth edge.[430] When the pane was thick, the cracks may have a feathered appearance.[431] Splinters will shoot back toward the heat force when the fracture occurs.

§ 24-8(B). Glass Fracture Findings.

Using the laws of physics outlined in the previous subsection, the analyst can reach a number of findings based on an examination of glass fragments.

By way of illustration, the analyst can reach some conclusions about the type of force that caused the fracture. As noted above, low-velocity, blunt force fractures, high-velocity fractures, and thermal fractures all have distinctive features. When those features are present, the analyst can at least fit the cause

430. Miller, *Forensic Glass Comparisons*, *in* FORENSIC SCIENCE HANDBOOK 139, 148 (R. Saferstein ed. 1982).

431. *Id.*

into one of those three categories. If the cause was a bullet, the analyst can reach some additional conclusions. Since the bullet's velocity determines whether there is a hole and, if so, the hole's shape, the analyst can estimate bullet speed. Moreover, when there were several shots, the analyst can sometimes opine as to the sequence of the shots. The cracks caused by subsequent shots will terminate at previously formed cracks. Thus, the interruption or intersection of fractures is a clue to the order of the shots.[432]

The analyst can also determine the direction of the origin of the force.[433] The striations on the radial fractures aid in making this determination. Some analysts use the Four R rule: "Ridges on radial cracks are at right angles to the rear (side opposite the impact)."[434] These striae take the form of conchoidal or shell-shaped arcs.[435] On radial fractures, the arcs bend away from the side where the force originated.[436] Some authorities assert that in contrast, the conchoidal marks on concentric fractures bend toward the side on which the force originated, but other analysts tend to ignore concentric fractures in determining the direction of force of the initial impact.[437] In part these analysts do so because they may not subscribe to the Four R rule.

Finally, the analyst may be able to estimate the distance between the origin of the force and the glass pane. However, the estimates are only rough approximations. One researcher, for instance, found little difference between bullet holes caused by discharge at five yards and holes caused by discharge at 20 yards.[438]

§ 24-9. Admissibility of Glass Fracture Analysis.

There are only a few cases dealing with glass fracture analysis. In *Dardy v. State*[439] the expert testified that a window was broken from the outside. He based his opinion in part on the fact that fragments were found on the inside but not on the outside. In an earlier case[440] the expert testified that the cause of the breaking of a window was a gunshot. The expert rested his opinion on the glass fracture pattern.

---

432. *Id.* at 150-51.

433. Locke & Uniknowski, *Breaking of Flat Glass) Part 2: Effect of Pane Parameters on Particle Distribution*, 56 Forensic Sci. Int'l 95 (1992); Locke & Scranage, *Breaking of Flat Glass) Part 3: Surface Particles from Windows*, 57 Forensic Sci. Int'l 73 (1992).

434. Miller, *supra* note 430, at 148.

435. Stone & Thornton, *supra* note 346, at 250.

436. *Id.*

437. *Id.*

438. McJunkins & Thornton, *supra* note 428, at 8.

439. 347 So. 2d 584 (Ala. Crim. App. 1977).

440. State v. George, 253 Or. 458, 455 P.2d 609 (1969). *See also* State v. Swallow, 405 N.W.2d 29 (S.D. 1987).

§ 24-10. Soil Analysis.

Soil seems even more omnipresent than hair or fiber. The primary problem of proof for the prosecution is often placing the defendant at the crime scene. Alternatively, the prosecution may use soil evidence to connect the victim's body to a particular site. Forensic geology played an important role in the investigation of the assassination of Italian Prime Minister Aldo Moro by the Red Brigades.[441] In the United States, the prosecution employed soil evidence for this purpose in the investigation of the killing of D.E.A. Special Agent Enrique Camarena.[442] In this light, soil has obvious potential as forensic evidence. Soil or earth material includes both organic and inorganic matter.[443] The organic matter might be microorganisms or decomposed vegetable material. The inorganic matter includes mineral particles resulting from the decomposition of rock. The earth material may also contain foreign matter such as glass, hair, or fiber.[444] There are numerous techniques for analyzing soil. By the use of these techniques, the analyst can reach a number of conclusions about the soil sample.

§ 24-10(A). Soil Sample Techniques.

Geological, mineralogical, and chemical techniques are used to analyze soil samples. The analyst does so to assess the following properties of the sample.

Color

One of the most obvious properties of a soil sample is its color. When two samples differ in color, in all probability they also differ in elemental composition.[445] At first blush, it might seem that the analyst's identification of

---

441. Lombardi, *The Contribution of Forensic Geology and Other Trace Evidence Analysis to the Investigation of the Killing of Italian Prime Minister Aldo Moro*, 44 J. FORENSIC SCI. 634 (1999).

442. Malone, *The Enrique Camarena Case: A Forensic Nightmare*, 58 F.B.I. LAW ENF. BULL. 1, 3 (Sept. 1989) ("[T]he color of the soil where the bodies had been deposited differed from the soil that had been recovered from the bodies. Therefore, 'known' soil samples from the drop site were taken to compare with soil removed from the victims. This led the forensic team to conclude that the bodies had been buried elsewhere, exhumed and transported to this site"). *See also* Hall, *The Forensic Utility of Soil*, 62 F.B.I. LAW ENF. BULL. 16 (Sept. 1993) (expert testimony connecting digging implements with the Staten Island burial site of five murder victims).

443. CUNLIFFE & PIAZZA, CRIMINALISTICS AND SCIENTIFIC INVESTIGATION 114 (1980).

444. F.B.I., HANDBOOK OF FORENSIC SCIENCE 45 (1979).

445. Murray, *Forensic Examination of Soil, in* FORENSIC SCIENCE HANDBOOK 653, 658 (R. Saferstein ed. 1982); Junger, *Assessing the Unique Characteristics of Close-Proximity Soil Samples: Just How Useful Is Soil Evidence?*, 41 J. FORENSIC SCI. 27 (1996) ("One hundred samples were collected from three different sites: a beach, an island isolated by a river, and a bus parking lot. Of the ... samples examined, over one-half could be discriminated by color alone"); Antoci &

color is a subjective decision. However, there is some uniformity in color assessments because many analysts use the color standards developed by Munsell Color Company in Baltimore, Maryland.[446] Under the standards, the analyst identifies the hue, value, and chroma of the color.[447] Hue refers to the dominant spectral color. The value represents the depth or lightness of the color. Finally, chroma is the color's relative purity. For example, on the Munsell scale, an analyst might record a color as 7.5YR5/2 (brown).[448] 7.5YR designates the hue, 5 represents the value, and 2 is the chroma.

Density

As in glass analysis, the density of the soil particle can be measured.[449] The parallel is complete because, as in the case of glass examinations, the analyst can use the density gradient column technique.[450]

Size Distribution

The analyst is also interested in the distribution of differently sized particles in the soil sample.[451] There are a number of techniques for separating out differently sized particles. In one technique, the analyst sends the sample through a series or nest of wire sieves.[452] In another method, the analyst measures the rate at which

---

Petraco, *A Technique for Comparing Soil Colors in the Forensic Laboratory*, 38 J. FORENSIC SCI. 437 (1993).

446. *Id.* at 659.

447. *Id.*

448. *Id.*

449. *Id.* at 661.

450. *Id.*

451. *Id.* at 665; Junger, *Assessing the Unique Characteristics of Close-Proximity Soil Samples: Just How Useful Is Soil Evidence?*, 41 J. FORENSIC SCI. 27 (1996) ("One hundred samples were collected from three different sites: a beach, an island isolated by a river, and a bus parking lot. Of the . . . samples examined, over one-half could be discriminated by color alone, the remainder needing only particle size distributions analysis for differentiation, negating the need for lengthy mineralogical examinations"); Wanogho, Gettinby, Caddy & Robertson, *Determination of Particle Size Distribution of Soils in Forensic Science Using Classical and Modern Instrumental Methods*, 34 J. FORENSIC SCI. 823 (1989) (comparing wet sieving, laser diffraction, Coulter counting, and microscopical image analysis as particle size distribution methods); Wanogho, Gettinby & Caddy, *Particle Size Distribution Analysis of Soils Using Laser Diffraction*, 33 FORENSIC SCI. INT'L 117 (1987).

452. Murray, *supra* note 445, at 665; Wanogho, Gettinby, Caddy & Robertson, *Some Factors Affecting Soil Sieve Analysis in Forensic Science. 1. Dry Sieving*, 33 FORENSIC SCI. INT'L 129 (1987); Wanogho, Gettinby, Caddy & Robertson, *Some Factors Affecting Soil Sieve Analysis in Forensic Science. 2. Wet Sieving*, 33 FORENSIC SCI. INT'L 139 (1987).

the various grains settle in a solution. The rate of settling is an indication of the size of the particles.[453]

Mineral Analysis

By identifying the minerals present in known and unknown soil samples, the analyst can frequently differentiate between samples.[454] One commentator has listed the most popular instruments for mineral analysis of soil samples: binocular microscope,[455] scanning electron microscope (SEM), and X-ray diffraction analysis (EDX).[456]

Chemical Analysis

Soils have many testable chemical properties. The same commentator lists three of the most important properties that analysts test for: pH (the acidity or alkalinity of the soil), saccharide content, and enzymatic characterization (due to the presence of microorganisms in the soil).[457]

§ 24-10(B). Significance of Analysis.

It would be ideal for the soil analyst if at every location, the soil were both unique and uniform. On that assumption, when two soil samples matched in their chemical and physical properties, the expert could conclude that the two samples were from the same location. There are indeed some studies finding that in certain respects such as pollen content, samples from the same localized area are similar to each other but differ from samples taken from other areas.[458] However, in the main the available data makes it questionable to assume that the soil at each site is unique or uniform. In § 24-2, we noted some of the weaknesses of

---

453. Murray, *supra* note 445, at 665.

454. Murray, *supra*, note 445, at 667; Marumo, Agr, Nagatsuka & Oba, *Clay Mineralogical Analysis Using the <0.05-mm Fraction for Forensic Science Investigation — Its Application to Volcanic Ash Soils and Yellow-Brown Forest Soils*, 31 J. FORENSIC SCI. 92 (1986).

455. Horrocks & Walsh, *Fine Resolution of Pollen Patterns in Limited Space: Differentiating a Crime Scene and Alibi Scene Seven Meters Apart*, 44 J. FORENSIC SCI. 417 (1999).

456. Murray, *supra* note 445, at 667-68. Hiraoka, *A Possible Approach to Soil Discrimination Using X-ray Fluorescence Analysis*, 39 J. FORENSIC SCI. 1381 (1994).

457. Murray, *supra* note 445, at 669. *See also* Reuland, Trinler & Farmer, *Comparison of Soil Samples by High Performance Liquid Chromatography Augmented by Absorbance Ratioing*, 52 FORENSIC SCI. INT'L 131 (1992).

458. Horrocks & Walsh, *Fine Resolution of Pollen Patterns in Limited Space: Differentiating a Crime Scene and Alibi Scene Seven Meters Apart*, 44 J. FORENSIC SCI. 417 (1999); Horrocks, Coulson & Walsh, *Forensic Palynology: Variation in the Pollen Content of Soil on Shoes and in Shoeprints in Soil*, 44 J. FORENSIC SCI. 119 (1999); Horrocks, Coulson & Walsh, *Forensic Palynology: Variation in the Pollen Content of Soil Surface Samples*, 43 J. FORENSIC SCI. 320 (1998).

hair evidence. The analyst cannot isolate a particular individual as the source of a human hair strand, and there is variation even among the same person's scalp hairs. Soil evidence suffers from the same weaknesses — but to a greater degree.

It cannot be demonstrated that the soil at any given location is unique to that location.[459] There is "almost an unlimited number of recognizable soil kinds"; and to make matters worse, soil composition can change "dramatically over short distances: both horizontally and vertically."[460]

Soil analysts acknowledge that they cannot prove that soil with any given set of properties can be found in only one location.[461]

Furthermore, there are grave doubts about the uniformity of soil at a particular location. In the case of man-made fibers, the manufacturer's quality assurance and control programs ensure that each fiber strand will be similar to the other strands. Nature has not implemented such a quality control program for soil. Soil can vary radically not only from point to point on the surface but even more so with depth.[462] At any site where soil is collected for forensic analysis, the commentators insist that investigators gather numerous samples and carefully record the site where each sample was found.[463] By studying all the samples found at the general location, the analyst gains a sense of the range of variation for soil at that site.

Using the currently available techniques, an analyst can conclude that the properties of two samples match and, therefore, the properties are consistent with the assumption of a common source or origin. However, given the weaknesses of soil evidence, it is difficult for an analyst to give testimony that would be more specific. Section 24-2 noted that some hair analysts believe that the specificity of hair evidence can be substantially increased by determining genetic markers such as blood types from hair samples. In the foreseeable future, soil analysis will not attain that degree of specificity. Nor is it likely that soil analysts will be able to

---

459. Murray, *supra* note 445, at 654.

460. *Id. But see* Marumo, Nagatsuka & Oba, *Rapid Clay Mineralogical Analysis for Forensic Science Investigation — Clay Mineralogy Over the Short Distances*, 33 J. FORENSIC SCI. 1360, 1367 (1988) (the researchers found that "it is possible to discriminate soil samples and further to estimate the sites in the region from which they were taken ...."); Hall, *The Forensic Utility of Soil*, 62 F.B.I. LAW ENF. BULL. 16, 18 (Sept. 1993) ("Laboratory personnel perform the examination by comparing the color, texture, and composition of soil samples. Because these characteristics result from locality-dependent factors ..., differences in the characteristics tend to dissociate two soil samples").

461. Stoneking v. United States, 232 F.2d 385, 392-93 (8th Cir.), *cert. denied,* 352 U.S. 835 (1956) (a concession made on cross-examination).

462. Hoffman, Brunelle & Snow, *Forensic Comparison of Soils by Neutron Activation Analysis and Atomic Absorption Analysis*, 60 J. CRIM. L., CRIMINOLOGY & POLICE SCI. 395 (1969).

463. CUNLIFFE & PIAZZA, CRIMINALISTICS AND SCIENTIFIC INVESTIGATION 116 (1980); CRIME LAB. DIV., WIS. DEP'T JUST., CRIMINAL INVESTIGATION AND PHYSICAL EVIDENCE HANDBOOK 106 (1969).

establish that even at a particular location, soil samples are as uniform as fibers. Soil evidence is useful, but it has limited probative value.

§ 24-11. Admissibility of Soil Evidence.

In light of the limitations of soil evidence, in most cases the analyst testifies only that the properties of a known and unknown sample are similar[464] and that the samples could have come from the same site.[465] In *Stoneking v. United States*[466] the analyst offered such testimony to link mud on the defendant's license plate to the soil at a particular location. Testimony, couched in such general terms, is as admissible in soil cases as it is in hair, fiber, and glass cases.

Surprisingly, however, the courts sometimes admit more definite or specific testimony. *State v. Rogers*[467] is a case in point. In *Rogers* the victim was raped. There was mud at the crime scene. The police obtained soil samples from the defendant's shoes and submitted the samples to the North Carolina State University. A soil analyst testified that in his opinion the soil on the defendant's shoes "certainly came from the same site."[468]

Miller v. State[469] is even more remarkable. There the soil analyst studied three characteristics of the soil samples: color, texture, and density. He found that the samples matched in all three respects. He assigned probabilities to the likelihood of random matches in each respect, multiplied the probabilities, and testified to the ultimate opinion that there was a one in one million chance that the soil samples came from different sources. Even if the testimony in *Rogers* is defensible, the testimony in *Miller* certainly seems assailable. Chapter 15 discusses statistical evidence. That chapter points out that the sources of individual probabilities must be trustworthy and that in the product rule, probabilities can be multiplied together only if they are independent. The testimony in *Miller* is challengeable on both grounds. There was no persuasive evidence that the analyst had conducted extensive, well-designed experiments to derive the individual probabilities. Moreover, there is a strong argument that the probabilities were not independent; it is likely that the chemical composition of the samples partially determined all three properties and, consequently, that the values of the three variables would move together to some extent. It is highly doubtful whether this testimony would pass muster under *Daubert*.

---

464. State v. Kelley, 674 S.W.2d 216, 219 (Mo. App. 1984).

465. Stoneking v. United States, 232 F.2d 385 (8th Cir.), *cert. denied,* 352 U.S. 835 (1956).

466. *Id.*

467. 275 N.C. 411, 168 S.E.2d 345 (1969), *cert. denied,* 396 U.S. 1024 (1970).

468. *Id.* at 432.

469. 240 Ark. 340, 399 S.W.2d 268 (1966).

Despite the difficulties illustrated in *Miller,* research is in progress to develop statistically valid methods of assessing soil comparisons.[470]

§ 24-12. Bloodspatter Analysis.

As we have seen, blood figures in genetic marker analysis, pathology, and toxicology. However, blood can also be treated as trace evidence. Geometric bloodspatter analysis treats blood in that fashion. Subsection 24-8(B) pointed out that glass fracture analysis entails the application of the laws of physics. Likewise, bloodspatter analysis consists in the application of rules of mathematics and physics to bloodspatters in order to reconstruct events.

In the view of some, the "seminal event in the history of [this]forensic science"[471] was an attempted use of bloodspatter analysis in the famous prosecution of Dr. Sam Sheppard for the murder of his wife Marilyn in Cleveland, Ohio. The defense moved to obtain a new trial on the basis of newly discovered evidence. In support of the motion, the defense filed an affidavit prepared by Dr. Paul Kirk of the University of California, Berkeley. According to the affidavit, the bloodspatters at the crime scene established that the assailant was a left-handed person.[472] At the time the motion was denied. However, the defense resorted to Dr. Kirk's analysis in 1966 when Sheppard gained a retrial and acquittal.[473]

Bloodspatter analysis is not an American creation. Early this century Dr. Paul Jeserich studied bloodstain patterns at murder scenes in Berlin.[474] During the

---

470. Wanogho, Gettinby, Caddy & Robertson, *A Statistical Method for Assessing Soil Comparisons*, 30 J. FORENSIC SCI. 864 (1985).

471. McCarty, *Body of Evidence: Mohammad Tamir Will Make History if He Can Prove Who Killed Marilyn Sheppard More than 40 Years Ago,'* SUNDAY MAGAZINE, PLAIN DEALER, NOV. 10, 1996, at 8.

472. State v. Sheppard, 100 Ohio. App. 399, 128 N.E.2d 504, 514 (Ohio 1955), *app. dismissed,* 164 Ohio St. 428, 131 N.E.2d 837 (1956). There is a detailed account of the case and the affidavit in JURGEN THORWALD, CRIME AND SCIENCE (1967). Dr. Kik "[a]pplied to the existing bloodstains the tried and true methods of determining the point of origin, distribution, and impact velocities of splashed blood." *Id.* at 151. Kirk concluded that the "[m]urderer must . . . have stood beside the victim's bed, or half kneeling on it, back to the foot of the bed, left side toward the east wall and the door of the wardrobe." *Id.* at 152. Kirk also reached the conclusion that the murderer wielded a weapon "[n]ot much more than twelve inches long, if that," like a "[l]eft-handed batter with a baseball bat." PAUL HOLMES, THE SHEPPARD MURDER CASE 221 (1961). With respect to one stain on the wardrobe in the bedroom, Dr. Kirk concluded that "[f]lowing blood from a wound is about the only reasonable manner in which this blood could have been placed." *Id.* at 223.

473. A. WINGATE, SCENE OF THE CRIME: A WRITER'S GUIDE TO CRIME-SCENE INVESTIGATIONS 186 (1992).

474. W. ECKERT & S. JAMES, INTERPRETATION OF BLOODSTAIN EVIDENCE AT CRIME SCENES 5 (1989).

1930's, a French scientist, Dr. Victor Balthazard, conducted experiments with bloodstain trajectories and patterns.

Although Dr. Kirk's 1955 affidavit spurred interest in the subject of blood dynamics in the United States, the turning point in America was the 1971 release of a landmark work by Herbert MacDonnell and Lorraine Bialousz, *Flight Characteristics and Stain Patterns of Human Blood*, published by the National Institute of Law Enforcement and Criminal Justice of the U.S. Department of Justice. MacDonnell began his research for the publication in 1969. He reports that at that time, "I found very little in the literature regarding bloodstain patterns."[475] However, as of 1996, he had "located over five hundred and fifty such references."[476] In addition to the 1971 work, there are now several texts devoted to the subject of bloodspatter analysis.[477] In 1983, the International Association of Bloodstain Pattern Analysis was founded.[478] Specialists in this field use the laws of physics and their knowledge of the properties of blood to make several determinations useful in forensic investigations. Notwithstanding their common reliance on well-settled laws of physics, blood spatter experts sometimes disagree.[479]

§ 24-12(A). The Properties of Blood.

A single drop of blood has a volume of approximately 0.05 ml. Drops of blood have surface tension. The drop is held together by cohesive forces that produce a surface resistant to penetration or separation. The tension gives each drop a surface "skin." This tension causes the drop to assume a spherical shape during

---

475. MacDonnell, *Crime Scene Evidence — Blood Spatters and Smears and Other Physical Evidence*, 1 QUINNIPAC HEALTH L. REV. 33, 38 (1996).

476. *Id.* at 38, 46-78. Pages 46-78 set out an extensive bibliography on blood spatter analysis.

477. T. BEVEL & R. GARDNER, BLOODSTAIN PATTERN ANALYSIS WITH AN INTRODUCTION TO CRIME SCENE RECONSTRUCTION (1997); W. ECKERT & S. JAMES, INTERPRETATION OF BLOODSTAIN EVIDENCE AT CRIME SCENES (1989); H. MACDONNELL, BLOODSTAIN PATTERNS (1993); H. MACDONNELL & L. BIALOUSZ, LABORATORY MANUAL ON THE GEOMETRIC INTERPRETATION OF BLOODSTAIN EVIDENCE (1971).

478. The IABPA has a Homepage, <Http://www.shadow.net/%7Enoslow/index.html>.

479. *A Battle of Blood Spatter Experts and the Shenanigans of a Texas Prosecutor*, 21 SCI. SLEUTHING REV. 18 (Summer 1997) (several blood spatter experts analyzed the physical evidence in the prosecution of Freda S. Mowbray for a shooting death, *Ex parte* Mowbray, 1996 Tex. Crim. App. LEXIS 253 (Dec. 18, 1996); one, Sergeant Hesskew of the Austin, Texas Police Department gave testimony which "emphatically 'contradicted' the accused wife's theory of the death of her husband by making it clear that she could not have been lying next to her husband when the gun unexpectedly went off;" the defense called "one Tom Bevel of the Oklahoma City Police Department.... Bevel's inspection of the evidence led him to conclude that suicide was more than a remote possibility"; Herbert MacDonell, "the granddaddy of blood spatter," also reached conclusions at odds with some of Hesskew's findings; The Texas trial court in its opinion granting Mowbray's petition for habeas corpus found that the prosecutor had "'knowingly suppressed MacDonell's report which supported [Mowbray's] theory of suicide.").

free fall when the drop falls from its source. During free fall, the terminal velocity is 25.1 feet per second (+/.05 feet). The drop will not rupture unless it is acted upon by some force or energy. The same tension causes the drop to resist breaking up even upon impact with a surface. As a general proposition, the smaller the spots of blood, the greater the energy of impact.

Blood also has the property of viscosity. Due to the friction of its molecules, blood has a resistance to flowing freely. As flow decreases, viscosity increases.

§ 24-12(B). Forensic Determinations.

As Dr. Kirk's affidavit illustrated,[480] using the laws of physics and the research conducted by authorities such as MacDonnell, a blood spatter analyst can make several determinations.

An analyst can determine whether blood was projected onto a surface or transferred. As Dr. MacDonnell explains, "Projected blood will be found down between the threads, transferred blood will not."[481] In one case, Dr. MacDonnell concluded that there were bloodstains on the defendant's shirt because he had leaned over bloody bed covers; the blood had been transferred onto his shirt rather than spattered onto the shirt during a beating.[482] This determination helps the trier of fact decide the defendant's role in the alleged crime.

An analysis can also determine whether blood was expirated or spattered.[483] A medium velocity impact spatter (MVIS) is ordinarily the result of an event such as a beating with a hammer or stabbing with a knife. The velocity is typically 25 feet per second. In an MVIS, the majority of the bloodstain spots have an average diameter of over one millimeter. In contrast, gunshots and explosions produce high velocity impact spatters (HVIS). In an HVIS, the blood is atomized into a mist-like spray; and the average diameter is well under one millimeter. Blood is expirated when it is blown out of the mouth or nose. Dr. MacDonnell describes one case:

> Careful examination of the bloodstains on the wall ... showed they all contained small air bubbles. Such bubbles will not be found in normal blood and are conclusive evidence of expired or aspirated blood.[484]

This determination helps the trier decide the cause of the bloodspatter — an axe, a shooting, or suicide.

---

480. *See* PAUL HOLMES, THE SHEPPARD MURDER CASE 221-23 (1961) and JURGEN THORWALD, CRIME AND SCIENCE 151-53 (1967).

481. MacDonnell, *supra* note 475, at 40.

482. *Id.*

483. *Id.* at 41.

484. MacDonnell, *supra* note 475, at 41.

An analyst can often determine directionality. A round bloodstain is an indication that the blood probably fell straight down. An elliptical stain indicates that the blood was moving forward as it was falling toward the surface. The stain has a tear drop shape. The pointed tail of the bloodstain usually points toward the origin; the sharp point faces the direction of travel of the drop before impact. As the angle of impact decreases from 90 degrees to 0 degrees, the resulting stain pattern becomes more elongated. By drawing straight lines showing the directionality of several blood spatters, the analyst can reconstruct a sequence of events. To visualize the lines, the analyst may employ string and endeavor to identify a point of convergence.[485]

The analyst can also reach findings as to distance. The analyst may need to perform a series of "blood drop versus distance" experiments in order to estimate distance. It is ideal if the analyst performs the experiments on the same surface involved in the alleged crime. However, even when the analyst can duplicate the surface, there are limits to the technique. According to some authorities, the bloodspatter pattern is of little value in estimating distance when the distance exceeds five or six feet.[486]

The analyst may be able to reach a conclusion as to the type of surface impacted. Hard, smooth, less porous surfaces produce little spattering. However, porous and irregular surfaces with protuberances cause extensive spattering.

The analyst can help the trier determine whether the site of the body's discovery was the primary or a secondary crime scene. Was the site the place where the wounds were inflicted or a place where the body was taken later?

The analyst can assist the trier decide whether an object was removed from the crime scene after the offense. Suppose, for instance, that except for one area, the whole scene is spattered. The arc indicates that something was removed from the scene after the incident.

§ 24-13. Admissibility of Bloodspatter Evidence.

§ 24-13(A). Qualifications of Expert.

The appellate courts give the trial judge wide discretion in determining whether the witness qualifies as an expert on bloodspatter analysis.[487] The courts have found a wide variety of witnesses qualified to testify as experts on blood spatter analysis: criminalists,[488] detectives,[489] F.B.I. agents,[490] investigators,[491]

---

485. *E.g.*, United States v. Phillip, 948 F.2d 241, 248-49 (6th Cir. 1991), *cert. denied*, 504 U.S. 930 (1992).

486. B. Fischer, Techniques of Crime Scene Investigation 219 (5th ed. 1993).

487. People v. Bolin, 18 Cal. 4th 297, 956 P.2d 374, 75 Cal. Rptr. 2d 412 (1998), *cert. denied*, 119 S. Ct. 1146 (1999); Farris v. State, 670 P.2d 995 (Okla. 1983).

488. United States v. Mustafa, 22 M.J. 165, *cert. denied*, 479 U.S. 953 (1986); Robinson v. State, 574 So. 2d 910 (Ala. 1990), *cert. denied* (Jan. 11, 1991); Droke v. State, 252 Ga. 472, 314

police officers,[492] pathologists,[493] and serologists.[494] It is ideal if the witness has formal education in physics. However, attendance at training programs on bloodspatter analysis is often held sufficient.[495]

§ 24-13(B). Validity of Underlying Scientific Theories.

There is now a large body of case law on blood spatter analysis.[496] To be sure, in the celebrated American case, *State v. Sheppard*,[497] the court attached little weight to Dr. Kirk's opinion. Moreover, on rare occasions, the courts have altogether excluded testimony about blood spatter analysis. For instance, in *People v. Owens*,[498] the court held that the prosecution had failed to sustain its burden of proving the general acceptance of blood spatter analysis.

However, decisions such as *Owens* are few and far between. The overwhelming majority of decisions uphold the admission of testimony about blood spatter analysis. Admissibility is the clearly prevailing view in both *Frye*[499] and *Daubert*[500] jurisdictions. The opinions tend to emphasize that bloodspatter analysis is an application of established propositions in well-recognized disciplines such as physics.[501] The opinions point to the research conducted by

---

S.E.2d 230 (1984); People v. Smith, 261 Ill. App. 3d 117, 633 N.E.2d 69, 198 Ill. Dec. 607, *app. denied*,157 Ill. 2d 518, 633 N.E.2d 69, 205 Ill. Dec. 181 (1994).

489. Fox v. State, 506 N.E.2d 1090 (Ind. 1987).

490. State v. Goode, 341 N.C. 513, 461 S.E.2d 631 (1995).

491. State v. Moore, 122 N.J. 420, 585 A.2d 864 (1991); State v. Myers, 301 S.C. 251, 391 S.E.3d 551 (1990).

492. Leonard v. State, 551 So. 2d 1143 (Ala. Crim. App. 1989); James v. State, 613 N.E.2d 15 (Ind. 1993).

493. State v. Satterfield, 3 Kan. App. 2d 212, 592 P.2d 135 (1979).

494. King v. State, 531 N.E.2d 1154 (Ind. 1988); State v. Moore, 458 N.W.2d 90 (Minn. 1990); State v. Mix, 239 Mont. 351, 781 P.2d 751 (1989).

495. Farris v. State, 670 P.2d 995 (Okla. 1983). *See also* Deel v. Jago, 967 F.2d 1079 (6th Cir. 1992) (the witness had a B.S. degree in Forensic Chemistry and had attended a one week workshop on bloodspatter analysis).

496. Annot., 9 A.L.R.5TH 369 (1995).

497. 100 Ohio App. 399, 128 N.E.2d 504 (1955), *app. dismissed*, 164 Ohio St. 428, 131 N.E.2d 837 (1956), *rev'd*, 384 U.S. 333 (1966).

498. 155 Ill. App. 3d 990, 508 N.E.2d 1088 (1987).

499. State v. Moore, 458 N.W.2d 90 (Minn. 1990); Farris v. State, 670 P.2d 995 (Okla. Crim. App. 1983); Lewis v. State, 737 S.W.2d 857, 860 (Tex. Ct. App. 1987).

500. United States v. Phillip, 948 F.2d 241, 248-49 (6th Cir. 1991), *cert. denied*, 504 U.S. 930 (1992); State v. Rodgers, 119 Idaho 1047, 812 P.2d 1208 (1991); State v. Hall, 297 N.W.2d 80 (Iowa 1980), *cert. denied*, 450 U.S. 927 (1981); Oregon v. Proctor, 94 Or. App. 720, 767 P.2d 453 (1989) (the novelty of a scientific technique goes to its weight rather than its admissibility).

501. State v. Rodgers, 812 P.2d 1208, 1212 (Idaho 1991); State v. Moore, 458 N.W.2d 90, 98 (Minn. 1990); Lewis v. State, 737 S.W.2d 857, 860 (Tex. Ct. App. 1987).

Dr. MacDonnell, the F.B.I., and Scotland Yard.[502] Several cases have announced that today the basic reliability of bloodspatter analysis is judicially noticeable.[503]

There are now several computer programs which apply rules of physics to bloodspatter analysis. Of course, before a result of using the program should be admitted at trial, all the formulae programmed into the software should be tested under *Daubert* or *Frye*.

§ 24-13(C). Proper Subjects for Bloodspatter Analysts.

The courts have permitted bloodspatter analysts to opine on a wide variety of subjects, including *inter alia*: whether the victim was standing when the first wound was inflicted,[504] whether the stains on a rug were consistent with the hypothesis that they were produced by the cleansing action of a mechanical rug shampooer on a bloody carpet,[505] whether an attack had occurred near a bed,[506] whether the bloodspatters on defendant's jeans were consistent with the hypothesis that he was in the vicinity of the victim when she was beaten,[507] whether the spatters on a defendant's trousers were consistent with the hypothesis that he was in close proximity to the victim at the time of a stabbing,[508] whether a blood drop had fallen straight down,[509] whether the victim had been shot at a certain height from the floor,[510] whether the stains on defendant's shirt were consistent with the administration of a beating with an object similar to a sledgehammer,[511] whether the stains on defendant's clothes were produced by merely hugging his wife's dead body,[512] whether a shot was fired at the victim from a certain direction,[513] whether the victim could have been standing upright when a gun discharged,[514] whether the stains on the defendant's clothing were consistent with nonviolent contact with the victim's blood,[515] how many times the victim was struck,[516] whether the linear blood smears on the floor

502. Farris v. State, 670 P.2d 995 (Okla. Crim. App. 1983).

503. People v. Haywood, 209 Mich. App. 217, 530 N.W.2d 497, *app. denied*, 450 Mich. 931, 543 N.W.2d 317 (1995); State v. Moore, 458 N.W.2d 90 (Minn. 1990).

504. State v. Breton, 235 Conn. 206, 663 A.2d 1026 (1995).

505. State v. Sirvi, 231 Conn. 115, 646 A.2d 169 (1994).

506. State v. Greenfield, 228 Conn. 62, 634 A.2d 879 (1993).

507. State v. Hoeplinger, 27 Conn. App. 643, 609 A.2d 1015 (1992).

508. People v. Railey, 159 Misc. 2d 393, 604 N.Y.S.2d 680 (1993).

509. Wilson v. Meeks, 52 F.3d 1547 (10th Cir. 1995), *aff'd*, 98 F.3d 1247 (10th Cir. 1996).

510. Gieffels v. State, 590 P.2d 55 (Alaska 1979).

511. State v. Graham, 422 So. 2d 123 (La. 1982).

512. Commonwealth v. Goins, 508 Pa. 270, 495 A.2d 527 (1985).

513. State v. Comfort, 113 A.D.2d 420 (N.Y. 1985).

514. State v. Moore, 458 N.W.2d 90 (Minn. 1990).

515. Lewis v. State, 737 S.W.2d 857 (Tex. 1987).

516. State v. Moore, 122 N.J. 420, 585 A.2d 864 (1991).

indicated that a body had been dragged,[517] whether certain bloodspatters were produced by the last shot,[518] whether the bloodspatters resulted from a blow to the head at the top of a flight of stairs or from falling down the stairs,[519] and whether the drops on the defendant's backpack came from two separate directions.[520]

Although these cases liberally admit bloodspatter testimony, there are limits imposed by the witness's expertise. By way of example, one Georgia case distinguished between the witness's scientific findings and the construction of a hypothetical sequence of events surrounding the shooting.[521] The court ruled that although the first type of finding is admissible, the witness overreached when the witness opined about a hypothetical scenario accounting for all the bloodspatters.

§ 24-13(D). Proper Bases for the Opinion.

The expert must not only base his or her opinion on a generally accepted or validated hypothesis. If the expert proposes to apply the hypothesis to the facts of the case, the expert must have a permissible source for information for his or her information about the specific facts of the case. Under Federal Rule of Evidence 703 as at common law, it is of course ideal when the expert has personal knowledge. For instance, the expert might have personally visited the crime scene. Alternatively, the expert may rely on a hypothetical question when the proponent presents admissible evidence of every hypothesized fact. Finally, under Rule 703 the expert may even rely on sources which are not independently admissible so long as it is the specialty's customary practice to consider that type of source. Suppose, for instance, that there are photographs of the spatters attached to the police report of the crime scene. Even if the proponent does not go to the length of laying a foundation for the admission of the photographs, it would be permissible for the analyst to rely on the facts depicted in the photographs.[522]

517. Fowler v. State, 566 So. 2d 1194 (Miss. 1990).

518. State v. Harris, 84 A.D.2d 63, 445 N.Y.S.2d 520 (1981) (the famous Scarsdale Diet Doctor murder prosecution), *aff'd*, 57 N.Y.2d 335, 442 N.E.2d 1205 (1982), *cert. denied*, 460 U.S. 1047 (1983).

519. United States v. Phillip, 948 F.2d 241, 248-49 (6th Cir. 1991), *cert. denied*, 504 U.S. 930 (1992).

520. Deel v. Jago, 967 F.2d 1079 (6th Cir. 1992).

521. Coleman v. State, 257 Ga. 313, 357 S.E.2d 566 (1987).

522. People v. Bolin, 18 Cal. 4th 297, 956 P.2d. 374, 75 Cal. Rptr. 2d 412 (1998), *cert. denied*, 119 S. Ct. 1146 (1999).

§ 24-13(E). Rule 403 Objections to Bloodspatter Testimony.

In many cases, a bloodspatter expert's testimony can be highly prejudicial. To illustrate his or her testimony, the expert often resorts to gory crime scene photographs. In one New Jersey case, the appellate court ruled that the trial judge should have barred the expert's testimony on the ground that the prejudicial character of the testimony outweighed its probative value.[523] The court emphasized that the testimony was merely cumulative on the issues of cause of death and extent of injuries. The court observed:

> Information about the parts of the house where the attack had taken place and the directionality of the blows, although startling, proves neither the intent nor the identity of the attacker Thus, it was only minimally probative of defendant's guilt.[524]

For the most part, though, Rule 403 objections to bloodspatter testimony have been unsuccessful. In rejecting Rule 403 objections, the courts have sometimes noted that many of the underlying scientific propositions have a simple, common sense basis.[525] Further, the jurors need not accept the expert's opinions at face value; the jurors themselves can inspect and examine the bloodstained objects to independently assess the opinions. For that reason, there is little risk that the testimony will "over-impress" the jurors.[526]

§ 24-14. Paint Analysis.

Like hair, fibers, and glass, paint can be used as associative evidence in a prosecution. Like those types of trace evidence, paint brings Locard's Exchange Principle into play: "every contact leaves a trace."[527] Paint evidence can be left on a person or surface in the form of a powder, chip, smear, or flake. In some cases, it is used as an investigative tool to help the police identify a suspect. For example, the analysis of a smear on the clothing of a hit-and-run victim might tell the police that they should be looking for a certain make and model of automobile. In other cases, paint evidence can be utilized for comparative purposes. Suppose, for instance, that the crime under investigation is a burglary. The crime scene investigation indicates that the burglar used a tool to pry open a painted door to the burgled residence. When the police arrest the defendant, they find a tool in his or her possession. The tool not only would have been suitable to

---

523. State v. Johnson, 120 N.J. 263, 576 A.2d 834 (1990).

524. *Id.* at 852.

525. State v. Hall, 297 N.W.2d 80 (Iowa 1980), *cert. denied*, 450 U.S. 927 (1981).

526. State v. Rodgers, 812 P.2d 1208, 1212 (Idaho 1991).

527. Castle, *The Forensic Examination of Paint*, 75 JOCCA-SURFACE COATINGS INT'L 247 (July 1992).

force the door open; there is also a paint smear on the tool. The police might submit paint samples from the door and the smear on the tool to the laboratory for comparative analysis.

§ 24-14(A). The Properties of Paint.

Although police ordinarily find their paint evidence in a dried state, paint itself is a liquid or semi-liquid. Paint has several components.

First, paint contains pigment giving it a color such as white, black, yellow, brown, red, green, or blue. As one might expect, different pigments have differing chemical composition.[528] For example, white pigments can be calcium carbonate, black amorphous carbon, and red ferric oxide.

Second, the paint includes a suspension medium for the pigment. The media fall into three categories: drying oil, solvent or spirits, and synthetic emulsions.[529] Enamels and exterior building paints fall into the first category. In the second category, drying results from evaporization of organic solvent. Synthetic emulsions consist of a polyvinyl acetate emulsified in water.

Paint can contain additional components. Thus, the paint might include: a drier to accelerate the hardening process, a filler to add lustre, or a thinner. Additional products such as resins must be included in water-based paints to increase their adhesiveness. Many of these additional components are organic in nature.

§ 24-14(B). Collecting Paint Evidence.

Evidence technicians who collect paint evidence should take special precautions to prevent the contamination of the evidence.[530]

Assume, for example, that the police find the paint on a crime scene surface and decide to chip the surface to obtain a sample for laboratory evaluation. It sometimes asserted that to chip the paint, the police ought to use a wooden implement such as a toothpick rather than a metal object such as a knife or razor blade.[531] The fear is that a metallic object might imbed fragments of the metal in the paint and distort the subsequent analysis of the sample. However, our reviewer is dubious of the assertion. First, he believes that any transfer of metal to the paint would be detected. Second, in his experience a toothpick will not remove the full thickness of the paint from an automobile.

---

528. A. Moenssens, J. Starrs, C. Henderson & F. Inbau, Scientific Evidence in Civil and Criminal Cases § 9.21 (4th ed. 1995).

529. *Id.* § 9.21, at 597.

530. Allen & Schnetz, *The Removal of Paint Smears from Tools and Clothing for Microscopical Examination and Analysis*, 52 Forensic Sci. Int'l 101 (1991).

531. A. Moenssens, J. Starrs, C. Henderson & F. Inbau, Scientific Evidence in Civil and Criminal Cases § 9.20, at 595 (4th ed. 1955).

Or suppose that at the crime scene, the police discover an object such as a garment or tool which appears to have paint powder on its surface. The police should place the object in a container such as a plastic bag and seal the bag; if they do so, any paint falling off the object will remain in the container.

Alternatively, assume that in a hit-and-run collision, there appears to be paint on a door or fender. The police might place a clean sheet of paper beneath the door or fender, tap the reverse side, allow the paint to fall onto the sheet, and then place the collected paint into a suitable container. Or they might use transparent pressure sensitive tape to remove the paint.[532]

If there are multiple paint samples at the scene, each sample should be placed in a separate container to preclude the occurrence of cross-contamination.

§ 24-14(C). Analytical Techniques.

There are numerous techniques for analyzing samples of paint evidence.[533] In the past, the following techniques have been in widespread use:

— Microscopic analysis. Many types of microscopes can be employed in the assessment of paint evidence, including optical microscopes, scanning electron microscopes (SEM),[534] and transmission electron microscopy (TEM). Even as simple an instrument as a traditional optical microscope would enable the analyst to identify the number, sequence, and color of each layer in a paint chip.

— Chromatographic techniques. Pyrolysis gas chromatography (PGC) is a popular technique for evaluating paint evidence.[535] This technique entails thermal degradation in the absence of oxygen. A small sample is heated without oxygen until it turns into a gas. The gas sample is then routed into the chromatographic column to determine the retention time of the compound--the time the compound requires to travel the column. Thin layer chromatography can also be useful.[536]

— Solubility tests. When there is a single layer of paint, a solubility test can give the analyst some insight into the type of paint.[537]

---

532. *Id.* § 9.20, at 596.

533. *Paint Examination Techniques Utilized in FBI Laboratory*, F.B.I. LAW ENF. BULL. (April 1973).

534. Ward & Carlson, *Paint Analysis Using the Scanning Electron Microscope*, CRIME LAB. DIG. 2 (Feb. 1983).

535. Cardosi, *Pyrolysis-Gas Chromatographic Examination of Paints*, 27 J. FORENSIC SCI. 695 (1982).

536. Home, Laing & Dudley, *The Discrimination of Modern Household Paints Using Thin Layer Chromatography*, 22 J. FORENSIC SCI. Soc. 147 (1982).

537. Thornton, Kraus, Lerner & Kahane, *Solubility Characterization of Automotive Paints*, 28 J. FORENSIC SCI. 1004 (1983).

— Infrared spectroscopy. Analysts can use infrared instrumentation to identify the organic components of a paint sample.[538] The instrument passes a beam of infrared energy through the sample and measures the amount of energy transmitted through the sample.[539] The amount of energy absorbed is a clue to identify the elemental composition of the sample.[540]

— Ultraviolet spectrophotometry. Like IR, UV can be employed in paint analysis.[541] Many paints contain phthalocyanine pigment, and that type of pigment is readily identifiable in UV analysis. UV analysis also permits the analyst to quantitate.

— Neutron activation analysis (NAA). At one time, some of the leading forensic laboratories utilized NAA in paint analysis.[542] However, it is rarely used in contemporary forensic practice. To begin with, the technique requires the availability of nuclear equipment which many laboratories lack. A further disadvantage is that subjecting the sample to NAA can interfere with subsequent analysis by rendering the sample radioactive.

The techniques listed above certainly do not exhaust the possibilities.[543] Within the past decade, several relatively new techniques have attracted special attention.

— Cathodoluminescence (CL).[544] Cathodoluminescence is a type of light emitted by certain materials when they are subjected to electron beam

---

538. Ryland, *Infrared Microspectroscopy of Forensic Paint Evidence*, *in* H. HUMECKI, PRACTICAL GUIDE TO INFRARED MICROSPECTROSCOPY (1995); Suzuki, *Infrared Spectra of U.S. Automobile Original Topcoats (1974-1989): V. Identification of Organic Pigments Used in Red Nonmetallic and Brown Nonmetallic and Metallic Monocoats — DPP Red BO and Thioindigo Bordeaux*, 44 J. FORENSIC SCI. 297 (1999); Zieba, *A Statistical Criterion for the Value of Evidence: Application to the Evaluation of the Results of Paint Spectral Analysis*, 17 FORENSIC SCI. INT'L 101 (1981).

539. Stoecklein, *Forensic Science: Paints, Varnishes, and Lacquers*, *in* ENCYCLOPEDIA OF ANALYTICAL SCIENCE 1628 (1995).

540. Zieba, *A Statistical Criterion for the Value of Evidence: Application to the Evaluation of the Results of Paint Spectral Analysis*, 17 FORENSIC SCI. INT'L 101 (1981).

541. Voskertchian, *Quantitative Analysis of Organic Pigments in Forensic Paint Examination*, 40 J. FORENSIC SCI. 823 (1995).

542. Krishnan, *Examination of Paints by Trace Element Analysis*, 21 J. FORENSIC SCI. 908 (1976); Snow & Washington, *Comparison of Paints by Neutron Activation Analysis. II. Colored Paints*, 54 J. ASSOC. OFF. ANAL. CHEM. 917 (1971); GENERAL GULF ATOMIC, FORENSIC NEUTRON ACTIVATION ANALYSIS OF PAINT 256 (GA-10142 June 30, 1970).

543. Allen, *The Examination of Thin Sections of Coloured Paints by Light Microscopy*, 57 FORENSIC SCI. INT'L 5 (1992); Laing, Dudley & Isaacs, *Colorimetric Measurements on Small Paint Fragments Using Microspectrophotometry*, 16 FORENSIC SCI. INT'L 159 (1980); Reeve & Keener, *Programmed Energy Dispersive X-Ray Analysis of Top Coats of Automotive Paint*, 21 J. FORENSIC SCI. 883 (1976).

544. L. OZAWA, CATHODOLUMINESCENCE: THEORY AND APPLICATIONS (1990).

irradiation. It is quite useful in comparing multilayered white or beige paint fragments. The analyst uses a cathode to bombard the sample with electrons. The bombardment excites the inorganic pigments in the paint sample to produce visible light or radiation of adjacent wavelengths.

— Pyrolysis Gas Chromatography-Mass Spectrometry (PGC-MS). As previously stated, PGC has long been utilized in paint examination. However, PGC has limitations. If the analyst employs only PGC, the test may yield a retention time shared by several compounds. By conjoining a PGC instrument to a mass spectrometer, the analyst can often differentiate between the compounds. When the instruments are conjoined, the GC column feeds directly into the mass spectrometer. The MS instrument bombards the gas with electronics to break down the molecules. The fragmentation pattern might be unique to a particular compound — a virtual "signature."[545]

— Fourier Transform Infrared Spectroscopy (FTIR). In 1983, the commercially available infrared microscope coupled to a Fourier transform infrared spectrophotometer (FTIR) made its advent.[546] Analysts adapted the new instrument to paint analysis.[547] FTIR can be used to assess very small samples. Moreover, although PGC-MS has limited utility in identifying inorganic paint components, FTIR can analyze inorganic as well as organic components of paint samples.

— Diffuse Reflectance Fourier Transform Spectroscopy (DRIFTS) is an excellent technique for assessing metallic paints.[548] Many automotive manufacturers use metallic paints as automotive finishes.

Proficiency tests of paint analysis indicate that there is a substantial margin of error in paint analysis. In the Crime Laboratory Proficiency Test, 18 paint samples were submitted to between 67 and 164 laboratories.[549] The participating laboratories were asked to perform such tasks as addressing the question of whether two samples could have come from a common origin. On one task, 78% of the responses erroneously concluded that two samples could have come from

---

545. Ryland, *Infrared Microspectroscopy of Forensic Paint Evidence*, *in* H. HUMECKI, PRACTICAL GUIDE TO INFRARED MICROSPECTROSCOPY 232 (1995).

546. *Id.* at 170.

547. Stoecklein, *Forensic Science: Paints, Varnishes and Lacquers*, *in* ENCYCLOPEDIA OF ANALYTICAL SCIENCE 1630-31 (1995).

548. Suzuki, *Forensic Science Applications of Diffuse Reflectance Infrared Fourier Transform Spectroscopy (DRIFTS). IV. Direct Analysis of Metallic Paints — Sampling Considerations*, 34 J. FORENSIC SCI. 164 (1989); Suzuki & Gresham, *Forensic Science Applications of Diffuse Reflectance Infrared Fourier Transform Spectroscopy (DRIFTS): I. Principles, Sampling Methods, and Advantages*, 31 J. FORENSIC SCI. 931 (1986).

549. J. Peterson & P. Markham, *Crime Laboratory Proficiency Testings Results, 1978-1991, II: Resolving Questions of Common Origin*, 40 J. FORENSIC SCI. 1009 (1995).

the same source.[550] In part as a response to these revelations, the Scientific Working Group for Materials Examination (SWGMAT) is developing guidelines for conducting these various analytical techniques. The working group is striving to both improve quality control at individual laboratories and refine protocols which can be used at all the laboratories employing a particular analytical technique.

§ 24-14(D). Forensic Determinations.

What findings can an analyst testify to after conducting the tests described in the preceding subsection? The "lack of statistical information on paint"[551] limits the analyst's ability to draw valid inferences from his or her findings.

At one level, the analyst can testify that the sample is a paint formulation used only by a particular make and model or automobile.[552] As a basis for such testimony, the analyst must have a database with which to compare the sample. Partial databases have been compiled in many countries, including the United States, the United Kingdom, and Canada.[553] Using such a database, the analyst might single out a particular make, model, and year automobile; and the attorney

---

550. *Id.* at 1021, 1028.

551. McDermott, Willis & McCullough, *The Evidential Value of Paint. Part II: A Bayesian Approach*, 44 J. FORENSIC SCI. 263 (1999).

552. Castle, *The Forensic Examination of Paint*, JOCCA-SURFACE COATINGS INT'L 249 (1992).

553. Suzuki, *Infrared Spectra of U.S. Automobile Original Topcoats (1974-1989): V. Identification of Organic Pigments Used in Red Nonmetallic and Brown Nonmetallic and Metallic Monocoats — DPP Red BO and Thioindigo Bourdeaux*, 44 J. FORENSIC SCI. 297 (1999); Suzuki & Marshall, *Infrared Spectra of U.S. Automobile Original Topcoats (1974-1989): IV. Identification of Some Organic Pigments Used in Red and Brown Nonmetallic and Metallic Monocoats — Quinacridones*, 43 J. FORENSIC SCI. 514 (1998); Audette & Percy, *A Rapid, Systematic, and Comprehensive Classification System for the Identification and Comparison of Motor Vehicle Paint Samples. I: The Nature and Scope of the Classification System*, 24 J. FORENSIC SCI. 790 (1979); Audette & Percy, *A Rapid, Systematic, and Comprehensive Classification System for the Identification and Comparison of Motor Vehicle Paint Samples. II: Paint Data Collected from Chrysler-Manufactured Cars*, 27 J. FORENSIC SCI. 622 (1982); Cousins, Holding, Locke & Wilkinson, *A Data Collection of Vehicle Topcoat Colours. 4. A Trial to Assess the Effectiveness of Colour Identification*, 43 FORENSIC SCI. INT'L 183 (1989); Locke, Wilkinson & Hanford, *A Data Collection of Vehicle Topcoat Colours. 2. The Measurement of Colour Samples Used in the Vehicle Refinishing Industry*, 37 FORENSIC SCI. INT'L 177 (1988); Ryland, *Infrared Microspectroscopy of Forensic Paint Evidence*, *in* H. HOMECKI, PRACTICAL GUIDE TO INFRARED MICROSPECTROSCOPY 174-76 (1995); Ryland, Kopec & Somerville, *The Evidential Value of Automobile Paint. Part II: Frequency of Occurrence of Topcoat Colors*, 26 J. FORENSIC SCI. 64 (1981); Suzuki & Marshall, *Infrared Spectra of U.S. Automobile Original Topcoats (1974-89): III. In Situ Identification of Some Organic Pigments Used in Yellow, Orange, Red, and Brown Nonmetallic and Brown Metallic Finishes — Benzimidazolones*, 42 J. FORENSIC SCI. 619 (1997); Taylor, Cousins, Holding, Locke & Wilkinson, *A Data Collection of Vehicle Topcoat Colours. 3. Practical Considerations for Using a National Database*, 40 FORENSIC SCI. INT'L 131 (1989).

could then introduce business records from the automobile manufacturer that it sold 300,000 vehicles of that make, model, and year.

At another level, the analyst might attempt to narrow the size of the class of potential sources by testifying that the sample was part of a particular batch of paint (one day's production) at the finishing plant. There might be only 300 cars with finishes from that paint batch. In order to give this testimony, the analyst would have to do further testing. For instance, the analyst might have used DRIFTS to establish both that the batch in question has a slightly different formulation than other formulations used on the same make, model, and year automobile and that other cars finished from the same paint batch have the same spectral pattern.

At still another level, the analyst might endeavor to lend support to the inference that the paint sample in question came from a particular automobile. In some cases, the testing will at least suggest that inference. For example, suppose that the automobile in question is an old one which has been frequently repainted. A paint chip might display the peculiar number and sequence of paints. Or the shape of the chip might appear to exactly fit a chip on the surface of the automobile in question. A fit can be as probative in this context as it is in glass fracture analysis.

In cases in which the sample is a multi-layer chip, an analyst might be tempted to use statistical techniques to give the jury a sense of how rare the chip is. For instance, after identifying the individual layers, the analyst might cite population frequencies for each type of paint, invoke the multiplication or product rule, and endeavor to testify that the product of multiplying the various frequencies is the random match probability for the chip. In one case, a defense expert witness proposed testifying along these lines.[554] However, the expert conceded that he lacked hard data for the individual frequencies. Given that record, the court excluded the testimony. The court remarked that "we find that any opinion he might have had regarding the probability that the paint samples found on the houses and the cloth matched would have been highly speculative, and with no scientific foundation." Section 15-7 of this treatise describes the type of foundation the proponent must lay before an expert should be permitted to testify to this type of opinion.

§ 24-15. Admissibility of Paint Evidence.

The courts' treatment of paint evidence has been similar to their handling of hair and fiber evidence. For the most part, the courts have been receptive to

---

554. State v. Spirko, 1989 WL 17734 (Ohio App. Mar. 6, 1989) (unpublished opinion), *aff'd*, 59 Ohio St. 3d 1, 570 N.E.2d 229, *cert. denied*, 502 U.S. 913 (1991).

testimony about paint examination.[555] The courts have routinely admitted the evidence in burglary and hit-and-run prosecutions where the evidence can be a crucial link between the defendant and the actus reus.

The courts have accepted testimony about sophisticated techniques such as spectroscopy[556] and neutron activation analysis[557] as well as simpler microscopic techniques.

In truth, the courts have been receptive to the point of being uncritical. In *State v. Raines*,[558] the defendants were charged with breaking and entering and possession of burglary tools. At trial, prosecution experts testified about the results of tests performed on paint samples from the victim's door and the defendants' crowbar. On appeal, the defense challenged the reliability of the expert testimony. The court rejected the challenge. In explaining its reasoning, the court focused almost exclusively on the expert witness's qualifications.[559] The court evidently felt no need to even discuss the question of the validity of the analytic methodology used by the expert. Thus, with the exception of cases in which the proponent has attempted to introduce statistical testimony quantifying the random probability of a paint "match,"[560] the courts have rejected the overwhelming majority of attacks on forensic paint evidence.

It remains to be seen whether the Supreme Court's enunciation of the new empirical validation test in *Daubert v. Merrell Dow Pharmaceuticals, Inc.*[561] will prompt the courts to rethink the liberal admissibility of paint evidence. As the sections of this treatise devoted to questioned document examination and trace evidence point out, in those areas some courts have reconsidered the

555.. Friendship Heights Assocs. v. Vlastimil Koubek, A.I.A., 785 F.2d 1154 (4th Cir. 1986); United States v. Longfellow, 406 F.2d 415 (4th Cir.), *cert. denied*, 394 U.S. 998 (1969); Pearson v. United States, 192 F.2d 681 (6th Cir. 1951); State v. Hansen, 199 Kan. 17, 427 P.2d 627 (1967); State v. Brown, 81 N.C. App. 622, 344 S.E.2d 817 (1986); State v. Steele, 1993 WL 52154 (Minn. App. 1993) (unpublished opinion); State v. Brooks, 960 S.W.2d 479 (Mo. 1997), *cert. denied*, 118 S. Ct. 2379 (1998); State v. Menard, 331 S.W.2d 521 (Mo. 1960); State v. Campos, 61 N.M. 392, 301 P.2d 329 (1956); State v. Walker, 6 N.C. App. 447, 170 S.E.2d 627 (1969); State v. Orricer, 80 S.D. 126, 120 N.W.2d 528 (1963); State v. Donnell, 598 S.W.2d 569 (Mo. Ct. App. 1980); Dees v. State, 753 S.W.2d 598 (Mo. Ct. App. 1988); People v. Fletcher, 66 Ill. App. 3d 502, 383 N.E.2d 1285, 23 Ill. Dec. 258 (1978); State v. Rhodes, 552 So. 2d 585 (La. App. 1989); Davis v. State, 455 So. 2d 213 (Ala. Crim. App. 1984); People v. Green, 28 Ill. 2d 286, 192 N.E.2d 398 (1963); State v. Fortson, 1990 WL 6837 (Tenn. Crim. App. 1990) (unpublished opinion).

556. State v. Vaccaro, 111 R.I. 59, 298 A.2d 788 (1973).

557. State v. Coolidge, 109 N.H. 403, 260 A.2d 547 (1969), *rev'd on other grounds*, 403 U.S. 443 (1971).

558. 29 N.C. App. 303, 224 S.E.2d 232 (1976).

559. *Id.*

560. State v. Spirko, 1989 WL 17734 (Ohio App. 1989) (unpublished opinion), *aff'd*, 59 Ohio St. 3d 1, 570 N.E.2d 229, *cert. denied*, 502 U.S. 913 (1991).

561. 509 U.S. 579 (1993).

admissibility issue and rejected testimony which would have been received as a matter of course under the prior *Frye* test.

There are at least indications that the defense bar will attack paint evidence more aggressively than it has in the past. In a 1996, post-*Daubert* prosecution, the defense offered parts of the Department of Justice's Office of Inspector General report about the F.B.I. laboratory to attack the credibility of a prosecution paint expert.[562] The relevant parts of the report of investigation concluded that in other tests, the expert in question had "violated FBI laboratory analysis protocol [and] issued scientific opinions without proper empirical bases...."[563]

These more aggressive defense attacks have already borne some fruit. The Virginia appellate court's 1996 decision in *Johnson v. Commonwealth*[564] is a case in point. There the defendant was convicted of hit-and-run driving causing a personal injury. At trial, the prosecution introduced testimony about a laboratory analysis of paint from the victim's and defendant's cars. The testimony was to the effect that the samples "matched in colors, types, textures, and layer sequence and were similar in inorganic composition. These paints could have had a common origin."[565] However, the court noted that the prosecution had failed to establish the population frequency of any of the listed characteristics. In large part for that reason, the court found that the testimony was legally insufficient to support a conviction. The court declared that "the paint evidence did not exclude reasonable possibilities other than guilt."[566] The court added that "[w]ithout expert testimony which explained the probability of two paint samples possessing similar properties, the jury had no standard to evaluate the weight or significance of such evidence."[567] If *Johnson* is any indication, in the future the courts may adopt a more skeptical attitude toward paint evidence and insist upon more elaborate foundations, as they have in many other areas of forensic science. After the Supreme Court's 1999 decision in *Kumho*,[568] it is clear that the proponent cannot escape from the requirement of showing the reliability of paint evidence by the simple expedient of labeling it nonscientific technical expertise rather than truly scientific testimony.

---

562. United States v. Gonzalez, 938 F. Supp. 1199 (D. Del. 1996), *aff'd*, 127 F.3d 1097 (3d Cir. 1997), *cert. denied*, 118 S. Ct. 1099 (1998).

563. 938 F. Supp. at 1202.

564. 1996 WL 31958 (Va. App. Jan. 30, 1996).

565. *Id.*

566. *Id.*

567. *Id.*

568. Kumho Tire Co., Ltd. v. Carmichael, 119 S. Ct. 1167 (1999).

§ 24-16. Selected Bibliography.

Hair, 5 AM. JUR. PROOF OF FACTS 569 (1960).

AMERICAN SOCIETY FOR TESTING MATERIALS, TENTATIVE METHODS FOR IDENTIFICATION OF FIBERS IN TEXTILES.

F. CUNLIFFE & P. PIAZZA, CRIMINALISTICS AND SCIENTIFIC INVESTIGATION (1980).

E. KORNREICH, INTRODUCTION TO FIBERS AND FABRICS (1966).

B. FISHER, TECHNIQUES OF CRIME SCENE INVESTIGATION (5th ed. 1992).

R. MURRAY & J. TEDROW, FORENSIC GEOLOGY (1992).

H. TUTHILL, INDIVIDUALIZATION: PRINCIPLES AND PROCEDURES IN CRIMINALISTICS (1994).

V. VALKOVIC, HUMAN HAIR (1988) (2 vols.).

TEXTILE INSTITUTE, IDENTIFICATION OF TEXTILE MATERIALS (7th ed. 1975).

Deadman, *Fiber Evidence and the Wayne Williams Trial (Part I)*, 53 F.B.I. LAW ENF. BULL. 12 (March 1984).

Deadman, *Fiber Evidence and the Wayne Williams Trial (Conclusion)*, 53 F.B.I. LAW ENF. BULL. 10 (May 1984).

Imwinkelried, *Forensic Science: Hair Analysis*, 27 CRIM. L. BULL. 447 (Sept.-Oct. 1991).

Imwinkelried, *Forensic Hair Analysis: The Case Against the Underemployment of Scientific Evidence*, 39 WASH. & LEE L. REV. 41 (1982).

McJunkins & Thornton, *Glass Fracture Analysis: A Review*, 2 FORENSIC SCI. 1 (1973).

Miller, *An Introduction to Fiber Evidence*, 1983 THE PRACTICAL PROSECUTOR 19.

Miller, *Forensic Glass Comparisons*, *in* FORENSIC SCIENCE HANDBOOK 139 (R. Saferstein ed. 1982).

Murray, *Forensic Examination of Soil*, *in* FORENSIC SCIENCE HANDBOOK 653 (R. Saferstein ed. 1982).

Stone & Thornton, *Glass Evidence*, *in* SCIENTIFIC AND EXPERT EVIDENCE 239 (2d ed. 1981).

Watkins & Watkins, *Identification of Substances by Instrumental Analysis*, 22 AM. JUR. PROOF OF FACTS 385 (1969).

CHAPTER 25

INSTRUMENTAL ANALYSIS*

§ 25-1. In General.

Various instrumental techniques for forensic analysis have been discussed throughout this text. One instrumental technique, neutron activation analysis (NAA), has so many applications and has attracted such publicity that a separate chapter, Chapter 11, is devoted to it. Other techniques have received little attention either because of their novelty or due to their limited application.[1] A

---

*The authors wish to express their appreciation to Professor Donald Land of the Chemistry Department, University of California, at Davis, who reviewed this chapter in the third edition of this treatise, and Dr. John Fairing of Scanning Microscopy International, Ballwin, Missouri, who reviewed this chapter in the first and second editions.

1. Grant, Moody, Hutcheon, Phinney, Haas, Volpe, Oldani, Whipple, Stoyer, Alcaraz, Andrews, Russo, Klunder, Andresen & Cantlin, *Forensic Analyses of Suspect Illicit Nuclear Material*, 43 J. Forensic Sci. 680 (1998); Sands, Hayward, Kirkbride, Bennett, Lacey & Batchelder, *UV-Excited Resonance Raman Spectroscopy of Narcotics and Explosives*, 43 J. Forensic Sci. 509 (1998); Hodge, *Satellite Data and Environmental Law: Technology Ripe for Litigation Application*, 14 Pace Envtl. L. Rev. 691 (1997); Young & Yohman, *Rapid, Noninvasive Contraband Detection by Acoustic Response*, 40 J. Forensic Sci. 470 (1995) (this article describes a new "method for the rapid detection of concealed contraband materials. This method exploits the difference in acoustic response between a hollow, contraband-laden host and a solid object of the same type"); The Rome Laboratory Law Enforcement Tech. Team, *The New Horizon: Transferring Defense Technology to Law Enforcement*, 65 F.B.I. Law Enf. Bull. 10, 13-15 (Apr. 1996) (new sensor technologies, including the use of radio frequency (RF) sensors for concealed weapon detection); United States v. Quinn, 18 F.3d 1461 (9th Cir.) (photogrammetry), *cert. denied*, 512 U.S. 1242 (1994); Graham, *Metal Detection: The Crime Scene's Best Kept Secret*, 64 F.B.I. Law Enf. Bull. 10 (Feb. 1995); Kalt-O'Bannon, *Scientific Dating and the Law: Establishing the Age of Old Objects for Legal Purposes*, 63 U.M.K.C. L. Rev. 93 (1994) (carbon-14 dating, accelerator mass spectrometry

number of other instrumental techniques have not received as much notoriety but nevertheless have wide-ranging applicability. Those techniques are discussed in this chapter.

If the expert has used one of these techniques, the attorney must determine not only whether the technique itself is trustworthy but also whether the expert used the technique properly in the instant case. It may be helpful to contact the American Society for Testing and Materials (ASTM). ASTM is headquartered at 100 Barr Harbor Drive, West Conshohocken, near Philadelphia, Pennsylvania. ASTM promulgates standards for the various instrumental testing techniques. For instance, volume 14.01 of the ASTM standards deals with chromatography, forensic sciences, and laboratory apparatus. If the expert has violated the ASTM standards, the violation calls into question the reliability of the expert's findings.

§ 25-2. Scanning Electron Microscopy (SEM).*

The light or optical microscope is commonly used in such forensic examinations as firearm, glass, and toolmark analysis.[2] The optical microscope enables the criminalist to view identifying characteristics that are invisible to the unaided eye. Optical microscopes are useful up to a magnification of about 1,000 times.[3] Some instruments have an upper limit of 2,000 times,[4] but magnifications up to 10,000 times are possible. Pictures at magnifications greater than 1,500, however, show "blank" magnification — that is, magnification without additional detail.

Microscopists are now using a new, more powerful instrument, the scanning electron microscope (SEM).[5] The SEM can produce magnifications exceeding 300,000 times. As in the case of the light microscope, there is a difference between the useful and possible magnifications. Magnifications exceeding

---

(AMS), thermoluminescent dating (TL), and dendochronology); Mahan, *Forensic Image Processing*, 10 CRIM. JUST. 2, 3 (Spr. 1995) ("In forensic image processing, evidentiary videotape is first converted to a digital format that is computer-readable. Digitized image frames are then merged together with algorithms that compensate for camera and subject motion. The resulting high-quality still image can be clarified with special algorithms to remove noise and blur.").

*Based in part on Imwinkelried, *The Forensic Uses of the Scanning Electron Microscope*, THE CHAMPION, Mar. 1981, at 2. Reprinted with permission of the National Association of Criminal Defense Lawyers.

2. Finch, *Histologic Examination of Trace Evidence*, 10 J. FORENSIC SCI. 253 (1965).

3. People v. Palmer, 80 Cal. App. 3d 239, 241 n.2, 145 Cal. Rptr. 466, 471 n.2 (1978). Optical microscopes also find enormous use at much lower magnifications from 10X on up. In practice, powers from 200 to 500 times are the most frequently used.

4. *Id.*

5. J. GOLDSTEIN & H. YAKOWITZ, PRACTICAL SCANNING ELECTRON MICROSCOPY (1975); O. WELLS, SCANNING ELECTRON MICROSCOPY (1974).

100,000 times ordinarily result in fuzzy pictures and yield no additional information. Even so, the SEM represents an "enormous improvement."[6]

The SEM industry is growing rapidly. Major anti-trust battles have already been waged over the SEM market.[7] The market is growing quickly precisely because SEM has numerous, useful applications. It has already been used in environmental litigation. For instance, in one case,[8] SEM was used to analyze the physical properties of Reserve Mining's discharges. Similarly, SEM has been employed in tort suits. *Breaux v. Louisiana Department of Highways*[9] is illustrative. In *Breaux,* a metallurgist utilized SEM to prove that a crack existed in an axle housing that caused a traffic accident.[10]

SEM's potential is not limited to civil cases; the technique also has criminal applications. In *People v. Marx,*[11] the court permitted an expert to use SEM in bitemark identification. More recently, in *People v. Palmer,*[12] a criminalist employed SEM to identify gunshot residue (GSR) particles. The court sustained the admission of the evidence; the court cited an Aerospace Corporation Report, stating that SEM "has been fashioned into the most definitive method of identifying and the most successful method of detecting gunshot residue to date."[13] Professor Judd reports finding 153 articles discussing possible courtroom applications of SEM.[14]

---

6. People v. Marx, 54 Cal. App. 3d 100, 111 n.16, 126 Cal. Rptr. 350, 356 n.16 (1975).

7. *E.g.,* Structure Probe, Inc. v. Franklin Institute, 450 F. Supp. 1272 (E.D. Pa. 1978), *aff'd,* 595 F.2d 1214 (3d Cir. 1979).

8. Reserve Mining Co. v. Environmental Protection Agency, 514 F.2d 492, 501-02 (8th Cir. 1975), *modified,* 529 F.2d 181 (8th Cir. 1976)..

9. 347 So. 2d 1290 (La. App. 1977).

10. *Id.* at 1292. *See also* Fromson v. Advance Offset Plate, Inc., 219 U.S.P.Q. 83 (D. Mass.), *vacated,* 720 F.2d 1565 (Fed. Cir. 1983); Rohm & Haas Co. v. Owen-Corning Fiberglass Corp., 196 U.S.P.Q. 726 (N.D. Ala. 1977); National Research Dev. Corp. v. Great Lakes Carbon Corp., 410 F. Supp. 1108 (D. Del. 1975); Moore v. Remington Arms Co., 100 Ill. App. 3d 1102, 56 Ill. Dec. 413, 427 N.E.2d 608 (1981); Rubright v. Codman & Shurtleff, 86 Ill. App. 3d 94, 41 Ill. Dec. 183, 407 N.E.2d 681 (1980).

11. 54 Cal. App. 3d 100, 111 n.16, 126 Cal. Rptr. 350, 356 n.16 (1975).

12. 80 Cal. App. 3d 239, 145 Cal. Rptr. 466 (1978).

13. *Id.* at 252-53, 145 Cal. Rptr. at 472.Germani, *Evaluation of Instrumental Parameters for Automated Scanning Electron Microscopy/Gunshot Residue Particle Analysis,* 36 J. FORENSIC SCI. 331 (1991); Varetto, *The Use of Plasma Ashing on Samples for Detection of Gunshot Residues with Scanning Electron Microscopy and Energy-Dispersive X-Ray Analysis (SEM/EDXA),* 35 J. FORENSIC SCI. 964 (1990); Zeicher, Foner, Dvorachek, Bergman & Levin, *Concentration Techniques for the Detection of Gunshot Residues by Scanning Electron Microscopy/Energy Dispersive X-Ray Analysis (SEM/EDX),* 34 J. FORENSIC SCI. 312 (1989); White & Owens, *Automation of Gunshot Residue Detection and Analysis by Scanning Electron Microscopy/Energy Dispersive X-Ray Analysis (SEM/EDX),* 32 J. FORENSIC SCI. 1595 (1987); Harris, *Analysis of Primer Residue from CCI Blazer Lead Free Ammunition by Scanning Electron Microscopy/Energy Dispersive X-Ray,* 40 J. FORENSIC SCI. 27 (1995); DeGaetano, Siegel & Klomparens, *A Comparison of Three Techniques Developed for Sampling and Analysis of Gunshot Residue by Scanning*

§ 25-2(A). SEM Technique.

There are three basic types of microscopes in widespread forensic use: optical, transmission electron (TEM), and scanning electron (SEM).[15]

Optical

The conventional optical microscope can be used in the transmission mode; for example, it can be employed to look through thin sections of stained

---

Electron Microscopy/Energy-Dispersive X-Ray Analysis (SEM-EDX), 37 J. FORENSIC SCI. 281 (1992).

14. Judd, *Scanning Electron Microscopy as Applied to Forensic Analysis, in* SCIENTIFIC AND EXPERT EVIDENCE 873, 874 (2d ed. 1981). *See also* Choudhry, *Comparison of Minute Smears of Lipstick by Microspectrophotometry and Scanning Electron Microscopy/Energy-Dispersive Spectroscopy*, 36 J. FORENSIC SCI. 366 (1991); Beam & Willis, *Analysis Protocol for Discrimination of Automotive Paints by SEM-EDXA Using Beam Alignment by Current Centering*, 35 J. FORENSIC SCI. 1055 (1990); Stowell & Card, *Use of Scanning Electron Microscopy (SEM) to Identify Cuts and Tears in a Nylon Fabric*, 35 J. FORENSIC SCI. 947 (1990); Ikeda, Watanabe, Harada & Suzuki, *A Scanning Electron Microscopy and Electron Probe X-Ray Microanalysis (SEM-EPMA) of Pink Teeth*, 33 J. FORENSIC SCI. 1328 (1988); Sehgal, Singh, Kumar, Jain, Grover & Dua, *Tool Mark Comparison of a Wire Cut Ends by Scanning Electron Microscopy — A Forensic Study*, 36 FORENSIC SCI. INT'L 21 (1988); Ueyama & Ishiyama, *The Characterization of Fragments from Electron Blasting Cap After Detonation by Scanning Electron Microscopy*, 35 FORENSIC SCI. INT'L 219 (1987); Moauro & Falso, *Identification of Ammunitions Used in a Lethal Robbery. Comparison Between Scanning Electron Microscopy/Energy Dispersive X-Ray Analysis (SEM-EDX) and Instrumental Neutron Activation Analysis (NAA) Measurements*, 38 J. FORENSIC SCI. 1237 (1993).

15. Although these are the three basic types of microscopes in common use, new types of microscopes are being developed. Allman, *The Journey to Inner Space*, 104 U.S. NEWS & WORLD REP. 66 (May 9, 1988). One is the scanning tunneling microscope. *Id.* "When two materials come close together, electrons will 'tunnel' or jump, from one to the other and create a tiny electric current." *Id.* In tunneling microscopy, the analyst places an electrically conductive probe, usually tungsten, near the sample. By measuring how the current changes as the probe moves over the surface, the analyst can determine the contours of the sample. Our reviewer adds that in scanning tunneling microscopy (STM), the variation of current through the tunneling gap is not linearly proportional to the distance and that therefore conversion from current to distance is complicated and reduces the accuracy of the results. The preferred method of operation uses a feedback loop to move the probe vertically so as to keep the tunneling current constant. This minute motion over subatomic distances is produced by a piezoelectric device (a crystal or ceramic the length of which changes according to the voltage applied). Similar piezoelectric devices are employed to move the probe over the sample surface.

A second type is atomic-force microscopy. *Id.* at 67. This technique "drags an ultrasharp diamond across the surface to 'feel' the electrons ...." *Id.* Researchers are using these two new microscopes to analyze organic molecules and other biological material such as DNA and blood cells.

The McCrone Research Institute of Chicago, Illinois, is one of the pioneers in microscopy research. The institute offers forensic microscopy courses, especially training in the use of the light microscope.

biological material. However, in materials analysis, the microscope is a surface tool; it enables the microscopist to view enlargements of the object's surface. The basic microscope consists of a round tube including a series of glass lenses, spaced varying distances apart. The lenses manipulate a light beam to produce the magnification. This type of microscope has limited resolving power. Resolving power refers to the sharpness of the image produced. Resolving power[16] is often measured in terms of Angstroms (Å), a ten-billionth of a meter or four billionths of an inch. The German physicist, Ernst Abbe, contended that the theoretical resolving power of an optical microscope is 1/125,000th of an inch or 2,000 Å;[17] the microscope could not distinguish objects separated by less than that distance or see objects smaller than that size. This limitation is due to the wavelength of light used in the microscope.

TEM

In contrast, TEM is analogous to medical X-ray. TEM shoots electrons through a sample and produces micrographs of the interior of the sample.[18] The SEM has characteristics of both the optical microscope and the TEM. Because electrons do not travel far through materials, the samples for TEM must be thinned to 50-5,000 Angstroms; and little information about surface structures is obtained. Thus, this technique is not generally useful for evidentiary analyses.

SEM

Like the optical microscope, SEM is a surface tool for studying topography and morphology.[19] Like the TEM, SEM uses a beam of electrons to produce its

---

16. Our reviewer points out that the actual resolution of a microscope is a function of three quantities: the angular aperture of the objective lens, the wavelength of the light used, and the refractive index of the media between the lens and the sample. These quantities are related by the Abbe equation and determine a mathematical limit to the resolution.

17. C. GILMORE, THE UNSEEN UNIVERSE (PHOTOGRAPHS FROM THE SCANNING ELECTRON MICROSCOPE) 6 (1974). Our reviewer points out that in the last 15 years, an enormous effort has been made to unify and standardize the units of measure in all branches of science. As a general proposition, the method is based on a system of units in which each unit differs from the next smaller one by a factor of one thousand. There are occasional exceptions such as centimeter and millimeter employed to make units more useful. Although Abbe originally used the Angstrom Unit, the Angstrom Unit is not a part of the new system and is no longer widely used. Many scientific journals do not even permit the use of that unit in articles published in those journals. The preferred unit is the nanometer (nm), which is one billionth of a meter or 40 billionths of an inch (*i.e.*, 1 nm = 10 Å).

The other unit of measure employed in microscopy is the micrometer (m) or micron. The micrometer is one millionth of a meter or 1/25,000 of an inch. Thus, 1,000 nm = 1 .

18. Structure Probe, Inc. v. Franklin Institute, 450 F. Supp. 1272, 1275 (E.D. Pa. 1978), *aff'd*, 595 F.2d 1214 (3d Cir. 1979).

19. *Id.*

micrographs.[20] However, in SEM, the electron beams do not pass through the sample. One commentator described the process in simplified fashion by asserting that the beams "are reflected back, through a process which is analogous to the manner in which the human eye forms an image of an object from light reflected from the surface of [an] object."[21] In fact, the reflected electrons play only a minor role in forming the SEM image, and the process differs markedly from the manner in which the human eye produces an image.

The process begins by focusing an electron beam, the primary beam, on the sample to be analyzed. The beam typically has an energy between 10,000 and 20,000 volts, but it can vary between 1,000 and 40,000 volts. The sample is placed in the SEM's specimen chamber. In the chamber, the sample is ordinarily mounted on an aluminum stub in a vacuum. The chamber can accommodate samples ranging in size from a few millimeters up to roughly one foot. An electron gun, which produces an electron beam, "shoots" the beam at the sample. In the form of a raster, the beam is usually scanned or swept over the surface of the sample.[22] When the beam strikes the surface, an interaction occurs. The interaction generates secondary electrons and X-rays. The X-rays can be analyzed to give elemental composition of microscopic particles, but the secondary electron emission is the most important interaction in the technique for image formation.

The secondary electrons emitted are collected and amplified to produce an image display on a cathode ray tube (CRT). This image is built up point-by-point. Each small part of the sample surface produces electrons, and those electrons are converted into a point on the CRT screen. The SEM continuously scans the electron beam over the entire surface of the sample, and this is synchronized with the beam on the CRT screen, thereby creating an image of the entire surface. The image is called a micrograph and appears as shades of black, gray, and white.

The micrograph has two notable characteristics. First, SEM micrographs achieve tremendous magnification or enlargement. For example, in his study of lines drawn by writing media, Waeschle used SEM at 20,000X magnification.[23] Professor Judd reported in 1981 that magnifications of 100,000X are normally

---

20. *Id.*

21. *Id.* Our reviewer cautions that this analogy is "far too simple." He cites Einstein's remark: "Everything should be made as simple as possible — but not simpler."

22. *Id.* Our reviewer points out that the newer SEMs with improved electron optics are capable of being used at voltages as low as 1,000 volts but with some decrease in resolution. He also notes that only a few special microscopes had accommodated a one-foot sample. In practice, the upper limit for a sample is usually 1/2 to 1 inch.

23. Waeschle, *Examination of Line Crossings by Scanning Electron Microscopy*, 24 J. FORENSIC SCI. 569 (1979).

available,[24] and in 1985 experts at Monsanto Chemical Company in St. Louis informed the authors that magnifications exceeding 300,000X are now possible. Furthermore, SEM has tremendous resolving power. Some experts formerly stated that its resolving power is 200 Å.[25] Today most top of the line SEMs are rated at 40 Angstrom resolution, and one is advertised at 20 Å. Coupled with its magnification capability, its resolving power makes SEM a powerful tool for studying surface topography.

Second, SEM has extraordinary depth of field. This advantage enables the microscopist to view a three-dimensional image of the sample. The image produced on the screen is thus quite similar to the image produced by the normal vision of the naked eye. The three-dimensional image is useful in such forensic examinations as bitemark identification.[26] By taking two photographs of the sample at different tilt angles, the expert can obtain true stereoscopic images. This capability makes the SEM an ideal instrument for studying surface morphology (structure).

§ 25-2(B). Forensic Applications.

SEM can be used to:

— identify blood stains and crusts of blood;
— view the minute features of suspected counterfeit coins;
— study the cystolithic hairs of cannabis and other plants;
— examine vehicle light filaments to determine whether a light was on at the time of an accident;
— identify fibers by their composition;
— study firing pin impression in detail;
— conduct micro-analysis of paint flakes, glass, and soils;
— view small features of hair strands;
— differentiate among brands of matches by studying the characteristics of their heads and sticks;
— examine surfaces in detail to locate dangerous conditions such as defects in welds;
— study identifying characteristics of brands of paper;
— help determine the sequence of the strokes on a written instrument;[27]
— study obliterated stamped serial numbers[28]

---

24. Judd, *Scanning Electron Microscopy as Applied to Forensic Analysis*, *in* SCIENTIFIC AND EXPERT EVIDENCE 873, 879-80 (2d ed. 1981).

25. C. GILMORE, *supra* note 17, at 6.

26. People v. Marx, 54 Cal. App. 3d 100, 111 n.16, 126 Cal. Rptr. 350, 356 n.16 (1975).

27. Blueschke & Lacis, *Examination of Line Crossings by Low KV Scanning Electron Microscopy (SEM) Using Photographic Stereoscopic Pairs*, 41 J. FORENSIC SCI. 80 (1996).

— examine toolmarks;
— view wounds to determine their age and cause, particularly high voltage injuries;
— identify particles as gunshot residue[29]
— examine incinerated teeth;[30]
— identify foreign material such as bone fragments on bullets;[31]
— analyze splinters from a wooden broomstick;[32]
— differentiate between plastic automobile bumper bars;[33]
— determine the direction of incised wounds caused by blades;[34] and
— to enhance images in conjunction with computers.[35]

---

28. Mongan, *Visualization of a Restored Serial Number Using Scanning Electron Microscopy (SEM)*, 41 J. FORENSIC SCI. 1074 (1996).

29. Wrobel, Millar & Kihek, *Comparison of Properties of Adhesive Tapes, Tabs, and Liquids Used for the Collection of Gunshot Residue and Other Trace Materials for SEM Analysis*, 43 J. FORENSIC SCI. 178 (1978).

30. Carr, Barsley & Davenport, *Postmortem Examination of Incinerated Teeth with the Scanning Electron Microscope*, 31 J. FORENSIC SCI. 307 (1986); Fairgrieve, *SEM Analysis of Incinerated Teeth As an Aid to Positive Identification*, 39 J. FORENSIC SCI. 557 (1994). *See also* Quatrehomme, Bolla, Muller, Rocca, Grevin, Bailet & Ollier, *Experimental Single Controlled Study of Burned Bones: Contribution of Scanning Electron Microscopy*, 43 J. FORENSIC SCI. 417 (1998).

31. DiMaio, Dana, Taylor & Ondrusek, *Use of Scanning Electron Microscopy and Energy Dispersive X-Ray Analysis (SED-EDXA) in Identification of Foreign Material on Bullets*, 32 J. FORENSIC SCI. 38 (1987). However, in Payne & Cromey, *Limitations of ZAF Correction Factors in the Determination of Calcium/Phosphorous Ratios: Important Forensic Science Considerations Relevant to the Analysis of Bone Fragments Using Scanning Electron Microscopy and Energy-Dispersive X-Ray Microanalysis*, 35 J. FORENSIC SCI. 560 (1990), the authors point out the danger of the widespread practice of embedding the sample in material such as epoxy resin. The analyst may misidentify the embedding material as a bone fragment.

32. Adelman, Peterson & Sorger, *Identification of Wooden Instruments by Scanning Electron Microscopy from Splinters Left in Victim*, 33 J. FORENSIC SCI. 787 (1988).

33. Parybyk & Kobus, *The Characterization of Plastic Bumper Bars Using Fourier Transform Infrared Spectroscopy (FTIS), Pyrolysis Gas Chromatography (PGC), and Energy Dispersive X-Ray Microanalysis Combined with a Scanning Electron Microscope (SEM-EDX)*, 35 J. FORENSIC SCI. 281 (1990).

34. Solano, Gomez & Banon, *Incised Wound Margins Caused by Steel Blades. Scanning Electron Microscopy to Determine Wound Directions*, 43 FORENSIC SCI. INT'L 21 (1989) (most entrance edges have a lateral accessory tail which exit edges lack).

35. Our reviewer points out that in conjunction with computers, SEM can be used to enhance, measure, and identify images. Computer enhancement of images has received an immense amount of attention during the last decade. The technique has tremendous potential, but there are also pitfalls. Images can be so radically transformed that the viewer loses perspective and can no longer interpret the image. Our reviewer gives this example. If one takes a photomicrograph of a flat surface with some smooth depressions but the picture is rotated through an angle of 180 degrees, the viewer will see hills rather than depressions. Without additional information, it is impossible to determine solely from the photograph which is the "true" image; we are conditioned to interpreting variations of light and shadow as though illuminated from above, not from below. This problem

Although this list is somewhat lengthy, the list is certainly not exhaustive.

§ 25-2(C). Admissibility of SEM Evidence.

To date, there have been only a few reported cases dealing with SEM. The first case is *People v. Marx.*[36] There the California Court of Appeal upheld the admission of bitemark identification testimony by several prosecution experts, including Dr. Sognnaes. At trial, Dr. Sognnaes testified that he had used SEM to view the samples.[37] He stressed that he resorted to SEM because of its powerful magnifications and its "unusual three-dimensional effect."[38] Without any extended analysis, the court sanctioned the admission of this testimony.

The second case is *People v. Palmer,*[39] also decided by the California Court of Appeal. In this case, criminalist Wilkaan Fong testified to the identification of gunshot residue, based on SEM viewing of particles on the defendant's right hand. As in *Marx,* the court sustained the admission of the SEM testimony. Although the court conceded that "[t]here are no reported cases dealing specifically with the admissibility of SEM for GSR particle analysis,"[40] it found that "[s]cientific journals have uniformly embraced this application ...."[41] The court reviewed some of the published studies dealing with the forensic application of SEM to GSR analysis and concluded that "there appears to be a unanimity of scientific opinion regarding the value and reliability of the SEM for GSR particle analysis."

Still another case is *State v. Allen.*[42] In *Allen,* the defendant was charged with a burglary and safecracking. In the process of breaking into the safe, the burglar left metal shavings of iron and manganese at the crime scene. The police found metal shavings on the defendant's shoes and gloves. An F.B.I. expert used SEM to compare the shavings on the defendant's clothing with the shavings left at the crime scene and testified that the two sets of shavings matched.

Although the prosecution can use *Marx, Palmer,* and *Allen* as precedent for the admission of SEM evidence, those cases have limited precedential value.

---

can be eliminated by taking a stereoscopic pair of pictures. H. ANDREWS & B. HUNT, DIGITAL IMAGE RESTORATION (1977); K. CASTLEMAN, DIGITAL IMAGE PROCESSING (1979); R. GONZALEZ & P. WINTZ, DIGITAL IMAGE PROCESSING (1977); Hawkes, Ottensmeyer, Saxton & Rosenfeld, *Image and Signal Processing in Electron Microscopy, in* SCANNING ELECTRON MICROSCOPY Supplement 2 (1988); W. PRATT, DIGITAL IMAGE PROCESSING (1978); A. ROSENFELD & A. KAK, DIGITAL PICTURE PROCESSING (2d ed. 1982).

36. 54 Cal. App. 3d 100, 126 Cal. Rptr. 350 (1975). *See also* Eltech Sys. Corp. v. PPG Indus., 710 F. Supp. 622, 629 n.4 (W.D. La. 1988), *aff'd,* 903 F.2d 805 (Fed. Cir. 1990).

37. 54 Cal.App.3d at 111 n.16, 126 Cal. Rptr. at 356 n.16.

38. *Id.*

39. 80 Cal. App. 3d 239, 145 Cal. Rptr. 466 (1978).

40. *Id.* at 252, 145 Cal. Rptr. at 472.

41. *Id.*

42. Slip op., Mar. 16, 1984, Tenn. Cr. App. (available onLEXIS).

None of the cases is a blanket approval of all SEM evidence; rather, they approve the admission of evidence of only particular SEM applications. Their limited precedential value is partially a product of the *Frye* test. Most jurisdictions still follow the rule enunciated in *Frye v. United States:*[43] To lay the foundation for scientific evidence, the proponent must establish that the technique has gained general acceptance within the relevant scientific field.[44]

The courts have construed *Frye* as requiring that the proponent prove general acceptance of each particular application of a scientific instrument. For example, before 1972, the Missouri courts had accepted evidence of the application of neutron activation analysis to hair.[45] Yet, in that year, the court refused to sustain the admission of evidence of the application of NAA to blood analysis.[46] The court reasoned that although there had been proof of general acceptance in the previous cases, there had been no proof of the general acceptance of NAA's application to blood analysis. Similarly, in *People v. Palmer,* the court continually referred to the application of SEM to GSR analysis.

§ 25-2(D). Weight of SEM Evidence.

Even if a court admits the SEM evidence, the defense can resort to weight attacks. The attack depends on whether the prosecutor is offering pure SEM evidence or evidence produced by an SEM/EDX instrument, a device with the additional capability of energy dispersive X-ray analysis.

Assume the former. In this case, the microscopist will testify that he viewed the micrograph and that the image displayed "appeared" to be gunshot residue or a type of paint.[47] The analyst might "arbitrarily" choose a certain number of points of similarity as a criterion for identification;[48] but there is no hard data dictating that number. The analyst's evaluation of an SEM micrograph is similar to the visual analysis of a firearm or toolmark impression. There is an element of subjectivity. To date, there has been no experimental verification of the need for a particular number of points of similarity, and the individual analyst's interpretive standards are experimental. Some advanced SEM instruments have storage capacity; therefore, on split screen, the SEM can produce micrographs of the unknown and knowns previously analyzed and stored. When the microscopist uses SEM with storage capability, the opinion will be more reliable. However,

---

43. 293 F. 1013 (D.C. Cir. 1923). For a discussion of *Frye,* see Chapter 1.

44. *Recent Development*, 64 CORNELL L. REV. 875, 878-79 (1979); Note, *Changing of the Standard for the Admission of Novel Scientific Evidence: State v. Williams*, 40 OHIO ST. L.J. 757, 769 (1979).

45. State v. Stout, 478 S.W.2d 368, 369 (Mo. 1972).

46. *Id.*

47. *E.g.,* People v. Palmer, 80 Cal. App. 3d 239, 250, 145 Cal. Rptr. 466, 471 (1978).

48. Grove, Judd & Horn, *Evaluation of SEM Potential in the Examination of Shotgun and Rifle Firing Pin Impressions*, 19 J. FORENSIC SCI. 441, 442 (1974).

even then there is an element of subjectivity in the witness's comparison of the two micrographs.

Alternatively, assume that the microscopist uses an SEM/EDX instrument. Subsection 25-2(A) pointed out that the scan of the sample causes X-ray emissions as well as secondary electron emissions. The X-rays emitted by each chemical element have a distinct energy and wavelength. An SEM/EDX also produces an analysis of the sample's elemental composition.[49]

The EDX attachment permits a more reliable determination of the sample's generic identity; the analyst can testify that the sample both appeared to be GSR and had the chemical composition of GSR. However, even this testimony is assailable. As the *Palmer* court indicated, the analyst must not only testify that the sample had the right chemical composition. The analyst must add that the levels of lead, barium, and antimony exceed "handblank" values: the levels that the subject may accumulate simply by industrial or occupational exposure to the same chemicals.[50] This is the same problem encountered in the early 1970s when prosecutors began resorting to NAA evidence. To properly determine the significance of the finding, the analyst needs a comparative data base — statistics showing the lead, barium, and antimony levels an innocent person might accumulate on his person in the routine course of his work.

There are other weight problems that arise even when the SEM has an EDX attachment. Specimens analyzed by SEM must ordinarily be conductive, although some new SEMs do not require conductive samples. If the samples are not conductive, the primary beam may deposit a static electric charge on the specimen. Such a charge can distort both the visual display and the compositional analysis. Some objects such as metal are naturally conductive. However, the analyst must coat other specimens with metal to make them conductive. The analyst usually employs a thin coating or plating of gold to drain off any charge

49. People v. Palmer, 80 Cal. App. 3d 239, 251, 145 Cal. Rptr. 466, 471 (1978). *See* Gettleman, Carr & Herschaft, *Identification of a Foreign Body Using Energy Dispersive X-Ray Analysis*, 26 J. Forensic Sci. 58 (1981); Tassa, Leist & Steinberg, *Characterization of Gunshot Residues by X-Ray Diffraction*, 27 J. Forensic Sci. 677 (1982); Tillman, *Automated Gunshot Residue Particle Search and Characterization*, 32 J. Forensic Sci. 62 (1987) ("SEM-EDX ... is potentially superior because it characterizes individual GSR particles both morphologically and elementally"). SEM/EDX analysis can be time-consuming; testing some samples can require eight hours. *Id.* at 62-63. However, researchers are attempting to perfect an automated SEM/EDX system. *Id.* at 63. Our reviewer points out that X-rays directly yield information only about the sample's elemental composition, not its chemical composition. In some cases, the analyst can infer how the elements are combined to form a chemical compound; but the chemical composition cannot be determined unequivocally. Platek, Ranieri & Wolnik, *A False Report of Product Tampering Involving a Rodent and Soft Drink Can: Light Microscopy, Image Analysis and Scanning Electron Microscopy/Energy Dispersive X-Ray Analysis*, 42 J. Forensic Sci. 1171 (1997).

50. 80 Cal. App. 3d 239, 253, 145 Cal. Rptr. 466, 472 (1978).

deposited on the specimen. Carbon can be used in lieu of gold. The use of carbon is standard when EDX analysis is performed.

Even if the analyst properly coats the specimen, the SEM/EDX technique has limitations. Unlike the TEM, SEM does not explore the interior of the sample to any great extent. The primary beam penetrates into the specimen, but the penetration is not deep. Thus, for all practical purposes, the SEM views only the surface of the specimen, and EDX analyzes only the elements closest to the surface. SEM/EDX does not enable the analyst to determine whether the interior of the sample is homogeneous.[51] Suppose, for instance, that an object is chrome-plated. Unless the analyst uses another technique to analyze the interior of the sample, he may reach an erroneous conclusion about the nature of the sample.

§ 25-3. Atomic Absorption Spectrometry (AAS).*

During the 1970s, neutron activation analysis (NAA) attracted much attention. In the 1980s, SEM promises to garner almost as much publicity. Unfortunately, the notoriety of these techniques sometimes obscures the utility of other, less well known, instrumental techniques. This section discusses one such technique, atomic absorption spectrometry (AAS).

Despite its relative obscurity, AAS has surfaced in several cases. For example, AAS has been employed to analyze waste in environmental lawsuits.[52] Prosecutors and defense counsel have resorted to AAS in criminal cases in federal and state courts.[53] The atomic absorption analysis can be "[t]he most damaging evidence" against the defendant.[54]

---

51. J. GOLDSTEIN & H. YAKOWITZ, *supra* note 5, at 445.

*Based in part on Imwinkelried, *Atomic Absorption Spectrometry*, THE CHAMPION, Sept.-Oct. 1982, at 10. Reprinted with permission of the National Association of Criminal Defense Lawyers.

52. United States v. Rohm & Haas Co., 353 F. Supp. 993 (S.D. Tex. 1973), *modified,* 500 F.2d 167 (5th Cir. 1974), *cert. denied,* 420 U.S. 962 (1975). *See also* Ezell v. General Motors Corp., 446 So. 2d 954 (La. App. 1984).

53. United States v. Stifel, 433 F.2d 431 (6th Cir. 1970), *cert. denied,* 401 U.S. 994 (1971); Dolvin v. State, 391 So. 2d 666, 676 (Ala. Crim. App. 1979), *aff'd,* 391 So. 2d 677 (Ala. 1980); Chatom v. State, 348 So. 2d 828 (Ala. Crim. App. 1976), *rev'd on other grounds,* 348 So. 2d 838 (Ala. 1977); Bell v. State, 339 So. 2d 96 (Ala. Crim. App. 1976); People v. Ellison, 100 Ill. App. 3d 282, 55 Ill. Dec. 733, 426 N.E.2d 1058 (1981); People v. Hanei, 81 Ill. App. 3d 690, 38 Ill. Dec. 1, 403 N.E.2d 16 (1980), *cert. denied,* 450 U.S. 927 (1981); Resnover v. State, 460 N.E.2d 922 (Ind.), *cert. denied,* 469 U.S. 873 (1984); State v. Shapiro, 431 So. 2d 372 (La. 1982); State v. Chatman, 156 N.J. Super. 35, 383 A.2d 440, *cert. denied,* 79 N.J. 467, 401 A.2d 223 (1978); State v. Sparks, 297 N.C. 314, 255 S.E.2d 373 (1979); State v. Crowder, 285 N.C. 42, 203 S.E.2d 38 (1974), *vacated in part,* 428 U.S. 903 (1976); Commonwealth v. Glass, 495 Pa. 405, 434 A.2d 707 (1981), *cert. denied,* 456 U.S. 932 (1982); Jones v. State, 70 Wis. 2d 41, 233 N.W.2d 430 (1975).

54. Chatom v. State, 348 So. 2d 828, 831 (Ala. Crim. App. 1976), *rev'd,* 348 So. 2d 838 (Ala. 1977).

§ 25-3(A). AAS Technique.

The Theory

The principle underlying the AAS technique is that the atoms of each chemical element absorb light selectively, that is, at a wavelength peculiar to the element.[55] The element's electrons can absorb only a certain quantum of energy and then move to a higher orbit or energy level.[56] The difference between the element's excited and ground (non-excited) states determines the wavelength of the light the element can absorb.[57] "The absorption is specific, since it takes place only when the irradiation wavelength is exactly equal to the difference in energies of the excited and ground states."[58]

The Instrument

The instrument implementing the theory is called an atomic absorption spectrometer. It was developed in 1955 by an Australian chemist, A. Walsh, as a means of elemental analysis.[59] The AA spectrometer is a common tool in metals testing laboratories.[60]

As previously stated, the technique is based on the theory that each chemical element will absorb only light of a peculiar wavelength. The instrument includes as one of its components a radiation source to generate the light to be absorbed.[61] If the purpose of the test is to detect copper, the analyst uses a hollow-cathode lamp that emits radiation at the wavelength unique to copper.[62] Or if the analyst is attempting to determine whether the unknown contains nickel, he uses a nickel lamp.[63]

There are two types of atomic absorption instruments. The first, conventional atomic absorption spectrometer (AAS), uses a hot flame to atomize the sample, that is, to vaporize the sample into free atoms.[64] The light is aimed at and passed

55. Midkiff, *Detection of Gunshot Residues: Modern Solutions for an Old Problem*, 3 J. POLICE SCI. & ADMIN. 77, 80 (1975).

56. Watkins & Watkins, *Identification of Substances by Instrumental Analysis*, 22 AM. JUR. PROOF OF FACTS 385, 477 (1969).

57. Krishnan, *Neutron Activation Analysis and Atomic Absorption Spectrometry*, *in* SCIENTIFIC AND EXPERT EVIDENCE, 279, 287 (2d ed. 1981).

58. *Id.*

59. Watkins & Watkins, *supra* note 56, at 476.

60. *E.g.*, People v. Hanei, 81 Ill. App. 3d 690, 694, 38 Ill. Dec. 1, 403 N.E.2d 16, 20 (1980), *cert. denied*, 450 U.S. 927 (1981).

61. Watkins & Watkins, *supra* note 56, at 478.

62. *Id.*

63. *Id.*

64. Midkiff, *supra* note 55, at 80.

through the flame.[65] If the sample contains the substance being tested for, its free atoms will absorb the light of appropriate wavelength.[66]

The second type of instrument is a flameless atomic absorption spectrometer (FAAS).[67] Like AAS, FAAS is a destructive technique.[68] Instead of a flame to atomize the sample, FAAS relies on a heated metal strip or carbon rod for atomizing.[69] FAAS instruments with electrically heated graphite tube atomizers are now common.[70] The flameless atomizer vaporizes the sample to form an atomic cloud.[71] The light beam passes through the cloud. FAAS has proven to be more sensitive than AAS and can be used to analyze smaller samples.[72]

Atomic absorption instruments yield both qualitative and quantitative analyses.[73] The instrument's capacity for qualitative analysis is evident. On each test, the analyst uses a particular radiation source generating light of a wavelength peculiar to the suspected chemical element; the analyst selects the hollow-cathode radiation tube designed to create that light.[74] Thus, the sample's absorption of that light is a specific test for the presence of the chemical element.[75]

The technique also has a capability for quantitative analysis.[76] The analyst usually prepares three standard solutions of the sample material but of varying concentrations of the suspected element.[77] The analyst tests each solution and notes the absorption. On older instruments, the absorbency (the percentage of absorption) is indicated by the deflection of a needle on a scale marked from 0 to 100 percent. Newer models display the percentage in illuminated digits.[78] The analyst uses the figures for the three standard solutions to plot a calibrated curve.[79] After testing the standard solutions, the analyst tests the unknown and then compares the unknown's absorbency with the curve and thereby determines the quantity.

---

65. *Id.*

66. *Id.*

67. *Id.* at 81.

68. Watkins & Watkins, *supra* note 56, at 482.

69. Midkiff, *supra* note 55, at 81.

70. *Id.*

71. State v. Chatman, 156 N.J. Super. 35, 38, 383 A.2d 440, 441, *cert. denied,* 79 N.J. 467, 401 A.2d 224 (1978).

72. Midkiff, *supra* note 55, at 81.

73. Watkins & Watkins, *supra* note 56, at 481.

74. *Id.*

75. *Id.*

76. *Id.*

77. *Id.*

78. *Id.* at 482.

79. *Id.* at 481.

Sample Preparation

The initial step in sample preparation is collecting the sample at the crime scene. *State v. Chatman*[80] describes the collection process. In *Chatman,* the court states briefly that the analyst wipes the test area "with cotton swabs saturated with a nitric acid solution."[81] In contrast, *State v. Crowder*[82] discusses the collection process in greater depth; the court quotes the instructions prepared by the North Carolina State Bureau of Investigation for collecting samples of gunshot residue:

> Instructions for collecting gunshot residue. North Carolina State Bureau of Investigation, Raleigh, North Carolina. The following procedure should be used to swab surfaces suspected of containing gunshot residue with the kit supplied by the North Carolina State Bureau of Investigation Chemical Laboratory.
>
> Number 1. Thoroughly wash your hands with soap and water and dry them with a clean towel prior to doing the wiping for gunshot residue.
>
> Number 2. Remove one of the cotton swabs from the plastic zip-lock bag and moisten it with four drops of two percent hydrochloric acid.
>
> Number 3. Use the moistened swab and thoroughly swab the back of the left hand including the back of the fingers.
>
> Number 4. Place the used swab into one of the clean zip-lock plastic bags. Seal the bag and label it in the following manner: a. Location of wiping (left back, right palm, etc.); b. name of suspect; c. date of wiping; d. your identification mark.
>
> Number 5. Using three additional swabs, moisten each one individually as in Step 2 and swab the left palm, right back, and right palm, respectively as in Step 3. These swabs should be placed in separate zip-lock bags and treated as in Step 4.
>
> Note: If at any time during the wiping procedure the hand of the wiper should come in contact with the cotton end of the swab or the suspect's hands, the hands should be thoroughly washed in soap and water before the next swab is used. In cases where the same person is wiping the hands of more than one suspect, it is necessary to wash your hands between each person.
>
> Number 6. Moisten one of the swabs with four drops of two percent hydrochloric acid and immediately place it in a separate zip-lock plastic bag. This bag should be labeled "control" as the swab will be analyzed to determine the purity of the materials used to collect the gunshot residue.

---

80. 156 N.J. Super. 35, 37, 383 A.2d 440, 441, *cert. denied,* 79 N.J. 467, 401 A.2d 224 (1978).
81. *Id.*
82. 285 N.C. 42, 203 S.E.2d 38 (1974), *vacated in part,* 428 U.S. 903 (1976).

> Number 7. Swab the inside of the cartridge casing (if available) with a cotton swab moistened with four drops of two percent hydrochloric acid and handle it as in Step 4. This step is particularly important since some types of ammunition do not contain antimony in their primer.
>
> Note: It is advisable not to handle the cartridge casing until the other wipings have been completed.
>
> When weapons and/or fired cartridge casings are being submitted to the firearms laboratory, do not follow Step 7. In these cases, the chemical laboratory will make a cartridge case wiping in the firearms laboratory. Indicate on the evidence sheet when this evidence has been submitted to the firearms laboratory.
>
> Number 8. Fill out the attached evidence sheets completely and enclose them in the mailing envelope with the wipings. The information on these sheets should include the type of weapon involved, the caliber and manufacturer of the ammunition, the condition of the weapon, and the amount of time elapsed between the firing of weapon and the wiping of the suspect's hands.
>
> Number 9. Seal all of the plastic bags used in the self-addressed envelope and mail them by first class mail. The envelope should be marked on the outside "Attention Chemical Laboratory — Gunshot Residue."
>
> Number 10. An official report will be mailed to the requesting officer within a reasonable period of time. If rush results are needed, this should be indicated by a personal telephone call to the chemical laboratory.

After the sample is collected and delivered to the laboratory, the analyst prepares the sample for insertion into the spectrometer. Liquid samples present no difficulty.[83] Solid material can be tested if the material can be dissolved in solvent.[84] The Perkin-Elmer Corporation has developed a technique for analyzing solids, such as ores, that are not readily soluble.[85] The technique involves mixing the solid with powder before atomizing the sample.[86] With this development, a wide range of liquids, soluble solids, and insoluble materials can now be analyzed in the spectrometer.[87] The analyst can use atomic absorption technology to test more than 66 metallic elements.[88]

---

83. Watkins & Watkins, *supra* note 56, at 483.
84. *Id.* at 480.
85. *Id.*
86. *Id.*
87. *Id.*
88. *Id.* at 118 (Supp. 1991).

§ 25-3(B). Forensic Applications.

The most commented-on application of AAS is gunshot residue analysis (GSR).[89] The primers of many bullets contain the elements antimony, barium, and lead. These elements usually deposit on a person's hand when a firearm is discharged as a result of blow-back from the muzzle, leakage around the cylinder of a revolver, or venting of an automatic.[90] AAS can identify those elements and measure the quantity in which they are present. With that information, AAS can help the analyst make a number of determinations:

First, whether there is gunshot residue on the person's hands. To make this determination, the analyst must compare the quantities of antimony, barium, and lead present with "handblank" values, the quantities that the person might innocently accumulate on his hand through environmental or occupational exposure.

Second, whether the residue was deposited by a handgun or longarm. Handguns tend to deposit more residue than longarms.[91]

Third, whether the person discharged a weapon or merely held the weapon. The distribution patterns differ. In a discharge there usually is more residue on the back of the firing hand while a person who merely handled a firearm ordinarily has more residue on his palm.[92]

Fourth, how far the firearm was from the target at the time of discharge. Analysts are now using AAS to aid in firing distance determinations.[93] The analyst employs AAS to analyze the barium and antimony in the primer particles around bullet entrance holes.[94] The quantity and distribution of the particles depend on the firing distance.

For the last three determinations, our reviewer adds a caveat. He emphasizes that it is important that the skin area swabbed (in terms of square inches) is nearly the same for all samples being compared.

Fifth, which company manufactured the bullet. In the early 1970s, Brunelle, Hoffman, and Snow reported the results of their research with .38 Special cartridges produced by the three leading domestic manufacturers (Winchester,

---

89. Sotera & Kahn, *Background Correction in AAS*, 14 AM. LAB. 100 (Nov. 1982). *See* People v. Ellison, 100 Ill. App. 3d 282, 426 N.E.2d 1058 (1981); State v. Shapiro, 431 So. 2d 372 (La. 1982).

90. Midkiff, *supra* note 55, at 77.

91. Krishnan, *Detection of Gunshot Residues on the Hands by the Trace Element Analysis*, SCIENTIFIC AND EXPERT EVIDENCE 315, 339 (2d ed. 1981).

92. *Id.* at 332-34.

93. Revreby, *Analysis of Long-Range Bullet Entrance Holes by Atomic Absorption Spectrophotometry and Scanning Electron Microscopy*, 27 J. FORENSIC SCI. 92 (1982).

94. *Id.*

Federal, and Remington).[95] Although AAS does not yield a conclusive identification, AAS of the antimony present is strong evidence of the identity of the manufacturer.[96]

Sixth, which batch of production the bullet came from. A batch is usually defined as one day of production by a particular manufacturer. As in the case of the identification of the manufacturer, the batch identification is not positive. However, Brunelle, Hoffman, and Snow were able to detect batch-to-batch differences with AAS.[97]

Although most reported studies deal with gunshot residue analysis, AAS has numerous other potential uses.[98] For instance, AAS is useful in poisoning cases.[99] In *People v. Hanei,*[100] AAS was used to unmask a case of thallium poisoning. AAS has also been adapted to the examination of soil, paints, and counterfeit money.[101]

§ 25-3(C). Comparison With Other Techniques.

AAS is superior to several, more widely known, techniques. It has distinct advantages over standard microscopic techniques. AAS is far superior when the questioned bullet has been mutilated by impact.[102] It is virtually impossible to compare a mutilated bullet by microscopic techniques.[103] In contrast, comparative AAS analysis of a test bullet with a mutilated, questioned bullet can yield valuable data.[104]

Similarly, AAS compares favorably with the dermal nitrate or paraffin test.[105] That test became popular during the 1930s as a technique for determining whether a person had recently discharged a firearm.[106] The analyst treated the back of the suspected firing hand with melted paraffin. As the paraffin cooled, it formed a cast or lift. The analyst peeled the cast away and sprayed it with diphenylamine-sulfuric acid or diphenyl-benzidine solution.[107] The theory was

95. Brunelle, Hoffman & Snow, *Comparison of Elemental Composition of Pistol Bullets by Atomic Absorption: Preliminary Study*, 53 J. Assoc. Off. Anal. Chem. 470 (1970).

96. *Id.* at 472.

97. *Id.*

98. Ramirez-Munoz, *Potentialities and Applications of Atomic Absorption Photometry in Criminology*, 5 Forensic Sci. Soc'y J. 151 (1967).

99. Watkins & Watkins, *supra* note 56, at 118-19 (Supp. 1991).

100. 81 Ill. App. 3d 690, 38 Ill. Dec. 1, 403 N.E.2d 16 (1980), *cert. denied,* 450 U.S. 927 (1981).

101. Watkins & Watkins, *supra* note 56, at 119-28 (Supp. 1991).

102. Brunelle, Hoffman & Snow, *supra* note 95, at 470.

103. *Id.*

104. *Id.*

105. Midkiff, *supra* note 55,, at 77.

106. *Id.*

107. *Id.*

that if the spraying developed dark blue spots, the test was positive for gunpowder nitrates.[108] However, as early as 1935, the F.B.I. cautioned that the test was not specific and that many substances other than gunpowder nitrates could produce a positive test.[109] The evidence of the test's unreliability steadily mounted; and as more courts held the test inadmissible, most law enforcement agencies abandoned the test.[110] AAS is not as prone to false positives as the dermal nitrate test.[111]

The growing rejection of the dermal nitrate test led to the emergence of the Harrison-Gilroy colorimetric test.[112] Like AAS, the Harrison-Gilroy test is designed to detect antimony, barium, and lead on the shooter's hands. The analyst swabs the hands with a cloth moistened with dilute hydrochloric acid. The analyst applies triphenylmethylarsonium iodide to the swab to detect any antimony present and employs sodium rhodizonate to identify barium and lead.[113] Unfortunately, like the dermal nitrate test, Harrison-Gilroy is subject to false positives.[114] The test is also subject to false negatives. The colorimetric reagents used in the test are relatively insensitive; they cannot detect the low concentrations of the elements found in many firing cases.[115] The technique's sensitivity is inferior to that of AAS.[116]

For certain elements, the sensitivity of AAS is also better than that of emission spectroscopy.[117] Researchers have compared the detection limits of the two techniques for numerous elements.[118] They have found that AAS has greater sensitivity for arsenic, thulium, vanadium, gallium, molybdenum, and zirconium.[119]

One of the few techniques that surpasses AAS is neutron activation analysis (NAA).[120] While AAS is more sensitive than either the Harrison-Gilroy test or emission spectrometry, the sensitivity of NAA exceeds that of AAS. In one court's words, NAA has "considerably higher sensitivity."[121] Just as they

---

108. *Id.*

109. *Id.*

110. *Id.* at 77-78.

111. *Id.* at 80-82.

112. *Id.* at 78.

113. *Id.*

114. Krishnan, *supra* note 91, at 316.

115. Midkiff, *supra* note 55, at 78.

116. *Id.*

117. Watkins & Watkins, *supra* note 56, at 118 (Supp. 1991).

118. *Id.*

119. *Id.*

120. Labowitz, *Instrumental Analysis: A Comparison of Neutron Activation Analysis and Atomic Absorption*, 4 Forensic Sci. Dig. 106 (1977).

121. Chatom v. State, 348 So. 2d 828, 833 (Ala. Crim. App. 1976), *rev'd,* 348 So. 2d 838 (Ala. 1977).

compared the detection limits of emission of spectroscopy and AAS, the researchers have matched AAS against NAA.[122] AAS is more sensitive for silver, zinc, and chromium, but NAA is superior for antimony, arsenic, and tin.[123] Moreover, NAA permits simultaneous multielement analysis.[124] AAS generally lacks that capability.[125] In AAS, the instrument mounts only one cathode lamp at a time, and each lamp tests solely for one element.

Nevertheless, a strong case can be made for AAS. The analyst can conduct an AAS test more quickly than an NAA test. An AAS test requires only a few minutes.[126] Even in rush cases, it often takes three days to complete an NAA test.[127] In addition, AAS tests are less expensive than NAA tests.[128]

§ 25-3(D). Admissibility and Weight of AAS Evidence.

As in the case of all scientific evidence, the proponent must lay a proper foundation for admission. The opponent has available admissibility and weight attacks.

The Witness's Qualifications

The opponent's first point of attack is the alleged expertise of the witness: Is that witness qualified to conduct and evaluate the AAS test? The opponent may "thoroughly question the expert concerning his training and experience...."[129]

The courts have been relatively liberal in holding witnesses qualified to conduct and interpret AAS tests. In *State v. Crowder*[130] the witness was "a forensic chemist ... with a Bachelor of Science Degree ... and a Master of Science Degree ... and with 50 semester hours of chemistry with major emphasis of study in the area of micro-biology and bio-chemistry." In *People v. Hanei,*[131] the court simply described the witness as "a chemist."

However, perhaps the best illustration of the courts' liberality is *State v. Chatman.*[132] Over defense objection, the trial court admitted prosecution evidence

---

122. Watkins & Watkins, *supra* note 56, at 126 (Supp. 1991).

123. *Id.*

124. Krishnan, *supra* note 91, at 322. *See also* State v. Noel, 303 N.J. Super. 435, 697 A.2d 157 (A.D. 1997) (upholding testimony about coupled plasma atomic emission spectroscopy analysis of lead bullets), *rev'd*, 157 N.J. 141, 723 A.2d 602 (1999).

125. *Id.*

126. Watkins & Watkins, *supra* note 56, at 477, 482.

127. Midkiff, *supra* note 55, at 80.

128. *Id.* at 82; Watkins & Watkins, *supra* note 56, at 395, 482.

129. Chatom v. State, 348 So. 2d 838, 841 (Ala. 1977).

130. 285 N.C. 42, 50, 203 S.E.2d 38, 44 (1974), *vacated in part,* 428 U.S. 903 (1976).

131. 81 Ill. App. 3d 690, 694, 38 Ill. Dec. 1, 5, 403 N.E.2d 16, 20 (1980), *cert. denied,* 450 U.S. 927 (1981).

132. 156 N.J. Super. 35, 383 A.2d 440, *cert. denied,* 79 N.J. 467, 401 A.2d 224 (1978).

of an AAS test, but precluded a defense witness from testifying to attack the manner in which the prosecution expert interpreted the result. The record indicated that the defense witness "had never performed this specific test. However, he stated that he had done extensive reading on the subject and was quite familiar with the problems surrounding its utilization through this reading and study."[133] The appellate court ruled that the trial court erred in rejecting the defense witness's testimony. The court declared that the defense witness had "the academic qualifications, the 'study without practice,' to permit his testimony on interpreting test results."[134]

Validity of the Technique

If the witness qualifies as an expert, the witness's testimony ordinarily proceeds in syllogistic fashion: a statement of the major premise (the general reliability of AAS); a description of the minor premise (the physical evidence subjected to AAS), and finally a statement of the conclusion (the expert's opinion).[135]

To establish the major premise, the proponent usually offers proof of both the technique's validity and its general acceptance within the relevant scientific community. The evidence of the validity of AAS analysis of gunshot residue in the reported cases provides the opponent with a surprisingly strong argument. In one leading Alabama case on AAS,[136] the prosecution expert gave the following testimony:

> Q. What is the accuracy percentage of this machine, of the test, in the last survey that you've made?
>
> A. I'm not certain, sir. On tests that I have run by myself where I know a gun has been fired, is that what you're asking? I would guess, sir, it's in the neighborhood of 75 to 80 percent of the time.[137]

The Supreme Court of Alabama reiterated that testimony in its 1977 decision, *Chatom v. State*.[138] The defense counsel pointed to the studies of the validity of polygraph that is routinely excluded and argued that "[t]he lie detector is better

---

133. *Id.* at 40, 383 A.2d at 442.

134. *Id.* at 41, 383 A.2d at 443.

135. Imwinkelried, *The "Bases" of Expert Testimony: The Syllogistic Structure of Scientific Testimony*, 67 N.C. L. REV. 1 (1988).

136. Chatom v. State, 348 So. 2d 828 (Ala. Crim. App. 1976), *rev'd on other grounds,* 348 So. 2d 838 (Ala. 1977).

137. *Id.* at 832.

138. 348 So. 2d 838, 840-41 (Ala. 1977).

than that."[139] Although the court rejected the argument, the more impressive statistics for polygraphy make the argument plausible.[140]

The proponent ordinarily presents proof of the test's general acceptance as well as its validity. The proponent offers this proof to comply with the *Frye* test:[141] In the majority of jurisdictions, both federal and state, to be admissible, a scientific technique must have gained general acceptance within the relevant scientific field.[142] Although the task of proving general acceptance can be burdensome, AAS should be able to pass muster. There is now voluminous technical literature on AAS.[143] Moreover, there are now many cases admitting AAS evidence.[144] Cumulatively, the technical literature and case law probably suffice to establish the general acceptance of AAS.

Material Subjected to AAS Test

The proponent must also establish the minor premise, namely, the identification of the physical evidence the AAS technique is applied to. The identification of the physical evidence usually presents two distinct problems.

One problem is the identification of the object on which the trace evidence is found. For example, in *People v. Hanei*[145] the suspected thallium poison was on a mortar and pestle owned by the defendant. The court demanded a chain of custody for the mortar and pestle as part of the foundation for the AAS evidence.[146]

The second problem is that the handling of the object can cause the loss of the trace evidence. For example, if a person has gunshot residue on his hands, the residue will gradually disappear in the course of normal activity such as rubbing one's hands.[147] The trace evidence can be "dislodged from the hands by washing, sweating, [and] rubbing on clothing or against other objects...."[148] Depending on the person's activity after discharging a weapon, the residue can remain as short a time as 30 minutes or as long a period as 24 hours.[149]

---

139. *Id.* at 840.

140. Abrams, *Polygraph Validity and Reliability: A Review*, 18 J. FORENSIC SCI. 313 (1973).

141. Frye v. United States, 293 F. 1013 (D.C. Cir. 1923).

142. Giannelli, *The Admissibility of Novel Scientific Evidence: Frye v. United States, a Half Century Later*, 80 COLUM. L. REV. 1197 (1980). For a discussion of *Frye, see* Chapter 1.

143. Watkins & Watkins, *supra* note 56, at 385, 515-16 (a listing of AAS technical references).

144. *E.g.,* State v. McCall, 698 S.W.2d 643 (Tenn. Crim. App. 1985).

145. 81 Ill. App. 3d 690, 38 Ill. Dec. 1, 403 N.E.2d 16 (1980), *cert. denied,* 450 U.S. 927 (1981).

146. *Id.* at 694, 403 N.E.2d at 20.

147. Chatom v. State, 348 So. 2d 828 (Ala. Crim. App. 1976), *rev'd on other grounds,* 348 So. 2d 838 (Ala. 1977).

148. Jones v. State, 70 Wis. 2d 41, 52, 233 N.W.2d 430, 436 (1975).

149. Krishnan, *supra* note 91, at 338. *See also* Chatom v. White, 858 F.2d 1479 (11th Cir. 1988) (The prosecution introduced the results of an atomic absorption test on a decedent's body to show

Ultimate Opinion

The first three elements of the foundation — the witness's qualifications, the reliability of the theory, and the integrity of the physical evidence — are points at which the opponent may attack the admissibility of AAS evidence. When we reach the final part of the expert's direct examination, the statement of the ultimate opinion, most of the available attacks are weight arguments.

In some cases, the defense counsel's primary concern is whether the technique yields false negatives. For example, in *Commonwealth v. Glass*[150] the defense contended that the decedent accidentally discharged a firearm. The prosecution introduced AAS evidence to show that there was so little antimony and barium on decedent's hands that he probably had not fired a weapon.

In a case such as *Glass* or a situation in which the defense claims that the decedent committed suicide, the defense must argue that AAS can fail to detect the primer elements even when they are present — a false negative. AAS has limited sensitivity. Moreover, interference is possible.[151] A common illustration of the interference problem is a sample that contains phosphates but is being analyzed for calcium.[152] Calcium and phosphates may form a stable compound, eliminating some of the calcium atoms necessary to absorb the radiation.[153]

In other situations, the defense counsel must attempt to establish a false positive. Even if antimony, barium, and lead are present in the appropriate quantities, their presence may not establish that the suspect discharged a firearm. As in the case of SEM/GSR analysis, the defense counsel has a number of possible arguments.

The defense counsel must make certain that all the characteristics of a positive test are present: All three elements (antimony, barium, and lead) are present; they are present in appropriate quantities, that is, quantities exceeding "handblank" values; the elements are located on the back of the suspected firing hand; and the quantities present on the back of the hand are greater than those on the person's palm.[154]

The defense counsel might attack the "handblank" standard the prosecution expert uses: Research on "handblank" values is ongoing. The defense may be

---

that the decedent had not fired a shot. The test was administered after the body was embalmed. The court held that the defense counsel's failure to object to the admission of the test results amounted to ineffective assistance of counsel), *cert. denied,* 489 U.S. 1054 (1989).

150. 495 Pa. 405, 434 A.2d 707 (1981), *cert. denied,* 456 U.S. 932 (1982).

151. Watkins & Watkins, *supra* note 56, at 480.

152. *Id.*

153. *Id.*

154. State v. Crowder, 285 N.C. 42, 53, 203 S.E.2d 38, 46 (1974), *vacated in part,* 428 U.S. 903 (1976).

able to find an expert willing to criticize the prosecution expert's standard as "antiquated and obsolete."[155]

Finally, the defense counsel can remind the jury that even when the prosecution expert uses the latest, most reliable "handblank" standards, the test is not conclusive. As previously noted, in *Chatom v. State*[156] the prosecution expert conceded that the "accuracy percentage" of AAS was "in the neighborhood of 75 to 80 percent."[157] AAS is a useful tool, but it is not infallible.

§ 25-4. Infrared (IR) Analysis.

As noted in Chapter 23, the IR spectrophotometer is one of the more specific tests for drug identification. IR technology has other applications.[158] For example, in environmental investigations, government inspectors use infrared photography.[159] Similarly, IR photography can be used in questioned document examination; an IR camera can detect words that were previously erased from a sheet of paper.[160] IR can be employed to analyze paint.[161] Law enforcement agencies use infrared equipment extensively in surveillance.[162] The equipment includes infrared night goggles[163] and scopes[164] patterned after weapons that the armed services developed for the Vietnam war. IR equipment can be employed to

---

155. Commonwealth v. Glass, 495 Pa. 405, 410, 434 A.2d 707, 709 (1981), *cert. denied,* 456 U.S. 932 (1982).

156. 348 So. 2d 828, 832 (Ala. Crim. App. 1976), *rev'd,* 348 So. 2d 838 (Ala. 1977).

157. *Id. See also Krishnan, Merits and Demerits of Forensic Activation Analysis When Compared to Other Trace Analysis Methods*, SCIENTIFIC AND EXPERT EVIDENCE 303, 312 (2d ed. 1981).

158. *E.g.*, Cantu & Prough, *Some Spectral Observations of Infrared Luminescence*, 33 J. FORENSIC SCI. 638 (1988).

159. Save Our Wetlands, Inc. v. Sands, 711 F.2d 634, 643 (5th Cir. 1983); Rademacher, *An Accurate Method of Focusing for Infrared Photography*, 33 J. FORENSIC SCI. 764 (1988).

160. United States v. Currier, 454 F.2d 835, 837 (1st Cir. 1972).

161. Suzuki, *Infrared Spectra of U.S. Automobile Original Topcoats (1974-89): II. Identification of Some Topcoat Inorganic Pigments Using an Extending Range (4000-220 cm) Fourier Transform Spectrometer*, 41 J. FORENSIC SCI. 393 (1996); Suzuki, *Infrared Spectra of U.S. Automobile Original Topcoats (1974-89): I. Differentiation and Identification Based on Acrylonitrile and Frerrocyanide C=N Stretching Absorptions*, 41 J. FORENSIC SCI. 376 (1996).

162. *E.g.,* United States v. Curtis, 562 F.2d 1153, 1155 (9th Cir. 1977), *cert. denied,* 439 U.S. 910 (1978); United States v. Coplen, 541 F.2d 211, 213 (9th Cir. 1976), *cert. denied,* 429 U.S. 1073 (1977).

163. United States v. Lace, 669 F.2d 46, 53 (2d Cir.), *cert. denied,* 459 U.S. 854 (1982).

164. United States v. Rivera, 654 F.2d 1048, 1049 (5th Cir. 1981), *vacated,* 684 F.2d 308 (5th Cir. 1982); United States v. Kerr, 876 F.2d 1440, 1442 (9th Cir. 1989) (the police employed an infrared sensing device to detect the exhaust produced by a combustion motor in a shed used to grow marijuana); *See also* State v. Noel, 303 N.J. Super. 435, 697 A.2d 157 (A.D. 1997) (upholding testimony about coupled plasma atomic emission spectroscopy analysis of lead bullets), *rev'd,* 157 N.J. 141, 723 A.2d 602 (1999).

detect emanations of suspiciously large amounts of heat, which suggest the use of growing lights to cultivate marijuana.[165]

165. United States v. Kuylo, 63 Cr.L. (BNA) 59 (9th Cir., Apr. 7, 1998) (the Agema 210 thermal imaging device); United States v. Cusumano, 83 F.3d 1247 (10th Cir. 1996); United States v. Depew, 992 F. Supp. 1209, 1211-12 (D. Mont. 1998) (the Agema Therma Vision 210 thermal imager); LaFollette v. Commonwealth, 915 S.W.2d 747 (Ky. 1996); Montana v. Siegal, 934 P.2d 176 (Mont. 1997); Commonwealth v. Gindlesperger, 706 A.2d 1216 (Pa. Super. 1997) (warrantless use of a thermal imaging (WASP) device to detect heat from a suspected marijuana growing operation in a residence was an unconstitutional search violative of the Fourth Amendment); Gibeaut, *High-Tech Heat Seeking: Warrantless Use of Detection Device Splits Appeals Courts*, 84 A.B.A. J. 34 (Aug. 1998) ("thermal imagers — devices similar to video cameras that can pick up infrared rays coming from structures and convert them to fuzzy visual images that distinguish warmer areas from cooler ones"); Colbridge, *Thermal Imaging: Much Heat but Little Light*, 66 F.B.I. LAW ENF. BULL. 18, 19, 21 (Dec. 1997) ("Most of the courts have decided targeting a building with a thermal imager is not a search under the Fourth Amendment"; however, there is a "minority view that the warrantless use of a thermal imager by the police violates the Fourth Amendment."); Laba, *If You Can't Stand the Heat, Get Out of the Drug Business: Thermal Imagers, Emerging Technologies, and the Fourth Amendment*, 84 CAL. L. REV. 1437 (1996); United States v. Robinson, 62 F.3d 1325 (11th Cir. 1995) (the use of an airborne thermal imaging device to scan a residence was not an unconstitutional search), *cert. denied*, 517 U.S. 1220 (1996); People v. Deutsch, 44 Cal. App. 4th 1224, 52 Cal. Rptr. 2d 366 (1996) (police must obtain a warrant before using a thermal imager to scan a residence; although the court acknowledged that "the bulk" of the case law is contra, the court opted for the view adopted by "[a] much smaller body of caselaw"); Wampler & Passanise, *The Increasing Used of Profiles and Prescribed Tactics in Drug Prosecutions*, 51 J. MO. BAR 288, 290 (Oct. 1995) (the instrument "measure[s] surface waste heat (excessive heat) emanating from a house. The heat is consistent with the use of halide lights to grow indoor marijuana;" FLIR devices "do not send beams or rays, but only detect temperature differences, showing little color for intense heat and darker shades of gray for cooler temperatures"); United States v. Ishmael, 48 F.3d 850 (5th Cir.), *cert. denied*, 516 U.S. 818 (1995) ; United States v. Myers, 46 F.3d 668 (7th Cir.), *cert. denied*, 516 U.S. 879 (1995); United States v. Zimmer, 14 F.3d 286 (6th Cir. 1994); United States v. Robertson, 39 F.3d 891 (8th Cir. 1994) (FLIR), *cert. denied*, 514 U.S. 1090 (1995); United States v. Pinson, 24 F.3d 1056 (8th Cir.), *cert. denied*, 513 U.S. 1057 (1994); United States v. Olson, 21 F.3d 847 (8th Cir.), *cert. denied*, 513 U.S. 888 (1994); United States v. Kyllo, 37 F.3d 526 (9th Cir. 1994) (the appellate court remanded to the trial judge to determine whether the scanning of the defendant's residence was a search within the purview of the fourth amendment); United States v. Ford, 34 F.3d 992, 995 n.3 (11th Cir. 1994) ("The majority of district courts and one other circuit that have considered this issue have held that thermal or infrared imagery is not an unreasonable search under the Fourth Amendment. Two district courts and one state supreme court have ruled that thermal imagery does constitute an unreasonable search"); United States v. Field, 855 F. Supp. 1518 (W.D. Wis. 1994) (obtaining a thermal image of a residence is a search, requiring a warrant); State v. Young, 123 Wash. 2d 173, 867 P.2d 593 (1994) (the warrantless infrared surveillance of the defendant's home constituted a search violative of the state constitution); State v. McKee, 181 Wis. 2d 354, 510 N.W.2d 807 (1993); Lappas, *Thermal Imaging and the Fourth Amendment*, 18 THE CHAMPION 14 (June 1994); United States v. Penny-Feeney, 773 F. Supp. 220 (D. Haw. 1991), *aff'd*, 984 F.2d 1053 (9th Cir. 1993); State v. Cramer, 851 P.2d 147 (Ariz. App. 1992); Steele, *Waste Heat and Garbage: The Legalization of Warrantless Infrared Searches*, 29 CRIM. L. BULL. 19 (Jan./Feb. 1993).

One of the most important types of infrared surveillance equipment is IR remote sensing.[166] IR sensing has great utility in the enforcement of environmental laws; IR equipment can enable an investigator to detect the release of pollution or changes in vegetation that would not be apparent from ordinary aerial photographs.[167] The military also employs IR remote sensing. The military adaptation of the equipment is known as FLIR (forward-looking infrared).[168] FLIR is a thermal imaging system. An enemy plane radiates heat in the form of photons, and FLIR detects and counts the photons radiated. FLIR then converts the photon count into an image on a screen.[169] After the United States Navy developed FLIR, law enforcement authorities began installing FLIR in planes, especially U.S. Customs aircraft conducting border surveillance.[170] The authorities use FLIR to track planes suspected of illegally importing contraband drugs into the United States.

FLIR has been used extensively.[171] However, in only one case has the government relied primarily on FLIR to identify the plane that flew in the

---

166. *See generally* Latin, Tannehill & White, *Remote Sensing Evidence and Environmental Law*, 64 CALIF. L. REV. 1300 (1976); New scanning technologies are being developed. Rovella, "*Smart" Metal Detectors*, NAT'L L.J., Aug. 25, 1997, at A6. They could be used for several purposes, including scanning persons entering courthouses. The technologies include magnetic gradient measuring, back-scattered X-ray imaging, and passive millimeter wave imaging. Hansen, *No Place to Hide*, 83 A.B.A. J. 44, 47 (Aug. 1997). In part, the advent of the new technologies is a result of funding by the United States Department of Justice's Concealed Weapon Detection Initiative. Dery, *Remote Frisking Down to the Skin: Government Searching Technology Powerful Enough to Locate Holes in Fourth Amendment Fundamentals*, 30 CREIGHTON L. REV. 353, 355 (1997). Some of the new instruments monitor persons for concealed weapons at fixed locations such as courthouse entrances while others can be used in the field. *Id.* at 355-56. The latter type of technology is illustrated by Millivision, developed by Millitech Corporation of South Deerfield, Massachusetts. The system "relies on the fact that the human body ... will 'naturally emit a broad spectrum of electromagnetic radiation.'" *Id.* at 356. For that reason, "the human body glows at the millimeter wave length level while most metallic and non-metallic objects do not." Consequently, "when the operator points their Millivision camera at a person, any weapons concealed under the individual's clothing are silhouetted against the glowing body." The instrument can detect metallic and plastic objects. *Id.* at 357. *See also* Jaynes, *Effective Use of Remote Sensing Products in Litigation Proceedings*, AM. SOC'Y PHOTOGRAMMETRY, 1983 Fall Convention 457-66 (1984).

167. Osterhoudt, *Remote Identification by Forward-Looking-Infrared: A Scientific Challenge*, P.L.I. NEWS (Nov. 21, 1977).

168. *Id.*

169. *Id. See also* United States v. Penny-Feeney, 773 F. Supp. 220 (D. Haw. 1991) (FLIR is "a passive, non-intrusive instrument that detects differences in temperature on the surface of objects being observed. It does not send any beams or rays into the area on which it is fixed or in any way penetrate structures within that area. The direction of the FLIR at objects in the absence of sunlight shows man-made heat sources on those objects as shading from white for intense heat to shades of gray for cooler temperatures"), *aff'd*, 984 F.2d 1053 (9th Cir. 1993).

170. *See* Osterhoudt, *supra* note 167.

171. United States v. Johns, 734 F.2d 657, 659 (11th Cir. 1984); United States v. Porter, 701 F.2d 1158, 1160 (6th Cir.), *cert. denied*, 464 U.S. 1007 (1983); United States v. Stone, 659 F.2d

contraband drugs. In that case, *United States v. Kilgus,*[172] the defense challenged the admissibility of the evidence to identify a particular plane. The defense presented expert testimony that in the current state of the art, FLIR imaging cannot distinguish between particular planes. FLIR imaging can differentiate between a plane and a boat or even between a DC-3 and a Lear jet — generic identification.[173] However, "the unrebutted testimony of the defense's expert was that the FLIR is not a generally accepted technique among the scientific community for the unique identification of remote objects."[174] Other courts,[175] including the Supreme Court,[176] have approvingly cited *Kilgus.*

Another IR technique is Diffuse Reflectance Infrared Fourier Transform Spectroscopy (DRIFTS) developed by Fuller and Griffiths.[177] The reflectance method is more sensitive than normal IR analysis using transmission through a pellet.[178] Some researchers report "a tenfold increase" in band intensity.[179] Before 1976, there was little research with DRIFTS because the equipment was not commercially available.[180] However, a good deal of experimentation is now in progress. The researchers are exploring the forensic potential of DRIFTS. DRIFTS seems well-suited for the analysis of tablets, capsules, powders,[181] and

569, 571 (5th Cir. 1981); United States v. Montgomery, 620 F.2d 753, 755 (10th Cir.), *cert. denied,* 449 U.S. 882 (1980); United States v. Young, 535 F.2d 484, 485 (9th Cir. 1976), *cert. denied,* 429 U.S. 999 (1976); United States v. Penny-Feeney, 773 F. Supp. 220 (D. Haw. 1991), *aff'd,* 984 F.2d 1053 (9th Cir. 1993).

172. 571 F.2d 508 (9th Cir., 1978); 19 SANTA CLARA L. REV. 491 (1979).

173. United States v. Kilgus, 571 F.2d 508, 510 (9th Cir. 1978); United States v. Sanchez, 829 F.2d 757 (9th Cir. 1987).

174. *Id.*

175. United States v. Tranowski, 659 F.2d 750, 757 (7th Cir. 1981).

176. Barefoot v. Estelle, 463 U.S. 880, 931 n.9 (1983) (Blackmun, J., dissenting).

177. Mazzella & Lennard, *Use of a Silicon Carbide Sampling Accessory for the Diffuse Reflectance Infrared Fourier Transform Analysis of Samples of Interest to Forensic Science*, 36 J. FORENSIC SCI. 556 (1991); United States v. McCaskey, 9 F.3d 368, 379 (5th Cir. 1993), *cert. denied,* 511 U.S. 1042 (1994); Kupstov, *Applications of Fourier Transform Raman Spectroscopy in Forensic Science*, 39 J. FORENSIC SCI. 305 (1994).

178. Suzuki & Gresham, *Forensic Science Applications of Diffuse Reflectance Infrared Fourier Transform Spectroscopy (DRIFTS): I. Principles, Sampling Methods, and Advantages*, 31 J. FORENSIC SCI. 931 (1986).

179. *Id.* at 932.

180. *Id.* at 931.

181. Suzuki & Gresham, *Forensic Science Applications of Diffuse Reflectance Infrared Fourier Transform Spectroscopy (DRIFTS): II. Direct Analysis of Some Tablets, Capsule Powders, and Powders*, 31 J. FORENSIC SCI. 1291 (1986); Levy, Ravreby, Meirovich & Shapira-Heiman, *A Survey and Comparison of Heroin Seizures in Israel During 1992 by Fourier Transform Infrared Spectrometry*, 41 J. FORENSIC SCI. 6 (1996) (heroin powder).

some foams.[182] The courts have already accepted testimony based on DRIFTS analysis.[183]

§ 25-5. Ultraviolet (UV) Analysis.

Like IR, UV has many applications other than as a drug identification technique. Police often "mark" or dust objects with special powders that fluoresce when excited by UV light.[184] When the criminal handles the object, the powder transfers to his or her hands. If the police arrest the criminal shortly after the transfer, the police can subject the defendant's hands to a UV test.[185] The police have used this technique on such objects as bags,[186] handles,[187] hashish,[188] marijuana,[189] packages,[190] suitcases,[191] tablets,[192] and towels.[193] In "controlled

---

182. Suzuki & Gresham, *Forensic Science Applications of Diffuse Reflectance Infrared Fourier Transform Spectroscopy (DRIFTS): III. Direct Analysis of Polymeric Foams*, 32 J. Forensic Sci. 377 (1987). *See also* Suzuki, *Forensic Science Applications of Diffuse Reflectance Infrared Fourier Transform Spectroscopy (DRIFTS): IV. Direct Analysis of Metallic Paints —Sampling Considerations*, 34 J. Forensic Sci. 164 (1989); Suzuki & Brown, *Forensic Science Applications of Diffuse Reflectance Infrared Fourier Transform Spectroscopy (DRIFTS): V. Direct Analysis of Metallic Paints — Screening of Panels*, 34 J. Forensic Sci. 180 (1989); Blackledge, *Viscosity Comparisons of Polydimethylsiloxane Lubricants in Latex Condom Brands via Fourier Self-Deconvolution of their FT-IR Spectra*, 40 J. Forensic Sci. 467 (1995).

183. People v. Roraback, 174 Misc. 2d 641, 666 N.Y.S.2d 397 (Sup. Ct. 1997) (the witness had used a Fourier Transform Infrared Spectrometer (FTIR) to establish that cement dust samples recovered from the defendant's van were consistent with safe lining cement which could have come from the victim's safe), *aff'd*, 668 N.Y.S.2d 781 (A.D. 1998).

184. Chatom v. State, 348 So. 2d 828, 832 (Ala. Crim. App. 1976), *rev'd,* 348 So. 2d 838 (Ala. 1977).

185. For a discussion of the question of whether this intrusion constitutes a search or seizure within the meaning of the fourth amendment, *see* Chapter 2. People v. Weekly, 42 Cal. App. 4th 310, 44 Cal. Rptr. 2d 322, 325 ("United States v. Richardson (6th Cir. 1968) 388 F.2d 842, 845 [ultraviolet examination of hands not a search]"), *superseded*, 47 Cal. Rptr. 2d 425, 906 P.2d 387 (1995); People v. Hull, 34 Cal. App. 4th 1448, 41 Cal. Rptr. 2d 99 (1995) (the police had placed ultraviolet-sensitive powder in a "bait vehicle;" a warrantless entry of a residence was justified because "the defendant ... could have used the time it took the officers to obtain a warrant to wash the powder off").

186. United States v. Richardson, 388 F.2d 842, 843 (6th Cir. 1968); People v. Gurtenstein, 69 Cal. App. 3d 441, 447, 138 Cal. Rptr. 161, 164 (1977), *cert. denied,* 434 U.S. 1035 (1978); Maumee v. Geiger, 45 Ohio St. 2d 238, 74 Ohio Op. 2d 380, 344 N.E.2d 133 (1976); United States v. Williams, 902 F.2d 678, 680 (8th Cir. 1990).

187. People v. Wesley, 80 Misc. 2d 581, 363 N.Y.S.2d 301 (1975), *rev'd on other grounds,* 88 Misc. 2d 177, 387 N.Y.S.2d 34 (1976).

188. United States v. Pratter, 465 F.2d 227, 229 (7th Cir. 1972); Commonwealth v. Dewitt, 226 Pa. Super. 372, 314 A.2d 27 (1973).

189. United States v. Coughlin, 338 F. Supp. 1328, 1329 (E.D. Mich. 1972).

190. People v. Lawton, 150 Cal. App. 2d 431, 433, 309 P.2d 862 (1957).

191. People v. Rodriguez, 151 Cal. App. 2d 598, 312 P.2d 272 (1957).

192. People v. Gallagher, 168 Cal. App. 2d 418, 420, 336 P.2d 259 (1959).

buys," purchases of drugs from suspected traffickers by police and police informants, the police often treat the currency before the buy. After the buy, the police subject the suspect's hands to UV light to prove that the suspect handled the marked bills.[194] Although many of the cases involve the use of fluorescent powders and UV instrumentation at a crime laboratory, there are variations of the procedure; some police departments use special ultraviolet pencils[195] and portable UV equipment.[196] Both paper currency[197] and coins[198] can be subjected to this UV treatment.

UV instrumentation has other forensic applications. For example, UV equipment can be used to detect the presence of bite marks[199] or body fluids,[200]

---

193. People v. Rosenberg, 59 Misc. 2d 1, 2, 297 N.Y.S.2d 860, 862 (1969), *aff'd,* 32 A.D.2d 1030, 303 N.Y.S.2d 1005 (1969), *aff'd,* 34 A.D.2d 961, 313 N.Y.S.2d 651 (1970); State v. Godwin, 13 N.C. App. 700, 701, 187 S.E.2d 400, 402, *cert. denied,* 281 N.C. 155, 188 S.E.2d 366 (1972).

194. United States v. Beechum, 582 F.2d 898, 904 (5th Cir. 1978), *cert. denied,* 440 U.S. 920 (1979); United States v. Prout, 526 F.2d 380, 383 (5th Cir.), *cert. denied,* 429 U.S. 840 (1976); Teasley v. United States, 292 F.2d 460, 464 (9th Cir. 1961); United States v. Coduto, 284 F.2d 464, 467 (7th Cir. 1960), *cert. denied,* 365 U.S. 881 (1961); Williams v. United States, 273 F.2d 781, 785 (9th Cir.), *cert. denied,* 362 U.S. 951 (1960); United States v. Secor, 280 F. Supp. 345, 347 (S.D.N.Y. 1966); People v. Ingle, 53 Cal. 2d 407, 412, 348 P.2d 577, 580, 2 Cal. Rptr. 14, 17, *cert. denied,* 364 U.S. 841 (1960); People v. Cervantes, 177 Cal. App. 2d 187, 189, 2 Cal. Rptr. 107, 108 (1960); People v. Adame, 169 Cal. App. 2d 587, 596, 337 P.2d 477, 483 (1959), *cert. denied,* 361 U.S. 969 (1960); People v. Martinez, 169 Cal. App. 2d 242, 244, 336 P.2d 988, 990 (1959); People v. Coagan, 28 Ill. App. 3d 634, 635, 328 N.E.2d 917, 918 (1975); People v. Marquis, 24 Ill. App. 3d 653, 657, 321 N.E.2d 480, 483 (1974); People v. Banks, 116 Ill. App. 2d 147, 150, 253 N.E.2d 631 (1969); People v. Almanza, 76 Ill. App. 2d 395, 222 N.E.2d 74, 75 (1966); People v. Baxter, 74 Ill. App. 2d 437, 442, 221 N.E.2d 16, 19 (1966); State v. Mears, 54 N.C. App. 666, 284 S.E.2d 158 (1981); State v. Conley, 32 Ohio App. 2d 54, 60, 61 Ohio Op. 2d 50, _, 288 N.E.2d 296, 300 (1971); State v. Welch, 441 A.2d 539, 540 (R.I. 1982).

195. Norris v. State, 259 Ark. 755, 757, 536 S.W.2d 298, 300 (1976), *cert. denied,* 435 U.S. 970 (1978).

196. People v. Martinez, 169 Cal. App. 2d 242, 244, 336 P.2d 988, 990 (1959).

197. United States v. Beechum, 555 F.2d 487, 490 (5th Cir. 1977), *cert. denied,* 440 U.S. 920 (1979).

198. People v. Murdick, 57 A.D.2d 650, 393 N.Y.S.2d 474 (1977).

199. West, Billings & Frair, *Ultraviolet Photography: Bite Marks on Human Skin and Suggested Technique for the Exposure and Development of Reflective Ultraviolet Photography*, 32 J. FORENSIC SCI. 1204 (1987); West & Barsley, *Ultraviolet Forensic Imaging*, 61 F.B.I. LAW ENF. BULL. 14, 14-15 (May 1992) ("In one method, known as reflective ultraviolet imaging, the wound is flooded with UV light, and the reflected ultraviolet image is photographed. An ultraviolet bandpass filter mounted on the camera lens blocks all light returning to the film except UV. Proper film selection ensures that only the UV light rays reach the film. In the second method, called fluorescent ultraviolet imaging, the wound is flooded with only UV light. However, a different filter is used to block all UV rays returning to the camera so that only the visible light colors fluorescing from the wound will be captured on the film").

200. People v. Voight, 72 Ill. App. 3d 472, 474, 29 Ill. Dec. 60, 391 N.E.2d 219, 220 (1979).

including seminal material.[201] Questioned document examiners use UV light in the analysis of ink[202] and paper.[203] Finally as Chapter 14 pointed out, UV is part of the trace metal detection technique (TMDT) to determine whether a person has recently held a metallic object such as a firearm.[204]

§ 25-6. Computerization.

The more advanced crime laboratories now use computers to perform functions other than merely generating data.[205] Suppose, for instance, that a laboratory links an infrared spectrophotometer to a computer. The IR spectrophotometer yields a spectrum. A library of standard spectra can be included in the computer's memory bank. With a proper program, the computer can be directed to search through the library to find a "matching" spectrum. Advances in computer graphics allow the technician to overlay the unknown spectrum on a known spectrum from the library. Computer-generated evidence, especially computer graphics, can have great appeal for a lay jury.[206] The computerization of an instrumental technique, however, does not make the technique infallible.

If the computer includes a library of spectra, the attorney must ascertain the source of the library. Did the laboratory itself build up the library by accumulating its own test results, or did the laboratory feed spectra from a text into the computer? If the laboratory itself created the library, it should be easy to determine the manner in which the library was collected. However, when the laboratory inserts a library from another source, the trustworthiness of that source must be investigated.

Next, the attorney will want to discover the program for searching for a "match." The program will include decisional criteria, rules that the computer uses in deciding whether two spectra match. Computerizing the search ensures that the criteria are consistently applied, but computerization in no way enhances the validity of the criteria. Whether applied by a computer or a human, the criteria must be accurate. Have the criteria been experimentally verified? Did the laboratory itself develop the criteria, or did the laboratory borrow the criteria from another source such as a treatise? If another source formulated the criteria, the reliability of that source must be investigated.

---

201. People v. Devine, 101 Ill. App. 3d 158, 162, 56 Ill. Dec. 731, 735, 427 N.E.2d 1277, 1281 (1981).

202. United States v. Bruno, 333 F. Supp. 570, 573 (E.D. Pa. 1971).

203. Hughes Tool Co. v. Meier, 489 F. Supp. 333, 339 (D. Utah 1977).

204. Reid v. State, 267 Ind. 555, 558, 372 N.E.2d 1149, 1151 (1978); People v. Lauro, 91 Misc. 2d 706, 711, 398 N.Y.S.2d 503, 506 (1977).

205. Nelburger, *Microcomputers in Forensic Science*, 30 J. FORENSIC SCI. 881 (1985).

206. M. DUMBROFF, DEMONSTRATIVE EVIDENCE ch. 9 (1983).

Even if the computer can perfectly overlay two spectra, the match may not indicate that the two substances are identical. Any spectrum merely measures certain properties of the substance analyzed. Are those properties peculiar to a particular substance? Is the test specific for that substance? If a spectrum depicts only nonspecific properties, the overlaid spectra are not conclusive evidence of the identity of the substance.

Finally, although computerization can eliminate some possible sources of human error in searching a library and matching spectra, sophisticated instrumentation interfacing a computer and an analytic tool such as an IR spectrophotometer requires constant, skilled maintenance. Computerization helps to minimize the possibility of error during the test or the interpretation of the test result. However, reliability is assured only if the complex instrumentation was in good working order.

§ 25-7. Selected Bibliography.

S. BASU & J. MILLETTE, ELECTRON MICROSCOPY IN FORENSIC, OCCUPATIONAL, AND ENVIRONMENTAL HEALTH SCIENCES (1986).

C. GILMORE, THE UNSEEN UNIVERSE — PHOTOGRAPHS FROM THE SCANNING ELECTRON MICROSCOPE (1974).

J. GOLDSTEIN & H. YAKOWITZ, PRACTICAL SCANNING ELECTRON MICROSCOPY (1975).

J. HICKS & D. YOUNG, DIRECTORY OF RARE ANALYSES 1987 (1987).

O. WELLS, SCANNING ELECTRON MICROSCOPY (1974).

S. GOROG, ULTRAVIOLET-VISIBLE SPECTROPHOTOMETRY IN PHARMACEUTICAL ANALYSIS (1995).

E. PUNGOR, A PRACTICAL GUIDE TO INSTRUMENTAL ANALYSIS (1995).

J. RUSS, THE IMAGE PROCESSING HANDBOOK (1995).

J. YINON, FORENSIC APPLICATIONS OF MASS SPECTROMETRY (1995).

Judd, *Scanning Electron Microscopy as Applied to Forensic Analysis*, *in* SCIENTIFIC AND EXPERT EVIDENCE 873 (2d ed. 1981).

Krishnan, *Neutron Activation Analysis and Atomic Absorption Spectrometry*, *in* SCIENTIFIC AND EXPERT EVIDENCE 279 (2d ed. 1981).

Krishnan, *Merits and Demerits of Forensic Activation Analysis When Compared to Other Trace Methods*, *in* SCIENTIFIC AND EXPERT EVIDENCE 303 (2d ed. 1981).

Krishnan, *Detection of Gunshot Residue on the Hands by Trace Element Analysis*, *in* SCIENTIFIC AND EXPERT EVIDENCE 315 (2d ed. 1981).

Watkins & Watkins, *Identification of Substances by Instrumental Analysis*, *in* 22 AM. JUR. PROOF OF FACTS (1969).

Latin, Tannehill & White, *Remote Sensing Evidence and Environmental Law*, 64 CAL. L. REV. 1300 (1976).

CHAPTER 26

ARSON*

§ 26-1. In General.

In the past two decades, there has been a growing realization of the magnitude of the problem of arson in the United States. One text states:

> Arson has become one of the most expensive crimes in the United States.... Its incidence is growing at an ever-increasing rate, and it may account for more than $2 billion a year in losses. About 15 percent of all building fires and one-fourth of dollar losses from building fires are attributed to arson.[1]

---

*The authors wish to express their appreciation to Special Agent David Campbell, North Carolina State Bureau of Investigation, who reviewed this chapter in the second and third editions of the treatise, and the late Captain John Imwinkelried, Retired, San Francisco Fire Department, who reviewed this chapter in the second edition.

1. STATE FARM INS. CO., TOUCHED OFF BY HUMAN HANDS 2. *See also* CROSBY, FISKE & FORSTER, HANDBOOK OF FIRE PROTECTION 1045-46 (Nat'l Fire Protection Ass'n 1941) ("While the number of fires which are of incendiary origin is a small proportion of the total, it is probable that a much larger proportion of the total losses is incendiary than is generally supposed. Various authorities have estimated that incendiary fire losses are from 10% to 40% of all losses. During a five-year period of all losses over $1000 in Elmira, N.Y., 54 per cent were incendiary or unknown;

The incidence of arson is especially likely to increase during periods of economic recession or depression.[2] If a business is failing but carries ample insurance, the owner may be tempted to resort to arson for profit; the owner might even increase his or her insurance coverage in anticipation of an arson fire. Worse still, fires result in a loss of human life and claim over 1,000 lives each year.

The law enforcement community has begun to appreciate the enormity of the arson problem. The Federal Bureau of Investigation reclassified arson as a Class I crime, the same category which includes murder and bank robbery. Unfortunately, there are still significant difficulties enforcing the arson laws. One study found that other major offenses such as murder, bank robbery, and grand theft auto have twice the arrest rate and four times the conviction rate of arson.[3] These difficulties are understandable. To begin with, most arsonists are careful enough to start their incendiary fires clandestinely. The fire frequently occurs at night. Furthermore, the fire itself consumes some of the physical evidence which might be used to convict the arsonist. In addition, the firefighting efforts may disrupt the physical evidence. Firemen may have to move evidence to get in position to fight the fire; and depending on the means used to extinguish the fire, the streams of water from the fire hoses may damage or wash away evidence.[4] Microbial activity can degrade any remaining evidence of accelerants.[5]

To overcome these difficulties, two types of experts — fire department investigators and crime laboratory analysts — have intensified their efforts in arson cases. Sections 26-2 through 26-6 of this chapter review the expert determinations which can be made by investigators and analysts. Section 26-7

---

in Portsmouth, Ohio, 68 per cent; in Glens Falls, N.Y., more than 50 per cent; in Brockton, Mass., 48 per cent"); Hammond & Sands, *Trial by Fire: Preparing to Defend an Arson Case*, 19 THE CHAMPION 4 (Apr. 1995) ("In the United States, one fire in every four is arson. Arson kills about 700 citizens annually. Furthermore, arson is responsible for 25 percent of all property damage.").

2. "A study of the relationship of monthly fire losses and of a business index for a 10-year period in Boston revealed that whenever a depression in business conditions occurred, there was a marked increase in fire losses. Depressions in business conditions of only 3 or 4 per cent were frequently followed by increases in fire losses of 40 to 180 per cent." INTERNATIONAL CITY MANAGERS' ASS'N, MUNICIPAL FIRE ADMINISTRATION 383 (5th ed. 1950).

3. LAW ENF. ASSIST. ADMIN., ARSON AND ARSON INVESTIGATION: A SURVEY AND ASSESSMENT 31 (1978).

4. United States v. Ryan, 9 F.3d 660, 663 (8th Cir. 1993) ("two experts testified that, depending upon the characteristics of the flammable liquids used, the amount of water applied, and the duration of the fire, flammable liquids can be diluted, can evaporate, or can be totally consumed by fire. Thus, the presence of flammable liquids is not always detectable, and the negative tests results not always conclusive"), *cert. denied*, 514 U.S. 1082 (1995). Malek v. Federal Ins. Co., 994 F.2d 49 (2d Cir. 1993) (a fire expert testified that either fire hoses had washed away the accelerants or they had burned off).

5. Kirkbride, Yap, Andrews, Pigou, Klass, Dinan & Peddie, *Microbial Degradation of Petroleum Hydrocarbons: Implications for Arson Residue Analysis*, 37 J. FORENSIC SCI. 1585 (1992).

surveys the legal restrictions on the admissibility and sufficiency of arson evidence.

§ 26-2. The Science of Fire.

Conducting an arson investigation can necessitate cooperation among many types of forensic scientists. Chapter 9 of this text discusses psychiatric and psychological evidence. Mental health experts frequently assist in the investigation and trial of arson cases. The arsonist may be a pyromanic,[6] who gains a thrill from watching the fire. Pyromaniacs have been known to start "vanity" or "hero" fires.[7] In this scenario, the arsonist not only starts the fire; he or she also reports the fire and even assists firemen in fighting the blaze — in the hope of obtaining "recognition or praise for his or her heroic efforts."[8] Chapter 19 of this text analyzes pathology evidence. The medical examiner plays an important role in the investigation of any fire resulting in the death of a human being.[9] During such investigations, the medical officer often calls on the services of the toxicologist,[10] whose expertise is discussed in Chapter 20.

The fire department investigator and the crime laboratory analyst also contribute to the efforts of this forensic team. The analyst may use instrumental techniques, such as those mentioned in Chapter 25, to evaluate trace evidence found at the fire scene. Chapter 24 discusses some of the methods of analyzing trace evidence. The fire department investigator can make additional determinations, based on his or her observations at the scene. To make those determinations, the investigator relies on scientific principles relating to the manner in which fires start, the phases which a fire then progresses through, and the way in which fire behaves or travels.

§ 26-2(A). The Triangle Needed to Start a Fire.

Oxidation is a type of chemical reaction.[11] Combustion is an oxidation process accompanied by heat and usually light as well.[12] More specifically, fire is a rapid, self-sustaining combustion which results in the evolution of heat and light.[13]

---

6. Gold, *Psychiatric Profile of the Firesetter*, 7 J. Forensic Sci. 404 (1962).

7. Mabley, *Establishing Arson*, 1984 The Practical Prosecutor, No. 2, at 17.

8. *Id.*

9. Dominguez, *Problems of Carbon Monoxide in Fires*, 7 J. Forensic Sci. 379 (1962); Rho & Hoffman, *The Investigation of Fatal Fires: Views of the Medical Examiner and Toxicologist Conclusion*, 55 F.B.I. Law Enf. Bull. 1 (Sept. 1986).

10. *Id.*

11. Berry, *Characteristics and Behavior of Fire*, 34 Def. L.J. 243 (1985).

12. *Id.*

13. *Id.*

Fire experts often refer to the fire triangle. Figure 26-1 depicts the triangle.[14] As the figure indicates, three elements are needed to trigger the combustion of a fire: oxygen, fuel, and heat.[15] One essential element is oxygen. The oxygen itself does not burn; however, it sustains the combustion.[16] A fire requires an atmosphere with at least 16% oxygen.[17] At sea level, ambient air contains 21% oxygen.[18] Thus, absent exceptional circumstances causing an oxygen-starved atmosphere, there is ordinarily ample oxygen for any fire.[19] The necessity for adequate oxygen can be illustrated by a simple example. It is common knowledge that you can put out a grease fire in a pan on a stove by placing a cover over the pan; doing so has the effect of putting out the fire because it cuts off the oxygen supply.[20]

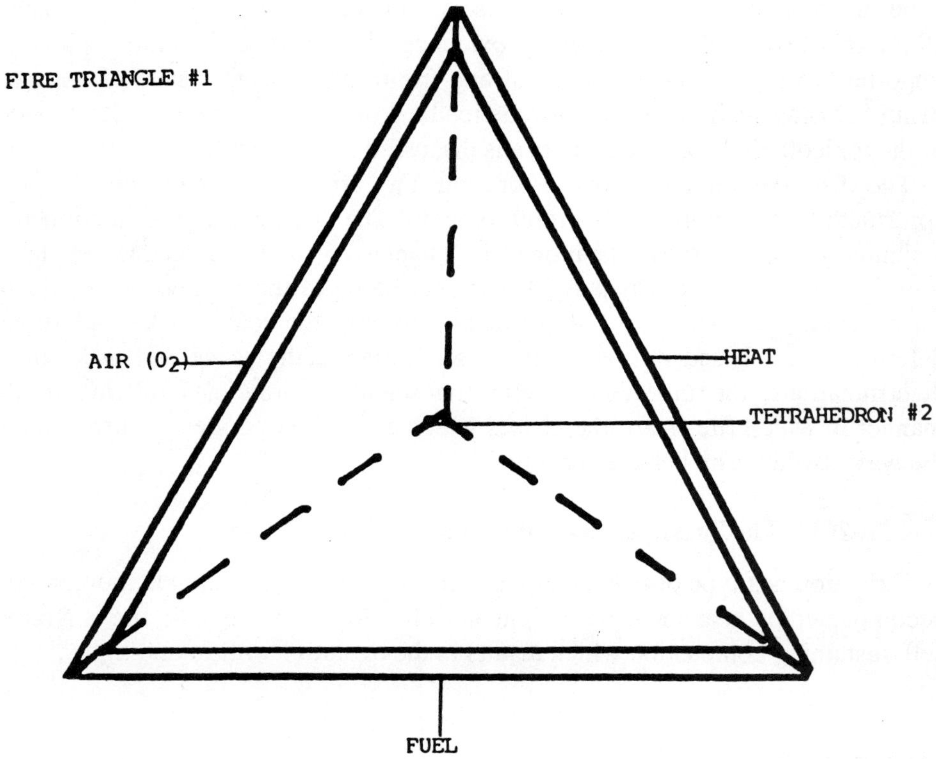

Figure 26-1

14. This diagram was prepared by Special Agent David Campbell. Reprinted with permission.
15. Berry, *Characteristics and Behavior of Fire*, 34 DEF. L.J. 243, 244 (1985).
16. *Id.*
17. *Id.*
18. *Id.*
19. *Id.*
20. *Id.*

Another essential — but commonly available — element is fuel. The fuel can be solid, liquid, or gaseous in form. Hence, virtually any material can function as a fuel.[21] However, as a general proposition, solids or liquids must be converted into vapor or gaseous form before combustion occurs.[22] Sufficient heat can vaporize solids and liquids and thereby convert the material into the gaseous state needed for combustion.[23] As in the case of the need for oxygen, the necessity for fuel can be illustrated by a simple illustration; if a fire is gas-fueled, you can extinguish the fire by shutting off the gas.[24] Fire investigators commonly classify fires on the basis of the type of fuel. Figure 26-2 describes the classification system.[25]

The third requisite for a fire is heat. "Since some kind of fuel and sufficient oxygen are almost always present, the investigator's main job is to find and establish [the] source of heat...."[26] The application of water is an effective way of fighting most fires precisely because water reduces heat.[27] There are numerous sources of heat energy.[28] Figure 26-3 lists some potential sources.[29]

The investigator must not only identify a source for the required heat; the investigator must also determine how the heat flowed to the fuel. There are several different methods of heat transferal.[30] In conduction, heat transfers when objects are in direct contact.[31] In convection, heat flows through a circulating medium such as an air current.[32] Finally, in radiation, heat transfers through electromagnetic waves.[33] This method explains how the heat from the sun reaches the earth's surface.

When all three elements — oxygen, fuel, and heat — concur, the result is a self-sustained interaction.[34] The chemical chain reaction is sometimes referred to as a tetrahedron.[35] The reaction continues so long as all three elements are

---

21. *Id.* at 245.

22. *Id.*

23. *Id.*

24. *Id.* at 246.

25. This diagram was prepared by Special Agent David Campbell. Reprinted with permission.

26. D. MABLEY, ARSON INVESTIGATION AND PROSECUTION 3 (1982).

27. Berry, *Characteristics and Behavior of Fire*, 34 DEF. L.J. 243, 246 (1985).

28. *Id.* at 247-50. Howitt, *The Surface Analysis of Copper Arc Beads — A Critical Review*, 42 J. FORENSIC SCI. 608 (1997) ("In the last few years it has become a popular idea to invoke the Auger analysis of arced copper wiring in order to say something about the likelihood that a fire was caused by some sort of electrical fault.").

29. This diagram was prepared by Special Agent David Campbell. Reprinted with permission.

30. Berry, *Characteristics and Behavior of Fire*, 34 DEF. L.J. 243, 247 (1985).

31. *Id.* at 250.

32. *Id.* at 251.

33. *Id.*

34. *Id.* at 246.

35. *Id.*

present. If any element is eliminated — by covering the pan fire, shutting off the gas, or dousing the area with water — the fire ceases.[36]

§ 26-2(B). The Phases of a Fire.

Many[37] fire experts maintain that after a "normal" structure fire starts, it progresses through a predictable series of phases.

CLASSIFICATION of FIRES

"CLASSIFIED ACCORDING TO TYPE OF FUEL"

CLASS A
WOOD PAPER CLOTH COAL PLASTICS

CLASS B
GASOLINE GREASE KEROSENE METHANE

CLASS C
ELECTRIC MOTORS TRANSFORMERS

CLASS D
MAGNESIUM SODIUM POTASIUM

Figure 26-2

---

36. *Id.*

37 Our reviewer points out that in recent years, a growing number of fire experts has moved away from the view that there are "distinct phases" in the development of the typical fire.

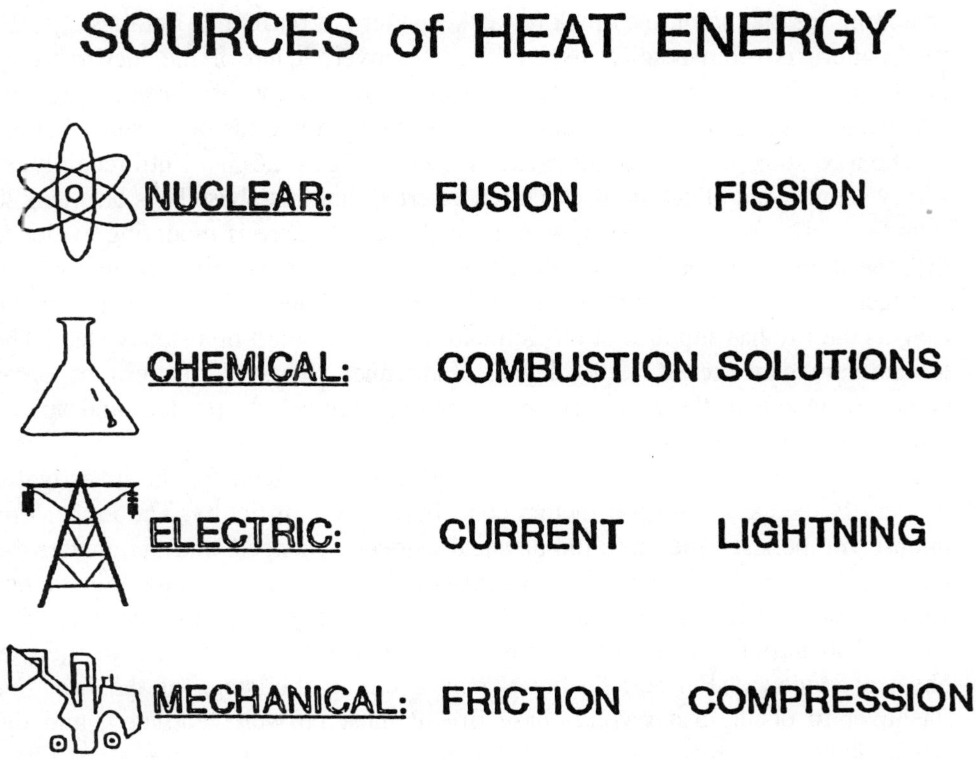

Figure 26-3

The initial phase is an incipient fire. Figure 26-4 depicts this stage.[38] It is sometimes stated that this phase lasts up to 20 minutes. However, that statement is imprecise; modernly, fire investigators appreciate that the duration of the phases of a given fire is highly variable. The length of time which the fire remains in a particular stage such as the incipient fire phase depends on such factors as the fire load, the arrangement of the fuel, and the type of construction. During this phase, most fires spread by radiation and direct flame impingement. The temperature can rise to 1,000 degrees Fahrenheit. In this early stage, extinguishing the fire can be simple for the firefighters; and if they succeed in putting out the fire during this stage, determining the cause of the fire can be a straightforward task for the investigator. As § 26-4 points out, to identify the cause, investigators typically search for a point of origin for the fire; and in

38. This diagram was prepared by Special Agent David Campbell. Reprinted with permission. Babrauskas & Krasny, *Upholstered Furniture Transition from Smoldering to Flaming*, 42 J. Forensic Sci. 1029, 1030 (1997) ("Out of a total of 102 items subjected to smoldering ignition in laboratory tests, 32% burned up partially or completely without erupting in flaming; 64% did go to flaming.... The mean smoldering-to-flaming transition observed in the laboratory tests was 88 min, the minimum 22 min, and the maximum 306 min.").

searching for that point, they look for a "V" pattern of burning.[39] In this stage, the "V" pattern is often readily discernible. Moreover, much of the incriminating physical evidence may still be intact. In this stage, to fight the blaze, firefighters can use hand lines which cause only minimal disruption to the physical evidence.

The next stage is a free-burning fire, shown in Figure 26-5.[40] Until recently, as a very rough generalization, it was often asserted that this phase lasts between 20 minutes and an hour. However, as previously stated, there is mounting evidence that the duration of each phase of a fire can be highly variable. In this phase, conduction, convection, and radiation all can contribute to fire propagation. So long as the fire has supplies of oxygen and fuel, it will burn in a steady state. The temperature can exceed 1,800 degrees Fahrenheit. The "V" pattern becomes etched in wood on the premises, and charring becomes deep. Heat and smoke lines appear on the walls.

If the fire is extinguished in this stage, it may be difficult for the investigator to identify the cause. Several factors contribute to this difficulty. The longer this intense fire persists, the more the physical evidence changes; and the greater the likelihood that the evidence will be destroyed. In addition, to combat this intense combustion, the firefighters may shift from hand lines to master streams. The force of a master stream can destroy, alter, or at least change the position of physical evidence. Further, flashover may occur in this stage of the fire. For flashover to occur in a second-phase fire, it must be well ventilated; and the temperature must reach between 1100 and 1300 degrees Fahrenheit.[41] Once flashover occurs, it burns the compartment or room from top to bottom, side to side, and end to end. The flashover can destroy evidence and obscure the point of origin of the fire.

---

39. United States v. Kladouris, 964 F.2d 658, 669 (7th Cir. 1992).

40. This figure was prepared by Special Agent David Campbell. Reprinted with permission.

41. Our reviewer states that 1100 degrees is the figure for a petroleum figure while 1300 degrees is the corresponding figure for a wood fire.

STAGES of FIRE
INCIPIENT STAGE
THE FIRST OR BEGINING STAGE
INCIPIENT PHASE
• SLIGHTLY OVER 100°
• RISING HOT GASES
• RISING AIR APPROXI-MATELY 20% OXYGEN

Figure 26-4

STAGES of FIRE
FREE-BURNING STAGE
RAPID HEAT BUILD-UP AND FLAME SPREAD
FREE BURNING
• APPROXIMATELY 1300°F
• HEAT ACCUMULATES AT UPPER AREAS
• REDUCED OXYGEN SUPPLY

Figure 26-5

If the fire has adequate supplies of oxygen and fuel, the combustion will continue indefinitely as a clear burning, unconfined fire. However, particularly when the fire is confined, the oxygen level may drop to less than the required 16% threshold. If that occurs, the fire will move into a third phase, namely a smoldering figure. Figure 26-6 depicts this stage.[42] The heat lines on the walls may burn as low as 12 inches from the floor. The damage to the structure is now extensive. Charring can become so deep that it will tend to hide the "V" pattern. The structure itself may begin to "huff and puff." A backdraft or smoke explosion can occur in this phase.

When the fire occurs in a tightly constructed, energy efficient building, it can enter a fourth phase. In this phase, the fire smolders for a substantial period of time — perhaps five or six days. The fire becomes cooler, and the heat dissipates due to lack of oxygen. When a fire enters this phase, pyrolysis is common. Pyrolysis is a chemical decomposition caused by exposure to heat in the absence of air. Pyrolysis can reduce physical evidence at the fire scene to charcoal and compound the difficulty of determining the cause of the fire.

§ 26-2(C). The Behavior or Movement of a Fire.

The preceding subsection set out a number of temporal generalizations about the sequence of a normal structure fire — the various phases through which the fire proceeds. Similarly, spatial generalizations are possible; there are several guidelines about the way in which a fire moves or travels through a structure.

Fire tends to propagate up and out rather than down. The fire involves hot gases, and hot vapors rise.[43] Consequently, the fire moves floor to ceiling and ground to roof. (When the physical evidence indicates that a particular fire traveled downward, the investigator almost automatically suspects that an arsonist caused the fire and set out "trailers" such as gas-soaked rags causing the fire to behave in this abnormal fashion).

Although fire tends to move vertically quickly, it tends to move horizontally slowly. (Again, if eyewitness accounts suggest that a particular fire moved very swiftly in a horizontal direction, the investigator will suspect arson).

When a fire's horizontal movement is obstructed, the fire will follow the path of less resistance; it will tend to spread out horizontally. It is sometimes said that faced with an obstruction, the fire "fans" or "mushrooms" out.[44] If the fire eventually consumes the obstruction, it may resume rapid vertical travel.

These guidelines are not hard-and-fast rules. The shape, composition, and ventilation patterns of the building in question and the presence of combustible

---

42. This figure was prepared by Special Agent David Campbell. Reprinted with permission.

43. Beland, *Comments on Fire Investigation Procedures*, 29 J. Forensic Sci. 190, 191 (1984) ("hot gases tend to rise and therefore a fire propagates upwards").

44. *Id.*

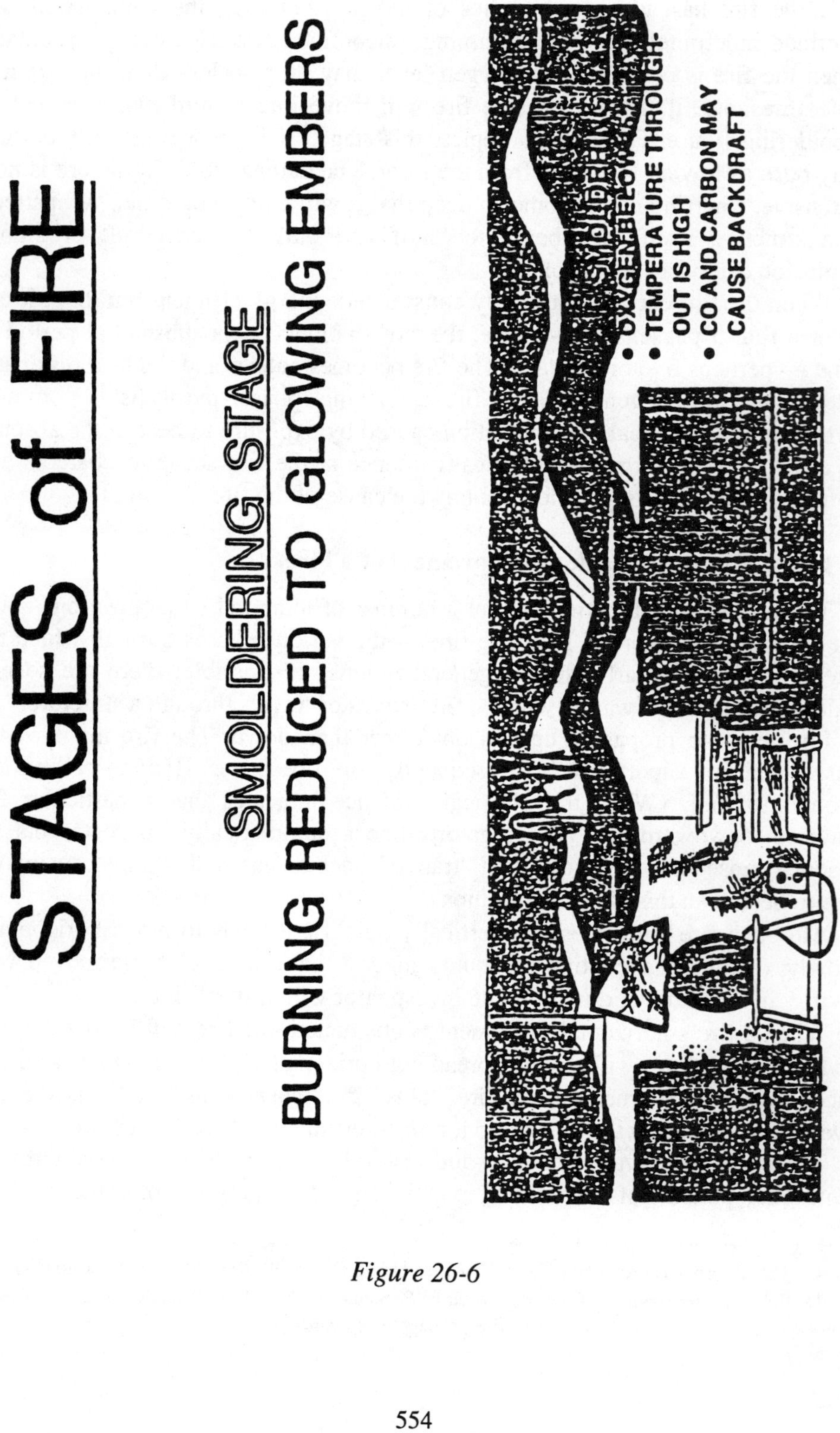
STAGES of FIRE
SMOLDERING STAGE
BURNING REDUCED TO GLOWING EMBERS
• TEMPERATURE THROUGH-OUT IS HIGH
• CO AND CARBON MAY CAUSE BACKDRAFT

Figure 26-6

material on the premises[45] can affect the behavior of a fire and cause the fire to travel in an unexpected manner. The temperature outside the building can likewise influence the behavior of the fire.[46] However, these guidelines are useful starting points for the investigator's analysis of the question of the cause of the fire.

§ 26-3. The Initial On-Scene Investigation by Fire Department Personnel.

It is critical that the investigation by fire department personnel begin as quickly as possible. Eyewitnesses may leave the scene shortly after they initially observe the fire. Firemen may inadvertently move items of physical evidence in the process of fighting the fire. Vapors from the fuel are an important clue, and vapors tend to evaporate quickly. Many accelerants have high evaporation rates during the first 30 minutes after the extinguishment of a fire; and within 24 hours, only faint traces may be left.[47]

The National Fire Protection Association (NFPA) has formulated guidelines for fire scene investigations.[48] As they comb through the fire scene for clues, investigators typically work backward. That is, they start at the area with the least damage and work toward the area of most severe damage. While they do so, they may take samples of trace evidence and vapor. They take extensive samples at the area they identify as the point of origin of the fire. However, they must not confine their sampling to that area. For comparison purposes, they should collect samples from other parts of the fire scene.

§ 26-4. The Expert Determinations Made by Fire Department Investigators.

Having studied the fire scene, an experienced fire department investigator can make a number of determinations. It must be emphasized that the investigator cannot draw these inferences with absolute confidence;[49] rather, the investigator employs generally reliable rules of thumb.[50]

---

45. *Id.*

46. Berry, *Characteristics and Behavior of Fire*, 34 DEF. L.J. 243, 263 (1985).

47. LAW ENF. ASSIST. ADMIN., ARSON AND ARSON INVESTIGATION: A SURVEY AND ASSESSMENT 73 (1978).

48. Ren & Bertsch, *A Comprehensive Sample Preparation Scheme for Accelerants in Suspect Arson Cases*, 44 J. FORENSIC SCI. 504, 514 n.1 (1999), citing NFPA 921 GUIDE FOR TIRE AND EXPLOSION INVESTIGATIONS (1995).

49. Beland, *Comments on Fire Investigation Procedures*, 29 J. FORENSIC SCI. 190, 195-96 (1984).

50. Tontarski, *A Review of Kirk's Fire Investigation*, 36 J. FORENSIC SCI. 1286 (1991).

§ 26-4(A). Where the Fire Began — The Point of Origin of the Fire.

In many cases, the key determination by the investigator is the identification of the point of origin of the fire. Once that point is identified, the investigator and laboratory analysts can concentrate their efforts to isolate the cause of the fire: The cause was the catalyst for the fire at the point of origin. In addition, the point of origin may be compelling evidence of the incendiary character of the fire. Suppose, for instance, that "the point of origin is in an 'unusual' location (*e.g.*, in the middle of a concrete floor with no nearby combustibles or possible accidental causes)."[51] Such an "unusual point of origin" virtually dictates the conclusion that the fire was initiated by an arsonist.[52]

There are several factors which the investigator takes into account in attempting to fix the point of origin of the fire. Most of the factors require a careful examination of the burn patterns on the premises.

The location of the apex of the "V"-shaped pattern. The normal fire creates an inverted conical burn pattern.[53] The apex of the cone usually indicates the point of origin of the fire.[54]

The location of the lowest level of burn. As previously stated, fires ordinarily propagate upwards. For that reason, the point of the lowest burning should be the point of origin of the fire.[55]

The point of deepest char. "The point of deepest char often indicates the origin of the fire."[56] The point of origin may burn the longest before the fire is extinguished, and consequently the char there ought to be the deepest. However, the investigator should not leap to "hasty conclusions" based solely on the depth of char.[57] The char in another area may be deeper than normal because of the presence of combustible material there, or the char at the point of origin may be shallower than normal because the firemen extinguished the fire there earlier.[58]

The area of greatest damage. The most extensive damage is likely to occur at the point of origin. The ceiling directly above that point may be the most severely damaged.[59] That may be the only section of ceiling which collapses. By the same token, surfaces facing the point of origin will probably be more seriously damaged than surfaces facing away from the point.[60] The "normal" ratio or rule of thumb of burning is that in a typical room with an eight foot ceiling, there are

51. D. Mabley, Arson Investigation and Prosecution 57 (1982).
52. *Id.*
53. Beland, *Comments on Fire Investigation Procedures*, 29 J. Forensic Sci. 190 (1984).
54. *Id.*
55. *Id.* at 191.
56. *Id.*
57. *Id.*
58. *Id.*
59. D. Mabley, Arson Investigation and Prosecution 57 (1982).
60. *Id.* at 58.

approximately three square feet of ceiling damage for every square foot of floor damage.

The size of the squares in "alligatorized" or "checked" wood. When wood burns, its surface has a tendency to form square blisters somewhat similar to the pattern on the skin of an alligator. This phenomenon is called "alligatorizing" or "checking." As the wood burns, the spaces between the squares become deeper; and the squares themselves shrink. The investigator can compare the size of the squares in various sections of the structure. The smallest squares are ordinarily present at the point of origin of the fire. Once again, however, the investigator must be cautious. The investigator must consider both the type and pre-condition of the wood. For instance, painted or lacquered wood alligatorizes at a different speed than untreated wood. The density of the wood can also affect the degree of alligatorizing.

The presence of small cracks in nearby glass. When glass is exposed to intense heat, the glass cracks or "crazes."[61] The presence of very small cracks in the glass may be indicative of very intense heat or a rapid buildup of heat[62] — either of which can occur at or near the point of origin of the fire.[63]

The amount of smoke deposit on glass. "Window glass near the fire's origin normally does not exhibit as much smoke deposit as glass farther away."[64]

The "spalling" of concrete. Under intense heat, concrete can crack or "spall." If there is spalling in only one section of a structure, the presence of the spalling points to the conclusion that the fire began in that section. Spalling must be "read" carefully; if true spalling has occurred, hydrocarbon rings or "ghosting" should be present.

The direction of distending of light bulbs. When light bulbs are subjected to sufficient heat, approximately 900 degree Fahrenheit, their shape distorts.[65] Many light bulbs warp at 900 degrees Fahrenheit. They may distend or point toward the source of the heat.[66] The source might be the fire at the point of origin.[67]

The "trailers" found on the premises. Arsonists sometimes use "trailers" or "trails" to direct the movement of the fire. For example, even if an arsonist starts the fire in one room, he or she might want to ensure that the fire spreads to another room. The other room might house records which the arsonist wants to

---

61. Mabley, *Establishing Arson*, 1984 THE PRACTICAL PROSECUTOR, No. 2, at 15. *But see* Lentini, *Behavior of Glass at Elevated Temperatures*, 37 J. FORENSIC SCI. 1358, 1362 (1992) (the researcher found that crazing occurs only when temperature is rapidly decreased; "[b]ecause crazing is actually a result of rapid cooling, it is likely to be a much less significant indicator of a fire's behavior than previously thought").

62. *Id.*

63. *Id.*

64. D. MABLEY, ARSON INVESTIGATION AND PROSECUTION 58 (1982).

65. Mabley, *Establishing Arson*, 1984 THE PRACTICAL PROSECUTOR, No. 2, at 15.

66. *Id.*

67. *Id.*

destroy or evidence of another crime which the arsonist wants to conceal. To increase the probability that the fire spreads in the desired manner, the arsonist may leave a trail of newspapers, wood shavings, accelerants, rope, or oily rags between the point of origin and the other area which the arsonist wants to burn. If part of the trailer survives the fire, its location can serve as a clue to the point of origin.

The location of smoke deposits on walls. If a room is distant from the point of origin, some deposits may be found only on the ceiling of the room.[68] In contrast, in rooms closer to the point of origin, smoke deposits will also be found on the lower levels of the walls.[69] The identification of the point of origin can be a difficult task. To begin with, the investigator cannot overlook the possibility that there were multiple points of origin. Indeed, the existence of multiple points of origin may be the most persuasive proof of the incendiary character of a fire. Drop down burning can create a misleading impression of multiple points of origin.[70] During a fire, a burning object may fall down and kindle a secondary fire.[71] The site of the secondary fire may have many of the appearances of a point of origin.[72]

§ 26-4(B). When the Fire Began.

The investigator can also draw inferences about the length of the fire from the burn pattern.[73] At one time, fire investigators relied on the rule of thumb that most woods burn approximately one inch in depth in 45 minutes. The investigator initially questioned the firefighters to fix the time when they extinguished the fire. After carefully measuring the depth of burn at its deepest point on the structure, the investigator estimated the burn time and then worked backwards from the time of the extinguishing of the fire to the approximate time when the fire began.[74] Modernly, however, there is evidence that various woods char at different rates even when they are subjected to the same, constant fire. For example, pine burns faster than oak or poplar.

§ 26-4(C). Why the Fire Began — The Cause of the Fire.

Having determined the point of origin of the fire, the investigator turns his or her attention to the task of identifying the cause of the fire: What occurred at the

---

68. D. Mabley, Arson Investigation and Prosecution 58 (1982).
69. *Id.*
70. *Id.* at 60.
71. *Id.*
72. *Id.*
73. Mabley, *Establishing Arson*, 1984 The Practical Prosecutor, No. 2, at 17.
74. *Id.*

point of origin to trigger the fire? Even without the aid of laboratory personnel, there are several clues which the investigator can evaluate.

The color of the smoke. The color of the smoke in the early stages of the fire may be indicative of what is burning.[75] When the combustion of an object is incomplete, smoke results. Smoke consists of unburned particles of the substance; the smoke is made up of carbon and ash particles. The ash particles give the smoke its color, and the color may help the investigator identify the burning material. The following combustible materials produce the following color of smoke:

Wood	Gray to Brown
Paper	Gray to Brown
Cloth	Gray to Brown
Gasoline	Black
Naptha	Brown to Black
Benzine	White to Gray
Lubricating Oil	Black
Lacquer Thinner	Brownish Black
Turpentine	Black to Brown
Acetone	Black
Cooking Oil	Brown
Kerosene	Black[76]

The color of the flame. Like the color of the smoke, the color of the flame can point to the identity of what is burning. In the early stages of a fire, the following combustible materials usually produce the following flame colors:

Wood	Red to Yellow
Paper	Red to Yellow
Cloth	Red to Yellow
Gasoline	Red to White
Naphtha	Straw to White
Benzine	Yellow to White
Lubricating Oil	Dark Red to Orange-Yellow
Lacquer Thinner	Red to Yellow
Turpentine	Yellow to White
Acetone	Blue to White
Cooking Oil	Red to Yellow
Kerosene	Dark Red to Orange-Yellow[77]

75. D. MABLEY, ARSON INVESTIGATION AND PROSECUTION 5 (1982).

76. CAMPBELL, FORENSIC EVIDENCE IN ARSON CASES (unpublished manuscript on file with the National College of District Attorneys, Houston, Texas).

77. *Id.*

In the later stages of a fire, the color of the flame indicates the intensity of the fire. The following colors roughly correlate with the following temperatures:

Reddish Glow --- about 500 degrees C
Light Red -- about 1,000 degrees C
Yellow-- about 1,100 degrees C
Blinding White --- reaching 1,500 degrees C[78]

Since certain fuels are more likely to generate a particular intensity of fire, these colors are also valuable clues for the investigator.

The odors present at the fire scene. The vapor odors at the fire scene may also assist the investigator in identifying the fuel and determining the cause of the fire. For example, the distinctive odor of sulphur may suggest that a sulphur candle was used to start the fire. Phosphorous has an odor similar to wet matches. Carbon-bisuphide has an odor like that of rotting cabbage.

Field chemical tests. Although the laboratory will later subject the physical evidence from the fire scene to sophisticated testing procedures, the investigator can conduct some simple field tests at the scene. For instance, to detect the presence of accelerants, the investigator can either dye the area or place a sample into a test tube full of reagent. If hydrocarbons are present, the reagent dye turns red. Such field tests are merely preliminary, screening tests. Most field tests are unspecific; they will yield false positives — positive outcomes even when accelerants are absent. In addition, many of the tests lack sensitivity; they produce positive test results only if massive concentrations of accelerant are present. Worse still, some field tests contaminate the sample and call into question the reliability of later testing.

§ 26-4(D). Whether the Fire Was Incendiary.

In an arson case, the ultimate determination for the investigator is whether the fire was incendiary: Did an arsonist deliberately start the fire? Or was the fire accidental or providential in character? It is conceivable that the fire might have been started by a worker's careless use of matches or even by lightning. In order to make this determination, the investigator endeavors to negatively eliminate other innocent explanations, and affirmatively demonstrate the incendiary character of the blaze.

Negatively eliminating other hypotheses.

There are numerous possible explanations for a fire: electrical system malfunction, careless play by children, reckless use of matches and cigarettes, overheating of machinery, and spontaneous combustion, to name only a few. The

---

78. Berry, *Characteristics and Behavior of Fire*, 34 DEF. L.J. 243, 258 (1985).

initial step in proving arson is working through a process of elimination to realistically negate these other potential explanations.[79]

In many cases, the defense suggests that the fire may have been started by negligent use of cigarettes. The investigator may be able to demonstrate that that suggestion is unrealistic:

> Cigarette fires have an "incubation period" of from 11/2 to 5 hours. Thus, a cigarette fire will not start within only a few minutes after the cigarette is discarded. [Furthermore, c]igarettes will not start a fire unless there is a substantial amount of insulating type material that can prevent generated heat from dissipating.[80]

The last sentence states the conventional wisdom. However,

> Recent studies conducted by the National Institutes of Standards and Testing (NIST) and by a variety of other laboratories around the United States have proven that a discarded cigarette butt can light a fire in a few minutes. Since this type of "scientific" evidence often has been used by prosecution experts to eliminate non-criminal explanations of a fire, evidence that these assumptions may be unreliable can be of great importance.[81]

Alternatively, the defense hypothesis might be spontaneous ignition. Again, the investigator can sometimes demonstrate that that hypothesis is unlikely:

> Like cigarette fires, spontaneous combustion will only occur in materials of sufficient density or quantity that they can generate and maintain heat. Additionally, spontaneous ignition only occurs in certain organic materials that are prone to oxidation, such as ... rags [soaked with linseed oil], sawdust, hay, etc. Prior to [open] flaming combustion, there will be a period in which heavy smoke and a very pungent odor are clearly evident to any persons who are present.[82]

The very rapidity of a fire may undermine an innocent explanation for the fire. Given modern construction standards and fire prevention devices, most structure blazes do not burn quickly. The investigator may have experience with a similar fire, that is, a fire at a building of roughly the same size and class as the structure in question and with comparable contents; that experience may enable the

---

79. D. Mabley, Arson Investigation and Prosecution 61 (1982).

80. *Id.*

81. Hammond & Sands, *Trial by Fire: Preparing to Defend an Arson Case*, 19 The Champion 4, 6 (Apr. 1995).

82. D. Mabley, Arson Investigation and Prosecution 62 (1982).

investigator to estimate the normal speed for such a fire. If a fire spreads with unusual speed, the speed itself is some evidence that the fire had an exceptionally favorable environment. In turn, the suggestion is that someone — the arsonist — prepared that environment.

Affirmatively establishing the hypothesis of arson.

There are many facts which would suggest arson even to an untrained layperson without the fire investigator's experience:

—There are signs of forceful entry into the structure.

—There are indications that another crime was committed on the premises. The purpose of the fire may have been to destroy the evidence of the commission of the other crime.

—Efforts were evidently made to impede the firefighters' access to the building. Large objects may have been placed near doors to make it more difficult for firemen to open the doors. Or ammonia may have been spread at entrances; ammonia has a pungent odor, its inhalation can cause choking, and its presence may indicate that someone wanted to deter firemen from entering the premises to extinguish the fire.

—Windows were left open, holes were bored in walls, or interior doors — especially firedoors — were tied open. The responsible person may have been attempting to improve ventilation to provide the fire with a better oxygen supply or to facilitate the spread of the fire throughout the structure.

—Valuable property was removed from the premises shortly before the fire. If inferior property was substituted, the substitution suggests insurance fraud.

—There was tampering with gas lines or electrical appliances on the premises. The tampering may have been calculated to improve the supply of heat or fuel for the fire.

—Burglar alarms or sprinkler systems were rendered inoperable.

—Blinds or shades were pulled down. Pulling down the window coverings would obstruct the outside view of the early stages of the fire.

The recognition of other indicia of arson requires the experience and expertise of the fire investigator:

—Indications of the use of timing devices. Arsonists often use timing devices to delay the start of the fire. A timing device not only allows the arsonist to reach safety before the fire begins; the device also may enable the arsonist to establish an alibi. There are numerous timing devices.[83] The

83. *Id.* at 7.

arsonist can wedge a lit cigarette protruding from a matchbook or a bundle of matches.[84] Or the arsonist might employ a picket delay.[85] In this technique, the arsonist tacks a thread to the ceiling, attaches burning material to the thread, and places flammable liquid under the material. When the thread burns, the burning material falls into the liquid and ignites the fire. In a residential structure, the arsonist might jam slices of bread into a toaster.[86] "After 6 minutes, smoke is seen. In about 12 minutes, the toast ignites...."[87] Candles can be used.[88] For example, the arsonist places the candle in a plastic dish filled with charcoal lighter. Depending on the composition, length, and diameter of the candle, it may take several hours for the candle to burn down. The rule of thumb is that a 3/4 to one inch thick candle burns at the rate of approximately an inch per hour.[89]

—The presence of "plants" at the point of origin of the fire. The arsonist may place additional fuel at the point of origin to feed the fire.[90] The arsonist might use newspapers, excelsior, or wood shavings.[91] If it would be unusual for that type of material to be left there in the normal course of activity on the premises, the location of the "plant" is evidence of the incendiary character of the fire.

—The presence of a "trail" or "trailers." While a "plant" helps start the fire, "trailers" direct the path of the fire.[92] Assume, for instance, that the arsonist decides to start the fire next to an electrical appliance in one room but he wants to ensure that the fire spreads to another room containing incriminating business records. The arsonist might connect the two rooms with a trail of an accelerant such as gasoline or kerosene or with rags, papers, rope, or toilet paper soaked with gasoline.[93] The investigator may find unburned parts of the trailers or residue. The use of trailers is strong evidence of arson.

—Multiple points of origin. Like the presence of trailers, multiple points of origin are powerful evidence of arson. As a matter of common human experience, it is simply unlikely that two or three accidental fires would begin on the same premises simultaneously. As noted in § 26-4(A), the

84. *Id.* at 7-8.
85. *Id.* at 8.
86. *Id.* at 10.
87. *Id.*
88. *Id.* at 11.
89. *Id.*
90. STATE FARM INS. CO, TOUCHED OFF BY HUMAN HANDS 10.
91. *Id.*
92. *Id.*
93. *Id.*

investigator must be cautious before concluding that there are several points of origin. Even if there is only one point of origin, during the fire debris may drop down, cause a secondary ignition, and create the misleading appearance of multiple points of origin. Or there may be a "missing link." While fighting a blaze, firemen may remove an object such as a burnt sofa. If the investigator does not discover that the sofa was originally in that location on the premises, the investigator may find an unburned area between two burnt areas — and mistakenly conclude that the two burned areas were separate points of origin. The path of the fire will seem to stop where the sofa once stood.

—The presence of unusual accelerants on the premises. Even before a laboratory analysis of trace evidence and vapors from the structure, the investigator may be able to determine that particular accelerants were present on the premises. As § 26-4(C) pointed out, the investigator may be able to make that determination based on the odors at the fire scene or the color of the smoke or flame. If it would be unusual for those accelerants to be located on those premises — abnormal for a residence or for the type of business conducted on the premises — the presence of accelerants suggests arson.

One of our reviewers, Agent Campbell, specifically asked us to add one comment at the end of this section. He points out that in the past 15 years, the composition of many items of common household items — mattresses, furniture, and the like — has changed from natural materials such as fiber and wood to plastic. While the burning of natural materials during an accidental fire might produce heat in the 1,300-1,500 degree Fahrenheit range, the burning of contemporary plastic materials often generates 2,000 degrees. This shift in the composition of furniture has complicated the fire investigator's task. Fifteen years ago, if the investigator encountered "indicators" of arson, he or she could be relatively confident in assuming that a flammable liquid had been poured in the area; the furniture normally present in a house could not have accounted for the indicators. Today, however, the investigator can no longer make that assumption. Consequently, the investigator must consider all the physical evidence at the fire scene rather than attaching inordinate weight to any single indicator."

Like the change in the composition of furniture, new research calls into question some of the received orthodoxy about fire investigation:

> [R]ecent studies and testing conducted in full-scale environments have demonstrated that most of these so-called accelerant fire indicators are often encountered in common household fires encountered without the aid of flammable substances. Some fire investigators have maintained that reliable inferences can be drawn from examining melted metal or by studying the

depth and general appearance of charred wooden objects. Scientists now know that neither of these [is] scientifically reliable as [an] indicator of arson. Yet, prosecution arson "experts" are still heard to say that, for example, "X alloy found in a melted object requires 2000 degrees temperature to melt, and only a flammable liquid burns that hot." In the fire in the hills of Oakland, California several years ago, investigators found precisely the indicators that might have led them at one time to incorrectly conclude that each of the Oakland home fires was fueled by large quantities of flammable liquids.[94]

§ 26-5. The Gathering of Physical Evidence by Fire Department Personnel for the Laboratory.

As previously stated, in addition to observing such matters as the color of smoke and burn patterns, the investigator can conduct some simple field tests at the fire scene. However, if the prosecution is to present a persuasive case in court, eventually more sophisticated tests will have to be conducted at the laboratory. Fire department personnel or special evidence technicians from the laboratory will have to collect physical evidence for subsequent laboratory analysis. The collection procedures entail photography, collection of vapors from the fire scene, and preservation of other physical evidence from the scene.

§ 26-5(A). Photography.

Both to support his or her own expert opinions and to permit independent evaluation by laboratory personnel, the investigator should ensure that adequate photographs of the fire scene are taken. It is ideal if some photographs can be taken during the fire.[95] Those photographs can capture the color of the smoke and flames. After the fire, there should be exterior as well as interior photographs. The exterior photographs "should be taken from all sides" of the structure.[96] Ideally, the exterior photographs should include one of the roof. The exterior photographs must be supplemented with interior shots.[97] There should be several shots at the suspected point of origin: all walls, the ceiling, and the floor. Photographs should also be taken of any plants, timing devices, and trailers.[98] Photographs of charred, blackened areas will be underexposed if the

---

94. Hammond & Sands, *Trial by Fire: Preparing to Defend an Arson Case*, 19 THE CHAMPION 4, 6 (Apr. 1995).

95. Tuttle, *Photography Plays Major Role in Arson Investigation*, POLICE 40 (Nov.-Dec. 1963).

96. Kennedy, *Photography in Arson Investigations*, 46 J. CRIM. L., CRIMINOLOGY & POL. SCI. 726, 731 (1956).

97. *Id.*

98. *Id.*

photographer follows the normal exposure guide.[99] Consequently, the photographer should take those shots with one or two more f-stops of exposure.[100] The photographer should consider holding the flash at an oblique angle to highlight important fire scene features such as concrete spalling.[101] It may also be advisable for the photographer to employ a small lens opening to enhance the sharpness and depth of field of the photographs.[102]

§ 26-5(B). Detecting Vapors from Accelerants.

Accelerants burnt during the fire may leave vapor traces which, when properly analyzed, will help identify the accelerant. The fire investigator attempts to detect and preserve these vapors. There are several types of vapor detectors.[103]

Perhaps the most common type of detector or "sniffer" is a catalytic combustion detector. The device captures a sample of the area where the investigator believes he or she smelled accelerant. The device passes the gas over a platinum catalyst coil. The gas is heated, and the heat changes the electrical resistance of the coil.[104] The degree of change is indicative of the elemental composition of the accelerant. These detectors have numerous advantages; they are sensitive down to one ppm (part per million), relatively inexpensive, and highly portable. However, they are subject to false positives; and at least some models have high sensitivity levels for certain common accelerants such as turpentine.

Portable gas chromatographs (GC) are increasingly in use. These devices are scaled down versions of the more sophisticated gas chromatographs used by the laboratories. The portable GC is more sensitive than the average catalytic combustion detector. However, the GC is bulkier, costlier, and requires a longer period of time to complete an analysis.

---

99. D. Mabley, Arson Investigation and Prosecution 33 (1982).

100. *Id.*

101. *Id.*

102. *Id.*

103. Rudolph, *Explosives Vapor Detectors*, 62 F.B.I. Law Enf. Bull. 19 (May 1993) (the article reviews the evolution of vapor detectors; the first detectors became commercially available in the early 1970's; these "first detectors worked on a technology known as electron capture, which is based on the principle that all explosives have a certain chemical nature (electronegative). When explosive vapors are introduced into the electron capture detector (ECD), the detector's standing current changes, and an electronic signal goes off"; these instruments detected few explosives other than dynamite and were prone to false positives; in the mid-1980's, researchers began developing a new type of detector "based on a technology called 'chemiluminescence.' This technology involves a specific chemical reaction that occurs with most nitrogen-based explosives;" these second-generation instruments both detect a wider range of explosive vapors and are sensitive to smaller particles).

104. Burd, *Detection of Traces of Combustible Fluids in Arson Cases*, 51 J. Crim. Law, Criminology & Pol. Sci. 263, 264 (1960).

Some investigators use flame ionization detectors. After mixing the sample with hydrogen, the detector burns the mixture. The burning ionizes the molecules of accelerant. The detector then measures the degree of ionization. The degree of ionization is a clue to the identity of the accelerant.

A few fire departments use advanced infrared or ultraviolet detectors. Infrared (IR) detectors in particular are highly reliable. They yield specific results for some accelerants, and they can be sensitive down to one part per ten million. However, like the other devices, IR detectors have their weaknesses. Samples must be purified before they are subjected to IR analysis, and water can be one of the worst contaminants. In addition, IR detectors are very expensive.

Ultraviolet (UV) detectors likewise hold promise.[105] In a UV test, the area where the accelerant was detected is darkened; and UV light is shone on the area. The accelerant may contain elements which glow on exposure to UV light. Although UV devices cannot detect some accelerants, UV detectors have strengths. They are not only portable and simple to operate. More importantly, they are nondestructive; the test does not contaminate the sample and interfere with subsequent laboratory analysis.

In addition to these detectors, sampling tubes and wires can be used to detect and capture accelerant vapors.[106] For example, the Curie point pyrolysis wire is coated with fine charcoal; and accelerant vapors are absorbed onto the charcoal.[107] Sampling tubes packed with porous polymers can likewise be utilized to collect vapors.[108]

Investigators are not limited to using instruments in detecting vapors; specially trained dogs can also be employed for this purpose.[109] Admittedly, there are doubts about the reliability of a dog's alert as proof of the presence of traces of flammable liquids,[110] and there is an element of subjectivity in determining whether the dog's conduct constitutes a positive alert. However, trained dogs are useful. According to our reviewer, the use of dogs is growing because the dogs are becoming more reliable. Until recently, many dogs had false positive rates of approximately 50%. However, our reviewer has had good experience with "food reward" dogs trained in Connecticut. He states that some of these dogs are 90-95% accurate.

---

105. LAW ENF. ASSIST. ADMIN, ARSON AND ARSON INVESTIGATION: A SURVEY AND ASSESSMENT 80 (1978).

106. Andrasko, *The Collection and Detection of Accelerant Vapors Using Porous Polymers and Curie Point Pyrolysis Wires Coated with Active Carbon*, 28 J. FORENSIC SCI. 330 (1983).

107. *Id.*

108. *Id.*

109. United States v. Marji, 158 F.3d 60, 62 (2d Cir. 1998).

110. Katz & Midkiff, *Unconfirmed Canine Acceleration Detection: A Reliability Issue in Court*, 43 J. FORENSIC SCI. 329 (1998) ("Canine handlers contend that the dog has greater sensitivity to typical accelerants than laboratory techniques but scientists counter that, while sensitive, the specificity of canine detection is unknown").

In the past, the investigators' primary activity at the first scene has been the detection and collection of evidence. However, advances in technology now permit the investigator to conduct some testing in situ. For instance, the compact Raman microscope enables the investigator to identify plastic explosives at the fire scene.[111]

§ 26-5(C). Preserving Evidence.

In addition to capturing vapors, the investigator may collect other physical evidence such as liquid residues[112] and the solid remains of plants or trailers at the fire scene. The fire may not have consumed all the accelerant used by the arsonist; particularly if the arsonist spread the accelerant on a wood floor, some of the accelerant may have seeped down between the cracks in the floor. At one time, many investigators inserted samples in glass jars for preservation of liquids and solids from fire scenes. However, that practice has largely been discontinued. The jars are not only breakable; the hydrocarbons in some volatile substances will react with the rubber or plastic lining in the lid and cause the seal to break.[113] Investigators then shifted to the use of paint cans. These cans can be closed with an air-tight seal and, at least in the short term,[114] the seal will not break.

Some jurisdictions employ non-metallic containers for physical evidence from fire scenes. Polyethylene containers are no longer in widespread use because they were found to be permeable to hydrocarbons.[115] Some authorities flatly assert that "[p]olyethylene containers should be avoided as evidence collection containers in arson cases. Significant accelerant loss and the possibility of sample contamination cannot be avoided with polyethylene containers."[116] Polyester bags have replaced polyethylene containers.[117]

---

111. Cheng, Kirkbride, Batschelder, Lacey & Sheldon, *In Situ Detection and Identification of Trace Explosives by Raman Microscopy*, 40 J. FORENSIC SCI. 31 (1995).

112. Jackowski, *The Incidence of Ignitable Liquid Residues in Fire Debris as Determined by a Sensitive and Comprehensive Analytical Scheme*, 42 J. FORENSIC SCI. 828 (1997) ("Flammable or combustible liquid residues were detected in 47.4% of the items, with petrol the most common ignitable liquid. As a group, fabric items, carpets, and plastics exhibited the highest incidence of flammable or combustible liquid residues, and ashen debris and soil the lowest.").

113. D. MABLEY, ARSON INVESTIGATION AND PROSECUTION 27 (1982).

114. *Id.* ("if liquids are put in the container and it is allowed to sit for a long period of time, the can may rust to an extent that it may eventually leak").

115. Tontarski, *Evaluation of Polyethylene Containers Used to Collect Evidence for Accelerant Detection*, 28 J. FORENSIC SCI. 440 (1983).

116. *Id.* at 444.

117. Kinard & Midkiff, *Arson Evidence Container Evaluation: II. "New Generation" Kapak Bags*, 36 J. FORENSIC SCI. 1714 (1991); Higgins, Higgins, Oakes & Braverman, *High-Speed Extraction of Accelerants from Arson Debris*, 29 J. FORENSIC SCI. 874, 880 (1984) ("The tests that have been discussed above, as well as many subsequent analyses, have shown the polyester bag to be an excellent alternative for the collection and analysis of both liquid and solid arson samples").

§ 26-6. Subsequent Laboratory Analysis of the Physical Evidence.

Sections 26-3 through 26-5 review the work of one type of expert, the fire department investigator. As § 26-5 notes, the investigator completes his or her work by collecting vapors and other physical evidence for laboratory analysis. The collection of that evidence sets the stage for the work of another type of expert, the laboratory analyst. Like the investigator, the laboratory analyst attempts to make a number of expert determinations: Does the physical evidence from the fire scene establish the presence of an accelerant? If the analyst answers that initial question in the affirmative, the analyst then proceeds to a number of increasingly specific questions which may or may not be answerable in a given case: Which accelerant is present? Which company manufactured the accelerant? Can the accelerant be tied to the defendant?[118] The analyst's ability to answer these questions depends on both the sophistication of the instrumentation available at the laboratory and the availability of comparative data. For example, to identify the manufacturer of the accelerant, the analyst must be in a position to compare the accelerant found at the crime scene with similar accelerant prepared by the same company.[119] Similarly, to connect the accelerant with the defendant, the analyst has to test specimens of similar accelerant found in the defendant's possession.[120] Of course, before testing the specimens, the analyst must extract the suspected accelerant from the physical evidence forwarded to the laboratory. Subsection 26-6(A) reviews the extraction procedures. After extraction, the analyst can subject the suspected accelerant to a variety of tests. Subsection 26-6(B) surveys the testing techniques most commonly used in arson cases.

§ 26-6(A). Extraction.

One extraction methodology is immiscible phase flotation. The analyst soaks the fire scene debris in water. The accelerant then floats to the top of the water. However, this method often yields a poor recovery of accelerant; the concentration of the accelerant must be high for this procedure to yield an adequate sample for subsequent testing.

Precisely because of the limitations of flotation extraction, most laboratories employ distillation extraction techniques.[121] Distillation extraction is especially popular when the analyst suspects that the accelerant was alcohol or another

118. Burd, *Arson and Fire Investigation: The Function of the Criminalist*, 7 J. FORENSIC SCI. 417, 425-26 (1962).

119. Midkiff, *Brand Identification and Comparison of Petroleum Products — A Complex Problem*, 26 THE FIRE AND ARSON INVESTIGATOR, No. 2 (Oct.-Dec. 1975).

120. *Id.* at 426.

121. *Id.* at 423. Lentini, *ASTM Standards for Forensic Sciences*, 40 J. FORENSIC SCI. 146 (1995) (the American Society for Testing and Materials has developed standard E 1385, prescribing practices for steam distillation).

water soluble liquid.[122] Steam distillation is an effective technique when the accelerant is a volatile petroleum product such as gasoline, kerosene, or fuel oil[123] with a low boiling point. Vacuum distillation is preferred when the accelerant has a high boiling point.

Solvent extraction techniques are also in use.[124] If the suspected accelerant is a heavy oil, the analyst may mix the fire scene debris with a volatile solvent such as carbon tetrachloride[125] or ethylene glycol.

While classical distillation and solvent extraction methods "were used primarily in the early years," "[m]ore recent methods focus around the principles of heated headspace enhancement."[126] There are dynamic (purge and trap) and static (carbon strip) methods. In the older, dynamic mode, "[h]eated headspace from a container of debris is pulled through a bed of granular charcoal."[127] That step is followed by a solvent extraction, ordinarily with carbon disulfide. In the static mode, "a carbon strip. . . is simply suspected in the headed headspace over the debris."[128]

Charcoal strips can also be employed.[129] Microextraction techniques are likewise available.[130]

§ 26-6(B). Analytic Techniques.

In many laboratories, the testing of arson debris proceeds through two stages.

Preliminary Tests

In the initial stage, the analyst makes several preliminary observations or measurements.[131] The preliminary tests may include the following procedures:[132]

---

122. *Id.*

123. *Id.*

124. *Id.* Lentini, *ASTM Standards for Forensic Sciences*, 40 J. FORENSIC SCI. 146 (1995) (the American Society for Testing and Materials has developed standard E 1386, prescribing practices for solvent extraction).

125. *Id.*

126. Ren & Bertsch, *A Comprehensive Sample Preparation Scheme for Accelerants in Suspect Arson Cases*, 44 J. FORENSIC SCI. 504 (1999).

127. *Id.*

128. *Id.*

129. Newman, Dietz & Lothridge, *The Use of Activated Charcoal Strips for Fire Debris Extractions by Passive Diffusion. Part 1: The Effects of Time, Temperature, Strip Size, and Sample Concentration*, 41 J. FORENSIC SCI. 361 (1996).

130. Ren & Bertsch, *A Comprehensive Sample Preparation Scheme for Accelerants in Suspect Arson Cases*, 44 J. FORENSIC SCI. 504 (1999) (discussing Solid Phase Micro Extraction (SPME)); Kirkbride, Klass & Pigou, *Application of Solid-Phase Microextraction to the Recovery of Organic Explosives*, 43 J. FORENSIC SCI. 76 (1998).

131. *Id.* at 423-24.

—Flash point determination. Even when the fire scene sample is small, the analyst can use microtechniques to approximate the accelerant's flash point.[133]

—Refractive index. The analyst employs a refractometer to make this measurement.[134]

—Specific gravity. If a gravitometer is available, the analyst can measure the specific gravity of the sample.[135]

—Unsaturated hydrocarbon test. A fraction of the sample is mixed with concentrated sulphuric acid. The test outcome enables the analyst to make a "very rough" estimate of "the quantity of unsaturated hydrocarbons present."[136]

More Sophisticated Tests

After the preliminary measurements, the analyst can administer more sophisticated tests. For the most part, these tests are procedures which research scientists have developed for other forensic tasks such as drug identification. Unfortunately, despite the encouragement of the Law Enforcement Assistance Administration, there has been relatively little scientific research into the phenomenon of fire.[137] Consequently, most of the arson testing techniques are procedures which laboratory analysts have simply adapted to use in arson cases.

Since the early 1960s, gas chromatography (GC) has been the most popular testing technique in arson cases.[138] For instance, GC can be utilized to identify

---

132. *Id.*

133. *Id.*

134. *Id.*

135. *Id.*

136. *Id.*

137. LAW ENF. ASSIST. ADMIN., ARSON AND ARSON INVESTIGATION: A SURVEY AND ASSESSMENT 32 (1978).

138. Barshick, *Analysis of Accelerants and Fire Debris Using Aroma Detection Technology*, 43 J. FORENSIC SCI. 284 (1998) ("Sample analysis is typically performed using gas chromatography"); Frenkel, Tsaroom, Aizenshtat, Kraus & Daphna, *Enhanced Sensitivity in Analysis of Arson Residues: An Adsorption-Tube/Gas Chromatograph Method*, 29 J. FORENSIC SCI. 723 (1984) ("[o]ne of the most popular analytical methods to date for the identification of fire residues"); Higgins, Higgins, Oakes & Braverman, *High-Speed Extraction of Accelerants from Arson Debris*, 29 J. FORENSIC SCI. 874 (1984) ("Since the early 1960s, gas chromatography has been used as a means of determining the presence of hydrocarbons in fire residues"); Gillette v. Tansy, 17 F.3d 308, 311 (10th Cir. 1994), *cert. denied*, 519 U.S. 1081 (1997); Lentini & Armstrong, *Comparison of the Eluting Efficiency of Carbon Disulfide with Diethyl Ehter: The Case for Laboratory Safety*, 42 J. FORENSIC SCI. 307 (1997); Schuberth, *Gas Residues of Engine Starting Fluid in Postmortem Sample from an Arsonist*, 42 J. FORENSIC SCI. 144 (1997); Hiley, *Dinitrosopentamethylenetetramine — A Potential Interference in the Detection of Explosive Traces*, 41 J. FORENSIC SCI. 975 (1996); Furton, Almirall & Bruna, *A Novel Method for the Analysis of Gasoline from Fire Debris Using Headspace Solid-Phase Microextraction*, 41 J. FORENSIC SCI. 12 (1996) (solid-phase

paraffin wax residue in fire remains.[139] Analysts are now using capillary column GC to achieve improved separations and increased sensitivity.[140] Section 23-2(D) of this text contains a detailed discussion of the strengths and limitations of GC.

The Vapor Trace Analyzer (VTA) is a modified GC[141] specially adapted for the analysis of arson and explosive residues. The suspected accelerant vapor passes through the VTA column. The analyst measures the amount of time which the vapor requires to travel through the column.[142] The VTA is subject to both false positives and false negatives. It can yield false positives with some shaving lotions, colognes, deodorants, and nitrobenzine (a common solvent).[143] Moreover, it has proved to be ineffective in identifying smokeless powders.[144]

Just as many drug identification tests now use high performance liquid chromatography (HPLC) rather than GC, HPLC has surfaced in arson casework.[145] HPLC can improve the separation of the vapors being analyzed and enhance the resolution of the chromatogram.[146] Like GC and HPLC, other modes of chromatography can be adapted to analyze arson debris.[147]

---

microextraction (SPME)); Kolla & Sprunkel, *Identification of Dynamite Explosives in Post Explosion Residues*, 40 J. FORENSIC SCI. 406 (1995) (gas-chromatography with chemiluminescence detection (GC-TEA)); Phelps, Chasteen & Render, *Extraction and Analysis of Low Molecular Weight Alcohols and Acetone From Fire Debris Using Passive Headspace Concentration*, 39 J. FORENSIC SCI. 194 (1994); Pinorini, Lennard, Margot, Dustin & Furrer, *Soot as an Indicator in Fire Investigations: Physical and Chemical Analyses*, 39 J. FORENSIC SCI. 933 (1994); Kolla, *Trace Analysis of Salt Based Explosives by Ion Chromatography*, 50 FORENSIC SCI. INT'L 217 (1991); Waters & Palmer, *Multiple Analysis of Fire Debris Samples Using Passive Headspace Concentration*, 38 J. FORENSIC SCI. 165 (1993). *See also* Ettling & Adams, *The Study of Accelerant Residues in Fire Remains*, 13 J. FORENSIC SCI. 76, 77 (1968).

139. Ettling, *Analysis of Paraffin Wax in Fire Remains*, 20 J. FORENSIC SCI. 476 (1975).

140. Reeve, Jeffrey, Weihs & Jennings, *Developments in Arson Analysis: A Comparison of Charcoal Adsorption and Direct Headspace Injection Techniques Using Fused Silica Capillary Gas Chromatography*, 31 J. FORENSIC SCI. 479 (1986).

141. Washington & Midkiff, *Systematic Approach to the Detection of Explosive Residues: Trace Vapor Analysis*, 56 J. ASS'N ANALYT. CHEMISTS 1239 (1973).

142. Wilson, *A Unified System for the Analysis of Light Petroleum Products Used as Fire Accelerants*, 10 FORENSIC SCI. 243 (1977).

143. Washington & Midkiff, *Systematic Approach to the Detection of Explosive Residues: Trace Vapor Analysis*, 56 J. ASS'N ANALYT. CHEMISTS 1239, 1240-44 (1973).

144. Kempe & Tannet, *Detection of Dynamite Residues on the Hands of Bombing Suspects*, 17 J. FORENSIC SCI. 323 (1972).

145. Aldridge & Oates, *Fractionation of Accelerants and Arson Residues by Solid Phase Extraction*, 31 J. FORENSIC SCI. 666 (1986).

146. *Id.* at 685.

147. Dhole, Kurhekar & Ambade, *Detection of Petroleum Accelerant Residues on Partially Burnt Objects in Burning/Arson Offences*, 35 SCI. JUST. 217 (1995); Hall & McCord, *The Analysis of Mono- and Divalent Cations Present in Explosive Residues Using Ion Chromatography with Conductivity Detection*, 38 J. FORENSIC SCI. 928 (1993); McCord & Whitehurst, *The Analysis and Characterization of TNT Using Liquid Chromatography with Photodiode Array Detection*, 37 J. FORENSIC SCI. 1574 (1992).

The parallel to drug identification testing continues. Subsections 23-3(A) and 23-3(C) point out that for specific drug identifications, laboratories are modernly turning to infrared (IR) techniques and gas chromatography/mass spectrometry (GC/MS). IR[148] and GC/MS[149] have similarly been adapted to arson cases. These procedures produce "more conclusive identification of the ... compounds present in these residues."[150]

There are also parallels between arson testing and general trace evidence testing. Section 25-2(D) of this treatise notes that energy dispersive X-ray analysis (EDX) is used to test trace evidence. EDX has also been utilized in some arson cases.[151] EDX is particularly useful in identifying gasoline accelerants.

Mass spectrometry (MS) is also used in fire investigation.[152] In particular, ion mobility spectrometry (IMS) has been adapted to arson analysis.[153] The analyst collects a sample onto a filter by wiping or vacuuming a surface. The filter is then inserted into the IMS. The IMS ionizes the sample. The ions are next gated into a drift tube. Substances have different, characteristic ion drift times. As the ions move through the tube, they are separated based upon size, shape, and mass.

---

148. Ettling, *Determination of Hydrocarbons in Fire Remains*, 8 J. FORENSIC SCI. 261, 262 (1963).

149. R. NEWMAN, M. GILBERT & K. LOTHRIDGE, GC-MS GUIDE TO IGNITABLE LIQUIDS (1998); Barshick, *Analysis of Accelerants and Fire Debris Using Aroma Detection Technology*, 43 J. FORENSIC SCI. 284 (1998); Nowicki, *Analysis of Fire Debris by Gas Chromatography/Mass Spectrometry (GC/MS): Case Studies*, 36 J. FORENSIC SCI. 1536 (1991); Trimpe, *Turpentine in Arson Analysis*, 36 J. FORENSIC SCI. 1059 (1991); Howard & McKague, *A Fire Investigation Involving Combustion of Carpet Material*, 29 J. FORENSIC SCI. 919, 921 (1984); R. NEWMAN, M. GILBERT & K. LOTHRIDGE, GC-MS GUIDE TO IGNITABLE LIQUIDS (1997); *Refining Fire Debris Analysis*, 21 SCI. SLEUTHING REV. 4-5 (Winter 1997) (discussing Sutherland, *The Analysis of Fire Debris Samples by GC/MS/MS*, 30 CAN. SOC. FOR. SCI. J. 185 (1997)); Keto, *GC/MS Data Interpretation for Petroleum Distillate Identification in Contaminated Arson Debris*, 40 J. FORENSIC SCI. 412 (1995); Grant, Whipple & Andresen, *Comprehensive Forensic Analyses of Debris from the Fatal Explosion of a "Cold Fusion" Electrochemical Cell*, 40 J. FORENSIC SCI. 18 (1995); Karkkainen, Seppala & Himberg, *Detection of Trace Levels of Gasoline in Arson Cases by Gas Chromatography-Mass Spectrometry with an Automatic On-Line Thermal Desorber*, 39 J. FORENSIC SCI. 186 (1994); Nowicki, *Automated Data Analysis of Fire Debris Samples Using Gas Chromatography-Mass Spectrometry and Macro Programming*, 38 J. FORENSIC SCI. 1354 (1993); Nowicki, *Addendum to "Automated Data Analysis of Fire Debris Samples Using Gas Chromatography-Mass Spectrometry and Macro Planning*," 39 J. FORENSIC SCI. 606 (1994).

150. Smith, *Mass Chromatographic Analysis of Arson Accelerants*, 28 J. FORENSIC SCI. 318 (1983).

151. Covey, *Application of Energy Dispersive X-Ray Spectroscopy in Fire Investigation*, 22 J. FORENSIC SCI. 325 (1977).

152. Gilbert, *The Use of Individual Extracted Ion Profiles Versus Summed Extracted Ion Profiles in Fire Debris Analysis*, 43 J. FORENSIC SCI. 871 (1998).

153. Fetterolf & Clark, *Detection of Trace Explosive Evidence by Ion Mobility Spectrometry*, 38 J. FORENSIC SCI. 28 (1993). Barringer Instruments, Inc., of South Plainfield, New Jersey, manufactures one IMS instrument, the IONSCAN.

The smaller ions drift faster and reach the IMS collector first. The analysis is fast, requiring only a fraction of a minute.

The cutting edge is aroma detection technology[154] such as the AromaScanner Electronic Aroma Detection Device manufactured by AromaScan, Inc., of Hollis, New Hampshire. The device contains

> an array of 32 electronically conducted, organic polymer sensors that respond to different volatile (and semi-volatile) chemicals to yield a unique "fingerprint" for each vapor sample.[155]

To date, the experience with the device has been mixed. The device has proven to be quite accurate with reference samples; but

> For actual fire debris samples . . ., wide variations in water content were shown to alter the sample humidity and variations in sample composition and concentration were shown to influence the sensor response.[156]

The researchers concluded that "[f]urther work is necessary . . . ."[157]

The American Society for Testing and Materials's Committee on Forensic Sciences has developed standards for arson testing.[158] The standards are E 1385-89 and 1412, 1413, and 1618. For example, E 1387 deals with gas chromatography, and 1618 concerns gas chromatraphy-mass spectrometry.

§ 26-7. Legal Restrictions on Arson Evidence.

§ 26-7(A). The Fourth Amendment.

As Chapter 2 notes, the fourth amendment forbids unreasonable searches and seizures. When fire or police department personnel enter a private structure, the entry can amount to a search within the purview of the fourth amendment.[159] Likewise, when they seize objects such as debris at the fire scene, their action constitutes an intrusion under the fourth amendment.[160] If an entry onto his real property or a seizure of his personal property violates fourth amendment standards, the defendant can move to suppress testimony about the search or

---

154. Barshick, *Analysis of Accelerants and Fire Debris Using Aroma Detection Technology*, 43 J. Forensic Sci. 284 (1998).

155. *Id.* at 285.

156. *Id.* at 292.

157. *Id.*

158. Lentini, *ASTM Standards for Forensic Sciences*, 40 J. Forensic Sci. 146 (1995).

159. Econ, *Search and Seizure Problems in Fire and Arson Investigations*, Police, Jan.-Feb. 1987, at 69.

160. *Id.* Hammond & Sands, *Trial by Fire: Preparing to Defend an Arson Case*, 19 The Champion 4, 4-5 (Apr. 1995) ("Fourth Amendment Considerations").

seizure.[161] As part of the foundation for her evidence, the prosecutor must therefore be prepared to establish compliance with fourth amendment standards.

The Intrusion onto Premises

The prosecutor can establish the legality of this intrusion by proving that the government personnel in question obtained a normal search warrant or by invoking a recognized exception to the warrant requirement such as the defendant's consent to a search.[162] If the courts have generally recognized an exception to the warrant requirement, in an appropriate case they will apply that exception to uphold a search or seizure in an arson prosecution.

However, by virtue of a line of Supreme Court authority spanning the 1960s through 1980s, there are two special doctrines applicable in arson cases. One doctrine permits a unique type of warrant. The United States Supreme Court announced the doctrine in two 1967 cases, *Camara v. Municipal Court of the City & County of San Francisco*[163] and *See v. City of Seattle.*[164] In the typical case of an intrusion onto private property, the police must seek a warrant;[165] and in order to obtain the warrant, they must show probable cause to believe that particular items subject to seizure such as contraband or evidence of a crime are located at certain premises.[166] On the one hand, in *Camara,* the Court ruled that absent exigent circumstances such as a fire, city health and safety inspectors must secure a warrant to enter private premises.[167] On the other hand, the Court modified the concept of probable cause in the context of a health or safety inspection. Writing for the majority, Mr. Justice White commented:

> There is unanimous agreement among those most familiar with this field that the only effective way to seek universal compliance with the minimum standards required by municipal codes is through routine periodic inspections of all structures.[168]

The justice argued that it would be impractical to apply the conventional probable cause standard here, since many dangerous conditions such as "faulty

---

161. D. MABLEY, ARSON INVESTIGATION AND PROSECUTION 15-16 (1982).

162. *Id.*

163. 387 U.S. 523 (1967).

164. 387 U.S. 541 (1967).

165. 2 E. IMWINKELRIED, P. GIANNELLI, F. GILLIGAN & F. LEDERER, COURTROOM CRIMINAL EVIDENCE § 1923 (3d ed. 1998).

166. *Id.* at § 1905.

167. Camara v. Municipal Court of the City & County of San Francisco, 387 U.S. 523, 534 (1967).

168. *Id.* at 535-36.

wiring" which might cause a fire "are not observable from outside the building...."[169] The majority then declared:

> Having concluded that the area inspection is a "reasonable" search of private property within the meaning of the Fourth Amendment, it is obvious that "probable cause" to issue a warrant to inspect must exist if reasonable legislative or administrative standards for conducting an area inspection are satisfied with respect to a particular dwelling. Such standards ... may be based upon the passage of time, the nature of the building (e.g., a multi-family apartment house), or the condition of the entire area, but they will not necessarily depend upon specific knowledge of the condition of the particular dwelling.[170]

In *See,*[171] the Court applied the *Camara* doctrine to a fire inspection.

The second special doctrine applicable in arson cases authorizes warrantless searches based upon exigent circumstances. While the Supreme Court announced the *Camara* doctrine in the 1960s, the Court recognized the second doctrine the following decade. The Court gave birth to the doctrine in 1978 in *Michigan v. Tyler.*[172] Mr. Justice Stewart authored the majority opinion. He wrote:

> A burning building clearly presents an exigency of sufficient proportions to render a warrantless entry "reasonable." Indeed, it would defy reason to suppose that firemen must secure a warrant ... before entering a burning structure to put out the blaze. And once in a building for this purpose, firefighters may seize evidence of arson that is in plain view. Although the Michigan Supreme Court appears to have accepted this principle, its opinion may be read as holding that the exigency justifying a warrantless entry to fight a fire ends, and the need to get a warrant begins, with the dousing of the last flame. [T]his view of the firefighting function is unrealistically narrow .... Fire officials are charged not only with extinguishing fires, but with finding their causes. Prompt determination of the fire's origin may be necessary to prevent its recurrence, as through detection of continuing dangers such as faulty wiring or a defective furnace. Immediate investigation may also be necessary to preserve evidence .... For these reasons, officials need no warrant to remain in a building for a reasonable time to investigate the cause of a blaze after it has been extinguished. And if the warrantless entry to put out the fire and determine

169. *Id.* at 537.
170. *Id.* at 538.
171. See v. City of Seattle, 387 U.S. 541 (1967).
172. 436 U.S. 499 (1978).

> its cause is constitutional, the warrantless seizure of evidence while inspecting the premises for these purposes also is constitutional.[173]

In a footnote,[174] the justice amplified the concept of a "reasonable time to investigate." He expressly stated that in the case of "a fire that spreads through a large apartment complex or that engulfs numerous buildings,"[175] "it may be necessary for officials ... to remain on the scene for an extended period of time repeatedly entering or re-entering the building or buildings, or portions thereof."[176] At the end of his opinion, the justice discussed the relationship between the exigent circumstances doctrine and the *Camara* doctrine recognized earlier. The justice stated that even after the lapse of a reasonable time to investigate the cause of the fire

> Thereafter, additional entries to investigate the cause of the fire may be made pursuant to the [special] warrant procedures governing administrative searches. See *Camara,* 387 U.S., at 534-539; *See v. Seattle,* 387 U.S., at 544-545 ....[177]

In the 1980s, the Supreme Court revisited the issue of searches in arson cases. In 1984, the Court handed down its decision in *Michigan v. Clifford.*[178] In *Clifford,* the Court both reaffirmed and clarified its earlier holdings in *Camara, See,* and *Tyler.* Justice Powell wrote the lead opinion. Initially, he reiterated the *Tyler* doctrine that during the fire and for a reasonable time thereafter, government officials may intrude upon the premises without obtaining a warrant. He emphasized that once that period of time has passed, further entries "generally must be made pursuant to a warrant ...."[179]

Justice Powell then addressed the question of the type of warrant and the type of probable showing needed:

> If a warrant is necessary, the object of the search determines the type of warrant required. If the primary object is to determine the cause and origin of a recent fire, an administrative warrant will suffice. To obtain such a

---

173. *Id.* at 509-10. United States v. Boettger, 71 F.3d 1410, 1416-17 (8th Cir. 1995) ("In the instant case, ... the required expertise was not close at hand. Lake Village did not have knowledgeable chemical explosive experts nearby.... This made necessarily for a longer delay. [S]uspending an investigation overnight because of adverse conditions does not end the exigency. The fireman posted outside ... did not end the possibility of another explosion occurring; only the chemicals' safe removal ended the exigency").

174. *Id.* at 510 n.6.

175. *Id.*

176. *Id.*

177. *Id.* at 511.

178. 464 U.S. 287 (1984).

179. *Id.* at 293.

> warrant, fire official need show only that a fire of undetermined origin has occurred on the premises, that the scope of the proposed search is reasonable and will not intrude unnecessarily on the fire victim's privacy, and that the search will be executed at a reasonable and convenient time.[180]

The justice next contrasted the situation in which "the primary object of the search is to gather evidence of criminal activity ...."[181] In that event, "a criminal search warrant may be obtained only on a showing of probable cause to believe that relevant evidence will be found in the place to be searched."[182]

Justice Stevens concurred in *Clifford.*[183] At the outset of his concurrence, he listed the points of law on which he concurred with the plurality. He agreed that: Firefighters have "the right ... to make a forceful, unannounced, nonconsensual, warrantless entry into a burning building;"[184] firemen have a "right to remain on the premises, not only until the fire has been extinguished and they are satisfied that there is no danger of rekindling, but also while they continue to investigate the cause of the fire;"[185] and "after investigators have determined the cause of the fire and located the place it originated, a search of other portions of the premises may be conducted only pursuant to a warrant ...."[186] However, he differed with the plurality over the issue of "whether a warrantless entry to make a post-fire investigation into the cause of a fire without the owner's consent is

---

180. *Id.* at 294.

181. *Id.*

182. *Id.*

183. *Id.* at 299 (Stevens, J., concurring).

184. *Id.*

185. *Id.* at 299-300.

186. *Id.* United States v. Mitchell, 85 F.3d 800 (1st Cir. 1996) (a fire investigator conducted a warrantless search of a commercial building the morning after the fire; the second search was merely a continuation of the warrantless search begun by a different fire investigator on the night of the fire; the initial search had been temporarily suspended on account of conditions at the scene, and the search was resumed at the first opportunity); United States v. Veltmann, 869 F. Supp. 929 (M.D. Fla. 1994), *aff'd*, 87 F.3d 1329 (11th Cir. 1996); Mazen v. Seidel, 185 Ariz. 195, 940 P.2d 923 (1997) (firefighters discovered a marijuana growing operation; they maintained the crime scene; the police then arrived, and they waited until narcotics detectives came and began actually moving the plants; the majority upheld the seizure of the plants; the majority argued that all the entries were part of the same temporal episode and that the police officers "stepped into the shoes" of the firefighters; two dissenters protested, writing:

> Because the purpose of this warrantless entry was unrelated to putting out the fire or investigating its cause, the search and seizure of the contraband does not fall within any clearly established exception to the Fourth Amendment and is invalid. The loss of a reasonable expectation of privacy in the storage unit attendant to the firefighter's lawful entry is not permanent. Under the majority's view, it continues at least as long as one state agent's presence on the property overlaps the later entries by other state agents for unrelated purposes.).

constitutional."[187] On that issue, Justice Stevens took the position that while the fourth amendment mandates a "traditional criminal search warrant in order to make an unannounced entry,"[188] a warrantless entry should be characterized "as reasonable whenever the inspector either has given the owner sufficient advance notice to enable him or an agent to be present, or had made a reasonable effort to do so."[189]

Justice Rehnquist filed a dissent in *Clifford.*[190] Then Chief Justice Burger and Justices Blackmun and O'Connor joined in the dissent. They took an even more permissive position than either the plurality or Justice Powell. In their view, on the facts in *Clifford,* there was no need for any type of warrant.[191]

Although *Clifford* is the controlling federal precedent, a state court is free to adopt a different, more rigorous view under its state constitution. Thus, alternatively, the defense may attack the legality of the intrusion onto the premises under the state constitution. In 1999, the Montana Supreme Court addressed the question of the validity of a warrantless entry by a sheriff's deputy after a fire.[192] The deputy entered to seize marijuana plants which firefighters had previously seen in plain view in a bedroom closet. The court surveyed the case law and concluded that there were three possible approaches: Once firefighters lawfully enter a home and observe evidence in plain view, the homeowner no longer has a reasonable expectation of privacy in the evidence;[193] the polar extreme view that even after the firefighters' lawful entry and observation, the homeowner has a protected expectation of privacy;[194] and a third, compromise position limiting the circumstances in which police may enter a home in the aftermath of a fire.[195] Under the compromise position, the relevant circumstances include the factor of whether the firefighters are still performing their customary work in the area of the home in which the evidence is seized. Expressly premising its decision on the Montana state constitution, the court opted for the second view. The court rejected the first, permissive view because that view seemingly permits unlimited re-entries of the home for purposes not reasonably anticipated by the victim of a fire. Since the police enter for a different reason than the firefighters, the court refused to hold that the police "step into the shoes" of the firefighters.

---

187. *Id.*

188. *Id.* at 303.

189. *Id.*

190. *Id.* at 305 (Rehnquist, J., dissenting).

191. *Id.* at 309-11.

192. State v. Bassett, 56 Mont. St. Rep. 447, 65 Cr.L. (BNA) 291 (Mont. Sup. Ct., May 24, 1999).

193. *Id.*, citing State v. Bell, 737 P.2d 254 (Wash. 1987).

194. *Id.*, citing United States v. Hoffman, 607 F.2d 280 (9th Cir. 1979). *Hoffman* was decided before *Clifford.*

195. *Id.*, citing Mazen v. Seidel, 940 P.2d 923 (Ariz. 1997).

The Subsequent Testing of Items Seized from the Premises

In addition to invoking the state constitution, a defense counsel might distinguish between the initial seizure of the samples and their subsequent scientific testing and argue that the testing represents a separate fourth amendment intrusion, requiring a distinct justification. Some authority supports that argument.[196] In a 1994 Connecticut case, *State v. Joyce*, under the state constitution the court applied the warrant requirement to later testing of burned clothing cut from a defendant's body by paramedics.[197] In 1997, a Connecticut court extended that holding to subsequent testing of charred wood flooring seized from the defendant's home during a fire investigation.[198] The majority premised its holding on a finding that the statutorily authorized cause-and-origin investigation had been completed before the testing was conducted.

In 1998, however, the same Connecticut court ruled that no warrant was needed before testing wood lawfully seized from a burned home.[199] The majority of the court distinguished its earlier *Joyce* decision. The majority noted that in *Joyce*, the basis for the lawful seizure of the evidence was the officers' community caretaking duty to safeguard the clothes. In contrast in the 1998 case the officers seized the samples of charred wood flooring pursuant to the statutes governing fire investigations. The majority further distinguished *Joyce* on the ground of "the nature and degree of the personal information that could be revealed by the evidence."[200] An analysis of the flooring would not reveal the same sort of intensely personal information which would be disclosed by testing a person's clothing. In concurrence, Justice McDonald argued that *Joyce* should be overruled as bad law. In dissent, Justice Berdon contended that *Joyce* was good law and the state statutes authorize warrantless searches only in exigent circumstances.

§ 26-7(B). The Limitations on the Admissibility of Expert Opinions.

In most cases in which a litigant puts an expert on the stand, the expert's direct testimony is syllogistic in structure.[201] After describing the credentials which qualify him or her as an expert, the witness: refers to a general explanatory theory or technique (the major premise), specifies the case-specific information

196. State v. Bernier, 46 Conn. App. 350, 700 A.2d 680 (1997), *rev'd*, 246 Conn. 63, 717 A.2d 652 (1998).

197. State v. Joyce, 639 A.2d 1007 (Conn. 1994), *cert. denied*, 118 S. Ct. 1523 (1998).

198. State v. Bernier, 46 Conn. App. 350, 700 A.2d 680 (1997), *rev'd*, 246 Conn. 63, 717 A.2d 652 (1998).

199. State v. Bernier, 63 Cr.L. (BNA) 569 (Conn. Sup. Ct., Aug. 4, 1998).

200. *Id.* at 570.

201. Imwinkelried, *The "Bases" of Expert Testimony: The Syllogistic Structure of Scientific Testimony*, 67 N.C. L. Rev. 1, 2-3 (1988).

which the theory or technique will be used to evaluate (the minor premise), and derives a conclusion or opinion by applying the major premise to the minor.[202] This section discusses the legal restrictions on each component of an arson expert's direct examination: the witness's qualification as an expert, the theories or techniques the expert relies on, the expert's minor premise, and the phrasing of the expert's ultimate opinion.

The witness's qualification as an expert. The profile of the ideal arson expert would include such qualifications as membership in the International Association of Arson Investigators[203] formal training at the annual arson investigation course offered by Purdue University,[204] and extensive, practical experience in a specialized arson squad.[205] However, a witness can qualify as an arson expert even if his or her qualifications fall far short of the ideal. To an extent, the required level of qualification is a variable function of the opinion which the witness wants to offer. Thus, while a fire captain was qualified "as a fire cause and origin expert," he could not opine that a heater had malfunctioned to start the fire.[206] Likewise, an experienced firefighter may testify to expert opinions on such questions as whether an accelerant "boosted" the fire in question;[207] but if the firefighter has not had any special training in arson investigation and detection, courts are generally reluctant to permit a fireman to opine directly that a fire was incendiary.[208] However, many courts routinely receive such opinions

---

202. *Id.*

203. STATE FARM INS. CO., TOUCHED OFF BY HUMAN HANDS 19.

204. INTERNATIONAL CITY MANAGERS' ASS'N, MUNICIPAL FIRE ADMINISTRATION 384 (5th ed. 1950); Smith v. Ford Motor Co., 882 F. Supp. 770, 772 (N.D. Ind. 1995) (the witness formed his own fire and accident investigation business; "From 1986 to 1988, Grinolds attended the North Dakota School of Science, taking four classes per week in fire science. His studies focused on structure and automobile fires, proper building construction, properties of fuels, and fire management. As a result of his efforts, Grinolds received certificates in fire management and fire science from the North Dakota School of Science").

205. *Id.*

206. Weigram v. Marley Co., 169 F.3d 514, 518 (8th Cir. 1999).

207. State v. Lytle, 214 Minn. 171, 7 N.W.2d 305 (1943); D. MABLEY, ARSON INVESTIGATION AND PROSECUTION 158 (1982).

208. State v. Hess, 9 Ariz. App. 29, 449 P.2d 46 (1969) (a course and two years' experience); State v. Williams, 654 S.W.2d 292 (Mo. App. 1983); State v. Purvis, 525 S.W.2d 590 (Mo. App. 1975) (battalion chief); Billings v. State, 503 S.W.2d 57 (Mo. App. 1973); Haynes v. County of Missoula, 163 Mont. 270, 517 P.2d 370 (1973); Commonwealth v. Smallwood, 465 Pa. 392, 350 A.2d 822 (1976) (seven years' experience); State v. Wilbur, 115 R.I. 7, 339 A.2d 730 (1975); Annot., *Expert Opinion as to Cause or Origin of Fire*, 88 A.L.R.2D 230, 254-56 (1963); People v. West, 264 Ill. App. 3d 176, 636 N.E.2d 1239, 201 Ill. Dec. 807 (the witness was not qualified to testify to an expert opinion as to the cause of the fire; the witness was not licensed to investigate fires, and the Illinois legislature obviously felt strongly that arson investigations must be conducted only by qualified, licensed individuals), *appeal denied*, 157 Ill. 2d 519, 642 N.E.2d 1300, 205 Ill. Dec. 183 (1994).

from an experienced arson investigator with specialized training.[209] Fire chiefs and marshalls with arson training may also venture such opinions.[210] Witnesses from other disciplines such as chemical engineering with relevant expertise may opine on such subjects as combustion and ignition.[211]

The validity of the theory or technique which the expert relies on. An arson investigator's major premise could be a theory about combustion. A laboratory analyst's major premise might be the accuracy of the Vapor Trace Analysis (VTA) analysis. In the minority of jurisdictions still subscribing to *Frye,* the expert's proponent will have to show the general acceptance of the theory or technique.[212] In *Daubert* jurisdictions,[213] the proponent will be obliged to demonstrate that the theory or technique has been experimentally validated.[214] According to our reviewer, the *Daubert* decision has already had a tremendous impact at the trial court level in fire cases. In his experience throughout the United States, the trial judges are much more insistent than in the past that the expert demonstrate that his or her theory has been validated in a "systematic, scientific" manner.

Under either test, the techniques mentioned in § 26-6(B) — notably gas chromatography, high performance liquid chromatography, infrared analysis, and gas chromatography/mass spectrometry — pass muster. One court has sustained the admission of testimony about canine behavior as an indicator of the presence of accelerants at the fire scene.[215]

---

209. Annot., *Expert Opinion as to Cause and Origin of Fire*, 88 A.L.R.3D 230, 253-54 (1963), State v. Hansen, 286 Minn. 4, 174 N.W.2d 697 (1970); D. MABLEY, ARSON INVESTIGATION AND PROSECUTION 158 (1982).

210. State v. Garrett, 682 S.W.2d 153, 155 (Mo. App. 1984) ("training in fire control, combat of fires and arson investigation at the University of Missouri at Columbia"); United States v. Markum, 4 F.3d 891, 896 (10th Cir. 1993) ("Experience alone can qualify a witness to give expert testimony. Chief Pearson worked as a firefighter and Fire Chief for 29 years"); Evans v. VanKleek, 110 Mich. App. 798, 314 N.W.2d 486 (1981).

211. People v. Gambrell, 429 Mich. 401, 415 N.W.2d 202 (1987); United States v. Kladouris, 964 F.2d 658, 668-70 (7th Cir. 1992) (although the expert could give "general kind of opinions about hydrocarbons and distillates," the expert could not testify about the significance of the burn pattern of the fire because the expert conceded "that he had never seen an inverted 'V' burn pattern").

212. *See* § 1-5, *supra.*

213. Weisgram v. Marley Co., 169 F.3d 514, 521 (8th Cir. 1999); United States v. Marji, 158 F.3d 60, 62-63 (2d Cir. 1998); Michigan Millers Mut. Ins. Corp. v. Benfield, 140 F.3d 915 (11th Cir. 1998).

214. *See* § 1-6, *supra.* Smith v. Ford Motor Co., 882 F. Supp. 770, 774 (N.D. Ind. 1995) (applying the *Daubert* test); State v. Marden, 673 A.2d 1304 (Me. 1996) (there was an insufficient showing of the basis for the detective's opinion about the different types of smoke odor; the detective claimed that he could determine that the odor emanated from wood and not cigarettes).

215. State v. Buller, 517 N.W.2d 711 (Iowa 1994). *But see* People v. Acri, 214 Ill. Dec. 761, 662 N.E.2d 115 (Ill. App. 1996) (a dog alert for accelerants at a fire scene is not generally accepted as reliable in the field of arson investigation unless the alert is confirmed by laboratory analysis;

The expert's minor premise. The expert produces his or her final opinion by applying the major premise to specific information in the case. An arson investigator might base an opinion about the identity of the accelerant causing the fire on an eyewitness report about the color of the flame and smoke in the initial stages of the fire. For his or her part, the laboratory analyst may base an opinion about the identity of the accelerant on the outcome of a GC test of particular physical evidence recovered from the fire scene. The eyewitness report and the physical object serve as the minor premise for the expert opinions.

Until recently, many jurisdictions prohibited experts from relying on hearsay reports which were not independently admissible.[216] Courts occasionally applied that prohibition in fire cases.[217] The prohibition may still be in effect in arson cases in some jurisdictions.[218] However, most jurisdictions have adopted a version of Federal Rule of Evidence 703, which governs the propriety of the expert's reliance on a hearsay report as part of his or her minor premise.[219] If the arson expert vouches that it is a customary practice of specialists in his or her field to rely on a particular type of information, the odds are that the court will allow the expert to use that kind of data as part of the basis for the expert's opinion.[220] There is authority squarely holding that Rule 703 permits the expert to rely on hearsay reports from private fire investigators.[221] Of course, the expert

---

without confirmation, testimony about the alert was properly excluded in an arson prosecution). *But see* Carr v. Georgia, 267 Ga. 701, 482 S.E.2d 314 (1997).

216. R. Carlson, E. Imwinkelried & E. Kionka, Evidence in the Nineties 533 (3d ed. 1991).

217. *E.g.,* Behr v. County of Santa Cruz, 172 Cal. App. 2d 697, 342 P.2d 987 (1959).

218. The official California Law Revision Commission comment to California Evidence Code § 801 approvingly cites the *Behr* case, mentioned in note 217, *supra.* Parker's Evidence Code of California § 801.

219. Almonte v. National Union Fire Ins. Co., 787 F.2d 763, 770 (1st Cir. 1986).

220. In some jurisdictions, the specialty's practice is dispositive; if the judge finds that it is in fact the specialty's custom to rely on a particular type of information, the judge must allow the expert to do so. *In re* Japanese Elec. Prods. Antitrust Litig., 723 F.2d 238, 275-79 (3d Cir. 1983), *rev'd sub nom.* Matsushita Elec. Indus. Co. v. Zenith, 475 U.S. 574 (1986). In other jurisdictions, the judge retains a residual power to second guess the reasonableness of the specialty's customary practice. *In re* "Agent Orange" Prod. Liab. Litig., 611 F. Supp. 1223, 1243-45 (E.D.N.Y. 1985), *aff'd,* 818 F.2d 187 (2d Cir. 1987), *cert. denied sub nom.* Lombardi v. Dow Chemical, 487 U.S. 1234 (1988).. However, even in these jurisdictions, the courts ordinarily defer to the specialty's custom. In effect, there is a rebuttable presumption that it is objectively reasonable for the expert to follow his or her specialty's customary practice. Ryan v. KDI Sylvan Pools, Inc., 121 N.J. 276, 579 A.2d 1241 (1990); Westfield Ins. Co. v. Harris, 134 F.3d 608, 613 (4th Cir. 1998) (under Rule 703, it was permissible for a fire marshal to rely on information furnished by private insurance investigators).

221. Westfield Ins. Co. v. Harris, 134 F.3d 608 (4th Cir. 1998).

must not only rely on a permissible kind of data; the expert must also have sufficient data to permit the expert to draw a reliable inference.[222]

The expert's ultimate opinion. At one time, some authorities suggested that an expert could not opine directly about an "ultimate fact" in the case.[223] Even when the courts avowed adherence to the ultimate fact rule, they permitted arson experts to go to the brink, so to speak, and testify on subjects short of the ultimate questions of whether the fire was incendiary and whether the defendant started the fire. Thus, the courts allowed experts to express opinions on topics such as where a fire began,[224] burn pattern,[225] burn rate,[226] and whether a fire was caused by sparks,[227] electrical malfunction,[228] a defective heating unit,[229] the ignition of gasoline,[230] careless smoking,[231] spontaneous combustion,[232] or accelerants.[233] However, a number of courts balked at permitting the expert to take the next step and testify directly to such ultimate issues as whether the fire was intentionally set[234] or had an incendiary origin.[235] If the opinion is otherwise admissible, it is

---

222. Breidor v. Sears, Roebuck and Co., 722 F.2d 1134, 1139-41 (3d Cir. 1983) (the trial judge erred in excluding the expert's opinion as to the cause of fire; since there was some evidence to support the expert's theory, the opinion was not excludable as speculative).

223. 1E. Imwinkelried, P. Giannelli, F. Gilligan & F. Lederer, Courtroom Criminal Evidence § 1403 (3d ed. 1998).

224. State v. Garrett, 682 S.W.2d 153, 155 (Mo. App. 1984); United States v. Ryan, 9 F.3d 660, 663 (8th Cir. 1993) ("at least six separate areas of fire origin"), *cert. denied*, 514 U.S. 1082 (1995); J. McNaught & J. Flannery, Massachusetts Evidence: A Courtroom Reference 14-7 (1988) (expert testimony is admissible on the "origination of a fire, Commonwealth v. Rhoades, 379 Mass. 810, 410 N.E.2d 342 (1980); Kenney v. Sears, Roebuck & Co., 355 Mass. 604, 246 N.E.2d 649 (1969)").

225. United States v. Lundy, 809 F.2d 392, 394-95 (7th Cir. 1987).

226. *Id.*

227. Annot., *Expert and Opinion Evidence as to Cause or Origin of Fire*, 88 A.L.R.2d 230, 269 (1963).

228. *Id.* at 275. United States v. Ryan, 9 F.3d 660, 663 (8th Cir. 1993) ("An electrical engineer also examined the fire scene and ruled out electrical cause and origin"), *cert. denied*, 514 U.S. 1082 (1995).

229. Annot., *Expert and Opinion Evidence as to Cause and Origin of Fire*, 88 A.L.R.2d 230, 278 (1963).

230. *Id.* at 280.

231. *Id.* at 282. United States v. Ryan, 9 F.3d 660, 663 (8th Cir. 1993) ("An electrical engineer also examined the fire scene and ruled out electrical cause and origin"), *cert. denied*, 514 U.S. 1082 (1995).

232. *Id.*

233. United States v. Triplett, 922 F.2d 1174 (5th Cir.), *cert. denied,* 500 U.S. 945 (1991).

234. Henderson v. State, 715 So. 2d 863 (Ala. Crim. App. 1997) (the court mentioned Evidence Rule 704 but added that "in the case of expert testimony, enforcement of this rule has been lax").

235. Annot., *Expert and Opinion Evidence as to Cause or Origin of Fire*, 88 A.L.R.2d 230, 264-65 (1963).

immaterial that the expert cannot vouch for his or her opinion as a "mathematical certainty."[236]

Just as Federal Rule of Evidence 703 expands the types of information which the expert may factor into his or her minor premise, Rule 704(a) purports to abolish the ultimate fact prohibition. The rule provides:

> Except as provided in subdivision (b), testimony in the form of an opinion or inference otherwise admissible is not objectionable because it embraces an ultimate issue to be decided by the trier of fact.

Since the adoption of Rule 704(a), "courts have generally not hesitated to ... permit expert testimony directly concerning the critical issue before the trier of fact."[237] Most jurisdictions now accept testimony by arson experts that a fire was incendiary in origin[238] or set deliberately.[239]

It would be a mistake, though, to assume that all courts permit expert opinions on these ultimate issues. Some jurisdictions are still resistant to opinions on the question of the incendiary character of the fire[240] or whether the fire was started intentionally.[241] Rule 704(b) strengthens the argument that an opinion on the latter question is inadmissible. That rule states:

> No expert witness testifying with respect to the mental state or condition of a defendant in a criminal case may state an opinion or inference as to whether the defendant did or did not have the mental state or condition constituting an element of the crime charged or of a defense thereto. Such ultimate issues are matters for the trier of fact alone.

The argument runs that in an arson case, the deliberate or intentional setting of the fire is "an element of the crime charged" and, thus, an improper subject for an expert opinion. Moreover, many, if not most, courts are still opposed to admitting expert opinions explicitly asserting that the defendant was the person who started

---

236. Bourdreau v. S/V Shere Khan C, 27 F. Supp. 2d 72, 80 (D. Me. 1998).

237. 2 G. JOSEPH & S. SALTZBURG, EVIDENCE IN AMERICA: THE FEDERAL RULES IN THE STATES § 53.3, at 2 (1987).

238. Almonte v. National Union Fire Ins. Co., 787 F.2d 763, 771 (1st Cir. 1986); Westfield Ins. Co. v. Harris, 134 F.3d 608 (4th Cir. 1998); United States v. Ryan, 9 F.3d 660, 663 (8th Cir. 1993) ("The fire marshal examined the debris and ... concluded that the fire was caused by arson."), *cert. denied*, 514 U.S. 1082 (1995); United States v. Markum, 4 F.3d 891, 895 (10th Cir. 1993) ("[w]hether the second fire was the result of arson").

239. American Home Assur. Co. v. Sunshine Supermarket, Inc., 753 F.2d 321 (3d Cir. 1985); Henderson v. State, 715 So. 2d 863 (Ala. Crim. App. 1997) (the court abrogated prior precedent and ruled that a fire marshal may testify that a fire was intentionally set).

240. People v. Rivera, 131 A.D.2d 518, 516 N.Y.S.2d 474 (1987).

241. *Id.* People v. Farnsley, 94 Mich. App. 34, 36, 287 N.W.2d 361 (1979) (the fire was deliberately set).

the fire in question.[242] Indeed, in one case, the court held that it was ineffective representation of counsel for the defense attorney to fail to object to such an opinion.[243]

§ 26-7(C). The Legal Sufficiency of Arson Evidence.

There is a presumption that a fire is accidental.[244] The prosecution must overcome that presumption[245] and establish that the fire was caused by criminal design.

There are three different settings in which a judge may have to evaluate the legal sufficiency of the prosecution's evidence of criminal design. First, the defense may move for a nonsuit or judgment of acquittal on the ground that the prosecution evidence of that element of the charged crime of arson is legally insufficient.[246] In this context, the legal sufficiency standard is the highest; the test is whether the prosecution's proof is sufficient to permit a rational trier of fact to find beyond a reasonable doubt every element of the charged crime, including the element that the fire was intentionally set.[247]

Second, the defense may argue that the prosecution's evidence is insufficient to corroborate an accomplice's testimony.[248] Some jurisdictions have common-law or statutory rules that a conviction may not rest on an accomplice's testimony unless the testimony is corroborated.[249] The corroborating testimony

---

242. Almonte v. National Union Fire Ins. Co., 787 F.2d 763, 770 (1st Cir. 1986); State v. Walters, 120 Idaho 46, 813 P.2d 857 (1990).

243. State v. Walters, 120 Idaho 46, 813 P.2d 857 (1990).

244. Comment, *Proof of the Corpus Delicti in Arson Cases*, 45 J. CRIM. LAW, CRIMINOLOGY & POL. SCI. 185, 186 (1954); INTERNATIONAL CITY MANAGERS' ASS'N, MUNICIPAL FIRE ADMINISTRATION 389, 391 (5th ed. 1950).

245. *Id.* at 389.

246. 2 E. IMWINKELRIED, P. GIANNELLI, F. GILLIGAN & F. LEDERER, COURTROOM CRIMINAL EVIDENCE §§ 2905, 2918-2921 (3d ed. 1998).

247. *Id.* at § 2919. Crowson, Cullum, Hiley & Lowe, *Survey of High Explosive Traces in Public Places*, 41 J. FORENSIC SCI. 980 (1996) ("The survey was carried out to determine the background levels of explosives traces in public places. Samples were taken at various transport sites. The survey showed that traces of the high explosives nitroglycerine (NG), trinitrotoluene (TNT), pentaerythritol tetranitrate (PETN), and cyclotrimethylene trinitramine (RDX) are rare within the general public environment").

248. D. MABLEY, ARSON INVESTIGATION AND PROSECUTION 148-49 (1982).

249. *Id.* (MINN. STAT. § 634.04); Orsini v. State, 281 Ark. 348, 665 S.W.2d 245 (ARK. STAT. § 43-2116), *cert. denied,* 469 U.S. 847 (1984); People v. Andrews, 49 Cal. 3d 200, 776 P.2d 285, 260 Cal. Rptr. 583, 591 (1989) (PENAL CODE § 1111), *cert. denied*, 494 U.S. 1060 (1990); People v. Razo, 217 Cal. App. 3d 616, 266 Cal. Rptr. 158, 163-64, *superseded*, 268 Cal. Rptr. 282, 788 P.2d 1154 (1990); McCleskey v. Kemp, 753 F.2d 877, 885 (11th Cir. 1985) ("In Georgia, an accomplice's testimony alone in felony cases is insufficient to establish a fact"), *aff'd,* 481 U.S. 279 (1987); Turner v. State, 452 A.2d 416 (Md. 1982); Martin v. Estelle, 691 F.2d 202, 204 n.1 (5th Cir. 1982) ("Under Texas law, a case may not be sent to the jury on the uncorroborated

must be substantial[250] and do more than merely create a suspicion of the defendant's guilt.[251] However, the prosecution may rely on circumstantial evidence;[252] and the corroboration need not, in itself, establish every element of the crime.[253] At the bare minimum, though, the corroborating evidence must connect the defendant to the crime.[254] The corroboration must make the accomplice's testimony implicating the defendant more likely than not.[255] The corroborating evidence need not be sufficient to convict;[256] and any inculpatory evidence, connecting the defendant to the commission of the offense, can suffice.[257]

Third, the defense may contend that the prosecution's evidence is sufficient to demonstrate the corpus delicti, which must be established before the judge may admit a defendant's confession.[258] Before the judge admits the defendant's confession admitting guilt, there must be proof that there was a fire and that the fire was set intentionally.[259] The legal sufficiency standard in this context is lax in several respects. To begin with, in the prior two settings — a directed verdict motion and an attack on the sufficiency of the corroboration of an accomplice's testimony -- the prosecution must present evidence linking the defendant to the crime. However, in this context, the corroborating evidence need not demonstrate the defendant's identity as the perpetrator.[260] Moreover, the required quantum of evidence is low. As in the case of the corroboration of an accomplice's testimony the corpus delicti evidence need not be sufficient to convict.[261] Depending on the jurisdiction, the prosecutor must present corroboration adequate to show either that a criminal act has occurred or merely that the confession is trustworthy.[262] The courts accept "a wide range of evidence" as sufficient proof of the corpus

---

testimony of an accomplice. *See* TEX. CODE CRIM. P. ANN. art. 38.14 ..."), *cert. denied,* 460 U.S. 1024 (1983).

250. Mackey v. State, 279 Ark. 307, 651 S.W.2d 82 (1983).

251. Redmon v. State, 282 Ark. 353, 668 S.W.2d 541 (1984).

252. Deleon v. State, 635 S.W.2d 771, 774 (Tex. App. 1982).

253. People v. Guiterrez, 232 Cal. App. 3d 1624, 284 Cal. Rptr. 230 (1991).

254. Henderson v. State, 279 Ark. 435, 652 S.W.2d 16, 19 (1983); Deleon v. State, 635 S.W.2d 771, 774 (Tex. App. 1982).

255. Torres v. State, 632 S.W.2d 844 (Tex. App. 1982).

256. Kennel v. State, 15 Ark. App. 45, 689 S.W.2d 5 (1985).

257. Graham v. State, 643 S.W.2d 920 (Tex. Crim. App. 1983).

258. 2 E. IMWINKELRIED, P. GIANNELLI, F. GILLIGAN & F. LEDERER, COURTROOM CRIMINAL EVIDENCE § 2321 (3d ed. 1998).

259. Comment, *Proof of the Corpus Delicti in Arson Cases*, 45 J. CRIM. LAW, CRIMINOLOGY & POL. SCI. 185 (1954).

260. 2 E. IMWINKELRIED, P. GIANNELLI, F. GILLIGAN & F. LEDERER, COURTROOM CRIMINAL EVIDENCE § 2321 (3d ed. 1998).

261. *Id.;* United States v. Garth, 773 F.2d 1469 (5th Cir. 1985), *cert. denied*, 476 U.S. 1140 (1986).

262. *Id.*

delicti.[263] Thus, the courts will receive evidence that: Wicks, candles, or timing devices were found at the fire scene; furniture or inventory had been removed from the premises; there had been previous threats against the owner; there were simultaneous, independent fires; furniture was arranged to impede the work of firemen; and there was another crime which the fire tended to cover up.[264]

In endeavoring to present legally sufficient evidence of an incendiary fire, the prosecution ought to combine the negative and affirmative approaches outlined in §26-4. The prosecutor should attempt to both eliminate natural and accidental causes[265] and show the incendiary character of the fire.[266] In most jurisdictions, expert testimony is admissible for both purposes;[267] and if the judge admits expert testimony of that tenor, the prosecution's evidence should be ruled legally sufficient. The evidence may be held sufficient even if the laboratory test results are negative for accelerants. As the laboratory analyst can explain, there are numerous reasons why the results can be negative in an arson fire: The fire may have consumed the accelerant, the accelerant might have evaporated after the fire, or samples may have been taken in the wrong place.

§ 26-8. Selected Bibliography.

W. BENNETT & K. HESS, INVESTIGATING ARSON (1984).
D. BERRY, FIRE LITIGATION HANDBOOK (1984).
L. GEDDES, HANDBOOK OF ELECTRICAL HAZARDS AND ACCIDENTS (1995).
C. HOBSON, FIRE INVESTIGATION: A NEW CONCEPT (1992).
KIRK'S FIRE INVESTIGATION (J.D. DeHaan, ed. 3d ed. 1991).
D. MABLEY, ARSON INVESTIGATION AND PROSECUTION (1982).
R. NEWMAN, M. GILBERT & K. LOTHRIDGE, GC-MS GUIDE TO IGNITABLE LIQUIDS (1997).
R. NOON, ENGINEERING ANALYSIS OF FIRES AND EXPLOSIONS (1995),
J. O'CONNOR, PRACTICAL FIRE AND ARSON INVESTIGATION (1986).
A. PATTON, FIRE LITIGATION SOURCEBOOK: TECHNICAL, MEDICAL AND LEGAL ASPECTS (2d ed. 1994) (2 vols.)
S. SWAB, INCENDIARY FIRES: A REFERENCE MANUAL FOR FIRE INVESTIGATORS (1983).
Beland, *Comments on Fire Investigation Procedures*, 29 J. FORENSIC SCI. 190 (1984).
Berry, *Characteristics and Behavior of Fire*, 34 DEF. L.J. 243 (1985).
Burd, *Arson and Fire Investigation: The Function of the Criminalist*, 7 J. FORENSIC SCI. 417 (1962).
Fladwed & Kirk, *Preparation and Trial of Arson Case*, 19 AMERICAN JURISPRUDENCE TRIALS 690 (1972).

263. Comment, *Proof of the Corpus Delicti in Arson Cases*, 45 J. CRIM. LAW, CRIMINOLOGY & POL. SCI. 185, 191 (1954).

264. *Id.* at 187 (collecting the cases).

265. People v. Rivera, 131 A.D.2d 518, 516 N.Y.S.2d 474 (1987).

266. Almonte v. National Union Fire Ins. Co., 787 F.2d 763, 770 (1st Cir. 1986).

267. *See* cases cited in notes 265-66, *supra.*

CHAPTER 27

ACCIDENT RECONSTRUCTION*

§ 27-1. In General.

Chapter 22 points out that within the past few years, legislators, courts, and prosecutors have adopted a more severe attitude toward drunk driving. Drunk driving often results in personal injuries to or the death of innocent victims. In the past, when such injuries or deaths ensued, prosecutors sometimes not only charged the driver with DUI; they also charged the defendant with more serious offenses such as manslaughter.[1] However, prosecutors filed such serious charges

---

*The authors wish to express their thanks to Professor John B. Kwasnowski, Western New England College, who reviewed this chapter in the second and third editions, and Mr. James Dedman III, Director of Training, National College of District Attorneys, who reviewed this chapter in the second edition of this treatise.

1. Huguley v. State, 39 Ala. App. 104, 96 So. 2d 315, *cert. denied,* 266 Ala. 697, 96 So. 2d 319 (1957) (manslaughter); People v. Haeassler, 41 Cal. 2d 252, 260 P.2d 8 (1953), *cert. denied,* 347 U.S. 931 (1954) (manslaughter); People v. Peoples, 212 Cal. App. 2d 581, 28 Cal. Rptr. 120 (1963)

only on rare occasions. A by-product of the national campaign against drunk driving has been a tougher attitude towards defendants whose drunken or otherwise careless driving leads to injury to others. In these cases, the filing of serious charges such as manslaughter is now far more commonplace; today some defendants are standing trial for second degree murder.[2] In other jurisdictions, the legislatures have created special vehicular homicide offenses.

Accident reconstruction testimony was once employed almost exclusively in civil actions. However, modernly, such testimony is also used extensively in criminal cases.[3] The toughened social attitude toward drunk and reckless driving has raised the stakes on those types of cases, and both prosecutors and defense counsel are increasingly turning to accident reconstruction expertise. Within the decade, the National College of District Attorneys has added a block of instruction on accident reconstruction to its curriculum. There is a growing realization that accident reconstruction analysis can be a very effective type of testimony in criminal as well as civil cases.[4]

(manslaughter); Jones v. State, 113 Ga. App. 667, 149 S.E.2d 426 (1966) (involuntary manslaughter); Collins v. State, 86 Ga. App. 157, 71 S.E.2d 99 (1952); People v. Dietschweiler, 21 Ill. App. 3d 707, 315 N.E.2d 585 (1974) (involuntary manslaughter); People v. Parr, 133 Ill. App. 2d 82, 272 N.E.2d 712 (1971); People v. Zimmerman, 385 Mich. 417, 189 N.W.2d 259 (1971) (negligent homicide); State v. Bosch, 125 Mont. 566, 242 P.2d 477 (1952); State v. Golub, 24 Or. App. 19, 544 P.2d 609 (1976) (criminally negligent homicide); State v. Betts, 235 Or. 127, 384 P.2d 198 (1963); Wallen v. State, 338 P.2d 170 (Okla. Crim. 1959) (manslaughter); State v. Read, 121 Utah 453, 243 P.2d 439 (1952) (involuntary manslaughter); State v. Lingman, 97 Utah 180, 91 P.2d 457 (1939); Lee v. State, 556 P.2d 217 (Wyo. 1976) (negligent homicide).

2. *See* People v. Fugatt, 229 Cal. App. 3d 240, 280 Cal. Rptr. 37, *opinion withdrawn,* 1991 Cal. LEXIS 3207 (Cal. 1991). The opinion was depublished and is no longer citable as authority, but the fact situation nevertheless illustrates that prosecutors are filing more serious charges in cases arising from traffic accidents.

3. Wilson v. State, 574 So. 2d 1324, 1335 (Miss. 1990) ("the testimony of accident reconstruction specialists is allowed in criminal cases in this State"); Kwasnoski, *Constructing Hypotheticals in Motor Vehicle Homicide Cases*, 16 THE CHAMPION 6 (Nov. 1992) ("The use of accident reconstruction technology in the prosecution and defense of motor vehicle homicide cases has dramatically increased over the last decade").

4. The reader should not assume, though, that the attorney should use such expert testimony to the exclusion of lay eyewitness testimony or that expert testimony is always needed to corroborate lay eyewitness testimony. The following is an illustrative closing argument attacking accident reconstruction testimony:

> Now these accident reconstruction experts . . . can be real helpful in the right type of case, and the plaintiff's expert is one of the best. In fact, we call on him for help sometimes in the right type of case. You know the kind I'm talking about, one of those collisions up on the interstate where there's a lot of ice and snow and lots of vehicles and maybe a tractor-trailer or two, and it's dark, and nobody really knows or remembers how it all happened, and you need someone to help re-create it--those types of cases. But not cases like this. In this case, we have an eyewitness. We don't need an accident reconstruction expert to tell us what he

§ 27-2. The Scientific Premises of Accident Reconstruction.

Accident reconstruction rests on principles and theories developed by the basic science of physics and the applied science of engineering.[5] In part, the discipline rests on the laws of mechanics and motion formulated by Sir Isaac Newton.[6] Those laws tell us the following:

—A body at rest tends to remain at rest. This is the law of inertia. "[A]ny body ... will remain still unless moved by some force."[7]

—A body in motion tends to remain in motion in a straight line at a uniform velocity. The body will move at a constant speed in a straight line "unless ... the body is acted upon ... by an unbalanced force."[8]

—If an unbalanced force acts on a moving body, the body accelerates in the direction of the force. The acceleration is directly proportional to the unbalanced force and inversely proportional to the mass of the body.[9] By way of example, a small push will move the object slowly or for a short distance. In contrast, a large push will move the object faster or for a greater distance.

—For every action, there is an equal and opposite reaction.[10] Thus, if a person throws a ball against a wall — the action — the ball will bounce back or react with the same amount of force it initially carried.

In addition to these laws, accident reconstruction experts rely on "hundreds of other equations."[11] Some of these equations have been deduced from the Newtonian laws of motion while others have been derived by empirical research.[12]

Accident reconstructionists use these laws and equations to determine how the accident happened.[13] Sections 27-4 through 27-9 of this chapter review some of the specific determinations which accident reconstruction experts can make. Of

---

thinks happened. We have an eyewitness to tell us what actually happened. No guesswork. No fancy math.

Burke, *Don't Expect the Expert*, 34 TRIAL 76 (Nov. 1998).

5. Baker, *Open Forum: Scientific Reconstruction of an Automobile Accident*, 25 INS. COUNSEL J. 433 (1958).

6. Zurmuhlen, *Automobile Accident Reconstruction*, 18 TRIAL LAW. Q. 49 (Winter 1987).

7. *Id.*

8. *Id.*

9. *Id.*

10. *Id.*

11. Badger, *Reconstruction of Traffic Accidents*, 9 AM. JUR. 3D PROOF OF FACTS 115, 140-45 (1990).

12. M. CHIECO & J. KWASNOSKI, ESTABLISHING LIABILITY IN VEHICULAR ACCIDENTS 234 (1989).

13. Schorr, *The Techniques of Traffic Accident Reconstruction*, 27 THE PRACTICAL LAW. 77 (Mar. 1, 1981).

course, before solving an equation, the expert must know what values to insert or "plug in" for the various variables in the equation.[14] The expert obtains those values by personally conducting a pretrial investigation of the accident, reviewing the written investigative reports, or directly contacting persons who have investigated the accident. The following section reviews that investigation.

§ 27-3. The Initial Accident Investigation.

Especially when the accident has caused serious personal injuries or death, there should be a careful inspection of both the accident scene and the involved vehicles.

A thorough accident scene inspection usually requires between two and six hours but, in a given case, can consume much more time. The inspector should examine: the location of objects such as vehicles and debris on the road; the placement of any marks on the road, including skidmarks, yaw marks, gouges, and scrapes; and damage to any roadside objects such as trees or embankments.

In the case of marks such as skids, the inspector must not only measure the mark; the inspector must also determine whether the mark is continuous. A break in the continuity of the mark may indicate that a vehicle "vaulted" through the air during the accident — an occurrence which can greatly complicate the process of making such determinations as estimating the speed of the vehicle. Further, the inspector must note whether the marks are linear or curved. If the vehicle struck a rigid barrier such as a brick wall and came to rest 20 feet from the wall, the inspector cannot assume that the vehicle rebounded from the wall in a straight line; after striking the wall, the vehicle's tires might have rotated. The curvature and/or appearance of the marks may evidence the rotation.

The inspector must not only note these items of information; more importantly, the inspector must record them for subsequent use by accident reconstruction experts, attorneys, judges, and juries. There are accepted methods of documenting and diagramming accident scenes. Two of the most widely used methods are triangulation and gridding. There are detailed, technical analyses of these techniques in *Motor Vehicle Accident Reconstruction and Cause Analysis* by Dr. Rudolf Limpert[15] and *Investigation and Prosecution of DWI and Vehicular Homicide* by John Kwasnoski, Gerald Patridge, and John Stephen.[16] In addition to diagramming the scene, the inspector can photograph the area. In doing so, the inspector should comply with accepted practices of

---

14. Badger, *Reconstruction of Traffic Accidents*, 9 AM. JUR. 3D PROOF OF FACTS 115, 188 (1990).

15. R. LIMPERT, MOTOR VEHICLE ACCIDENT RECONSTRUCTION AND CAUSE ANALYSIS § 32-4.2 (3d ed. 1989).

16. J. KWASNOSKI, G. PARTRIDGE & J. STEPHEN, INVESTIGATION AND PROSECUTION OF DWI AND VEHICULAR HOMICIDE Ch. 6 (1998).

photogrammetry which are also addressed in the Limpert text.[17] If the inspector does so, at a later point in time an accident reconstruction expert can use known dimensions depicted in the photographs to estimate unknown measurements such as the length of skidmarks shown in the photographs.

The inspector should make a particularly detailed examination of the vehicles involved in the accident. This examination can easily require an hour or two. In the course of the examination, the inspector should study, *inter alia:* the tires — whether they are inflated or flat and whether their tread is deep or shallow; any damage to the tires or rims; the angle of the damage to the vehicle; areas of damage and disrepair; the steering axle; the brake assembly, including drums and pads or discs; any leaking seals or excessive grease; the suspension and frame, including springs, shock absorbers, assembly bolts, tierods, and spring hangers; and the condition of vehicle controls such as the gear selector, light control, radio, and wipers.[18] It is critical that the inspector examine all sides of these components[19] and the undercarriage of the vehicle.[20]

There are checklists which the inspector can use to ensure that she gathers all the information which the accident reconstruction expert could later need.[21]

§ 27-4. Determining the Role of the Accident Participant: Driver, Passenger, or Pedestrian.

Armed with sufficient physical facts about the accident scene, the accident reconstruction expert can draw many inferences about various aspects of the accident. For example, the expert may be able to determine both whether a person was involved in a traffic accident[22] and, if so, the person's role in the accident.[23] Suppose, for instance, that the police find both the defendant and a decedent at an accident scene. An hour before the accident, the two were drinking together; and they left the bar together. The defendant owns the car involved in the accident, but he claims that the decedent was driving. It is

---

17.. R. LIMPERT, *supra* note 15, at § 32-5. United States v. Quinn, 18 F.3d 1461 (9th Cir.) (approving the use of photogrammetry in a different context), *cert. denied*, 512 U.S. 1242 (1994).

18. Zurmuhlen, *Automobile Accident Reconstruction*, 18 TRIAL LAW. Q. 49, 52-54 (Winter 1987).

19. *Id.* at 54.

20. Badger, *Reconstruction of Traffic Accidents*, 9 AM. JUR. 3D PROOF OF FACTS 115, 152 (1990).

21. J. KWASNOSKI, G. PARTRIDGE & J. STEPHEN, INVESTIGATION AND PROSECUTION OF DWI AND VEHICULAR HOMICIDE ch. 6 (1998); Van Kirk, *A Scientific Approach to Documenting Evidence for Accident Reconstruction*, 29 J. FORENSIC SCI. 806 (1984).

22. Tomczak & Buikstra, *Analysis of Blunt Trauma Injuries: Vertical Deceleration Versus Horizontal Deceleration Injuries*, 44 J. FORENSIC SCI. 253 (1999) (the nature of the injuries can indicate whether the injuries resulted from vertical deceleration (falling) or deceleration in a horizontal plane (an automobile accident)).

23. Fox v. Dannenberg, 906 F.2d 1253 (8th Cir. 1990).

undisputed that the defendant was present at the time of the accident, but the crucial question is whether the defendant was behind the wheel.[24] There are several factors which an expert can weigh to determine the defendant's role in the accident.

On the one hand, the expert cannot rely solely on the final resting place of the bodies of the participants. The force of the accident may have throw the participants around the interior of the vehicle or even entirely out of the vehicle.

On the other hand, the following factors are helpful clues to identifying the role of each participant in the accident:

Typical injury patterns.[25] A pedestrian is likely to sustain lower leg bruises or even open fractures due to impact with the vehicle's bumper. The location of these injuries should roughly correspond with the height of the bumper. The bumper injuries tend to be lower if the driver applied the brakes before impact, since the front of the automobile dips. The absence of bumper injuries suggests that the pedestrian was side-swiped. Injuries to the abdominal area, hip, and buttocks are likewise common. Even when the visible injuries appear superficial, there may be serious subcutaneous hematomas, deep pockets of blood, or torn tissue. If the body is thrown from the hood onto the street, the body may have severe head or neck injuries. When the body is thrown violently onto the pavement, the body may have road burns; and the clothing may suffer friction tearing.

A passenger's head often impacts the windshield during an accident and causes the windshield to form a spiderweb fracture pattern. Windshield injuries are often deep. In contrast, the shattering of tempered side windows tends to cause angled, dicing cuts. If the passenger is not wearing a seat belt, his or her entire body may fly forward; and the dashboard tends to force the kneecap between the femoral condyles.

The driver will frequently sustain closed chest injuries caused by the steering wheel. Impact with the steering wheel can result in multiple rib fractures, pulmonary tears and contusions, and cardiovascular injuries. If the driver's face comes into contact with a padded steering wheel or dashboard, the face may exhibit abrasions, lacerations, and fractures.

---

24. J. Tarantino, *How the Accident Reconstruction Expert Can Contribute to DUI Defense*, 6 D.W.I. J. 6, 7 (Apr. 1991). *See also* J. KWASNOSKI, G. PARTRIDGE & J. STEPHEN, INVESTIGATION AND PROSECUTION OF DWI AND VEHICULAR HOMICIDE ch. 6 (1998).

25. *See generally* DEDMAN, ISSUES AND EXPERTS IN VEHICULAR HOMICIDE ACCIDENT RECONSTRUCTION 10-12 (unpublished manuscript on file with the National College of District Attorneys, Law Center, University of Houston). Dell'Erba, Di Vella & Giardino, *Seatbelt Injury to the Common Iliac Artery: Case Report*, 43 J. FORENSIC SCI. 215 (1998); Rosenbluth & Hicks, *Evaluating Low-Speed Rear-End Impact Severity and Resultant Occupant Stress Parameters*, 39 J. FORENSIC SCI. 1393 (1994); Estate of Sohni v. Byrne, Orange County Sup. Ct., N.Y., No. 1982/90, Nov. 7, 1991, 35 A.T.L.A. L. Rep. 154 (May 1992) (an accident reconstruction expert explained how Newton's laws of motion determined the injury patterns to the various vehicle occupants).

Matching injuries to trace evidence within the vehicle. The expert can attempt to correlate the injuries sustained by the accident participant and the trace evidence at the accident scene. For example, in a given case, it might be clear that something — presumably impact with the passenger's head — caused a dent in the dashboard. If the defendant is the only accident participant who sustained that type of head injury, the injury is some evidence that the defendant was the passenger rather than the driver.

Textile-plastic fusing (TPF).[26] This phenomenon is usually referred to as textile-plastic or fiber-plastic fusing. During a collision, a vehicle occupant's hair or fibres from his or her clothing may come into contact with parts of the vehicle's interior such as upholstery, roof, head liner, pillar covers, and dashboard.[27] These parts of the interior are thermal plastic material. If part of a person's body strikes this material, the material can momentarily soften; and hairs or fibres from the body can become imbedded in the thermal surface.[28] The imbedded hair and fibre is a contact trace, evidencing contact with the person's body. The imbedded hair or fibre can later be matched with the person's hair or clothing.

Other clues. There might be fingerprints on the steering wheel. Similarly, there may be pedal imprints on the bottom of the driver's shoes. When the driver realizes that a collision is imminent, the driver may press down on the brakes; and that the pressure created by the impact may leave a pedal imprint on the sole of that person's shoe.

It should be evident at this point that the determination of the accident participant's role can require the expertise of several disciplines: fingerprint examiners, trace evidence analysts, and forensic pathologists.

§ 27-5. Determining the Vehicle's Direction of Travel.

The question facing the accident reconstruction expert may be the direction of travel of the vehicle. What path or trajectory did the vehicle take? Given enough physical evidence from the accident scene, the expert may be able to answer this question as well.[29] The accident reconstruction expert attempts to determine the vector which the vehicle was proceeding along. In doing so, the expert relies heavily on roadway marks. In §§ 27-6 and 27-8 of this chapter, we shall define and discuss skidmarks, yaw marks, and gouge marks. The expert identifies all the

---

26. J. Tarantino, Strategic Use of Scientific Evidence § 14.33 (1988).

27. *Id.*

28. Masakowski, Enz, Cothern & Rowe, *Fiber-Plastic Fusions in Traffic Accident Reconstruction*, 31 J. Forensic Sci. 903 (1986).

29. Box v. California Date Growers Ass'n, 57 Cal. App. 3d 266, 129 Cal. Rptr. 146 (1976). *See* B. Jefferson, Synopsis of California Evidence Law § 29.3, at 450 (1985).

marks, ensures that they are attributable to the vehicle in question, and connects the marks.

The key problem can be attributing the marks to the vehicle. Even when only one vehicle was involved in the accident, attribution can be a difficult task. When the accident occurs on a well-traveled road or highway, there is always the possibility that an earlier vehicle left the mark on the road surface. Attribution can be especially difficult when several cars were involved in the accident. When a vehicle's front wheels rest at the very end of a skidmark and several witnesses to the accident verify that the vehicle has not been moved, it is obvious that the skidmark is attributable to that vehicle. However, when the mark is a gouge into the road surface, the expert should carefully match the shape of the gouge to a part of the vehicle which may have caused the mark. Even when there is a virtually perfect physical match, there is always the chance that the mark antedated the accident.

§ 27-6. Determining the Vehicle's Velocity.

In addition to identifying the direction of the vehicle, the expert often needs to determine the speed or velocity with which the vehicle was moving in that direction. Technically, there is a distinction between speed and velocity.[30] As one commentator has stated, "[S]peed is 'rapidity in moving' [without regard to direction], where velocity is the 'time rate of change of position of a body in a specified direction.'"[31] For the balance of this chapter, we shall use the expression, "velocity." In some cases, the expert is interested in the velocity of a vehicle after impact. There are recognized formulae for computing that velocity. Figure 27-1 sets out two of the formulae.[32] However, in most cases — especially prosecutions — the expert is more concerned about determining the velocity of the vehicle before impact. It is ideal if a police officer happened to be nearby and used radar, discussed in Chapter 28, to clock the vehicle. However, even absent a

30. Badger, *Reconstruction of Traffic Accidents*, 9 AM. JUR. 3D PROOF OF FACTS 115, 140 (1990).

31. *Id.*

32. DEDMAN, ISSUES AND EXPERTS IN VEHICULAR HOMICIDE ACCIDENT RECONSTRUCTION (unpublished manuscript on file with the National College of District Attorneys, Law Center, University of Houston). Reprinted with permission. Many of the formulae for computing post-accident speed require data about the distance the vehicle traveled after the collision and before coming to rest. Section 27-3 of this chapter pointed out that when the inspector is conducting the initial accident scene investigation, the inspector must carefully note whether marks such as skids are linear or curved. That point is relevant here. The inspector should not assume that the vehicle traveled in a straight line between the point of impact and the point where the vehicle finally came to rest; depending on the angle of impact, the vehicle may have rotated before coming to the point of rest. If so, the vehicle will have traveled farther — perhaps much farther — than the straight line distance. Applying the formula to the straight line distance will yield an underestimate of the correct speed.

radar reading, an accident reconstruction expert can draw conclusions about the pre-impact velocity from several types of data, including skidmarks, yaw marks, and the damage to the vehicles.

§ 27-6(A). Skidmarks.

Assume that before collision, the driver attempts to apply his or her brakes. The wheels consequently lock rather than continue rotating. A locked wheel can produce skidmarks.[33] The abrasive action between the sliding tire and the road surface can generate temperatures between 200 and 1,000 degrees F.[34] Rubber particles are torn off the tire and deposited on the road surface.[35] In order to estimate speed from these skidmarks, the expert must determine both the length of the skidmarks and the drag factor for the road surface.

Ascertaining the skidmark length and drag factor

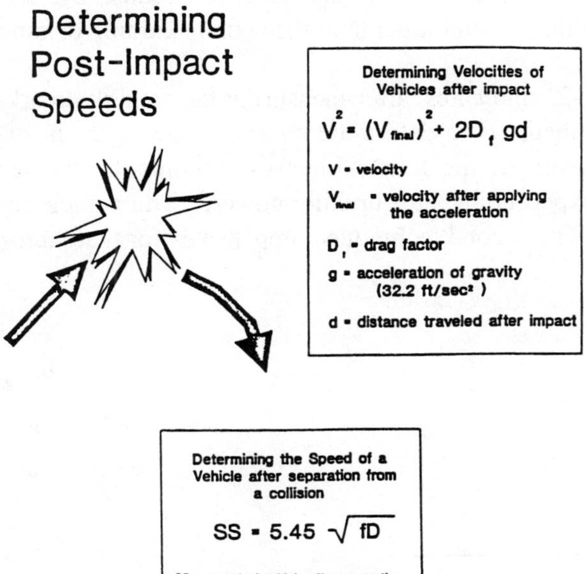

Figure 27-1

33. Badger, *Reconstruction of Traffic Accidents*, 19 AM. JUR. 3D PROOF OF FACTS 115, 136 (1990).

34. A. MOENSSENS, J. STARRS, C. HENDERSON & F. INBAU, SCIENTIFIC EVIDENCE IN CIVIL AND CRIMINAL CASES § 11.03 (4th ed. 1995).

35. *Id.*

Skidmark length. It is vital that the length of the skidmarks be measured accurately. The skidmarks should not be merely paced off. Experience indicates that although the person measuring the skidmarks may think he is consistently taking a 36 inch pace, the pace is often only 32 inches.[36] The person making the measurement may have to get down on hands and knees[37] to see parts of the skidmark and use a rolling wheel or tape[38] to make accurate measurements.

The expert should measure the skidmarks left by all four wheels. At first blush, it may appear that there are only two skidmarks. However, if the car proceeded along a straight vector, the rear wheel skidmarks may overlap the front wheel skidmarks. In that case,

> the measurement started when the rear tires began to leave marks, and the measurement ends where the front tires stopped. If this is a case of one set of skidmarks overlapping another, the driver has been "cheated" by the length of the wheel base of the vehicle, because the measured skidding distance is that much longer than the actual skidding distance was.[39]

As Figure 27-2[40] indicates, after measuring the four skidmarks, the expert can use one of two methods to determine overall skid length. In one technique, the expert simply averages the four skidmarks to compute the mean. In the other technique, the expert adjusts for braking power.[41] The vehicle may pitch forward during braking. The second technique compensates for that factor.[42]

---

36. Caufield, *Cross-Examination of Accident Reconstruction Expert by Defense Attorney to Refute Opinion of Speeding and Inattentiveness Based on Formulas*, *in* R. HABUSH, ART OF ADVOCACY: CROSS EXAMINATION OF NON-MEDICAL EXPERTS 41-20 (1991).

37. Badger, *Reconstruction of Traffic Accidents*, 19 AM. JUR. 3D PROOF OF FACTS 115, 137 (1990).

38. M. CHIECO & J. KWASNOSKI, ESTABLISHING LIABILITY IN VEHICULAR ACCIDENTS 310 (1989).

39. Badger, *Reconstruction of Traffic Accidents*, 9 AM. JUR. 3D PROOF OF FACTS 115, 138 (1990).

40. DEDMAN, ISSUES AND EXPERTS IN VEHICULAR HOMICIDE ACCIDENT RECONSTRUCTION (unpublished manuscript on file with the National College of District Attorneys, Law Center, University of Houston). Reprinted with permission.

41. *Id.* at 7.

42. *Id.*

Methods to Compute 4 Wheel Skid Length

Averaging

Right Front	27.5
Right Rear	22
Left Front	26
Left Rear	24
	99.5

99.5 / 4 = 24.875 feet

4 Wheel Skid Distance of 24.875 feet

Brake Power

Right Front	27.5 x 30% = 8.25
Right Rear	22 x 20% = 4.4
Left Front	26 x 30% = 7.8
Left Front	24 x .20% =4.8
	25.25

4 Wheel Skid Distance of 25.25 feet

Figure 27-2

Drag factor. Just as there is a technical distinction between speed and velocity, there is a distinction between drag factor or friction number[43] and friction coefficient.[44] When the surface is inclined or wet and one or more of the wheels do not brake, the factor and the coefficient can differ. However, if the road surface in question is dry and level and the brakes on all four wheels locked, the coefficient and the factor are identical.[45] They both represent "the resistance of sliding of two surfaces in contact: the force parallel to a surface required to keep an object sliding on that surface divided by the force of the object against the surface."[46] In other words, it is "the horizontal force required to cause an object to move in the direction of the force, divided by the weight of the object being moved."[47] The formula is:

$$f = F / W$$ [48]

---

43. The expressions, "drag factor" and "friction number," are sometimes used as if they are synonymous. However, our reviewer cautions against confusing the two concepts. The friction number is the drag factor multiplied by 100. He states that the expressions should not be used interchangeably.

44. Badger, *Reconstruction of Traffic Accidents*, 9 AM. JUR. 3D PROOF OF FACTS 115, 175-76 (1990).

45. *Id.* at 175.

46. *Id.* at 176.

47. *Id.*

48. *Id.* at 146.

If the force required were 19 pounds and the weight dragged were 25 pounds, the drag factor would be 0.76.[49]

There are several methods of determining drag factor.[50] One is the use of a drag sled or box.[51] Or the expert can employ an accelometer[52] or electronic instrument attached to the vehicle involved in the accident or a substitute test vehicle.[53] Alternatively, the expert can perform test skids with either the same vehicle or a similar exemplar vehicle.[54] In many cases, the person investigating the accident unfortunately does not bother to measure drag factor of the road. Instead, the person relies on published charts of average drag factors for certain types of surfaces. Figure 27-3 is illustrative.[55] The difficulty is that some of these charts were generated in the late 1950s and early 1960s when rubber tire compounds were different and many road surfaces were aggregate.[56] Further, motor vehicle braking systems were not as refined then.[57] Moreover, little is known about the manner in which some of these charts were prepared.[58] Nevertheless, in many cases — occasionally because the road in question has been resurfaced since the accident — the expert relies on generalizations from such a chart rather than a measurement carefully performed at the accident scene. The expert should consider a range of drag factors, since the true drag factor might fall outside the published chart values.

Estimating velocity

After determining the skidmark length and drag factor, the expert can estimate the velocity of the vehicle leaving the skidmarks in one of two ways.

Formulae for computing velocity from skidmarks. One way is to use a recognized equation and solve the equation for velocity. There are numerous equations which the expert can solve for velocity once she knows the values for skidmark length and drag factor. For example, one equation is:

---

49. *Id.* at 190.

50. *See* J. Kwasnoski, G. Partridge & J. Stephen, Investigation and Prosecution of DWI and Vehicular Homicide ch. 6 (1998).

51. Badger, *Reconstruction of Traffic Accidents*, 9 Am.Jur.3d Proof of Facts 146, 188 (1990).

52. *Id.* at 147.

53. *Id.*

54. *Id.*

55. R. Limpert, Motor Vehicle Accident Reconstruction and Cause Analysis 276 (3d ed. 1989). Reprinted with permission.

56. Badger, *Reconstruction of Traffic Accidents*, 9 Am. Jur. 3d Proof of Facts 115, 146 (1990).

57. *Id.*

58. *Id.*

$$S = \sqrt{30fd}$$

In this formula, S is the velocity, f is the drag factor, and d is the skidmark length. Another formula is:

$$v = \sqrt{2gfd}$$

In this equation, v is velocity in feet per second before the skid, g is the acceleration of gravity (32.2 feet per second squared), f is the drag factor, and d is the length of the skidmark.

Nomograph charts. Just as the expert can use a chart to estimate drag factor, the expert can resort to a chart to estimate velocity after determining the values for skidmark length and drag factor. These charts are referred to as speed calculators or nomographs. Figure 27-4 is a nomograph chart.[59]

Average Sliding and Peak Friction Coefficients for Passenger Car Tire

Surface Condition	Sliding Friction	Peak Friction
Concrete/Asphalt, polished to new, dry:	0.65 - 0.90	0.80 - 1.00
wet:	0.45 - 0.70	0.60 - 0.75
Gravel, loose to packed:	0.40 - 0.70	- - - - - - -
Gravel, some grass:	0.35 - 0.40	0.40 - 0.50
Meadow, wet:	0.15 - 0.20	0.20 - 0.25
Meadow, dry, firm, short grass:	0.35	0.45
Off-road shoulder, firm, dry:	0.35	0.40
Soil, loose, moist, tires sink down appr. 2 in.:	0.60	0.70
Asphalt, wet leaves:	0.60	0.60
Road, snow covered:	0.30	0.30
Ice:	0.15	0.15

Figure 27-3

59. Cook, *Speed Calculations and the Expert Witness*, 42 NEB. L. REV. 100, 126 (1962). Reprinted with permission.

A "straight line [is] drawn to connect assumed values on [the] two scales"[60] on the edges of the chart. The skidmark length column is on one edge, and the drag factor column is on the other. The expert connects the pertinent values in the two columns with a straight line. The line intersects the speed column in the middle of the nomograph, and the point of intersection is the velocity estimate.

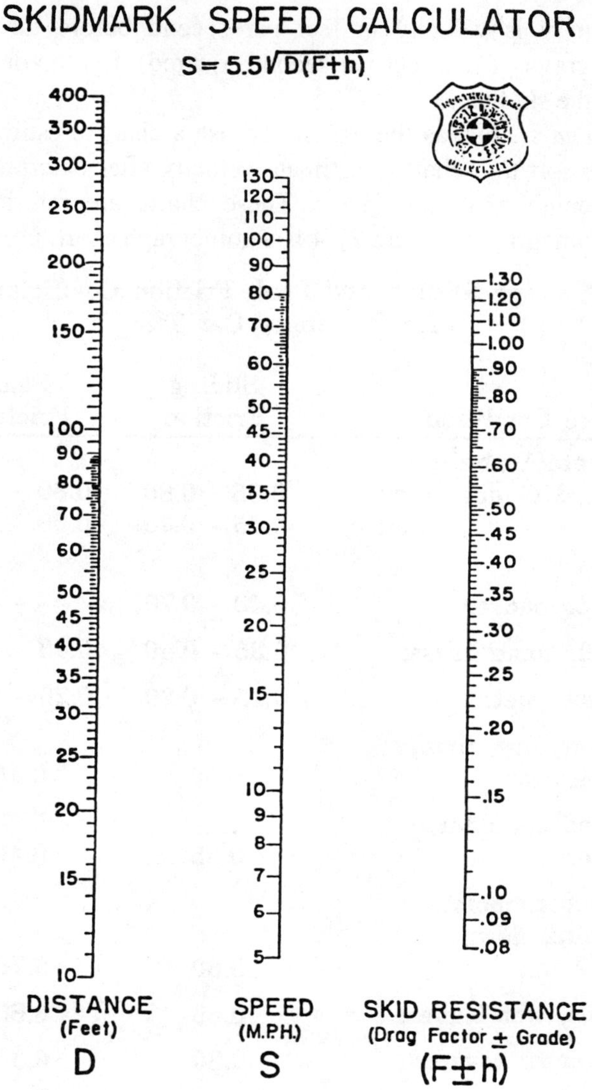

Figure 27-4

60. Baker, *Practical Use of Speed Charts*, 2 DEF. L.J. 156, 163 (1957).

There are several caveats about this method of determining velocity. The drag factor in particular is "susceptible to ... variation."[61] There can be substantial imprecision in the estimate when the expert relies on a drag factor chart rather than meticulously measuring the factor at the accident scene.

The estimate is likely to be the minimum speed for the vehicle.[62] Studies by Professors Reed and Keskin at the University of Texas suggest that "at least 20% of the vehicle's kinetic energy is lost before skidding commences."[63] In the earliest braking stage, a vehicle sometimes leaves only the faint shadow of a skidmark.[64] Twenty percent of the vehicle's energy can be "dissipated during this shadow period ...."[65]

Due to these uncertainties, many accident reconstructionist experts concede that velocity determinations based on skidmarks are merely "ballpark" figures.[66] Rather than citing a single estimate, some reconstruction experts prefer to report a range of probable velocities.[67]

§ 27-6(B). Yaw Marks.

When the vehicle brakes, the resulting road mark is a skidmark or scuffmark. Assume, however, that before the accident, the driver was endeavoring to negotiate a curve. The driver begins to realize that he or she is losing control of the vehicle but tries to steer through the curve.[68] Centripetal force (friction) tends to keep the vehicle on the road and in the curving movement while centrifugal force pushes the car on a tangent away from the curve.[69] This maneuver results in a different type of road mark. The mark is called variously a yaw mark, scrub, scuff, or sideslip.[70] The tire is still rotating but sliding. More precisely, the tire is rotating in one direction but sliding in another. The resulting mark is an arc portion of a circle[71] — the circle the vehicle would have completed if it continued the arc. In a skidmark, the striations are usually parallel to the mark.[72] In contrast, in a yaw mark, the striations can be oblique to the mark.[73]

---

61. Cook, *Speed Calculations and the Expert Witness*, 42 NEB. L. REV. 100, 112 (1962).

62. M. CHIECO & J. KWASNOSKI, ESTABLISHING LIABILITY IN VEHICULAR ACCIDENTS 404 (1989).

63. *Id.* at 404.

64. *Id.* at 311.

65. *Id.* at 312.

66. Badger, *Reconstruction of Traffic Accidents*, 9 AM. JUR. 3D PROOF OF FACTS 115, 189 (1990).

67. *Id.* at 174.

68. *Id.* at 136.

69. *Id.*

70. *Id.*

71. *Id.* at 137.

72. *Id.* at 136-37.

73. *Id.* at 137.

When the investigator finds a yaw mark at the accident scene, the investigator should of course record all the relevant dimensions of the mark. However, in truth, for the velocity estimate, the length of the mark is less important; but it should still be measured and recorded.[74] It is much more important to determine the radius of the curve.[75] Figure 27-5[76] depicts that determination. The expert initially establishes a chord on the curve by drawing a straight line from one point on the curve to another.[77] The expert then draws another straight line from the midpoint of the chord perpendicularly to the yaw arc. That line represents the middle ordinate. Knowing the width of the vehicle's track, the expert can now solve the equation on Figure 27-5 to determine the radius of the yaw arc.

Figure 27-6[78] sets out the formula which the expert can then use to estimate the critical speed of the vehicle. That speed is the maximum velocity which the vehicle can maintain before it begins to yaw or slide at the curve.[79] In the view of some authorities, "[a] speed correctly determined from a yaw mark is generally more accurate than one from a skidmark."[80]

§ 27-6(C). Damage to the Vehicles.

Subsections 27-6(A)-(B) both deal with inferences about velocity from highway marks. This subsection also deals with a velocity inference; but, in this case, the inference is drawn from the damage to the objects involved in the accident.

---

74. M. Chieco & J. Kwasnoski, Establishing Liability in Vehicular Accidents 407 (1989).

75. *Id.*

76. Dedman, Issues and Experts in Vehicular Homicide Accident Reconstruction (unpublished manuscript on file with the National College of District Attorneys, Law Center, University of Houston). Reprinted with permission.

77. *Id.* at 339.

78. Dedman, Issues and Experts in Vehicular Homicide Accident Reconstruction (unpublished manuscript on file with the National College of District Attorneys, Law Center, University of Houston).

79. *Id.* at 8.

80. Badger, *Reconstruction of Traffic Accidents*, 9 Am. Jur. 3d Proof of Facts 115, 137 (1990).

$$\text{Radius} = C^2/8m + m/2 - T/2$$

C = Chord
m = middle ordinate
T = width of axle

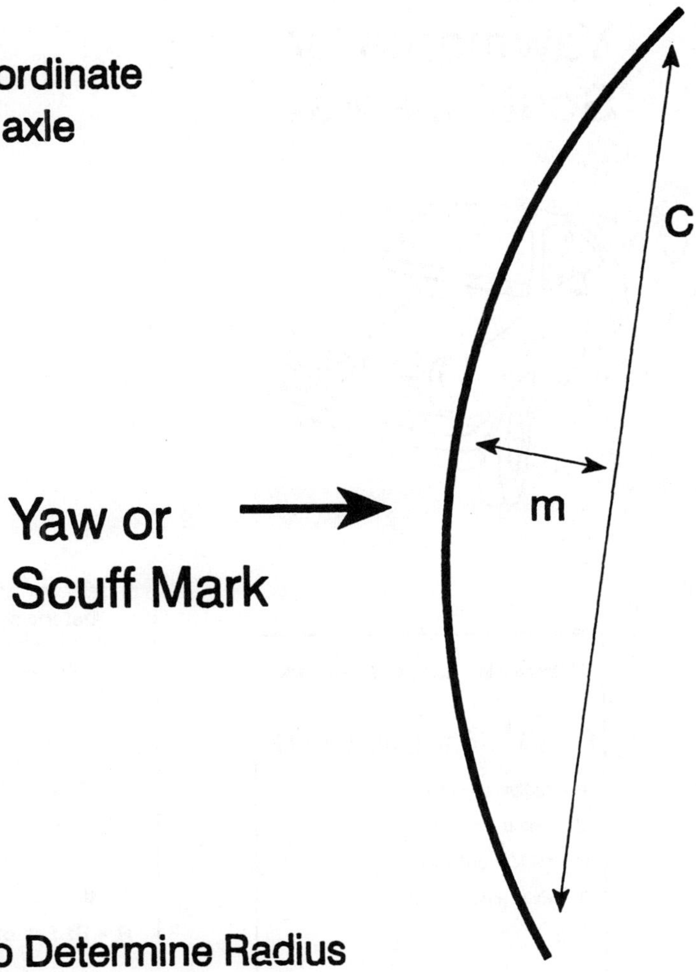

Method to Determine Radius
of Yaw Arc to Compute
"Critical Speed"

Figure 27-5

Formulae for Speed with Yawmarks or Scuff marks

Determining Radius of Yawmark

$$R = C^2/8m + m/2 - T/2$$

R = radius of curve

C = chord

m = middle ordinate

T = axle width (track)

Determining Critical Speed (Maximum Speed at which a vehicle can make a turn)

$$V = \sqrt{gfR}$$

V = Critical Speed

g = acceleration of gravity (32.2 ft/sec²)

f = drag factor of road

R = Radius of curve

Figure 27-6

The key to drawing the inference is the law of the conservation of energy:

> [W]hen two or more vehicles or a single vehicle and another object collide, the conservation of energy principle states that the total linear energy of the

system before the collision equals the total linear energy after the collision.[81]

Hence, the energy of the system before the collision must be equal to "the energy of the bodies after the process, plus (or minus) the work or energy put into the system (or taken out)."[82] The pertinent formula reads:

$$E \text{ before} = E \text{ after} \pm \text{Work in (out)}$$

To determine the pre-collision energy, the expert uses this formula:[83]

$$KE = \frac{1}{2} MV^2$$

In this formula, KE is kinetic energy, M is the mass of the vehicle, and V is velocity in feet per second. Mass is determined by dividing weight by gravity.[84] As previously noted, the acceleration due to gravity is 32.3 feet per second per second.

Collecting the necessary data. In effect, the expert works backward to solve the first equation for the pre-collision velocity. To do so, the expert needs to gather several items of information:

—The weight of the vehicle before collision. The expert should include the weight of any occupants or objects in the vehicle before collision. The expert can have the vehicle weighed after the accident. If parts of the vehicle broke off during the collision, those parts should be collected and weighed as well although this may not make a significant difference. Alternatively, the expert can use the weight stated in the manufacturer's specifications.

—The energy dissipated in the braking action prior to collision.[85] When the vehicle leaves skidmarks, the expert can employ the length of the skidmarks to compute the energy dissipated in the braking process.

—The energy dissipated in post-collision movement. This action is referred to as separation movement.[86]

---

81. M. CHIECO & J. KWASNOSKI, ESTABLISHING LIABILITY IN VEHICULAR ACCIDENTS 343 (1989).

82. R. LIMPERT, MOTOR VEHICLE ACCIDENT RECONSTRUCTION AND CAUSE ANALYSIS 247 (3d ed. 1989).

83. Zurmuhlen, *Automobile Accident Reconstruction*, 18 TRIAL LAW. Q. 49, 50 (Winter 1987).

84. *Id.*

85. DEDMAN, ISSUES AND EXPERTS IN VEHICULAR HOMICIDE ACCIDENT RECONSTRUCTION 2 (unpublished manuscript on file with the National College of District Attorneys, Law Center, University of Houston).

86. *Id.* at 3.

—The energy spent in damaging one or both vehicles during the collision. Even if they are struck during the collision, some rubber parts of the vehicle may be capable of absorbing the impact and then making an elastic rebound to their original shape. Most parts, however, will suffer plastic deformation. The extent of the "crush" or plastic deformation is indicative of the amount of energy expended in damaging the vehicles.

The person inspecting the damaged vehicle must carefully measure the crush in inches.[87] As Figure 27-7[88] indicates, the inspector prepares a crush profile of the damage. The inspector draws a straight line along the undamaged plane of the vehicle.[89] At regular intervals, the inspector measures the distance perpendicularly from the plane to the indented damage. The Society of Automotive Engineers has developed a system for classifying and assigning numerical values to damage of vehicles.[90] The system is described in a document known as SAE J224 entitled Collision Deformation Classification[91] and is used as an input to some computer softwares.

Inferring velocity from the data. Having collected this information, the expert can then estimate speed in one of two ways. The expert can manually calculate the speed by using equations for deriving pre-collision speed from vehicle damage.[92] Some of these equations are based on the empirical research of Rodolf Limpert;[93] but our reviewer cautions that in some instances, Limpert's research data is rather old. Or the expert can use computer software programs specially designed for this purpose.[94] Subsection 27- 10(G) describes some of the leading programs.

It is important to remember that if the accident involved two vehicles, their combined kinetic energy is the cause of the damage. The damage therefore reflects the speed of both vehicles.[95] In most cases, the expert is ultimately interested in determining the speed of the individual vehicles. That computation is a simple matter if the witnesses to the accident establish that one of the

---

87. Badger, *Reconstruction of Traffic Accidents*, 9 AM. JUR. 3D PROOF OF FACTS 115, 184 (1990).

88. DEDMAN, ISSUES AND EXPERTS IN VEHICULAR HOMICIDE ACCIDENT RECONSTRUCTION (unpublished manuscript on file with the National College of District Attorneys, Law Center, University of Houston).

89. *Id.* at 12.

90. M. CHIECO & J. KWASNOSKI, ESTABLISHING LIABILITY IN VEHICULAR ACCIDENTS 291 (1989).

91. *Id.* at 291, 416.

92. *Id.* at 234.

93. *Id.* at 234, 357-58.

94. *Id.* at 345-48.

95. Badger, *Reconstruction of Traffic Accidents*, 9 AM. JUR. 3D PROOF OF FACTS 115, 186 (1990).

vehicles was stationary at the time of the collision.[96] Skidmarks will often permit the expert to determine the minimum velocity of one of the vehicles, and in some cases this allows an inference to be made about the speed of the other vehicle.

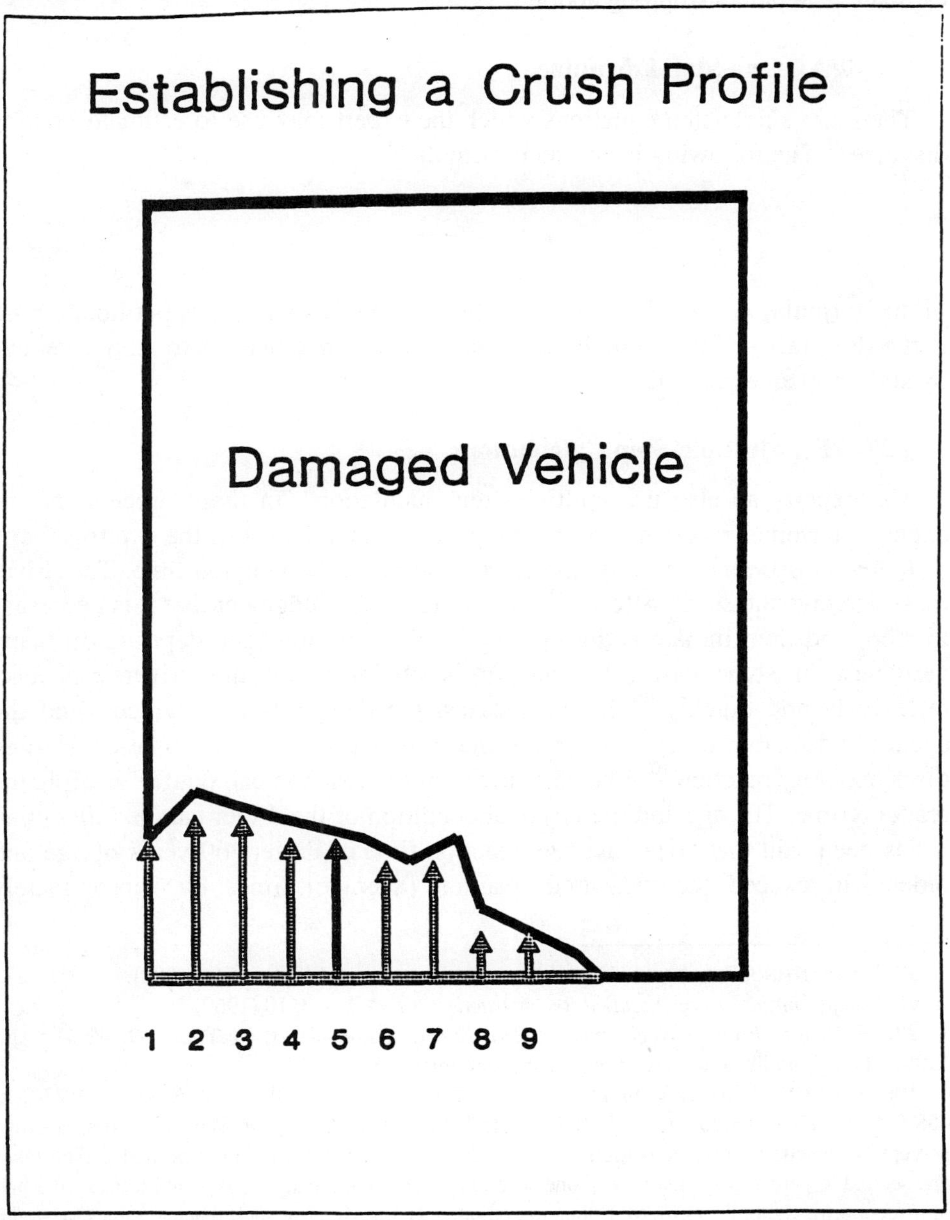

Figure 27-7

96. *Id.*

§ 27-7. Determining the Vehicle's Stopping Distance.

There are several methods which an accident reconstruction expert can use to estimate a vehicle's stopping action.

§ 27-7(A). One-Step Formulae.

There are single-step equations which the expert may use to estimate braking distance.[97] The following is one such formula:[98]

$$x_b = \frac{S^2}{30F}$$

In this formula, x_b is the braking distance, S is the speed in miles per hour, and F is the drag factor. This formula calculates the distance needed to stop a vehicle by sliding in an emergency-stop.[99]

§ 27-7(B). Multiple-Step Calculations.

The expert can also use multiple-step calculations. In these procedures, the expert determines reaction and braking distances and then adds the two together.

Reaction distance. Initially, the expert estimates the reaction time. The driver must perceive the scene before him or her, reach the judgment that it is necessary to stop, and then initiate action to stop.[100] The reaction time depends on many variables. In some cases, the danger is obvious; and the driver can react reflexively and quickly.[101] In other cases, the danger is less evident; and the eventual decision to stop may be the product of a more time-consuming discriminatory reaction.[102] The complexity of the reaction can double or triple the reaction time. The age and the physical condition of the driver can be influential. It has been said that "[t]he average reaction time of drivers 60 years of age and older will exceed the measured reaction [average] times by approximately

---

97. J. Tarantino, Strategic Use of Scientific Evidence § 14.23, at 549 (1988).

98. Baker, *Limitations on Accident Reconstruction*, 8 Def. L.J. 3, 10 (1960).

99. *Id.* Felton, *Proving Negligence in Rear-End Collision Cases*, 31 Trial 39, 40-41 (Apr. 1995) (stating and illustrating the use of a one-step formula).

100. R. Limpert, Motor Vehicle Accident Reconstruction and Cause Analysis § 23-2, at 458 (3d ed. 1989); Boodoo v. Cary, 21 F.3d 1157, 1160 (D.C. Cir.) ("Dr. Wu assumed an average perception, reaction, brake-activation time ('PRB').... In Dr. Wu's opinion, a normal person takes one second to perceive a danger ('P'), one second to react to that danger ('R'), and it takes one-half of a second for the brakes of a Metrobus to activate ('B'). Assuming such reaction times, it would have taken about 2.5 seconds (P + R + B) for the bus to begin skidding"), *amended*, 1994 U.S. App. Lexis 23,991 (D.C. Cir. June 7, 1994).

101. Badger, *Reconstruction of Traffic Accidents*, 9 Am. Jur. 3d Proof of Facts 115, 154 (1990).

102. *Id.*

75%,"[103] but our reviewer cautions that the available data does not permit such an exact statement. In most instances, it is impossible to know the actual reaction time of the driver. For that reason, the expert will fall back to relying on an assumed "normal" reaction time. Courts differ over this question. In the past, some have assumed reaction times of at least half a second or a full second.[104] However, three quarters of a second appears to be the most popular assumption.[105]

After assuming the appropriate reaction time or range of possible times, the expert calculates the reaction distance — the distance the vehicle traveled during the reaction time. The expert might use the skidmark length to estimate the speed of the vehicle. A rule of thumb then comes into play: "[A] car travels in feet per second approximately one and one-half times its speed in miles per hour. In other words, if a car is traveling 50 M.P.H., it is traveling at the rate of 75 feet per second."[106] In reality, the conversion factor is 1.46666[107] or 1.47.[108]

In a given case, the expert might assume that the reaction time was three seconds and that during that time, the velocity of the vehicle was 50 miles per hour or 75 feet per second. Multiplying 3 by 75, the expert would estimate the reaction distance as 225 feet.

Braking distance. The expert adds braking distance to the reaction distance. Ideally, the expert will have personally measured the skidmarks at the accident

---

103. R. LIMPERT, MOTOR VEHICLE ACCIDENT RECONSTRUCTION AND CAUSE ANALYSIS § 23-2, at 459 (3d ed. 1989).

104. Cook, *Speed Calculations and the Expert Witness*, 42 NEB. L. REV. 100, 107 n.31 (1962).

105. *Id. See also* J. KWASNOSKI, G. PARTRIDGE & J. STEPHEN, INVESTIGATION AND PROSECUTION OF DWI AND VEHICULAR HOMICIDE ch. 6 (1998); M. CHIECO & J. KWASNOSKI, ESTABLISHING LIABILITY IN VEHICULAR ACCIDENTS 379 (1989); State v. Manning, 612 S.W.2d 823, 826 n.4 (Mo. App. 1981); McCreary v. Conroy, 611 S.W.2d 234 (Mo. App. 1980); Gassiraro v. Merlo, 589 S.W.2d 632 (Mo. App. 1979); Hill v. Barton, 579 S.W.2d 121, 132 (Mo. App. 1979); Felton, *Proving Negligence in Rear-End Collision Cases*, 31 TRIAL 39, 41 (Apr. 1995) ("'Perception time is defined as the interval between first possible sighting of the obstacle and accelerator release.' Stated simply, it is the time it takes a driver to perceive a danger and begin to react. It is widely accepted that perception time for the average rider is at least three-quarters of a second. Studies show that many variables affect perception time; the three-quarters of a second is a minimum. Some drivers, under some conditions, may have a perception time of up to 2 seconds or more. 'Reaction time,' also called response time, 'is defined as the interval between release of the accelerator and contact with the brake pedal.' It is the time it takes a driver to react by applying the brakes after perceiving a danger. The reaction time of an average driver is three-quarters of a second, and many courts will take judicial notice of that fact....").

106. A. MORRILL, TRIAL DIPLOMACY § 4.32, at 68 (2d ed. 1972); Corrigan, *Using Judicial Notice in a Personal Injury Case*, J. MO. BAR 179, 180 (Apr.-May 1991); Felton, *Auto Accident Analysis*, TRIAL 60, 65 (Feb. 1991).

107. Baker, *Reconstruction of Traffic Accidents*, 9 AM. JUR. 3D PROOF OF FACTS 115, 140 (1990).

108. Baker, *Practical Use of Speed Charts*, 2 DEF. L.J. 156, 157 (1957).

scene or have access to reliable skidmark measurements. The sum of those two numbers is the stopping distance.

§ 27-7(C). Charts.

As in the case of estimates of velocity based on skidmark length, the expert can use a chart to estimate stopping distance.[109] (Our reviewer adds the caveat that such charts may assume a drag factor which differs significantly from the true drag factor.) Figure 27-8 is a chart prepared by the National Safety Council. In some jurisdictions, the legislature has decreed that the courts must take judicial notice of the contents of a specified chart. For example, Code of Virginia § 46.2-880 formerly provided:

MOTOR VEHICLE STOPPING DISTANCES

PASSENGER CARS

Speed: Miles per Hour	Speed: Feet per Second	Driver † Reaction Distance	Vehicle ‡ Braking Distance	TOTAL * STOPPING DISTANCE
10	15	11	6	17
15	22	17	14	31
20	29	22	25	47
25	37	28	39	67
30	44	33	55	88
35	51	39	78	117
40	59	44	105	149
45	66	50	136	186
50	73	55	188	243
55	81	61	230	291
60	88	66	300	366
65	95	72	380	452
70	103	77	455	532

† Driver reaction distance based on reaction time of ¾ second, a typical reaction for most drivers under most traffic conditions.

‡ Vehicle braking distance based on provisions of the Uniform Vehicle Code for 20 MPH, adjusted where necessary at higher speeds to conform to studies of the U.S. Bureau of Public Roads.

* If perception time is determined to be an appreciable factor for a particular situation, the distance travelled during this time should be added to the total stopping distance. After estimating perception time, the corresponding distance may be determined by reference to the second column which shows the feet travelled per second for the various speeds.

Figure 27-8

109. *Id.* at 171.

46.1-195. Tables of speed and stopping distances. — (a) All courts shall take notice of the following tables of speed and stopping distances of motor vehicles, which shall not raise a presumption, in actions in which inquiry thereon is pertinent to the issues:

SPEED IN		AVERAGE STOPPING DISTANCES			TOTAL STOPPING DISTANCES: DRIVER AND	
Miles Per Hour	Feet Per Second	Automobile Brakes (In Feet)	Truck Brakes (Brakes on All Wheels) (In Feet)	Average Driver Reaction Time (3/4 Second) (In Feet)	Automobiles (In Feet)	Trucks (In Feet)
10	14.67	5	7	11	16	18
15	22.0	12	17	16	28	33
20	29.34	21	30	22	43	52
25	36.62	32	47	27	59	74
30	44.0	47	67	33	80	100
35	51.3	63	92	38	101	130
40	58.7	82	120	44	126	164
45	66.0	104	152	50	154	202
50	73.3	128	187	55	183	242
55	80.7	155	227	61	216	288
60	88.0	185	270	66	251	336
65	95.3	217	316	71	288	387
70	102.6	252	367	77	329	444
75	109.9	289	422	82	371	504
80	117.2	328	480	88	416	568
90	132.0	425	607	99	524	706
100	146.0	514	750	109	623	859

(b) The courts shall further take notice that said tables are the result of experiments made with motor vehicles, unloaded except for the driver, equipped with four-wheel brakes, in good condition, on dry, hard, approximately level stretches of highway free from loose material. (Code 1950 (Supp.), § 46-212.2; 1956, c. 600; 1958, c. 541.)

By its terms, § 46.2-880 referred to "average" stopping distances — rather than the actual stopping distance of the vehicle and driver in question. It is generally understood that there is a large element of uncertainty in stopping distance estimates. At one time, many courts adopted the position that "judicial notice of stopping distance is never appropriate due to variable road conditions and car qualities."[110] Some courts went farther and excluded braking distance charts.[111] The prevailing contemporary attitude is that judicial notice is permissible, but the consensus is that the court "will not take judicial notice of

110. Recent Case, *Judicial Notice — Disputability and Appellate Practice Regarding Judicial Notice of Stopping Distances*, 38 Mo. L. Rev. 678, 683 n.37 (1973).

111. Annot., *Admissibility of evidence, in automobile negligence action, of charts showing braking distance, reaction times, etc.*, 9 A.L.R.3d 976, 978 (1966).

the precise distance within which a motor vehicle can be stopped."[112] Rather, the court may notice "that a vehicle traveling at a certain speed can be stopped within a [certain] number of feet, and likewise, that an automobile cannot be stopped within a [specified] number of feet."[113]

A good stopping distance chart will specify its underlying assumptions about reaction time and drag factor.[114] If it is clear that those assumptions do not hold true in the instant case, "special calculations" should be made.[115]

§ 27-8. Determining the Point of Impact.

In many cases, the pivotal question is where a collision occurred — the point of impact. Suppose, for example, that the defendant is charged with involuntary manslaughter. The prosecution's theory of the case might be that the defendant was grossly inattentive and permitted his vehicle to drift into the oncoming traffic lane. To establish this theory, the prosecution will have to prove that the point of impact was in the other driver's lane. Locating the point of impact can be one of the most difficult determinations for an accident reconstruction expert.[116]

§ 27-8(A). The Relevant Individual Factors.

In attempting to locate the point of impact, the expert can consider several factors. One factor, gouge marks, relates to subsurface damage to the roadway. Several other factors, including skidmarks and scuff marks, concern marks left on the roadway surface itself. Finally, still other factors, notably debris, the final resting place of the vehicles, and the damage to the vehicles, relate to objects resting on the surface.

Gouge marks. At the point of maximum engagement between the vehicles, one or both of the vehicles may dig into the roadway surface with considerable force. Parts of the vehicles such as bolts and bumpers can be forced downward. These

---

112. Corrigan, *Using Judicial Notice in a Personal Injury Case*, J. MO. BAR 179, 180 (Apr.-May 1991). *See* State v. Manning, 612 S.W.2d 823, 826 n.4 (Mo. App. 1981) ("we cannot take judicial notice of the exact distance within which a particular automobile may be stopped under given conditions").

113. Corrigan, *Using Judicial Notice in a Personal Injury Case*, J. MO. BAR. 179, 180 (Apr.-May 1991). *See also* State v. Manning, 612 S.W.2d 823, 826 n.4 (Mo. App. 1981) ("the limits above within which a stop can be made"); Recent Case, *Judicial Notice — Disputability and Appellate Practice Regarding Judicial Notice of Stopping Distances*, 38 MO. L. REV. 678, 683 n.37 (1973) ("a court ... may judicially notice that a vehicle travelling at a certain speed can be stopped within certain limits").

114. Baker, *Practical Use of Speed Charts*, 2 DEF. L.J. 156, 171 (1957).

115. *Id.*

116. Badger, *Reconstruction of Traffic Accidents*, 9 AM. JUR. 3D PROOF OF FACTS 115, 132 (1990).

parts of the vehicle can scoop or chop out sections of the road surface.[117] If there are several gouge marks at a particular location on the road, the presence of the marks is circumstantial evidence of the location of the impact point; but it does not conclusively prove that that was the point of impact.

It is not enough for the expert to find a gouge mark in the roadway surface. The expert must initially decide whether the mark was caused by the accident she is investigating. It may be impossible to make that decision if there is a significant delay in investigating the accident. Later traffic could conceivably cause the gouge. The gouge might even result from a tow truck removing the damaged vehicles from the scene. In addition, assuming that the expert is satisfied that the accident in question caused the mark, whenever possible the expert ought to match the mark to a part of the vehicle in question. The expert might find, for instance, that the configuration of a particular gouge matches the shape of a nut on a cross-beam of the vehicle. If the nut has a ground-down appearance, its appearance is further evidence that that nut caused the gouge mark.

Even when the expert finds a gouge and can attribute it to a specific part of a vehicle, the expert cannot leap to the conclusion that the site of the mark is the point of impact. Gouges can occur elsewhere.[118] By way of example, a gouge might result when a vehicle tips over or pitches after the collision.[119]

Skidmarks. While a gouge mark removes part of the road surface, a skidmark is left on the surface. Skidmarks can be cogent evidence of the point of impact.[120] Skidmarks might indisputably cross the center line. Moreover, the distance between the parallel marks might dictate the conclusion that the skidmarks were left by the defendant's vehicle rather than by the other vehicle involved in the accident. In these circumstances, the expert could confidently infer that impact occurred at the terminal point of the skidmarks.

The great probative value of skidmarks as evidence of point of impact underscores the need for a prompt investigation of the accident scene. Skidmarks are temporary conditions. Weather conditions such as rain can wear the rubber particles off the roadway surface. Passing traffic can cause the skidmarks to fade; but the skidmarks are darkest at the end of skidding where impact occurred. Unless there is a prompt investigation of the scene, the expert may be unable to rely on skidmarks at the scene as proof of the point of impact in the accident in question.

---

117. M. Chieco & J. Kwasnoski, Establishing Liability in Vehicular Accidents 390 (1989).

118. *Id.* at 270.

119. *Id.*

120. Briggs v. Burk, 174 Kan. 440, 257 P.2d 164 (1953); Chesshir v. Nall, 218 S.W.2d 248 (Tex. Civ. App. 1949).

Scuff or offset marks. If two vehicles collide head-on and the colliding slides overlap, the force of the collision is centered; the force acts in a straight line through the center of gravity of each vehicle. The vehicles might be forced forward or backward, but they will not rotate.

However, if the collision is not head-on or the overlap is incomplete, the vehicles tend to rotate. During the rotation, the vehicles may leave scuff or offset marks on the roadway surface. The scuff marks will circle around the point of impact. The location of these marks, called impact scuffmarks, can be valuable evidence of the impact point.[121]

Before treating such a mark as proof of the impact point, the expert must determine both that the mark is a scuff and that the mark is attributable to the accident in question. Characterizing the mark as a scuff is a relatively simple determination. The appearance of a scuff mark differs from that of a skidmark. A skidmark results from a tire sliding forward. In a skidmark, the striations are parallel to the sides of the mark. However, scuff marks are caused by tires sliding and slipping sideways. Understandably, the striations in scuff marks are at an angle to the sides of the mark.

As in the case of skidmarks, unless there is a prompt investigation, it may be difficult for the expert to confidently attribute the mark to the accident she is investigating. When there is a significant delay between the accident and the investigation, there is a possibility that later traffic caused the mark. The delay may even have the effect of making it difficult or impossible to find the mark. As in the case of skidmarks, subsequent weather conditions and passing traffic can erase or obscure the scuff.

Debris. The expert must not only consider damage to and marks left on the road surface; the expert should also evaluate the significance of objects resting on the surface such as debris. When vehicles collide, debris scatters around the point of impact.[122] Some of the debris will be trapped under or between the colliding vehicles. Other debris may be concentrated around the impact point. If all the accident debris is found in one traffic lane, the location of the debris is evidence that impact occurred in that lane.[123]

However, it is the rare case in which the expert will base a point of impact determination solely on the location of debris. The debris might be scattered in an erratic pattern. Debris can fan out widely after the collision:

---

121. Stark's Adm'x v. Herndon's Adm'r, 292 Ky. 469, 166 S.W.2d 828 (1942).

122. M. Chieco & J. Kwasnoski, Establishing Liability in Vehicular Accidents 389 (1989).

123. Anderson v. Kearly, 312 Mich. 566, 20 N.W.2d 728 (1945).

> At a speed of 30 mph, debris from two feet off the ground would scatter by as much as fifteen feet, making any definite location of an impact [by debris alone] uncertain.[124]

Thus, even if the debris scatters in a roughly circular pattern and the apparent center of the pattern is in one traffic lane, the center may not be the impact point. Worse still, the debris may be distributed roughly equally between the two lanes.[125] In short, as proof of the impact point, debris is often inconclusive evidence.

The final resting position of the vehicles. At the very least, the final resting place of the vehicles is relevant evidence of the point of impact. If the vehicles are resting facing each other with almost all the debris concentrated between the vehicles, their position and that of the debris point to the conclusion that the area between the vehicles was the impact point.

However, reliance on the vehicles' resting position as proof of impact point can be hazardous. The first hazard is the resting position at the time of the accident investigation may not be the position the vehicles were in immediately after the accident. If the accident occurred on a main traffic artery at rush hour, the police may be virtually compelled to move the vehicles when they arrive on the scene. Passing drivers may move the vehicles on their motion to prevent a traffic jam. The tow truck driver may move the vehicles even before taking them from the accident scene.

Even when the accident reconstruction expert is assured that the present location was the location immediately after the accident, it can be difficult to base a point-of-impact determination on the resting place. It is true that if there is a head-on collision between two vehicles with exactly the same momentum, the vehicles should come to rest at the impact point. However, the collision may not be head-on. In this event, the vehicles may rotate after collision. Even if there is a head-on collision, the vehicles rarely have exactly the same momentum at impact; they are likely to have different weights and velocities — the variables which determine momentum. In this event, the vehicles will move away from the impact point after collision. Moreover, vehicles are somewhat elastic and, thus, will rebound slightly from a collision.

Thus, in order to properly evaluate the significance of the vehicles' final resting position in the typical case, the expert will have to gather other evidence. Since the weight and velocity of the vehicles determine their momentum, the expert should make every effort to determine weight and velocity. Hence, the expert ought to attempt to ascertain the weight of the two vehicles. The expert

---

124. M. Chieco & J. Kwasnoski, Establishing Liability in Vehicular Accidents 389 (1989).

125. Satovich v. Lee, 385 Pa. 133, 122 A.2d 212 (1956).

should consider the weight of the vehicle, its passengers, and cargo. If the accident debris includes parts of the vehicle which broke off during impact, the weight of the debris must be added. When the vehicle in question is no longer available, the expert should consult the manufacturer's specifications for that model of vehicle.

Furthermore, the expert should try to determine the pre-impact velocity of the vehicles. The expert can rely on the methods described in § 27-6 of this chapter. If the expert can determine the weight and pre-impact velocity of the vehicles, the expert can make a much more intelligent assessment of the significance of the vehicles' resting place as proof of the location of the impact point.

The damage to the vehicles. In the typical case, it would be foolhardy for the expert to rely heavily on this factor as evidence of the impact point. To begin with, the damage evident to the vehicle may not have been caused by the accident. The damage might be pre-existing; the vehicle might have sustained the damage before the accident. Or the damage may have resulted after the accident. After striking the other vehicle, the damaged vehicle might have bounced into a traffic light or embankment. (To some extent, the expert can call upon the services of trace evidence analysts to decide whether the accident caused the damage in question. For example, the presence of specks of paint from the other vehicle in a particular dent may help establish that the dent was caused by colliding with the other vehicle).

Moreover, even when the expert is reasonably certain that the damage resulted from the accident, the damage usually has limited probative value as proof of the impact point. The extent and nature of the damage are highly probative of the position of the vehicles with respect to each other. However, a point-of-impact investigation focuses on a different question — namely, the relation of the vehicles with respect to the road surface. It would be highly speculative to base a point-of-impact finding solely on evidence of the damage to the vehicles in most cases.

§ 27-8(B). The Assessment of the Cumulative Significance of the Factors.

It is certainly permissible for the expert to weigh the totality of the evidence. In the ideal case, all the relevant factors point to the same impact point. If so, the expert can reach a relatively firm conclusion about the point of impact. In other cases, a particular factor such as the location of the skidmarks may be entitled to great weight. That factor could easily lead the expert to discount a contrary inference suggested by other factors such as the position of the vehicles at the time of the accident investigation.

However, it must be frankly conceded that in some cases, even an expert cannot reach a confident conclusion as to the point of impact. That outcome is especially likely when there is a substantial time lapse between the collision and the accident investigation. When there is such a delay, it may be difficult attributing gouges or roadway marks to the accident. The difficulty of attribution may preclude the accident reconstruction expert from drawing a firm inference about the impact point.

§ 27-9. Other Determinations.

Sections 27-4 through 27-8 discuss the most common determinations which the accident reconstruction expert is called upon to make. However, those determinations do not exhaust accident reconstruction expertise. The other possibilities include:

—*Determining whether a defect in a vehicle caused a particular accident.*[126] Thus, a witness with the appropriate training and experience can determine whether a deficiency in the chassis, steering system, or electrical system could have contributed to the accident.[127]

—*Determining whether a particular driver could have perceived a dangerous condition in time to have avoided the accident.* The issue may be point of initial perception: At what point on the highway could the driver have first seen the condition? A related problem is sightline: Even if the condition would otherwise have been within the range of visibility, at the time of the accident was an object present — such as a large truck — which obstructed the driver's view of the condition?

—*The behavior of vehicles during attempted turns which lead to accidents.* Section 27-5 discusses the methods which the expert can use to determine the vehicle's path when the vehicle is traveling in a straight line. In many cases resulting in accidents, one or both vehicles are attempting a turn just before collision. Although the vehicles are not proceeding along a straight line vector, the physical evidence at the accident may enable the expert to reconstruct the path of the vehicles.[128]

—*The operational condition of various parts of the vehicle.* For instance, if the filament coil of the front light bulb displays particular oxidization

126. Doupnik v. General Motors Corp., 225 Cal. App. 3d 849, 275 Cal. Rptr. 715, 727 (1990). *But see* People v. Fugatt, 229 Cal. App. 3d 240, 280 Cal. Rptr. 37 (in a vehicular homicide case, the defense proffered expert testimony about alleged defects in the gas tank and backseat of the vehicle; the testimony was irrelevant because at most, the testimony would have established a concurrent cause which would not have relieved the defendant of criminal responsibility), *opinion withdrawn,* 1991 Cal. LEXIS 3207 (Cal. 1991). *Fugatt* was ordered depublished and may no longer be cited as authority.

127. *See* R. LIMPERT, MOTOR VEHICLE ACCIDENT RECONSTRUCTION AND CAUSE ANALYSIS chs. 2-15 (3d ed. 1989); J. TARANTINO, STRATEGIC USE OF SCIENTIFIC EVIDENCE §§ 14.02-14.15 (1988).

128. Jones v. Garnes, 395 S.E.2d 548 (W. Va. 1990).

colorings, the coloring indicates that the light was flashing just before the accident.[129]

§ 27-10. The Admissibility of Accident Reconstruction Testimony.

§ 27-10(A). In General.

It would be a mistake to think that expert testimony is the only type of opinion evidence admissible on accident reconstruction issues. Federal Rule of Evidence 701 authorizes the receipt of lay opinion testimony, and lay witnesses are sometimes permitted to testify to inferences relevant in accident reconstruction cases.[130] However, when the propriety of a particular inference is a key issue in an accident reconstruction case, a prudent attorney will almost always proffer supporting expert testimony. The case law on accident reconstruction testimony in civil cases is voluminous,[131] and it is well-settled that this species of expert testimony is also admissible in criminal cases.[132]

Although modern courts are generally receptive to accident reconstruction testimony, their receptivity is a relatively recent development. Initially, the courts viewed accident reconstruction evidence with distrust.[133] The courts were dubious of the alleged expertise of "accidentologists"[134] and questioned whether the lay jurors needed expert assistance to draw reliable inferences from the primary facts.[135] The courts asserted that accident reconstruction "is more art than

---

129. Baudoin & Lavabre, *A Particular Case of Oxidation Colors on Bulb Filament After a Car Crash*, 41 J. FORENSIC SCI. 304 (1996).

130. *E.g.*, Lievrouw v. Roth, 157 Wis. 2d 332, 459 N.W.2d 850 (1990) (an accident victim was allowed to testify that he believed he faced an emergency). *But see* Pomella v. Regency Coach Lines, Ltd., 899 F. Supp. 335, 341 n.5 (E.D. Mich. 1995) ("Wilson is competent to testify to the facts (*i.e.*, perceived time and distance), but any conclusions as to whether, given these facts, the bus could have stopped, must be established by expert testimony").

131. Badger, *Reconstruction of Traffic Accidents*, 9 AM. JUR. 3D PROOF OF FACTS 115, 130 (1990).

132. Wilson v. State, 574 So. 2d 1324, 1335 (Miss. 1990) ("the testimony of accident reconstruction specialists is allowed in criminal cases in this State").

133. *E.g.*, Wright v. Flagg, 508 S.W.2d 742 (Ark. 1974); Woodward v. Blythe, 249 Ark. 793, 462 S.W.2d 205 (1971); Watts v. Handley, 427 S.W.2d 272 (Mo. App. 1968); Housman v. Fiddyment, 421 S.W.2d 284 (Mo. App. 1967); Penn v. Hartman, 525 S.W.2d 773 (Mo. App. 1975); Sheets v. Davenport, 181 Neb. 621, 150 N.W.2d 224 (1967); McFall v. Shelley, 70 N.M. 390, 374 P.2d 141 (1962).

134. Zachery v. Wheeler, 511 F. Supp. 591 (E.D. Tenn. 1981).

135. *Id.*; Upshur v. Shepherd, 538 F. Supp. 1176 (E.D. Pa. 1982), *aff'd*, 707 F.2d 1395 (3d Cir. 1983); People v. Zimmerman, 385 Mich. 417, 189 N.W.2d 259 (1971); Getter v. Wal-Mart Stores, Inc., 829 F. Supp. 1237, 1238 (D. Kan. 1993) (the jury did not need the benefit of the forensic engineer's testimony; "the normal life experiences and qualifications of the jury would permit it to draw its own conclusions...."), *aff'd*, 66 F.3d 1119 (10th Cir. 1995), *cert. denied*, 516 U.S. 1146 (1996).

science."[136] These courts reasoned that since most lay jurors are experienced drivers, the choice of inferences to be drawn from the primary facts should be "solely the province of the jury."[137]

Gradually, the courts lessened their hostility toward accident reconstruction testimony. They grudgingly acknowledged that expert testimony on this subject ought to be admissible when lay eyewitness testimony was either unavailable[138] or conflicting.[139] In these situations, there was a greater need for expert evidence.[140]

Within the recent past, however, there has been a marked shift away from the necessity test for the admissibility of expert testimony.[141] The courts have moved toward a more lax helpfulness standard of admissibility.[142] In the accident reconstruction cases, that trend was evident even before the passage of the Federal Rules of Evidence. In the early 1960s one commentator asserted:

> The trend is to allow expert opinion testimony reconstructing motor vehicle accidents from physical evidence, provided the expert witness is sufficiently qualified in the particular field [and] has before him enough physical evidence to provide him with the important variables involved....[143]

The enactment of the Federal Rules of Evidence in the 1970s and their adoption by 40 states has accelerated that trend. Under Federal Rule 702, the decisive question for the trial judge ruling on the admissibility of expert testimony is whether the evidence "will assist the trier of fact."

---

136. Tokio Marine & Fire Ins. Co. v. Grove Mfg. Co., 958 F.2d 1169, 1174-75 (1st Cir. 1992).

137. Venable v. Stockner, 200 Va. 900, 108 S.E.2d 380 (1959); A. MOENSSENS, J. STARRS, C. HENDERSON & F. INBAU, SCIENTIFIC EVIDENCE IN CIVIL AND CRIMINAL CASES § 11.08 (4th ed. 1995); A. MOENSSENS, F. INBAU & J. STARRS, SCIENTIFIC EVIDENCE IN CRIMINAL CASES § 17.08, at 737 n.43 (3d ed. 1986).

138. *E.g.,* McGrath v. Rohde, 53 Ill. 2d 56, 289 N.E.2d 619 (1972); Plank v. Holman, 46 Ill. 2d 465, 264 N.E.2d 12 (1970); Dobkowski v. Lowe's, Inc., 20 Ill. App. 3d 275, 314 N.E.2d 623 (1974); Dauksch v. Chamness, 11 Ill. App. 3d 346, 296 N.E.2d 592 (1973); National Bank of Bloomington v. Pickens, 8 Ill. App. 3d 58, 289 N.E.2d 64 (1972); McMahon v. Coronet Ins. Co., 6 Ill. App. 3d 704, 286 N.E.2d 631 (1972); Payne v. Noles, 5 Ill. App. 3d 433, 283 N.E.2d 329 (1972); Siltman v. Reeves, 131 Ill. App. 2d 960, 269 N.E.2d 728 (1971); Allstate Ins. Co. v. Sunbeam Corp., 865 F. Supp. 1267, 1274-75 (N.D. Ill. 1994) (Illinois law), *aff'd*, 53 F.3d 804 (7th Cir. 1995).

139. Adkins v. Chicago, R. I. & P.R.R., 2 Ill. App. 3d 906, 274 N.E.2d 507 (1971), *rev'd,* 54 Ill. 2d 511, 301 N.E.2d 729 (1973), *cert. denied*, 424 U.S. 943 (1976).

140. A. MOENSSENS, J. STARRS, C. HENDERSON & F. INBAU, SCIENTIFIC EVIDENCE IN CIVIL AND CRIMINAL CASES § 11.08 (4th ed. 1995); A. MOENSSENS, F. INBAU & J. STARRS, SCIENTIFIC EVIDENCE IN CRIMINAL CASES § 17.08, at 786-87 n.38 (3d ed. 1986); Badger, *Reconstruction of Traffic Accidents*, 19 AM. JUR. 3D PROOF OF FACTS 131 (1990).

141. 1 C. MCCORMICK, EVIDENCE § 13 (5th ed. 1999).

142. *Id.*

143. *Reconstruction of Accident*, 10 PROOF OF FACTS 137, 144 (1961).

> Opinion testimony concerning point of impact or other accident reconstruction has been more liberally received under the rule than previously. Under the rules, the courts have not categorically prohibited police officers, engineers or other qualified experts from testifying on such issues as accident causation and point of impact. Although many appellate courts continue to express skepticism concerning accident reconstruction testimony of this sort, admissibility has been left to the trial judge's discretion. Some appellate courts have gone so far as to find an abuse of discretion when the trial judge refused to allow such testimony.[144]

After noting that "prior to the enactment of" its code patterned after the Federal Rules of Evidence "our cases looked with disfavor on reconstruction of accidents by expert testimony," the Arkansas court added that "we have liberalized that position somewhat since the" adoption of the new code.[145]

Under the Federal Rules of Evidence and the majority view at modern common law, there is no rigid barrier to the admissibility of accident reconstruction testimony. To be sure, at least when lay eyewitness testimony is available,[146] a few courts still resist the receipt of opinions on impact point for the stated reason that those opinions "invade[] the province of the jury."[147] However, by and large, expert accident reconstruction testimony is admissible if the proponent lays a sufficient foundation. Most of the remaining subsections of § 27-10 touch upon the elements of that foundation. When an expert appears at trial, the testimony usually has a syllogistic structure.[148] After establishing her qualifications as an expert, the expert: testifies about a general theory or technique (the major premise), specifies the case-specific information she contemplates applying the theory or technique to (the minor premise), and arrives at an opinion (the conclusion) by applying the major premise to the minor.

---

144. 2 G. JOSEPH & S. SALTZBURG, EVIDENCE IN AMERICA: THE FEDERAL RULES IN THE STATES § 51.3, at 5 (1988); Allstate Ins. Co. v. Sunbeam Corp., 865 F. Supp. 1267, 1275 (N.D. Ill. 1994) (in contrast to Illinois law, "[u]nder Rule 702 of the Federal Rules of Evidence, all we need to ask is whether the expert's specialized knowledge will help the court understand the evidence or determine a fact in issue"), *aff'd*, 53 F.3d 804 (7th Cir. 1995). J. WEINSTEIN & M. BERGER, WEINSTEIN'S EVIDENCE para. 702[02], at 702-28 (1994) ("in automobile accident cases, the trial judge has been affirmed regardless of whether he admitted or excluded the proffered expert testimony of an 'accidentologist'").

145. Price v. Watkins, 283 Ark. 502, 678 S.W.2d 762, 764 (1984).

146. Gust v. Jones, 162 F.3d 587, 594 (10th Cir. 1998) ("it is not an abuse of discretion to exclude proffered expert testimony 'when the normal life experiences of the jury would permit it to draw its own conclusions . . . based upon the lay testimony of eyewitnesses'").

147. Housman v. Fiddyment, 421 S.W.2d 284, 290 (Mo. 1967). *See also* Kunce v. Breen, 671 S.W.2d 23, 26 (Mo. App. 1984); Lopez v. Dodson, No. 900339 (Va. Nov. 9, 1990).

148. *See generally* Imwinkelried, *The "Bases" of Expert Testimony: The Syllogistic Structure of Scientific Testimony*, 67 N.C. L. REV. 1 (1988).

Subsection 27-10(B) deals with the accident reconstruction expert's qualifications, § 27-10(C) with the expert's major premise, § 27-10(D) with the minor premise, and § 27-10(E) with the phrasing of the expert's conclusion.

§ 27-10(B). The Qualification of the Witness as an Expert.

In the early part of his or her direct testimony, the proffered witness testifies to the credentials which allegedly qualify the witness as an expert on accident reconstruction. It is, of course, ideal if the witness has both formal training and practical experience in accident reconstruction. However, under Federal Rule of Evidence 702, the witness need not possess both to qualify for expert status; in pertinent part, the rule refers to "a witness qualified as an expert by knowledge, skill, experience, training, or education ...." The operative connective in the phrase is "or," and consequently a witness can conceivably qualify as an expert on the basis of either practical experience standing alone or formal training standing alone.[149] Under Rule 702,

> There is a decided tendency to permit the fact finder to hear the testimony of persons having superior knowledge [to the lay jurors] .... If there is a reasonable basis for saying a witness knows more of the subject at hand than a person of ordinary knowledge, his evidence is admissible.[150]

There is agreement that the witness qualifies as an expert if the witness has formal training in such highly pertinent subjects as physics, mechanics, and the laws of motion. Thus, a witness may testify as an expert on accident reconstruction if he or she: possesses relevant academic degrees;[151] is a college

---

149. 2 G. Joseph & S. Saltzburg, Evidence in America: The Federal Rules in the States § 51.3, at 3-4 (1987); Scott v. Yates, 71 Ohio St. 3d 219, 643 N.E.2d 105 (1994) (the majority held that the trial judge abused his discretion in permitting the introduction of the investigating officer's opinion as to point of impact; the officer "testified that he was unfamiliar with the theory of conservation of momentum and consequently did not know how it might affect the post-impact course of motor vehicles involved in a crash. Nor did he know the formula for calculating the speed of motor vehicles, either before or after the impact, or what effect speed would have upon the post-impact course of vehicles. He frankly admitted that he was not an accident reconstructionist...." The dissent argued that the majority unduly emphasized the officer's lack of formal education; the dissent contended that the officer had the requisite "superior knowledge not possessed by ordinary jurors").

150. Killian v. Hill, 32 Ark. App. 25, 26-29, 795 S.W.2d 369, 370-71 (1990). *See also* State v. Love, 100 N.C. App. 226, 232-33, 395 S.E.2d 429, 433 (1990) ("As long as study, experience, or both makes the witness better qualified than the jury to draw appropriate inferences from the facts, he may be qualified as an expert").

151. Mannino v. International Mfg. Co., 650 F.2d 846 (6th Cir. 1981) (biomechanical engineer); Campbell v. Clark, 283 F.2d 766 (10th Cir. 1960) (civil engineer); Marks v. Mobil Oil Corp., 562 F. Supp. 759 (E.D. Pa. 1983) (a doctorate in mechanical engineering), *aff'd,* 727 F.2d 1100 (3d Cir. 1984); J. Tarantino, Strategic Use of Scientific Evidence § 14.32, at 558 (1988) ("a Bachelor

professor teaching in a relevant field;[152] or has attended and graduated from a specialized accident reconstruction course such as the Northwestern University Traffic Institute.[153]

The point of disagreement among the courts is whether, without a showing of formal training, a police officer experienced in investigating traffic accidents can testify on accident reconstruction subjects.[154] The early view was that without some special training, even extensive experience alone did not qualify the officer as an expert on these subjects.[155] In the words of one court,

> As for regular police officers, sheriffs, mechanics, etc., it generally may be said that they lack such training ... as would qualify them to make a scientific analysis from physical evidence, regardless of how many accident scenes one may have examined.[156]

---

of Science degree in aeronautical engineering and mathematics, a Master of Science degree in engineering mechanics, and a doctorate in mechanical engineering"); Tarantino, *How the Accident Reconstruction Expert Can Contribute to the Defense*, 6 D.W.I.J. 6, 7 (Apr. 1991) ("an advanced degree and training in engineering, physics, mathematics or ergonomics"); Cook, *Speed Calculations and the Expert Witness*, 42 NEB. L. REV. 100, 117 (1962), citing Storbakken v. Soderberg, 246 Minn. 434, 75 N.W.2d 496 (1956) (a Bachelor of Science in Civil Engineering).

152. Cook, *supra* note 151, at 121; Peil v. Kohnke, 50 Wis. 2d 168, 184 N.W.2d 433 (1971) (physics professor); J. TARANTINO, STRATEGIC USE OF SCIENTIFIC EVIDENCE § 14.32, at 558 (1988) ("a professor of mechanical engineering").

153. Cook, *Speed Calculations and the Expert Witness*, 42 NEB. L. REV. 100, 121 (1962); Kosieradzki, *Cross-Examining the Accident Reconstructionist*, 31 TRIAL 44 (Apr. 1995) ("In 1985 the National Highway Traffic Safety Administration provided a grant to develop minimum criteria for the training of police traffic accident reconstructionists. From that grant grew the Accreditation Commission for Traffic Accident Reconstruction. The commission developed a training and accreditation process to certify qualified accident reconstructionists. As of 1994, 46 percent of those who took the exam failed on the first attempt, 35 percent on the second, and 46 percent on the third. No retests are allowed after the third try. Many reconstruction witnesses do not hold this accreditation.").

154. J. TARANTINO, STRATEGIC USE OF SCIENTIFIC EVIDENCE § 14.32, at 558 (1988); Scott v. Yates, 71 Ohio St. 3d 219, 643 N.E.2d 105 (1994) (the majority held that the trial judge abused his discretion in permitting the introduction of the investigating officer's opinion as to point of impact; the officer "testified that he was unfamiliar with the theory of conservation of momentum and consequently did not know how it might affect the post-impact course of motor vehicles involved in a crash. Nor did he know the formula for calculating the speed of motor vehicles, either before or after the impact, or what effect speed would have upon the post-impact course of vehicles. He frankly admitted that he was not an accident reconstructionist...." The dissent argued that the majority unduly emphasized the officer's lack of formal education; the dissent contended that the officer had the requisite "superior knowledge not possessed by ordinary jurors").

155. Eckis v. Graver Tank & Mfg. Co., 289 F.2d 335 (9th Cir. 1961); Lee v. Terminal Transp. Co., 269 F.2d 97 (7th Cir. 1959); Walden v. Wylie, 645 S.W.2d 246 (Tenn. App. 1982).

156. Trailways, Inc. v. Clark, 794 S.W.2d 479, 483 (Tex. App. 1990) (quoting Note, *Opinion Testimony of Expert "Accident Analyst" Reconstructing Collision Admissible*, 38 TEX. L. REV. 503, 506 n.14 (1960)).

Under this view, the witness's proponent must demonstrate that the witness possesses additional qualification in the form of "scientific, technical or specialized knowledge"[157] gained by formal training in accident investigation[158] at a police academy[159] or university.[160] The hostility toward accident reconstruction testimony is so deep-seated in some jurisdictions that these courts have ruled officers unqualified even when they had tens of hours of classroom instruction in accident reconstruction.[161] The courts are especially skeptical of accident reconstruction testimony when the record indicates that the expert is a professional witness.[162]

Today the prevailing view is that standing alone, practical experience and generalized training can qualify a police officer to testify on at least some accident reconstruction questions.[163] The courts embracing this view have held that even if an experienced police officer lacks the formal training necessary to testify as an expert on the full range of accident reconstruction issues, the officer may opine on such questions as speed estimates based on skidmarks[164] and point of impact.[165] The adoption of Federal Rule of Evidence 702 has given impetus to the prevailing view.[166] In one opinion permitting an officer to opine on the subject of point of impact, the court conceded that it had earlier declared that "officers cannot testify as to the point of impact."[167] However, the court stressed

157. Hatfield v. Andermatt, 54 Ohio App. 2d 188, 561 N.E.2d 1023, 1026 (1988).

158. Ernst v. Ace Motor Sales, Inc., 550 F. Supp. 1220 (E.D. Pa. 1982), *aff'd,* 720 F.2d 661 (3d Cir. 1983).

159. Mosser v. Fruehauf Corp., 940 F.2d 77 (4th Cir. 1991); Vanhook v. Stanford-Lincoln County Rescue Squad, Inc., 678 S.W.2d 797 (Ky. App. 1984).

160. Mosser v. Fruehauf Corp., 940 F.2d 77 (4th Cir. 1991); B. & J. Byers Trucking, Inc. v. Robinson, 281 Ark. 442, 665 S.W.2d 258 (1984).

161. *E.g.,* Southwood v. Harrison, 638 S.W.2d 706 (Ky. App. 1982).

162. Tokio Marine & Fire Ins. Co. v. Grove Mfg. Co., 958 F.2d 1169, 1174 n.3 (1st Cir. 1992) ("The fact that a person spends substantially all of her time consulting with attorneys and testifying in trials is not a disqualification, but it is not an automatic qualification guaranteeing admission of expert testimony"; "[i]n a field like accident reconstruction that is more art than science, the trial judge has particular liberty to eschew 'professional witnesses'").

163. Kelsay v. Consolidated Rail Corp., 749 F.2d 437 (7th Cir. 1984); May v. Strecker, 453 N.W.2d 549, 555 (Minn. App. 1990) (collecting cases dealing with "practical experience"); Jones v Garnes, 395 S.E.2d 548, 550 (W.Va. 1990) ("he had investigated several hundred to one thousand accidents"); Comment, *The Highway Patrol Officer as Expert Witness*, 44 MONT. L. REV. 251, 253 (1983) ("experience in investigating accidents and general training").

164. Trailways, Inc. v. Clark, 794 S.W.2d 479, 483 (Tex. App. 1990).

165. Loseke v. Mables, 217 Ill. App. 3d 521, 160 Ill. Dec. 471, 577 N.E.2d 796 (1991).

166. 2 G. JOSEPH & S. SALTZBURG, EVIDENCE IN AMERICA: THE FEDERAL RULES IN THE STATES § 51.3, at 5 (1987); 2 G. JOSEPH & S. SALTZBURG, EVIDENCE IN AMERICA: THE FEDERAL RULES IN THE STATES § 51.3, at 81 (1991 Cum. Supp.).

167. Smith v. Davis, 281 Ark. 122, 663 S.W.2d 165 (1983).

that "[a]ll" of those decisions "were before the adoption of" that state's current code patterned after the Federal Rules of Evidence.[168]

Of course, the witness must confine his or her opinion to the area of his or her expertise. A witness experienced in fire reconstruction is unqualified to venture opinions reconstructing a traffic accident if the witness: only recently shifted his professional emphasis to accident reconstruction, never taught accident reconstruction, has no certification in accident reconstruction, has not completed the requirements for certification by the Association of Accident Reconstructionists, and has never conducted any experiments in the field of accident reconstruction.[169] By the same token, a witness qualified to opine as to how an accident occurred might lack the medical training to venture a further opinion as to the cause of a person's personal injuries[170] or whether changing the manner in which an accident occurred would have prevented the accident from being fatal.[171]

§ 27-10(C). The Validity of the Scientific Theories Which the Expert Relies Upon.

After qualifying as an expert, the witness turns to his or her major premise; the expert will typically expressly or implicitly invoke a general explanatory theory to evaluate the specific facts in the pending case. For example, the expert might rely on one of the general laws of motion described in § 27-2 or a specific equation relating to accident reconstruction.[172] Depending on the jurisdiction, the proponent of the witness will have to elicit foundational testimony either that the theory is generally accepted within the pertinent specialty or that the theory has been experimentally validated.[173]

---

168. *Id.*

169. Wilson v. Woods, 163 F.3d 935 (5th Cir. 1999).

170. Smelser v. Norfolk Southern Ry. Co., 105 F.3d 299 (6th Cir.), *cert. denied*, 118 S. Ct. 67 (1997).

171. Behn v. State, 621 So. 2d 534 (Fla. Dist. Ct. App. 1993).

172. Badger, *Reconstruction of Traffic Accidents*, 9 AM. JUR. 3D PROOF OF FACTS 115, 140-45 (1990). *See also* United States v. Quinn, 18 F.3d 1461 (9th Cir.) (approving the use of photogrammetry in another context), *cert. denied*, 512 U.S. 1242 (1994).

173. *See* §§ 1-5 and 1-6 of this text, *supra.* Wilson v. Woods, 163 F.3d 935 (5th Cir. 1999); Desrosiers v. Flight Intern. of Florida, Inc., 156 F.3d 952 (9th Cir. 1998) (the applicability of *Daubert* to accident reconstruction testimony in an action arising from a fatal airplane crash); Demaree v. Toyota Motor Corp., 37 F. Supp. 2d 959 (W.D. Ky. 1999); Pinsker v. Cohen, No. CV 95-12419 (Super. Ct., Maricopa County, Ariz., Sept. 22, 1997) (the biomechanic's opinion was inadmissible under *Frye*; the biomechanist cited a study supporting his theory, but the database was quite small; the theory was not sufficiently broad-based and had not been sufficiently professionally reviewed to have gained general acceptance).

In practice, opposing counsel rarely attack the expert's major premise.[174] Many of the basic propositions in accident reconstruction are so well-settled that the proponent does not even have to present live foundational testimony; the judge can judicially notice the validity of the proposition.[175] Many, if not most, of the commonly used equations such as those set out in Limpert's text[176] have been derived empirically.[177] Whether the court applies the *Frye* general acceptance test or the *Daubert* validation standard, the expert's major premise will probably pass muster.[178] In a *Daubert* jurisdiction, the proponent might succeed on the alternative ground that the empirical validation test is confined to "scientific knowledge" under Rule 702 and that the expert's theory qualifies as nonscientific "technical knowledge."[179] In *Kumho Tire Co., Ltd. v. Carmichael*,[180] a 1999 decision, the Supreme Court held that under Federal Rule 702, the judge must subject the reliability of even nonscientific expert testimony to a "*Daubert*-style scrutiny."[181] However, *Kumho* is based on statutory interpretation rather than constitutional law; and consequently even in the 40 jurisdictions with codes patterned after the Federal Rules of Evidence, the state courts are free to recognize a sharper distinction between scientific and nonscientific expert testimony.

---

174. Badger, *Reconstruction of Traffic Accidents*, 9 AM. JUR. 3D PROOF OF FACTS 115, 188 (1990).

175. Springer v. United States, 641 F. Supp. 913 (D.S.C. 1986), *aff'd*, 819 F.2d 1139 (4th Cir. 1987); Holst v. United States, 755 F. Supp. 260 (E.D. Mo. 1991); State v. Manning, 612 S.W.2d 823, 826 n.4 (Mo. App. 1981); Corrigan, *Using Judicial Notice in a Personal Injury Case*, J. MO. BAR 179, 180 (Apr.-May 1991); Recent Case, *Judicial Notice — Disputability and Appellate Practice Regarding Judicial Notice of Stopping Distances*, 38 MO. L. REV. 678 (1973).

176. R. LIMPERT, MOTOR VEHICLE ACCIDENT RECONSTRUCTION AND CAUSE ANALYSIS (3d ed. 1989).

177. M. CHIECO & J. KWASNOSKI, ESTABLISHING LIABILITY IN VEHICULAR ACCIDENTS 234 (1989).

178. State v. Patrick, 358 N.W.2d 426, 428 (Minn. App. 1984) (citing the Minnesota version of Federal Rule 702, the court upheld the admission of speed estimates). *But see* People v. Jakupcack, 275 Ill. App. 3d 830, 656 N.E.2d 442 (1995) (an accident reconstruction expert's opinion must be based "upon scientific theories which have gained general acceptance in his field"; in the instant case, the expert used a peculiar concept of an in-line accident which was supported by only his own self-serving statement), *app. denied*, 165 Ill. 2d 558, 662 N.E.2d 428 (1996).

179. Lauria v. National Railroad Passenger Corp., 145 F.3d 593 (3d Cir. 1998); Carmichael v. Samyang Tire, Inc., 131 F.3d 1433 (11th Cir. 1997), *rev'd sub nom.* Kumho Tire Company, Ltd. v. Carmichael, 119 S. Ct. 1167 (1999); Imwinkelried, *The Next Step After Daubert: Developing a Similarly Epistemological Approach to Ensuring the Reliability of Nonscientific Expert Testimony*, 15 CARDOZO L. REV. 2271 (1994); Comment, *Inconsistent Gatekeeping in Federal Courts: Application of Daubert v. Merrell Dow Pharmaceuticals, Inc., to Nonscientific Expert Testimony*, 30 LOY. L.A. L. REV. 1379 (1997).

180. 119 S. Ct. 1167 (1999).

181. *Id.* at 1179.

In this light, it is understandable that the courts have permitted experts to opine on a wide range of accident reconstruction topics, including:[182] the identity of the driver;[183] speed estimates premised on the length of skidmarks;[184] speed estimates based on the damage to the vehicles[185] and the conservation of momentum theory;[186] point of impact;[187] the movement and position of vehicles during collisions;[188] the cause of an accident;[189] and the possibility that a defective part of the vehicle was responsible for the accident.[190]

§ 27-10(D). The Type, Quantity, and "Fit" of the Expert's Information About the Accident in Question.

The next component of the expert's reasoning process is the minor premise, the information about the specific accident he or she proposes evaluating. While the opposing attorney rarely attacks the expert's major premise, the attorney often attacks the admissibility and weight of the expert's minor premise.[191] The expert's equation may be unassailable, but the "[c]alculated results are only as

---

182. Richard v. Scott, 79 Cal. App. 3d 57, 144 Cal. Rptr. 672 (1978) (speed estimates based on skidmark length, point of impact, the position of vehicles, and the condition of pavement).

183. Fox v. Dannenberg, 906 F.2d 1253 (8th Cir. 1990).

184. Richard v. Scott, 79 Cal. App. 3d 57, 144 Cal. Rptr. 672 (1978); Trailways, Inc. v. Clark, 794 S.W.2d 479, 483 (Tex. App. 1990); Rogers v. Gonzales, 654 S.W.2d 509 (Tex. App. 1983); Parker, *Automobile Accident Analysis by Expert Witnesses*, 44 VA. L. REV. 789, 796 (1958) (collecting cases).

185. *Id.* at 794-96 (collecting the cases); Annot., *Expert or opinion evidence as to speed based on appearance or condition of motor vehicle after accident*, 93 A.L.R.2D 287 (1964); Annot., *Expert or opinion evidence as to speed based on appearance or condition of automobile after accident*, 133 A.L.R. 726 (1941).

186. Storbakken v. Soderberg, 246 Minn. 434, 441, 75 N.W.2d 496, 501 (1956); Cook, *Speed Calculations and the Expert Witness*, 42 NEB. L. REV. 100, 117 (1962).

187. Butler v. Dowdy, 304 Ark. 481, 803 S.W.2d 534, 536 (1991); Parker, *Automobile Accident Analysis by Expert Witnesses*, 44 VA. L. REV. 789, 796-97 (1958) (collecting the cases); Annot., *Admissibility of opinion evidence as to point of impact or collision in motor vehicle accident case*, 66 A.L.R.2D 1048 (1959). *But see* Note, *Opinion and Demonstrative Evidence: Automobile Accident Reconstruction*, 14 WASHBURN L.J. 264, 272 (1975) ("The jurisdictions are divided on the admissibility of expert opinion concerning point of impact"); Dyer v. R.E. Christiansen Trucking, Inc., 318 Or. 391, 868 P.2d 1325 (1994); Link v. McCoy, 39 Mich. App. 120, 197 N.W.2d 278 (1972); Motorists Mut. Ins. Co. v. Howard, 21 Mich. App. 146, 175 N.W.2d 351 (1970); LaFave v. Kroger Co., 5 Mich. App. 446, 146 N.W.2d 850 (1966).

188. Annot., *Admissibility of opinion evidence as to whether vehicle involved in collision was standing still or moving,* 33 A.L.R.2D 1250 (1954).

189. May v. Strecker, 453 N.W.2d 549, 555 (Minn. App. 1990); Annot., *Admissibility of opinion evidence as to the cause of an accident or occurrence*, 38 A.L.R.2D 13 (1954).

190. Annot., *Admissibility and weight of evidence as to condition of automobile or parts thereof after accident, on issue as to responsibility for accident*, 129 A.L.R. 438 (1040).

191. Badger, *Reconstruction of Traffic Accidents*, 9 AM. JUR. 3D PROOF OF FACTS 115, 188 (1990).

accurate as the data from which they are calculated."[192] Simply stated, this is another illustration of the "garbage in, garbage out" rule:[193] If the expert inserts unreliable values for the variables in an otherwise perfect equation, the expert's ultimate opinion will be unreliable. For that reason, in many cases the expert's minor premise becomes the opposing attorney's principal target. The opponent can question the quality, quantity, or "fit" of the information comprising the minor premise.

The quality of the information comprising the minor premise. At one time, the quality of the information in the expert's minor premise was a profitable target for the opposing attorney.[194] Prior to the enactment of the Federal Rules of Evidence, in many jurisdictions an expert could factor information into his or her minor premise only if the information was independently admissible.[195] When the information in question was subject to a hearsay objection, the opponent could therefore preclude the expert from relying on the information as part of the basis of his or her opinion. At common law, the courts frequently sustained the objection that an accident reconstruction expert could not rely on statements by third parties who had observed the accident.[196] The statements fell within the definition of hearsay, and there was no applicable hearsay exception.

However, as § 5-4 of this text notes, Federal Rule of Evidence 703 overturned the traditional, common-law view. Rule 703 announces that an expert may rely on technically inadmissible information as a basis for an opinion if the information is "of a type reasonably relied upon by experts in the particular field in forming opinions or inferences upon the subject ...." The Advisory Committee Note to Rule 703 states that "the language" of the statutory text "would not warrant admitting in evidence the opinion of an 'accidentologist' as to the point of impact in an automobile collision based on statements of bystanders, since [the] requirement [of reasonable reliance] is not satisfied." The courts differ over the interpretation of the term "reasonably" in the statute. Some courts equate the term with customarily; under this interpretation, if the judge finds as a matter of fact that specialists within the expert's discipline routinely rely on this kind of source of information, the judge must permit the expert to do so.[197] However,

---

192. Cook, *Speed Calculations and the Expert Witness*, 42 NEB. L. REV. 100, 112 (1962).

193. Ballard, *The Computer as Expert Witness: Accident Reconstructions by Computers Can Be Powerful Evidence for Juries*, 5 CAL. LAW. 26, 28 (Aug. 1985).

194. Dallas & Mavis Forwarding Co. v. Stegall, 659 F.2d 721 (6th Cir. 1981) (a state highway trooper proposed resting an impact point opinion in part on biased eyewitness accounts of the accident).

195. 1 C. MCCORMICK, EVIDENCE § 15 (5th ed. 1999).

196. Bullard v. Stonebraker, 101 Ariz. 584, 422 P.2d 700 (1967); Gray v. Woods, 84 Ariz. 87, 324 P.2d 220 (1958); Steed v. Cuevas, 24 Ariz. App. 547, 540 P.2d 166 (1975); Killingsworth v. Nottingham, 18 Ariz. App. 356, 501 P.2d 1197 (1972); Brayman v. National State Bank, 180 Colo. 304, 505 P.2d 11 (1973); Ruby v. Easton, 207 N.W.2d 10 (Iowa 1973).

197. 2 G. JOSEPH & S. SALTZBURG, EVIDENCE IN AMERICA: THE FEDERAL RULES IN THE STATES

other jurisdictions accord the trial judge residual discretion to second-guess the specialty's practice and find that even customary reliance is objectively unreasonable.[198] However, even in the latter jurisdictions, in deciding whether the expert's reliance on a type of data is reasonable, the trial judge considers the specialty's customary practice.[199] Some courts in these jurisdictions have gone to the length of recognizing a rebuttable presumption that it is reasonable for the witness to rely on a type of source of information customarily considered by experts in his or her specialty.[200] The net result of the adoption of Rule 703 is that with one exception, it is now far more difficult for the opposing attorney to successfully challenge the type of information which the expert proposes including in his or her minor premise.

The exception comes into play when the expert relies on information about the physical condition of the involved vehicles if the information was gathered a substantial period of time after the accident. Assume that there was a significant time lapse between the accident and the inspection of the vehicle which yielded the information. The time lapse raises the possibility that the physical condition of the vehicle changed in the interim. For example, emergency personnel may have caused additional damage to the vehicle in the process of removing an injured person from the vehicle; to do so, they may have used hammers, crowbars, or "the jaws of life." Another possibility is that the tow truck driver who removed the vehicle from the accident scene might have caused further damage to the vehicle. If the accident reconstructionist mistakenly assumes that the further damage is attributable to the accident, he or she may reach an erroneous conclusion about the speed of the vehicle. Given that possibility, the

---

§ 52.3, at 93-95 (1991 Cum. Supp.).

198. *Id.* Pomella v. Regency Coach Lines, Ltd., 899 F. Supp. 335, 341-43 (E.D. Mich. 1995) (the expert's assumption about the coefficient of fraction was "too speculative;" the expert's opinion assumed that "the coefficient of friction on westbound I-94 on January 10, 1993 was greater than or equal to a value taken from a textbook's table for the coefficient of friction for wet pavement.... Plaintiff's evidence might be acceptable if the conditions on I-94 were established and uniform, but the facts of this case are otherwise. The testimony of the eyewitnesses establishes that the condition on I-94 on the date of this accident was anything but uniform. It is undisputed that it had snowed and that there was snow on the ground.... McQuire and Newcomb testified that they encountered ice...."); Dallas & Mavis Forwarding Co. v. Stegall, 659 F.2d 721, 722 (6th Cir. 1981) (the expert gathered most of the information from the account of a biased eyewitness; "The trial process is better served when a biased eyewitness is required to testify directly and to be subject to cross-examination. To permit his opinion to be heard through the testimony of an [expert] would cloak it with undeserved authority that could unduly sway a jury"). The courts also differ over the question of whether Rule 703 permits the proponent to formally introduce technically inadmissible information and quote or present it to the jury. Kosieradzki, *Cross-Examining the Accident Reconstructionist*, 31 TRIAL 44, 44-45 (Apr. 1995).

199. Chicago v. Anthony, 136 Ill. 2d 169, 144 Ill. Dec. 93, 554 N.E.2d 1381, 1389, *cert. denied,* 498 U.S. 900 (1990).

200. Ryan v. KDI Sylvan Pools, Inc., 121 N.J. 276, 579 A.2d 1241 (1990).

proponent of the reconstructionist's opinion should be prepared to show a chain of custody for the vehicle between the time of the accident and the time when the information about the vehicle's physical condition was gathered. Chapter 7 discusses chain of custody in detail.

The quantity of the information comprising the minor premise. Given Federal Rule of Evidence 703, many opposing attorneys have shifted the focus of their attack on the expert's minor premise to the quantity of the expert's information about the accident in question. Even if it is permissible for the expert to rely on this type of information, the rub may be that he or she does not have *enough* information to form a trustworthy opinion.[201] In most cases in which an accident reconstruction expert cannot reach an opinion with any degree of confidence, the root cause is "lack of facts" about the accident.[202] The opponent can certainly attack the weight of the expert's opinion on the ground that the opinion rests on limited or arguably insufficient data.

More importantly, though, notwithstanding Rule 703, the opponent can attack the admissibility of the expert opinion on that ground. Rule 703 speaks only to the type of information which the expert contemplates relying upon; the rule does not purport to regulate the adequacy of the quantity of the information. However, as at common law,[203] the courts in Federal Rules jurisdictions continue to exclude expert opinions when the witness's minor premise includes inadequate data.[204] Rule 703 may not explicitly bar the opinion, but the opponent has a powerful, common-sense argument that the opinion runs afoul of Rule 702 — an opinion resting on a demonstrably inadequate basis "will [not] assist the trier of fact ...."

Accident reconstruction testimony can be excluded on this basis.[205] Suppose, for example, that the expert proposes relying on a particular equation but there is a missing variable[206] — the expert concedes that to apply the equation, she will

201. Badger, *Reconstruction of Traffic Accidents*, 9 AM. JUR. 3D PROOF OF FACTS 115, 127 (1990). *In re* Air Crash Disaster: Polec v. Northwest Airlines, Inc., 86 F.3d 498 (6th Cir. June 6, 1996) (it is doubtful that it is reasonable for an expert to rely on rumors about what another expert said); Paz v. Sherwin-Williams, 917 F. Supp. 51 (D.D.C. 1996) (there was no competent eyewitness testimony supporting the expert's assumption, and there was contrary eyewitness testimony); Sparks v. Gilley Trucking Co., 992 F.2d 50, 53-54 (4th Cir. 1993); Dallas & Mavis Forwarding Co. v. Stegall, 659 F.2d 721, 722 (6th Cir. 1981) (the accidentologist did not have any physical evidence and derived the information basically from the story of a biased eyewitness).

202. Baker, *Limitations on Accident Reconstruction*, 8 DEF. L.J. 3, 19 (1960).

203. Everett v. Bishop, 680 S.W.2d 779 (Mo. App. 1984) (a hypothetical question must include enough facts to permit the witness to reach a trustworthy conclusion).

204. 2 G. JOSEPH & S. SALTZBURG, EVIDENCE IN AMERICA: THE FEDERAL RULES IN THE STATES § 52.3, at 95-96 (1991 Cum. Supp.) (collecting the cases).

205. Logsdon v. Baker, 366 F. Supp. 332 (D.D.C. 1973), *vacated,* 517 F.2d 174 (D.C. Cir. 1975); Abramson v. Levinson, 112 Ill. App. 2d 42, 250 N.E.2d 796 (1969), *cert. denied,* 39 U.S. 950 (1970); Spraker v. Lankin, 218 Kan. 609, 545 P.2d 352 (1976); Parker v. Hohman, 250 A.2d 698 (Me. 1969).

206. A. MOENSSENS, J. STARRS, C. HENDERSON & F. INBAU, SCIENTIFIC EVIDENCE IN CIVIL AND

simply have to invent a value for that variable. In this situation, many courts would bar the expert's opinion.[207] Standing alone, the final resting place of the vehicles involved in the accident is insufficient to support an opinion as to the point of impact. Many courts also carefully scrutinize the adequacy of the basis for the expert's conclusion when the expert intends to infer velocity from the damage to the vehicles.[208] Similarly, there is authority that an expert cannot base a speed estimate solely on debris left by the accident.[209] In all these cases, the opponent can assume *arguendo* that the expert is considering a proper kind of information but argue alternatively that the expert has neglected to collect enough information to permit the formation of a reliable opinion.

The *"fit" of the information comprising the minor premise.* The information comprising the minor premise should "fit" the major premise. The major premise is conditional in nature: *If* conditions A, B, and C concur, *then* consequence D should follow. The conditions are facts about the accident. For example, when Professor Limpert conducted his experiments to derive formulae describing vehicle behavior, he controlled certain variables such as the size of the vehicle during the experiments. Before the expert can properly use such formulae to evaluate the facts in the instant accident, the expert should ensure that the facts obtained during the accident match or fit those which obtained during the original experiments validating the formula.

Many of the formulae commonly used in accident reconstruction are based on experiments conducted in the 1970s. There are marked differences between the average car sold in the 1970s and the typical car being marketed today. For example, many modern cars have more rigid sides; for obvious safety reasons, manufacturers are building more cage structure into the sides of their vehicles. However, modern vehicles tend to have more collapsible front ends than the typical car on the road in the 1970s. If a formula derived in the 1970s is designed to estimate speed from the extent of damage to the side or front of a vehicle, the application of the formula to an accident involving a differently designed vehicle is questionable. Even if the trial judge admits the expert's opinion based on the formula, the opposing attorney can effectively attack the weight of the opinion.

CRIMINAL CASES §§ 11.08, 11.10 (4th ed. 1995); A. MOENSSENS, F. INBAU & J. STARRS, SCIENTIFIC EVIDENCE IN CRIMINAL CASES § 17.08, at 787 n.43 (3d ed. 1986), citing Thorpe v. Commonwealth, 223 Va. 609, 292 S.E.2d 323 (1982).

207. *See* § 15-7(B) of this text, *supra.*

208. Adams v. Smith, 479 S.W.2d 390 (Tex. Civ. App. 1972); Flores v. Barlow, 354 S.W.2d 173 (Tex. Civ. App. 1962); Jackson v. Trogan, 364 Mich. 148, 157, 110 N.W.2d 612 (1961) (the expert may not infer speed solely from data about the force of the impact). The expert needs additional data such as the weather conditions, skid marks, the coefficient of friction on the street, the efficiency of the brakes, and the weight of the vehicle. People v. Ebejer, 66 Mich. App. 333, 340-43, 239 N.W.2d 604 (1976).

209. Mills v. Redwing Carriers, Inc., 127 So. 2d 453 (Fla. App. 1961); Kratzer v. King, 401 S.W.2d 405 (Mo. 1966).

§ 27-10(E). The Ultimate Fact Prohibition.

Just as Rule 703 has relaxed the limitations on the expert's minor premise, Rule 704 has liberalized the restrictions on the phrasing of the expert's conclusion. At common law, many courts paid at least lipservice to the so-called "ultimate fact" prohibition forbidding the expert from testifying to an opinion which coincided with an ultimate issue in the case.[210] To an extent, the case law applied the prohibition to accident reconstruction testimony.[211] However, Rule 704(a) provides:

> Except as provided in subdivision (b), testimony in the form of an opinion or inference otherwise admissible is not objectionable because it embraces an ultimate issue to be decided by the trier of fact.

The import of this language is that it is now "meritless" for the opponent to object exclusively on the ground that the expert's proffered opinion coincides with an ultimate issue in the case.[212] Construing this language, several courts have allowed accident reconstruction experts to testify to highly conclusory opinions such as statements that a factor was "a major contributing cause" of an accident[213] or that one driver failed to yield the right-of-way.[214] Some courts have expressly ruled that an expert may opine on mixed questions of law and fact.[215]

Yet even in jurisdictions which have adopted Rule 704, some courts balk at admitting such conclusory opinions. For instance, one court indicated that it would not permit an expert to testify directly on the question of whether a driver "made an illegal legal turn."[216] These courts reason that notwithstanding Rule 704, highly opinionated conclusions are not "otherwise admissible." These courts believe when the witness opines on a mixture of fact and law, the witness is venturing beyond the area of his or her expertise. As one text explains, Rule 704

> is not a license for experts to testify on questions of law. If the witness has an adequate background in physics and the laws of motion, the witness can qualify as an expert in accident reconstruction. Given that expertise, the

---

210. 1 C. McCormick, Evidence § 12 (5th ed. 1999).

211. A. Moenssens, J. Starrs, C. Henderson & F. Inbau, Scientific Evidence in Civil and Criminal Cases § 11.08 (4th ed. 1995); A. Moenssens, F. Inbau & J. Starrs, Scientific Evidence in Criminal Cases § 17.08, at 787 (3d ed. 1986) (citing Bieghler v. Kleppe, 633 F.2d 531 (9th Cir. 1980), the authors assert that "[s]ome courts have shown a little reluctance to admit accident reconstruction expert testimony that goes to the ultimate issue").

212. Jones v. Garnes, 395 S.E.2d 548, 550 (W. Va. 1990).

213. May v. Strecker, 453 N.W.2d 549, 555 (Minn. App. 1990).

214. Jones v. Garnes, 395 S.E.2d 548 (W. Va. 1990).

215. Puente v. A.S.I. Signs, 821 S.W.2d 400, 402 (Tex. App. 1991); Harvey v. Culpepper, 801 S.W.2d 596, 601 (Tex. App. 1990).

216. Butler v. Dowdy, 304 Ark. 481, 803 S.W.2d 534, 536 (1991).

> witness can testify about such factual questions as point of impact and velocity. However, the proponent should not attempt to elicit an opinion that a particular driver acted "negligently" or violated a specific section of the Vehicle Code. Those questions are mixed questions of law and fact, and the legal component of the questions exceeds the scientific expertise of the witness.[217]

In one case, an appellate court ruled that even a forensic pathologist could not opine on the question of whether an automobile collision was the result of an accident or the result of recklessness.[218]

§ 27-10(F). The Admissibility of Accident Reports.

At trial, the proponent of expert accident reconstruction testimony might attempt to introduce a police report of the accident investigation. The proponent might proffer passages in the report as substantive evidence to corroborate the expert's opinion, or the proponent could adduce the expert's testimony that the contents of the report are one of the bases of the expert's opinion.[219] These attempted uses of the report at trial can trigger both hearsay and privilege objections.

Hearsay. If the proponent is content to elicit the expert's testimony that he or she relied on the report, there is no tenable hearsay objection. The evidence is not hearsay, since the proponent is putting the report to a nonhearsay use:

> An accepted nonhearsay use of evidence is showing the effect of the statement on the hearer's or reader's state of mind — sometimes referred to as a mental input theory of logical relevance. Out-of-court reports used as a basis for an expert's opinion under Rule 703 are admitted on this theory. The reports are not admitted to establish the truth of the report. Rather, it is logically relevant that the expert received the report. The receipt of the information contained in the report makes the expert's opinion better grounded and more trustworthy.[220]

---

217. E. IMWINKELRIED, R. WYDICK & J. HOGAN, CALIFORNIA EVIDENTIARY FOUNDATIONS 261 (2d ed. 1994). The 1977 Committee Comment to Minnesota Rule 703 specifically states: "[A] distinction should be made between opinions as to factual matters, and opinions involving a legal analysis or mixed questions of law and fact. Opinions of the latter nature are not deemed to be of any use to the trier of fact."

218. State v. Jamerson, 63 Cr.L. (BNA) 65 (N.J. Sup. Ct., Mar. 25, 1998).

219. *E.g.,* Cravens v. County of Wood, Ohio, 856 F.2d 753 (6th Cir. 1988) (under Rule 703, a highway patrol officer testifying as an expert witness could base his opinion in part on the official accident report and accompanying photographs).

220. R. CARLSON, E. IMWINKELRIED & E. KIONKA, EVIDENCE IN THE NINETIES 578 (3d ed. 1991).

On the opponent's request, the judge would give the jury a limiting instruction defining the proper use of the evidence.

When the expert mentions the report as one of the bases of his or her opinion, though, it is unclear whether the proponent may introduce the report itself into evidence. The courts are divided over this question.[221] "Some trial judges apparently construe Rule 703 as permitting both the formal admission of the reports and their submission to the jury."[222] To resolve the controversy in that state, the Minnesota drafting committee revised its version of Rule 703 to add the following provision:

> (b) Underlying expert data must be independently admissible in order to be received upon direct examination; provided that when good cause is shown in civil cases and the underlying data is particularly trustworthy, the court may admit the data under this rule for the limited purpose of showing the basis of the expert's opinion.

There is a pending amendment to Federal Rule of Evidence 703 to the same effect; but even if the amendment is adopted, it probably will not take effect until December 2000.

Suppose that the proponent wants to offer the contents of the report as substantive evidence to corroborate the expert's testimony. As § 6- 2 of this text notes, the passages representing the investigating officer's firsthand knowledge fall within the recognized hearsay exceptions for business entries (Federal Rule of Evidence 803(6)) and official records (Rule 803(8)).[223] Furthermore, under the Supreme Court's 1988 decision in *Beech Aircraft Corporation v. Rainey,*[224] reliable findings of fact within the report can qualify for admission under Rule 803(8)(C).

There are two caveats to introducing the reports as substantive evidence under these hearsay exceptions. First, only civil parties and the criminal defense can resort to the theory of admissibility that the passage is a finding of fact admissible under 803(8)(C). That subdivision begins with the language, "in civil actions and proceedings and against the Government in criminal cases ...." The clear implication is that the prosecution cannot avail itself of this theory.

---

221. Carlson, *Collision Course in Expert Testimony: Limitations on the Affirmative Introduction of Underlying Data,* 36 U. FLA. L. REV. 234, 235, 242-43 (1984); Rice, *Inadmissible Evidence as a Basis for Expert Opinion Testimony: A Response to Professor Carlson,* 40 VAND. L. REV. 583 (1987); People v. Anderson, 113 Ill. 2d 1, 495 N.E.2d 485, *cert. denied,* 479 U.S. 1012 (1986).

222. R. CARLSON, E. IMWINKELRIED, E. KIONKA & K. STRACHAN, EVIDENCE: TEACHING MATERIALS FOR AN AGE OF SCIENCE AND STATUTES 632 (4th ed. 1997).

223. *See* Lievrouw v. Roth, 157 Wis. 2d 332, 459 N.W.2d 850 (Ct. App. 1990) (portions of the WISCONSIN MOTORIST'S HANDBOOK were admissible under that state's version of Rule 803(8)(C)).

224. 488 U.S. 153 (1988).

Second, when the report is a police report, the criminal defense may argue that even the passages reflecting the investigating officer's personal knowledge are barred by Rule 803(8)(B). That subdivision "exclud[es] ... in criminal cases matters observed by police officers and other law enforcement personnel ...." Section 6-2 of this text discusses this exclusionary provision. As that section explains, the courts have divided over the correct interpretation of the provision. A court subscribing to the minority, *Oates*[225] view might uphold the defense argument.

Privilege. Even if the proponent can overcome any hearsay objections, there may be an insuperable privilege objection. Many jurisdictions have created a special statutory privilege for accident reports.[226] The rationale for the privilege is that the privilege encourages citizens furnishing information to the police to be candid; if the reporting citizen realizes that the report is inadmissible against him or her, the citizen is more likely to file a full, frank report.[227] California Vehicle and Safety Code § 20013 provides that "[n]o ... [required] accident report shall be used as evidence in any trial, civil or criminal ...."[228]

Assuming that there is a statutory required reports privilege in the jurisdiction question, the proponent may still succeed in defeating or circumventing a privilege objection. The scope of the privilege may be limited in several respects. To begin with, the privilege might protect only the data furnished by the private citizen reporting to the police. The privilege may not extend to other data which the investigating officer gathers firsthand. In addition, in many jurisdictions, the courts have construed the privilege as cloaking only the written report itself. This construction permits the introduction of testimony about the driver's oral statements to the police.[229]

§ 27-10(G). Computerized Accident Reconstruction.

Many of the subsections of this chapter deal with equations for solving various accident reconstruction problems. Although the expert can solve the problem

225. United States v. Oates, 560 F.2d 45 (2d Cir. 1977).

226.1 C. McCormick, Evidence § 112 (5th ed. 1999); Comment, *The Required Report Privileges*, 56 Nw. U. L. Rev. 283 (1961); Lusby v. Union Pac. R.R. Co., 4 F.3d 639 (8th Cir. 1993) (discussing 23 U.S.C.A. §§ 130 and 409, which bar the admission of certain railroad reports).

227. 1 C. McCormick, Evidence § 112 (5th ed. 1999)..

228. *See also* Graham v. Collier, 688 F. Supp. 146 (D. Del. 1988) (discussing the Delaware statute); Dresser, *Use of Scientific Tests in the Defense of Personal Injury Actions*, 5 Def. L.J. 135, 137-38 (1959) (discussing the Iowa statute).

229. People v. Misner, 134 Cal. App. 2d 377, 285 P.2d 928 (1955); Grocers Wholesale Cooperative Inc. v. Nussberger Trucking Co., 192 N.W.2d 753 (Iowa 1971); 1 C. McCormick, Evidence § 112, at 412 n.3 (4th ed. 1992)); Annot., *Admissibility of police officer's testimony at state trial relating to motorist's admissions made in or for automobile accident report required by law*, 46 A.L.R.4th 291 (1986).

manually, a computer could obviously work the equation more quickly.[230] Furthermore, even if the relevant equations yield answers to questions about the behavior of the vehicles in question, oral testimony about the answers may have little impact on the trier of fact. Based on those answers, it would be more persuasive to prepare a film or videotape depicting the behavior of the vehicles.[231] Preparing a videotape in the conventional manner could be time-consuming, but again computerization can speed the preparation process.[232]

In our computerized age,[233] it was predictable that computer technology would eventually be adapted to speed both the process of working accident reconstruction equations and that of preparing visual accident simulations.[234] The United States Department of Transportation, independent research institutions, and private firms all have played a part in adapting computer technology for these purposes.[235] Several programs are now available:

—AICALC. This program was developed by the Northwestern University Traffic Institute.[236]

—CRASH (CALSPAN Reconstruction of Accident Speeds on the Highway) 3. This is the third version of a software package prepared for the United States Department of Transportation.[237] CALSPAN, headquartered in Buffalo, New York, conducts crush damage research at Cornell Aeronautical Laboratories.[238]

—EDCRASH. This program is similar to CRASH. EDCRASH was developed by Engineering Dynamics in Oregon.[239]

—IMPACT (Improved Mathematical Predictions of Automobile Collision and Trajectory). This program was created by Dynamic Analysis Corporation in Concord, Massachusetts.[240]

---

230. Badger, *Reconstruction of Traffic Accidents*, 9 AM. JUR. 3D PROOF OF FACTS 115, 178 (1990).

231. *E.g.,* Brandt v. French, 638 F.2d 209 (10th Cir. 1981) (a film and slides simulating the accident).

232. Seither, *Software: Expert Witness*, FORBES 202 (Sept. 24, 1984).

233. People v. Collins, 68 Cal. 2d 319, 438 P.2d 33, 66 Cal. Rptr. 497 (1968) ("our computerized society").

234. Chi & Vossoughi, *Engineering Aspect of Automobile Accident Reconstruction Using Computer Simulation*, 30 J. FORENSIC SCI. 814 (1985).

235. Ballard, *The Computer as Expert Witness: Accident Reconstructions by Computers Can Be Powerful Evidence for Juries*, 5 CAL. LAW. 26 (Aug. 1985); Wallace, *Reconstructing Traffic Accidents Through the "Eye" of the Computer*, 18 TRIAL 24, 25 (Apr. 1982).

236. M. CHIECO & J. KWASNOSKI, ESTABLISHING LIABILITY IN VEHICULAR ACCIDENTS 421 (1989).

237. *Id.*

238. *Id.* at 423.

239. *Id.*

240. Ballard, *The Computer as Expert Witness: Accident Reconstructions by Computers Can Be*

—SMAC (Simulation Model of Automobile Collision). This program was developed by CALSPAN for the National Highway Traffic Safety Administration.[241]

These are not the only programs currently available. Other programs include CRUNCH, TRAJECTORY, and WRECKER. The various programs perform many accident reconstruction calculations, including estimations of velocity from crush damage.

Both the mathematical models and the programs which go farther and prepare visual simulations based on the modeling are admissible with a proper foundation.[242] The foundation varies, depending on whether the proponent proffers the animation as purely demonstrative evidence or as substantive proof. The proponent might offer the animation simply as demonstrative evidence to help illustrate a witness's testimony. If so, the foundation is minimal.[243] The witness merely testifies that the animation fairly, accurately depicts the manner in which the witness believes the accident occurred, the version of the accident described in the witness's other testimony.[244] When the animation is proffered on this theory, however, on timely request the judge must give the jury a limiting instruction as to the evidentiary status of the animation; and in many jurisdictions, the exhibit cannot accompany the jury into the deliberation room.[245]

Powerful Evidence for Juries, 5 CAL. LAW. 26 (Aug. 1985).

241. J. TARANTINO, STRATEGIC USE OF SCIENTIFIC EVIDENCE § 14.29 (1988).

242. People v. McHugh, 124 Misc. 2d 559, 476 N.Y.S.2d 721, 722-23 (Sup. Ct. 1984); J. TARANTINO, STRATEGIC USE OF CIRCUMSTANTIAL EVIDENCE § 14.30 (1988); Haldeman & Adelman, *Planning Demonstrative Proof*, 11 LITIGATION 8 (Summer 1985).

243. Comment, *Admission of Computer Generated Visual Evidence: Should There Be Clear Standards?*, 6 SOFTWARE L.J. 325, 333-34 (1993). *See generally* E. IMWINKELRIED, EVIDENTIARY FOUNDATIONS 106-15 (4th ed. 1998) (the foundations for computer animations offered as illustrative or substantive evidence); Note, *Computer Generated Accident Reenactments: The Case for Their Admissibility and Use*, 15 REV. LITIGATION 203 (1996)..

244. Pierce v. State, 671 So. 2d 186 (Fla. Dist. Ct. App. 1996) (citing *McHugh, infra), on remand*, 718 So. 2d 806 (Fla. Dist. Ct. App. 1997); People v. McHugh, 124 Misc. 2d 559, 476 N.Y.S.2d 721, 722-23 (1984) ("The evidence sought to be introduced is more akin to a chart or diagram than a scientific device. Whether a diagram is hand drawn or mechanically drawn by means of a computer is of no importance. What is important is [that] the presentation ... fairly and accurately reflect the oral testimony offered and that it be an aid to the jury's understanding of the issue"); Dilworth, *Computer Animations Reach Criminal Court*, 28 TRIAL 26 (Sept. 1992) (in People v. Mitchell, No. 12462, Cal. Marin County Super. Ct., Feb. 19, 1992, the prosecution introduced an animation depicting a shooting; the crime scene reconstruction expert testified that the animation accurately reflected his testimony.) Some commentators use "animation" as a term of art signifying a depiction offered solely as demonstrative evidence and employ "simulation" when the proponent claims that the depiction is accurate and qualifies for admission as substantive proof. Karnavas & Jason, *Courtroom Computer Animation and Simulation*, 20 THE CHAMPION 5, 6 (Jan./Feb. 1996).

245. United States v. Wood, 943 F.2d 1048 (9th Cir. 1991); ME. R. EVID. 616; Brain &

If the proponent wants the jury to have an opportunity to view the animation during deliberation,[246] the proponent should proffer the animation as substantive evidence. On this theory, the proponent must lay a more extensive foundation. The foundation consists of proof of both the validity of the technology and the reliability of the assumptions about the accident in question —the foundational elements discussed in §§ 27-10(C)-(D). When the proponent offers testimony based on a mathematical model, the proponent must identify the formulae programmed into the model and demonstrate that the formulae satisfy the general acceptance or validation standard. Prior to trial, the proponent should review both the program itself and any user's manual for the program. The program or manual may indicate that there are limitations on the proper use of the program. Some programs, for instance, are designed to analyze accidents involving passenger cars rather than trucks.[247]

If the proponent also wants to offer a computer-generated simulation of the accident, the proponent must take the additional step of establishing the validity of the program which converts the answers yielded by the formulae into a visual display.[248] In any event, the proponent must identify the case-specific information input to the program and prove that that information is an acceptable basis for an opinion under Rule 703.[249] The software may supply "default values" for variables which are different from the actual facts in the case.[250] In some cases, even a slight change in the numerical value input for the variable can significantly change the outcome.[251]

Broderick, *The Derivative Relevance of Demonstrative Evidence: Charting Its Proper Evidentiary Status*, 25 U.C. DAVIS L. REV. 957, 965-66 (1992); Henke, *Admissibility of Computer-Generated Reconstructions and Simulations*, 35 TRIAL LAWYER'S GUIDE 434, 444 (1991).

246. *Id.* at 437. Some commentators use "animation" as a term of art signifying a depiction offered solely as demonstrative evidence and employ "simulation" when the proponent claims that the depiction is accurate and qualifies for admission as substantive proof. Karnavas & Jason, *Courtroom Computer Animation and Simulation*, 20 THE CHAMPION 5, 6 (Jan./Feb. 1996); Livingston v. Isuzu Motors, Ltd., 910 F. Supp. 1473, 1494-95 (D. Mont. 1995) (the court upheld the admission of a CGA under *Daubert*; Dr. Nalecz "stated that the computer program is made up of various physical laws and equations commonly understood in science;" "Peer review of Dr. Nalecz's computer simulation methodology included several lectures and presentations to members of the scientific community. Dr. Nalecz identified peers within his discipline who have worked with him and evaluated his work. He testified that he had presented his theories both in publications and lectures").

247. J. TARANTINO, STRATEGIC USE OF SCIENTIFIC EVIDENCE § 14.30, at 556-57 (1988).

248. People v. McHugh, 124 Misc. 2d 823, 476 N.Y.S.2d 721, 722-23 (Sup. Ct. 1984).

249. Seither, *Technology Software: Expert Witness*, FORBES 202, 203 (Sept. 24, 1984) ("the GIGO questions — garbage in, garbage out").

250. Kwasnoski, *Constructing Hypotheticals in Motor Vehicle Homicide Cases*, 16 THE CHAMPION 6, 8 (Nov. 1992) (even the user of the software may be unaware of the default values included in the software program).

251. *Id.* at 10.

§ 27-11. Selected Bibliography.

J. BAKER & L. FRICKE, TRAFFIC ACCIDENT INVESTIGATION MANUAL (1986).

T. BOHAN & A. DAMASK, FORENSIC ACCIDENT INVESTIGATION: MOTOR VEHICLES (1995).

J. BROWN & K. OBENSKI, FORENSIC ENGINEERING RECONSTRUCTION OF ACCIDENTS.

M. CHIECO & J. KWASNOSKI, ESTABLISHING LIABILITY IN VEHICULAR ACCIDENTS (1989).

J. COLLINS, ACCIDENT RECONSTRUCTION (1980).

A. DAMASK & J. DAMASK, INJURY CAUSATION ANALYSES: CASE STUDIES AND DATE SOURCES (1990).

L. FRICKE, TRAFFIC ACCIDENT RECONSTRUCTION (1990).

G. LACY, M. BARZELAY & M. MINZER, SCIENTIFIC AUTOMOBILE ACCIDENT RECONSTRUCTION (1981).

R. KUHLMAN, KILLER ROADS: FROM CRASH TO VERDICT (1986).

J. KWASNOSKI, G. PARTRIDGE & J. STEPHEN, INVESTIGATION AND PROSECUTION OF DWI AND VEHICULAR HOMICIDE (1998).

R. NOON, ENGINEERING ANALYSIS OF VEHICULAR ACCIDENTS (1994).

R. NOON, INTRODUCTION TO FORENSIC ENGINEERING (1992).

R. RIVERS, TRAFFIC ACCIDENT INVESTIGATORS HANDBOOK (1973).

M. SCHWARTZ & N. SCHWARTZ, ENGINEERING EVIDENCE (3d ed. 1996).

Badger, *Reconstruction of Traffic Accidents*, 9 AM. JUR. 3D PROOF OF FACTS 115 (1990).

R. LIMPERT, MOTOR VEHICLE ACCIDENT RECONSTRUCTION AND CAUSE ANALYSIS (4th ed. 1994).

Baker, *Limitations on Accident Reconstruction*, 8 DEF. L.J. 3 (1960).

Cook, *Speed Calculations and the Expert Witness*, 42 NEB. L. REV. 100 (1962).

Kohlman, *Computer Reconstruction of Highway Accidents*, 13 CAL. TRIAL LAW ASS'N J. 65 (Fall 1974).

Kriger, *New Dimensions in Litigation: Computer-Generated Video Graphics Enter Courtroom Scene*, 25 TRIAL 69 (Oct. 1989).

Zurmuhlen, *Automobile Accident Reconstruction*, 18 TRIAL LAW Q. 49 (Winter 1987).

Note, *Opinion and Demonstrative Evidence: Automobile Accident Reconstruction*, 14 WASHBURN L.J. 264 (1975).

CHAPTER 28

THE MEASUREMENT OF SPEED*

§ 28-1. In General.

The National Safety Council estimates that speeding contributes to 65% of all the traffic accidents and 50% of all traffic fatalities.[1] Those statistics alone make the scientific methods of measuring speed a critical topic. However, there is another reason why this topic is so important. As the Wisconsin Supreme Court remarked in *State v. Hanson*:[2]

> For the average law-abiding American citizen, minor traffic offenses constitute the only contact such persons will have with the law enforcement and judicial systems. Public confidence rests upon the fairness of such proceedings.[3]

The legitimacy[4] of the legal system depends on the existence of a widespread public perception that the system operates fairly, and in part that perception is shaped by the average citizen's experience with the enforcement of speed limits.

There are numerous scientific methods for determining speed. By applying the principles of physics to physical evidence such as skidmarks and the damage to

---

*The authors wish to express their appreciation to Dr. John Kwasnoski of Western New England Technical Consultants in Ludlow, Massachusetts, who reviewed this chapter in the second and third editions of this treatise and Professor David Kaye, College of Law, Arizona State University, who reviewed this chapter in the first edition.

1. Note, *Radar Speed Detection: Homing in on New Evidentiary Problems*, 48 FORDHAM L. REV. 1138, 1164 n.172 (1980).

2. 85 Wis. 2d 233, 270 N.W.2d 212 (1978).

3. *Id.* at 246, 270 N.W.2d at 219.

4. Imwinkelried, *A Sociological Approach to Legal Ethics*, 30 AMER. U. L. REV. 349, 351-52 (1981).

the vehicles, accident reconstructionists can make speed estimates after the accident.[5] Such evidence is frequently offered in civil tort actions. (Chapter 27 discusses accident reconstruction testimony in detail.) In criminal prosecutions, the evidence usually consists of a speed estimate made at or near the time of the offense. Since 1902 when the British tribunals first accepted stopwatch evidence,[6] courts have accepted a myriad of scientific techniques for clocking speeders. The principal weapons in the police arsenal against speeders are VASCAR and radar. Every year over 8.5 million speeding tickets are issued on the basis of radar clockings.[7]

Many jurisdictions now use moving radar in addition to stationary radar. As its name suggests, moving radar enables a police car to clock a suspected speeder while the police car itself is moving along the highway. Moving radar has been in use in the United States for little more than two decades.[8] Its use has spawned a national controversy.[9] In the so-called Miami radar trial of 1979, a Dade County, Florida, trial judge ruled radar evidence inadmissible.[10] As part of the aftermath of the trial, the Florida legislature passed a statute, upgrading radar equipment and training in that state.[11] The preamble to the Florida statute specifically states that "the reliability of present day radar is subject to question...."[12] In the wake of those developments, the Commerce Department's National Bureau of Standards

---

5. J. BAKER, TRAFFIC ACCIDENT INVESTIGATION MANUAL (1975); Herman v. Lee, 210 Neb. 563, 316 N.W.2d 56 (1982). *See* Osner v. Boughner, 180 Mich. App. 248, 446 N.W.2d 873 (1989) (a state trooper who had received basic and advanced training in accident investigation), *appeal granted in part*, 435 Mich. 861, 457 N.W.2d 344 (1990), *vacated*, 437 Mich. 951, 467 N.W.2d 592 (1991); State v. Minor, 47 Ohio App. 3d 22, 546 N.E.2d 1343 (the witness relied on a coefficient of friction from *Road and Track* magazine), *cause dismissed*, 38 Ohio St. 3d 702, 532 N.E.2d 1317 (1988); Miller v. Stiglet, Inc., 523 So. 2d 55, 57-58 (Miss. 1988) (a majority of jurisdictions now allow the use of accident reconstruction testimony); Cook, *Speed Calculations and the Expert Witness*, 42 NEB. L. REV. 100 (1962); Ryder, *Vehicle Accident Reconstruction*, 93 CASE & COMMENT 8, 10-12 (Sept.-Oct. 1988) (discussing both the use of the concepts of kinetic and crush energy to compute speed based on the deformation of the structure of the vehicle and the use of the concept of friction or rubbing force to calculate speed based on the length of skidmarks); Zurmuhlen, *Automobile Accident Reconstruction*, 18 TRIAL LAW. Q. 49 (Winter 1987) (discussing the application of Newton's Laws of Motions to accident reconstruction). *But see* Drope v. Owens, 298 Ark. 69, 765 S.W.2d 8 (1989) (sustaining the exclusion of accident reconstruction testimony).

6. Gorham v. Brice, 18 T.L.R. 424 (K.B. Div. 1902); Commonwealth v. Whynaught, 377 Mass. 14, 16, 384 N.E.2d 1212, 1214 (1979); State v. Frandsen, 391 N.W.2d 59 (Minn. App. 1986).

7. Schuon, *Police Radar Examined Amid Debate*, N.Y. TIMES, Nov. 27, 1979, at C1.

8. FLA. RADAR COMM'N, FINAL REPORT 9 (1981) (hereinafter cited as FLORIDA REPORT).

9. *Id.* at 2.

10. *Id.* at 1-3.

11. *Id.* at 49-53.

12. *Id.* at 49.

and the International Association of Chiefs of Police (IACP) undertook testing programs to improve the accuracy of radar.[13]

This chapter reviews the dispute over scientific techniques for measuring speed. An overview of the instruments themselves, notably VASCAR, stationary radar, moving radar, and laser speed gun, is found in the next section. Other sections consider operational conditions that can affect the instruments, operator qualifications, working order of the instruments, and the legal sufficiency of the evidence to support a speeding conviction.

§ 28-2. Scientific Instruments.

There are numerous devices for measuring the speed of a moving automobile. The technology is constantly evolving.[14] One device is the foto patrol or photo speed recorder.[15] The device takes several pictures of a moving auto, compares the size of the auto in each picture, and on the basis of the comparison estimates the automobile's speed.

Another instrument is a Prather speed device or electronic timer. This device is based on the following formula: Rate of speed equals the distance traveled divided by the time:

$$r = \frac{d}{t}$$

The police place two rubber air hoses or enoscopes a predetermined distance apart on the road; for example, the distance might be 88 or 176 feet. Thus, the distance is known. When the car wheels roll over each hose, the hose activates a stopwatch in a control box. After the car passes over the second hose, the control box has both the distance and time. The control box then registers the speed of the vehicle.

In a growing number of jurisdictions, the police are using a third type of device — small hand-held radar units such as the Decatur Ragun[16] and the Speed Gun.[17] However, by far the most common instruments are VASCAR, stationary

13. U.S. DEP'T COMM. NEWS, March 23, 1978, at 1.

14. Working in cooperation with the Swedish National Police Board, Sensys Traffic AB has developed a new radar technique which supposedly both reduces interference problems and more effectively distinguishes between vehicles. *New Swedish Radar*, RADAR REP., Nov. 1991, at 2.

15. Commonwealth v. Whynaught, 377 Mass. 14, 16, 384 N.E.2d 1212, 1214 (1979); Commonwealth v. Buxton, 205 Mass. 49, 91 N.E. 128 (1910). *See also* Note, *Evidence in Speeding Prosecutions*, 35 ALB. L. REV. 573, 579-80 (1971).

16. State v. Boyington, 153 N.J. Super. 252, 379 A.2d 486 (1977). *See Some New Technologies Keeping An Eye on Your Speed*, RADAR REP., Wint. 1998/99, at 2.

17. United States v. Fields, 30 Crim. L. Rep. (BNA) 2459 (S.D. Ohio Feb. 4, 1982) (concluding that the Speedgun Eight cannot be operated in a reliable manner). *But see* People v. Donohoo, 54 Ill. App. 3d 375, 369 N.E.2d 546 (1977).

radar, moving radar, and devices employing laser technology.

§ 28-2(A). VASCAR.

VASCAR is an acronym for Visual Average Speed Computer and Recorder. It has two advantages over conventional, stationary radar. First, only one police car is required to use VASCAR. When stationary radar is utilized, two police cars are ordinarily needed: a radar car and a chase car. Second, VASCAR can be employed while the police car is moving, thus allowing the police car to detect and deter speeding on a longer stretch of highway than stationary radar. These advantages account for the use of VASCAR in 35 states.[18]

Like the Prather device, VASCAR relies on the following formula:

$$\text{rate of speed} = \frac{\text{distance}}{\text{time}}$$

The VASCAR device collects data for the distance and time variables and then computes the average speed by dividing distance by time. The device has four modules or components. One is an odometer component, which is connected to the transmission and collects the distance data. Another component is the control module, which contains on-off toggle switches for distance and time. A third component is a computer module. The computer has memory units to store distance and time data; the memory unit can usually store up to 5.5 miles of distance data and 6.5 minutes of time data. It is programmed to divide automatically distance by time. The final component is a display module which reads out the average speed calculated by the computer. The operator feeds in the time of the target vehicle (the vehicle suspected of violating the speed laws) and a distance covered by both the target and patrol vehicle.

There are five basic scenarios for using VASCAR: The patrol car can follow the target vehicle to retrace its path; the target vehicle can follow the patrol vehicle; the patrol vehicle can approach the target vehicle from the opposite side of the highway; the target vehicle may pass in front of a patrol vehicle stopped at a T intersection; or the target vehicle can travel a premeasured distance (a distance that the officer measured earlier with a certified measuring tape).[19]

A simple example illustrates the use of VASCAR. Suppose that the target vehicle passes a patrol vehicle stopped at a T intersection, and the officer suspects that the target vehicle is speeding. As soon as the target vehicle passes a reference point on the road (a shadow, tree, pole, overpass, or sign), the officer flips the time toggle switch on. When the target vehicle passes a second reference point, the officer flips the time switch off. The patrol vehicle now begins pursuit.

---

18. E. Henry, Defense of Speeding — VASCAR Evidence (1974).

19. *See* F. Council, Testing of the In-the Field Accuracy of the VASCAR and TDS Speed Detection Devices 2-4 (1970).

When the patrol vehicle passes the first reference point, the officer flips the distance switch on. The officer flips the switch off when the patrol vehicle reaches the second reference point. The computer now has the distance and time data and will read out the target vehicle's average speed on the display screen. It is immaterial whether the officer feeds in the time or the distance data first.

In conjunction with the National Highway Traffic Safety Administration, Ohio State University studied the accuracy of VASCAR.[20] One of the lead researchers was Thomas Santer, a professor of statistics at O.S.U. In Professor Santer's words, the objective of the study was to determine "the magnitude of error in the operation" of VASCAR units.[21] The research generally indicated that VASCAR is reliable; but as the ensuing paragraphs indicate, there are possibilities for human error in the VASCAR technique--notably mistakes in perception or reaction time.

Admissibility and Weight of VASCAR Evidence

In the early cases involving VASCAR evidence, the courts insisted on expert testimony concerning the accuracy of VASCAR.[22] In 1972, in *People v. Leatherbarrow,*[23] a New York court refused to take judicial notice of the reliability of VASCAR; the court held that expert testimony was still necessary.[24]

Almost three decades have passed since the New York court rendered its decision in *Leatherbarrow.* New Jersey courts now extend judicial notice to VASCAR.[25] Furthermore, some states have enacted statutes that appear to sanction the admission of VASCAR evidence. For example, the Virginia statute refers not only to radar devices using "radio microwaves" but also to "other electrical device[s]."[26] The statute provides that clockings produced by these electrical devices "shall be accepted as prima facie evidence of the speed of such motor vehicle in any court or legal proceeding where the speed of the motor vehicle is in issue."[27] As Chapter 1 points out, if there is "legislative recognition"

---

20. *Study to Determine VASCAR Accuracy,* RADAR REP., Feb. 1991.

21. *Id.*

22. State v. Schmiede, 118 N.J. Super. 576, 289 A.2d 281 (1972); People v. Persons, 60 Misc. 2d 803, 303 N.Y.S.2d 728 (Spec. Sess. 1969); Tiffin v. Whitmer, 32 Ohio Misc. 169, 60 Ohio Op. 2d 367, 290 N.E.2d 198 (1970).

23. 69 Misc. 2d 563, 330 N.Y.S.2d 676 (Cty. Ct. 1972).

24. *See also* People v. Conlon, 109 Misc. 2d 729, 731, 440 N.Y.S.2d 831, 833 (Dist. Ct. 1981).

25. State v. Finkle, 128 N.J. Super. 199, 319 A.2d 733, *aff'd,* 66 N.J. 139, 329 A.2d 65 (1974), *cert. denied,* 423 U.S. 836 (1975); State v. Salup, 128 N.J. Super. 209, 319 A.2d 739 (1974); Note, *supra* note 1, at 1148-49 n.74. Wisconsin is in accord. State v. Frankenthal, 113 Wis. 2d 269, 335 N.W.2d 890 (1983).

26. VA. CODE § 46.2-882.

27. *Id.*

of the validity of a scientific technique, the proponent need not lay a *Daubert* or *Frye* foundation.

In jurisdictions accepting VASCAR evidence, admissibility in a particular case depends on satisfying other foundational requirements. Thus, if there is insufficient proof that the VASCAR unit was in proper working order at the time of the clocking, VASCAR evidence is inadmissible.[28] The operator may ensure the unit's working order by testing the instrument "in accordance with the manufacturer's recommendations, using a certified stopwatch at a distance premeasured by a certified steel tape."[29] The proponent will also have to demonstrate that the operator was qualified.[30]

Even when VASCAR evidence is admissible, it may be vulnerable to a weight attack. VASCAR is more subject to human error than stationary or moving radar. The operator must flip the time and distance switches to feed the data into the VASCAR computer. An error in perception or reaction time can result in an inaccurate reading. Suppose, for instance, that the operator errs in perception and mistakes one pole or other reference point for another; the operator could easily commit such an error if the day is overcast or night is approaching. The result might be that too much distance is fed into the computer; when the distance is overstated, the computer will read out an erroneously high speed for the target vehicle.[31] Or assume that the operator acts too quickly and throws the time toggle switch off before the target vehicle reaches the second reference point. The result would be that the time is understated, and again the computer will read an erroneously high speed for the target vehicle. Due to these possibilities for error, many jurisdictions carefully test the officer's proficiency during initial training. In some jurisdictions, the officer must pass a final proficiency test to be certified as a VASCAR operator. In the test, the officer cannot commit an error greater

---

28. St. Louis v. Martin, 548 S.W.2d 622 (Mo. App. 1977); Note, *supra* note 1, at 1148-49 n.74.

29. State v. Frankenthal, 113 Wis. 2d 269, 270, 335 N.W.2d 890, 891 (1983).Systems Innovation, Inc., supplies and calibrates the VASCAR equipment in Pennsylvania. *Pennsylvania Officials Criticize VASCAR-Plus Calibration*, RADAR REP., Feb. 1988, at 1. At a news conference, the Pennsylvania Auditor General Donald Bailey charged that the company had falsified calibration records. *Id.* The company denied the allegations and filed a damages action in federal court against Mr. Bailey. *VASCAR Company Fights Back Against Pennsylvania Auditor General*, RADAR REP., May 1988, at 3.

30. Note, *supra* note 1, at 1154 n.108 ("VASCAR certification ... [requires] approximately sixty hours of instruction.").

31. Henry offers the following formula for computing the speed error when the operator misjudges the distance:

$$\text{Speed error} = \text{VASCAR speed readout} \times \frac{\text{(Distance misjudged)}}{\text{(Clocked distance)}}$$

E. HENRY, *supra* note 18, at 5-10.

than two miles per hour, and the officer's average error cannot exceed 0.75 miles per hour.[32]

§ 28-2(B). Stationary Radar, Including Photo Radar.

"Radar" is an acronym for radio direction and ranging. It gained notoriety during World War II because of its military applications. Unlike military radar, police radar is based on the Doppler shift or effect principle. The military uses a pulse type of radar.[33] The unit sends out a beam at regular intervals. In contrast, police radar units include a transmitter that emits a continuous beam of microwaves.[34] The unit generates undulating patterns called cycles.[35] The frequency or number of waves per second is stated in hertz (Hz).[36] When the microwaves strike a reflective object such as a battleship, they bounce back to the source. By measuring the time for the wave to reflect back to the radar unit, the operator can determine the distance of the object from the radar unit — a common military use.[37]

The Doppler principle also enables the operator to determine the speed of the object. The Doppler effect is an everyday experience. When an ambulance is approaching, for example, its siren has a higher frequency and pitch. The pitch sounds lower as the ambulance recedes. Similarly, when an object is moving toward the radar unit, the microwaves reflecting back have a higher frequency. Conversely, if the object is moving away from the radar unit, the frequency is lower.[38] According to one court, the radar computes the speed by employing the following formula:[39]

---

32. *Id.* at 5-2-3.

33. Trichter & Patterson, *Police Radar 1980: Has the Black Box Lost Its Magic?*, 11 St. Mary's L.J. 829, 833 (1980).

34. *Id.* at 834.

35. State v. Wojtkowiak, 170 N.J. Super. 44, 48, 405 A.2d 477, 479 (1979), *rev'd on other grounds,* 174 N.J. Super. 460, 416 A.2d 975 (1980).

36. *What You're Up Against*, Radar Rep., Nov. 1992, at 1 ("Traffic radar began on X band (10.525 gigahertz (GHz)) close to 30 years ago, and this frequency is still used widely today. K-band (24.150 GHz) has been around for about 20 years and is popular as a short-range unit.... The newest types of radar operate on the wide Ka band (34.2-35.2 Ghz)"); *Stalker Comes to Delaware*, Radar Rep., Sep. 1996, at 2 ("The Stalker is a wideband Ka radar with a 6,000-foot range and the ability to track the speeds of vehicles both in front of and behind the police car. The unit will work in a police cruiser moving as slow as 1 mph, as opposed to 20 mph for other moving-mode radars").

37. Ill. Dep't Law Enf., Moving Radar: An Assessment of Its Role in Traffic Law Enforcement 5 (1981) (hereinafter cited as Illinois Report).

38. State v. Wojtkowiak, 170 N.J. Super. 44, 49, 405 A.2d 477, 479 (1979), *rev'd on other grounds,* 174 N.J. Super. 460, 416 A.2d 975 (1980).

39. *Id.* at 49, 405 A.2d at 480.

$$f_{dop} = \frac{2vf}{c}$$

In the formula, f_{dop} signifies the changed frequency of the reflected microwaves, 2 is a constant, v is the speed of the object, f is the frequency of the microwave originally emitted from the transmitter, and c is the speed of light.[40] By controlling the frequency emitted from the transmitter and measuring the changed frequency reflected back to its receiver, the radar unit computes the unknown variable, (v), the speed of the object.[41] The computer inserts the appropriate values for all the other variables and solves the formula for v.[42] However, according to one of our reviewers, Professor David Kaye, the correct formula is:

$$f = [1 - 2\,v/c]f$$ [43]

Photo Radar

"Photo radar" is a modification of stationary radar. Photo radar operates in this fashion:

> The photo radar unit — consisting of an integrated package of traffic radar, camera, and computer — is mounted in the rear of a vehicle. The law officer parks the vehicle next to an expressway and adjusts the angle of the radar antenna according to the lane of traffic he plans to monitor. Then he sets the speed at which he wants passing vehicles to activate the system. When a vehicle passes at or above the preset speed, the radar unit triggers the camera. [T]he photo show[s] ... the vehicle, its license plate [and] the face of the operator .... The device also imprints on the negative the speed, date, time, and location.[44]

The owner of the vehicle is later sent a letter, notifying the owner of the speeding violation.

The system is manufactured by a Texas company, Traffic Monitoring Technologies.[45] The system was originally used in Galveston County, Texas;[46] but two communities in that county, Friendswodd and LaMargue, have since discontinued use of photo radar.[47] Similarly, after a test project, King County,

40. *Id.*

41. *Id.*

42. Kopper, *The Scientific Reliability of Radar Speedmeters*, 33 N.C. L. REV. 343 (1955).

43. Correspondence with Professor David Kaye, Arizona State University College of Law.

44. *The Menace of Photo Radar*, RADAR REP., Oct. 1987, at 1.

45. *Id.*

46. *Id.*

47. *Hometown Gives Photo Radar the Boot*, RADAR REP., Apr. 1988, at 1.

Washington, abandoned use of photo radar.[48] Likewise, while police in Peoria, Arizona once employed photo radar, its use was discontinued after local residents voted against the use of the system.[49] Campbell, California followed suit and ceased its use of photo radar.[50] However, the system is in use on a routine or experimental basis in: Paradise Valley and Scottsdale, Arizona; Danville, Folsom, Glendale, Los Altos, National City, Pasadena, Riverside, Roseville, and San Jose, California; Batavia Lake Forest and Glen Ellyn, Illinois; St. Paul, Minnesota; Beaverton and Portland, Garland, Huntington, Wellington, and West Valley, Utah; and Spokane, Federal Way and Tacoma, Washington.[51] State police in Maryland and Virginia are testing photo radar on the Capital Beltway in the Washington, D.C. area.[52] Ithaca, New York is also contemplating testing photo radar.[53]

Admissibility and Weight of Stationary Radar Evidence

As we shall soon see, there is only a small body of case law addressing the admissibility of photo radar. In contrast, there is a wealth of authority analyzing the admissibility and weight of the more traditional modes of stationary radar. In part because of the favorable reputation enjoyed by military radar, the courts were eager to embrace the police use of stationary radar units. In 1955, *State v. Dantonio*[54] first extended judicial notice to the reliability of stationary radar

48. *Id.*; RADAR REP., May 1989, at 2; RADAR REP., Dec. 1988, at 1.

49. *Peoria Voters Give Photo Radar the Boot*, RADAR REP., May 1991, at 1.

50. *California City Shuts Down Photo Radar*, RADAR REP., Spr. 1998, at 1.

51. *California City Shuts Down Photo Radar*, RADAR REP., Spr. 1998, at p. 2; Cooper, *Photo Radar: Is It Big Brother? Speeders in Roseville, Folsom Will Soon Find Out*, THE SACRAMENTO BEE, July 26, 1990, at 1; Grab, *Photo-Radar: What's Wrong With This Picture?*, 19 GLENDALE L. REV. 51 (1991); *Photo Radar: Where It Is & Where It's Not*, RADAR REP., May 1996, at 1 (the article lists the following locations where photo radar is currently being used: British Columbia, Canada; Campbell, California; Paradise Valley, Arizona; Madison, Wisconsin; Pasadena, California; Portland and Gresham, Oregon; Sandy, Utah; and West Valley, Utah). The Roseville city council has voted to discontinue the use of photo radar in that jurisdiction. *Roseville Says Goodbye to Photo Radar*, RADAR REP., May 1992, at 2. Similarly, the Kansas City, Missouri council rejected photo radar. *Kansas City Rejects Photo Radar*, RADAR REP., Dec. 1992, at 2; *Photo Radar Moves East . . . .*, RADAR REP., Nov. 1991, at 1; *This Is a Test*, RADAR REP., Sep. 1991, at 2; *Utah Photo Radar Ban Fails*, RADAR REP., Apr. 1991; *The Photo Radar Scorecard*, RADAR REP., July 1990; *Photo Radar Is Busting Out All Over*, RADAR REP., Apr. 1990, at 2; *Hometown Gives Photo Radar the Boot*, RADAR REP., Apr. 1988, at 1.

52. *Maryland, Virginia Begin Beltway Photo Radar Testing*, RADAR REP., Dec. 1989, at 2.

53. *Ithaca Wants Photo Radar Test*, RADAR REP., May 1997, at 4.

54. 18 N.J. 570, 115 A.2d 35 (1955). *Accord* State v. Tomanelli, 153 Conn. 365, 216 A.2d 625 (1966); People v. Abdallah, 82 Ill. App. 2d 312, 226 N.E.2d 408 (1967); People v. Barbic, 105 Ill. App. 2d 360, 244 N.E.2d 626 (1969); State v. Gerdes, 291 Minn. 353, 191 N.W.2d 428 (1971);

evidence. The prevailing view today is that the validity of stationary radar is judicially noticeable and, hence, the proponent need not present expert testimony vouching for the general validity of stationary radar.[55] Under the prevailing view, the radar evidence is admissible as substantive evidence of the driver's speed. One court has developed an alternative theory for the admissibility of the evidence; the Maine Supreme Judicial Court has held that radar evidence may be admitted for the limited purpose of showing the basis of an accident reconstruction expert's opinion.[56] Another jurisdiction has gone to the length of holding that radar testimony is not only admissible but also necessary; this jurisdiction has construed its radar statutes as manifesting a legislative intention that standing alone, a police officer's opinion of a car's speed is insufficient to support a judgment of conviction.[57]

The one dissenting voice questioning the validity of stationary radar has been the trial court in the 1979 Miami radar trial, *State v. Aquilera.*[58] There the court found that there are numerous possible causes of erroneous radar speed estimates and that officers using radar have not had sufficient training to avoid and recognize the causes. The court conceded that "more of these errors pertain to radar in the moving mode than in the stationary mode"[59] but concluded that enough errors affected stationary radar to warrant excluding that evidence as well.

State v. Graham, 322 S.W.2d 188 (Mo. 1959); East Cleveland v. Ferell, 168 Ohio St. 298, 7 Ohio Op. 2d 6, 154 N.E.2d 630 (1958); ILLINOIS REPORT, *supra* note 37, at 6, 85.

55. 2 C. MCCORMICK, EVIDENCE § 204 (5th ed. 1999). Federal Rule of Evidence 201(b)(2) sets out a relatively liberal standard for judicial notice of, for example, scientific propositions. The basis for judicial notice codified in 201(b)(2) is sometimes referred to as "verifiable certainty." However, the statute does not use the expression, "certainty." In Daubert v. Merrell Dow Pharmaceuticals, Inc., 509 U.S. 579 (1993), the Supreme Court asserted that even in the hard sciences, "arguably, there are no certainties . . . ." The Court frankly acknowledged the uncertainty inherent in the scientific enterprise. One of the consequences should be an increased willingness to resort to judicial notice. Imwinkelried, *Evidence Law Visits Jurassic Park: The Far-Reaching Implications of the Daubert Court's Recognition of the Uncertainty of the Scientific Enterprise*, 81 IOWA L. REV. 55, 71-73 (1995).

56. State v. Herbest, 551 A.2d 442, 445 n.3 (Me. 1988). The court relied on its state version of Federal Rule of Evidence 703. The rule specifically states that an expert may rely on information which is not independently admissible. FED. R. EVID. 703, 28 U.S.C.A.

57. Commonwealth v. Martorano, 387 Pa. Super. 151, 563 A.2d 1229 (1989), *app. denied*, 525 Pa. 597, 575 A.3d 563 (1990).

58. 48 Fla. Supp. 207 (1979).

59. *Id.* at 210. *Compare* Goodson, *Technical Shortcomings of Doppler Traffic Radar*, 30 J. FORENSIC SCI. 1186 (1985) *with* Benson, *Discussion of "Technical Shortcomings of Doppler Traffic Radar*," 32 J. FORENSIC SCI. 9 (1987) (Deputy Benson of the Traffic Homicide Section of the Pima County's Sheriff's Department in Tucson, Arizona argues that many law enforcement agencies have upgraded the radar training to enable officers to overcome the shortcomings identified in the 1985 article).

Although all but one of the 18 Dade County, Florida trial courts followed *Aquilera,* the decision has had negligible impact outside Florida.[60] In most jurisdictions, the sources of error identified in *Aquilera* can serve as attacks on the weight of stationary radar evidence but do not bar its admission. Some of the alleged problems with stationary radar, that were identified during the *Aquilera* trial, include the following:

Beam Range and Width. Early police radar units had a relatively short range, a short "zone of influence." In contrast, modern units have an extensive range and a relatively wide beam, compared to the narrower beam radar units used in Europe. At its source, the beam may be only a few inches wide. However, the beam spreads out from its point of origin in the transmitter. As one commentator has pointed out, a modern unit may have a range of 7,500 feet. On the assumption that the beam angle is 19 degrees,

> At a range of 100 feet, the beam width was 34 feet; at 500 feet, it was 172 feet; at 1,000 feet, it was 344 feet; at 5,000 feet, it was 1,720 feet; and at 7,500 feet, it was 2,580. At half a unit's range, therefore, its zone of influence would easily include over ten lanes of traffic. With such a wide area for the operator to observe, the (*Aquilera*) court concluded that the chance of misidentification was simply too great to permit operator testimony based on radar.[61]

The combination of a long range and a wide beam raises the possibility that the operator may misidentify the car causing the reading on the display screen. As discussed in the next section, it was once assumed that radar always registered the closest car — the "nearest car" or "first car in line" theory. That assumption is incorrect. The radar registers the strongest signal reflected back to the receiver. The strength of this signal depends not only upon the distance between the receiver and the object but also upon the object's reflective qualities. In turn, those reflective qualities — its reflective cross-section — are affected by the size and shape of the object. If a small, curved car is followed by a huge truck with large flat surfaces facing the patrol car, the signal reflecting back may be the signal bouncing off the truck rather than the car. There are methods that a knowledgeable, skilled operator can use to determine whether the car first in line is causing the radar reading; but the long range and wide beam of most American radar units increase the possibility of misidentification of the target vehicle.

The Cosine Error. It would be ideal if the operator could aim the radar unit's transmitter directly at the target vehicle — at a 90 degree angle to the approaching front edge of that vehicle. As a practical matter, however, it is impossible to do so; the operator would have to place the transmitter in the

---

60. Trichter & Patterson, *supra* note 33 at 854.

61. *Id.* at 855.

middle of a traffic lane. Doing so would be hazardous to both the operator and traffic. For that reason, the officer usually locates the transmitter a few feet off the highway. Thus, there is an angular disparity between the linear axis of the signal and the linear axis of the target vehicle's path, as shown in Figure 28-1:

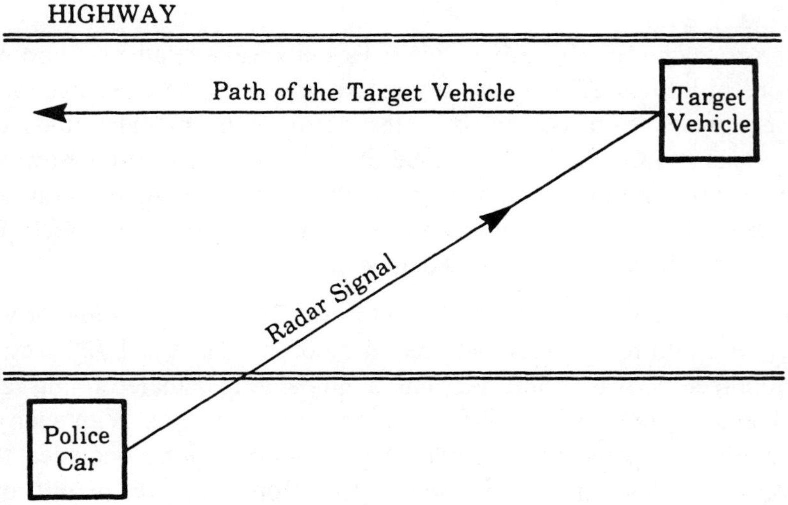

Figure 28-1

Due to the disparity, the radar unit's receiver reads a component of the target vehicle speed, but not the full speed — the cosine or angular effect error or distortion.[62] When the operator is using stationary radar, this error usually favors the target vehicle; since the radar registers only a component or part of the speed, the radar understates the true speed of the target vehicle. As discussed in the next section, the cosine error can have the opposite impact on a moving radar reading and overstate the target vehicle's speed. The cosine error "takes its name from the trigonometric function related to the principle. The indicated or display speed can be computed for any angle by multiplying the cosine of the angle by the true speed."[63] For example, if the true speed is 30, the following angles would result in the indicated display speeds: at 0 angle, 30 mph; at 5, 29.89; at 10, 29.54; at 20, 28.19; at 45, 21.21; and at 60, 15.[64]

62. *Id.* at 851.

63. Fuhrman, *The Mistakes Radar Makes — Part 4: Stationary Radar Cosine Error*, RADAR REP., June 1991, at 3.

64. *Id.* Fuhrman also provides the data for 40, 50, and 60 miles per hour. If the true speed is 40, the display speeds at the various angles would be 40, 39.85, 39.39, 37.59, 28.28, and 20. If the true speed is 50, the display speeds would be 50, 49.81, 49.24, 46.99, 35.36, and 25. If the true speed is 60, the display speeds would be 60, 59.77, 59.09, 56.38, 42.43, and 30.

Catch-Up. This problem arises when the police car using stationary radar accelerates from a dead stop.[65] The acceleration speed may be erroneously added to the supposed speed of the target vehicle.[66] The operator should either lock the speed in before accelerating or disregard the readings immediately after starting up.

In addition to the above problems, stationary radar may produce an erroneous reading due to interference or poor maintenance. The problem of interference is discussed in § 28-3, and proper maintenance of radar equipment is analyzed in § 28-5.

The Admissibility of Photo Radar Evidence

There has been little litigation involving the technique of photo radar.[67] The Utah legislature has enacted a statute restricting the use of photo radar.[68] The Arizona Supreme Court has declined to review a case challenging the legality of photo radar.[69] However, the Alaska courts have ruled on the subject.[70] In two decisions, the Alaska Court of Appeals has rejected photo radar. In the more recent decision, handed down in November 1997, the court noted that the lower court record contained conflicting expert testimony over the validity of photo radar and that much of the favorable expert testimony had been supplied by American Traffic Systems of Arizona, the developer of the system. Moreover, one Canadian court has ruled photo radar evidence unreliable and inadmissible.[71]

---

65. Trichter & Patterson, *supra* note 33, at 850.

66. *Id.*

67. *See generally* Grab, *Photo-Radar: What's Wrong With This Picture?*, 10 GLENDALE L. REV. 51 (1991).

68. *Photo Radar Moves East ...*, RADAR REP., Nov. 1991, at 1. UTAH CODE ANN. § 41-6-52.5(2) reads:

> Photo radar may not be used except:
> a)(i) in school zones; or (ii) in other areas approved by a local authority's governing body based on a demonstrated public safety need;
> b) when a peace officer is present with the photo radar unit; (c) when signs are posted on the highway providing notice to a motorist that photo radar may be used; and
> d) when use of photo radar by a local authority is approved by the local authority's governing body.

69. *Arizona Supreme Court Declines to Review Photo Radar*, RADAR REP., June 1989, at 2 (Roseanne Cortright of Phoenix filed suit to challenge the use of photo radar in Paradise Valley).

70. *Alaska Court Gives Photo Radar The Cold Shoulder*, RADAR REP., Winter 1998, at 5.

71. *Photo Radar Ruled "Unreliable,"* RADAR REP., Oct. 1990 ("A provincial judge in Calgary has ruled that the photo radar system used in that city is unreliable. 'The Multanova device is not by itself, or as operated by the Calgary police service, a technically fit and proper device — at all times and without fail — capable of accurately measuring and recording the speed of a motor vehicle,' wrote Judge Bernard Laven.... Laven agreed with the defense that the Multanova is incapable of distinguishing which vehicle is speeding if other vehicles are in its view").

§ 28-2(C). Moving Radar.

Moving Radar Technology

When police use stationary radar, they ordinarily assign two police cars to each traffic patrol. One officer operates the stationary radar, and the other officer staffs the chase car. When the first officer detects a target vehicle speeding, he or she radios the officer in the chase car and provides the officer with a description of the target vehicle.[72] The officer driving the chase car pursues and apprehends the driver of the target vehicle. As in VASCAR, only one car is needed with moving radar. The same officer who monitors the moving radar pursues the target vehicle and issues the speeding citation. Thus, moving radar allows the officer to patrol a longer stretch of highway.

Moving radar differs from stationary radar in design as well as in operation. A moving radar unit has two transceivers because it emits two beams. The low beam is designed to reflect off stationary objects near the patrol vehicle; when that beam reflects back to the receiver, that component registers the speed of the patrol vehicle. A second, higher beam is aimed above and beyond the low beam; it is aimed at the target vehicle. When the high beam reflects back to its receiver, the return frequency represents the sum of the speeds of the patrol and target vehicles — known as the closing speed. When the unit has computed the closing speed and the patrol vehicle's speed, simple subtraction of the latter from the former yields the speed of the target vehicle. By turning off the low beam, the officer may use a moving radar unit as stationary radar. When the officer is employing both beams, the unit is said to be in its moving or verifying mode.

The typical moving radar unit has several unique features. One feature is an Auto Lock, which enables the officer to preset the unit for a certain speed such as 65 miles per hour. Whenever the unit encounters a speed equalling or exceeding the preset speed, the unit registers and locks that speed into the display panel. When the Auto Lock is off, the unit is said to be in a manual mode. A related feature is the Alert Tone; the tone sounds when the Auto Lock activates. A Read Through Lock differs radically from an Auto Lock. A Read Through Lock

---

72. *Here's a Quick Roundup of What's New on the Technology Front*, RADAR REP., Mar. 1995, at 1-2 ("Police in at least seven states are using Kustom Signals' new Eagle series radar, which employs digital signal processing, that the manufacturer claims more accurately identifies the fastest vehicle in traffic. Instead of fixating on the strongest target (usually the biggest or closest vehicle) in a group, the Eagle is said to be able to cut through the 'noise' to find which car is going the fastest. This makes it almost impossible for a speeder to hide in the radar shadow behind a large truck ... Digital processing makes the Eagle–moving-mode unit available in X, K, and Ka bands–able to identify the reflected signal of each vehicle.... The unit tracks the strongest signal, but with the press of a button it begins following the fastest vehicle within range. The signal can then be locked in and shown in a separate display on the radar unit").

enables the officer to lock one recorded speed into the unit while continuing to clock the speed of the target vehicle. This feature allows an officer to verify the identity of the suspected target vehicle without losing a previously registered high reading. Still another feature is a Doppler Audio Tone. The quality of the tone helps the officer determine whether the registered reading was produced by a transient condition, such as momentary radio interference, or by the speed of the target vehicle. The tone is relatively steady when the target vehicle is maintaining a constant speed or slowly changing speeds, but a transient condition such as brief radio interference produces a warbling or variable sound.[73]

The unit might also have an Anti-Detection Switch. Many drivers have installed radar detectors or Fuzzbusters in their cars. To thwart these devices, radar manufacturers have added the antidetection switch to their units. The switch suppresses the beam of microwaves until the officer visually detects a target vehicle. By throwing the antidetection switch, the officer can bounce a beam off the target vehicle and obtain a radar speed estimate before the Fuzzbuster alerts. Finally, the unit may incorporate a new type of microcircuitry known as Phase Lock Loop (PLL).[74] PLL permits the unit to lock onto a target vehicle's reflected signal far more quickly than the older radar units.[75] Some experts contend that PLL enables the newer moving radar units to lock onto a signal in a few hundredths of a second.[76] A very brief signal produced by transient interference would not have registered on an older radar unit; but if the officer is using a moving unit with PLL, the unit will lock onto the signal, and the signal would then trigger both the Auto Lock and the Alert Tone.

Admissibility and Weight of Moving Radar Evidence

As should be expected, the shift to the moving radar units has led to attacks on the admissibility of moving radar evidence even in jurisdictions that readily accept stationary radar evidence. The attacks have resulted in a split of authority among the courts. Although most jurisdictions have not yet passed on the admissibility of moving radar evidence, the majority of those that have considered the issue have judicially noticed the reliability of moving radar.[77]

---

73. ILLINOIS REPORT, *supra* note 37, at 15.

74. Trichter & Patterson, *supra* note 33, at 842.

75. *Id.*

76. *Id.*

77. State v. Primm, 4 Kan.App.2d 314, 606 P.2d 112 (1980); State v. Musgrave, 169 N.J. Super. 204, 404 A.2d 650, *rev'd on other grounds*, 171 N.J. Super. 477, 410 A.2d 64 (1979); State v. Shelt, 46 Ohio App.2d 115, 75 Ohio Op. 2d 103, 346 N.E.2d 345 (1976); Akron v. Gray, 60 Ohio Misc. 68, 10 Ohio Op. 3d 303, 397 N.E.2d 429 (1979); ILLINOIS REPORT, *supra* note 32, at 6-7, 85. *See also* State v. Newton, 421 A.2d 920 (Del. Super. 1980); *Massachusetts Court Admits Moving Radar as Evidence Though Questions of Accuracy Remain*, RADAR REP., Feb. 1991 ("A Massachusetts district court judge in December issued the state's first written decision admitting

However, that view is far from universal. A number of jurisdictions judicially notice the reliability of moving radar only when the operator uses the unit in the manual mode and deactivates the Auto Lock.[78] Other jurisdictions have flatly refused to judicially notice the reliability of moving radar.[79] Still other courts have not only insisted upon the presentation of expert testimony to vouch for moving radar; but even after hearing the testimony, these courts have ruled the evidence inadmissible.[80] That was the outcome in *Aquilera*,[81] the celebrated Florida radar case.

In some cases, attacks on the admissibility of moving radar evidence have been premised on statutory arguments. In many jurisdictions, statutes provide that the police may use only models of radar units that have been approved for use by a designated state agency, such as a department of motor vehicles or transportation.[82] Since a statutory argument is involved, counsel need not assert or prove that the particular model is unreliable. The only questions are the legal issue — whether the statute was intended to bar evidence of radar readings by unapproved models — and the factual issue — whether the model used has been

---

moving radar as evidence in speeding cases. However, the judge also left open the possibility for challenges of the accuracy of this type of traffic radar. In *Commonwealth v. Carol Sliwa*, Judge James Dohoney of the Southern Berkshire District ruled that moving radar technology is generally accepted in the scientific community. Though he suggested that traffic radar is subject to a variety of errors and identification problems, he said none of those factors was present in the Sliwa case. The state's Supreme Judicial Court recognized the validity of stationary radar in a 1979 case, *Commonwealth v. Whynaught*"); People v. Knight, 72 N.Y.2d 481, 530 N.E.2d 1273, 534 N.Y.S.2d 353 (1988) ("insofar as the underlying scientific principles of moving and stationary radar are the same, evidence derived from either should be admissible without the need for expert testimony"); State v. Calvert, 682 S.W.2d 474, 477 (Mo. 1984) (listing cases from other jurisdictions accepting moving radar evidence); State v. Moore, 700 S.W.2d 880 (Mo. App. 1985); State v. Bechtel, 24 Ohio App. 3d 72, 24 Ohio B.R. 126, 493 N.E.2d 318 (1985); Washington County v. Leudtke, 135 Wis. 2d 131, 399 N.W.2d 906 (1987).

78. State v. Wojtkowiak, 170 N.J. Super. 44, 63, 405 A.2d 477, 487 (1979), *rev'd on other grounds,* 174 N.J. Super. 460, 416 A.2d 975 (1980); Note, *supra* note 1, at 1162 n.159.

79. People v. Conlon, 109 Misc. 2d 729, 440 N.Y.S.2d 831 (Dist. Ct. 1981) (the MR-9 unit); People v. Winter, N.Y.L.J., Jan. 30, 1979, at 12, col. 4 (App. Term 1979); People v. Mangelberg, N.Y.L.J., Nov. 21, 1977, at 14, col. 5 (App. Term 1977); People v. Lampert, N.Y.L.J., May 31, 1977, at 14, col. 2 (App. Term 1977); State v. Freeman, 24 Ohio Misc. 7, 24 Ohio B.R. 131, 493 N.E.2d 571 (1985); Kirtland Hills v. Logan, 21 Ohio App. 3d 67, 21 Ohio B.R. 71, 486 N.E.2d 231 (1984); State v. Colby, 14 Ohio App. 3d 291, 14 Ohio B.R. 348, 470 N.E.2d 924 (1984); State v. Doles, 70 Ohio App. 2d 35, 24 Ohio Op. 3d 25, 433 N.E.2d 1290 (1980); State v. Hanson, 85 Wis. 2d 233, 270 N.W.2d 212 (1978); Note, *supra* note 1, at 1148-49 n.74.

80. State v. Aquilera, 48 Fla. Supp. 207 (1979); People v. Bellizi, 108 Misc. 2d 209, 441 N.Y.S.2d 147 (Sup. Ct. 1980) (insufficient evidence of the reliability of moving radar when the police car and the target vehicle are traveling in opposite directions).

81. State v. Aquilera, 48 Fla. Supp. 207 (1979).

82. *See* Commonwealth v. Beatty, 310 Pa. Super. 128, 456 A.2d 216 (1983).

properly approved. Several courts have sustained this defense argument.[83] To make matters more difficult for the prosecution, some courts have held that courts may not judicially notice the agency's approval of a particular model.[84] The prosecution must present evidence of the approval.[85]

At one time the federal government considered issuing performance standards for radar units. On January 8, 1981, the National Highway Traffic Safety Administration (NHTSA) published proposed standards in the Federal Register.[86] The regulations would have prescribed specifications for radar units as well as methods of field testing the units. Under the proposed regulations, states would have had to purchase only complying units to maintain their eligibility for certain federal assistance. However, on November 19, 1981, the NHTSA terminated the rule-making proceedings.[87] In doing so, the NHTSA noted "the concern of three of the commentators in these proceedings ... over the possibility that the issuance of the standard will trigger challenges in the courts of pre-standard radar devices. Although the draft standard did not propose to address pre-standard radar, the development of a Qualified Products List (QPL) could have been interpreted as a statement of disapproval of the quality of existing radar units."[88] The NHTSA stated that the termination of the rule-making proceeding was "in keeping with this [Reagan] Administration's commitment to giving State and local governments as much flexibility as possible ...."[89] The NHTSA's action foreclosed the possibility that defense counsel could use national radar standards as the basis for an argument to exclude speed readings by radar units that did not comply with these standards.

As in the case of stationary radar, defense counsel can make weight attacks as well as admissibility attacks. Some of the weight attacks against stationary radar are also available against moving radar, but there are several attacks peculiar to moving radar.

---

83. Commonwealth v. Nardei, 278 Pa. Super. 420, 420 A.2d 612 (1980); *Florida Ticket Dismissed Over Uncertified Radar*, RADAR REP., Sept. 1992, at 2 ("Because permanent certification for the Kustom Pro 1000 radar gun fell through the cracks, hundreds of Florida speeding tickets could be void. A St. Lucie County judge in July dismissed Kenneth Conner's citation ... because the unit was not on Florida's list of approved radars"; in January 1990, the Department of Highway Safety gave the unit interim approval, but a final approval was never formally published). *See also* Wiggins v. State, 249 Ga. 302, 304-05, 290 S.E.2d 427, 430 (1982); Commonwealth v. Perdok, 411 Pa. 301, 192 A.2d 221 (1963).

84. Commonwealth v. Beatty, 310 Pa. Super. 128, 456 A.2d 216 (1983). However, Federal Rule of Evidence 201(b)(2) sets out a rather liberal standard for judicial notice. A court might reach a different result under that statute.

85. Wiggins v. State, 249 Ga. 302, 305, 290 S.E.2d 427, 430 (1982).

86. 46 Fed. Reg. 2097 (Jan. 8, 1981).

87. 46 Fed. Reg. 56,823 (Nov. 19, 1981).

88. *Id.* at 56,823-24.

89. *Id.* at 56,824.

Beam Range and Width. In some cases, the courts seem to assume that the car closest to the patrol vehicle is necessarily the car that produced the speed reading.[90] That assumption is incorrect. Radar registers the strongest frequency reflected — which may not be the reflection from the closest vehicle.[91] "[I]t is possible that a larger target rather than the one closest to the transmitter can be 'locked' into the machine and tracked. An illustration of the phenomenon is the very small but first-in-line vehicle being followed closely by a very large truck. The larger truck could very well be the 'target' vehicle rather than the first-in-line smaller automobile."[92] To ensure that the closest vehicle is the target, the operator continues to monitor the suspected target until it passes; if the reading disappears when the suspected target passes, the operator knows that the target has been correctly identified. The operator can use the Read-Through-Lock to hold the initial speed reading while he continues to monitor the suspected target until it reaches the front bumper of the patrol vehicle.[93] If the operator neither continued tracking nor used a Read-Through-Lock, misidentification of the target can occur.

The Cosine Error. In stationary radar, the cosine distortion usually benefits the defendant. In moving radar, the distortion will have no effect if the cosine error affects the low and high beams equally. However, when the error affects only the low beam, the error can disadvantage the defendant. If the low beam understates the patrol vehicle's speed, the radar unit will overstate the target vehicle's speed when it subtracts the supposed patrol car speed from the closing speed. There are two ways in which the cosine error can affect the low beam. The unit's antenna could be improperly aligned, or the low beam might momentarily reflect off a nearby surface at an extreme angle.[94] Many radar units have a display of the

---

90. *E.g.*, State v. Harper, 382 A.2d 263, 264 (Del. 1978).

91. State v. Newton, 421 A.2d 920, 922 (Del. 1980).

92. *Id.*

93. *Id.*

94. ILLINOIS REPORT, *supra* note 37, at 17. This error is also discussed in Fuhrman, *Mistakes Radar Makes — Part 5: Moving Radar Cosine Error*, RADAR REP., July 1991, at 3. The author states that "[w]hen the unit is misaligned 20 degrees to the left to improve readings across an interstate median, a true 55 mph patrol speed will be reduced to 51 mph. If the angle is 30 degrees, 55 mph will read as 47 mph by the radar unit." The author adds:

> Even w]hen the patrol speed computation is correct, the Cosine Effect can still cause an error in the target speed. The median of a divided highway is wide enough to create a large angle between the radar beam and the target vehicle. The closing speed computation will be reduced by the cosine of this angle. The target speed indication will be reduced by the amount of the error created by the angle. A curve in the road can cause a similar situation to arise. If you are approaching a moving radar unit from around a curve, you are not traveling a straight line toward the radar beam. The target speed will be reduced by the cosine of the angle created by the curve. With moving radar, this is the only Cosine Effect error that works to the favor of the motorist.

patrol speed registering on the low beam. An attentive operator should constantly compare that speed to the speed registered by his speedometer; a discrepancy would alert the operator to the possibility of a cosine error.[95] An inattentive operator, however, might not notice the discrepancy.

The Auto Lock. The use of an Auto Lock in a unit with phase lock loop circuitry increases the likelihood that the operator will erroneously attribute an excessive speed to the target vehicle. When the operator relies on Auto Lock and Alert Tone, the operator begins searching for a target after the violation has supposedly occurred. The initial reading may simply indicate transient interference; the PLL registers the speed estimate so quickly that even a transient reading may activate the Auto Lock and Alert Tone. A careless operator might rely on the erroneous, initial reading and issue a citation on the basis of the momentary false signal.[96] Any sources of interference mentioned in § 28-3 could cause the false signal.[97] The trend is to prohibit the operator from relying on these features.[98] Five states, including Florida, prohibited radar operators from using these features.[99]

Power Surge Created by the Antidetection Switch. The switch allows the unit to be on and warmed up without emitting microwaves.[100] Occasionally, when the operator flips off the antidetection switch, there is a power surge that produces an abnormally high beam frequency.[101] When this beam reflects off the target and returns to the unit, the result is an exaggerated speed reading.[102] In its tests, though, the National Highway Traffic Safety Administration found the problem to be minimal. Power surge did not create false reading during any of the tests.[103]

Id.

95. ILLINOIS REPORT, *supra* note 37, at 17. However, as a practical matter, when the patrol car is moving, it may be difficult for the patrol car driver to both monitor that display and drive safely. Fuhrman, *The Mistakes Radar Makes — Part 5: Moving Radar Cosine Error*, RADAR REP., July 1991, at 3.

96. Trichter & Patterson, *supra* note 33, at 849.

97. *Id.* at 850.

98. ILLINOIS REPORT, *supra* note 37, at 12.

99. *Id.* at 27; FLORIDA REPORT, *supra* note 8, at 9, 51 (FLA. STAT. ANN. § 316.1096(2)(c)) now provides that moving radar evidence is admissible only if the operator "is using radar which has no automatic speed locks and no audio alarms unless disconnected or deactivated").

100. Trichter & Patterson, *supra* note 33, at 853.

101. *Id.*

102. *Id.*

103. NAT'L HIGHWAY TRAFFIC SAFETY ADMIN., U.S. DEP'T TRANSP., POLICE TRAFFIC RADAR: ISSUE PAPER 9 (1980) (hereinafter cited as NHTSA REPORT).

Ghosting. Ghosting occurs when the beam returned to the receiver has reflected off surfaces other than the target vehicle. One report describes the phenomenon in this manner:

> Here the portion of the signal reflected from the target has bounced from a stationary or slowly moving object back to the target then to the radar (or from radar to object to patrol car to target to radar). The second reflection increases the frequency of the signal, thereby increasing the speed computed by the radar.[104]

The beam returned to the receiver represents the sum of two reflections and can inflate the estimate of closing speed and target vehicle speed. However, in most cases, a skilled operator is able to detect the problem. The ghost reading may be transitory and erratic; the variable sound of the Audio Doppler will help the operator recognize the signal as a ghost reading.[105] Moreover, a ghost reading is usually weak; and a stronger signal, including the true returning signal, will quickly replace it.[106] When the beam reflects off the target twice, the reading may be twice the target speed — for example, 130 miles per hour rather than 65; and it will be obvious that the reading is in error.[107]

Although the ghost reading is usually readily recognizable as such, there are exceptions. The Illinois State Police report one situation in which a strong ghost reading registered and the speed estimate was within reason.[108] In that situation, a slowly moving train was headed in the same direction as the patrol vehicle.

Shadowing. Shadowing occurs when the low beam reflects off a large, slow-moving object traveling in the same direction as the patrol vehicle.[109] The low beam should reflect off a stationary object. When the low beam accidentally reflects off a moving object such as a truck moving parallel to the patrol car, the unit registers an erroneously low speed for the patrol car. The patrol car's speed relative to the other moving object is slower than the patrol car's speed relative to stationary objects. Since the patrol car estimate is too low, the unit overestimates the target speed; the unit subtracts an underestimated patrol speed from the total closing speed. In its tests, the National Highway Traffic Safety Administration reported that shadowing affected most of the units tested. In some cases, the shadowing effects were "very severe."[110] As previously noted, many moving

104. ILLINOIS REPORT, *supra* note 37, at 18.

105. State v. Wojtkowiak, 170 N.J. Super. 44, 61, 405 A.2d 477, 486 (1979), *rev'd on other grounds,* 174 N.J. Super. 460, 416 A.2d 975 (1980).

106. *Id.;* ILLINOIS REPORT, *supra* note 37, at 18-19.

107. *Id.*

108. *Id.*

109. *Id.* at 17.

110. NHTSA REPORT, *supra* note 103, at 3.

radar units have a separate display for the registered patrol vehicle speed. An attentive operator can compare the registered speed with his speedometer and detect the error.[111] An experienced operator will be especially leery of shadowing when the patrol vehicle is passing a truck.

Panning. Panning occurs when the radar antenna is pointed at the control unit.[112] The antenna pans across the control unit and can cause an unpredictable reading.[113] In its testing, the National Highway Traffic Safety Administration found that "[u]sing the radar in this fashion always produced an erroneous reading."[114] The solution is to train the officer never to aim the antenna at its radar console. In addition, the Audio Doppler Tone can assist the operator in identifying the signal as a panning effect. The Tone should give off a sound similar to that heard when a microphone is held up to a speaker.

Scanning. In this phenomenon, the operator quickly rotates the antenna through the horizontal or vertical.[115] The unit reads the motion of the radar as a speed, registering the movement of the unit rather than the speed of the target vehicle. The operator can eliminate the problem by facing the antenna toward the target before making a reading.[116] The National Highway Traffic Safety Administration reported that "[a]lthough erroneous readings were observed for some of the radars during these (scanning) tests, this interference was not observed when the radars were tracking a target during operational testing."[117]

Batching. Batching is similar to "catch-up" in stationary radar; it occurs when the patrol vehicle rapidly accelerates or decelerates while operating the moving radar. The radar unit does not respond instantly to the changed patrol speed. Suppose, for example, that the patrol vehicle quickly speeds up. The unit may still register the previous, slower patrol speed while later reading the higher, combined closing speed. The result is an overestimation of the target vehicle's speed. An experienced operator can avoid and detect batching. First, the operator should maintain a constant speed while operating the radar unit or disregard any speeds registered during rapid acceleration of the patrol vehicle. If the radar unit has a separate display for the patrol speed, the operator can compare that speed with the speedometer during acceleration. Finally, improved circuitry has helped to reduce batching.[118] Batching is sometimes called target speed bumping.[119]

---

111. Illinois Report, *supra* note 37, at 18.

112. *Id.* at 16.

113. *Id.*

114. NHTSA Report, *supra* note 103, at 6.

115. Illinois Report, *supra* note 37, at 16.

116. *Id.*

117. NHTSA Report, *supra* note 103, at 7.

118. Illinois Report, *supra* note 37, at 18.

119. *Id.*

Mirror Switch Aiming. The National Highway Traffic Safety Administration described this problem as follows: "This method of operating ... permits the operator to place the radar in his rear view mirror looking backwards while he looks frontwards...."[120] The operator may misread the speed reflected in his mirror.[121] If the operator locks the speed into the unit, he will discover the error when checking the display screen in writing the ticket. In the NHTSA's tests, this method of using moving radar did not produce any erroneous readings.[122]

The consensus of the official agencies investigating the state of police radar seems to be that skilled, knowledgeable operators can avoid or detect all the problems outlined above.[123] Although there are situations such as rapid acceleration or passing large, slow-moving vehicles that can lead to erroneous readings, "experience should quickly expose such situations."[124] One report asserts that if the operator is properly trained and attentive, none of the phenomena listed above "will ... interfere with the correct identification of a violator or the measurement of the speed of his vehicle."[125] The theme through all these reports is that a properly trained operator can avoid or detect these phenomena. Radar training is discussed in detail in § 28-4.

§ 28-2(D). Laser Speed Gun.

Laser Technology, Inc. of Englewood, Colorado, has developed a laser speed gun.[126] Kustom Signals of Lenexa, Kansas markets a competing laser device.[127] Laser is an acronym for Light Amplification by Stimulated Emission of Radiation. The police officer aims the gun with a telescopic sight. The gun then emits pulses from an infrared laser diode.[128] "The time it takes for reflections to return indicates how far away the car is from the gun. Computing the rate at which the distance changes yields a speed reading."[129] The laser gun has a

---

120. NHTSA REPORT, *supra* note 103, at 9-10.

121. *Id.*

122. *Id.* at 10.

123. *Id.* at 19.

124. State v. Wojtkowiak, 170 N.J. Super. 44, 62, 405 A.2d 477, 487 (1979), *rev'd on other grounds,* 174 N.J. Super. 460, 416 A.2d 975 (1980).

125. ILLINOIS REPORT, *supra* note 37, at xii.

126. *Laser on the Market*, RADAR REP., Oct. 1990; *Laser Thwarts Auto Radar Detectors*, 166 POPULAR MECHANICS 11 (Sept. 1989).

127. *Shedding Some Light On Lasers — Part II*, RADAR REP., Aug. 1992, at 1.

128. *Shedding Some Light on Lasers*, RADAR REP., July 1992, at 2 (conventional radar technology relies on a radio wave, while laser instruments use optical or light energy).

129. *Id. Laser Inconsistencies Highlighted in New Jersey*, RADAR REP., Oct. 1997, at 3 (between September 1996 and July 1997, the New Jersey Department of Transportation tested the accuracy of the LTI 20-20 Marksman; "officials tested the laser gun against conventional radar and a speed detector used by the New Jersey Department of Transportation, taking more than 1,100 readings in

narrower beam than a radar speedmeter[130] and "needs only a $^1/_2$ second to take a reading ...."[131] "In theory, the narrow beam and sighting system should result in fewer target-identification problems than radar, while the avoidance of microwave technology should mean the laser is susceptible to fewer sources of interference."[132] The "[c]laimed accuracy" of the LTI 20-20 UltraLyte "is +/- 1 mph, with a speed acquisition time of 0.4 seconds."[133]

Although the laser speed gun has obvious advantages, it also has limitations. To begin with, it can be used only in a stationary position.[134] In addition, it has a shorter range than most radar units.[135] Further, there are some doubts about its reliability.[136] Finally, "[p]riced at $3,500-$4,500, the laser is about three times

---

all. Only two of the laser measurements were more than 1 mph different from the radar readings, officials claimed.").

130. *Should Lasers Be Used for Speed Detection?*, RADAR REP., June 1991, at 1 ("The beam width of the laser is 3.5 feet at a range of 1,000 feet. At the same distance, traffic radar's microwave beam is 200-400 feet wide"); *Shedding Some Light on Lasers*, RADAR REP., June 1992, at 2 ("Radio waves are very large, with wavelengths measured in inches to hundreds of feet, while light waves are typically a few millionths of an inch. The 900 nanometer laser from the laser speed guns translates to thirty-five millionths of an inch wavelength. The size of the beams emitted is ... a major difference between laser and radar. Each beam is made up of many pulses, and in the case of radar, this beam is normally about 19 degrees wide. This translates to a radar beam 550 feet wide one mile from the source. A laser beam is more like one-sixth of a degree wide, which is 19 feet (2 lanes) wide at one mile").

131. *Should Lasers Be Used for Speed Detection?*, RADAR REP., June 1991, at 1 ("a speed reading in 0.3 seconds").

132. *Id.*

133. *Some New Technologies Keeping An Eye on Your Speed*, RADAR REP., Wint. 1998/99, at 2.

134. *Should Lasers Be Used for Speed Detection?*, RADAR REP., June 1991, at 1; *Shedding Some Light on Lasers — Part III*, RADAR REP., Oct. 1992, at 1.

135. *Id.*

136. *Laser Inconsistencies Highlighted in New Jersey*, RADAR REP., Oct. 1997, at 3 (during a lengthy five week hearing in a New Jersey prosecution, defense attorney Sohail Mohammed presented testimony about a test of the laser gun against a speed detector; "In one [instance], the laser clocked a vehicle at 73 mph, while the speed detector indicated 58"; prosecutor Michael Rubbinaccio attributed some of the apparent discrepancies to typographical errors in recording the data); *Laser Loses Again in Ohio*, RADAR REP., Nov. 1995, at 3 (Henry Roberts, a retired optics engineer from Fairlawn, New Jersey, has studied the laser speed gun; "Among the problems Roberts cites: [1] To get an accurate laser reading, the operator must keep the gun locked onto the target so long that he moves the device to track the vehicle. Yet the manual cautions against moving the gun while taking a reading. [2] Even the slightest amount of fog on the optics will cause mistaken readings. This can happen easily as the operator, sitting in an air-conditioned car, rolls down the window to aim the laser in the hot sun. [3] Shooting toward the sun can yield distorted readings caused by infrared rays."); *Shedding Some Light on Lasers*, RADAR REP., June 1992, at 2 ("Laser beams are ... much more affected by the atmosphere than radio waves."); *Shedding Some Light on Lasers — Part III*, RADAR REP., Oct. 1992, at 1 ("[T]he laser gun is highly affected by the atmosphere, especially cloudy or humid days; ... and it is degraded when used

more expensive than ... radar ...."[137]

The acceptance of the laser gun has been limited. The Michigan State Police tested an early model of the gun but decided against adopting the gun for routine use.[138] However, the Cedar Rapids, Iowa police department adopted the gun.[139] The gun has been purchased or is already in use in areas in Georgia, Iowa, Louisiana, Maryland, Michigan, New Jersey, New York, Ohio, Oregon, Rhode Island, South Carolina, Tennessee, Texas, Virginia, and Washington.[140]

In most states, "courts have yet to recognize speed readings from the laser as reliable evidence in speeding cases."[141] The defense has prevailed in several trial

---

through windshields or other glass."); *The Laser Speed Gun: An Update*, RADAR REP., Dec. 1991, at 1 ("a laser speed gun used during ESPN's broadcast of last summer's NASCAR race at Watkins Glen showed speed readings fluctuating by as much as 30-40 mph. This can happen when the beam moves from one part of the target vehicle to another (for example, from the windshield to the grill").

137. *Should Lasers Be Used for Speed Detection?*, RADAR REP., June 1991, at 1.

138. *Laser Speed Gun Fails Michigan Test*, RADAR REP., Aug. 1989, at 3 ("Inaccurate and cumbersome was the Michigan State Police reaction to testing with the much-heralded laser speed gun").

139. *Laser & Photo RADAR Roundup*, RADAR REP., Jan. 1991.

140. *The Laser Speed Gun: An Update*, RADAR REP., Dec. 1991, at 1. More than 200 police forces around the world now have the laser. *Shedding Some Light on Lasers — Part III*, RADAR REP., Oct. 1992, at 1. There are 600 laser speed guns in use in 31 states and several Canadian provinces. *Laser/Super-Wideband Update: Are You At Risk?*, RADAR REP., Mar. 1993, at 1; *Shedding Some Light on Lasers — Part II*, RADAR REP., Aug. 1992, at 2.

141. *Laser Speed Guns: Who's Got 'Em*, RADAR REP., Oct. 1991, at 3. *Connecticut Member Beats the Laser*, RADAR REP., Sept. 1997, at 2 (in a recent Connecticut prosecution, the magistrate dismissed the citation under § 14-219c of the state's motor vehicle law; "The law in question addresses the use of monitoring devices, including lasers, to support a conviction, and establishes five conditions that must be met before any speed reading is acceptable as prima facie evidence. Among them: adequate training and experience on the officer's part, the monitoring device was in proper working condition, the unit was used in a location where any possibility of distortion would be minimized, and if it was moving radar, that the patrol car's speed also was verified. But it was the expert's final provision on which the magistrate apparently based his decision. Under item 5 of Section 14-219c, the unit must have been 'expertly tested within a reasonable time following the arrest, and such testing was done by means which do not rely on the internal calibrations' of the device."); *A Second Look for New Jersey Lasers*, RADAR REP., Apr. 1997, at 2 ("A New Jersey judge has agreed to review new test data the state says will prove the accuracy of laser speed guns. Last June, Superior Court Judge Reginald Stanton forced the New Jersey State Police to shelve their LTI 20/20 Marksman lasers after ruling he was unconvinced, based on the testimony presented during a lengthy hearing, that the units can provide accurate and reliable evidence. Michael Rubbinaccio, the municipal prosecutor for Parsippany and Rockaway townships involved in last year's court action, says new data show the lasers are accurate within 1 mph."); *Colorado Driver Defeats Laser Ticket*, RADAR REP., Sept. 1995, at 3 (the driver "defeated a laser-based speeding ticket in Boulder, Colorado, successfully arguing that the calibration on the Kustom Signals ProLaser II was invalid"; the gun was certified when it was shipped, but that certification

court tests of laser evidence, and in a 1999 case the Georgia intermediate appellate court concluded that the prosecution had failed to present an adequate foundation establishing the reliability of a laser device.[142]

However, it has been said that "[w]hen the prosecution has mounted a serious effort to prove that the device can measure vehicular speed accurately, the evidence has been deemed admissible."[143] In early 1995, for instance, a New York court ruled laser readings admissible. In the court's words, "the use of the LTI 20-20 device is based upon well accepted scientific principles and can be accepted ... as an accurate method of measuring the speed of a moving vehicle...."[144] The Maryland Court of Appeal issued a similar ruling.[145] In 1998, a

---

had expired); *Laser Loses Again in Ohio*, RADAR REP., Nov. 1995, at 3 ("A Medina judge recently threw out a speeding ticket because the Ohio Patrol trooper failed to calibrate the speed gun properly before he clocked ... Joseph Coticchia allegedly traveling 88 mph on Interstate 71.... The ruling by Judge Dale Chase came as part of a growing wave of laser challenges in Ohio.... The Mentor Municipal Court has ruled that lasers are not reliable."); *New York Court Throws Out Laser Ticket*, RADAR REP., Apr. 1995, at 3 ("A Long Island village justice has dismissed a laser-based speeding citation on the basis that laser speed readings have not yet been generally accepted as reliable evidence in New York state. People v. Michelle D. Foran.... In his November 8, 1994 decision, Village Justice Pfeffer indicated that he searched the LEXIS legal database and found no court decision in New York which addressed laser use. '[G]iven the fact that the use of laser testing has not yet reached the level in which any court of this state has reported the allowance of its use without some evidence of the underlying principles and reasonable scientific acceptance of the technique, the burden was on the people to provide appropriate evidence."). *Laser Evidence Not Admissible*, RADAR REP., Nov. 1993, at 2 ("A Michigan judge decided earlier this year that while the ... LTI 20-20 laser speed gun is potentially quite accurate, the evidence provided by experts to prove laser's reliability was less than convincing. In Michigan v. Kinczkowski (case 92-20510), Judge Thomas Brookover of the 48th Judicial District ruled that before laser-based speed readings can be admitted as evidence, the LTI 20-20 must be tested by an independent entity...."; although the prosecution presented the testimony of Dr. P. David Fisher of Michigan State University, Dr. Fisher "performed his speed tests with a radar gun that was not calibrated and failed to take his readings in a consistent manner"; Judge Brookover found that Fisher's test was "seriously flawed."). *But see Laser/Super-Wideband Update: Are You At Risk?*, RADAR REP., Mar. 1993, at 1 ("To date no court has decided in favor of the defendant in a laser-based speeding case."); *Lasers in Honolulu*, RADAR REP., Oct. 1993, at 3 ("The lasers have withstood court challenges in Hawaii").

142. Izer v. State, 236 Ga. App. 282, 511 S.E.2d 625 (1999).

143. 2 MCCORMICK, EVIDENCE § 204 (5th ed. 1999), citing *In re* Admissibility of Motor Vehicle Speed Readings Produced by the LTI Marksman 20-20 Laser Speed Detection System, 714 A.2d 381 (N.J. Super. Ct. 1998), People v. DePass, 629 N.Y.S.2d 367 (Village Ct. 1995), and Goldstein v. State, 664 A.2d 375 (Md. 1995).

144. People v. Depass, 165 Misc. 2d 217, 629 N.Y.S.2d 367 (Village Ct., Roslyn Harbor, 1995). A ruling on laser evidence was recently handed down in nearby New Jersey. *Court to Consider Laser Admissibility in New Jersey*, RADAR REP., Mar. 1996, at 2 (a New Jersey Superior Court in Morristown, New Jersey, "has agreed to consolidate some 40 speeding cases" from two municipal courts raising the question of the admissibility of laser evidence). The case involved the LTI 20-20 Marksman laser speed gun. Superior Court Judge Reginald Stanton ruled "June 13 that speed

New Jersey Superior Court ruled that under certain operational conditions, laser speed guns can yield reliable, admissible readings.[146] The court imposed the following conditions:

—The operator must have received appropriate training;
—The operator performed all manufacturer-recommended checks before using the laser;
—Speed readings made in snow or heavy rainfall must be supported by expert testimony; and
—Any speed measurements made at distances exceeding 1,000 feet similarly must be supported by expert testimony.[147]

§ 28-3. Operational Environment.

Both transient and relatively permanent conditions in the environment can distort a speed reading.

Transient Conditions

This section focuses on the environment in which radar is used. The conditions of usage,[148] that is, external or outside factors in the environment,[149] can interfere

---

readings from the lasers cannot be used as evidence to prosecute pending or future speeding cases in Rockaway Township and Parsippany municipal courts because he is not convinced that laser readings are accurate or reliable." *New Jersey Judge Declares Lasers Unreliable*, RADAR REP., July 1996, at p. 2.

145. Goldstein v. State, 339 Md. 563, 664 A.2d 375 (1995) ("With respect to the technique, there was no actual dispute. The defense effectively conceded that the use of lasers to measure speed is generally accepted within the relevant scientific community. With respect to the design of the LTI 20-20 itself, the *Frye-Reed* inquiry was unnecessary. The *Frye-Reed* test was designed to apply to scientific theories and processes, not to brand-name products. If every brand of every instrument were subject to a discreet *Frye-Reed* evaluation, trial courts would be mired in hearings concerning devices incorporating scientific principles, possibly including calculators and magnifying glasses").

146. *New Jersey Judge Changes Mind About Lasers*, RADAR REP., Spr. 1998, at pp. 2-3. Judge Reginald Stanton issued the ruling on March 20, 1998. The case involved the LTI 20/20 Marksman.

147. *Id.* at 2. The trial judge was impressed by additional testing of the laser:

> The New Jersey Department of Transportation and the state police conducted almost 2,000 tests, clocking vehicles with lasers, radar and other devices . . . . The timings took place at a racetrack and on Interstate 95 under a variety of conditions and distances. In the final tally, the laser and the comparison measurement device were more than 1 mph apart in just 16 of 1,908 tests, or 0.8%. Defense attorneys . . . brought in a witness who used the test data to show that accuracy was affected by rain . . . .

Id. at 3.

148. Comment, *Operation and Use of Police Radar in Kentucky*, 7 NO. KY. L. REV. 429, 435 (1980).

with the operation of the unit. The factors fall into three categories: internal electronic interference (interference within the patrol vehicle); external electronic interference; and external, nonelectronic interference.

The National Highway Traffic Safety Administration reported that in its tests, internal electrical interference affected the operation of several of the radar units tested.[150] There are numerous potential sources of interference or "noise" within the patrol vehicle: the air conditioner,[151] the radiator fan, the police radio,[152] the auto ignition,[153] a CB radio within the patrol vehicle,[154] the windshield wiper motor,[155] and the alternator.[156] These problems can be eliminated or minimized. For example, proper mounting and placement of the radar unit within the vehicle help to prevent interference by components such as the air conditioner.[157] In addition, a knowledgeable operator will not transmit on the police or a CB radio while the radar is operating.[158]

Although the NHTSA found that internal interference affects radar units more frequently than external electrical interference,[159] in one respect external interference is more troublesome: It is more unpredictable than internal interference, and the operator has no control over the causes of external interference. Those possible causes include: diathermy or X-ray equipment, low-

---

149. State v. Weatherwax, 635 S.W.2d 34, 35 (Mo. App. 1982).

150. NHTSA REPORT, *supra* note 103, at iii.

151. FLORIDA REPORT, *supra* note 8, at 6; Fuhrman, *The Mistakes Radar Makes — Part 6: Mechanical Interference and Tuning*, RADAR REP., Aug. 1991, at 3 ("one potential source of interference is the patrol car's AC/heater fan. Depending upon the type of radar unit, two piece or single, and the dash construction, the fan reflection can vary from weak to strong. The operator must use care to avoid positioning the antenna too close to the patrol car fan. This requires operator consideration because the fan location is not obvious. Just placing the antenna away from the vents or ducts is not enough. The operator should test by turning the fan 'on' and 'off' and operating the fan at various speeds to ensure 'ghost' readings are not encountered").

152. NHTSA REPORT, *supra* note 103, at 15; State v. Wojtkowiak, 170 N.J. Super. 44, 56, 405 A.2d 477, 485 (1979), *rev'd on other grounds,* 174 N.J. Super. 460, 416 A.2d 975 (1980).

153. Note, *supra* note 1, at 1144.

154. NHTSA REPORT, *supra* note 103, at iii.

155. NAT'L HIGHWAY TRAFFIC SAFETY ADMIN., U.S. DEP'T TRANSP., PERFORMANCE STANDARDS FOR SPEED MEASURING RADAR DEVICES, 46 Fed. Reg.
097, 2102, 2107 (Jan. 8, 1981).

156. NHTSA REPORT, *supra* note 103, at 16.

157. *Id.* at 19-20; Fuhrman, *The Mistakes Radar Makes — Part 6: Mechanical Interference and Tuning*, RADAR REP., Aug. 1991, at 3 ("The operator must use care to avoid positioning the antenna too close to the patrol car fan. This requires operator consideration because the fan location is not obvious. Just placing the antenna away from the vents and ducts is not enough. The operator should test by turning the fan 'on' and 'off' and operating the fan at various speeds to ensure 'ghost' readings are not encountered").

158. ILLINOIS REPORT, *supra* note 37, at 14.

159. NHTSA REPORT, *supra* note 103, at iii.

strung power lines,[160] airport radar, aircraft radio,[161] ventilating fans, rotating ventilation turbines, rotating signs,[162] CB radios in the vicinity of the patrol vehicle,[163] garage door openers,[164] neon lights,[165] security alarms,[166] electrical storms,[167] and microwave ovens.[168] In some instances, external interference is foreseeable. For example, in a particular area where there are numerous neon lights, patrol vehicles may have encountered interference in the past. Some police departments maintain records of these areas and instruct their operators to avoid them or be alert to the possibility of interference when they are operating a radar unit in the area. Other sources of external interference, however, cause erroneous readings that are both temporary and unforeseeable. To combat this problem, Florida police now equip their units with a special radio frequency interference (RFI) sensor to "detect the presence of such interfering RF signals and ... inhibit any speed display when such signals are present."[169] The Audio Doppler Tone can also help the operator identify external interference.[170] An RFI source such as an X-ray machine or a garage door opener is likely to produce a sudden or intermittent signal.[171] The Tone would register that type of signal with a warbling or variable sound.[172] In contrast to the unsteady tone produced by external interference, the Doppler tone caused by a speeding car is steady or slowly changing.[173]

Lastly, there may be external, nonelectronic interference with the radar unit. Objects such as pedestrians, birds, tall weeds, trees, buildings, and billboards have occasionally reflected the radar beam. Climatic conditions including sleet, snow, rain, and thick dust have sometimes produced similar distortions.

In most jurisdictions, these sources of interference can be used only as a basis for attacking the weight of radar evidence; without more, their mere existence

---

160. State v. Wojtkowiak, 170 N.J. Super. 44, 59, 405 A.2d 477, 485 (1979), *rev'd on other grounds,* 174 N.J. Super. 460, 416 A.2d 975 (1980).

161. Trichter & Patterson, *supra* note 33, at 840.

162. Fuhrman, *The Mistakes Radar Makes — Part 6: Mechanical Interference and Tuning,* RADAR REP., Aug. 1991, at 3 ("mechanical interference due to nearby moving objects").

163. State v. Wojtkowiak, 170 N.J. Super. 44, 59, 405 A.2d 477, 485 (1979), *rev'd on other grounds,* 174 N.J. Super. 460, 416 A.2d 975 (1980).

164. Schuon, *Police Radar Examined Amid Debate,* N.Y. TIMES, Nov. 29, 1979, at C3.

165. Trichter & Patterson, *supra* note 33, at 840.

166. Schuon, *Police Radar Examined Amid Debate,* N.Y. TIMES, Nov. 29, 1979, at C3.

167. Trichter & Patterson, *supra* note 33, at 840.

168. *Id.*

169. FLORIDA REPORT, *supra* note 8, at 17.

170. *Id.* at 6, 9, 17.

171. *See* State v. Musgrave, 169 N.J. Super. 204, 208, 404 A.2d 650, 652, *rev'd on other grounds,* 171 N.J. Super. 477, 410 A.2d 64 (1979).

172. ILLINOIS REPORT, *supra* note 37, at 14.

173. *Id.* at 20.

does not bar the admission of the evidence. Even when the defense can demonstrate the presence of sources of possible interference[174] such as other police radios within inches of the radar unit,[175] the prosecution need not prove that the sources had no effect on the unit.[176] The testing done by the National Highway Traffic Safety Administration lends support to this view. The NHTSA reported that in its tests, although external CB transmissions affected one radar unit, other possible sources of external interference resulted in "no observed degradation in the performance of any of the units...."[177]

However, there is a minority view. For instance, the Wisconsin courts have required the prosecution to establish that "the device was used in an area where road conditions were such that there is a minimum possibility of distortion."[178] The New York courts have adopted the same position as Wisconsin.[179] A Kansas court has also approvingly referred to the Wisconsin rule.[180] Yet even in Wisconsin, the rule is applied laxly. For example, in one case there were power lines nearby where the operator used an MR-7 moving radar unit. The court nevertheless held the radar evidence admissible.[181] As additional states deploy moving radar, this issue may become more controversial. When the patrol vehicle is using moving radar, the vehicle covers more ground, and the radar unit is more likely to encounter random interference than when stationary radar is used.

As previously stated, a New Jersey Superior Court has passed on the admissibility of laser speed gun readings.[182] Although Judge Stanton ruled the evidence admissible, he recognized the possibility that weather conditions might distort the readings. In particular, he required that readings made in snow or heavy rainfall be supported by expert testimony.

Relatively Permanent Conditions

The above paragraphs discuss transient environmental factors which can distort the radar reading. Permanent environmental factors can also be relevant. In some jurisdictions, statutes require engineering surveys before determining the

---

174. State v. Murray-Miller, 143 Vt. 210, 465 A.2d 237 (1983).

175. People v. Boalbey, 90 Ill. App. 3d 738, 46 Ill. Dec. 113, 413 N.E.2d 553 (1980).

176. State v. Murray-Miller, 143 Vt. 210, 465 A.2d 237 (1983).

177. NHTSA REPORT, *supra* note 103, at iii.

178. State v. Hanson, 85 Wis. 2d 233, 245, 270 N.W.2d 212, 218 (1978).

179. People v. Knight, 72 N.Y.2d 481, 530 N.E.2d 1273, 534 N.Y.S.2d 353 (1988) ("Since the potential for error is greater, the prosecution will bear a greater burden of proof .... [T]he evidence should show that ... the radar was used in an area posing minimal risk of misidentification or distortion (*i.e.*, from heavy traffic, large trucks or large roadside objects such as billboards)").

180. State v. Primm, 4 Kan. App. 2d 314, 317, 606 P.2d 112, 115 (1980).

181. State v. Mills, 99 Wis. 2d 697, 699, 299 N.W.2d 881, 882 (1981).

182. *New Jersey Judge Changes Mind About Lasers*, RADAR REP., Spr. 1998, at pp. 2-3.

appropriate posted speed for a stretch of highway. Absent a current, appropriate survey, radar readings at that site may be inadmissible on the theory that the stretch of highway is an unfair "speed trap."[183]

§ 28-4. Operator Qualifications.

Assume for purposes of this section that the trial court has judicially noticed the reliability of the VASCAR , radar model, or laser device used to clock the defendant[184] or that the prosecutor has presented expert testimony to vouch for the reliability of the model.[185] In some jurisdictions, after the prosecutor has established the reliability of the model, the prosecutor does not have to prove the operator's qualifications as part of the foundation for the radar reading; the operator qualifications go to the weight but not the admissibility of the evidence.[186] However, in most states, as part of the foundation, the prosecutor must establish the qualifications of the person who operated the unit at the time the speed was clocked. Federal Rule of Evidence 702 purports to require a showing of the witness's expert status. In any state with an evidence code patterned after the Federal Rules, the wording of Rule 702 would seem to dictate the conclusion that a showing of the witness's qualifications is necessary.

---

183. People v. Studley, 44 Cal. App. 4th Supp. 1, 52 Cal. Rptr. 2d 461 (Cal. Super. 1996); People v. Earnest, 40 Cal. Rptr. 2d 304 (App. Dep't Super. Ct. 1995); People v. Ellis, 40 Cal. Rptr. 2d 111 (App. Dep't Super. Ct. 1995); People v. Conzelman, 33 Cal. App. 4th Supp. 6, 39 Cal. Rptr. 2d 156 (App. Dep't Super. Ct. 1994) (citing CAL. VEH. CODE §§ 40802(b), 40803(b), and 40804(a)); People v. Goulet, 13 Cal. App. 4th Supp. 1, 17 Cal. Rptr. 2d 801 (App. Dep't Super. Ct. 1993). *See also* Kiwatch, *Speeding Offenses and Radar Speed Traps*, 24 CACJ/FORUM, No. 3, at 35, 37 (1997) (the author points out that in a speeding prosecution, CAL. VEH. CODE § 40803(b) "puts the burden of producing the engineering and traffic survey on the prosecution. The prosecution's burden ... is not satisfied by mere evidence that such a document exists; it must be produced in court (People v. Earnest (1995) 33 Cal. App. 4th Supp. 18, 40 CR 2d 304). And the document which is produced is not sufficient if it is just a summary of the survey; it must be a copy of the actual survey document (People v. Ellis (1995) 33 Cal. App. 4th Supp. 25, 40 CR 2d 1111). In order to be usable at trial the survey must be admissible in evidence. Often you'll find the citing officer did not take part in the survey, and that there is no original certification to authenticate the copy procured in court."); Kuwatch, *Illegal Detentions for Speeding: What Remedies Are There?*, 24 CACJ/FORUM, No. 4, at 35 (1997). In 1998, California Vehicle Code § 40802 was amended to permit the use of engineering and traffic surveys that are up to 10 years old but only if certain specified conditions are satisfied. Kuwatch, *"Radar Speed Trap" Definition Amended*, 26 CACJ/FORUM, No. 2, at 79-81 (1999).

184. Masquelette v. State, 579 S.W.2d 478, 481 (Tex. Crim. App.) *cert. denied,* 444 U.S. 986 (1979).

185. *E.g.,* State v. Newton, 421 A.2d 920, 921 (Del. Super. Ct. 1980) (testimony of an employee of M.P.H. Industries, Inc., the manufacturer of the K-55 radar unit); State v. Harper, 382 A.2d 263, 264 (Del. Super.Ct.1978) (testimony of the vice-president of M.P.H. Industries, Inc.).

186. *See* Note, *supra* note 1, at 1155 n.111 (citing cases from Minnesota and Wisconsin).

The courts have traditionally been liberal in assessing the qualifications of the operators of VASCAR and radar units.[187] If judicial notice or expert testimony has already established the reliability of the model, the operator need not be an expert in electronics, physics, or radar; the operator does not have to be able to explain either the theoretical principles underlying the instrument or its internal functioning.[188] One of the early proponents of radar evidence, Kopper, claimed that a police officer could be trained to operate a radar unit in one and a half to two hours.[189] Most courts have accepted that claim at face value. For example, courts have ruled officers qualified to operate stationary radar when the officer received only one and a half hours of formal training.[190] The courts have been almost as lax in the case of moving radar. They have deemed operators qualified who had a mere two[191] or three[192] hours of formal training followed by some field practice. In a leading VASCAR case,[193] a single day's training, followed by a month of practice, was held sufficient.

In some cases, the defense can mount a statutory attack on the operator's qualifications. *Commonwealth v. Schmitzer*[194] is a case in point. Just as state statutes often require that the police use radar models approved by a state agency, some statutes restrict the types of officers who may operate radar. For example, the Pennsylvania Vehicle Code provides that "[e]lectronic devices such as radio-microwave devices (commonly referred to as electronic speed meters or radar) may be used only by members of the Pennsylvania State Police ...."[195] In *Schmitzer* a local police officer issued a traffic citation based on a radar reading, but the court held the radar testimony inadmissible because the "legislature has not extended the right to use radar to local police ...."[196]

---

187. Comment, *Proposal for a Uniform Radar Speed Detection Act*, 7 U. MICH. J.L. REFORM 440, 445 (1974).

188. People v. Flaxman, 74 Cal. App. 3d Supp. 16, 23, 141 Cal. Rptr. 799, 803 (1977); State v. Stoll, 464 A.2d 64 (Conn. Super. Ct. 1983); State v. Harper, 382 A.2d 263, 264 (Del. Super. 1978); State v. Primm, 4 Kan. App. 2d 314, 606 P.2d 112 (1980); State v. Mills, 99 Wis. 2d 697, 704, 299 N.W.2d 881, 882 (1981); Note, *supra* note 1, at 1155.

189. Kopper, *supra* note 42, at 353.

190. State v. Graham, 322 S.W.2d 188, 196 (Mo. App. 1959); Note, *supra* note 1, at 1155 n.109.

191. State v. Musgrave, 169 N.J. Super. 204, 208, 404 A.2d 650, 653, *rev'd on other grounds,* 171 N.J. Super. 477, 410 A.2d 64 (1979).

192. State v. Wojtkowiak, 170 N.J. Super. 44, 63, 405 A.2d 477, 487 (1979), *rev'd on other grounds,* 174 N.J. Super. 460, 416 A.2d 975 (1980).

193. State v. Schmiede, 118 N.J. Super. 576, 289 A.2d 281 (1972).

194. 286 Pa. Super. 138, 428 A.2d 610 (1981).

195. PA. CONS. STAT. tit. 75, § 3368(c)(2).

196. Commonwealth v. Schmitzer, 428 A.2d 610, 612 (Pa. Super. Ct. 1981); People v. Depass, 165 Misc. 2d 217, 629 N.Y.S.2d 367 (Village Ct., Roslyn Harbor, 1995) (as part of his testimony laying the foundation for a laser reading, "[t]he training officer explained that before taking the

There have also been some successful common-law challenges to the qualifications of radar operators. Even the National Highway Traffic Safety Administration has acknowledged that "[t]he quality of operator training often has not kept up with the technological advances."[197] The moving radar unit of today is a far more sophisticated device than the primitive stationary radar unit that Kopper was familiar with. The modern unit has features — and vulnerabilities — that did not exist in 1955. In *State v. Aquilera*[198] the defense argued that Florida radar operators had insufficient training to avoid and detect the interferences that cause erroneous speed estimates. After wading through over 2,000 pages of testimony and 33 exhibits, the court agreed.[199] In the *Sanders* case, decided in the Superior Court of King County, Washington, on March 10, 1982, Judge David Summers issued a 12-page opinion accepting a similar argument.[200] Judge Summers noted that in Washington, there were no minimum qualifications for either radar operators or radar instructors at the police academy. The limited training of police radar operators may well have been a factor influencing the New Jersey Superior Court to limit its acceptance of moving radar to cases in which the radar is used in the manual mode.[201]

The successful attacks on operator qualifications gave added impetus to the trend toward improved operator training.[202] The National Highway Traffic Safety Administration has developed a model, 40-hour training course for operators.[203] The course includes 24 hours of classroom instruction and 16 hours of supervised field practice.[204] Several states, including Arkansas and Florida, implemented 40-hour training programs. The Florida statute prescribing the program specifically states that the training must emphasize the "recognition of potential errors of said speed measuring devices."[205] Operators are not only being trained how to operate the unit; they are now trained to recognize spurious readings and the conditions such as interference that cause spurious readings.[206] As a further guarantee of operator competence, the NHTSA recommends recertification testing every three

---

laser course an officer must first be certified in the use of radar devices"). *See also* Commonwealth v. DePasquale, 509 Pa. 183, 501 A.2d 626 (1985).

197. NHTSA REPORT, *supra* note 103, at 1.

198. 48 Fla. Supp. 207 (1979).

199. *Id.*

200. MONDAY A.M.: THE NEWSLETTER OF THE RADAR DETECTOR INDUSTRY, ID #321, published by Electrolert, Inc., 4949 So. 25-A, Tipp City, Ohio 45371.

201. State v. Wojtkowiak, 170 N.J. Super. 44, 62-63, 405 A.2d 477, 487 (1979), *rev'd on other grounds,* 174 N.J. Super. 460, 416 A.2d 975 (1980).

202. ILLINOIS REPORT, *supra* note 37, at 10.

203. NAT'L HIGHWAY TRAFFIC SAFETY ADMIN., U.S. DEP'T TRANSP., PERFORMANCE STANDARDS FOR SPEED MEASURING RADAR DEVICES, 46 Fed. Reg. 56,823-24 (Nov. 19, 1981).

204. NHTSA REPORT, *supra* note 103, at 4.

205. FLA. STAT. § 943.14 10(a), *quoted in* FLORIDA REPORT, *supra* note 8, at 51-52.

206. ILLINOIS REPORT, *supra* note 37, at 26.

years.[207] Five states have instituted annual refresher training for their operators.[208] In its opinion admitting moving radar evidence, the New Jersey court added that "it is the court's view that periodic follow-up training be instituted in order to verify continuing qualification as a [radar] operator."[209]

§ 28-5. Proper Working Order Requirement.

The final element of the foundation for radar evidence is proof that the instrument was in proper working order. In most jurisdictions, such evidence is essential not only to complete the foundation for the admission of radar evidence but also to support a speed conviction based on radar.

§ 28-5(A). Admission of Radar Evidence.

In some jurisdictions, proof of the instrument's working order is not an essential element of the foundation.[210] In these jurisdictions, the fact that the instrument is untested affects the weight but not the admissibility of the evidence. There is authority supporting this view in seven states, including New York.[211] However, this is a minority view.[212]

All speed measuring devices are factory tested before they are released for sale, but most jurisdictions demand proof of subsequent testing to verify that the device is still in proper working order later at the time of the clocking.[213] This requirement raises several issues.

Types of testing. In the past, courts have accepted five different methods of verifying the working order of the instrument.[214] One procedure is the run-

207. NHTSA REPORT, *supra* note 103, at 4.

208. ILLINOIS REPORT, *supra* note 37, at 25.

209. State v. Wojtkowiak, 170 N.J. Super. 44, 62-63, 405 A.2d 477, 487 (1979), *rev'd on other grounds,* 174 N.J. Super. 460, 416 A.2d 975 (1980).

210. Note, *supra* note 1, at 1151 n.83, citing People v. Abdallah, 82 Ill. App. 2d 312, 226 N.E.2d 408 (1967); State v. Shimon, 243 N.W.2d 571 (Iowa 1976); State v. Gerdes, 291 Minn. 353, 191 N.W.2d 428 (1971); People v. Dusing, 5 N.Y.2d 126, 155 N.E.2d 393, 181 N.Y.S.2d 493 (1959); State v. Bonar, 40 Ohio App. 2d 360, 69 Ohio Op. 2d 310, 319 N.E.2d 388 (1973); State v. Sprague, 113 R.I. 351, 322 A.2d 36 (1974); State v. Hanson, 85 Wis. 2d 233, 270 N.W.2d 212 (1978).

211. *See* cases cited in note 210, *supra.*

212. Commonwealth v. Whynaught, 377 Mass. 14, 18 n.3, 384 N.E.2d 1212, 1215 n.3 (1979).

213 Trichter & Patterson, *supra* note 33, at 842 n.78 ("An operator of a speed measuring device does not actually 'calibrate' by following any of the testing procedures. The radar unit is calibrated at the factory during manufacture; these testing procedures do no more than verify proper calibration").

214. *Id.* at 842. *See* State v. Calvert, 682 S.W.2d 474, 477 (Mo. 1984) (a certified speedometer, an internal tuning fork, and two external forks); *"Ghost Car" Calibration,* RADAR REP., Aug. 1994, at 3 ("The National Institute of Standards and Technology is busy developing a 'ghost car' to

through, which is based on a comparison between the radar's display screen and a previously calibrated speedometer. There are two techniques for conducting a run-through. While one police car is stopped with its radar unit operating, another police car drives through the zone of influence. The officer operating the moving car checks his speedometer and radios the speed to the officer in the other car who is monitoring the radar. Or the officer can point the stationary unit forward and aim it at stationary objects while the police car is moving.[215] The radar and the speedometer should register the same speed.[216] In either technique, the officer relies on the accuracy of the speedometer. Even speedometers that are periodically maintained can be inaccurate. Some automotive experts estimate that the average margin of error for an American-made car traveling at 50 miles an hour is seven percent.[217] Yet there is authority that the speedometer used to verify the accuracy of the radar unit need not be separately checked or certified.[218]

Another verification procedure is the use of external tuning forks. When struck, the tuning fork produces a frequency corresponding to a particular speed. The speed is usually engraved on the fork. The operator strikes the fork on a nonmetallic object such as plastic or wood, waits three seconds, and then holds the vibrating fork in front of the radar unit. Each fork tests the accuracy of the unit at only one speed; and forks test the accuracy of only the unit's receiver, not the transmitter. Furthermore, the same manufacturer that made the unit usually supplies the forks. One court has held that reliance on the fork supplied with the unit amounts to bootstrapping:

> The use of ... a tuning fork furnished by the manufacturer is tantamount to allowing the machine to test itself. A tuning fork furnished by the manufacturer is but an extension and part of the total speed measuring apparatus which is furnished by the manufacturer upon delivery. The test of the device by a tuning fork which comes from the same source as the device effectively rules out the use of any independent testing mechanism.[219]

It is ideal if the tuning fork has been recently calibrated. The calibration can occur either before or after the clocking of the defendant.[220] One state, Nebraska, requires the prosecution to show both that the tuning fork was particularly

---

calibrate police radar. The device is said to use Doppler radar signals to simulate a car moving at the legal speed limit and links with any type of radar unit. The device is intended to ensure that a radar unit's readings reflect a target vehicle's true speed").

215. Trichter & Patterson, *supra* note 33, at 845.

216. *Id.*

217. *Id.* at 846.

218. Washington County v. Luedtke, 135 Wis. 2d 131, 399 N.W.2d 906 (1987).

219. State v. Allweiss, # 80-463-134U (Fla. 1980), *quoted in* FLORIDA REPORT, *supra* note 8, at 63, 69.

220. City of Aurora v. McIntyre, 719 P.2d 727 (Colo. 1986).

designed to test that model of radar unit and that the tuning fork itself has been tested, calibrated, or certified as reliable.[221]

A third verification procedure is the use of a tuning fork built into the unit or an internal oscillator. The signal or tone generated by the oscillator corresponds to a common speed such as 55 or 60 miles an hour. This procedure suffers from the same weakness as the use of external tuning forks but to a greater degree. As in the case of an external tuning fork, the internal oscillator tests the accuracy of only the receiver and at only one speed. When the operator is using external forks, the operator has the option of employing other forks to test other speeds. Moreover, there is substantial authority that relying on the internal oscillator is insufficient. The courts have split over the issue,[222] but there is precedent that the use of the internal tone button is bootstrapping.[223] Since the oscillator is internal and could be damaged by jostling the radar unit, the bootstrapping argument is stronger here than in the case of external forks furnished by the identical manufacturer.

Another verification procedure is testing the internal electronic functions of the unit, sometimes referred to as a bench test. The testing is done by an electronics expert at the technical shop or motor pool.[224] In some jurisdictions, state statute or administrative regulation requires that the tester possess at least a Second Class Radiotelephone License issued by the Federal Communications Commission.[225]

A final procedure is testing one radar unit against another.[226] The units can be operated one at a time or simultaneously. Just as a run-through assumes the working order of the speedometer, this technique presumes the working order of the control radar unit that the other unit is tested against. The advantage of this procedure is that it supposedly tests the entire unit, not merely the receiver.

Similar issues can arise in connection with the laser speed gun. In a 1995 case, although upholding the admission of laser evidence, the court required proof that

221. State v. Lomack, 239 Neb. 368, 476 N.W.2d 237 (1991).

222. Commonwealth v. Whynaught, 377 Mass. 14, 20 n.6, 384 N.E.2d 1212, 1216 n.6 (1979).

223. United States v. O'Shea, 952 F. Supp. 700, 702-03 (D. Colo. 1997) (the case involved the Kustom KR-105P; reviewing the Colorado case law, the court remarks that the Colorado courts have been "unwilling to allow use only of internal tests for a radar device;" here "no outside test was used to calibrate the accuracy of the radar unit on the day in question. There was no evidence of anything having been done to verify the accuracy of the radar unit, except for the so-called internal tests. [T]here was insufficient evidence to establish that the internal tests were sufficient to insure proper calibration on the date in question"); State v. Gerdes, 291 Minn. 353, 357, 191 N.W.2d 428, 431 (1971); State v. Kramer, 99 Wis.2d 700, 299 N.W.2d 882 (1981); Note, *supra* note 1, at 1154 n.105.

224. *E.g.*, State v. Hunziker, 638 S.W.2d 793, 794 (Mo. App. 1982).

225. *E.g.*, Wiggins v. State, 249 Ga. 302, 290 S.E.2d 427 (1982), citing GA. CODE ANN. §§ 68-2101, 68-2103, and 68-2107.

226. Trichter & Patterson, *supra* note 33, at 847.

the device was in proper working order. The court stated that "the user is required to conduct certain tests periodically during each day of use. The court specified several tests, including:

1) the operator turns on the device and insures that the digital readout display is working properly;
2) the operator performs an alignment test for the scope annexed to the device to insure that the bulls-eye of the scope is properly centered on an object, both vertically and horizontally, when the device's "on-target" tone is heard;
3) the operator stands a premeasured 100 feet away from an object and then measures the distance with the laser device. This measures both the laser operation, the clock action, and the computer since all must be synchronized for the correct response; [and]
4) the operator applies the laser gun to two preset distances, 100 and 125 feet away. This then displays a velocity reading as if the device was measuring two locations of a vehicle. This shows that the calculation means are properly functioning.[227]

Number of tests. Is one test sufficient? This question has produced a sharp "divergence in views."[228] One view is that a single test — one run-through or the use of one tuning fork — suffices.[229] Another view is that a single test is adequate only if the accuracy of the testing device itself was verified.[230] Thus, the proponent would have to show that the speedometer of the car used in the run-through had recently been calibrated or that the tuning fork had been tested and certified for accuracy. A third view requires the operator to use multiple tests although the testing devices themselves need not have been tested for

227. People v. Depass, 165 Misc. 2d 217, 629 N.Y.S.2d 367 (Village Ct., Roslyn Harbor, 1995).

228. Commonwealth v. Whynaught, 377 Mass. 14, 18, 384 N.E.2d 1212, 1215 (1979).

229. *Id.* at 18 n.4, 384 N.E.2d at 1215 n.4, citing both cases and Annot., 47 A.L.R.3D 822 (1973); State v. Tailo, 70 Haw. 580, 779 P.2d 11 (1989) (when a police officer testifies that he used a tuning fork to verify the working condition of a radar gun, a presumption arises that the tuning fork was accurate).

230. People v. Walker, 199 Colo. 475, 610 P.2d 496 (1980); State v. Allweiss, #80-463-134U (Fla. 1980), quoted in FLORIDA REPORT, *supra* note 8, at 63, 67; Myatt v. Commonwealth, 11 Va. App. 163, 397 S.E.2d 275 (1990) (the police officer testified that the radar device responded appropriately to a tuning fork, and the prosecution proffered a certificate of the accuracy of the tuning fork. However, standing alone, the officer's testimony was insufficient; and the certificate was inadmissible hearsay. *Myatt* was governed by the unamended version of VIRGINIA CODE § 46.2-882. Although the statute was amended in 1990 to extend to certificates of the accuracy of the tuning fork, the unamended version of the statute applied only to certificates of the accuracy of speedometers used to calibrate the radar device). *See also* United States v. Wornom, 754 F. Supp. 517, 520 (W.D. Va. 1991) (discussing Myatt).

accuracy.[231] These jurisdictions reason that even when the testing devices have not been retested, common experience dictates that it is unlikely that all the devices would be unreliable to the same degree.[232] The strictest view requires several tests using testing devices that have also been tested.[233]

The last view raises an additional issue. If the accuracy of the testing devices must also be established, the possibility of an infinite regress arises; the opponent can next argue that the proponent must establish the accuracy of the means used to verify the testing devices, and so on. As one court has remarked, "we must have a point of faith somewhere."[234] Despite the practical necessity for a point of faith, some courts refuse to draw the line at the radar unit itself and demand at least proof of the accuracy of the testing devices. The leading case espousing this view is *Ballwin v. Collins.*[235] There are also scattered dicta supporting the strict view.[236] However, "[m]any courts have rejected the strict view."[237] For instance, in one case[238] the operator used a digital frequency counter to verify the accuracy of the radar unit. The court held that the prosecutor did not have to present evidence that the counter itself had been tested for accuracy.[239]

Time and place of test. The prevailing view is that the unit must be tested at a place and time reasonably close to the site and time of the clocking of the defendant's car.[240] These courts require testing within "a reasonable time frame,"

---

231. People v. Walker, 199 Colo. 475, 610 P.2d 496 (1980); State v. Readding, 160 N.J. Super. 233, 389 A.2d 512 (1978); State v. Kramer, 99 Wis. 2d 700, 706, 299 N.W.2d 882, 885 (1981). *See* Myatt v. Commonwealth, 11 Va. App. 163, 397 S.E.2d 275, 280-81 (1990) (Cole, J., dissenting) ("Our sister states are almost unanimous in holding that when two tuning forks are used to ascertain the accuracy of a radar unit, no additional proof of the accuracy of the tuning forks is necessary because each tuning fork corroborates the accuracy of the other. I would follow the overwhelming weight of authority in the United States and hold that a radar unit's accuracy is established by proof that two tuning forks and the internal system of the radar unit were used as corroborating devices...."); State v. Creel, 490 So. 2d 711, 714 (La. App. 1986) (two tuning forks); State v. Bechtel, 24 Ohio App. 3d 72, 24 Ohio B.R. 126, 493 N.E.2d 318 (1985) (two tuning forks).

232. *See* cases cited in note 231 *supra.*

233. ILLINOIS REPORT, *supra* note 37, at 7.

234. State v. Graham, 322 S.W.2d 188, 197 (Mo. App. 1959).

235. 534 S.W.2d 280 (Mo. App. 1976); Note, *supra* note 1, at 1150 n.82 & 1154 n.104. *See also* State v. Bollinger, 550 S.W.2d 214, 215 (Mo. App. 1977).

236. State v. Stoll, 39 Conn. Supp. 313, 464 A.2d 64 (1983), citing State v. Tomanelli, 153 Conn. 365, 216 A.2d 625 (1966).

237. Note, *supra* note 1, at 1151 n.82, citing Nebraska, New Jersey, New York, and Rhode Island case law.

238. City of Kansas City v. Tennill, 630 S.W.2d 173 (Mo. App. 1982).

239. *Accord* State v. Hunziker, 638 S.W.2d 793, 796 (Mo. App. 1982).

240. People v. Wilson, 97 Ill. App. 3d 505, 53 Ill. Dec. 80, 423 N.E.2d 272 (1981); Schaumburg v. Pederson, 60 Ill. App. 3d 630, 18 Ill. Dec. 99, 377 N.E.2d 252 (1978); State v. Weatherwax, 635 S.W.2d 34, 35 (Mo. App. 1982) ("reasonably close to the time of the arrest"). *See also id.* at 38 (Pritchard, J., dissenting) (citing cases from Connecticut, New York, and Virginia).

but they do not prescribe "precise time limitations."[241] When the test occurs before the clocking, these courts sometimes invoke the presumption of the continued existence of a fact or condition after it comes into existence.[242] If the unit was tested and found accurate and there are no intervening events that call into question the unit's continued accuracy, the court assumes that the unit was still accurate at the time of the subsequent clocking. Courts have sustained the admission of the radar evidence even when the defense established that the radar unit malfunctioned after the clocking.[243]

In some jurisdictions, however, courts have announced stricter rules to govern the adequacy of the testing. For example, there is authority that the unit must be tested at the site[244] of the clocking.[245] In addition, some jurisdictions either require testing both before and after the clocking or prescribe specific time limitations for testing. Some authorities declare that "it is well settled that the radar unit must be shown to have been tested both before and after it has been set up."[246] Testing before and after the clocking is a common practice in many jurisdictions,[247] and some jurisdictions have elevated this practice to the status of a requirement.[248] They will exclude radar evidence when, for example, there is "no testimony of testing subsequent to the incident."[249] By statute, some jurisdictions specify time limits for testing. For example, the Pennsylvania statute provides that the unit must have been calibrated within 60 days before the clocking.[250]

Applicability of technical rules of evidence. The radar unit's working order is a preliminary fact upon which the admissibility of the ultimate evidence, the radar speed estimate, is conditioned. In some jurisdictions, the formal rules of evidence

---

241. State v. Kramer, 99 Wis. 2d 700, 707, 299 N.W.2d 882, 886 (1981).

242. State v. Weatherwax, 635 S.W.2d 34, 37 (Mo. App. 1982) (Pritchard, J., dissenting).

243. State v. Dahlgren, 627 S.W.2d 53 (Mo. 1982) (en banc).

244. Jackson v. Langford, 648 S.W.2d 927, 929 (Mo. App. 1983), citing St. Louis v. Boecker, 370 S.W.2d 731 (Mo. App. 1963). *But see* State v. Weatherwax, 635 S.W.2d 34, 37 (Mo. App. 1982) (Pritchard, J., dissenting) (arguing that the language in *Boecker* about testing at the site is dictum).

245. Trichter & Patterson, *supra* note 33, at 838-39 (Texas law requires proof of the accuracy of the radar unit "on location," citing Wilson v. State, 168 Tex. Crim. 439, 328 S.W.2d 311 (1959)).

246. A. Moenssens, F. Inbau & J. Starrs, Scientific Evidence in Criminal Cases § 13.09, at 694 (3d ed. 1986).

247. State v. Doria, 135 Vt. 341, 342, 376 A.2d 751, 752 (1977); McEntire, *Successfully Trying a Speeding Case,* Colo. Law., Oct. 1981, at 2561 n.5.

248. Comment, *supra* note 148, at 436.

249. People v. Cunha, 93 Misc. 2d 467, 468, 402 N.Y.S.2d 925, 926, (Dist. Ct.), *aff'd,* 96 Misc. 2d 522, 409 N.Y.S.2d 387 (1978).

250. Pa. Cons. Stat. Ann. § 3368(b).

do not apply to the proof of certain types of preliminary facts.[251] Federal Rules of Evidence 104(a) is illustrative; the rule reads:

> Preliminary questions concerning the qualifications of a person to be a witness, the existence of a privilege, or the admissibility of evidence shall be determined by the court, subject to the provisions of subdivision (b). In making its determination, it (the court) is not bound by the rules of evidence except those with respect to privileges.[252]

In *State v. Cardone*[253] the court held that the last sentence of the rule applies to the preliminary fact of the unit's working order. Hence, in attempting to prove the unit's condition, the prosecutor may resort to affidavits and certificates that would otherwise be excluded as hearsay.[254] Likewise, if the prosecutor attempted to introduce one officer's testimony about a run-through, that officer could relate the other officer's statements over a hearsay objection. The hearsay objection would not be well taken when the evidence is offered solely for the purpose of laying the admissibility foundation.

Other jurisdictions subscribe to the contrary view applying the formal rules of evidence to proof of the unit's accuracy.[255] Suppose, for instance, that the prosecutor relies on proof of a run-through to establish the accuracy of the unit. The prosecutor calls the driver of the chase car to the witness stand and attempts to elicit testimony that in a radio conversation with the radar operator during the run-through, the operator stated that the radar was registering 60 miles an hour. This testimony would be objectionable on hearsay grounds.[256]

---

251. 1 C. McCormick, Evidence § 53 (5th ed. 1999).

252. Fed. R. Evid. 104(a).

253. 146 N.J. Super. 23, 368 A.2d 952 (1976), *cert. denied,* 75 N.J. 3, 379 A.2d 234 (1977).

254. *Id.* at 28-29, 368 A.2d at 954-55. *See* 1 J. Weinstein & M. Berger, Weinstein's Evidence § 104 [02], at 104-25 n.26 (1982).

255. Note, *supra* note 15, at 579 n.52; E. Imwinkelried, R. Wydick & J. Hogan, California Evidentiary Foundations 3-4 (2d ed. 1994).

256. State v. Hebert, 437 A.2d 185, 186 (Me. 1981); People v. Offerman, 204 Misc. 769, 125 N.Y.S.2d 179 (Sup. Ct. 1953). However, even though this testimony falls within the definition of hearsay, in some jurisdictions the testimony would fall within the present sense impression hearsay exception. The operator is saying that the radar is registering 60 miles an hour at the very time that he or she is monitoring the radar. However, this argument would be unavailable in many jurisdictions. To begin with, some jurisdictions still do not recognize the present sense impression exception. Further, other jurisdictions such as California restrict the exception to statements describing or explaining the declarant's own conduct. Cal. Evid. Code § 1241. In this hypothetical, the operator is describing an external event rather than his or her own conduct. Finally, some jurisdictions apply the exception only when the in-court witness also witnessed the event described by the declarant. Waltz, *The Present Sense Impression Exception to the Rule Against Hearsay: Origins and Attributes*, 66 Iowa L. Rev. 869, 889-98 (1981). The opponent's ability to cross-examine the in-court witness then serves as a doublecheck of the accuracy of the

If the jurisdiction applies the rules of evidence to this foundational element, there are two methods by which the proponent can satisfy those rules. One method is to invoke a special statutory hearsay exception for documents establishing the accuracy of the unit. Several jurisdictions have enacted statutes providing that a certificate of accuracy from a specified testing agency is admissible to show the unit's working order.[257] A Pennsylvania statute provides that "[a]n official certificate from an official inspection station, showing that the calibration and tests required by this subsection were made within the required period, and that the radar apparatus was accurate or was adjusted for accuracy, shall be competent and prima facie evidence of ... the accuracy of the radar apparatus ...."[258]

The second method is to comply with the normal evidentiary rules. By way of example, the prosecutor might offer habit evidence that the operator routinely uses two tuning forks to test the device before clocking any passing cars.[259] Moreover, when the officer who drove the chase car attempts to testify about the other officer's description of the reading on the radar during the run-through, the prosecutor might argue that the other officer's statement qualifies as a contemporaneous statement or present sense impression; the other officer was describing the radar reading at the very time that he or she observed the reading.[260] If the proponent offers documentary evidence such as a report from a testing station or the manufacturer, the proponent may be able to invoke the

---

declarant's perception. In this hypothetical, the other officer is another police car and, hence, cannot perceive the speed displayed on the radar unit in the other car.

257. FLA. STAT. ANN. § 316.1905 (formerly § 316.058); PA. STAT. ANN. tit. 75, § 3368(d); VA. CODE § 46.2-882; Comment, *supra* note 148, at 449.

258. PA. STAT. ANN. tit. 75 § 1002(d.1)(a), construed in Commonwealth v. Perdok, 411 Pa. 301, 192 A.2d 221 (1963).

259. *E.g.,* FED. R. EVID. 406; Russell v. Pitts, 105 Ga. App. 147, 123 S.E.2d 708 (1961) (customary sterilization procedures in medical center).

260. *See* FED. R. EVID. 803(1). *But see* Waltz, *The Present Sense Impression Exception to the Rule Against Hearsay, Origins and Attributes*, 66 IOWA L. REV. 869 (1981) (arguing that Rule 803(1) should be construed as continuing the common-law requirement that the witness on the stand has observed the event that the out-of-court declarant described in the contemporaneous statement.) Several courts require corroboration as part of the foundation for the admission of a present sense impression. Note, *Res Gestae, The Present Sense Impression Exception and Extrinsic Corroboration Under Federal Rule of Evidence 803(1) and Its State Counterparts*, 17 FORDHAM URB. L.J. 89 (1989).

hearsay exceptions for business entries,[261] public records,[262] or recorded recollection.[263]

§ 28-5(B). Sufficiency of Radar Evidence.

If the radar evidence is admissible, the next issue is whether standing alone, that evidence is sufficient to sustain a jury finding that the defendant was driving at the speed indicated by the radar unit. Again, there is a division of authority.

As noted in the last subsection, in some jurisdictions the radar evidence is admissible even when the unit was untested. However, in many of these jurisdictions, the untested radar unit's reading standing alone is insufficient to sustain a conviction.[264] There must be corroboration for the untested unit's reading;[265] the prosecutor must supplement the radar reading with independent evidence.[266]

A second view is that so long as the radar evidence is admissible, it is sufficient to support a conviction. Five states have enacted statutes providing that a radar reading is prima facie evidence of the defendant's speed.[267] Two states have opted for a compromise view that to sustain a conviction, the speed reading must exceed the applicable speed limit by a certain number of miles per hour, six

---

261. Webster v. State, 528 P.2d 1179 (Alaska 1974), *cert. denied,* 423 U.S. 836 (1975); People v. Stribel, 199 Colo. 377, 609 P.2d 113 (1980); Wiggins v. State, 249 Ga. 302, 305, 290 S.E.2d 427, 430 (1982); People *ex rel.* Katz v. Jones, 10 Misc. 2d 1067, 171 N.Y.S.2d 325 (1958); FED. R. EVID. 803(6); Note, *supra* note 15, at 577; Annot., 77 A.L.R.3D 115, 159 (1977).

262. FED. R. EVID. 803(8).

263. FED. R. EVID. 803(5). *See* United States v. Marshall, 532 F.2d 1279 (9th Cir. 1976) (chemist's report admitted as recorded recollection).

264. Note, *supra* note 1, at 1151, 1159; Note, *supra* note 15, at 576-77.

265. Commonwealth v. Whynaught, 377 Mass. 14, 384 N.E.2d 1212 (1979); State v. Gerdes, 291 Minn. 353, 359, 191 N.W.2d 428, 431 (1971); People v. Magri, 3 N.Y.2d 562, 147 N.E.2d 728, 170 N.Y.S.2d 335 (1958).

266. Trichter & Patterson, *supra* note 33, at 841.

267. ME. REV. STAT. ANN. tit. 29, § 1254; NEB. REV. STAT. § 39-664; N.D. CENT. CODE § 39-03-15; VA. CODE ANN. § 46.2-882; W. VA. CODE ANN. § 17C-6-7; Comment, *supra* note 169, at 449; Note, *supra* note 1, at 1152. *See* Myatt v. Commonwealth, 11 Va. App. 163, 397 S.E.2d 275, 276-77 (1990) ("The result of the use of radar to check the speed of a motor vehicle is prima facie evidence of the speed of that motor vehicle. VA. CODE § 46.2-882. That follows from the 'natural and rational evidentiary relation' between the results of a radar check of speeding and the actual speed of the motor vehicle. Expert testimony is not admissible to contest the [general] reliability of the use of radar for this purpose. However, evidence may be introduced to show that a particular radar reading may have improperly recorded the speed of a vehicle which it had been used to measure. Such evidence is admissible to rebut the prima facie presumption created by the statute").

in one case and 10 in the other.[268] As a matter of case law, other courts have decided that standing alone, a radar reading is adequate to support a conviction, at least when there is no rebuttal evidence in the record.[269]

Although most courts have routinely rebuffed attacks on the legal sufficiency of radar evidence to sustain speeding convictions, the time may be ripe for a renewed defense attack. As noted in other chapters, in 1979 the Supreme Court toughened the standard for assessing the legal sufficiency of prosecution evidence. In *Jackson v. Virginia*[270] the Court announced that the cumulative probative value of prosecution evidence must be sufficient to remove any lingering doubt from the mind of a hypothetical, rational juror. Before *Jackson* was decided, most courts had required only substantial evidence — a permissive inference — to support jury findings on appeal in criminal cases.

The advent of the more rigorous *Jackson* standard coincides with the emergence of a more skeptical judicial attitude toward radar evidence. Until the late 1970s, most courts viewed radar evidence uncritically as if radar units "carried some Divine imprimatur."[271] Beginning in the late 1970s, however, the courts began hearing expert testimony questioning the reliability of speed detection devices, especially moving radar. In 1978 in a Wisconsin case,[272] there was expert testimony that moving radar readings are inaccurate 15-20% of the time. The following year, 1979, witnessed the Miami radar trial in which the court concluded that "the reliability of the radar speed measuring devices as used in their present modes ... has not been established."[273] One year later, the Florida legislature passed reform legislation with an introductory statement that "the

268. GA. CODE ANN. § 68-2101(a) (10 mph above the speed limit); PA. STAT. ANN. tit. 75, § 3368(c)(2) (six mph above the speed limit); Note, *supra* note 1, at 1152. N.C. GEN. STAT. § 8-50.2(a) reads: "The results of the use of ... speed measuring devices shall be admissible as evidence of the speed of an object in any criminal or civil proceeding for the purpose of corroborating the opinion of a person as to the speed of an object based upon the visual observation of the object by such person." In State v. Jenkins, 80 N.C. App. 491, 342 S.E.2d 550 (1986), the court held that the use of the term, "corroborating," in the statute manifested a legislative intention that standing alone, a radar speed measurement cannot support a speeding conviction. A Pennsylvania Superior Court reached the same conclusion. Commonwealth v. Martorano, 387 Pa. Super. 151, 563 A.2d 1229 (1989) ("we ... hold that a police officer's uncorroborated testimony as to speed is insufficient to support a conviction ...;" "the Pennsylvania legislature fully intended to require the use of speed timing devices when a driver is charged with violating Section 3362"), *app. denied*, 525 Pa. 597, 575 A.2d 563 (1990).

269. East Cleveland v. Ferell, 168 Ohio St. 298, 7 Ohio 2d 6, 154 N.E.2d 630 (1958); Comment, *supra* note 187, at 449 n.88.

270. 443 U.S. 307 (1979). The defendant cited *Jackson* in State v. Creel, 490 So. 2d 711, 716 (La. App. 1986).

271. Trichter & Patterson, *supra* note 33, at 830.

272. State v. Hanson, 85 Wis. 2d 233, 270 N.W.2d 212 (1978).

273. State v. Aquilera, 48 Fla. Supp. 207 (1979).

reliability of present day radar is subject to question ...."[274] Even if radar evidence is admissible, a plausible argument can be made that the evidence is legally insufficient to convict at least without corroboration that the instrument was in good working order and properly utilized.

§ 28-6. Selected Bibliography.

J. BAKER, TRAFFIC ACCIDENT INVESTIGATION MANUAL (1975).

M. CHIECO & J. KWASNOSKI, TRIAL PREPARATION MANUAL: ESTABLISHING LIABILITY IN VEHICULAR ACCIDENTS (1989).

FLORIDA RADAR COMMISSION, FINAL REPORT (1981).

L. FRICKE, THE TRAFFIC ACCIDENT INVESTIGATION MANUAL (1990).

E. HENRY, DEFENSE OF SPEEDING — VASCAR EVIDENCE (1974).

ILLINOIS DEPARTMENT OF LAW ENFORCEMENT, MOVING RADAR: AN ASSESSMENT OF ITS ROLE IN TRAFFIC LAW ENFORCEMENT (1981).

R. LIMPERT, MOTOR VEHICLE ACCIDENT RECONSTRUCTION AND CAUSE ANALYSIS (3d ed. 1989).

J. MCCAHEY, J. CAMPBELL, P. FISHER & D. MANSFIELD, DEFENSE OF SPEEDING, RECKLESS DRIVING AND VEHICULAR HOMICIDE (1984).

J. MESSINA, HANDLING MOTOR VEHICLE ACCIDENT CASES (1990).

NATIONAL HIGHWAY TRAFFIC SAFETY ADMINISTRATION, UNITED STATES DEPARTMENT OF TRANSPORTATION, POLICE TRAFFIC RADAR: ISSUE PAPER (1980).

Kopper, *The Scientific Reliability of Radar Speedometers*, 33 N.C. L. REV. 43 (1955).

Trichter & Patterson, *Police Radar 1980: Has the Black Box Lost Its Magic?*, 11 ST. MARY'S L.J. 829 (1980).

Note, *Radar Speed Detection: Homing in on New Evidentiary Problems*, 48 FORDHAM L. REV. 1138 (1980).

274. FLA. STAT. § 316.1906, quoted in FLORIDA REPORT, *supra* note 8, at 49.

TABLE OF CASES

A

B

C

D

E

F

H

I

J

K

L

M

N

O

P

Plunkett v. State, 719 P.2d 834 (Okla. Crim. App. 1986) — § 4-5(C), n. 108; § 4-5(E), n. 164; § 17-8(C), n. 231

Pointer v. Texas, 380 U.S. 400 (1965) — § 6-4, n. 135

Polk v. State, 612 So. 2d 381 (Miss. 1992) — § 4-5(C), n. 116; § 4-5(D), nn. 135, 136; § 4-5(E), n. 219; § 18-5(A), nn. 150, 158; § 18-5(B), n. 200

Pollard v. State, 549 So. 2d 593 (Ala. Crim. App. 1989) — § 20-5(B), n. 185

Pomella v. Regency Coach Lines, Ltd., 899 F. Supp. 335 (E.D. Mich. 1995) — § 27-10(A), n. 130; § 27-10(D), n. 198

Porter v. State, 94 Nev. 142, 576 P.2d 275 (1978) — § 9-2(C), n. 45

Porter v. United States, 409 F. Supp. 757 (Cust. Ct. 1976) — § 15-4(B), n. 115

Porterfield v. State, 150 Ga. App. 303, 257 S.E.2d 372 (1979) — § 8-4(C), n. 217

Portis v. State, 418 So. 2d 924 (Ala. Crim. App. 1982) — § 19-10(B), n. 353

Postell v. State, 663 S.W.2d 552 (Tex. App. 1983) — § 24-3, n. 230

Pote v. State, 695 P.2d 617 (Wyo. 1985) — § 12-6(B), n. 189

Pouncy v. Prudential Ins. Co., 668 F.2d 795 (5th Cir. 1982) — § 15-1, n. 11

Pouncy v. State, 353 So. 2d 640 (Fla. App. 1977) — § 5-10, nn. 194, 197

Powell v. Alabama, 287 U.S. 45 (1932) — § 4-6(A), n. 328

Powell v. Texas, 492 U.S. 680 (1989) — § 2-2(C), nn. 64, 68

Prater v. State, 307 Ark. 180, 820 S.W.2d 429 (1991) — § 1-10, n. 420; § 4-5(C), n. 116; § 4-5(E), nn. 198, 223; § 18-4(B), n. 83; § 18-5(A), n. 150; § 18-5(C), n. 216

Preston v. State, 444 So. 2d 939 (Fla. 1984) — § 24-7, n. 401

Prewitt v. State, 460 So. 2d 296 (Ala. Crim. App. 1984) — § 12-5(A), n. 80

Price v. State, 269 Ga. 222, 498 S.E.2d 262 (1998) — § 3-4, n. 72; § 6-1, n. 17; § 6-4(B), n. 187

Price v. Watkins, 283 Ark. 502, 678 S.W.2d 762 (1984) — § 27-10(A), n. 145

Prime v. State, 767 P.2d 149 (Wyo. 1989) — § 12-5(B), n. 118

Prince v. Superior Court, 8 Cal. App. 4th 1176, 10 Cal. Rptr. 2d 855 (1992) — § 3-7, n. 127; § 4-5(L), nn. 311, 312; § 4-6(A), nn. 343, 344

Products v. Proctor & Gamble Co., 871 F. Supp. 739 (D.N.J. 1994) — § 15-4(B), n. 113

Proffitt v. United States, 582 F.2d 854 (4th Cir. 1978) — § 4-3, n. 40; § 4-6(A), nn. 329, 340

Provenzano v. Singletary, 148 F.3d 1327 (11th Cir. 1998) — § 4-5(F), n. 251

Prudential Ins. Co. v. Gibraltar Fin. Corp., 694 F.2d 1150 (9th Cir. 1982) — § 15-4(B), n. 103

Pruett v. Norris, 153 F.3d 579 (8th Cir. 1998) — § 12-6(B), n. 189

Pudwill v. Brown, 294 N.W.2d 790 (S.D. 1980) — § 20-5(B), n. 180

Puente v. A.S.I. Signs, 821 S.W.2d 400 (Tex. App. 1991) — § 27-10(E), n. 215

Puett v. Superior Court, 96 Cal. App. 3d 936, 158 Cal. Rptr. 266 (1979) — § 4-5(E), n. 185

Pulakis v. State, 476 P.2d 474 (Alaska 1970) — § 8-4(B), nn. 162, 193; § 8-4(C), n. 207

Purnell v. City of Akron, 925 F.2d 941 (6th Cir. 1991) — § 18-5(A), n. 150

Pyle v. Kansas, 317 U.S. 213 (1942) — § 3-12, n. 187

Pyron v. State, 237 Ga. App. 198, 514 S.E.2d 51 (1999) — § 9-5(D), n. 255

Q

R

S

T

U

V

Y

Z

INDEX

A

N

PSYCHOLOGICAL AND SOCIAL SCIENCE EVIDENCE—Cont'd

U

V

Y

9407